Library of
Davidson College

Anglo-Scottish Literary Relations
1430–1550

Anglo-Scottish Literary Relations 1430–1550

GREGORY KRATZMANN
LECTURER IN ENGLISH
LA TROBE UNIVERSITY

CAMBRIDGE UNIVERSITY PRESS
CAMBRIDGE
LONDON · NEW YORK · NEW ROCHELLE
MELBOURNE · SYDNEY

Published by the Press Syndicate of the University of Cambridge
The Pitt Building, Trumpington Street, Cambridge CB2 1RP
32 East 57th Street, New York, NY 10022, USA
296 Beaconsfield Parade, Middle Park, Melbourne 3206, Australia

© Cambridge University Press 1980

First published 1980

Printed in Great Britain by The Anchor Press Ltd
Tiptree, Essex

Library of Congress cataloguing in publication data
Kratzmann, Gregory Charles 1949–
Anglo-Scottish literary relations, 1430–1550
Bibliography: p.
Includes index.
1. Scottish poetry – To 1700 – History and criticism. 2. English poetry – Middle English, 1100–1500 – History and criticism. 3. English poetry – Early modern, 1500–1700 – History and criticism. 4. Literature, Comparative – English and Scottish. 5. Literature, Comparative – Scottish and English.
I. Title.
PR8519.K7   821'.2'09   78-74537
ISBN 0 521 22665 1

for Chasely

Contents

		page
	Preface	ix
	Texts and Abbreviations	xi
1	Influences and perspectives	1
2	*The Kingis Quair* and English poetry	33
3	Henryson and English poetry	63
4	*The Palice of Honour* and *The Hous of Fame*	104
5	Dunbar and Skelton	129
6	Two *Aeneid* translators – Surrey's debt to Douglas: Wyatt and Henryson	169
7	*Ane Satyre of the Thrie Estaitis* and English drama	195
8	The two traditions	227
	Notes	263
	Select bibliography	275
	Index	279

Preface

This book is a study of literary influences. In it I have attempted to show how a number of Scots poets, most of whom had some connection with the Stewart courts, drew upon English literature to enrich the quality of their own 'making'. The Scots poets are frequently – and rightly – thought of as a homogeneous group: it may even be justifiable to think of several of them as 'Chaucerians', depending upon how the label is applied. The existence of a political border between the northern and southern parts of 'Albion iland braid' did not prevent Scots poetry from becoming known in England, and I have tried to show how some of it influenced at least two English poets of the early sixteenth century.

The greatest danger involved in a study of this kind is the tendency to minimise the individual merits of writers, and to regard 'influences' as being worthy of attention in their own right. I have tried to avoid this pitfall, but nevertheless I am acutely aware that there is more to be said about the distinctive qualities of many of the works discussed in this book. In writing about such an extensive period, it has been necessary to be very selective, and I have no doubt that there is more to be said about the interrelations of late medieval English and Scots literature. The book will have served its purpose if it promotes informed critical comment on the subject, including qualification of and disagreement with the views which I have expressed.

I am indebted to many other reapers in this field of literature: fortunately it is so fertile that its harvest will never be 'lad awey'. Like most students of the period, I have learned much from the work of C. S. Lewis, John MacQueen, Denton Fox, Derek

Pearsall and Priscilla Bawcutt. I am particularly glad to acknowledge the assistance given me over several years by Professor John MacQueen, who supervised my thesis at Edinburgh University: his criticisms of my work have invariably been relevant and incisive. Professor Denton Fox was kind enough to read the typescript in its final form, and has made several valuable suggestions. I am also pleased to acknowledge the assistance given me, as questions answered or as comments offered, by Dr J. A. C. Stevenson, Professor James Kinsley, Mrs Priscilla Bawcutt, Dr Ian Jamieson, Dr W. S. Ramson, Miss J. M. Hughes and Mrs Janet Williams. Mrs Joyce Arey has typed the manuscript accurately and patiently. To my wife, Chasely Kratzmann, I owe more than I can express.

May, 1979
Melbourne

Texts and Abbreviations

Listed, in alphabetical order, are the works most frequently quoted from in the chapters which follow.

The Bannatyne MS.	*The Bannatyne Manuscript*, ed. W. Tod Ritchie (4 vols., STS, 1927–32).
Chaucer, Geoffrey	*The Works of Geoffrey Chaucer*, ed. F. N. Robinson, 2nd edn (Cambridge, Mass., 1957).
Douglas, Gavin	*Virgil's 'Aeneid' Translated into Scottish Verse by Gavin Douglas*, ed. D. F. C. Coldwell (4 vols., STS, 1957–64). Page-numbers refer to vol. II. *The Shorter Poems of Gavin Douglas*, ed. Priscilla Bawcutt (STS, 1967). Quotations from *The Palice of Honour* follow the Edinburgh text of the poem.
Dunbar, William	*The Poems of William Dunbar*, ed. W. Mackay Mackenzie, 1932; rev. edn (London, 1970).
Henryson, Robert	*Robert Henryson: Poems*, ed. Charles Elliott, 2nd edn (Oxford, 1974).
James I	*The Kingis Quair of James Stewart*, ed. Matthew P. McDiarmid (London, 1973).
Lindsay, David	*The Works of Sir David Lindsay of the Mount*, ed. Douglas Hamer (4 vols., STS, 1931–6). Vol. I contains the texts of the

	poems, vol. II the Bannatyne and Charteris texts of *Ane Satyre of the Thrie Estaitis*. My quotations from *Ane Satyre* follow the Charteris text.
Skelton, John	*The Poetical Works of John Skelton,* ed. A. Dyce (2 vols., London, 1843). Quotations from *Magnyfycence* follow R. L. Ramsay's EETS edition (1910).
Surrey, Henry Howard, Earl of	*Poems,* ed. Emrys Jones (Oxford, 1964).

ABBREVIATIONS

EETS	The Early English Text Society (o.s. original series; e.s. extra series)
JEGP	*The Journal of English and Germanic Philology*
MLN	*MLN*; formerly *Modern Language Notes*
MLR	*The Modern Language Review*
NM	*Neuphilologische Mitteilungen*
N&Q	*Notes and Queries*
PBA	*Proceedings of the British Academy*
PMLA	*Publications of the Modern Language Association*
RES	*The Review of English Studies*
SLJ	*Scottish Literary Journal*
SSL	*Studies in Scottish Literature*
STS	*The Scottish Text Society*

I

Influences and perspectives

John Skelton, the brilliantly irascible Tudor laureate, wrote several attacks upon the Scots. One of them is directed at a Scot called Dundas, who wrote a witty little gibe in Latin, based on the legend that Englishmen had been cursed with tails as a result of their impious treatment of St Augustine. Skelton is moved to defend the honour of his countrymen, and he does so by means of a fairly crude appeal to national feeling:

> Dundas, sir knaue,
> Why doste thow depraue
> This royall reame,
> Whose radiant beame
> And relucent light
> Thou hast in despite,
> Thou donghyll knyght?
> But thou lakest might,
> Dundas, dronken and drowsy,
> Skabed, scuruy, and lowsy,
> Of vnhappy generacion
> And most vngracious nacion.

It may come as a surprise to realise that Skelton seems to have learned some of his poetic craft from writers of that same 'vngracious nacion', which he attacks even more vigorously in that series of malicious poems which commemorate the rout of the Scots at Flodden. Yet the violence of Skelton's feeling is all that is really surprising: throughout the fifteenth century and well into the sixteenth it was by no means unknown for poets from one extremity of 'Albion iland braid' (Douglas, *Eneados*, Prol. 1) to borrow and adapt from works written in the other. Surrey's translation of two books of the *Aeneid* shows beyond any doubt

that its author, who accompanied his father to Solway Moss in
1542, saw nothing amiss in borrowing from the literature of a
country which his own approached at best with polite suspicion,
at worst with munitions. Over a century before, James I of
Scotland, who had been a prisoner in England for eighteen years,
dedicated *The Kingis Quair* to the memory of Gower and Chaucer:
the praise of Chaucer at least is not surprising, since James's style
is heavily influenced by poems such as *Troilus and Criseyde* and *The
Knight's Tale*. James's admiration for English cultural achievement, like the interest in Scots poetry which is evident in poems
by Skelton, Surrey and Wyatt, indicates very clearly that the
Heliconian springs are not always to be separated from the murky
waters of national ambition and intrigue. It is easy to over-
emphasise the strength and the uniformity of nationalistic feeling
in this period. Skelton's *Against the Scottes* brought criticism from
readers in England, although Skelton's response is characteristically indignant – those who dare to 'wrangyll' in this way are the
enemies of the English king. A few years before, his contemporary Alexander Barclay (who may have been 'borne beyonde the
cold river of Twede', but who wrote in England) saw nothing
amiss in following a eulogy of Henry VIII with some stanzas
commending James IV as a pattern of chivalric virtue.[1] For their
part, the Scots makars of the reign of James IV are silent on the
subject of the 'auld enemy' to the south.

Fifteenth- and early sixteenth-century Scottish poetry – the
work of James I, Henryson, Dunbar, Douglas, Lindsay and of
other poets not always identifiable by name – is extraordinarily
rich and varied in terms of genre, stylistic range and sheer imaginative power. It is small wonder that the eighteenth-century antiquary Alexander Campbell described the period of the makars as
'the augustan age of poetry in Scotland'.[2] In crossing the literary
frontier from Scotland to England we pass, in C. S. Lewis's
memorable phrase, 'from civilization to barbarism'[3] – from poetry
which manifests its vitality through persistent and various reinterpretation of convention to verse which is for the most part
dull and narrowly derivative, conforming to the standards of
sober didacticism fixed by the massive productions of Lydgate.

The fact that generations of literary historians have made claims for the influence of Chaucer on the Middle Scots poets, to the extent of suggesting that most of it could not have been written but for Chaucer's example, perhaps indicates some embarrassment that the breadth of Chaucer's vision made so little impact upon the poets of his own country. Since the influence of English poetry upon Scots has long been recognised – even if often misunderstood and overemphasised – it seems strange that the possibility that Scots poetry may in turn have some influence on the way English poets wrote has seldom been discussed. There can be no doubt that the English influence upon the makars is larger than the later impact which Scots writing had upon English, in terms of both the quantity and the quality of what was written, but nevertheless there are signs of indebtedness to Scots poetry in works by Skelton, Surrey and Wyatt: Skelton's indebtedness shows itself in the characteristics of the 'Skeltonic' style, Surrey's in his dependence on Douglas's *Eneados*, and Wyatt's (a less significant matter) in his use of a Henrysonian fable for some of the details of a verse epistle. The one-sidedness of the usual view of Anglo-Scottish literary relationships in the fifteenth and early sixteenth century doubtless has something to do with the unequal fortunes of Scots and English as literary languages in more recent times – the Union of the Crowns inevitably weakened the status of written as well as spoken Scots, at home as well as in England. Literary 'revivals' have never restored the balance, and today even well-educated English readers tend to assume that Scots has always been a subservient language. It is also assumed, at least by most literary historians, that political tensions between the two kingdoms throughout the period brought about a state of cultural *apartheid*. J. M. Berdan, who expresses the quaint view that the Scots poets could have brought no new impulse to English writing because they 'represent derivatives from Chaucer', asserts also that the two countries 'were separated by a sort of no-man's land'.[4] There may have been a physical no-man's land between the two countries – in the shape of the Borders, where there were always factions hostile to one another and the kings of Scotland and England alike – but the barriers to communication between the courts of Edinburgh and London were fewer than one might suppose.

Although smaller and less affluent than its neighbour, Scotland was an independent kingdom, with an important role to play in maintaining the precarious European balance of power. During the reigns of the Stewart monarchs exigencies of state and the vicissitudes of personal fortune involved a great deal of coming and going between north and south, and far from being a deterrent to cultural interchange, political circumstances seem to have fostered it. The most spectacular example concerns the negotiations which preceded the marriage of James IV to Margaret Tudor, and the union of the Thistle and the Rose itself in 1503. William Dunbar, who commemorated the marriage in one of his best-known poems in the high style, was himself absent in England just prior to the marriage, and he may well be both the author of the poem *To the City of London* and the 'Rymer of Scotland' to whom Henry VII made two quite lavish payments.[5] When Margaret came to Edinburgh to be married, her escort was led by the Earl and Countess of Surrey, grandparents of the poet Henry Howard. The career of James's English queen, who if we are to judge from some of Dunbar's addresses seems to have shown some favour towards him, involves figures who are perhaps better known to literary than to political historians. When she fled from Scotland in 1515 as the wife of Archibald Douglas, she was met in England by Skelton's poet-antagonist, Sir Christopher Garnesche, who escorted her to her brother's court.[6] Margaret is known to have been favourably disposed for a time to her husband's uncle, the poet Gavin Douglas, whose great translation of the *Aeneid* was to prove so useful to Surrey. Becoming the victim both of his own ambition and of the rift between Margaret and his nephew, Douglas found himself a virtual exile in London in 1522: he had been urging Angus's cause with Wolsey, when 'yon young wytles fwyll' suddenly capitulated to Margaret's faction in Scotland.[7] Before Douglas's death in London in the same year, he came to know the humanist historian Polydore Vergil, to whom he gave stern advice about the interpretation of early Scottish history.

The Paston letters offer an equally interesting example, from half a century earlier, of how exile due to political circumstances might further cultural communication. Thomas Boyd, made Earl of Arran after his marriage to the sister of James III, was compelled to flee from Scotland after his family had fallen from favour. John Paston wrote to his brother in London, commending Arran in superlative terms, and remarking that he had borrowed their sister's 'book . . . of the Sege of Thebes', which 'when he hathe doon with it, he promysyd to delyver it yow'.[8] Unfortunately there is no record in the letters of the Scots nobleman's reaction to Lydgate's monumental book.

Gavin Douglas and William Dunbar were not the only Scots poets whom political circumstance — in the shape of either diplomatic negotiation or exile — brought to London. Richard Holland, author of *The Buke of the Howlat*, was forced to flee to England along with the members of the house he served, and was expressly excluded from the pardon extended to the Douglases in 1482.[9] David Lindsay, principal poet of the court of James V and an important household official, visited England in more peaceful circumstances, probably on several occasions. Affairs of state, although the most fully documented occasions of travel between England and Scotland, were not the only reasons for which Scotsmen travelled to England and Englishmen to Scotland. In the fifteenth century, after the foundation of universities at Glasgow and Aberdeen, it became increasingly uncommon for Scots students to attend English universities, yet a sixteenth-century title of a poem by Dunbar suggests that he visited Oxford: this is supported by the claim which the poet makes in another poem, that he passed 'into evry lusty toun and place/Off all Yngland, from Berwick to Kalice' when he wore the habit of a friar (*How Dumbar wes Desyrd to be Ane Freir*, 34). The most intriguing instance of a learned Scot's sojourn in England concerns the period of John Skelton's tutorship of the young sons of Henry VII. After the sudden death of Prince Arthur in 1502 Skelton was dismissed, together with a Scot, whose name has not been recorded. The queen's privy purse expenses simply record a payment of 20*s*. to Lady Bray, 'for money by hur given to a

Scottisheman scole maister to the prince at his departing'.[10] The position of tutor to the English heir-apparent was a high one indeed for a Scot to have held. He may have been Walter Ogilvie, a classicist of some renown, who earlier in the same year had addressed a panegyric to Henry VII, mentioning the illustrious pedigree of Prince Arthur. Whatever his identity, one may be excused for speculating on the nature of his relations with Skelton during the short period in which they were colleagues.

Instances of travel between the northern and southern kingdoms can be multiplied, but enough have been given to illustrate that even at times when the 'auld alliance' between Scotland and France was very strong, there were opportunities for cultural communication between Scotland and England. It is hardly surprising that Chaucer's poetry should have been so well known in Scotland, given that several decades of English manuscript production separate it from the most flourishing period of Middle Scots poetry. The advent of the printing press in England no doubt increased the availability of English works in Scotland, and there are signs that the transmission of texts was sometimes very rapid. It is not possible to date Henryson's *Morall Fabillis* with absolute precision, but he must have obtained copies of both Caxton's *Reynard* and his *Aesop* within a short time of their coming from the press. There was a copy of Caxton's *The Booke of the Ordre of Chyvalry* in Edinburgh in the year of its publication: in 1483 James, Earl of Buchan, appeared before the Lords Auditors on the charge that he had stolen this and two other 'Inglis bukis' from Edinburgh Castle.[11] When at the beginning of his *Aeneid* translation Douglas disparages Caxton's 'Virgill in Eneadoss', remarking with justifiable asperity that Caxton and Virgil are 'na mair lyke than the devill and Sanct Austyne', he seemed to assume that some members of his audience at least knew Caxton's book. Printing did not come to Scotland until relatively late, not until 1507, when Walter Chapman and Andrew Myllar were authorised by a royal charter to 'bring hame ane prent': this press did produce literary works, but it main purpose was to facilitate the dissemination of Scottish laws, liturgical practices and hagiography. It must be

Influences and perspectives

assumed that most Scots literary works which reached England were in manuscript. Several of them were printed in London: the long devotional poem, *The Contemplacioun of Synnaris*, by Wynkyn de Worde in 1499; *The Testament of Cresseid* by William Thynne as part of his 1532 edition of Chaucer's works; Lindsay's *The Testament and Complaynt of the Papyngo* by John Byddell in 1538; Douglas's *Eneados* and *The Palice of Honour* by William Copland in 1553. Since such a relatively large number of Scots poems were printed in England, it is safe to assume that others were known, in manuscript, to English readers and poets. It is probable that writers such as Hawes, Barclay, Bradshaw and Nevill were acquainted with some Scots poems, and the absence of signs of borrowing from northern literature in their works is almost as interesting as the fact that Skelton and Surrey *do* borrow from the Scots.

The omission is connected with one of the most striking characteristics of fifteenth- and early sixteenth-century English verse – its conservatism and introspection. The reason for the dull uniformity of most southern poetry cannot be simply that there was a dearth of good poets: the enormous prestige of Lydgate's work must be taken into account, along with the related phenomenon (of which Lydgate's poetry is part effect, part cause) of the sober tastes of a newly-expanded reading public, at a time when the court did little to foster literary novelty. Most Scots poetry would not have conformed to an English poet's notion of what a poem should be – long, avoiding both excessively elaborate and vulgar language, tonally uniform, thoroughly and obviously sententious. The Chaucerian view that a poem might be both edifying and entertaining seems to have eluded Lydgate and his followers completely, if we are to judge from their own poetic practice. Just as most English poets chose not to imitate or to adapt from the Scots, so too Scots poets chose to ignore post-Lydgatian developments in English literature. In both cases, explanation is to be found not in ignorance, nor in the absence of channels of communication, but in different standards of taste and literary decorum. Chaucer's work was of course widely read and presumably enjoyed in sixteenth-century England: perhaps later poets felt that Chaucer's venerable status gave him a latitude and freedom denied to them. Certainly the Scots appear to have inherited many of the qualities which modern readers value in Chaucer's poetry, at a time when their contemporaries in England were the heirs of Lydgate. It is impossible to appreciate just how radical were the literary borrowings which occurred across national boundaries after the later years of the fifteenth century, unless we understand the extent to which the English and Scots traditions were separate and different. This is a matter to which I shall return in a few pages, and again in the final chapter.

Since the influence of southern English poetry upon the Scots is larger than the later influence of Scots writing upon English, it may be appropriate to place it in context, as one of a number of 'foreign' literatures which Scots poets chose to read and adapt to enrich their own writing. The narrow fifteenth-century English view of what was valuable and worth adapting from in the literary past was not shared by the Middle Scots poets, who wrote within a tradition which was nourished from many sources. As a foreign influence on Scots poets' choice of style and subject matter, the courtly poetry of southern England is rivalled only by English alliterative verse. It is inevitable that this kind of poetry should have found its way into Scotland, as it flourished in the north. Because alliteration is so thoroughly a part of Middle Scots poetic style by the end of the fifteenth century, it is not usually thought of as a mode foreign to Lowland writers, but as there is no evidence of any strong alliterative impulse at work in fourteenth- and early fifteenth-century Scots poetry, it is reasonable to infer that English alliterative poetry made its influence felt in Scotland long after it had ceased to be a significant force in England.[12] In Scottish poetry there is an impressive amount of alliterative rhymed stanzaic verse – *The Awntyrs of Arthure*, *The Buke of the Howlat*, *Golagros and Gawaine*, *The Taill of Rauf Coilȝear*, Henryson's *Sum Practysis of Medecyne*, Douglas's eighth *Eneados* Prologue, and several comic pieces. Lindsay employs the alliterative bob-and-wheel stanza at the beginning of *Ane Satyre of the Thrie Estaitis*, and alliterative effects are used repeatedly throughout the play. It is very likely that the allegorical action of the discredited vices winning the guidance of the Three Estates – Flatterie of both the spiritual and temporal estates, Dissait of the Merchants, and Falset of the craftsmen – was inspired by the episode in *Piers Plowman* which tells how Fals, Fauel and their associates attempt to escape the king's wrath by winning the protection of various sections of society (B, II, 210–36). Langland's Mede and Lindsay's Sensualitie are very closely related. For both, sexuality is hardly to be distinguished from the profit motive, and neither has any difficulty in subverting the spiritual estate. There can be little doubt that *Piers Plowman*, which survives in so many manuscripts, was known to a poet who was so conscious of the need for reform as Lindsay: the poem was certainly known in some form in Scotland, as Douglas alludes in *The Palice of Honour* to the episode of the halfacre (1714). In *The Tretis of the Tua Mariit Wemen and the Wedo*, Dunbar uses alliteration systematically, although here the stanzaic form is discarded. Alliteration is used incidentally in many other poems for the sake of variety and emphasis. By the end of the fifteenth century, alliteration had been thoroughly naturalised into Scots verse, and it is hardly surprising that James VI and I, in *Ane Schort Treatise Conteining some Reulis and Cautelis to be obseruit and eschewit in Scottis Poesie*, should set out guidelines for the use of 'Rouncefallis or Tumbling verse'.[13] Alliterative effects are to be found occasionally in English poetry of the same period, but there is no equivalent to the Scots poets' thorough and imaginative exploitation of the technique. It is ironically appropriate that, at the beginning of the sixteenth century, Skelton attempts to reintroduce into English poetry what the Scots poets had taken over from the fourteenth-century poets of northern England.

As well as the two kinds of English influence, the Chaucerian–Lydgatian and the alliterative, there is a variety of continental influences on Middle Scots poetry. Chaucer's poetry, which assimilates continental genres, themes and stylistic devices into English, no doubt provided an important precedent for the makars: the *Morall Fabillis* and *The Palice of Honour*, for example, illustrate a talent for adaptation and synthesis which is reminiscent of the literary synthesis illustrated in *The Parlement of Foules* and *Troilus and Criseyde*. The French influence is, however, present in earlier Scots poetry which owes nothing to Chaucer, namely in Barbour's *Bruce* and *The Buik of Alexander*: the conventions of French romance are as important as 'background' for Barbour's style as those of Chaucerian poetry are for the style of the later makars. In the fifteenth century, the influence of French romance continues to be important, in both alliterative (*Golagros and Gawaine*) and non-alliterative poetry (*Lancelot of the Laik*). *The Palice of Honour* shows a knowledge of various French allegorical poems from the thirteenth century to Douglas's own lifetime, and not surprisingly the influence of the *Roman de la Rose* is discernible in the work of James, Dunbar, Douglas and others. There are traces of borrowing from various kinds of *chanson* throughout the fifteenth and sixteenth centuries: Clapperton's *In Bowdoun on Blak Monunday*, for example, is a near relative of the French *chanson à mal mariée*. In drama, the second part of *Ane Satyre* suggests that Lindsay may have been aware of the work of Pierre Gringore.

The influence of Latin literature, both classical and medieval, is just as important for Scottish poetry as it is for the poetry of Chaucer and Lydgate. Latin was the literature of European learning and of Christian worship, and it is inevitable that a wide variety of Latin works – poetry, prose treatises and commentaries of various kinds – should have been known and used by Scottish writers. Andrew of Wyntoun, at the beginning of his *Oryginall Cronycle*, explains that among the *auctors* he had read are Orosius, Peter Comestor and Martinus Polonus: chronologically, these range from the fifth to the thirteenth centuries. *The Kingis Quair* reflects a thorough knowledge of Boethius's *De Consolatione Philosophiae*, although it is possible that the influence of Boethian thought is indirect – i.e. transmitted via Chaucer's translation and *Troilus and Criseyde*. In fable composition, one of *The Tales of the Five Beasts* is a loose translation of Nigel de Longchamps's *Speculum Stultorum*. The primary source of several of Henryson's *Fabillis* is a work from the same period, the twelfth-century verse *Romulus* of Gualterus Angelicus, and there is evidence that Henryson drew on other Latin writings from Augustine and Aquinas to Boccaccio and Nicholas Trevet. The culmination of that familiarity with Latin literature which was fostered by grammar-school and university curricula is Gavin Douglas's translation of Virgil into Scots. The influence of vernacular Italian literature on Scots poetry of the fifteenth and early sixteenth centuries is relatively slight: as R. D. S. Jack explains, the force of Italian writing is felt much more strongly after the middle of the sixteenth century.[14]

The literary influences at work on Middle Scots poetry are by no means entirely 'foreign': the inspiration for many Scots poems comes from within the vernacular tradition – i.e. from other works written in Scots. For example, the great historical romance of the fourteenth century, Barbour's *Bruce*, may be regarded as the instigator of a distinctively Scots sub-genre which includes Hary's *Wallace* in the fifteenth century and Lindsay's *Squyer Meldrum* in the sixteenth. The number of fifteenth-century collections of tales or fables which incorporate some kind of narrative frame suggests that this, too, is a kind of poetry which was especially popular among Scots writers, and it is reasonable to infer that the interest in one collection of this kind led to the composition of others. A more clearly definable generic continuity is provided by the history of the 'flyting' – Dunbar and Kennedy, Lindsay and James V, Montgomerie and Polwart, and *The flytting betuix the sowtar and the tailʒor* (Bannatyne MS., CCIII). (The 'flyting' is essentially a contest or duel of abuse, in which one poet challenges another by insult and awaits a reply.) The fertilising impulse of the national tradition, the degree to which Scots poets were stimulated by work written by predecessors and contemporaries among their own countrymen, may be apprehended in other ways – for example, through the interest shown in distinctive styles of poetic language and in ways of juxtaposing these, through experimentation with idiosyncratic stanza forms, and with the potentialities of various kinds of tonal variation. The evidence of such resemblances is supported by what some of the poets have to say about their fellow-poets. Dunbar's sonorous roll-call of dead and dying poets in *The Lament for the Makaris*, Douglas's triumphant introduction of the poets of 'this cuntre' to 'the Court Rhetoricall' in *The Palice of Honour*, and David Lindsay's moving tribute to

Douglas in *The Testament of the Papyngo*, all reinforce the impression of keen interest in, and respect for, the local tradition.

The influence of vernacular writing on Middle Scots poetry is rivalled in importance only by that of southern English poetry. In her study of French influences, Janet M. Smith concedes that 'it is seldom possible to point to direct borrowings unless the Scots poet is simply translating his original'[15] and this is also true, in general, of the use which the Scots poets make of Latin literature. The prominence of the English influence is due, in some measure, to the fact that the spoken language of Scotland was similar to that of southern England. The author of *The Complaynt of Scotlande* makes the astringent observation that 'there is nocht tua nations vndir the firmament that ar mair contrar and different fra vthirs nor is inglis men and scottis men, quhoubeit that thai be vitht [both] in ane ile, and nychtbours, and of ane langage'.[16] The historical circumstance that the spoken and written languages were sufficiently close in terms of vocabulary, accidence and phonology for the speakers of one country to be able readily to understand those of the other, taken in association with the geographical proximity alluded to in the *Complaynt*, provides a perfectly logical explanation of why English literary influences should be more obvious and more pervasive than others, despite any antipathies based on national feeling. The linguistic proximity is close enough for poets to be able to describe the language in which they write as 'Inglis': Dunbar, for instance, praises Chaucer as the sovereign light of 'oure Inglisch' (*The Goldyn Targe*, 259), and Lindsay, in a eulogy permeated by nationalistic sentiment, exalts Gavin Douglas as the finest flower of 'our Inglis rethorick' (*The Testament of the Papyngo*, 24). When Scots poets such as James I, Henryson, Douglas, Dunbar and Lindsay praise writers other than the revered Latin masters, they turn to one or all of the Chaucer–Gower–Lydgate triad rather than to Guillaume de Lorris or Dante, and in this they reflect the practice of English poets in the same period.

Only the slightest acquaintance with the poetry of the Scots makars is necessary, of course, to enable one to understand that the poetic language of Henryson and Dunbar is not identical with that of Chaucer or Lydgate: Scots has a multiplicity of words and forms which have no exact counterparts in southern English. The Middle Scots poetic lexicon is fuller and more diverse even than the range of language used by Chaucer. Its basis is the spoken language, a dialect closely related to the northern form of Middle English: both derive from the Northumbrian dialect of Old English. Scots developed its own distinctive features of sound and sense. The spoken language, and to a greater extent the written, was augmented during the fourteenth century and increasingly in the fifteenth by words and forms drawn from French, from the Scandinavian languages and (to a lesser extent) from Gaelic.[17] At the beginning of his *Aeneid* translation, Douglas pays tribute to the range of this spoken language:

> And ȝit forsuyth I set my bissy pane
> As that I couth to mak it braid and plane,
> Kepand na sudron bot our awyn langage,
> And spekis as I lernyt quhen I was page.
> (I, Prol., 109–12)

He goes on to explain that although it contains many borrowings from French, Latin and English already, he has felt obliged, in the interests of 'fowth' [fullness, amplitude] and clarity, to make more (113–20). Despite the very considerable differences between Douglas's 'Scottis' and the language of his contemporaries in the south, it is clear that the two are sufficiently close for literature of the one country to have been readily understood in the other. Although pride in his linguistic and poetic inheritance no doubt played a large part in sustaining Douglas in his heroic labour of translation, he obviously intended his work to be read in its existing form outside Scotland:

> Throw owt the ile yclepit Albyon
> Red sall I be, and sung with mony one.
> (*Conclusio*, 11–12)

His confidence was not misplaced, although it is interesting to see that when Surrey borrowed from Douglas he did not understand some of the more 'braid and plane' Scots words.

It is important that the ways in which various Scots poets use their knowledge of English poetry to creative advantage should be seen against the background of what is known about the taste for English poetry in Scotland in the period. The most obvious indication of this taste is the occurrence of English poems, 'translait' into Scots, in a number of Scottish manuscripts and prints. The largest single source of such works, in which Scots words and forms are substituted for southern ones, is the manuscript which contains *The Kingis Quair*. MS. Selden Arch. B. 24 is a Chaucerian miscellany, probably made for Henry, Lord St Clair, to whom Gavin Douglas dedicates his *Aeneid* translation: as well as *Troilus and Criseyde*, *The Parlement of Foules* and *The Legend of Good Women*, it contains two poems in the courtly idiom of Chaucer's dream visions, Lydgate's *The Complaint of the Black Knight* and Clanvowe's *The Cuckoo and the Nightingale* (*The Boke of Cupide*), as well as a fragment of Walton's Boethius translation and two short works by Hoccleve. 'Translation' is probably too emphatic a way of describing the process by which English word-forms and spellings are replaced by Scots ones, since all of these poems contain a large number of distinctively English features. A similar kind of 'scotticising' is illustrated by a slightly later version of *The Complaint of the Black Knight* (in the guise of *The Maying or Disport of Chaucer*), which was among the first products of the Chepman and Myllar press in 1508. Included in this print is a Scots version of Lydgate's *Ryme without Accord*, which is also in both the Bannatyne and Maitland Folio manuscripts. George Bannatyne, or the scribes of his 'copeis awld, mankit [battered] and mvtillait', translates a variety of other English pieces into Scots from a printed text, mistakenly ascribing some of them to Chaucer:[18] Chaucer's genuine work is represented by the *Canticus Troili* from Book I of *Troilus and Criseyde* (CCLXXXIII), and an expanded version of the admonitory lyric *Lak of Stedfastnesse* (LXXIX). The dream visions and *The Canterbury Tales* must have been sufficiently well known in printed texts in the Scotland of the 1560s for Bannatyne to have omitted them, and in any case their length would probably have made them unsuitable for his purposes. Lydgate is represented in Bannatyne by extracts from *The Temple of Glas* and *The Complaint of the Black Knight* (the latter ascribed, as by sixteenth-century English editors, to Chaucer), a Passion lyric and a dietary.[19] There are no surviving manuscripts, in Scots or English, of Lydgate's long historico-moral works, and it is rather surprising to find a Scots version of two stanzas from *The Fall of Princes* in a sixteenth-century collection of Gaelic poetry.[20] MS. Arundel 285, a pre-Reformation collection of devotional poems, contains a Scots version of the fifth part of Lydgate's *Testament*, and there are other religious poems and 'ballatis full of wisdome and moralitie' in Scots which are translations of southern works. There are, for example, fifteenth-century English versions of the verse *God is a substance for evir durable*, which Tod Ritchie mistakenly attributes to George Bannatyne (II), and of the poem which begins 'I saw ane rob riche of hew' (CCXXVII).[21] There are probably many more translations of this kind, contained in the Bannatyne and other manuscripts. Amid the few known mid-sixteenth-century English poems in Bannatyne are some of Heywood's epigrams (CCXXIV). English lyric poetry is more important for the development of the Scots lyric after the middle of the century than before, but English love-lyrics were undoubtedly known in Scotland. Song books are the kind of production which Scotland's two English queens, Joan Beaufort and Margaret Tudor, may be expected to have brought with them to Edinburgh. One of the 'ballattis of luve' preserved by Bannatyne, *Allace depairting, grund of wo*, is a skilful amalgam of two fifteenth-century English lyrics.[22] It is quite probable that Alexander Scott, writing later in the sixteenth century, had connections with the Wyatt circle in England.[23] Wyatt's own *I am as I am and so will I be* is contained, in Scots translation, in the Bannatyne MS. (CCCXXII). English poems were also read in Scotland in their original form, in both manuscript and print, and there can be no doubt that Henryson, Dunbar and Douglas read Chaucer in 'sudron'. We have already seen that books from Caxton's press were known in Scotland. It is also reasonably certain that there were handsome 'presentation' manuscripts of English poetry at the Scottish court, the kind that would have changed hands at an occasion such as the wedding of James IV to Margaret Tudor. In 1652 the Provost of Queen's College, Oxford, wrote to the antiquary John Selden to inquire after 'A Copy of Chaucer wch came out of Scotland': this may be the book referred to in the sale catalogue of the library of John Maitland, first Duke of Lauderdale, as 'The Works of Sir Geoffrey Chaucer, curiously writ upon Vellum and gilded, very ancient'.[24] It is known that Robert Maxwell, Bishop of Orkney, owned 'ane Inglis buke of Gowere', and that David Paniter gave copies of both Chaucer and Gower to John Sinclair, Dean of Restalrig.[25] These were probably much less splendid productions, and prints rather than manuscripts.

These surviving records of English poetry in Scotland suggest that Chaucer, and to a lesser extent Lydgate, were the most popular 'sudron' poets among the Scottish audience, until well into the sixteenth century. This taste is paralleled by the practice of the poets themselves: those of the makars who make creative use of English poetry turn to Chaucer, and the influence of post-Lydgatian poetry is negligible. When they allude to the three 'fathers' of English poetry, a distinction is frequently made between the first member and the other two. In Dunbar's tribute at the end of *The Goldyn Targe*,

> O reverend Chaucere, rose of rethoris all,
> As in oure tong ane flour imperiall,
> That raise in Britane evir, quho redis rycht,
> Thou beris of makaris the tryumph riall;
> Thy fresch anamalit termes celicall
> This mater coud illumynit have full brycht:
> Was thou noucht of oure Inglisch all the lycht,
> Surmounting eviry tong terrestriall,
> Alls fer as Mayis morow dois mydnycht?
>
> O morall Gower, and Ludgate laureate,
> Your sugurit lippis and tongis aureate,
> Bene to oure eris cause of grete delyte;
> Your angel mouthis most mellifluate
> Oure rude language has clere illumynate,
> And faire ourgilt oure speche, that imperfyte
> Stude, or your goldyn pennis schupe to wryte;
> This Ile before was bare and desolate
> Off rethorike or lusty fresch endyte.
>
> (253–70)

celicall heavenly; *schupe* set about

the distinction is made by means of the stanza division, and the slackening of the hyperbole in the Lydgate–Gower stanza. All three are praised, no doubt sincerely, for their achievements in enriching and 'illuminating' the language which is the poet's raw material, but Chaucer is undoubtedly given pride of place. Gower and Lydgate may well have great delight to Dunbar's ears, but the terms in which the tribute is couched tell us something about his attitude to Lydgate at least. The diction and imagery of the passage clearly suggest that it was modelled on Lydgate's tributes to his master. In the Prologue to *The Siege of Thebes*, for example, Chaucer is styled 'Floure of Poetes', and attention is drawn to his 'sugrid mouth' and power to 'enlumyne' (cf. *GT*, 254, 263). The following lines from *The Life of Our Lady* are even closer to Dunbar: Chaucer is addressed as 'The noble rethor Poete of bretaine',

> That made firste to distille and reyne
> The gold dewe droppis of speche and eloquence
> Into oure tounge thour3 his excellence
> And founde the flourys first of rethoryk
> Oure rude speche oonly to enlumyne.
>
> (5–9)

Dunbar 'outdoes' Lydgate quite self-consciously in the elaborate mode of the tribute, heightening the English poet's level of language still further, and combining it with incidental alliteration and a more sonorous metre. Denton Fox comments that 'The Middle Scots poets are addicted to praising Chaucer, Lydgate, and Gower, surely, because they wish to announce that they are following in their footsteps, and that they too are modern, sophisticated, and technically skilful poets.'[26] The stanzas from *The Goldyn Targe* are a demonstration of Dunbar both following Lydgate's footsteps and leaving some much more elegant ones of his own. The inference to be drawn, I think, is that Dunbar saw his verse as belonging in the company of Chaucer's work rather than Lydgate's: outdoing Lydgate appears to have been quite congenial to Dunbar's talent. The Scots poets may well have admired 'morall Iohne Goweir', but there is little sign in their work that his poetry stimulated any kind of imaginative response. Gower is the master of the plain style in Middle English didactic poetry, and it would be difficult to discern any signs of influence from either his restrained style or his sober and conventional habits of thought.

Like Dunbar, Douglas probably mentions Chaucer's achievement in order to invite favourable comparison with his own. In the first *Eneados* Prologue, there is an address to,

> venerabill Chauser, principal poet but peir,
> Hevynly trumpat, orlege and reguler,
> In eloquens balmy, cundyt and dyall,
> Mylky fontane, cleir strand and royss ryall,
> Of fresch endyte, throu Albion iland braid.
>
> (339–43)

orlege timepiece; *reguler* regulator; *cundyt* conduit; *dyall* dial; *royss* rose

Recognition of Chaucer's superiority to Gower and Lydgate is implicit in the place he is given among the British contingent at the 'Court Rethoricall' in *The Palice of Honour*:

> ȝit saw I thair of Brutus' Albyon
> Geffray Chauceir, as *A per se sans peir*
> In his vulgare, and morall Iohne Goweir.
> Lydgait, the Monk, raid musing him allone.
>
> (918–21, my italics)

In *The Testament of the Papyngo*, Lindsay gives priority to Chaucer in conventional fashion, simply by placing his name before those of Gower and Lydgate. This is more like Dunbar's practice in *The Lament for the Makaris*, but there, as in *The Goldyn Targe*, Dunbar registers his preference very clearly:

> He hes done petuously devour,
> The noble Chaucer, *of makaris flour*,
> The Monk of Bery, and Gower, all thre.
>
> (49–51, my italics)

Professor Fox is quite right to suggest that the Scots poets appear to have regarded Gower and Lydgate as 'lesser luminaries', but his unwillingness to see the implications of these explicit statements extending into the creative practice of the poets concerned should be questioned. He notes that 'the late medieval writers did not know very much, perhaps often did not care very much, about the canons of these three poets, so that they did not make clear or accurate distinctions between them', and that their interest in the literary past was strictly utilitarian:

> They did not wish to make comparative evaluations, but to use the new modes of poetry which Chaucer, Gower, and Lydgate had introduced, and to steal from them anything that seemed useful: diction, rhetoric, genres. Lydgate, voluminous, dilute, and easy to improve upon, was in many ways more immediately useful to his successors than Chaucer who, like other poets of the very first rank, did not always have a beneficent influence on his followers.[27]

It is of course quite likely that they were unaware that a poem such as *The Complaint of the Black Knight* was not by Chaucer, but there is very little evidence of this kind of indiscriminate borrowing from English poetry. There are, notably in the work of James I and Dunbar, some instances of 'improvement' upon Lydgate – Dunbar's tribute at the end of *The Goldyn Targe* is a good example – but there is good reason to believe that these poets and others found Chaucer's poetry more valuable and more stimulating than Lydgate's. It is suggestive that neither James I nor Henryson allude to Lydgate at all. Henryson's failure to do this is perhaps not surprising, since the framework of the *Fabillis* does not permit any direct reference to an *auctor* other than 'Aesop', but the omission of Lydgate's name at the end of the *Quair* is puzzling, since at several points in the poem James reworks passages from at least two of Lydgate's poems. The failure to mention Lydgate as a master of the art of cloaking 'moralitee' in 'eloquence ornate' may be due to the fact that Lydgate was still alive when the poem was written,[28] but there is an equal possibility that the omission reflects a critical judgement that Lydgate does not share the 'superlatiue' status of his predecessors. (*The Kingis Quair*, st. 197, 5.)

The implications of the tributes are to a large extent supported by the number of Chaucer's works which are used, relative to the number of Lydgate's, and by the fact that the Lydgatian influence is different in kind from the Chaucerian. Nearly all of Chaucer's major poems, from the dream visions to *The Canterbury Tales* and *Troilus and Criseyde*, were used in various ways by Scots poets. *Troilus and Criseyde* is of paramount importance, since both James I and Henryson draw upon it extensively to enrich their own statements about the nature and value of sexual love. At a more utilitarian level, Lindsay reworks the famous image of the woodbind in Book III of *Troilus* to pay a witty compliment to a real-life Troilus *nouveau* in his *Squyer Meldrum* (987–91; cf. *TC* III, 1230–2). This kind of borrowing from Chaucer, which consists of reworking a motif or an image in a new and distinctive context, is practised by most of the makars, and all categories of Chaucerian narrative are used in this way. There are also more complex forms of reference to Chaucer, and in subsequent chapters I shall argue that at least three of the makars allude to Chaucer's poems in such a way that the new poems may be read as critical commentary on their sources. There are no signs that Lydgate's poetry elicited this quality of imaginative response. Poems by Lydgate are used in one of the ways that Chaucer's work is used, as an incidental source of images and subject matter, and significantly these poems are the ones which represent Lydgate at his most 'Chaucerian'– *The Flower of Courtesy*, *The Complaint of the Black Knight*, and *The Temple of Glas*, the poems which were thought to have been written by Chaucer himself. *The Kingis Quair*, for example, contains a skilful and witty adaptation of one of the episodes in *The Temple of Glas*, while *The Quare of Jelusy* (the least memorable of all the Scots poems in the courtly allegorical mode) illustrates a much more derivative handling of Lydgate's poem, in metres which are reminiscent of Lydgate's at their most awkward.[29] Lydgate's influence may be discerned in other ways in the work of later Scots poets, notably in their use of aureate language, but it should be remembered that the poems which are written in this mode constitute only a tiny proportion of Lydgate's vast output. Although they were probably known to Scots poets of the fifteenth and early sixteenth centuries, Lydgate's longer and more ambitious historico-religious pieces – *The Troy Book*, *The Fall of Princes*, *The Siege of Thebes* – do not seem to have had any significant effect on their own choice of subject matter, form or style. We might expect to find substantial signs of Lydgatian influence in the longest and most consciously didactic of Scots court poems, Lindsay's *Ane Dialog betuix Experience and Ane Courteour*, but if there is any English influence at all on this poem, it is probably from Hoccleve's *The Regement of Princes*, which also features the form of the dialogue. Lindsay's main sources, however, are a group of Latin chronicles and prose treatises, and clearly he had sufficient confidence in his own abilities as a moralist and *translateur* to have avoided the use of Lydgatian models. For the makars, Lindsay included, Chaucer's poetry is a more fruitful source of inspiration than Lydgate's.

The term 'Scottish Chaucerian' has frequently been applied to James I, Henryson, Dunbar and Douglas, considered either singly or collectively, but its use has seldom been informed by proper discrimination about the ways in which Chaucer's work was used by these poets, or about the reasons for their esteem of Chaucer. Like most of the labels used by literary historians, it is of very limited value. There can be no suggestion that it describes work which is narrowly derivative or imitative of Chaucer's poetry, echoing its subject matter, form and techniques without any enlivening sparks of originality. The Scots poets assimilate Chaucer's work in much the same way that Chaucer himself assimilates poetry by Guillaume de Lorris, Dante, Machaut and Deschamps: in both cases it is possible to point to words, lines, verse forms, themes and images taken over from an earlier poem, and in both cases it is clear that the new poetry is very different in spirit from its source. The nature of this creative assimilation of Chaucer differs markedly from one Scots poet to another, so that the way in which James I, for example, draws upon his work is very different from the use which Dunbar makes of it. The Chaucerianism of *The Kingis Quair* is largely a matter of its extensive imitation of Chaucer's language and techniques. The poem contains several passages of close verbal reminiscence, but these similarities appear calculated to reflect a very different attitude to experience, in particular the experience of love. James's attitude to Chaucer is essentially critical, as he offers an alternative perspective on themes and ideas drawn from his predecessor's work. The same can be said of Henryson, who in *The Testament of Cresseid* continues Chaucer's story of Troilus and Criseyde using the same stanza form and certain recognisably Chaucerian techniques, but introducing an allegorical dimension and a moral perspective which are the products of his own invention. Henryson's departures from Chaucer are an integral part of his poem's meaning, and considered together, they amount to critical commentary on *Troilus and Criseyde*. Despite the very considerable differences between these two Scots poems and the Chaucerian works to which they allude, the *Quair* and the *Testament* could not have existed independently of their sources, of which *Troilus and Criseyde* is the most important. Elsewhere in Scots poetry the influence of Chaucer appears in a more diffuse form, in the use of subject matter, themes, stylistic devices and poetic structures, without the degree and kind of close reference exhibited in the *Quair* and the *Testament*. The meaning of *The Palice of Honour* is enriched when we recognise how closely it is related to *The Hous of Fame*, but it would be wrong to suggest that Chaucer's influence on Douglas's style is a very potent one. Conversely, the style of *The Unicorn's Tale* is modelled on that of *The General Prologue* and some of Chaucer's *Tales*, but we do not need to have read Chaucer to be able to understand and enjoy the story. No Scots poet felt obliged to consult Chaucer before taking up his pen. Henryson's *Orpheus and Eurydice* and the *Morall Fabillis*, for example, draw upon a great variety of source material, little of it English, and only a handful of Dunbar's many poems show any close link with Chaucer's work. However valuable Chaucer may have been to the so-called Chaucerians of Scotland, their attitude to him is one of healthy independence. Although Douglas claims a subordinate place to Chaucer in the hierarchy of poets,

> For as he standis beneth Virgill in gre,
> Vndir hym alsfer I grant my self to be,
> (1, Prol., 407–8)

he has no scruples about taking Chaucer to task for his claim, in *Tho Legend of Dido*, to be a faithful follower of Virgil (405–49). From the point of view of the accurate translator, Chaucer has indeed 'gretly Virgill offendit' by taking liberties with the presentation of Aeneas, and Douglas's 'excuse' of Chaucer – 'For he was evir (God wait) all womanis frend' – ironically highlights the offence. There is no parallel in contemporary English writing to

this shrewd rebuke of Chaucer, which leaves no doubt at all about
Douglas's estimation of his own poetic abilities. Douglas is not
the first Scot to refer to Chaucer in this way. Henryson's allusion
to Chaucer in his account of the 'uther quair',

> Quha wait gif all that Chauceir wrait was trew?
> Nor I wait nocht gif this narratioun
> Be authoreist, or fenyeit of the new
> Be sum poeit, throw his inventioun.
>
> (64–7)

suggests that in writing the poem Henryson wished to invite
direct comparison between his own work and Chaucer's. John
MacQueen observes that 'in the most Chaucerian of his works,
Henryson is not the disciple, rather he regards himself with some
justification as a fellow innovator with Chaucer'.[30]

'Chaucerianism' is defined in this way by a recent editor of
Henryson:

the expression stands for an amalgam of things: a capacity for humour,
urbanity, and sympathy held in near-perfect balance for most of the
time; a fluent narrative art using a variety of measures and manipulated
by a changing yet always identifiable *persona*; a faculty for juxtaposition
(whether for immediate effect or to carry broad thematic points); an
ability to produce rich patterns of responses (manifested sometimes in
piquant lexical complexities, but more often in the handling of the
sentence itself).[31]

Elliott sees in both the *Testament* and the *Fabillis* some of the salient
textural characteristics of Chaucer's verse. Similar comparisons
can be made between Chaucer's poetry and the work of James I,
Dunbar and Douglas, all of whom are as different from one another as they are from Chaucer. Are the details of a comparison
such as this so general, then, as to render the term 'Scottish
Chaucerian' entirely useless? I think not, even though it is obviously inadequate as a critical account of what is most distinctive
about the work of each of these poets. As a way of denoting the
general standard of much Scots poetry, however, the term is not
misleading, and its use need not imply any dependence on Chaucer.
There is no reason to discard 'Scottish Chaucerian' altogether, as
Professor F. H. Ridley advocates in an essay which protests at

some of the inaccuracies which have resulted from its use.³² Certainly, nobody has ever considered calling Spenser and Shakespeare 'English Chaucerians' because they borrowed from Chaucer, but then Spenser and Shakespeare did not respond to Chaucer's work as closely as some of the Scots poets did, nor does the texture of their writing have very much in common with that of Chaucer. It may well be, as Louis Golding suggests, that the Middle Scots poets might have had a happier fate if they had been born in China³³ – but they were not.

Lydgate looms much larger as an influence on the style and subject matter of fifteenth- and sixteenth-century poetry in England, and as I shall attempt to show in the final chapter, this is one of the major reasons for the great differences between contemporary English and Scots poetry. The question of why Chaucer's poetry was so much more important than Lydgate's for the development of the Scots tradition cannot be answered decisively, but neither can it be ignored. It is not sufficient to observe that a succession of talented poets in Scotland responded to Chaucer's poetry simply because it was so much richer and more diverse than any previous or subsequent non-alliterative poetry. The degree of interest in Chaucer is partly due to the fact that the Scots poets were trying to achieve in their form of 'Inglis' what Chaucer had been the first to achieve in 'sudron': an assimilation of continental poetic forms and techniques into new poetry which would dignify the vernacular. In English, Chaucer is the supreme 'Grant translateur', and it is almost inevitable that poets in Scotland who wished to communicate with a cultivated native audience in their own language should have been impressed by Chaucer's example. Like Chaucer, a succession of poets after James I are engaged upon what H. A. Mason (in a different context) calls 'a critical-creative activity, a process of assimilation in which the native digestion system is as important as the foreign matter assimilated'.³⁴ Scottish literature does not, of course, begin with *The Kingis Quair*, but this poem is the first to be written in the Chaucerian style of courtly allegory which descends from the *Roman de la Rose*. For the poets writing later in the fifteenth century, Chaucer's poetry is an example rather than a model: that is to say, they are concerned less

Influences and perspectives

with imitation than with introducing into their own language forms of poetry similar to those which Chaucer had earlier introduced into English. It is more than likely that the synthesising mode of Chaucer's poetry influenced the manner in which poets such as Henryson, Dunbar and Douglas approached the literary past. Like Chaucer, they are engaged in exploring the potentialities of well-worn forms such as the dream vision, and like him they have the ability to incorporate matter, thought and styles drawn from a wide variety of sources. The Scots have few points of contact with Lydgate in this approach to the literary past: Lydgate's relationship to tradition is much less imaginative, and is more inclined to paraphrase or amplification of a single *auctor*.

Recognition of Chaucer's priority and superiority to Lydgate as a 'translateur' of continental forms into English goes some way towards explaining why poets using a different but related literary language should have paid more attention to his work. There is a second reason for this, namely that the makars recognised that the milieu in which Chaucer composed his work was in some respects much closer to their own than to that of Lydgate. Two related factors must be considered here. The first is that Chaucer was a court poet, writing from the cultural hub of his country: H. S. Bennett provides a brief but illuminating review of the variety of social and cultural forces with which Chaucer must have been in contact at the courts of Edward III and Richard II.[35] The second is the nature of the relationship between the poet and his public, and the effect which this may be assumed to have had on Chaucer's style. Undoubtedly Chaucer expected his poetry to be read privately by 'silent' readers like himself,[36] but his writing was also conditioned by the demands of reading aloud. Court poetry is a form of communal recreation, in which entertainment is to be combined with edification. This is illustrated by the scene which Pandarus interrupts in *Troilus and Criseyde*:

> and he forth in gan pace,
> And fond two othere ladys sete, and she,
> Withinne a paved parlour, and they thre
> Herden a mayden reden hem the geste
> Of the siege of Thebes, while hem leste. (II, 80–4)

The illumination in the Corpus Christi *Troilus* manuscript, showing the figure of the poet reading aloud to an audience of courtiers, is perhaps a symbolic representation of the social composition of Chaucer's audience, but it is just as likely that it presents an accurate picture of the way in which poetry was usually read and enjoyed. The central organising principle of *The Canterbury Tales* makes great poets out of figures drawn from all levels of society, but the fiction of an oral tale-telling competition is a reminder that most forms of medieval literature, from romance to sermon, originated in a performing relationship between a speaker and an audience. The poetry itself provides the strongest testimony to its manner of presentation: again and again Chaucer addresses an audience which is physically present – 'But wherefore that I speke al this?', 'I wol yow seyn', 'This trowe I, knoweth al this compaignye', and so on. So prevalent is the tendency that it is impossible to believe that oral conventions are being used anachronistically. Lydgate is an inferior poet: no amount of historical argument can explain away a deficiency of invention and craft. Yet the fact that he wrote within a milieu which was fundamentally different from Chaucer's explains to some extent the difference in the texture of most of his verse. Unlike Chaucer, Lydgate was not a court poet, writing with the advantage of his predecessor's centrality in the world of literature and human affairs. A series of dedications to notable personages such as Humphrey of Gloucester, Henry VI and the Earl of Warwick should not prevent recognition that Lydgate's vocation lay elsewhere. The abbey of Bury St Edmunds did not isolate its inhabitants from the realities of the larger world – it would be wrong to entertain a sentimental view of Lydgate as successor to Chaucer's ideal monk, 'Upon a book in cloystre alwey to poure' – but at the same time it is clear that monastic status separated Lydgate from what cultural court life there was. W. F. Schirmer observes:

Chaucer's select audience, with its taste sharpened on French literature, and its delight in allusions, wit, and irony had ceased to exist. The court of the sober-minded Henry IV no longer had the same brilliance as under the romantic Richard II, during whose unhappy reign many of the finest works of Middle English literature were composed. With the fading of semi-French culture the lay poet gave way to the cleric.³⁷

Lydgate has the prestige of the poet who writes to be 'published' to an audience considerably wider, and as literacy progressed more socially diverse, than Chaucer's courtly audience. Well-to-do readers, some of them aristocrats, some rural gentry, some burgesses, could obtain their copies of his latest work from commercial scriptoria like that of John Shirley. Derek Pearsall suggests that literature was a status symbol for this new audience, that they 'preferred a big book to a good one'.³⁸ It may well be that the phenomenon of a new reading public contributed to a decline in the standards of poetry, but it is more certain that the changed circumstances of presentation contributed to the stylistic difference between Chaucer's poetry and Lydgate's. The diffuseness of syntax, the extended amplifications, the monotonous rhythms, and the absence of significant variations of tone and language in Lydgate's longer works are all parts of a composite deficiency – the lack of any sense of the poet's presence in his work. However this judgement cannot be applied to all of Lydgate's verse. Some of the shorter religious and didactic pieces are pleasing examples of their kind, and the works in the Chaucerian mould, although lacking Chaucer's feeling for dramatic situation, have a certain formal elegance. It is interesting to observe that a sixteenth-century Scots reader of the Chepman and Myllar print of the *Complaint* describes it as 'liber probus atque amabilis atque pro auriculis audiendus'. What is absent from most of Lydgate's enormous output are the changes of tone and language, the shifts of irony and the broader humour which contribute so much to the life of Chaucer's poetry.

It is necessary to turn to Scots poetry of the fifteenth and early sixteenth centuries to find the equivalent of that sense of authorial presence which makes Chaucer's work so different from most of Lydgate's. In a great deal of Scots writing, as in Chaucer's work, authorial presence makes itself felt in two ways, through the movement of the verse, and through what the 'I' of the poet tells us about himself and his reactions to his subject matter. The first is largely a matter of rhythm, and it consists in establishing a balance between speech rhythms and the demands of a metrical pattern. This is a feature of most Middle Scots poetry, and it is accompanied, as in Chaucer, by skilful and sometimes surprising variations of tone and language. It is not of course necessary that poets should also attempt to characterise themselves in their work for it to have a convincing sense of 'voice'. Barbour, for example, is not given to personal reminiscence or even to extensive comment on his material, yet the *Bruce* fulfils very well his introductory promise that stories 'said on gud maner,/Have doubill plesance in heryng' (4-5). Nevertheless, a large amount of Middle Scots poetry is marked by strong and interesting self-depictions which are essential to the development of 'sentence'. In Scotland, the dream-vision form flourishes at a time when its use has deteriorated into a series of wearisome clichés in English writing. The *sine qua non* of the genre is the recording of an experience which purports to be the poet's own: the rhetorical strategy is that of a confidence offered by the poet to his audience – 'This is how I came to write as I do rather than in any other way.' Handled skilfully, this kind of first-person framework heightens the verisimilitude of what is told by giving it a dimension of human interest. Chaucer's great achievement in the use of the form handed on to him by the French poets, from Guillaume de Lorris to Machaut, is to focus attention throughout the poem on the situation of the dreamer, even in passages of description and in lengthy dramatic sequences which do not actively involve him. At the end of the lengthy 'parliament' episode in *The Parlement of Foules*, for example, there is a return to the predicament of the poet *vis à vis* 'commune profit', and, at a less serious level, the eagle's long monologue on sound in *The Hous of Fame* derives most of its comic force from the poet's eloquent silence. There is very little of this kind of dramatic effect about the 'I' of Lydgate's poetry. In his most Chaucerian pieces, *The Temple of Glas* and *The Complaint of the Black Knight*, the characterisation of the poet is of the most conventional kind. This 'I' exists only as a compound of stylised literary characteristics – Lydgate the Courtly Lover – with the result that there is very little sense of dramatic interaction, either between the poet and his subject, or between the poet and his audience. Yet these works are not bad poetry in the way that *The Pilgrimage of the Life of Man* is: the lifelessness of the narrator, even when he is describing a state of mental and emotional disturbance, must be due in some measure to the fact that Lydgate simply did not know how to translate Chaucer's spoken nuances into poetry for private reading. In Scots poetry, use of the dream-vision form is almost invariably accompanied by authorial self-depictions which invite the interest and the involvement of the audience in what is being narrated. *The Kingis Quair*, *The Testament of Cresseid*, the Prologue to *The Taill of the Lyoun and the Mous*, *The Palice of Honour*, *The Thrissil and the Rois*, Lindsay's *Dreme* . . . all are works in which a sense of human drama involving the poet is evoked in order to enrich meaning. Detailed discussion of particular poems is reserved for the following chapters, but it is appropriate to observe at this point that the first-person effects in these poems are frequently adaptations of similar passages in Chaucer's poems. The Chaucerian device of the poet's reflections about a newly-read book as a way of beginning a poem is used by James I and Henryson; the broadly comic and ironic self-depreciation which has given rise to the term 'naïve narrator' finds an appreciative echo in both the *Quair* and *The Palice of Honour*; the reluctance pose of *The Parlement of Foules* and *The Hous of Fame* is given an original twist by Dunbar in a poem of celebration. Even if these and other links between Chaucer and the Scots were not to be taken into account, it would still be reasonable to suggest that they found his work especially relevant because of the kind of relationship between writer and audience which it implies.

Not all Scots poetry of this period was written with a 'gentill' audience in mind, but a remarkable amount of it proclaims its connection with the court. James I, whose literary tastes are praised by the historians Bower and Major,[39] is the court poet *par excellence*: *The Kingis Quair* suggests the kind of community of feeling between poet and audience which underlies *Troilus and Criseyde*. Dunbar combined the functions of cleric with those of court poet in the household of James IV, and we do not need the Treasurer's Accounts to tell us how closely Dunbar's life was connected to the life of the court. Douglas was himself 'of noble

strynd', and his dedication of *The Palice of Honour* to the king
suggests the kind of audience for which he wrote the poem.
Lindsay's poetry, written in and after the reign of James V, shows
a keen familiarity with the affairs of court and state. There is no
internal evidence to suggest that Henryson was a 'courtman', but
there is reason to believe that both *Orpheus and Eurydice* and *The
Testament of Cresseid* were written with a court audience in mind:
the former begins with a reflection on 'nobilnes and grit magni-
ficens' which has little point in a non-courtly context, and the
latter culminates in a thinly-veiled warning to the ladies of the
court. There is reasonable evidence of Henryson's association
with Dunfermline, the abbey of which had a royal guest-house,
and it would have been quite natural for the poet's abilities to be
brought to the attention of James III: the historian Lindesay of
Pitscottie chronicles the king's love of learning and the arts.[40]
The existence in Scotland of a court environment in which the
arts were valued was a safeguard to the life of poetry, and it is
apparent that the tradition of poetry in performance survived
until well into the sixteenth century. There is no Scots equivalent
to the Corpus Christi illumination, but the poetry provides its
own evidence. For example, James tells his 'litill tretisse' that the
'tong' of the reader (one other than the poet himself) will remedy
its defects (*KQ*, st. 194). At the beginning of Book III of *The Palice
of Honour*, Douglas implores the Muses,

> Sum gratious sweitnes in my breist Imprent
> Till mak the heirars bowsum and attent
> Reidand my writ, Illuminate with ʒour loir
> (1293–5)

bowsum amenable; *Reidand . . . loir* When I read out what I have written,
illuminated by your teaching

Douglas seems to have intended his translation of the *Aeneid* to
be used in schools and 'red on hight' to 'onletterit folk', but the
address to Lord St Clair,

> That Virgill mycht intill our langage be
> Red lowd and playn be ʒour lordschip and me,
> And other gentill companʒeonys quha sa lyst

leaves little doubt that the educated as well as the uneducated enjoyed spoken poetry. Dunbar's petitionary poems are the most striking examples of the contribution of the speaking voice to what had been written and revised in privacy. The 'performance' quality of so much Scottish poetry does not imply an inability for private reading in the vernacular: the members of Dunbar's audience, for example, were almost certainly more literate than the courtiers of Richard II.[41] It is reasonable to infer that at the court of James IV the tradition of recitation before a listening audience was strengthened by the fact that books in the vernacular, whether in Scots or English, were not as readily available as they were in contemporary England.

Although Chaucer's poetry is by no means the only influence at work on the Scots poetry of the fifteenth and early sixteenth centuries, it is the most important single foreign influence, not least because it appears to have served as a touchstone of excellence for the makars. The fact that no Scots writer was so daunted by Chaucer's example as to fall into the error of servile imitation testifies to the survival of Chaucer's *kind* of talent in the courts of Scotland. The ability to adapt and select – from Chaucer, from Lydgate, from continental poetry, from earlier writing in Scots – in order to vivify a work with its own 'moralite' and tone produces a complex and varied body of poetry which has few points of contact with the literature of England in the same period. It is wholly appropriate that Skelton, the first truly inventive English poet since Chaucer, should have turned to Scottish poetry as part of an effort to infuse some new life into English letters. My concern in the chapters which follow is to show how imaginative the makars were in their borrowings. As long ago as 1908, G. Gregory Smith warned of the dangers of a comparative approach to late medieval Scottish literature:

It has become a commonplace to say of the [Scots] poets that they, best of all Chaucer's followers, fulfilled the lessons of the master-craftsman; and it has long been customary to enforce this by contrasting the skill of Lydgate, Occleve, and their contemporaries in the south, with that of James I, Henryson, Dunbar, and Gavin Douglas. The contrast, however, does not help us to more than a superficial estimate; it may lead us to exaggerate the individual merits of the writers and to neglect such important matters as the homogeneity of their work.[42]

I have been unable to do justice to all the individual merits of the Scots poets – that would require a whole series of books. Nevertheless, some attempt is made in the chapters which follow to suggest some of the distinctive qualities of individual poems, and to give some idea of that strength of local tradition in the two parts of 'Albion iland braid' which makes Scottish literature so different from English work in the same period.

2

The Kingis Quair and English poetry

The Kingis Quair of James I[1] is the first Middle Scots poem to show any marked affinities with the poetry of Chaucer and with early fifteenth-century writing in the Chaucerian mode. Written some time after the king's marriage and return to Scotland in 1424, and before his death in 1437, the poem predates by more than half a century the efflorescence of Scots poetry which began during the reign of James III. The time gap makes it necessary to be cautious about James's influence on poets such as Henryson and Dunbar, but the possibility that his choice of a Chaucerian style had some effect on the way later poets wrote cannot be dismissed. Like so many works from that later 'augustan' age of Scots poetry, the *Quair* is a court poem, one which implies that it was composed to be read aloud – in performance – as well as privately. Even at its most insistently rhetorical, the rhythms of the poem accommodate themselves to those of the speaking voice. 'Say' is a frequently-used verb, and at the end of the poet implores his 'reder' to remedy the poem's defects with his 'tong'. This prompts A. C. Spearing to observe that 'we have left behind the intimate link of poet and listeners at the Ricardian court',[2] but we need to keep in mind that Chaucer, at the end of *Troilus and Criseyde*, also recognises that his 'litel bok' will be 'red' by others (v, 1797). Like Chaucer, James realises that poetry is to be enjoyed not only in performance but also in private reading. It is difficult to imagine that a reigning monarch would have addressed a poem based on personal experience to anything less than an audience of courtiers, but it does contain several references which combine to leave little doubt about the matter: to illustrate the universality of Fortune's operations the ranks of 'prynce' and 'page' are chosen (st. 9); towards the conclusion the poet addresses, echoing Chaucer, his 'brethir that bene in this place' (st. 184), and covertly, the queen herself (st. 195). The dialogue between Venus and the dreamer implies an intention on James's part to found a new tradition of courtly poetry, on his return 'doune to ground ageyne', through the goddess's command that her supplicant should actively encourage the spread of 'The songis new, the fresch carolis and dance' (st. 121). It may be significant that part of the speech (the conceit of the rain as Venus's tears) is an elegant variation on a theme borrowed from *Lenvoy de Chaucer a Scogan*, a poem which contains references which are unmistakably personal and topical. *The Kingis Quair* appears to reflect a desire on the part of its author to enrich his kingdom with some of the more positive knowledge gained during his enforced sojourn in England. In this sense it is the literary counterpart of James's attempt to introduce a bicameral parliament on the English model, adapted to suit the traditions of his own country.

The most recent editor of the *Quair* suggests that 'More, perhaps, might have been made of the eighteen years of exile and frustration.'[3] The desire to know more about the Scottish king's eighteen years' imprisonment in England is of course perfectly understandable, given that so little is known about the details of his captivity. There are however very sound aesthetic reasons for James's reticence, and to insist on a strictly autobiographical interpretation is to misunderstand the terms in which the poem is introduced — as an 'auenture' with a philosophical import. In view of the likelihood that the poem was written for the edification of a comparatively small court, there is a further reason for keeping autobiographical detail to a minimum. Presumably its original audience would have brought to their experience of the poem a knowledge of its background in the personal experience of the poet, which would have come into force as soon as allusions to the childhood journey, the capture at sea 'by fors ... Off inymyis' (st. 24, 4–5), and the imprisonment 'Nere by the space of ȝeris twise nyne' (st. 25, 5) were made. They would also have appreciated the ingenuity shown in the treatment of historical fact. In the poem James refers to his 'folk' (st. 27), the companions of his captivity, some of whom would have been among its first audience – men such as William Giffart, given a pension by the Scots parliament in 1424, Thomas Myrton, who became treasurer, and Walter Ogilvy, who although never a prisoner himself, was a frequent ambassador during the years of captivity.[4] It may be no coincidence that the manuscript which contains *The Kingis Quair* belonged to Henry, Lord St Clair: his great-grandfather was the Earl of Orkney who led James's escort on the fateful voyage, while his maternal grandmother was Margaret Douglas, eldest sister of James I. If my assumptions about the relationship between poet and audience are correct, his task in writing the poem would have been to curb rather than to give rein to any autobiographical impulse, in order to facilitate the presentation of his generalising 'sentence'.

Although most of the details of James's captivity in England are shrouded in obscurity, it is clear that he was not made particularly comfortable: he was perpetually short of money, and the bed-linen of one of his fellow-prisoners had not been renewed for two years. Walter Bower's account of the king's prodigious achievements in learning in a country whose language was strange to him ('etsi linguam quam non noverat audivit'),[5] which implies the ready accessibility of tutors in the households of Henry IV and V, should be treated with suspicion. Nevertheless, English court life did play a part in his confinement: James was with the court at Croydon in 1412, and later at Windsor; he was at the coronation of Queen Catherine, and in 1420 and 1421 was with Henry on campaign in France. Political expediency undoubtedly prompted such public exhibitions of the King of Scots, but it is more important here to observe that although a prisoner, there would have been some opportunity for James to encounter in manuscript or perhaps even in performance such expressions of English culture as the poetry of Chaucer and Lydgate. Parts of the *Quair* are conscious reworkings of their work, and from this we must infer that James had with him in Scotland copies of the relevant poems, in manuscripts similar to that which contains the *Quair* itself. There can be no doubt that the *Quair* was written in Scotland, despite the Selden colophon, 'maid quhen his Maiestie was in England'. The king and queen came to Scotland only a few weeks after their marriage, and the poem's strongly retrospective tone (e.g. sts. 192–3) is simply not consistent with a date of composition prior to 1424. The poems of Chaucer were probably already known in Scottish court circles, since transmission of texts could easily have been effected through the normal channels of diplomatic exchange, but until the composition of the *Quair* there is no Scots work written in accordance with similar artistic principles. It is written in the seven-line *Troilus and Criseyde* stanza and contains a wealth of echoes of the language, themes and devices of a number of late fourteenth- and early fifteenth-century poems. The vocabulary of the poem is clearly different from that of the later work of Henryson and Dunbar, which abounds in distinctively Scots dialectical forms. Factors such as these have led commentators to regard it as a southern composition. Skeat described the language of the poem as an 'artificial dialect',[6] and in the influential view of Sir William Craigie it is basically Chaucerian English, contaminated by scribal interference.[7] In his study of fifteenth-century English poetry, Derek Pearsall refers to 'the fact proved by Craigie to the satisfaction of all but the most fanatical Scottophile, that the language of the poem is the Southern English of Chaucer'.[8] The language of the poem, with its mixture of southern and northern words and forms, is what one would expect of a man who had been exposed to English speech and English writing over a long period, but who nevertheless had never lost touch with the language of his own country by virtue of his association with the older Scots who shared his captivity. The southern element is of course much stronger than it is in the work of Henryson and Dunbar, but one does not need to be 'the most fanatical Scottophile' to see the poet's native linguistic inheritance at work in association with the language of the southern court and its literature. The accumulation of possessive pronouns in the account of the transition from reading Boethius to creative activity,

> Therefore I lat him pas, and in *my* tong
> Procede I will agayn to *my* sentence
> Of *my* mater, and leve all incidence,
>
> (st. 7, 5–7, my italics)[9]

is not simply fortuitous. Despite the preceding disclaimer 'my scole is ouer ʒong', the poet's 'sentence' and 'mater' are his own, and they are set forth in a language – 'my tong' – which would easily have been understood by his Scots audience.

A considerable part of the modern critical interest in the nexus between the *Quair* and its Middle English antecedents was anticipated by the late nineteenth-century scholar Henry Wood, who wrote an exhaustive account of the verbal parallels between the Scots poem and Chaucerian poetry in English. (The Chaucer canon had not of course been clearly defined at the time.) The most interesting aspect of Wood's essay is that it suggests that the use which James made of Chaucer and others was other than narrowly mechanical. The resemblances between the work of James I and Chaucer, he says, are

less a question of particular passages, than of Chaucer's whole personality, as we see it in his works. The character which shows itself to us in the King's Quair is a similar one, although not so many sided and far less experienced; and everything indicates that the younger poet felt himself powerfully attracted towards the elder, and educated himself under the influence of the latter's works to ways of thought and expression, to which he otherwise never could have attained in such a degree.[10]

What Wood touches on here is the importance of tone, of the quality of the author's presence in his work, as a determinant of meaning. Even in the more rhetorically elevated sections of the *Quair*, the verse moves easily and creates that sense of relaxed and intimate contact between poet and audience which is so pervasive in Chaucer's poetry: in both cases, the effect is created largely through rhythmical variation and modulation between different levels of language. This quality is accompanied, in both cases, by a strong sense of the poet's continued involvement as an 'I' figure in his narrative, even in descriptive passages which seem to bear little relevance to his stated interests and concerns. There are parallels to be drawn between the *Quair* and late Middle English works such as *Pearl* and Gower's *Confessio Amantis* in these respects, but the affinity with Chaucer is more significant because of the presence of verbal parallels and the use of similar stylistic devices. Although James's manner of writing is to a very large extent modelled on Chaucer's practice, there can be no suggestion that the 'I' of the *Quair* could ever be mistaken for Chaucer's authorial voice, in any of its moods. Two passages, one from the beginning of the poem and the other from near the end, illustrate very well both the indebtedness to Chaucer and James's independence of Chaucer in the use of the first person. The narrative of the Scots poem is, from the outset, centred unobtrusively but quite firmly on the experience of one man. The poet tells how, one restless night, he came to a reckoning with himself, by examining the shape of his life,

> all myn auenture
> I gan ourehayle, that langer slepe ne rest
> Ne myght I nat, so were my wittis wrest,
>
> (st. 10, 5-7)

and how reflection was translated into creative activity by the commanding voice of the matins bell – 'Tell on, man, quhat the befell' (st. 11, 7). The earlier reference to the poet's sleeplessness, in stanza 2, shows a knowledge of the technique of self-introduction which Chaucer uses in *The Book of the Duchess*. There, by hinting at an interesting personal history, the poet sharpens the interest of his audience in the narrative to come – we feel that this must have some bearing on the speaker's state of mind. The same kind of effect is created by the passage in the *Quair*, although there is the important difference that James excludes from his self-introduction all of the ambiguity which surrounds Chaucer's account of his sleeplessness. Instead of mystifying allusions to a 'seknesse', the cause of the sleeplessness is dealt with in a comparatively dismissive way:

> Fell me to mynd of mony diuerse thing,
> Off this and that, can I nought say quharefore
> Bot slepe for craft in erth myght I no more.
>
> (st. 2, 2-5)

From the beginning of the poem, James places the narrative of his personal 'auenture' within a framework of wider human experience. One of the ways in which this is done is through the account of the reading which the poet does to alleviate his sleeplessness. The idea of taking up a book, like the motif of sleeplessness, is borrowed from Chaucer – from *The Book of the Duchess* and *The Parlement of Foules*.[11] Like Chaucer, James uses it as part of a *sententia*, the general potentialities of which are explained thus by Geoffroi de Vinsauf in the *Poetria Nova*:

> If the first part of the work aims at even greater splendour ... let a well-known *sententia* incline in no respect to the particular, but rather raise its head higher, to something universal ... Let the *sententia* stand above the given theme, but glance straight at it; let it say nothing outright, but develop its thought therefrom.[12]

The allusion to Boethius, whose virtuous youth 'Was in his age the ground of his delytis' (st. 6, 2) is seen to be particularly appropriate as a counterpoint to the poet's own experience: love, of a kind acceptable to a Christian philosopher, is to be the source of the deliverance from the uncertainties of 'sely ȝouth'. James's use of *De Consolatione* is much more directly related to thematic concerns than is Chaucer's rambling and facetious treatment of Ovid in *The Book of the Duchess*: it has more in common with the account of the *Somnium Scipionis* in *The Parlement of Foules*, which introduces the theme of the relation between individual desire and common profit, amplified in the following section of the poem. The *Quair* differs greatly from both Chaucerian poems, however, in the clear and unequivocal way in which it relates what is read to the career of the narrator. In the *Parlement*, Chaucer is unwilling to commit himself to the extent of admitting that his own professed disquiet, expressed so memorably in the introductory stanzas, is connected either with his choice of reading or with the subsequent 'sweven': in the end, the reader is left to infer for himself the nature of that 'certeyn thing' which the poet was so anxious to learn. By contrast, the author of the *Quair* is concerned to explain precisely why a reading of Boethius brought about not sleep, but a renewed state of intellectual ferment. He ponders the general moral proposition of the unreliability of Fortune:

> For sothe It is, that on hir tolter quhele
> Euery wight cleuerith in his stage,
> And failyng foting oft quhen hir lest rele,

> Sum vp, sum doune; is none estate nor age
> Ensured more, the prynce than the page,
> So vncouthly hir werdes sche deuidith,
> Namly in 30uth that seildin ought prouidith.
>
> (st. 9)

tolter shaky; *werdes* destinies

Having resolved to write a poetic account of his own experience, he returns to this theme of Youth's vulnerability to the assaults of Fortune as a way of beginning his 'buke' (sts. 14–15). The point that his own experience illustrates the general proposition, and hence that he intends his audience to see him as a typical human figure, is made very clearly:

> I mene this by my self as in partye.
> Though nature gave me suffisance in 30uth,
> The rypenesse of resoune lakkit I
> To governe with my will.
>
> (st. 16, 1–4)

James's purposefulness as a narrator is in marked contrast with the *ennui* and uncertainty of the Chaucerian narrator. In the *Quair*, reading is not shown to be conducive to the passive state of dreaming, but rather to the immediate and strenuous business of writing.

The second instance of creative departure from a Chaucerian model of first-person narrative concerns the prayer to Venus on behalf of other lovers, towards the conclusion of the poem. Several commentators have observed the sustained echo of Chaucer's bidding prayer for lovers, in the Proem to Book 1 of *Troilus and Criseyde*, but there has been no appreciation of the critical purpose reflected in James's reworking. It is impossible to know for certain whether the first audience of the *Quair* recognised the delicately witty commentary on Chaucer's point of view, but it is quite possible that they had the same knowledge of Chaucer's great poem of courtly love that Henryson was to assume in his audience half a century later. In the first few stanzas of *Troilus and Criseyde*, the poet establishes with tact and subtlety the nature of his relationship to both subject matter and audience. The key to this relationship, which combines compassion with detachment, is given by the parody of the papal title *servus servorum Dei*:

> For I, *that God of Loves servantz serve*,
> Ne dar to Love, for myn unliklynesse,
> Preyen for speed, al sholde I therfore sterve,
> So fer am I from his help in derknesse.
>
> (1, 15–18)

This implies not only a priestly lack of direct experience but also an authority to make pronouncements on matters of love which is of the same order as the pope's authority to make pronouncements on matters of faith. The poet remains aloof from the joys and sorrows of 'Loves folk', and it is for this reason rather than because of his 'unliklynesse' that he does not pray himself to the 'God of Love'. (The nearest he comes to a commitment to experience is the exclamation during the account of the Trojan lovers' 'hevene blisse' in Book III – 'Why nad I swich oon with my soule ybought . . . ?') The deity in whose service Chaucer writes is addressed variously as 'God', 'God of Love', and 'Love', and this has the effect of suggesting that there may be a direct relationship between secular and Christian love. This suggestion is confirmed at the conclusion of the poem, where it is made clear that human love is divinely ordained. 'Trouthe in love' is a state to be striven for and cherished when found, but the high priest of love can offer the men and women of his audience little hope for enduring and honest sexual relationships.

The point of the reworking of Chaucer's introduction in *The Kingis Quair* is to display secular love from a different perspective. James's attitude to his subject matter implies criticism of Chaucer's posture as narrator. Unlike his predecessor, James addresses the love deity directly:

> Beseching vnto fair Venus abufe
> For all my brethir that bene in this place,
> This is to seyne, that seruandis ar to lufe.
>
> (st. 184, 1–3)

His conception of brotherhood is less equivocal than that of Chaucer's 'I', who will show only the detached solicitude of a 'brother dere'. The narrator of the *Quair* is one who has experienced love himself – in both its joyful and its sorrowful aspects – and this direct experience is opposed to the Chaucerian aloofness. A pontifical authority in the affairs of lovers is inadequate: the actual experience provides a more trustworthy authority. James's use of Chaucer's lines,

> *For so hope I my sowle best avaunce,*
> To prey for hem that Loves servauntz be,
> And write hire wo, and lyve in charite,
>
> (47–9)

is very illuminating:

> And eke I pray for all the hertis dull,
> That lyven here in sleuth and ignorance
> And has no curage at the rose to pull,
> Thair lif to mend, *and thair saulis auance*
> With thair suete lore, and bring thame to gude chance.
>
> (st. 186, 1–5; my italics)

Chaucer is here consigned to the company of those with 'hertis dull'. James wittily suggests that his predecessor, as a mere mortal, claims too much for himself by adopting a papal charity towards lovers, and that the human soul can be better advanced by submitting to the experience of love. Whereas Chaucer can offer only the consolation of other-worldly felicity to those unhappy in love ('So graunte hem soone owt of this world to pace'), the fortunate lover–poet of the *Quair* offers the hope of grace in this world. Not surprisingly, he shares Chaucer's sentiment towards lovers who are 'at ese', using almost the identical words – 'To graunt thame all, lo, gude perseuerance' (cf. *TC*, 'That God hem graunte ay good perseveraunce'). James's prayer for lovers is, like the introduction and the conclusion of Chaucer's poem, a way of showing the applicability of the story to the lives of the audience. The two poems reach the same philosophical position i.e. that human love is a natural and desirable thing, provided that there is a recognition of the transcending power of Christian love. But where Chaucer lays the emphasis of his 'moralitee' upon the great difficulty of winning the 'hevene' of honest sexual love from which the lover may progress to the Christian heaven, James is concerned to show that the search for a worldly felicity similar to his own is well worth making. It is not too much to say that his adaptation of Chaucer's lines effectively redresses the balance of *Troilus and Criseyde*. The *Kingis Quair* demonstrates that not all women are Cressids, and that the fulfilment of an honest desire can be achieved by every lover. James's concern is with the flower of love 'that now from day to day/Flourith ay newe' (st. 193, 6–7), whereas Chaucer's is with the symbolic meaning of the flower's decay.

The same process of adjustment of a Chaucerian perspective underlies his description of the temple of Venus:

> And in a retrete lytill of compas,
> Depeyntit all with sighis wonder sad,
> Nought suich sighis as hertis doith manace
> Bot suich as dooth lufaris to be glad,
> Fond I Venus vpon hir bed.
>
> (st. 96, 1–5)

These lines are modelled equally on the descriptions of Venus's temple in *The Knight's Tale* and *The Parlement of Foules*:

> First in the temple of Venus maystow se
> Wroght on the wal, ful pitous to biholde,
> The broken slepes, and the sikes colde,
> The sacred teeris, and the waymentynge,
> The firy strokes of the desirynge
> That loves servantz in this lyf enduren
>
> (*KnT*, 1918–23)

> Withinne the temple, of sykes hoote as fyr
> I herde a swogh that gan aboute renne,
> Whiche sikes were engendered with desyr,
> That maden every auter for to brenne
> Of newe flaume, and wel espyed I thenne
> That al the cause of sorwes that they drye
> Cam of the bittere goddesse Jelosye.
>
> (*PF*, 246–52)

Here James's lines bear the same kind of relation to their Chaucerian source as do the account of the poet's reading and the prayer for lovers. In each case, the Scots poet's attitude to his subject matter is shown to be more positive, more affirmative, than

Chaucer's tone. Whereas in Chaucer's poetry the kind of physical passion which is represented by the worship of Venus is seen to have an attractiveness which is fraught with peril for the spiritual and indeed the physical wellbeing of the lover, in *The Kingis Quair* the value of such love is unhesitatingly affirmed, at the same time as its sanctions are scrupulously defined.

The rhetorical strategy of the poem consists of the creation of a first-person *exemplum*: the personal 'auenture' is told in such a way as to stress its applicability to the lives of other lovers, and to invite their involvement in the narrative. James invites the participation of his audience through the relaxed and sometimes even conversational movement of his verse, with its frequent questions ('But now, how trow 3e . . .?', 'Quho suld me wite [reproach] to write thar-of, lat se?'), asides, and calls for attention ('But now to purpose of my first entent', 'And quhat I met I will 3ow now deuise'). This quality of the verse no doubt owes something to the real relationship between the poet and his audience, but it also reflects a lesson well learned from Chaucer's style of direct address, which is always directed at stimulating or maintaining interest in what is being said. This affinity with Chaucer is of course reinforced by James's use of the stanza form of *Troilus* and *The Parlement of Foules*. Although James's debt to Chaucer in the matter of intimacy of address is very considerable, it is equally clear that James chose not to follow the Chaucerian manner of self-characterisation. The 'sentence' of the *Quair* is developed largely through the poet's representation of himself as 'I', through the interplay between present and past levels of awareness: the introductory proposition about 'sely 3outh' in its relation to Fortune is amplified from the perspective of one who has been enlightened by grace and experience, and who offers his personal experience as a guide to others. That James intended to set himself forth as a representative figure, everyman as well as an individual, is shown in the explanation which follows the apostrophe to youth in stanza 14 (see p. 40). MacQueen does no injustice to the subtlety and liveliness of the poem when he says that its theme 'may be briefly described as the liberation of Youth by Love and Philosophy from its bondage to Fortune'.[13] The depiction of an

'I' who is shown to be the subject of universal moral laws places the *Quair* in the tradition of first-person narrative to which such English poems as *Pearl*, *Piers Plowman*, *Confessio Amantis*, and *The Temple of Glas* belong. In Book 1 of Gower's poem, comments on the binding and blinding properties of love are followed by the poet's declaration that experience qualifies him to be a teacher and exemplar to 'hem that ben lovers aboute':[14]

>   Fro point to point I wol declare . . .
>   That every man ensample take
>   Of wisdom which him is betake,
>   And that he wot of good aprise
>   To teche it forth, for such emprise
>   Is forto praise; and therfore I
>   Woll wryte and schewe al openly
>   How love and I togedre mette,
>   Wherof the world ensample fette
>   Mai after this, whan I am go,
>   Of thilke unsely jolif wo.
>   (73–88)

The view of love which emerges from the *Confessio Amantis* is of course more sober than the 'sentence' of the *Quair*, but the same kind of rhetorical technique is used in both poems – the poet figures are shown in the process of acquiring wisdom and in neither case is individuating detail permitted to obscure their universal applicability as 'mirrors' for the edification of others. The protagonists of the Scots poem is a more interesting figure in many ways than Gower's 'I' – largely because of the conciseness and fluency of James's style – but it would be more in the spirit of the poem to call him Amans than it would to call him James Stewart. The lover's vision, which places sexual love in the context of the divine universal scheme, expresses his representative nature very clearly. Venus exacts his service to her law by extracting the promise that when he returns to the world he will be a model of courtly virtue (sts. 120-1), and Minerva, the direct descendant of Boethius's Lady Philosophy, speaks to him as a type of 'all ȝe creaturis/Quhich vnder vs beneth haue ȝour duellyng' (st. 145, 1-2). The positivism of the *Quair* – that unequivocal commitment to accepted moral principles, which finds lyrical expression in the reworking and expansion of the Chaucerian prayer for lovers – is inseparable from the manner in which James chooses to present himself as narrator, speaking directly to his audience, and as actor within his recollected experience.

Chaucer's poetry does not conform to the tradition of explicit didacticism and 'everyman' narrators: his experiments with the first person in *Troilus and Criseyde* and the *Tales* as well as in the dream visions, are highly individualistic interpretations of the conventions, giving rise to the detachment and scepticism which have been discussed so closely in modern criticism.[15] The habitual Chaucerian position is such as to induce the reader to draw his own conclusions from the various groupings of 'matere' within each poem: for example, in the *Parlement*, about whether it is possible for any reconciliation between sensual love and the common good to be made. A complementary aspect of Chaucer's withdrawal is his unwillingness, as a character within his own dream visions, to be involved in action or 'experience' of any kind – one thinks immediately of the dreamer's fear outside the gate to the garden of love in the *Parlement*, and his extreme reluctance to be carried aloft to the abode of Fame. It is impossible to classify the dreamer in any of the visions as an embodiment of youth, or the model courtly lover, or even as an everyman figure. Neither is he simply a *naïf* or a buffoon: there are elements of *naïveté* and buffoonery, but the figure who awakens with such serious perplexity in the *Parlement*, and who dissociates himself from those who pay court to Fame, defies simple categorisation. As a narrator, too (i.e. outside the dramatic 'action' of the various dreams), Chaucer again and again prefers irony and ambiguity to clear statements of commitment to any systematic view of experience. In only one place, the celebrated conclusion of *Troilus and Criseyde*, does Chaucer come out with a clear and strong affirmation of principle. But even this passage produces a characteristically Chaucerian effect, that of posing for the audience the problem of how to reconcile the apparent discrepancy between the view of love which pleads 'Repeyreth hom fro worldly vanyte' and that which sees the love of Troilus and Criseyde as 'hevene blisse'.

James's poetic sensibility is much more orthodox than Chaucer's, and the originality of the *Quair* is connected more with the synthesis and arrangement of inherited thought and style than with any infusion of personality. This does not necessarily imply any deficiency of ability or imagination on his part. A. C. Spearing's comment on the difference between the nature of the dream experience in the *Quair*, affirmed as a sign from the heavens, and that of Chaucer's dreams, always ambiguous, may be extended to characterise two different approaches to poetry: '[James's] certainty ... is unChaucerian; but it derives from a clear understanding of the significance of Chaucerian uncertainty.'[16] James takes Chaucer's work as a point of departure in the *Quair*, using some of its themes and techniques to develop an idea of his own, one which is firmly grounded in accepted systems of belief. His relationship to Chaucer in this respect is very similar to that reflected in Henryson's *The Testament of Cresseid* and Douglas's *The Palice of Honour*, poems which in their different ways also illustrate that affirmation and certainty can be expressed without sacrificing either subtlety or invention.

One recent editor of the *Quair* has been quite justifiably criticised for remarking dismissively on its 'naïve authorial charm'.[17] The comment is misguided because it confuses the dreamer and character within an unfolding action – the poet's recollected self – with the poet who interprets his experience from the dual vantage-point of a wise, contented maturity and a close familiarity with literary and philosophical tradition. The 'thought' of the poem – which involves the exploration of a Boethian theme in the context of a courtly love relationship, a combination which may well have been suggested by Chaucer's practice in *The Knight's Tale* and *Troilus and Criseyde* – is presented through the sustained juxtaposition of these two levels of awareness, so that to hear only one authorial voice in the poem is to miss the essentially dramatic tenor of James's 'sentence', in which so much of its originality lies. The poem is presented as the outcome of the poet's review of his life ('and all myn auenture/I gan ourehayle'), and its action creates very effectively the illusion that he is reliving his experience in imagination. The distance between wise maturity and 'sely

30uth' is exemplified dramatically in the two attitudes to Fortune expressed within twenty lines. In the present, the speaker understands the intransigence of worldly affairs made manifest in his capture so long ago – 'Fortune it schupe [devised] non othir wayis to be' (st. 24, 7): at the time, though, he was totally ignorant of Fortune's nature:

> Quhat schall I seyne, quhat resoune may I fynd
> That fortune suld do so?
>
> (st. 27, 4–5)

Imprisonment provides the context for the complaint, but not its real cause, which is that he fails to comprehend Fortune's subordination to God, 'of the whiche lord it is a sovereyn fredom to ben governed by the brydel of hym and obeye to his justice' (Chaucer's *Boece*, Book I, Prosa 5, 23–5). An essential part of the lesson he has to learn about understanding his fortune concerns the proper use of free will. His position is analogous to that of the Boethian prisoner, to whom Philosophy explains 'For it is set in your hand (as who seith, it lyth in your power) what fortune yow is levest (that is to seyn, good or yvel).' The prisoner sets himself on the road to enlightenment when he assents to the power of love. The passage in which this is recounted illustrates an interesting fusion of the poet's present and past levels of awareness:

> And though I stude abaisit tho alyte,
> No wonder was, for quhy my wittis all
> Were so ouercome with plesance and delyte,
> Onely throu latting of myn eyen fall,
> That sudaynly my hert become hir thrall
> For euer of free wyll.
>
> (st. 41, 1–6)

The prominence given to free will in this otherwise conventional enough 'power of the eyes' scene is a remarkable departure from the Chaucerian treatment of the same theme.[18] In *The Knight's Tale*, which affords several parallels with the *Quair*, the prisoner–lovers have no power to resist: their world is heavily deterministic – 'We faren as he that dronke is as a mous.' Although the *Canticus Troili* contains a pledge to serve the God of Love (Book I, 422–3), the context makes it very clear that Troilus has very little choice in the matter of falling in love. Clearly, James's adaptation of Boethian thought for the purposes of a love-poem is more optimistic in temper than Chaucer's.

James uses various stylistic devices, learnt from English poetry, as a way of 'characterising' his youthful self and thereby suggesting the distance between youth and maturity. For example, in that part of the action which precedes the vision, the prisoner–lover's despair and lack of knowledge are conveyed through the use of short interrogative and exclamatory periods. The questioning of fortune is followed by an anxious meditation on the nature of love:

> Quhat luf is this that makis birdis dote?
> Quhat may this be, how cummyth it of ought?
> Quhat nedith it to be so dere ybought?
>
> (st. 36, 3–5)

A similar series of urgent questions marks his response to the sight of the lady in the garden (sts. 42–3), and to the nightingale who apparently refuses to sing (sts. 57–8). The sequence culminates in an impassioned questioning of the very value of life,

> Than said I thus, 'Quhareto lyve I langer,
> Wofullest wicht and subiect vnto peyne?
> Of peyne, no! God wote, ʒa, for thay no stranger
> May wirken ony wight, I dare wele seyne!
> How may this be, that deth and lyf, bothe tueyne,
> Sall bothe atonis in a creature
> Togidder duell, and turment thus nature?'
>
> (st. 68)

wirken work upon

The double sorrow of the youthful prisoner is evoked with some immediacy and realism, but at the same time the figure has an allegorical function. He is a member of that large fraternity of courtly lovers in medieval literature, and as such his characteristics – single-minded devotion to the lady, a sense of isolation, readiness to despair – are similar to those of the hero of the *Rose*, Gower's Amans, Chaucer's Troilus and the Man in Black, and the unfortunate lovers of Lydgate's *The Temple of Glas*. Even the combination of physical imprisonment and subjection to love has a literary precedent in *The Knight's Tale*. In each poem there is a young prisoner who sees in May from his place of incarceration a young woman walking in an adjoining garden. So beautiful is she that the prisoner mistakes her for a goddess. Palamon exclaims 'I noot wher she be wooman or goddesse,/But Venus it is soothly, as I gesse' (1101–2): James's 'I' asks,

> A, suete, ar ȝe a warldly creature,
> Or hevinly thing in liknesse of nature?
>
> Or ar ȝe god Cupidis owin princesse,
> And cummyn are to louse me out of band?
> (st. 42, 6–7; st. 43, 1–2)

Both poems introduce the paradox that falling in love appears to worsen the plight of the prisoner: Palamon laments that his torment has been doubled, while the prisoner in the Scots poem complains that life will have no further point if Venus does not intervene (st. 69).

The first encounter of James I with Joan Beaufort almost certainly did not take place in the extravagantly literary circumstances outlined in the *Quair*. Reality has been bypassed to make the experience intelligible to the poet's audience, and to enable them to make a ready identification, on the basis of their familiarity with other courtly poems, with the lover–prisoner in the poem. James's use of literary convention to create a generalised portrait of himself is illustrated not only by his use of *The Knight's Tale*, but also by his reworking of a passage in the fifteenth-century English poem *The Flower of Courtesy*, ascribed by John Stow to Lydgate.[19] Here the poet represents himself as the suffering lover of literary convention, drawing a contrast between his own painful introspection on St Valentine's day and the spontaneous joy of the birds,

> alas! what may this be,
> That every foul hath his libertee
> Frely to chesen after his desyre
> Everich his make thus, fro yeer to yere?
> (53–6)

The Kingis Quair and English poetry

> But man aloon, alas! the harde stounde!
> Ful cruelly, by kyndes ordinaunce,
> Constrayned is, and by statut bounde,
> And debarred from alle such plesaunce.
> What meneth this? What is this purveyaunce
> Of god above, agayn al right of kynde,
> Withoute cause, so narewe man to bynde?
>
> (64–70)

He goes on to lament the 'fellness' of Fortune. The subject matter is conventional enough, but verbal and stylistic parallels suggest that James used this complaint as a model for his own:

> Quhat haue I gilt to faille
> My fredome in this warld and my plesance,
> Sen euery wight has thereof suffisance
> That I behold, and I, a creature,
> Put from all this? Hard is myn auenture!
>
> The bird, the beste, the fisch eke in the see,
> They lyve in fredome, euerich in his kynd,
> And I, a man, and lakkith libertee!
> Quhat schall I seyne, quhat resoune may I fynd
> That fortune suld do so?
>
> (st. 26, 3–7; st. 27, 1–5)

The lament in the *Quair* has a greater dramatic impact than its model, partly because it is more concise, partly because of its context in a developing human drama. (*The Flower of Courtesy* is a rather static dramatic monologue.) The solitary outpourings of the young man in the *Quair* are carefully organised. The passage adapted from the *Flower* refers specifically to his literal loss of liberty through imprisonment: it is followed by musings about the relationship between liberty and love (sts. 37–8), which conclude with the resolution that he would be prepared to serve that Lord who has the power 'To bynd and lous' (st. 39, 3). After seeing the lady and submitting willingly to Love, he laments because his imprisonment now seems to be an obstacle to a specific kind of freedom, the freedom to pursue his love-suit (sts. 68–70).

The tendency towards rhetorical excess in direct speech suggests a gently ironic indulgence on the part of the poet. The audience is invited to smile at the youthful lover's envy of his lady's 'lytill hound',

> Than wold I say, and sighe therewith alyte,
> 'A, wele were him, that now were in thy plyte!'
>
> (st. 53, 6–7)

and at the immediate reversion to the mode of agitated questioning when he awakes 'Fulfilld of thoght',

> 'A! merci, lord, quhat will 3e do with me?
> Quhat lyf is this? Quhare hath my spirit be?
> Is this of my forethought impressioune,
> Or is it from the hevin a visioune?'
>
> (st. 175, 4–7)

This contains an echo of *The Hous of Fame*, where the dreamer exclaims in astonishment, 'O Crist! . . . that art in blysse,/Fro fantome and illusion/Me save!' (492–4). The irony should not, however, be overemphasised. Norton-Smith not only confuses poet and character in his comment on the lover's plea to the nightingale (sts. 54–9), but also fails to appreciate the allusion which gives the episode its point: 'James's unique attractiveness may be summed up in his indulgent concern about the nightingale's failure to sing and in his serious and irrelevant search for the reason.'[20] The key is contained in the lover's challenge to the nightingale,

> Quhat, wostow than sum bird may cum and stryve
> In song with the, the maistry to purchace?
> Suld thow then cesse? It were gret schame, allace.
>
> (st. 59, 3–5)

The 'sum bird', unidentified in the *Quair*, is the cuckoo, traditional enemy of the nightingale, as one of Venus's pairs of contraries makes clear (st. 110, 3). There may be an allusion here to an English Chaucerian poem, Clanvowe's *The Cuckoo and the Nightingale* (*The Boke of Cupide*).[21] The narrator in this work tells how, among lovers,

> hit was a comvne tale
> That it wer good to her the nyghtyngale
> Rather than the leude cukkoo synge.
>
> (48–50)

When he (a lover himself) hears the song of the cuckoo, he calls out to the nightingale, in much the same way that the prisoner in the *Quair* does,

> 'A! good nyghtyngale,' quod I then,
> 'A lytell hast thou be to longe hen,
> For her hath be the lewede cukkow,
> And songen songes rather then hast thou.'
>
> (101-4)

The song of the cuckoo, as the ensuing bird dialogue makes clear, is a song in condemnation of love. The narrator's anxious hope that the nightingale should have 'maistry', and his close affinity with her, are strongly reminiscent of the situation in the *Quair*. If the cuckoo were to come to sing first, it is highly unlikely that the love-suit could prosper. As well as Clanvowe's destructive bird, it is worth recalling Chaucer's cuckoo, who is totally selfish and takes the view that others may be 'soleyn al here lyve' (*PF*, 605-7). In the *Quair* the lover's plight is so desperate because the song of the bird is the only means by which he can communicate with the lady in the garden.[22]

The exclamatory tenor of the prisoner–lover's rhetoric is not carried to such an extreme that he is made to appear ridiculous. At only one point during the poem does the young man become a figure of fun, in the account of the exchange between him and the goddess Fortune, which is inspired by a scene in *The Parlement of Foules*. The dreamer's guide Africanus is clearly amused by his pupil's fear and inability to take any positive course of action, and he provides some humorous reassurance,

> It stondeth written in thy face,
> Thyn errour, though thow telle it not to me;
> But dred the not to come into this place,
> For this writyng nys nothyng ment bi the,
> Ne by non, but he Loves servaunt be:
> For thow of love hast lost thy tast, I gesse,
> As sek man hath of swete and bytternesse.
>
> But natheles, although that thow be dul,
> Yit that thow canst not do, yit mayst thow se.
>
> (155-63)

James's appreciation of Chaucer's self-depreciation may be seen in the goddess Fortune's wry amusement at her supplicant's earnestness. After making a rather obvious pun from the chess metaphor with which he ends his plea,[23] she suggests that he might just as well have kept silent,

> 'Off mate?' quod sche. 'O verray sely wreche!
> I se wele by thy dedely colour pale,
> Thou art to feble of thy self to streche,
> Vpon my quhele to clymbe or to hale
> Withoutin help, for thou has fundin stale
> This mony day withoutin warldis wele,
> And wantis now thy veray hertis hele.'
>
> (st. 169)

fundin stale found [a] prison (also the sense of 'stalemate')

In both passages, the idea of *ennui* caused by deprivation of the 'taste' of love is treated humorously. The parallel with the *Parlement* is continued in the comically undignified treatment meted out to the dreamers by their respective guides. Chaucer is 'shof in at the gates wide' by Africanus (154), while Fortune's pupil receives equally undignified but more painful treatment,

> 'Fare wele,' quod sche, and by the ere me toke
> So earnestly that therewithall I woke.
>
> (st. 172, 6–7)

Elsewhere James does not attempt this kind of broad humour, but the overtly Chaucerian treatment of the narrator does nothing to detract from the seriousness of the quest or from the tonal unity of the poem. One of the most pleasing aspects of this unity is the ease with which the poem's two speaking voices merge. Just as the mature narrator is capable of sympathetic involvement with his youthful self, the young lover survives in the man who reads Boethius and moralises about the ignorance of Youth. Some of his exclamations about past experience suggest that he is imaginatively reliving it as he writes – comments such as 'O happy exercise' (st. 29, 5), 'Now, gif there was gud partye, god it wote!' (st. 48, 7), and the series of inset poetic tributes after stanza 189 leave no doubt that he has retained the enthusiasm of youth. One of James's principal achievements is the creation of a persona which convincingly illustrates the distance between maturity and youth, but at the same time has a consistency and continuity which give a sense of realistic depth to the portrait.

There can be little doubt that many of the details of the narrative were drawn from the poet's personal experience – for example, the departure from his country as a child, the capture at sea, the eighteen years' imprisonment, the company of his own people, and the love-suit associated with his liberation. It is important to recognise these facts for what they are, but it is even more important to understand the manner in which autobiographical truth is selected and formalised to enrich the texture of a poem which sets out to demonstrate the universal applicability of an individual 'auenture'. This process is illustrated by the treatment of the sea voyage and the capture on 'the wawis weltering to and fro'. The literal voyage is mentioned only after the stanzas in which maritime imagery is used in the twin contexts of the voyage of life and the creative process (sts. 15–18): the personal experience is thus fixed in the perspective of experience in a wider sense. The Romantic notion of the intimate and exclusively personal autobiography is entirely foreign to James's manner of writing, which is firmly in the tradition of autobiography illustrated by poems such as *Pearl, Piers Plowman* and *Confessio Amantis*. In all of these poems autobiographical detail – the age of the child in *Pearl*, the poet's name and details of his way of life in *Piers Plowman* (C, Passus VI) and the *Confessio* (Book VIII) – is apparently provided to lend a dimension of verisimilitude, an appeal to the audience's personal knowledge of the poet in order to verify the truth of his 'sentence'. It is impossible for the literary historian to decide that the personal experience of any later medieval poet provided the inspiration for his work. Even in works such as *Pearl* and the *Quair*, where this appears to be the case, it is clear that the personal element has been heightened and formalised to a large extent, with the aid of literary tradition, in order to make the experience recounted accessible to a general audience. Recent criticism has been reluctant to see the 'I' of the *Quair* in this context of autobiography in late Middle English dream-vision poetry. Most commentators have been swayed by the rhetoric of C. S. Lewis, who sees in the *Quair* 'the poetry of marriage emerging from the poetry of adultery': 'In our own language, the author, who had long desired to write but spent much ink and paper "to lyte effect", had suddenly perceived that his own story, even as it stood in real life, might pass without disguise into poetry.'[24] This is extraordinary, first because of the poet's deliberate use of poetic convention in his self-representation, secondly because the poem says nothing directly about marriage and very little about wooing. M. P. McDiarmid accepts Lewis's view, however, taking other commentators to task for what he regards as their excessive emphasis on the conventional bases of the poem's thought. The complaint that what is missing from these accounts is 'the author and subject of the *Quair*, James Stewart',[25] prompts a lengthy Skeatian paraphrase of the narrative, one which insists on the autobiographical significance of details which the poet has left carefully general. Thus Venus's injunction to the dreamer (st. 123) means 'Obey my law and when you have left the world you and your wife will share my heaven perpetually', the gilly-flower means the 'queen's flower', and 'lufis 3ok' (st. 193, 2) means marriage specifically.[26] The poet probably did have marriage in mind when he wrote, but there is a deliberate ambiguity in his choice of language. Thus the phrase 'lufis 3ok' includes not only marriage, but also any virtuous bond which exists before or apart from marriage. The allusion to 'souirane' (st. 181, 7) is almost certainly directed at the queen herself but at the same time it carries unmistakable overtones of the lady's place in the courtly love relationship. James's approach here is very like Chaucer's in *The Book of the Duchess*, where the bereaved John of Gaunt is represented as a young man who possesses all the characteristics of the model courtly lover. No explicit reference is made to marriage, the relationship between the bereaved knight and his lady being evoked in terms of an 'atempre' form of courtly love. Chaucer's method may have been partly motivated by tactful respect for a patron's sorrow, but it does have the effect of generalising the situation described so that an inclusive statement about the nature of suffering and loss emerges from the dream dialogue. James, like Chaucer, places a barrier between himself and his audience in the treatment of biography, in order to induce them to go beyond their knowledge of his personal career and domestic felicity, to recognise him as a convincing exemplar of familiar aspirations and states of mind.

The creation of an authorial portrait in which the individual is successfully amalgamated with the typical is not the only means used by the author of the *Quair* to generalise the meaning of the 'auenture'. There are several passages, mainly descriptive in nature, which draw upon earlier English poetry to develop the theme of Fortune's operations as they apply to lovers. The most extended of these is the account of Venus's 'glade empire' (sts. 77–93), which has as its source a long *descriptio* in Lydgate's *The Temple of Glas*.[27] In this work, which draws heavily upon Chaucer, the poet represents himself as an unhappy and therefore sleepless lover, who is transported in a dream to the Temple of Venus, where he beholds first various groups of unhappy lovers making their plaints, and then the resolution of a particular case of unfortunate love, involving a beautiful lady and an ideally courteous knight. The poem is little more than a sequence of set-pieces, and the first-person framework is merely a formal unifying device, somehow extraneous to the matter of the poem. In the Epilogue Lydgate does attempt to recall the opening situation and to relate himself to the matter of his dream. The attempt does not succeed, not only because of the heavily stereotyped characterisation of the poet as lover, but also because there is no sense within the body of the narrative of the narrator's presence as dreamer and beholder. James succeeds where Lydgate fails, in making the substance of the vision both encyclopaedic and relevant to the situation of the dreamer. Lydgate tries to make his description say too much: his list of complaints about misfortune in love appears calculated to cover *any* eventuality, and the effectiveness of two fairly specific kinds of grievance – being forced into unwanted marriages and into the religious life – is dissipated by continuation of the catalogue of more general complaints. As elsewhere in Lydgate's poetry, the use of the catalogue as a form of *amplificatio* involves monotony and a progressive deterioration of meaning. His living company of 'mani a thousand of louers' is introduced by an equally verbose list of famous lovers of history and legend, whose names are painted on the wall of the temple. With a shrewd glance at the prolixity of his model, James declines to name any of his 'mony a mylioune':

> Off quhois chancis made is mencioune
> In diuerse bukis, quho thame list to se,
> And therefore here thaire namys lat I be.
>
> (st. 78, 5–7)

The rambling account in *The Temple of Glas* of the various kinds of complainants is carefully reduced and structured in the *Quair*. Where Lydgate has a catalogue of multiple causes for complaint against Venus, James makes a twofold division of 'loves folk': on the one side of a 'trevesse' or curtain there are those who have won a measure of immortality through their true service to love. These are divided into three 'stages': on the highest one are the old people who have served Venus truly all their lives, then come the young folk who show true 'curage', and on the lowest stage are those lovers who are clerics visited by Repentance. On the other side of the division are those who have not had the opportunity to love, and here James introduces Lydgate's two most specific groups of unfortunates. In the *Quair* the description of the inhabitants of the temple is carefully ordered: the architectural device of the 'trevesse' contributes to this effect, and the explanation by the mysterious voice of what the various groups represent (sts. 83–92) follows the order in which he beholds them. The structural technique of the episode seems to be modelled on Chaucer's method in Book III of *The Hous of Fame*, where those who have won fame are situated on pillars of different kinds, while the supplicants are separated from them and divided into several groups. Unlike Lydgate, James makes his persona an actor as well as a beholder in the temple of Venus: the voice addresses him directly. The episode is made relevant to the situation of the 'I' in two ways: first, the point that a desire to serve Venus is not always accompanied by good fortune is made (recalling the earlier references to Fortune), and beyond this, there is the clear suggestion that the poet is to be regarded as one who will occupy a position on the highest 'stage' of love, with the 'agit folk' who have given true and lifelong service. (The scene is recalled later, when Venus promises him that if he and his lady are faithful to her, they will live with her forever more 'as goddis in this place'.) The strong retrospective effect of the poem – Maturity reviewing Youth – implies that the poet is no longer in his first youth when he addresses his audience, and hence there is an implied affinity between the narrator and those who occupy the privileged place of the highest stage,

>   agit folk with hedis hore and olde,
>   ȝone were the folk that neuer change wold
>   In lufe, bot trewly seruit him alway,
>
>   (st. 83, 4–6)

which is absent in the original of the description. Also relevant to the situation of the poet is the fact that poets, specifically those who extol the virtue 'of lufe in thaire suete layes', are included in this honoured company of the first stage. This is another of James's particularising additions to the list in *The Temple of Glas*.

A later passage of amplifying description – the account of the 'lusty plane' which is the dominion of Fortune (sts. 152–7) – is a skilful and inventive adaptation of two Chaucerian passages which also have the quality of *paysage moralisé*. The first of these is the description of the well-ordered dream garden in *The Book of the Duchess* (416–20; 427–33); the second, the account of the garden in which Venus and Nature dwell in *The Parlement of Foules*. Like Chaucer, James employs the catalogue form to emphasise the sense of ordered variety and plenitude in the scene. The difference is, as MacQueen points out, that whereas Chaucer describes the realm of Nature, James associates Nature with Fortune. In *The Book of the Duchess*, the suffering knight turns his back on the world of ordered Nature to bewail the cruelty of Fortune in depriving him of his lady. There is a similar dualism in the *Parlement*, one which centres on the natures of the two goddesses in the dream garden: 'the gift of Nature appears to be fruitful and happy, as opposed to unsuccessful and miserable, love, which last is controlled by Venus'.[28] In the *Quair* there is a striking reconciliation of Fortune, Nature and Venus. Fortune fulfils the role of Chaucer's beneficent goddess Nature, at the centre of an ordered creation, as the agent of the divine Reason. The poet is guided into the land of Fortune – i.e. the world – after he has been instructed on the related themes of endurance in love, self-knowledge, and an understanding of Fortune, by Venus and Minerva. The descent 'doune to ground ageyne' is the logical outcome of the advice which is given by the two goddesses, who act in concert with Fortune, and the descriptive passage thus becomes a way of articulating the poet's philosophy. James draws on the Chaucerian passages to imply a contrast in context between them and his own description. Chaucer's poems explore discord and division, and few reconciliations are suggested. In the *Quair*, on the other hand, the poet chooses to express an optimistic view of love and destiny. In his captivity (which is both literal and metaphorical), the poet laments his isolation from the free harmony of 'The bird, the beste, the fisch eke in the see', and this return to the world is presented in terms of an imminent reunion, through the intercession of Fortune, with the rest of ordered creation. The poet's concern for structural coherence and for relevant detail are illustrated by the boundaries of the dream journey: the dream has begun, in misery, when the poet is confined within a tower, and it comes to an end with the promise of happiness when he visits another 'round place and a wallit'.

The most recent criticism of the *Quair* makes plausible claims for the existence of a structural scheme based on numerological principles.[29] Although we may well have undervalued James's ingenuity, it is difficult to believe that the complicated system of number symbolism was accessible to more than a few members of the contemporary court audience. I suspect that then, as now, the most satisfying aspect of the poem's structure was its demonstration, through the continuing emphasis upon the poet's experience, of the interdependence of present and past. The lyrical stanzas towards the close of the poem, in which thanks are offered to the gods, the nightingale, the castle wall and the lady (sts. 187–93), are both a celebration of divine providence and an answer to the perturbation about Fortune's role in the shaping of life, expressed at the beginning of the poem. The resolution of the questions about youth's susceptibility and about the shape of the individual life through time is accomplished by the act of writing, for which an intelligent use of memory is shown to be essential. A. C. Spearing observes that there is an element of confusion in the Prologue to the *Quair*, implying that this confusion marks the presentation of the 'I' throughout the poem. 'The speaker of the prologue is divided between two roles, being experienced as a lover but immature as a poet . . . James is by no means merely imitating earlier dream-poets, but he is not sufficiently the master of the conventions of dream-poetry to re-shape them radically.'[30] The comment reflects an inadequate appreciation of a structural technique which is essentially dramatic in nature. The distrust, expressed in the Prologue, of the book's source of inspiration – the 'fantasye' of the speaking bell – and the appeal for 'wynd' to fill out poetic sails, are variations of the modesty-*topos*, ways of attracting the involvement of the audience in what is to follow. As well as articulating its philosophical 'sentence', the poem advances the charming fiction of a connection between personal fulfilment through love and the ability to write good poetry. Immediately after the account of the dove who arrives upon his awakening from the dream with her tangible promise of reward comes the question, 'Quhat nedis me aponn so littil evyn/To writt all this?' (st. 182, 2–3). The poet's answer is disarmingly simple:

> Quho that from hell war croppin onys in hevin
> Wald efter o thank for joy mak sex or sevin!
> And euery wicht his awin suete or sore
> Hes maist in mynde, I can say ȝou no more.
>
> (st. 182, 4–7)

war croppin onys had crept [but] once

In the concluding address to the poem itself, the poet's lady, in a line which recalls the maritime imagery of the introductory remarks on literary creation, is described as the 'gyd and stere' of his poetic endeavours. The artistic fiction embodied here is the same as that contained in Chaucer's address to lovers in the Prologue to *The Legend of Good Women*, where he claims that those who have experience of love reap the field of poetry ('makyng') before the arrival of the poet who does not have the benefit of their 'sentement' (F, 68–72). The device is thoroughly conventional, but like so many of the other conventional features of the *Quair*, it is used in a fresh and imaginative way. It is this aspect of James's traditionalism, his fascination with the possibilities of a literary inheritance of which the elements can be unified and revitalised through the medium of a speaking voice, which shows, even more convincingly than any verbal borrowings, the existence of a talent comparable with Chaucer's own. He is a much more conservative poet, who attempts none of Chaucer's startling juxtapositions of matter, technique and tone, but the ease and grace with which he applies his knowledge of literature to the expression of personal experience makes James better qualified than any of his English contemporaries to receive the kind of praise which William Webbe gives to Chaucer:

who could with more delight prescribe such wholsome counsaile and sage aduise, where he seemeth onelie to respect the profitte of his lessons and instructions? . . . so that this is the very grounde of right poetrie, to give profitable counsaile, yet so as it must be mingled with delight.[31]

3

Henryson and English poetry

(i) *The Testament of Cresseid* and *Troilus and Criseyde*

'Thus endeth the fyfth and laste booke of Troylus: and here foloweth the pyteful and dolorous testament of fayre Creseyde' – so William Thynne introduced *The Testament of Cresseid* to English readers in 1532. Whether Thynne, and subsequent generations of Chaucer editors, believed (or intended their public to believe) that the *Testament* was the work of Chaucer cannot be known, but sixteenth- and seventeenth-century readers could have been excused for accepting the authorship implied by the placing of the poem between *Troilus and Criseyde* and *The Legend of Good Women*. The Thynne text of the *Testament* has, as one might expect, been considerably anglicised, but the connections between the poem and *Troilus and Criseyde* go far beyond linguistic similarities. Henryson's treatment of the Trojan love-story is profoundly original, but some of its most distinctive effects cannot be properly appreciated unless the reader has the same close knowledge of *Troilus and Criseyde* which the poet himself possessed. The *Testament* does not illustrate the extent of verbal borrowing from Chaucer which we find in *The Kingis Quair*, but the poems are alike in that they explore and develop Chaucerian themes, using recognisably Chaucerian stylistic devices. The meaning of the *Testament* is dependent on that of *Troilus and Criseyde* – intentionally so, and in this respect the poem is not self-contained in the way that *The Kingis Quair* is. In marked contrast to this critical and allusive kind of Scots Chaucerianism is Henryson's method in his *Morall Fabillis*, where he draws upon his reading of a wide variety of 'source' material, written in Latin, French and English.

So much at ease with Chaucer's poetry is Henryson that he dares to cast doubt upon the English poet's handling of Boccaccio's story as a way of introducing his own: the ironic question 'Quha wait gif all that Chauceir wrait was trew?' is a landmark among his English contemporaries' fulsome and repetitive expressions of their inferiority to the master of poets. Henryson provides a brief résumé of part of Chaucer's final book – Criseyde's reception by Diomede, Troilus's hope which rapidly gives way to despair and grief (43–56) – relying on his audience to know the preceding action. More important perhaps, he relies on their ability to recognise a major departure from Chaucer's narrative. Troilus's discovery of Criseyde's infidelity, his death and ascent to the heavens are ignored, and Henryson turns, through the device of the 'uther quair', to the subject of Criseyde's life among the Greeks, taking up from where Chaucer had left off. Troilus, in Chaucer's poem, is unquestionably the dominant figure: the 'double sorwe' about which the poem is structured centres upon his experience of love, and most of Book v is devoted to an account of his torment. Troilus's idealism, his 'worthiness', is emphasised throughout, and he is clearly much less culpable than Criseyde. There is a development from scornful disregard of Love to a willing subjection to its promptings, attainment of its supreme felicity giving way to an anguish which culminates in the knowledge of his beloved's perfidy: after death, this bitter knowledge is replaced by recognition of what natural love means *sub specie aeternitatis*. From the point of view of moral development, Criseyde is a much more static figure, since from beginning to end her behaviour is regulated to a considerable extent by her need for protection and security. Henryson's point of departure is to show his heroine undergoing change, coming to recognise, as Chaucer's hero does so theatrically, the meaning and the errors of the past. Twice in the *Testament* the epithet 'worthie' is used, as it is in *Troilus and Criseyde*, of Troilus. Henryson's repetition of the adjective in the lines,

> I tuik ane quair, and left all uther sport,
> Writtin be *worthie* Chaucer glorious,
> Of fair Creisseid, and *worthie* Troylus,[1]

denotes not clumsiness, but a critical perception of how closely Chaucer's point of view is identified with that of his hero in Books IV and V. With an artless 'quha will luik' (which points to familiarity with *Troilus and Criseyde* among the contemporary audience),² the Scots poet turns to the 'double sorwe' of the lady – the 'wofull end of this lustie Creisseid,/And quhat distres scho thoillit [endured] and quhat deid' (69–70). This last line is to be read, I believe, with a strong accent on the personal pronoun – 'And quhat distres *scho* thoillit . . .' The poem presents the story of Cresseid as part of an elaborately articulated *argumentum*, illustrating the destructive and painful consequences which ensue from untruth in love. Its greatness comes from the combination of elaborate artistry, intellectual control and 'greit humanitie' with which the moral theme is presented.

Henryson's concluding stanza leaves no doubt of his didactic purpose, even though the 'moralitie' is not cast formally as a *moralitas* as it is in the *Fabillis* and *Orpheus and Eurydice*:

> Now, worthie wemen, in this ballet schort,
> Maid for your worschip and instructioun,
> Of cheritie, I monische and exhort:
> Ming not your lufe with fals deceptioun.
> Beir in your mynd this schort conclusioun
> Of fair Cresseid – as I have said befoir;
> Sen scho is deid, I speik of hir no moir.

This complements the moving speech in which Cresseid proclaims her function as an example and a warning to others,

> Lovers be war and tak gude heid about
> Quhome that ye lufe, for quhome ye suffer paine:
> I lat yow wit thair is richt few thairout
> Quhome ye may traist to have trew lufe agane (561–4)

> Becaus I knaw the greit unstabilnes,
> Brukkill as glas, into myself, I say,
> Traisting in uther als greit unfaithfulnes –
> Als unconstant and als untrew of fay –
> Thocht sum be trew, I wait richt few ar thay:
> Quha findis treuth lat him his lady ruse!
> Nane but myself as now I will accuse. (568–74)

ruse praise

With new self-knowledge, Cresseid generalises from her own experience ('into myself, I say'), stating that many other women are as unfaithful as she has been. It is important to recognise the thematic continuity between the *Testament* and *Troilus and Criseyde*, since it reflects an affinity of temper and moral outlook between the two poets. In Denton Fox's view, Henryson follows Chaucer inasmuch as his poem, like Chaucer's, emphasises 'the vanity of sexual love'.[3] Sexual love in Henryson's poem is of course shown to be mutable, simply because mutability is a condition of human life: the imagery of the seasons and of natural growth expresses this idea quite clearly.[4] But if we read the poem as an outright condemnation of love, we undervalue the meaning of the passages quoted above. The distinction between 'trew' and 'fals' in love is heavily emphasised at the end of the poem, and Cresseid dies torn by the memory of her abuse of Troilus's 'trew lufe'. The question of justice, of truth and falsehood in love, is at the core of the poem's meaning. The narrator introduces the notion of Cresseid's 'gilt' (90) in a context which makes the fact of her untruth palpably obvious, and her behaviour at her father's house, hiding herself away so that the facts will not be 'demed' by the people, and hysterically cursing the gods, suggests at least that she has become repulsive to herself. In her blasphemy Cresseid attributes the blame ('wyte') for her wretchedness to the gods of love, and it is for what this act signifies – a refusal to recognise that she is bound to accept the constraints imposed by 'devyne sapience' on 'all things generabill' – that she is found guilty and sentenced by the parliament-court. The legal terminology in which this, the longest episode in the poem, abounds is echoed in Cresseid's bitterly poignant self-reproach, uttered when she is brought to recognise the difference between Troilus's conduct as a lover and her own. 'Nane but myself as now I will accuse.' The poem presents the view that deception in love, because it is essentially self-deception, leads to pain and self-destruction. Truth in love is comparatively rare ('thair is richt few thairout/Quhome ye may traist to have trew lufe agane'), and for this very reason it is to be cherished and preserved when found.

To what extent, then, is Henryson echoing or developing a

thematic concern of *Troilus and Criseyde*? In this connection it is helpful to recall what Chaucer has to say about the meaning of the poem in the Prologue to *The Legend of Good Women*, where he pleads in defence against the charge of heresy levelled at him by the God of Love:

> Ne a trewe lover oght me not to blame,
> Thogh that I speke a fals lovere som shame.
> They oghte rather with me for to holde,
> For that I of Creseyde wroot or tolde,
> Or of the Rose; what so myn auctour mente,
> Algate, God woot, yt was myn entente
> To forthren trouthe in love and yt cheryce,
> And to ben war fro falsnesse and fro vice,
> By swich ensample; this was my menynge.
> (F, 466–74)

Troilus and Criseyde is a complex and ambiguous poem, and one of its most perceptive critics has cautioned that 'The thematic material ... – the conception of love, the moral and philosophical content – is woven through, and is not detachable as a coherent, separate "message".'[5] Admittedly, Chaucer's presentation of sexual love amplifies the complexity of the subject through reference to divergent systems of thought, but there is no reason to believe that the poet is not being serious when he says, as a character in a later poem, that his intent was 'To forthren trouthe in love and yt cheryce'. Henryson's earnest address to 'worthie wemen' seems to have been modelled on Chaucer's plea that 'every gentill womman' should understand that Criseyde's untruth is not universal (v, 1772–8). Chaucer attempts to extend the applicability of the message by implying that not all men are as true as Troilus: 'N'y sey nat this al oonly for thise men,/But moost for wommen that bitraised be/Thorugh false folk' (v, 1779–85). The address to both sexes is implied also in the *Testament*: Cresseid speaks to 'lovers' rather than simply to men when she advises caution in the choice of a partner. The only difference is in the comparative awkwardness of Chaucer's transition from addressing one sex to addressing the other.

Troilus and Criseyde does not present an ascetic view of life, one which encourages the avoidance of sexual love. Henryson, more perceptive than some of his critics, recognises that Chaucer's 'menynge' is rather to uphold honesty, and this moral emphasis is sustained in the alternative ending of *Troilus and Criseyde* which he offers. The *Testament*, like the *Troilus*, does not confuse transience with illusion: love, like life itself, cannot endure forever, but it is not to be shunned for this reason. Cresseid's blasphemy reflects her mistaken belief that her beauty, her ability to love and her capacity for attraction, are ordained to flower forever – 'Ye gave anis [once] ane devine responsaill/That I suld be the flour of luif in Troy', she complains to Cupid and Venus (127–8), apparently unaware of the irony in her reference to Troy. Her conception of love is illusory, because self-delusive, and too late she recognises her fault in abusing the true love of Troilus. What is condemned is not the sexual love itself, but the deception made manifest by Cresseid's 'leving unclene and lecherous'. In Chaucer's narrative, both lovers are deceived in their belief that sexual love is life's dominant controlling force: both elevate emotional experience to a position inadmissible in either Christian or Platonic-Stoic philosophy. It is important, if we are to understand *Troilus and Criseyde* and Henryson's appreciation of it, to recognise that what is condemned at the end of Chaucer's poem is not sexual love itself but a complete and single-minded devotion to it – 'The blynde lust, the which that may nat laste' (v, 1824). The value of love is expressed in the very image which evokes its transience ('This world, that passeth soone as floures faire') and there is also recognition of its naturalness ('In which that love up groweth with youre age').

One of the most striking differences in Henryson's treatment of the themes of self-deception and unfaithfulness is his avoidance of Chaucer's explicitly Christian framework of reference. At the end of his story Chaucer quite consciously underlines its pastness, its remoteness from the Christian dispensation under which he and his audience live – 'Lo here, of payens corsed olde rites'. The final standpoint is at marked variance with the attempt throughout the poem to secure a high degree of audience involvement in the story, and the effect of the emphatically Christian conclusion is to suggest that the Christian must use his free will to ensure that his emotional conduct is within the bounds prescribed by Divine Law. Laying the heart 'al holly' on Christ, and setting 'al oure herte on heven' does not exclude sexual experience grounded on truth, provided that the human love does not take precedence over the spiritual. The ending brings into sharp focus the references to God which punctuate the poem, compelling the reader to observe their ambivalence. Thus the 'Love' and 'God' of the first proem refer to both Cupid and the Christian God, and the God who 'loveth, and to love wol nought werne' (III, 12) is both the blinding force of pagan cosmology and the God of Aquinas. Chaucer relies here on the standard medieval interpretation of the gods, inviting his audience to recognise that the powers of the Trinity encompass – 'circumscrive' – the functions of those deities addressed by poets and philosophers. He uses Christianity, the courtly love code, and the Boethian system as perspectives on the narrative, and ultimately the reader is left to make the necessary reconciliations and syntheses, with the knowledge that the Christian revelation is the exclusive and ultimate sign of Truth.

Whereas Chaucer comes to view transient worldly experience from the standpoint of the eternal verities of Christian revelation, Henryson's focus is constantly upon human conduct in this life. The Scots poet shares his predecessor's concern for integrity in the conduct of sexual affairs, but the way in which this theme is treated differs from Chaucer's. There is no explicit reference to the Christian God at all. Cresseid blasphemes against Venus and Cupid, the gods who regulate sexual affairs. What Henryson understands by love is made quite clear by the symbolic action of the parliament dream-vision: Cupid summons the seven planets, 'participant of devyne sapience', requesting that they should take action to correct an injury which has been done to them as well as to himself (292–3). The planet gods and their interrelations signify, as MacQueen explains, 'one aspect of the moral, but also ... the physical law of the universe, a law which is most clearly expressed for the twentieth-century reader by such terms as time and change, growth and decay'.[6] Love is hence not conceived as *amour courtois* (although some of the conventions of courtly love are used), but as love in its much more general application to 'all thing generabill'. By paying insufficient attention to the telling link between Cupid and the forces of time and change, some critics have taken the view that Cresseid's behaviour must be judged in terms of courtly morality.[7] Henryson sees human love in considerably wider and more universally relevant terms, although like Chaucer he applauds Troilus's constancy in terms of the courtly standard (554–60). Cresseid's sin is twofold: a rejection of Troilus's faithful love, and a presumption that it is natural to exchange one partner for another as circumstances decree. It is not primarily against the love deity (because of the context in which Henryson places Cupid), but against Nature, the laws that regulate human behaviour. Nor is her sin treated as one specifically against the Christian God: her presumption is of course a sin 'against God's holy laws'[8] but the planet symbolism compels us to see it as being *primarily* a sin against Nature. It is according to the laws of Nature that she is punished. The punishment is unpleasant, as the vivid descriptions of Cresseid's diseased appearance testify, but it is also eminently natural. Henryson emphasises this by his ironic (because so obviously contradictory) appeal for mercy,

> O cruell Saturne, fraward and angrie,
> Hard is thy dome and to malitious!
>
> Withdraw thy sentence and be gracious –
> As thou was never.
>
> (323–8)

Time, clearly enough, is by its very nature unmerciful. Cresseid's transformation is ugly, but it is the logical outcome of her ugly abuse of her sexuality: by Henryson and his audience, just as by the sixteenth-century poetasters who were fascinated by the more sensational aspects of the poem, leprosy was thought to be a venereal disease.[9]

The sombreness of some of the planet-gods who pronounce sentence on Cresseid, and the fact that the moral balance of the group appears to incline in favour of these darker forces, have led to certain critical misunderstandings of Henryson's moral outlook. In his stimulating essay on the conciseness of Henryson's style, A. C. Spearing suggests that the poem raises disturbing questions about the presence of justice in the universe. Cresseid is seen as the victim of the 'overwhelming' power of forces beyond her control, forces which epitomise 'the threatening, the destructive, the malicious'.[10] It is necessary for this view that the planet-gods and Cresseid's disease should be regarded as essentially non-symbolic. The reasons given for regarding Jupiter and Mercury as sinister forces are not convincing, and it is excessively literal-minded to dissent from the view that Cresseid's leprosy is a venereal disease on the grounds that there are no symptoms before she curses Cupid: surely her cry (uttered *before* her dream) that the 'seid of lufe . . . with froist is slane' betokens an awareness that she has become repulsive to herself. Failure to recognise fully the implications of Henryson's symbolism underlies a slightly different view, that in the *Testament* Henryson 'questions the divine order quite peremptorily'.[11] A third interpretation, by which cruelty is seen not merely as a cosmic principle but as the distinguishing feature of Henryson's attitude to women,[12] begs the all-important question of Cresseid's painful but intensely moving regeneration. Her final speech is an affirmation of the 'womanheid' and the 'wisdom' which the poet sets out to 'excuse' (87–8), and through it is evinced an enormous growth in moral and spiritual stature. Is Cordelia's murder in the last scene of *King Lear* just cause for labelling Shakespeare a misogynist? Cresseid dies amid unbearable suffering, but this is no reason to charge the poet with being inhumane.

What distinguishes the *Testament* from *Troilus and Criseyde* is not a questioning of God's justice versus an affirmation of it, but rather Henryson's un-Chaucerian willingness to maintain a rigorous focus on the unpleasant consequences of wilful and concupiscent behaviour. This insistence on the facts of temporal experience is the ground for the kind of tropological reading which MacQueen advocates: the story of Cresseid as an instance of the painful consequences of the divorce of Appetite from Moral virtue.[13] (This approach to the poem extends, but is by no means necessary to, our understanding of it.) In her final meeting with Troilus, Cresseid remembers all that he represents, and this recalls the parting scene in *Troilus and Criseyde*, where Chaucer's heroine declares the ground of her affection for Troilus – 'moral vertue, grounded upon trouthe' (IV, 1672). In the *moralitas* of *Orpheus and Eurydice*, the characteristics of Appetite are described:

> Quhile to ressone it castis the delyte,
> Quhyle to the flesche it settis the appetyte.
>
> (433–4)

What Cresseid recognises before her death is that she has misused Appetite by loosening the bond with Moral Virtue, a bond in which sexual love was controlled by intellect and reason. No similar kind of allegorical reading of *Troilus and Criseyde* is possible, partly because it is a much more diffuse poem than the *Testament*, partly because of Chaucer's removal of his hero to a vantage-point from which he is able to laugh at the whole of human life: the clear implication is that Troilus has placed too high an evaluation upon a transitory good, and for this reason the temptation to identify Chaucer's Troilus with an ideal of moral behaviour does not occur. In depicting the moral regeneration of his heroine – the recognition that she has been in error – Henryson makes a significant departure from his model. At the end of his poem Chaucer quite deliberately alienates his audience's sympathy for Troilus: the hero's death is not dwelt upon, and his recognition of the nature of earthly love is the kind that can only come after death. It is rather difficult to extend sympathy and compassion to a figure who rejects them by his laughter. It has been suggested that Cresseid 'goes through precisely the same cycle' (i.e. as Chaucer's Troilus does), of 'abandonment, suffering, death, wisdom, and salvation'.[14] Surely, though, it is quite obvious that wisdom for Cresseid comes before her death, not after it. The effect of this radical change of emphasis, illustrated by Cresseid's 'Nane but my self as now I will accuse', is to give her a moral stature and a capacity for attracting our sympathy which she has never had in *Troilus and Criseyde*, and which even Chaucer's Troilus does not achieve. That Henryson does not translate his heroine literally to a supra-worldly vantage-point strongly suggests that he intended a comparison with Chaucer's treatment of

Troilus. When this comparison is made, we see that Henryson's faith in the potential of the human spirit to recognise the extent of its past error has no counterpart in Chaucer's poem. The view that compared with Chaucer, Henryson is a harsh and even a vindictive moralist is misguided, to say the least.

The question of salvation for Cresseid is largely irrelevant to the interpretation of the poem, although Henryson does hint strongly, in the bequeathing of her spirit to Diana, that she is to be granted an after-life. This act, it may be noted, should not be interpreted as a condemnation of sexual love. The value which Cresseid endorses at her death is rather the kind of chastity in love which is adhered to by Troilus, 'Honest and chaist in conuersatioun'. Cresseid's vow, which indicates a growth of spirit beyond the confines of blind sexuality, has its counterpart in Troilus's ascent 'to the holughnesse of the eighthe spere'. It is tempting to believe that the much more subdued treatment of Cresseid's fate after death reflects some criticism on Henryson's part of Chaucer's heavily theatrical method of bridging the gap between the conclusion of Troilus's story and the Christian exhortation to his audience.[15] The fact that Henryson does not proceed, as Chaucer does, to place his *exemplum* of the necessity for truth in love within an insistently Christian framework of reference, is the most significant indication of the independence of his artistic vision. The *Testament* is far from being an un-Christian poem: the case is rather that Henryson has sufficient confidence in his audience's powers of understanding to depend on them to recognise that the temporal laws which Cresseid abuses are part of the divinely ordained scheme which, just as it has punished a false lover's sin through pain and death, will sanction the existence of human love which is conducted in the knowledge that it cannot endure forever.

In the *Testament*, as in *Troilus and Criseyde*, there are numerous references to Fortune, both in the form of authorial comment and in the speech of the characters. The idea of Fortune's control over sublunary affairs, whether as blind fate or as agent of divine providence, is so common in late medieval literature that it would be unwise to suggest that Henryson borrowed it from *Troilus and*

Criseyde. There are clear indications, though, that certain aspects of Chaucer's treatment of the theme of Fortune impressed Henryson sufficiently for him to incorporate them into the *Testament*. The most noteworthy instance of Henryson's appreciation of Chaucer's complex treatment of the subject is his reworking of these lines in the Prologue to Book IV, which is ostensibly an account of the goddess's fickleness:

> From Troilus she gan hire brighte face
> Awey to writhe, and tok of hym non heede,
> But caste hym clene out of his lady grace,
> And on hire whiel she sette up Diomede.
>
> (8–11)

There is here an identification between Criseyde and Fortune, suggested by the image of the 'brighte face', and by the beginning of the following stanza:

> For how Criseyde Troilus forsook,
> Or at the leeste, how that she was unkynde,
> Moot hennesforth ben matere of my book.
>
> (15–17)

The implication of this passage, like that of the other references to Fortune, is that Fortune exists only as a way of describing the consequences of the operation of free will. Henryson develops Chaucer's identification of the human character with the female deity through his description of the goddess Venus. The attribution to Venus of two faces,

> Under smyling scho was dissimulait,
> Provocative with blenkis amorous,
> And suddanely changit and alterait,
> Angrie as ony serpent vennemous,
> Richt pungitive with wordis odious:
> Thus variant scho was, quha list tak keip,
> With ane eye lauch, and with the uther weip,
>
> (225–31)

associates her firmly with that other 'vnstabill' goddess, Fortune.[16] There is also an implicit identification here between Venus–Fortune and Cresseid, whose eyes have also shot forth 'blenkis amorous', and who has changed, becoming 'Richt pungitive' in her act of blasphemy. Cresseid, of course, has two faces, one fair and the other painfully disfigured, and there is the sharp irony that, unlike Venus, she does not have the power to change her 'bitter and sour' countenance at her own will. It is worth remembering, too, that medieval art sometimes portrayed Fortune as a harlot in the court:[17] there is an obvious parallel with the woman who wanders 'into the court commoun'. In Cresseid's enlightenment, when she admits that she 'clam' upon the 'fickill' wheel, there is the recognition that by her selfish sexuality she has tried to imitate the behaviour natural to the goddess.[18]

The narrative stance which Henryson adopts in the *Testament* is carefully developed to complement the implied *moralitas* about the need for integrity in love. The tone of the narrator is often ironic in the same way that Chaucer's voice is in *Troilus and Criseyde*, and the similarity shows the extent of Henryson's sensitivity to the nuances of Chaucer's style. There are, however, two important differences in Henryson's self-characterisation; unlike Chaucer, he depicts himself as an old man, and as one who has in his time been the servant of Venus. These distinguishing features of Henryson's 'I' have important implications for interpretation of the *Testament*, and perhaps too for determining Henryson's attitude towards Chaucer's relationship to his subject matter. The first two lines of the *Testament* are a variant on the rhetorical dictum about the decorum which should govern a teller's relation to his tale, and obviously they correspond to Chaucer's,

> For wel sit it, the sothe for to seyne,
> A woful wight to han a drery feere,
> And to a sorwful tale, a sory chere.
>
> (*TC*, I, 12–14)

Henryson, as he presents himself in the *Testament*, is a very appropriate 'feere' for both his central character and his audience, and the place which he holds in the narrative may be interpreted in two related ways. The first of these concerns our understanding of Cresseid and her error: the opening lines are an invitation to observe the extent of 'correspondence' and 'equivalence' between present and past, and the very conciseness of the poem is an inducement to examine the author's self-portrait for what it has to say about his subject matter. The figure who is prevented by the cold (both external and internal) from praying to Venus is clearly associated with the character whose story he is about to tell. Like Cresseid, the narrator goes to an 'oratur' in order to address the love-deity: the awareness that the physical facts of existence make it impossible to associate himself with Venus, which leads him to embark upon a more natural occupation, is in marked contrast with Cresseid's attitude when she goes to pray. She blames the God of Love, and by extension Nature itself, because she is unable to recognise the sober truths of mutability. Her inability to continue in love is not, however, the result of age, but of her defiance of natural law. The link between heroine and narrator is underlined by the metaphors of flowering and fading which are applied to both, in the context of the 'doolie [woeful] sessoun' in which the narrative is set. Henryson implicitly associates himself not only with Cresseid, but also with Troilus, relying again on his audience's familiarity with *Troilus and Criseyde*. Throughout his poem Chaucer demonstrates the fervour of his hero's affection, and Henryson's lines,

> Thocht lufe be hait, yit in ane man of age
> It kendillis nocht sa sone as in youtheid,
> Of quhome the blude is flowing in ane rage,
>
> (29–31)

draw a parallel between the different operations of Nature in age and youth. There is no disapproval implied here of the urgency of those feelings which Troilus experiences, and this is in accordance with the attitude to love which emerges from the poem. Henryson's sentiments are echoed in more explicit form in the sixteenth-century poem *O man transformit and vnnaturall* which George Bannatyne includes in that section of his anthology called 'the contempt of Blyndit Luve', attributing it to one Weddirburne.[19] The poem (which seems to show some knowledge of the *Testament*) is informed by a morality which is heavy-handed and uncompromisingly severe, but its author does not condemn the sexuality of youth:

Henryson and English poetry

> Quhan ȝung men dois sic thing It is na schame
> Becauss ȝowthheid garris thair blude flow & rege
> bot auld menis Lust proceidis of daft dotage.
>
> (75-7)

A secondary aspect of the thematic function of Henryson's self-portrait is that in it is set forth an example of how sexuality should be regulated according to the capacity of nature. Henryson does not bring any compulsion to bear on his audience in this respect – for example, he does not urge, as Cresseid does, 'in your mynd ane mirrour mak of me' – but the invitation is nevertheless implied. It will be recalled that at the close of the *Confessio Amantis* Gower reveals himself as an old man, turning away from allegiance to Venus in order to undertake the study of moral virtue. Like Gower, Henryson recognises the necessity to curb the impulses of nature: more honest than Cresseid, he understands that love cannot be obtained at will, and turns away to the pleasures of the fire, a book and a drink. Again, Weddirburne makes explicit the moral significance of Henryson's engaging personal aside in this exhortation to old men:

> And sen thy blude Is becum cawld and dry
> And als thy flesche and banis consumys for eild
> Thairfoir thow sowld leif wantone chevalry
> Off venus warkis And to gif our þe feild
> And nevir to beir in amoris speir nor schield
> Bot rathir at ane hett fyre the to hold
> Wt ane sydgoun to keip the fra þe cold
>
> Thow hes mair mistir of ane dowbill cap
> Nor of þe farest lady in to france
> Wt mittanis warme thy tendir handis to hap
> Nor for to se thy deir lufe sing or dance
> Restoratyvis be wyiss menis ordinance
> Wt sweit confectionis sowld be thy confort
> Rathir nor wt fresche ladeis for till sport.
>
> (78-91)

mistir need

Weddirburne is a more doctrinaire moralist than Henryson: he urges that old men 'sowld be to ȝung men gud exempill' by contemplating with 'bukis and beidis' (41-2). In the *Testament*, the book which the narrator chooses to read is hardly the kind which needs to be followed with the aid of 'bedis', but in its concern for issues temporal and eternal *Troilus and Criseyde* is just as serious as any devotional work.

We have already seen how in *The Kingis Quair* James implies some criticism of Chaucer's pose of withdrawal and detachment in *Troilus and Criseyde*. The Chaucerian narrator will come no nearer to the experiences described than to exclaim, in the account of the first night of love, 'Why nad I swich oon with my soule ybought,/Ye, or the leeste joie that was theere?' (III, 1319–20). Perhaps by portraying himself as he does in the *Testament*, Henryson is following his royal predecessor in suggesting to his audience that a man who has experienced sexual love has greater authority to write about it than one who assumes a position of priestlike remoteness. The narrator's past experience of love is not specifically discussed, but the allusion is sufficient for an audience to understand that he has a special competence to write a continuation of Chaucer's story. The Chaucerian withdrawal for which Henryson substitutes a pose of experience is of course not to be confused with the objective tendency of Chaucer's style in *Troilus and Criseyde*, which is marked by an extensive use of dialogue and description without authorial comment. Like Chaucer, Henryson is sufficiently confident to allow his story to 'tell itself' with a minimum of explanation: the result, in both poems, is to give a special importance to passages in the first person.

Although Henryson distinguishes himself from Chaucer in the details of his self-representation, his comments on his heroine show a keen understanding of the ironical authorial commentary in *Troilus and Criseyde*. Like Chaucer, Henryson uses a technique of exposing moral fault through expressions of apparent sympathy and protectiveness. After the brief reference to Cresseid's expulsion from the court, the narrator launches into what is ostensibly an exclamation of pity for Cresseid as the victim of malignant Fate:

> O fair Creisseid, the flour and *A per se*
> Of Troy and Greece, how was thow fortunait!

> To change in filth all thy feminitie,
> And be with fleschelie lust sa maculait,
> And go amang the Greikis air and lait
> Sa giglotlike, takand thy foull plesance!
> I have pietie thow suld fall sic mischance!
>
> Yit nevertheles, quhatever men deme or say
> In scornefull langage of thy brukkilnes,
> I sall excuse, *als far furth as I may*,
> Thy womanheid, thy wisedome and fairnes –
> The [quhilk] Fortoun hes put to sic distres
> As hir plesit, and nathing throw the gilt
> Of the, throw wickit langage to be spilt.
>
> (78–91; 87, my italics)

There is a complex dramatic irony at work in this passage: at the same time that the narrator appeals for sympathy for Cresseid as a passive victim, he conveys a strong sense of disgust at her wilful self-abuse. 'Fortunait' in line 79 (which surely means 'treated by Fortune' rather than the more neutral 'fated')[20] is made to alliterate with words that have overtones of moral judgement (*f*ilth', *f*eminitie', *f*leschelie lust', *f*oull plesance') in the lines which follow. They recall the lines in which Chaucer's heroine pleads the value of her 'honeste' when Troilus proposes escape,

> That floureth yet, how foule I sholde it shende,
> And with what filthe it spotted sholde be,
> If in this forme I sholde with yow wende.
>
> (IV, 1577–9)

It is no coincidence that Henryson repeats some of Chaucer's alliterating words ('flour', 'foull', 'filth'): recollection of Chaucer's lines heightens the significance of the passage in the *Testament*, since Chaucer's heroine sees 'filth' as the outcome of an act of will on her part. In the *Testament*, as in *Troilus and Criseyde*, it is the heroine, not Fortune, who transforms 'feminitie' into 'filth' by an act of choice. The credibility of Henryson's insistence on Fortune's responsibility for Cresseid's moral degeneration is undercut by the accompanying suggestion that responsibility lies with her: as we read this passage, we suspect that his tone is ironical, and suspicion becomes certainty as the poem proceeds. Henryson's rhetorical strategy in these lines is that of showing us Cresseid's predicament at her own evaluation. When she sees for the first time the physical manifestations of her guilt, she blames Fortune, just as earlier she has blamed Venus and Cupid for her isolation:

> Fell is thy fortoun, wickit is thy weird;
> Thy blys is baneist, and thy baill on breird
>
> (412–13)
>
> Fortoun is fikkill, quhen scho beginnis and steiris.
>
> (469)

thy baill on breird your misery increases

Before her death she comes to see that she, and not Fortune, has been 'fikkill'. This recognition is of course foreshadowed by the identification of Cresseid with Fortune in the description of Venus.

It is important to recognise that Henryson does not say that he will attempt to exonerate Cresseid: 'excuse' in line 87 has rather the sense of 'to defend'. The narrator says only that he will defend Cresseid's womanhood, fairness and wisdom as far as he is able – 'als far furth as I may', and this important limitation upon his ability to defend is itself a recognition of her guilt. Henryson's skilful assimilation of Chaucer's delicately ironical tone may be seen when we compare lines 85–91 of the *Testament* with some of Chaucer's comments upon Criseyde. At the beginning of Book IV of *Troilus and Criseyde*, for example, the narrator explains,

> For how Criseyde Troilus forsook,
> Or at the leeste, how that she was unkynde,
> Moot hennesforth be matere of my book,
> As writen folk thorugh which it is in mynde.
> Allas! that they sholde evere cause fynde
> To speke hire harm, and if they on hire lye,
> Iwis, hemself sholde han the vilanye.
>
> (15–21)

What may appear to be a plea on Criseyde's behalf is in fact an admission of her culpability. 'Unkynde' means unnatural as well as inconsiderate, and the anticipation of her reputation in literature points toward her fault rather than away from it. What Chaucer regrets is that there should ever have been cause to castigate his heroine: no attempt is made to conceal the fact that the cause exists. A similar kind of effect is created in these lines which follow the account of Criseyde's transfer of allegiance,

> Ne me ne list this sely womman chyde
> Forther than the storye wol devyse.
> Hire name, allas! is punysshed so wide,
> That for hire gilt it oughte ynough suffise.
> And if I myghte excuse hire ony wise,
> For she so sory was for hire untrouthe,
> Iwis, I wolde excuse hire yet for routhe.
>
> (v, 1093–9)

Like Henryson, Chaucer suggests only that he would like to defend Criseyde, not that he is actually doing so: 'I wolde excuse hire' corresponds very closely to 'als far furth as I may'. Moreover, Henryson repeats Chaucer's ironic disclaimer of knowledge: compare 'Men seyn – I not – that she yaf hym hire herte' (*TC*, v, 1050), with 'And sum men sayis into the court commoun' (*Testament*, 77). In both cases the effect is not to question, but rather to affirm the veracity of received opinion.

Ironical authorial commentary on the heroine in both poems produces the complex effect of both underlining the moral fault and expressing pity for her. Like Chaucer, Henryson is a clear-sighted but by no means cold-blooded or vindictive moralist: there is pity for the woman because she is the victim not of cosmic injustice, but of her own egotism. In the *Testament*, the combination of accusation and sympathy is apparent not only in the passage discussed above, but also in the address to 'cruell Saturne' (323–9). The context establishes that Saturn is not in fact 'to malitious', and that it is not in the nature of time to show mercy to anybody. It would be difficult to deny Cresseid pity, but the line 'Quhilk was sa sweit, gentill and amorous' is a reminder that sweetness and 'gentilnesse' were attributes of the lady who gave her love to Troilus so long before, attributes which she clearly does not possess when she returns to her father after being expelled from the Greek court. To suggest that the poem is anchored in 'the inescapable factuality of physical and mental anguish'[21] is to undervalue its 'sentence', the dimension of justice which is so firmly focussed through the presence of the narrator. It has been suggested that the 'I' of the *Testament* is a dramatic character, readily distinguishable from his creator – 'an unintelligent, low-minded and agreeable old man', 'an example of foolish and sinful attachment to sensuality', who is stupidly and passionately involved with the plight of his heroine.[22] This view of the narrator confuses the occasional ironic tone of voice with an attempt at large-scale characterisation, and it is impossible to reconcile with it first-person passages such as the learned comment based on Aristotelian psychology (505–11), and the final admonitory stanza.

As narrator, Henryson addresses his audience with urbane assurance, showing compassion for the central figure and at the same time relying on his audience to appreciate the occasional irony of tone. To this extent his method is very similar to Chaucer's, although Henryson does advance the distinctive authority of age and experience in love. His resignation, his wry acceptance of the limitations of mortality, are implicitly set against Cresseid's determination to be above mutability, and in this important respect Henryson's persona introduces a moral dimension which is not part of the discursive and enigmatic Chaucerian self-characterisation. Professor Spearing uses the contrast between Henrysonian directness and conciseness on the one hand and Chaucerian indirectness and diffuseness on the other as the basis of his contention that Henryson's poem could not have been written with oral delivery in mind.[23] This I believe to be insupportable: the difference between the two 'I' figures reflects a different kind of sensibility, a different kind of 'invention'. Henryson is not the author of an epic romance. He is telling only one part of a story, and his theme of justice in the universe does not permit the Chaucerian range of tonal variation.

Compared with *The Kingis Quair*, the *Testament* contains very few verbal borrowings from *Troilus and Criseyde*, or for that matter from any other poem by Chaucer. Apart from the passages which are recalled for ironic effect, commented on above, the only borrowings of interest are the epithets used to describe the characters: Troilus, for example, is 'worthie' (*Testament*, 41, 485: *TC*, I, 226; V, 1766, 1829) and Cresseid is 'bricht of hewe' (*Testament*, 44: *TC*, IV, 663; V, 1573). The language of the *Testa-*

ment is thus very different from that of Lydgate's handling of the Troilus and Cressida story in the *Troy Book*: Lydgate's practice is to quote almost *verbatim* from Chaucer. It is difficult to comment on Henryson's language accurately, since the surviving texts of the poem have been subject to sixteenth-century modernisation and (in the case of Thynne's print) to a degree of anglicisation. Nevertheless, it is clear that his language and orthography are predominantly Scots rather than English, and there are instances of translation from Chaucerian English into Scots: for example, Chaucer's form 'brotel' (*TC*, v, 1832) becomes 'brukkill' in the *Testament* (569). What is most Chaucerian about Henryson's style is its ability to encompass, without apparent effort, a range of words from the learned to the colloquial, giving the overall effect of a form of heightened speech. Like Chaucer, he uses insistently rhetorical effects very sparingly: in both poems, for example, the *ubi sunt* formula is subordinated to a more varied style of complaint (*Testament*, 407–69; *TC*, v, 218–45). Perhaps the greatest tribute to Henryson's skill in versification is the brilliant effect to which he puts the highly intricate stanza form of Anelida's complaint in *Anelida and Arcite*. There, the nine-line stanzas rhyming *aabaabbab* are remarkable only as a technical *tour de force*, but in Cresseid's complaint they acquire the dignity of a suitable emotional and dramatic context. In this respect Henryson may be seen to have 'outdone' his model.

The close connection between the Scots and the English poems, focussed by the characterisation of the protagonists, the partially Chaucerian treatment of the Henrysonian narrator and the treatment of Fortune in both poems, is reinforced by several allusions in the *Testament* to certain narrative and descriptive details of *Troilus and Criseyde*. The most famous of these is Cresseid's anguished recollection of her failure to observe the symbolic value, the 'takning', of the ring and the brooch given to her so long before by Troilus (582, 589). She, but not the audience of the poem, remains unaware that for Troilus the brooch which she gave to Diomede has become the token of her untruth in love, because he has seen it on the armour captured from Diomede (*TC*, v, 1660–6). Another of several less overt references to

Chaucer's poem is the description of Cresseid's physical transformation. This recalls some of the details in Book IV of the 'alteration' of Chaucer's heroine when she learns that she must leave Troy: her 'sonnysshe heeris' are disarrayed (116), her eyes encircled by a 'purpre ryng' (869), her clear voice 'broken . . . al hoors forshright' (1147). Henryson intensifies the details of disfigurement (*Testament*, 337–9, 443–5), and by recalling Chaucer's description he underlines the extent of Cresseid's fall. In the Middle English poem, physical alteration is the 'sothfast tokenyng of hire peyne' at leaving Troilus (870), but in the *Testament* the change betokens a serious moral disarray. A similar contrast between present and past is established by the stanza which describes how Troilus comes to remember the figure of Cresseid as he looks upon her in deformity:

> The idole of ane thing in cace may be
> Sa deip imprentit in the fantasy
> That it deludis the wittis outwardly.
>
> (507–9)

The passage recalls Chaucer's account of the 'imprinting' itself when Criseyde returns Troilus's gaze in the temple,

> And of hire look in him ther gan to quyken
> So gret desir and such affeccioun,
> That in his hertes botme gan to stiken
> Of hir his fixe and depe impressioun.
>
> (I, 295–8)

The reminiscence of the moment when the love affair began intensifies the pathos of a 'recognition' scene in which neither of the actors is able to recognise the other.

Another of the references to *Troilus and Criseyde* reflects, in a direct and even humorous way, Henryson's keen appreciation of his predecessor's subtle distortion of the so-called 'authority *topos*'. Chaucer frequently claims to be taking the details of his story from an older work by 'myn auctour called Lollius' (I, 394). Perhaps he did, by misunderstanding Horace's 'Trojani belli scriptorum, maxime Lolli', assume that there was a Trojan historian called Lollius, but for obvious reasons he could not have had the work before him as he wrote. Like any reputable medieval poet, Chaucer wanted his audience to believe that he wrote supported by the authority of 'these olde wyse', but that he valued rhetorical advantage more than scrupulous scholarship is all too obvious in his failure to name Boccaccio, the major source for *Troilus and Criseyde*. This is an elaborate literary joke, and Henryson shows his appreciation of it by repeating the authority *topos* in the *Testament*, in the allusion to the 'uther quair' taken up after reading the book written 'be worthie Chaucer glorious'. (It has been suggested that this mysterious other book might have existed, because of a reference to a 'common' Cresseid in the prose *Spektakle of Luf*, of 1492: it seems much more likely, however, that the author of this had read Henryson's poem.[24]) Henryson's reference to the 'uther quair' expresses more than his appreciation of the Chaucerian rhetorical trick, since it is by way of introducing a manifesto about the value of originality – 'inventioun' – to apply not only to his own work, but also to Chaucer's achievement. The device of taking up a book as a way of introducing an original poetic composition is also used by the author of *The Kingis Quair*, and it is possible that Henryson may have taken this over, together with the authority-in-love stance, from the earlier Scots poem.

In the *Testament* Henryson creates an *exemplum* for his audience, an illustration of the pain and sorrow which inevitably follow untruth in love. This lesson is developed in a variety of ways, some of them highly original: for example, the creation of an allegorical sub-structure, the juxtaposition of poet and heroine, and the allusions to Chaucer's poem. The thematic emphasis on truth in love is essentially the same as that of *Troilus and Criseyde*, and Henryson draws, in an imaginative and very distinctive way, on aspects of Chaucer's style. This can be seen in the manner of the narrator, in the system of ironic references to Fortune, in the allusion to authority, and in a willingness to allow meaning to develop through description and direct speech. Henryson's major contribution to the story of the Trojan lovers lies in his handling of the heroine. Cresseid's story moves us as it does not so much because she suffers, as because she grows in moral stature to the point where she understands the nature and extent of her error. F. H. Ridley comments, that 'While Chaucer's heroine ends as she began, "slydinge of corage" and totally unaware of it, Henryson's learns and changes, her mind's eye ironically becoming ever clearer as her physical eyes become blurred with disease.'[25] This regeneration is significant in the general sense that it reflects Henryson's faith in the ability and willingness of mankind to respond in this life to the Good, even when it has fallen to the point of apparent despair. Henryson's human optimism has no counterpart in *Troilus and Criseyde*. Chaucer's translation of Troilus to the heavens suggests no comparable faith in man's ability to attain self-awareness in this life. Henryson would doubtless have agreed with Chaucer that, viewed from the perspective of eternity, human love is a thing of small value ('The more of age the nerar hevynnis blisse'), but his willingness to retain a this-worldly focus on his 'matere' evinces a humaneness which we glimpse less clearly at the end of *Troilus and Criseyde*. Irrespective of whether she achieves any sort of spiritual salvation, Henryson's heroine possesses at the moment of her death the power to draw not only our sympathy but also our awed respect. She is the most impressive heroine of all British medieval literature, and it is possible that it was to Henryson rather than to Chaucer that the honour of being remembered as 'all womanis frend' should have been given.[26] It is one of the most bizarre accidents of literary history that Henryson's story should have been embellished as it was by the English poetasters of the sixteenth century, all of them fascinated by the repulsive physical details of Cresseid's punishment.[27]

(ii) The English affinities of the *Morall Fabillis*

If ever any demonstration that Middle Scots poetry was in no way dependent on English literature for its inspiration were to be sought, it would readily be found in *The Morall Fabillis of Esope the Phrygian*. Whereas the *Testament* was designed to be seen in close relationship to *Troilus and Criseyde*, and even to comment on Chaucer's work, the *Fabillis* proclaim their place in a tradition of European writing, to which the English contribution is relatively small. Henryson calls his work 'ane maner of translatioun': the *Fabillis* are in no sense literal translations, but rather highly creative expansions and adaptations of material inherited from such diverse sources as the twelfth-century Latin verse *Romulus* of Gualterus Anglicus, its derivatives the French *Isopets*, the French beast-epic *Roman de Renart*, and the sermon *exempla* of Odo of Cheriton.[28] None of Henryson's thirteen fables depends for its meaning on a knowledge of sources or analogues, although no doubt a contemporary audience would have delighted in some of the variations which are played on familiar fable narratives and themes. Although the poems are wholly intelligible and enjoyable in their own right, our appreciation of their merits is deepened when we look at them in the context of earlier fable-writing in English. This would be worth doing even if it could be shown beyond doubt that the Scots poet was entirely ignorant of the exercises in the same genre which had been written by Chaucer, Lydgate and Caxton. The fact that Henryson probably had read the 'sudron' pieces makes it even more interesting to read the *Fabillis* in the context which these provide.

Inevitably, Henryson's achievement as a fabulist has been compared with Chaucer's, since both wrote versions of the fable of the wily cock who manages to deceive his captor the fox. *The Nun's Priest's Tale* was known in fifteenth-century Scotland, and there can be little doubt that it had been read by one whose knowledge of *Troilus and Criseyde* was so considerable. Comparison between the two fables has sometimes been influenced by the close relationship between the *Testament* and *Troilus*, and the assumption has been made that the Scots poet *must* have been influenced by Chaucer's treatment of the fable of the cock and the fox. It is unlikely that anyone would still suggest that Henryson 'perhaps allowed his admiration for the "flower" of "Makaris" to override too much his own personality',[29] but attempts have been made to show that Henryson drew extensively on *The Nun's Priest's Tale* to enrich the texture of his narrative in the first part of the miniature beast-epic called, in the Bannatyne MS., *The Tod*. The two versions do admittedly share several details which are not present in any other of the known occurrences of the fable, but the narrative parallels, in themselves, are not conclusive evidence that Henryson borrowed from Chaucer. The genealogy of a fable is rarely simple: there are at least four versions of the cock-and-the-fox fable written before *The Nun's Priest's Tale*, and there may well have been more composed both before and after Chaucer's tale, and no longer in existence. It has been suggested that the fact that Henryson makes the owner of the cock a poor widow rather than a rich farmer (as in the *Roman de Renart*) implies indebtedness to Chaucer.[30] This may be the case, but it seems just as likely that Henryson took this particular detail from a version of the story (perhaps never written down) which has not survived.[31] The most that can be claimed is that it is at least likely that Chaucer's poem gave Henryson the idea for some of the narrative details of his own work. This kind of borrowing is not that upon which any theory of substantial indebtedness could be based. If Henryson did use his knowledge of Chaucer in this way it is certain that he altered and embellished the details which attracted him. Perhaps the most interesting correspondence of detail between *The Cock and the Fox* and *The Nun's Priest's Tale* concerns the test prescribed by the fox as the means by which Chanteclere is to prove that he is superior in crowing to his father. In the English version the fox praises the father cock, challenging the son to 'countrefete' his gymnastic virtuosity:

> And for to make his voys the moore strong,
> He wolde so peyne hym that with bothe his yen
> He moste wynke, so loude he wolde cryen,
> And stonden on his tiptoon therwithal.
>
> (VII, 3304–7)

In the Scots fable the imitation test is significantly altered and amplified. The cock is again challenged to stand on tiptoes to crow, but the basis of the challenge is different, because Henryson's avian hero is accused of being inferior to his sire ('changit and degenerate'). The dramatic effect of the test is greater than in *The Nun's Priest's Tale* because when the cock has crowed in the manner specified, the fox offers an irresistible bait to his vanity:

> 'Weill said, sa mot I the!
> Ye ar your fatheris sone and air upricht:
> Bot off his cunning yit ye want ane slicht:
> For,' quod the tod, 'he wald – and haif ne dout –
> Baith wink and craw and turne him thryis about.'
>
> (469–73)

There follows a stanza of authorial moralising upon the dangers of such 'Unwarlie winkand', the effect of which is to throw into sharp relief the tersely monosyllabic account of the actual capture:

> And suddandlie, be he had crawin ane note,
> The foxe wes war and hint him be the throte.
>
> (479–80)

Henryson's handling of this part of the story is more circumstantial and more dramatic, and it provides an amusingly effective literal background for the address to 'puft-up pryde' in the *moralitas*:

> Quha favoris the on force man haif ane fall:
> Thy strenth is nocht, thy stule standis unstabill.
>
> (594–5)

If indeed he had Chaucer in mind as he wrote, the additions are in the direction of heightened realism, and they contribute to the themes of degeneracy and false family pride, which are explored further in the second and third parts of *The Tod*.

There is an affinity of style between *The Cock and the Fox* and *The Nun's Priest's Tale* which suggests more strongly than any correspondence of narrative detail that there is a direct link between the two poems. Henryson echoes the mock-heroic and parodic effects which are integral to the *Tale*, when like Chaucer he characterises a hen as a courtly heroine. Chaucer's Pertelote is 'curteys, discreet, and debonaire', and when Chauntecleer is taken her grief is reported in suitably elevated terms (3355–73). In the Scots fable, a lofty lament comes from the beak of Pertok:

> 'Allace,' quod Pertok makand sair murning,
> With teiris grit attour hir cheikis fell,
> 'Yone wes our drowrie and our dayis darling,
> Our nichtingall and als our orloge-bell,
> Oure walkryfe watche, us for to warne and tell
> Quhen that Aurora with hir curcheis gray
> Put up hir heid betwix the nicht and day.' (495–501)

It must be added that Henryson parodies courtly rhetoric in his treatment of Pertok for a different reason. Whereas Chaucer plays on the disparity between the farmyard reality and an inflated mode of expression to achieve an effect which is near to farce, Henryson uses parody as a vehicle for moral judgement: like the fox, his avian heroine is described (in the Bannatyne text) as 'willye' and her inflated lament, like her sister Toppok's sermonising, is a cover for her real feelings about Chantecleir's disappearance. Henryson's description of the Widow's extreme reaction to the rape of the cock,

> As scho wer woid, with mony yell and cry,
> Ryvand hir hair, upon hir breist can beit;
> Syne paill of hew, half in ane extasy,
> Fell doun for cair in swoning and in sweit
>
> (488–91)

can did

has the same mock-heroic flavour as Chaucer's account of the hens' reaction. Throughout the fable the epithet 'gentill' is applied to Chantecleir: this is very close to Chaucer's practice, and there is a further parallel with the characterisation of Troilus, who is described as 'worthie' in both *Troilus and Criseyde* and the *Testament*. In the Scots poem the concept of 'gentillesse' is shown to bear a much more direct relation to the capture of the protagonist than it does in *The Nun's Priest's Tale*. As in the account of the posture in which the crowing is to be performed, Henryson translates what is given as descriptive detail in Chaucer's poem into the dramatic action of his own. The fox is able to gull Chantecleir because he approaches him as a feudal inferior – as the elderly 'servitour' of the cock's 'progenitouris' – and the foolish bird is almost literally mesmerised by this particular appeal to his vanity. The brilliantly comic scene in which the fox disguises only very slightly the facts about his behaviour in the past and his present intention ('Syne at the last the sweit swelt in my arms' . . . 'To mak yow blyith I wald creip on my wame') is essential to the 'moralitee' of the poem and to that of the miniature beast-epic which it introduces. The fox, who is the central character of the following fable, would also 'fane pretend to gentill stait' (711), and here the consequences of presumption are shown to be more serious than they are in *The Cock and the Fox*. The moral element of Chaucer's tale (insofar as this can be separated from the tale's rich vein of verbal comedy) concerns the absurdity of false knowledge: Chauntecleer is blinded by his own chauvinistic display of 'ensamples' and 'auctoritees', and vanity prevents him from recognising their applicability to himself. Like the fox in the third part of *The Tod*, Chauntecleer does not appreciate the meaning of the proverb *Felix quem faciunt aliena pericula cautum*.

Although some kind of direct link between *The Cock and the Fox* and *The Nun's Priest's Tale* probably does exist, it is impossible to define it accurately, and what is more remarkable is Henryson's independence of Chaucer. As is so frequently the case in the relationship of Middle Scots poems to English sources, the *varius sis* offers more insights into the nature of the Scots work than the *tamen idem* aspect of the classical axiom. There are differences between *The Cock and the Fox* and *The Nun's Priest's Tale* in terms of theme and moral interpretation, tone and style, and narrative detail. Chaucer's fable is by no means devoid of moral meaning, but throughout there is at least an equal emphasis on various kinds of stylistic excess. The life of this *Tale* stems from its prodigious use of various kinds of *amplificatio* – these include several passages of description in the high style, a proliferation of *exempla*, and an abundance of apostrophe and *exclamatio*. The meaning of *The Nun's Priest's Tale* depends on its manner as much as on its matter: Chaucer is drawing attention to the dangers of an undiscriminating use of the 'colours' prescribed in treatises such as Geoffroi de Vinsauf's *Poetria Nova*. Some of these devices are, of course, used to convey the absurdity of vainglory, and the unspecified 'fruyt' of the Nun's Priest's mock *moralitas* is the subject to which Henryson turns at the end of his tale – 'Fy! puft-up pryde! Thow is full poysonabill!/Quha favoris the on force man haif ane fall' (593–4). As we have already seen, Henryson uses parody for the purposes of moral discrimination rather than for literary satire. *The Cock and the Fox* differs from *The Nun's Priest's Tale* in giving equal emphasis to the sins of pride and flattery: this is shown by the detail that the fox's temptation speech is considerably longer than its Chaucerian counterpart, and its psychology of flattery much more elaborate. The result of the greater emphasis given to flattery in the Scots poem is that the fox's concluding plea and the cock's indignant refusal acquire a force which the corresponding lines in *The Nun's Priest's Tale* do not have. The greater seriousness of Henryson's moral purpose is also apparent in the obituaries delivered by the three hens. Each exemplifies some facet of pride: Pertok in her presumption to a courtliness which is foreign to her nature, Sprutok in her strongly appetitive complacency, and Toppok in her sanctimonious pose as interpreter of God's purpose.

The tone of Henryson's poem is, in general terms, much more serious than that of *The Nun's Priest's Tale*. This is partly due to the greater emphasis given to questions of personal morality, and partly to the fact that in Henryson's poem the *moralitas* is the logical culmination of the tale itself, rather than an artful parody of the conventional way of concluding a fable. The expression of the conviction that there is an urgent need to avoid sinful self-deception has no counterpart in Chaucer's poem. Henryson's greater seriousness is not altogether a matter of greater explicitness in discussing aspects of morality: the *moralitas* of *The Cock and the Fox* carefully refrains from reference to the episode of the hens. (This kind of understatement would probably be given the label 'Chaucerian' by those who applaud the indirectness of Chaucer's method.) The omission is an example of the intellectual wit which Henryson displays in his handling of the *moralitas* convention. Elsewhere in the *Fabillis* – for example, in *The Cock and the Jasp* and *The Trial of the Fox* – the moral application is not what we would have expected, and the result is to compel reinterpretation of the *taill* itself in terms of its *moralitas*. Humour, as distinct from this kind of intellectual manipulation, is part of the technique of *The Cock and the Fox*, but it is different in kind from that of *The Nun's Priest's Tale*. There is none of the broad comedy which comes from Chaucer's use of mock-heroics, or from a detail such as Pertelote's request that her husband should take 'som laxatyf'. Henryson's comic effects are less obtrusive, sometimes playing on the connotations of a single word, as in the fox's 'Syne at the last the *sweit* swelt in my arme' (445), where the rhetoric of courtly love is overshadowed by the gastronomical reference. (The fox is later to confess 'me think that hennis ar sa honie-sweit'.)

The style of the *Morall Fabillis* has been fairly described as 'Chaucerian', inasmuch as it combines qualities such as wit, control, demand for the co-operation of the audience and fluency of metre and diction,[32] but it is essential to recognise that neither in *The Cock and the Fox* nor anywhere else in the *Fabillis* is there any attempt to *imitate* Chaucer's style. As a way of describing Henryson's style, 'Chaucerian' has a limited usefulness, simply because there are so few correspondences of detail. No doubt Henryson's reading of Chaucer sharpened his awareness of the effectiveness of variations between one tone and level of language and another, but in this respect Chaucer is only one of a number of possible literary models, continental, English and (not least) Scots. Alliteration is one of the most important aspects of Henryson's fluency of metre and diction: it is used, for example, to intensify the colloquial flavour of passages of dialogue, to make moralising more emphatic, and, in the two nature prologue fables, *The Taill of the Lyoun and the Mous* and *The Preiching of the Swallow*, to give vigour and sharpness to what might otherwise be fairly conventional descriptions of the natural world. The respect for the value of alliteration is one which Henryson shares with his fellow-makars in Scotland rather than with Chaucer or Lydgate. The flexibility of Henryson's verse is also conditioned by the fact that, like Chaucer, he was writing with the demands of performance in mind. The frequent use of understatement at points of crisis in the narrative is one of the ways in which Henryson's poetry, like Chaucer's, achieves the effect of speech. H. Harvey Wood sees in the authorial comment at that stage of *The Twa Mice* when the diners are interrupted by the spenser – 'Thay taryit not to wesche [wash], as I suppose' (295) – an instance of 'Henryson's most Chaucerian gift, although it should be recognised as one distinctively Scottish . . . his power of turning from pathos to humour, from the sublime to the ridiculous, in a line or phrase which breaks in upon the narrative like a spoken comment in the voice of the poet'.[33] The comment may, as Wood suggests, belong to the same order of art as Chaucer's chat with the eagle in *The Hous of Fame*, but it is much more closely related to the art of these lines from *The Bruce*, which describe the Irish king's attempt to drown Edward Bruce and his men:

> He maid thame na gud fest, perfay,
> And nocht for thi yneuch had thai.
> For thouch thame failit of the met,
> I warne yhow weill thai war weill wet.
>
> (XIV, 363–6)

fest feast; *for thi* therefore; *met* meat

This kind of understatement is one of Henryson's favourite forms of humour, and while he no doubt appreciated its occurrence in Chaucer's poetry, his own practice reflects a relish for one of the habits of his own spoken language. As for so many other features of his style, no assumption of specific indebtedness to Chaucer should be made.

Unlike his contemporary Robert Henryson, the late fifteenth-century Scots author of *The Unicorn's Tale* did choose to write a beast-fable in a style that is readily identifiable as Chaucerian. The poem is one of five, known as *The Tales of the Five Beasts*, which together form a miniature *speculum principis*.[34] *The Unicorn's Tale* is a free adaptation of lines 1251–1502 of the twelfth-century Latin ecclesiastical satire, the *Speculum Stultorum* of Nigel de Long-champs, monk of Canterbury.[35] The episode concerns a cock's revenge on a boy who had long ago injured his leg by throwing a stone: when chicken and boy are grown, the cock refuses to wake the young man on the morning of his presentation to a lucrative benefice. In the Latin original the wiliness of the cock in gaining his sweet revenge is presented as a subject for admiration: this 'sentence' is preserved in the allusion which Chaucer's fox makes to the story in *The Nun's Priest's Tale*:

> I have wel rad in 'Daun Burnel the Asse,'
> Among his vers, how that ther was a cok,
> For that a preestes sone yaf hym a knok
> Upon his leg whil he was yong and nyce,
> He made hym for to lese his benefice.
>
> (*CT* VII, 3312–16)

The unknown author of the Scots version of the story gives it a more serious application, reminiscent of the *moralitas* of Henryson's fable *The Lyoun and the Mous*. He who is 'lord and rewlare of of this land' is warned of the consequences which may follow the oppression of the poor and the apparently powerless (270–9).

The reworking of the Latin source to highlight a Henrysonian moral application is in the best traditions of medieval fable composition. Even more interesting to the student of 'Chaucerianism' is the style in which the recasting is accomplished, for despite its context in a *speculum principis*, *The Unicorn's Tale* proclaims itself indirectly as a latter-day Canterbury Tale, one which incorporates the authorial 'voice' of *The General Prologue*. The first echo of Chaucer is the Scots poet's choice of setting: the clerk Gundulfus is trained at 'Oxinfurd', the whole action of the fable takes place in Kent (136, 151, 163), and the venue for the awaited ceremony is 'Rochister' (197, 211). It is just possible that the Scots fable is a translation of an English version of the episode in the *Speculum Stultorum*, but since no such tale or reference to it exists, it seems hardly necessary to posit an intermediate source. Why should a Scots poet give an English habitation to his work – and a Kentish one at that – if not to announce his appreciation of *The Canterbury Tales*? In most of the *Tales*, the setting is sketched in the introductory lines, and three of the 'English' ones (those of the Miller, the Reeve and the Summoner) give quite precise regional *loci*. Some idea of the way in which the Scots poet has assimilated the 'introductory' mode of Canterbury narrative may be gained by setting the Unicorn's beginning beside that of the Summoner:

> Before this tyme in Kentschire it befell,
> A bonde thare was, his name I can nocht tell,
> Gundulfus was his sonis name I ges,
> Of tender age of nyne ȝeris ald he wes
>
> (*UT*,1–4)

> Lordynges, ther is in Yorkshire, as I gesse,
> A mersshy contree called Holdernesse,
> In which ther wente a lymytour aboute,
> To preche, and eek to begge, it is no doute.
>
> (*CT* III, 1709–12)

The Scots poet has very skilfully reproduced Chaucer's artfully ingenuous way of leading his audience into the narrative, by a mixture of precision and indefiniteness in introducing the geographical setting and the principal character. His use of decasyllabic couplets, exhibiting regularity of stress and placing heavy emphasis upon the rhyme words, shows an obvious affinity with Chaucer's versification.

The account of Gundulfus's assault upon the chicken is permeated by a distinctively Chaucerian style of irony. The child is the self-appointed guardian of his father's grain, which is in constant danger of attack 'Ffra cokis, crawis, and vther foulis wyld':

> So on a day this litill prety child
> Seand thir birdis lukand our the wall
> Toward the grangis, Gundulfus gois withall,
> And with the casting of a litill stone,
> Of ane littil bird the theis bone
> Brokin he has in sounder at a cast.
>
> (143–8)

The repetition of 'litill', with its associated bathos, recalls Chaucer's use of the adjective in *The Prioress's Tale* (*CT* VII, 503, 509, 516, 552, 587), where it epitomises the teller's fatuous involvement in her story of the 'litel clergeon'. A similar kind of tongue-in-cheek irony is produced by the repetition: Gundulfus's vigilance, like the piety of the Prioress's hero, is strangely unchildlike. The portrait of the chicken who grows to rule the roost has affinities with the account of Chauntecleer in *The Nun's Priest's Tale*. Here the resemblance is also one of tone, as both are mock-heroic. When the chick is injured there is universal lamentation – 'Sore for him wepit all the hennis of Kent' – and he is borne to a garden couch, to be helped 'throu comfort and throu medecyne' (151–4). Admittedly the tone is lower than that of the passage in *The Nun's Priest's Tale* which compares the sorrowing hens to the matrons of Troy and Rome, but the effect is very similar. The Scots cock, like Chauntecleer, is described in superlatives – 'The cruellest of all the cokis of Kent' (463). The chivalric touch echoes the account of Chaucer's bird, who 'looketh as it were a grym leon' (VII, 3179). Both poems sound a humorous note of lifelong avian

Henryson and English poetry

romance, although in the Scots poem Chaucer's courtly lovers have become models of wedded felicity:

> And he had Copok to be his wyf,
> And he had chosyn hir for term of lyf,
> And scho agane till him hire treuth plicht,
> To luf him best of ony erdly wicht.
> And so at evyne apon his perke he gat,
> On his richt hand dame Copok nixt him sat.
>
> (164–9)

The picture of the pair sitting side by side on the perch appears to derive from *The Nun's Priest's Tale* (2884–5). Also developed from Chaucer are the dramatic characterisations of the fowls. Coppok, like Pertelote, is a vigorous scold: she upbraids her husband for his refusal to crow in the same way that her English predecessor rebukes Chauntecleer for his faith in dreams (*NPT* 2908–21):

> Slepe ʒe schir! get wp for Cristis saik,
> ʒour houre is gone, quhy syng ʒe nocht, for shame!
>
> (225–6)

Like Chauntecleer, the Scots cock adopts an attitude of lordly condescension in reply, and both address their hens as 'madame' or 'dame' (*UT* 233, 239; *NPT* 2970, 3122, 3158). There is no precedent for this kind of presentation in the *Speculum Stultorum*. The bird characterisations of *The Unicorn's Tale* are even closer to those of *The Nun's Priest's Tale* than are Henryson's portraits of Chauntecleir and Pertok in *The Cock and the Fox*.

The following account of Gundulfus's accomplishments, the most extensive addition to the episode as it is told in the *Speculum*, is a remarkably sensitive imitation of Chaucer's manner in *The General Prologue*:

> He was na master in diuinite
> Bot he wald preche in to that science hie.
> Weile couth he cast the bukis of decres,
> Bot tharin nothing had he of his greis.
> Prentis in court he had bene for a ʒere,
> He was a richt gud syngare in the quere.
> He couth wele reid and sumpart write and dyte,
> And in his grammere was he wele perfyte.

> He was na gret bachillare in sophistry,
> With part of pratik of nygramansy,
> Of phesik he baire ane vrinale,
> To se thire folk gif thai war seike or hale.
> And in his clething was he wele besene,
> Ffor govne and hude was all of Lyncome grene.
> Gret was the joy that in the place was than,
> To se the meting of that noble man.
>
> (178–93)

greis degrees

John Norton-Smith's comment on the 'negligently planned neutrality' of Chaucer's method in the pilgrim portraits is directly relevant to the technique used in the portrait of Gundulfus: 'an "ymage" or "peynture" emerges as a bundle of qualities or adjuncts with the whole moral character and coherent temperament cunningly left out or only obliquely indicated'.[36] The Scots poet successfully re-creates the Chaucerian pose of the genial but shrewd reporter, willing to applaud façade and social accomplishment, at the same time as he suggests the moral implications of the deficiency in application. Gundulfus's nearest Canterbury relatives are the Friar, both 'wantowne and merye' and 'a ful solempne man', and the Summoner, with his 'fewe termes' of Latin, 'That he had lerned out of som decree'. There are of course affinities with other pilgrims, such as the Squire, the Sergeant and the Physician. The poet makes little overt critical comment, but through the accumulation of detail emerges a picture of a dilettante, concerned to be seen as the universal scholar, but in reality setting as much store by courtly as by intellectual achievement. Just as in most of the Canterbury portraits, the *ethopoeia* concludes with an account of the figure's attire. The epithet 'noble' in the last line of the passage quoted above provides a telling anti-climax. Both here and in the telling of the sad end to the clerk's undignified scramble for preferment – 'And in the myre this worthy clerk lay still' (253) – is to be seen a keen appreciation of Chaucer's use of such adjectives in *The General Prologue* (e.g. 'Unto his ordre he was a noble post' . . . 'Was nowher swich a worthy vavasour'). In the portrait of Gundulfus, the 'voice' of *The General Prologue* is re-created not only by the accumulation of details and by the general mood of approbation, but also through the handling of the decasyllabic couplet. The insistent rhymes reinforce the impression of artlessness, of the narrator's apparent sympathy for his character. The effect is, as so frequently in Chaucer's pilgrim portraits, an ironic one. For example, the clerk's skill in physic is brought into question by the mention of 'nygramansy', which also glances at his deficiency as a sophistic philosopher. The rhyme effect is very similar to that of *The General Prologue*, 413–14, where 'surgerye' and 'astronomye' are connected. The inversion in 'Weile couth he cast . . .' (180) is another Chaucerian touch: as in the description of the Physician (417–18), it is part of a strategy of deflation. Although the passage in *The Unicorn's Tale* does not attempt such Chaucerian subtleties as the 'split' couplet and humorous effects which derive from the introduction of apparently inconsequential details, the imitation of the style of *The General Prologue* is remarkably successful.

C. S. Lewis, in his remarks on Chaucer's influence on fifteenth-century poetry, notes that 'Chaucer's comic and realistic style is imitated by Lydgate in the Prologue to the *Book of Thebes*, and by an unknown poet in the Prologue to the *Tale of Beryn*, but this is a small harvest.'[37] Neither of these pedestrian English pieces employs the decasyllabic couplet of *The General Prologue*, so on the grounds of versification, as well as those of tone and descriptive detail, the neglected Scots poem has the strongest claim to being considered the inheritor of what is probably the most memorable of the Canterbury styles. *The Freiris of Berwick*, which Pinkerton thought to be the work of Dunbar, is another Scots poem which invites comparison with the *Tales* – specifically, with the 'cherles tales' of the Miller and the Reeve. There are, however, no close verbal parallels between these and the Scots poem. The affinity is one of tone and structural sophistication, and it does not necessarily argue any indebtedness to Chaucer.

The indebtedness of the *Morall Fabillis* to Chaucer's poetry is relatively slight: where Henryson appears to have taken over a Chaucerian detail for his own story, the transference inevitably involves a great deal of alteration to meet the demands of a new and distinctive narrative context. And so it is with style: Henryson's way of writing probably owes much to his appreciation of Chaucer's variety and flexibility, but again the influences are assimilated to the extent that it is almost impossible to point to specific borrowings. It is obvious from parts of the authorial commentary in *The Testament of Cresseid* that Henryson could imitate Chaucer's 'voice' if he wanted to, in much the same way that the author of *The Unicorn's Tale* does. Since Henryson chose not to follow Chaucer closely in any part of the *Fabillis*, we can hardly be surprised to find that there are no very close links between the Scots work and those of Lydgate and Caxton, even though it is extremely probable that they were known to Henryson. Lydgate's *Isopes Fabules*, written early in the fifteenth century, is the earliest known composition of its kind in English.[38] Like the *Morall Fabillis*, it is a small collection (an *Isopet*) of moralised tales belonging to the vast repository of European Aesopic material. Efforts have been made to show the existence of verbal parallels between Lydgate's work and Henryson's,[39] but these are too general to provide convincing evidence of borrowing – the parallels are even more tenuous than those which exist between the description of Saturn in the *Testament* and a similar passage in *The Assembly of Gods*, a pseudo-Lydgatian work of the early fifteenth century. Any relationship which does exist between the two fable collections is one of form. Lydgate's are introduced by a general Prologue which leads naturally into the fable of the cock and the jewel, and in this respect Henryson's practice is obviously very similar. Four of the Scots fables – *The Cock and the Jasp*, *The Frog and the Mouse*, *The Sheep and the Dog*, and *The Wolf and the Lamb* – have counterparts in the English fables. It is possible that Henryson may have been inspired by his reading of Lydgate to 'outdo' the English collection, although of course no proof can be offered for this conjecture. The only lesson that Henryson could have learned from Lydgate is the negative one of what should be avoided rather than imitated. At its best, Lydgate's verse is plodding and undistinguished, reflecting his usual inability to develop narrative or character: the stories are a feeble framework upon which is erected a series of trite and repetitive *moralitates*. The fables offer nothing to compare with the ironic and dramatic effects of the later Scots ones, and in the relationship of tale to *moralitas* there is no equivalent to the Henrysonian combination of wit and moral seriousness. What distinguishes Henryson's 'moralitee' from Lydgate's is not its nature (both poets are conventional and conservative moralists), but rather the intellectual energy and verbal dexterity with which it is expressed.[40] A similar distinction can be made between the *Morall Fabillis* and William Caxton's two prose translations, *The History of Reynard the Fox* and *Aesop*.

The literary value of Caxton's works rests in their swiftness of pace and deft touches of *fabliau*-style humour rather than in any complexity of style or meaning, and no one could seriously suggest that Henryson could have learned anything about good writing from either of them. Caxton's racy and unpretentious stories are attractive in a way that Lydgate's are not, so perhaps it is not surprising that Henryson may have taken over some of their narrative details. Henryson and the English printer were contemporaries, and substantial correspondences of detail suggest that two of the *Fabillis*, *The Fox and the Wolf* and *The Trial of the Fox* (Parts II and III of *The Tod*) show the influence of parts of Caxton's *Reynard*, published in 1481, and that another two, *The Wolf and the Wether* and *The Fox, the Wolf, and the Husbandman*, show the influence of Caxton's *Aesop* and may therefore be dated after 1484. The clustering of parallels between Henryson's works and Caxton's does seem conclusive, although it is of little interest apart from the assistance which it provides in the dating of some of the *Fabillis*.[41] His approach to the English prose works is similar to the use to which he puts Chaucer's infinitely superior *Tale*, that of taking up a number of interesting details in the handling of a familiar story, submitting them to the subtle alchemy of his own 'inventioun'.

There is no English poetry of the late fifteenth century – fable collection or otherwise – which approaches the combination of stylistic variety, humour, moral rigour and intellectual control illustrated by the *Fabillis*. Since the *Testament* was discovered and anglicised comparatively early by an English publisher, it may appear strange that the *Fabillis* were not printed in England until

1577. Perhaps one of the reasons for their late appearance in the south is their uncompromising Scottishness: it is understandable that the *Testament* could be received as the work of Chaucer, but no translator, however ingenious, could disguise the origins of the northern Aesop. One thinks immediately of their distinctively Scots legal vocabulary, and to the allusions to socio-political institutions and circumstances in Scotland. Richard Smith completed his translation 'in the Vale of Aylesburie the thirteenth of August 1574', and it was printed in London in 1577 as *The Fabulous tales of Esope the Phrygian, Compiled moste eloquently in Scottische Metre by Master Robert Henrison, & now lately Englished*.[42]

In his dedication, Smith conjectures that political prejudices are responsible for the neglect of Scots work:

But whether most men haue that nation in derision for their hollowe hearts and vngratefull mindes to this countrey alwayes had (a people verie subject to that infection) or thinking scorne of the Authour or first inuentor let it passe.

Despite his nationalism and his many shortcomings as a translator, Smith was sensitive enough to recognise the value of Henryson's work, 'verie eloquent and full of great inuention'. The translation is prefaced by a dialogue between 'Aesop' and Smith in St Paul's churchyard, and the model for this is Henryson's own Prologue to *The Taill of the Lyoun and the Mous*. Aesop, who is 'Apparalled both braue and fine,/After the Scottish guise', requests to meet someone who would teach him 'to speake English'. Smith protests that his abilities are merely those of the servant of Pan who plays an 'oaten pipe', and he tries to direct the northern visitor first to 'the Innes of Court and Chaucery/where learned haue to do', and then to the poets who employ an elegant lyric style. Henryson–Aesop will have none of this, preferring to entrust his work to one whose style is unpretentious. He laments the fact that readers of poetry (by implication, English readers) undervalue the work of northern poets:

> 'They do not care for Scottish bookes,
> They list not looke that way:
> But if they would but cast their lookes
> Some time when they do play,

> Somewhat to see perhaps they might
> That then would like them wel,
> To teach them treade thair way aright
> To blisse, from paines of hel.'

The printer replies that he can tarry no longer:

> 'If not', sayth Esope, 'then adew,
> Into Scotland I'le returne'.

Although it is itself of little literary value, the dialogue is of interest because it provides one of the few sixteenth-century English comments on Scottish literature. Smith goes so far as to suggest that Henryson's work is superior to some of the English poetry of his day: he is not specific, but it is tempting to believe that after printing George Gascoigne's *Posies* and *The Steel Glas*, Smith turned to Henryson's *Fabillis* with a sense of relief.

4

The Palice of Honour and *The Hous of Fame*

Gavin Douglas is the author of two very different poems, *The Palice of Honour* and a translation of the *Aeneid* which has long been recognised as a masterpiece of the translator's art. The earlier poem, completed about 1501, contains some clever advance publicity for the planned classical translation: when the poet has become a member of the 'Court Rethoricall', that illustrious company of classical and modern poets whose abilities befit them to journey to the court of Honour, he promises Venus to 'put in Ryme' an unnamed book, remarking to his audience,

> Tuitchand this buik perauenture ʒe sall heir
> Sum time efter, quhen I haue mair laseir.
>
> (1756–7)

At the conclusion of the *Eneados* he proclaims that he is now 'fully quyt' of his 'ald promyt'. The difference between the earlier and the later poem is analogous to the difference between *The Testament of Cresseid* and the *Morall Fabillis*. The *Palice*, like the *Testament*, is closely related to a Chaucerian work, whereas the *Eneados*, like Henryson's 'maner of translatioun', has few direct connections with English poetry. Like his fellow makars, Douglas had a wide and sensitive knowledge of English letters, but was in no way dependent on Chaucer or any other southern poet for his inspiration. In the *Eneados* he reproves Chaucer, as 'principall poet but peir', for distorting Virgil's meaning in his Legend of Dido: this mixture of admiration and critical sensitivity is anticipated by his practice in *The Palice of Honour*.

The *Palice* has been rightly described by Denton Fox as 'a very useful commentary on *The Hous of Fame*'.[1] The parallels between the two are so striking as to suggest that Chaucer's poem provided Douglas with ideas that could be developed and elaborated in his own work, but nevertheless full recognition should be given to two important aspects of the Scots poem in its relation to Chaucer. The first is that the *Palice* is, in the words of its most recent editor, 'remarkable both for its wealth of literary allusion and for the way in which almost every theme or episode has some precedent in earlier medieval poetry'.[2] The poem is a *summa* of nearly two centuries of writing in the genre of the vision allegory, and it is probable that one of Douglas's reasons for writing it was to display a thorough accomplishment in the tradition instigated by the *Roman de la Rose*. The various gardens in which the poet finds himself, the processions or 'triumphs' which recur throughout the vision, the guide who accompanies the poet, the *grundmotif* of the journey, the catalogues of famous personages, and the elaborate descriptions of allegorical landscapes and architecture, are all thoroughly traditional, and illustrate the breadth of the poet's literary heritage. Although there are no parallels in French or Italian poetry which are as close as those which exist between the *Palice* and *The Hous of Fame*, it is possible that Douglas was even more widely read than Chaucer. The second feature of the *Palice* which must be kept in mind when one is investigating its relation to Chaucer's work is that it is in many ways quite unlike *The Hous of Fame*. Both are digressive and episodic to a remarkable extent, but where Chaucer's poem is casual to the point of apparent carelessness, Douglas's is finely and elaborately wrought. Where the tone of Chaucer's writing is at many points notoriously difficult to comprehend, Douglas's attitude to his subject matter and his audience is seldom in any doubt. Both of these differences, the structural and the tonal, are related to the different verse forms which are employed. *The Hous of Fame* is written in octosyllabic couplets, which frequently give an effect of artless *naïveté* which is far removed from the sonorous finality of Douglas's ingeniously contrived stanzas, with their longer line and self-consciously ornate and 'poleit' eloquence. There is certainly nothing Chaucerian about the texture of Douglas's verse, and it is possible that his masterly display of high-style virtuosity is part of the implied commentary on the art of *The Hous of Fame*. This is at least conceivable, since both poems are to a very large extent *about* the art of poetry. Their resemblances are thematic and structural rather than stylistic, and when considered together point to the conclusion that the Scots poet regarded his work, in part at least, as a response to Chaucer's views about the proper allegiances of the literary artist, the problems which he confronts in reconciling the demands of life with those of art, and the nature of poetic composition.

The Palice of Honour and *The Hous of Fame* are unique in British dream-vision poetry because of their formal division into three books, each of which is preceded by a piece of commentary (customarily a proem or an invocation) on some aspect of the art of poetry. (The Scots poem has the fourth division of a Prologue, in which the occasion of the 'visioun' is set forth.) The elaborate rhetorical preliminaries of Chaucer's Book I lead into the account of how the poet fell asleep one day in December and found himself in the temple of Venus, elaborately decorated with a fresco illustrating the *Aeneid*. The poet relates the story of Dido and her lost fame, and tells how upon leaving the temple he was suddenly in a desert, 'Withouten toun, or hous, or tree,/Or bush, or grass, or eryd lond (484–5), from which he is rescued by a golden eagle who reveals himself as the emissary of Jove. Book II is a richly humorous account of the loquacious eagle's attempts to instruct the quivering 'Geffrey' *en route* to their destination, where the poet is promised reward for his poetic services to Venus and Cupid, in the shape of actual 'tydynges' of 'Loves folk'. The matter of Book III is the account of Fame's abode and of her treatment of the companies of supplicants who entreat her quixotic favour. The scene shifts to the house of Rumour in which the long promised 'love-tydynges' have their place, and the poem breaks off after the mention of that 'man of gret auctorite' whose identity has so long been debated. The *Palice* is almost exactly the same length as Chaucer's unfinished poem, but its action is considerably more diverse. The dream landscape in which the poet finds himself after his rather undignified swoon in the ideally beautiful and productive May garden of the Prologue is a 'desert place/Amyd a Forest by a hyddeous flude'. From his hiding place in a withered stump he beholds the various companies who are on their way to the palace of Honour, and is powerfully attracted by Venus and her magnificent retinue. In the garden of the Prologue he has been moved to doubt and fear by the song in praise of fecundity, and now he is moved to sing a lay of his own in which he condemns Venus and Cupid roundly. For this act of blasphemy he is hauled before the goddess and her court, and threatened with death. (There are several echoes of *The Testament of Cresseid*.) Book II opens with the arrival of the 'Court Rethoricall', the very sight of which gives the prisoner cause for hope: Calliope intercedes successfully on his behalf, and he is entrusted to her care. He joins the literary company on a lightning tour of the world, and they pause for rest and poetic recreation at 'the Musis Caballine Fontane'. The final section is concerned with the remainder of the journey to Honour, with the many 'wonderis' of the court itself, including the brilliant visage of the deity which precipitates the dreamer's second swoon. After his guardian nymph has explained the nature of Honour he is admitted to another experience, the sight of the Garden of Rhetoric, and his unsuccessful attempt to cross over into it causes his awakening in the garden where the vision began.

Although the structure and subject matter of the *Palice* are dictated by the needs of Douglas's own *argumentum*, the poem contains several episodes which correspond with Chaucer's narrative, in terms both of detail and position within the tripartite construction which the poems share: for example, the desert is mentioned at the end of Book I, just as it is in the English poem (Douglas's *descriptio* is reserved for the beginning of the next book); Venus is figured in both first books – through the court in the *Palice*, through the temple in *Fame*; in Book II there is the account of the journey 'Als swift as thocht' (1077) which corresponds to the journey in *Fame*, during which the traveller associates his altitude with the processes of thought (973–8). Book III of the *Palice*, like the corresponding section of Chaucer's poem, opens with the dreamer's ascent of a forbidding mountain which forms the foundation for a splendid palace, and in both third books there is extensive description of both the architectural and the musical attractions of the courts of Honour and Fame. The French poems on the theme of Honour – works by Froissart, Molinet and Saint-Gelais – do not correspond to this extent with *The Palice of Honour*, and there can be no doubt that Douglas drew more extensively on *The Hous of Fame* than on any other single poem. More interesting than the mere existence of these and other parallels between the two dream visions are the uses to which Douglas puts his reading of Chaucer. His practice, like Henryson's in the *Morall Fabillis* (and that of any medieval poet worthy of a place in the 'Court Rethoricall') is to transform his borrowings so that they fit easily and naturally into a new and individual poetic context.

Both poems employ the central motif of the poet's dream journey, and in both 'sentence' emerges from the ordering of episodes and passages of description: connections of various kinds are implied through context and verbal detail, and the reader is left to explore the implications of these connections for himself. Close attention to the desert episodes which come at the end of the first third of both poems shows how sensitively Douglas has understood Chaucer's method, and indicates endorsement of the view implicit in this stage of the Chaucerian 'argument'. At one level the desert episode in *The Hous of Fame* provides a convenient setting from which the bewildered poet can be rescued, thereby permitting the poem's narrative line to be maintained. Nor surprisingly, however, it has a significance which goes further than narrative expedience, one related to the poet's evaluation of art. The dream traveller's admiration for the artifice of the temple of Venus – an artifice which is at once pictorial and literary, because of its Virgilian subject matter – is beyond doubt (470–3), but the bemused reflection which follows his praise for the 'ymages',

> But not wot I whoo did hem wirche,
> Ne where I am, ne in what contree,

suggests a desire to know about the life which has made the artistic creation possible. He responds to the desert as to an unnatural place:

> Ne no maner creature
> That ys yformed be Nature
> Ne sawgh I me to rede or wisse.
> 'O Crist!' thoughte I, 'that art in blysse,
> Fro fantome and illusion
> Me save!'
>
> (489-94)

Significantly, he does not retreat for consolation to the ordered world of the temple, and there is the clear implication that art, even as represented by the Virgilian story, might have at best a limited meaning unless the beholder (or reader) has some context of immediate human experience in which to place his appreciation. At the beginning of the *Palice* the waking poet responds with delight to the ordered beauty and plenitude of the May garden – so intense is his response that he seems to be in a dream (60) before the swoon itself occurs. The natural world is for him a living artifact, in which flowers are precious stones, the leaves 'natures Tapestreis', and the dew drops of silver, but his sense of the harmony between nature and art is destroyed by the song, with its theme of what mankind owes to the season:

> In the is amorous lufe and Harmonie
> With Incrementis fresche in lustie age.
> Quha that constranit ar in luifis rage,
> Addressand thame with obseruance airlie,
> Weill auchtis the till gloir and Magnifie.
>
> (84-8)

auchtis ought

The poet-figure has arisen early to do his 'obseruance' (6), and he is thrown into a state of agitated confusion because he fears that his worship is insufficient without physical participation in the scene. He pleads for guidance from Nature and Venus so that he can respond, *as an artist*, to the richness of the life about him:

> Recounsell me out of this greit affray
> *That I may sing* ʒow *laudis day be day.*
>
> (94-5, italics mine)

The 'dreidfull terrour' is represented in the forceful literal terms of the desert, the obverse of the ideal May garden ('Ver translait in winter furious'): the dream landscape is an emblem of the poet's world when the nexus between art and nature has been broken, apparently through the arbitrary workings of cruel Fortune. The ways in which the themes of the artist's relationship to life are introduced are different in the two poems – Douglas's treatment is fuller and more explicitly personal – but the technique is the same: in the *Palice*, as in *The Hous of Fame*, the question of the poet's allegiance to the experience of life as it exists outside his specific vocation is put forward by a suggestive contrasting of settings. (The process by which landscape settings are juxtaposed so as to reinforce and amplify the developing 'sentence' of the poem is carried much further in the *Palice*: the structure is circular, in that at the conclusion of the vision the poet is returned with knowledge and renewed confidence to the garden in which the vision began, where he feels regretful that he could not have remained forever in the stable and immutable garden of rhetoric.)

The connection between the poet's experience of life and his creative capacities, implied by transitions between ordered settings and wastelands, is amplified in both poems through allusion to the relationship between poet and goddess of love. Both Chaucer and Douglas create humorous effects as they explore quite serious questions concerning the proper relation between the individual poet and the experience of that 'ioly wo' enshrined by tradition and courtly taste as the stock-in-trade of the secular author. Chaucer's view on the subject, expressed ironically in *The Hous of Fame* as elsewhere in his poetry, would seem to be that aloofness from love 'in dede', perhaps even abstinence, is by no means a handicap to the writing of poetry. In Book II of *Fame* the condescending voice of the eagle is used to draw the attention of Chaucer's audience to the solitude in which the poet exists as a reader of old books and a maker of new poetry: so absorbing is the labour of creation that the poet has no contact with his 'verray neygheboros'. What the eagle and his master Jove find particularly regrettable is that one who 'ever mo of love enditest' is set apart not only from the experience of love but even from first-hand information of the servants of Venus and Cupid (616–40). Of course Chaucer exaggerates his 'abstynence' and physical 'unliklinesse' to humorous effect, perhaps even to the extent of suggesting that he is subdued by a nagging wife (561–6), but the nature of the dream journey which he is compelled to undertake implies that the joke has a serious edge. The desert scene, like the spectator's keen 'entente . . . for to pleyen and for to lere' amid the whirligig human confusion of the House of Rumour, suggests that human contact is essential to the poet, but there can be little doubt about the strength of Chaucer's affirmation of his self-sufficiency as an artist. Fame, in the sense of personal renown, is shown to be the purpose of most human activity, and in the House of Rumour even the most meaningless and trivial records of everyday life aspire to a place of permanent fame. The poet, when asked if he has 'com hider to han fame', makes an unequivocal denial of any interest in personal recognition:

> I cam noght hyder, graunt mercy,
> For no such cause, by my hed!
> Sufficeth me, as I were ded,
> That no wight have my name in honde.
> I wot myself best how y stonde;
> For what I drye, or what I thynke,
> I wil myselven al hyt drynke,
> Certeyn, for the more part,
> As fer forth as I kan myn art.
>
> (1874–82)

Despite the syntactical obscurity of the last two lines it is clear that a contrast is being drawn 'between the personal mortality of the man and the potential durability of that part of his experience and intelligence . . . which he can convert into poetry'.[3] Achievement in the course of active ordinary life is dismissed as having at best a transient value, and even the art of love cannot be excepted. There is an echo in the poet's disclaimer of interest in personal fame of Dido's bitter comment on love:

> Now see I wel, and telle kan,
> We wrechched wymmen konne noon art;
> For certeyn, for the more part,
> Thus we be served everychone.
>
> (334–7)

Love, as it is displayed in the treatment of the Virgilian story, is seen to be fraught with the same uncertainty as the various attempts to win fame, and indeed Dido's lament about the trials of serving Venus looks forward to Book III – 'O wikke Fame! for ther nys/Nothing so swift, lo, as she is!' The whole movement of the poem affirms the validity of the poet's allegiance to Venus as a *literary* emblem. In the Proem of Book II Venus ('faire blisfull, O Cipris') is invoked as a muse, and in the narrative of Book I she is addressed as 'my lady dere' (213). Venus, as mother of Virgil's hero and powerful force in the action of the epic, is a fitting object for the poet's devotion: the *Aeneid* is imaged as her poem, for the painted action which begins 'I wol now singen, yif I kan,/The armes, and also the man' takes place within her temple. The immediate concern of the contemporary poet–interpreter is with the uncertain fame, the 'untrouthe', of love, and the words which he utters late in his journey suggest that the promised 'preve by experience' is of doubtful value:

> For wel y wiste ever yit,
> Sith that first y hadde wit,
> That somme folk han desired fame
> Diversly, and loos, and name.
>
> (1897–1900)

The journey to Fame and the goings-on at her court have little to teach one who has applied himself so well to 'olde bokes' such as the two which are mentioned in Book II, 'Virgile in Eneydos' and Ovid's *Heroides* (378–9). Chaucer's emphasis on 'auctorite' as a reliable guide to understanding and writing is of course reiterated throughout his poetry: in *Troilus and Criseyde*, he observes the universal law of that 'blissful light, of which the bemes clere/ Adorneth al the thridde heven faire' not as lover, but as high priest of Love. Obviously it would be absurd to take Chaucer's protestations that he is ignorant of love 'in dede' at face value, but they do serve to affirm the value of detachment and study as ways in which the practising poet may comprehend experience in general and the works of Venus in particular.

The Palice of Honour offers an extended illustration, through the poet's 'aventure' within the dream, of the way in which the

Palice of Honour and Hous of Fame

demands of Venus are reconcilable with those of art, and although the details are different the resolution is remarkably similar to that which is offered more obliquely in *The Hous of Fame*. The dreamer is delighted by the art of music which heralds the coming of 'the Court sa variabill' (486–525), and even the wasteland is made to seem transformed with 'Carpettis fair' (660–2). That he regards himself less as the servant of Venus than as the servant of poetry, however, is implied by the excitement which he experiences at the sight of the Muses' court:

> The suddane sicht of that firme Court foirsaid
> Recomfort weill my hew, befoir was faid.
> Amid my spreit the Ioyous heit redoundit,
> Behalding how the lustie Musis raid
> And all thair Court, quhilk was sa blyith and glaid,
> Quhais merines all heuines confoundit.
>
> (889–94)

The problem of his 'obseruance' is solved by the pact which Calliope's intercession makes possible. He is to serve Venus not as lover but as poet, and later at the court of Honour is given that 'nixt ressonabill command' which proclaims itself twelve years later as the translation of Virgil.

It may be no accident that Douglas, like Chaucer, chooses the *Aeneid* as the illustration of his vocational allegiance to Venus. Other factors doubtless helped to shape Douglas's decision to translate the *Aeneid*, but the example of Chaucer as an interpreter of Virgil – relating the story of Dido in both *The Hous of Fame* and *The Legend of Good Women* – should not be overlooked. In both the English and the Scots dream visions, the writer's allegiance to Venus is closely linked with demonstration of the traditional basis of poetic art. In Chaucer's poem the literature of the past is to be esteemed not only for its formal beauty (represented by the elaborate 'olde werk' of the architectural surround), but also for its usefulness to the modern poet. The interpretative retelling of the Dido story is an extended illustration of the famous 'olde feldes . . . newe corn' metaphor, designed to reinforce and complement the eyewitness account of Fame's spectacular intransigence in Book III. The equivalent to the temple-of-Venus episode in *Fame* is the account of Venus's mirror in the *Palice*. At his destination, the palace of Honour, the poet encounters Venus for the second time, and he devotes twenty-eight stanzas to telling what he saw in the mirror before her throne (1468–1728). Calliope's tutelary nymph is ironically matter-of-fact about this 'royall Relick', saying only that it reflects what the beholder wishes to see, that it 'Signifyis na thing ellis to vnderstand/Bot the greit bewtie of thir Ladyis facis,/Quhairin louers thinks thay behald all graces' (1762–4). The implication is that the poet of Venus has a superior and wider-reaching power of observation. He sees the whole range of human experience preserved by written authority. Biblical history, pagan epic and legend, and more homely local events – 'All plesand pastance and gammis that micht be' – are present to his sight and ready for him to draw upon.[4] Significantly Douglas, like his English predecessor, devotes a section to paraphrase of the *Aeneid*, and soon afterwards Venus presents him with the commission of translating it. The mirror itself illustrates what is meant by the earlier description of poetry as 'Ioyous discipline,/Quhilk causes folk thair purpois to expres/In ornate wise' (846–8). The delightful variety of matter which it reflects is shaped and disciplined by the circular 'bordour' of ornate decoration. In a similar way, the 'ymages' from the *Aeneid* which the dreamer beholds in *The Hous of Fame* are contained and illuminated by the richly formal setting of the temple. The second (related) meaning of the mirror episode is hinted at by the command of Calliope's nymph, which precedes it – 'Quhat now thow seis, luik efterwart thow write' (1464). Just as lovers are restored after 'the Tornament' by beholding the faces of their ladies, so too is the poet strengthened and inspired by his contact with books. In neither poem is the demonstration of the traditional basis of poetry very successful: Chaucer's treatment of the Dido story is perfunctory and curiously flat, while the Venus's mirror episode suffers from Douglas's fascination with catalogue and *repetitio*.[5]

The trial scene in the *Palice* is modelled on the dreamer's encounter with the God of Love in the Prologue to *The Legend of Good Women*, which in its concern with the responsibilities of the poet has close affinities with *The Hous of Fame*. In both Chaucer's poem and the *Palice*, there is the charge of poetic blasphemy against the love deity, and similarly the irony that fear robs both poets of all eloquence. Calliope plays the role of Alceste in Chaucer's poem: she is the poet's advocate, who intervenes with the angry god, using the argument that it would be degrading to the divine estate to punish an insignificant man for 'sa small ane cryme' (*LGW* Prol. F, 384–410; *PH*, 955–63). A similar argument is used, in his own defence, by Henryson's mouse in *The Taill of the Lyoun and the Mous*. Venus, clearly, is much more exacting than Alceste, since she orders from the penitent poet a work more ambitious in its scope than 'A glorious legende/Of goode wymmen'. Douglas follows Chaucer here, in indulging in witty self-advertisement of his special status as a poet who has been specifically 'authoreist' by the love deity, even if as punishment. In Chaucer's poem the nature of this authority is exposed to some delicately ironic criticism: the God of Love and his consort are physically very impressive, but their reliability as arbiters of literary taste is highly questionable: Chaucer's translation of the *Roman de la Rose* and *Troilus and Criseyde* are dismissed absolutely as heresy against the law of Love (F, 327–34), while his most ascetic productions are advanced in his defence (424–30). Love's powers are clearly not of the intellectual kind, and it is small wonder that 'wise folk', such as the poet, find it easy to 'withdrawe' from the experience of worship. It is very likely that Chaucer's wry satire of the God of Love prompted Douglas to a similar essay in literary humour, begun in the *Palice* and completed in the *Eneados*. The prisoner of Venus releases himself by questioning her wisdom as a patron: the son of Venus is glorified as the exemplar of pagan heroic virtue, but a medieval poet who is also a churchman can have very little good to say about the mother. Within the palace itself, Venus occupies an ambivalent position with respect to Honour – within the walls, yet outside the gates of Honour's actual dwelling. In the fourth *Eneados* Prologue Venus and her works are roundly condemned, in a tone which echoes part of the conclusion of *Troilus and Criseyde*:

> Lo, quhow Venus can hir seruandis acquyte!
> Lo, how hir passionis vnbridillis all thar witt!

In the concluding remarks that his promise 'as twichand Venus' is now fulfilled, Douglas advises Henry St Clair to 'lat dame Venus have guid nycht adew'. Clearly the cultivation of letters is a preferable pursuit for gentle Scots, just as Chaucer claims it is for him.

The view of the relation between experience – in particular the experience of love – and literary creation which emerges from Douglas's poem endorses the view implicit in *The Hous of Fame*. There is more to be said about the implied commentary on Chaucer's work in the context of those concepts which give the poems their titles. It begins with the difference between the pinnacles on which the two dwellings are built: Fame's palace stands on the 'feble fundament' of a partially melted mount of ice, whereas Honour is founded on a 'Roche of slid, hard marbell stone'. Fame, in the English poem, is the sister of Fortune (1547), so it is hardly surprising that the rewards of her petitioners should be given in an arbitrary and irrational way. The poem is a kind of meditation on that question posed by the astonished dreamer at the foot of Fame's mountain of ice: 'What may ever laste?' (1147). The quest for renown in everyday life, even in dedicated service of Love, is seen to be fraught with uncertainty. Those who dedicate themselves to the complex task of interpreting and recording the flux of experience in art have a better chance of success, but even here there can be no hope of lasting personal renown. The authors of 'hy and gret sentence', who on their metal pillars offer the spectator the only stability in Fame's bizarre court, bear on their shoulders the fame of their subject matter, which is in itself no easy burden (1473-4). In Douglas's third book a clear and unequivocal answer is given to the question posed in *The Hous of Fame*, in the form of the careful distinction which Calliope's nymph makes between honour and fame. In the realm of Honour even the most powerful temporal rulers,

> Allanerlie sall for vertew honourit be.
> For eirdlie gloir is nocht bot vanitie
> That as we se sa suddanelie will wend,
> Bot verteous Honour neuer mair sall end. (1977-80)

Allanerlie only

The hollowness of Fame as a goal is further underlined by the nymph's explanation that when rulers die all that may remain is 'fame of thair Estaitis', and that nothing but 'verteous warkis' may accompany them after death – 'Ay vertew ringis [reigns] in lestand [lasting] Honour cleir' (1990–8). Honour is a more beneficent and positive force than Chaucer's ever-fluctuating goddess, who refuses to recognise even in their own lifetimes the works of virtuous men (1615–21), much less grant them eternal renown. Where Chaucer leaves his audience to draw their own conclusions about the delusiveness of temporal fame, Douglas makes a firm statement about the proper goal of all human endeavour. Honour cannot be attained without the exercise of Christian virtues and responsibilities, as the account of the Prince's allegorical household makes clear: this must have had a special force for the contemporary audience, as the offices of Honour are those of the Scots royal household:

> His Comptrollar is cleipit Discretioun.
> Humanitie and trew Relatioun
> Bene Ischaris of his Chalmer morne and ewin.
>
> (1801–3)

The Christian significance of Honour is further underlined by the association with redemption through Christ (1387–95), and the deity's power to condemn to eternal punishment those who are without virtue (2053–6). It is true, as Priscilla Bawcutt suggests, that there seem to be 'unresolved contradictions in Douglas's thought' in relation to Honour,[6] as evidenced by the high value given to deeds of martial valour – some very sophisticated reasoning would be necessary to justify the admission of Achilles and Semiramis, for example, to the Christian heaven. Not too much emphasis should be placed, however, on the possible implication of the different readings of line 1921 which the two texts of the poem offer – 'a god armypotent' as opposed to 'ane God Omnipotent'. That the poet intended an identification of Honour with the Christian God rather than Mars is quite obvious because of the mention of Christ, the imagery of the final prayer to Honour, and the poet's acknowledgement of 'The glorious Lord ringand in persounis thre' (776) who has made 'Intercessioun' for him. (All

E

of these exist in both the Edinburgh and the London texts.) Through his definition of Honour, Douglas offers an alternative to the ironic account of misdirected endeavour in *The Hous of Fame*, wherein Chaucer's indirectness and unwillingness to provide a religious perspective for his subject matter is replaced by a strong affirmation of the value which 'neuer mair sall end'. Throughout the first two books of both poems, we are prepared, like the poet–travellers themselves, to receive 'tydynges' which are specially relevant to the poet's task of commemorating experience in art. In place of Chaucer's disavowal of interest in personal renown and a rather tentative affirmation of the enduring qualities of literature, we are offered in the *Palice* a confident statement that it is the poet's task to be virtuous in the conduct of his own life, and to pay special attention to the quest for honour as the subject matter for poetry. To the kind of interpretation proposed here it might be objected that the fact that Douglas's conclusions about value in art and life are different from Chaucer's need not imply any direct reference to *The Hous of Fame*, especially as the English poem is nowhere explicitly alluded to. Since the *Palice* plays so many variations on Chaucerian themes relating to the nature of poetry and the function of the poet, however, it seems more likely that Douglas does in fact invite comparison between his own 'sentence' and Chaucer's, just as James I does by reworking a crucial passage of *Troilus and Criseyde*, and Henryson by his continuation of Chaucer's poem.

One of the ways in which Honour differs from Fame is that it is both the goal and the source of all virtuous activity – 'Of worschip kend the glorious end and rest' (2119), as well as the 'greit puissance' which makes all achievement possible (2121). The quest for Honour through poetic composition is placed within the perspective of other roads to Honour – notably those of virginity, faithful love, martial valour and 'sapience' in general. Fame, although capable of fortuitously bestowing *laus* or *gloria* ('Clere Laude'), is more closely allied to that most untrustworthy of all phenomena, rumour. There is no question in Chaucer's poem of fame being a source of guidance or inspiration: this is demonstrated by the witty fiction that it is Chaucer's reputation as a hardworking poet which brings him to the attention of Jove, thence to the throne of Fame – an experience which teaches him little beyond what he already knows from his reading and observation. Douglas seems to have been impatient of Chaucer's irony and scepticism, or at least anxious to show that the central quest for illumination which is the subject matter of Chaucer's poem as well as his own could be placed in a religious context. Through his portrayal of Honour, Douglas claims a loftier place for poetry and for the office of poet than Chaucer is willing to advance. The scene in which his dream self faints away before the 'glorious visage' of the deity suggests, albeit humorously and modestly, that the poet has a status equivalent to that of the seer. (This view of poetry as prophesy, whatever Chaucer may actually have thought of it, is held up to humorous scrutiny through the mockserious invocation of Apollo at the beginning of the 'lytel laste bok' of *Fame*.) The 'revelation' scene of Douglas's poem stands in marked contrast with the Chaucerian dreamer's long and intensive scrutiny of the enthroned Fame and her operations: the English poet is in no danger of fainting, and his vision brings not the swoon of fearful ecstasy but a speech of commonsense irritation (1873–7). Chaucer makes extensive use of the *Divine Comedy*, transmuting Dante's high seriousness into comic irony, and it is hardly surprising that his poem does not echo Dante's triumphant affirmation of the poet's office as the recorder of divine truth. (*En route* to his destination the poet acknowledges God's greatness, but in the context of his own feebleness.) Douglas is closer to Dante than to Chaucer in this respect, and his expression of intense regret that he was not granted the vision of Honour's vengeance (2107–12) denotes, not a nasty temperament, but a lost opportunity to celebrate the workings of Justice.

    Although the *Palice* is not pervasively ironic in the manner of Chaucer's poem, Douglas follows Chaucer in stressing the commemorative value of poetry. The view of literature as a vehicle for the preservation of the truths of experience as perceived at a particular time and place is of course a commonplace of medieval critical theory, but what is interesting about the connection between the two vision poems is their similarity of emphasis.

Douglas, like Chaucer, places particular stress on historical narrative in prose as well as poetry. The named writers in the statuesque assembly at the court of Fame are all historians: the presence of 'Venus clerk', Ovid, is by no means incongruous, as Chaucer knew him also as the author of historical and mythographic work. In the *Palice* many kinds of writers are present in the Muses' court, but the emphasis is upon the recorders of history, headed by Homer, Virgil and Ovid: this is in keeping with the veneration of Calliope as chief of the Muses, 'For scho of Nobill fatis hes the steir/To write thair worschip, victorie and prowes/in Kinglie stile, quhilk dois thair fame Incres' (875–7). Neither Douglas nor Chaucer celebrate their own national histories in verse, but their elevation of this kind of writing is readily explicable in terms of the variety of subject matter explored by many of the authors they mention, a variety which gave both of them inspiration for their own work. In his comments on the present in which he is attempting to record poetically what is ostensibly his experience, Douglas follows Chaucer again in giving strong emphasis to the difficulty of creating an accurate record for 'remembrance'. The apostrophe at the beginning of Part 1,

> Thow barrant wit, ouirset with fantasyis,
> Schaw now the craft, þat in thy memor lyis.
> Schaw now thy schame, schaw now thy bad nystie,
> Schaw thy endite, reprufe of Rethoryis
>
> (127–30)

nystie folly

is closely related to Chaucer's,

> O Thought, that wrot al that I mette,
> And in the tresorye hyt shette
> Of my brayn, now shal men se
> Yf any vertu in the be,
> To tellen al my drem aryght.
>
> (523–7)

Neither is a simple *captatio benevolentiae*: both reflect a concern for clear and accurate expression, although what precedes the Chaucerian statement – comparison of the vision with the great visions of the Bible and classical literature – is hardly to be taken at face value. Douglas's plea to the Muses to lend 'a recent, schairp, fresche memorie' (1291) repeats the theme of the passage above, while the appeal for 'facund castis [figures] Eloquent' (1290) and 'gratious sweitnes' (1293) emphasises the need for 'craft'. Both poets express their awareness that poetry may be misunderstood and misrepresented. Just as Chaucer calls down a curse upon 'mysdemers', Douglas voices a fear that 'Ianglaris suld it bakbite and stand nane aw' (1268). Expressions of lack of ability, of the need for external guidance and for the favourable disposition of the audience are of course part of the stock-in-trade of late medieval poets, and there can be no suggestion that in this respect Douglas gained his inspiration from Chaucer alone. What is important to note is that Douglas uses the *topoi* in much the same way that Chaucer does in *The Hous of Fame*, to draw attention to some of the poet's fundamental problems in a work in which poetry and the role of the poet are major themes.

In the introductory account of the Muses' court, poetry is defined as 'Ioyous discipline' (846), which recalls the classical *dulce et utile* and its Chaucerian equivalent, the combination of 'sentence' in poetry with 'solaas' and 'mirthe'. Douglas's practice in the *Palice* shows that, like Chaucer, he believed that there was a place for humorous effects in the long narrative poem. In the Scots poem, these have little in common with the elaborate and puzzling game which Chaucer intermittently plays with his audience, but Douglas does follow Chaucer quite closely in characterising his dream persona as one whose timidity invites our amusement. Douglas's 'I' is even more fearful than Chaucer's: at least the poet recently emerged from the temple of Venus has good reason to be startled out of his wits by the 'grymme pawes' and 'sharpe nayles longe' of the eagle which has snatched him so unexpectedly, but the 'grym monstures' of Douglas's wilderness do seem to be only yelling fish. Such is his 'megirnes and pusillamitie' that 'The stichling of a Mous out of presence / Had bene . . . mair vgsum than the Hell' (308–9). When confronted by the angry Venus, his main fear is that he will be metamorphosed:

> Bot sair I dred me for sum vther Iaip,
> That Venus suld throw hir subtillitie
> In till sum bysning beist transfigurat me
> As in a Beir, a Bair, ane Oule, ane Aip.
> I traistit sa for till haue bene mischaip
> That oft I wald my hand behald to se
> Gif it alterit, and oft my visage graip.
>
> (738–44)

bysning monstrous

The inspiration for this is the quaking poet's inability to accept the eagle's genial reassurances in *The Hous of Fame*:

> 'O God!' thoughte I, 'that madest kynde,
> Shal I noon other weyes dye?
> Wher Joves wol me stellyfye,
> Or what thing may this sygnifye?'
>
> (584–7)

In both passages the humour is enriched by the dreamers' recollection of classical and biblical precedents for such transformations: Chaucer thinks of Enoch, Elijah, Romulus and Ganymede (588–92), while Douglas remembers the fates of Acteon, Io, Lot's wife and Nebuchadnezzar (745–58).[8] As in *The Hous of Fame* and *The Parlement of Foules*, the timorousness of the poet in *The Palice of Honour* makes it necessary for his guide to behave boisterously. The nymph who drags the stupefied poet up the mountain by his hair, and who pushes him through the palace gates scolding,

> Quhat deuill . . . hes thow nocht ellis ado
> Bot all thy wit and fantasie to set
> On sic doting?
>
> (1866–8)

is a direct descendant of the eagle who says of Fame's house, 'Hyt is nothing will byten the' (1044). Douglas's 'I', like Chaucer's, 'sweats' in fear (*HF* 1043; *PH* 1868). The passage in *The Palice of Honour* also recalls the scene in *The Parlement of Foules* in which Africanus unceremoniously pushes the dreamer through the gates of the garden of love.

One of the minor literary themes of *The Hous of Fame* concerns the use of scientific subject matter in poetry: the eagle's long discourse on the theory of sound (729–852) is brilliantly justified by its dramatic context. Douglas's appreciation of the passage is clearly indicated by his own discourse on sound, prompted by the music which heralds the arrival of Venus's court (364–81). Like Chaucer's digression, that in *The Palice of Honour* is given a humorous edge by being self-depreciatory. The abrupt breaking-off – 'Aneuch of this – I not quhat it may mene' – creates much the same effect as the unspoken terror of the poet during the eagle's sonorous 'demonstracion'. Another way in which Chaucer's self-characterisation as an actor within his own dream appears to have fired Douglas's imagination concerns the use of autobiography. As well as drawing attention to his office as poet, as Chaucer does in *The Hous of Fame* and the Prologue to *The Legend of Good Women*, Douglas invites his audience to recognise the implications of his clerical status. The trial scene echoes the Chaucerian treatment of the theme of potential conflict between the impulses of the clerk and those of the lover, but introduces the crucial fact that he is a churchman. No doubt the contemporary audience would have appreciated even more than we do the speech in which the poet tries to plead privilege of clergy before Venus (691–702). The nymph's rejoinder to the angry poet, who threatens to strike her after she has taunted him with effeminacy,

> 'Soft ȝow,' said scho, 'thay ar not wise that stryifis,
> For kirkmen war ay gentill to thair wyifis',
>
> (1943–4)

is in the same spirit of comedy as the reference in *The Hous of Fame* to the familiarity of the eagle's voice. This kind of 'personal' comic effect is made possible for Douglas only because, like Chaucer, he enjoyed an easy and intimate rapport with his audience.

In terms of its structure, its arguments concerning the proper relationship between the artist and experience, and its implied comments on various aspects of the nature of poetry, *The Palice of Honour* reflects a close appreciation of *The Hous of Fame*. Yet no reader can fail to be aware of the radical difference in verbal texture between the two. The stylistic difference is itself a commentary on Chaucer's poem, provided that we are able to accept that, like

Chaucer, Douglas was thoroughly engaged in illustrating a theory of decorum, a connection between the matter and the manner of poetic art. The substitution of the journey to Honour for the journey to Fame, and the careful elaboration of the difference between the two concepts, is the starting-point of this demonstration. In his reading of Chaucer's poem, Douglas may have been more penetrating than many of its modern critics, by recognising that its meaning exists as an experiment in imitation, wherein the nature of Fame is embodied through tone and style. Fame, as she is displayed in Book III, is the deity who presides over the confusion of human activity and ambition, imaged in the poem through the endless variety of sounds which seek her court as their 'propre mansyon'. It is entirely natural that a poet should find his way there, since his craft, perhaps more than any other sort of human activity apart from music, is concerned with sound. *En route* to Fame, the dreamer recollects the words of Boethius about the capacities of thought assisted by Philosophy (972-8): like the Boethian traveller he sees 'cloude' beneath him, but the destiny of the English poet, far from being the immutable home of the philosopher's soul, is a world in which the confusions and ambiguities of the real world are magnified to truly bizarre proportions. For Dido, as for the airborne dreamer, all things seem clouded ('kevered with the myst'). The problem of accurate perception, of distinguishing true from false, becomes the subject matter of a comic poem, highlighted dramatically in its idiosyncratic art. The first proem sets the tone for what is to come, by presenting us with a massive sentence of fifty lines in which the various conflicting theories about the causes of dreams are rehearsed. Chaucer offers it as a dramatisation of his own perplexity – 'But why the cause is, noght wot I' – but by the end it is the audience which is more confused. The subsequent invocation, with its solemn threat of a curse on 'mysdemers', suggests that what is to come will be awe-inspiring, to say the least, so the self-consciously banal paraphrase of Virgil has a strong flavour of anti-climax. This is the key to the rhetorical strategy of the poem. Book II, in its tempering of the eagle's heavily pedagogic 'sentence' with the 'solaas' provided by the dramatic framework, is

Chaucerian comedy at its finest, but there is nothing in it to justify either the preliminary comparison with the great biblical and classical visions, or the lofty invocation. The rhetorical preliminaries of the 'lytel laste bok' (which even in its unfinished state is as long as the first two together) promise a 'sentence' which is so sublime in itself that it compels the abandonment of 'craft': here, too, our expectations are disappointed, for in place of the grand and final revelation for which the conventional form of the educative dream vision prepares us, we are offered the long and tedious tableau of the petitioners before Fame. The fact that the 'action' in the court is so repetitive as to make it difficult to distinguish between one company and the next is an essential element of the implied comment about the arbitrary nature of Fame. The lengthy list of musicians in the service of Fame at the beginning of the book, like the catalogue of dream theories at the beginning of the first book, emphasises through its very form the difficulty of separating the genuine from the counterfeit. By the time the poem breaks off its audience has, like Dido and the poet-dreamer in their different ways, been made to experience confusion. The poem is a comic demonstration of the 'illusion' which coexists with life's unlimited variety, and an explanation of why the poet, whose responsibility it is to separate truth from illusion and to create order from chaos, may look so 'fully daswed'.

The *Palice of Honour* ends with three highly-wrought exclamatory stanzas written after the dream in honour of Honour: by their intricate verse form, which combines internal- with end-rhyme, their insistent alliteration and assonance, and their religious imagery, they strive to embody the grandeur of the concept they celebrate. The surprisingly subdued last line, 'For I apply, schortlie, to thy deuise [for in short, I submit myself to your design]' may be read not just as a comment on 'thir versis thre', but on the poem as a whole. The *Palice* is probably the first, and certainly the longest Middle Scots poem to be written in the high aureate style, and since it is directed to a king it is appropriate that its words

> Suld conform to that manis dignitye
> Quhamto our wark we direct and endyte.
> (*Eneados* IX Prol., 34–5).

As well as the consideration due to the nature of its audience, the poem's level of style seems to be a commentary on the manner of *The Hous of Fame*: just as Douglas defines Honour in his third book as a superior goal to Fame, so too he chooses a loftier style to complement and celebrate his subject matter. There is certainly an affinity between the two poems, in the extent to which manner and matter are related: of no other late medieval 'Inglis' poems can it be said that 'craft' is so closely linked with 'sentence' that the two elements may be frequently indistinguishable. Where Chaucer's experiment in matching style to subject matter leads to some very flat poetic terrain, Douglas's essay in the high style follows the opposite, but equally dangerous path to a consistently elevated poetic edifice. Whereas the rhetorical preliminaries of Chaucer's poem are part of a strategy of anti-climax, Douglas strives to match the style and substance of his books to the portentous implications of their prologues. There is no place in the Scots poem for ironic obfuscation, and the action of the vision is a carefully orchestrated progression towards the final revelation of what Honour means to the practising poet. (One critic complains of 'a lack of climax', but only because he regards the end of the journey as the vision of the deity, rather than of the garden of rhetoric.)[9] The most striking feature of Douglas's language and imagery is its display of learned, polysyllabic terms, many of which have been coined from Latin: these tend to cluster within the descriptive parts of the poem, although they occur throughout. Douglas's handling of aureate vocabulary is highly successful because his 'poleit' effects are placed within the setting of a cultivated middle style which draws freely on homely vernacular speech. Douglas's aureate language is a less conspicuous part of the poem's stylistic 'fowth [fullness, amplitude]' than the various kinds of structural amplification in which the *Palice* abounds. A detailed analysis of these effects is beyond the scope of this chapter, but those in search of them will find nearly all of the rhetorical colours detailed in the early medieval handbooks. Mrs Bawcutt points out that Douglas's favourite rhetorical colour is *repetitio*[10] – the echoing of the same word or phrase at the beginning of consecutive lines, accompanied usually by parallel grammatical structure: in these lines the device merges with that of *exclamatio*,

> Quhat sang! Quhat Ioy! Quhat harmonie! Quhat licht!
> Quhat mirthfull solace, plesance all at richt!
> Quhat fresche bewtie! Quhat excelland estait!
> Quhat sweit vocis! Quhat wordis suggurait!
>
> (403ff.)

The most insistent form of *amplificatio*, however, is the catalogue, as Denton Fox observes:[11] the poem contains lists of wise men (250–62), musical instruments (501–5), precious textiles (537–43), lovers (562–89), place names (1086–1133), poets (896–924), and heroes (1194–1215). In this context it is interesting to see that Chaucer's gallery of famous poets grows from twelve to thirty-six in the *Palice*. Douglas's fondness for detailed description contrasts with Chaucer's practice in *The Hous of Fame*: for example both palaces have richly ornamented gates of gold, but Chaucer's perfunctory and generalised ten-line account (*HF* 1294–1304) is replaced in the Scots poem by a lengthy and detailed description (1834–63). All of Douglas's rhetorical effects are heightened by the unusually elaborate stanza form, in which rhymes are limited to a bare minimum. Books I and II employ the *Anelida and Arcite* model, the third book the equally complicated stanza of *The Complaint of Mars*. It would appear that Douglas's choice of the two forms which Chaucer uses only for shorter poems was intended to draw attention to his own facility in the 'Ioyous discipline' of poetry.

The ornate style of the *Palice* is surprisingly successful – the Venus's-mirror episode is the only part of the poem where the catalogue form becomes seriously strained, but even then it is possible to see that the episode plays a part in the developing argument. The central situation of the fearful dreamer–poet's quest for Honour is never neglected, and full use is made of the potential for humorous effect which it offers. Douglas's restraint in describing the garden in which grow 'the sweit flureist flouris of Rethoreis' is masterly. A more elaborate *descriptio* would inevitably have duplicated some of the effects of the *locus amoenus* Prologue, and the middle style provides an effective foil for the following hymn to Honour, a triumphant résumé of the poem's most elaborate rhetorical effects. Nowhere is the high style an impediment to narrative coherence or to meaning. C. S. Lewis, the first modern critic to express an enjoyment of Douglas's poem, damns with faint praise when he describes it as 'sheer wonderland, a phantasmagoria of dazzling lights and eldritch glooms, whose real *raison d'être* is not their allegorical meaning, but their immediate appeal to the imagination'.[12] *The Palice of Honour* is a more accomplished poem than *The Hous of Fame*: Chaucer's poem has passages of undeniable brilliance, but no amount of exposition can disguise either its essentially fragmentary nature, or the sheer dullness of much of Books I and III. Douglas's work is an ordered yet varied celebration of the concept of Harmony, which stands as a counterpart to Chaucer's disordered and anti-climactic anatomy of disorder. There is nothing in *The Palice of Honour* to rival the extended high comedy of Chaucer's Book II, yet as a whole the Scots poem is arguably a more successful work than Chaucer's.

5
Dunbar and Skelton

(i) Dunbar and English poetry

The poetry of William Dunbar, like that of his contemporaries Douglas and Henryson, has the ease and assurance conferred by familiarity with European literary tradition. It reflects the intelligent eclecticism which marks the writing of his Scots contemporaries, and although Dunbar is not a learned poet in the manner of the other two, his work like theirs shows an acquaintance with classical Latin poetry, French amatory poetry, secular and devotional lyrics in Latin, and the alliterative poetry of his own country which had come originally from northern England. *The Lament for the Makaris* leaves no doubt about Dunbar's respect for his 'brether' makars in Scotland and his consciousness of a local tradition, but it is important to remember that the roll-call of dead and dying poets is headed by Chaucer, 'of makaris flour'. The English trio are the only non-Scottish writers (apart from Homer and Cicero) whom Dunbar acknowledges by name, and the poems themselves support the suggestion of *The Lament* and *The Goldyn Targe* that English poetry, in particular the poetry of Chaucer, is the most important external influence on Dunbar's work. That said, it is necessary to add that there are probably no two medieval poets more unlike than Chaucer and Dunbar – the one versatile but customarily unostentatious as a stylist, exploring a variety of themes through characterisation, irony and disposition of his 'matere' in long poems, the other equally versatile, but usually a self-conscious virtuoso, his preference being for statement rather than allusion, and for shorter rather than longer poetic forms. Several of Dunbar's poems suggest knowledge of works by Chaucer and Lydgate, but the differences between particular English and Scots poems are invariably more instructive than the similarities. There is no equivalent in Dunbar's poetry to the kind of influence which is discernible as verbal echo in *The Kingis Quair*, or as critical response to Chaucerian poems in the *Testament* and *The Palice of Honour*. Only a few of Dunbar's many poems are related to particular English works, although it may be that Chaucer and perhaps also Lydgate influenced Dunbar in more general ways which it is difficult to define with any precision.

Dunbar's *The Tretis of the Tua Mariit Wemen and the Wedo* and *Of Sir Thomas Norny* are closely related to two of *The Canterbury Tales*, the Wife of Bath's Prologue and Tale, and the pilgrim-poet's own 'drasty speche', *Sir Thopas*. The *Tretis* and the Wife's Prologue belong to a long tradition of anti-feminist satire, represented by the collection of writings which the Wife of Bath's most recent husband possesses 'bounded in o volume', and by more recent literature such as sections of Jean de Meun's continuation of the *Roman de la Rose* and the French *chansons à mal mariée*. This extensive tradition may explain some, but not all, of the resemblances between the English and the Scots poems: the rich irony of Dunbar's 'uncouth aventur' does seem to have been augmented by his reading of Chaucer. At the simplest level of meaning, both poems amplify a familiar satirical view of women and matrimony, expressed thus in the lesson which Chaucer's knight-errant learns from the crone:

> Wommen desiren to have sovereynetee
> As wel over hir housbond as hir love,
> And for to been in maistrie hym above.
>
> (1038–40)

In both poems this 'moralitie', and much more, is presented in memorable dramatic form, through the presentation of those two highly experienced embodiments of 'sovereynetee', the Wedo and the Wife of Bath. Both are preachers of the art, and their autobiographies draw on the manner of the medieval sermon. The Wife's specious use of biblical authority at the beginning of her story has its counterpart in the Wedo's appeal for divine guidance before she begins,

> God my spreit now inspir and my speche quykkin,
> And send me sentence to say, substantious and noble;
> Sa that my preching may pers your perverst hertis,
> And mak yow mekar to men in maneris and conditiounis.
> (247-50)

The self-appointed sexual divines presume to make general pronouncements upon female psychology, speaking as the representatives of 'we women':

> We love no man that taketh kep or charge
> Wher that we goon; we wol ben at oure large.
>
> Deceite, wepyng, spynnyng God hath yive
> To wommen kyndely, whil that they may lyve
> (WB Prol., 321-2, 401-2)

>   for certis, we wemen
> We set us all fra the syght to syle men of treuth:
> We dule for na evill deid, sa it be derne haldin.
> Wise wemen has wayis and wonderfull gydingis
> With gret engyne to bejaip ther jolyus husbandis;
> And quyetly, with sic craft, convoyis our materis
> That, under Crist, no creatur kennis of our doingis.
> (*Tretis*, 448-54)

syle mislead; *dule* grieve; *derne haldin* held secret

Dunbar follows Chaucer in creating a further dramatic irony which is inherent in the relationship between speaker and audience. The Wife's assertion of female sovereignty is given a dramatic edge by her tilts at three male members of the Canterbury company, the Pardoner, the Friar and the Clerk, two of whom make some attempt at retaliation: indeed the whole of the Clerk's tale of Grisilde is offered as revenge on the Wife and 'al hire secte' (E, 1170-1212). Dunbar provides a similar dramatic and ironic context for his essay in sexual politics by the device of presenting the poem itself to an audience which includes men – 'Quhilk wald ye waill to your wif, gif ye suld wed one?' The women are so frank in their disclosures only because they believe that 'ther is no spy neir', while all the time a clerk who represents 'the kyn of Adam' is listening behind the hedge. The fact that both poems provide an ironic link between speaker and audience suggests that Dunbar's distinctive use of the convention of poet as spectator may have derived its inspiration from Chaucer's practice.

There are several correspondences of narrative detail between the Wife's autobiography and that of the Wedo: this is hardly surprising, since both figures provide what they regard as a *summa* of female sexual experience, but some of them indicate that Dunbar may have borrowed from Chaucer. For example, the two characters' attitudes to religious observance are very similar. Both take advantage of the opportunity for personal display which is offered by 'preichingis and pilgrimages' (*WB* Prol., 556–8; *Tretis* 70–2). Alice feigns grief at her husband's funeral – 'for it is usage' (580) – to cover her search for a new 'paire / Of legges and of feet so clene and faire' (597–8). Similarly, the Wedo attends mass to make fresh conquests (534–5), wetting her cheeks with a sponge to win the sympathy of her late husband's friends (436–43). A more interesting point of resemblance between the poems is the presence in both of them of an ironic tension created by the juxtaposition of two conventional ways of writing about sexual relationships, the modes of courtly romance and of *fabliau*. In the case of the Wife of Bath, the contrast is between the framework of the Prologue and that of the Tale. Her choice of metaphor is one of the ways in which her sensuality is expressed: she accepts the validity of her old husband's simile of the cat (348–56), going on to liken herself to a horse (386), and later to draw attention to her 'coltes tooth' (602). This kind of reference is directly opposed to the courtly mode of her tale, which explores the nature of 'gentillesse'. The Tale is permeated by the irony that its teller fails to live up to the definition of gentleness advanced by the crone – 'Thanne am I gentil, whan that I bigynne / To lyven vertuously and weyve synne' (1175–6). In the *Tretis*, courtly conventions and the courtly ethic are invoked in the introductory descriptive passage, in the concluding *demande d'amour*, and in the Wedo's reference to the central tenet of feminine pity,[1]

> Bot mercy in to womanheid is a mekle vertu,
> For never bot in a gentill hert is generit ony ruth.
>
> (315–16)

On the other level, there is a profusion of animal references, applied to men and women alike: man is likened to a horse (114, 354–7), a worm (89), a 'dotit dog' (186),[2] while women are urged to recognise their diabolical potential:

> Be dragonis baith and dowis ay in double forme,
> And quhen it nedis yow, onone, note baith ther strenthis.
> (263–4)

onone anon

Although the juxtaposition of courtly and animal definitions of sexuality suggests that Dunbar drew on Chaucer's poem, the nature and the effects of the contrast are very different from those of the Wife of Bath's Prologue and Tale. The *Tretis* is a poem of extremes, in a way that Chaucer's poem is not. In the transition from the Wife of Bath's Prologue to her Tale there is no abrupt heightening or refinement of rhetoric to highlight the gulf between the world of boisterous sexual conflict and the world which has 'gentillesse' as its supreme value: both parts are written in the familiar Canterbury middle style of eloquence. In the Scots poem, by contrast, there is a startling jump from the ornate *descriptio* of the 'thre gay ladeis' to the self-consciously coarse mode of the first confession. The Wife has no reticence about discussing male and female sexual functions, but her language does not pass the bounds of mild vulgarity established by the 'cherles tales' of the Miller and the Reeve. Her expressions of pride in her 'likerous tayl' and in her power over a husband who might have 'pissed on a wal' are far removed in both rhetoric and thought from even the milder sections of disclosure in the Scots poem:

> I have ane wallidrag, ane worme, ane auld wobat carle,
> A waistit wolroun, na worth bot wourdis to clatter;
> Ane bumbart, ane dron bee, ane bag full of flewme,
> Ane skabbit skarth, ane scorpioun, ane scutarde behind.
> (89–92)

wallidrag sloven; *wobat* caterpillar; *wolroun* mongrel; *bumbart* drone; *skarth* cormorant; *scutarde* one who evacuates

The accretion of unpleasant physical detail in the *Tretis*, emphasised by the pervasive use of alliteration, is quite un-Chaucerian, and is even more outrageous in effect than the most graphic sections of Gluttony's confession in *Piers Plowman*. Dunbar's poem, like Chaucer's Prologue and Tale, contains an element of conventional satire on the kin of Eve, but in neither poem is satire the predominant effect. Chaucer's Prologue and Tale are very closely linked, and their combined 'sentence' is the portrait of the Wife herself – lustful, aggressive and avaricious, but at the same time appealing in her vitality and in her wistful attempt to challenge the power of time 'that al wole envenyme'. Dunbar may well have appreciated the delicate psychological realism of Chaucer's satire, but he makes no attempt to imitate it. The marital sufferings of the first two of Dunbar's women compel a limited amount of sympathy, but with the Wedo's sermon the poem moves into the realm of fantasy.[3] The portrait of woman's cruelty and depravity is just as unreal in its own way as the description of idealised Nature and idealised feminine beauty with which the poem opens. There is nothing in the Wedo's confession which corresponds in tone to the warmth which Dame Alice feels for her most recent husband, or to her nostalgia for youth. Both the nature of the 'legeand' and the manner of its expression become so grotesque that it is impossible to infer that any very serious 'moralitie' about women, marriage or sexuality in general is intended. The poem is a species of court entertainment, with the same kind of verbal and vituperative appeal as the 'flyting'. The taste for this kind of poetry is as distinctively Scots as the taste for sustained alliteration in the fifteenth century, and one suspects that Chaucer and his audience would have found it rather difficult to comprehend.

Dunbar's shorter poem, *Of Sir Thomas Norny*, was also written as court entertainment: this is the implication of the reference to 'Pesche and Yull' (49), seasons which were especially festive occasions in the household of James IV.[4] The hero of the poem was one of the royal fools, so a degree of complicity on his part may be assumed. Like Chaucer's *Sir Thopas*, it exploits the conventions of the tail-rhyme romance to humorous effect, and it may be safely assumed that Dunbar knew and used it as a model for his own poem. Like Chaucer, Dunbar uses the verse form and other characteristics of a popular genre – the minstrel's call for attention, recitation of the hero's pedigree, a formalised account of 'aunters [adventures]' in love and war, comparison with the famous heroes of the past – for a purpose other than the conventional one of glorification. It has been suggested that in writing a humorous tail-rhyme romance which employs a larger than usual proportion of southern words and forms, Dunbar was reminding his audience of *Sir Thopas*.[5] Such a comparison may well have been intended (indeed it is an approach which would have been familiar to those who knew *The Testament of Cresseid* and *The Palice of Honour*), but if so the audience would have been conscious as much of differences between the two poems as of their similarities.

Chaucer's poem is a parody, which invites its audience to observe the potential for monotony and anti-climax which is inherent in the tail-rhyme form, with its well-worn formulae, its insistent rhymes and its breathless transitions from long lines to short. *Sir Thopas* is a masterpiece of irrelevance, and although there is an element of satire in the fact that the effeminate knight-errant has a decidedly bourgeois cast, the appeal of the tale has less to do with any social realities than with the comic dislocation of a familiar literary form. Dunbar's poem is satirical rather than parodic: it uses the form of tail-rhyme romance to ridicule the exploits of those who would be seen as exemplars of chivalry even though they lack the necessary qualifications of noble birth and high courage. (The poem seems to be grounded on some event, the significance of which is no longer apparent, involving the Quenetyne and Curry who are mentioned so unfavourably.) Whereas Chaucer exploits the anti-climactic tendency of the 'tail' for parodic effect, Dunbar's end lines have a sharper, sarcastic edge:

> He hes att werslingis bein ane hunder,
> Yet lay his body never at under:
> He knawis giff this be leis.
>
> (22–3)

werslingis wrestling-matches

The Scots poem is topical in a way that Chaucer's work is not, in making a particular person the subject of comic deflation, a kind of entertainment which, if we are to judge from several of Dunbar's other poems, was very congenial to his audience. The pungency of its effects is far removed from Chaucer's delicate and subtle ironies, and in this respect *Sir Thomas* bears a relationship to *Sir Thopas* similar to that which exists between *The Tretis* and the Wife of Bath's Prologue and Tale.

The relationship between two of Dunbar's poems and two of *The Canterbury Tales* may be only one indication of Chaucer's influence. It is possible that Chaucer's poetry exerted a more profound and pervasive influence on Dunbar's style and choice of poetic form, as Denton Fox has suggested. As an indication of borrowing from Chaucer, he cites 'Dunbar's prevailingly syllabic metrics . . . and his willingness to accept into his poetry rhetorical figures and learned words', and his fondness for what are called 'Chaucerian genres' – 'allegorical poems about spring and love, dream visions, moral lyrics, and witty begging poems'.[6] There is simply no way of testing the extent of Dunbar's borrowing from Chaucer in either of these respects, but it is probably not of the proportions that Professor Fox implies. Allowance must be made for Dunbar's originality, for his undoubted acquaintance with poetry other than Chaucer's, and for what might be considered the secondary influence of Chaucer's achievement – the extent to which Dunbar's practice was conditioned by that of other writers, Scots and English, who had themselves been influenced by Chaucer. The willingness to accept rhetorical figures and learned words may argue an appreciation of Chaucer's flexible approach to language, but it is impossible to be more specific: all medieval poetry, after all, demonstrates the use of rhetorical figures, and Dunbar's use of a learned high style has more in common with the practice of Lydgate. Like Chaucer, Dunbar is a master of tonal variation, moving easily from one register of language to another within the same poem, and making extensive use of a middle style of poetic eloquence. The same kind of comparison with Chaucer can, however, be made in respect of James I, Henryson or Douglas. Like his fellow-makars Dunbar was able to reconcile the traditions of stress and syllabic metre, and the effect is sometimes reminiscent of Chaucer, although the frequent use of octosyllabic couplets with a regular four-stress line indicates a metrical affinity with Wyntoun and Barbour rather than Chaucer. It is only in the area of Dunbar's rhetorical and metrical differences from Chaucer that confident judgements may be made. There is no Chaucerian counterpart to the yoking together of rhetorical extremes in poems such as *The Tretis* and *The Fenyeit Freir*, to the sustained use of the aureate style in *The Goldyn Targe* and the poems of religious celebration, and to the intensive exploitation of abusive rhetoric in *The Flyting* and several of the complaint poems. The intensity of Dunbar's effects is usually emphasised by the fact that most of his poems are short: Chaucer's preference is for longer forms of narrative which allow the maximum scope for conversational and dramatic effects. If we are to judge from variety of metre and stanzaic form, Dunbar was fascinated by the possibilities of poetic form: this is apparent, too, in his use of many different genres. His poetry is rivalled only by *The Canterbury Tales* in the extent to which it illustrates the power of an individual talent to reshape and revive inherited forms and conventions. Dunbar expresses his admiration for Chaucer's 'illumination' of poetic language, and no doubt he was impressed too by Chaucer's achievement as a 'translateur' of continental poetic forms into English. His own choice of genres, however, affords very little in the way of recognisable indebtedness to Chaucer. A full century after his death, the 'Chaucerian genres' had been thoroughly integrated into the native poetic tradition, and in any case the greater part of Dunbar's work belongs to genres which were not used by Chaucer (localised satires and celebrations, religious lyrics).

The brevity and compression of Dunbar's dream visions are in marked contrast with the discursive and leisurely Chaucerian manner, but one of them, *The Thrissil and the Rois*, contains an interesting adaptation of a distinctively Chaucerian first-person technique. In this poem, which commemorates the union of the Scottish Thistle with the English Rose in the marriage of James to Margaret Tudor, Dunbar represents himself as one who is reluctant to rise from his bed in May to perform the poet's duty of 'indyting' when urged to do so by the lady who personifies the season:

> 'Quhairto,' quod I, 'sall I uprys at morrow,
> For in this May few birdis herd I sing?
> Thai haif moir caus to weip and plane thair sorrow,
> Thy air it is nocht holsum nor benyng . . .'
>
> (29–32)

Like Henryson in the opening of the *Testament*, Dunbar is doing more here than simply highlighting the difference between the literary climatic ideal and the reality of the Scottish spring. The primary effect of his reluctance, and the fact that May binds him to his promise 'for to discryve the Ros of most plesance', is to distance the poet from the idealised celebration of the vision. The note of disquiet is sounded again at the end of the poem, when he reports that he awoke 'halflingis in affrey'. There is a parallel to this way of providing a counterpoise to the harmonious celebration of the dream in the Chaucerian manner of withdrawal in *The Parlement of Foules*. There, too, the poet is awakened by the 'shoutyng' of the birds, and his hope to find 'some thyng for to fare / The bet' has the similar effect of suggesting the distance between the ideal dream world and the world of waking reality. Chaucer's technique is well adapted to the subject matter of *The Thrissil and the Rois*: Dunbar uses it to give an edge of complexity to what would otherwise be what has been described as poetry of 'statement' and 'surfaces'.[7] Just as the Scottish landscape and climate cannot, even in spring, live up to the ideal of the *locus amoenus*, so too James IV cannot be the ruler of the just and harmonious kingdom portrayed in Nature's heraldic pageant.

Although Dunbar's work is very different from Chaucer's – in terms of subject matter, style, scale and indeed of the kind of creative treatment which all of these reflect – it is inevitable that the comparison with Chaucer will be made, because of Dunbar's imaginative power and technical proficiency. The term 'Scottish Chaucerian' is of very limited use as an approach to the distinctive qualities of his poetry, but one suspects that Dunbar would have approved its use as praise for the standard of his 'making'. Since his borrowings from Chaucer are relatively slight – even after allowance has been made for a diffuse and scarcely tangible stylistic debt – it may seem surprising that he drew anything at all from Chaucer's prolific, popular, but vastly inferior, English follower. Claims have been made that Dunbar is a 'Scottish Lydgatian',[8] but he would probably have repudiated the label in stern 'flyting' style. To see that Dunbar is in no sense a disciple of Lydgate, one has only to compare his work with that of his English contemporary Stephen Hawes, who does imitate Lydgate's uniformity of tone, the diffuse syntactic structures, the use of 'cloudy fygures' of allegory, and even his prolixity. Dunbar's conciseness and control mark him as a very different kind of poet, but nevertheless there are certain parallels between his work and Lydgate's which suggest interest in part at least of Lydgate's vast output. Several of Dunbar's poems belong to genres used by Lydgate. Both write short satirical pieces directed at particular individuals or occupational groups, following them up with ironical palinodes: the poems addressed to James Doig and to the tailors and soutars have Lydgatian equivalents in the *Ballade on an Ale-Seller* and *Ballade per Antiphrasim*.[9] Many of Dunbar's didactic poems which incorporate refrains and catalogues have counterparts in what Lydgate's editor refers to as 'little homilies with proverbial refrains'. Both write occasional poetry and works of religious celebration. All of these genres are thoroughly conventional, and in itself the correspondence is no proof that Dunbar was inspired by Lydgate. Nevertheless, there are occasional echoes of detail which suggest that Dunbar may have taken over themes and techniques from Lydgatian works. This passage from *Of Deming*, for example,

> Be I bot littill of stature,
> Thay call me catyve createure;
> And be I grit of quantetie,
> Thay call me monstrowis of nature;
> Thus can I not undemit be
>
> (26–30)

is obviously related to some lines from Lydgate's *A Wicked Tunge Wille Sey Amys*:[10]

> Ʒif thow be fatte owther corpolent,
> Than wille folke seyn thow art a grete glotoun,
> A deuowrer or ellis vinolent;

> ȝif thow be lene or megre of fassioun,
> Calle the a negard yn ther oppynyoun,
> ȝitte suffre hem speke and triste right wel this,
> A wicked tonge wille alwei sei a-mys.
>
> (43–9)

The common subject matter, together with the use of a *pro* and *contra* arrangement, does suggest that the Scots knew Lydgate's lines, although the differences of effect are more revealing than the similarities. The Scots passage is much sharper in outline than the English: the syntax is tighter, and the use of the short line makes the answering effect more striking, giving the effect of an exasperated speaking voice. The use of the first person instead of the second also contributes to a gain in immediacy.

Dunbar's remarkable power in adapting from and combining conventions in order to make an individual poetic statement is well illustrated by the relationship between *The Lament for the Makaris* and three of Lydgate's works, *Timor Mortis Conturbat Me*, the *Daunce Machabree*, and the *Testament*.[11] Again, the question of precise indebtedness is complicated by the traditional nature of all three, but if Dunbar did not draw on Lydgate's poems, it is clear that he knew others which were very much like them. The *Lament* has as literary background three kinds of didactic poem on the theme of the imminence of death: the mortality poem in which the speaker is an old or sick man,[12] the meditation with liturgical refrain (exemplified by Lydgate's *Timor Mortis*), and the much rarer Dance of Death. Lydgate's *Testament*, part celebration of the majesty of Christ, part carefully generalised personal confession, is of the first kind: the effect of the revelation that the poet is 'Gretly feblysshed of old infirmite' as he writes is to give the poem a distinctive authority which is independent of the literal truth of the statement. Dunbar's *Lament* may well have been inspired by a specific private experience, but if so the articulation of the experience was shaped to a considerable extent by literary tradition: the mood of the *Lament*, which begins 'I that in heill wes and gladnes, / Am trublit now with gret seiknes, / And feblit with infermite' suggests strong personal feeling,[13] but this is more a matter of technique than of autobiographical detail. The Scots poem, like Lydgate's *Testament* and *Timor Mortis*, has a significance which is as much public as private, as its conclusion makes clear:

> Sen for the deid remeid is none,
> Best is that we for dede dispone,
> Eftir our deid that lif may we;
> *Timor mortis conturbat me.*
>
> (97–100)

The corresponding lines in the English poem are as follows:

> Enpreente this mateer in your mynde,
> And remembre wel on this lessoun,
> Al wourldly good shal leve be hynde,
> Tresour and greet pocessioun.
> So sodeyn transmutacioun
> Ther may no bettir socour be
> Than ofte thynke on Cristes passioun
> Whan *timor mortis conturbat me.*
>
> (121–8)

The difference between the two is one of technique. Dunbar's stanza is concise and understated, and its use of 'we' in the second last line avoids Lydgate's awkward transition from second-person address to the '*me*' of the refrain. Like Lydgate, Dunbar uses the refrain from the Office for the Dead to give authority and sonority, but the shorter stanza in the Scots poem gives the further effect of imitating the insistent rhythm of the *Totentanz*. The second similarity between the two poems is the extensive use of catalogue. Lydgate begins with the proposition that there would have been no *timor mortis* but for Adam's transgression, and proceeds to give a long list of the biblical figures claimed by Death: to this is added the Nine Worthies, and a ménage of biblical and romance heroines. In all, the list occupies some fifty lines, and is typically Lydgatian in its inclusiveness. Its counterpart in the *Lament* is a specific and localised list of poets, most of whom must have been known to Dunbar's audience. Dunbar's list is arranged to produce a powerful cumulative effect, beginning with the triad of English poets, going on through the company of deceased Scots makars to Walter Kennedy 'In poynt of dede', and concluding with the poet's own *timor mortis*:

> Sen he hes all my brethir tane,
> He will nocht lat me lif alane,
> On forse I man his nyxt pray be;
> *Timor mortis conturbat me.*
>
> (93–6)

There is no comparable sense of involvement and personal relevance in Lydgate's poem, although it is only fair to point out that nothing of the kind is attempted.

The central image of Lydgate's *Daunce Machabree* – a loose translation from French, and the only known poem of its kind in English – is the figure of Death who speaks to and claims figures from all ranks of society. Literary criticism has a limited relevance to the poem, as it exists in isolation from what was almost certainly its visual complement, a mural painting of the characters in the dance. Presumably the London mural was a larger version of the ceiling decoration in the Lady Chapel at Roslin near Edinburgh, which shows some twenty-three figures, some of whom are clutched by a skeleton.[14] The figures in the St Clair chapel are not accompanied by inscriptions, but their existence suggests that other versions of the *Totentanz* may have been known to Dunbar. Lines 17–44 of the *Lament* recall Lydgate's poem most clearly, although they are not divided into speeches of claim and reply. Instead there is a description of Death's remorseless activity, in which the techniques of parallelism and listing are very prominent:

> On to the ded gois all Estatis,
> Princis, Prelotis, and Potestatis,
> Baith riche and pur of al degre;
> *Timor mortis conturbat me.*
>
> He takis the knychtis in to feild,
> Anarmit under helme and scheild;
> Victour he is at all mellie;
> *Timor mortis conturbat me.*
>
> That strang unmercifull tyrand
> Takis, on the moderis breist sowkand,
> The bab full of benignite;
> *Timor mortis conturbat me.*

> He takis the campion in the stour,
> The capitane closit in the tour,
> The lady in bour full of bewte;
> Timor mortis conturbat me.
>
> (17-32)

campion champion; *stour* battle

Given the comprehensiveness of Lydgate's list, it is hardly surprising that there should be some overlapping with the Scottish one: both include knight, baby, captain, lady and clerk. Of rather more interest are Lydgate's 'scientists' – the astronomer, the magician and the physician – who correspond to Dunbar's,

> Art-magicianis, and astrologgis,
> Rethoris, logicianis, and theologgis
>
> In medicyne the most practicianis,
> Lechis, surrigianis, and phisicianis.
>
> (37-8, 41-2)

The resemblances may be wholly coincidental, but it is possible that Dunbar expanded the English list in the direction of those 'servitouris' who enjoyed the particular favour of James IV. Rather surprisingly, in view of his usual preference for the general and the universal, Lydgate departs from his original at one point to include a real person at the court of Henry V. After claiming the minstrel, Death turns to

> Maister Jon Rikelle some tyme tregetowre
> Of nobille harry kynge of Ingelonde.
>
> (st. 65)

It is just possible that this piece of local detail in the *Daunce Machabree* may have given Dunbar the idea for his list of poets dead and about to die.

The borrowings from literary tradition as it is represented by Lydgate's poems are combined with original subject matter – the list of poets – and incorporated into a powerfully original poetic structure. The *Lament* portrays an inexorable movement from the universal to the particular and personal: it begins with a general statement about 'the stait of man', illustrating this with the examples of several kinds and ranks of humanity. Emphasis is placed on those courtiers who are also men of learning, from whom it is an inevitable step to the poets and to a poignantly understated treatment of the *ars longa, vita brevis* theme. The poem stresses the mortality of poets very clearly, but there is also an implied contrast between the poets and the 'estaitis' mentioned earlier. Poets, unlike even the most learned or valiant courtiers, have the opportunity to create something which defeats Death and oblivion and hence to ensure the perpetuity of their names: the *Lament* enacts this by naming them and no one else. Dunbar's proud boast in the *Remonstrance to the King* – 'Als lang in mynd my wark sall hald . . . As ony of thair werkis all' (28–33) – comes immediately to mind, but in the *Lament* confidence in this measure of immortality is heavily outweighed by the personal fear of death. In the second last stanza the poet speaks as Death's next victim – 'On forse I man his nyxt pray be' – and the imminence of the mocking figure of Lydgate's poem is keenly felt. The poem does not end here, though: in the last stanza the personal meditation merges into a subtle form of didacticism by its use of the first person plural – 'Best is that *we* for dede dispone.' The rhetorical strategy is the same as that which underlies the presentation of the speaker in a contemporary English mortality lyric:[15]

> I wende to dede, clerk full of skill,
> Þat cowthe with wordes men mate & stylle.
> So sone has þe dede me made ane end –
> Bes war with me! to dede I wende.

In *The Lament*, the powerful evocation of the poet's *timor mortis* prompts his audience to identify strongly with him, and hence to be inclined to accept his advice about the need to 'dispone' for death. There is nothing in the poetry of Lydgate, not even the avowedly autobiographical *Testament*, which is remotely comparable with the fusion of the individual and the universal in the *Lament*.

The comprehensiveness of Lydgate's poems, their pedantic and seemingly exhaustive working-out of conventional themes and devices of style, appears to have made some of them valuable to Dunbar as sources of imagery, although not as models to be imitated. Both *The Goldyn Targe* and *The Thrissil and the Rois*, for example, contain images which seem to have been borrowed from the long and pedestrian allegory, *Reson and Sensuallyte*.[16] In the *Targe*, several details from the English poem come together in lines which have a similar moral context: the image of the dew, the treatment of Nature and the description of her mantle, the ship and the musical catalogue.[17] In *The Thrissil and the Rois* the figure of May wears the mantle given her by Nature in the *Targe* (87–90):

> Hevinly of color, quhyt, reid, broun, and blew,
> Balmit in dew and gilt with Phebus bemys,
> Quhill all the hous illumynit of hir lemys.
>
> (19–21)

lemys beams

The context suggests that the image has been developed from Lydgate's Dame Nature, who wears a mantle 'Wrought of foure elementys' (*RS*, 351). Dunbar's May, like Lydgate's Nature, visits the poet in his chamber, illuminating it with her radiance (*TR* 21, *RS* 214–24), and from *Reson and Sensuallyte* seems to have been developed the idea of the goddess's chastisement and instruction of the poet-figure. May addresses him as 'slugird', bidding him 'awalk anone for schame', and to participate in the spirit of the spring morning by writing something in her honour. Lydgate's Nature says,

> My childe . . . thou art to blame,
> And vn-to the yt is gret shame,
> Thy self so longe to encombre,
> Thus to slepe and to slombre
> This glade morwe fresh and lyght.
>
> (445–9)

She is more high-minded than Dunbar's goddess, pressing on her poet the 'occupacioun' of right living rather than the writing of a mere poem. In *The Thrissil and the Rois* the poet's reluctance to perform his task is Dunbar's own invention, and it contributes, as I have explained, to an effect which is more characteristic of Chaucer than of Lydgate. As in the borrowings for *The Goldyn Targe*, Dunbar takes a few details from Lydgate, altering them to accord with his own thematic purpose. The accounts of nature in Dunbar's two courtly allegories reflect his appreciation of other

Lydgatian poems. The charming portrait of the regal month in the *Targe*, for example,

> There saw I May, of myrthfull monethis quene,
> Betuix Aprile and June, her sistir schene,
> Within the gardyng walking up and doun
>
> (82-4)

echoes the details of a similar metaphor in the *Testament* (329-31), and there is the same sort of relationship between the elaborate accounts of the dawn in the *Targe* and *The Flower of Courtesy*.[18] This poem, which was also known to James I, is an extensive piece of Chaucer imitation, and the following passage shows the influence of a kind of imagery, found in *The Knight's Tale*, *Troilus and Criseyde*, and the Prologue to *The Legend of Good Women*:

> And yet I was ful thursty in languisshyng;
> Myn ague was so feruent in his hete
> Whan Aurora, for drery complaynyng,
> Can distyl her chrystal teeres wete
> Vpon the soyle, with syluer dewe so swete,
> For she durste, for shame, not apere
> Vnder the lyght of Phebus beames clere.
>
> (36-42)

Dunbar's lines are closer to those of Lydgate (or his imitator) than they are to any of the Chaucerian passages:

> Anamalit was the felde wyth all colouris,
> The perly droppis schake in silvir schouris,
> Quhill all in balme did branch and levis flete;
> To part fra Phebus did Aurora grete,
> Hir cristall teris I saw hyng on the flouris,
> Quhilk he for lufe all drank up wyth his hete.
>
> (*GT*, 13-18)

flete waver, move

Both use the metaphor of Aurora and Phoebus, with the dew as the lover's tears ('crystal' and 'silver'), and both play on the connection between moisture and heat, rhyming 'swete' and 'hete'. The Lydgatian lines are an elegant example of this kind of description, but Dunbar succeeds in making his model even more expressive. This is done partly by alliteration, and partly by the emphasis given to the mythological reference: Lydgate's Aurora weeps 'for shame', but in the *Targe* her tears are those of parting, which her lover acknowledges by drinking them with his 'hete'. Beside this ingenious and evocative image, the lover's tears of Lydgate's poem appear pallid and conventional. The elaborate descriptions of Nature in the *Targe* and *The Thrissil and the Rois*, like those in *The Palice of Honour*, may be seen as part of a conscious attempt to outdo the achievements of Lydgate within the same rhetorical mode. Comparison between short extracts can illustrate the greater degree of mannerism in Dunbar, but not the increase in the scale of his effects: for example, the lines from *The Flower of Courtesy* constitute the poem's only stanza of pure description, whereas in the *Targe* there are some seven stanzas devoted to the setting.

Dunbar's choice of a richly elaborate high style for large sections of his two major secular dream allegories may well have been influenced by Gavin Douglas's practice in *The Palice of Honour*: it was probably Douglas rather than Dunbar who introduced the aureate style into Scots secular poetry. Dunbar reserves his most ornate and artificial effects – polysyllabic Latinate diction, alliteration and internal rhyme, elaborate syntactic structures – for poems of religious celebration, and in this respect he appears to have followed Lydgate, or at least the English school of aureate religious poetry which is represented so well by Lydgate's Marian hymns. Dunbar's *Ane Ballat of Our Lady* and Lydgate's *Ave Regina Celorum* have a common source in early medieval Latin hymnody, but it is more than likely that in writing this kind of devotional poem Dunbar was responding to what he knew of English exercises in the genre. Like Lydgate, Dunbar matches fragments from the Latin prayer with a heavily Latinate style of English vocabulary. The difference between the two poems is one of intensity of effect: the Scots poem is ostentatiously Latinate (John Metham, who remarked on Lydgate's 'halff chongyd Latyne', would have been intrigued by a line such as 'Hodiern, modern, sempitern'),[19] and even more exclamatory in tenor than the English. The internal rhymes and the displacement of conventional syntax give the poem an urgent, thrusting movement which is absent from similar English hymns. Dunbar pushes language to the very limit of intelligibility, but the poem is more than 'sheer lovely verbal noise for its own sake'[20] because of its theological occasion of joyful celebration.

However interesting they may be as indications of Dunbar's ability to revitalise conventional genres, images and rhetorical techniques, none of the affinities with Lydgate's poetry suggest that it influenced Dunbar's writing to any great extent. Lydgate's poetry may have had a greater utilitarian value than Chaucer's for Dunbar, but he is no more a 'Lydgatian' than a 'Chaucerian'. The high aureate mode of *Ane Ballat*, and the lower but still elaborately refined mode of the courtly allegories provide the strongest suggestions of Lydgate's influence, but these works are only a fragment of Dunbar's large and varied achievement. His borrowings are transmuted to suit the demands of new poetic contexts of which brevity and technical excellence are guiding principles. Dunbar's attitude to Lydgate's poetry was probably very close to that of his exact contemporary in England, the 'laureate' Skelton: both wrote the kinds of occasional poetry for which Lydgate was so well respected, and both were influenced, if indirectly, by Lydgate's enrichment of language in the higher reaches of poetic style. They are, however, more lively poets, and neither attempts the soberly ambitious labour of a *Troy Book* or a *Fall of Princes*. These obvious differences aside, both Dunbar and Skelton seem to respect Lydgate's poetry. Skelton's praise is never so fulsome as the tribute at the end of *The Goldyn Targe*, but he does include Lydgate in the English contingent at the Palace of Fame. In *Phyllyp Sparowe*, Jane acts as a spokesman for the poet when she makes this comparison between Chaucer and Lydgate:

> Also John Lydgate
> Wryteth after an hyer rate;
> It is dyffuse to fynde
> The sentence of his mynde,
> Yet wryteth he in his kynd,
> No man that can amend
> Those maters that he hath pende;
> Yet some men fynde a faute,
> And say he wryteth to haute. (804–12)

Dunbar is not so outspoken, yet the differences between his own practice and that of Lydgate suggest that he too chose not to imitate the Monk of Bury's particular brand of 'hautness' and diffuseness.

(ii) Skelton and Scottish poetry

The strongest non-Scottish affinities of Dunbar's poetry are not with Chaucer and Lydgate, but with Skelton. Dunbar has been labelled as the 'Scottish Skelton',[21] although strangely enough nobody has ever thought to call Skelton the 'English Dunbar'. The individuality of their poetic voices is beyond dispute, but nevertheless there are marked similarities between them. Skelton, like Dunbar, has a strong respect for conventional forms, and finds it easy to take up (no doubt sincerely) traditional attitudes and time-honoured techniques. Both write occasional poems, religious and secular, and both experiment with the forms and techniques of allegory, the dominant mode of poetry in the later Middle Ages. The results are sometimes very similar, although this may not necessarily imply the indebtedness of one poet to the other. Skelton, like Dunbar, uses personification allegory very seldom: an early poem, *The Bowge of Courte*, his most fully sustained exercise in this style, provides a fascinating parallel with *The Goldyn Targe*. In terms of both subject matter and style the poems are very different: Dunbar's is an elliptical and highly stylised account of the battle between the forces of Reason and Beauty, whereas Skelton's is a satire of court life, developed in a predominantly naturalistic dramatic style. The poems are strangely alike, however, in that they use the dream vision form, and its convention of the poet's presence as an actor within his dream, to make quite complex statements about fear and alienation. The 'action' of Dunbar's poem is contrivedly formal, and this throws into sharp relief the poet's cry of despair when his ally is overcome: 'Quhy was thou blyndit, Resoun? quhi, allace!' (214). The fear of irrational sensual love is imaged by the first reference to the ship – 'As falcoune swift desyrouse of hir pray' (54) – and by the violent 'crak' which brings his vision to an end (243). Dunbar's

'I' does not correspond directly to any of the customary allegorical abstractions of courtly poetry. Because he is so unwilling, he is not like the Amans of the *Rose*, and there is a strange sense of distance between him and Reason, his ally in the psychomachia. If he can be labelled at all, it must be as Fear or Dread. Skelton's allegory is less allusive and considerably more realistic, yet the poem conveys a sense of menace which is remarkably reminiscent of Dunbar. Skelton's persona is described more fully than the protagonist of *The Goldyn Targe*, yet he has the same passiveness, the same inability to take decisive action. One of the most original aspects of the poem is the allegorical role assigned to the poet, that of Drede, but Skelton differs here from Dunbar only in being more explicit. The conclusion of *The Bowge of Courte* is similar in content and mood to the scene in *The Goldyn Targe* which precipitates the poet's awakening; both, it is interesting to note, involve the idea of attack and the image of the ship. These poems are very different from Chaucer's dream visions. In his self-depictions, Chaucer too manages to create the effect of estrangement – and sometimes also of fear – but his work differs from Dunbar's in being more realistic and more leisurely, and from Skelton's in showing a different balance between description and dialogue. Chaucer's genial humour and self-depreciation are quite foreign to Dunbar and Skelton alike. Dunbar may have known Skelton's poem (which by 1500 had been printed by Wynkyn de Worde), but it would be rash to assume direct influence.

The Goldyn Targe and *The Bowge of Courte* are both marked by a blend of conservatism and intense individuality. This finds a different kind of expression in parody: Dunbar and Skelton partake of a talent, comparatively rare in late medieval English and Scots poetry, for transplanting conventional forms of devotional expression into incongruous settings. Skelton's thorough exploitation of the Office for the Dead in *Phyllyp Sparowe*, his mock-heroic poem about the death of a pet, has a Scots counterpart in *The Dregy of Dunbar*, in which Dunbar uses the Matins from the Office for the Dead to express his horror at the rigours of court life away from Edinburgh. The poems have their distinctive merits, but the rhetorical strategy which pervades them is the same – the application to trivial local occasion of devotional forms of which the *raison d'être* is their relevance to the life of the soul. A related comic impulse works within Skelton's *Epitaphe* for two citizens of Diss and Dunbar's *The Testament of Mr Andro Kennedy*, poems written predominantly in Latin, burlesques of pious commemorations. Skelton embellishes all the worst attributes of the deceased worthies of Diss, paying particular attention to the drinking habits of John Clarke:

> *Fratres, orate*
> For this knauate,
> By the holy rode,
> Dyd neuer man good:
> I pray you all . . .
> With, fill the blak bowle
> For Jayberdes sowle.
> *Bibite multum*:
> *Ecce sepultum*
> *Sub pede stultum* . . .
> With hey, howe, rumbelowe.
>
> (44-55)

The mood of these lines is reminiscent of Kennedy's desire to be remembered for good drinking rather than good works:

> A barell bung ay at my bosum,
> Of warldis gud I bad na mair;
> *Corpus meum ebriosum*,
> I leif on to the toune of Air;
> In a draf mydding for ever and ay
> *Ut ibi sepeliri queam*,
> Quhar drink and draff may ilka day
> Be cassyne *super faciem meam*.
>
> (33-40)

leif leave, bequeath; *draf mydding* midden (of dregs); *cassyne* cast

In none of these poems which exploit the comic potential of a discrepancy between form and subject matter is there ever any attempt to question the authority of the devotional forms themselves. Both poets were priests, and their orthodoxy is beyond question, despite the pungency of so much of their writing.

Much of Dunbar's poetry, and even more of Skelton's, has an

unmistakably personal edge, and the mood which both of them express most frequently is that of indignation. Skelton is uncompromisingly vicious towards enemies of the state, in particular the Scots, and although the mood of rabid patriotism was apparently foreign to Dunbar there is one work, the *Epetaphe for Donald Owre*, which rivals *Against the Scottes* in its crude mockery of a defeated enemy. (Dunbar's sentiments about 'helandmen' were doubtless very similar to Skelton's sentiments about Scots in general.) Poems such as *Colyn Cloute*, *Speke, Parrot*, and *Why Come Ye Nat to Courte?* are overtly political in their concentration upon what Skelton comes to see as the responsibility of one man, Wolsey, for all the evils of society. Dunbar is no poet of the 'common weill', but he has Skelton's directness in attacking those who dissemble in the interests of self-advancement. (Skelton appears to have been well satisfied with his 'laureate' status: unlike Dunbar, he does not use complaint as an occasion to dramatise any feelings of neglect.) There is also a similarity between the ways in which corruption is assailed. Skelton, like Dunbar, is fond of driving home an attack by piling up verbal effects to the point where sound fuses with sense. In this part of *Colyn Cloute*, for example, a battery of parallelism, repetition, alliteration and sustained rhyme is used to castigate the bishops for their failure to control,

> Suche maner of sysmatykes
> And half heretykes,
> That wolde intoxicate,
> That wolde conquinate,
> That wolde contaminate,
> And that wolde vyolate,
> And that wolde derogate,
> And that wolde abrogate
> The Churchis hygh estates.
>
> (702–10)

Here and elsewhere in Skelton's poetry the sound enacts the reeling disorder of the sense, and the effect is remarkably similar to that of Dunbar's lists of upstarts, such as the one in *Complaint to the King* which begins,

> Bot fowll, jow-jowrdane-hedit jevillis,
> Cowkin-kenseis, and culroun kevellis;
> Stuffettis, strekouris, and stafische strummellis;
> Wyld haschbaldis, haggarbaldis, and hummellis ...
>
> (15–18)

Dunbar's spectacular 'flyting' style is at a more colloquial level of diction, but the remorseless accretion of detail suggests an obvious affinity with Skelton.

The fact that Skelton's poetry has so much in common with Dunbar's is doubtless to some extent a matter of historical chance – they wrote at court, they were both priests, their temperaments were probably similar, and as poets they were engaged in the imaginative exploitation of a weight of inherited convention. There is, however, a more direct and immediate connection between some at least of their poems. There is a very good reason to believe that Skelton knew some Scots poetry, and that on one occasion at least his work was influenced by Dunbar's. Skelton's *Poems against Garnesche*, composed some time after 1513, constitute one half of a 'flyting': regrettably, Christopher Garnesche's initial challenge and his subsequent poems have not survived. This is the first instance of this bizarre form of court entertainment in English, and in both form and style its Scots inspiration is apparent. The source of Skelton's poems (and no doubt also of the lost Garnesche works) is almost certainly *The Flyting of Dunbar and Kennedie*, which was printed by Chepman and Myllar in 1508. In this 'flyting' each antagonist has the support of a 'commissar', or second: Sir John Ross sides with Dunbar, 'Quinting' (possibly Quentin Shaw) with Kennedy. In the English contest, Garnesche has the assistance of one 'Greasy Gorbellied Godfrey', although the laureate Skelton (as one might expect) answers his challengers unaided. The presence of the poet's assistant is also characteristic of the French *serventois* and *jeu-parti*, but the Scots poems differ from these and from other forms of medieval abuse poetry in their sheer intensity of effect. In tone and style Skelton's poems are much closer to the Scots 'flyting' than to other forms of debate. They are linked too by their occasion as court entertainment. The *Flyting* contains allusions which are clearly directed at a court audience: for example, each poet refers to the other's supposed offences against the royal house, and Kennedy pleads for the intervention of his 'Hye Souverane Lorde' (481–2). Skelton protests as he takes his leave that he would have exercised his talents in other ways, 'But for to serue the kinges entent / Hys noble pleasure and commandemennt' (177–8).

There are several close verbal parallels between the Garnesche poems and the Dunbar–Kennedy 'flyting',[22] but the essence of Skelton's use of the Scots work lies not in specific borrowings but in more general imitation of its techniques. Like the Scots, Skelton refrains from using his sharpest missiles at the beginning of the attack. Dunbar begins his side of the *Flyting* with a general statement of his complaint against Kennedy and Quentin. The pace is quickened by Kennedy's rejoinder, which begins the attack proper with a swift burst of alliteration:

> Fantastik fule, trest weill thow salbe fleyit,
> Ignorant elf, aip, owll irregular,
> Skaldit skaitbird, and commoun skamelar.
>
> (35–7)

skaitbird skate; *skamelar* sponger

Skelton's first two poems use alliteration for scurrilous abuse, but he follows the Scots in keeping his attack at a relatively impersonal level at the beginning. Dunbar's second poem expands upon his opponent's infamy: Kennedy is a highland traitor, who would have poisoned 'our Lordis cheif' in Paisley, he is a beggar, a stealer of hens.... Kennedy retaliates by attacking the supposedly English sympathies of his opponent – Dunbar is the worst kind of traitor, and a pardoner and coward into the bargain. Kennedy's attacks on Dunbar's cankered ancestry have their counterpart in Skelton's third poem, where he raises the matter of Garnesche's lowly origins:

> Whan ye war yonger of age,
> Ye war a kechyn page,
> A dyshwasher, a dryvyll,
> In the pott your nose dedde sneuyll.
>
> (III, 24–7)

(This apparently brought retaliation, for in the last poem Skelton begins a fresh attack with the question 'Dysparage ye mynauncetry?' IV, 63.) In both English and Scots poems, personal attacks which have at least a plausible basis in reality are set against torrents of abuse which move, like the Wedo's confession in the *Tretis*, into the realm of fantasy:

> Mauch muttoun, byt buttoun, peilit gluttoun, air to Hilhous;
> Rank beggar, ostir dregar, foule fleggar in the flet;
> Chittirlilling, ruch rilling, lik schilling in the milhous;
> Baird rehator, theif of natour, fals tratour, feyindis gett ...
> (241-4)

Mauch thief?; *air* heir (topical reference); *ostir dregar* oyster-dredger; *fleggar* flatterer; *flet* inner part of house; *ruch rilling* rough shoe; *rehator* enemy; *feyindis gett* offspring of a fiend

Towards the end of the third poem, Skelton turns his 'serpentis and ... gunnys' on Garnesche,

> Thou tode, thow scorpyone,
> Thow bawdy babyone,
> Thow bere, thow brystlyd bore,
> Thou Moryshe mantycore,
> Thou rammysche stynkyng gote,
> Thow foule chorlyshe parote,
> Thou gresly gargone glaymy,
> Thou swety slouen seymy,
> Thou murrionn, thow mawment ...
> (III, 162-70)

The accumulation of short phrases, the alliteration, and the insistent rhymes of the *Flyting* are all there, but Skelton breaks up the long Scots line into his preferred form of the short line. In the *Flyting*, verbal pyrotechnics of this kind are reserved for the conclusions of the attacks which one poet makes upon the other. Skelton does not seem to have understood the principle of orchestration involved here: the lines quoted above are followed by a less concentrated form of attack, which weakens their effect.

Since the object of a 'flyting' match was presumably to demonstrate one's superior skill in abuse, it is not surprising to find that Skelton's poems, like those of Dunbar and Kennedy, contain both disparagement of his opponent's abilities and defence of his own.

He alleges that Garnesche learned his craft from a baker of pies (III, 111), and charges him with monotony of effect:

> Ye rayl, ye ryme, with, Hay, dog, hay!
> Your chorlyshe chauntyng ys all o lay.
> Ye, syr, rayll all in deformite:
> Ye haue nat red the properte
> Of naturys workys, how they be
> Myxte with sum incommodite.   (IV, 5–10)

Certainly Skelton's own contributions are varied, both in verse form and tone, but when it comes to explicit self-defence Skelton appeals to his status as 'poete lawreate' (IV, 80–4), and as former royal tutor – 'The honor of Englond I lernyd to spelle, / In dygnyte roialle that doth excelle' (IV, 95–6). This form of self-advertisement has none of the wit with which the Scots proclaim their superiority, Dunbar by his claim to make 'fairar Inglis' than Kennedy's with 'ane pair of Lowthiane hippis' (110–12), Kennedy by his polished but equally outrageous claim to have drunk from the fountain of eloquence 'Quhen it was purifit wyth frost, and flowit cleir' (337–40). Skelton was, no doubt, the victor in his contest with Henry VIII's former gentleman-usher, but it is hard to imagine that he could have vanquished either Dunbar or Kennedy on the 'flyting' field. The Garnesche poems are entertaining enough, but they lack the rich abusive variety, the delight in the inexhaustible fertility of language, which makes the Scots poems so memorable.

In one of Skelton's anti-Scottish poems (a group which includes *Against the Scottes* and *Howe the douty Duke of Albany*), there is evidence of a poetic confrontation between Skelton and a Scot – probably Sir George Dundas, a graduate of St Andrews and of Montacute College, who had ties with the English court by virtue of his membership of the Order of St John. In three terse and witty Latin hexameters, Dundas alleges that Englishmen have tails, and that for this reason they are 'gens sine laude'.[23] The legend about the Englishman who pinned a tail on St Augustine, thereby inflicting his countrymen with the witty punishment of God, is used by both Dunbar and Kennedy in the *Flyting* (125–6; 350–1). Skelton's defence is predictably peppery:

> Skelton laureat
> After this rate
> Defendeth with his pen
> All Englysh men
> Agayn Dundas,
> That Scottishe asse
>
> (19–24)
>
> Dundas, dronken and drowsy
> Skabed, scuruy, and lowsy,
> Of vnhappy generacion
> And most vngracious nacion.
>
> (50–3)

Neither poem meets the requirements of a full-scale 'flyting', but there is a nice irony in the fact that in *Against Dundas* Skelton uses a version of the abusive style which he had adapted from the literature of that same 'most vngracious nacion'.

The genre to which *The Flyting of Dunbar and Kennedie* belongs should be seen in its local context, as the most spectacular kind of Scots comic poetry to rely for effect on sustained verbal grotesquerie. A pervasive sense of the absurd and the outrageous, promoted by techniques such as the piling up of epithets, lists, word-play of various kinds, obtrusive alliteration and rhyme, runs through poems such as *Colkelbie Sow*, *The Cursing of Sir Johine Rowlis*, the *Dreme* of 'Lichtoun Monicus', *Lord Fergus Gaist*, Henryson's *Sum Practysis of Medecyne*, and *Christis Kirk on the Grene*. The *Flyting* is not the only specimen of the rich fund of late medieval Scots comic poetry to have reached the attention of Skelton. We have no way of knowing how many of these works were known to him, but there are signs that he may have been influenced to a very considerable extent by one of them, *Colkelbie Sow* – if not by the version which is preserved in the Bannatyne MS. (CCCCI), by one which is very close to it. It is not surprising that the poem – or more specifically, the first of its three parts, which tells the story of the first of Colkelbie's three pennies – should have been known to Skelton, since it seems to have been very popular in Scotland. Modern commentators, swayed unduly by Skelton's vituperative comments on the Scots, have been reluctant even to consider the possibility of such a northern influence: C. S. Lewis, for example, mentions the interesting parallel between Skelton's metre and that of some Scots comic poems, but discounts any direct relationship by remarking that 'Skelton himself would rise from the grave to bespatter us with new Skeltonics if we suggested that he had learned his art from a Scotchman.'[24] There is good reason to believe that in writing *Elynour Rummyng*, the poem which more than any other earned him Pope's ringing condemnation of 'beastly Skelton', he was influenced not only by the subject matter but also by the style of the first part of *Colkelbie Sow*. Professor Lewis's horror at this suggestion might not, *sub specie aeternitatis*, be shared by the poet himself. There can be little doubt about the priority in time of the Scots poem: linguistic evidence suggests a date of *c.* 1490 for the surviving text.[25]

The *prima pars* of *Colkelbie Sow* is the story of a harlot's proposed banquet, and the disorder which ensues when the farm animals and in turn their owners arrive on the scene. By Dunbar's time the mention of the event seems to have been sufficient to denote a riotous assembly of rogues: in *Remonstrance to the King* he disparages idle courtiers as 'the uther fulis nyce, / That feistit at Cokelbeis gryce [pig]', and in listing them uses what was probably recognisable to his audience as a 'Colkelbie style', distinguished by ostentatious rhymes and patterns of alliteration and assonance (39–49). The subject matter of *Elynour Rummyng* also concerns a riotous company, the women who come to sample the dubious delights of Elynour's ale-vat. Skelton's choice of subject may have been influenced by his knowledge of a real hostelry run by a real Eleanor at Leatherhead,[26] but a literary inspiration from the Scots poem is equally likely. (There are parallels with another English poem about a group of drunken women, but this is almost certainly later than Skelton's work.)[27] As in *Colkelbie Sow*, there is an extensive use of proper names. The Scots poet individualises the members of the porcine company who go to rescue the pig – 'Wrottok', 'Writhneb', 'Hogy', 'Baynell', 'Sigill Wrigill' – and soon after there follows the list of their owners,

> Gilby on his gray meir
> and fergy on his sow fair
> hoge hygin be þe hand hint
> And symy that was sone brint
> Wᵗ his lad loury . . .
>
> (210ff)

hint held; *sone brint* soon burnt

Similarly, Elynour's customers are introduced by name,

> Thyther cometh Kate,
> Cysly, and Sare . . .
>
> (118-19)
>
> And than came haltyng Jone . . .
>
> (326)
>
> Than thyder came dronken Ales . . .
>
> (351)
>
> Than sterte in mad Kyt . . .
>
> (412)

In *Colkelbie Sow* it is difficult to distinguish the swine from their owners, because animals and humans have similar names: 'Hogy' (163) has his human counterpart in 'Hoge' (212), and the swineherds have as their captain 'Sweirbum with his snowt' (277). In Skelton's poem there is also a literal enough herd of pigs (169-86), and here too the human rioters are identified with swine by metaphor (20, 233-4, 554). (The work mentioned in *The Garlande of Laurell* as *The Gruntyng and the Groynninge of the Gronnyng Swyne*, which has not come down to us, may have been even more closely related to *Colkelbie* in terms of its subject matter.) Considered in isolation, this kind of parallel between the English and the Scots poem is no evidence of indebtedness, but it becomes more important when seen in conjunction with other more striking similarities. One of these is structural. *Colkelbie Sow* is divided into three 'fitts', or *passus*, and in turn the first of these is divided into blocks of matter which correspond to the 'caisses' mentioned by the author in his prologue. First there is the account of the harlot's 'mangery', then the attack of the pigs, followed by the chase of the owners, the revelries, the battle, and a short account of the subsequent career of the piglet. There is almost no narrative progression: the poet's interest is not so much in telling a story as in verbal humour, the imitation in words of the hurly-burly scenes described. The only concession to narrative coherence is an occasional introductory comment about the next block of 'matere': e.g.

> Is not this a nyce caiss
> Bot ʒit a fer werss it waiss
> A new noyment and nois
> W^t a rumour vprois . . .
>
> (194–7)

> And ʒit this is a strange caiss
> Bot eftirward . . .
>
> (437–8)

Elynour Rummyng has the same kind of static quality. Skelton is more interested in evoking a sense of chaotic activity than in developing narrative, and he too divides his material into structural blocks, introduced by comments such as 'Nowe in cometh another rabell' (382), and 'Another sorte of sluttes' (436). Both poems are set within a framework of oral delivery: Skelton begins with the traditional minstrel's call for silence, and the Scots poem purports to be an entertainment suitable for a feast.

Because *Elynour Rummyng* is written in the style which we have come to associate with the name of the poet, the stylistic parallels between it and *Colkelbie* are of very great interest: obviously, if the Scots poem is a likely influence upon the style of *Elynour Rummyng* it follows that it may have shaped the development of the 'Skeltonic' mode in other works which do not have the affinity of subject matter and structure. Various sources have been proposed for the Skeltonic, such as the Anglo-Saxon alliterative line,[28] medieval Latin rhymed prose,[29] and a kind of Latin rhymed verse.[30] Indeed all of these are persuasive, especially when consideration is given to Skelton's own prose and verse in Latin, but it is worth remembering Professor H. L. R. Edwards's view of the nature of literary growth, that 'a new verse form, like a new animal, has more ancestors than one'.[31] My own suggestion is that in the first section of *Colkelbie Sow* Skelton found a vernacular model for effects of a similar kind to those which he knew from his reading of Latin. All of the prominent stylistic features of *Elynour Rummyng* are present in the Scots poem. Both poems are written in short lines which have two, and occasionally three, heavy stresses, with a variable number of unstressed syllables. If this were the only parallel, it could be explained quite convincingly as two independent adaptations of the old alliterative line. This seems improbable, however, since both poems have the unusual feature of long strings of words which have the same rhyme. The following lines, from the guest list for the harlot's banquet, typify the Scots poet's fondness for ostentatious rhymes:

> On apostita freir
> A peruerst perdonair
> And practand palmeir
> A wich and a wobstare
> A milygant and a mychare
> A fond fule a fariar
> A cairtar a cariar
> A libbar and a lyar . . .
>
> (52–9)

wobstare weaver; *milygant* scoundrel; *mychare* thief; *libbar* gelder

In all there are some forty words in this list which rhyme in 'air'. The effect is intentionally humorous – we see it again in the description of the rustics' dances:

> Maister myngeis the mangeis
> Maister tyngeis la tangeis
> Maister totis la toutis
> And rousty rottis the routis
> Maister Nykkis la nakkis
> And Schir Iakkis la Iakkis . . .
>
> (341–6)

In *Elynour Rummyng* Skelton attempts this same kind of verbal humour, in passages such as this:

> This ale, sayde she, is noppy;
> Let vs syppe and soppy
> And not spyll a droppy
> And so mote I hoppy
> It coleth well my croppy.
>
> (557–61)

Like the *Colkelbie* poet, Skelton uses couplets extensively, to act as a foil to the 'hirdy girdy' of the rhyme leashes: the intensive verbal effects account for a relatively small proportion of both poems. Another of these effects is parallel syntactic structure, an apparently endless progression of lines which have the same word order and extensive repetition, although not necessarily the rhyme-runs. These lines are from the account of the rustics' dances in *Colkelbie*:

> Sum trottit tras and trenass
> Sum balterit the bass
> Sum perdowy Sum trolly lolly
> Sum cok crow thow quhill day
> Sum lincolne sum lindsay . . .
>
> (300ff)

tras . . . trenass . . . bass . . . perdowy kinds of dance; *thow quhill* thou till

Skelton uses the same kind of construction in *Elynour Rummyng*:

> Some brought walnuttes,
> Some apples, some peres,
> Some brought theyr clyppynge sheres,
> Some brought this and that,
> Some brought I wote nere what,
> Some brought theyr husbandes hat,
> Some podynges and lynkes
> Some trypes that stynkes.
>
> (437-44)

This fondness for listing, which takes the form of a pell-mell accretion of words, is another link between the two poems. Although Skelton does not use alliteration to the same extent as the Scots poet, it occurs sporadically in association with other onomatopoeic effects. Both delight in piling up strident and giddy sound effects: for long stretches sound is largely synonymous with sense – the verse strives to imitate the chaos and the incessant movement of the scenes described, and the effect is one of verbal fantasy. This is not to suggest that the mood of *Elynour Rummyng* is identical with that of the first part of *Colkelbie*. Skelton's occasional descent to a style of brutal naturalism does suggest an element of satire, in the manner of Dunbar's picture of woman in the

Tretis: the mood of the Scots poem is one of pervasive gaiety, and the *sententiae* 'That foly is no sapience' (492) and 'That oft of littil cumis mich' (544) are sufficient to discourage any attempt to find serious meaning. Nevertheless, the predominant impulse of Skelton's poem is verbal entertainment rather than moral persuasion, in keeping with his comment *hæc loca plena jocis* and the abrupt conclusion,

> For my fyngers ytche;
> I haue wrytten to mytche
> Of this mad mummynge
> Of Elynour Rummynge.

This is very similar to the author's *apologia* in *Colkelbie*: in the Prologue he insists that he has written to appease his 'awin spereit', and at the beginning of the second part craves pardon for 'thir mokking meteris and mad matere'. Skelton's most distinctive use of 'these mocking metres' and their associated effects is for the purpose of attack upon the abuses of political power, in *Colyn Cloute* and *Why Come Ye Nat to Courte?* In these poems he makes no apology for writing 'too much', and actively exploits the opportunity which the style offers for apparently endless continuation of effect, thereby creating a new style of poetic complaint distinguished by its minimal interest in conventional form. Self-consciously 'tattered and iagged' and 'rudely rayne beaten', the style is powerfully effective as the vehicle for disgust and indignation, especially as it defies any attempt at critical definition. Understandably this Skeltonic manner quickly becomes tedious and overblown in the hands of a less gifted poet such as the author of *The Image of Ipocrysy*.[32]

The proliferation of parallels thematic, structural and stylistic between *Elynour Rummyng* and the first part of *Colkelbie Sow* points very strongly to the direct influence of one poem upon the other. There is good reason to believe that *Elynour Rummyng* may have been the first, or at least one of the first, of Skelton's long poems in the short-line style: like *Phyllyp Sparowe*, it lacks the *Orator regius* signature which is paraded in the later works. On the basis of verbal parallels with later poems and of a possible topical reference, some critics have suggested that the poem was written relatively late in Skelton's career, but such evidence is at best doubtful.[33] If we can accept the influence of the Scots poem upon *Elynour Rummyng*, it follows that we must allow for its indirect influence upon other poems written in the same style. The question of dating *Elynour Rummyng* has little bearing on the relationship between *Colkelbie* and other poems by Skelton, since it is quite feasible that the adaptation of the style to different purposes – delicate and witty burlesque in *Phyllyp Sparowe*, political invective in *Colyn Cloute* and *Why Come ye Nat to Courte?* – may have come earlier rather than later than the 'mad mummynge'. Other influences no doubt assisted in the formation of Skelton's favourite style, but the proliferation of parallels between *Elynour Rummyng* and the Scots poem suggests a link between the two which is as strong and as direct as the link between the *Poems Against Garnesche* and *The Flyting of Dunbar and Kennedie*. This connection makes it possible to see several of Skelton's poems, like works by Dunbar, as developments within a tradition of comic writing which is as distinctively Scots as the 'flyting'. Indeed the 'flyting' mode is the most elaborate form of this tradition, which is distinguished by its insistent sound effects and its keen interest in the absurd. Whereas Skelton uses the techniques of poems such as the *Flyting* and *Colkelbie* in both humorous and unequivocally serious contexts, Dunbar works within the tradition as a comic satirist. Several of his poems share the spirit of other poems in Scots. The mock-solemnity of the *Dregy*, for instance, recalls the mood of *The Cursing of Sir Johine Rowlis*, a poem which in its lavish details of the torments of hell has close affinities with Dunbar's *The Dance of the Sevin Deidly Synnis* and *The Sowtar and Tailyouris War*. Another of Dunbar's poems in the 'eldritch' vein, *The Birth of Antichrist*, echoes the bizarre comedy of *The Manere of the Crying of Ane Playe* and *The Gyre Carling*. As I have already suggested, there is a debt to *Colkelbie* in the list of rogues in *Complaint to the King*: here, and more dramatically in the burlesque dance and tournament poems, we see the keen interest in scenes of crowded activity which is reminiscent of *Colkelbie*, *Christis Kirk on the Grene*, and *Peblis to the Play*.

Although Skelton's use of the tradition represented by poems such as these leads, in the political works, to effects which are far removed from those of comedy, his knowledge of and willingness to experiment with a style foreign to his own literary milieu suggests that his creative sympathies lay with poets whose nationality made them the enemies of the Tudor state. Certainly his artistic allegiances were not with English contemporaries such as Hawes and Barclay, who continued to look to Lydgate as a model of poetic excellence. Seen from the point of view of the whole body of his writing, Skelton's indebtedness to either Chaucer or Lydgate is relatively slight, less substantial even than Dunbar's indebtedness to them. The Tudor laureate was rightly praised by Bradshaw as 'inuentiue Skelton',[34] but this invention is at its weakest in the late poem which shows, paradoxically, the strongest signs of influence from earlier English poetry. The movement of the rhyme-royal sections of *The Garlande of Laurell* recalls Lydgate's metre at its shambling worst, and the Chaucerian theme of the dream encounter with Fame is treated with the minimum of imagination. There are several aspects of the *Garlande* which suggest *The Palice of Honour* rather than *The Hous of Fame* – for example, the introductory setting of the sinister wood, the dramatic situation in which one goddess supports the poet when charges are made against him by another, the nature of the list of poets with its combination of ancients and moderns, and the description of the palace. It is by no means unlikely that Skelton knew Douglas's poem, but it is clear that if he did borrow from it he failed to match either Douglas's intellectual ingenuity or his poetic craftsmanship. If comparisons with Scots poetry help to illuminate some of the distinctive excellences of Skelton's writing, they also serve to emphasise his comparative lack of interest in tonal variation and technical subtlety. C. S. Lewis's view of the technical difference between Skelton and Dunbar – that the one has the charm of the gifted amateur, whereas the other is the complete professional[35] – is true of the difference between Skelton and any of the other makars.

There might be further evidence of Skelton's borrowing from Dunbar if the poem which begins 'Doverrit [stupefied] with dreme, devysing in my slummer' (*A General Satyre*) could be shown to be the work of Dunbar.[36] (Bannatyne ascribes it to him, Maitland to one Sir James Inglis.) There is an affinity between this poem and the ten stanzas which conclude *Speke, Parrot*. Here Skelton throws aside the riddling, obfuscating style of his parrot persona, stating the resolve to 'Sette asyde all sophysms, and speke now trew and playne'. So abrupt is the change of style that the stanzas amount to a separate poem, which like the Scots work belongs to the well-established genre of the general complaint: both enumerate social evils such as the self-seeking behaviour of clergy and nobility, disregard of law and the plight of the poor, and extravagance of dress. This resemblance is largely *sui generis*, but there is a closer connection between the two poems, one of style, which does suggest that one influenced the other. Both make very effective use of parallelism and of a specific kind of antithesis:

> So mony preistis cled up in secular weid,
> With blasing breistis casting thair clathis on breid,
> It is no neid to tell of quhome I mene;
> So quhene to reid the deirgey and the beid
> Within this land was nevir hard nor sene.
>
> Sa mekle tressone, sa mony partiall sawis,
> Sa littill ressone to help the common cawis,
> That all the lawis ar not sett by ane bene;
> Sic fenyeit flawis, sa mony waistit wawis
> Within this land was nevir hard nor sene.
>
> (*GS*, 11–15, 26–30)
>
> So many complayntes, and so smalle redresse;
> So myche callyng on, and so small takyng hede;
> So myche losse of merchaundyse, and so remedyles;
> So lytell care for the comyn weall, and so myche nede;
> So myche dow3tfull daunger, and so lytell drede;
> So myche pride of prelattes, so cruell and so kene;
> Syns Dewcalyon's flodde, I trowe, was nevyr sene.
>
> (*SP*, 463–9)

With blasing . . . breid With blazing breasts (i.e. gaudy clothes) flaunting their robes about; *quhene* few; *deirgey* dirge; *fenyeit flawis* (probably) feigned defects in legal documents; *wawis* walls

Borrowing is suggested also by verbal correspondences between the refrains, and by a few other verbal echoes. Both works give special prominence to the decline in the standards of poetry as a manifestation of the general decay. Who, though, is indebted to whom? Linguistic evidence suggests that *A General Satyre* could not be the work of Dunbar, and that it was written closer to the middle years of the sixteenth century, and therefore after Skelton's poem. A form of 'fucksailis' has its first recorded use in Skelton's *Colyn Cloute* (*c.* 1520), of 'ketchepillaris' in a public record of 1539, and of 'rubeatouris' in *Ane Satyre of the Thrie Estaitis*. The strongest argument for later dating derives from the references to new fashion in dress. Historians of fashion seem agreed that the vogue for 'fartingaillis' (71) – Spanish hooped skirts – did not reach Britain until the mid-1540s.[37] The poet's jibe at 'fowill tailis' which sweep the ground and raise dust is reminiscent of Lindsay's attack in the *Supplication . . . in contemptioun of Syde Taillis*, written about 1540. It would seem that the Scots poet, whose identity remains shadowy, was inspired to adapt Skelton's poem to suit local conditions: naturally enough there is no counterpart to the personal attack on Wolsey, and it is hardly surprising to find such a distinctive detail as the comparison of rogues in high places to those who thronged about 'Cowkelbyis gryce'. The poem is in no sense an imitation of the stanzas from *Speke, Parrot*. Its range of attack is wider, and it is technically more fluent. *A General Satyre* belongs to a higher order of art than the second Scots adaptation of verses which have been attributed to Skelton. The thirteen stanzas in the Bannatyne MS. which begin 'O god that in tyme all thingis did begin' (CXXVIII) incorporate the short English poem which early editions of Skelton entitle *On Tyme*. The Scots poem is undistinguished in every way, and the relevant stanzas are no more than a loose Scots rendition of the English verses. It is barely plausible that the borrowing should have been in the other direction – that is, that Skelton should have been moved to abbreviate and sharpen a mediocre and rambling Scots poem. The process of reworking is probably like that evident in the sixteenth-century revision of Henryson's *The Garmont of Gud Ladeis*, also in the Bannatyne manuscript (CCLXXVI).

Skelton's writing occupies a unique and important position in Anglo-Scottish literary relationships. Like Dunbar, he is conscious of his place in a tradition which acknowledges the seminal importance of Chaucer and Lydgate, and his work, like that of his Scots contemporary, shows some signs of their influence. Both Skelton and Dunbar are strongly original, and their individuality is apparent in the transformations which inherited genres, themes and techniques undergo in their hands. There is good reason to suppose that Skelton's creativity, like Dunbar's, was fostered by his knowledge of late medieval Scots poems which owe little, if anything at all, to the examples of Chaucer and Lydgate. It is not surprising that Skelton's poetry should have had no more influence than it did on Scots poetry of the sixteenth century, since the northern writers presumably had sufficient guidance from the sources which had attracted Skelton himself. His contribution to Scots literature is the part which his morality drama *Magnyfycence* played in shaping the first part of Sir David Lindsay's great play, *Ane Satyre of the Thrie Estaitis*.

6

Two *Aeneid* translators - Surrey's debt to Douglas: Wyatt and Henryson

Gavin Douglas's translation of the *Aeneid* was completed, he tells us, 'Apon the fest of Mary Magdelan, / Fra Crystis byrth, the dait quha lyst to heir, / A thousand fyve hundreth and thretteyn ȝeir.' In England in 1513, the king requested the printing of the *Troy Book*, Lydgate's extremely popular translation of Guido delle Colonne's thirteenth-century account of the Troy story, written nearly a century before. Douglas's translation of Virgil into Scots reflects the kind of historical interest in the story of Troy which was current in England, as it had been for several centuries, but more than this, it reflects an interest among his Scots contemporaries in the most celebrated Latin epic dealing with the matter of Troy. Douglas explains that the translation was undertaken at the request of his kinsman Henry, Lord St Clair:

> That Virgill mycht intill our langage be
> Red lowd and playn by ȝour lordschip and me,
> And other gentill companȝeonys, quha sa lyst;
> Nane ar compellit drynk not bot thai haue thryst.
> (Directioun, 85-8)

The *Eneados* might not have come into being but for the existence of this 'thryst' for a vernacular Virgil on the part of some at least of Douglas's circle. In England and Scotland alike, Virgil was being read in Latin by intellectuals, responding and contributing to the continental revival of interest in classical texts. The fact that by 1513 less learned Scots were able to enjoy an accurate vernacular rendition of Virgil rather than a pedestrian translation of an earlier medieval version of the Troy story is testimony not only to Douglas's enterprise and skill, but also to the superior vitality of the Scots poetic tradition. In some respects the *Eneados* is a medieval poem (the last great medieval poem), but in the quality of the translator's conception of his task – a continuing attempt to render Virgil's meaning accurately and sensitively – the poem is unquestionably of the Renaissance. In contemporary England, the highest achievement of the poetic translator's art is to be found in *The Ship of Fools* and the *Eclogues* of Lydgate's follower Alexander Barclay. Their originals are satires with a decidedly medieval cast, and although Barclay had some acquaintance with both Virgil's *Eclogues* and the *Aeneid*, it is clear that he would not have presumed to take Virgil as a model.

The *Eneados* of Gavin Douglas has affinities with a long and varied tradition of classical commentary and exegesis. Douglas's aim as a translator is to use his learning in order to make Virgil's meaning as accessible as possible to his audience. His prime duty, as he explains in the first Prologue, is to his original:

> Quha is attachit ontill a staik, we se,
> May go na ferthir bot wreil about that tre:
> Rycht so am I to Virgillis text ybund,
> I may nocht fle less than my falt be fund.
>
> (p. 11, 297–300)

wreil reel

Douglas's 'text' was not of course the text of Virgil as we know it, but one which showed the evidence of several centuries of corruption. Priscilla Bawcutt, to whose detailed and lucid account of both Douglas's Virgilian heritage and the nature of his translation I am indebted, gives good reasons for identifying Douglas's text as the 1501 edition of the *Aeneid* made by the Flemish scholar-printer Badius Ascensius.[1] This edition, typical of many, contains as well as the text a large amount of paraphrase and commentary, Ascensius's own as well as the work of earlier scholars such as Servius and Donatus. There are signs that Douglas followed Ascensius's commentary not only in interpreting difficult sections of the classical Latin, but also for simpler stretches of the text, and that his practice as a translator was influenced to some extent by Ascensius's practice as a commentator. Both show a pedagogic concern for accurate interpretation of Virgil's *sens*: both amplify, by providing both synonyms and the metaphorical as well as the literal meanings of words and phrases. Expansions of this kind are of course also undertaken by Douglas because of his sense of the gulf between classical Latin and his own language:

> Sum tyme the text mon haue ane expositioun,
> Sum tyme the collour will causs a litill additioun,
> And sum tyme of a word I mon mak thre
>
> Sum tyme I follow the text als neir I may,
> Sum tyme I am constrenyt ane other way
>
> For thar be Latyn wordis mony ane
> That in our leyd ganand translatioun hass nane
> Less than we mynyss thar sentens and grauyte
> And ȝit scant weill exponyt.
>
> (pp. 12–13, 347–66)

leyd language; *ganand* appropriate

In order to make a 'ganand translatioun', it is necessary for him to supplement the resources of Scots with 'Sum bastard Latyn, French, or Inglis', and for this there was ample precedent in earlier and contemporary Scots poetry which was not translation. Douglas draws upon his wide knowledge of vernacular poetry, both Scots and English, to render the sense rather than the precise letter of his original. Stylistically, the Scots tradition had a profound influence on the texture of Douglas's translation: its most obvious influence is seen in Douglas's pervasive use of alliteration, but more important even than this is the contribution made by that variety and range of language – the apparently effortless combination of words drawn from many sources, learned and 'lewed', literary and non-literary – which is characteristic of the finest makar poetry. No doubt Douglas's style was influenced by his reading of works such as *Troilus and Criseyde*, *The Knight's Tale*, and *The Legend of Good Women*, but the Chaucerian influence has been so thoroughly assimilated that we recognise its existence only through the occasional word and phrase in Douglas's poem, and by grammatical and syntactic anglicisms.[2] Chaucer provided Douglas with very little guidance in the matter of interpreting Virgil's *sens*. There may be traces of the vigorous descriptive mode of Chaucer's *Legend of Dido* in the corresponding section of

Douglas's Book IV, but his comments on Chaucer's interpretation of the Dido story suggest that however greatly Douglas admired the English poet's eloquence, his position as the accurate translator of the classical text committed him to disapprove of Chaucer's un-Virgilian approach. Douglas recognised that Chaucer was superior as an artist to both Caxton and Lydgate, the translator of Guido, but clearly he had no more to learn from Chaucer's scholarship than from theirs. Douglas's intellectual affinities are with scholars and commentators such as Badius Ascensius and Cristofero Landino, although without the guidance of vernacular poetry, Chaucerian and local, his work would indeed have been as he describes it mock-modestly in the first Prologue – 'ignorant blabryng imperfyte', unworthy of comparison with Virgil's 'flude of eloquens'.

For sixty years Douglas's *Eneados* was the only complete British translation of Virgil's epic. It was printed in England in 1553, and it was not until 1573 that there was a full translation by an English poet – Thomas Twyne's continuation of Phaer's *Seven First Books of the Eneidos*. There are other English translations of sections of the *Aeneid*, the first of which is Surrey's translation of Books II and IV, made some thirty years after the *Eneados*. Surrey's work shows beyond any doubt that he knew the Scots translation, and that he used it as a guide to his own distinctive rendition of two of Virgil's books into English. The evidence suggests that the *Eneados* was just as important to Surrey as Ascensius's commentary on Virgil's Latin had been to Douglas. Like Skelton in his borrowings from Scots poetry, Surrey does not mention Douglas explicitly. Sixteenth-century poets, like those of earlier times, saw no obligation to record indebtedness to other writers, and it would be wrong to see any impure motive in the omission. Nevertheless, we might be excused for seeing the shadow of one: it does not seem likely that Surrey, any more than Skelton, would have felt inclined to acknowledge the achievement of a Scot, however admirable. The means by which Surrey came to know Douglas's poem are unknown, but in view of his close association with the court circle as companion to the Duke of Richmond, it is hardly surprising that the Scots manuscript came to his attention. After

Douglas's death in London in 1522, copies of what he calls his 'bettir part' were no doubt eagerly received by the group of humanist scholars who had close associations with the royal household. It is possible, too, that Surrey came to know the work through the associations of Margaret Douglas, the king's niece, daughter of Margaret Tudor in her second marriage to the Earl of Angus, who was Gavin Douglas's nephew. Margaret Douglas was a member of the court circle which provided the audience for Wyatt's poetry, and her clandestine marriage to Surrey's uncle Thomas Howard provoked the king's wrath and her husband's downfall.

The frequency with which words, phrases and even whole lines of the *Eneados* are echoed in the English translation suggests that Surrey worked, quite literally, with a copy of Douglas at his elbow. In her edition of Surrey's translation, Florence H. Ridley shows quite conclusively that he borrowed extensively from the relevant books of the *Eneados*: in the text she italicises those words and phrases taken over from the Scots, after taking into account that some apparent borrowings may in fact be independent translations from Virgil and from commentaries such as that of Ascensius.[3] In all nearly 900 instances of verbal borrowing are adduced in the text of Surrey's poem which Tottel printed in his *Miscellany*. The extent to which Surrey drew upon Douglas's translation may be even greater than this suggests, since the other two extant versions of Book IV indicate an even higher proportion of Scots words. Ridley effectively discounts the arguments that one of Surrey's editors may have 'scotticised' the work on the basis of his own reading of Douglas, and that the similarities between the two translations may be explained as common use of commentaries. In the frequency of its verbal borrowings, the closest analogy to Surrey's use of Douglas is perhaps the use which James I, the most obviously 'Chaucerian' of the Scots poets, makes of Chaucer's poetic language in *The Kingis Quair*. Yet like James, Surrey works with an original purpose. The fact that he translates only two of Virgil's Books (those which have the strongest emotive colouring), suggests that he regarded himself as an experimenter rather than one, like Douglas, who was concerned to convey the whole 'history' of Aeneas as Virgil represents it. The dimensions of Surrey's translation imply that he was not writing, as Douglas was, with a view to the capabilities and critical judgements of a large audience, and no doubt for this reason he felt it unnecessary to set out a theory of translation in the way that Douglas does in his first Prologue. The verse itself suggests, however, that Surrey's emphasis as a translator was not the same as that outlined by Douglas:

> So thocht in my translatioun eloquens skant is,
> Na lusty cast of oratry Virgill wantis;
> My studyus brayn to comprehend his sentens
> Leit me nevir taist hys flude of eloquens.
>
> (p. 11, 307-10)

Allowance must be made, here as elsewhere, for the implications of the modesty-*topos*: Douglas was undoubtedly conscious both of the need for 'eloquens' and of the interdependence of style and meaning. But the translation itself bears out the implications of this statement of the theory. Consistently, Douglas's endeavour is directed at Virgil's 'sentence', his meaning, rather than at sustained imitation of the Latin style. In his translation of two Books of the *Aeneid*, Surrey's main aim seems to have been to reproduce in English something of the distinctive quality of Virgil's 'eloquens'. This is not to suggest that Surrey was insensitive to Virgil's meaning – any more than Douglas was insensitive to Virgil's style – but merely to point to a different order of priority. Surrey's translation is the first English poem to be written in blank verse. Whether this medium was inspired directly by Virgil's hexameters or indirectly by the *versi sciolti* of his Italian translators it is not possible to say, but through it Surrey endeavours to imitate both the conciseness and the compact verbal texture of the Latin. Emrys Jones draws attention to the element of 'pure verbality' in Surrey's translation: 'words, phrases, and sentences occupy more attention, they themselves become aesthetic objects. The reader senses a continual striving after balance, parallelism, antithesis, symmetry, and pleasurable asymmetry.'[4] He notes that Douglas's style is less obtrusive, that in reading the *Eneados* we have more freedom to concentrate on the narrative. We do no injustice to Surrey's very considerable achievement as an innovative 'classical' poet by recognising that he was free to experiment because he did not have Douglas's pedagogic responsibility to an audience.

Douglas's conservatism – or perhaps more accurately, his medievalism – as a translator of Virgil is most apparent in his choice of the decasyllabic couplet as a medium. This is the metrical form used by Lydgate in the *Troy Book*, but Douglas's practice probably owes more to the example of Chaucerian works such as *The Knight's Tale* and *The Legend of Good Women*, and to the *Wallace*. In these and other vernacular poems he found a style which was eminently suitable for a long narrative incorporating a large amount of dramatic speech. The necessity to observe both rhyme and a predominantly 'natural' word order would have made any sustained attempt to imitate the texture of Virgil's verse impossible. It is surprising to find that one of the aspects of Douglas's translation which Surrey found sufficiently attractive to imitate on occasion is its sound: consider, for example, his use of the first few lines of Douglas's Book II: the Scots,

> The Grekis chiftanys, irkit of the weir
> Bypast or than samony langsum 3eir,
> And oft rebutyt by fatale destany
> Ane huge horss, lyke ane gret hil, in hy
> Craftely thai wrocht
>
> (p. 66, 1–5)

becomes in English,

> *The Grekes chieftains, all irked with the war*
> Wherin they wasted had so many yeres
> *And oft repulst by fatal destinie,*
> *A huge hors* made, *hye* raised like a *hill.*
>
> (18–21: italics correspond with Ridley's treatment of the text.)

The verbal similarities are self-evident, and it cannot be argued that they are simply fortuitous: no two wholly independent translators could have arrived at almost the same rendition of the Latin. Surrey repeats both the 'double translation' of 'fatisque' in the third line, and the alliteration of the following line, although he did not understand that Scots 'in hy' means 'in haste', not 'on high'. He echoes not only Douglas's words, but the word order and rhythm of the Scots lines. In both, the first three lines are basically iambic, with the same kind of variation in lines 2 and 3, and an accumulation of six heavy stresses in line 4. Other examples of sound borrowing may be found, but they are not as extensive as this one:[5] the most interesting is Surrey's echo of Douglas's

> O wytles lufe! quhat may be thocht or do,
> At thou constrenys nocht mortell myndis tharto?
>
> (p. 177, 9–10)
>
> O witlesse love, what thing is that to do
> A mortal minde thou canst not force thereto!
>
> (IV, 540–1)

(Virgil's 'improbe Amor, quid non mortalia pectora cogis'.) It would appear that in Surrey's endeavour to reproduce the cadence of Douglas's lines he unwittingly incorporated a couplet into his blank verse.

The sections of the *Eneados* from which Surrey borrows whole lines in which the rhythms of the Scots translation are echoed tend to be those in which Douglas is at his most concise. Surrey's borrowings from the more characteristic parts of Douglas's translation, in which the Latin text is amplified and particularised to a considerable extent, are very selective, and illustrate clearly that Surrey's conception of translation was very different from Douglas's. Comparison of the English and Scots translations of the Latin frequently suggests that Surrey was trying to effect a compromise between Virgilian conciseness and the vivid particularity of Douglas's language. This can be seen when we set side by side the two renditions of the Latin similes. Here, for example, are the figurative accounts of the fury of Pyrrhus and his band:

> Not sa fersly the fomy ryver or flude
> Brekkis our the bankis on spait quhen it is wode,
> And, with hys bruoch and fard of watir brown,
> The dykis and the schoris bettis doun,
> Ourspredand croftis and flattis with his spait,
> Our al the feildis that thai may row a bayt,
> Quhil howsys and the flokkis flyttis away,
> The corn grangis and standand stakkis of hay.
>
> (Douglas, p. 90, 101–8)

> *Not so fercely* doth overflow the feldes
> The *foming flood*, that *brekes out his bankes*,
> Whoes rage of waters beares away what heapes
> Stand in his way, the coates, and eke the herdes
> (Surrey, II, 639–42)

brusch and fard rush and charge; *flattis* plains

The brevity of Surrey's passage marks the difference of approach: clearly the model here is the conciseness of the Latin,[6]

> non sic, aggeribus ruptis cum spumeus amnis
> exiit oppositasque evicit gurgite moles,
> fertur in arva furens cumulo camposque per omnis
> cum stabulis armenta trahit.   (II, 496–9)

It is not difficult for Surrey to follow Virgil in the matter of length, but he fails to capture the allusiveness of the Latin – a matter of both sense and rhythm. Virgil's simile is an uninterrupted sweep of words. The alliteration at the end of Surrey's second line intensifies the pause after 'bankes', and this break in the flow of the simile detracts from its force: there is a further loss in vigour in the removal of the verbs from their positions at the beginning of the lines ('exiit', 'fertur'). There is nothing in the English to correspond to Virgil's 'gurgite', with its connotations of excess and indulgence, so appropriate in the context of Pyrrhus's fury. Surrey's lines are stately and elegant, but their extensive alliteration is no substitute for the mimetic effect which Virgil creates through his taut rhythms and by more insistent patterns of sound. The underlined words in the quotation indicate that the alliteration, as well as some of the vocabulary, is taken over from Douglas. But no further did Surrey go in his borrowing, preferring a clipped brevity to the Scots poet's detailed and imaginative expansion of the original. Douglas conjures up for his audience the picture of a real river 'in spait', using a series of familiar words – 'dykis', 'schoris', 'croftis', 'flattis', 'feildis', 'howsys', 'flokkis', 'grangis', 'stakkis' – to evoke the scale of the destruction. Although the passage is longer and more particular than the Latin, Douglas successfully re-creates Virgil's onomatopoeic sweeping effect: from the first line to the last there is no interruption to the sibilant thrust of the utterance – a remarkable achievement, considering that Douglas writes in what is basically a two-line sense unit. Moreover, he is sensitive to Virgil's choice of words: the list of objects swept away, and the use of 'wode' to describe the torrent, successfully re-create the sense of 'gurgite'. As in the Latin, additional emphasis is gained by the placing of the verb at the beginning of the line (102, 105). Here, as in the other similes, Douglas's expansion results in an increase of particularity which is nevertheless faithful to Virgil's 'sentens'. In comparison, Surrey's attempt to maintain a classical economy appears cautious and even pallid.

C. S. Lewis describes Surrey's translation as 'Virgil in corsets'.[7] This is not altogether unfair, because although Surrey's lines have a commendable conciseness and elegance of form, they seldom re-create the flexibility and the energy of the corresponding sections of the Latin text. Only occasionally does Surrey catch something of what Ridley calls 'the sinuous sweep of Vergilian statement'.[8] It may seem paradoxical that Douglas, who does not attempt to imitate the verbal texture of his original, should frequently create stylistic effects which are more readily comparable with Virgil's 'eloquens'. The limitations imposed by the use of rhyme should not be overestimated: Douglas's couplets are very flexible, and display an accomplished use of enjambment and various kinds of metrical variation. By comparing two quite extensive passages, it is possible to see how Douglas's translation may be just as polished, just as sonorous, as Surrey's more consciously 'classical' approach. Because, as Professor Jones observes, 'Surrey tends to be more successful in speeches that are oratorical in cast than in passages of elaborate description or narrative', I have chosen to concentrate on two versions of a dramatic speech, Aeneas's account of the return of the dead Hector to announce the imminent destruction of Troy (*Aeneid* II, 274-97).

> Ha, walloway, quhat harm and wo eneuch!   44
> Quhat ane was he, how far changit from ioy
> Of that Hector, quhilum returnyt to Troy
> Cled with the spulӡe of hym Achillys,
> Or quhen the Troiane fyry blesis, I wyss,
> On Grekis schippis thyk fald he slang that day
> Quhen that he slew the duke Prothesylay!   50

Hys fax and berd was fadyt quhar he stude
And all hys hayr was glotnyt ful of blude.
Full mony woundis on his body bayr he,
Quhilk in defens of hys natyve cuntre
About the wallys of Troy ressavyt he had.　　　　55
Me thocht I first wepyng and na thing glaid
Rycht reuerently begouth to clepe this man,
And with sik dolorus wordis thus began:
'O thou, of Troy the lemand lamp of lycht,
O Troiane hope, maist ferm defens in fyght,　　　60
Quhat has the tareit? Quhy maid thou this delay,
Hector, quham we desyrit mony a day?
From quhat cuntre this wyss cummyn art thou?
That eftir feil slauchter of thi frendis now
And of thi folkis and cite efter huge payn,　　　65
Quhen we beyn irkit, we se the heir agayn!
Quhat hard myschance fylyt so thi plesand face?
Or quhy se I tha feil woundis, allace?'
Onto thir wordis he nane answer maid,
Nor to my voyd demandis na thyng said,　　　70
Bot with ane hevy murmour, as it were draw
Furth of the boddum of his breste weil law,
'Allace, allace, thou goddes son,' quod he,
'Salf thi self from this fyre and fast thou fle.
Our ennemyss has thir worthy wallys tane;　　　75
Troy from the top down fallys, and all is gane.
Enewch has lestit of Priamus the ryng,
The fatis wil na mair it induryng.
Gif Pergama, the Troiane wallys wyght,
Mycht langar haue beyn fendit into fyght,　　　80
With this rycht hand thai suld haue be defendit.
Adew, fair weil, for euer it is endit.
In thi keping committis Troy but less
Hir kyndly goddis clepit Penates;
Tak thir in falloschip of thi fatis all,　　　85
And large wallis for thame seik thou sall,
Quhilk at the last thi self sall beld vp hie
Eftir lang wandryng and errour our the see.'
Thus said Hectour, and schew furth in his handis
The dreidfull valis, wymplis and garlandis　　　90
Of Vesta, goddes of the erth and fyre,
Quhilk in hir tempil eternaly byrnys schyre.

(pp. 79–80)

begouth began; *lemand* gleaming; *weil law* low down; *lestit* lasted; *schyre* clear

This corresponds to Surrey's,

>   Ay me, what one! that Hector how unlike
>   Which erst *returnd clad with Achilles spoiles*,
>   Or when he threw into the Grekish shippes   350
>   The Troian flame! so was his beard defiled,
>   His crisped lockes al clustred with his blood,
>   With all such wounds as many he received
>   *About the walls of* that *his native town*.
>   Whome franckly thus me thought I spake unto,   355
>   With bitter teres and dolefull deadly voice:
>   'O Troyan light! O only hope of thine!
>   What lettes so long thee staid? or from what costes,
>   Our most desired Hector, doest thou come?
>   Whom, after slaughter of thy many frends,   360
>   And travail of thy people and thy town,
>   Alweried, lord, how gladly we behold!
>   What sory *chaunce* hath staind thy lively *face*?
>   Or *why see I these woundes, alas* so wide?'
>   He answeard nought, nor in my vain demaundes   365
>   Abode, but *from the bottom of his brest*
>   Sighing he sayd: 'Flee, flee, O goddesse son,
>   And save thee from the furie of this flame.
>   Our enmies now ar maisters of the walles,
>   And *Troye* town now *falleth from the top*.   370
>   Sufficeth that is done *for Priams reigne*.
>   If force might serve to succor Troye town,
>   This right hand well mought have ben her defense.
>   But Troye now commendeth to thy charge
>   Her holy reliques and her privy gods.   375
>   Them joyne to thee, *as felowes of thy fate*.
>   *Large walles* rere thow *for them*: for so *thou shalt*,
>   After time spent in th'overwandred flood.'
>   This sayd, he brought fourth Vesta in his hands,
>   Her fillettes eke, and everlasting flame.   380

Surrey's concern for conciseness here impedes the achievement of a sense of spoken eloquence, which is such a striking feature of the Latin. His lines are for the most part elegant and graceful, but there is little of that effect which is produced by Douglas's balancing of the demands of prosody against a feeling for the rhythms and the idiom of speech. 'Ay me, what one!' is perfectly acceptable as a literary exclamation, the equivalent of Virgil's 'ei mihi, qualis erat', but it lacks the force of Douglas's colloquial, 'Ha, walloway, quhat harm and wo eneuch!' The 'when he' of Surrey's line 350 is syntactically awkward, and appears to have been inserted to satisfy the metrical demand of the line. The 'quhen' of Douglas's line 48, on the other hand, introduces a clause which balances the adverbial construction of the preceding lines, creating an appropriate sonority. The meaning of Surrey's first four lines is perfectly clear (despite their slightly awkward word order), but in the attempt to maintain the *brevitas* and the word order of the Latin 'quantum mutatus ab illo / Hectore, qui redit exuvias indutus Achilli / vel Danaum Phrygios iaculatus puppibus ignis' (274–6), Surrey fails to reproduce the flow of the utterance which in the Latin contributes to an effect both elegiac and strongly dramatic. Douglas's rendition of the passage is more copious, but it does catch the movement and the feeling of the original. 'Thyk fald' (49) is a characteristic 'particularisation' of Virgil, but it effectively complements the sense. Later, Douglas again catches the mood of the Latin when he comes to translate Aeneas's agitated questioning of his visitor. In the Scots, as in the Latin, the speaker's agitated and slightly reproachful frame of mind is realised by a series of short questions. In place of Douglas's,

> Quhat has the tareit? Quhy maid thou this delay,
> Hector, quham we desyrit mony a day?
> From quhat cuntre this wyss cummyn art thou?

Surrey offers the more compressed

> What lettes so long thee staid? or from what costes,
> Our most desired Hector, doest thou come?

In the interests of condensation, the English line creates an imbalance of stress and hence of meaning: the accumulation of heavily-accented syllables in 'doest thou come' produces an unfortunate anti-climactic effect. Douglas, by contrast, effectively conveys the poignancy of Virgil's 'quibus Hector ab oris / exspectate venis?' Surrey's imitation of Virgil's short sense-units produces a staccato effect which misses most of Virgil's sense of

G

drama (see especially lines 374–8). Douglas's translation is much more fluid, with variation from the two-line unit of meaning. The rhymes are not allowed to intrude: the sense of the couplet is frequently completed in the following line (79–81, 85–7, 89–91), and there are departures from the basic iambic pattern which mean that stress does not always fall upon the last syllable of the line. In the passage quoted, as throughout the *Eneados*, the poet's feeling for the rhythms of speech helps to save the rhyming from monotony.

The English translation contains a number of verbal borrowings from the Scots. Both their incidence and their general nature typify Surrey's practice throughout the translation. Close examination of the more extended of them shows that what is taken over into the English translation is seldom accompanied by the poetic implications of the Scots original. Surrey's 'Which erst returnd clad with Achilles spoiles', for example, carries little of the allusiveness of the Scots 'quhilum returnyt to Troy': the stress placed on 'quhilum' by the medial pause after 'Hector' effectively reproduces the sense of Virgil's 'mutatus', opposing the victorious past to the inglorious present. A little later, 'About the walls of that his native town' echoes Douglas's 'of his natyve cuntre / About the wallys of Troy', an amplification which Douglas makes to obtain the sense of Virgil's allusive 'patriam'. The more concise English line carries no comparable emotive association. Although he is a master in the art of amplification, Douglas has the ability to use language concisely, to make a single word convey more than one meaning. This is apparent in the line 'Or quhy se I tha feil woundis, allace?' where 'feil' seems to have the double sense of 'many' and 'mortal'. Since there is no Virgilian counterpart to either sense, it is obvious that Surrey is following Douglas when he too amplifies the Latin – 'Or why see I these woundes, alas so wide?' (This double meaning is also implicit in the use of the word in line 64.) It is not difficult to see why Surrey was attracted by Douglas's translation of 'sed graviter gemitus imo de pectore ducens':

> Bot with ane hevy murmour, as it were draw
> Furth of the boddum of his breste weil law . . .

Surrey's 'but from the bottom of his brest / Sighing he sayd' repeats both words and alliteration from the Scots, but has no counterpart to the assonance and the slow-paced movement which contribute so much to Douglas's imaginative re-creation of the Virgilian *sens*. The danger that conciseness may be the enemy of sense is further illustrated by the English translation of 'sat patriae Priamoque datum' – 'Sufficeth that is done for Priams reigne.' 'Reigne' here has been taken over from Douglas's more copious translation, but again Surrey misses what gives the Scots lines both energy and accuracy – in this case, an amplification of the starkly monosyllabic 'all is gane' in line 76, which uses very simple language and a highly dramatic opposition of passive and active sense-structures to convey the idea of fatality. By comparison, Surrey's line is awkwardly archaic. Douglas re-creates the portentous climax of the Latin verse paragraph by a characteristically amplified translation which pays careful attention to stress and movement. 'Eftir lang wandryng and errour our the see', prominent because it is the culmination of a four-line utterance, is given further emphasis by the accumulation of heavy stresses and the decisive pause before 'Thus said Hectour'. Surrey's line, 'After time spent in th'overwandred flood' is closer to Virgil from a purely literal standpoint, but it lacks the associative power of 'magna pererrato statues quae denique ponto', which Douglas so skilfully re-creates. It is Douglas rather than Surrey who manages to convey the sense of awe before the emblems of divinity. Surrey's lines 379–80 have a certain spare beauty, but they convey little of the mystery of Douglas's sonorous expansion of 'et manibus vittas Vestamque potentem / aeternumque adytis effert penetralibus ignem' (296–7). Recognition of Douglas's achievement in creating such equivalents to the allusiveness of Virgil's style should make us question the argument that Douglas's expansions of the Latin 'make the poem more lively, probably, than it was originally, but at the sacrifice of some of the melancholy and elegiac tone'.[9] Neither translation is even in quality, however, and there are a few sections of Surrey's poem which are more powerful than the corresponding parts of the *Eneados*.[10] Among Surrey's finest lines is the farewell speech of Creusa at the end of

Book II. This is one of the rare occasions on which the translation achieves a fusion of conciseness and Virgilian eloquence. Beside the splendidly defiant,

> Ne I, a Troyan lady and the wife
> Unto the sonne of Venus the goddesse,
> Shall goe a slave to serve the Grekish dames,
>
> (1045–7)

Douglas's translation seems rather pedestrian. Surrey's account of Aeneas's grief, which is entirely true to the spirit of the original, is one of the finest things in English blank verse:

> Thrise raught I with mine arms t'accoll her neck,
> Thrise did my handes vaine hold th'image escape,
> Like nimble windes, and like the flieng dreame.
>
> (1054–6)

In the conclusion to Book II, Surrey works independently of Douglas's translation, and this is exceptional. Elsewhere he borrows frequently, and his practice suggests that he found the Scots poem useful because of the vigour and the precision of its language. This is apparent in the borrowings from the Hector passage and from the epic simile, both of which have been discussed. In Book IV, he follows Douglas's imaginatively localised account of the Bacchae:

> Scho wyskis wild throu the town of Cartage,
> Syk wyss as quhen thir nunnys of Bachus
> Ruschis and relis
>
> (p. 171, 40–2)

> Then ill bested of counsell rageth she,
> And *whisketh* through the town like *Bachus nunne*.
>
> (IV, 388–9)

Here the onomatopoeic 'wyskis' and the anachronistic description transfer easily into English. Douglas makes full use of the opportunities offered by Virgil's similes for vividly localised descriptive effects, and it is hardly surprising to find Surrey borrowing from the Scots for another such passage earlier in Book IV. His description of the Trojans rebuilding the fleet,

> Like ants, when they do spoile the *bing* of corne,
> (IV, 529)

is derived from Douglas's

> Lyke emmotis grete
> Quhen thai depulʒe the mekill *byng* of quhete.
> (p. 176, 79–80)

Here Surrey prunes the Scots passage quite successfully, except for his substitution of the vague 'do spoil' for Douglas's precisely descriptive 'despoil'. Throughout, the English translation is enlivened by repetition of many of those felicitous 'litill additiouns' which permeate Douglas's Virgil. Attention has been drawn above to the 'Bacchus' nun' passage, and some further examples of this kind of borrowing may be observed. One of the most effective is Douglas's allusion to the dead Priam ('sine nomine corpus') – 'A corps but lyfe, renown or other fame' (p. 93, 87), which becomes in Surrey's translation 'A body now without renome and fame' (II, 729). Other such expansions include Douglas's description of the horse – 'suttell hors of tre' (p. 77, 73; cf. Surrey II, 303), the detail 'Standing wod wraith' in the account of Juno's rage (p. 96, 96; cf. Surrey II, 805), and the epithet 'the grysly' in the reference to Erebus (p. 182, 76; cf. Surrey IV, 684). Surrey tends to prune Douglas's amplifications, but the fact that he repeats them at all suggests that he, too, recognised that expansion was necessary for clarity and immediacy. It is interesting to note that Surrey makes 'litill additiouns' of his own.

Surrey's transference of Scots words into English is not always successful, and there are signs that he did not always understand the sense both of Douglas's 'haymly playn termys famyliar' and of more elevated northern diction. Scots 'regrait', for example, in the line 'With this regrait our hertis sterit to piete' (p. 69, 27), becomes 'regrete' in English (II, 93): for the sense 'renewal of weeping' is substituted the less forceful 'expression of regret'. The same failure to capture the nuances of Scots may be seen in Surrey's use of Douglas's line 'Kest vp the portis and yschit furth to play' (p. 66, 26). It becomes 'The gates cast up, we *issued* out to play' (II, 37), and the word is deprived of its Scots sense of 'to run forth unrestrained', which is so appropriate in the context of release from the confinement imposed by a long war. In some cases Surrey's use of northern expressions produces an awkwardly artificial effect, as in the following:

> Our first labor thus *lucked* well with us,
>
> (II, 494)

for,

> The first lawbour thus *lukkit* weil with wss
>
> (p. 85, 43);

> Some to the ground were *lopen* from above,
>
> (II, 741)

for,

> Sum to the erd *loppin* from hie towris of stane
>
> (p. 93, 12);

> From heaven she sent the goddesse Iris downe,
> The *throwing* sprit and jointed limmes to loose,
>
> (IV, 926–7),

for,

> Hir mayd Irys from the hevyn hess send
> The *throwand* sawle to lowyss
>
> (p. 192, 102).

That Surrey should have attempted to enliven his translation in this way is in itself unexceptionable, but the attempt is not altogether successful because the colloquial flavour of the Scots words is lost in the englishing. Borrowing of this kind is the opposite of what Dunbar does in *The Goldyn Targe* and what Douglas himself does in the *Eneados* and *The Palice of Honour*: i.e. taking over southern English words of a learned or decorative kind, and combining these with familiar Scots terms. There are fewer dangers inherent in the practice of the Scots poets than in Surrey's use of a vocabulary which is alien to his own spoken language, although of course Surrey must be given credit for the attempt to make his poetic language more flexible. On occasion he completely misunderstands a word or a phrase in Douglas, and consequently there is a shift and a weakening of meaning. Attention has already been drawn to Surrey's interpretation of 'in hy', and some further examples may be noted here. Douglas's account of the departure of the nurse,

> Hychit on furth with slaw payss lyke a *trat*,
>
> (p. 189, 114)

becomes in Surrey's translation, 'redouble gan . . . / Her steppes, forth on an aged womans trot' (IV, 857-8): here the English poet seems to have mistaken the Scots 'trat' (old woman) for a translation of 'gradum'. In a similar way, Douglas's line,

> Amyd the flambis and armour I *in preste*,
>
> (p. 82, 76)

becomes 'Amid the flame and armes ran I *in preasse*' (II, 430), which clearly does not mean the same thing. Here Douglas is closer to Virgil's 'in flammas et in arma feror' (II, 337), and Surrey's reading misses the sense of energetic movement. Misunderstanding of a part of speech alters Douglas's 'oft with rycht handis gryp the battalyng *wald* [would]' (p. 88, 14) to the less kinetic, 'their right hands/Griped for hold th'embatel of the *wall*' (II, 573-4).

The most interesting feature of Surrey's purely verbal borrowing from the *Eneados* is its comprehensiveness. Not only especially striking words, phrases and lines, but also some of the less distinctive sections of Douglas's translation are echoed.[11] It is easy to understand why Surrey should have been struck by Douglas's rendition of 'tot vigiles oculi subter' in the description of Fame – 'Als mony walkryfe eyn lurkis thar vndir' (p. 165, 17). In the English translation this becomes 'As many waker eyes lurk underneath', and a few lines later there is a repetition of Douglas's evocative 'By nycht scho fleys amyd' (Surrey IV, 237). It is less easy to understand, however, why Surrey should have gone on to echo Douglas's 'with mony a taill' and 'this rumour' (p. 165, 31-2), which are an accurate but unexceptional rendition of Virgil's sense. (There is no Latin equivalent to 'this rumour'.) Surrey's translation abounds in such minor borrowings from Douglas, and coincidence cannot account for all of them. Their significance lies in indicating the degree to which Surrey relied on the older translation, and their frequency is evidence for Mrs Bawcutt's theory that Surrey used the Scots translation as an aid to understanding Virgil's Latin.[12]

Although in this respect Surrey may have been in a similar position to the modern student who reads Virgil with the aid of a Loeb Classics translation, it is very clear that he put his close knowledge of the *Eneados* to creative use. Surrey uses the older translation to enrich the verbal texture of his own. Obviously he admired the vigour and the variety of Douglas's language, even if he did not understand the meaning of all of the words which he borrowed. That he felt the need to introduce unfamiliar northern diction into his poem suggests that his own literary tradition was unable to give him the necessary support in the matter of linguistic variety. Post-Chaucerian English poetry offers no equivalent to the verbal range of Scots poetry, in which there is a place for all kinds of language, from 'harsk' colloquialism to polished and ostentatiously 'literary' effects. This variety exists not only between one kind of poem and another, but also within individual works, where unity is frequently provided (as in the *Eneados*) by imitation of the rhythms of speech. This kind of tradition was not available to Surrey in his own language: the 'new company of courtly makers' in the reign of Henry VIII to which Puttenham alludes had learned to make use of spoken rhythms in poetry, but what was appropriate for poetic language was governed by a decorum which was much more narrow than that followed by the Scots poets. Puttenham observes that northern language is the 'purer English Saxon, yet it is not so Courtly nor so currant [smooth-flowing] as our Southerne English is'.[13] The Elizabethan critic's standard of taste is partly moulded by the practice of Wyatt and Surrey, whose poetic language conforms to the ideal of speech for men 'ciuill and graciously behauoured and bred'. Although its borrowing from the Scots helps to provide life and variety, Surrey's *Aeneid* translation suggests that there were serious obstacles in the way of rendering Virgil's 'hie profund sentens' into a poetic idiom which reflects such a high evaluation of the 'courtly' and the 'currant'. No English translation of the later sixteenth century exhibits anything comparable to the amplitude and variety of Douglas's language, although it is interesting to note that later poets prefer to follow Douglas's method of expansion and amplification rather than Surrey's more severely classical approach. Barnabie Googe showed sound critical sense in recognising the superiority of Gavin Douglas as a translator in his *Epytaphe of Maister Thomas Phayre*:[14]

> The noble H. *Hawarde* once,
>   that raught eternall fame,
> With mighty Style, did bryng a pece
>   Of *Virgils* worke in frame,
> And *Grimaold* gaue the lyke attempt,
>   and *Douglas* wan the Ball,
> whose famouse wyt in Scottysh ryme
>   had made an ende of all.

Perhaps Googe's judgement was affected by personal feeling, but for whatever reason he registers his preference for Phaer's incomplete translation, claiming for it a 'greater grace' than Virgil's Latin. Few modern readers would find the marks of a distinguished poetic sensibility in the thumping fourteeners of Phaer's seven books, but nevertheless this work, completed by Twyne, came to be more popular in England than Douglas's *Eneados*. This is probably to be explained more by the difficulty of Douglas's language for a non-Scottish audience than by any nationalistic considerations. There is little sign that the *Eneados* provided any sort of creative stimulus to English poets other than Surrey. Thomas Sackville, in the Induction to *The Mirror for Magistrates*, echoes Douglas at several points, but these borrowings are significant only inasmuch as they reflect knowledge of the translation. It is worth noting in this context that Sackville may also have read Lindsay: the details of the winter setting for the dream allegory are reminiscent equally of Douglas's seventh Prologue and the Prologue to Lindsay's *Dreme*.

Surrey's creative use of Scots poetry has a precedent not only in Skelton's practice, but also in the use which Wyatt seems to have made of one of Henryson's fables. There is evidence that

The Taill of the Uponlandis Mous and the Burges Mous provided, if not the inspiration, at least guidance for both the philosophical emphasis and some of the narrative detail of Wyatt's satiric verse epistle, *My mothers maydes*.[15] The claim for Wyatt's knowledge of and indebtedness to Henryson cannot be proved (in the way that Surrey's debt to Douglas can) because of the traditional nature of the story: the Aesopic fable is a genre of venerable antiquity, and Wyatt probably knew several versions of the tale of country mouse who learns a hard lesson about the vanity of ambition. Horace's version (in Satire II, vi) would almost certainly have been known to Wyatt, as would Caxton's retelling in his translation of a French *Aesop*. There were undoubtedly oral versions of the tale which have not come down to us. Denton Fox draws attention to one of them, which exists only as a phonetically transcribed fragment in a sixteenth-century Danish manuscript.[16] This song, or one like it, might account for Wyatt's opening lines – 'My mothers maydes when they did sow and spynne, / They sang sometyme a song of the feld mowse.' If the narrative had a popular inspiration, however, the form of the poem clearly did not, and it seems likely that in beginning as he does Wyatt had a literary precedent in mind: Horace, for example, puts the tale into the mouth of one Cervius, who is fond of telling homely 'grandmothers' stories' after dinner. Patricia Thomson raises the theory that Wyatt may have worked from a folksong original also known to Henryson, as a way of explaining the similarities between Henryson and Wyatt, but at the same time admits that it 'leaves still unexplained Wyatt's reconstruction of Aesop's story as one of sin and freewill, and the philosophical gravity with which he moralizes its theme'.[17] These two aspects of Wyatt's poem are also characteristic of Henryson's treatment of the fable, and considered together with the similarities of narrative detail, they suggest that Wyatt was familiar with the Scots fable. His treatment of the story is different in some respects from Henryson's – most notably in the omission of the town mouse's initial visit to her sister, which in Horace and Henryson alike provides the motivation for the country-dweller's journey, but from the beginning Henryson, too, draws our attention to the philosophical question of fallen man's use of his free will.

The Taill of the Uponlandis Mous and the Burges Mous represents Henryson's juxtaposition of animal and human worlds at its ironic and entertaining best: the mice are mice, but at the same time they have the aspirations and susceptibilities of humans. We are prompted to see them, specifically, as types of fallen humanity, through the presentation of them as 'outlawis' and 'pykeris', having no title to any possessions of their own. (This is Henryson's view of both mice, not simply the town-dweller who sustains herself so lavishly in the merchant's house: see lines 168, 203.) The burgess mouse's determined assault on her sister's self-content is a miniature drama of free will. Her methods are formidably varied (refusal to eat, veiled insult, the promise of luxury, dismissal of danger), and eventually the rural mouse's commonsense and sound judgement are undermined. In the town, the country-dweller again questions the wisdom of her sister's way of life, and again fails to act according to the dictates of conscience. Even after the terrifying interruption of the spenser, when the country mouse protests her desire to be at home and her inability to eat, she allows herself to be persuaded back to the table by 'wordis hunny sweit' – the result is a near escape from death, in the shape of 'Gib Hunter, our jolie cat'. The *moralitas* is not so much an explanation as an amplification of the *taill*. Henryson does not attach precise significations to the details of the narrative, but as MacQueen suggests, there are hints within the *taill* that the cat may be identified with Fortune and death, and the human intruder who precedes the cat and should act as a warning, as divine providence.[18] Certainly this witty and undisguisedly 'artificial' identification of metaphysical realities with aspects of the animal–human world is characteristic of other fables in the collection, and the warning in the *moralitas* – 'The cat cummis, and to the mous hes ee' – is an invitation to such an allegorisation. The main emphasis of the *moralitas*, the desirability of contentment 'with small possessioun', complements the moral about the proper use of conscience and free will which emerges from the *taill*.

Wyatt's treatment of the fable proceeds in a different way. His country mouse, more than Henryson's, is prompted to the visit by envy: the material hardship of her life seems to make contentment impossible. But like Henryson's character, her most serious error consists in refusal to heed a warning, in the shape of the fear which her sister endures as the outcome of her choice to live as she does. (The aspect of warning, which contributes so much to the philosophical import of both Henryson's and Wyatt's fables, is not prominent in other known versions of the fable.) The implications of the country mouse's plight are ironically emphasised in the line, 'And made her there against her will remain' (67): the possibility of such ruin is implicit in her own initial assertion of will. Like Henryson, Wyatt stresses the power of fortune or chance over those who are tempted away from the life of severe self-sufficiency: the Scots mouse is saved only 'throw fortune and gude hap' (302, 335), while her less fortunate English sister suffers through the same equally arbitrary power of 'sorry chaunce' (50, 63). The moralisation of the stories in both poems is more extensive than in other known versions, and here too there are points of contact. Like Henryson, Wyatt admonishes mankind severely and in general terms,

> O wantoun man! that usis for to feid
> Thy wambe, and makis it a god to be,
> Luke to thy self!
>
> (*The Twa Mice*, 381–3)

> O wretched myndes, there is no gold that may
> Graunt that ye seke!
>
> (*My mothers maydes*, 75–6)

and both comment on the susceptibility of all estates to change. Sententiousness of this kind is no doubt partly *sui generis*, but the fact that Wyatt follows Henryson in presenting the familiar story as an *exemplum* of the consequences of misdirected will does suggest indebtedness. Wyatt's poem is not in any sense an imitation of Henryson's fable, however: the tone of his moralising is unrelievedly sombre, and the concluding prayer sounds a note of bitterness which is far removed from Henryson's genial exaltation of the virtues of the simple life. Wyatt reinterprets the Boethian emphasis of the Scots fable in a manner which accords with the world-weary introspection of the fable's companion piece, *Myne owne John Poyntz*.

This view of the relation between the two poems – that Henryson's fable in all probability provided a stimulus to Wyatt's extensively philosophical handling of the story – argues for a closer connection than that suggested by Patricia Thomson. Her view is that 'Henryson . . . accounts, not so much for the moral and psychological essence of Wyatt's satire, as for some of its lively touches.'[19] Wyatt's poem features neither the elaborate episodic structure nor the extensive use of description and direct speech which contribute so much to the life of the Scots poem, but nevertheless there are signs that he borrowed some of Henryson's details. Henryson's fable features the mice as sisters, and the cat as agent of destruction. Both of these details are found in Wyatt's poem: his mouse-eye view of the cat ('two stemyng Ise / In a rownde hed with sherp erys') provides in fact the only humorous touch. Both English and Scots mice have the power of human speech, but cry 'peip' to attract attention (H, 187, 808: W, 42). In Henryson's poem, 'thay drank the watter cleir / Insteid off wyne' (272–3), and in Wyatt's, 'they drancke the wyne so clere' (47): both rhyme 'clear' with 'cheer'.

Wyatt's probable indebtedness to Scots poetry is a less significant matter than the indebtedness of Scots lyric poets to the work of both Wyatt and Surrey. There can be little doubt that Alexander Scott, like Alexander Montgomerie and other poets of the latter part of the sixteenth century, read English lyrics appreciatively.[20] Many of Scott's poems, for example, have a simplicity and directness which is reminiscent of Wyatt, and it is possible to point to techniques such as the clipped statement, the alternation of short lines with long, and the 'witty' refrain, which recall Wyatt's manner very clearly. Poems such as Scott's *It cumis you luvaris to be laill* and *The answeir to the ballat of hairtis*[21] possess a quality of witty detachment similar to that which informs Wyatt's *My pen, take payn a lytyll space* and *Blame not my lute*.[22] The vogue for sonnet composition among poets associated with the court of James VI almost certainly owes something to English fashion, although the Castalians experimented independently with continental models. As in the case of the relationship of the older makar poetry to the work of Chaucer, there is little sign that Scots lyric poets were slavish imitators of their Tudor and Elizabethan counterparts: the relationship is probably best described as one of 'affinity and guidance'.[23] Yet it must be acknowledged immediately that there are no Scots rivals to the finest achievements of English lyric poetry in the sixteenth century. One searches in vain for any equivalent to the earlier efflorescence of 'Chaucerian' poetry in Scotland.

7

Ane Satyre of the Thrie Estaitis and English drama

Ane Satyre of the Thrie Estaitis, Sir David Lindsay's wide-ranging appeal for the reordering of church and state, is the earliest surviving Scots play. We should resist the temptation to see it in a position of splendid isolation, even if we are unable to study and enjoy it in the context of a national dramatic tradition. The public records of the fifteenth and early sixteenth centuries show that plays of various kinds were performed in Scotland, both at court and in the burghs.[1] If some of these texts were to come to light, it could probably be shown that Lindsay's great play has affinities with other dramatic works in Scots – just as his poetry has affinities with the poetry of an earlier generation. If Lindsay's practice as a poet is any guide, we would expect his play to be related to others which had some connection with the court. His entire career was spent in the royal service, and indeed one of the earliest records of Lindsay at court concerns a payment made in 1511 for taffeta 'to be ane play coit [coat] to David Lindesay for the play playt in the King and Quenis presence in the Abbay'. The surviving texts of *Ane Satyre* are connected with the performances at Cupar (1552) and Edinburgh (1554), and a link with other Scots drama can be postulated only on the assumption that the 'interluyde' played before the king, queen and council at Linlithgow in 1540 was not in fact the work of Lindsay. This production, which is known only by notes sent to Cromwell by Sir William Eure, apparently had the spectacularly persuasive effect of inducing James V to threaten to send six of his proudest bishops 'vnto his vncle of england [Henry VIII]' if they did not 'reforme thair facions and maners of lyving'.[2] The 'nootes of the interluyde' suggest several close parallels – in terms of character-names and dramatic action – with the later versions of Lindsay's play, and it is highly probable that the Linlithgow play was the work of Lindsay. The evidence for relating Lindsay's play to other vernacular plays is almost non-existent. What, though, of the possible connections between *Ane Satyre* and non-Scottish drama? Several critics have remarked on the parallels between the Scots play and the *Jeu du Prince des Sotz* of Pierre Gringore, acted in Paris in 1511.[3] It seems very likely that Lindsay knew Gringore's play, and that he adapted several features of it for the second part of *Ane Satyre*: both plays satirise corruption in church and state through the dramatic spectacle of a parliament-court presided over by a king, who hears the complaints of Common Weal (La Commune) against the spiritual and temporal estates (Clergy and the Seigneurs). Many of the complaints alleged against the estates in the French play recur in *Ane Satyre*, although in itself this is no evidence of borrowing: more important is the close resemblance between Gringore's Pugnicion Divine and Lindsay's Divine Correctioun. The two plays are, however, very different, and it is clear that if Lindsay did borrow from Gringore, he did so imaginatively, in accordance with his own conception of dramatic structure.

The English affinities of *Ane Satyre* have received very little critical attention. Dr Mill, for example, confines herself to the observation that 'both in its setting and in its clear development of the Vice role *Ane Satyre of the Thrie Estaitis* is in the tradition of the English moralities'.[4] It is the purpose of this chapter to suggest that the play has links not only with the English secular morality tradition, but also with a particular English play, Skelton's *Magnyfycence*. Skelton's political morality was probably written in 1516, and had been printed by 1532. It is possible that Lindsay became acquainted with the late laureate's 'goodly Interlude and a mery' during the course of his official duties in 1535, when he was one of the party sent to receive the Order of the Garter on behalf of James V.[5] *Ane Satyre* occupies a unique place in British secular drama of the earlier sixteenth century. It is distinguished by the comprehensiveness of Lindsay's vision, by the variety of its characters and its dramatic effects, and by the technical proficiency of its verse. Anges Mure Mackenzie remarks on how thoroughly aspects of dramatic tradition have been assimilated to Lindsay's purposes, with the result that the play as a whole defies precise categorisation in terms of the conventional genres. She is clearly suspicious of any attempt to separate any fusion of tradition and individual talent into its component parts.[6] I do not claim that a knowledge of Skelton's play – or, for that matter, of any other play – is necessary to our understanding of *Ane Satyre*, but nevertheless I think it worth considering the relation between the English play and the Scots, because there are signs that Lindsay knew Skelton's work, and that he drew upon it in writing his own play. Furthermore, an understanding of the relation between the two plays may help us to appreciate more fully the distinctiveness of Lindsay's achievement.

The term 'interlude' was loosely used in the sixteenth century to describe virtually any kind of dramatic entertainment, irrespective of length or subject matter.[7] The whole of the play performed at Linlithgow in 1540 is described as an 'interluyde', for example, even though it contains other interludes within it. The first part of *Ane Satyre*, which in the 1602 text concludes shortly after the reformation of the king, resembles *Magnyfycence* in being the kind of interlude which has its roots in the morality play. The earliest known English moralities (from the beginning of the fifteenth century) develop the venerable tradition of personification allegory in dramatic terms, and they differ from the older miracle plays in being concerned not with the stages of man's redemption through Christ, but rather with demonstrating the connection between right conduct and salvation. Grace is celebrated in the morality plays as well as in the miracles, but the morality emphasis is on the potentialities of free will. Typically, a character who represents *Humanum Genus* (with a name such as Mankind, Everyman, or Free Will) is shown to make the wrong choices, forsaking the sound and sober counsels of Reason for the blandishments offered by more vivacious forces such as Sensuality and Pride. Having succumbed to temptation – which is almost invariably portrayed as false appearance – his period of pleasure is very soon over: the legions of vice are seldom able to agree among themselves in their task of subversion, and man soon finds himself confronted by the alarming spectacle of Adversity (Death, Old Age). When ruin is imminent or actually present, man is saved through divine intervention: there is usually a return to measured life in the world, although sometimes, as in *The Castle of Perseverance* and *Everyman*, redemption is not won until the end of life. (*Everyman* is atypical of the English moralities in that it is not built around their pattern of temptation and conflict.) The 'moralite' announced by Mercy at the end of *Mankind*[8] is entirely typical:

> Now, for hys lowe that for vs receyuyd hys humanite,
>   Serche your condicyons with dew examinacion!
> Thynke & remembyr the world ys but a wanite,
>   As yt ys prowyd daly by diuerse mutacyon.
>
> Mankend ys wrechyd, he hath sufficyent prowe;
>   There-fore God [kepe] ʒow all, per suam misericordiam,
> That ye may be pleseres with the angell[es] abowe,
>   And hawe to ʒour porcyon vitam eternam. Amen!
>
>   (900–7)

The morality interludes of the fifteenth and early sixteenth centuries are prevailingly universal in their depictions of the conflict between the forces of vice and virtue for the soul of the protagonist, but just as in poems such as *Confessio Amantis* and *Piers Plowman*, local and topical elements frequently reinforce and give point to the larger allegorical significance. Indeed most of the plays derive their force from this intersection of the timeless with the topical. In *Wisdom*, for example, the presentation of the universal human soul is such that it enables the dramatist to focus upon the corruption of the clergy, and upon the need for clerical and judicial reform, at a time when the growth of the Tudor bureaucracy gave increasing scope for ambitious clergy to become involved in the affairs of state. Less insistently topical works such as *Mankind*, *Hickescorner*, and *Youth* present what D. M. Bevington calls 'the evils of increasing social mobility and resultant disruption of moral values'.[9] In these plays, immoderation of spirit is commonly signified through excess in dress and language. In *Mankind*, for example, the trio New Gyse, Nowadays, and Nought, who are the servants of the Devil and the enemies of Mercy, ape the guise of courtiers, providing most of the life of the play by their vigorous cursing and boisterous action. The focus of Medwall's *Nature* is more insistently upon courtly extravagance. Pride, *alias* Worship, is the leader of the vices: he is of 'noble progeny', and his code is one of total self-indulgence. Medwall was chaplain to Henry VII's chancellor John Morton, and it is highly probable that his depiction of the vices had reference to the profligacy of some of the older noble families whose power the king's taxation measures were intended to curb.[10] The play concludes with a plea for moderation in the use of worldly goods, when Man is constrained (ironically, by Liberality) to take the middle way between penury and prodigality.

In its emphasis upon Measure in the conduct of the noble life, Skelton's *Magnyfycence* has more in common with Medwall's *Nature* than with any other known English morality interlude. (It is almost certain that Skelton knew the older play, which was printed about the time at which his own play was written.) Skelton's major innovation within the morality tradition, a matter which is directly relevant to the link between *Magnyfycence* and the first part of *Ane Satyre*, is in the substitution of a prince for the everyman–mankind protagonists of earlier morality plays. (A king is the central figure of the early fifteenth-century morality fragment *Pride of Life*, but he is figured solely as the epitome of worldly achievement: no attention is given to his proper function as a ruler.) *Magnyfycence* belongs to the wider literary tradition of the *speculum principis*, and the opening debate between Felycyte and Lyberte, its reconciliation by Measure, and the ordering by Magnyfycence of his trio of servants, serve to define the play's central character and to introduce its allegorical action. Magnyfycence is an idealised governor, whose conduct is guided at all times by measure:

> There is no prynce but he hath nede of vs thre,
> Welthe, with Measure, and plesaunt Lyberte.
>
> (159–60)

Unless Measure keeps Lyberte (Free will) in check, there can be no Felycyte (19–21), nor indeed can Magnyfycence properly exist. The prince makes these conditions of his estate clear when he orders his household:

> For dowtlesse I parceyue my Magnyfycence
> Without Measure lyghtly may fade,
> Of to moche Lyberte vnder the offence;
> Wherfore, Measure, take Lyberte with you hence,
> And rule hym after the rule of your scole.
>
> (227–31)

Felycyte, Measure and Lyberte are thus defined as the qualities which combine to form the 'character' of Magnyfycence, and the action of the play outlines the process by which the prince's rightful magnificence does fade when he succumbs to temptation, thereby misusing his free will. The vices of *Magnyfycence* have a distinctly courtly cast, and in this they are the descendants of Medwall's subversives and the trio of roisterers in *Mankind*. Magnyfycence is undermined first by Fansy, who presents himself as Largesse, 'encreace of noble fame' (271). Four other conspirators, Counterfet Countenaunce, Crafty Conueyaunce, Clokyd Colusyon and Courtly Abusyon, are introduced successively by Fansy to the prince, and under their guidance he liberates Lyberte from the surveillance of Measure. Magnyfycence is reduced to the level of Foly, and Waste succeeds Thrift in the kingdom (1444). Inevitably the prince is robbed of his felicity and is visited by Adversity and Poverty. Magnyfycence repents ('Alasse my Folly, alasse my wanton Wyll', 2062), is spurned by his false counsellors, and visited by Dyspare and Myschefe. The temptation in adversity balances the earlier temptation in prosperity and again, the protagonist is ready to succumb. But at the crucial moment Good Hope, Redresse and Cyrcumspeccyon intervene through the grace of God to restore the balance of moral forces which had formerly existed in the character of the prince. The play concludes with the clearly secular spectacle of the regenerate prince returning 'Home to [his] paleys with Ioy and Ryalte' (2562), in the company of his wise counsellors.

The extent to which the action and characters of *Magnyfycence* mirror a real situation and actual people is crucial to any interpretation of the play, and it is necessary to raise it here in order to compare Lindsay's treatment of historical fact with Skelton's. With very few exceptions, Skelton scholars have echoed R. L. Ramsay's view of the play's topical significance, which holds that the morality play foreshadows the verse satires against Wolsey. The general outline of the proposed historical identification is summarised thus by I. A. Gordon: 'Magnyfycence represents Henry VIII, and the vices and virtues in the play are the two parties among the councillors – those, headed by Wolsey, advocating a campaign of showy extravagance, and those in favour of a more economical policy, of whom the chief was Thomas Howard, the Earl of Surrey.'[11] In his study of the play, W. O. Harris argues vigorously against both this kind of historical identification and the philosophical tradition of Aristotelian liberality which has often been assumed to underlie Skelton's concept of Magnificence. He suggests that the play should be seen as counsel to understand and observe Fortitude, described by one of Skelton's contemporaries as the cardinal virtue which gives man 'contempt both of prosperyte and aduersyte'.[12] This philosophical reading has much to recommend it, not least because it provides a rationale for the last 700 lines which relate the temptation in adversity (frequently dismissed as a concession to morality tradition), and for the insistence upon the workings of Fortune at the end of the play. Harris's rebuttal of the conventional historical approach is well founded: here it may be sufficient to observe only that at the time *Magnyfycence* is assumed to have been written there does not seem to have been any deep conflict between Henry's councillors. There may have been some resentment by Howard (the Lord Treasurer) of Wolsey's ascendancy, but the rift between them took place after 1520, the time of the popular antagonism to Wolsey of which poems such as *Speke, Parrot* and *Colyn Cloute* are expressions. It is doubtful whether before 1516 Wolsey did advocate a policy of 'showy extravagance': he may even on occasion have tried to curb the young king's expensive bellicosity. It is worth remembering one of the earliest letters written by Wolsey to his patron Bishop Fox, in 1511: in it he mentions Howard, 'by whos wanton meanys his grace spendyth mych money and ys more dysposyd to ware than paxe'.[13] Some historians have given support to this view of Howard's policy in the years which followed, and the evidence suggests that it might be possible to reverse the terms of the historical situation which has been proposed for *Magnyfycence*.

Are we to accept, then, that Skelton's play is exclusively philosophical in its terms of reference, that it forms a dramatic counterpart to the *Speculum Principis* which Skelton had written several years before for his prince? Professor Harris's view that the play is a counsel to Fortitude is persuasive, especially as it reveals the fallacies and inconsistencies inherent in the old view that the play represents a conflict between the king's virtuous and vicious advisers, one faction headed by Norfolk, the other by an embryonic arch-villain Wolsey. It is probable, nevertheless, that the play does contain a dimension of topical meaning, existing with and reinforcing the larger pattern of philosophical meaning. Since the greater part of Skelton's poetry reflects a close involvement with the happenings and personalities of the world around him, it is surely worth pondering the question of why he chose to write a play with a king as its central character. As Occupacioun explains in *The Garlande of Laurell*, the play has a universal applicability: 'who pryntith it wele in mynde / Moche dowblenes of the worlde therin he may fynde' (1196–7). Harris describes *Magnyfycence* as 'a morality play designed for the "salvation" of a king':[14] like a great deal of court literature, it implies an awareness of two audiences, one immediate and local, the other universal. Presumably Skelton would not have written the play had he not felt that Henry had some need of the kind of advice which it offers. Although Magnyfycence is not Henry VIII, but rather the image of a potentially ideal ruler, wise and responsibly liberal towards his subjects, Henry is the logical point of reference in a play which refers repeatedly to 'Englonde' and the court, and which contains a reference to the recent death of the French king. Despite a high degree of abstraction and conceptualisation, the play does have some bearing upon historical reality. Wolsey's spectacular rise from a relatively insignificant position as royal almoner to the chancellorship was made possible only by his shrewd calculation of the royal character: Henry was soon impatient with the tedious routines of kingship, and Wolsey was only too willing to perform the duties which irked his master. The young king's negligence was well known, and there are several records in the vein of the papal envoy's report: 'He devotes himself to accomplishments and amusements day and night, is intent on nothing else, and leaves business to Wolsey, who rules everything.'[15] To a conservative like Skelton, who had worked in the household of the conscientious Henry VII, the king's attitude must have smacked of Idleness, the arch-enemy of royal Fortitude. In *Magnyfycence*, Folly boasts that he has the power to make fools of kings by teaching them 'howe they sholde syt ydyll / To pyke theyr fyngers all the day longe' (1222–3). In the play, the chief manifestation of the prince's deviation from the path of Measure is the warlike posture he adopts in the monologue, his longest single speech (1457–1514); here he prides himself on being above Fortune, the superior of all the great warrior-kings of history. The play itself does not prepare us for the emphasis on military might, and the speech seems to depend for effect upon a knowledge of contemporary events. Magnyfycence's boast that there are 'none so hardy of them with me that durste crake, / But I shall frounce them on the foretop and gar tham to quake' (1513–14) is an accurate account of Henry's attitude to the European powers in the years prior to 1516, and the parallel can hardly have been lost upon the contemporary audience. The king is the focus of Skelton's concern 'vnder pretence of play', but the insistence on the *parvenu* status of the courtly vices, and in one case, an apparent reference to a particular upstart 'set in auctorite' (1242–52), may suggest that Wolsey too was being satirised under the veil of dramatic 'dowblenes'. The toppling of the play-prince would seem to be a 'myrrour', a warning to Henry of what might well happen if he did not set his house in order. The reinstatement of Measure and the coming of Perseueraunce and Cyrcumspeccyon, similarly, represent the poet's ambition for the future of his sovereign and former pupil.

The first part of *Ane Satyre* resembles *Magnyfycence* in that it features a king as protagonist within the framework of the traditional morality conflict between vices and virtues. Lindsay's King Humanitie, as his name suggests, is an abstraction, but like the king in Skelton's play he is presented in such a way as to suggest some of the characteristics of a real king – James V. Despite the fact that the temper of Lindsay's play is very different from that of *Magnyfycence*, the topical element in its portrait of kingship, taken in association with a number of parallels in terms of characterisation and action, is sufficient to suggest the influence of one play upon the other.

The surviving texts of *Ane Satyre* relate to performances in 1552 and 1554, and the question of the extent to which King Humanitie is to be seen as a representation of James V at a particular stage of his career is directly relevant to the dating of the play. John MacQueen argues for a closely historical interpretation of the first part of the play, identifying Humanitie with the young James V, and two of the vices with the Treasurer and Secretary of the time: on the basis of this and the close verbal parallels with poems written before 1530, he suggests that the play was written in the early 1530s, truncated for the 1540 Linlithgow performance, and revised some twelve years later.[16] It is possible that the kingship morality of the surviving texts did exist in an earlier form: as a *speculum* addressed to a living prince, such a play would have had the historical immediacy of Lindsay's *Dreme* and the *Complaynt*, and indeed of *Magnyfycence*. In this context, MacQueen indicates that Correctioun's advice to the play king, to be chaste until a suitable 'Queene of blude-royall' is found (1745–9), is 'very relevant to the period before James's first marriage in 1537'.[17] The qualities of the play king who is *tanquam tabula rasa* and quite unrealistically passive are, however, moulded considerably by the tradition of morality characterisation, and it is hazardous to insist on an exclusive identification with the young James V. Anna Jean Mill and Vernon Harward, favouring a date in the middle of the century for the surviving texts, argue that King Humanitie represents a generalised and typical King of Scots,[18] but allow for a partial identification with James, the king whom the playwright knew so well in his own lifetime: Harward suggests that 'Lindsay found a congruence between the erring young King of Scots in past history and the traditional morality protagonist. King Humanitie is not to be identified specifically with James V, although the latter shared the youthfulness and indulgence of his predecessors and of the morality protagonist.'[19] Lindsay's approach is not unlike that which shapes the characterisation of the 'I' in *The Kingis Quair*. Both poem and play invite associations with real lives, but at the same time check the impulse towards exclusively biographical interpretation.

In its combination of the general and the particular, the depiction of King Humanitie is close to that of Magnyfycence: just as Skelton alludes obliquely to the nature of Henry VIII, so too Lindsay invites his audience to recognise in Humanitie some of the traits of James V. The temptation of the king in the Scots play is specifically a sexual temptation, and in this regard it seems unlikely that a contemporary audience would fail to have recalled the propensities of their last king. In 'Ane Exhortatioun to the Kingis Grace' at the end of the *Dreme*, Lindsay reminds James of the ruinous consequences of sexual immoderation. The warning, repeated in *Ane Satyre*, is obviously applicable to a king who is known to have had at least five mistresses, all with powerful family connections.[20] Lindesay of Pitscottie, like the poet, identifies sexual indulgence with misgovernance and ill counsel: he observes that if James had 'ressawit goode consall of wyse and godlie men and spetiallie of his great lordis and keipit his body from harlotrie and had left the evill consall of his papistis bischopis and gredie courteouris, he had ben the most nobillist prince that ever rang in the realme of Scotland'.[21] James's policy was frequently swayed by influential prelates, and it is probably no accident that the most insidious of the vices in the play, Flatterie, should undermine Humanitie by adopting a clerical disguise. The surviving texts of the play contain many references to events of the middle years of the century, and although the possibility of an early version of the morality plot cannot be ruled out, it is very likely that Lindsay wrote the play as a whole near to the time of the Cupar performance. There is nothing inherently improbable about allusion to the career of a king who in 1552 had been dead for a decade. Dr Mill points out that the play does not depend for its success on the recognition of topical overtones, but that nevertheless the 'then last king of Scotland and tales of his minority would surely not so soon fade from the minds of his people'.[22] The first part of the play presents the reformation of King Humanitie as the necessary prelude to the spiritual regeneration of society at large, and the topical significance of the depiction of kingship is largely connected with James's failure as a reformer. In the *Complaynt*, Lindsay could congratulate the king upon the success of many of his policies, at the same time reminding him of the urgent need for reformation of the spiritual estate:

> Swa is thare nocht, I vnderstand,
> Withoute gude ordour in this land,
> Except the spiritualitie.
> Prayand thy grace thareto haue ee.
>
> (409–12)

James did not correct the abuses to which Lindsay refers in the *Complaynt*,[23] and the worldliness and negligence of the church in Scotland were exacerbated by his death. *Ane Satyre of the Thrie Estaitis* is a misleading title, inasmuch as the main thrust of Lindsay's satire is directed at the spiritual estate. It is probable that the play's depiction of sweeping correction was intended to show the audiences of Cupar and Edinburgh not only the pressing need for change, but also to remind them of their last king's failure to accomplish reform where it was most necessary: there may well be an implicit appeal for the Queen Regent to promote the reformation which her husband had at least begun. As a satirist, Lindsay's optimism is considerable, as in the mid-sixteenth century there was no immediate prospect of another king of Scotland, at least one who was a Stewart by birth. There is about Rex Humanitas, with his overtones of the last male Stewart, also something of the quality of *rex quondam rexque futurus*. He is about to appear, announces Diligence at the beginning of the play, having 'bene absent this monie ʒeir', but although the absence has been the cause of 'misreull' and injustice, it is characterised as no more than a sleep (24). The source of Lindsay's hope, in the play as in *The Buke of the Monarche* (his last poem, completed in 1553), would seem to be in the 'Kyng and Gouernour' to be brought home from France in the future by the heir to the realm (16). Although the absence of a king is a cause for sorrow in *The Monarche*, Lindsay in his last poem is clearly optimistic about the future of kingship in Scotland. Experience speaks for the poet when he says,

> I traist to se gude reformatione
> From tyme we gett ane faithfull prudent king
> Quhilk knawis the treuth and his vocatione.
>
> (2605–7)

This hope is also given expression through the presentation of Rex Humanitas.

Although the presentation of kingship in *Ane Satyre* is distinctive, Lindsay's depiction of a play king has a close parallel in the portrayal of Magnyfycence. Lindsay's character, like Skelton's, is a type which has connections with other morality protagonists, but both are presented in such a way as to suggest associations with historical figures, thereby contributing to the topical value of the allegorical action. There are several other similarities of characterisation and plot construction which, considered together, reinforce the likelihood that Lindsay knew and borrowed from Skelton's play. The structural pattern of the protagonist's career – innocence, temptation, fall and misrule, correction and repentance – is common to *Magnyfycence* and *Ane Satyre*, but it is not necessary to assume that Lindsay borrowed this from Skelton, since it is the framework of all the 'mankind' morality plays. The prominence given to the physical presence of Sensualitie, the specific occasion of temptation in Lindsay's play, is reminiscent more of Medwall's *Nature* than of *Magnyfycence*, where the prince's mistress does not actually appear. It is possible, however, that some of the details of Humanitie's seduction are developed from the scene in *Magnyfycence* where Courtly Abusyon succeeds in arousing the prince's sexual curiosity. In both plays, the inexperienced rulers are seduced by the sugary rhetoric of their false advisers rather than by the conventional means of Presence and Sweet-Looking. Skelton carefully draws attention to the extravagance of Courtly Abusyon's rhetoric through the compliment paid by the rapt Magnyfycence – 'Pullyshed and fresshe is your ornacy' (1529–31). There is a strong element of parody in the following speech, where the elevated rhetoric of courtly love is twisted to serve the designs of the procurer:

> fasten your Fansy vpon a fayre maystresse
> That quyckly is enuyued with rudynes of the rose,
> Inpurtured with fetures after your purpose,
> The streynes of her vaynes as asure inde blewe,
> Enbudded with beautye and colour fresshe of hewe,
> As lyly whyte to loke vpon her leyre,
> Her eyen relucent as carbuncle so clere,
> Her mouthe enbawmyd, dylectable, and mery,
> Her lusty lyppes ruddy as the chery.   (1550–8)

The effect is ironically complemented by the crudely enthusiastic vigour of the prince's reply (1560–9). There is a very similar juxtaposition of high and low styles in the descriptions of the lady with which Solace and Placebo ply King Humanitie: e.g.

> To luik on hir is great delyte,
> With lippis reid and cheikis quhyte:
> I wald renunce all this warld quyte
>   For till stand in hir grace:
> Scho is wantoun and scho is wyse
> And cled scho is on the new gyse
> It wald gar all ȝour flesche vp ryse,
>   To luik on hir face.   (198–205)

> That perfyt patron of plesance,
>   Ane perle of pulchritude:
> Soft as the silk is hir quhite lyre,
> Hir hair is like the goldin wyre:
> My hart burnis in ane flame of fyre
>   I sweir ȝow be the Rude.
> I think scho is sa wonder fair,
> That in earth scho hes na compair.
> War ȝe weill leirnit at luifis lair
>   And syne had hir anis sene,
> I wait, be cokis passioun,
> ȝe wald mak supplicatioun,
> And spend on hir ane millioun
>   Hir lufe for till obteine.   (339–52)

lyre skin

Lindsay's speech is prefigured by the semi-dramatic account of temptation and procuration in the *Complaynt* (237–52), but the rhetoric of the scene in *Ane Satyre* is considerably more elaborate. Both plays present their audiences with the unedifying spectacle of ruler rewarding panders in exchange for securing female favours: King Humanitie, like Magnyfycence, has to be told about the necessity for payment (*Satyre*, 397–405; cf. *Magnyfycence*, 1570–82). Skelton's parodic effects pale into insignificance beside the triumphant *introit* of Sensualitie ('Luifers awalk! behald the fyrie spheir'), although in fairness it should be said that the introduction of a similar figure might have distorted the thematic emphasis of the play. There is sufficient resemblance between the two temptation scenes – the pandering efforts of false courtiers who seduce by rhetoric, the undercutting of the elaborate language by crude reality – to suggest that the scenes which explore Humanitie's affair with Sensualitie may have grown out of the relationship between Magnyfycence and Courtly Abusyon.

Perhaps the strongest evidence for the influence of Skelton's play upon *Ane Satyre* concerns the relationship between the two groups of vices. Just as Skelton replaces the traditional mankind protagonist with a type character who represents secular authority, so too he enlarges upon the 'nowadays' vices of plays such as *Nature* and *Mankind*, giving a more emphatically courtly emphasis to vice than in any earlier morality. Fansy, the embodiment of hare-brained irresponsibility and the instigator of the prince's downfall, introduces himself as a courtier – 'Yet amonge noble men I was brought vp and bred' (261) – and posing as Largesse he is made a knight (520–1). The four vices represent current varieties of social evil whose highest aspiration is to subvert and dispossess those of high rank: it is no accident that these figures have counterparts in Skelton's quasi-dramatic poetic satire *The Bowge of Courte*. When Foly appears, he too boasts that his greatest achievement is to bring into his company 'cayser . . . or kynge' (1215–16). In *Ane Satyre*, Flatterie, Falset and Dissait represent similar kinds of social evil to which court life is especially prone. That Dissait is intended to be recognised as a courtier is clear by the allusion to his apparel (676–7). At the end of the play, their accomplice Folie boasts of his power over 'princelie and imperiall fuillis' (4558). It is interesting to observe that like Skelton, Lindsay depicts his vice characters in such a way that the wide-ranging consequences of regal misrule are amplified. In *Magnyfycence*, the conspirators are given monologues in which their effect on the body politic is made abundantly clear. Counterfet Countenaunce's 'bastarde ryme', for example, explores the pervasiveness of counterfeit moral values: merchants, courtiers, tradesmen, maidens, wives and clerics alike are intent upon deceiving others in all that they do or say (410–93). Later, one of his fellows, representing an even more sinister kind of falsehood, boasts,

> By Cloked Colusyon, I say, and none other,
> Comberaunce and trouble in Englande fyrst I began.
>
> (714–15)

In the first part of *Ane Satyre*, the corruption among the Three Estates is highlighted by the particular social connections of each of the vices. Dissait is 'counsallour to the Merchand-men' (656), to whom he flees at the coming of King Correctioun (1520–5), when Flatterie and Falset go to dwell with the spiritual estate and the 'men of craft' respectively (1514–19, 1529–31). The point is visually underlined in the second part of the play, when the trio reappear leading the Three Estates 'gangand backwart'. Lindsay represents the sins of the realm in a direct and concrete way in a play which has a much wider scope than *Magnyfycence*, but nevertheless his method of alluding to the illnesses of society in Part 1 is very close to the method of Skelton's play.

The use of physical disguise for satirical purposes in Lindsay's play offers a further parallel with *Magnyfycence*. Disguise is, of course, one of the standard elements in the emergence of drama, and in earlier morality plays it is frequently used to illustrate the idea of Evil's superficial attractiveness. In *Wisdom*, for example, Lucifer appears wearing the dress of a devil over a flashy gallant's robe, explaining to the audience that when he removes his 'proper' habit, Anima will be seduced by his glorious brightness. In *Nature*, the Seven Deadly Sins assume euphemistic aliases in order to deceive Mankind: e.g., Pride becomes 'Worship', Wrath,

'Manhood', and Sloth, 'Ease'.[24] Skelton's contribution to the morality disguise *topos* is to increase both the element of business involved and the moral implications of the physical disguise. As Ann Wierum shows, Skelton's exploitation of disguise as costume, rather than as simple name-changing, goes further than earlier uses of the theatrical metaphor.[25] When Skelton's Clokyd Colusyon enters for the first time, the others pretend not to be able to recognise him because he is wearing clerical garb:

> Se howe he is wrapped for the colde.
> Is it not a vestment?
>
> (603)
>
> Tushe! it is Syr John Double-Cope.
>
> (605)

To match his physical disguise, the others give him the alias 'Sober Sadnesse' (681). The element of play-acting which accompanies the changes of name and costume is emphasised in the scenes in which the vices discuss their new identities in tones of delighted self-satisfaction (e.g. 516–28, 669–84). Lindsay enlarges upon the Skeltonic combination of name-changing and physical disguise, embellishing the stage business involved and boosting the comic element. Flatterie hits on the idea of a double disguise as a way of deceiving Humanitie, and appeals to the audience for the necessary props:

> Wee man turne our claithis, & change our stiles,
> And disagyse vs, that na man ken vs.
> Hes na man Clarkis cleathing to len vs?
>
> (720–2)

Dissait struts about with cocky delight (729–32), and not to be outdone, disparages Flatterie's 'gay garmoun'. The *pièce de resistance*, however, is Flatterie's metamorphosis into a friar: Lindsay may have derived the notion from Skelton's Sober Sadnesse ('Syr John Double-Cope'), but his exploitation of the comic and satirical potential of disguise is more thorough than Skelton's. The conspiracy scene in *Ane Satyre* concludes with a mock-baptism, in which the vices solemnly bestow new names upon one another (779–800). The idea for a parody of ritual in this context may have come from *Magnyfycence*, where, after receiving his new name of Consayte, Foly thanks Fansy, who has given him the name – 'God haue mercy, good godfather' (1313). The exchange between Dissait and Falset during the ceremony,

> DISSAIT. I neid nocht now to cair for thrift,
> Bot quhat salbe my Godbairne gift?
> FALSET. I gif 30w all the Deuilis of hell
>
> (787–9)

is reminiscent of the scene in *Magnyfycence* where the vanquished prince is cursed ritualistically by the vices (2252–61). Both plays present the ineptitude of some of the conspirators in a spirit of broad comedy. In *Magnyfycence*, the appearance of Counterfet Countenaunce before his appointed time threatens to overturn Fansy's attempt to subvert the prince. Magnyfycence, who has accepted Fansy's claim to be Largesse and is about to read the counterfeit letter, overhears Counterfet Countenaunce as he tries to attract the attention of his accomplice. For one perilous moment it seems that Magnyfycence will trust his own ears rather than accept Fansy's explanation that the voice called to 'a Flemynge hyght Hansy' (328), but Fansy succeeds in quelling his doubts (330). Again Counterfet Countenaunce risks discovery, by appearing just as Fansy is about to depart with the deluded prince, with the result that he is furiously rebuked (396–400). In *Ane Satyre*, similarly, the plot is threatened at its inception through the ineptitude of one of the plotters, Falset, who forgets his new name at the crucial moment of his introduction to Humanitie. After three questions from the king about his identity, Falset frantically ad-libs – 'Marie thay call me thin drink I trow' (853) – and eventually Flatterie has to introduce him. As in *Magnyfycence*, the situation is saved only by some ingenious rhetoric (862–7).[26]

The presentation of fool characters as vices in the two plays constitutes another important parallel between them. A. J. Mill, relating the sermon of Folie at the end of Part II of *Ane Satyre* to the *sermon joyeux* of contemporary French drama, suggests that the English morality was comparatively uninfluenced by fool literature.[27] Here she overlooks the fools in *Magnyfycence,* and like subsequent commentators fails to notice that in both Skelton's play and *Ane Satyre* the physical presence of court fools is vital to the dramatic presentation of folly in kingship. In Lindsay's play, just as in Skelton's, there are two fool characters (apart from the fool in the Cupar banns), specifically court fools rather than merely the adherents to multiple forms of folly who are satirised in Brant's *Narrenschiff* and its various translations. There are unmistakable allusions in *Magnyfycence* to the court-fool's garb worn by Fansy and Foly: Foly greets his brother, 'What, frantyke Fansy! in a foles case?' (1047), and a little later one of the other characters makes a remark which reveals that Foly is similarly attired (1177). Both characters carry purses or wallets (347, 1103), and in one scene they are accompanied by animals (923, 1044), 'the natural appurtenances for the domestic or court fool'.[28] Their speech, too, marks them as members of the class of professional fools. When Fansy first enters, he addresses the prince in the tones of insolent familiarity permitted only to a court fool, and later he explains to Crafty Conueyaunce that Foly will treat Magnyfycence in the same way (1168–9). Ramsay observes that there is an important difference between Skelton's two fools: Fansy is a type of the natural fool, 'frantyke' and wildly capricious by nature, whereas Foly is an allowed fool, one who has sufficient intellect to assume the guise of the buffoon in order to make fools of others. It is Foly who brings Magnyfycence to his moral nadir, entertaining him with a torrent of sheer nonsense (1803–42). The significance of this spectacle, in which the prince plays the fool (1805), is explained by Foly's boast of his power over kings (1214–16).

The characters Flatterie and Folie in *Ane Satyre* are closely related to Skelton's Fansy and Foly. Flatterie's boisterous entry leaves no doubt that he is playing the part of the court fool:

> Quhat say ȝe sirs am I nocht gay?
> Se ȝe not Flatterie, ȝour awin fuill,
> That ȝeid to mak this new array?
> Was I not heir with ȝow at ȝuill?
>   (628–31)

ȝ*eid* went

Like Fansy in *Magnyfycence*, he regales his listeners with a racy anecdote about the dangers he has passed through in order to be present. Flatterie's account of his dangerous sea journey has the same outrageous tone as Fansy's story about escaping from France (*Satyre*, 603–35; cf. *Magnyfycence*, 347–61). Like Fansy, Flatterie is actively engaged in conspiracy: in both plays, the fool-conspirators take the initiative in deception. They are the first of the vices to appear, and it is they who set the conspiracy in motion. The fool's guile is praised by Counterfet Countenaunce,

> Fansy hath cachyd in a flye net,
> This noble man Magnyfycence,
>
> (403–4)

and in *Ane Satyre* the whole idea of the disguise plot is hatched by Flatterie (719–24). Lindsay's fool does not, admittedly, have the caprice which marks Fansy as a specific kind of court fool. Indeed, Flatterie has more in common with Skelton's Clokyd Colusyon, who, also disguised as a friar, achieves his end by a similar means:

> To flater and to flery is all my pretence
> Among all suche persones as I well vnderstonde
> Be lyght of byleue and hasty of credence.
>
> (738–40)

Lindsay's second fool, Folie, is also immediately recognisable as a court entertainer: at his first entry he expects recognition from the audience (4272–9), and later he produces from his purse a 'pillok' with which to divert the ladies. The latter is clearly a variant of the traditional fool's bauble. Folie affects an insolent style of address to those in authority (4316–17), like the two fools in Skelton's play. It is interesting to observe that, like his namesake in *Magnyfycence*, Folie feigns dumbness and stupidity when it suits him to do so. Here Diligence attempts to make him rise and hasten to the king:

> DILIGENCE Get vp. Me think the carle is dum.
> FOLIE Now bum balerie bum bum.
>
> (4400–1)

This exchange recalls the dialogue between Foly and Fansy in which Foly feigns deafness in order to parry his companion's indignant inquiries about the dog (*Magnyfycence*, 1059–66, 1085–97). Lindsay did not need literary precedents to enable him to depict the antics of a court fool, since he would have been quite familiar with the behaviour of fools in the Scottish royal household,[29] but nevertheless it seems likely that he was impressed by the idea of putting court fools into a play, and that he recognised the dramatic force of Skelton's distinction between two kinds of stage court fool. In *Ane Satyre*, Flatterie represents a particular kind of folly, to which those in high places are particularly susceptible, whereas Folie is the embodiment of a wide range of sinful inclinations. The essential difference between the allegorical significations of the two figures is highlighted in dramatic terms by Folie's entry as soon as Flatterie departs in search of new pupils (4271.) Folie's sermon (4466–4512) and the subsequent dialogue with Diligence (4513–4612) make it abundantly clear that Folie is a composite of all the vices: he sells 'Folie Hats' not only to flatterers, but also to lechers, pilferers and the followers of Pride in all its forms among the three estates. Folie's 'self-revelation' speech is reminiscent of the passage in *Magnyfycence* in which Foly boasts about the various kinds of fools who flock to his 'scolys' (1220–34, 1239–52). 'Princelie and imperiall fuillis' are singled out for special attention in the last stage of Folie's address (4554–85), where he exults, like Skelton's Foly, in his power over even the greatest temporal rulers. The parallel between the form of Folie's address and the French *sermon joyeux* should, as A. J. Mill suggests, be kept in mind, but it should also be remembered that Skelton's Foly casts himself in the role of the preacher, without actually using the sermon form in the play. This is clearly implied by the account of how he wins over the gullible – 'Fyrst I lay before them my bybyll.' (1221). There is nothing especially novel in the message about the pervasiveness of Folly, nor even in the definition of Folly as a composite of all sinful inclinations,[30] but the insistence in both plays upon the prevalence of Folly in royal courts, put in the mouth of the Vice himself, does suggest very strongly that Lindsay was influenced by Skelton. Because Folie's sermon is placed at the very end of *Ane Satyre* in the only surviving text of the complete play, it serves as a remarkably effective warning about the fragility of good order, a state which depends for its continuation upon the vigilance and fortitude of princes.

In *Ane Satyre*, as in *Magnyfycence*, the subversion of the prince proceeds from misuse of his free will. King Humanitie rebukes his false servants for their advice, affirming both his obedience to God and his readiness to make his own moral decisions:

> Becaus I haue bene to this day
> *Tanquam tabula rasa*:
> That is als mekill as to say,
> Redie for gude and ill.
>
> (223–6)

Skelton's ruler is also 'redie' in this sense, and the first scene of the play develops the idea that his capacity to follow the Good depends upon the maintenance of a proper relationship between Wealth, Measure and Liberty. This first scene illustrates the conflict within Magnyfycence between Liberty and Restraint, at the same time as it illustrates two opposing theories of statecraft. Liberty's recalcitrance (205–10, 232) is a clear portent of the prince's susceptibility. This scene has a counterpart in the first episode of *Ane Satyre*, where Humanitie is easily won over by his 'Wantonnes' to the society of Sensualitie: Wantonnes, Placebo and Solace represent both easy-living courtiers and the propensities of the central morality character. The action of both plays demonstrates that initial blindness and wilfulness – in *Magnyfycence*, a disposition towards unrestrained liberty, and in *Ane Satyre*, a fondness for sexual indulgence – are inevitably followed by errors of judgement which endanger the very position and authority of the ruler. Although Skelton does not introduce the physical equivalent of Lindsay's Sensualitie into his play, he places some emphasis on the undesirable preoccupation with the flesh which follows when the restraint of Measure is removed: when Liberty appears after having been 'liberated' by the conspirators, he is singing a bawdy song (2064–77). Lindsay follows Skelton in ascribing a 'neutral' moral quality to the defects of his young monarch. Liberty's explanation of his own nature,

> For I am a vertue yf I be well vsed,
> And I am a vyce where I am abused,
>
> (2101–2)

is relevant also to the minions of Lindsay's king. A prince must be permitted some liberty, but desire or will must always submit to the restraint of the divinely-appointed faculty of Reason or Measure. King Humanitie's error, like that of Magnyfycence, lies in his failure to recognise the need for restraint: Wantonnes and Solace are not in themselves vicious tendencies, provided that they are not abused, thereby preparing the way for the assaults of more serious vices. Correctioun is prepared to recognise sexuality, provided that it is kept within lawful bounds (1745–9), and he is surprisingly lenient in his treatment of Wantonnes and Solace:

> Princes may sumtyme seik solace,
> With mirth and lawfull mirrines,
> Thair spirits to reioyis.
>
> (1842–4)

This implicit distinction between natural impulses, in themselves only potentially vicious, and the active vice (synonymous with folly) which proceeds from immoderation, constitutes one of the most important parallels between the allegorical schemes of the two plays.

A further similarity between the plots of *Magnyfycence* and *Ane Satyre* is that both incorporate physical confrontations between good and evil counsellors, in which the latter are victorious. Having deluded Magnyfycence, Clokyd Colusyon and Courtly Abusyon proceed to displace Measure, who seeks to approach the prince through the intercession of Clokyd Colusyon. The false courtier confesses his ruse to Magnyfycence and explains that the supplicant is not 'mete' company for him (1652–3), with the result that Measure is unceremoniously banished. In the corresponding scene in *Ane Satyre*, Humanitie, who like Magnyfycence has been beguiled by false appearance, empowers his new officials to treat with Gude Counsell. The vices, of course, have no intention of allowing him to approach the royal presence, and *'thay hurle away Gude-Counsall'* (928–77). Humanitie, although negligent, is less culpable than Skelton's prince, since he does not know the identity of the wronged adviser. The idea of banishment plays a much more important part in Lindsay's play, since the scene involving Gude Counsell is followed by similar episodes in which Veritie and Chastitie are forcibly prevented from coming to the king.

Again at the level of action, it is interesting to observe that Lindsay, like Skelton, portrays the young king's false advisers as common thieves. Magnyfycence is robbed not only of his 'Felycyte' (1864), but also of his money and silver plate (2163–8): this of course is particularly appropriate in a play which reflects an interest in fiscal morality. When Lindsay's vices know that reformation is at hand, Flatterie makes a rapid exit, while Falset and Dissait steal the king's box: says Falset,

> Lo heir the Box now let vs ga:
> This may suffice for our rewairds.
>
> (1544–5)

In *Ane Satyre*, as in *Magnyfycence*, the theft of royal property is followed by a brawl. Clokyd Colusyon and Crafty Conueyaunce have a heated argument about which of them is the more daring thief (2171–97), and they are soon joined by Counterfet Countenaunce (2198–236). Falset and Dissait fall to abuse and clouts over a similar issue of priority, and eventually Dissait captures the box (1556–71). Lindsay goes further than Skelton by introducing a character called Thift, whose spiritual affinity with the two courtiers is dramatically illustrated in the hanging scene of Part II.

The most important parallels between *Magnyfycence* and *Ane Satyre* are sufficiently striking in terms of what is known about the development of the morality genre to suggest that Lindsay adapted and borrowed from Skelton's play. Such features include the choice of a theme which is predominantly secular and political rather than religious, the depiction of an idealised yet recognisably historical king as morality protagonist, the method by which he is tempted, the characteristics of the vices, the predominance given to the theme of folly, and various details of dramatic action. Despite these similarities, however, the first part of *Ane Satyre* is very different in spirit from *Magnyfycence*. If *Magnyfycence* is a source (as I believe it is) it is clear that Lindsay used it very selectively, with a constant eye upon a structural and thematic design of his own devising. His practice as a dramatist, in this sense, reflects the approach to the literary past in his poems, and the attitude of earlier Scots poets to the work of Chaucer. The kingship morality of *Ane Satyre* is a prelude to the considerably longer 'parliament' section, which Diligence calls 'The best pairt of our play'. The two are connected by the magisterial figure of Divine Correctioun, who instigates first the 'awakening' of the king, then the reformation of the estates, and also by the linked interludes involving the Pauper and the Pardoner. Characters from the first part figure prominently in the 'social' action of the second: the vices Flatterie, Falset and Dissait reappear in new roles, as leaders of the three estates, and later two of them are spectacularly hanged; Sensualitie figures prominently as the companion of Spiritualitie; Veritie and Chastitie are freed from the stocks and come to seek redress from King Humanitie; Gude Counsell fulfils the function denied to him by the misguided king in the first part of the play, and Diligence plays an active part in the setting up of the new regime. *Ane Satyre* is a much more comprehensive play than *Magnyfycence*, in terms of theme, range of characters and technical variety. The satirical dimension of Skelton's play – represented by the success of the disguise plot, and by the conspirators' boasts of being omnipresent in society – has some immediate local relevance, but the manner of its expression tends toward the level of generality which is characteristic of medieval complaint literature. Lindsay's satirical method, by contrast, is insistently local and topical. In the second part of the play there is an exhaustive attack upon the corruption of the Scottish church. Here too there are attacks upon the legal system (3053–84), and upon the injustices of the scheme of land tenure (2571–7): there are references to domestic discord in the borders

(2582–6), and to international politics (3562–3, 4564–79). The first part is not so overtly topical, but even here there are some incisive satirical thrusts, such as Gude Counsall's lament that he has been 'fleimit [expelled] lang tyme space' out of Scotland (578–9), and Solace's gibe at the king, 'Speir at the Monks of Bamirrinoch / Gif lecherie be sin' (261–2). *Magnyfycence*, with its exclusively courtly milieu, its small range and number of characters, and its paucity of dramatic action, was almost certainly written to be performed indoors before a small and socially restricted audience. *Ane Satyre*, on the other hand, is a national drama: this is reflected in the scope of its thematic concerns, in the number and social variety of its characters and in the fact that the two surviving texts are associated explicitly with outdoor performance.

It is perhaps unfair to compare the whole of *Ane Satyre* with *Magnyfycence*, since the second part of the Scots play is different in scope and spirit from anything Skelton ever wrote. But even if we compare only Part 1 of *Ane Satyre* with the English work it is clear that Lindsay's play is the more vigorous and theatrically effective. A large part of Skelton's play is devoted to exchanges among the vices, mainly of an abusive kind: there is a proliferation of exclamations, oaths, curses and nonsense dialogues such as the scene in which Foly gulls Fansy (1044–1154). Their rhetorical point is not just to entertain, but also to highlight the moral implications of 'low' language. The most striking scene is that in which Magnyfycence descends to the linguistic level of Foly (1803–42). Yet in the play, as in much of Skelton's poetry, the excess of 'vyle termes' becomes repetitive and tedious. Interspersed with the vices' repartee is a series of monologues in which they disclose their natures to the audience. Although these are written in a variety of verse forms, their number, and the fact that they are placed so predictably within the dialogue, combine to detract from the life of the play. The two groups of vices in the Scots play have a less tortuous style of speech, and part of the reason that the scenes which involve them are so funny is that their interchanges are not allowed to run on for too long. Lindsay has a keener sense of theatre than Skelton, and even the longest speeches in *Ane Satyre* have the quality of dialogue. Gude

Counsall, for example, begins his introductory speech with a prayer, and then turns to address his audience ('My Lords, I came nocht heir to lie'), inviting their involvement in the action to follow. Flatterie bursts in immediately (602) with a vigorously scatalogical account of his travels, addressing the audience first ('Se ʒe not Flatterie, ʒour awin fuill?'), and then bellowing for his 'fallowis'. The contrast between the sober gravity of Gude Counsall's speech and the raucous vulgarity of Flatterie's is a very telling dramatic illustration of the opposite forces which contend for Rex Humanitas. One of Lindsay's most effective alterations to the pattern of the morality plot is his consolidation of the various proponents of reform (in *Magnyfycence*, Aduersyte, Pouerte, Good Hope, Redress, Cyrcumspeccyon and Perseueraunce) into the single imposing figure of Divine Correctioun. Instead of presenting a lengthy account of the punishment and reformation of the misguided ruler, as Skelton does, Lindsay shows Correctioun *threatening* Humanitie with punishment:

> I haue power greit Princes to doun thring,
> That liues contrair the Maiestie Divyne,
> Against the treuth quhilk plainlie dois maling:
> Repent they nocht I put them to ruyne.
>
> (1713–16)

thring thrust; *maling* malign

Correctioun's contemptuous dismissal of Sensualitie ('Swyith [quickly] harlot. Hence without dilatioun.') is sufficient warning, and the subsequent docility of Humanitie is more effective as a token of a reformed spirit than a lengthy speech would have been.

Although he insists that *Ane Satyre* is, in terms of political satire and sheer theatricality, a better play than *Magnyfycence*, Ramsay holds to the view that Skelton's play is incontestably superior in terms of its construction.[31] It is true that the plot of *Magnyfycence* is carefully designed to illustrate the successive stages of the protagonist's career, but it does not follow that this balanced and logical form is superior to the much more flexible structure of *Ane Satyre*. The introduction of the farcical 'interluyde' involving the wives of the Sowtar and the Tailor has little to do with the theme of Humanitie's reformation, but it is dramatically appropriate because it provides comic relief and at the same time broadens the social dimensions of the play. The same can be said of the episode of the Old Man and his wife in the Cupar banns (preserved in the Bannatyne MS.), and it is important to note that even this hilariously farcical episode carries a moral which is highly relevant to both parts of the play: in the words of the Clerk, 'Thay ar not sonsy that so dois ruse [deceive] thame sell' (181). The episodes which involve the Pauper, the Pardoner, and the Sowtar and his wife, reveal corruption of various kinds in Church and State, and hence are important as illustrations of themes which are raised in a more elevated context elsewhere in the play. Nowhere do elements of crude humour and farce undermine the seriousness of Lindsay's plea for reform and hence lay the play open to the charge of structural imbalance. The fact that *Magnyfycence* has fewer characters than the Scots play (even after allowing for the practice of 'doubling' which Lindsay may well have followed) can hardly be an argument for greater structural cohesiveness. In terms of lucid plot construction, *Ane Satyre* is in no way inferior to *Magnyfycence*, despite the fact that the 'raw materials' of the Scottish plot are much more diverse. It need hardly be stressed that Lindsay's play includes characters and scenes which have no counterpart in Skelton's morality because its whole *raison d'être* – the need for wide reform throughout various grades of society – is much more ambitious and more complex than the moral impulse underlying Skelton's play.

Several critics have detected the influence of Lindsay's panoramic play in a variety of sixteenth-century English dramas advocating religious and social reform. The attitude of mind which has predisposed commentators to find traces of Lindsayan themes, characters and techniques in English plays is summed up in this comment by J. A. Lester:

> The Scotchman's play was trenchant and witty to a degree far surpassing contemporary English drama, and attacked abuses which did not exist alone north of the border, but were objects of satire in every country which felt the Reformation. It would, then, be strange if Ward's opinion, that this work was without influence on contemporary English drama, were founded on fact.[32]

With one probable exception, A. W. Ward's view that Lindsay's play did not influence secular drama in English is accurate.[33] The play most frequently singled out as exhibiting the influence of *Ane Satyre* is John Bale's *Kynge Johan*. Historical fact poses an insurmountable obstacle to this theory, unless one can believe that *Ane Satyre* was written in the 1530s, since *Kynge Johan* existed before 1536, the date of Bale's *Anglorum Heliades*, which includes in the list of his own works notice of the play *Pro Rege Ioanne*.[34] It is unlikely, moreover, that Bale's play influenced *Ane Satyre* in any way, even though Lindsay may have been aware of its existence. Hamer notes that there is no trace of similarity with the Scots play 'beyond a common hatred of Church abuses, the wrongs of the poor, the name of Verity, and the fact that both plays were written in two parts'.[35] Bale's choice of a chronicle form (an innovation in English secular drama) to a large extent dictates his choice of characters. It is difficult to imagine that a play which purports to depict the struggle between monarchy and the Church in the reign of the historical King John could have been written without representations of Prelacy, Nobility and Commons. Bale's extensive use of disguise suggests the literary influence of Skelton. (As in *Magnyfycence*, the impostors have polysyllabic double names: Sedition dupes the estates in the clerical disguise of 'Good Perfeccyon', and Dissimulation assumes the alias 'Monastycall Devocyon' in the scene in which he poisons the king.) The most striking parallel between Bale's play and *Ane Satyre* – the fact that both are 'estates' dramas – might lead one to conjecture that the second part of the Scots work had been influenced by Bale, were it not for the existence of the much stronger link between *Ane Satyre* and Gringore's play.

Considered as propaganda for the Tudor split with Rome, Bale's play must be conceded a certain crude effectiveness. Yet simply because it is a propaganda piece, there are very few points of contact with *Ane Satyre*. The hour of the Protestant reformation had not yet come in Scotland when Lindsay wrote his play, and although he directs some keen criticisms at the Papacy and the higher clergy he never descends, as Bale does, to vilifying the Old Religion. Lindsay is not the servant of a particular regime or a set of doctrines, and his satire is more comprehensive, in terms of both tone and social range. There is no place for humour or even for compassion in Bale's zealous Protestant *Weltanschauung*. F. P. Wilson provides an accurate summing-up of the essential differences between the plays: 'There is a world of difference between the humane and humorous genius of Lindsay, with his wide sweep and genuine sympathy for the suffering poor, and the bitter doctrinaire spirit of Bale. We cannot imagine Bale sparing even a reformed Wantonness, Placebo, and Solace.'[36] The action and characterisation of Lindsay's play are not directed, as they are in *Kynge Johan*, at depicting a struggle to the death between high-minded Monarchy and villainously corrupt Papacy.

William Bullein's allusion to Lindsay in *A Dialogue Against the Feuer Pestilence* (1564) demonstrates that *Ane Satyre* was known in the south before its publication in 1602, but the vogue in England for secular plays which advocated reform of various kinds is more likely to have been stimulated by 'native' dramatists such as Skelton and Bale. There are, however, some scenes in the anonymous Catholic morality *Respublica*[37] which constitute the exception to the theory put forward by Ward and Hamer, that Lindsay's play had no discernible effect on English drama. *Respublica* celebrates through its character Nemesis, 'the mooste highe goddesse of correccion' (1783), the accession of Mary in 1553, but like *Ane Satyre* it focusses on oppression and injustice rather than on doctrinal controversy. The central character of the play is the 'commonwealth', Lady Respublica, who is sadly misled by a company of vices under the leadership of Avarice. There are two scenes which recall both the mock-christening episode in *Ane Satyre*, and the scene in which Falset almost ruins the whole disguise plot by forgetting his new name when he is introduced to Humanitie. In the first act of *Respublica*, Avarice confides to his companions Adulation, Insolence and Oppression his plan to ruin Respublica (sc. iii), and explains to them how they can assist (sc. iv). It becomes clear that the plot has no chance of success unless all of them assume new names, and Oppression informs Avarice, 'Thowe must newe christen vs' (377). Amidst considerable argument, Insolence is renamed Authority, while Adulation and Oppression become Honesty and Reformation: Avarice himself takes the name of Policy. Adulation, however, is slow of study, and he has to learn the new names by rote, a syllable at a time (389–413). Avarice's warnings,

> And whan yowe are [in] your Robe, keape yt afore close
> (429)

> All folke wyll take yow, if theye piepe vnder youre gowne,
> for the veriest catif in Countrey or towne
> (431–2)

suggest that as in *Ane Satyre*, the new names are accompanied by changes of clothing. When the cloaked vices come into the presence of Respublica and are introduced by Avarice, the doltish Adulation threatens to reveal all by speaking *in propria persona* (560–1), but Avarice, like Lindsay's stage-manager Flatterie, manages to retrieve the situation (562, 565). The combination of mock-christening and threatened revelation at the crucial moment when disguised Vice confronts *naïf* Virtue suggests that Lindsay rather than Skelton provided the model for the scene in *Respublica*, the comic spirit of which is reminiscent of the scene in *Ane Satyre*. The episode as it exists in Lindsay's play is elaborated and expanded, notably in the characterisation of the chief vice, and it is in no sense a close imitation.

That Lindsay's play should have had such a slight influence on English drama is not surprising, in view of the increasing vogue for plays which were comparatively short and suitable for indoor production. Charteris's claim that the Edinburgh performance of *Ane Satyre* lasted 'fra ix houris afoir none, till vi houris at euin'[38] may not be accurate, but it could not be acted out in its entirety in under four hours. Any potential adaptor of *Ane Satyre* would have been intimidated not only by its length, but also by its demand for an outdoor setting on a scale which no English play after *The Castle of Perseverance* seems to require. The fact that Lindsay advocates reforms which were appropriate to Scotland in the 1540s and 1550s, but certainly not to a 'reformed' England, is possibly another reason for its being considered remote and perhaps irrelevant in an English context. One recalls George Bannatyne's reason for recording only certain extracts from the play in 1568: the 'grave mater pairof' is omitted 'becaws the samyne abvse Is weill reformit in scotland praysit be god'.

8

The two traditions

The fact that Chaucer's poetry should have been a fertilising influence upon Scots poetry of the late fifteenth and early sixteenth centuries is not very surprising. The Scots makars recognised in Chaucer a poet who had dignified and enriched vernacular literature by an intelligent assimilation of various continental genres, styles and techniques. He answered, we may safely conjecture, to their conception of what a poet should be – a careful literary craftsman, aware equally of the potentialities of his own language and of his place as an innovator within a European literary tradition. Like Lydgate, they were keen that their own poetic achievements should be seen as part of a Chaucerian tradition of vernacular writing. More discriminating than Lydgate, they did not see length and unrelieved high seriousness as the hallmarks of good poetry. As I have already suggested, Chaucer's work was more attractive than Lydgate's to poets such as James I, Henryson, Dunbar and Douglas because it had been composed within a milieu similar to their own – one in which the demands of performance continued to be felt. No amount of argument can explain away the gulf between good and mediocre art, but it may well be that the distance of the late fifteenth-century Scots poets from Chaucer's work – one of time, language and nationality – facilitated an independence and objectivity which Lydgate could not easily have possessed because of his proximity to Chaucer.

That Lindsay should have borrowed from Skelton is perhaps more surprising. So too it is hardly to be expected that Skelton should have been influenced by Scots comic poetry, or that Surrey should have made such extensive use of Douglas's

Eneados. These instances of borrowing across national cultural boundaries are so interesting because they are so rare: they defy the pattern of local cohesiveness which is such a striking feature of the development of both Scottish and English literature in the period. The rarity of such cultural exchange between England and Scotland is not to be explained by the theory that writers in one country were ignorant of literary developments in the other. The fact that Dunbar, Douglas and Lindsay do not refer, either directly or indirectly, to the work of English authors such as Hawes, Barclay, Bradshaw and Nevill need not imply that the English work was unknown to them. The tributes which the Scots pay to the Chaucer–Gower–Lydgate triumvirate, which are paralleled by similar expressions in post-Lydgatian English poetry, are in fact the only clue to the Scots' knowledge of southern writing. (The idea that silence need not imply ignorance is reinforced by Skelton's practice: the Tudor poet is completely silent about the course of his own country's poetry after the death of Lydgate.) Similarly, the failure of early sixteenth-century poets to refer to Henryson, Dunbar or Douglas must not be taken as an indication that they were unaware of the northern tradition. National hostilities were by no means a barrier to cultural communication: the visits of Englishmen to the Scots court and of Scotsmen to the centre of power in England were frequent, and in some cases involved poets themselves. Perhaps the clearest testimony to this awareness concerns the publication of Scottish works in England.

The borrowings across national boundaries which take place after the late fifteenth century – those of Skelton, Surrey and Lindsay – are remarkable not only for the different kinds of creative impulse which they reflect, but also because they cut across definite trends of literary development. The history of each national literature throughout the fifteenth and earlier sixteenth centuries exhibits a high degree of continuity: English poetry is to a very large extent conditioned by earlier English poetry, Scots poetry by what had been written in Scots, even though poets in southern England and lowland Scotland can have been by no means ignorant of one another's work. Unless this cohesiveness and continuity is properly understood, it is difficult to comprehend just how radical the borrowings discussed in the preceding chapters are. The importance of local literary influences on both English and Scottish poetry is itself a subject for a book-length study, and in the following pages I can do no more than indicate some of the more striking aspects of this internal continuity. Inevitably, I have had to be very selective, so it may be necessary to provide some perspective for what follows. The comments on Scots poetry apply, in the main, to the work of those poets whose work has been discussed in this book, and they focus upon the genre of vision narrative. This was the most widely used literary form, in England no less than in Scotland, throughout what has been called the 'transitional period' between writing which is unmistakably medieval in spirit and writing which is equally unmistakably of the renaissance. Poetry of other kinds was of course written – comic verse of a particularly high standard, epic poetry, translation of various kinds and lyric. The second quarter of the sixteenth century is a period of efflorescence for the English lyric, one associated with the names of Wyatt and Surrey. The lyric was not subject to the same degree of decline which marks other forms of English poetry after 1400, and there is nothing in what survives of Scots lyric poetry (for example, in Bannatyne's 'ballattis of luve') to equal Wyatt or Surrey at his best. But a great many English lyric poems suffer from one of the faults of the longer forms of poetry – a deficiency of metre. We need to remember that the author of the celebrated 'natural-sounding' *They flee from me, that sometime did me seek* is also the author of the *Song of Iopas*, written in the extraordinarily cumbersome poulter's measure. As late as 1586, it was possible for William Webbe to rail against 'the canckred enmitie of curious custome'[1] which had marred the development of English metre.

It might be argued that just as I have not discussed in detail what most modern readers find to be the finest achievements of early sixteenth-century English poetry, I have glossed over the existence of inferior poetry in Scots. There is, after all, much in the Bannatyne and other manuscripts which could never be mistaken for the work of Henryson, Dunbar or Douglas. These deficiencies I acknowledge: but in spite of them, and in spite of the general superiority of English lyric poetry to Scots, the concentration on the longer non-lyric form seems justified, on the grounds of their great popularity throughout the period. The publication in 1554 of *The Fall of Princes*, 'in aedibus Richardi Totteli', is eloquent testimony to the conservatism of English taste. Lydgate's translation of Laurence de Premierfait's prose paraphrase of Boccaccio's *De Casibus Virorum Illustrium* is the longest English essay on the characteristically medieval theme of Fortune's 'variaunce': written in the 1430s, it had been printed four times between 1494 and 1558. In the following year Tottel printed a work almost equally old-fashioned, Hawes's *The Passetyme of Pleasure*. Fame has enrolled Tottel as the printer of *Songes and Sonettes* and Surrey's *Aeneid* translation, but it is necessary to remember that he published Lydgate and Hawes as well.

The extent to which Chaucer's work provided a stimulus to the writing of new poetry is an important aspect of the continuity of Middle Scots literature. For poets of the late fifteenth century, Chaucer's poetry possessed the attraction of having become part of their own literary tradition. Although Henryson, Dunbar, Douglas and others had independent access to manuscripts and prints of Chaucer's work, they had in *The Kingis Quair* an important precedent for composing poetry in the Chaucerian mode. This statement raises, of course, the question of the extent to which the *Quair* was known in Scotland in the century after its composition. The absence of any allusion to the poem in specific terms should not be taken as an indication that it was unknown to the later makars. The manuscript in which the poem is preserved and attributed to the king was compiled no later than 1505, and it is extremely unlikely that the possession of a high-ranking nobleman could have remained unknown to contemporary poets: Henry Lord St Clair, whose name and coat of arms appear in the manuscript was 'neir coniunct in blude' to Gavin Douglas, who tells how he translated the *Aeneid* at his kinsman's request. The poem was, however, almost certainly known to other poets before the compilation of the manuscript. Henryson's *Fabillis* offer several suggestions that he knew *The Kingis Quair*. Minerva's speech on free will is echoed in *The Preiching of the Swallow*,² and in *The Taill of the Lyoun and the Mous*, the narrator makes the sign of the cross, just as James represents himself as doing at the beginning of his 'buke'³ (*KQ*, st. 13, 7; cf. *LM* 1345). The catalogue of beasts in the third part of *The Tod* is reminiscent of a similar list in the earlier poem. In *Lancelot of the Laik*,⁴ probably written during the reign of James III, there appear to be other echoes of the *Quair*. This poem, also preserved in the Selden MS., is a not-very-competent translation of the thirteenth-century French prose romance *Lancelot del Lac*. Its best poetry is contained in passages of direct speech, notably in the soliloquies of Lancelot, which have as their occasion the 'double peine and wo' (physical imprisonment and thraldom to love) suffered also by the protagonists of *The Knight's Tale* and *The Kingis Quair*. Verbal parallels suggest indebtedness to James rather than to Chaucer. Lancelot's apostrophe to his heart in the second lyric, for example,

> Bot hart, sen at yow knawith she is here,
> That of thi lyue and of thi deith is stere,
> Now is thi time, now help thi self at neid
>
> (1018–20)

recalls both James's 'Bot hert, quhere as the body may nought throu...' (st. 63, 4) and the address to the nightingale, 'Here is in fay the tyme and eke the space' (st. 59, 2). The theme of heavenly predestination from birth,

> I curss the tyme of myne Natiuitee,
> Whar in the heuen It ordinyd was for me,
> In all my lyue neuer til haue ees
>
> (703–5)

echoes a prominent concern of the *Quair*. The fact that *Lancelot* is written in a heavily anglicised form of Scots (evident, for example, in the use of 'ith' instead of terminations in 'it' and 'is', and of the prefixes 'y' and 'wh' for normal Scots 'quh') may well denote an attempt to imitate the language of the *Quair* rather than that of Chaucer's poetry.

At the end of the Prologue to the translation, the *Lancelot* poet pays tribute to another poet whom he refuses to name. Presumably, the refusal had point only because the contemporary audience was aware of this author's identity.

> Bot first I pray, and I besek also,
> One to the most compilour to support,
> Flour of poyetis, quhois nome I wil report
> To me nor to non vthir It accordit,
> In to our rymyng his name to be recordit;
> For sum suld deme It of presumpsioune,
> And ek our rymyng is al bot derysioune,
> Quhen that remembrit is his excellens,
> So hie abuf that stant in reuerans.
> Ye fresch enditing of his laiting toung
> Out throuch yis world so wid is yroung,
> Of eloquens, and ek of retoryk,
> Nor is, nor was, nore neuer beith hyme lyk,
> This world gladith of his suet poetry.
> His saul I blyss conseruyt be for thy;
> And yf that ony lusty terme I wryt
> He haith the thonk yerof, & this endit.
>
> (318–34)

laiting Latin, polished

If Chaucer is intended here, the reticence is difficult to understand, given the fifteenth-century vogue for acknowledging Chaucer as the father of British eloquence. But reluctance to name James I is easier to comprehend. If he were to invite comparison between his own work and that of a recent monarch, the charge of 'presumpsioune' might easily be made. A similar kind of delicacy in the matter of claiming association with the royal poetic talent may perhaps explain the absence of James from Dunbar's roll-call of poets in *The Lament for the Makaris*. This suggestion is just as valid as those advanced by McDiarmid: 'That Dunbar . . . makes no mention of him might be variously explained; it may simply illustrate the fact that kings are most naturally remembered as kings, or be due to a feeling that too much would have to be said if he were cited at all.'[5] *Lancelot of the Laik* offers strong evidence that the *Quair* was known to at least one late fifteenth-century poet other than Henryson. Some two generations later, in *The*

Testament of the Papyngo, Lindsay invites his audience to remember James I not only as a just and prudent ruler, but also as a writer – 'Gem of Ingyne . . . and flude of Eloquence' (431–2).

The main contribution which the *Quair* makes to the naturalisation of Chaucer into the Scots tradition is its demonstration of the value of engaging authorial presentation in first-person poetry. Since considerable attention has been given in previous chapters to the contribution which authorial self-depiction makes to the poetry of James, Henryson, Dunbar and Douglas, I intend to show only how several uses of a particular technique suggest how one Scots poet could inspire others. In *The Kingis Quair* there is an adaptation of the central dramatic episode of the Prologue to *The Legend of Good Women*. Just as the God of Love commands Chaucer to write the histories of faithful women as his penance, the Scots Venus orders her subject to encourage the dissemination of 'songis new', as the return for her assistance in the love-suit. (The *Quair* itself proclaims the poet–dreamer's promise fulfilled, by the several lyrics which are set into the narrative.) It is clear that *The Legend of Good Women* was also known to the author of *Lancelot of the Laik*. Here too the love-deity orders the composition of a certain kind of poem – significantly, a kind other than the love-lyric,

> for thir sedulis and thir billis are
> So generall, and ek so schort at lyte,
> And swne of thaim is lost the appetit.
>
> (142–4)

Sedulis . . . billis schedules . . . bills (kinds of poem); *swne* soon

Possibly this was intended to remind his audience of the *Quair*, to indicate that James's hint to other court poets had been fulfilled to the extent that the love-lyric had become a hackneyed form.

In all three poems – the Prologue to *The Legend of Good Women*, *The Kingis Quair*, and the Prologue to *Lancelot of the Laik* – the dramatic device of the love-deity's command to write a certain kind of poem is a way of introducing a fictional 'historical' dimension. The effect is to foster a sense of personal intimacy between poet and audience: put very simply, it is as though the poets are allowing those about them into a confidence. The literary public of any age is interested in personal background (even when they are aware of poetic fiction), and the situation in which the poet is told what he is to write must have had a particular appeal to those familiar with the realities of patronage. The device is used in a more complicated way in *The Palice of Honour*, in Douglas's account of his allegiance to Venus. The love-lyric 'Vnwemmit [unharmed] wit deliuerit of dangair' and the promise to translate 'ane buk' for Venus may have a significance other than that of illustrating the poet's distinctive allegiance to Love. It is likely that Douglas deliberately echoes the 'poet's-command' sections of *The Kingis Quair* and *Lancelot of the Laik*, as well as Chaucer's Prologue. By so doing, he shows his audience that he is helping to sustain the life of the poetic genres recommended by his predecessors. The lyrics throughout the poem, and the surrounding frame of the first-person allegorical narrative, are in the tradition of the *Quair*, while the task of translation is the supreme example of the creative activity which the God of Love's messenger recommends in *Lancelot* – the contribution of a long poem 'Of love, or armys, or of sum othir thing'. By appreciating the reference to earlier Scots poems as well as to Chaucer's poem, we are made aware of Douglas's claim for a place in a distinctively Scottish tradition. Use of the interview device does not stop with *The Palice of Honour*. The dialogue between the poet and reproachful May in *The Thrissil and the Rois* is another interesting development. As I have suggested, Dunbar's professed reluctance to write in praise of love is a way of qualifying the celebratory effect of what follows. The result is reminiscent of Chaucer's manner in *The Parlement of Foules*, but the dramatic situation itself has probably been adapted from *The Palice of Honour*, which had been completed in 1501.

Douglas's adaptation of a poem by Henryson in the Prologue to the final book of the *Eneados* is anticipated by his practice in *The Palice of Honour*. The court-of-Venus episode contains reminiscences not only of the Prologue to *The Legend of Good Women*, *The Kingis Quair*, and *Lancelot of the Laik*, but also of *The Testament of Cresseid* and *Orpheus and Eurydice*. The poet's curse 'Wo worth

Cupyd and wo worth fals Venus' (634) recalls Cresseid's angry outburst, and the list of musical instruments and terminology recalls a similar passage in *Orpheus and Eurydice*. The latter parallel is all the more marked because Douglas, like Henryson, concludes with a disclaimer of musical knowledge:

> Off sic musik to wryt I do bot doit,
> Thairfoir of this mater a stray I lay,
> For in my lyfe I cowth nevir sing a noit
> (OE, 240–2)

> Na mair I vnderstude thir numbers fine,
> Be God, than dois a gekgo or a swine.[6]
> (PH, 517–18)

gekgo gecko

The abrupt transition, in both poems, from elegantly rhetorical catalogue to ironically personal statement, serves to remind us of the poets' continued presence in their poems. The Prologue of *The Taill of the Lyoun and the Mous* and Douglas's thirteenth *Eneados* Prologue are related to the first-person passages discussed earlier in that they are dramatic vignettes which introduce poems through the fiction that compulsion has been brought to bear upon the teller. Henryson tells how he dreamt that a richly dressed man, bearing the implements of a writer, came to greet him in the wood. The poet acknowledges him as 'maister', and asks who he is. His delight when the stranger replies, 'Esope I hecht; my writing and my werk / Is couth and kend to mony cunning clerk' (1375–6), is a felicitous personal touch, since of course he is addressing one of those cunning clerks. He agrees only reluctantly to the younger poet's request that he should tell 'ane prettie fabill', because he feels that if 'haly preiching' falls on deaf ears there can be no point in using poetic fiction for the purposes of correction. At the conclusion of the fable itself, the younger poet presses him to provide explication:

> Quod I: 'Maister, is thair ane moralitie
> In this fabill?' 'Yea, sone,' he said, 'richt gude.'
> 'I pray yow, schir,' quod I, 'ye wald conclude.'
> (1570–2)

The use of this kind of first-person framework, reverted to in ths last stanza of the *moralitas*, gives a special prominence to thie fable. Unlike the others, *The Taill of the Lyoun and the Mous* purports to be the actual words of Aesop. The framework also enables comment about the worth of different kinds of rhetorical utterance to be made: i.e. that 'haly preiching' should be a more effective means of persuasion than the poetic fable. As MacQueen suggests, Aesop's aesthetic judgement is probably a way of drawing attention to *The Preiching of the Swallow*.[7] It is difficult to identify the source (if indeed there is one) of Henryson's poet-dialogue. The idea may well have been suggested by *The Fall of Princes* or its Latin original, in which a procession of famous figures comes to tell the recording poet of their treatment by Fortune. Occasionally, Lydgate catches something of the liveliness of Boccaccio's passages of dialogue: the Prologue to Book VIII, for example, relates a debate within the mind of 'Bochas' about the value of continuing the book, and goes on to record the rebuke administered by Boccaccio's 'maister', Petrarch. (Lydgate is not himself an actor in any 'imaginary conversation', as one critic claims.)[8] Henryson may have borrowed the interview-*topos* directly from Boccaccio, but a source in earlier Scots poetry seems more likely.

The Prologue to Book XIII of the *Eneados* is closely modelled on Henryson. (It is hardly necessary to argue that Douglas is a more creative imitator than the English printer Richard Smith.) Like the earlier poet, Douglas records how he wandered alone through the flowering landscape, falling asleep under a tree (a 'greyn lawrer' rather than a hawthorn, appropriate to his status as the translator of Virgil). He, too, is approached by an old man, whom he identifies as a fellow-poet: the description of the headress – 'Lyke to sum poet of the ald fasson' (88) – echoes Henryson's line, 'His bonat round and off the auld fassoun' (1353). The newcomer is Virgil's fifteenth-century continuator Maphaeus Vegius, who comes to rebuke Douglas for his failure to translate 'The thretteyn buke ekit Eneadan'. When the younger poet gives his reasons for the omission Maphaeus sets upon him:

> 'Thou salt deir by that evir thou Virgill knew.'
> And, with that word, doun of the sete me drew,
> Syne to me with hys club he maid a braid,
> And twenty rowtis apon my riggyng laid,
> Quhill, 'Deo, Deo, mercy,' dyd I cry
> And, be my rycht hand strekit vp inhy,
> Hecht to translait his buke
>
> (145–51)

of the sete from the bench; *braid* sudden movement; *rowtis* thumps

The spectacle of brute force overcoming the poet's moral and artistic scruples is of course richly entertaining, and it has no counterpart in Henryson's encounter with the much more courteous Aesop. But Douglas follows Henryson in exploiting the situation of a dialogue between poets to suggest a difference between two kinds of writing: not, as in the *Fabillis*, the difference between sermon and poetic fable, but between two attitudes to classical poetry. One is the exact and sensitive approach of the faithful translator of Virgil, the other is the interpretative approach taken by a humanist continuator. The dialogue mirrors Douglas's doubt concerning the propriety of appending a 'schort Christyn wark' to his translation of the *Aeneid*, and at the same time it emphasises in a very diverting manner the fundamental difference between Book XIII and the remainder of the translation. By protesting that he was forced into submission, Douglas provides a skilful and witty defence against criticism by scholars for the inclusion of a spurious book: 'Lat clerkis ken the poetis different' (195). It is possible that Prologue XIII contains a further debt to Henryson. Douglas shows how his activity as a poet takes place in a context of universal activity and celebration: in his dedication to his task, he resembles the other human figures in the June landscape, the rural labourers:

> Sone our the feildis schynys the lycht cleir,
> Welcum to pilgrym baith and lauborer;
> Tyte on hys hynys gaif the greif a cry,
> 'Awaik on fut, go till our husbandry.'
>
> (169–72)

Tyte . . . a cry Quickly the steward called to his servants

Douglas's lines contain more descriptive detail, but they suggest nevertheless the situation of the poet-figure at the beginning of *The Preiching of the Swallow*, in particular his 'grit joy' at the sight of the workers sowing the seed (1720–6).

All of these passages about the writing of poetry illustrate a prevailing interest in the human and dramatic. Poetry is felt to be a spoken as well as a written art, and for this reason the presence of the speaker is evoked with great immediacy. This conception of poetry, held by James I, Henryson, Dunbar, Douglas and other Scots poets, helps to impart a new vigour and interest to their handling of well-worn medieval genres, in particular to their handling of various kinds of allegory. Pearsall's definition of the characteristic temper of fifteenth-century poetry – 'Moral earnestness, love of platitude and generalisation, a sober preoccupation with moral and ethical issues (often combined with a taste for the extravagantly picturesque and decorative)'[9] – applies to a great deal of Scots as well as to English poetry, but there is the important difference that the Scots makars make their presence felt in their moralising, and in their self-characterisations. The influence of Lydgate was not felt so strongly in Scotland as it was in England: Chaucer was more useful than Lydgate to poets who worked within a tradition of performance. Lydgate's poetry forms a literary watershed between Scotland and England, and the fact that it was imitated so extensively in the south but not in the north helps to explain why the work of Hawes and Barclay is so different from that of Henryson and Douglas. Nearly all of Lydgate's poetry is anonymous in tone, irrespective of whether or not it is written within a first-person framework, and this impersonality is the poet's most important legacy to later English writing. The view that Lydgate is the pattern of a new orthodoxy of literary taste, 'though as symptom rather than cause',[10] demands some qualification. Lydgate helped to mould the taste for the sober and the explicit, and it would be difficult to overestimate his influence on later English poetry.

The Lydgatian influence can be gauged in various ways, and in relation to various genres. My concern here is to illustrate that continuity of conception about the nature of poetry which is exhibited in the development of allegorical poetry in England. Lydgate's chief contribution is made not through love-allegory, but rather through those poems which explore a wide variety of ethical and religious themes, using the extended metaphor of a journey of discovery. In poems such as *Reson and Sensuallyte* and *The Pilgrimage of the Life of Man*, for example, Lydgate represents himself as a generalised *humanitas* figure engaged in a quest for knowledge. There are occasions when his voice catches the rhythm of speech (as occasionally within the dialogue between the poet and Venus in *Reson and Sensuallyte*, 2117–700), but in general no attempt to generate any kind of interaction between the first-person frame and the scheme of narrative allegory which is developed within it. The poet's concern is with the amplification and explication of his subject matter, and any commentary on it is of an abstract and sententious kind. There is the barest minimum of individuating detail in Lydgate's self-characterisations, and an absence of irony and humour.

The pervasiveness of the abstract, generalising and heavily explicit of poetic allegory in fifteenth-century England has been a major obstacle to critics who have attempted to define the Lydgate canon. H. N. MacCracken excludes from it works such as *The Assembly of Gods* and *The Court of Sapience*, even though there are several sixteenth-century attributions of these to Lydgate. The arguments for and against his authorship have tended to centre upon metre, compared with that of works which are generally accepted as genuine.[11] Metrically, *The Assembly of Gods* is often hopelessly confused, whereas *The Court of Sapience* is usually regular. The vices of the one and the virtues of the other have their respective precedents in Lydgate's poetry. Within the compass of a single poem such as *The Temple of Glas* it is possible to find smooth and competent lines beside lines which defy any attempt at scansion, and if metre alone were to be used as a touchstone there seems to be no good reason why the two poems should not be given to Lydgate rather than to a disciple. Both echo the encyclopaedic allegorical approach and the plodding explicitness of the 'translations', *The Pilgrimage* and *Reson and Sensuallyte*. Like these poems which are accepted as genuine

Lydgatia, they take the form of a series of static allegorical scenes. The overall theme of the *Assembly* is the apparent irreconcilability of Reason and Sensuality, which is amplified in turn by a lengthy 'parliament of gods' scene, a *psychomachia* (the battle between the hosts of Vice and Virtue), a pictorial representation of the History of Man, and a concluding debate in which Reason and Sensuality resolve their differences in common fear of Death. The elements of the *Court* are equally varied: a theological debate among the Four Daughters of God (which recalls Chapters XI–XIV of *The Life of Our Lady*), a miniature lapidary, an account of the Cardinal Virtues and the seven 'Sciences liberall', and several allegorised descriptive passages. These two poems, like *Reson and Sensuallyte* and the monumental *Pilgrimage*, must be conceded the merit of comprehensiveness: their 'doctryne' is presented through a wide variety of figurative schemes. What makes them so different from *The Palice of Honour*, which is equally comprehensive, is their failure to make any dramatic advantage out of the *grundmotif* of the poet's journey. When the 'I' addresses his audience directly, it is in a serious and wholly impersonal voice. The moralising is worthy, but unvarying in its tone, and there is no attempt at even rudimentary characterisation within the framework of the reported action. This implies the lack of any sense of direct contact between poet and audience, and uncertainty about the reader's powers of comprehension accounts in some measure for the explicitness of approach. At the end of *The Assembly of Gods*, the figure of Doctrine provides an exhaustive *moralitas* which explains the allegorical significance of almost every detail of the preceding narrative. This is a different kind of explicitness from that which marks the nymph's sermon in Douglas's poem, since here the audience is invited to observe for themselves how the various stages of the poet's journey are related to the unifying theme of Honour.

The Lydgatian combination of explicitness and comprehensiveness in the handling of allegory is carried on in the work of Stephen Hawes, which convincingly bears out the sincerity of its author's repeated claims to be considered as the humble disciple of Lydgate:

> To folowe the trace and all the parfytenesse
> Of my mayster Lydgate with due exercyse
> Suche fayned tales I do fynde and deuyse.
>
> (PP 47–9)

The narrative scheme of Hawes's most ambitious work, *The Passetyme of Pleasure*,[12] is original in that it fuses the 'life of man' allegorical scheme with the framework of the chivalric quest. In style, subject matter and tone, the *Passetyme* is related to *The Court of Sapience*, which Hawes attributes to Lydgate (*PP*, 1356–8). Hawes's most notable borrowing is the expansion of the section which deals with the getting of Sapience through dedicated application to the liberal arts and other kinds of learning (*CS*, sts. 221–328). Over one-fifth of the *Passetyme* is devoted to telling of Graunde Amoure's visits to the chambers of Grammar, Logic, Rhetoric, Arithmetic, Music, Geometry and Astronomy in the Tower of Doctrine. The poem goes on to tell of the narrator's wooing of the lady La Belle Pucelle, which takes him on a journey to the Tower of Chivalry. Before attaining the lady's favour he is called upon to slay two allegorical giants, one with three heads, the other with seven: obligingly, the monsters provide their own instant expositions, written on banners attached to their heads. Hawes's flaccid structural scheme has room not only for monsters and companies of graceful female personifications, but also for Old Age, Death, Eternity and the Nine Worthies. The long poem is devoid of the continuity which might have been achieved by some 'humanising' of its central character, and in the absence of this Hawes is forced to resort to explaining what is to come and to making pocket summaries of what has gone before. The editor of the poem observes with justified asperity that 'the reader is repeatedly confronted with a twice-told tale'.[13]

In his defence of poetry in the section on Rhetoric, invention is defined as the process of,

> Clokynge a trouthe with colour tenebrous
> For often vnder a fayre fayned fable
> A trouthe appereth gretely profytable.
>
> (712–14)

(The definition is reminiscent of the theory announced in the Prologue of the *Morall Fabillis*: although there is no trace of a Henrysonian influence on Hawes, it is possible that the *Fabillis* were known to him.) The *Passetyme* and shorter poems such as *The Example of Vertu* and *The Conforte of Louers*[14] illustrate that Hawes followed his own precept by consistently amplifying his subject matter in the manner approved by literary tradition:

> For to inuencyon it is equypolent
> The mater founde ryght well to comprehende
> In suche a space as it is conuenyent
> For properly it doth euer pretende
> Of all the purpose the length to extende
> So estymacyon maye ryght well conclude
> The parfyte nombre of euery symylytude.
>
> (743–9)

This view of poetry, as well as being pertinent to Hawes's own work, is a commentary on the Lydgatian tradition to which it belongs: the highest form of literary art is that which cloaks an edifying morality in the guise of a protracted personification allegory. The tradition is carried on in shorter poems such as *The Castell of Labour*[15] and Nevill's *The Castell of Pleasure*: the first of these (which is possibly the work of Alexander Barclay) uses the dream-vision framework and personification allegory to exalt the spiritual value of work, while the second seems indebted to the chivalric strain of the *Passetyme* and *The Conforte of Louers*. There are verbal parallels and similarities of narrative detail between *The Castell of Pleasure* and Hawes's work, but even more conclusive is the heavily sententious and totally impersonal manner in which Nevill, like Hawes, treats an allegory of love. Barclay's major contributions to the genre of the long didactic poem, *The Ship of Fools* and the *Eclogues*, represent departures from the usual 'cloudy figures' of allegory: the translation of Brant's *Narrenschiff* is cast in the form of a long series of sermons, while the *Eclogues* use dialogue to develop their 'sentence'. Although there are lively and entertaining passages in both poems, the prevailing technique is one of repetitious and anonymous sermonising. Barclay may have been born a Scot, but there can be no doubt that he learned his poetic craft south of the border.

The continuity of fifteenth- and early sixteenth-century poetry in England which is reflected in the continuing respect for non-personal, non-dramatic allegorical forms can be illustrated in various other ways. With the exaltation of moral improvement as the *raison d'être* of poetry comes a distrust of humorous effects in serious poetry. Again, Lydgate is important both as direct influence on later poets and as an arbiter of the kind of taste for which they wrote. The way in which Lydgate praises Chaucer's achievement in the Prologue to *The Fall of Princes* (274–357) and in the Prologue to *The Siege of Thebes* (18–57) leaves little doubt that his response to Chaucer was wider than modern criticism has usually been prepared to allow,[16] but at the same time it is clear that Lydgate found it very difficult to imitate Chaucer's lightness of touch in his own work – at least in his longer poems. In the Prologue to *The Siege of Thebes* Lydgate struggles to follow the humorous drama which centres on the directness of the Host in *The Canterbury Tales*, but the effect is crude and clumsy. Calling upon Lydgate for a tale, the Host, who will hear of 'non holynesse', requests 'somme thyng that draweth to effekke / Only of Ioye' (167–71). It is understandable that the poet should begin 'with a pale cheere', for the comic mode is foreign to his talent. This is not to suggest that Lydgate's political history is dull: Pearsall rightly commends it for its 'deep moral concern, good sense, and a sober solemnity of style'.[17] It is clear that Lydgate felt that there was something profoundly improper about humorous effects in a serious poem. Perhaps the monastic temperament is partly responsible for this, but the reason for the sober uniformity of tone is more likely to be the poet's sense that the distance between himself and his readers called for a stricter sense of decorum in the matter of tone than Chaucer had found it necessary to observe in the company of his courtly audience.

In *The Passetyme of Pleasure*, Hawes launches an attack on contemporary poets who disdain to follow his and his master's example:

> They fayne no fables pleasaunt and couerte
> But spend theyr tyme in vaynfull vanyte
> Makynge balades of feruent amyte
> As gestes and tryfles without fruytfulness
>
> (1389–92)

The complaint is carefully general, but it is tempting to see a reference to the poet who dared to suggest that Lydgate's style was 'to haute', and who drew upon a whole battery of 'vyle termes' as well as upon the sober language of the Lydgate tradition. The vehement attack in Barclay's Fourth Eclogue[18] on poets who are,

> auoyde of honestie,
> Nothing seasoned with spice of grauitie,
> Auoyde of pleasure, auoyde of eloquence,
> With many wordes, and fruitlesse of sentence,
>
> (699–702)

with its gibe at the 'Poete laureate' in the service of 'stinking Thais' (685–6), is quite clearly a reference to Skelton's departures from respectable models of poetic eloquence. The poet-shepherd Minalcas takes upon himself the task of reforming the young shepherd's tastes, which run to 'merry fits' about the delights of the ale-house (719–26), through his own 'ballade extract of sapience' (759–90). At the end of *The Ship of Fools*, Barclay defies his audience even more openly to prefer Skeltonic newfangleness to his own elevated productions:

> Wyse men loue vertue wylde people wantones
> It longeth nat to my scyence nor cunnynge
> For Phylyp the Sparowe the Dirige to synge.

Barclay's references to Skelton indicate a satiric talent of sorts, which reveals itself occasionally throughout *The Ship of Fools*: the portrait of the foolish book-owner who boasts, 'I am content on the fayre coverynge to loke' (sts. 23–35) is the most memorable of these passages. In spite of his fondness for sustained pedantic moralising, Barclay must be given credit for a humorous sensibility which is rare in English poetry of that period. When a note of comedy is sounded in the longer works of the fifteenth and early sixteenth centuries, the effect is usually one of incongruous vulgarity. Mention has already been made of the schoolboy jesting which precedes Lydgate's sober history of the siege of Thebes, and it is indicative of the tonal continuity within post-Lydgatian English poetry that this kind of comic effect is not uncommon. The 'low' comedy of the Godfrey Gobelive episodes in the *Passetyme*, for example, might have been effective in a separate poem, but in context it is incongruous even as light relief. A similar startling juxtaposition of the sententious and the bawdy can be found in the later sixteenth-century 'folly' works in the tradition of *The Ship of Fools*, Robert Copland's *Jyl of Braintford's Testament* and *The Hye Way to the Spyttel Hous*. The sparseness of any subtle humorous effects comparable with the gradations of irony and satire in the poetry of Henryson and Dunbar is symptomatic of the strength of Lydgate's precept.

The topics of authorial presence, tonal variety and variation of language and metre are inextricably linked. That continuity within the English tradition which I have attempted to illustrate can also be seen in the language and versification of most of the poetry of this period. What is chiefly remarkable about the language of most fifteenth- and early sixteenth-century poetry is its gravity and uniformity of level. The subject requires much fuller discussion than I am able to provide here, but in general it should be evident that successive English poets followed Lydgate's example in striving for refinement of English poetic diction. Hawes praises Lydgate for his use of Latin:

> From whens my master Lydgate deryfyde
> The depured rethoryke in Englyshe language
> To make our tongue so clerely puryfyed
> That the vyle termes shoulde nothynge arage
> As lyke a pye to chattre in a cage
> But for to speke with Rethoryke formally
> In the good ordre withouten vylany.
>
> (PP, 1163–9)

It is not difficult to understand why the tribute should have been made. The refinement of language to which borrowing from Latin contributes, and the organisation of words into elegant formal patterns may produce an effect which is impressive in its gravity and uniformity of tone – one thinks immediately of Lydgate's poems of religious celebration. But Lydgate's verse also illustrates the danger of separating a 'depured' rhetorical mode from the vocabulary and rhythms of a spoken language. His longer poems show an avoidance of any kind of 'talking' style. The only variation from the sober and measured middle style is in the direction of heightening, and in a poem of any length the inevitable result is tonal monotony. Lydgate's metre is usually deficient not in being confused, but rather in being insufficiently varied. *The Kingis Quair* illustrates a sustained use of a vocabulary which is neither insistently colloquial nor elaborately formal, but it avoids the monotony of *The Temple of Glas* because of the author's Chaucerian feeling for spoken effects. For Hawes, Barclay and a host of other English poets, Lydgate's vocabulary and versification were influential models. Most post-Lydgatian poetry fails to reproduce even the measured solemnity of the master's eloquence. The work of Lydgate's followers shows a widening of the gulf between literary and spoken language, and one suspects that to Hawes at least the use of any kind of colloquial effect of diction or rhythm in a non-satirical context would have been as deplorable as the use of 'vyle termes'. Barclay's poetic vocabulary is more varied and more particular, but his sense of rhythm is equally deficient. The mere fact that the subject matter of his two long poems is linked to an objectively real world is no guarantee against monotony. The metrical incompetence which negates any attempt to enliven poetry through variation of language cannot be explained adequately by theories about the instability of the spoken language and the decline of inflections.[19] A more convincing explanation is to be found in the breaking of the old link between poetry and performance which removed the obligation upon poets to control their rhythms. This factor is also relevant to the syntactic confusion which is common in post-Lydgatian verse: convoluted arrangement of words is not such an obstacle to the reader as it is to the listener.

The interest in refinement of language and sobriety of tone is accompanied by the elevation of amplification to the position of a guiding principle in poetic composition. The control which

Chaucer exercises over his subject matter is demonstrated by variations in vocabulary, tone and rhythm: later poets seem to have ignored this kind of control in their pursuit of an ideal of 'prolixitee'. We see this in the endless moralising, the interminable allegorical figures, the sustained use of a restricted level of poetic language, disordered metre and syntax, and in a failure to observe discipline in the use of rhetorical colours. Hawes's lines on Measure, for example, show an absurdly extravagant use of anaphora:

> Where that is mesure / there is no lackynge
> Where that is mesure / hole is the body
> Where that is mesure / good is the lyuynge
> Where that is mesure / wysedome is truely
> Where that is mesure / werke is dyrectly
> Where that is mesure / natures werkynge
> Nature encreaseth by ryght good knowlegynge.
>   (PP, 2591–7)

(Note also lines 2598–604, 2619–39.) The separation between style and subject matter here is of course a wholly unintentional irony. Although most of Skelton's poetry is radically different from the work of his contemporaries, its strident lack of control makes it very much part of the English tradition. I refer particularly to the sustained rhymes of poems such as *Colyn Cloute* and *Elynour Rummyng*, the fondness for prolonged parallelism, and that pervasive disregard of structure which gives his work its curiously 'open-ended' effect. As C. S. Lewis remarks, 'There is no building in his work, no planning, no reason why any piece should stop just where it does.'[20] It is important to remember that the Scottish works which feature effects of this kind have a comic and burlesque character. His 'helter-skelter' lines are something entirely new in English poetry, but the lack of discipline which they embody is one of the strongest features of the poetry against which they react.

Not all fifteenth- and early sixteenth-century English poetic allegory is in the mould of Lydgate's longer poems. There is an English Chaucerian tradition also, represented in those erotic allegories included in sixteenth-century editions of Chaucer –

works such as *The Flower and the Leaf*, *The Assembly of Ladies*, *The Cuckoo and the Nightingale*, and *The Court of Love* – which display a lightness of touch, a feeling for structure and rhythm, which are absent from the other allegories of the period. Their value and interest, like the merits of *The Complaint of the Black Knight* and *The Temple of Glas*, cannot be denied, but at the same time it is important to recognise that this kind of writing is by no means characteristic of the period, and that none of these poems reflect the quality of creative interpretation of Chaucer which is to be found in *The Kingis Quair*, *The Testament of Cresseid* and *The Palice of Honour*. Skeat makes the interesting suggestion that *The Court of Love*, probably written in the mid-sixteenth century, is indebted to Scottish poetry, in particular to *The Kingis Quair*. It is, however, highly unlikely that such a link exists, for what may appear to be verbal parallels between the two amount to no more than independent borrowing from the courtly poetry of Chaucer and Lydgate. Like James, the English poet draws upon the hall-of-Venus episode in *The Temple of Glas* (CL, 218–66): at every point, the *Court* is closer to its English antecedent than to *The Kingis Quair*. Skeat comments on the 'smoothness of rhythm and the frequent modernness of form, quite different from the halting lines of Lydgate and Hawes', suggesting that 'the author may have learnt his metre from Scottish authors, such as Henryson and Dunbar'.[21] Although he probably did know some Scots poetry, the model for his versification is more likely to have been Lydgate at his best in the courtly pieces. The use of aureate words such as 'celsitude' and 'pulcritude' need not point to borrowing from Scots, as Skeat claims: it seems just as likely that these words were taken from Hawes (*PP* 80) or from one of the other English poets interested in extending the range of Lydgate's Latinate vocabulary.

The strongest testimony to the survival in England of the taste for poetry which is encyclopaedic in scope and unrelievedly serious in tone is *The Mirror for Magistrates*. The controlling idea of the *Mirror* is the illustration of Fortune's power over rulers. The model for this work, which was printed in varying forms no less than eight times between 1555 and 1587, is *The Fall of Princes*.

(The *Fall* belongs to the genre of the *speculum*, which is related to allegory in that it depicts 'ensamples', although without the usual allegorical component of plot.) The first edition of the *Mirror*, printed by John Wayland in 1555, was quite clearly conceived as a continuation of Lydgate's poem, which was also printed by Wayland. (Tottel had printed the *Fall* in the previous year.) The printer declares his intention to supplement Lydgate's work with material drawn from recent history:

> To which I haue added a continuacion of that Argument, concernynge the chefe Prynces of thys Iland, penned by the best clearkes in such kinde of matters that be thys day lyuing, not vnworthy to be matched with maister Lydgate.[22]

This *schema* was continued by Baldwin in his edition of 1559, and for the next three decades a succession of poets contributed new 'tragedies' in the Lydgatian mould. Metrically, most of them are more proficient than Lydgate's verse, but tonally they are very similar.

The continuity which is apparent within the Scots literary tradition is just as strong as the continuity within English poetry of the fifteenth and early sixteenth centuries, but it is of a totally different character. I have drawn attention throughout this study to the strong sense of authorial presence in Scots verse. Even without the evidence provided by a series of different uses of a particular first-person technique such as the one discussed earlier in this chapter, the strength of the sense of 'voice' in Scots poetry would be the mark of a continuity which is just as remarkable as the pervasive anonymity of contemporary English poetry. The cohesiveness of the Scots tradition is not to be illustrated by reference to a series of long and sober allegorical exercises. Although there is no reason why *The Pilgrimage of the Life of Man* and later *The Passetyme of Pleasure* should not have been read in Scotland, it is clear that there was no attempt made by poets to imitate their prosaic long-windedness. The continuity of the allegorical mode in Scotland is a matter of its very diversity. Warton was right to praise the makars for 'their striking specimens of allegorical invention, a species of composition for some time almost totally extinguished in England'.[23] 'Invention' is surely the key word here. *The Kingis Quair* illustrates the adaptation from Chaucerian and Lydgatian sources of a new kind of allegory, based on an identifiable personal life. Henryson's contribution is a non-explicit species of allegory: non-explicit, in the sense that his *moralitates* frequently appear to contradict the literal and emotional logic of his 'fenyeit fabillis', thereby making demands on the intellectual capacity of his audience. In *The Testament of Cresseid*, there is no overt interpretation of the episode in which the planetary deities confer to decide the heroine's fate: the grouping of the figures, and their individual attributes, provide the key to the allegorical significance of the episode. Henryson's brevity and understatement are in marked contrast with the technique of *The Assembly of Gods*. The scene in which the court of gods confers about the punishment of Eolus serves the same allegorical function as the scene in the *Testament* – highlighting the inevitability of natural law – but it is considerably longer, and is followed by a wholly superfluous explanation by Doctrine (1625–729). Dunbar works within shorter allegorical forms, but a poem such as *The Goldyn Targe* indicates that he shared Henryson's confidence in the power of his audience to extract the full weight of meaning without authorial prompting. As a translator who realises that he has no warrant to 'moralise' Virgil in the body of his text, Douglas frequently reminds his audience that the task of detailed interpretation is for them to undertake:

> Reid, reid agane, this volume, mair than twyss:
> Consider quhat hyd sentence tharin lyis;
> Be war to lak, less than 3e knew weil quhat;
> And gif 3ou list not wirk eftir the wiss,
> Heich on 3our hede set vp the foly hat.
>
> (VI, Prol. 12–16)

war to lak wary of reproach

Douglas's predecessors seem to have shared his confidence in the ability of their audience to seek out and to find their 'hyd sentence'.

The Palice of Honour, inasmuch as it employs the framework of a poet's journey in search of knowledge, belongs to the same general category of vision-allegory as *The Passetyme of Pleasure*, but there is a wide gulf between the two. Where Hawes is painstakingly explicit at every turn of his narrative, Douglas constructs his poem so that the audience is able to infer the relation between each of its parts, with passages of explicit moralising being worked into the dramatic framework. *King Hart* is also related to the *Passetyme* in that it is a 'life-of-man' allegory. In mood and technique, however, it is quite different. There is a bare minimum of description and an absence of authorial commentary: its appeal stems from a combination of vigorous dramatic effect and rapid narrative pace. The affinities of *King Hart* are with other Scots brief allegories such as *The Goldyn Targe* and *Bewty and the Prisoneir*. Like them, it is a vigorously told psychomachia, and the closeness of the relationship is indicated by the echo of Dunbar's terse account of the blinding of Reason (*GT*, 203–4) in the description of Discretioun's fate (*KH*, 281–5). It is very likely that Thomas Vaux's *The assault of Cupide*,[24] a short poem in Tottel's *Miscellany*, was modelled on one or both of the Scots allegories. The English poem is written in the same terse style, and it too employs the central metaphor of the battle against the forces of Beauty, which leads to the imprisonment of the lover.

Although the fifteenth century in England saw the composition of a great many religious and secular lyrics (some of which are of a very high standard), the longer forms of poetry predominate. Scottish literature has its share of long poems, but with the obvious exceptions of the historical romances and the *Eneados*, there is no poetic work with the sprawling dimensions of *The Pilgrimage of the Life of Man*, the *Passetyme*, and *The Ship of Fools*. The willingness shown by successive poets to experiment with shorter forms is one mark of the versatility of the Scots tradition as compared with the English. Dunbar's experimentation with a wider variety of genres is the most striking example of this, but his range is by no means exceptional. There is good reason to doubt Henryson's authorship of all of the shorter poems attributed to him,[25] but even so his output is even more varied than the use of several kinds of allegorical narrative suggests. If Douglas had written only *The Palice of Honour* and the *Eneados*, the contrast between the two styles of composition, discursive allegory and accurate translation, is great enough to leave no doubts about his adaptability. It is possible that James I provided a precedent for later court poets in the variety of his own writing. Even if *Peblis to the Play* is not the work of James, recognition must be given to Major's account of the variety of the king's writing in the vernacular.[26] An integral part of the court literary tradition in Scotland is the assimilation of strongly comic matter which English taste would no doubt have dismissed as being 'vyle' or 'upland', and hence offensive to a cultivated audience. The poem about a farcical tournament between low-life characters has a firm place in the Scots tradition. *Peblis to the Play* is related to other works by court poets – *The Sowtar and Tailyouris War*, Lindsay's *The Iusting betuix Watsoun and Barbour*, and Scott's *Iusting and Debait*. The fourteenth-century northern English *Turnement of Tottenham*,[27] which may be the ancestor of all of the Scots pieces, differs from them in having no obvious associations with courts and court poets. The popularity of this comic genre among 'serious' poets is a reminder that the distinction between courtly and popular taste in Scotland is not always an easy one to make.

I have mentioned several aspects of the traditionalism of Middle Scots poetry – the strong sense of authorial presence and control, inventiveness in allegorical composition, and within the output of individual poets, a high degree of variety in subject matter and tone. All are features of Chaucer's work, and the Scots court poetry discussed in this book may be described as 'Chaucerian' inasmuch as it shows a respect for the standards of Chaucer's poetry. Another aspect of the tradition is a feeling for verbal texture: the attention shown to detail at the level of the individual line is in marked contrast to the diffuseness of most post-Chaucerian English poetry. The difference becomes apparent when (for example) the introductory stanzas of *The Example of Vertu* and *The Goldyn Targe* are compared. Each passage is a development of the Lydgatian style of aureate description. Hawes's lines are syntactically and metrically haphazard,[28] and their polysyllabic terminations strengthen the effect of ponderous circumlocution:

> Whan the golden sterres clere were splendent
> In the firmament puryfyed clere as crystall
> By imperyall course without incombrement
> As Iuppyter and Mars that be celestyall.
>
> (36-9)

Dunbar uses an even more elaborate style of aureation, creating an evocative tension between imported polysyllabic diction and native monosyllables in the line 'Up sprang the goldyn candill matutyne'. This tension between the aureate and the familiar is the key to the choice of diction in the stanzas which follow, and the effect is to give an impression of the abundant life contained within the overall harmony of Nature. The idea is reinforced by alliteration, and by the carefully controlled rhythms: variation from the iambic norm of the ten-syllable line is made to intensify the sense of rapid movement. I have suggested earlier that the juxtaposition of Scots words against the Latinate coinings is part of an attempt to outdo the verbal brilliance of Lydgate's aureate effects. It is possible that the idea of intensifying the alliterative element in the English passages of nature description came to Dunbar from the Prologue to *The Lyoun and the Mous*. Henryson's lines show how evocative the combination of alliteration with a relatively simple vocabulary can be. The Scots tradition of experimentation with this descriptive convention is also illustrated by *The Palice of Honour* and Douglas's twelfth *Eneados* Prologue. The conclusion to the latter shows quite clearly that Douglas set out to surpass all that had been written before in a similar vein:

> The lusty crafty preambill, 'perle of May'
> I the entitel, crownyt quhil domysday,
> And al with gold, in syng of stait ryall
> Most beyn illumnyt thy letteris capital.

syng sign

The twelfth Prologue is a triumphant affirmation of the resources of the poet's 'Scottis', and of his place in a developing literary tradition:[29] Douglas borrows from his own poem 'maid weil twelf ȝheris tofor', and from *The Goldyn Targe* and *The Thrissil and the Rois*: the indebtedness can be traced to the level of word and image, but it is more important to observe that Douglas amplifies

K

the various elements which contribute to the rich verbal texture of his models. There is development and extension of the two extremes of Dunbar's vocabulary, the aureate and the familiar, as part of a more detailed and more extensive *descriptio*. In each of his poems Dunbar devotes a stanza to describing the rising of the sun (*GT* 1–9, *TR* 50–6): in *Eneados* XII, a similar description occupies some forty lines. Douglas's use of Scots words to balance his aureation in the account of the sun is even more remarkable than Dunbar's: for example,

> Defundand from his sege etheryall
> Glaid influent aspectis celicall;
> Befor hys regale hie magnificens
> Mysty vapour vpspryngand, sweit as sens,
> In smoky soppys of donk dewis wak,
> Moich hailsum stovys ourheldand the slak.
>
> (41–6)

Glaid influent glad influence; *soppys* clouds; *wak* wet; *Moich . . . slak* Moist wholesome vapours covering the valley

The transition from aureate to simple diction is made without any deflation of tone: the continuity is provided by the rhythmic sweep of the lines and by the use of alliteration. Into the idealised literary landscapes of the two Dunbar poems and the *Palice* are introduced homely and familiar details. The cock may indeed be 'Phebus red fowle' (155), but he is a cock for all that, and like the grandiloquent roosters of the *Morall Fabillis* he is glimpsed scratching for his food 'Amyd the wortis and the rutys gent [fair]' (155–8). The presence of lowly creatures such as the cock, the gasping corby and the 'cowschet' in the company of the more poetic grades of 'Dame Naturis menstralis' illustrates the poet's concern for variety of subject matter. This is also apparent in his treatment of the human figures in the scene: as well as the singing nymphs and the sorrowful lovers of courtly tradition, there is a pair of roisterers who whisper of some 'schamefull play' (187–224). The variety of subject matter is complemented by variety of style. In language, a heightened form of polite speech is enlivened by variations to the aureate mode, to the 'busteous' manner of some traditional alliterative poetry, and to simple colloquialism. There is also tonal variation within the overall celebratory mode:

note, for example, the contrast between the two types of dramatic utterance, the vaguely sinister human dialogue, and the harmonious *sermocinatio* of the birds which follows it (213-24, 252-66). Douglas's praise of Virgil for his range and versatility – 'He altyrris his style sa mony way ... Lyke as he had of euery thyng a feill' (v, Prol. 33-8) – quite justifiably invites comparison with his own achievement.

Most of the other *Eneados* prologues, like the twelfth, serve both as introduction to the books which follow and as critical commentary.[30] At another level, the prologues are a remarkable tribute to the strength and continuity of the Scots poetic tradition, and to the flexibility of 'Scottis' as a medium for all kinds of poetic discourse. There is more variety in these prologues – of subject matter, genre, style and language – than there is in the whole corpus of fifteenth- and early sixteenth-century English poetry, and considered together, they affirm both the inventiveness of the poet and the value of inspiration from other Scots poetry. Even the most uniformly 'elevait' of them, the second and the tenth, preserve the illusion of spoken address from poet to audience. In the second Prologue there is movement from the grandly formal mode appropriate to an invocation to the 'auld fader of malancoly' into a simpler homiletic style, in which various sections of the audience are singled out. (This kind of direct address, which occurs in several of the prologues, recalls the manner of some of Henryson's *moralitates*.) The first few stanzas of Douglas's meditation on the Trinity (Book x) provide even stronger evidence of Henryson's influence: the theme of apprehending the Creator through the Creation is explored in the first thirteen stanzas of *The Preiching of the Swallow*, and the tonal similarity between the two passages is immediately obvious. The sense of the poet's presence in his work which is fostered by rhythm and direct appeal to his audience is strengthened in other prologues by Douglas's self-dramatisations. Earlier in this chapter his use of Henryson's Prologue to *The Lyoun and the Mous* for Prologue XIII was discussed: the influence of Henryson's self-portrayal in *The Testament* is apparent in the Prologue to Book VII, where the poet tells of his attempts to dispel 'the peralus persand cald'. That willingness to discuss the background to the writing of poetry – whether it be real or fictional – is, as I have tried to show elsewhere, one of the most significant features of the interest in the personal and the dramatic which is so pervasive in Scots poetry.

The eighth Prologue puts a complaint about the times into a dramatic setting, through the medium of the alliterative line and the traditional alliterative stanza form. Two quite separate forms of Scots poetry are brought together here. The subject matter of the poem, the degeneracy at work within all levels of society, is also that of several poems by Dunbar: the similarity is enhanced by the use of the 'Sum . . . sum' construction which is featured in *Tydingis fra the Sessioun*, and by the alliterative vernacular vocabulary. The stanza form is basically the same as that of alliterative romances such as *Golagros and Gawayne* and *The Awntyrs of Arthure*. Douglas's choice of style is both a way of giving fresh interest to the well-known general complaint theme and of showing that the old alliterative metre and vocabulary are worthy of a place in a developing literary tradition. In England alliteration came to be regarded as having a purely ornamental value, as a device to be used occasionally for emphasis. No poet who claimed to use the literary language of Chaucer and Lydgate would have deigned to use the old provincial style of 'rum, ram, ruf'.

Thorough investigation of the links which exist between Douglas's prologues and earlier Scots poetry is beyond the scope of this study, and I have tried merely to give some idea of the extent to which Douglas's writing is inspired and supported by the work of Henryson, Dunbar and poets whose names have not survived. The sense of belonging to a local community of poets, it is reasonable to infer, helped to sustain Douglas in his herculean task of rendering Virgil into his 'lewit barbour tong'. It is significant that both prologues and translation contain relatively few verbal reminiscences of either Chaucer or Lydgate: the poetry of Henryson and Dunbar, written in his own language, has a much more immediate relevance. It is not to be wondered at, then, that there is no sign of influence from contemporary English poetry which is of scarcely greater merit than Caxton's 'buke of Inglys gross'. The work of 'venerabill Chauser, principal poet but peir' undoubtedly played some part in developing Douglas's literary taste, but the work of other Scots poets, Chaucerian or otherwise, is a more important influence on the *Eneados*. Like his predecessors, Douglas is highly selective about what English work he chooses to adapt for his own writing. More is taken from Chaucer than from Lydgate, and nothing at all from the post-Lydgatians.

Lindsay's poetry, like Douglas's, affirms the cohesiveness of the Scots tradition. In his tribute to the literary past in *The Testament of the Papyngo*, 'Chawceir, Goweir, and Lidgate laureate' are the first to be mentioned, but having praised their example he goes on to lament the loss of a large company of Scots makars. The tribute to Douglas – 'in our Inglis rethorick, the rose' – leaves no doubt about where his strongest allegiance lies (22–36). The poem demonstrates the extent to which Lindsay's writing has been influenced by earlier poems in Scots. The elaborate account of the *locus amoenus* (101–42), for example, reflects a clear debt to both Douglas and Dunbar. Lindsay's innovation is to weave this kind of description into the fabric of a mock-heroic poem: the elaborate introduction prepares us for something other than the fall of an overweening, overweight parrot. The poem belongs to the 'fall of princes' genre, but English poems of the kind offer nothing like Lindsay's delightful mixture of absurdity and pathos. The papyngo's complaint against Fortune contains several echoes of Cresseid's complaint in the *Testament*: even more strongly reminiscent of Henryson is the Papyngo's own testament, in particular its conclusion:

> Bot, sen my spreit mon fra my body go,
> I recommend it to the quene of farye,
> Eternallye in tyll hir court to carye,
> In wyldernes, among the holtis hore.
> Than scho inclynit hir hed, and spak no more.
>
> (1132–6)

holtis hore grey woods

Lindsay re-creates the sober and poignant mood of Henryson's lines to good effect, by following the testament with the horrific account of the dismemberment of the corpse by the bird clerics –

a passage which owes something, I think, to *The Buke of the Howlat*. Among the several other borrowings from earlier Scots poetry is the account in the Second Epistle of one of the kinds of court vice:

> Pandaris, pykthankis, custronis, and clatteraris
> Loupis up frome laddis, syne lychtis amang lardis;
> Blasphematours, beggaris, and commoun bardis
> Sum tyme in courte hes more auctoritie,
> Nor devote Doctouris in Divinitie.   (390–4)

custronis wasters

Lindsay takes over this mode from Dunbar (*Complaint to the King, Remonstrance to the King*) and uses it to add variety to a less spectacular complaint style. *The Buke of the Monarche*, Lindsay's last poem, shows a decline from the standard of his earlier poetry. The poem, a lengthy account of kingship abused and misused, eschews tonal variation in the interest of moral persuasion, and in this respect it has more in common with poems by Hoccleve and Lydgate than it does with the work of Dunbar and Douglas. One of its more appealing features is the framework of nature description. The Prologue, with its elaborate account of the sun's rising, is modelled on Douglas's 'perle of May', and in the concluding stanzas there are echoes of the thirteenth *Eneados* Prologue.

At the beginning of this chapter I suggested that the infrequency with which both English and Scots poets from the late fifteenth to the mid-sixteenth century draw upon each other's work need not imply total ignorance of the other literary tradition. Given the sheer dullness of most English poetry of the period, it is not difficult to understand why the Scots tended to ignore it as they did. It is natural, though, to wonder why the wide-ranging excellence of Scots poetry seems to have stimulated no poets other than Skelton, Surrey and possibly Wyatt. There is no single satisfactory answer, but the very weight of Lydgate's example as a writer of uniformly sober didactic poems is part of the reason for the ossification of English poetry. The growing interest in the standardisation of language – both spoken and literary – is a related factor. The Lydgatians would have found it difficult to comprehend, much less to imitate, the breadth and range of

Scots poetic vocabulary. In the *Poems Against Garnesche* Skelton strenuously exploits the colloquial vocabulary at his disposal, yet he fails to match the abusive profuseness of *The Flyting*. The relative poverty of English may account, at least as much as the wish to write an elegantly concise translation of Virgil, for Surrey's failure to echo any more of Douglas's vocabulary than he does.

In Barclay's fourth Eclogue, Minalcas explains that the continued life of poetry depends upon the interest of princes:

> Than standeth the Poet and his Poeme arere,
> When princes disdayne them for to reade or here.
> (655–6)

Barclay and Hawes, like Lydgate, make claims upon the attention of their monarchs, and it is clear that they hoped that their 'hye stile of eloquence' would be read at court. But it is difficult to find, even in the much more topical and outspoken poetry of Skelton and in the work of the Henrician courtier–poets, any equivalent to the sense of easy and intimate address from poet to prince which is so strongly present in Scots poetry. (Wyatt's epistolary satires, addressed to friends and fellow-courtiers, are remarkable among contemporary English writing, in the sense which they convey of a spoken communication between poet and audience.) The Scots frequently complain of neglect at the royal hands, but the subject matter and tone of much of their work suggest strongly that as poets they enjoyed a freedom of expression which no Lancastrian or Tudor monarch would have suffered. The fact that they wrote for the edification and amusement of a small court for whom the hearing of poetry was at least as important as the reading of it may have limited the appeal of their work to poets who occupied a peripheral place in the life of a larger and more complex court. Anthony à Wood writes of how Henry VII would listen to Hawes reciting from memory passages of Lydgate.[31] If there is any truth in the account, it is a remarkable tribute both to the poet's powers of memory and to the king's powers of concentration. It is not difficult to see how an English poet writing for such sober royal tastes might have been appalled by a Scots poet's freedom of expression.

The sense of being part of a community of writers, present and past, courtly and non-courtly, is still persistent among Lindsay's contemporaries and successors. In the Prologue to *The Seven Sages*, for example, John Rolland tells how he sought the advice of four famous court poets – Lindsay, John Bellenden, William Stewart and Bishop Durie – about how to compose a new poem. The result, *The Court of Venus*, abounds in reminiscences of poems by Henryson, Douglas, Dunbar and Lindsay, but in its ponderous handling of the structural convention of the journey and in the mechanical approach to love-allegory, the poem is closer to *The Court of Love*. Rolland, like the sixteenth-century imitator of *The Temple of Glas*, is writing in a self-consciously archaic way, and it must be acknowledged that the English poem is more graceful and more witty. Although there is much in later Scots poetry that is genuinely new and inventive, there is a marked decline from the high standards of the early sixteenth century. One of the marks of this decline is the prolixity and tonal monotony of poems such as *The Buke of the Monarche*, *The Court of Venus* and *The Cherrie and the Slae*. It is difficult to avoid the suspicion that later poets began to look back for inspiration, not only to Scots poetry, but also to the English literature which their predecessors had chosen to ignore, at least as models for imitation. Another sign of this turning to southern poetry, as Jack points out,[32] is the appearance of features of Lydgatian versification in the work of Stewart, Fowler and Alexander Craig.

The Essayes of a Prentise shows a strong concern for continued experimentation in the art of vernacular poetry: although James was by no means ignorant of older vernacular forms and techniques (the 'flyting', alliteration), his tastes were European rather than Scots, and it is natural that he should have looked to French and Italian poetry as the inspiration of new literary forms in Scots. By the time the king's treatise had been written, English poetry had begun to undergo a renaissance which eclipsed the literary revival at the Scots court, and it is inevitable that his removal to London should have hastened the decline of Scots poetry which had begun even before the Scottish reformation. The nature of the shaping influence of politics upon poetry at the beginning and end of the Middle Scots court tradition is a fascinating accident of literary history. Political circumstance – in the shape of incarceration at the English court – provided the unlikely occasion for a Stewart king's apprenticeship to English poetry, an apprenticeship which was to have consequences for the poetry of his own country. Nearly two centuries after the return of James I to Scotland, his descendant, another poet-king, travelled south to claim the throne of England, there by hastening the demise of a literary tradition which had been nourished by the political 'infortune' of the first James.

Notes

1 Influences and perspectives

1. *The Ship of Fools*, ed. T. H. Jamieson (2 vols., Edinburgh, 1874), II, sts. 1570–5. The comment about Barclay's birthplace comes from William Bullein's *Dialogue Against the Fever Pestilence*, ed. M. W. and A. H. Bullen (EETS, 1888), 17, lines 30–1.
2. *An Introduction to the History of Poetry in Scotland* (Edinburgh, 1798), p. 57.
3. *English Literature in the Sixteenth Century, excluding Drama* (Oxford, 1954), p. 120.
4. *Early Tudor Poetry* (New York, 1920), pp. 416–17.
5. J. W. Baxter, *William Dunbar: A Biographical Study* (Edinburgh, 1952), pp. 90, 94. R. L. Mackie argues convincingly for Dunbar's authorship of the poem in *King James IV of Scotland: A Brief Survey of His Life and Times* (Edinburgh, 1958), p. 95n.
6. J. S. Brewer, *The Reign of Henry VIII, 1509–30*, ed. J. Gairdner (2 vols., London, 1844), I, 218–19.
7. *The Poetical Works of Gavin Douglas*, ed. J. Small (4 vols., Edinburgh, 1874) I, civ. See also Priscilla Bawcutt, *Gavin Douglas: A Critical Study* (Edinburgh, 1976), I, 10–22.
8. *The Paston Letters: A. D. 1422–1509*, ed. J. Gairdner (6 vols., London, 1904), V, 144.
9. F. J. Amours (ed.), *Scottish Alliterative Poems in Riming Stanzas* (2 vols., STS, 1897), I, xxvi.
10. *Privy Purse Expenses of Elizabeth of York*, ed. N. H. Nicolas (London, 1830), p. 28.
11. Discussed by Andrew Crawfurd in *Northern Notes and Queries*, LIII (1851).
12. W. A. Craigie, 'The Scottish alliterative poems', *PBA* XXVIII (1942), 217–36.
13. *The Poems of King James VI of Scotland*, ed. J. Craigie (2 vols., STS, 1955–8), I, 81.
14. *The Italian Influence on Scottish Literature* (Edinburgh, 1970), pp. 9–14, 15–16.
15. *The French Background of Middle Scots Literature* (Edinburgh, 1934), p. xxi.
16. Ed. J. A. H. Murray (EETS, 1872), p. 106.
17. For more detailed accounts of Middle Scots poetic language, see M. A. Mackay, 'The Scots of the makars', in A. J. Aitken (ed.), *Lowland Scots: papers presented to an Edinburgh conference* (Edinburgh, 1973), pp. 20–30; A. J. Aitken, 'Variation and variety in written Middle Scots', in A. J. Aitken *et al.* (eds.) *Edinburgh Studies in English and Scots* (London, 1971), pp. 177–209. Both articles provide essential qualifications to the view of G. Gregory Smith, that Middle Scots is an 'artificial, created and literary language', in *Specimens of Middle Scots* (Edinburgh and London, 1902), pp. xi–xii.
18. English pieces wrongly ascribed to Chaucer by Bannatyne include an extract from *The Complaint of the Black Knight* (CCCLXXI), sections of *The Remedy of Love*

(CCCXLI, CCCXLIII), and Hoccleve's *The Letter of Cupid* (CCCLXI). These poems, together with several others which Bannatyne attributes to Chaucer, were included in Thynne's edition of Chaucer. Denton Fox gives good reasons for his suggestion that Bannatyne worked from the 1545 Thynne text: 'Manuscripts and prints of Scots poetry in the sixteenth century', in A. J. Aitken, *et al.* (eds.), *Bards and Makars* (Glasgow, 1977), pp. 158–60.

19 The Passion lyric (XXI) and the dietary (LXXXVIII) are both in the Makculloch MS. also: *Pieces from the Makculloch and the Gray MSS.*, ed. G. Stevenson (STS, 1918), X, XIV.
20 Cited by Fox, in his edition of *The Testament of Cresseid* (London and Edinburgh, 1968), pp. 6–7.
21 *Religious Lyrics of the Fifteenth Century*, ed. Carleton Brown (Oxford, 1939), nos. 56, 183.
22 Discussed by John MacQueen in his edition of Scots love-lyrics, *Ballattis of Luve* (Edinburgh, 1970), pp. xxviii–xxx.
23 *Ibid*, p. xxxvi. See also MacQueen, 'Some aspects of the early renaissance in Scotland', *Forum for Modern Language Studies* III (1967), 201–22.
24 Ethel Seaton, 'That Scotch copy of Chaucer', *JEGP* XLVII (1948), 352–6.
25 J. Durkan and A. Ross, *Early Scottish Libraries* (Glasgow, 1961), p. 7.
26 'The Scottish Chaucerians', in D. S. Brewer (ed.), *Chaucer and Chaucerians: Critical Studies in Middle English Literature* (London, 1966), p. 170.
27 *Ibid*.
28 J. Norton-Smith (ed.), *The Kingis Quair* (Oxford, 1971), p. xiii.
29 *Miscellany Volume*, ed. J. T. T. Brown (STS, 1933). McDiarmid comments on the superficiality of English usages in the *Quare* and *Lancelot of the Laik* (*The Kingis Quair*, Introduction, p. 31).
30 *Robert Henryson: A Study of the Major Narrative Poems* (Oxford, 1967), p. 55.
31 Elliott, *Robert Henryson: Poems*, p. vii.
32 'A plea for the Middle Scots', in Larry D. Benson (ed.), *The Learned and the Lewed: Studies in Chaucer and Medieval Literature* (Cambridge, Mass., 1974), pp. 175–96.
33 Ridley, 'A plea for the Middle Scots', p. 181.
34 *Humanism and Poetry in the Early Tudor Period* (London, 1959), p. 24.
35 *Chaucer and the Fifteenth Century* (Oxford, 1947), pp. 1–11.
36 H. J. Chaytor suggests that even as late as 1500, such accomplished silent readers were comparatively rare: *From Script to Print* (London, 1945), p. 17. See also Ruth Crosby, 'Chaucer and the custom of oral delivery', *Speculum* XLIII (1938), 413–32. Nevertheless, the implications of statements such as 'Turne over the leef and chese another tale' (*CT*, IA, 3177) should not be forgotten.
37 *John Lydgate: A Study in the Culture of the XVth Century*, trans. A. Keep (London, 1961), p. 35.
38 'The English Chaucerians', in Brewer, *Chaucer and Chaucerians*, p. 201.
39 Bower, *Scotichronicon*, Book XVI, c. xxx, ed. W. Goodall (Edinburgh, 1759); *A History of Greater Britain by John Major*, trans. and ed. A. Constable (Edinburgh, 1892), p. 366.
40 *The History and Chronicles of Scotland*, ed. A. J. G. Mackay (3 vols., STS, 1899, 1911), I, 163.
41 For a discussion of literacy in Scotland in this period, see John Durkan, 'Education in the century of the Reformation', in David McRoberts (ed.), *Essays on the Scottish Reformation, 1513–1625* (Glasgow, 1962), pp. 145–68.
42 'The Scottish Chaucerians', in *The Cambridge History of English Literature*, vol. II, (Cambridge, 1908), p. 239.

2 'The Kingis Quair' and English poetry

1. I do not intend to discuss the question of authorship. The view that the *Quair* may not have been written by James I, put by J. T. T. Brown, *The Kingis Quair: A New Criticism* (Glasgow, 1896), A Lawson (ed.), *The Kingis Quair and the Quare of Jelusy* (London, 1910) and W. M. Mackenzie (ed.), *The Kingis Quair* (London, 1939), is convincingly countered by McDiarmid. He argues that the language is consonant with a date of composition in the first half of the fifteenth century, and that the historical details given accord with what is known of James's capture and captivity (McDiarmid, *The Kingis Quair*, Introduction, pp. 28–33, 38–42). Equally important are the two ascriptions to James in the manuscript, and Major's testimony (*ibid*, pp. 46–8).
2. *Medieval Dream-Poetry* (Cambridge, 1976), p. 186.
3. McDiarmid, *The Kingis Quair*, p. 60.
4. For a detailed account of James I's captivity see E. M. W. Balfour-Melville, *James I, King of Scots* (London, 1936).
5. *Scotichronicon*, Book XVI, c. XXX.
6. W. Skeat (ed.), *The Kingis Quair* (STS, 1911), Introduction, p. xxiv.
7. 'The language of *The Kingis Quair*', *Essays and Studies* XXV (1939), 30.
8. 'The English Chaucerians', p. 227. See also Norton-Smith, *The Kingis Quair*, Introduction, p. xxix, and Fox, 'The Scottish Chaucerians', p. 164.
9. I prefer the manuscript reading, 'my sentence' to McDiarmid's emendation 'the sentence'.
10. 'Chaucer's influence upon King James I of Scotland as poet', *Anglia* III (1880), 226.
11. John Preston notes merely that James's use of the reading device as an introduction is the product of literary convention: '"Fortunys exiltree": a study of *The Kingis Quair*', *RES* n.s. VII (1956), 341. The motif does, however, seem to have been originated by Chaucer: see M. W. Stearns, 'Chaucer mentions a book', *MLN* LVII (1942), 28–31.
12. In *Three Medieval Rhetorical Arts*, trans. J. B. Kopp and J. J. Murphy (Berkeley and London, 1971).
13. See J. MacQueen, 'Tradition and the interpretation of the *Kingis Quair*', *RES* n.s. XII (1961), 119.
14. *The English Works of John Gower*, ed. G. C. Macaulay (2 vols., EETS, 1900–1).
15. See, for example, E. T. Donaldson, 'Chaucer the pilgrim', *PMLA* LXIX (1954), 928–36; Spearing, *Medieval Dream-Poetry*, pp. 48–110; R. O. Payne, *The Key of Remembrance: A Study of Chaucer's Poetics* (New Haven and London, 1963), pp. 220–32.
16. *Medieval Dream-Poetry*, p. 182.
17. Norton-Smith, *The Kingis Quair*, p. xvii: cf. McDiarmid, *The Kingis Quair*, p. 64n.
18. See A. von Hendy, 'The free thrall: a study of *The Kingis Quair*', *SSL* III (1965), 141–51.
19. The poem, and the question of Lydgate's authorship, are discussed by Derek Pearsall, *John Lydgate* (London, 1970), pp. 97–103. It is worth mentioning the possibility that *The Flower of Courtesy* may have been influenced by the *Quair*, rather than the *Quair* by the *Flower*. There is no external evidence of the date at which the English poem was composed – there are no manuscripts, and it first appears in Thynne's 1532 edition of Chaucer. Because it so closely resembles *The Complaint of the Black Knight* and *The Temple of Glas* in language, style and subject matter, the poem has been estimated to belong to the period pre-1420 (Pearsall, *John Lydgate*, p. 84). The evidence is at best inconclusive, and although it seems more likely that James would have reworked the English poem, the indebtedness may be in the other direction.

20 Norton-Smith, *The Kingis Quair*, p. xv.
21 *The Works of Sir John Clanvowe*, ed. V. J. Scattergood (Cambridge, 1975).
22 See also G. C. Kratzmann, 'The nightingale and the cuckoo: literary reminiscence in *The Kingis Quair*', *SLJ* 11 (1975), 70–1.
23 The image of love as a game of chess is probably borrowed from *The Book of the Duchess*, where Fortune is adversary rather than benefactress: 618–19, 652–64. See also Lawson, *The Kingis Quair and The Quare of Jelusy*, pp. lxi–lxii.
24 *The Allegory of Love* (Oxford, 1936), pp. 236–7. See also Mackenzie, *The Kingis Quair*, pp. 26–7, 38; Kurt Wittig, *The Scottish Tradition in Literature* (Edinburgh and London, 1958), p. 34; James Kinsley, 'The mediaeval makars', in James Kinsley (ed.), *Scottish Poetry: A Critical Survey* (London, 1955), p. 12.
25 McDiarmid, *The Kingis Quair*, p. 49. It should be noted, however, that McDiarmid's own interpretation of the poem's philosophical content does not differ materially from those of MacQueen and Preston.
26 McDiarmid, *The Kingis Quair*, pp. 53–4.
27 Ed. J. Schick (EETS, 1891).
28 'Tradition and the interpretation of the *Kingis Quair*', pp. 122–4.
29 J. MacQueen, 'The literature of fifteenth-century Scotland', in Jennifer M. Brown (ed.), *Scottish Society in the Fifteenth Century* (London, 1977), pp. 187–92.
30 *Medieval Dream-Poetry*, p. 183.
31 *A Discourse of Englishe Poetrie*, ed. E. Arber, English Reprints Series (Westminster, 1895), p. 41.

3 Henryson and English poetry

1 I prefer Charteris's reading 'worthie' in line 43 to Thynne's 'lustie'. See also line 485.
2 J. A. W. Bennett argues that Henryson could not have assumed a good knowledge of *Troilus and Criseyde* on the part of his audience. If this is the case, it is difficult to explain why Henryson should have made what Professor Bennett admits is a 'subtle and discriminating' use of motifs from Chaucer's poem: 'Henryson's *Testament*: a flawed masterpiece', *SLJ* 1 (1974), p. 5.
3 Fox, *The Testament of Cresseid*, pp. 56–7.
4 MacQueen, *Robert Henryson*, pp. 60–1.
5 P. M. Kean, *Chaucer and the Making of English Poetry* (2 vols., London and Boston, 1972), I, 148.
6 MacQueen, *Robert Henryson*, p. 70.
7 Dolores L. Noll, '*The Testament of Cresseid*: are Christian interpretations valid?', *SSL* IX (1971), 16–25: C. W. Jentoft 'Henryson as authentic "Chaucerian": narrator, character, and courtly love in *The Testament of Cresseid*', *SSL* X (1972), pp. 100–1.
8 E. M. W. Tillyard, *Five Poems, 1470–1870* (London, 1948), p. 16.
9 See Fox, *The Testament of Cresseid*, pp. 24–30.
10 *Criticism and Medieval Poetry*, rev. edn (London, 1972), p. 180.
11 Douglas Duncan, 'Henryson's *Testament of Cresseid*', *Essays in Criticism* XI (1961), 129.
12 Tatyana Moran, '*The Testament of Cresseid* and *The Book of Troylus*', *Litera* VI (1959), 18–24.
13 MacQueen, *Robert Henryson*, pp. 88–93.
14 Fox, *The Testament of Cresseid*, p. 56.
15 See also J. MacQueen, 'The case for early Scottish literature', in Aitken *et al.*, *Edinburgh Studies in English and Scots*, p. 240.
16 H. R. Patch, *The Goddess Fortuna in Medieval Literature* (New York, 1927), pp. 42–3.
17 *Ibid*, pp. 56–7.

18 See also E. Duncan Aswell, 'The role of Fortune in *The Testament of Cresseid*', *Philological Quarterly* XLVI (1967), 482.
19 *The Bannatyne MS.*, CCCLXXVIII.
20 Cf. Fox, *The Testament of Cresseid*, p. 93, note to line 62.
21 Spearing, *Criticism and Medieval Poetry*, p. 184.
22 Fox, *The Testament of Cresseid*, pp. 53, 55.
23 *Criticism and Medieval Poetry*, p. 162.
24 B. J. Whiting, 'A probable allusion to Henryson's *Testament of Cresseid*', *MLR* XL (1945), 46–7.
25 'A plea for the Middle Scots', p. 190. This article contains an up-to-date and useful account of critical studies of the *Testament*.
26 Gavin Douglas, *Eneados*, Book I, Prol., 449.
27 See Hyder E. Rollins, 'The Troilus–Cressida story from Chaucer to Shakespeare', *PMLA* XXXII (1917), 383–429.
28 See I. W. A. Jamieson, 'The poetry of Robert Henryson: a study in the uses of source material' (unpub. Ph.D. dissertation, Edinburgh, 1965), and MacQueen, *Robert Henryson*, Appendices I and II.
29 T. F. Henderson, *Scottish Vernacular Literature: A History*, 3rd edn (Edinburgh, 1910), p. 117.
30 Donald MacDonald, 'Henryson and Chaucer: cock and fox', *Texas Studies in Language and Literature* VIII (1966), 454. This article discusses a number of parallels between the English and Scots poems, using them as evidence for Henryson's indebtedness to Chaucer. The argument cannot be conclusive, however, because although Henryson almost certainly knew *NPT*, it is possible that he knew another version (or versions) of the fable.
31 Evidence for the existence of this version is provided by the late thirteenth-early fourteenth-century Ormesby Psalter, which contains an illumination of an unaccompanied woman bearing a distaff, chasing a fox which is carrying away a cock (K. Varty, *Reynard the Fox: A Study of the Fox in Medieval English Art* (Leicester, 1967), p. 38, plate 28). Note also that in *The Kingis Quair* the fox is referred to as 'the wedowis inemye' (st. 156, 4).
32 Elliott, *Robert Henryson: Poems*, p. vii.
33 H. Harvey Wood (ed.), *The Poems and Fables of Robert Henryson*, 2nd edn (Edinburgh and London, 1958), p. xv.
34 The poem is preserved in the Asloan MS., ed. W. A. Craigie (STS, 1922–4). It has also been edited by David Laing (with revisions by John Small) in *Select Remains of the Ancient Popular and Romance Poetry of Scotland* (Edinburgh and London, 1885), pp. 278–93. Quotations are from this edition.
35 *Nigel de Longchamps Speculum Stultorum*, ed. J. H. Mozley and R. R. Raymo (Berkeley and Los Angeles, 1960).
36 *Geoffrey Chaucer* (London and Boston, 1974), p. 114.
37 *The Allegory of Love*, p. 162. See also Denton Fox, 'Chaucer's influence on fifteenth-century poetry', in Beryl Rowland (ed.), *Companion to Chaucer Studies* (Toronto, 1968), p. 394; Norton-Smith, *Geoffrey Chaucer*, p. 108.
38 *The Minor Poems of John Lydgate*, ed. H. N. MacCracken (EETS, 1934), vol. II, no. 24.
39 M. Plessow, 'Geschichte der Fabeldichtung in England bis zu John Gay', *Palaestra* XLI (Berlin, 1906), xlvii; G. Gregory Smith (ed.), *The Poems of Robert Henryson* (3 vols. in 2, STS, 1906–7, 1909–10), I, p. xxxix. See also David K. Crowne, 'A date for the composition of Henryson's *Fables*', *JEGP* LXI (1962), 588–90.
40 See also Derek Pearsall's observations on the differences between Lydgate's approach and Henryson's in *John Lydgate*, pp. 194–8.

41 See MacQueen, *Robert Henryson,* Appendix III; Crowne, 'A date for the composition of Henryson's *Fables',* pp. 583–8. Denton Fox argues, on the other hand, that 'there is no good proof that Henryson had any knowledge of Caxton's *Reynard* or *Aesop*' in 'Henryson and Caxton', *JEGP* LXVII (1968), 587. Fox's objections do not seem to me to be valid: see my doctoral dissertation, 'Anglo-Scottish literary relationships, 1430–1550' (Edinburgh, 1975), fols. 170–5.
42 The only known copy of Smith's print is housed in the National Library of Scotland. The dialogue is included in Harvey Wood's edition of Henryson.

4 'The Palice of Honour' and 'The Hous of Fame'

1 'The Scottish Chaucerians', p. 193. Fox discusses the parallels of narrative detail between the two poems. See also P. Lange, 'Chaucer's Einfluss auf die Originaldichtungen des Schotten Douglas', *Anglia* VI (1883), 46–95.
2 Bawcutt, *The Shorter Poems of Gavin Douglas,* p. xxix. See also her discussion of the poem's literary background in *Gavin Douglas,* pp. 50–1, and her essay, 'The "Library" of Gavin Douglas', in Aitken *et al., Bards and Makars,* pp. 107–26.
3 Payne, *The Key of Remembrance,* pp. 86–7.
4 G. B. Kinneavy expresses a similar view when he notes that the account of the vision may be a way of representing the restoration of the poet's imaginative faculty: 'The poet in *The Palice of Honour*', *Chaucer Review* III (1968), 280–303.
5 See also Bawcutt, *Gavin Douglas,* p. 63.
6 *Ibid,* pp. 62–3.
7 J. A. W. Bennett discusses the Virgilian antithesis between *laus/gloria* and *fama* in *Chaucer's 'Book of Fame'* (Oxford, 1968), p. 39.
8 Bawcutt rightly stresses the Ovidian affinities of Douglas's 'transformations', (*Gavin Douglas,* p. 59). It is likely, however, that the immediate inspiration is Chaucerian.
9 Fox, 'The Scottish Chaucerians', p. 196. Note, however, Fox's sensitive appreciation of Douglas's 'scene-shifting' effects (p. 199).
10 *The Shorter Poems of Gavin Douglas,* p. xlvii. Mrs Bawcutt's analysis of Douglas' rhetorical effects in her chapter on the *Palice* is invaluable.
11 'The Scottish Chaucerians', p. 198.
12 *The Allegory of Love,* p. 290.

5 Dunbar and Skelton

1 See James Kinsley, '*The Tretis of the Tua Mariit Wemen and the Wedo*', *Medium Aevum* XXIII (1954), 31–5. Kinsley discusses the poem as an 'essay in contrasts'.
2 Bawcutt suggests *The Parson's Tale* as a source for the dog image, in *N & Q* XI (1964), 332–3.
3 I am unable to agree with Tom Scott's autobiographical reading of the *Tretis* in *Dunbar: A Critical Exposition of the Poems* (Edinburgh and London, 1966), p. 204.
4 See Mackie, *James IV of Scotland,* pp. 122–4.
5 Elizabeth R. Eddy, '*Sir Thopas* and *Sir Thomas Norny*: romance parody in Chaucer and Dunbar', *RES* n.s. XXII (1971), 401. See also F. B. Snyder, '*Sir Thomas Norray* and *Sir Thopas*', *MLN* XXV (1910), 78–80.
6 'The Scottish Chaucerians', pp. 186–7.
7 *Ibid.*
8 Pierrepont H. Nichols, 'William Dunbar as a Scottish Lydgatian', *PMLA* XLVI (1931), 214–24. See also R. D. S. Jack, 'Dunbar and Lydgate', *SSL* VIII (1971), 215–27.
9 MacCracken, *The Minor Poems of Lydgate,* vol. II, nos. 9–10.

Notes to pp. 139–160

10 *Ibid.* vol. II, no. 76. See Jack, 'Dunbar and Lydgate', p. 222.
11 *Ibid.* vol. II, no. 73 (*Timor Mortis Conturbat Me*); *The Dance of Death*, ed. F. Warren and B. White (EETS, 1931); MacCracken, vol. I, no. 68 (*Testament*).
12 See, for example, Carleton Brown (ed.), *Religious Lyrics of the XIVth Century*, 2nd edn, rev. G. V. Smithers (Oxford, 1952), no. 6. The technique is discussed by Rosemary Woolf, *The English Religious Lyric in the Middle Ages* (Oxford, 1968), pp. 102–6, 332–4.
13 See Scott, *Dunbar*, p. 251.
14 For a detailed description of the Roslin *Totentanz*, see John Thompson, *Guide to Rosslyn Chapel and Castle* (Edinburgh, 1922), pp. 60–2.
15 Brown, *Religious Lyrics of the Fifteenth Century*, no. 158.
16 *Reson and Sensuallyte*, ed. E. Sieper (EETS, 1901).
17 Jack ('Dunbar and Lydgate') discusses these parallels in some detail, suggesting that Dunbar's list of deities is a condensation of a much longer 'list' in *RS*. His theory of a gaffe on Dunbar's part, caused by a misreading of *RS*, and evident in the inclusion of Apollo and of Pallas and Minerva as separate deities, is questionable. I suggest that line 78, as printed by Chepman and Myller, should read 'Thetes, and prudent Pallas Minerva'. There is nothing incongruous about the inclusion of Apollo among the ladies – it sustains the reference to light at the beginning of the poem, and emphasises the link between light and sexuality. There is no actual 'list' in *RS* at all, and Lydgate nowhere uses the name 'Apollo'.
18 MacCracken, *The Minor Poems of Lydgate*, vol. II, no. 4. Pearsall discusses the question of authorship (*John Lydgate*, p. 97).
19 *John Metham's Works*, ed. H. Craig (EETS, 1906), 'Amoryus and Cleopes', 2194.
20 Scott, *Dunbar*, p. 304.
21 G. Gregory Smith, *Scottish Literature: Character and Influence* (London, 1919), p. 13. See also Lewis, *English Literature in the Sixteenth Century*, p. 17 (disagreeing with the label).
22 Listed by F. Brie, 'Skelton-Studien', *Englische Studien* XXXVII (1907), 1–86.
23 Brie suggests that one Adam Dundas may have been the author. This Dundas, an agent of Albany, was in England in 1523, but it is hardly likely that he would have drawn attention to himself by writing lampoons. Skelton's 'dunghill knight' points to Sir George Dundas. For an account of the latter's career, see C. M. MacDonald, 'The struggle of George Dundas for the preceptory of Torphichen', *Scottish Historical Review* XIV (1916), 19–48.
24 *English Literature in the Sixteenth Century*, p. 136.
25 E. F. Guy, who edits the poem, suggests a date of *c.* 1490: 'Some comic and burlesque poems in two sixteenth century manuscript anthologies' (unpub. Ph.D. dissertation, Edinburgh, 1952), fol. 306G.
26 H. L. R. Edwards, *Skelton: The Life and Times of an Early Tudor Poet* (London, 1949), p. 115.
27 The claim that *ER* is indebted to *Gossip's Meeting* is made by M. Pollet in *John Skelton: Poet of Tudor England*, trans. J. Warrington (London, 1971), p. 106. The anonymous poem, among the contents of Richard Hill's commonplace-book, is probably of the sixteenth century rather than the fifteenth. Fifteenth-century dating is claimed, without support, by Thomas Wright (ed.), *Songs and Carols ... from a MS. of the Fifteenth Century*, Percy Society publications, vol. XXIII (London, 1847).
28 Ian A. Gordon, *John Skelton, Poet Laureate* (Melbourne and London, 1943), p. 194.
29 William Nelson, *John Skelton, Laureate* (New York, 1939), pp. 90–3.
30 Edwards, *Skelton*, pp. 87–8.

31 *Ibid.*
32 Dyce, *Works of Skelton*, II, 413–47.
33 Edwards, *Skelton*, pp. 122–3; Pollet, *John Skelton*, pp. 104–5.
34 *The Life of St Werburghe*, ed. C. Horstmann (EETS, 1887), line 199.
35 *English Literature in the Sixteenth Century*, p. 97.
36 Professor James Kinsley, Dunbar's most recent editor, argues convincingly that the poem should not be attributed to Dunbar: 'On editing Dunbar', a paper read at the First International Conference on Medieval and Renaissance Scottish Literature (Edinburgh, September 1975).
37 See C. W. Cunnington *et al.*, *A Dictionary of English Costume 900–1900* (London, 1960), p. 77, and M. C. Linthicum, *Costume in the Drama of Shakespeare and his Contemporaries* (Oxford, 1936), pp. 179–82.

6 Two 'Aeneid' translators – Surrey's debt to Douglas: Wyatt and Henryson

1 *Gavin Douglas*, pp. 98–100.
2 *Ibid*, pp. 144–50.
3 F. H. Ridley (ed.), *The 'Aeneid' of Henry Howard, Earl of Surrey* (Berkeley and Los Angeles, 1963). Ridley extends and redefines the view about Surrey's indebtedness to Douglas, advanced by G. F. Nott (ed.), *The Works of Henry Howard*, 2 vols. (London, 1815), I, cciii–ix. For a detailed account of the critical history of the subject, see Ridley, 'Surrey's debt to Gavin Douglas', *PMLA* LXXVI (1961), 25–33. In an essay which predates her book, Bawcutt discusses the differences between Douglas and Surrey as translators, although not the direct relation between the two: 'Douglas and Surrey: translators of Virgil', *Essays and Studies* XXVII (1974), 52–67.
4 *Surrey: Poems*, p. xvii.
5 See Ridley, *The 'Aeneid' of Henry Howard*, pp. 43–4, for other examples.
6 Quotations from the *Aeneid* follow the Loeb Classics revised edition (Cambridge, Mass., and London, 1956).
7 *English Literature in the Sixteenth Century*, p. 234.
8 *The 'Aeneid' of Henry Howard*, p. 33.
9 Coldwell, *Virgil's 'Aeneid' Translated into Scottish Verse, by Gavin Douglas*, I, 59.
10 See also Emrys Jones's comparisons of Surrey and Douglas, for a view which is generally more sympathetic to Surrey than my own: *Surrey: Poems*, pp. 134–40.
11 See the lists of parallels compiled by M. M. Gray, *TLS* (3 October 1936); and Edith Bannister, *TLS* (24 October 1936).
12 *Gavin Douglas*, p. 198.
13 *'The Arte of English Poesie' by George Puttenham*, ed. G. Willcock and A. Walker (Cambridge, 1936), pp. 60, 145.
14 *Barnabe Googe: Eglogs, Epytaphes, & Sonettes*, ed. E. Arber, English Reprints Series (Birmingham, 1871), pp. 72–3.
15 *Collected Poems of Sir Thomas Wyatt*, ed. Kenneth Muir (London, 1949), no. 197.
16 'A Scoto-Danish stanza: Wyatt, Henryson, and the two mice', *N & Q* CCXVI (1971), 203–7. Professor Fox thinks it extremely unlikely that there is any direct connection between Wyatt's poem and Henryson's, and suggests that the parallels between the two might be explained by a common source in the song to which the Scoto-Danish fragment belongs. In view of the extreme brevity of the fragment however, it seems just as likely that Wyatt knew and drew upon Henryson's poem.
17 *Sir Thomas Wyatt and His Background* (Stanford, 1964), p. 267. H. A. Mason (*Humanism and Poetry in the Early Tudor Period*, p. 227) will not allow of any indebtedness of Wyatt to Henryson.

18 MacQueen, *Robert Henryson*, pp. 126-7.
19 Thomson, *Wyatt and His Background*, p. 266.
20 Jack, *The Italian Influence on Scottish Literature*, pp. 29, 42.
21 Most conveniently consulted in MacQueen, *Ballattis of Luve*, nos. XXX, XXXVII.
22 Muir, *Collected Poems of Wyatt*, nos. 103, 132.
23 This is the way Thomson describes the relationship of Wyatt's poetry to earlier English lyric poetry (*Wyatt and His Background*, p. 126).

7 'Ane Satyre of the Thrie Estaitis' and English drama

1 The records of various kinds of drama are listed and discussed by A. J. Mill, *Medieval Plays in Scotland* (Edinburgh and London, 1927), Appendix 1.
2 The 'nootes', together with Eure's letter, are given by Hamer, *Works of Lindsay* II, 2-6.
3 J. A. Lester, 'Some Franco-Scottish influences on the early English drama', *Haverford Essays: Studies in Modern Literature* (Haverford, Pa., 1909), pp. 132-3; A. J. Mill, 'The influence of continental drama on Lyndsay's *Satyre of the Thrie Estaitis*', MLR XXV (1930), 425-42; Smith, *The French Background*, pp. 126-30; E. K. Chambers, *The Medieval Stage* (2 vols., Oxford, 1903), II, 157.
4 'The influence of continental drama on Lyndsay's *Satyre*', p. 425.
5 Hamer, *Works of Lindsay*, IV, xx-xxi.
6 'The background and the play', in James Kinsley (ed.), *Ane Satyre of the Thrie Estaits* (London, 1954), pp. 16-17.
7 For a fuller discussion see the Introduction to Glynne Wickham's edition, *English Moral Interludes* (London, 1976), pp. vi-viii.
8 Ed. J. M. Manly, *Specimens of the Pre-Shaksperean Drama* (2 vols., Boston, 1897; repr. 1967), vol. I.
9 *Tudor Drama and Politics: A Critical Approach to Topical Meaning* (Cambridge, Mass., 1968), p. 41.
10 *Ibid*, p. 52.
11 *John Skelton, Poet Laureate*, p. 137.
12 *Skelton's 'Magnyfycence' and the Cardinal Virtue Tradition* (Chapel Hill, 1965). Chapters 3 and 4 are particularly valuable.
13 Cited by Harris, *ibid*, p. 39.
14 *Ibid*, p. 155.
15 Cited by A. F. Pollard, *Henry VIII* (London, 1902), p. 96.
16 '*Ane Satyre of the Thrie Estaitis*', *SSL* III (1966), 135-42.
17 *Ibid*, p. 138.
18 A. J. Mill, 'The original version of Lindsay's *Satyre of the Thrie Estaitis*', *SSL* VI (1968), 69-70; V. Harward, '*Ane Satyre of the Thrie Estaitis* again', *SSL* VII (1970), 141-2. The arguments advanced by MacQueen, Mill and Harward, are summarised by J. S. Kantrowitz, 'Encore: Lindsay's *Thrie Estaitis*, date and new evidence', *SSL* X (1972), 18-32. Kantrowitz supports the mid-century dating of Mill and Harward, on the basis of topical references which include mention of the 'Pater Noster controversy' of 1549.
19 Harward, '*Ane Satyre* again', p. 143.
20 See J. S. Kantrowitz, *Dramatic Allegory: Lindsay's 'Ane Satyre of the Thrie Estaitis'* (Lincoln, Nebraska, 1975), pp. 36, 58, 19n.
21 *History and Chronicles of Scotland*, I, 408-9.
22 'The original version of Lindsay's *Satyre*', p. 70.
23 See Gordon Donaldson, *Scotland: James V to James VII* (Edinburgh, 1971), pp. 54-5, 58.
24 For other examples of false-naming, see B. Spivack, *Shakespeare and the Allegory of Evil* (New York, 1958), pp. 155-60.

25 '"Actors" and "play-acting" in the morality tradition', *Renaissance Drama* III (1970), 195.
26 Wierum remarks on the close similarity between these two scenes, apparently without reckoning on the likelihood of indebtedness (*ibid*, p. 203).
27 'The influence of continental drama on Lyndsay's *Satyre*', p. 436.
28 Discussed by Ramsay in his edition of *Magnyfycence*, p. xlvi. See also pp. xcix–ci.
29 Towards the end of his speech, Folie refers to 'Gillymouband' and 'gude Cacaphatie' (4608, 4610). The Treasurer's Accounts confirm the existence of 'a fule callit Gillemowband': Hamer, *Works of Lindsay*, IV, 240.
30 In *Mundus et Infans*, Conscience explains to Mankind that flattering Folly is but another name for the Seven Deadly Sins (458–61).
31 Ramsay, *Magnyfycence*, p. ix.
32 'Some Franco-Scottish influences on the early English drama', p. 137.
33 *A History of English Literature to the Death of Queen Anne* (2 vols., London, 1875), I, 132.
34 '*King Johan*' by John Bale, ed. J. H. P. Pafford (Oxford, 1931), p.xx.
35 *Works of Lindsay*, IV, 160.
36 *The English Drama, 1485–1585* (Oxford, 1969), p. 36.
37 Ed. L. A. Magnus (EETS, 1905).
38 Hamer, *Works of Lindsay*, IV, 139.

8 The two traditions

1 *A Discourse of English Poetrie*, p. 18.
2 MacQueen, *Robert Henryson*, pp. 154–6.
3 In place of Bannatyne's 'Syne maid a corss', Bassandyne gives the weaker Protestant, 'Syne cled my heid'.
4 Ed. M. M. Grey (STS, 1912). On the question of dating, see B. Vogel, 'Secular politics and the date of *Lancelot of the Laik*', *Studies in Philology* XL (1943), 1–13
5 *The Kingis Quair*, p. 46.
6 The reading of line 518 given by the London text is superior to that of the Edinburgh text.
7 *Robert Henryson*, p. 168.
8 Cf. Bawcutt, *Gavin Douglas*, p. 189.
9 *John Lydgate*, p. 68.
10 *Ibid*.
11 For a fuller discussion than I am able to provide here, see O. L. Triggs (ed.), *The Assembly of Gods* (EETS, 1896), pp. xiv–xx, and E. P. Hammond (ed.), *English Verse between Chaucer and Surrey* (Durham, N.C., 1927), pp. 258–60.
12 Ed. W. E. Mead (EETS, 1928).
13 *Ibid*, p. cvi.
14 Ed. W. F. Gluck and A. B. Morgan (EETS, 1974).
15 Ed. A. W. Pollard (Edinburgh, 1905).
16 See W. S. Ramson, 'In praise of Chaucer', *Proceedings and Papers of AULLA* XII (Sydney, 1970), pp. 456–76.
17 *John Lydgate*, p. 156.
18 *The Eclogues of Alexander Barclay*, ed. B. White (EETS, 1928).
19 Cf. N. F. Blake, 'The fifteenth century reconsidered', *NM* LXXI (1970), 146–57.
20 *English Literature in the Sixteenth Century*, p. 142.
21 Skeat (ed.), *Chaucerian and Other Pieces* (Oxford, 1897), pp. lxxvi–lxxx.
22 *The Mirror for Magistrates*, ed. Lily B. Campbell (Cambridge, 1938), pp. 5–6. See also Lewis, *English Literature in the Sixteenth Century*, pp. 240–6.
23 *The History of English Poetry*, ed. W. C. Hazlitt (4 vols., London, 1871), III, 204.

24 *Tottel's Miscellany*, ed. Hyder E. Rollins rev. edn (2 vols., Cambridge, Mass., 1965), I, no. 211.
25 See I. W. A. Jamieson, 'The minor poems of Robert Henryson', *SSL* IX (1971), 125–47.
26 Major, *A History of Greater Britain*, p. 366.
27 *Remains of the Early Popular Poetry of England*, ed. W. C. Hazlitt (4 vols., London, 1864–6), III.
28 C. S. Lewis provides an interesting, if ingenious, explanation of this 'broken-backed' line which is so common in fifteenth-century English poetry: 'The fifteenth-century heroic line', *Essays and Studies* XXIV (1938), 28–41.
29 Cf. Penelope Starkey, 'Gavin Douglas's *Eneados*: dilemmas in the nature prologues', *SSL* XI (1973), 92.
30 See also Bawcutt, *Gavin Douglas*, p. 165.
31 Cited by W. Murison, *CHEL* II, 224.
32 'Dunbar and Lydgate', pp. 215, 218.

Select bibliography

It is possible to list here only a small proportion of the works cited in the Notes. Additional bibliographical information will be found in vol. 1 of *The New Cambridge Bibliography of English Literature*, ed. George Watson (Cambridge, 1974). For recent work on Scots literature, consult the *Annual Bibliography of Scottish Literature*, comp. James Kidd and Robert H. Carnie (supplement to *The Bibliotheck*, 1969–). See also Peter Heidtmann, 'A bibliography of Henryson, Dunbar, and Douglas, 1912–68', *Chaucer Review* V (1970), 75–82.

Aitken, A. J. 'Variation and variety in written Middle Scots', in Aitken *et al.* (eds.), *Edinburgh Studies in English and Scots*. London, 1971. pp. 177–209.
Aswell, E. Duncan. 'The role of Fortune in *The Testament of Cresseid*', *Philological Quarterly* XLVI (1967), 471–87.
Bawcutt, Priscilla. *Gavin Douglas: A Critical Study*. Edinburgh, 1976.
Bennett, H. S. *Chaucer and the Fifteenth Century*. Oxford, 1947.
Bennett, J. A. W. 'The early fame of Gavin Douglas's *Eneados*', *MLN* LXI (1946), 83–8.
'Henryson's *Testament*: a flawed masterpiece', *SLJ* I (1974), 5–16.
Berdan, J. M. *Early Tudor Poetry*. New York, 1920.
Bevington, D. M. *Tudor Drama and Politics: A Critical Approach to Topical Meaning*. Cambridge, Mass., 1968.
Blake, N. F. *Caxton and His World*. London, 1969.
'The fifteenth century reconsidered', *NM* LXXI (1970), 146–57.
Brewer, D. S. 'Images of Chaucer, 1386–1900', in Brewer (ed.), *Chaucer and Chaucerians: Critical Studies in Middle English Literature*. London, 1966. pp. 240–70.
Craigie, W. A. 'The language of the *Kingis Quair*', *Essays and Studies* XXV (1939), 22–38.
'The Scottish alliterative poems', *PBA* XXVIII (1942), 217–36.
Crosby, Ruth. 'Chaucer and the custom of oral delivery', *Speculum* XLIII (1938), 413–22.
Crowne, David K. 'A date for the composition of Henryson's *Fables*', *JEGP* LXI (1962), 588–90.

Dickinson, W. Croft. *Scotland from the Earliest Times to 1603*. London, 1961.
Donaldson, Gordon. *Scotland: James V to James VII*. Edinburgh, 1971.
Duncan, Douglas. 'Henryson's *Testament of Cresseid*', *Essays in Criticism* XI (1961), 128–35.
Durkan, John. 'The cultural background in sixteenth-century Scotland', in David McRoberts (ed.), *Essays on the Scottish Reformation, 1513–1625*. Glasgow, 1962. pp. 274–331.
Eddy, Elizabeth R. 'Sir Thopas and Sir Thomas Norny: romance parody in Chaucer and Dunbar', *RES* n.s. XXII (1971), 401–9.
Edwards, H. L. R. *Skelton: The Life and Times of an Early Tudor Poet*. London, 1949.
Fox, Denton (ed.). *Testament of Cresseid*. London and Edinburgh, 1968.
'The Scottish Chaucerians', in Brewer, *Chaucer and Chaucerians*, pp. 164–200.
'Chaucer's influence on fifteenth-century poetry', in Beryl Rowland (ed.), *Companion to Chaucer Studies*. Toronto, 1968. pp. 385–402.
'Henryson and Caxton', *JEGP* LXVII (1968), 586–93.
'Manuscripts and prints of Scots poetry in the sixteenth century', in A. J. Aitken *et al.* (eds.), *Bards and Makars*. Glasgow, 1977. pp. 156–71.
Gordon, Ian A. *John Skelton, Poet Laureate*. Melbourne and London 1943.
Harris, W. O. *Skelton's 'Magnyfycence' and the Cardinal Virtue Tradition*. Chapel Hill, 1965.
Hyde, Isabel. 'Primary sources and associations of Dunbar's aureate imagery', *MLR* LI (1956), 481–92.
Jack, R. D. S. 'Dunbar and Lydgate', *SSL* VIII (1971), 215–27.
Jamieson, I. W. A. 'The poetry of Robert Henryson: a study in the uses of source material'. Unpub. Ph.D. dissertation, Edinburgh, 1965.
'The minor poems of Robert Henryson', *SSL* IX (1971), 125–47.
Kantrowitz, J. S. *Dramatic Allegory: Lindsay's 'Ane Satyre of the Thrie Estaitis'*. Lincoln, Nebraska, 1975.
Kinneavy, G. B. 'The poet in *The Palice of Honour*', *Chaucer Review* III (1968), 280–303.
Kinsley, James. 'The medieval makars', in Kinsley (ed.), *Scottish Poetry: A Critical Survey*. London, 1955.
Lewis, C. S. *English Literature in the Sixteenth Century, excluding Drama*. Oxford, 1954.
MacDonald, Donald. 'Henryson and Chaucer: cock and fox', *Texas Studies in Language and Literature* VIII (1966), 451–61.

'Chaucer's influence on Henryson's Fables: the use of proverbs and sententiae', *Medium Aevum* XXXIX (1970), 21–7.
Mackay, M. A. 'The alliterative tradition in Middle Scots verse'. Unpub. Ph.D. dissertation. Edinburgh, 1975.
MacQueen, John. *Robert Henryson: A Study of the Major Narrative Poems.* Oxford, 1967.
'Tradition and the interpretation of the *Kingis Quair*'. *RES* n.s. XII (1961), 117–31.
'*Ane Satyre of the Thrie Estaitis*', *SSL* III (1966), 129–43.
'Some aspects of the early renaissance in Scotland', *Forum for Modern Language Studies* III (1967), 201–22.
Mill, A. J. *Medieval Plays in Scotland.* Edinburgh and London, 1927.
'The original version of Lindsay's *Satyre of the Thrie Estaitis*', *SSL* VI (1968), 67–75.
Nichols, Pierrepont H. 'William Dunbar as a Scottish Lydgatian', *PMLA* XLVI (1931), 214–24.
Payne, R. O. *The Key of Remembrance: A Study of Chaucer's Poetics.* New Haven and London, 1963.
Pearsall, Derek. *John Lydgate.* London, 1970.
'The English Chaucerians', in Brewer (ed.), *Chaucer and Chaucerians.* pp. 201–39.
Preston, John. '"Fortunys exiltree": a study of *The Kingis Quair*', *RES* n.s. VII (1956), 339–47.
Ridley, F. H. (ed.). *The 'Aeneid' of Henry Howard, Earl of Surrey.* Berkeley and Los Angeles, 1963.
'A plea for the Middle Scots', in Larry D. Benson (ed.), *The Learned and the Lewed: Studies in Chaucer and Medieval Literature.* Cambridge, Mass., 1974. pp. 175–96.
Rollins, Hyder E. 'The Troilus–Cressida story from Chaucer to Shakespeare', *PMLA* XXXII (1917), 383–429.
Scheps, W. 'Chaucerian synthesis: the art of *The Kingis Quair*', *SSL* VIII (1971), 143–65.
Spearing, A. C. *Criticism and Medieval Poetry.* Rev. edn London, 1972.
Medieval Dream-Poetry. Cambridge, 1976.
Speirs, John. *The Scots Literary Tradition: An Essay in Criticism.* 2nd edn London, 1962.
Thomson, Patricia. *Sir Thomas Wyatt and His Background.* Stanford 1964.
Wilson, F. P. *The English Drama, 1485–1585.* Oxford, 1969.
Wood, Henry. 'Chaucer's influence upon King James I of Scotland as poet', *Anglia* III (1880), 223–65.

Index

alliterative poetry: as influence on
  Scots literature 8; pervasiveness
  of in Scotland 8–9
Anglicus, Gualterus
  Romulus 10
Assembly of Gods, The 100, 239–40,
  250
Assembly of Ladies, The 248
Awntyrs of Arthure, The 8, 256

Badius Ascensius, Jodocus 170–1, 172
Bale, John
  Kynge Johan 223–4
Bannatyne MS. 14–15, 76, 87, 226,
  229
Barbour
  Bruce 10, 28, 94, 137
Barclay, Alexander 2, 7, 165, 228, 238
  Eclogues 170, 242, 259
  Ship of Fools, The 170, 242, 244–5,
  251
Bawcutt, Priscilla 105n, 117, 170, 188
Beaufort, Joan (wife of James I) 15
Bellenden, John 260
Bennett, H.S. 25
Berdan, J.M. 3
Boccaccio, Giovanni 230, 236
Boethius 10, 39, 48, 69, 124
Bower, Walter 29, 35
Boyd, Thomas (Earl of Arran) 5
Bradshaw, Henry 7, 165, 228
Brant, Sebastian
  Narrenschiff 213
Buke of the Howlat, The see Holland,
  Richard
Bullein, William 224
Byddell, John 7

Campbell, Alexander 2
Castell of Labour, The 242

Caxton, William
  Aesop 6, 101, 190
  Eneydos 6, 172, 256
  Reynard 6, 101
Charteris, Henry 225
Chapman, Walter (and Andrew Myllar)
  14, 27, 153
Chaucer, Geoffrey: 'English
  Chaucerians' 247–8; influence on
  Scots poetry 3, 16–24, 31, 227,
  230, 238, 248, 256; poems in Scots
  manuscripts 14
  Anelida and Arcite 83, 127
  Book of the Duchess, The 38, 56–7,
  59–60
  Canterbury Tales, The 26, 46, 243;
    General Prologue 95, 97–9; *Kn T*
    43, 48, 50, 146, 171, 175, 231;
    NPT 87–92, 94, 96–7; *Pr T* 96;
    Sir T 130, 134–6; *WB* Prol. and
    Tale 130–4
  Complaint of Mars, The 127
  Hous of Fame, The 22, 28, 58, 112;
    and *The Palice of Honour* 105–28
  Legend of Good Women, The 22, 63,
    113, 171–2, 175: Prologue 67, 113,
    114, 123, 146, 233–4
  Lenvoy a Scogan, 34
  Parlement of Foules, The 28, 39, 43,
    53–4, 122, 138, 234
  Troilus and Criseyde 20, 40–3, 112,
    171; and *The Testament of Cresseid*
    63–86, 90
Christis Kirk on the Grene 157, 164
Clanvowe, Thomas
  Cuckoo and the Nightingale, The 52–3,
  248
Colkelbie Sow 157–64
Complaynt of Scotlande, The 12
Contemplacioun of Synnaris, The 7

Copland, Robert 245
Copland, William 7
Court of Love, The 248, 260
Court of Sapience, The 239–40
Craig, Alexander 260
Cromwell, Thomas 195
Cursing of Sir Johine Rowlis, The 157, 164

Dante
  Divine Comedy 119
Douglas, Archibald (Earl of Angus) 4, 173
Douglas, Gavin 1, 2, 4, 137, 227, 250–1, 260
  Eneados 3, 7, 11, 13, 18, 113, 114, 169–89, 227, 230, 236–7, 250, 253–6
  Palice of Honour, The 9, 10, 11, 18, 22, 30, 47, 104–28, 130, 147, 165, 186, 234–5, 240, 253
Dunbar, William 2, 4, 245, 258, 260; and Chaucer 129–39, 227; and Lydgate 139–49, 227; and Skelton 149–58, 166, 167–8
  Ane Ballat of Our Lady 147–8
  Bewty and the Prisoneir 251
  Birth of Antichrist, The 164
  Complaint to the King 164, 258
  Dance of the Sevin Deidly Synnis, The 164
  Donald Owre 152
  Dregy 150
  Dunbar at Oxinfurde 5
  Fenyeit Freir of Tungland, The 137
  Flyting of Dunbar and Kennedie, The 137, 153–7, 259
  Goldyn Targe, The 16–17, 129, 137, 145–6, 147, 148, 149, 186, 250, 251, 252–3
  How Dumbar wes Desyrd to be Ane Freir 5
  Lament for the Makaris, The 11, 129, 140–4, 232
  Of Deming 139–40
  Remonstrance to the King 144, 158, 258
  Sir Thomas Norny 134–6
  Sowtar and Tailyouris War, The 164
  Testament of Mr Andro Kennedy 151
  Thrissil and the Rois, The 137–8, 145, 147, 234, 253
  Tretis of the Tua Mariit Wemen and the Wedo, The 130–4, 137, 155
  Tydingis fra the Sessioun 256

Dundas, George 1, 156
Durie, Bishop 260

Edwards, H. L. R. 160
Elliot, Charles 23
Eure, William 195
Everyman 198

Flower and the Leaf, The 248
Fowler, William 260
Fox, Denton 17, 18–19, 66, 72n, 79n, 136, 190
Freiris of Berwick, The 99
French poetry as influence on Scots 10
Froissart, Jean 108

Garnesche, Christopher 4, 153–6
Gascoigne, George 103
General Satyre, A 165–7
Golagros and Gawayne 10, 256
Golding, Louis 24
Googe, Barnabie 189
Gordon, I. A. 160n, 201
Gower, John
  Confessio Amantis 16, 17–18, 37, 45, 55, 77, 198
Gringore, Pierre
  Jeu du Prinz des Sotz 10, 196, 223
Gualterus Anglicus 10, 87

Harris, W. O. 201–2
Harward, Vernon 204–5
Hawes, Stephen 7, 165, 228, 238, 247, 259
  Conforte of Louers, The 242
  Example of Vertu, The 242, 252
  Passetyme of Pleasure, The 230, 243–4, 245, 249, 251
Henry VII 4, 5–6, 199, 203, 259
Henry VIII 2, 154, 195, 201–3
Henryson, Robert 2, 3, 8, 9 10, 30, 136, 227, 230, 242, 248, 253, 260
  Garmont of Gud Ladeis, The 167
  Morall Fabillis 3, 6, 9, 10, 19, 22, 23, 63, 86–103, 104, 108, 231; *Cock and Jasp* 92, 100; *Fox, Wolf, and Husbandman* 101; *Lion and Mouse* 29, 95, 102, 115, 231, 235, 253, 255; *Preiching of the Swallow* 231, 236, 238, 255; *Tod, The,* 87–93, 97, 101; *Twa Mice* 93, 190–3; *Wolf and Wether* 101
  Orpheus and Eurydice 22, 65, 72, **234**

Index

Sum Practysis of Medecyne   157
Testament of Cresseid   8, 21–2, 23, 47,
    63–86, 100, 102, 104, 130, 138,
    234, 248, 256, 257
Heywood, Thomas   15
Hickescorner   19
Hoccleve, Thomas   14, 21, 258
Holland, Richard   6, 258
Homer   120
Horace   190

Image of Ipocrysy, The   163
Inglis, Sir James   166

Jack, R. D. S.   11, 260
James I, King of Scotland   33–4, 252
    Kingis Quair, The   2, 10, 19, 20, 29,
    32–62, 63, 78, 85, 130, 136, 173,
    205, 227, 230, 231–4, 246, 248, 250
James III, King of Scotland   231
James IV, King of Scotland   134, 137,
    138
James V, King of Scotland   6, 195,
    196, 204, 205–6
James VI and I   9, 193, 260–1
Jones, Emrys   174, 178

Kennedy, Walter
    Flyting of Dunbar and Kennedie, The
    153–7
King Hart   251
Kingis Quair manuscript (MS Arch
    Selden B. 24)   14

Lancelot of the Laik   231–3
Landino, Cristoforo   172
Latin poetry as influence on Scots
    10–11
Lester, J. A.   222
Lewis, C. S.   2, 56, 99, 128, 158, 165,
    178
'Lichtoun Monicus'   157
Lindsay, David   2, 5, 228, 257–8, 260
    Buke of the Monarche, The   206–7,
    258, 260
    Complaynt   204, 206, 209
    Dreme   189, 205
    Iusting between Watsoun and Barbour   252
    Satyre of the Thrie Estaitis, Ane   8,
    10, 167, 168, 195–226
    Squyer Meldrum   11, 20
    *Supplication . . . in contemptioun of Syde
    Taillis*   167

Testament of the Papyngo, The   7, 12,
    18, 257–8
Longchamps, Nigel de
    Speculum Stultorum   10, 94
Lydgate, John: influence on English
    poetry   7, 165, 238–48, 258–9;
    influence on Scots poetry   20, 24,
    25, 26–7, 238; poems in Scots
    manuscripts   14–15
Ave Regina Celorum   147
Ballade on an Ale-Seller   139
Ballade per Antiphrasim   139
Complaint of the Black Knight, The   14,
    19, 248
Daunce Machabree   140, 142–3
Fall of Princess   230, 236, 243, 248–9
Flower of Courtesy, The   50–1, 146–7
Isopes Fabules   100–1
Pilgrimage of the Life of Man, The
    239, 240, 249, 251
Reson and Sensuallyte   145, 239, 240
Testament   140, 146
Timor Mortis Conturbat Me   140–3
Troy Book   148, 169
Wikked Tunge Wille Sey Amys, A   139

McDiarmid, Matthew   34n, 56, 232
Mackenzie, A. M.   197
MacQueen, John   23, 44, 59, 60n,
    66n, 69, 71, 191, 204, 236
Major, John   29, 315
Mankind   198–9, 209
Maphaeus Vegius   236
Margaret Tudor (wife of James IV)
    4, 15, 137, 173
Mary Tudor   224
Mason, H. A.   24
Maxwell, Robert   16
Medwall, Henry
    Nature   199, 200, 207, 209, 210
Metham, John   147
Mill, A. J.   195n, 196, 204, 206, 212,
    215
Mirror for Magistrates, The   189, 248–9
Molinet, Jean   108
Montgomerie, Alexander   193, 260
morality plays (English)   197–9, 209

Nevill, William   7, 228
    Castell of Pleasure, The   242
Norton-Smith, J.   47n, 98

Odo of Cheriton   87

Ogilvie, Walter 6
'O god that in tyme all thingis did begin' (Bannatyne CXXVIII) 167
'O man transformit and vnnaturall' (Weddirburne?) 76–8
Ovid 120

Paniter, David 16
Paston letters 5
Pearl 37, 55
Pearsall, Derek 27, 36, 238, 243
Peblis to the Play 164, 252
Phaer, Thomas 172, 189
Piers Plowman 9, 45, 133–4, 198
Pinkerton, John 99
Pitscottie, Lindesay of 30, 205
Puttenham, George 188

Quare of Jelusy, The 20

Ramsay, R. L. 201, 213, 221
Respublica 224–5
Ridley, F. H. 23, 86, 173, 178
Rolland, John
 Court of Venus, The 260
 Seven Sages, The 260
Roman de la Rose 24, 105, 130, 150
Roman de Renart 87
Roslin Chapel 142

Sackville, Thomas 189
St Clair, Henry, Lord 30, 35, 116, 169, 230
Saint-Gelais, Octavien 108
Schirmer, W. F. 26–7
Scott, Alexander 193, 252
Selden, John 16
Skeat, W. W. 36, 248
Skelton, John: and Dunbar 148–57, 165, 167–8; and Lydgate 165; the 'Skeltonic' 3, 160–4, 247
 Against Dundas 1, 156–7
 Against the Scottes 1–2, 152
 Bowge of Courte, The 149–50, 209
 Colyn Cloute 152, 163, 201
 Elynour Rummyng 158–64
 Garlande of Laurell, The 165, 202
 Magnyfycence 196–223
 On Tyme 167

Phyllyp Sparowe 148, 150, 163
Poems against Garnesche 153–6, 259
Speke, Parrot 152, 166–7, 201
Why Come Ye Nat to Courte? 152, 163
Smith, G. Gregory 31–2
Smith, Janet M. 12
Smith, Richard 102–3
Spearing, A. C. 61, 71
Spektakle of Luf 85
Stewart, William 260
Surrey, Henry Howard, Earl of 1–2, 229; use of Douglas's *Eneados* 172–89, 227
Surrey, Thomas Howard, Earl of 201–2

Tale of Beryn, The 99
Tales of the Five Beasts 10
 The Unicorn's Tale 22, 94–9
Thomson, Patricia 190, 193
Thynne, William 7, 63
Tottel, Richard 173, 230, 249, 251
Turnament of Tottenham, The 252
Twyne, Thomas 172, 189

Vaux, Thomas 251
Vergil, Polydore 4
Vinsauf, Geoffroi de 39, 91
Virgil
 Aeneid, translated by Douglas and Surrey 169–89

Wallace 11, 175
Warton, Thomas 249–50
Webbe, William 62, 229
Wilson, F. P. 224
Wisdom 210
Wolsey, Thomas 4, 152, 201, 202, 203
Wood, Anthony à 259
Wood Henry 37
Wood, H. Harvey 93
Wyatt, Thomas 2, 15, 173, 188, 229
 My mothers maydes (and Henryson's *Twa Mice*) 189–93
Wyntoun, Andrew of 10, 137

Youth 198

LIBRARY OF DAVIDSON COLLEGE

Mixing in Convective Supernova

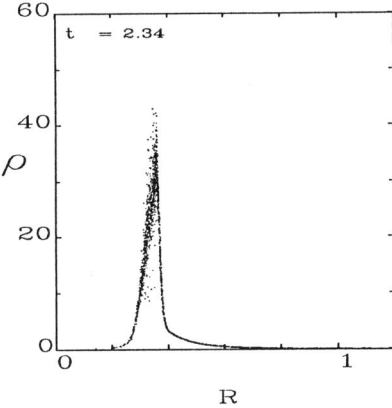

Fig.1. The projected radial density profile of *"blast wave solution"*. As in 1-D calculation, the topology of the expansion is not a shell but a sphere with the limb enhanced by shock front.

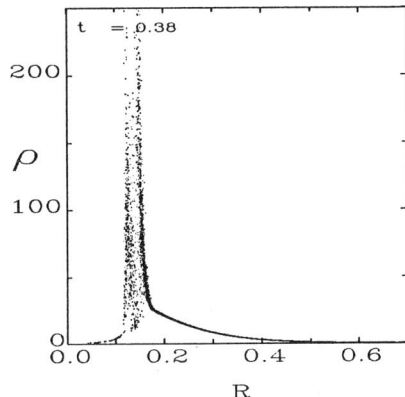

Fig.2. The radial density profile shows two discontinuity in 3-D explosion of *"bubble solution"*. The shock front and the contact discontinuity are the characteristic of Sedov solution in steep density gradient.

causes the effective mixing in the shell. The typical unstable wavelength, in the nonlinear stage, is determined by the thickness of the spherical shell as in Fig 4. The mixing motion in the nonlinear stage is resolved with $N = 10^6$ particles. The ejected gas, plotted with a certain density level, seems very clumpy. While, due to the phase cancellation of complicated fragments, there is no dominant contribution to the degree of polarization. The initial random fluctuations are introduced as a numerical noise ($\lesssim 1\%$) when we construct the 3-D equilibrium

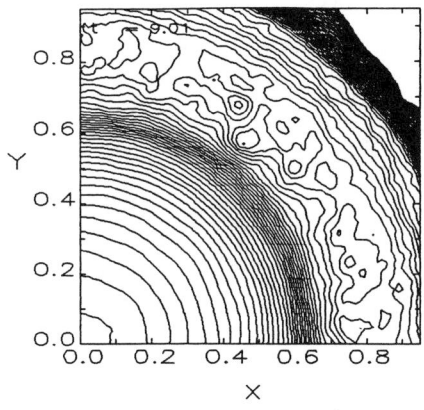

Fig.3. The density contour of *"blast wave solution"*. Only the narrow region of shocked gas is unstable as indicated by linear stability analysis.

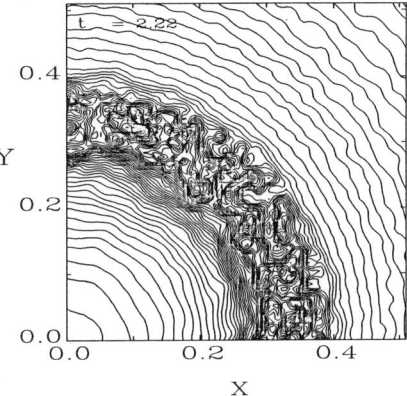

Fig.4. The density contour of *"bubble solution"* in contour level of 10% spacing. The convective motion in the whole shell makes the clumpy structure.

spheres by relaxation. However, we found that the fluctuation of the hot bubble at the initial is more important than the fluctuation in the outer envelope. In this way, the fragmentation and the mixing of the ejecta is reconfirmed.

We have to be careful to discuss Rayleigh–Taylor instability of compressible gas. It is different from the ordinary growth of density fluctuations. Since the boundary of density jump is disturbed by instability, focusing on the density at a certain position, the fluctuation appears as if there is no stage of linear growth. The buoyancy of hot blob makes this nonlinear growth possible, which is inhibited in 1-D simulations as a shell crossing of fluid element. In 3-D spaces, it means the existence of interior motion of hot blobs in the shocked shell. This means the heavy elements which locate at the center of progenitor can appear at the surface of supernova most effectively. The mixing motion of gas element is most effective in the wholly convective case. We can interpret this interchange motion as a result of convection.

Our 3-D SPH makes the fluid motion clear: the mixing is not the result of fragmentation but the fragmentation is the result of wholly convective motion. The evolutions of off-central point explosions are almost spherically symmetric as a whole, but they are found to be convective and to grow non-spherical structures on the shell. The inner hot blobs creep out the outer mass shell. Our former results should be distinguished from the relatively stable *"blast wave solutions"*. To investigate the mixing degree, 3-D Lagrange method is preferable and the Euler methods need much efforts to treat multi-fluids system and difficulty to get void structure. The advantage of our SPH is that most of particles are used to resolve this interesting discontinuous region.

REFERENCES

Arnett, D., Fryxell, B.A., and Müller, E., 1989, *Asrtrophys. J. Lett.*, in press.
Barret, P., 1987, *ESO Workshop on SN1987A (ed. I.J.Danziger)*, 174.
Benz, W., Thielemnn, F.K., 1989, *Asrtrophys. J. Lett.*, in press.
Erickson, E.F., Haas, M.R., Colgan, S.W.J., Lord, S.D., Burton, M.G., Wolf, J., Hollenbach, D.J., and Werner, M., 1988, *Asrtrophys. J. Lett.*, **330**, L39.
Itoh, M., Kumagai, S., Shigeyama, T., Nomoto, K., and Nishimura, J., 1987, *Nature*, **330**, 233.
Müller, E., Hillebrandt, W., Orio, M., Höflich, P., Mönchmeyer, R., and Fryxell, B.A., 1989, *Astr. Astrophys.*, in press.
Nagasawa, M., Nakamura, T., and Miyama, S.M., 1988, *Publ. Astron. Soc. Japan*, **40**, 691.

Mixing in SN 1987A
Willy Benz & F. C. Thielemann

1. Introduction

Many supernova remnants (like e.g. Cas A, Kirshner and Chevalier 1977) show evidence that some form of mixing has to take place in the ejecta. While there existed some theoretical indications that this mixing is due to instabilities associated with the propagation of a shock wave (e.g. Falk and Arnett 1973, Gull 1973, Chevalier and Klein 1978) it has usually been related to the expansion into the interstellar medium. SN1987A now showed clearly that mixing has to take place already during the supernova explosion itself (or possibly very shortly thereafter). Several independent observations lead to such a conclusion: the early appearance of x-rays and gamma-rays, the spread of expansion velocities seen in line widths of infrared observations and in the gamma ray lines of ^{56}Co, and the details of the rise of the light curve after the initial adiabatic decline and a flattened rather than a sharp maximum before the exponential decline of ^{56}Co.

This extensive mixing must have resulted from hydrodynamic instabilities taking place within the first two or three weeks after the explosion. Two major driving mechanisms were suggested: 1. Rayleigh-Taylor instabilities associated with the additional expansion of the central nickel bubble triggered by the energy release from the radioactive decay of ^{56}Ni and ^{56}Co (Arnett 1988, Woosley 1988). 2. Instabilities associated with the propagation of the shock through the star itself, dependent on the detailed internal structure of the progenitor (Chevalier 1976) or associated with the reverse shock originating at the inner edge of the hydrogen envelope (Shigeyama, Nomoto, Hashimoto 1988). Both driving mechanism are discussed.

2. The Ni-Bubble

We followed the homologous expansion phase of SN1987A from 1.1 days to 160 days after the explosion by modelling the inner 6M$_\odot$ numerically with a 3D Smooth Particle Hydrodynamics code. The initial conditions were taken from Woosley (1988) on which small (2-4%) random density perturbations were superimposed. 0.07 M$_\odot$ of ^{56}Ni were deposited in the center and a nuclear network for the Ni-decay chain added to the code as in Benz, Hills, and Thielemann (1989). Various numbers of particles were used, ranging from 10 000 for the whole sphere to 40 000 in one octant.

After 160 days only small density fluctuations (clumping) of less than a factor 2 (peak to peak) emerged. Fig. 1 shows density contours in a 2D slice which contains the center of the explosion. Contrary to prior suggestions the Ni-Co-decay energy, when superimposed onto a strong spherical expansion, is not sufficient to result in large

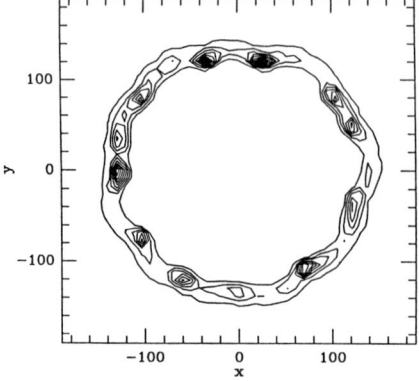

Fig. 1: Isodensity contours after 160 days. The density contrast is of about a factor 2 peak to peak.

enough density inversions which can cause Rayleigh-Taylor instabilities and mixing within the first three weeks.

This picture might change if, as it turns out to be the case, strong instabilities are already associated with the propagation of the blast wave *inside* the star itself resulting in a strongly inhomogeneous abundance and density distribution, even before Ni-decay. The additional energy release by the radioactive decay of the nickel can in this case quite conceivably have more dramatic consequences. We address this question in the following sections.

3. 3D Calculations of Blast Wave Propagation

Nagasawa *et al.* (1988) followed the propagation of a supernova blast wave by depositing the appropriate amount of energy in the center of a n=3 polytrope of $10M_\odot$. Their simulations, done with a 3D SPH code, resulted in rapid and severe clumping (density fluctuations of 400%) regardless of the explosion energy. Since the same calculations done by Müller *et al.* (1989) and by Clancy and Bowers (this volume), but using classical Eulerian finite-difference methods, did not result in any major clumping or instabilities (density fluctuations less than 15-20%), it became clear that the stability of blast waves propagating in even simple density distribution is by far not definitively established.

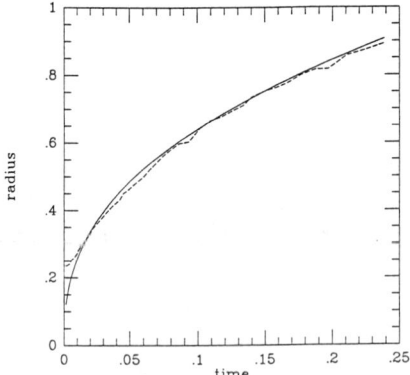

Fig. 2: Location of the shock in a blast wave propagating in a constant density medium.
solid line : exact
dashed line : numerical

In order to establish that SPH is able to accurately model the propagation of spherical blast waves, we modelled a central explosion in a constant density medium.

Constant, as well as simple power law, density distributions are ideal testing grounds for numerical calculations as the analytical solutions are available (Sedov 1959). In Fig. 2 we plot the location of the shock as a function of time for both the analytical and numerical solution in the case of a strong explosion in a constant density medium. Notice that for this case, the analytical solution is completely determined, no scaling is therefore necessary. Clearly, the agreement between both (once the initial conditions are forgotten) is very good.

As a second test we have run the same polytrope explosion simulation as Nagasawa *et al.* (1988), using from 10000 particles for the whole star up to 40000 particles in one octant only. These simulations did not show the extensive clumping and mixing claimed by Nagasawa *et al.* (1988) but rather confirm the results obtained by the Eulerian finite-difference methods. The 2% density perturbations that were introduced in the initial configuration resulted indeed in 15-20% density fluctuations at the end of our simulation (see Fig. 3). Extensive clumping might, however, be obtained when using highly perturbed initial conditions or unrealistic explosion energy deposition schemes.

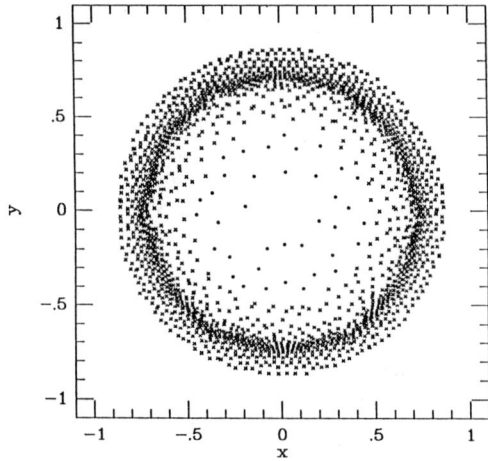

Fig. 3: Blast wave in a n=3 polytrope. Shown are the particles in a small slice through the central plane.

The search for instabilities in SN1987A has to be performed with a realistic supernova progenitor model, rather than a polytrope. Arnett, Fryxell, and Müller (1989) could indeed show in 2 and 3D numerical simulations that instabilities were growing in the high density shell left behind the shock. They identified the finger-like structures obtained with a classical Rayleigh-Taylor instability. Ebisuzaki, Shigeyama, and Nomoto (1989) performed a linear stability analysis of a spherical explosion using the usual Rayleigh-Taylor criterion (see section 4) and were able to show that essentially the mass zones between the metal-He and He-H interfaces are unstable.

4. Stability Analysis

Chandrasekhar (1961) discussed the stability of an initially static, incompressible fluid in a gravitational field. In the case of supernova explosions, gravity is negligible and pressure gradients provide the required relative acceleration. The criterion for a Rayleigh-Taylor instability to develop in this case can be written as

$$\frac{\mathcal{R}}{\mathcal{P}} < 0, \qquad (1)$$

where $\mathcal{P} = \frac{1}{P}\frac{\partial P}{\partial z}$ and $\mathcal{R} = \frac{1}{\rho}\frac{\partial \rho}{\partial z}$ are the reciprocals of the pressure and density scale heights, respectively. As emphasized by Bandiera (1984) and Benz and Thielemann (1989) a local linear stability analysis show that for a compressible fluid instabilities will develop and grow exponentially provided the Scharzschild criterion is met

$$\frac{\mathcal{R}}{\mathcal{P}} < \frac{1}{\gamma}, \qquad (2)$$

where γ is the adiabatic index of the gas. Comparing equations (1) and (2), it appears that the incompressible Rayleigh-Taylor criterion is more stringent than the actual stability criterion for a compressible fluid. Consequently for a compressible fluid, instabilities, i.e. convective motions, will set in even if condition (1) is not satisfied. Taking the limit $\gamma \longrightarrow \infty$ in (2), that is assuming incompressibility, we indeed recover the classical criterion (1). We conclude that applying the Rayleigh-Taylor criterion (1) to determine the stability of compressible fluid flows can be misleading since instabilities will occur for situations predicted to be stable. Stability of compressible fluids should be checked using (2). Whether these instabilities are called Rayleigh-Taylor or convection, is only of a semantic interest, but to keep with astronomical traditions, we probably should call them convective instabilities.

We have performed explosion simulations with a 1D Lagrangian hydrodynamics code, using the stellar model for the progenitor of SN1987A with a $10M_\odot$ H-envelope by Nomoto *et al.* (1988). We deposited 10^{51} erg in the center and followed the blast wave propagation through the entire star. For simplicity we adopted a polytropic equation of state with $\gamma = \frac{4}{3}$ and neglected radiation transport over the time scale considered. When zones were found unstable, according to (1) or (2) an estimated time integrated growth rate was computed (Benz and Thielemann 1989). The results are presented in Fig. 4 against the Lagrangian mass coordinate of ejected mass (excluding the $1.6M_\odot$ neutron star - Thielemann, Hashimoto, Nomoto 1990) for a time corresponding to one hour after the explosion. The dotted curve gives the integrated Rayleigh-Taylor growth rate, whereas the solid line corresponds to the integrated convective instability growth rate. Notice the large spikes at the metal-He and He-H interfaces. When using instability criterion (2) rather than (1), the growth of the perturbations in the center is substantially larger although still not as large as at the metal-He interface, and the barrier at $3M_\odot$ is partially removed. Therefore convective motions will lead to substantial mixing inside the inner core, and even into the hydrogen envelope but with a significantly smaller growth rate. This makes it possible for some material (most probably only a small fraction) originating from the inner core to be convected into the envelope and conversely, for some hydrogen from the envelope to be transported into the core.

Further improvements in understanding the quantitative extend of the mixing and the nonlinear behavior of the instabilities have to come from a global stability analysis including boundaries (Goodman 1989) and multi-dimensional, high-resolution numerical simulations of realistic stellar explosions similar to the ones by Müller *et al.* (1989) and Arnett, Fryxell and Müller (1989). We are currently investigating these questions with a 3D Smooth Particle (SPH) code.

This research was supported in part by NASA grant NGR 22-007-272, NSF grant 86-12647 and the National Center for Supercomputer applications at the University of Illinois (AST 890009N). One of us (W.B.) also acknowledges partial support from

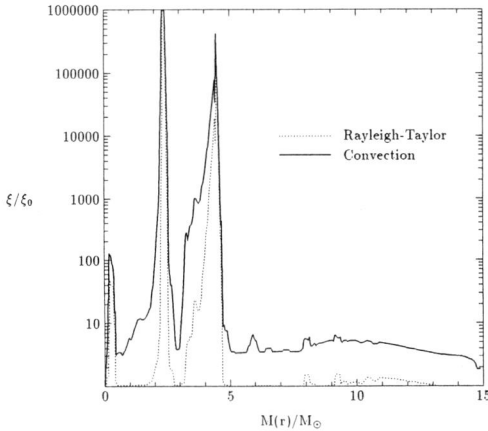

Fig. 4: Integrated growth rate for the convective (solid line) and Rayleigh-Taylor (dashed line) instabilities

the Swiss National Science Foundation and from the Milton Fund.

References

Arnett, W.D. 1988, *Ap. J.* **331**, 377

Arnett, W.D., Fryxell, B., Müller, E. 1989, *Ap. J. Lett.* **341**, L63

Bandiera, R. 1984 *Astron. Astrophys.* **139**, 368

Benz, W., Hills, J. G., and Thielemann, F.-K., 1989, *Ap. J.* **342**, 986

Chandrasekhar, S. 1961, *Hydrodynamic and Hydromagnetic Stability*, (Dover, New York)

Chevalier, R.A. 1976, *Ap. J.*, **207**, 872

Chevalier, R.A., Klein, R.I. 1978, *Ap. J.*, **219**, 994

Ebisuzaki, T., Shigeyama, T., Nomoto, K. 1989, *Ap. J. Lett.*, in press

Falk, S.W., Arnett, W.D. 1973, *Ap. J. Lett* **180**, L65

Goodman, J. 1989, preprint

Gull, S.F. 1973, *M.N.R.A.S.* **161**, 47

Kirshner, R.P., Chevalier 1977, *Ap. J.* **218**, 142

Müller, E., Hillebrandt, W., Orio, M., Höflich, P., Mönchmeyer, R. 1989, *Astron. Astrophys.*, **220**, 167

Nagasawa, M., Nakamura, T., Miyama, S. 1988, *Publ. Astron. Soc. Japan* **40**, 691

Nomoto, K., Hashimoto, M., Shigeyama, T., Kumagai, S. 1988, *Proc. Astron. Soc. Australia* **7**, 490

Sedov, L.I. 1959, *Similarity and Dimensional Methods in Mechanics* (Academic Press, New York)

Shigeyama, T., Nomoto, K., Hashimoto, M. 1988, *Astron. Astrophys.* **196**, 141

Thielemann, F.-K., Hashimoto, M., Nomoto, K. 1989, *Ap. J.* **348**, in press

Woosley, S.E. 1988, *Ap. J.* **330**, 218

Rayleigh-Taylor Instability in Supernova 1987A: Dependence on the Presupernova Model

T. Ebisuzaki, T. Shigeyama, & K. Nomoto

1. Rayleigh-Taylor Instability

The Rayleigh - Taylor instability is the most probable mechanism to mix the ejecta of SN 1987A as suggested from observations. Although the gravity is negligible in the explosion, acceleration of the matter acts as an effective gravity and can be responsible for the Rayleigh - Taylor instability. The growth rate, $G_{\rm RT}$, of this instability is estimated as

$$G_{\rm RT} = \sqrt{-\frac{\rho_+ - \rho_-}{\rho_+ + \rho_-}\frac{1}{\rho}\frac{dP}{dr}k}, \qquad (1)$$

where k is the wave number of the perturbation and ρ_+ and ρ_- are the densities in the upper and lower layers. Equation (1) shows that the layer is Rayleigh - Taylor unstable when $(dP/dr)(d\rho/dr) < 0$.

Ebisuzaki, Shigeyama, and Nomoto [1; hereafter ESN] performed a linear stability analysis of the explosion using the realistic hydrodynamical model 14E1 [2, 3], where the ejected masses of the hydrogen-depleted core and the hydrogen-rich envelope are 4.4 $M_\odot$ and 10.2 $M_\odot$, respectively, and the kinetic energy of explosion is 1×10^{44} J. The model 14E1 with mixing of hydrogen and ^{56}Co well reproduces the light curves in the optical/infrared, X-ray, and gamma-ray regions [4, 5].

Figure 1 shows the evolution of the pressure profile of the exploding star. The dashed lines indicate the H/He interface and He/Metal interface. Before the explosion, pressure gradient is negative being balanced with gravitational attraction (stage 0). After the blast shock passed, the layer expands to decrease the pressure rapidly. When the blast shock is propagating through the hydrogen-rich envelope with a much less steep pressure gradient, an inwardly propagating reverse shock (R) forms (stages 2 and 3). The layer between the blast wave (B) and the reverse shock (R) is decelerated and thus has a positive pressure gradient. When the blast shock reaches the surface layer with a steep pressure gradient, an inward-moving rarefaction wave forms and produces a negative pressure gradient that accelerates the matter outward (stage 5). As a result of this complicated pressure evolution, the H/He interface is first accelerated, then decelerated, and finally accelerated again; i.e., the pressure gradient changes its sign twice. The He/Metal interface also experiences similar acceleration and deceleration.

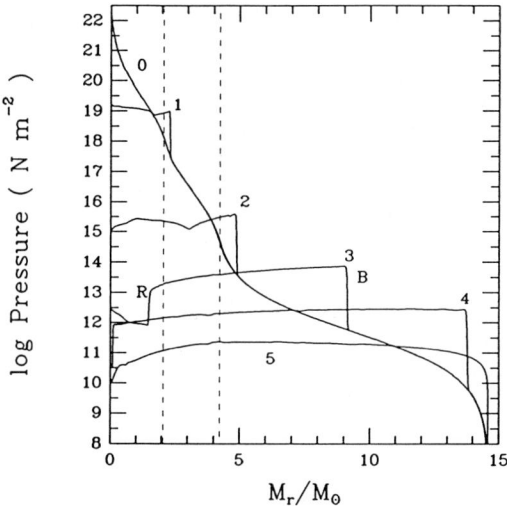

Figure 1: Change in the pressure profile in the ejecta of model 14E1. Stage numbers correspond to (0) $t = 0$, (1) 9.0 s, (2) 166 s, (3) 1060 s, (4) 3330 s, and (5) 6710 s after the explosion. The two dashed lines indicate the H/He and He/Metal interfaces. The letters B and R indicate the positions of the blast shock and the reverse shock, respectively. The pressure gradient is positive between the blast and reverse shocks.

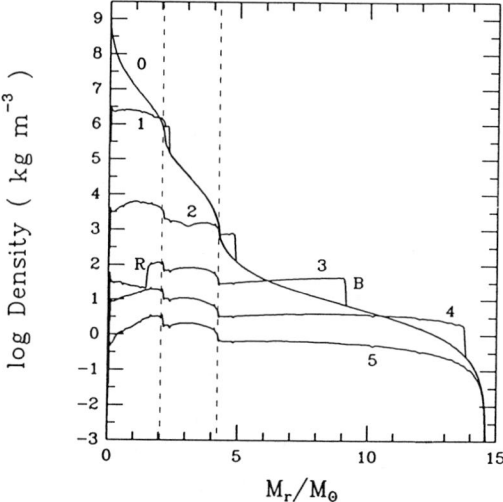

Figure 2: The same as Figure 1 but for the change in the density profiles. The density steeply decreases outward at the H/He and He/Metal interfaces (dashed lines).

Figure 2 shows the time evolution of the density profile. Near the H/He and the He/Metal interfaces (dashed lines), the density steeply decreases with radius because of the changes in the mean molecular weight, μ, and the specific entropy, s. Such distributions of μ and s originate from the presupernova model. During the hydrodynamical stages of explosion, the sign of the gradients of μ and s and, hence, of density near the composition interfaces do not change.

Figures 1 and 2 clearly show that pressure gradient is positive during the deceleration phase (stages 2 - 4 for the H/He interface), while the density gradient remain negative near the H/He and He/Metal interfaces. These layers are Rayleigh - Taylor unstable.

The distribution of the amplification factor ζ/ζ_0 at $t = 18,000$ s is plotted against M_r in Figure 3 for $l = 20$ (solid curve). Here the amplification factor is given as

$$\zeta/\zeta_0 = \exp(\int_0^t \mathrm{Re}(G_{\mathrm{RT}})dt') \qquad (2)$$

and well exceeds 100 near the H/He interface.

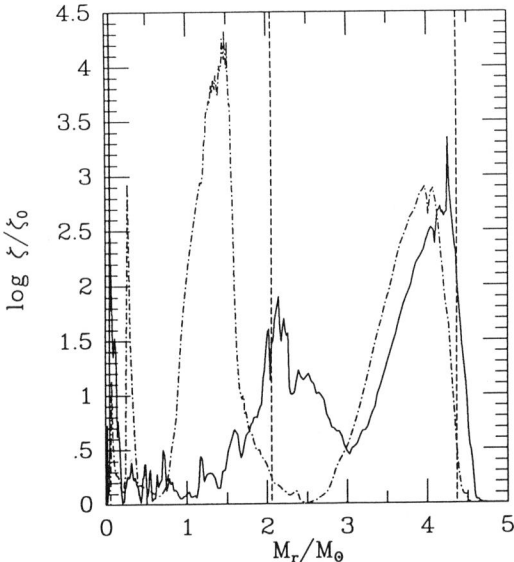

Figure 3: Amplification factor (ζ/ζ_0) at $t = 18,000$ s is plotted against mass (M_r). The H/He and He/Metal interfaces are Rayleigh - Taylor unstable and the amplification factors are well above 100 for both $l = 10$ and 20.

2. Dependence on the Presupernova Structure

Arnett, Fryxell, and Müller [6; hereafter AFM] performed two-dimensional simulations of the explosion for the 15 $M_\odot$ progenitor model of SN 1987A (Arnett [7]). They found a pronounced nonlinear growth of the Raleigh - Taylor instability around the He/Metal interface, which is basically in agreement with the linear stability analysis. However, the instability around the H/He interface is *not* significant, which is *not* consistent with the above linear analysis.

Hachisu *et al.* [8] have also carried out a two-dimensional simulation for the model 14E1 and found that the instability develops more rapidly at the H/He interface than at the He/Metal interface. Their results are consistent with ESN's linear analysis.

The difference between the two models can be seen from linear stability analysis for the Arnett's [7] progenitor model with the mass cut at $M_r = 0$. The amplification of the perturbation (Eq. 2) is larger at the He/Metal interface than at the H/He interface as shown by the dash-dotted curve in Fig. 3.

This difference may stem from the difference in i) the initial models and ii) the assumed mass cut that divides the neutron star and the ejecta:

i) Compared with model 14E1 which has a 6 $M_\odot$ helium core [9], Arnett's (1987) 15 $M_\odot$ model has a smaller helium core (4 $M_\odot$) that is more centrally concentrated; the density gradient is much steeper around $M_r = 1.5 M_\odot$, i.e., the density changes by a factor of ~ 1000 over the narrow region from the He/Metal interface to the outer part of the central core.

ii) AFM [6] deposited energy at the center of the progenitor model, i.e., the mass cut is $M_r \sim 0$ neglecting the neutron star residue. After the shock passage, only the central region suffers from rarefaction and the density gradient is much steeper around $M_r = 1.5 M_\odot$ than in the model that has a mass cut around $M_r \sim 1.2 M_\odot$ (see Fig. 6 of Arnett [7]). (The mass cut for 14E1 is 1.6 $M_\odot$.)

These differences yield much larger density contrast at the He/Metal interface in Arnett's model than 14E1. Equation (1) gives a higher growth rate for a larger density contrast, if k and the pressure gradient is fixed.

As can be seen in the above example, the development of the Rayleigh - Taylor instability in the supernova explosion is quite sensitive to the density structure of the progenitor. Since ^{56}Ni is synthesized near the mass cut, the above differences could yield a significant difference in the mixing process of ^{56}Ni. Further systematic studies are necessary to figure out how the Rayleigh - Taylor instability depends on the structure of the progenitor model.

REFERENCES

(1) Ebisuzaki, T., Shigeyama, T., and Nomoto, K. 1989, *Ap. J. (Letters)* , in press (ESN).
(2) Shigeyama, T. 1989, Ph.D. Thesis, University of Tokyo.
(3) Shigeyama, T., and Nomoto, K. 1989 *Ap. J.,* submitted.
(4) Nomoto, K., Shigeyama, T., and Kumagai, S. 1989, in *Particle Astrophysics* , ed. E.B. Norman (Singapore: World Scientific), in press.
(5) Nomoto, K., Shigeyama, T., and Kumagai, S. 1989 in this volume.
(6) Arnett, D., Fryxell, B. and Müller, E. 1989, *Ap. J. (Letters)* , **341** , L63 (AFM).
(7) Arnett, D., 1987, *Ap. J.* , **319** , 136.
(8) Hachisu, I, Matsuda, T., Nomoto, K. and Shigeyama, T. 1989, *Ap. J. (Letters)* , submitted.
(9) Nomoto, K., Hashimoto, M. 1988, Physics Report, **163,** 13.

SECTION V
X-RAYS AND γ-RAYS FROM SN 1987A

SMM γ–Ray Observations of SN 1987A
Mark D. Leising & Gerald H. Share

Supernovae have long been considered important sites of nucleosynthesis of many nuclides found in nature, including some thought to be ejected in the form of radioactive parents. These unstable progenitors can reveal themselves through their power input to the ejecta [1], or more directly through their emission of signature γ-ray line photons [2]. Supernova 1987A has yielded an awesome quantity of data which has for the most part confirmed theories of Type II supernovae, as is demonstrated by many articles in these Proceedings. Among the important observations was the the precise agreement between the decline of the "bolometric" light curve and the 113 day exponential decay of ^{56}Co [3,4], implying the production of its radioactive parent ^{56}Ni by the explosion. The ^{56}Co nucleus was further implicated by observations of large abundances of the element cobalt in infrared lines [5,6]. The direct observation of γ-ray lines from ^{56}Co decay (e.g., [7]) laid to rest any doubts about its production in the explosion. It is the detection of these γ-ray lines by the γ-ray spectrometer (GRS) on the Solar Maximum Mission (SMM) satellite we discuss here. We also describe how the time evolution of the fluxes in these lines can be used to probe the distribution of the ^{56}Co within the ejecta. These γ-ray light curves show that the radioactivity is found over a large range of optical depths in the ejected matter, a conclusion consistent with many other observations discussed in this volume.

I. Data Analysis   SMM was launched in February 1980 to observe the Sun and has operated for most of the time since then. The GRS [8] has been used successfully to detect cosmic γ-ray emission [9]. Here we use data accumulated by the GRS since 1984. This analysis is described in detail elsewhere [10]. Basically, each one-minute spectrum accumulated with the Large Magellanic Cloud (LMC) visible to the detector is corrected by subtracting spectra taken under similar background conditions before 1987, and by also subtracting similarly corrected spectra accumulated during the same orbit but with the LMC occulted by the Earth. These difference spectra are then summed over periods of about 36 days. (For about 17 days out of each 53 day orbital precession period, there is little or no time when the Earth blocks the LMC.) Each such summed spectrum is then fit over two energy intervals, 0.7 to 1.5 MeV, and 2.3 to 3.6 MeV, with models of smooth continua and gaussian peaks. The peak positions were chosen at energies of instrument calibration source lines and at the energies of four lines of ^{56}Co decay, namely 0.847, 1.238, 2.599, and 3.250 MeV (the last is a composite of three lines).

The resulting best-fit intensities of these four lines are shown versus time in Fig. 1. For each line the intensities before the outburst of SN 1987A (day 2611) are consistent with zero counts. All four show positive excesses after July 1987. Figure 2 shows the sum of all spectra from August 1987 through May 1988, in which at least four lines from ^{56}Co

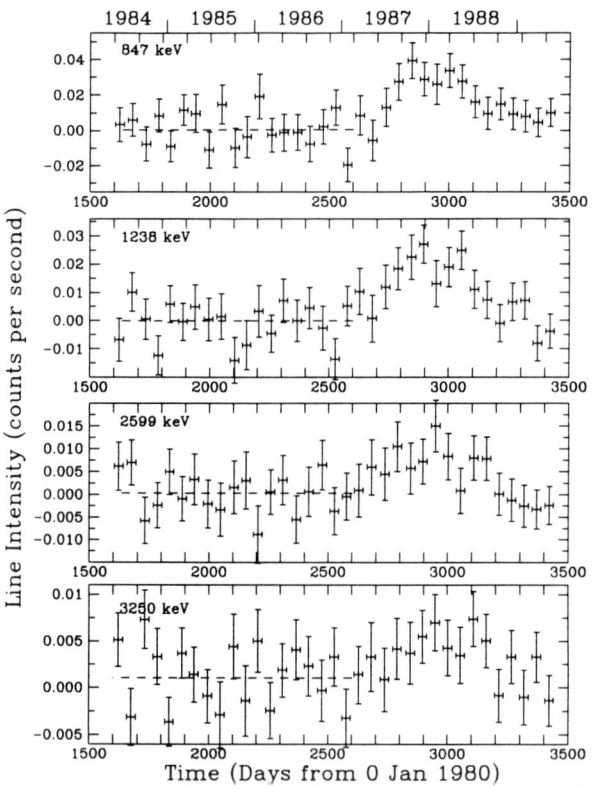

Figure 1. The count rates in each of four ^{56}Co lines versus time. The dashed lines are the mean counts in each line before February 1987. Each mean is consistent with zero. Errors are statistical only.

decay are apparent. Other features of this spectrum are from known background or celestial sources. Figure 3 shows the measured fluxes in the four ^{56}Co decay lines for the time after the explosion of SN 1987A. Generally the 0.847 and 1.238 MeV fluxes are consistent with those measured by balloon experiments [11-15]. The results presented here are also consistent with earlier analyses of some of the same data [7,16].

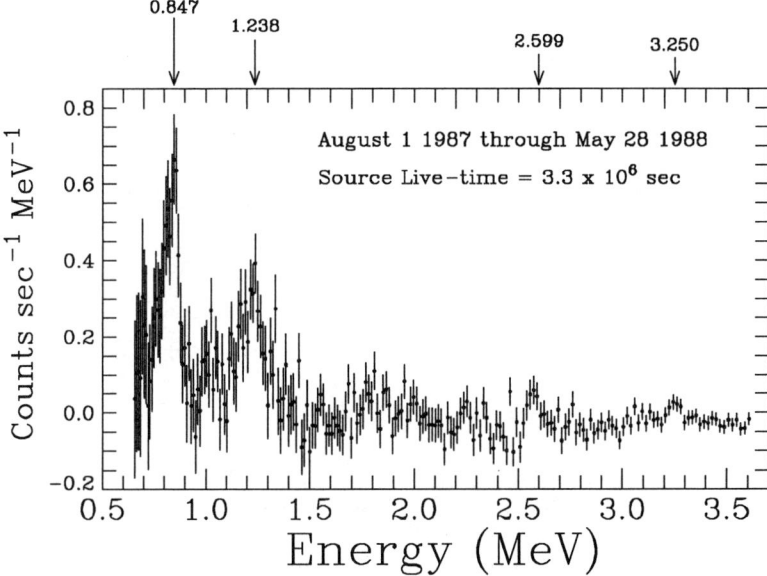

Figure 2. The mean of all SN 1987A spectra from August 1987 through May 1988. This is the time over which significant fluxes are found in the lines.

II. Discussion The γ-ray light curves can be understood in terms of a simple description of a supernova envelope. The escaping fluxes depend only on the amount of ^{56}Ni initially produced and the column depth of scatterers between the ^{56}Co and the observer at a given time. Conventional descriptions of supernova ejecta, with the ^{56}Co located entirely at the inner edge, cannot fit the γ-ray fluxes, or the shape of the peak of the optical light curve [17-19]. The γ-ray light curves can be satisfactorily described only by models where the ^{56}Co is distributed over a large range of optical depths (e.g., [10,20]), but given the precision of the γ-ray measurements, many different such models can fit the data. For example, it was shown that two different distributions of ^{56}Co mass versus optical depth gave equally good fits to the γ-line fluxes [10]. One model had two "spikes" in the ^{56}Co mass distribution, with ~5% of the ^{56}Co at very low optical depth and ~95% located at large depth as in the pre-SN 1987A picture. Another successful model utilized a continuous distribution of ^{56}Co in optical depth.

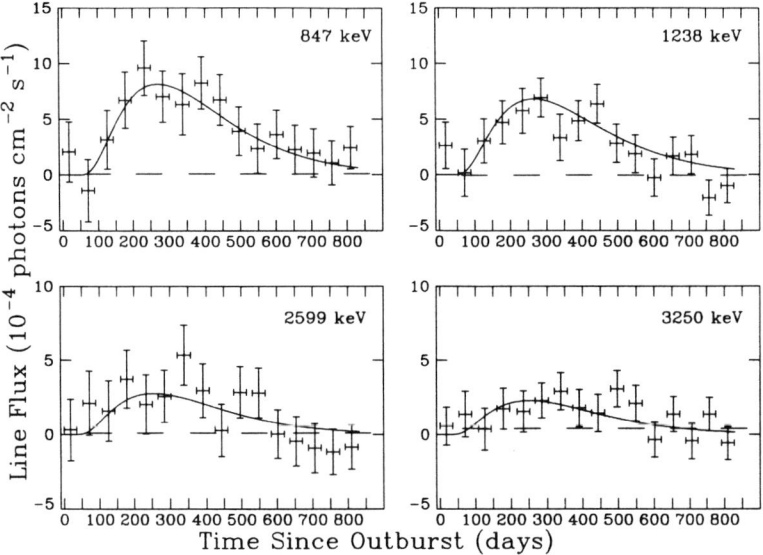

Figure 3. The measured fluxes in four ^{56}Co lines versus time since the explosion (crosses) and the flux in each line from the best fit of equation (1) (solid lines). For reference, the mean measured fluxes before the explosion are also shown (dashed lines).

Here we describe the latter model in some detail. Consider the case where the emitting nuclei are distributed over a region of the inner ejecta of finite thickness (e.g., homogeneous "mixing" of the ^{56}Co). The outer envelope, overlying the mixed region, will exponentially attenuate the escaping γ-rays, and its thickness will decrease as 1/time^2. Because of the finite optical thickness of the inner zone, the outer, unmixed, zone will effectively "see" only the outermost unit optical depth of the mixed region. The fraction of the mass (and therefore number of ^{56}Co nuclei) within this depth will increase with time, approximately proportional to time^2 (this approximation becomes less good at later times). Obviously the fraction visible will increase only until all of the inner zone is thin. Thus the emerging luminosity in a line of energy E is

$$L_E(t) = b_E L_o (e^{-t/\tau_{Co}} - e^{-t/\tau_{Ni}}) e^{-\frac{\sigma_E}{\sigma_{847}}(t_{o,847}^2 / t^2)}$$
$$\times \frac{\sigma_{847}}{\sigma_E} (t^2 / t_{i,847}^2) \qquad \text{for } t < t_{i,847} , \tag{1}$$

where b_E is the branching ratio of the line, L_o is the total (input) 847 keV line intensity at t=0, τ_{Co}=113 days, τ_{Ni}=8.8 days, the σ's are the total Klein-Nishina scattering cross-sections, $t_{o,847}$ is the time at which the escape of 847 keV photons through the outer shell is 1/e of the input luminosity (i.e., when the effective optical depth of the unmixed shell at 847 keV is unity) and $t_{i,847}$ is the time when the inner, mixed, region becomes thin to 847 keV γ-rays. Assuming we know the initial ^{56}Ni mass (which we fix at 0.07 M$_\odot$) and distance (we assume 50 kpc), this function requires only two parameters to define the γ-ray light curves at all energies.

We fit the four light curves of Fig. 3 simultaneously with this function and find an acceptable fit (reduced $\chi^2 = 0.7$), shown as the solid curves in Fig. 3. The single function seems to fit all four lines equally well, and so is an acceptable description of the average depth of the γ-emitters. The best-fit values of the parameters are $t_{o,847}$=124±31 days and $t_{i,847}$=1860±111 days. That is, nearly the entire ejecta must be mixed to explain the γ-ray data. This outer zone is only as thick as 1/3 M$_\odot$ of hydrogen expanding at 3000 km s^{-1}! Clearly the data require some of the ^{56}Co at very low optical depth at very early times. This model also requires a very thick, either massive or slow moving, mixed region to keep the fluxes low after the initial peak. Because it is encouraging for future work, we note that with the mass of ^{56}Ni as a free parameter in the fit, we find a value in reasonable agreement with that determined from the optical light.

A significant component of the bolometric luminosity, especially at later times is the hard emission, at X-ray and γ-ray energies. So far, efforts to account for all the expected ^{56}Co decay power in the bolometric luminosity have utilized only theoretical estimates of the X-ray and γ-ray luminosities (e.g., [3]). We have measured only a few of the ^{56}Co γ-ray lines, but we can infer from models, such as the above one, the escape of all lines. Also, we can obtain the escape fraction of γ-rays from any species (e.g., ^{57}Co) at a given time from (1). With the aid of Monte Carlo simulations of Compton scattering and photoelectric absorption we can also calculate the emerging continuum luminosity. Shown in Fig. 4 are the γ-ray line and continuum luminosities, based on this model, and the total ^{56}Co decay power.

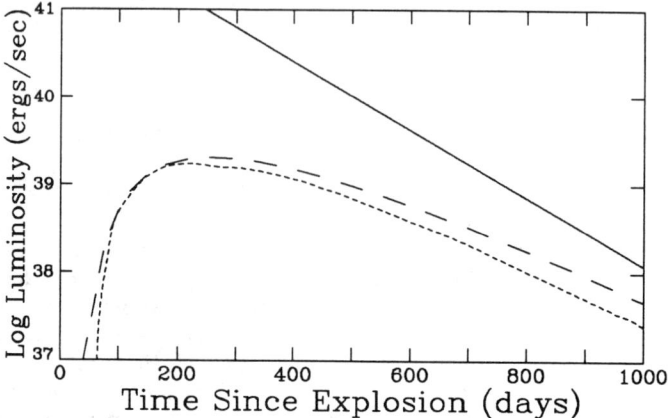

Figure 4. The total γ-ray line luminosity from (1) versus time (dashed line); the > 10 keV continuum luminosity, from Monte Carlo simulation (dotted line); and the ^{56}Co decay power (solid line).

Shown in Fig. 5 is the flux of ^{57}Co 122 keV γ-rays predicted by equation 1 assuming that 1.7×10^{-3} $M_\odot$ of ^{57}Ni was ejected by the explosion (i.e., that the solar ratio of ^{56}Fe/^{57}Fe holds for the ejection of the unstable progenitors). Theoretical estimates of the mass of ^{57}Ni ejected range from this value to 2.5 times greater (e.g., [19,21]). The ejected mass of ^{57}Ni is important because it reflects both the neutron richness of the burning region and the division between the ejected and accreted portions of the star. It is possible that the ^{57}Co mass will be measured from its influence on the bolometric light curve, as was that of ^{56}Co. However, it is becoming increasingly difficult to measure the true bolometric light curve. The determination of this mass from γ-rays requires a measurement of the line flux and an estimate of its attenuation by the ejecta. The model discussed here has the greatest attenuation at late times of those with which we have successfully fit the earlier ^{56}Co γ-line fluxes. Even so, the 122 keV line and its Compton scattered continuum fluxes are marginally detectable by future experiments [22,23] if they are launched on current schedules. The attenuation can be derived from measurements of the line to continuum ratio or from multiple observations of the line fluxes, considered in the context of simple models of the ejecta.

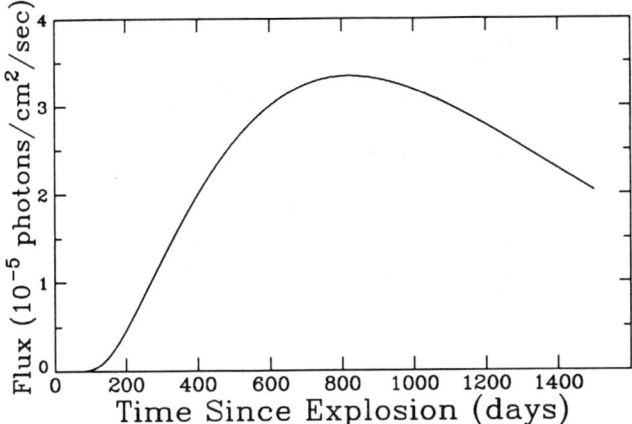

Figure 5. The 122 kev line flux versus time, assuming 1.7×10^{-3} $M_\odot$ of ^{57}Ni ejected, from (1). This is about the minimum flux expected at late times, as this model has larger attenuation than others and most calculations suggest more ^{57}Ni is ejected.

III. Conclusions   With the *SMM* GRS, we have detected significant γ-ray line fluxes from the decay of radioactive ^{56}Co in the ejecta of SN 1987A, and monitored their evolution over two years. This has allowed us to infer the thickness of the envelope and, to a degree, the distribution of ^{56}Co within it. It is clear that the ^{56}Co was distributed over a large range of depths in mass in the ejecta, although the statistical precision of the data do not allow us to probe that distribution in detail. We have also derived the luminosity in all the >10 keV emission from ^{56}Co in a semi-empirical manner. Finally we note that although γ-ray spectroscopy has added insight into this supernova, type I supernovae emit relatively more information regarding their nature in γ-rays. At distances of 10 to 20 Mpc, where they are likely to be found, type I supernovae will be detectable with near-future γ-ray experiments at levels of significance comparable to those in this work. We are therefore hopeful that we will learn much about these objects, such as the mass of radioactivity ejected and something of their structure, from γ-ray measurements made in the next decade.

References

1. S.A. Colgate, C. McKee: *Ap. J.* **157**, 623 (1969).
2. D.D. Clayton, S.A. Colgate, G.J. Fishman: *Ap. J.* **155**, 75 (1969).
3. P.A. Whitelock *et al.*: These proceedings and references therein.
4. N.B. Suntzeff *et al.*: These proceedings and references therein.

5. W.P.S. Meikle: These proceedings and references therein.
6. D.M. Rank: These proceedings and references therein.
7. S.M. Matz et al.: *Nature* **331**, 416 (1988).
8. D.J. Forrest et al.: *Solar Physics* **65**, 15 (1980).
9. G.H. Share et al.: *Ap. J.* **326**, 717 (1988).
10. M.D. Leising et al.: in preparation (1989).
11. W.R. Cook et al.: *Ap. J. Lett.* **334**, L87 (1988).
12. W.R. Mahoney et al.: *Ap. J. Lett.* **334** L81 (1988).
13. W.G. Sandie et al.: *Ap. J. Lett.* **334**, L91 (1988).
14. A.C. Rester et al.: *Ap. J. Lett.* **342**, L71 (1989).
15. J. Tueller et al.: These proceedings.
16. S.M. Matz, G.H. Share, E.L. Chupp: *AIP Proceedings* **170**, 51 (1988).
17. W.D. Arnett: These proceedings.
18. K. Nomoto: These proceedings.
19. S.E. Woosley: These proceedings.
20. P.A. Pinto: These proceedings.
21. F.-K. Thielemann et al.: submitted to *Ap. J.* (1989).
22. P. Durouchoux: These proceedings.
23. J.D. Kurfess: *AIP Proceedings* **170**, 368 (1988).

X-Ray Observation of SN 1987A from GINGA

Yasuo Tanaka

1 Introduction

X-rays from SN1987A (hereafter abbreviated as SN) were detected first time in July 1987 from Ginga. The first result was published by DOTANI et al. [1], hereafter refered to as Paper I. In Paper I, it was shown that X-rays from the SN appeared to consist of two separate components; a hard component which was essentially flat in the range 10 - 40 keV and a soft component which rose towards low energies. The observed intensity of the hard component was in general agreement with the result of an independent observation from the Kvant experiments by SUNYAEV et al. [2], which measured the spectrum up to about 1 MeV. However, the Kvant observation did not confirm the soft component.

In this paper, we report on the X-ray intensity history of the SN obtained from the continued Ginga observations over 900 days after the outburst. After the error box was determined, we employed the pointing mode only (see Paper I). The X-ray light curves are obtained in two energy bands, 6 - 16 keV and 16 - 28 keV. These two energy bands are so chosen that the separation of the hard and soft comoponents is optimum, since the observed energy spectrum indicates that the hard X-ray component turns down below 20 keV. The results on the X-ray energy spectrum will be reported separately.

In obtaining the X-ray intensity of the SN, there are three different sources of systematic errors in addition to the statistical errors. These are (1) the cosmic-ray induced background, (2) the absolute pointing direction, and (3) the contributions from neighbouring sources in the field of view. The last one will be discussed in the next section. The results published in Paper I were also re-examined for these systematic errors.

A background measurement was performed immediately before or after each SN observation. In addition, the background rate <u>during</u> each SN observation can be estimated independently by an empirical method established by HAYASHIDA et al. [3]. This method also provides an estimate of the systematic error in the background estimation, which is about 1% of the background counts. The directly measured background and that estimated from this empirical method are in agreement within this systematic error. The systematic error is usually much larger than the statistical error, and is incorporated in the present errror estimation.

The error in the pointing direction influences not only the aspect determination for the SN but also the corrections for the nearby source contaminations. The error in the pointing direction estimated from the comaprison of the gyro data with the star tracker data is found to be at most 1.5 arcminutes. Although this error is not of statistical nature, we include the effect corresponding to an offset of ± 1.5 arcmin. in the error estimation.

2 Corrections for Nearby Sources

The region of the SN is populated with many X-ray sources as shown in Fig. 1 (LONG, HELFAND and GRABELSKY [4]). Among these sources, LMC X-1 and four supernova remnants SNR0540-69, N132D, N157B and SNR0519-69 (source No. 26 from the <u>Einstein</u> survey by LONG, HELFAND and GRABELSKY [4]) are relatively intense, and their contributions are corrected for. LMC X-1 is by far the brightest among them and also time variable. We therefore attempt to keep LMC X-1 outside the field of view. The exposure to LMC X-1 has been less than 2 %, with only one exception for the observation of July 4, 1987 in which the exposure was about 9 %. In this way, the contribution of LMC X-1 turns out to be much smaller than that of the SNR0540-69.3 described below. The contamination by LMC X-1 through reflection on the collimator walls is absolutely negligible in the range above 6 keV. Since the intensity of LMC X-1 at the time of each observation is unknown, we employ a large enough systematic error in order to cover the maximum variation based on the results from the frequent LMC X-1 observations from Ginga.

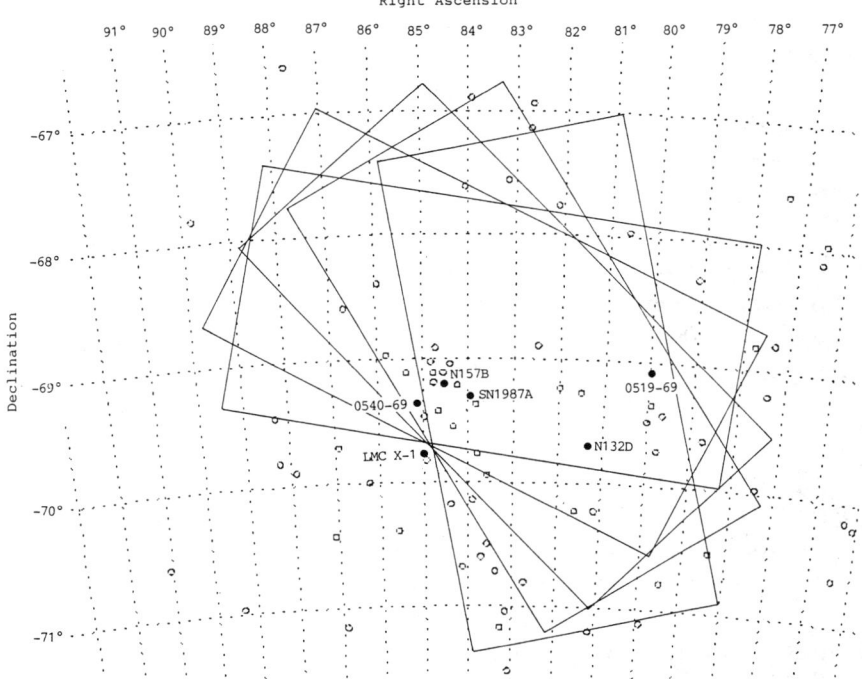

Fig. 1. The sky region of the Large Magellanic Cloud including SN1987A. X-ray sources detected from the Einstein survey (LONG et al. [4]) are indicated, and various orientations of the Ginga field of view employed for the SN observations are also illustrated.

Contributions of the supernova remnants SNR0540-69.3, N132D, N157B and SNR0519-69 were individually estimated for every SN observation. The spectrum of each of these SNR's was determined from separate Ginga observations with various pointings, putting the SN outside the field of view. However, the statistical uncertainties at high energies remain fairly large, since these sources are all weak for the Ginga sensitivity. We therefore determined the acceptable range of intensity for each source using two different model spectra, power-law model and thin thermal model. Power-law model gives higher flux estimates at high energies than the thin thermal model.

Among these sources, SNR0540-69.3 requires the largest correction, because this source, located only half a degree away from the SN, is the strongest in the energy range concerned and known to possess a hard spectrum (CLARK et al. [5]). This SNR includes a 50 ms. pulsar and is similar to the Crab Nebula in several respects (SEWARD et al. [6]). This pulsar component is measured in every SN observation, and an accurate intensity was obtained. The power-law index determined over the range 1 - 24 keV was 1.77 ± 0.09 in good agreement with that obtained in the Einstein energy range [6]. In the overlapping energy range, the measured fluxes from Ginga and the Einstein Observatory also agree with each other within statistical errors. The pulsed fraction in the range 1.7 - 4 keV is 27 ± 4% according to SEWARD et al. [6]. For obtaining a high estimation, we assume that the pulsed fraction is constant over the entire energy range. However, the pulsed fraction may increase with energy as in the case of the Crab Nebula. For a low estimation, we assume a thin thermal spectrum with kT = 10 keV for the remnant. In this case, the flux in the range 16 - 28 keV is essentially due to the pulsed component alone.

N157B is a SNR whose spectrum is similarly hard to SNR0540-69.3 in the Einstein energy range [5]. We assume the intensity of N157B to be approximately one quarter of SNR0540-69.3, the ratio in the Einstein range [5], over the entire energy range of Ginga.

N132D is a bright, oxygen rich SNR similar to Cas A. According to the result of the Einstein observation by CLARK et al. [5], the energy spectrum is composed of a soft (kT = 0.57 keV) component dominating in the low energy range and a hard (kT = 4.0 keV) component. However, an extrapolation of their best-fit model gives a much smaller flux than measured from Ginga, although the Ginga field of view includes another weaker source SNR0519-69. Since the Einstein spectrum of N132D [5] is very steep, a straight extrapolation of this spectrum from the Einstein range to the Ginga range is subject to a large ambiguity. We estimated the intensities of these two SNR's from our own Ginga observations assuming the same spectral shape for both and employing the intensity ratio of eight to one obtained from the Einstein observation [4]. A high estimation is obtained from the best-fit power law with a slope of 2.2, and a low estimation is given by an acceptable thin thermal spectrum with kT = 10 keV.

Thus obtained high and low estimates of the source intensities are given in Table 1. Contributions from these sources quickly diminishes towards higher energies. The other sources in the field of view are much fainter and estimated to be negligible. The diffuse background intensity in the SN region above 6 keV was determined for a field directly north of the SN, which excluded all major sources listed above.

Table 1. Estimated Fluxes of the Nearby Sources

Source Name	6 - 16 keV (counts/s)		16 - 28 keV (counts/s)	
	High Estimate	Low Estimate	High Estimate	Low Estimate
LMC X-1	20.30 ± 12.2		0.65 ± 0.48	
N132D	1.27	0.54	0.06	0.005
SNR0540-63	5.40	4.30	0.45	0.10
SNR0519-69	0.16	0.07	0.008	0.00
N157B	1.24	0.99	0.10	0.00
Diffuse Bkgd.	0.16		0.02	

3 X-Ray Light Curves of the SN

The light curves of the SN so far obtained are shown in Fig. 2(a) and 2(b) for the soft X-ray band in 6 - 16 keV and the hard X-ray band in 16 - 28 keV, respectively. The flux from the SN is plotted for two cases in which the high estimates (open circles) and the low estimates (crosses) of the nearby source intensities are employed. (See Table 1.) The 1σ errors (including all systematic errors) are shown on only one side of the individual data points. For an approximate conversion of a count rate (counts/sec) to an energy flux in units of 10^{-12} ergs/cm²sec, multiply 4.6 for the soft X-ray band and 32 for the hard X-ray band.

The first positive detection of hard X-rays from the SN was on July 4, 1987 (131 days after outburst). The difference between the open circle and the cross in each observation is mostly due to the different intensity values of SNR0540-69.3 employed. The observed light curve indicates that the intensity in the hard X-ray band increased gradually by roughly a factor of two from July through December, 1987. In January 1988, hard X-ray intensity increased by a factor of two, which was however much less pronounced than the increase in the soft X-ray band. From the study of the energy spectrum, this increase in the hard X-ray band is explained as due to a spill over from the soft X-ray band. Excluding this period, the maximum of the hard X-ray intensity seems to have occurred near the end of 1987. Since then, the hard X-ray intensity has been steadily decreasing with time. If one assumes an exponential decline, the decay constant lies

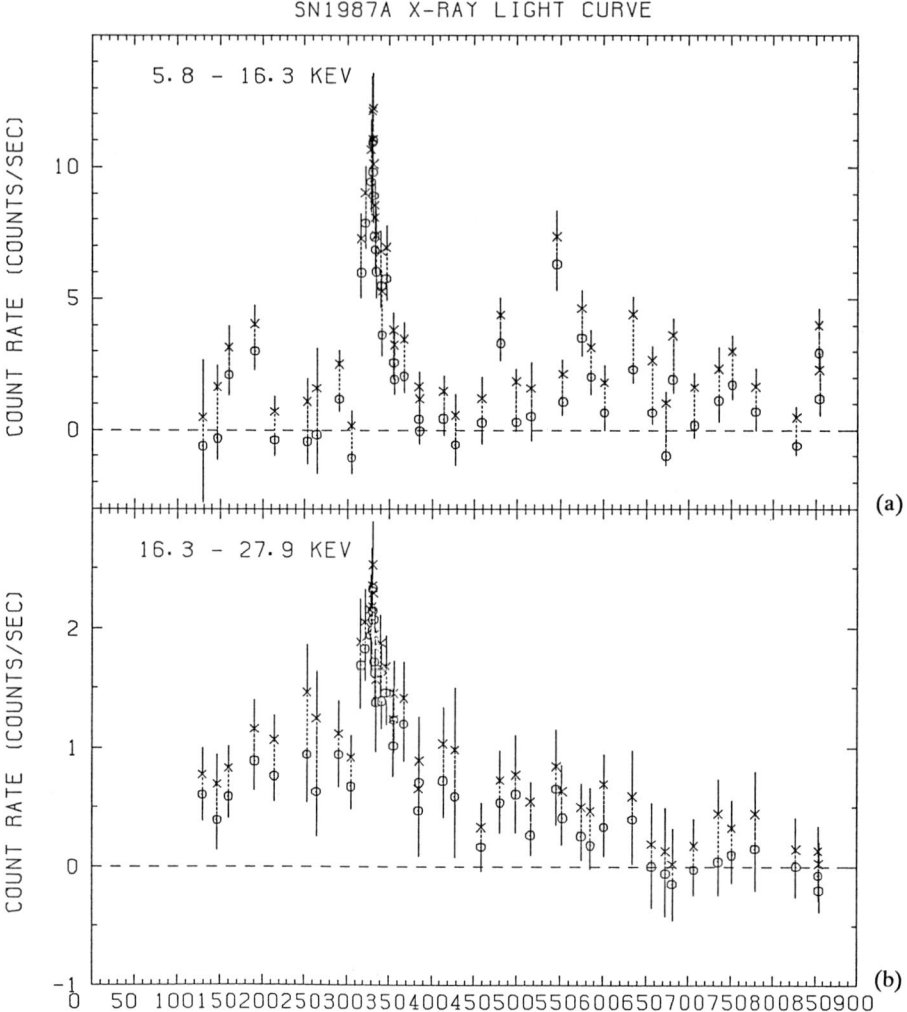

Fig. 2. The X-ray light curves of SN1987A in two energy ranges; (a) the soft X-ray band in 6 - 16 keV, and (b) the hard X-ray band in 16 - 28 keV. Open circles and crosses correspond to the cases in which the high estimates and the low estimates of the nearby source intensities are employed for the corrections, respectively. The error bars shown on only one side include all systematic errors.

in the range between 200 and 350 days. The flux approached to the detection limit around Januray 1989. Later, the average hard X-ray flux over the last two hundred days (650 - 850 days) is lower than the detection limit.

In the soft X-ray band, the difference between the open circle and the cross is due mostly to that between the high and low intensity values of SNR0540-69.3 and/or N132D employed, depending on the orientaion of the field of view. On January 7, 1988 (318 days), a dramatic intensity increase was detected. The intensity increased further and stayed at the maximum level from January 19 (330 days) through 22 (333 day). The intensity started to decrease from January 23 (334 days) steadily through March 14 (357 days) and came back to the general level of 1987. We shall hereafter call this event the "January flare". The light curve in the soft X-ray band for the part of the January flare is shown in Fig. 3. For this flare, we were able to determine the line position of the source by means of an aspect switching method, as drawn in Fig. 4. In addition, the spectrum during the flare was very hard, much harder than that of any known class of galactic X-ray sources. From these results, we conclude that the source of the flare is SN1987A.

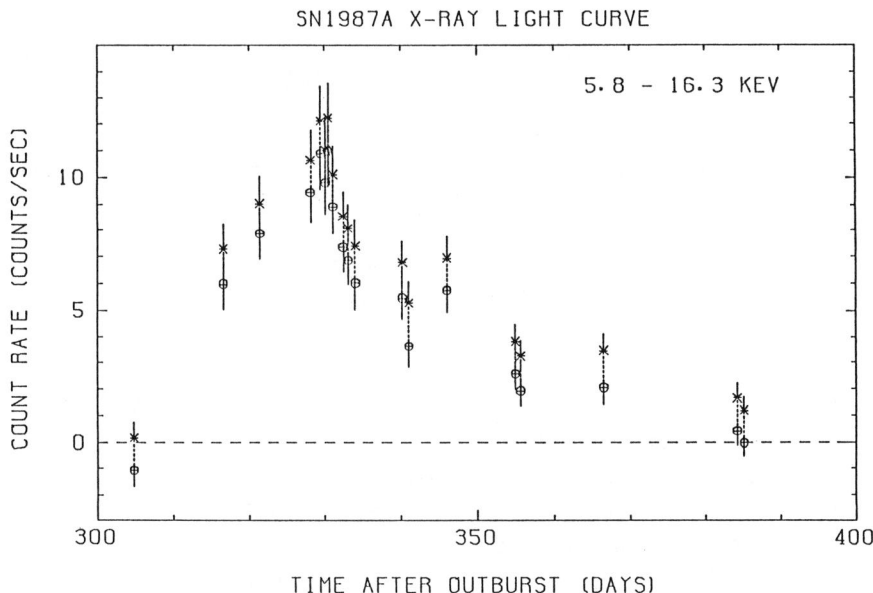

Fig. 3. The X-ray light curves during the January flare. See the caption for Fig. 2.

Besides the January flare, a significant soft X-ray flux was observed occasionally. For the crosses in which the high estimations of the nearby source intensities are used, about two thirds of the points are consistent to be null. On the other hand, there are several points for which the

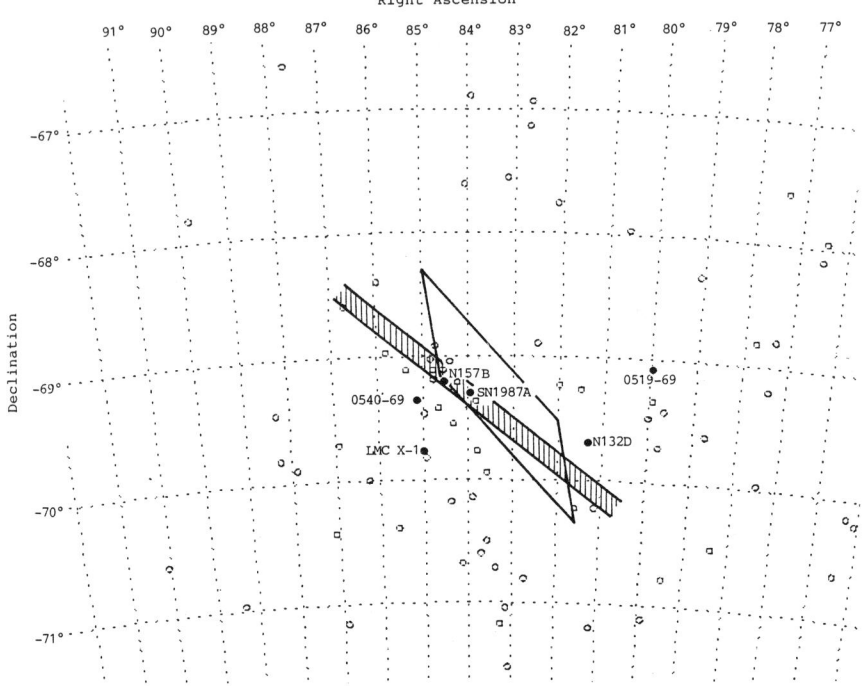

Fig. 4. The line position of the January flare (hatched) and the error box of the variable soft X-ray source.

observed soft X-rays are quite intense. The presence of a variable soft X-ray source in the region of SN1987A is beyond doubt. The soft X-ray intensity is highly variable on a time scale of the order of a day.

The accurate source position has not been determined yet. In order to obtain the source position, we are currently performing aspect switching observations. In this mode, the pointing direction is switched back and forth by 0.2°. The line position of the source can be determined from the amount of change in the count rate, when a significant soft X-ray flux is present. A two-dimensional error box will be obtained from the crossing of line positions determined at different orientaions of the field of view. At present, thus localized source region shown in Fig. 4 includes the SN. Yet, the error box is still fiarly large, and we cannot firmly exclude the possiblity that some other highly variable source which was not detected by LONG et al. [4] exists near the SN.

Search for pulsar with a high time resolution mode has been continued.

The result so far is negative. It is to be noted, however, that, if the pulsation period were shorter than 2 milliseconds, it would not be possible for Ginga to detect the pulsar due to the limitation of the time resolution.

Summary of the Observational Results

Hard X-rays from the SN is consistent to be of Co^{56} origin from the shape of the energy spectrum and the long, smooth decay. However, they emerged much earlier and lasted much longer than originally predicted. In addition, a soft X-ray flare occurred in the SN in January, 1988. Variable soft X-ray flux is also observed occasionally in the SN region, although we still reserve conclusion of the SN origin. No X-ray pulsation is detected as yet.

Acknowledgment

The author is indebted to the Ginga Team for making frequent observations of SN1987A posible in spite of extremely tight schedule of Ginga. This analysis was performed by K. Hayashida, H. Inoue, M. Itoh and the author.

References

1. T.Dotani et al.: Nature **330**, 230 (1987).
2. R.Sunyaev et al.: Nature **330**, 227 (1987).
3. K.Hayashida et al.: Publ. Astron. Soc. Japan **41**, 373 (1989).
4. K.S.Long, D.J.Helfand and D.A.Grabelsky: Astrophys. J. **248**, 925 (1981).
5. D.H.Clark et al.: Astrophys. J. **255**, 440 (1982).
6. F.D.Seward, F.R.Harnden Jr. and D.J.Helfand,D.J.: Astrophys. J. Letters **287**, L19 (1984).

High Resolution Observations of Gamma-Ray Line Profiles from SN 1987A

J. Tueller, S. Barthelmy, N. Gehrels, M. Leventhal, C. J. MacCallum, & B. J. Teegarden

Supernova 1987A was a unique opportunity for gamma-ray astronomers to observe freshly synthesized radioactive material from a type II supernova. Gamma-ray lines were first detected by the spectrometer on the SMM satellite (MATZ et al. [1,2]), which was the only instrument to provide a continuous monitor of the gamma-ray line light curves. Unfortunately, no high resolution satellite instrument was in space to make the critical continuous measurements of the shape of the gamma-ray lines, which are necessary to extract direct information about the distribution of ^{56}Co in the expanding supernova shell. Balloon-borne instruments were able to partially fill this gap with a few snapshots of the line profile (see Table 1). The Gamma-Ray Imaging Spectrometer (GRIS) was the most sensitive of a new generation of high resolution spectrometers which were rushed to completion in time to observe SN1987A (see TUELLER et al. [3] for a description of the instrument).

The gamma-ray measurements have forced revisions of the relatively simple pre-existing models of the supernova, which predicted a delay of about a year before the hydrogen envelope of SN1987A would be thin enough to allow the escape of gamma rays. Figure 1 summarizes the gamma-ray line flux measurements and illustrates the discrepancy with the initial models (5L). To allow the early escape of gamma-rays from the supernova, mixing was introduced to get the radioactive elements up near the surface where the optical depths are low. The 10HMM model is representative of these spherically-symmetric homogeneous mixed models and Fig. 1 illustrates that it can produce an acceptable fit to the gamma-ray line light curves. Gamma rays in this energy range interact by Compton scattering, thus the scattering cross-sections are not dependent on ionization state of the scattering medium and photons are usually scattered far away from the energy of the line. As a result, the line profiles can be calculated by a straightforward integration of the distribution of ^{56}Co multiplied by the transparency, which is determined by the mass distribution. The gamma-ray line profiles yield a direct measure of the distribution of radioactive material in the supernova without the complications of ionization state and resonant scattering effects that confuse the interpretation of line profiles from atomic transitions. While different in detail, all of these mixed models make qualitatively similar predictions of the gamma-ray line shape. Because the ^{56}Co is mixed far into the fast moving hydrogen envelope, large Doppler shifts, up to 3000 to 4000 km s^{-1}, will be observed at the edges of the lines. Because the source is optically thick and homogeneous, only the blueshifted photons from the approaching surface can reach the observer and, therefore, the line centroid will be blue shifted.

On day 433 (after the core collapse) the 847 and 1238 keV lines from ^{56}Co were observed by GRIS at 2.3 and 4.3σ significance. On day 613, the lines at 847, 1238, and 2599 keV were observed at 4.6, 3.4, and 1.9σ respectively. The combined significance for the three line complex in both flights is 7.8σ. Gaussian profiles yield acceptable least-squares fits to the lines. Figures 2, 3, and 4 are plots of photon spectra for the spring 1238 keV line and the fall

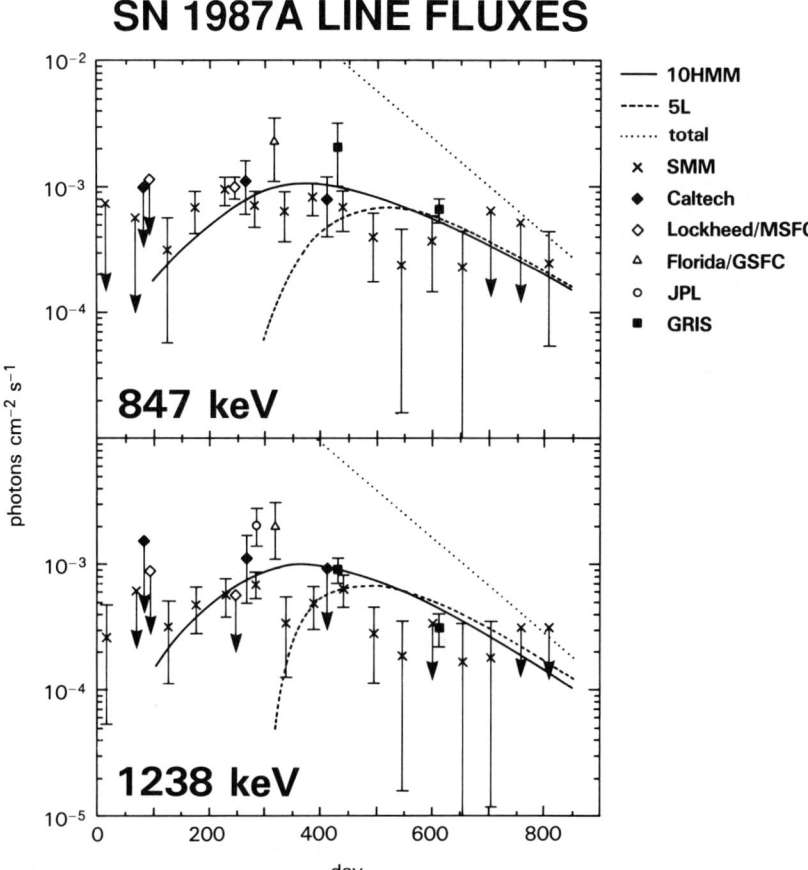

Figure 1. The GRIS line flux measurements are shown with theoretical predictions and the measurements of other instruments. The GRIS fluxes on day 433 are 21.+12.,-9. and 9.1±2.1 x10^{-4} photons cm^{-2} s^{-1} for the 847 and 1238 keV lines. On day 613 the fluxes are 6.5±1.4 and 3.1±0.9 x10^{-4} photons cm^{-2} s^{-1} for the 847 and 1238 keV lines. All of the measurements are in reasonably good agreement with the 10HMM model. (solid line: 10HMM model; dashed line: 5L model without mixing; dotted line: unattenuated line flux; all models from PINTO and WOOSLEY [6,7]; SMM: LEISING [8]; Caltech: COOK et al. [9,10,11]; Lockheed/MSFC: SANDIE et al. [12,13]; Florida/GSFC: RESTER et al. [14]; JPL: MAHONEY et al. [15]) This figure is from TUELLER et al. [5].

Table 1. SN1987A High Resolution Measurements

Group	Day	847 keV Line		1238 keV Line	
		Centroid (keV)	FWHM (keV)	Centroid (keV)	FWHM (keV)
Lockheed, MSFC	248-250	~844	~12	—	—
JPL	287	—	—	1240.8 ± 1.7	8.2 ± 3.4
Florida, GSFC	319-322	844.1 ± 1.0	6.0 ± 2.6	1239.0 ± 1.7	10.4 ± 3.4
GSFC, Bell Labs, and Sandia Labs	433	844.6 ± 1.2	8.7 +4.9,-3.3	1235.0 ± 2.2	14.8 ± 5.2
	613	844.2 ± 1.3	10.8 +2.9,-2.4	1233.5 ± 1.8	11.0 +3.7,-3.1

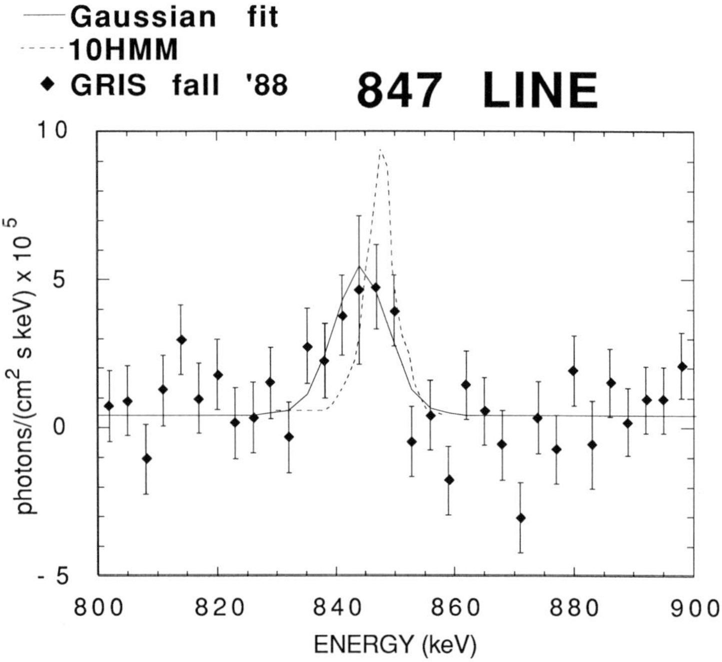

Figure 2. GRIS data for the 847 keV line from the decay of ^{56}Co in SN87A is shown for day 613. The top-of-atmosphere photon spectrum is shown in 3 keV bins which are larger than the FWHM resolution of the instrument. The solid line is a best fit to a Gaussian line profile. The dashed line is the predicted line profile for the 10HMM model. Although this model and similar spherically symmetric mixed models predict the line flux correctly there is a clear discrepancy with the measured line profile.

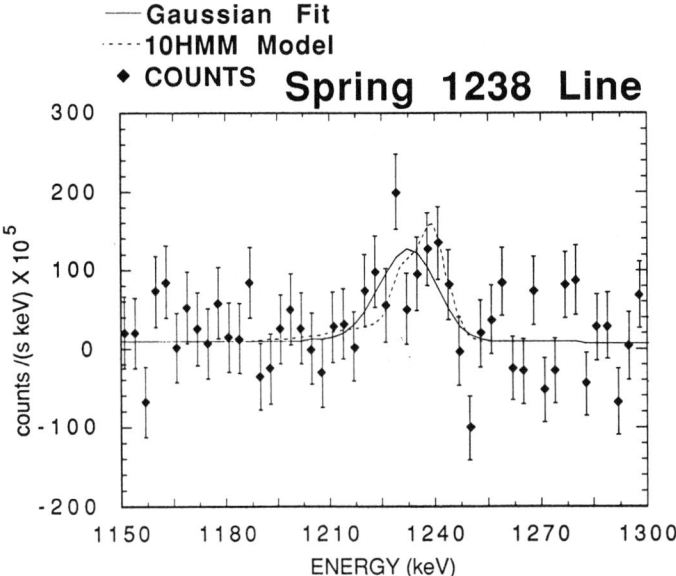

Figure 3. GRIS data for the 1238 keV line on day 433 is shown. The 10HMM model has been folded with the instrument response function to account for the spring flight resolution problem.

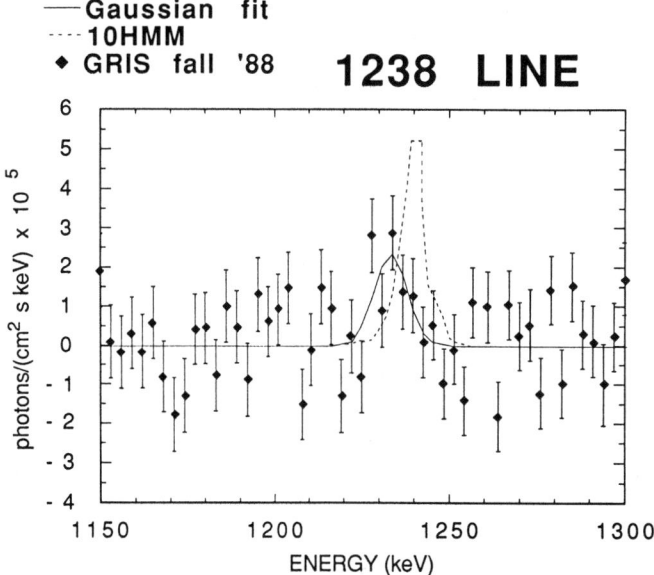

Figure 4. GRIS data for the 1238 keV line on day 613.

847 and 1238 keV lines. On each plot the the best fit Gaussian line profile (solid line) and the 10HMM line profile (dashed line) are shown. The observed lines are not blueshifted and are broader than the 10HMM prediction. The combined significance of the differences between our data and the 10HMM model is 4.9σ for the line centroids and 3.0σ for the widths. (The spring 847 keV line was not included because potentially significant systematic uncertainties have not been evaluated.) For the details of the data analysis see TEEGARDEN et al. [4] and TUELLER et al. [5]. Table 1 is a summary of the line profiles from all the high resolution measurements of SN1987A gamma-ray lines. At 847 keV, all of the instruments are in good agreement: the centroid of the line is redshifted from the rest energy of 846.0 keV (corrected for LMC redshift) and the width is consistently broader than the value of <5.5 keV predicted by the 10HMM model. While the situation at 1238 keV is less consistent, the GRIS results are the most statistically significant and are in excellent agreement with the 847 keV line profiles. The line centroids are redshifted from the rest energy of 1237.2 keV and the widths are consistently broader than predicted by 10HMM (<7.3 keV). The JPL results for the 1238 keV line are in better agreement with the 10HMM model, but they are only different from the GRIS values at the ~2σ level of significance. Although the results of the Florida/GSFC collaboration at 1238 keV do not appear to be consistent with their own 847 keV line profile, the uncertainties assigned by the authors to the line centroids are significantly smaller than the conventional value of FWHM/(2.36 x significance). This suggests that a more conservative analysis might find that these results are consistent. We conclude that the consensus of the high resolution gamma-ray line measurements contradicts predictions of the line profiles by 10HMM and similar models.

The observed gamma-ray lines have the profile of an optically thin source, but the fluxes are ≲30% of the emission of 0.075 $M_\odot$ of ^{56}Co determined from the bolometric light curve. The line widths imply velocity dispersions of ~3500 km s^{-1} in the distribution of radioactive material, which is much larger than predicted by unmixed models. To be consistent with the gamma-ray results, a theory must explain optically thin emission for the lines at times when most of the gamma rays are still absorbed in the source and when a uniform hydrogen envelope would still be optically thick. It must also explain the acceleration of a significant fraction of the ^{56}Co to velocities characteristic of the outer regions of the expanding supernova shell. To accommodate the apparent contradictions and explain the shape of the gamma-ray lines will require new and more complex models for SN1987A, such as a theory combining mixing and fragmentation.

References

1. S. M. Matz et al.: Nature 331, 416 (1988).
2. S. M.Matz, G. H.Share, and E. L. Chupp in Nuclear Spectroscopy of Astrophysical Sources (AIP Conf. Proc. 170), ed. N. Gehrels and G. H. Share (New York,AIP 1988), p. 51.
3. J.Tueller et al. in Nuclear Spectroscopy of Astrophysical Sources (AIP Conf. Proc. 170), ed. N. Gehrels and G. H. Share (New York,AIP 1988), p. 439.
4. B. J. Teegarden et al.: Nature, 339, 122 (1989).
5. J. Tueller et al.: submitted to Ap. J. Let. (1989).
6. P.Pinto and S. E.Woosley: Ap. J., 329, 820 (1988).
7. P.Pinto and S. E.Woosley: Nature, 333, 534 (1988).
8. M. Leising: private communication (1989).
9. W. R. Cook et al.: IAU Circ., 4400 (1987).
10. W. R. Cook et al.: IAU Circ., 4584 (1988).
11. W. R. Cook et al.: Ap. J. Let., 334, L87 (1988).
12. W. G. Sandie et al:: IAU Circ., 4463 (1987).
13. W. G.Sandie et al.: Ap. J. Let., 334, L91 (1988).
14. A. C. Rester et al.: Ap. J. Let., 342, L71 (1988).
15. W. A.Mahoney et al.: Ap. J. Let., 334, L81 (1988).

An Observation of SN1987A with a New High Resolution Gamma-Ray Spectrometer

J. Matteson, M. Pelling, B. Bowman, M. Briggs, R. Lingenfelter, L. Peterson, R. Lin, D. Smith, K. Hurley, C. Cork, D. Landis, P. Luke, N. Madden, D. Malone, R. Pehl, M. Pollard, P. von Ballmoos, M. Neil, & P. Durouchoux

1. Introduction

The discovery (Matz et al. [1]) of gamma-ray line emission at 847 and 1238 keV from radioactive ^{56}Co in the recent supernova SN1987A proved that explosive nucleosynthesis occurred in this supernova. Gamma-ray light curves derived from these and subsequent observations (Cook et al. [2], Mahoney et al. [3], Sandie et al. [4], Rester et al. [5], Teegarden et al. [6]) have a broad plateau from August 1987 to October 1988, with an 847 keV flux of $\sim 7\times10^{-4}$ ph/cm^2-sec (Tueller et al. [7]). The early detection of gamma rays required the inclusion of mixing or clumping in the models, (e.g. Pinto and Woosley [8] and Chan and Lingenfelter [9]). The gamma-ray fluxes are predicted, e.g. Bussard et al. [10], to peak at about day 400 and then decrease, by a factor of ~ 6 at day 800, as the effect of increasing transparency becomes dominated by radioactive decay. Then they should depend primarily on the amount of ^{56}Co produced and little on the degree on mixing since most of the ^{56}Co should be exposed. Thus measurements of the ^{56}Co gamma-ray line fluxes and profiles will continue to be important during the decline of SN1987A.

Radioactive ^{57}Co is also expected to have been produced in SN1987A initially as ^{57}Ni by neutron rich nucleosynthesis in the deepest layers of the ejecta (Clayton [11]). Its production ratio, ^{57}Ni/^{56}Ni has been estimated (Woosley and Pinto [12], Kumagi et al. [13]) to lie between the solar value of the decay products, ^{57}Fe/^{56}Fe = 0.024 (Cameron [14]), and about twice this value. Depending on the mixing, velocity and mass of the overlying ejecta, the ^{57}Co's 122 keV gamma -rays are expected to have a broad maximum from about day 700 to 1600, with a peak flux from 5 to 15×10^{-5} ph/cm^2-s.

Observations of these phenomena require high resolution gamma-ray spectroscopy with a sensitivity to narrow lines of $\sim 10^{-4}$ ph/cm^2-s. Below we describe a new instrument with these capabilities and its 22 May 1989 observation of SN1987A.

2. The 12-Detector Germanium Spectrometer

This new balloon-borne, high resolution gamma-ray spectrometer was developed (Matteson et al. [15]) by a collaboration of US and French scientists in order to observe astrophysical sources of gamma-ray lines, with a sensitivity of $\sim 10^{-4}$ ph/cm^2-s, and to prove new instrumental techniques that may be applied to future space missions. Gamma rays are detected in high purity germanium detectors which measure ~ 55 mm in length and ~ 55 mm in diameter. They are cooled to 85 K by liquid nitrogen and have an energy resolution of 1 keV below 100 keV and 2 keV at 1 MeV. The detectors' total volume is 1568 cm^3 and total area is 285 cm^2. The instrument's new techniques include detector β-decay background rejection by detector segmentation and pulse shape discrimination (Roth et al. [17], Smith et al. [18]), a large array of 12 detectors and the use of 5 cm thick bismuth germanate (BGO) for the anticoincidence shield. The detectors' inner electrodes are segmented, providing a 1.2 cm thick front segment and a 4.3 cm thick rear segment. Segmentation provides information on the energy losses' axial position and dispersion. Pulse shape discrimination is used to determine the radial dispersion of energy losses. The position and dispersion data are then used to discriminate against β-decays (single site events) while accepting gamma rays (multiple site and front segment events). Data for accepted energy losses are telemetered in an event-by-event format at 40 kbps.

The sides and rear of the anticoincidence shield containing 51 BGO bars, with a maximum size of 5×7×21 cm, each with its own 2 inch photomultiplier tube (PMT). The excellent light collection geometry results in an anticoincidence threshold of 30 keV even though BGO's light output is only ∼ 10 percent of NaI. Conventional CsI(Na), 10 cm thick, is used for the front of the shield. It has apertures over each detector which define a 20° FWHM field of view and nine 2 inch PMTs, which also give a 30 keV threshold. The BGO and CsI weigh 240 and 55 kg, respectively, and the entire instrument weighs 540 kg. Alt-azimuth pointing control is provided by the balloon gondola, whose complete weight, including the instrument, is 1134 kg.

3. Balloon Flight and Instrument Performance

The 12-Detector Germanium Spectrometer had its first balloon flight from Alice Springs, Australia on 22 May 1989, day 819 of SN1987A. Four of its detectors had fully operational segmentation and pulse shape discrimination. Carried on a Raven 28 million cubic foot balloon, it floated at 3.5–4.7 g/cm^2 for 17.4 hours and observed SN1987A for 9.9 hours, the Galactic Center for 6.3 hours, and the Crab Nebula and the transient x-ray source 0535+26 for 1.3 hours. Observations were performed by a series of target and background pointings, each for 20 minutes. Pointing aspect was verified by a star camera.

The instrument and gondola performed extremely well. The only problems were the failure of two detectors and the presence of spurious peaks below 200 keV in the background spectra. The causes for these are under investigation, and the latter is certain to be due to recovery from large energy losses. Neither problem had a significant effect on the scientific results. The background levels at 122, 847 and 1238 keV were 4×10^{-4}, 4×10^{-5} and 2×10^{-5} c/cm^2-s-keV, respectively. The background reductions from segmentation and pulse shape discrimination have not yet been exploited.

4. Preliminary Scientific Results

Preliminary analysis of the SN1987A data has been performed. We expect the final results to be up to a factor of 2 more sensitive due to finer energy resolution, which will result from more accurate gain corrections, the use of all the data, lower background through the use of segmentation and pulse shape discrimination and detector-to-detector anticoincidence, which will reduce the background by ∼ 20 percent.

The 2σ limits on broad (FWHM/E = 1 percent) gamma-ray line emission from SN1987A are 2×10^{-4} ph/cm^2-s at 122 keV from ^{57}Co, and 3.4 and 2.4×10^{-4} ph/cm^2-s at 847 and 1238 keV, respectively, from ^{56}Co. The ^{57}Co flux limit is a factor of 1.5 above the prediction of Kumagi et al. [13]. It can be interpreted to limit the ^{57}Co/^{56}Co ratio to < 0.086, or 3.6 times the solar value for ^{57}Fe/^{56}Fe. Here we assume the same optical depth at 122 and 847 keV. The 2σ limits on the two ^{56}Co gamma-rays have been combined using the branching ratios for their production and assuming that lines have about the same optical depth. This yields an equivalent limit at 847 keV of 2.4×10^{-4} ph/cm^2-s, which is a factor of ∼ 3 below the plateau of 847 keV flux measurements from August 1987 to October 1988, showing that the flux decreased after October 1988. This flux limit is only 0.75 of the flux that would be expected if the supernova ejecta were completely transparent, exposing the entire 0.075 M$_\odot$ of ^{56}Co, as determined from the bolometric light curve. Thus the optical depth for the 847 keV line must still have been > 0.3 on day 819, indicating that the decrease in the optical emission at about that time did not result from greatly increased gamma ray escape. This limit is nonetheless still a factor of 1.7 above the 10HMM model prediction (Pinto and Woosley [8]).

Acknowledgements

The successful development and balloon flight of the 12-Detector Germanium Spectrometer was the result of the work of many people. The authors express their appreciation for the efforts of F. Duttweiler, C. James, G. Huszar, D. Gruber, D. Philips, G. Beriones and G. Allen at UCSD, H. Primbsch, S. McBride, J. Penegor, and B. Campbell at UCB, G. Vedrenne, F. Cotin, J. Couteret and J. Coutelier at CESR and J. Poulalion at CEN–Saclay. The balloon flight and supporting logistics were ably handled by R. Kubara, D. Gage and D. Ball of NSBF and R. Sood of UNSW. This work was supported under NASA Grant NAGW-449.

References

1. Matz, S. M., et al. 1988, *Nature*, **331**, 416.
2. Cook, W. R., et al. 1988, *Ap. J. (Letters)*, **334**, L87.
3. Mahoney, W. A., et al. 1988, *Ap. J. (Letters)*, **334**, L81.
4. Sandie, W.G., et al. 1988, *Ap. J. (Letters)*, **334**, L91.
5. Rester, A.C., et al. 1989, *Ap. J. (Letters)*, in press.
6. Teegarden, B.J., et al. 1989, *Nature*, published.
7. Tueller, J., et al. 1989, in *Proceedings of the Gamma-Ray Observatory Workshop*, in press.
8. Pinto, P.A., and Woosley, S.E. 1988, *Nature*, **333**, 534.
9. Chan, K. W., and Lingenfelter, R. E. 1988, in *Nuclear Spectroscopy of Astrophysical Sources*, ed. N. Gehrels and G. Share (New York: Am. Inst. Phys.), p. 110.
10. Bussard, R. W., Burrows, A., and The, L.S. 1989, *Ap. J.*, **341**, 40.
11. Clayton, D. D. 1974, *Ap. J.*, **188**, 155.
12. Woosley, S.E., and Pinto, P.A., 1988 in *Nuclear Spectroscopy of Astrophysical Sources*, ed. N. Gehrels and G. Share (New York: Am. Inst. Phys.), p. 98.
13. Kumagi, S., et al. 1989, *Ap. J.*, in press.
14. Cameron, A. G. W. 1982, in *Essays in Nuclear Astrophysics*, ed. C. A. Barnes and D. N. Schramm (Cambridge: Cambridge Univ. Press) p. 23.
15. Matteson, J. L., et al. 1985, in *19th Internat. Cosmic Ray Conf. Papers*, **3**, 326.
16. Matteson, et al. 1989 in *21st Internat. Cosmic Ray Conf. Papers*, in press.
17. Roth, J., Primbsch, J.H., and Lin, R.P. 1984, *IEEE Trans. Nuc. Sci.*, **31**, 367.
18. Smith, D.M., et al. 1988, in *Nuclear Spectroscopy of Astrophysical Sources*, ed. N. Gehrels and G. Share (New York: Am. Inst. Phys.), p. 484.

Pre-Discovery Hard X- and Gamma-Ray Luminosity of SN 1987A from Optical Spectra

N. N. Chugai

Modelling of the emergent hard X- and gamma-ray emission in SN1987a is an important diagnostic tool for ^{56}Co distribution in the envelope as well as for the envelope structure (SUNYAEV et al. [1]; KUMAGAI et al. [2]; GREBENEV and SUNYAEV [3], and ref. there). The time of apearence of escaping gamma-rays is crucial point for the model. GRAHAM [4] proposed to estimate pre-discovery gamma-ray flux from HeI 10830 A scattering line, which had been recognised as a probe of ^{56}Co decay in SNII just before detection of this line in SN1987A (CHUGAI [5]). In the present paper I use Hα absorption to probe escaping gamma-rays. New estimates of gamma-ray flux dramatically exceed those by GRAHAM [4]. This controversy stems from previously missed processes, namely, Penning ionization and radiative transition $2^3S - 2^3P - 1^1S$, which strongly depopulate 2^3S level of He.

1. Non-Thermal Ionization and Excitation of H and He

In outer layers presumably transparent to gamma-rays ($\tau_\gamma < 1$) the energy deposition rate [ergs cm^{-3} s^{-1}] due to Compton scattering is

$$\epsilon = (4\pi)^{-1}(vt)^{-2}\eta\langle\sigma_\gamma\rangle(n_H + 2n_{He})L_\gamma, \qquad (1)$$

where $4\pi\eta$ is a ratio of the average intensity of gamma-rays to the flux (we adopt $\eta = 1.4$), $\langle\sigma_\gamma\rangle = 0.13\sigma_T = 0.86 \times 10^{-25}$ cm^2 is the cross-section $\sigma_C(\Delta E/E)$ weighted over the gamma-ray spectrum. Primary (Compton) electrons loose their energy "on the spot" on ionization and excitation of H and He, and heating of thermal electrons. The characteristic rate of non-thermal ionization is $\zeta^0 = \epsilon_H w_H n_H^{-1}$ [s^{-1}], where $w_H = 36$ eV is the average energy spent on creation of H$^+$ ion (cf. DALGARNO and Mc CRAY [6]). Taking into account main processes of the degradation of the deposited energy and adopting ionization degree x_H $10^{-3} - 10^{-2}$, and hydrogen abundance X=0.6 one obtains rates of non-thermal ionization, ζ, and excitation, ξ, of hydrogen and helium:

$\zeta_H = 1.14\zeta^o$, $\zeta_{He} = 0.14\zeta^o$,
$\epsilon_H = 0.77\zeta^o$, $\epsilon_{He}(2^3S) = 0.0265\zeta^o$. (2)

In the "two level plus continuum" approximation values n_e and n_2 are defined by equations (we assume $n_e = n_H$ and $v = r/t$)

$dn_e/dt = -3n_e/t + \zeta_H n_H + P_2 n_2 - \alpha_B n_e^2$,

$n_2(A_{2q} + P_2 + A_{21}\beta_{12}) = \epsilon_H n_H + \alpha_B n_e^2$, (3)

where $A_{2q} = 2$ [s^{-1}] is the Einstein coefficient for the two-photon transition 2-1 (2s and 2p states are farely mixed), P_2 is the photoionization rate in a given point, β_{12} is Lα escape probability. In steady-state regime (i.e for $n_e/\zeta_H n_H \ll t$), equations (3) can be reduced to

$n_2(A_{2q} + A_{21}\beta_{12}) = (\zeta_H + \epsilon_H) n_H$. (4)

The equation for He^+ concentration is

$dn_{He^+}/dt = -3n_{He^+}/t + \zeta_{He} n_{He} - \alpha_B^{He} n_e n_{He^+}$, (5)

while for the population of 2^3S level of HeI the equation is

$n_{He}(2^3S)(C + C_P + R) = \epsilon_{He} n_{He} + \alpha(^3L) n_e n_{He^+}$, (6)

where $C = q n_e$ is the rate of collisional transition $2^3S - 2^1S$, $q = 1.9 \times 10^{-8}$ cm^{3}s^{-1} (cf. OSTERBROCK [7]), $C_P = \langle \sigma_P u_{th} \rangle n_H$ is the rate of Penning process $He(2^3S) + H - He + H^+ + e$, equal to 3×10^{-9} cm^{3}s^{-1} for T=5000 K (OLSON [8]; BELL [9]; SHAW et al. [10]). R is the rate of two-stage radiative transition $2^3S - 2^3P$,

$R = B_{23} f_\nu^c (4\pi)^{-1} (D/vt)^2 e^{0.92A(\lambda)} A_{32}^{-1} A_{31} \beta_{13}$, (7)

where f_ν^c is the continuum flux at $\lambda = 10830$ A, determined from IR spectra, see: BOUCHET et al. [11]; ELIAS et al. [12] (distance D = 50 kpc and A_V = 0.6 mag are adopted here). Both, Penning process and two-stage radiative transition, dominate depopultion of 2^3S due to electron collisions in the outer layers (v>4000 km/s) of SN1987A at the relevant epoch.

2. Density in the Outer Layers of SN1987A

Data on hard X- and gamma-rays from SN1987A (cf. COOK et al. [13]; MATZ et al. [14]; GREBENEV and SUNYAEV [3]) imply that in mid-October 1987 gamma-ray luminosity of SN1987 was $L_\gamma = 4 \times 10^{39}$ ergs s^{-1} (cf. GREBENEV and SUNYAEV [3]). With the known value of L_γ one can find from (1) and (2) concentration of hydrogen in the outer layers for a given n_2. On the other hand, n_2 can be obtained from the blue wing of Hα or Hβ absorption. On 13 Oct. 1987 according to Hβ profile in spectrum of SN1987A (cf. CATCHPOLE et al. [15]) n_2 in the range 4000<v< 7000 km/s can be described by $n_2 = 0.26(v/5000$ km/s$)^{-10}$ (CHUGAI [16]). This result and the analysis of hydrogen excitation lead to the density in the range of velocities 4000-7000 km s^{-1}

$$n_H = 0.8 \times 10^8 (v/5000 \text{ km s}^{-1})^{-m}(t/232 \text{ d})^{-3},$$

where 5<m<6. For X=0.6, Y=0.4 one obtains at v=5000 km s^{-1} on 232 day the density $\rho = 2.2 \times 10^{-16}$ g cm^{-3}, which is only two times lower than the density in the model by SHIGEYAMA et al. [17].

3. Hα Absorption as an Indicator of Gamma-Ray Escape

The relative intensity in the blue wing of Hα absorption ($v_z = -7000$ km s^{-1}) at the epoch 20 - 150 days after explosion in accordance with the spectra of SN1987A (MENZIES et al. [19]; CATCHPOLE et al. [20]; CATCHPOLE et al. [15]), as well as the model curves (with and without nonthermal excitation) are shown in Fig 1. Equations (3) were solved for the ionization degree $x_H = 0.00124$ on 25 day. $P_2 = 2.9(t/100$ d$)^{-2}(v/7000$ km/s$)^{-2}$ s^{-1} was adopted in accordance with the UV data in the range 2500-3400 A from IUE (KIRSHNER [21]) and ASTRON (BOYARCHUK et al. [22]). The dependence of ζ_H on time was parametrized as

$$\zeta_H = 2\zeta_H^o (t/50 \text{ d})^K [1 + (t/50 \text{ d})^{K-1}]^{-1},$$

where parameters K and ζ_H^o were determined from the best fit of Hα absorption evolution (see Fig. 1).

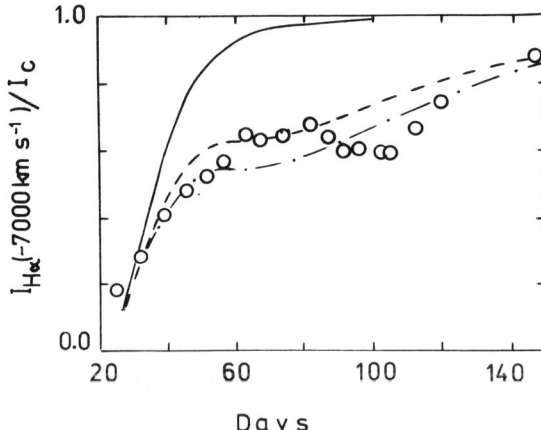

Figure 1. Evolution of intensity of Hα absorption at $v_z = -7000$ km/s. Circules: data from SAAO (see text); solid line: model without non-thermal excitation; dashed line: model with non-thermal excitation, $\zeta_H^o = 4.65 \times 10^{-10}$ s^{-1}; and dash-dotted line: with non-thermal excitation, $\zeta_H^o = 5.8 \times 10^{-10}$ s^{-1}

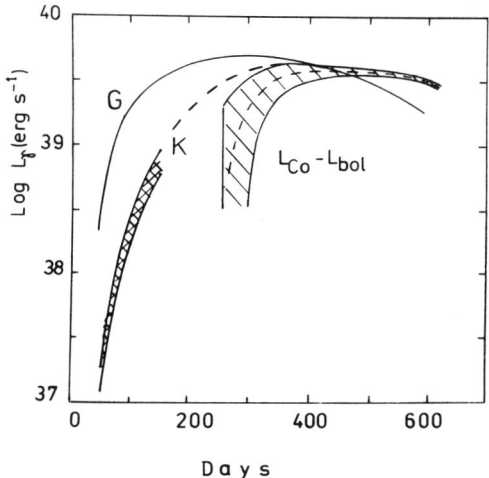

Figure 2. Evolution of gamma-ray luminosity of SN1987A. Cross-hatched field: this work; line-hatched field: from WHITELOCK et al. [23]; curve G: model by GREBENEV and SUNYAEV [3]; K: model by KUMAGAI et al. [2]

Figure 1 shows that model without non-thermal excitation fails for t>40 days. Models with non-zero ζ_H^0, 5.8×10^{-10} and 4.65×10^{-10} s^{-1}, (in Fig. 1 the case m=6, k=4 is shown) fit better (especially latter case). For m=5 best fit values are k=4 and $\zeta_H^0 = 3 \times 10^{-10}$ s^{-1}.

With known n_H and ζ_H the hard X- and gamma-ray luminosity of SN1987A was found from (1). Two extreme set of parameters (a) m=5, $\zeta_H^0 = 3 \times 10^{-10}$ s^{-1}, and (b) m=6, $\zeta_H^0 = 4.65 \times 10^{-10}$ s^{-1} give lower and upper curves $L_\gamma(t)$ in Fig. 2. For t>250 days evolution of $L_\gamma(t)$ is given according to WHITELOCK et al. [23]. Gamma-ray luminosity calculated by KUMAGAI et al. [2] (K) and by GREBENEV and SUNYAEV [3] (G) are presented at this plot too.

Pre-discovery (untill Jul-Aug 1987) gamma-ray luminosity is substantially higher than that suggested by early behavior of L_γ curve given by WHITELOCK et al. [23]. Yet, the model calculations (both suggest mixing of ^{56}Co, up to 4200 km s^{-1} in K, and up to 5000 km s^{-1} in G model) generally agree with the high early gamma-ray luminosity implied by hydrogen lines.

4. HeI 10830 A Line and Escaping Gamma-Rays

On 76, 105, and 135 day gamma-ray luminosity found from Hα, respectively, 10^3, 10^2, and 10 times exceeds those found by GRAHAM [4] from HeI 10830 A line. This discrepancy was removed by taking into account Penning process (He*+H) and radiative mechanism of the 2^3S depopulation. For two sets of parameters m, k, and ζ_H^0, corresponding to upper and lower limit for

Table 1. Theretical and "observed" values of $n_{He}(2^3S)$

t	L_γ, 10^{38} ergs/s		$n(2^3S)$, cm^{-3}		
days	m=5	m=6	m=5	m=6	obs.
76	0.63	1.0	0.012	0.018	0.008
105	2.0	2.9	0.018	0.025	0.02
135	4.5	7.1	0.026	0.039	0.03

$L_\gamma(t)$ implied by Hα (see Fig. 2 and Table 1), equations (3,5) and (7) were solved to find n_e, n_{He^+}, and $n(2^3S)$ on 76, 105 and 135 days at the level v=7000 km s^{-1}. Results are presented in the fourth and fifth column of Table 1. Values of $n_{He}(2^3S)$, found from profiles of HeI 10830 A in the spectra published by ELIAS et al. [12] for the same level v=7000 km s^{-1}, are given in the last column. Agreement between theoretical and "observed" values of $n(2^3S)$ is fairly good, thus supporting reliability of pre-discovery gamma-ray luminosity found from hydrogen lines.

References

1. R. A. Sunyaev et al.: Nature 330, 227 (1987).
2. S. Kumagai et al.: Astr. Ap. 197, L7 (1988).
3. S. A. Grebenev, R. A. Sunyaev: Preprint IKI No. 1560 (1989).
4. J. R. Graham: Ap. J. (Letters) 335, L53 (1988).
5. N. N. Chugai: Pisma Astr. Zh. 13, 671 (1987).
6. A. Dalgarno, R. A. Mc Cray: Ann. Rev. Astr. Ap. 10, 375 (1972).
7. D. Osterbrock: In Astrophysics of gaseous nebulae (Freeman, San Francisco 1974).
8. R. E. Olson: Phys. Rev. 6A, 1031 (1972).
9. K. L. Bell: J. Phys. B. 3, 1308 (1970).
10. M. J. Shaw et al.: Chem. Phys. Lett. 8, 148 (1971).
11. P. Bouchet et al.: ESO Preprint No. 592 (1988).
12. J. H. Elias et al.: In CTIO 25th Aniversary Symposium (San Francisco 1988).
13. W. R. Cook et al.: Ap. J. (Letters) 334, L87 (1988).
14. S. M. Matz et al.: Nature 331, 416 (1988).
15. R. M. Catchpole et al. Mon. Not. R. astr. Soc. 231, 75P (1988)
16. N. N. Chugai: Pisma Astr. Zh. 14, 1079 (1988).
17. T. Shigeyama et al.: Astr. Ap. 196, 141 (1988).
18. W. D. Arnett: Ap. J. 331, 377 (1988).
19. J. W. Menzies et al.: Mon. Not. R. astr. Soc. 227, 39P (1987).
20. R. M. Catchpole et al.: Mon. Not. R. astr. Soc. 229, 15P (198
21. R. P. Kirshner: Preprint of Harvard-Smithsonian Center for Astrophysics No. 2888 (1989).
22. A. A. Boyarchuk et al.: Pisma Astr. Zh. 13, 739 (1987).
23. P. A. Whitelock et al.: Preprint SAAO No. 631 (1989).

Future Missions for Gamma-Ray Astronomy — Sigma and the Nuclear Astrophysics Explorer

P. Durouchoux & J. Matteson

1. Introduction

Continuing progress in gamma-ray astronomy requires new instruments which provide significant improvements in sensitivity, angular resolution and energy resolution. The Gamma-Ray Observatory, scheduled for launch in June 1990, will obtain a substantial improvement in sensitivity over earlier space missions. However, in the MeV energy range its angular resolution, $\sim 5°$, will not be adequate to resolve dense source regions and locate sources with high accuracy, and its energy resolution, $E/\Delta E \sim 10$, will not be adequate to resolve gamma-ray lines and measure their profiles. In this paper we describe two future instruments which will obtain much better angular and energy resolution while maintaining high sensitivity. The SIGMA was launched on the USSR's GRANAT spacecraft on 1 December 1989. It will obtain 13 arc minute resolution imaging in the 30 keV to 2 MeV range. The Nuclear Astrophysics Explorer is a possible NASA Explorer mission which could be launched in the late 1990's. It would perform high resolution spectroscopy in the 15 keV to 10 MeV range, with an energy resolution of 2 keV at 1 MeV, i.e. $E/\Delta E = 500$.

2. SIGMA

The SIGMA telescope is the first space instrument that obtains high quality imaging in the low energy gamma-ray range. Developed in France, it is expected to operate for several years and has the following features.

- a wide operational bandwidth, 30 keV – 2 MeV, which will link high energy x-ray and gamma-ray astronomy.
- good angular resolution, typically 13 arc minutes, within a field of view measuring 4.7° x 4.3°, fully coded, or 11.5° x 10.6°, partially coded. Stronger sources will be positioned to $\sim$1 arc minute.
- moderate energy resolution, 30% to 6%, depending on energy.
- high sensitivity for both continuum, of the order of a few times 10^{-7} to few times 10^{-6} ph/cm^2-s-keV, and line measurements, $\sim 3 \times 10^{-5}$ ph/cm^2-s.

2.1 Description of SIGMA

A cross section of the SIGMA telescope is shown in Fig. 1. Its four key subsystems, the coded mask, position sensitive detector, detector electronics and anticoincidence shield are described below.

Coded Mask – This consists of 49 x 53 elements, based on a 29 x 31 Hadamard matrix. The elements are made of tungsten, measuring 9.4 x 9.4 x 15 mm thick. The thickness has been choosen in order to give good absorption of photons in the overall energy range. These elements are attached to a carbon-Nomex honeycomb plate which provides the necessary stiffness and transparency to gamma-rays. The mask is located 250 cm above the detector plane,

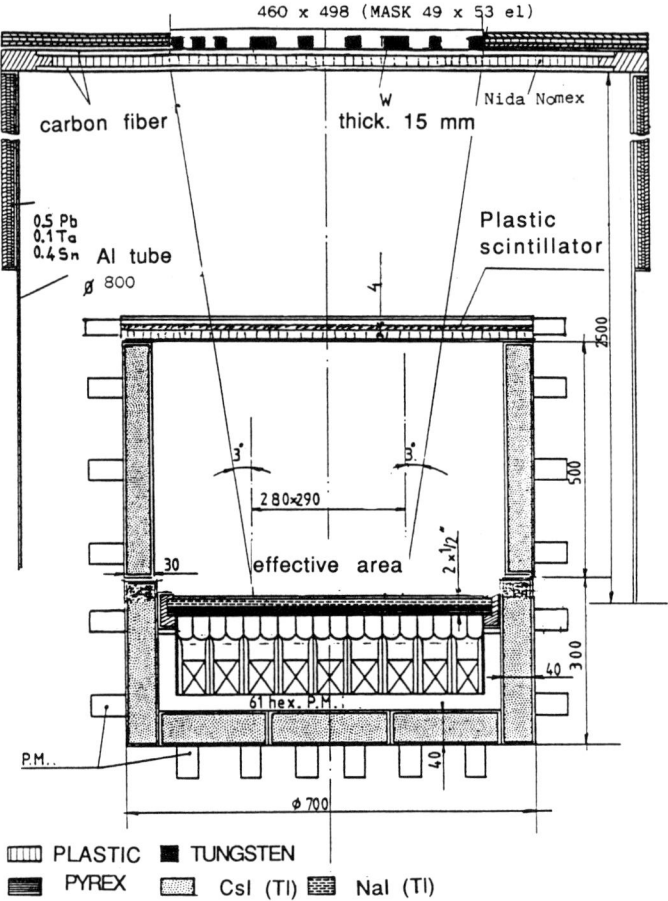

Figure 1. A cross section of the SIGMA instrument.

attached to a tube which provides the requisite stiffness to achieve the required alignment accuracy.

Detector – This is directly derived from a medical camera, and consists of a NaI crystal, 57 cm diameter x 1.25 cm thick, which is viewed by 61 hexagonal photomultiplier tubes (PMTs).

Detector Electronics – These process the signals from the PMTs to determine the coordinates of the sites of the photon interactions and their energy losses. The coordinate data are collected in a 232 x 248 element matrix.

Anticoincidence Shield – This shields the detector in order to reduce the background from gamma-rays and charged particles. It contains CsI crystals, with a thickness of 3 to 4 cm on the sides and 4 cm on the bottom. A thin plastic scintillator is located at the top of the shield.

2.2 Performance

The sensitivity of SIGMA depends on the background, which is directly dependent on the orbit. SIGMA is in a high altitude, highly eccentric orbit with a 2000 km perigee, 200000 km apogee and 4 day period. This has higher background than the typical low altitude orbit, but allows a continuous observations during the 3 days of each orbit above 60000 km. In the range 20-100 keV, the sensitivity is of the order of few milli-Crab. Table 1 gives the continuum sensitivity and Table 2 gives the line sensitivity. The continuum sensitivity and spectra of selected sources are shown in Fig. 2.

Table 1. 3σ **Continuum Sensitivity for 1 and 10 day Observations**

E (keV)	Sensitivity (ph/cm^2-s-keV)	
	(1 day)	(10 days)
20–30	1.7×10^{-5}	5.4×10^{-6}
30–50	7.5×10^{-6}	2.4×10^{-6}
50–100	3.7×10^{-6}	1.2×10^{-6}
100–300	1.6×10^{-6}	5.0×10^{-7}
300–500	2.0×10^{-6}	6.5×10^{-7}
500–1000	1.3×10^{-6}	4.2×10^{-7}
1000–2000	1.0×10^{-6}	3.2×10^{-7}

Table 2. 3σ **Line Sensitivity (10 day Observation)**

E (keV)	Sensitivity (ph/cm^2-s)
30	3.3×10^{-5}
70	2.5×10^{-5}
200	3.9×10^{-5}
511	1.6×10^{-4}

The sensitivity to the 122 keV gamma-ray from ^{57}Co gamma-ray is of the order of 3×10^{-5} ph/cm^2-s, which is below the theoretical predictions for SN1987A. At 511 keV the sensitivity is a factor of ~ 10 below the maximum flux reported from the Galactic Center region. This should allow maps to be obtained which will provide < 2 arc minute localization of the variable point source of 511 keV gamma-rays.

The angular resolution results from the distance between the mask and the detector, 250 cm, and the size of the mask elements, 9.4 mm. The nominal resolution is 13 arc minutes. Strong sources can be localized to about 10 times this accuracy, i.e. ~ 1 arc minute.

Gamma-ray bursts will be detectable with SIGMA, both with the detector and the shield. For the detector, with an area of 400 cm^2 in the energy range 20-100 keV, a sensitivity of 1.6×10^{-8} erg/cm^2 is expected for time bins of 0.25 s.

2.3 Observation Program

SIGMA will perform observations of a wide range of galactic and extragalactic objects including active galaxies and quasars, clusters of galaxies, selected regions of the galactic plane, interstellar clouds, supernova remmants, the COS-B sources, radio pulsars, known x-ray sources and targets of opportunity such as supernovae and novae. Most observations will require from 1 to 10 days, depending on the sensitivity desired.

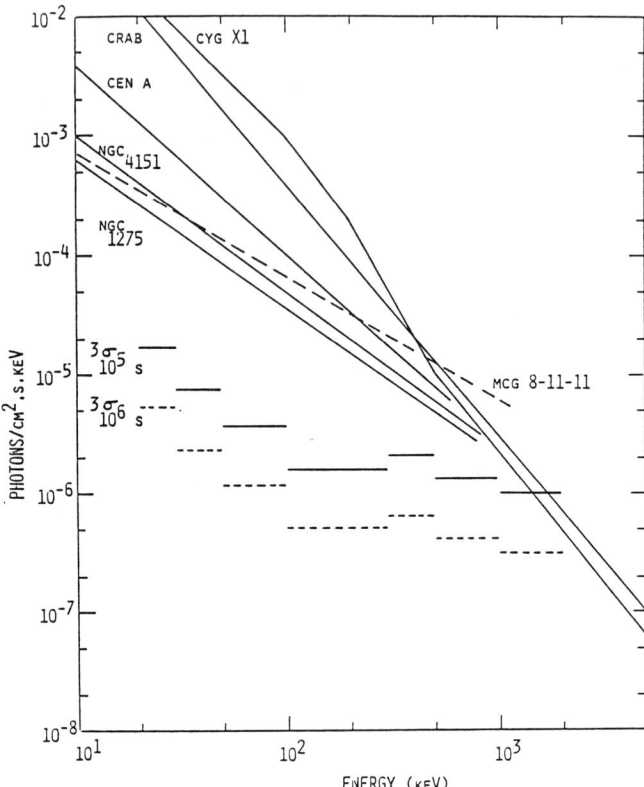

Figure 2. SIGMA continuum sensitivity for 1 and 10 day observations and the spectra of selected sources.

The study of active galaxies and quasars is one of the major objectives of the mission. The unambiguous identification of a large number of active galaxies will lead directly to the compilation of a gamma-ray luminosity function for these objects in the region of the spectrum where their luminosity is maximum. SIGMA will also study their variability both in hard x-rays and gamma-rays, as well as the correlation of these variations.

A survey of the central region of the Galaxy is scheduled, in particular at the annihilation energy of 511 keV. Due to the expected point source flux at this energy, $\sim 1 \times 10^{-3}$ ph/cm^2-s, SIGMA should be able to localize the point source with an accuracy of $\sim$2 arc minutes, which is equivalent to 5 pc at the center of the Galaxy. This goal is very important in terms of understanding the object, which might be at the galactic nucleus itself.

2.4 Status and Plans

The SIGMA was launched on the USSR's GRANAT satellite on 1 December 1989 and is operating nominally, with a slightly lower than expected background. The planned operational life is 18 months, but the onboard consumables permit the mission to be extended by a few years. No Guest Observer program is officially set up, but people interested in collaboration should contact one of the two French PI's:

Future Missions for γ-Ray Astronomy

J. Paul
CEN/SACLAY
SAP/GERES
91191 Gif Sur Yvette
Cedex, France

P. Mandrou
CESR
9, avenue du Colonel Roche
31400 Toulouse
France

3. The Nuclear Astrophysics Explorer

The Nuclear Astrophysics Explorer (NAE) is a concept for a future NASA Explorer mission which would obtain high resolution, $E/\Delta E \sim 500$, observations of gamma-ray lines, at a sensitivity of $\sim 3 \times 10^{-6}$ ph/cm^2-s, or 100 times below the presently known fluxes, in order to study many fundamental problems in astrophysics. In July 1989 NASA's Explorer Concept Study Program completed a 1-year feasibility study of the NAE and three other missions. Two of these were to be selected for development for missions in the mid 1990's. Although the NAE was not selected, there is strong interest within NASA and the US and international scientific communities in performing the NAE mission. The late 1990's would be the earliest date for this. The scientific motivation, instrument concept, mission concept and expected results, and status and plans are discussed below.

3.1 Scientific Motivation

Gamma-ray lines are the most direct probe of cosmic nuclear processes. High resolution spectroscopy of these lines can provide basic information on fundamental astrophysical problems such as nucleosynthesis, supernovae dynamics, neutron star and black hole physics, and particle acceleration and interactions. Gamma-ray line observations have, in fact, already made major contributions to our understanding of a variety of astrophysical objects and phenomena. Table 3 contains a summary of these observations, which were made with instruments that had relatively low sensitivity, greater than $\sim 2 \times 10^{-4}$ ph/cm^2-s, and, in many cases, low energy resolution, $E/\Delta E \sim 10$.

Gamma-ray lines are known to be produced in astrophysical objects by electron-positron annihilation, radioactive decay, nuclear excitation, neutron capture and cyclotron processes in strong magnetic fields, i.e. transitions between quantized electron energy levels. The observed lines' energies and production processes are listed in Table 3. Lines can be produced when the temperature exceeds $\sim 10^8$ K, energy exceeds ~ 1MeV/nucleon or magnetic field exceeds $\sim 10^{12}$ gauss. Although these are extreme conditions by terrestrial standards, they occur frequently in the cosmos. Unique astrophysical information is encoded in gamma-ray lines; not only do their energies indicate the presence of specific nuclei and excitation processes, electron-positron pairs or the magnetic field strength, but the line parameters, i.e. intensities, energy shifts from rest values, widths and profiles, carry information on abundances, bulk velocities, gravitational potentials, densities, temperatures, the spectra of the exciting particles and the magnetic field geometry. The literature contains many reviews of gamma-ray line astrophysics [1-9].

The observations summarized in Table 3 have lead to many important conclusions and promise a wealth of new information when new instruments are flown in space. Some of these are discussed further below.

Electron-positron pair plasmas are expected to form at the extreme densities and temperatures of matter accreting onto black holes. Electron-positron annihilation radiation is the signature of this phenomenon, appearing as a broad line shifted above 511 keV. This feature has been observed in the spectra of Cyg X-1 and the Galactic Center, both of which also contain a narrow 511 keV annihilation line as well. These sources have been observed to vary on 6-month time scales, but the variability has not been resolved and its connection to underlying mechanisms is unknown. Electron-positron annihilation and the decay of radioactive ^{26}Al, which has a 740,000 year half-life, have been observed to occur in the central 5 kpc of the Galaxy, producing gamma-rays at 511 and 1809 keV. The latter proves that nucleosynthesis is an ongoing process in the Galaxy and the former is thought to be primarily due to the decay of nucleosynthetic ^{56}Co produced in supernovae [54]. This produces positrons, some of which escape the remnant and have lifetimes of 10^5 to 10^6 years in the interstellar medium.

These gamma-rays provide tracers of the sites and nature of galactic nucleosynthesis in the present epoch and the physical conditions of the interstellar medium [55]. The latter results from the dependence of the profile of the 511 keV line and associated positronium continuum on the physical conditions of the annihilation medium. Gamma-rays from radioactive ^{56}Co synthesized in the recent Type II supernova SN1987A proved that explosive nucleosynthesis of heavy elements occurred in this supernova and the line profile requires that the ejecta is fragmented [37,38]. Gamma-rays from radioactive material synthesized in supernovae and novae can be used as diagnostics of the yield, expansion and energetics of these events. ^{44}Ti is expected to be produced in significant quantities in supernovae [56] and its 54 year half life allows its gamma-rays to be used as tracers of the undiscovered ~ 10 galactic supernovae thought to have occurred in the past 500 years. About 5 of these should be discovered by the NAE. Assuming half a solar mass of ^{56}Ni is produced in a Type I supernova, the NAE should be able to observe the ^{56}Co gamma-rays from these events out to distances of 20 Mpc, i.e. the Virgo cluster, with 1 week time resolution for several months after the optical outburst.

Gamma-ray lines due to nuclear excitation, neutron capture and electron-positron annihilation are diagnostics of particle acceleration to high energies, 10-100's of MeV, and their subsequent interactions. Solar flares are copious producers of these lines, which have been interpreted to study the spectrum of the accelerated particles and the abundances in the solar atmosphere. With future high resolution measurements many more lines will be observed and they will be used to determine the geometry of the accelerated particles confinement, transport and interactions. Nuclear excitation must also occur throughout the Galaxy due to cosmic ray interactions with the interstellar medium. The predicted fluxes [57] are below present detection capabilities, but the NAE should detect the stronger lines and use them to obtain new information on the abundances of the interstellar gas and dust, and the flux and spectrum of the low energy, <100 MeV, cosmic rays, which cannot penetrate the solar system.

Absorption and emission lines in the 20 to 70 keV range, interpreted as due to cyclotron absorption and emission in intense, $\sim 10^{12}$ gauss, magnetic fields have been observed in the spectra of many objects thought to be neutron stars, e.g. gamma-ray bursters, X-ray pulsators and the pulsar in the Crab Nebula. Since the transport of radiation is strongly dependent on photon energy, propagation direction and electron temperature [58,59], the lines are sensitive diagnostics of the geometry of the magnetic field and the conditions in it.

Generally only the intensities and energies of gamma-ray lines have been determined to a useful accuracy and the information carried by the other line parameters has not yet been exploited. However, observations with the NAE would obtain detailed measurements of the parameters of known lines and many weaker lines as well. It would simultaneously obtain 1) a hundred fold improvement in sensitivity to point sources of narrow lines, i.e. $\sim 3 \times 10^{-6}$ ph/cm^2-s, and a diffuse flux sensitivity of $\sim 2 \times 10^{-5}$ ph/cm^2-s-rad, 2) an energy resolution that is less than most lines' predicted widths in order to determine energy shifts, widths and profiles, i.e. $E/\Delta E \sim 500$, and 3) an angular resolution of a few degrees in order to map diffuse emission, resolve source complexes and locate sources. With these capabilities the NAE could effectively pursue all the presently defined objectives of high resolution gamma-ray spectroscopy.

3.2 Instrument Concept

The NAE instrument concept is shown in Figure 3 and its parameters are given in Table 4. It contains 9 large, ~ 300 cm^3 each, Ge detectors in a heavily shielded 3 x 3 array. These are cooled by a Stirling Cycle mechanical refrigerator. The detectors have very low background, because of 4 essential features. 1) They use position sensitivity, obtained through axial segmentation and pulse shape discrimination, to discriminate against induced β-decay radioactivity in the detectors themselves. Here the multiple-site signature of Compton scattered gamma-rays is distinguished from the single site signature of β-decays, which are a major background component in heavily shielded instruments. 2) A 10 cm thick anticoincidence shield made of bismuth germanate (BGO), which greatly attenuates the background

Table 3.   Astronomical Gamma Ray Line Observations

Process	Observed Energy	Source	Flux, ph/cm²-s	Ref
e± **Annihilation**	511	Galactic Center	$0.6\text{-}1.8\times10^{-3}$	10-15
Radiation	511	Interstellar Gas	$\sim2\times10^{-3}$/rad	15-17
	511	Solar Flares	up to ~0.1	18-19
	400-460	Gamma Ray Bursters	up to 70	21-23
(Redshifted)	~400	CrabPulsar Transient	$2\text{-}7\times10^{-3}$	24,25
	~413	10June74 Transient	7×10^{-3}	26,27
	500-2000	Cygnus X-1	up to 2×10^{-2}	28-31
Radioactive Decay				
^{56}Co$(\epsilon\gamma,\beta^+\gamma)^{56}$Fe	847	Supernova 1987A	$\sim10^{-3}$	32-39
	1238	″ ″	$\sim10^{-3}$	32,33-39
	2598	″ ″	$\sim10^{-3}$	36,39
^{26}Al$(\beta^+\gamma)^{26}$Mg	1809	Interstellar Gas	4.8×10^{-4}/rad	40,41
Nuclear Excitation				
^{56}Fe (p,p′γ)	847	Solar Flares	up to ~0.05	18-20
^{24}Mg (p,p′γ)	1369	″ ″	up to ~0.08	18-20
^{20}Ne (p,p′γ)	1634	″ ″	up to ~0.1	18-20
^{28}Si (p,p′γ)	1779	″ ″	up to ~0.08	18-20
^{12}C (p,p′γ)	4438	″ ″	up to ~0.1	18-20,42
^{16}O (p,p′γ)	6129	″ ″	up to ~0.1	18-20
Neutron Capture				
^{1}H (n,$\gamma)^2$H	2223	Solar Flares	up to ~1	18-20,42,43
^{1}H (n,$\gamma)^2$H	2223	10June74 Transient	1.5×10^{-2}	26,27
(Redshifted)	1790	″ ″	3×10^{-2}	26,27
^{56}Fe (n,$\gamma)^{57}$Fe	5947	″ ″	1.5×10^{-2}	26,27
(Redshifted)				
Cyclotron Emission	20-70	Gamma Ray Bursters	up to 3	22,44-46
& Absorption in	20-58	X-Ray Pulsators	$1\text{-}3\times10^{-3}$	47-51
$\sim10^{12}$ **gauss fields**	73-79	Crab Pulsar Transient	4×10^{-3}	25,52,53

due to ambient gamma-rays. Its transmission is 1 percent at 1 MeV. 3) A 10° FWHM field of view, defined by apertures in the BGO shield, reduces the 1 MeV background due to aperture gamma-rays to the level of the residual, non-rejected detector radioactivity. 4) The low inclination, low altitude orbit, e.g., 10° inclination and 500 km altitude, has a small exposure to the background producing fluxes of trapped protons, cosmic rays and their secondaries.

Imaging and aperture chopping, for suppression of background systematics, are simultaneously obtained through the use of a 25-element coded mask/antimask system. The mask and antimask codes, or patterns, form complementary 5 x 5 arrays, which are produced by open elements and 7 cm thick BGO elements that are nearly opaque to gamma-rays. They pro-

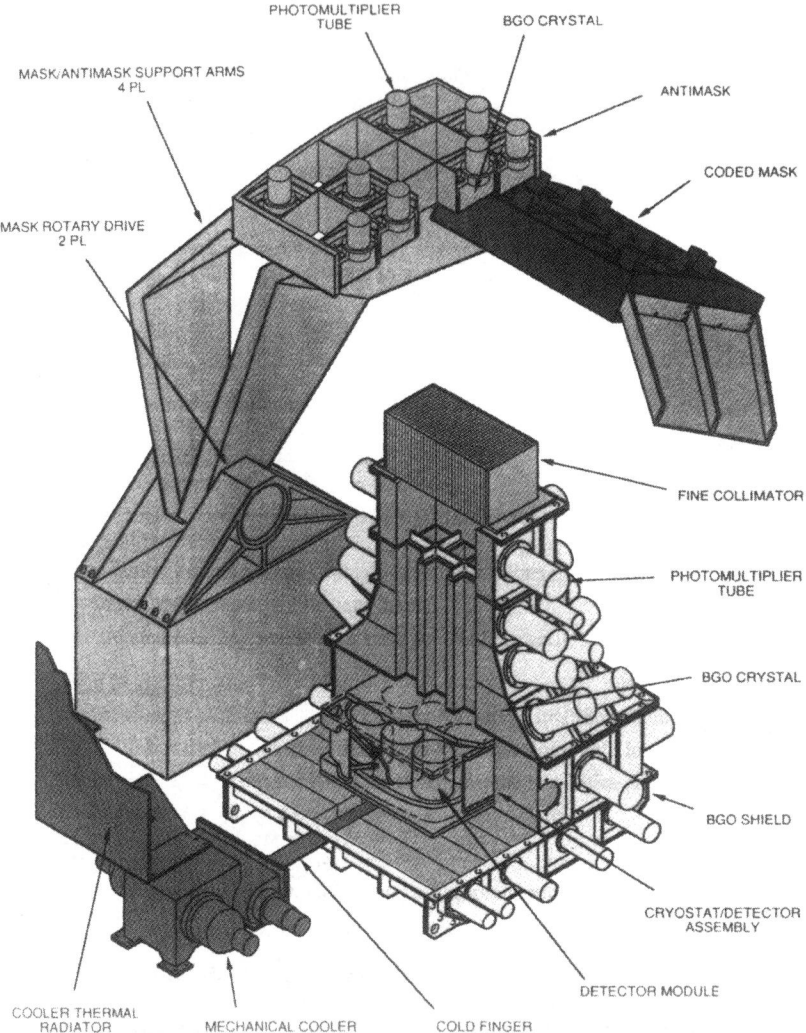

Figure 3. The Nuclear Astrophysics Explorer instrument concept. The BGO anticoincidence shield and cryostat are shown in a cutaway view to allow the germanium detector modules to be seen. The mask/antimask system is also cutaway. Its support arms extend to a second rotary drive (not shown) at the right side of the instrument.

duce shadowgrams on the detector array which are deconvolved by matrix multiplication to produce a sidelobe-free 2-D image of point and point-like sources with 4° angular resolution.

Table 4. NAE Instrument Concept Parameters

Energy Range	15 keV to 10 MeV
Energy Resolution	2 keV at 1 MeV
Sensitivity, 3σ	3×10^{-6} ph/cm^2-s in 10^6 sec
Detector System	9 cooled Ge detectors, 300 cm^3 each
Anticoincidence Shielding	10 cm thick bismuth germanate (BGO)
Imaging and Aperture Modulation System	25 element mask/anti-mask system, 7 cm thick bismuth germanate
Field of View	10° FWHM (Image Mode, Knife-Edge Mode)
	20° FWOM (Image Mode, Knife-Edge Mode)
	1° FWHM (Fine Collimator Mode)
Angular Resolution	4° FWHM (Image Mode)
	2° FWHM (Knife-Edge Mode)
Instrument Size	1m(W) x 1.3m(L) x 1.8m(H)
Cryostat Thermal Load	0.5 W at 85 K
Cryostat Cooling System	Mechanical refrigerator, thermoelectric cooler
Power	242 W
Mass	1500 kg
Bit Rate	8 kbps (av), 25 kbps (peak)
Pointing Requirement	0.05°, unrestricted viewing in any direction
Orbit Requirement	low exposure to trapped radiation and cosmic rays, e.g. <10° incl. x 500 km alt.

The mask and antimask are alternately placed in the aperture during imaging observations. This is performed with a few minute cycle in order to suppress the systematic effects of varying background caused by changing cosmic ray cutoff energies around the orbit. The mask/antimask combination can also be moved together in and out of the aperture to obtain either 1) a "knife-edge" which is smoothly moved over the aperture to produce a 1-D image with 2° angular resolution, in order to study complex source regions and better locate sources or 2) a totally blocked or totally open aperture, in order to modulate and detect diffuse flux with high efficiency. A 1° FWHM collimator that is effective below 150 keV can be placed in the aperture to improve the sensitivity and angular resolution at low energies.

As a consequence of its very low background, the NAE would become background limited at very low flux levels, $\sim 1 \times 10^{-5}$ ph/cm^2-s at 1 MeV. It would obtain sensitivity to larger fluxes very rapidly. Only 1/2 hour would be required to reach $\sim 3 \times 10^{-4}$ ph/cm^2-s, the limiting flux for previous instruments, and 1 day to reach $\sim 1 \times 10^{-5}$ ph/cm^2-s. With 10^6 sec of good data, a sensitivity of $\sim 3 \times 10^{-6}$ ph/cm^2-s would be reached. Even better sensitivity could be obtained with longer observations, for example, of the galactic plane. The NAE's sensitivity versus energy is shown in Figure 4 along with those of the Gamma-Ray Spectrometer on the HEAO-3, which used high resolution Ge detectors, $E/\Delta E \sim 300$, and the Oriented Scintillation Spectrometer Experiment (OSSE) on the GRO, which uses lower resolution NaI detectors, $E/\Delta E \sim 15$.

At 1 MeV the NAE would have a sensitivity and energy resolution that are 10 and 30 times better than the OSSE. Its sensitivity would be 100 times better than the HEAO-3. The very good sensitivity predicted for the NAE is the result of careful consideration of the many factors which affect sensitivity. The most significant of these, in comparison with the HEAO-3, are: 6 times more detector volume, 6 times more observing time (due to pointed observations), 2 times more useful data and ~ 100 times lower background per unit detector

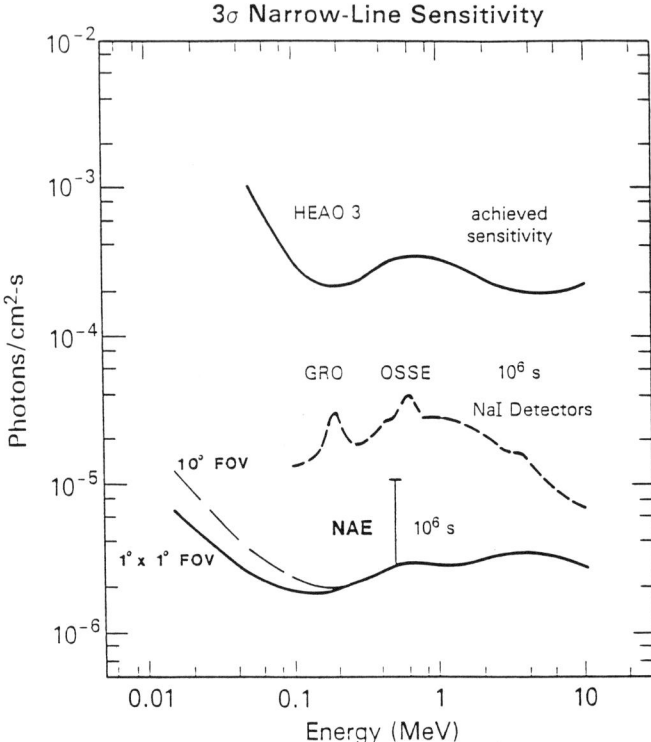

Figure 4. The predicted sensitivity of the Nuclear Astrophysics Explorer to narrow gamma-ray lines in a 10^6 sec observation. Shown for comparison are the predicted sensitivity of the OSSE instrument on the Gamma-Ray Observatory, in 10^6 sec, and the achieved sensitivity of the Gamma-Ray Spectrometer on the HEAO-3, which typically obtained $\sim 2 \times 10^5$ sec on a source. The NAE sensitivity is 100 times below the known gamma-ray line fluxes.

volume (primarily due to a much better orbit, much thicker gamma-ray shielding, and the rejection of β-decay background).

3.3 Mission Concept and Expected Results

The NAE's sensitivity and versatility will allow it to be used to pursue many astrophysical problems with relatively brief observations, e.g. a few hours to a few days. Therefore, the observing program would extend beyond the mission development team and involve a large number of scientists who would use the NAE as a facility. In a 2-year mission scenario the following observational program could be accomplished.

3.3.1 Galactic Plane Survey and Mapping (6 months)

A complete survey of the galactic plane would be performed with 5 days of observations at each 10° step in longitude. Mask/antimask and blocked/open modes would be used to detect and map the diffuse emission with 10° and 4° resolution, allowing the total galactic flux to be determined and separated into its diffuse and point-like, < 4°, components. The galactic 511 and 1809 keV gamma-rays would be detected at $\sim 50\sigma$ and $\sim 20\sigma$ significance in each 10°

step. A sensitive, high-contrast map would result which could be used to determine (1) the sites and rates of nucleosynthesis; longitude from the map, distance from the lines' Doppler velocities, determined to < 30 km/sec, and the galactic rotation model known from 21 cm observations, (2) the nature of the mixing of nucleosynthetic material into the Galaxy and temperature of the electron-positron annihilation regions from the line widths and profiles, (3) the sites and nature of $\sim$ 5 undiscovered galactic supernova which have occurred in the past $\sim$ 500 years from their ^{44}Ti gamma-ray emission, (4) the scale height and velocity dispersion of the postulated high-velocity plasmas in the galactic disk, bulge and corona.

3.3.2 Detailed Mapping of Selected Regions (2 months)
The knife-edge mode would be used to obtain 2° resolution images at multiple position angles to resolve source complexes and better locate point sources. The vicinity of the Galactic Center is already known to be a region where this will be required. The knife-edge mode would also be used to map the latitude distribution of galactic gamma-rays with high precision, in order to determine their scale height and study their possible association with various galactic components.

3.3.3 Extragalactic Supernovae (6 months)
About 4 Type I supernova/year are expected at distances out to the Virgo cluster, $\sim$ 20 Mpc, and at this distance the 847 keV line flux from ^{56}Co decay should be detected for several months with $\sim$ 1 week time resolution. Measurements of line widths will test models of supernova explosions and measurements of their intensities, profiles and time evolution will give information on the nucleosynthetic yield, and the energetics and mass distribution of the ejecta.

3.3.4 Galactic Novae (2 months)
Several galactic novae within 2 kpc are expected to be discovered during a 2 year mission. These will be close enough for sensitive tests of the predicted nucelosynthesis of ^{22}Na (2.6 year half-life) by searching for its 1275 keV gamma-ray. The predicted ^{22}Na yield is sensitive to the thermal history and dynamics of a nova outburst, so it is expected to vary greatly from one nova to the next. The NAE sensitivity corresponds to a yield of $\sim 6 \times 10^{-9}$ M$_\odot$ for a nova at 2 kpc, which is 100 times below present limits.

3.3.5 Observations of Known Point Sources (8 months)
Many known galactic gamma-ray sources will require regular monitoring to observe unpredictable temporal changes that are known to occur but have not been resolved. The Galactic Center region and Cygnus X-1 are two of the best known in this class. Other objects, such as X-ray binaries, have their unique, predictable variability that requires observations at specific times. External galaxies which have energetic nuclei characterized by high energy, nonthermal radiation, i.e. the active galactic nuclei, are prime candidates for observations. Models predict a massive, accreting black hole at the nucleus with an associated electron-positron plasma or relativistic particle jets which transport energies over vast distances. In either scenario gamma-ray lines are expected [60] and their discovery would place the theoretical ideas on a much firmer footing. The sun is known to be a source of intense gamma-ray line fluxes during solar flares which often last for tens of minutes. The NAE would perform dedicated solar observations when a large flare is deemed likely.

3.3.6 Benefits of an Extended Mission
An extended mission lasting much longer than 2 years is very desirable scientifically and technically feasible. The latter follows from the lack of consumables in the instrument and spacecraft concepts and the detectors' > 10 year resistance to radiation damage. In a 5 to 10 year scenario much more extensive observations could be performed of objects where

unpredictable variability will carry key information. We already know that this is true of active galaxies, and the Galactic Center and Cyg X-1. An extended mission will allow the galactic plane survey to be repeated several times in order to obtain information on source variability, with variable sources being selected for follow up observations. A large number, ~ 20, of extragalactic Type I supernovae would be observed, providing definitive information on their range of nucleosynthetic yield and explosion mechanism(s). The likelihood of the mission overlapping solar maximum, the only time when gamma-ray producing flares are frequent, would be greatly increased and long periods, many months to years, of dedicated solar viewing could be obtained. In this scenario ~ 30 large flares would be expected, with hundreds to thousands of photons counted in the 15 strongest lines in each flare.

3.4 Status and Plans

In October 1989 NASA announced that the NAE was not selected for development. However, strong interest was expressed in the NAE and the Astrophysics Division of NASA is planning to continue the support of technology and instrument development as well as observational programs in high resolution gamma-ray spectroscopy. The next round of future Explorer selections is planned to begin with a Spring 1991 request for proposals for 1 year feasibility studies. The NAE will be proposed at that time and the earliest it could be launched is the late 1990's. In November 1989 a European-US collaboration submitted a proposal to ESA for a "Blue Box" mission in the late 1990's. This would combine ESA and NASA Explorer resources in a mission named INTEGRAL. This joins the NAE instrument with the Gamma-Ray Imager from the ESA/GRASP mission concept, which was studied in 1987-88.

Acknowledgements

Many people contributed to the development of the SIGMA and the NAE concept. We wish to acknowledge the contributions to the NAE concept by B. Teegarden, W. Mahoney, N. Gehrels, R. Lingenfelter, R. Ramaty, J. Higdon, M. Leventhal and R. Muller. This work was supported in part by NASA contract NAS5-30338 and NASA grant NAGW-449.

References

1. D. D. Clayton: in Gamma-Ray Astrophysics, eds. F. W. Stecker and J. I. Trombka (NASA SP-339, Washington, DC, 1973) p. 263.
2. R. Ramaty, R. E. Lingenfelter: Ann. Rev. Nucl. Part. Sci. 32, 235 (1982).
3. J. L. Matteson: Adv. Space Res. 3, No. 4, 135 (1983).
4. R. E. Lingenfelter and R. Ramaty, in Conference Papers of 19th International Cosmic Ray Conference, Vol. 5, 1985, p. 19.
5. L. E. Peterson: in Nuclear Spectroscopy of Astrophysical Sources, eds. N. Gehrels and G. H. Share (AIP, New York, 1988) p.1.
6. R. E. Lingenfelter: in Nuclear Spectroscopy of Astrophysical Sources, eds. N. Gehrels and G. H. Share (AIP, New York, 1988) p. 17.
7. E.L. Chupp: in Nuclear Spectroscopy of Astrophysical Sources, eds. N. Gehrels and G. H. Share (AIP, New York, 1988) p. 24.
8. R. Ramaty and R.E. Lingenfelter: Nature, 278, 127 (1979).
9. R. E. Lingenfelter and R. Ramaty: Physics Today, 31, No. 3, 40 (1978).
10. R. C. Haymes et al.: Ap. J. 201, 593 (1975).
11. M. Leventhal et al.: Ap. J. (Letters) 225, L11 (1978).
12. G. R. Riegler et al.: Ap. J. (Letters) 248, L13 (1981).
13. G. R. Riegler et al.: Ap. J. (Letters) 294, L13 (1985).

14. M. Leventhal et al.: Nature, 339, 36 (1989).
15. J. L. Matteson et al.: IAU Circular No. 4889 (1989).
16. G. H. Share et al.: Ap. J. 326, 717 (1988).
17. W. A. Mahoney: in Nuclear Spectroscopy of Astrophysical Sources, eds. N. Gehrels and G.H. Share (AIP, New York, 1988) p. 149.
18. E. L. Chupp et al.: Nature 241, 333 (1973).
19. M. Yoshimori et al.: Solar Physics 86, 375 (1983).
20. E. L. Chupp et al.: Ann. Rev. Astr. Ap. 22, 359 (1984).
21. E. P. Mazets et al.: Nature 282, 587 (1979).
22. E. P. Mazets et al.: Nature 290, 378 (1981).
23. B. J. Teegarden and T. L. Cline: Ap. J. (Letters) 236, L67 (1980).
24. M. Leventhal et al.: Ap. J. 216, 491 (1977).
25. C. A. Ayre et al.: Mon. Not. R. Astr. Soc. 205, 285 (1983).
26. A. S. Jacobson et al.: in Gamma-Ray Spectroscopy in Astrophysics, eds. T. L. Cline and R. Ramaty (NASA TM 79619, Greenbelt, MD, 1978) p. 228.
27. J. C. Ling: in Gamma-Ray Transients and Related Astrophysical Phenomena, eds. R. E. Lingenfelter, H. S. Hudson and D. M. Worrall (AIP, New York, 1982) p. 143.
28. P. L. Nolan and J. L. Matteson: Ap. J. 265, 389 (1983).
29. J. C. Ling et al.: Ap. J. (Letters) 321, L117 (1987).
30. J. C. Ling: in Nuclear Spectroscopy of Astrophysical Sources, eds. N. Gehrels and G.H. Share, (AIP, New York, 1988) p. 315.
31. J. C. Ling, W.A. Wheaton: Ap. J. 343 (1989).
32. M. Matz et al.: IAU Circular No. 4568 (1988).
33. W. Sandie et al.: IAU Circular No. 4526 (1988).
34. W. R. Cook et al.: IAU Circular No. 4527 (1988).
35. W. A. Mahoney et al.: IAU Circular No. 4584 (1988).
36. A. C. Rester et al.: IAU Circular No. 4535 (1988).
37. S. Barthelmy et al.: IAU Circular No. 4593 (1988).
38. B. J. Teegarden, et al.: Nature 339, 122 (1989).
39. J. Tueller, et al.: in Proceedings of the Gamma-Ray Observatory Workshop, ed. N. Johnson (1989) p. 4-258.
40. W. A. Mahoney et al.: Ap. J. 286, 578 (1984).
41. G. H. Share et al.: Ap. J. (Letters) 292, L61 (1985).
42. H. S. Hudson et al.: Ap. J. (Letters) 236, L91 (1980).
43. T. Prince et al.: Ap. J. (Letters) 255, L81 (1982).
44. B. R. Dennis et al.: in Gamma-Ray Transients and Related Astrophysical Phenomena, eds. R. E. Lingenfelter, H. S. Hudson and D. M. Worrall (AIP, New York, 1982) p. 153.
45. G. J. Hueter in High Energy Transients in Astrophysics, ed. S. E. Woosley (AIP, New York 1984) p. 373.
46. T. Murakami et al.: Nature, 355, 234 (1988).
47. J. Trümper et al.: Ap. J. (Letters) 219, L105 (1978).
48. W. A. Wheaton et al.: Nature 282, 240 (1979).
49. D. E. Gruber et al.: Ap. J. (Letters) 240, L127 (1980).
50. J. Tueller et al.: Ap. J. 279, 177 (1984).
51. G. S. Maurer et al.: Ap. J. 254, 271 (1982).
52. J. C. Ling et al.: Ap. J. 231, 896 (1979).
53. M. S. Strickman et al.: Ap. J. (Letters) 253, L23 (1982).
54. R. E. Lingenfelter, R. Ramaty: in High Resolution Gamma-Ray Cosmology, eds. D.B. Cline and E. Fenyves, Nuclear Physics B Proc. Suppl. 10B (North Holland, Amsterdam, 1989) p. 67.

55. R. E. Lingenfelter, R. Ramaty: in Proceedings of the 21st International Cosmic Ray Conference, paper OG7.2–6, in press.
56. S. E. Woosley, et al.: Ap.J. 301,601 (1986).
57. R. Ramaty, B. Kozlovsky, and R.E. Lingenfelter: Ap.J. Supp., 40, 487 (1979).
58. R. W. Bussard: Ap.J. 237 970 (1980).
59. E. Nagel: Ap.J. 251 288 (1981).
60. J.L. Matteson: in Electron-Positron Pairs in Astrophysics, eds. M.L. Burns, A.K. Harding and R. Ramaty (AIP, New York, 1983) p. 292.

SECTION VI

THE NEUTRON STAR IN SN 1987A AND OTHER SUPERNOVAE

The Sub-Millisecond Pulsar in SN 1987A: A Review of the Discovery Data After Six Months

Saul Perlmutter, Richard A. Muller, Carlton R. Pennypacker, & Timothy P. Sasseen

1. THE PULSAR DISCOVERY

1.1. Experiment Design

Two years ago, when Supernova 1987A was discovered, we were presented with an unusual opportunity to catch a pulsar at its birth. It was of course not known how long it would take before the expanding supernova photosphere would become transparent enough to see into a pulsating center. In collaboration with researchers from the United States, Canada, Chile, and Australia, we began an optical search for pulsations in SN 1987A about a month after the supernova discovery, and this search set upper limits on pulsed light until January, 1989 (PENNYPACKER et al. [1]).

The experiment itself is very simple: A silicon photodiode detector collects light from 2-, 3- or 4-meter telescopes in Chile and Australia (PENNYPACKER et al. [1]). The voltage from the photodiode is digitized at 5 or 10 kHz, based on a stable clock, and the resulting data are written to magnetic tape. The analysis of these data tapes is performed at Los Alamos on the Cray XMP computers. This is necessary because we search many 10^8-point modified Fourier transforms, each with a different pulsar slow-down rate (dP/dt). The Cray CPU time for the analysis is comparable to the time for the observation at the telescope, and in the two years of observations since the discovery of SN 1987A, we have used hundreds of hours of Cray time.

1.2. The Observed Signal

On January 18, 1989 we observed the supernova for seven hours at the Cerro Tololo 4-meter telescope, with a sampling rate of 5 kHz.(MIDDLEDITCH et al. [2], KRISTIAN et al. [3]). The Fourier transforms of these data show a very strong peak at 1968.63 Hz that reaches as high as 600 times the background noise level in this frequency region. As shown in Figure 1, the signal amplitude stays relatively constant for the first half of the observation and then increases by a factor of three in the last half. This means that the fraction of the light from the supernova that is pulsed varies from one part in 300 to one part in 100. (Note that these numbers have been re-calibrated to account for instrument inefficiencies since the first reports. See MIDDLEDITCH et al. [5]) This corresponds to about 100 times the optical luminosity of the Crab pulsar at the same distance.

Twelve minutes after the seven hours of observation of the supernova we observed Globular Cluster NGC 3201; this serves as an instrument check. No pulsations were seen near 1968 Hz in a half-hour observation of this object, at a limit 12 times less than the weakest SN 1987A pulsations (the arrow in Figure 1), indicating that the SN 1987A pulsations were not instrumental artifacts.

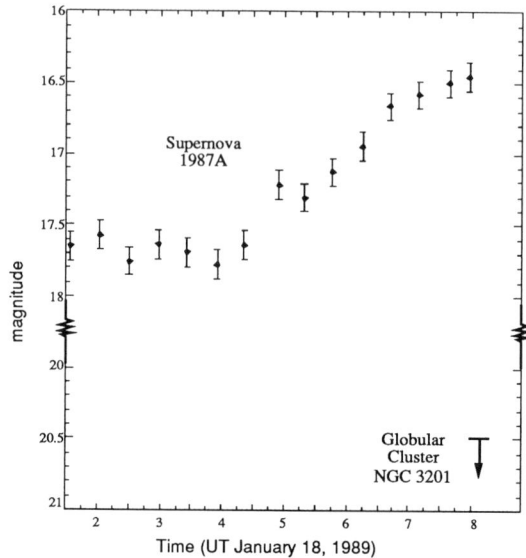

Figure 1. The magnitude of pulsed light from Supernova 1987A versus time for seven-hour observation on January 18, 1989. The arrow shows (on a "broken" magnitude axis) the upper limit on pulsed light from an observation on globular cluster NGC 3201. (These magnitudes are newly calibrated for instrument inefficiencies. See MIDDLEDITCH et al. [5].)

The SN 1987A signal at 1968.63 Hz was also visible in higher harmonics. Since the Nyquist frequency of 2.5 kHz is below the second harmonic, it is necessary to look at the "folded" frequency where the aliased harmonics should appear. The second harmonic of the 1968.63 Hz signal is very strong and tracks the fundamental in amplitude, while the third harmonic is visible towards the end of the observation when the signal was stronger. After correcting for the effects of aliasing and the rolloff of the photodiode amplifier, the ratios of the power in the first three harmonics, 1 : 1.8 : 1.6, is similar to those of the Crab pulsar in its optical light, 1 : 1.92 : 1.36. Figure 2 shows the SN 1987A pulse profile reconstructed from these first three harmonics, with the analogous curve for the Crab pulsar drawn for comparison.

We conclude from this data that we are seeing pulsations from SN 1987A. In the 36 previous observations in the two years since the supernova was discovered, no comparable signal was seen. The largest Fourier-transform peaks in these two years were 6σ events (PENNYPACKER et al. [1]), while the 1968.63 Hz signal increased from 11σ to 37σ during the January 18 observation.

1.3. A Pulsar at 1968 Hz

If we interpret this signal as a classical rotating-neutron-star pulsar, we find it to be a surprising object. At this rotation frequency, the star's self-gravitation is barely stronger than its centrifugal force: it is almost flying apart (more about this later). The velocity at the equator is about 40% of the speed of light—this is a highly relativistic object. The kinetic energy of rotation is on the order of 10^{53} ergs, comparable to the total amount of energy released in the supernova collapse/explosion.

A pulsar rotating this fast inside SN 1987A must have a small magnetic field, or else the supernova would appear brighter than it does ($L_{1987A} \approx 3 \times 10^{38}$ erg/sec). The least luminosity that could be emitted from a pulsar with a dipole magnetic field B would be:

$$L_{\text{dipole}} \propto B^2 \omega^4$$

where ω is the pulsar rotation frequency. For comparison, the Crab pulsar, which is believed to power the Crab nebula with a luminosity of 5×10^{38} erg/sec, has a rotation frequency of 30.2 Hz and a magnetic field strength of 4×10^{12} Gauss. Scaling from the Crab pulsar, we find that the SN 1987A pulsar must have a magnetic field a factor of (1968 Hz / 30 Hz)^2 smaller, or about 10^9 Gauss. This is of course an upper limit.

1.4. Follow-up Observations and Other Group's Observations

The natural question at this point is, have we seen the pulsar again? In the six months since the January 18 observation, we have observed SN 1987A on about 16 separate nights, for a total integrated observation time of approximately 20 hours. None of the resulting data sets have shown significant pulsations at frequencies near 1968 Hz. The limits set by these observations are all about 20.5 magnitude, a factor of 13 below the weakest January 18 pulsations.

Ours was not the only group searching for a pulsar in SN 1987A. A European group, observing in Chile, and an Australian group also had searches underway. In fact, Peterson and Manchester, in Australia, observed the supernova on the same night that we found the pulsar. Their system sampled the signal at 100 kHz, although they originally analyzed their data in 1 kHz bins. (Our experiment was apparently the only one that was sensitive to a pulsar faster than previously known pulsars.) Peterson and Manchester later reanalyzed their data with shorter time bins to look for the 1968 Hz signal, but found no signal. The significant difference between their experiment and ours is probably their choice of a blue-pass filter, blocking light redwards of 4800 Å. According to the SN 1987A atmosphere models of PINTO, AXELROD, and WOOSLEY [4], the atmosphere becomes much more transparent for wavelengths longer than 8000–9000 Å where our silicon photodiode still had sensitivity. It appears likely that a detector with sensitivity at even longer wavelengths would be appropriate for this search.

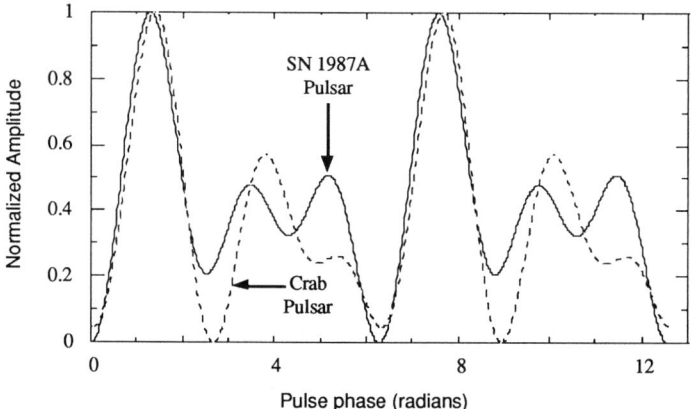

Figure 2. Pulse profiles synthesized from the first three harmonics. The solid line is the pulse profile of the signal in SN 1987A and the dotted line is the profile of the Crab Pulsar.

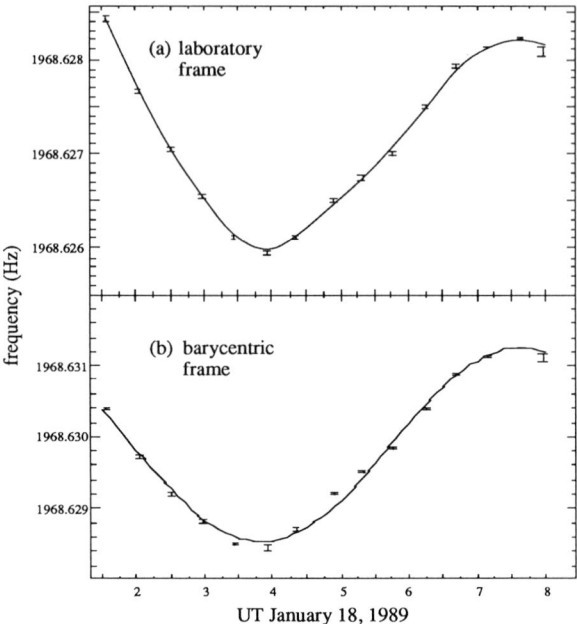

Figure 3. a) Observed frequency versus time for seven-hour run on January 18, 1989. The solid line is to guide the eye. b) Same as a), but corrected for the Doppler shift due to the rotation of the Earth about its axis and about the Sun. The solid line is the best fit sine function. (Based on KRISTIAN et al. [3].)

1.5. Frequency Modulation

The signal at 1968.63 Hz is very narrow in frequency; it is stable to better than a part in 10^6. There is, however, a very small frequency modulation observable over the 7 hours of data, at the millihertz level. Figure 3a shows this modulation. The timescale of this frequency drift was difficult to understand until we corrected the frequencies for the doppler shifts due to the Earth's rotations about its axis and about the Sun. As Figure 3b shows, this corrected frequency modulation is close to a sine wave, which would be the doppler modulation for an orbiting companion in a circular orbit.

The 7 hours of data contain a strong enough signal that we can do a more detailed analysis by breaking the data into 56 seven-minute segments (MIDDLEDITCH et al. [5]). For each segment we can find the frequency and phase of the 1968.63 Hz signal so precisely that the exact number of cycles in each seven minute segment can be found and linked to the next segment. We can then calculate the arrival time of the pulsar pulse that occurred closest to the middle of each segment, and use this as an independent "pulsar clock." Since this clock is very stable, a plot of "pulsar time" versus lab-clock time is essentially a straight line. The deviations from this straight-line can be magnified as in Figure 4 to show the pulses arriving a few milliseconds early and then a few milliseconds late as the pulsar moves forward and back, perturbed (apparently) by the 7-hour orbit of a companion.

If the deviation is due to an orbiting companion, what are its properties? Using Kepler's Law and the 7-hour period, we can easily find the semi-major axis, R, of the companion's orbit. Scaling from the Earth's orbit about the Sun, we find

$$R \approx \left(\frac{7 \text{ hours}}{365 \text{ days}}\right)^{2/3} [\text{AU}] \approx 10^{-2} \text{ AU}$$

in Astronomical Units, the distance from the Earth to the Sun. This is approximately $R \approx 10^{11}$ cm. The modulation amplitude of $\sim 1.4 \times 10^{-3}$ Hz corresponds to a doppler velocity of (~ 0.2 km/sec) / sin i, where i is the inclination angle of the orbit to our line of sight. Taking sin i to be of order unity, this gives a semi-major axis for the pulsar about the center-of-mass, $r \approx 10^8$ cm. The ratio of these semi-major axes is of course the ratio of the masses of the pulsar and its companion, about 1 to 1000. For a neutron star with a typical mass of 1.4 solar masses, this makes the companion slightly more massive than Jupiter.

Pulsars with a short-period companion are not completely unknown. Recently, FRUCHTER, STINEBRING, and TAYLOR [6] discovered pulsar PSR 1957 +20, with a 9-hour orbit. The companion of PSR 1957 +20 (or its surrounding ionized region) appears to eclipse the pulsar as it passes in front. So far the data for the SN 1987A pulsar shows no significant evidence of a similar eclipse by its companion, so we are probably not looking at an orbit edge on.

2. IMPLICATIONS

2.1. Problems for Current Pulsar Models

If the signal described in the preceding section is a pulsar, it presents a number of puzzles for current pulsar theories. First, there is the surprising period—shorter than any other known pulsar by a factor of three. This short period suggests a low magnetic field, a second puzzle. Third is the problem of the companion orbiting so close to the pulsar.

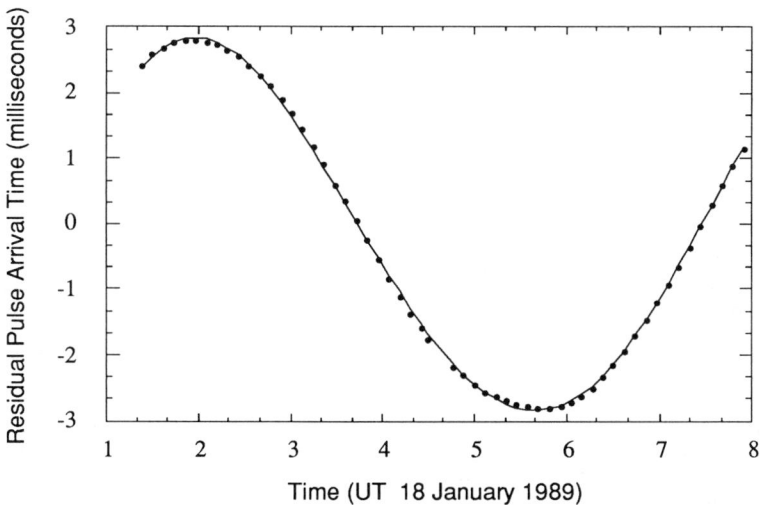

Figure 4. Residuals from fit of pulse arrival times to straight line ($f_0 t + \varphi_0$). The error bars are smaller than the data points. The solid line is the best fit Keplerian orbit with a 7.1 hour period and eccentricity $e = 0.093$. (Based on MIDDLEDITCH et al. [5].)

Fourth, and perhaps most perplexing, why were the pulsations so bright, and why are they not visible now?

Most fast pulsars are currently believed to have been "spun up" over millions of years by accreting matter from an orbiting companion. The SN 1987A pulsar, however, has had only two years to reach its current period. WOOSLEY and CHEVALIER [7] have suggested that an accretion-driven spin-up did occur within the first few hours after the explosion. When the expanding shock wave hits the hydrogen envelope of the progenitor star, a reverse shock forms, which can throw material back down onto the neutron star. Woosley and Chevalier point out that the progenitor star for SN 1987A is thought to be much smaller than is typical before a supernova explosion, and therefore there is much denser debris to be thrown back by the reverse shock wave. This scenario might also explain the weak magnetic field, since material accreting on the neutron star with a disordered magnetic moment can bury its magnetic field (WOOSLEY and CHEVALIER [7]).

WANG et al. [8] have proposed a fundamentally different model to explain the short pulse period, and to avoid the problem of a weak magnetic field. They point out that the half-millisecond period is very close to the natural period of radial oscillation of a neutron star. If an optical pulse could be generated by some mechanism every time the star "breathed" out or in, this would avoid the necessity of considering high spin rates or weak magnetic fields. One constraint on this model is that the optical-pulse mechanism must generate the interpulse structure that is visible in Figure 2, or, equivalently, the dominant power at the second harmonic.

The radial oscillation model will be easily tested when and if the pulsar is reobserved, since a rotating neutron star should slow down as it radiates energy, while an oscillating neutron star should remain at the same (or higher) frequency with a reduced amplitude of oscillation. It is possible that the oscillation observed on January 18 has already damped out, and that we are now waiting for another star-quake to "ring the bell" of the neutron star and thus produce more optical pulsations. If the neutron star is oscillating at 1968 Hz *and* rotating (at a slower rate) then we should also be able to see frequency-modulation sidebands about the main Fourier peak.

With either a rotating or oscillating pulsar model it is still difficult to understand how a companion can exist at a distance of only 10^{11} cm from the pulsar. This is well within the progenitor star's radius and the companion is unlikely to have survived the supernova explosion. Aside from the energy released in the explosion, enough mass is lost from the region inside of 10^{11} cm that a bound object should become unbound. Alternatively, we can look for mechanisms that could create such an object after the explosion. (The other pulsar with a similar orbit, PSR 1957 +20, has been explained by postulating a companion star spiraling its way in towards the pulsar over many millions of years, ablating mass as it goes. Clearly this is not a viable solution in the case of SN 1987A.)

Why have we--and other groups--been unable to reobserve the 1968 Hz pulsations? For the reasons given above and in MIDDLEDITCH et al. [5], it is difficult to attribute this signal to a spurious local source, and we have been forced to ask what is going on at SN 1987A that could be hiding or suppressing the signal source. It is possible that we saw the signal through a momentary clearing in the opaque debris surrounding the pulsar, and that dust has been forming to add to this shroud. If this is the case, a detector more sensitive in the IR may help. Given that the pulsations were intrinsically much brighter than the Crab's, and that the amplitude changed by a factor of three in three hours, it is also plausible that we observed a flare-up in the pulse emission mechanism. If this is the case the observing task is a little more daunting, since we are then spot checking the pulsar with the hope of catching another flare-up.

2.2. Nuclear Equations of State

A pulsar rotating at 1968 Hz puts strong constraints on the nuclear equation of state, the equation that describes the compressibility of matter at nuclear densities. This is because

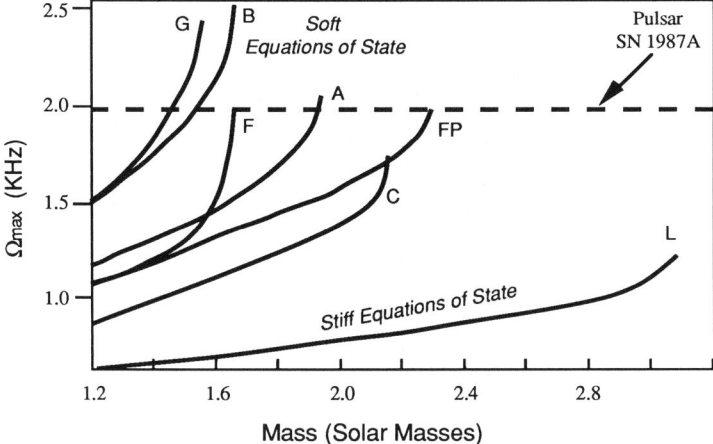

Figure 5. The maximum rotation frequency versus neutron star mass, for a sampling of equations of state. (Based on figure from FRIEDMAN, IPSER, and PARKER[9].)

the compressibility of a neutron star sets a limit on the maximum rotation frequency of the star: A "stiff," incompressible equation of state gives a larger star for a given mass, while a "soft," compressible equation of state allows a star of the same mass to "pull itself in" to a smaller radius. The smaller star can rotate faster before its surface becomes unbound or unstable.

The neutron star mass is the other factor in the calculation of a rotational "speed limit." For a given equation of state, a more massive star will be smaller and thus able to spin faster. One cannot however add mass indefinitely in a stellar model to permit higher and higher angular velocities, because above a certain mass the star collapses into a black hole. Figure 5, based on a figure from FRIEDMAN, IPSER, and PARKER [9], shows these competing factors for a few different equations of state. The stiff equations of state give a lower maximum velocity, Ω_{max}, than the soft equations of state, and for each equation of state increasing the mass increases Ω_{max}. The endpoint for each curve is at the maximum mass that the equation of state could support against gravitational collapse, even with the help of centrifugal force from a 1968 Hz rotation.

If the pulsar in SN 1987A is rotating at 1968 Hz, then the only viable nuclear equations of state are those that appear above the horizontal line in Figure 5. This rules out all of the stiff equations of state. Of the equations shown, only models B, G, F, and A of FRIEDMAN, IPSER, and PARKER [9] allow such a rapidly rotating neutron star. However, as their paper points out, models B and G are not stiff enough to support the mass of the binary pulsar, PSR 1913 +16, which rotates much more slowly. Equations F and A are probably also unacceptable, because 1968 Hz is so near their endpoint that nonaxisymmetric instabilities may set in. These are, however, only a sampling of possible phenomenological equations of state, and there could exist other equations between curves A and B that do satisfy all the constraints (see LATTIMER *et al.* in this volume for more discussion on this point).

It is of course possible to avoid these tight limits on nuclear equations of state if the pulsar turns out to be a radially oscillating neutron star, as described above.

2.3. Gravitational Radiation

The power emitted in gravitational radiation from a rotating neutron star with a finite quadrupole moment scales as $P_{grav} \sim \omega^6$. The SN 1987A pulsar should thus be the most efficient gravitational radiator of any known pulsar—unless it is symmetric about its spin axis. (Compared to the much nearer Crab pulsar, it would be radiating 10^8 times more power for the same quadrupole moment.) In fact, a 1968 Hz pulsar would be so efficient that any asymmetries in its mass distribution would be damped out in a time-scale of seconds. To be emitting gravitational radiation now, asymmetries would therefore have to be continuously regenerated through some dynamical mechanism. KLUZNIAK et al. [10] have suggested that Chandrasekhar-Friedman-Schutz gravitational instabilities would be such a mechanism for this pulsar. So far, however, one can only set limits on the total amount of gravitational radiation based on the lack of significant slowing in the pulsar period ($dP/dt < 3 \times 10^{-14}$ s s^{-1}).

The next generation of gravitational wave antennas might be sensitive enough to detect these waves, particularly if they can be tuned to a specific pulse period. Unfortunately, the Chandrasekhar-Friedman-Schutz mechanism does not generate gravitational radiation at the pulsar rotation period, so it is more difficult to look for this particular source of gravity waves.

3. CURRENT PROGRESS

3.1. Further Analysis of Pulse Arrival-time Residuals

Figure 4 showed the residuals from a two-parameter straight-line fit to the pulse arrival times. If we fit five more parameters to account for the orbit (MIDDLEDITCH et al. [5]), as shown by the solid line in Figure 4, we are left with the residuals of Figure 6. The plotting scale has once again been magnified to show the very small (~30 microsec RMS) deviations. At this scale the error bars are finally larger than the plotting points, and it is clear that the points are not statistically scattered about the zero line. We are currently examining possible explanations for the systematic drifting of these residuals, including systematic error in the laboratory clock, random perturbations at the pulsar, and periodic events at the pulsar.

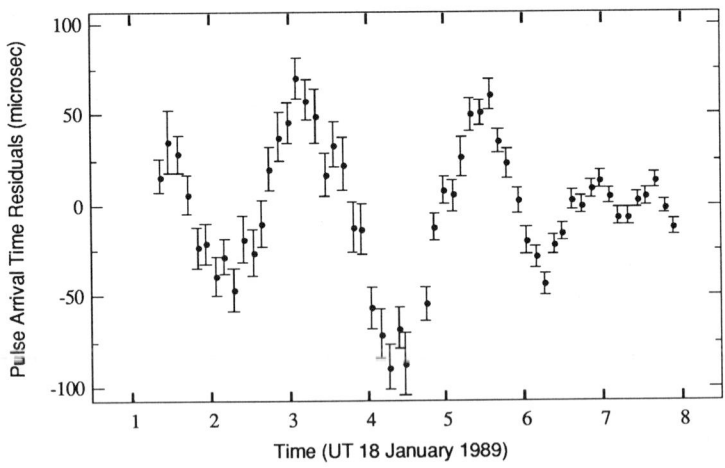

Figure 6. Residuals from the fit of a Keplerian orbit to pulse arrival times versus Universal Time. (Based on MIDDLEDITCH et al. [5].)

Clock Error. The clock used to record the data was a Datum model 9110 quartz crystal with a factory-specified limit on its frequency drift of 5 parts in 10^9 per day. Its stability was determined by comparison with a rubidium standard clock to be within 5 parts in 10^{10} and 3 parts in 10^9 for time intervals of minutes and several days, respectively. The drift in Figure 6 is at the part in 10^8 level, at least an order of magnitude larger than the clock's stability; thus we conclude that the clock could not have been the cause.

Random Perturbations at the Pulsar. Similar systematic drifting of pulse-arrival-time residuals have been found in the analysis of the Crab Pulsar's optical pulsations (GROTH [11], BOYNTON et al. [12]). In the case of the Crab, the time scale of the drifts turned out to depend on the length of the data set. This led GROTH [11] to observe that since their analysis fit the data to a second-degree polynomial $(1/2\,[df/dt]_0 t^2 + f_0 t + \varphi_0)$, the residuals can only be characterized by a third-degree (or higher) polynomial. Thus any random perturbations in the frequency of the pulsar (due to material accreting on the pulsar, for example) would result in residuals with three or more zero crossings.

In the case of the data from SN 1987A, the seven parameter fit to an orbit is more complicated than a sixth-degree polynomial, so it is not obvious how the residuals should look if there are random frequency perturbations at the pulsar. The number of zero crossings is, however, comparable to the number of parameters fit. We have therefore performed Monte Carlo simulations by adding the effect of a random walk in frequency to a perfect Keplerian orbit's pulse arrival times. After fitting a new orbit (seven parameters) to these simulated data sets, we found that the residuals did show systematic drifts similar to the true data, for certain values of the random walk parameters. Figure 7 shows the residuals from one of the first five random-walk data sets that was generated this way. Although these Monte Carlo residuals look similar, they do not appear to the eye to be as regular in their zero crossings, so we have also considered the alternative possibility that the perturbing events are periodic.

Periodic Events at the Pulsar. The residuals in Figure 6 appear to vary with a period of approximately 2 hours. Fitting an additional five parameters for a second companion's orbit gives the excellent fit shown in Figure 8, but is probably ruled out because of the immense densities necessary for such a companion to survive the tidal forces from the pulsar. A precession of the neutron star's spin axis about its symmetry axis could also produce the 2 hour period (NELSON, FINN, and WASSERMAN [13]). The fit to precession, with four additional parameters, appears almost the same as Figure 8, reminding us that is difficult to

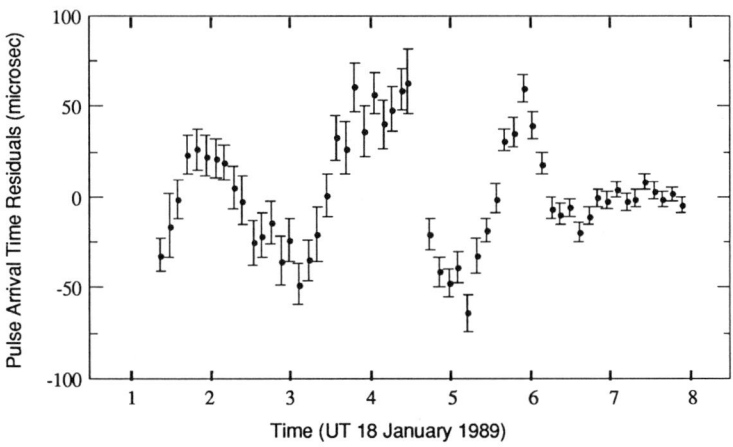

Figure 7. Same as Figure 6, but for Monte Carlo simulated data.

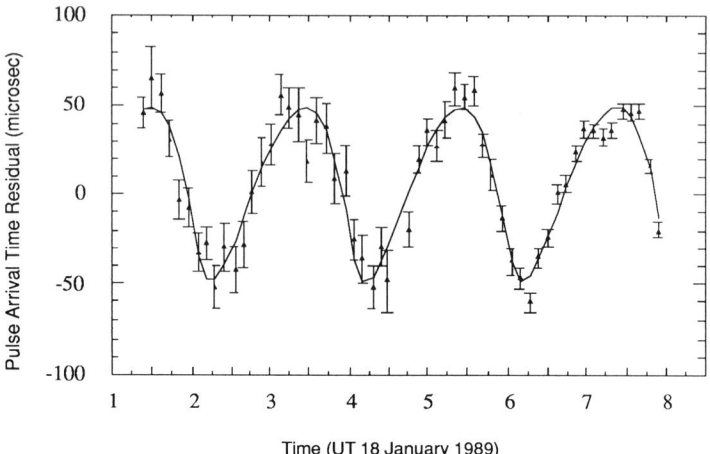

Figure 8. Pulse arrival-time deviations due to the second orbit in a 2-orbit fit of pulse arrival times versus Universal Time. (Based on MIDDLEDITCH et al. [5].)

distinguish these periodic models based on 11- and 12-parameter fits.

The pulsed amplitude data provides some additional support for the hypothesis that there are 2-hour periodic events at the pulsar. After the slow trends (e.g. the three-hour brightening) are removed with a cubic fit, the Fourier transform of the amplitude shows a peak at 1.95 ± 0.1 hours with more than six times the mean power (MIDDLEDITCH et al. [5]). The probability of such a peak to occur by chance within an error-bar of the 2-hour period seen in the pulse-arrival-time data is less than 1%. The peak should not be due to the cubic fit itself since the characteristic residual for such a cubic should have power around a 4-hour period (4 zero-crossings).

In conclusion, I should stress that however one interprets the small microsecond drift in residuals, this is a small perturbation on the smooth curve of the millisecond residuals, which fit a 7.5 hour Keplerian orbit very well. In particular, it is important to note that the mechanism of BOYNTON et al. [12] for creating spurious sinusoidal modulations through multi-parameter fits, which we considered for the microsecond residuals, is not a serious concern for the millisecond residuals, since the 7-hour modulation appears in the frequency-vs-time plot even when no parameters are fit.

3.2. Observing Plans

We are continuing to search in SN 1987A for a signal near 1968.63 Hz, as well as any other periodic signal. Currently, hour-long observations are made every few weeks at Cerro Tololo in Chile during "bright time" (when the moon is bright), and once a month at Siding Springs in Australia.

We are also constructing a new detector and data acquisition system. This system will be able to sample up to 50 kHz, and the detector will be sensitive to 1.8 microns. We will thus be able to see the (apparently) more powerful second harmonic of the 1968 Hz signal, and observe through the wavelengths where the supernova remnant is probably more transparent. We intend to be using this more sensitive system within the next few months.

This work has been supported in part by the National Science Foundation, the Ann and Gordon Getty Foundation, the Institute of Geophysics and Planetary Physics, of Los Alamos National Laboratory, and the U.S. Department of Energy under contract number DEAC03-76SF00098.

REFERENCES

1. Pennypacker, C., et al., *Astrophys. J. Lett.*, **340**, L63 (1989).
2. Middleditch, J., et al., *IAU Circ.* No. 4735 (1989).
3. Kristian, J., et al., *Nature*, **338**, 234, (1989).
4. Pinto, P., Axelrod, and Woosley, S. E., private communication (1989).
5. Middleditch, J., et al., *LBL Report*, No. LBL-27347, June, 1989, submitted to *Science* (1989).
6. Fruchter, A. S., Stinebring, D. R., and Taylor, J. H., *Nature*, **333**, 237 (1988).
7. Woosley, S. E., and Chevalier, R. A., *Nature*, **338**, 321 (1989).
8. Wang, Q., et al., *Nature*, **338**, 319 (1989).
9. Friedman, J. L., Ipser, J. R., and Parker, L., (Preprint, 1989).
10. Kluzniak, W., et al.,*Nature*, **339**, 19 (1989).
11. Groth, E. J., Ph.D. Thesis, Princeton University (1971).
12. Boynton, P. E., et al., *Astrophys. J.*, **175**, 217 (1972).
13. Nelson, R. W., Finn, L. S., and Wasserman, I., (Preprint, 1989).

Implications of a Fast Pulsar for the Equation of State

James M. Lattimer

The recent observation of a sub-millisecond pulsar [1] in the remnant of SN1987A with period $P = 0.508$ ms is very exciting because the possibility exists of pinning down the equation of state (EOS) of supra-nuclear density matter, *if the pulsations are due to rotation*. The neutrinos detected by Kamioka [2] and IMB, [3], although basically confirming the standard theoretical models of neutron star birth, did not give an accurate enough estimate of the neutron star's binding energy or mass to constrain the EOS. The maximum rotation rate of a star must be less than or equal to the Keplerian rate, Ω_K, at which the equatorial surface velocity equals the orbital velocity of a particle at the equator. Recent general relativistic instability analyses [4] demonstrate that the maximum rotation rate cannot be less than about $0.9\Omega_K$. If there exist physical mechanisms for increasing the neutrino fluxes of young neutron stars, such as quarks or meson condensates, the maximum rotation rate becomes nearly equal to Ω_K.

In general, Ω_K is larger for more compact neutron stars with higher central densities. Thus, the maximum rotation rate is an increasing function of the "softness" of the EOS. The observed period of 0.508 ms, if due to rotation, sets one limit to the EOS. In addition, the masses (1.44 M$_\odot$ and 1.38 M$_\odot$) of the components of the binary pulsar PSR 1913+16 [5] set a lower limit to the maximum mass of a neutron star. The maximum mass is a decreasing function of the "softness" of the EOS, and therefore establishes a second constraint. These two constraints will restrict the EOS to lie in a narrow range.

The calculations of the maximum rotation rate and the maximum mass permitted by a given EOS has to be done with full general relativity. It has been shown, however, that an approximate formula [6] for the Keplerian rotation rate in terms of the maximum mass properties of the non-rotating star is extremely accurate [7]. It is

$$\Omega_K = 7.7 \times 10^3 \left(\frac{M_{max}}{M_\odot}\right)^{1/2} \left(\frac{R_{max}}{10 \text{km}}\right)^{-3/2} \text{s}^{-1}. \qquad (1)$$

The subscripts "max" refer to the maximum mass non-rotating star of a given equation of state. This formula is, in fact, accurate to within 4% for all equations of state we have tested, except that of a completely incompressible fluid (for which the coefficient 7.7 is 9.6). In addition, the general relativistic calculations of Friedman, Ipser and Parker [8] follow this formula to within the same accuracy. The challenge for an EOS is therefore to compress at least 1.44 M$_\odot$ within a radius limited by $\Omega_K = 2\pi/P \geq 1.237 \times 10^4 \text{s}^{-1}$, which implies $R_{max} \leq 8.2\sqrt{M_{max}/1.44 \text{ M}_\odot}$ km. By employing the schematic equation of state developed by Prakash, Ainsworth and Lattimer [9], we have shown that this constrains the EOS to be *both* relatively soft around nuclear densities *and* quite stiff at higher densities.

The softness around nuclear densities may have two possible sources: a low value for the nuclear compression modulus $K \leq 160 \pm 20$ MeV, or a phase transition in the range 1–3 times nuclear saturation density ($n_s = 0.16$ fm^{-3}). The high density (above 5–6 times n_s) equation of state, on the other hand, must be very nearly at the causal limit $\partial P/\partial \epsilon = 1$, where P is the pressure and ϵ is the energy density. Even with a phase transition, the nuclear compression modulus cannot be much larger than 200 MeV if both rotation and mass constraints are to be satisfied by the EOS. Interestingly, the phase transition apparently cannot be to a quark phase of matter, because in this case the high density EOS is very subcausal ($\partial P/\partial \epsilon = 1/3$).

Our results for the case without any phase transitions are shown in Figure 1. The graphs on the left display the case that the high density equation of state is exactly causal above the transition density n_t. The only other significant parameter of the EOS is the compression modulus K. The upper left graph shows the Keplerian rotation rate Ω_K in units of 10^4s^{-1} as a function of the two EOS parameters. At best, Ω_K must be less than about 160 MeV in order to satisfy the SN1987A rotation rate (1.237×10^4s^{-1}). The lower left graph shows the maximum mass of non-rotating stars as a function of the EOS parameters. The small region to the right of the curve 1.44 M$_\odot$ is excluded by the PSR 1913+16 constraint. The graphs on the right display contours of $\Omega_K = 1.237$ and $M_{max} = 1.44$ M$_\odot$ for various values of the parameter $s = \partial P/\partial \epsilon$, which defines the EOS above n_t. The case $s = 2$ is included only for reference, since in reality the EOS cannot violate causality. It is clear that for s less than unity the allowable phase space in K and n_t rapidly shrinks: the rotation constraint implies that the maximum allowable value of K drops, and the binary pulsar mass constraint increases the size of the excluded region. By $s = 1/2$, there are no more acceptable solutions, ruling out quarks ($s = 1/3$).

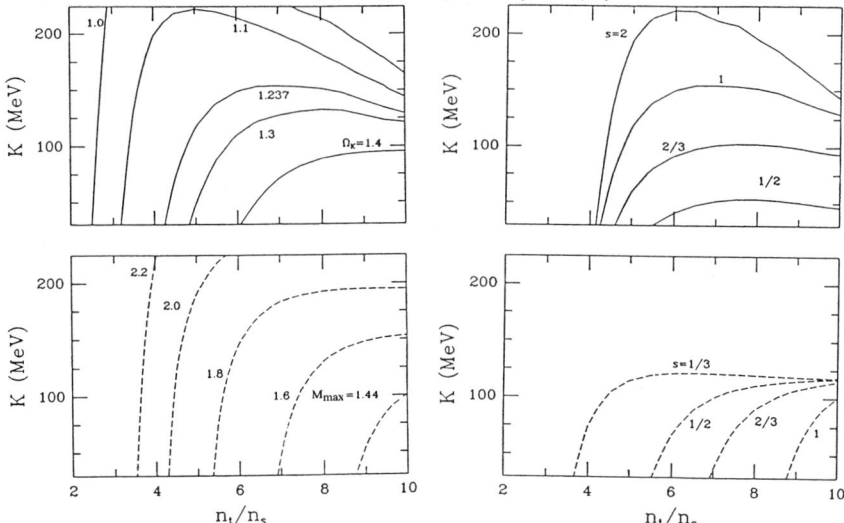

Fig. 1: Left: Contours of $\Omega_K/10^4$s^{-1} (upper) and $M_{max}/$ M$_\odot$ (lower) as functions of K and n_t for the case $s = \partial P/\partial \epsilon = 1$. Right: Contours of $\Omega_K/10^4$s$^{-1} = 1.237$ (upper) and $M_{max}/$ M$_\odot = 1.44$ (lower) as functions of s.

Friedman, Ipser and Parker [8] and we [7] have examined the rotational properties of a number of published equations of state. Only equations of state with very small values of K and $s \simeq 1$ are successful. Therefore, we feel that although a schematic equation of state was used to derive Figure 1, the results are, in fact, rather general.

The effect of phase transitions is, generally speaking, to lower the effective value of the nuclear compression modulus. It is difficult to express this quantitatively, however, because the compression modulus is defined at n_s and phase transitions, if they occur, set in at higher densities. Nevertheless, from our own experience with specific models for phase transitions (pion condensates [10]; kaon condensates [11]; Chiral parity doubling transitions [12]), they are only effective in permitting rapid rotation if they occur below 3– 4 n_s, if K is not too large, and if the high density equation of state is nearly causal. Therefore, qualitatively, the results expressed in Figure 1 remain valid even if phase transitions occur.

The constraint that the high density equation of state must be nearly causal seems to rule out a phase transition to quark matter at moderate densities. The EOS models containing quark cores that have been published [13] all fail to attain sufficiently rapid rotation. But what if the entire star is made of quark matter?

Witten [14] explored the structure of neutron stars using the self-bound equation of state $P = (1/3)(\epsilon - \epsilon_o)$ that is applicable in the case of massless quarks of both 2 and 3 flavors. The constant $\epsilon_o = 4B$, where B is the MIT bag constant. The linear dependence of pressure on the energy density has the interesting consequence that non-rotating configurations with maximum mass scale with ϵ_o according to $M_{max} \propto \epsilon_o^{-1/2}$ and $R_{max} \propto \epsilon_o^{-1/2}$. For $\epsilon_o = 224$ MeV fm^{-3}, $M_{max} = 2.033$ M$_\odot$ and $R_{max} = 11.09$ km. The success or failure of these models depends crucially on the value of ϵ_o. In the bag model, ϵ_o is bounded from above by the condition that quark matter be bound at low densities: $\epsilon_o \leq 366$ MeV fm^{-3}. This implies that $M_{max} \geq 2.6$ M$_\odot$, $R_{max} \geq 14.2$ km, and, therefore, $\Omega_K \leq 1.20 \times 10^4$s^{-1}. Therefore, even a quark star, subject to the matter being self-bound, cannot satisfy the rotation constraint.

This work was supported in part by the DOE under grant DE–FG02–87ER40317.

References
1. C. Kristian et al., Nature 338, 234 (1989).
2. K. Hirata, et al., Phys. Rev. Lett. 58, 1490 (1987).
3. R. M. Bionta, et al., Phys. Rev. Lett. 58, 1494 (1987).
4. J. R. Ipser and L. Lindblom, Phys. Rev. Lett.62, 2777 (1989).
5. J. M. Weisberg and J. H. Taylor, Phys. Rev. Lett.52, 1348 (1984).
6. P. Haensel and J. L.Zdunik, Nature, submitted (1989).
7. J. M. Lattimer, M. Prakash, D. Masak and A. Yahil, Ap. J., submitted (1989).
8. J. L. Friedman, J. R. Ipser and L. Parker, Astrophys. J. 304, 115 (1986);
 J. L. Friedman, J. R. Ipser and L. Parker, Phys. Rev. Lett. 62, 3015 (1989).
9. M. Prakash, T. L. Ainsworth and J. M. Lattimer, Phys. Rev. Lett. 61, 2518 (1988).
10. W. Weise and B. E. Brown, Phys. Lett. 58B, 300 (1975).
11. G. E. Brown, K. Kubodera, M. Prakash and M. Rho, Nucl. Phys. A479, 175c (1988).
12. T. Hatsuda and M. Prakash, Phys. Lett. 224B, 11 (1989).
13. W. B. Fechner and P. C. Joss, Nature 274, 347 (1978);
 P. Haensel, J. L. Zdunik and R. Schaeffer, A. and Ap. 160, 121 (1986).
14. E. Witten, Phys. Rev. D30, 272 (1984).

Surface Structure of Neutron Stars and Nuclear Reactions with High Magnetic Fields

Ikko Fushiki

There is considerable evidence for the existence of strong magnetic fields at the surfaces of some neutron stars. The strengths of magnetic fields at neutron star surfaces have been estimated for over three hundred known pulsars and lie between $10^{10.36}$ G to $10^{13.33}$ G (MANCHESTER and TAYLOR [1]). In a strong magnetic field, the electron motion perpendicular to the field lines is quantized to discrete Landau orbitals (LANDAU and LIFSHITZ [2]) and the electrons behaves as a one–dimensional gas rather than a three–dimensional gas. Many calculations of the properties of bulk matter in such fields have been performed, beginning with the work of RUDERMAN [3] and KADOMTSEV and KUDRYAVTSEV [4]. Subsequently a variety of techniques has been applied to calculate the energy of bulk matter.

An important question is whether or not matter in a high magnetic field can have a zero pressure state with lower energy per atom than the energy of an isolated atom, since some pulsar emission mechanisms (RUDERMAN and SUTHERLAND [5]) work only if such a bound state exists. The question is a difficult one because the energy differences are so small, but the most recent Hartree–Fock calculations for chains of atoms (NEUHAUSER, KOONIN, and LANGANKE [6]) suggest that for magnetic fields B in excess of 1×10^{12} G for $Z > 2$ and for $B > 5 \times 10^{12}$ G for $Z > 4$ no such bound state exists. The purpose of this work is not to discuss in detail the possibility of the existence of such a bound state, but rather to show that the magnetic field has a large effect on the equation of state and the surface structure of neutron stars, irrespective of whether or not there is a bound state of condensed matter.

In the surface of the neutron star the Tolman–Oppenheimer–Volkov equation of hydrostatic equilibrium becomes simply (GUDMUNDSSON, PETHICK, and EPSTEIN [7])

$$\frac{dP}{dz} = \rho g_s , \qquad (1)$$

where z is the proper distance below the surface of the star and g_s is the surface gravity including the general relativistic corrections. The Gibbs-Duhem relation then has the form

$$dP = n_{\text{atom}} d\mu_{\text{atom}}, \qquad (2)$$

where n_{atom} is the number density of atoms and μ_{atom} is the chemical potential of an atom. From Eqs. (1) and (2) one finds (FUSHIKI, GUDMUNDSSON, and PETHICK [8])

$$\mu_{\text{atom}}(z) = \mu_{\text{atom}}(0) + (Am_p g_s)z, \qquad (3)$$

where m_p is the proton mass. The knowledge of the chemical potential as a function of density thus gives immediately the density profile of the star.

We calculate the equation of state in the Thomas-Fermi (TF) approximation, and in the Thomas-Fermi approximation with exchange, the so-called Thomas-Fermi-Dirac (TFD) approximation. Our work differs from earlier work in that we derive new results for the exchange energy of the uniform electron gas, which we use in the TFD calculations. In Fig. 1 we show a plot of the density versus zg_{14}, where g_{14} is the surface gravity in units of 10^{14} cm s^{-2} (A neutron star with a mass of 1 $M_\odot$ and a radius of 10 km has a surface gravity of 1.56×10^{14} cm s^{-2}). The results for the TFD (thick continuous lines) and TF (thick dashed lines) approximations are given for $A = 56$, $Z = 26$ with $B = 10^{11}$, 10^{12} and 10^{13} G in Fig. 1. In addition to these results we show those for the non-magnetic free gas (line with thin long and short dashes) and a non-interacting electron gas in a magnetic field (thin dashed lines) in Fig. 1. We notice that the surface structure of the neutron star is insensitive to exactly which approximation one uses except at the very lowest densities.

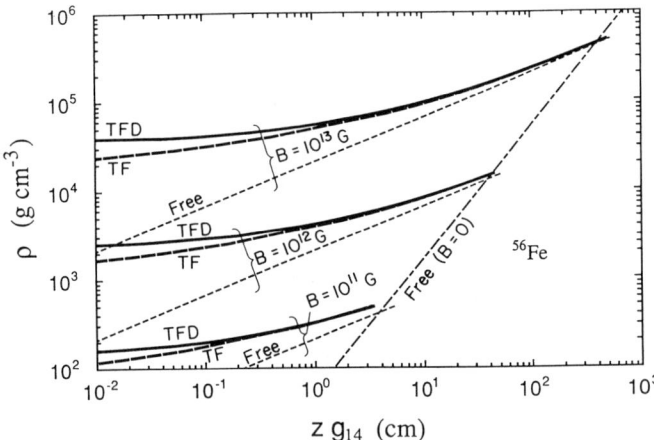

Fig. 1. Density of a neutron star for pure ^{56}Fe as a function of zg_{14} where z is the depth below the surface and g_{14} is the acceleration in units of 10^{14} cm s^{-2} (This is taken from Fig. 6. of Ref. [8]).

In the presence of a magnetic field, density of matter at a given depth is higher than in the absence of a field. For example, the density rises to $\sim 4 \times 10^3$ g cm^{-3} within 1 cm of the surface of a neutron star with $B = 10^{12}$ G while for the non-magnetic free gas the density is less than 10^2 g cm^{-3} at $z = 1$ cm. Since the surface density of a neutron star which is governed by a strong magnetic field ranges from $\sim 10^3$ to $\sim 10^6$ g cm^{-3}, the surface structure is going to influence the relation between the surface and interior temperature of the star (see [7]). This relationship is important for model calculations of neutron star cooling when one wants to compare theoretical results with observations of thermal X-ray emission from the stellar surface.

The rate of nuclear reactions in high-density matter is affected by the fact that the clouds of electrons surrounding nuclei alter the interactions among nuclei. As a consequence of the electron clouds, the reaction rate is increased by a factor which is conventionally written as $e^{-U_{sc}/k_B T}$, where U_{sc}, a negative quantity, is the so-called screening potential and T is the temperature. If the electron distribution is rigid, the screening potential is simply given by the difference of the lattice energies and it is independent of the magnetic field. However, the electrons are not rigid and they respond to the ionic potential. Their compressibility depends on the magnetic field, and this leads in turn to a field dependence of the screening potential. The change in the screening potential due to the compressibility of the electrons for a high magnetic field is (see [8])

$$\delta U_{sc} \doteq -254 \left[(Z_1 + Z_2)^{7/3} - Z_1^{7/3} - Z_2^{7/3} \right] \overline{\left(\frac{A}{Z} \right)}^{-4/3} \rho^{-4/3} B_{12}^2 \text{ keV}, \qquad (4)$$

where $\overline{(A/Z)}$ is the average A/Z ratio which corresponds to the mean molecular weight per electron. The densities at which hydrogen burning by the CNO cycle occurs in X-ray burst sources are of order 10^5 g cm^{-3}, and if the magnetic field were as high as 5×10^{13} G, the value at which relativistic effects begin to play a role, the screening correction for proton capture on ^{14}N would be 4.5 keV, while in the absence of a magnetic field it is only 0.23 keV. Since temperatures of hydrogen induced X-ray bursts are around 2×10^7 K $\simeq 2$ keV (FUSHIKI and LAMB [9]), screening corrections can be significant in the case of very high magnetic fields, even though they are negligible in the zero field case.

REFERENCES

1. R. N. Manchester, J. H. Taylor: Astron. J., 86, 1953 (1981).
2. L. D. LANDAU, E. M. LIFSHITZ: In Quantum Mechanics, 3rd ed. (Pergamon Press, Oxford), p. 457 (1977).
3. M. A. Ruderman: Phys. Rev. Lett., 27, 1306 (1971).
4. B. B. Kadomtsev, V. S. Kudryavtsev: Soviet Phys., JETP, 35, 76 (1972).
5. M. A. Ruderman, P. G. Sutherland: Ap. J., 196, 51 (1975).
6. D. Neuhauser, S. E. Koonin, K. Langanke: Phys. Rev., A36, 4163 (1987).
7. E. H. Gudmundsson, C. J. Pethick, R. I. Epstein: Ap. J., 272, 286 (1983).
8. I. Fushiki, E. H. Gudmundsson, C. J. Pethick: Ap. J. 342, 958 (1989).
9. I. Fushiki, D. Q. Lamb: 1987, Ap. J. Lett., 323, L55 (1987).

Multigroup Simulation of Protoneutron Star Cooling

Hideyuki Suzuki & Katsuhiko Sato

As well known, the data of the neutrino burst from SN1987A observed by KAMI-OKANDE-II and IMB show good agreement with the theoretical model of protoneutron star cooling developed by mainly BURROWS and LATTIMER[1]. Although they used the energy-integrated scheme for neutrino transfer, it is not very insufficient because of the small statistics of the data as for SN1987A. But situations would be changed when the neutrino burst from the next Galactic supernova is detected by the future experiment such as SUPERKAMIOKANDE. Since several thousands of events will be detected, we can analyze the neutrino spectrum. That means multigroup simulation of the protoneutron star cooling is required to get useful information about equation of state of high density matter, supernova mechanism, neutrino interaction and so on. This is one of the main reasons why we are doing multigroup simulation of the protoneutron star cooling.

Our code is a spherical symmetric Lagrange mesh code with implicit method. We calculate neutrino transfer with the multigroup flux limited diffusion scheme and calculate the protoneutron star structure by solving Oppenheimer-Volkoff equation with Henyey method. That is, we assume the hydrostatic structure of the protoneutron star and our simulation is corresponding to the cooling stage which starts about 1 second after the bounce. Three types of neutrinos (ν_e, $\bar{\nu}_e$, 'ν_μ' = $1/4$ (ν_μ, $\bar{\nu}_\mu$, ν_τ, $\bar{\nu}_\tau$)) are included and general relativistic effects for neutrino transfer such as red shift are also included. The special feature of our code is flexibility. Our code consists of many module and it is very easy to change the EOS, flux limiter and so on. As for the EOS, however, in the present simulations we use the table calculated with Hartree-Fock method by R. Wolff. Matter is composed of free neutrons, free protons, α particles, a representing species of nuclei, electrons, positrons and photons.

The following neutrino interactions are included in the source term of the spectral change with the assumption of spherical symmetry.

$$e^- \; p \longleftrightarrow \nu_e \; n \; , \; e^+ \; n \longleftrightarrow \bar{\nu}_e \; p \; , \; e^- \; A \longleftrightarrow \nu_e \; A'$$
$$e^+ \; e^- \longleftrightarrow \nu \; \bar{\nu} \; , \; \nu \; e^{\pm} \longleftrightarrow \nu \; e^{\pm}$$

We mainly use the energy-dependent interaction rate summarized in BRUENN's paper[2]. We would stress that we treat the neutrino-electron scattering and pair process in a full manner and not use the Fokker-Planck approximation. Isoenergetic neutrino scattering off n, p, α, A are included only as the opacity source.

Up to now, we calculated two models. Model C40B is started from an artificial initial model with the baryon mass of $1.7 M_\odot$ which is somewhat cold model. We use the flux limiter almost same as BRUENN's[2]. 40 radial grids and 12 energy grids are used and we terminate the simulation at 15.6sec. The initial model for another model, MW88, is constructed from the data given by WILSON[3]. From his data of 0.4sec after bounce, the entropy distribution and the electron fraction distribution within the baryon mass of $1.62 M_\odot$ are used for the construction of initial model. In the case of model MW88, we adopt the almost same flux limiter as MAYLE & WILSON's[4]. Furthermore the radial(84) and energy(16) grids resemble theirs. Note that since we do not have the same EOS as Wilson's, we use Wolff's table and the constructed structure is different from theirs.

Model C40B shows good agreement with the results of BURROWS[5] as for the $\bar{\nu}_e$ luminosity curve and the $\bar{\nu}_e$ mean energy. But the evolution of the inner structure of the protoneutron star is somewhat different from their early work[1]. We also calculate the neutrino energy spectrum and get the information about the evolution of the spectral shape such as $< E^2 > / < E >^2$. We will investigate the evolution of the structure and spectra systematically since now.

Figure 1 shows the comparison between the neutrino mean energy of our model MW88 and MAYLE & WILSON's[3]. Our simulation results in lower mean energy than theirs. Specially our 'ν_μ' is much lower. As for the luminosity curve, while 'ν_μ' has the smallest luminosity among the three in our results, 'ν_μ' is highest in their result. (The difference between our luminosity and theirs for ν_e and $\bar{\nu}_e$ is small.) What is the origin of these differences? Although we do not know the code dependence and it may be effects of matter accretion in Mayle & Wilson's simulation, we think one of the main reasons is the difference of EOS.

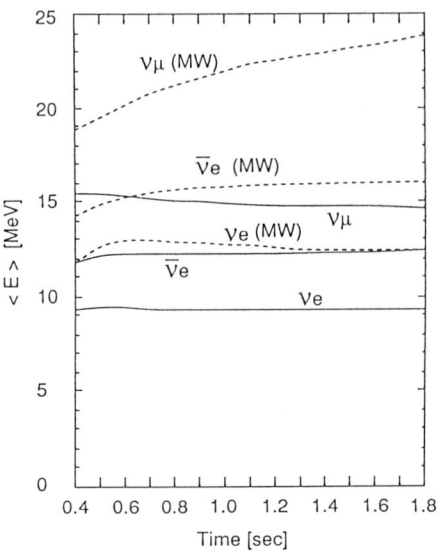

Figure 1. Mean energy of the neutrino flux. Solid lines are our model MW88 and dashed curves are Mayle & Wilson's.

In Fig.2 we plot the matter pressure of the two EOSs along the same array of density, electron fraction and entropy, $P(\rho_B, Y_e(\rho_B), S(\rho_B))$. Wolff's EOS is stiffer than Wilson's. For example it has three times higher pressure than Wilson's at $\rho_B = 8.407 \cdot 10^{14} \text{g/cm}^3$, $Y_e = 0.2921$, $S = 1.19$. Stiffness of the EOS results in the low temperature in the protoneutron star because of less contraction. In our initial model maximum temperature is less than 30MeV but in the data of Wilson's it is nearly 50MeV. Since the production rate of 'ν_μ' is very sensitive to the temperature, we can interpret the low mean energy of 'ν_μ' as the effect of stiff EOS.

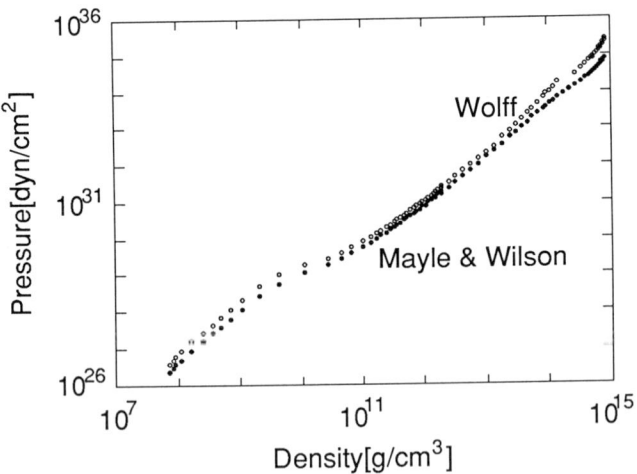

Figure 2. Comparison of the two EOSs. Matter pressure corresponding to the same sets of density, electron fraction and entropy.

The authors thank M. Fukugita, R. Wolff, R. Mayle and J. Wilson for offering us their data, H.-T. Janka for many discussions and KEK for supporting our computation. This research is supported in part by the Grant-in Aid for Scientific Research Fund from the Ministry of Education, Science and Culture(01629504,01790167) and the Japan-U.S. Cooperative Science Program(MPCR-185).

References

1. A. Burrows and J. M. Lattimer, Ap. J. **307**, 178 (1986).

2. S. W. Bruenn, Ap. J. Suppl. **58**, 771 (1985).

3. J. R. Wilson and R. W. Mayle, preprint (1988), and private communications.

4. R. W. Mayle, J. R. Wilson and D. N. Schramm, Ap. J. **318**, 288 (1987).

5. A. Burrows, Ap. J. **334**, 891 (1988).

SECTION VII
EXPLOSION MECHANISMS AND NEUTRINO BURSTS

Neutrino Astrophysics: New Adjunct of Astronomy and Elementary Particle Physics
Alfred K. Mann

Neutrinos, the neutral, elementary fermions with very small, perhaps zero mass, are the only known particles to interact only weakly (and gravitationally) with matter. Nevertheless, they carry energy and linear and angular momentum, as well as a quantum number denoting their lepton nature. Due to these properties neutrinos constitute a unique probe of stellar interiors because, unlike photons, they can emerge promptly from the central regions of stars and transmit direct information relating to, e.g., relaxation times or processes in those regions. Moreover, traversal of the stellar interiors with their extreme values of temperature and density provides a means of searching for as yet undetected intrinsic properties of neutrinos. Accordingly, neutrino astrophysics is an adjunct of both astronomy and elementary particle physics.

The data of neutrino astrophysics are in part neutrino flux limits acquired from searches for energetic neutrinos from distant point sources, e.g., SN1987A; from a search for relic antineutrinos (with energies from a few to 20 Mev) from all part supernovae; and from searches for neutrinos as or from dark matter candidates. More interesting are the data on atmospheric (cosmic ray induced) neutrinos and the positive observations of low energy anti-neutrinos from SN1987A and their implications; and, of comparable interest, measurement of the magnitude and direction of the flux of neutrinos from the Sun. Observation of neutrinos from the Sun in turn permits tests for possible correlations of the solar neutrino flux with intense solar flares and with the solar magnetic cycle.

Each of the subjects above is material for an extended seminar and consequently only a representative sample could be discussed in a short talk. For the purpose of a talk at the Santa Cruz Workshop on Supernovae it seemed appropriate to treat briefly the less familiar material, for example, the limiting flux values from the searches for neutrinos and implication of neutrinos from the Sun. This was intended as an overview of the progress of neutrino astrophysics during the last few years. Much of this material has been published recently, and rather than reproduce it in this proceedings of the Supernovae Workshop, it appears reasonable simply to give in addition to the summary in this abstract a few references for the reader who may wish to pursue the subject further.

References

Search for distant point sources: Y. Oyama *et al.,* Phys. Rev. Lett., **59,** 2604 (1987); R. Svoboda *et al.,* Astrophys. J., **315,** 420 (1987); Y. Oyama *et al.* Phys. Rev., **D39,** 1481 (1989).

Search for relic anti-neutrinos from past supernovae: W. Zhang *et al.* Phys. Rev. Lett., **61,** 385 (1988); A. K. Mann and W. Zhang, to be published in Proc. of the NASA Workshop on Physics and Astrophysics from a Lunar Base, Stanford University, May, 1989 (in press).

Solar neutrinos: R. Davies, Jr. in Proc. Conf. on Neutrino Physics and Astrophysics, Boston, 1988. Ed. by J. Schneps *et al.* World Scientific, 1989 (p. 518); K. S. Hirata *et al.* Phys. Rev. Lett., **63,** 16 (1989); R. Davis, Jr., A. K. Mann, and L. Wolfenstein, Ann. Rev. Nucl. and Particle Science, **38,** 467 (1989).

Calculations of Neutrino Heating Supernovae
Ronald W. Mayle & James R. Wilson

I. Physical and Numerical Model

The numerical model is based on a fully general relativistic treatment of hydrodynamics and neutrino flow. The neutrino time evolution is approximated by a flux limited diffusion equation. The neutrinos are described by three functions, one representing electron neutrinos, another electron antineutrinos and a third to represent muon and tauon neutrinos and their antiparticles; these functions depend on time, space and neutrino energy. All neutrino-matter interactions thought to be important in the collapse and explosion process are included. The equation of state for matter below nuclear density is represented by the species: photons, electrons, positrons, neutrons, protons, helium nuclei and heavy nuclei. The heavy nuclei have properties dependent on the chemical potentials of the other constituents; Saha equations are solved to determine the abundance of all particles. A simple nuclear burn model consisting of He, C, O, Ne, Si, and Ni is used to carry matter up "iron" (nuclear statistical equilibrium); after matter has burned to "iron" it is assumed to be in statistical equilibrium thereafter. When the star becomes convectively unstable by either the Le Doux or the salt finger criteria, convection is treated in the mixing length approximation.

II. Collapse and Bounce

After the inner part (1.2 - 1.5 solar masses) of a massive star burns to "iron", the core cools by neutrino emission and consequently increases in density due to slow contraction. When densities reach about 10^9 [gm/cc] electron capture on heavy nuclei and the accompanying energy loss becomes fast enough that the core begins to collapse dynamically. The central part of the iron core contracts homologously with the in fall velocity proportional to the distance from the center of the star. The size of this homologous core is about the

Chandrasekhar mass (M_{ch}) = 5.8 Y_e^2 solar masses, where Y_e is the number of electrons per baryon. In what follows we will give results of a collapse calculation using as initial data the evolved core of a 20 solar mass stellar model of SN1987a supplied by T.A. Weaver and S. Woosley. This model had an initial iron core mass of about 1.45 solar masses.

At the start of the collapse $Y_e \approx .43$ giving M_{ch} = 1.12 solar masses; by the time nuclear density is reached at the center of the core $Y_e \approx .30$ and M_{ch} = 0.53 solar masses. The entropy per baryon starts at about 1.0 and rises to 1.5 as the density passes from 10^{11} to 10^{12} [gm/cc]. The star passes from being transparent to neutrinos for $\rho < 10^{11}$ [gm/cc] to being diffusive for $\rho > 10^{12}$ [gm/cc]. In the range $10^{11} < \rho < 10^{12}$ [gm/cc] the neutrinos are very interactive with the matter but not able to stay in equilibrium; this leads to the entropy increase. After the density rises above 10^{14} [gm/cc] the entropy slowly falls due to neutrino cooling. It is found that Ye $\approx Y_1$ (Y_1 is the lepton number per baryon) for $\rho < 10^{11}$ [gm/cc] and ($Y_1 - Y_e$) is constant for $\rho > 3 \times 10^{12}$ [gm/cc] reflecting again the transition of the state of the neutrinos from complete non interaction to complete equilibrium with the matter. The fraction of baryon matter contained in heavy nuclei is .98 at the start of collapse. Due to the rise in temperature and density during the core contraction, this fraction drops to about .75, keeping the pressure lower than it would have been without the break up of the heavy nuclei and allowing the collapse to accelerate.

Just before bounce, the core has attained the maximum in fall kinetic energy of 1.1×10^{52} [ergs]; below the sonic point (the position in the star where the sound speed equals the in fall velocity) the matter is collapsing homologously. The position of the sonic point is close in mass to $M_{ch} \approx .50$ solar masses. Outside the sonic point the matter is falling in supersonically with more than half the free fall velocity. After the central density exceeds nuclear matter density, $\approx 2.4 \times 10^{14}$ [gm/cc] at $Y_1 = .37$, the pressure rises very rapidly and the collapse decelerates; the peak central density reached is 5.6×10^{14} [gm/cc]. The inner sonic core rebounds and starts a pressure wave moving out into the supersonic in falling material. At a mass of about 0.60 solar masses the pressure wave turns into a shock wave. Some fraction of the maximum in fall kinetic energy of 1.1×10^{52} [ergs] should be available for energizing the outward moving shock wave. However, the shock has to proceed through nearly 0.9 solar masses of in falling iron; to dissociate one solar mass of iron requires about 1.65×10^{52} [ergs] of energy. In addition to the energy expended dissociating iron the neutrino luminosity is very high, peaking at close to 10^{54} [ergs/sec]. The integral over the first 10 [ms] after bounce of the neutrino luminosity just outside the shock front minus the luminosity at the neutrinosphere (the point in the star inside of which the neutrino mean free path is less than the neutrinosphere radius) is 3.2×10^{51} [ergs]. The combination of energy losses to iron dissociation and neutrino emission weakens the shock so that after a few tens of milliseconds it turns into an almost stationary accretion shock at a radius of about 4×10^7 [cm].

III. Late Time Neutrino Heating

After a few tenths of seconds the first phase of neutrino heating occurs. Well outside the neutrinosphere we can approximate the neutrino energy exchange with the matter in the following manner. The heating rate is given by

$$\dot{E}_+ = K(T_p) L / 4\pi R^2 \tag{1}$$

where L is the total luminosity in electron neutrinos and electron antineutrinos. The opacity, $K(T_p)$, is evaluated at the neutrinosphere temperature T_p and is proportional to the square of the temperature. Since the major source of opacity in this phase of neutrino heating is the emission and absorption of electron neutrinos and antineutrinos on free baryons, the opacity is also proportional to the free baryon mass fraction (this is not explicitly shown in the notation). The cooling rate is given by

$$\dot{E}_- = - K(T_m) a'c \, T_m^4 \tag{2}$$

where T_m is the matter temperature at the point of interest, a' is the radiation constant for Fermi particles (7/8 the photon radiation constant 'a'), and c is the speed of light. If we let $L = 4\pi R_p^2 \, a' \, c \, T_p^2 / 4$ then the net heating rate becomes

$$\dot{E}_{net} = a' \, c \, K(T_p) \, T_p^4 [\; (R_p/ 2R_m)^2 - (T_m / T_p)^6 \;] . \tag{3}$$

Thus if the matter temperature is low enough compared to the neutrinosphere temperature a positive net heating can occur.

At the times under consideration the matter falling through the shock wave is iron; the kinetic energy dissipated in the shock is approximately the gravitational energy since the shock position is nearly constant. So we may write

$$\frac{GM}{R} \approx \left(\frac{3}{2} f + 3 \, Y_e \right) kT + f \, I \tag{4}$$

where the first two terms on the left are the thermal energy of free baryons and electrons; in the last term I is the dissociation energy and f is the degree of dissociation. For our example calculation M ≈ 1.5 solar masses, Y_e ≈ 0.5 so we have with R_7 equal to the radius in units of 10^7 [cm] and temperatures and energies measured in [MeV]

$$\frac{20}{R_7} \approx 1.5 \, (\, 1. + f \,) \, T + 8.4 \, f \; . \tag{5}$$

At the densities just below the shock (10^8 to 10^9 [gm/cc]) the decomposition temperature is about 1 to 2 [MeV]. Above a radius of about 3×10^7 [cm] the material is predominately undecomposed iron and helium which have smaller opacities for neutrino interactions than free baryons; heating will not occur in this region. The heating is a maximum at about 2×10^7 [cm].

This phase of neutrino heating does not occur immediately after bounce. As time progresses the density of in falling matter decreases which lowers the temperature at which decomposition occurs. Also the proto-neutron star contracts with time and the neutrinosphere temperature increases. These two effects lead to the heating phase being delayed for several tenths of a second after bounce. When neutrino heating occurs the heated matter expands; the amount of material in the heating region decreases due to the expansion thus resulting in a decrease of the heating rate. The heating rate is high from about 0.3 to 0.5 seconds after core bounce . The accretion shock wave begins moving outward rapidly again after 0.5 seconds passing through the iron and into the predominately silicon-oxygen region; in this region the shock raises the temperature sufficiently to burn some of the Si-O to nickel. After the shock passes a radius of about 2×10^8 [cm] the density becomes too low and the shock too weak to induce nuclear burn. The amount of Ni^{56}, which is an observable, produced depends directly on the energy deposited in this first phase of neutrino heating. The energy contained in the hot bubble between the neutrinosphere and the shock is still much less than the gravitational binding energy of the matter above the shock. Further energy deposition is needed.

After the hot bubble has expanded a different kind of neutrino heating can occur, neutrino-antineutrino annihilation. This was discussed as an explosion mechanism by GOODMAN, DAR and NUSSINOV [1]; COOPERSTEIN, VAN DEN HORN and BARON [2] dismissed neutrino-antineutrino annihilation as being a small effect since the annihilation can only occur near the neutrinosphere and if the density in this region is too high the deposited energy is immediately re-radiated by electron-positron capture on protons and neutrons. However,

Calculations of Neutrino Heating Supernovae

after the first phase of neutrino heating the density gradient outside the neutrinosphere becomes progressively steeper and eventually becomes sufficiently so that matter on the surface of the proto-neutron star is heated and blown off.

The cross section for neutrino antineutrino annihilation depends on the neutrino energy, ε_ν, and the angle, θ_ν, between the neutrino and antineutrino in the combination $\varepsilon_\nu^2(1 - \cos\theta_\nu)^2$. The cross section is thus proportional to the square of the collision energy in the center of mass frame of the colliding neutrino and antineutrino. In the numerical computer model we carry only the energy density of neutrinos, F_0, as a function of the neutrino energy. We must infer the angular distribution indirectly. In the diffuse limit we approximate the angular distribution by

$$F(R,\varepsilon,\mu) = F_0(R,\varepsilon) + \frac{3D\mu}{c}\frac{\partial F_0(R,\varepsilon)}{\partial R} \tag{6}$$

where D, the flux limited diffusion coefficient, depends on $\lambda \left|\frac{\partial \log F_0}{\partial R}\right|$ with λ being the neutrino mean free path (see BOWERS and WILSON [3]) and μ the cosine of the angle of the neutrinos with respect to the radial direction. Integration of the cross section over μ gives the angular factor

$$Q_1 = 1 - \frac{3}{2}\frac{D\bar{D}}{c^2}\left|\frac{\partial \log F_0}{\partial R}\right|\left|\frac{\partial \log \bar{F}_0}{\partial R}\right| \tag{7}$$

where the bars over D and F_0 denote the flux limited diffusion coefficient and the distribution function for the antineutrinos. In the limit of an infinitely sharp neutron star boundary the angular integration gives a factor

$$Q_2 = (1 - x)^2(5 + 4x + x^2) / 8 \tag{8}$$

with $x = \sqrt{1 - (R^*/R)^2}$ where R^* is the radius of the neutron star which we will take as the neutrinosphere radius. We use the larger of Q_1 and Q_2 for our angular factor; in the limit where Q_2 dominates the net heating per unit volume goes as $(1/R)^8$ for large R.

A a time of 0.9 [sec] after bounce the density above the neutrinosphere falls with radius as $(1/R)^{27}$. The second phase of neutrino heating is just getting underway. At a density a little under 10^{10} [gm/cc] the neutrino-antineutrino annihilation energy deposition becomes greater than the electron-positron annihilation energy loss to neutrino production. The energy deposition rate is not high, only a few times 10^{50} [ergs/sec], but it will continue as long as the proto-neutron star is emitting energy in neutrinos.

An additional neutrino process also occurs at late times when matter in the bubble region has heated sufficiently that most of its internal energy is in photons and electron and positron pairs. As soon as this happens we may write

$$E = \frac{11}{4} \frac{a T^4}{\rho} \tag{9}$$

$$n_p = \frac{7}{4} \frac{aT^3}{3k} \tag{10}$$

$$\sigma_e = \frac{5}{4} \sigma_0 \frac{\varepsilon_\nu T}{(m_e c^2)^2} \tag{11}$$

$$\dot{E} = \sigma_e\, n_p\, L\, /\, 4\pi R^2 = \frac{11}{4} a \dot{T}^4 \tag{12}$$

$$\frac{\dot{T}^4}{T^4} = \frac{5}{12} \frac{\sigma_0}{k} \frac{\varepsilon_\nu}{(m_e c^2)^2} \frac{L}{4\pi R^2} \equiv \frac{1}{\tau} \tag{13}$$

where a is the photon radiation constant, k is Boltzmanns constant, c is the speed of light, m_e is the mass of an electron, $\sigma_0 = 1.7 \times 10^{-44}$ [(cm)^2] is a fundamental weak interaction cross section (see TUBBS and SCHRAMM [4]), ε_ν is the neutrino energy, n_p is the number of electron-positron pairs, L is the neutrino luminosity, E is the internal energy of matter per gram and R is the radius. At a time of 2.5 sec after bounce at a radius of 10^7 [cm] t = 0.5 [sec]. This pair heating does not produce much total energy deposition but it takes matter heated by the other two neutrino heating processes and raises the entropy per baryon to a few thousand. The calculation was carried out to a time of 3.6 [sec] after bounce. At that time the density near 10^7 [cm] had fallen to about 100 [gm/cc].

The calculation becomes very expensive in computer time so it was not completed. We extrapolate the energy production rate to estimate the final explosion energy. Not until 2.5 sec after bounce is there a net explosion energy since the initial binding energy of the hydrogen helium envelope is negative. At 3.6 sec the net explosion energy is 0.3×10^{51} [ergs] and about two thirds of the final binding energy (3×10^{53} [ergs]) of the neutron star has been emitted in neutrinos that have escaped the star. At this time we find the ratio of the rate of energy deposition from neutrino-antineutrino annihilation reactions to the total neutrino luminosity to be 0.02. If we assume that the energy deposition efficiency for the remaining energy to be emitted in neutrinos is the average (0.01) found in the interval from 2.5 to 3.6 seconds then the final explosion energy should be about 1.4×10^{51} [ergs].

IV. Comparison of Calculations and Observations

As stated earlier the calculation described above was based on a stellar evolution calculation made by Weaver and Woosley for a 20 solar mass star that is thought to be similar to the progenitor of SN1987a. We estimate the explosion energy to be about 1.4×10^{51} [ergs]. From the immediate post explosion light curve an estimate of the explosion energy of 0.6 to 2.0×10^{51} [ergs] has been derived (see for example SHIGEYAMA, NOMOTO and HASHIMOTO [5] and WOOSLEY [6]). From the late time photon luminosity of the supernovae the Ni^{56} production is estimated to be about $.075 \pm .020$ solar masses. Our calculation gave .065 solar masses of Ni^{56}. One half of the Ni^{56} is produced during in fall by adiabatic compressional heating and the rest is produced by shock heating after the shock wave passes the burn front. The density of the in fall burn is about 3×10^6 [gm/cc] while the preshock burn density is around 2×10^6 [gm/cc]. At the end of our calculation the baryonic mass of the neutron star is 1.63 solar masses. To calculate the neutrino signal we took the star shortly after bounce and removed all the matter outside 1.63 solar masses and then calculated the neutrino emission assuming the star is in quasi static equilibrium. To check the mean energy of the electron antineutrinos we folded our energy spectrum with the detector efficiencies of the IMB detector (see BIONTA et al. [7]) and the Kamiokande-II detector (see HIRATA et al. [8]). Our mean neutrino energy weighted by the detector efficiency for the Kamiodande-II detector is 20.2 [MeV] while the average energy of the antineutrinos detected is 15.4 [MeV]. The numbers for the IMB detector are 27.9 [MeV] for the predicted average energy and 32.5 [MeV] for the average detected particle energy. To examine the temporal emission of the neutrinos we combined the events of the two detectors with equal weight (we counted an IMB event as 11/8 of a Kamiokande-II event since IMB saw 8 events and Kamiokande-II saw 11) to produce a cumulative count curve versus time. We find good agreement between the calculated emission folded with an average detector efficiency (to take into account the two different detector efficiencies) and the combined observational emission (cumulative count curve). Thus we have good overall agreement of observation and calculation. The final neutron star gravitational mass we estimate to be 1.45 solar masses; however, this is not observable.

V. Equation of State Considerations

In Section I of this paper the sub nuclear density equation of state we use is described. Above nuclear density we use a zero temperature equation of state plus a thermal component. The zero temperature nuclear EOS was suggested by H.A. Bethe who used results described in MUTHER, PRAKASH and AINSWORTH [9]. The internal energy per baryon, E_0 (in units of [MeV]), of the zero temperature component of our EOS is taken to be

$$E_0 = -16 + \frac{1}{9} K_0 (\eta^\gamma - 1 + \gamma(\eta - 1))/(\eta \gamma (\gamma - 1)) + E_{SYM} \tag{14}$$

$$E_{SYM} = 16 (1 - 2 Y_e)^2 \eta (1 + 72/(1 + 4\eta)) \tag{15}$$

where $K_0 = 200$ [MeV], $\gamma = 2.75$, and $\eta = \rho/\rho_N$ with $\rho_N = 2.656 \times 10^{14}$ [gm/cc]. This equation of state produces a cold neutron star with a gravitational mass of 1.40 solar masses and a baryon mass of 1.64 solar masses ; the binding energy is 3.04×10^{53} [ergs].

The presence of pions, which is ignored in the present calculations, will make an appreciable change in the EOS. Estimates using a model similar to that described in the work of FRIEDMAN, PANDHARIPANDE and USMANI [10] show that a lowering of the peak temperature seen in our model calculations by 10 [MeV] could be expected (inclusion of an effective nucleon mass would raise the temperature). The neutrino opacity would increase by as much as a factor of two if pions were included in the EOS. The biggest effect expected is from the reduction of the electron density by the conversion of electrons to negative pions. The effect of this latter process on the cooling of the proto-neutron star is hard to estimate at present.

The present calculation appears to account for SN1987a quite adequately. One concern we have at present if whether we have treated the prompt shock propagation well. It is necessary that the prompt shock go out to a distance of about 4×10^7 [cm] and remain there long enough (around 0.5 [sec]) for the first heating to occur. Another concern is whether our algorithm for neutrino-antineutrino annihilation is sufficiently accurate outside the neutrinosphere. We are working with H.-T. Janke on this latter problem.

This work was performed under the auspices of the USDOE at Lawrence Livermore National Laboratory under contract no. W-7405-ENG-48.

References

1. Goodman, Dar and Nussinov: Ap. J., 314, L10 (1987).
2. Cooperstein, van den Horn and Baron: Ap. J., 309, 653 (1987).
3. Bowers and Wilson: A. J. Suppl. 50, 115 (1982).
4. Tubbs and Schramm: Ap. J., 201, 467 (1975).
5. Shigeyama, Nomoto and Hashimoto: Astron. Astrophys, 196, 141 (1988).
6. Woosley: Ap. J., 330, 218 (1988).
7. Bionta et al.: Phys. Rev. Lettr. 58, 1494 (1987).
8. Hirata et al.: Phys. Rev. Lettr. 60, 1999 (1987).
9. Muther, Prakash and Ainsworth: Phys. Lettr. B, 199, 469 (1987).
10. Friedman, Pandharipande and Usmani: Nuc. Phys. A372, 483 (1981).

Initial Models and the Prompt Mechanism of SN II

E. Baron & J. Cooperstein

1 Introduction

Massive stars ($M \gtrsim 10 - 12\ M_\odot$) become catastrophically unstable when the fuel in their central regions is exhausted. The innermost $1-2\ M_\odot$ of fusion ashes (iron peak elements burnt to nuclear statistical equilibrium (NSE)) is the *iron core*. It resembles a white dwarf star dominated by the pressure of relativistic electrons, albeit a hot one. An isolated white dwarf can not support more than the appropriate Chandrasekhar mass for its composition, but the compact core of the massive star must support the overlying burning shells. Before it evolves completely to the low–temperature white dwarf configuration it loses this ability, is overwhelmed by gravitation and collapses. It is generally agreed that a Type II supernova explosion ensues but there is no general agreement about the details of the process. In fact at present there exist no self–consistent calculations of the explosive stage which adequately explain observed explosion features.

There are two well developed theories of the central moments of the explosion. In the first, the prompt mechanism, which has been studied by many authors, the star implodes to supranuclear densities and then resists further compression. The inner core rebounds and launches a shock wave which then propagates through the star and eventually erupts through the photosphere producing the supernova display. In the second theory, the delayed mechanism[1,2,3,4] there is insufficient energy in the initial shock wave to propagate all the way to the edge of the star. Instead it falters and becomes an accretion shock. However, about one second after the central bounce, it is revived by deposition of a small percentage of the energy leaving in neutrinos, and resumes its outward motion. The result is a weaker explosion than in the prompt mechanism. In this talk, we will focus on the prompt mechanism.

It is generally agreed[5,6,7,8] that using the best input physics available and initial models that result from current presupernova evolution calculations the prompt shock mechanism does not work. The prompt shock wave stalls and dies either to be revived by the delayed mechanism or to be engulfed when enough matter rains through it to drive the proto-neutron star to a black hole.

Stellar evolution calculations are not, however, without uncertainties. The treatment of convection is notoriously uncertain, as well as the complicated silicon burning stage (cf. refs.[9,10]). Recently[11], the electron capture and beta decay rates used in the presupernova calculations have been re-examined and it has been suggested that the models may be considerably cooler than current models. In this paper we examine the effect of varying the initial iron core on the viability of the prompt shock wave. Lower mass iron cores require the shock to traverse, and hence, dissociate less iron significantly reducing the energy losses of the shock. Colder cores have fewer free protons. Free protons copiously capture electrons on infall, reducing the final trapped lepton fraction and hence, the mass point where the shock forms. Thus, we consider smaller, colder cores in hopes of delineating the range of successful prompt shock waves. We find that cold initial cores of mass $M \sim 1.12\ M_\odot$ can produce reasonably strong explosions.

2 Construction of Models

Ideally, to construct a series of initial models we would tell the stellar evolutionist that we would like a core of such and such a description and that if she would change her assumptions about this piece of physics she could produce for us an iron core meeting our specifications. This method is, however, not feasible. To construct a run of models would take an enormous amount of computer time as well as frustration. Instead, we construct our own "fake" models taking guidance from the results of pre-supernova evolution calculations.

In order to construct an initial model we must specify both the composition and profile of the thermodynamic variables and the density structure and velocity profile. Now, iron cores are essentially destabilized hydrostatic stars, since the pressure of the hydrostatically stable core of the star has just been reduced by a combination of photodisintegration and electron capture. Therefore we build models that are in hydrostatic equilibrium and destabilize them. Examining the results from stellar evolution calculations we find that the models are destabilized rather uniformly. In order to accomplish this uniform destabiliztion we have chosen to build hydrostatic models using a somewhat reduced gravity. Thus, when gravity is restored in the hydrodynamical calculation the model collapses with a very uniform pressure deficit. In order to accomplish this we build models using a Tolman, Oppenheimer, Volkov code, but with Newton's constant somewhat reduced; i.e., we take

$$G = g_{\text{eff}}\ G_0, \tag{1}$$

where G_0 is the actual value and $g_{\text{eff}} < 1$.

To complete the specification of the models, we must choose a central density, a composition profile, and a temperature or entropy profile. We choose to work with the entropy since that stays roughly constant during the collapse. Figure 1 displays the entropy and Y_e profiles of the results of pre-supernova evolution calculations of 13 $M_\odot$ model of NOMOTO and HASHIMOTO[9], the 15 $M_\odot$ model of WOOSLEY and WEAVER[10], and the 18 $M_\odot$ model of WEAVER and WOOSLEY[12]. Certain general features of the entropy profile are immediately apparent. There is a roughly linear rise in the entropy in the center up to mass point M_1 which corresponds to the convective silicon burning core. In the two models of WOOSLEY and WEAVER which had a silicon burning shell ignite after core silicon exhaustion there is a steeper rise up to mass point M_2, followed by a flat region up to mass point M_3, then there is another steep rise up to mass point M_4 after which the entropy is roughly constant; this is the silicon burning shell at the onset of instability. It is important to note that on quite general grounds the entropy must follow this stepwise rising pattern, with a high outer entropy if the core is to have a high enough pressure at its edge to support the overlying layers of the star, which contain the bulk of the mass. The Y_e profile is somewhat simpler since it is determined only by the time available since the iron is produced for electron captures to occur, and is flat prior to that. Thus, the Y_e rises roughly linearly up till mass point M_3 and has a steep rise to some value near 0.5 at M_4. We use these schematic profiles in constructing our models, as displayed by the solid line in Figure 1. Table 1 displays the parameters used to construct the various models we have used. We have yet to specify the central density which is needed to completely determine our models. This we specify implicitly by demanding that the temperature at mass point M_4 is high enough to ignite silicon burning which we take to be 0.35 MeV.

3 Results

Regardless of how our initial models have been constructed, they can be taken as given and then hydrodynamics pursued. Indeed, this is exactly what is done when the numerical simulations take as input the results of detailed presupernova investigations. Complete details of the construction of the models are given in BARON and COOPERSTEIN[13]. Table 2 gives the parameters used in the equation of state at high density which we take to be the BCK form[14,15]. Note that we use a rather stiff equation of state except in models 106 and 110.

Computational details of our hydrodynamic program have been given elsewhere[5]. In Table 3 we list the results from the calculations we have performed. We see that only models 109 and 110 have more than 10^{50} ergs of outgoing kinetic energy, although calculations 102 and 104 also have shock waves that are still propagating when the calculations were stopped, once the shocks had reached about 2000 km.

3.1 Model 103

Model 103 is our benchmark model, and is constructed to be essentially a smaller version of the $1.28 M_\odot$ iron core, corresponding to a $15 M_\odot$ main sequence star constructed by WOOSLEY and WEAVER[10]. This model has a relatively stiff high density equation of state and neutrino electron scattering (NES) is included in the neutrino transport. We see from Table 3 that the shock wave just makes it to the beginning of the silicon shell at about 550 km before it stalls and becomes an accretion shock.

3.2 Model 102

In model 102 we study the effects of neutrino electron scattering on the infall and subsequent shock propagation. Our results confirm the work of BRUENN[16,7] and MYRA and BLUDMAN[6]. Model 102 is identical to 103 except that in model 102 NES has not been included in the neutrino transport. We see from Table 3 that

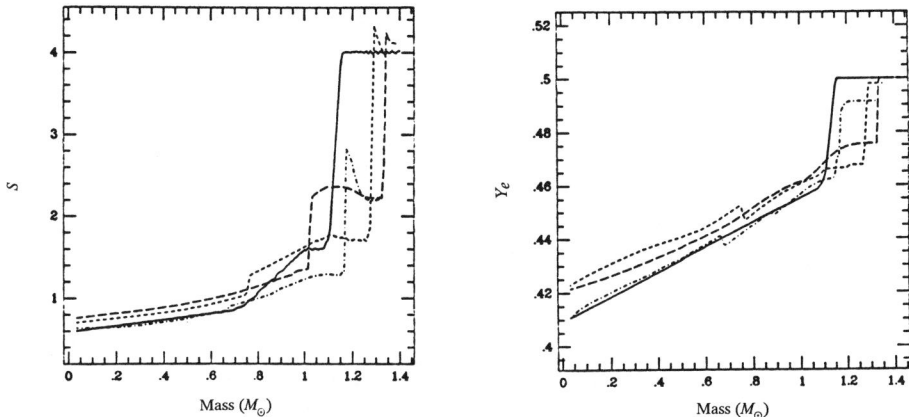

Figure 1:
The profiles of S and Y_e of our "benchmark" model (solid line) (used in calculations 102, 103, and 106) are compared to the pre-supernova calculations of the Woosley and Weaver (1988) $15 M_\odot$ model (short dashed line), the $18 M_\odot$ model of Weaver and Woosley (1988) (long dashed line) and the Nomoto and Hashimoto (1988) $13 M_\odot$ model (dot-dashed line).

Model	102, 103, 106	104	105	107	109, 110
M_1	0.72	0.72	0.72	0.72	0.72
M_2	1.00	1.00	0.90	1.00	1.00
M_3	1.10	1.10	0.975	1.05	1.10
M_4	1.15	1.15	1.00	1.10	1.15
$M_{\text{iron core}}$	1.125	1.125	0.988	1.075	1.125
S_c	0.60	0.50	0.60	0.60	0.50
S_1	0.86	0.70	0.86	0.86	0.63
S_2	1.60	1.60	1.30	1.60	1.60
S_4	4.00	4.00	4.00	4.00	4.00
$\langle S \rangle_{M \leq M_3}$	0.94	0.83	0.84	0.91	0.80
Y_{ec}	0.41	0.42	0.40	0.41	0.415
Y_{e3}	0.46	0.46	0.46	0.46	0.46
Y_{e4}	0.50	0.50	0.50	0.50	0.50
$\langle Y_e \rangle_{M \leq M_3}$	0.435	0.440	0.430	0.435	0.438

Table 1: Initial model compositions

The masses M_{1-4} are the points where the entropy and Y_e profile change as discussed in the text. $M_{\text{iron core}}$ is the mass of the iron core. S_c and Y_{ec} are the central values of S and Y_e. The other values of S and Y_e refer to those values at the mass points with the same subscripts. Also listed are the average values of S and Y_e where averages are taken for mass points inside of M_3. The masses are given in units of $M_\odot$, and the entropy is in k_B^{-1} per nucleon.

Model	K_0	γ	W_s	NES	$\rho_{10}^{(c)}$	g_{eff}
102	180	3.0	31.5	off	0.538	0.975
103	180	3.0	31.5	on	0.538	0.975
104	180	3.0	31.5	on	0.500	0.975
105	180	3.0	31.5	on	0.150	0.950
106	180	2.5	31.5	on	0.538	0.975
107	180	3.0	31.5	on	0.250	0.975
109	180	3.0	31.5	on	2.000	0.975
110	180	2.5	31.5	on	2.000	0.975

Table 2: Model parameters

The parameters used in each calculation. K_0 is the incompressibility of symmetric matter at saturation in MeV and γ is the high density adiabatic index. W_s, the symmetry energy is measured in MeV, NES refers to whether the effects of neutrino electron scattering are included, and $\rho_{10}^{(c)}$ is the initial central density in units of 10^{10} g cm^{-3}. g_{eff} is discussed in the text.

Model	102	103	104	105	106	107	109	110
R_{dead}	–	566.1	–	318.3	1117.3	263.2	–	–
M_{dead}	–	1.167	–	1.125	1.208	1.125	–	–
E_{ν_e}	7.08	3.39	5.92	1.16	6.18	0.87	4.69	4.61
$E_{\bar{\nu}_e}$	5.21	1.36	4.05	0.03	4.24	0.01	2.95	2.90
$E_{\nu_{\text{pair}}}$	7.13	1.98	6.20	0.20	6.17	0.13	3.96	4.64
E_{kin}	0.01	–	0.01	–	–	–	0.14	0.26
u_{max}	0.49	–	0.66	–	–	–	1.59	2.05
R_s	2104	–	1754	–	–	–	2682	3159
M_s	1.267	–	1.208	–	–	–	1.192	1.200

Table 3: Results of hydrodynamical simulations

The results at the end of the calculation are described for each model. The radius (in km) and mass point (in $M_\odot$) at which the wave stalls are listed as R_{dead} and M_{dead} respectively. The total amount of energy lost in electron type neutrinos, electron type anti-neutrinos, and μ and τ pair neutrinos is listed as E_{ν_e}, $E_{\bar{\nu}_e}$, $E_{\nu_{\text{pair}}}$. The energies are given in units of 10^{51} ergs. If the shock wave is still propagating at about 2000 km the maximum outward velocity at that time, (in units of 10^9 cm s^{-1}) is listed as u_{max}, the total out going kinetic energy is E_{kin} (in units of 10^{51} ergs), and the radius (in km) and mass point (in $M_\odot$) of the shock wave are listed as R_s and M_s, respectively.

model 102 produces a significantly more powerful shock wave than 103, the shock wave still propagating at 2100 km, albeit weakening significantly. The effects of NES reduce the final Y_l by about 0.02 which is quite significant. BRUENN[7] finds that NES reduces the final Y_l by about 0.04. However, with NES included both our calculations and those of BRUENN find a total final Y_l of about 0.365, i.e. BRUENN finds significantly less capture on infall with no NES than we do. The difference is due to differing treatments of neutrino transport, but it is important to note that we agree when NES is included.

3.3 Model 106

Model 106 is another variation on our "benchmark" model, 103. In this calculation we study the effects on the shock propagation of softening the high density equation of state. Model 106 had the value of the parameter γ in BCK eos reduced from $\gamma = 3$ to $\gamma = 2.5$, producing a soft but not excessively soft equation of state. It is well known (BCK) that softening the high density equation of state strengthens the shock wave. We see that although the shock wave is indeed strengthened, propagating out to over 1100 km, versus 550 in the stiffer case (103) the shock is still not strong enough to produce an explosion. In fact, comparing 102, 103 and 106 we see that the harmful effects of NES are not completely overcome by the somewhat softer equation of state.

3.4 Model 104

Model 104 is significantly colder in the central regions than our "benchmark" model. This extra cooling could occur, for example, if beta decays on heavy nuclei play an more important role than has been assumed in current stellar evolution calculations[11]. The effect on the collapse of having such a low initial entropy is to reduce the fraction of free protons. This reduction in the free proton abundance substantially quenches the amount of electron capture on free protons and thus leads to a higher final trapped lepton fraction at bounce. Whereas the previous models that we have considered are both hot enough and have a low enough initial Y_e that the effects of electron capture on heavy nuclei would probably not give a large contribution to the total reduction in the final trapped lepton fraction. In this model, the initial Y_e is high. The available nuclei have states for which allowed transitions can proceed, and because there are very few free protons, electron capture on nuclei could become a more important source of lepton number reduction. In these calculations we have not included the effects of such captures on heavy nuclei and so we must temper our conclusions until this process is properly included in such cold models. Another possibly harmful effect which has yet to be included is neutrino downscattering due to the neutral current process $A(\nu,\nu')A^*$ where A is a heavy nucleus[17]. This has effects similar to those of NES, however, the size should be smaller and in combination with NES it may not be much of an enhancement. In any event, it is clear that this model produces a weak explosion; while not strong enough to actually be a supernova, it shows that such a cold core is helpful.

3.5 Models 105 and 107

In models 105 and 107 we examine the effect of making the iron core smaller simply by altering the positions of the silicon burning shells, that is by moving them in. The results are interesting and perhaps somewhat paradoxical. The trapped lepton fraction at bounce is significantly lower in these models than for model 103. Both the shock waves make it out of the putative iron core and die in fact at the same mass point $1.125 M_\odot$. Specifically how changing the location of the burning shells makes a difference on the final trapped lepton fraction is not obvious. This reduction in the lepton fraction does not occur until the center reaches about 10^{13} g cm^{-3} so it must alter the flow of neutrinos, but exactly how this occurs is not clear, and we have not yet arrived at a satisfactory explanation of this complicated behavior. Comparing the initial density profiles the models appear more favorable than 103, yet they fare worse.

3.6 Models 109 and 110

These models represent more extreme versions of Model 104. The mass of the iron core is kept fixed, as is the central entropy. It is the slope of the entropy in the initially convective core that is reduced. The average Y_l is substantially higher in model 109. This is reflected in the strength of the shock wave. Models 109 and 110 have reached the end of the computational grid with substantial velocities. An estimate of the total energy in the shock wave for model 109 is about 0.5×10^{51} ergs and 1.3×10^{51} ergs for model 110. Model 110 is stronger simply because the high density equation of state was softer for that model. In these models the same caveat about electron capture on heavy nuclei that we noted in our discussion of model 104 applies. It is still gratifying to see that the prompt mechanism can work on some models with conservative input physics.

4 Discussion and Conclusions

The above hydrodynamical results seem to show that the single most important factor determining the sucess or failure of the shock wave is the value of the final trapped lepton fraction Y_l in the homologous core of the star. The models that are cold initially and hence are subject to less electron capture on infall produce viable shock waves. These models are uncertain, however, as to the effects of capture on heavy nuclei as discussed above. A variety of agencies may affect the final Y_l, including the outer regions of the core, in a complicated fashion. Regardless of the actual cause of the variation, small changes in Y_l lead to large changes in the shock's strength. Primarily this is because the shock formation point moves inward with decreasing Y_l[18,19] as has been well studied. Our results agree with the conclusions of BRUENN[8] who also studied the effects of reducing the entropy and mass of the initial model.

Our results clearly show that the mass of the iron core, at least as we have defined it, does not allow one to easily predict the effect on the shock wave when compared with some other core. In fact, our calculations seem to show that there is a minimum mass below which the effects of reducing the mass still further become detrimental. This can be seen in table 3 by comparing our "benchmark" model 103 with models 105 and 107 which all have smaller iron cores, but the shock is weaker in these models. We have no unambiguous explanation for this effect and the possibility remains that it is the result of our assumptions, although the same effect occurs with models that come from the results of stellar evolution calculations. It would seem that it may be possible that iron cores with masses below about 1.1 $M_\odot$ could produce strong shock waves, but such models would have to look very different in their entropy and composition structure than those we have considered.

Acknowledgement

We wish to thank Morry Aufderheide, for allowing us to use the results of our joint unpublished work on neutrino electron scattering, Paul Schinder for providing us with his results on plasmon emission rates, Ken Nomoto and Stan Woosley for providing us with the results of their calculations and useful discussions, and Hans Bethe for helpful discussions. The calculations reported herein were performed at the National MFE computer center under auspices of the Nuclear Physics division, US Department of Energy.

This work has been supported in part by the U.S. Department of Energy under contract no. DE-AC02-76CH00016 and grant DE-FG02-88ER40388.

References

[1] H. A. Bethe and J. R. Wilson, Astrophys. J. **295**, 14 (1985).

[2] R. Mayle, PhD thesis, University of California, Berkeley, 1985, issued as Livermore Report UCRL-53713.

[3] R. Mayle and J. R. Wilson, Astrophys. J. **334**, 909 (1988).

[4] J. R. Wilson, in *Relativistic Astrophysics*, edited by J. Centrella, J. LeBlanc, and R. Bowers (Jones and Bartlett, Boston, 1985).

[5] J. Cooperstein and E. Baron, in *Supernovae*, edited by A. Petschek (Springer-Verlag, New York, 1989) [in press].

[6] E. S. Myra and S. A. Bludman, Astrophys. J. **340**, 384 (1989).

[7] S. Bruenn, Astrophys. J. **340**, 955 (1989).

[8] S. Bruenn, Astrophys. J. **341**, 385 (1989).

[9] K. Nomoto and M. Hashimoto, Phys. Repts. **163**, 13 (1988).

[10] S. E. Woosley and T. A. Weaver, Phys. Repts. **163**, 79 (1988).

[11] M. B. Aufderheide, G. E. Brown, D. B. Stout, T. T. S. Kuo, and P. Vogel, (1989) [preprint].

[12] T. A. Weaver and S. E. Woosley, (1988) [private communication].

[13] E. Baron and J. Cooperstein, Astrophys. J. (1989) [submitted].

[14] E. Baron, J. Cooperstein, and S. Kahana, Nucl. Phys. **A440**, 744 (1985).

[15] E. Baron, J. Cooperstein, and S. Kahana, Phys. Rev. Lett. **55**, 126 (1985).

[16] S. Bruenn, Astrophys. J. Suppl. **58**, 771 (1985).

[17] W. Haxton, Phys. Rev. Lett. **60**, 1999 (1988).

[18] A. Burrows and J. M. Lattimer, Astrophys. J. **270**, 735 (1983).

[19] J. Cooperstein, H. A. Bethe, and G. E. Brown, Nucl. Phys. **A429**, 527 (1984).

Supernova Calculations and the Hot Bubble
Stirling A. Colgate

The recent calculations of James Wilson and Ronald Mayle (1989) showed that the mechanism of supernova explosions caused by collapse to a neutron star now appears to be both understood conceptually and modeled convincingly up to 3.4 s following collapse. In particular they show the formation of a hot, high entropy bubble that continues to push on the shocked matter for a time long enough that the subsequent history is not in significant doubt. The hot bubble is formed primarily due to mu, tau neutrino antineutrino annihilation as first proposed by Goodman, Dar, and Nussinov (1987). The hot bubble that separates the neutron star from the ejected matter has high entropy, 10^2 to 10^4, measured in units of the Boltzmann constant, k per free nucleon. This high entropy means that for every nucleon there are many photons and electrons (pairs) and so the molecular weight is small and the scale height is large even at modest temperatures, $\leq 1 MeV$. Such a photon gas can "push" simultaneously on both the neutron star surface as well as on the expanding matter. It extends to a radius of $10^9 cm$ so that no fallback or reimplosion of any significant fraction of the ejected matter will take place. The kinetic and internal energy minus the gravitational energy of matter whose total energy is positive is $0.35 \times 10^{51} ergs$ at 3.4 s. They expect this to increase to 1 to $1.5 \times 10^{51} ergs$ by the end of the calculation, typical of Type II supernova.

It has long been my major concern (Colgate 1971) that despite a very strong shock wave a significant fraction of the ejected matter would subsequently fall back onto the neutron star. This fraction, several solar masses or more, would fall back in a time of about a half an hour despite an initial large (greater than escape) velocity leading to a black hole.

The reason for the large fallback mass is two-fold. First, normal matter falling onto a neutron star will be cooled by neutrino emission in a few tens of seconds from the high temperature, 1 to 2 MeV, that is created when this matter is shocked and compressed at the neutron star surface. Hence, the pressure that might ordinarily extend from the neutron star surface to the shocked matter, forming a piston to maintain the shock, disappears. The neutron star then acts like a black hole. Second, the internal energy in shocked material is always equal to the kinetic energy of motion of the same matter (behind a strong shock). Hence, despite the radially outward velocity that exists behind a strong ejection shock there is always enough heat to allow for an expansion inwards or backwards (in one dimension) at a velocity equal to the shock created outward velocity. The radially inward velocity of the rarefaction wave overcomes the original outward radial velocity of the shocked matter. When one adds to this backwards expansion the strong gravity existing in the central regions, the rarefaction velocity is quite sufficient to insure reimplosion even for the most energetic shocks whose total energy greatly exceeds that initially needed to eject matter from the star. Third, if the pressure deficit at the neutron star surface, due to neutrino cooling, occurs significantly later than the formation of the strong outward going shock, then the resulting rarefaction wave moving in the co-moving matter will always catch up to the shock wave and weaken it. (The flow behind a shock wave is always subsonic.) Thus we require a positive pressure extending from the neutron star surface to the shock until the shock reaches the outer low density layers of the star where the entropy generated by the shock alone is very large.

With spherical convergence the problem is more complicated due to what is known as Bondi accretion. Here if the shocked matter has a very high entropy or sound speed, the accretion or rarefaction flow tends to "choke" at a smaller radius corresponding to where the gravitational potential is equal to the specific internal energy (sound speed)^2 of the shocked matter. For example if the shock wave were four times stronger, i.e. has four times more energy per mass than is required to unbind the matter, then the radius at which the accretion would be choked by Bondi accretion (Bondi 1952) is no smaller than half the radius of the shock wave, and hence, would only reduce the flow by a factor of between two to four. Thus, there has always been the need to prevent the fallback of matter after being shock ejected from the neutron star.

The reason that measuring entropy in photons per nucleon is conceptually convenient is the following: the gravitational binding of a nucleon to the neutron star is approximately 1/10 its rest mass or 100 MeV per nucleon. (The neutron star cools in a second such that its radius is $\simeq 10^6 cm$.) Consequently, at temperatures typical of the neutron star surface, namely an MeV or 10^{10} degrees, the scale height of normal matter, i.e. just nucleons, would be roughly 1/100 of the neutron star radius. And so, despite the high temperature, nucleonic matter would be tightly bound to the neutron star, and the "push" 100 scale heights away at the shock contact surface would be trivially small (e^{-100}). Hence, one requires an extremely lightweight low atomic number gas to push equally against both the neutron star surface and the contact surface, i.e. the piston, of the ejection shock. Such a lightweight gas is the photon-pair dominated gas that forms at high temperature provided it is nucleon deficient. A measure of this deficiency is that there must be at least 100 photons with their associated electron pairs per nucleon such that the energy density per nucleon is greater than the nucleon binding energy to the neutron star or hence, entropies of the order of 100 to 1000 at $T \simeq 1 MeV (\rho_{nucleon} \leq 10^6\ g\ cm^{-3})$. This is just the entropy range formed in the hot bubble in Wilson's and Mayle's recent calculations.

Older calculations of Wilson (1985) and in (Bethe and Wilson 1985) showed a weaker hot bubble, $s \leq 100$ whose existence was dependent sensitively upon input parameters. Instead the present calculation which utilize a more exact treatment of neutrino-neutrino annihilation shows a much higher entropy, larger hot bubble.

The hot bubble is aided by the bounce shock, which temporarily reduces the flow of matter onto the neutron star. At the same time the neutrino emission that carries the heat of the binding energy of the neutron star is emitted in neutrinos in all flavors: electrons, muons and taus and their antiparticles. The density of nucleons ($\rho_{nucleon} \leq 10^9$ g cm^{-3}) following the bounce shock is not in itself enough to absorb these neutrinos and cause it to heat into a hot bubble. Instead, the neutrino number density itself from the heat flux is far greater than ($\times 100$) the nucleon component, and as was first shown by Goodman et al. (1987), these neutrinos and particularly the very hottest neutrinos, the mu's and tau's ($T \simeq 10 MeV$) that carry the most energy, annihilate on each other into electrons that create the hot bubble ($\nu_{\mu,\tau} + \bar{\nu}_{\mu,\tau} \rightarrow e^+ + e^-$). The energetic electron pairs immediately thermalize resulting in a photon plus pairs plus nucleon gas. As Wilson and Mayle have discussed, the extreme energy dependence of this neutrino-neutrino annihilation process requires that the neutrinos preferentially annihilate in nearly head-on collisions or at least with extreme angular dependency of the order of the eighth power of the angle. Hence, only when the neutron star surface has become extremely sharp, that is a very small scale height at the mu tau neutrino photosphere, will the neutrino-neutrino annihilation start heating the external low density matter to form the bubble. This happens some few tenths of a second following the bounce and thus forms a hot cavity that expands rapidly driving the ejection shock. Once the hot bubble starts to form, then the pairs, associated with the high temperature gas, become the dominant particle for neutrino interaction and so once started, the hot bubble is further heated by the entire neutrino flux only a small fraction of which has annihilated to form the initial hot bubble. This further heating produces at the end of 3.6 seconds a hot bubble whose entropy is as high as 10^4 in places and whose temperature adjacent to the contact surface i.e. the piston driving the shock is now low enough, a few hundred keV, that its subsequent cooling by neutrino emission is negligible.

Mixing Behind the Shock

The consequence of the hot bubble is that it will mix at the contact surface of the expanding shocked matter. This shocked matter has considerably lower entropy than the hot bubble. To investigate the degree of this mixing there are several surprising simplifications to the problem. These are (1) the expected mixing is close to the thickness of matter behind the shock and (2) the shock entropy increases due to the decreasing density of the envelope and the two entropies: that of the expanding hot bubble and that of the material behind the shock will become equal somewhere near the boundary between helium and hydrogen or when $\rho \simeq 1$ g cm^{-3}. Thus the outer mass fraction of ejected hydrogen will be unmixed, and that inside everything will be mixed.

Turbulent Mixing

Read and Youngs (1984) developed measurements and theory that shows the Rayleigh Taylor unstable mixing leads to a turbulent boundary layer separating the two fluids. This is the nonlinear limit of growth from a thermal noise spectrum of an initial interface with no other initial perturbations and infinite Reynolds numbers. They found that the thickness grew as a function of acceleration and time as

$$\Delta x = 0.07 a t^2 \tag{1}$$

where a is the acceleration. Since the displacement of the interface increases as

$$x = 1/2 a t^2, \tag{2}$$

the thickness of the layer becomes 1/7 of the displacement. As an aside, the mechanism of growth is that the spikes and bubbles of the nonlinear limit of the dominant growing wavelength excite eddies of equal scale, some of which coalesce by inverse turbulent cascade and thereby excite the next larger wavelength perturbation, etc. In the case of the stellar shock, the slowing down of the contact surface between the hot bubble material at higher entropy and the shocked matter at lower entropy is what drives the instability. This slowing down is due to the increasing mass of the matter external to the shock. In general the effect of gravity is less than the deceleration due to increasing mass behind the shock, but contributes at the early phase of the expansion.

Acceleration of Contact Surface

We assume that the hot bubble has been formed and expands adiabatically. Both the hot bubble as well as the material behind the shock is radiation domination and so $\gamma = 4/3$. Hence, in a homologous expansion no pressure gradient is formed across the contact surface due to different adiabats.

The acceleration of the contact surface then is due to a decreasing shock velocity and gravity. The contact surface is always close to the shock, $\Delta R \simeq R/(3\eta)$ because the compression ratio, $\eta = \frac{\gamma+1}{\gamma-1} = 7$ is large and the entropy gradient is weak.

The density distribution is close to polytropic external to the core and so to good approximation

$$\rho = \rho_o (R/R_o)^{-3} \tag{3}$$

$\rho_o = 4 \times 10^4 \ g \ cm^{-3}$ at $R_o = 2.5 \times 10^9 \ cm$. This gives a logarithmically increasing mass as $M = 1.25 M_\odot$ at a surface $R = 2 \times 10^{12} \ cm$ including the neutron star. With this distribution there also exists $1.25 M_\odot$ of matter inside R_o of the hot bubble that has collapsed to the neutron star. The Wilson, Mayle calculations put this mass at $1.63 M_\odot$ which is within the accuracy of the approximation. If we take $10 M_\odot$ ejected with 1.5×10^{51} ergs - typical of the models (Woosley 1988, Arnett 1989, Nomoto 1989) then the surface velocity of the equivalent uniform density sphere is

$$(u_{surf}^2/2)(5/3)M_{ej} = 1.5 \times 10^{51} ergs \tag{4}$$

or $u_{surf} = 3 \times 10^8 \ cm \ s^{-1}$. The fluid velocity behind the ejection shock that gives rise to this free surface velocity is closely one half of the surface velocity, contrary to simple energy conservation (Colgate and White 1966). Hence, the fluid velocity behind the shock near the surface is $\simeq 1.5 \times 10^8$ cm s^{-1} neglecting the speed-up of the shock in the final density gradient. The corresponding velocity at the radius of $R_o = 2.5 \times 10^9$ cm will be larger by the square root of the internal mass ratio or by $(\ln R_s/R_o)^{\frac{1}{2}} = 2.6$ in order to conserve energy. Thus $u_o = 4 \times 10^8$ cm s^{-1}. The corresponding internal energy of the hot bubble is then $3P_o \times Vol$ where $P_o = \rho_o u_o^2 \times 7/6 = 7.4 \times 10^{21} dynes\ cm^{-2}$, or $W_{bubble} = 1.4 \times 10^{51} ergs$. The sum of internal and kinetic energy behind the shock at $u_o = 4 \times 10^8$ cm s^{-1} and $M_o = 1.6 M_\odot = 0.5 \times 10^{51} ergs$ or a total of $1.8 \times 10^{51} ergs$. Roughly $0.8 \times 10^{51} ergs$ is retained as binding energy giving the self-consistent value of final kinetic energy of $1 \times 10^{51} ergs$.

Entropy and Mixing

Using this model we can calculate the entropy. If we use the variable $S = P/\rho^{4/3}$, then for a bubble entropy of 10^2 the minimum value necessary to retain a pressure against the neutron star in units of k, the Boltzmann constant, then $s_b = 1.4 \times 10^{17}$. The entropy behind the shock in the same units

$$s_o = \frac{\rho_o u_0^2 (\eta/\eta - 1)}{(\rho_o \eta)^{4/3}} = 8.7 \times 10^{-2} u_o^2 / \rho_o^{1/3} = 4 \times 10^{14}. \tag{5}$$

Thus the shock entropy and the bubble entropy become equal when

$$s_b = s_{shock} = s_o (\rho_s/\rho_o)^{1/3} \ln(R_s/R_o)$$

Since $(\rho_s/\rho_o)^{1/3} = R_s/R_o$, we obtain a radius $R_s = 80 R_o = 2 \times 10^{11}$, or where the stellar envelope density is $\rho_s = 0.05\ g\ cm^{-3}$.

The integral of the acceleration determines the degree of mixing up to this point in the envelope. If the velocity had decreased to zero in this distance and neglecting gravity, the mixed layer would be $1/7$ the radius. However, the velocity decrease is only half and so the acceleration is reduced in half so that roughly the mixed zone is only $1/2$ or $R/14$. On the other hand, for a uniform density sphere of matter compressed by η will appear as a layer $\Delta R/R = (1/3\eta)$ thick or $R/21$. Hence, a strong shock will be compressed to a thin layer in a uniform medium and somewhat thicker with our density distribution $\rho \propto R^{-3}$. Thus the mixing will penetrate close to the shock. A decreased mixing can also be expected due to the decreasing entropy of the bubble itself due to mixing with the lower entropy shocked matter. Thus more detailed calculations are warranted, but it appears that one can expect the hot bubble to mix out to roughly the helium-hydrogen zone in the star, $\rho \simeq 1\ g\ cm^{-3}$ and possibly somewhat further. This is just what is required to give the gamma ray transparency from $^{56}Ni \rightarrow ^{56}Co \rightarrow ^{56}Fe$ decay.

It is noteworthy that the astrophysical attempt to understand the explosion of supernovae using the caculational tools developed for nuclear weapons is now a tradition of 30 years at Lawrence Livermore Laboratory (Colgate and White 1966). The existence of the Z particle which permits neutrino-neutrino annihilation was not known at that time. Demonstrating the solution to the problem at LLL is a tribute to this long dedication.

References
1. J. R. Wilson and R. Mayle: Proceedings of the NATO Conf. "The Nuclear Equation of State," (Springer-Verlag, Berlin, 1984).
2. S. A. Goodman, A. Dar, and S. Nussinov: Ap. J. 314, L7 (1987).
3. S. A. Colgate: Ap. J. 163, 221 (1971).
4. H. Bondi: M.N.R.A.S (1952).
5. J. R. Wilson: In Numerical Astrophysics, ed. J. Centrella, J. LeBlanc, and R. Bowers (Jones and Bartlett, Boston 1985) p. 422.
6. H. Bethe and J. Wilson: Ap. J. 295, 14 (1985).
7. K. I. Read: Physica 12D, (North-Holland, Amsterdam) p. 45-58 (1984).
8. D. L. Youngs: Physica 12D (North-Holland, Amsterdam) p. 32-44 (1984).
9. S. A. Colgate and R. H. White: Ap. J. 143, 626 (1966).
10. S. E. Woosley: Astrophys. J. 330, 218 (1988).
11. W. D. Arnett: In Supernova 1987A in the Large Magellanic Cloud, ed. M. Kafatos and A. Michalitsianos (Cambridge: Cambridge University Press) p. 301 (1988).
12. K. Nomoto, T. Shigeyama, M. Hashimoto: In SN 1987A, ed. I. J. Danziger, ESO, Garching, p. 325 (1987).

Effects of Rotation on Collapsing Stellar Iron Cores

Ralph Mönchmeyer

O- and B- main sequence stars are found to rotate in general and it cannot be excluded that rotation may significantly influence the collapse of iron cores of Type II Supernova progenitor stars. Mönchmeyer and Müller have, therefore, numerically investigated the effects of angular momentum conservation on the axisymmetric collapse of a model iron core with a mass of 1.36 $M_\odot$. Several cases with parameterized initial angular momentum distributions have been considered. For details of the input physics, of the numerical scheme and the results see MÖNCHMEYER and MÜLLER [1], [2], MÖNCHMEYER [3], HILLEBRANDT et al. [4]. In the following some major results of these calculations will be summarized.

I. General Effects due to Rotation

During collapse the iron core splits up into a subsonically contracting "inner core" [IC] and a supersonically falling outer core. The mass of the IC depends both on its average electron concentration and on its angular momentum and may be up to 10% larger than in a nonrotating model. Without rotation the collapse of the IC is stopped in a "core bounce", only, when nuclear densities are reached at the core center. In rotating models, instead, even a small amount of initial rotational energy (about 1% or more of the initial potential energy of the core) may cause a bounce at subnuclear central densities, if the adiabatic index γ given by the equation of state [EOS] of iron core matter is close to the value 4/3 for densities $\rho \lesssim 10^{14}\,\text{gcm}^{-3}$.

Further effects due to centrifugal forces during collapse are the following : i) The equatorial diameter of the IC may become a factor of 2 larger than the polar diameter. ii) Centrifugal deceleration may reduce the kinetic infall energy (i.e. the kinetic energy minus the rotation energy) of the IC at bounce significantly in comparison to nonrotating models. (see ref. [3]). iii) In contrast to the oblate deformation of the isopycnic surfaces the surfaces of constant angular velocity Ω have at and after bounce an overall cylindrical shape inside the IC. There the Ω–profile eventually exhibits an exponential decline with the distance from the axis. At the polar edges of the IC the evolution of local Ω-maxima causes the generation of dips in the density stratification. iv) The profile of the infall velocity becomes very asymmetric. At bounce the maximum infall velocity in the equatorial plane roughly reaches only half the value of the maximum infall velocity on the axis.

A deformed shock front is generated at the surface of the IC at bounce. The shape of the outward propagating shock surface is determined by the density and velocity stratification outside the IC and details of the EOS. The large infall velocities of the supersonic matter near the axis lead to the generation of polar entropy blobs behind the shock front, which rise and expand due to buoyancy forces. The resulting inclination of isopycnic and isobaric surfaces may drive circulation flows in the shock heated matter. The shock is mainly weakened by energy losses due to the photo–disintegration of nuclei. At larger radii the shock dissipation of kinetic energy decreases because of the decreasing infall velocities in the supersonic flow. In one of the calculated models the resulting unstable entropy gradient triggered the evolution of a Rayleigh - Taylor - instability on timescales $\Delta t < 5$ ms. The corresponding mixing of high with low entropy material leads to a contraction of the shock heated matter in the gravitational field and weakens the shock. Nevertheless the shock front can reach a larger mass coordinate in rotating than in nonrotating models (see II.).

Post bounce oscillations of the IC with amplitudes larger than in the nonrotating case were found in all rotating models. The frequencies and amplitudes of the oscillation modes depend strongly on the stiffness of the EOS at maximum central density and on the kinetic infall energy of the IC at bounce. In a specific case, in which the collapse was stopped at a central density of $1.6 \cdot 10^{14}$ gcm^{-3} nonlinear, large scale volume oscillations occured : The shock was driven outward by the vehemently expanding IC until a minimum central density of only $7 \cdot 10^{12}$ gcm^{-3} was reached. In all cases the oscillations are damped by the generation of non-radial pressure waves, which are emitted from the surface of the IC and eventually catch up with the shock. The IC thus transfers energy to the shock until the IC approaches a state of rotational equilibrium after a model dependent damping time between 5 ms and 50 ms. The gravitational waves of the collapsed cores reflect the bounce and post bounce dynamics in a model specific, characteristic way.

Iron cores that bounce at central densities around (or below) 10^{13} gcm^{-3} produce only weak shocks and evolve into matter accreting configurations in rotational equilibrium. How their stability is influenced by neutrino transport processes on timescales of several hundred milliseconds remains to be investigated. In any case it can be shown that the deformation of the neutrino emitting region ("neutrinosphere") in the shock heated matter of collapsed rotating cores leads to a significant dependence of the observable neutrino flux on the inclination angle between the observer's line of sight and the rotational axis of the core (JANKA and MÖNCHMEYER [5]).

II. Consequences for the Shock Propagation

The shock can propagate to the surface of the iron core with large velocities, only, if the energy transferred to the shock heated matter is sufficient both to compensate energy losses (e.g. due to disintegration of nuclei) and to supply at least the minimum internal energy necessary to establish an equilibrium stratification of the shocked matter against the gravitational forces and the ram pressure at the shock surface. Otherwise the hot matter behind the shock will stop to expand. Therefore, rotation seems to be fatal for the shock propagation, because centrifugal forces reduce the kinetic infall energy (i.e. a major source of the initial shock energy and the energy dissipated by the shock) throughout the core in comparison to nonrotating models. The quantity that measures the energy transferred from the IC to its surroundings is the binding energy of the IC, i.e. the sum of its gravitational, internal and rotational energy. In all rotating models the binding energy of the IC in the final rotational equilibrium state was found to be smaller than in the nonrotating case but it was at least larger than the kinetic infall energy of the rotating IC at bounce. The latter holds especially in models, in which the post bounce oscillations of the IC have large amplitudes.

Some effects of rotation can, however, strengthen the shock : The virial theorem shows that the stabilizing effects of rotation on a gas in hydrostatic equilibrium are comparable to those of a gas with $\gamma = 5/3$. Centrifugal forces reduce the average ram pressure of the supersonic matter at the shock surface. In addition the gravitational energy of the matter outside the IC is smaller in rotating than in nonrotating models due to the larger radial extensions of rotating cores at and after bounce. According to the virial theorem the thermal energy needed to establish hydrostatic equilibrium in the shock heated matter (with $\gamma > 4/3$) outside the IC is, therefore, significantly reduced in rotating cores. It follows that the thermal energy deposited in the shock heated matter can much more efficiently be transformed into expansion work than in nonrotating cores. The shocks, therefore, reached in all calculated rotating models at least a mass coordinate of 1.3 $M_\odot$, slightly larger than in the nonrotating case.

In a specific model characterized by a maximum central density of $1.6 \cdot 10^{14}\,\text{gcm}^{-3}$ at bounce and extreme large scale oscillations after bounce the shock had even penetrated the silicon shell and reached a mass coordinate of 1.42 $M_\odot$, when the calculation was stopped. Although even in this case no strong explosion is to be expected, further calculations are necessary to clarify the role of rotation for the final evolution of massive stars and supernova explosions.

References

1. R.Mönchmeyer, E.Müller: NATO ASI C 262, eds. H.Ögelman, van den Heuvel, E., Kluwer, Dordrecht, 549 (1989)

2. R.Mönchmeyer, E. Müller: Astron. Astrophys. 217, 351 (1989)

3. R.Mönchmeyer: Proc. MPA P1, 92 (1989)

4. W.Hillebrandt, E. Müller, R. Mönchmeyer: NATO ASI, "The Nuclear Equation of State", ed. W.Greiner, Plenum, NY (1989) in press

5. H.T.Janka, R.Mönchmeyer: Astron. Astrophys. 209, L5 (1989)

Neutrino Inelastic Scattering and Prompt Shocks in Core Bounce Supernovae

Alak Ray

Attempts to numerically simulate "prompt explosions" in core bounce supernovae -believed to be due to a shock delivering sufficient energy at the base of the envelope, have been largely unsuccessful (COOPERSTEIN and BARON [1]). The primary reasons for the shock's failure in these models are two-fold: (1) energy loss from the shock radiated in neutrinos and (2) energy loss due to dissociation of iron group nuclei into helium and that of the latter into nucleons as the shock moves into the outer core and heats the matter to high temperatures. However, a significant fraction of the energy of the electron type neutrinos radiated in a few milliseconds burst may not be lost and can possibly go into preheating iron nuclei outside the shock front. If sufficient heat is deposited by the burst neutrinos, the material ahead of the shock will pre-dissociate before the shock actually arrives. Thus, "prompt" preheating by neutrinos would be a net energy saver for the shock. The energy of complete dissociation of $M_{Fe}/M_\odot$ of iron group nuclei into nucleons is $E_D = 1.7 \times 10^{52}$ erg $(M_{Fe}/M_\odot)$. As the typical energy of explosion in a type II SN is a few times 10^{51} erg, predissociation of approximately one tenth of a solar mass of heavy nuclei is significant.

When the shock breaks out of the neutrinosphere, a burst of neutrinos is radiated much in the same way as the ultraviolet flash that occured in SN1987A when the the shock reached the photosphere of the progenitor star. Since the burst duration is so short, the radiation of $\approx 3 \times 10^{51}$ erg leads to an extraordinary peak luminosity (e.g. $L_{\nu_e} \approx 5 \times 10^{53}$ erg/s as in MAYLE et al [2]). At this early stage the mu tau neutrino luminosity is still small enough so that the preheating is primarily due to electron type neutrinos. To evaluate the preheating due to the ν_e we use the recently reprted rates by HAXTON [3] who includes both charged and neutral current cross-sections on light and heavy nuclei with their giant resonances in first - forbidden transitions (see also DOMOGATSKII and NADYOZHIN [4]). The hydrodynamic model calculation used here is from MAYLE et al [2] for neutrinos from a 25 $M_\odot$ star (model 25 C). The shock break out time is 4 ms when the neutrinosphere radius is at 70 km and the peak luminosity occurs at 10.5 ms after bounce.

Very soon after the shock breakout, there are two components of the ν_e emission: (1) the direct blackbody emission from the neutrinosphere and (2) the emission from a thin shell behind the shock due to the rapid electron capture on protons just behind the shock in the entering material. These two components have been investigated analytically by BETHE, APPLEGATE and BROWN (BAB) [5] and by BURROWS and MAZUREK [6]. After shock breakout and neutrinospheric decay, the electron capture neutrinos take over and continue to dominate for 20 to 30 ms after which the long term core deleptonization flux takes over. The main part of the electron captures take place between densities $10^{11} - 10^{10}$ gmcm^{-3} in the timescale of interest ($\tau_{cap} \propto (X_e\rho)^{-5/3}$). Fast shocks generate stronger shell sources. The initial neutrinospheric emission is argued to be blackbody in nature in these analyses [5]. A luminosity, half of the peak luminosity of 5×10^{53} erg/s from a neutrinosphere of radius

70 km implies a neutrino temperature close to that for BAB's x parameter of 0.5 (i.e. 6.4 MeV). In one set of our calculations we take a neutrinosphere radius and temperature of 70 km and 6.5 MeV respectively. Even though the shell emission due to electron capture from a particular density zone may be non-thermal (and are richer in high energy particles compared to a Fermi Dirac distribution of temperature T_ν and zero η_ν), taken together, the energy spectrum of neutrinos, a jumble of such emission spectra coming from different density and temperature zones can be described by an effective temperature. We also take the neutrinosphere stationary at 70 km since it moves far less than the shock during the ν_e burst.

Any mass zone overlying the position and mass coordinate of the shock when the ν_e burst is over is heated purely by the burst neutrinos and can be termed as a region of pure preheating, i.e. unaffected by shock heating. By the time the neutrino burst is clearly over the shock is about 180 km from the center [2]. The net heating rate at a distance R from the center is (BETHE and WILSON [7]):

$$\dot{E} = K(T_\nu) \left[\frac{fL_\nu}{4\pi R^2} - \left(\frac{T}{T_\nu}\right)^2 acT^4 \right] \mathrm{erg\,gm}^{-1}\mathrm{s}^{-1} \qquad (1)$$

The preheating causes a change in composition in any given mass zone. Thermodynamic evolution of matter in these zones is tracked as in our earlier work (RAY and KAR [8]). The equilibrium fractions of the four components (Fe, He, n, p) at temperature T are found by solving the Saha equations for iron and alpha dissociation. Given a net heat deposition $\dot{E}\,\Delta t$ in a time step, the change in entropy is:

$$T\Delta S = \dot{E}\Delta t - \frac{Q_\alpha}{4}\Delta X_\alpha - \frac{Q_{Fe}}{56}\Delta X_{Fe} \qquad (2)$$

where Q_α (=28.3 MeV) and Q_{Fe} (=124.4 MeV). (Neutrino - nucleus inelastic scattering cross sections are used in calculating the factor $K(T_\nu)$ in eq.(1)). The temperature change is calculated along with the two independent baryon fractions self-consistently. The total entropy of the system at a given mass zone contains the contribution from the four types of baryonic matter (see e.g.,FULLER [9]), their nuclear excitation entropy and radiation and (relativistic) electron entropies. Included in this temperature change calculation is the density change of a given zone after core bounce. This density dependance outside the shocked zone is: $\rho_1 = A_1 t^{-1} r^{-3/2}$, with $A_1 = 1.2 \times 10^{18}$cgs units (BETHE and WILSON [7]). The calculation of heating is continued till $\approx$ 18 ms after bounce in which roughly 3.5×10^{51}ergs of ν_e energy is radiated away. The initial core entropy ahead of the shock is taken as a constant to a first approximation and the initial composition profile calculated. Since the initial core entropy depends on the previous stages of evolution, (i.e. presupernova and collapse phases) we take it as a variable parameter in our calculations.

The optical depth at the neutrinosphere does not abruptly drop to zero at $r = R_\nu$; in reality there is an extended neutrinosphere. As in the case of stellar atmospheres this renders the neutrino distribution more isotropic through partial reprocessing of the inner flux and increases the neutrino number density over what it would have been otherwise. We take into account the isotropy of the distribution by multiplying the heating rate in eq (2) by a factor $f = (1 + 3\,(R_\nu/r)^2)$ to test the effects of the fuzzy neutrinosphere. Detailed computations of the reprocessed flux cofirms this to be a good approximation [10]. The heating rate at a radius of e.g. 240 km at the shock breakout time for $T_\nu = 6.5$ MeV is dominated by the heating on iron nuclei. This situation changes dramatically during the peak of the ν_e burst when almost the entire heating is due to the nucleons. The results of the preheating calculations are summarized in Table I. In order to see the effects of neutrino energy spectrum on the predissociation of nuclei, we have used three temperatures for the neutrinos: 6.5 MeV, 5 MeV and 4 MeV.*The radius and mass upto which matter is completely dissociated into nucleons are quite sensitive to the difference of neutrino temperatures and energies.* The isotropy factor introduced by the factor f in eq (2) produces only minor changes in the masses of iron and helium dissociated and the dissociation energy. In addition, in the case of a higher initial entropy in the core, although the initial heating rates are somewhat higher due to the presence of a higher fraction of free nucleons, the initial entropy conditions are quickly forgotten and the dissociation energy remains close to the case for a lower entropy.

An energy of the order of 10^{51} ergs is substantial in the energy budget of the shock which is expected to produce prompt explosions. Even in the case of a neutrino temperature of 5 MeV this is in excess of 10^{51} ergs and is a reasonable fraction of the energy in the ν_e pulse. However, lower neutrino temperatures make a less effective coupling of the neutrino energy to matter ahead of the shock, although the energy of dissociation for $T_\nu = 4$ MeV is not negligible and since it is delivered at the appropriate place in the star, it can possibly improve situations for shock propagation. To conclude, preheating of unshocked matter by neutrinos can contribute substantially towards shock survival and propagation in a prompt explosion *depending on the neutrino energy spectrum*. Detailed hydrodynamical simulations need to include this effect and determine the ν_e burst energy spectrum carefully.

A detailed version of this work done with Kamales Kar will be published elsewhere. I was supported in part by a grant from the National Science Foundation.

TABLE 1

NEUTRINO PREHEATING AHEAD OF SHOCK

$\frac{T_{\nu_e}}{MeV}$	$\left(\frac{T}{10}\right) r_7^{3/4}$	$\frac{E_{in}^{th}}{foe}$	$\frac{R_{He}}{km}$	$\frac{R_{Fe}}{km}$	$\frac{\Delta M_{He}}{M_\odot}$	$\frac{\Delta M_{Fe}}{M_\odot}$	$\frac{E_D}{foe}$
$S_i = 1.2 k_B$/nucleon							
6.5	0.5	4.7	270	380	0.08	0.2	2.5
6.5 (f=1)	0.5	4.7	250	360	0.06	0.175	2.2
5.0	0.38	2.75	230	300	0.04	0.11	1.4
4.0	0.31	2.0	200	240	0.02	0.05	0.7
$S_i = 2.5 k_B$/nucleon							
6.5	0.5	4.7	275	385	0.085	0.205	2.6

REFERENCES

1. J. Cooperstein and E. Baron, to appear in this Proceedings.
2. R. Mayle, J.R. Wilson and D.N. Schramm, Astrophys. J. **318**, 288 (1987).
3. W.C. Haxton, Phys. Rev. Lett. **60**, 1999 (1988).
4. G.V. Domogatskii and D.K. Nadyozhin, Soviet Astronomy **22**, 297 (1978).
5. H.A. Bethe, J.H. Applegate and G.E. Brown, Astrophys. J. **241**, 343 (1980).
6. A. Burrows and T.L. Mazurek, Nature **301**, 315 (1983).
7. H.A. Bethe and J.R. Wilson, Astrophys. J. **295**, 14 (1985).
8. A. Ray and K. Kar, Astrophys. J. **319**, 143 (1987).
9. G.M. Fuller, Astrophys. J. **252**, 741 (1982).
10. H.T. Janka, Private Communication (1989).

A Look at Dissipation in Stellar Collapse
Edward A. Baron

1 Introduction

The possible discovery[1,2] of an optical pulsar in SN 1987A (PSR 1987A) having a period of ~ 0.5 ms raises many exciting issues. Not the least of these is the effect of the rotation on the actual mechanism of the explosion. The distribution of angular momentum in the iron core prior to collapse is completely unknown.

One natural possibility is that the iron core is rotating rigidly with an angular velocity

$$\Omega_{ic} = (\frac{R_{ns}}{R_{ic}})^2 \Omega_{ns} \qquad (1)$$

where ic refers to quantities of the iron core and ns refers to quantities of the neutron star. Taking $\Omega_{ns} = 1.2 \times 10^4$ s^{-1}, the value appropriate to PSR 1987A, this gives $\Omega_{ic} = 1$ s^{-1}, an enormously fast rotation rate. While this model seems quite näive, the iron core is very similar to a white dwarf and white dwarfs are known to rotate rigidly although somewhat more slowly.

Another possibility[3] is that the iron core is rotating slowly and the mantle is rotating rapidly. In this scenario, the core collapses to nuclear matter density and the neutron star is "spun up" by the accretion of $\sim 0.2\ M_\odot$ of material at the Keplerian velocity. This structure could arise, for example, by the transfer of angular momentum out of the core due to convection. The efficiency of this process is unknown.

A third possibility is a combination of the previous two. Core silicon burning does not occur throughout what is to become the final iron core, but stops at between 0.8 and 1.0 $M_\odot$. The rest of the iron core is built up later through shell burning events. Now it is possible that the convective core silicon burning could serve to sweep the angular momentum from the inner 0.8-1.0 $M_\odot$ of the iron core. In this scenario the inner part of the core is rotating slowly, while the outer part of the iron core is rotating rapidly.

Current one-dimensional calculations of iron core collapse fail to provide a convincing mechanism for turning the collapse into a successful explosion. Given the state of one dimensional calculations and the impetus supplied by the observation of PSR 1987A, it is natural to investigate the effects a large rotational energy might have upon the collapse of the iron core. Two dimensional calculations have been performed by several groups[4,5,6,7,8,9]. These calculations have shown that with rapid rotation nuclear matter densities may not be reached. General relativistic effects remain beyond the reach of current 2-d codes and they have also had to treat neutrino transport in a simplified manner.

In this talk I present a summary of some schematic calculations I have done with Stan Woosley that will be published in detail elsewhere[10]. We study the effect of various angular momentum distributions as well as the effect of dissipation of the kinetic energy of differential rotation. These calculations are carried out in a one dimensional framework and are only schematic. They serve to illustrate the possible size of effects and are useful bases upon which more detailed and correct calculations can be built.

2 Calculations

In the case that convection during silicon core burning is very effective at transferring angular momentum it might be thought that one can produce a strong shock wave by bouncing at supernuclear density, while at the same time strengthen the shock by keeping the outer parts of the iron core at low density due to centrifugal forces. It turns out that this is not the case. As an example we took the WEAVER and WOOSLEY[11] 18 $M_\odot$ model as an initial model. We gave it 3×10^{49} erg s of angular momentum, distributed in the core for $M \geq 0.8$. While, this is marginally helpful (the shock goes 30 km further than the non-rotating case the shock still dies at around 220 km, inside the iron core. Basically, the outer part of the core doesn't collapse enough for the centripetal acceleration to be important.

Now, let us turn our attention to models where differential rotation leads to dissipative heating in the iron core. We study the effect of dissipation in a phenomenological manner. Since dissipation will heat the matter, and will be proportional to the difference in the velocity across a surface, we simply add a term to the pressure, analogous to the pseudoviscosity used to model shock waves. The form we take for the dissipation term is

$$q_{vis} = q <R>^2 |\Omega_j^2 - \Omega_{j-1}^2|/V, \qquad (2)$$

where $<R>$ is the radius at the center of the zone, V is the specific volume and Ω_j is the angular velocity of the zone, Ω_{j-1} is the angular velocity of the adjacent zone, q is simply a scale factor that we will take to be in the range 0–10. To gain some feeling for the size of q, we can examine the total work done by the dissipative term in a calculation for which $q = 1$. We find that the total work done in a zone is less than 10^{49} ergs, or between 1 and 100 percent of the maximum rotational kinetic energy of a zone. Another measure is the maximum value of the ratio q_{vis}/p, where p is the pressure in a zone. We find for $q = 1$ that $q_{vis}/p < 0.5$, corresponding to a weak shock wave. Thus, it seems reasonable to take q in the range 0–10.

Table 1 describes the models we have calculated and Table 2 displays the results. We see that the two models are reasonably vigorous explosions. The difference between them is only that neutrino electron scattering (NES) is included in model 111 and not in model 101. NES does not hurt the shock wave, in fact, since it was run a bit longer model 111 is a stronger explosion.

We have shown in our schematic calculations that dissipation of the kinetic energy could provide a potent energy source for the shock wave. In fact, dissipation is a continuous source of energy that could act as a pre-heater for the delayed mechanism as well as an energy booster over long times.

Dissipation in Stellar Collapse

Model	Description	NES	Ω_0 s^{-1}	$L_{tot}/10^{49}$ erg s	q	ρ_{dis}
101	Rigid Rotation	off	1.0	1.0	8	$5(10^{11})$
111	Rigid Rotation	on	1.0	1.0	8	$5(10^{11})$

Table 1: Summary of models run with dissipation

NES refers to whether or not the effects of neutrino electron scattering were included. The value of q refers to the coefficient of the dissipative term, and the value of ρ_{dis} refers to the value of the central density when the dissipation term was turned on since we expect models to be stable against turbulence initially.

Model	101	111
ρ_c^{max}	4.51	4.41
R(1.1)	169.1	172.7
u(1.1)	-1.3	-1.3
ρ(1.1)	8.3(9)	8.0 (9)
T(1.1)	1.08	1.07
R_s	12.4	12.9
M_s	0.65	0.55
R(2.7)	10.8	12.9
M(2.7)	0.55	0.55
ρ_c^{equil}	2.5	2.5
E_{kin}	0.2	0.27

Table 2: Summary of results for dissipative models

The table lists various quantities of the models, ρ_c^{max} is the maximum central density at bounce in units of 10^{14} g cm^{-3}, R(1.1), u(1.1), ρ(1.1), and T(1.1) are the radius (in km), velocity (in 10^9 cm s^{-1}), density (g cm^{-3}), and temperature (in MeV), at the mass point $M = 1.1\ M_\odot$, listed for each model at bounce. R(2.7) and M(2.7) are the radius and mass point where the shock forms, R_s and M_s are the radius and mass point of the shock wave at bounce, ρ_c^{equil} is the value of the central density after rebound, and E_{kin} is the kinetic energy (in units of 10^{51} ergs) in the shock wave if the shock wave makes it to the end of the numerical grid.

Acknowledgement

I would like to thank Stan Woosley for letting me present our joint work and Jerry Cooperstein for the use of the hydrodynamical code that we have developed together as well as many helpful discussions. These calculations were performed at the National MFE Computer Center and I thank the US DOE for a generous allocation of computer time.

This work has been supported in part by the U.S. Department of Energy under grant DE-FG02-88ER40388.

References

[1] J. Middleditch et al., IAU Circ. No. 4735 , (1989).

[2] J. Kristian et al., Nature **338**, 234 (1989).

[3] S. E. Woosley and R. A. Chevalier, Nature **338**, 321 (1989).

[4] P. Bodenheimer and S. E. Woosley, Astrophys. J. **269**, 381 (1983).

[5] J. LeBlanc and J. R. Wilson, Astrophys. J. **161**, 541 (1970).

[6] R. Mönchmeyer and E. Müller, in *Timing in Neutron Stars* (Reidel, Dordrecht, 1988).

[7] E. Müller and W. Hillebrandt, Astr. Astrophys. **103**, 358 (1981).

[8] E. Müller, M. Różyczka, and W. Hillebrandt, Astr. Astrophys. **81**, 288 (1980).

[9] E. M. D. Symbalisty, Astrophys. J. **285**, 729 (1984).

[10] E. Baron and S. E. Woosley, (1989) [preprint].

[11] T. A. Weaver and S. E. Woosley, (1988) [private communication].

Shock Simulation in Type II Supernovae: A Collection of Recipes
Maurice B. Aufderheide

It is safe to say that the central riddle of type II supernovae, how a collapsing iron core manages to form a proto-neutron star and a strong shock wave blowing apart the star, has not yet been solved. Yet it is clear from SN 1987A that such events do occur. Although this central problem has not yet been solved, it is possible to study the physics outside the core by generating a shock wave by hand. There are several ways of doing this and the question is whether they are equivalent and when do these artificial methods approach what might really be seen in supernovae? In this study these questions will be discussed. They will be explored in greater detail in a forthcoming paper[1].

Before discussing different generation methods, it is necessary to examine how one can characterize the shocks generated. One method which is commonly used is to measure the "energy of the shock". This quantity is not uniquely defined and each group has its own definition. One possible definition is to quote the initial energy deposited in generating the shock. Another definition is to quote the kinetic energy of the shocked material after the shock has reached hydrogen envelope. Another measure is to compute the total energy in escaping zones, less the total energy which was present in the initial model. All of these are useful measures, but they will not yield the same values. However, one does expect a one-to-one mapping between them.

Another method which can be used for characterization is to compare temperature versus Lagrangian mass coordinate generated in various shocks. One can compare the peak temperatures reached as a function of enclosed mass in the shocked material. One can also examine temperature versus time profiles at particular points within the star. These diagnostics allow one to examine the strength and shape of the generated shock wave and its effect upon nucleosynthesis. In Figure 1 (see the last page for all plots), peak temperatures are plotted as a function of enclosed mass for two shocks of differing energy. All simulations reported here were performed upon the NOMOTO SN 1987A model[2]. The mass range plotted is the prime nucleosynthetic region. The solid line corresponds to a shock energy of 1 foe (10^{51} ergs), while the dashed line is a shock with energy of 2.9 foes. These energy assignments are obtained using the third method discussed above. Note that tripling the shock energy results in peak temperature increases of $.5 \times 10^9$ K to 1×10^9 K.

Having discussed how to characterize shocks, it is now possible to compare methods of generation. One method is to deposit a lot of kinetic energy somewhere in the outer iron core and let the shock be generated as a result of the collision with surrounding material. A second way is to deposit the energy as a surplus of internal energy in a layer of the core[3]. This layer will then expand, generating a shock wave. The third way to make a shock is to specify a violent trajectory, R(t), for a particular mass point (a piston) which forces it to smash into the surrounding material. If one knew the trajectory of such a point in the actual, self-consistent case, this is all that would be necessary to generate the actual shock wave. Such a trajectory is not known at present, so some prescription must be chosen. WOOSLEY and WEAVER have such a prescription[4] and this method will be used for comparison here.

One must be careful in the area just outside the shock initiation region because nucleosynthetic results may be unphysical. This is an artifact of the original artificiality of each method. A physically self-consistent shock wave carries its energy partitioned between kinetic and internal energy. Each initiation starts with this partition skewed unphysically. As the shock propagates, smashing into new material, the energy is gradually partitioned properly. One can think of the shock wave "maturing". The region in which the shock has sorted itself out will be called the mature region and the volume between the shock initiation point and the mature region will be called the adolescent region. Within the adolescent region the temperature profiles will not be consistent with the energy attributed to the shock wave, since either too much or too little of the shock's energy will be in internal energy. Because of the dubious temperature profiles, the abundances determined in the adolescent region will also be suspect.

This effect can be seen in Figures 2 and 3. In both graphs, peak temperature is plotted versus enclosed mass. In Figure 2, two kinetic energy bombs with an energy of 1 foe are compared. The solid line is a shock started at $.6M_\odot$, while the dashed line is a shock started at $1.32M_\odot$. Note that this shock exhibits low temperatures until roughly $1.55M_\odot$, after which the profiles agree. $1.32M_\odot$ to $1.55M_\odot$ is the adolescent region for the second shock wave. Notice that this implies that the first shock had matured by the time it reached roughly $.83M_\odot$. In Figure 3, two internal energy bombs with an energy of 1 foe are compared. The solid line is a shock started at the center of the star, while the dashed line is a shock started at $1.43M_\odot$. Note here that the second shock is immature until roughly $1.66M_\odot$, and that here the immaturity is exhibited by higher temperatures. It is interesting that in both cases, the adolescent region extends $.23M_\odot$. One should not trust nucleosynthetic results in these regions for such shock waves. If one does desire accurate results in such areas, one must move the shock initiation point back far enough that the adolescent region does not intersect with the region of interest. Immaturity in piston generated shock waves has not yet been examined.

A comparison of the three initiation methods is also interesting. In Figure 4, peak temperatures are again plotted versus mass for shocks with energies of 1 foe. Maturity has been verified for each shock wave. The solid line is a kinetic energy bomb, the dashed line is a WOOSLEY-WEAVER piston, and the dotted line is an internal energy bomb. Note the agreement between the first two methods. Note also that the internal energy bomb exhibits lower temperatures until roughly $2.2M_\odot$. This last shock wave would produce $.04M_\odot$ less of ^{56}Ni than the first two shocks using the THIELEMANN et. al. rule of thumb for the synthesis of ^{56}Ni[5]. This is over half of what was seen in SN 1987A and is not trivial matter. It is worrisome that, given the same amount of energy, significantly different temperature profiles can produced.

This may indicate that in the silicon and oxygen shells there is not a unique shock solution corresponding to a given energy. If this is true, reliable simulation of the nucleosynthesis of iron group elements will have to wait for the solution of the core collapse-explosion problem.

Acknowledgement: I would like to thank my collaborators, E. Baron, F.-K. Thielemann, and J. Cooperstein for allowing me to discuss results of our work.

This work has been supported by the U.S. Department of Energy under contract no. DE-AC02-76CH00016, and grant no. DE-FG02-88ER40388

References

[1] M. B. Aufderheide, E. Baron, F. K. Thielemann, and J. Cooperstein, in preparation, 1989.

[2] K. Nomoto and M. Hashimoto, Phys. Rept. **163**, 13 (1988).

[3] T. Shigeyama, K. Nomoto, and M. Hashimoto, Astron. and Astrophys. **196**, 141 (1988).

[4] S. E. Woosley and T. A. Weaver, in *Essays in Nuclear Astrophysics*, edited by C. A. Barnes, D. D. Clayton, and D. N. Schramm, p. 377 (Cambridge Univ. Press, 1982).

[5] F. K. Thielemann, M. Hashimoto, and K. Nomoto, preprint, 1989.

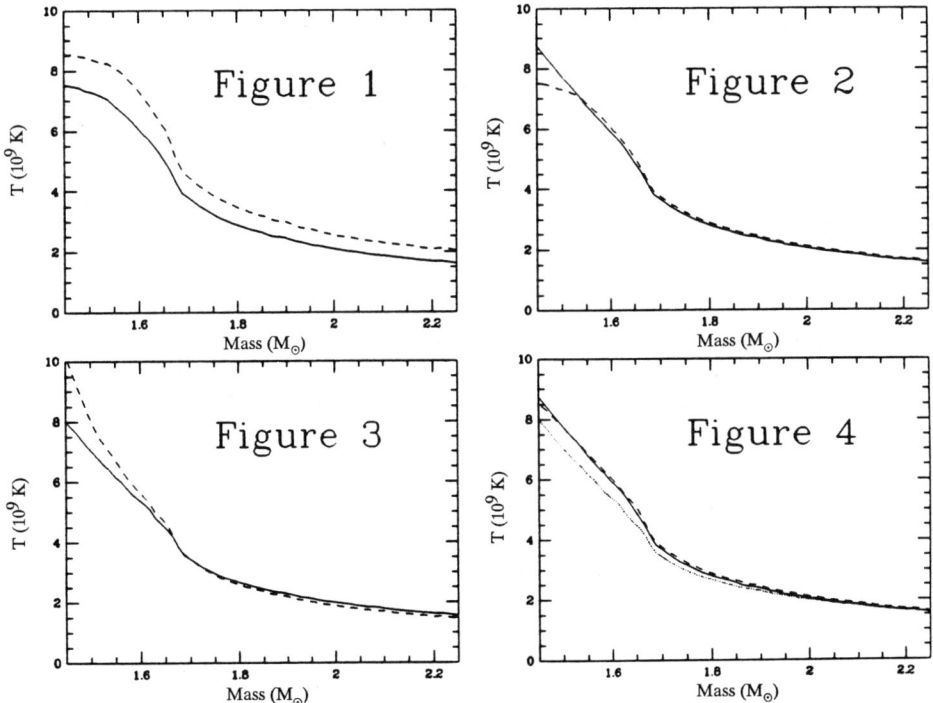

Is There Life After Fuller, Fowler & Newman?
Maurice B. Aufderheide

Weak interactions have been an important part of nuclear astrophysics ever since hydrogen burning in the sun was elucidated. In type II supernovae, $\beta^{\pm}$ decay and electron capture are extremely important because they determine the electron fraction per nucleon (Y_e) of the iron core. The mass of the iron core and the Lagrangian position of shock formation both vary as Y_e^2[1],[2]. Also, these reactions create neutrinos which, before core collapse, are able to carry core energy off to infinity. These rates are thus crucial ingredients of the stellar evolution calculation which is the initial model for a type II supernova simulation.

The inclusion of these rates is difficult to achieve because one must compute them for a large number of potentially important nuclei, over a large range of temperature, density, and Y_e. This monumental work has been undertaken several times in the past. The most recent effort was made by FULLER, FOWLER, and NEWMAN in the early 1980's[3],[4], [5],[6]. They tabulated $\beta^{\pm}$ decay and electron capture rates for nuclei with mass number up to 60 over a wide range of temperature, density, and Y_e. In their calculations, they included the effects of the Gamow-Teller and the isobaric analog resonances. These rate tables are the ones currently employed in the stellar evolution codes of NOMOTO[7] and WOOSLEY and WEAVER[8].

The study reported here is an investigation whether nuclei with masses heavier than 60 could have a significant effect upon the presupernova evolution of the iron core[9]. It is a sensitivity study for nuclei with $60 < A \leq 70$, during the hydrostatic silicon burning stages of the core's evolution. This is the most active part of the core's life as far as the pre-collapse history is concerned. It is characterized by densities of 10^6 g/cm^3 to 10^9 g/cm^3, temperatures of 2 billion K to 5 billion K and electron fractions ranging from .5 down to .42. In this study, only the strongest allowed Gamow-Teller transition was included for each nucleus. Because a lot of the Gamow-Teller strength has been neglected, these rates will be underestimates; however, if large effects are uncovered here, they will certainly be important after a full calculation is performed. This study is therefore a prelude to an exhaustive calculation.

The electron capture rate on a nucleus A due to a transition i can be written as:

$$\lambda_i^A(e.c.) = Factors \times B(GT) \int_L^\infty \frac{p_e^2 (\Delta E + \epsilon_e)^2 F(Z, \epsilon_e) dp_e}{1 + exp[(\epsilon_e - \mu_e)/k_B T]} \qquad (1)$$

where B(GT) is the Gamow-Teller matrix element for the transition, ΔE is E$_{mother}$

$-E_{daughter}$, μ_e is the electron chemical potential, and T is the temperature. $F(Z,\epsilon_e)$ is the Fermi function, which includes the effect of the nuclear Coulomb field on the electron wave function. $\mathcal{L}$ is the lower limit of the electron momemtum. For $\Delta E \geq -m_e$, $\mathcal{L}$ is zero, while for $\Delta E < -m_e$, $\mathcal{L}$ is $\sqrt{\Delta E^2 - m_e^2}$. The β^- decay rate can similarly be written as:

$$\lambda_i^A(\beta^-) = Factors \times B(GT) \int_0^{\sqrt{\Delta E^2 - m_e^2}} \frac{p_e^2(\epsilon_e - \Delta E)^2 F(Z,\epsilon_e) dp_e}{1 + exp[(\mu_e - \epsilon_e)/k_B T]}. \quad (2)$$

where all factors are defined as above, except that Z is now the charge of the daughter nucleus. Such transitions affect the evolution of the electron fraction in the following way:

$$\frac{dY_e}{dt}\Big|_i^{(Z,A)} = \pm \lambda_i^A Y_{(Z,A)} \quad (3)$$

$Y_{(Z,A)}$ is the number fraction of the mother nucleus. The plus sign applies for β^- decay, while the minus is used for electron capture or β^+ decay. To estimate the effect a transition will have upon the electron fraction, form $\Delta Y_e = \pm \lambda_i^A Y_{(Z,A)} \Delta t$ where Δt is the characteristic time of the silicon burning stages, 10^5 to 10^6 seconds.

This last expression shows that, in order for a reaction to really affect the core, the product of the abundance and the rate must be greater than $10^{-8} sec^{-1}$. Computing the reaction rate is not enough; the species could still be abysmally rare. On the other hand, a mother nucleus could become abundant at a time when the rate is small. In this study the abundance of each nucleus was estimated by determining its abundance in nuclear statistical equilibrium (NSE) for a given temperature, density, and electron fraction. Of course this might yield abundances which are somewhat large during early stages of silicon burning, because NSE has not yet been achieved. But it provides an order of magnitude estimate.

Using these tools, the strongest transitions on nuclei with A between 60 and 70 were sought. Electron captures on nuclei which were on the neutron-poor side of the valley of β stability were ignored for now because they would only be abundant for values of Y_e near .5. This corresponds to the early stages of hydrostatic Si burning, during which the material is not yet in NSE and is mostly silicon and sulfur. The strongest electron capture transition which was found was $^{66}Cu + e^- \longrightarrow {}^{66}Ni + \nu_e$. This is a transition between the 1^+ ground state of ^{66}Cu and the 0^+ ground state of ^{66}Ni. The value of ΔE is -.747 MeV[10] and the β^- decay in the reverse direction has been measured, providing the desired matrix element by detailed balance. At a temperature of 4×10^9K, a density of 10^8 g/cm^3, and and electron fraction of .44, the change in Y_e is:

$$\Delta Y_e = 3.5(-3)\frac{1.3(-5)}{66}10^6 = 7(-4). \quad (4)$$

This is not very large. This was the largest effect found for electron capture reactions. Inclusion of the full Gamow-Teller strength could make these rates larger.

When one considers the possible β^- decays, one sees a vastly different picture. The contributions of these rates is largely determined by the size of ΔE in the reaction. In the region of atomic mass studied here, the $^{64}Co \longrightarrow {}^{64}Ni + e^- + \bar{\nu}_e$ reaction is the largest because of its huge mass difference of 7.818 MeV[10]. The ratio of Z to A for ^{64}Co is low (.422), which ensures that it will only contribute at $Y_e \leq .44$. This corresponds to the last stages of silicon burning. If one estimates the change in electron fraction due to this single reaction, one obtains

$$\Delta Y_e = 2.09 \frac{6.3(-5)}{64} 10^5 = .2. \qquad (5)$$

This would be an huge effect on the electron fraction. If one tries to estimate the thermal effects of these decays, one obtains a similarly large effect. These results are so large that it is clear that the nonlinearity of the iron core's response will regulate the effect of these decays. Although it is difficult to predict what the inclusion of such reactions will do in detail, it is clear that they will alter the evolution of the iron core. With the inclusion of the full Gamow-Teller strength in the electron capture rates, even these marginal rates will begin to make significant contributions.

In conclusion, even with deliberate underestimates of the rates for nuclei with A between 60 and 70, it has been shown that some electron captures may make a small contribution to core evolution and that several of the β^- decays will have a large effect on the core's evolution. This shows that there is a need for a full calculation of these rates and inclusion of these rates into present stellar evolution codes. There is life after FULLER, FOWLER, and NEWMAN and it is time to get to work.

Acknowledgement: I would like to thank my collaborators, G. E. Brown, T. T. S. Kuo, D. B. Stout, and P. Vogel for allowing me to discuss results of our work.

This work has been supported by the U.S. Department of Energy under contract no. DE-AC02-76CH00016.

References

[1] A. Burrows and J. Lattimer, Ap. J. **270**, 735 (1983).

[2] J. Cooperstein, H. A. Bethe, and G. E. Brown, Nuclear Physics **A429**, 527 (1984).

[3] G. M. Fuller, W. A. Fowler, and M. J. Newman, Ap. J. Suppl. **42**, 447 (1980).

[4] G. M. Fuller, W. A. Fowler, and M. J. Newman, Ap. J. **252**, 715 (1982).

[5] G. M. Fuller, W. A. Fowler, and M. J. Newman, Ap. J. Suppl. **48**, 279 (1982).

[6] G. M. Fuller, W. A. Fowler, and M. J. Newman, Ap. J. **293**, 1 (1985).

[7] K. Nomoto, Ap. J. **277**, 791 (1984).

[8] T. A. Weaver, S. E. Woosley, and G. M. Fuller, in *Numerical Astrophysics*, edited by J. Centralla, J. LeBlanc, and R. Bowers, p. 374 (Jones and Bartlett, 1985).

[9] M. B. Aufderheide, G. E. Brown, T. T. S. Kuo, D. B. Stout, and P. Vogel, in preparation.

[10] C. M. Lederer and V. S. Shirley, editors, *Table of Isotopes* (John Wiley, 1978) 7th edition.

Nucleosynthesis in Non-Spherical Supernova Explosion and Observations

Valeri M. Chechetkin, Andrei A. Denissov, & Yuri P. Popov

During the last two decades many investigators had taken attempts to construct Supernova models, that will be able to describe observed physical pattern of this phenomena. Most of them considered models of collapsing iron core of massive star, that were supposed to be a mechanism for Type II Supernova (see HILLEBRANDT [1] and references there). But despite the fact that some of them were very sophisticated one (includes rotation, relativity effects, neutrino transport and some other physical processes), models of this class have failed to explain some aspects of Type II Supernova and Type I Supernova. That was the reason why thermonuclear model of Supernova explosion was suggested by FOWLER and HOYLE [2], ARNETT [3] and others for Type I Supernova.

But the main unresolved question in this model is the question about mode of burning that should realize in supernova explosion – deflagrational or detonational one. The mode depends on many factors, including degree of degeneration of electron gas, initial temperature distribution and chemical composition. WOOSLEY [4] and BLINNIKOV and KHOKHLOV [5] have studied formation of detonational wave depending on instantly burning mass. IVANOVA et al [6] have studied dependence of the mode on instantly burning mass and found that not only detonational mode may take place, but also deflagrational burning can appear. But all these models were spherically symmetric, so rotation was not included in them. Including rotation into thermonuclear model is a further step towards real physical situation, since we know, that most of compact Supernova remnants rotates quite rapidly.

In our study two-dimensional calculations of burning of a rotating CO core were carried out. As an initial configuration a degenerate CO core with a mass of 1.4 M_O and a central density of $2 \cdot 10^9$ g cm^{-3} was assumed. We have considered solid-state rotating core with several angular velocities. At the initial moment roughly 20% of the total core mass was instantly burned off and 10^{50} erg of nuclear energy was released, generating the detonation wave.

Figure 1 shows propagation of the detonation front through the stellar core for the variant with rapid rotation. Angular velocity equal roughly 0.5 of critical value $(G \cdot M/r^3)^{1/3}$, where G is gravitational constant, M - stellar mass, r - equatorial radius of the core. The detonation burning in external layers of the core occurs in over-compressed mode. Such a detonation wave has a tendency to be dumped in case when supporting pressure profile behind the burning front is decreased. One can see from Fig 1 that burning front first reaches the surface of core in polar regions. It leads to appearance of a rarefaction wave going from poles to equatorial region, so the detonation wave may damp here under certain conditions and unburned remnant will appear.

So the main difficulty in our simulation arise from impossibility to calculate detonation and deflagration wave using the same code. Now we couldn't determine in simulation the mode of burning really exist in the model described earlier, it is possible only to postulate existence one of the modes and calculate process of explosion. So, there appear necessity for special computational algorithms, that should give us possibility to simulate all types of modes of burning.

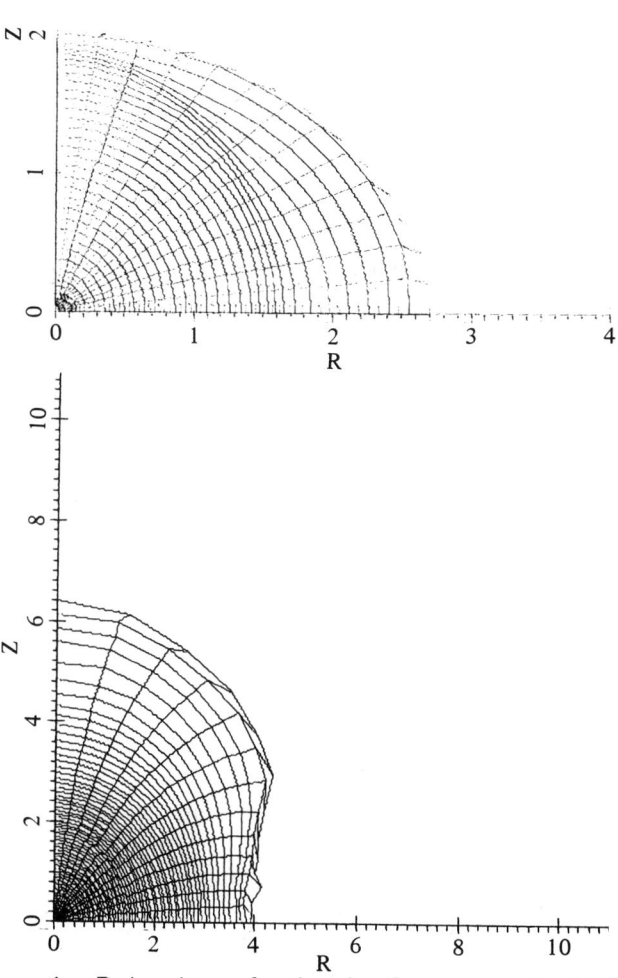

Figure 1. Detonation front at the moment 0.110 sec from the begining of explosion; matter expandes along the polar axis at the moment 0.190 sec. Z is axis of rotation, R - axis is located in equatorial plane. All distances are shown in 10^8 cm units.

What astrophysical consequence follow from the results which include a possibility of formation of unburned carbon-oxygen remnant? With further evolution such a remnant will resemble a colder region against a hotter region with increased content of primary matter from degenerate stellar core. Similar structures have been observed in young supernova remnants (LOSINSKAYA [7], CHUGAI [8].

Some interesting conclusions from the results of our simulation may be done for the resent Supernova 1987A in Large Magellanic Cloud. It is known from observations that presupernova SK-69202 has rotate quite rapidly (WEISS, HILLEBRANDT, TRURAN [9]). Explosion along polar directions may lead to mixing of core and envelope matter, which leads to appearance of large amounts of radioactive Ni^{56} in envelope. Such a process should "trigger" hard X-ray emission from supernova remnant.

References

1. Hillebrandt W., Preprint MPI-PAE/Astro 279, (1981).
2. Fowler W.A., Hoyle F., Astrophys. J. Suppl. 9, 201, (1964)
3. Arnett W.D., Astrophys. Space Sci., 5, 180, 1969.
4. Woosley S.E., Ann. Rev. Astron. Astrophys., 24, 205, (1986).
5. Blinnikov S.I., Khokhlov A.M., Pis'ma Astr. Zh., 12, 318, (1986).
6. Ivanova L.N., Imshennik V.S., Chechetkin V.M., Astrophys. Space Sci., 31, 477, (1974).
7. Losinskaya T.A., Stellar winds and supernova remnants, Nauka, Moscow, (1986).
8. Chugai N.N. Astr. Circular No. 1469, (1986).
9. Weiss A., Hillebrandt W., Truran J.W. Astron. Astrophys. 197, L11 (1988).

Relativistic Neutrino Transport in Stellar Collapse

Sidney A. Bludman & Paul J. Schinder

1. POLAR-SLICED GENERAL RELATIVISTIC HYDRODYNAMICS

In stellar core collapse, the initial bounce shock energy derives from core compression almost high enough to form an event horizon and black hole. We are interested in maximizing this compression in order to make a strong supernova explosion and also in collapses that, after emitting an observable neutrino signal, accrete enough matter to form a black hole rather than remnant neutron star. We have therefore developed a neutrino radiation hydrodynamics [1,2,4 that gives complete coverage of the space-time domain of outer communication as seen by a distant observer.

1.1 Reasons for an Improved General Relativity

Previous relativistic stellar collapse calculations have used comoving (Lagrangian) Gaussian normal coordinates in which the metric

$$ds^2 = -\alpha^2 dt^2 + \Gamma^{-2} dR^2 + R^2 d\Omega$$

is diagonal and R is the areal radius. These coordinates are "synchronous" in the sense that as soon as any trapped surface begins to form, they become singular everywhere in a finite time. Because we consider only spherical collapse, the gravitational field is always non-dynamic.

1.2 Advantages of Polar Slicing

In order to allow evolution to proceed until <u>each</u> mass zone approaches the horizon, we have performed the coordinate shift

$$dR = \dot{R} dt + R' dr = R'(\beta^r dr + dr) \tag{1}$$

on each time slice, so that the metric becomes

$$ds^2 = -(\alpha^2 - \beta^2)dt^2 + 2\beta_r dr dt + (R'/\Gamma)^2 dr^2 + R^2(r,t)d\Omega,$$

in which the shift $\beta^r = \dot{R}/R', \beta_r = (R'/\Gamma)^2 \beta^r$, dots and primes represent partial derivatives with respect to t and r respectively. In these comoving polar-sliced coordinates, the lapse function is determined by

$$\frac{\alpha'}{\alpha} = R'\frac{M + 4\pi R^3(P + \tilde{P})}{R^2(1 - 2M/R)} \qquad (2)$$

where $\tilde{P} \equiv (P + \rho)U^2/(1 - 2M/R - U^2)$ is the contribution to the pressure by fluid flow with velocity $U = \partial R/\alpha \partial t$. Because $d\alpha/\alpha = dP/(P+\rho)$, when the fluid is stationary ($\beta^r = 0, R = r$) Eq. (2) reduces to the Tolman-Oppenheimer-Volkov equation. The advantage of these non-normal coordinates is that they are non-singular everywhere outside the apparent horizon (outermost trapped surface): because these coordinates are non-synchronous, each mass zone carries its own clock, so that evolution continues in outer mass zones even as it slows down in inner mass zones, as they approach the apparent horizon, which is never reached in finite time.

1.3 Implicit Hydrodynamics

In order to economically follow the core evolution through quasistatic stages (as in shock revival and later neutrino cooling), we have also converted our code from explicit to implicit hydrodynamics. An implicit code escapes the Courant time step restriction and is always numerically stable. We solve the large set of non-linear equations self-consistently at each time step, by not only inverting numerically but also by calculating the many differential coefficients numerically. Our code is therefore (a) comoving, to give maximum coverage of material zones, (b) polar-sliced, to give maximum coverage of space-time, and (c) implicit, to allow efficient calculation over long times.

1.4 Adiabatic Hydrodynamic Tests

Our implicit polar-sliced code tested well in three adiabatic hydrodynamic calculations: relaxation to equilibrium of a stable polytrope, collapse to a black hole of an unstable polytrope, collapse of an initially homogeneous dust cloud from rest to a black hole.

2. GENERAL RELATIVISTIC RADIATION TRANSPORT

2.1 Exact Solutions of the Transport Equation

Almost all previous calculations of radiation transport during stellar collapse assumed some form of diffusion approximation. Because this reduces a hyperbolic wave equation to a parabolic equation, any diffusion approximation is inherently non-relativistic. Although the flux can be limited so as to maintain causality, any flux limited approximation is ad hoc and of uncertain accuracy in regions intermediate between the diffusion and free-streaming regions. This semi-transparent intermediate region is crucial in all radiation transport problems and especially so in supernovae in this region, the angular distribution of the emergent radiation is determined and the weak coupling between neutrinos and the outer collapsing core will or will not explode matter.

For these reasons, we believe an exact treatment of neutrino transport to be necessary for an ultimate understanding of the supernova explosion mechanism. In spherical symmetry, the relativistic phase-space distribution function f(t,r,E/μ) depends on two coordinates (t,r) and two momentum variables (E,μ), $\mu \equiv \cos\vartheta$ being the direction cosine of the neutrino momentum with respect to the radius vector and the neutrino energy E depending upon the gravitational field. The transport equation is a partial differential equation which can be solved at each time step: (1) by finite difference methods in the spatial elements r, μ, provided sufficient computing power exists; (2) By the method of characteristics, provided there is sufficient symmetry in the problem. The first method [3] is being pursued with A. Mezzacappa and will not be described here. Instead, we describe the second method, a relativistic generalization of the tangent ray method, which reduces the partial differential equation to a system of ordinary equations [4].

The spherical symmetry can always be used to eliminate the variable μ from the transport equation, which now reads for rays characterized by the constant angular momentum $L = RE\sin\vartheta$,

$$\gamma^{-1}\{[1+\beta\mu]\frac{\partial}{\partial r} + \frac{\Gamma\gamma^2}{R'\alpha}\mu\frac{\partial}{\partial R} - [\mu A + \mu^2 B + \frac{\dot{R}}{R}(1-\mu^2)]E\frac{\partial}{\partial E}\}f$$
$$= \eta/E^3 - \chi f \equiv \chi(S-f), \qquad (3)$$

where the source function $S \equiv \eta/E^3\chi, \eta$ is the emissivity, χ the total absorption coefficient and

$$A \equiv \frac{\Gamma\gamma}{R'\alpha}[\gamma' + \frac{\partial}{\partial t}(\frac{\beta r}{\gamma})]$$

$$B \equiv \frac{1}{\gamma^2}[\beta_r\alpha\frac{\partial}{\partial t}(\frac{\beta r}{\alpha}) + \alpha^2\frac{\partial}{\partial t}(\frac{R'}{\Gamma})]$$

$$\gamma^2 \equiv \alpha^2 - \beta^2, \quad \beta^2 \equiv \beta_r\beta^r = (\dot{R}/\Gamma)^2 \quad (4)$$

depend on the gravitational field.

2.2 Stationary Transport in Static Gravitational Fields

We now restrict ourselves to stationary transport in a static gravitational field described by time-independent metric coefficients $\Gamma, \alpha = \gamma$ so that $\beta_r = 0$, $r = R$. (Although a dynamic phenomenon when radiation transport in a collapsing star is treated by operator splitting, the gravitational field is held fixed during each transport step.) The stationary transport equation is now

$$\Gamma\{\mu\frac{\partial}{\partial R} + (1-\mu^2)(\frac{1}{R} - \frac{\alpha'}{\alpha})\frac{\partial}{\partial \mu} - \mu(\frac{\alpha'}{\alpha})E\frac{\partial}{\partial E}\}f = \chi(S-f). \quad (5)$$

The terms in α'/α describe gravitational red shift and angular abberation. The characteristic equations of Eq. (5) are

$$\frac{dR}{\Gamma\mu} = \frac{d\mu}{\Gamma(1-\mu^2)(\frac{1}{R} - \frac{\alpha'}{\alpha})} = \frac{-dE}{\Gamma\mu E(\alpha'/\alpha)} = \frac{df}{\chi(S-f)} \equiv d\lambda, \quad (6)$$

where λ is the arc length along a characteristic ray, so that the transport equation is

$$\frac{df}{d\lambda} = \Gamma\mu\frac{df(R, E_\infty b)}{dR} = \chi(S-f), \quad \mu \equiv \sqrt{1-(\alpha p/R)^2}. \quad (7)$$

Each ray is now parametrized by two constants obtained by integrating the first two equations in Eq. (4):

$$\alpha E = E_\infty, \quad \frac{R\sin\vartheta}{\alpha} = p, \quad (8)$$

the neutrino energy at infinity and the impact parameter p = angular momentum/E_∞. In the non-relativistic regime (weak gravitational fields $\alpha, \Gamma \to 1$), the neutrino energy E would be constant along characteristic trajectories which are straight lines $R\sin\vartheta = p$. Strong gravitational fields increase the neutrino energy as they propagate blue shift inwards on trajectories that bend inwards toward the radial direction as $\alpha(R)$ increases inwards.

3. VARIABLE EDDINGTON FACTOR METHOD FOR STATIONARY TRANSPORT

3.1 Radiation Moment Equations in Stars

We are generally most interested in the mean intensity and flux $J \equiv 2\pi \int E^3 f d\mu$ $H = 2\pi \int E^3 F \mu d\mu$. These could be obtained directly from the zeroth and first angular moments of the transport equation, which for stationary transport in a static background geometry with isotropic absorptivity χ and source function S, are

$$\Gamma \frac{d}{dR}(\alpha R^2 H) = R^2 \alpha (4\pi E^3 S - J) \tag{9}$$

$$\Gamma[\frac{dK}{dR} + \frac{3K-J}{R}] \equiv \frac{\Gamma}{q}\frac{d}{dR}(q f_K J) = -\chi H, \tag{10}$$

provided we knew the second moment $K \equiv 2\pi \int E^3 f \mu^2 d\mu$ or Eddington factor $f_K \equiv K/J = \langle \mu^2 \rangle$. In these equations, the relativistic effects are carried by the metric coefficients Γ, α and the sphericity effects are contained in the sphericity factor q(R) defined by

$$\frac{d \ln q}{d \ln R} \equiv \frac{3 f_K - 1 + (R\alpha'/\alpha)}{f_K}. \tag{11}$$

The radiation angular distribution can only be obtained by solving the original transport equation subject to appropriate boundary conditions on the flux H(R). Even if the Eddington factor $f_K(R)$ could somehow be prescribed, the flux boundary values $H(0)$ and $H(R_s) \equiv f_H(R_s) J(R_s)$ are needed before Eqns. (9) and (10) can be (trivially) integrated.

In the variable Eddington factor method, some approximate $f_K(R)$ is used to calculate $J(R)$ from Eqns. (9) and (10) which is then inserted in the transport equation source term $S[J(R)]$ to approximately solve for the distribution function and an improved value for $f_K(R)$. This procedure of using the moment equations to iteratively solve the transparent equation accelerates the numerical convergence of the solution which is otherwise poor.

3.2 Conservative Scattering and Power Law Operators

We now consider flux-conservative scattering in which $S = J/4\pi E^3$ so that $\alpha R^2 H =$ constant. This is the case for pure isotropic coherent scattering in a gray structure in radiative equilibrium. In terms of $\mathcal{J} \equiv 4\pi r^2 J, \kappa \equiv 4\pi R^2 \mathcal{H} =$ luminosity / 4π, the moment equations (9) and (10) now are

$$\alpha \mathcal{H} = \text{constant} \tag{12}$$

$$\frac{(\Gamma\alpha)R^2}{q}\frac{d}{dR}\left(\frac{q}{R^2}f_K\mathcal{J}\right) = -\chi(\alpha\mathcal{H}). \tag{13}$$

In the diffusive region $f_K \approx 1/3, q \propto \alpha^3$,

$$\Gamma\frac{d}{dR}(\alpha^3 J) = 3\chi(\alpha^3 H) \tag{14},$$

this reduces to planar scattering. In the free-streaming region $(f_K \approx 1, q \propto \alpha R^2$,

$$\Gamma\frac{d}{dR}(\alpha\mathcal{J}) = -\chi(\alpha\mathcal{H}). \tag{15}$$

We now consider the (Kosirov) power law opacity $\chi(R) = R_o^{n-1}/R^n$ with scale height $h(R) \equiv (-d\ln\chi/dR)^{-1} = R/n$. For $n > 1$, the optical thickness to the center is infinite. For large n, the opacity decreases from a large value just inside R_o to a small value just outside R_o. The neutrinosphere is therefore located at radius R_o and of thickness R_o/n.

We distinguish three different kinds of stellar atmospheres by the ratio of stellar radius R_S to neutrinosphere radius R_o: (1) $R_s/R_o >> 1$, extended atmospheres; (2) $R_s/R_o \approx 1$, semiplanar atmosphere; (3) $R_s/R_o << 1$, planar atmosphere. Except in spherical shells, planar atmospheres (3) do not occur astrophysically. This case is nevertheless interesting formally because, in the limit $R_s/R_o \to 0$, it reduces the spherical problem to the classical Milne problem of conservative scattering in a semi-infinite planar medium. The Eddington approximation $f_K = 1/3$ is then a good approximation nearly up to the boundary.

Case (2), with large n, is realized in the very thin atmosphere surrounding a neutron star (X-ray bursters, Goodman-Dar-Nussinov heat deposition in a stalled shock, cooling neutron stars). Because absorption is very non-gray in these situations, surface cooling and back-warming are important, so that the neutrinosphere does not radiate as a black-body.

3.3 Sphericity Effects in an Extended Atmosphere

Although our ultimate interest is in the semiplanar atmospheres surrounding compact objects, our methods will be most severely tested in (1), extended atmospheres where the sphericity effects become important, so that f_K, f_H approach each other and approach unity as R_s/R_o or n increases. Because non-relativistic numerical solutions are well known [4,5], we have used this case (1) to test our relativistic tangent-ray method.

Choosing starting values $f_K = 1/3, f_H = 1/2$, we iterated between the moment equations (9), (10) and the transport equation (7). Using variable spatial zoning to give adequate coverage in

both the interior and the atmosphere, after less than 5 iterations, we obtained good agreement with the Hummer-Rybicki solutions. The Eddington factor $f_K(R) \equiv K/J$ and streaming function $f_H(R) \equiv H/J$ are plotted in Fig. 7, 13, 14, 15 of ref. 3 and will not be repeated here. They show (f_K, f_H) changing over from interior values $(1/3, 0)$ to surface values $(f_K(R_s), f_H(R_s))$ in the outermost mean free path. In a weak gravitational field, these surface values are [4,6]:
(1) For the planar atmosphere $R_s/R_o = 0.1, (f_K(R_s), f_H(R_s)) =$ (0.414, 0.581), (0.448, 0.616), (0.529, 0.685) for n = 3, 2, 3/2 respectively.
(2) For the semiplanar atmosphere $R_s/R_o = 1, (f_K(R_s), f_H(R_s))$ = (0.63, 0.78), (0.67, 0.80), (0.68, 0.81) for n = 3, 2, 3/2.
(3) For the extended atmospheres $(R_s/R_o, n) = (10,2), (100, 3/2), (30, 2), (10, 3), (f_K(R_s), f_H(R_s)) =$ (0.930, 0.959), (0.943, 0.966), (0.974, 0.985), (0.982, 0.990) respectively.

The emergent Eddington factors all fall within a few percent of the linear trajectory $f_K(R_s) = -\frac{1}{3} + \frac{4}{3}f_H(R_s)$, i.e. although the Kosirov opacities depend on two parameters (R_o, n), the surface Eddington factors both depend on one parameter. In the semiplanar atmosphere outside the stalled shock, we expect $f_H(R_s) \sim 0.75, f_K(R_s) \sim 0.5$, a radiation pattern that is sufficiently forward-peaked to disfavor appreciable neutrino momentum deposition by the Goodman-Dar-Nussinov $\nu + \bar{\nu} \to e^- + e^+$ mechanism.

We now digress to discuss the origin of "universal" Eddington trajectories and their limited applicability.

3.4 Maximum Entropy Methods

Maximum entropy methods have been used [6, 7] to derive the most probable gray atmosphere angular distribution consistent with two specified angular moments J, H. For non-degenerate neutrinos or photons, these methods lead to a Boltzman distribution of direction cosines, $f(\mu) = e^{\eta}e^{a\mu}$, that depends on only two parameters η and a. The Eddington ratios depend only on a, which ranges from zero to infinity as the angular distribution ranges from isotropic to free-streaming. Eliminating a, a universal Eddington trajectory $f_K = f_K(f_H)$ is obtained that is expected to be most probable for each depth in all radiation fields.

Because boundary conditions are ignored, allowing μ to range over the full interval $-1 \le \mu \le 1$ everywhere, the full-range moments of MINERBO [7] give only a fair approximation: $f_K(f_H)$ is underestimated in an extended atmosphere, especially at depth, and overestimated in a planar atmosphere, especially near the surface. By allowing only the half-range $0 \leq \mu \leq 1$, Rybicki (1984) [9] obtained half-range moments

$$J, H, K = e^{\eta} \int_o^1 \mu^l e^{a\mu} d\mu \quad l = 0, 1, 2$$

and Eddington factors

$$f_H(R_s) = \frac{1}{J}\frac{dJ}{da} = \frac{1}{1-e^{-a}} - \frac{1}{a} \tag{16}$$

$$f_K(R_s) = \frac{1}{J}\frac{d^2J}{da^2} = \frac{1}{1-e^{-a}} - \frac{2}{a}f_H, \tag{17}$$

that well represent the emergent radiation field for all the Kosirov models considered. Graphically eliminating $a = a(R_o, n)$ [8], we find the trajectory is approximately linear $f_K(R_s) \approx -\frac{1}{3} + \frac{4}{3}f_H(R_s)$, to within a few percent.

What use is the Eddington trajectory of the emergent radiation? The streaming function $f_H(R_s)$ still must be obtained by solving the transport equation subject to appropriate boundary conditions. Nevertheless, a good initial guess for $f_K(R)$ in the moment equations (9) and (10) allows a good starting approximation for the source function in the transport equation whose iterative solution then converges rapidly.

3.5 Stationary Transport in Strong Gravitational Fields

After testing the tangent-ray method in the non-relativistic Kosirov problem, we studied [4,10,11] the stationary radiation transport out of two 1.65 $M_\odot$ polytropic stars with $P = K\rho^2$ and power-law opacity $\chi(R) = R_o/R^2$ in an extended atmosphere $R_s = 10R_o$. (Although compact objects have semiplanar atmospheres, we chose an extended atmosphere to test our treatment of sphericity effects.)

The two 1.65 $M_\odot$ stars chosen were (1) A "white dwarf" of central density $\rho_c = 10^9 \text{gcm}^{-3}$ and stellar radius $R_s = 1370$ km; as indicated by the central values for the relativity index $(P/\rho c^2)_c = 8.9 \times 10^{-4}$ and lapse $\alpha_c = 0.996$ and by the surface red-shift $(GM/RC^2)_s = 0.0018$, this is a non-relativistic or weak gravity case. (2) A "neutron star" of $\rho_c = 4 \times 10^{15} \text{gcm}^{-3}$, $R_s = 9.08$ km which, because $(P/\rho c^2)_c = 0.45$, $\alpha_c = 0.326$, $(GM/Rc^2)_s = 0.269$, is practically maximal for a stable polytrope with causal equation of state, this is a strong-gravity case.

We found that strong gravity enhanced the sphericity q(r) in Eq. (11) by about a factor two and reduced the mean intensity J and the luminosity $4\pi\mathcal{H}$ by the red-shift factor $\alpha(R)$ and the surface Eddington factor $f_K(R_s)$ by about 20%.

4. CONCLUDING SUMMARY

We have (1) prepared an implicit hydrodynamics code to simulate stellar core collapse and bounce shock for long times; (2) gone to asynchronous coordinates that are polar-sliced and co-moving, so as to allow maximum coverage of space-time and of material zones. This adiabatic hydrodynamics code has been tested in the collapse of a polytrope and of a dust cloud to a black hole; (3) prepared the formalism for treating general relativistic radiation hydrodynamics by variable Eddington factor methods in order to accurately describe neutrino momentum deposition in semi-transparent material regions. We have generalized the tangent ray method (method of characteristics) to radiation transport in curved space-time. This code has been tested in stationary transport in a static geometry with power-law (Kosirov) opacity.

We intend to go on to (1) compare exact solutions of the transport equations by the method of characteristics and by finite differences; (2) compare the neutrino fluxes emerging from slow collapse into a black hole with that from collapse to a remnant neutrino star; (3) study the late time evolution of the bounce shock and the cooling of the nascent hot neutron star by the radiation of neutrinos of all flavors.

References

1. P. J. Schinder, S. A. Bludman and T. Piran, Phys. Rev. D **37**, 2722, (1988).

2. P. J. Schinder, Phys. Rev. D **38**, 1673, (1988).

3. A. Mezzacappa and R. A. Matzner, Astrophys. J **343**,853, (1989).

4. P. J. Schinder and S. A. Bludman, Astrophys. J **356**, 350, (1989).

5. D. G. Hummer and G. B. Rybicki, M.N.R.A.S. **152**, (1971).

6. P. G. Martin and C. Rogers, Astrophys. J. **284**, 317, (1984).

7. G. N. Minerbo, J. Quant. Spectros. Rad. Transf. **20**, 541, (1978).

8. A. Fu, Astrophys. J. **323**, 227, (1987).

9. Referred to in ref. 6, 8.

10. S. A. Bludman and P. J. Schinder in Proc. XIV Texas Symposium on Relativistic Astrophysics, Proc. N.Y. Academy of Sciences (1989).

11. S. A. Bludman in Proc. Workshop on Particle Astrophysics: Forefront Experimental Issues, edited by E. B. Norman (World Scientific, 1989).

Neutrino Transport in Supernovae and Protoneutron Stars by Monte Carlo Methods

H.-Thomas Janka

The still unsolved puzzle of how to make a type II supernova explosion from the collapse of a massive star's iron core, the detection of 19 neutrino events associated with SN 1987A in the IMB and Kamiokande 2 experiments (BIONTA et al. [1], HIRATA et al. [2]) and, most currently, the idea of making nucleosynthesis by non-conservative scattering of neutrinos off heavy nuclei (EPSTEIN et al. [3]; WOOSLEY et al. [4]) keeps interest in neutrino emission from newly formed neutron stars very vivid.

Although considerable effort has been payed to neutrino transport during stellar core collapse and neutron star formation, still a number of questions are not answered yet. E.g. it is not yet clear how the spectra of the various neutrino kinds can be described, how the released gravitational binding energy is shared between the different neutrino types and how efficiently neutrinos can deposit energy during the shock propagation phase. Transport methods employed in hydrodynamical codes are constrained in accuracy by the need of computational fastness. So most of the workers in the field employ flux-limiters of some kind. However, it is clear that such an approach will lead to uncertainties and errors which have to be checked and, if possible, reduced. In order to do this and to try to investigate the points mentioned above we employed a Monte Carlo (MC) method for simulating neutrino transport. Some of the results will be shortly described here.

1. Spectra

Spectra of all types of neutrinos were found to be different from a black body distribution. Although they are actually non-thermal it is possible to approximate them very closely by Fermi-Dirac functions employing 'effective degeneracy' parameters η_ν^{eff}. Typical values for these were found to be $\eta_{\nu_e}^{\text{eff}} \approx 3 - 3.5$ for electron-type neutrinos, $\eta_{\bar\nu_e}^{\text{eff}} \approx \eta_{\nu_x}^{\text{eff}} \approx 2 - 2.5$ for electron antineutrinos and neutrinos of other flavors ($\nu_x \hat{=} \nu_\mu, \bar\nu_\mu, \nu_\tau, \bar\nu_\tau$). These numbers seem to be quite general and turned out to hold roughly for all investigated cases, i.e. for core collapse models of the 1.36 $M_\odot$ iron core of a 20 $M_\odot$ star (stiff equation of state) at stages 12 and 315 milliseconds after core bounce (HILLEBRANDT [5]; JANKA and HILLEBRANDT [6], [7]) and for the Kelvin-Helmholtz cooling phase of a 1.64 $M_\odot$ protoneutron star (soft equation of state) at times 3.32, 5.77 and 7.81 seconds after bounce (WILSON [8]). So we conclude that they reflect general properties of neutrino-matter interaction and do not sensitively depend on specific features of the background model and its physical (and numerical) description (JANKA and HILLEBRANDT [7]). The inferred narrowing of the energy distributions leads to a strong suppression of the high energy tails. This is important for the evaluation of neutrino detections (JANKA and HILLEBRANDT [7]) as well as for the strongly energy dependent reactions between neutrinos and heavy nuclei that are supposed to be responsible for nucleosynthesis during a supernova explosion.

2. Flow Pattern

Using flux-limiting causes severe uncertainties in the absolute values of the luminosities and the local 'flow pattern' of the radiation field. By the latter we mean the distribution of the outgoing particle flow in angle. As a rough measure for its degree of anisotropy one can use the first and second Eddington moments, $\langle z^1 \rangle \equiv j/(n \cdot c)$ and $\langle z^2 \rangle$, respectively (j being the flux density, n the local energy or particle density and c the speed of light). Let us estimate the errors due to a 'vacuum description' of the radiation field outside the neutrino sphere (COOPERSTEIN et al. [9]), when a number for the local energy deposition by neutrino-antineutrino annihilation is to be derived. We will adopt the notation employed in COOPERSTEIN et al. [10]. Assuming vanishing phase space blocking, separability in energy and angle and coincidence of neutrino and antineutrino spheres they get for the local energy deposition rate:

$$Q_{e^+e^-} = \frac{4\,G^2}{9\,\pi} D\,\varepsilon_\nu\,\varepsilon_{\bar{\nu}}\,(\omega_\nu + \omega_{\bar{\nu}}) \cdot \chi \quad , \tag{1}$$

where ε_ν, $\varepsilon_{\bar{\nu}}$ are the energy densities, $\omega_\nu = T_\nu \cdot \frac{F_4(\eta_\nu)}{F_3(\eta_\nu)}$ are energy moments of the neutrinos, and χ is given by

$$\chi = \frac{3}{4} \cdot \left[1 - 2\langle z^1 \rangle \langle \bar{z}^1 \rangle + \langle z^2 \rangle \langle \bar{z}^2 \rangle + \frac{1}{2}(1 - \langle z^2 \rangle)(1 - \langle \bar{z}^2 \rangle) \right] \quad . \tag{2}$$

Assuming vacuum outside an isotropically emitting neutrino sphere of radius R_ν implies that $\varepsilon_\nu^{\text{vac}}(z) = 2 \cdot (1 - z) \cdot L_\nu/(4\pi R_\nu^2 c)$ (L_ν = neutrino luminosity) and $\langle z^1 \rangle_{\text{vac}} = \frac{1}{2}(1+z)$ and $\langle z^2 \rangle_{\text{vac}} = \frac{1}{3}(1+z+z^2)$ for $z \equiv \sqrt{1-(R_\nu/r)^2}$, so $\chi_{\text{vac}} = \frac{1}{8}(1-z)^2(5 + 4z + z^2)$. Most of the annihilation heating will occur at radii between R_ν and $1.1R_\nu$, i.e. for z-parameters between 0 and 0.417. Therefore deviations from the vacuum description due to non-vanishing neutrino-matter interactions outside the 'neutrino sphere' (which is an artifact by definition rather than a physical sphere, anyway) will be very important. MC simulations (JANKA and HILLEBRANDT [6]) suggest that they are significant, indeed. It was found that having a density profile according to $\rho \propto r^{-n}$ a very good description is given by $\varepsilon_\nu(z)^{\text{MC}} = 2(1-z)\left(1+(1-z^2)^{(n-1)/2}\right) \cdot L_\nu/(4\pi R_\nu^2 c)$, i.e. $\langle z^1 \rangle_{\text{MC}} = \frac{1}{2}\frac{1+z}{1+(1-z^2)^{(n-1)/2}}$. In addition $\langle z^2 \rangle_{\text{MC}}$ increases much slower than in the vacuum case. So we end up with a local ratio of

$$\frac{(Q_{e^+e^-})_{\text{MC}}}{(Q_{e^+e^-})_{\text{vac}}} \cong \frac{\chi_{\text{MC}}}{\chi_{\text{vac}}} \cdot \left[1 + (1 - z^2)^{(n-1)/2} \right]^2 \quad , \tag{3}$$

where we used equality of the quantities L_ν, $L_{\bar{\nu}}$ and ω_ν, $\omega_{\bar{\nu}}$ in the nominator and denominator, an assumption which turns out to be actually not true, when e.g. flux-limited diffusion results are compared to MC studies (see 3.). Inserting typical numbers for the region of interest ($z \lesssim 0.5$), $\langle z^1 \rangle \approx \langle z^2 \rangle \approx z \approx \frac{1}{3}$ we find for density profiles of $n = 4, 10, 20$:

$$\frac{(Q_{e^+e^-})_{\text{MC}}}{(Q_{e^+e^-})_{\text{vac}}} \approx \frac{0.8333}{0.3580} \cdot (3.378, 2.524, 1.760) = 7.864, 5.874, 4.096 \ . \quad (4)$$

Although these results were derived on grounds of a vacuum approximation outside an artificially defined 'neutrino sphere', it must be expected that also flux-limited diffusion cannot do any better due to its inability of describing the angular distribution of the radiation field especially in situations of rapid variations in space and time.

3. Luminosities

The possibility of a direct conclusion from the MC transport results on influences due to flux-limiting and discretization in energy space is most easily possible in the case of muon neutrinos, because their number flux is conserved at densities below 10^{13} g cm^{-3}, where (in the 'late' protoneutron star models discussed here) their emission and annihilation processes are essentially unimportant. At the inner boundary of the stellar window where the transport is followed explicitly by the MC code we impose an isotropic ν_μ-distribution according to the given local neutrino density resulting from WILSON's [6] data. Without including general relativistic effects the multigroup flux-limited diffusion scheme yields particle fluxes of $J_{\nu_\mu}^{\text{MFL}} \approx 1.03 \cdot 10^{56}, 3.26 \cdot 10^{55}, 2.78 \cdot 10^{55}$ s^{-1} and average energies of $\langle \epsilon_{\nu_\mu} \rangle^{\text{MFL}} \approx 23.6, 32.7, 30.8$ MeV for times $t = 3.32, 5.77, 7.81$ seconds after core bounce, whereas with the MC treatment we find $J_{\nu_\mu}^{\text{MC}} = 1.27 \cdot 10^{56}, 4.19 \cdot 10^{56}, 5.90 \cdot 10^{55}$ s^{-1} and $\langle \epsilon_{\nu_\mu} \rangle^{\text{MC}} = 24.5, 27.0, 25.5$ MeV, respectively. Roughly, the differences increase as the neutron star becomes more compact, i.e. the density decline near its surface gets steeper.

4. General Relativistic Effects

Gravitational redshift and light bending effects were included into the MC transport code. Ray bending and time dilatation yield a reduction of the local Eddington moment $\langle z^1 \rangle$ by about 15–30% in the diffusion regime (where $\langle z^1 \rangle \lesssim 0.1$), decreasing to 1–2% when free streaming is achieved ($\langle z^1 \rangle \gtrsim 0.5$). Accordingly, the local neutrino concentrations in the free streaming region are smaller by 15–30%, too. Gravitationally redshifted energies are lower by 5–10% at the protoneutron star 'surface'. Altogether the emitted fluxes turn out to be reduced by 20–40%. For an observer at infinity an additional reduction by 20–35% occurs, so that including general relativity causes the observable fluxes in particle number to be only 60–80% and in energy only 40–60% of those obtained in the Newtonian case.

It is the aim of this short contribution to point out that there are significant uncertainties in the presently used approximate treatments of neutrino transport in hydrodynamical core collapse simulations. They are of a size which makes them important when neutrino detections are to be evaluated and when dynamical consequences of neutrinos for the supernova are to be investigated.

References

1. R. M. Bionta, G. Blewitt, C. B. Bratton, D. Casper, A. Ciocio, R. Claus, B. Cortez, M. Crouch, S. T. Dye, S. Errede, G. W. Foster, W. Gajewsky, K. S. Ganezer, M. Goldhaber, T. J. Haines, T. W. Jones, D. Kielczewska, W. R. Kropp, J. G. Learned, J. M. LoSecco, J. Matthews, R. Miller, M. S. Mudan, H. S. Park, L. R. Price, F. Reines, J. Schultz, S. Seidel, E. Shumard, D. Sinclair, H. W. Sobel, J. L. Stone, L. R. Sulak, R. Svoboda, G. Thornton, J. C. van der Velde, C. Wuest: Phys. Rev. Lett. 58, 1494 (1987).

2. K. Hirata, T. Kajita, M. Koshiba, M. Nakahata, Y. Oyama, N. Sato, A. Suzuki, M. Takita, Y. Totsuka, T. Kifune, T. Suda, K. Takahashi, T. Tanimori, K. Miyano, M. Yamada, E. W. Beier, L. R. Feldscher, S. B. Kim, A. K. Mann, F. M. Newcomer, R. Van Berg, W. Zhang, B. G. Cortez: Phys. Rev. Lett. 58, 1490 (1987).

3. R. I. Epstein, S. A. Colgate, W. C. Haxton: Phys. Rev. Lett. 61, 2038 (1988).

4. S. E. Woosley, D. H. Hartmann, R. D. Hoffman, W. C. Haxton: The ν-Process, preprint (1989).

5. W. Hillebrandt: in High Energy Phenomena around Collapsed Stars, ed. by F. Pacini, (Dodrecht, Reidel 1987) (p. 73).

6. H.-T. Janka, W. Hillebrandt: Astron. Astrophys. Suppl. 78, 375 (1989).

7. H.-T. Janka, W. Hillebrandt: Astron. Astrophys. (1989), in press.

8. J. Wilson: private communication (1988).

9. J. Cooperstein, L. J. van den Horn, E. A. Baron: Astrophys. J., 309, 653 (1986).

10. J. Cooperstein, L. J. van den Horn, E. A. Baron: Astrophys. J. (Letters), 321, L129 (1987).

The SN 1987A Neutrino Signal and the Future
Adam Burrows

1. Introduction

As brilliant as SN1987A was and is in light, on February 23, 1987 at $7^h 35^m 41^s$ universal time, startling proof was obtained that photons were not its most spectacular radiation. It was then that two massive underground detectors, the Irvine-Michigan-Brookhaven (IMB) detector in the U.S. [1] and the Kamiokande II (KII) detector in Japan [2], registered supernova neutrinos for the first time. Within only about ten seconds, the general theory developed by a generation of astrophysicists over the past thirty years connecting supernova explosions and the death of massive stars with prodigious neutrino bursts was transformed into a concrete fact, and extragalactic neutrino astronomy was born. Neutrinos interact very weakly with matter and can penetrate with ease the earth, the sun, and even the envelope of the 15 to 20 solar mass ($M_\odot$) blue star that exploded as SN1987A. The transparency of the progenitor star to the neutrinos we now know are generated in its heart as it dies makes a supernova's neutrino signal the only good diagnostic of the violent internal convulsions that attend stellar death.

The supernova trigger is otherwise shrouded in mystery by the profound opacity of the star to photons. In theory, the ~1.5 $M_\odot$ core of a massive star (>8 $M_\odot$) whose thermonuclear life may have lasted ~10^7 years collapses within one second to a "protoneutron-star" (PNS), whose subsequent transformation into a dense neutron star proper (later, perhaps a pulsar) takes seconds. It is during the birth of the neutron star that the neutrinos are emitted. The shock wave generated during these seconds travels from the core to the stellar surface in between an hour and a day and disassembles the star in an explosion that lasts months to years. This explosion is the supernova. Though 10^{49} ergs (~2.5×10^{26} megatons of TNT equivalent) is eventually radiated in supernova light and the kinetic energy of the supernova debris is ~10^{51} ergs, more than one hundred times again as much energy (>10^{53} ergs) is liberated in the brief, but massive burst of neutrinos. During such a burst, the supernova core is as bright in neutrinos as the entire observable universe is in optical light. It was such a neutrino burst from SN1987A that was detected simultaneously in North America and Asia on February 23, 1987, and it is such bursts, their detection, and what we can learn from them that is the subject of this paper.

2. Neutrinos from Supernovae: Theory

Neutrinos dominate the emissions from the high-energy density plasma in the core of a massive star before and after collapse almost by default. Since the electrodynamic interaction is much stronger than the weak interaction, the photon production rate in this hot, dense "pit" far exceeds that of neutrinos. However, once created, a photon can travel no more than a few angstroms before being absorbed. It is completely trapped in the "matter," which is actually a soup of heavy nuclei, alpha particles, electrons, positrons, free neutrons and protons, and photons in thermal equilibrium. The neutrinos, on the other hand, once created can much more easily stream unimpeded out of the core. By surveying all the particles in the particle physicist's zoo, one arrives at the conclusion that, of the known particles, only neutrinos are both copiously produced and weakly coupled in the hot core of a massive star. Hence, neutrinos dominate the luminosity of a massive star in the advanced stages of its life. Even though the core neutrino luminosity of a massive star just _before_ core collapse can be ten orders of magnitude greater than its surface photon luminosity, this neutrino luminosity and the average per neutrino energy during pre-supernova stages are still not adequate to trigger extant or projected terrestrial neutrino detectors. However, once the core has grown to the "critical" Chandrasekhar mass of $\sim 1.5~M_{\odot}$ and can no longer support itself against gravity, it implodes to even higher densities and temperatures. It is under these extreme conditions that the neutrino luminosities and energies are finally adequate to be detected on Earth from anywhere in our galaxy, the LMC, or the Small Magellanic Cloud (SMC).

Before we address this neutrino burst, we must first describe collapse dynamics. After some ten or twenty million years, the core of a massive star (Mass > 8.0 $M_{\odot}$) has exhausted its thermonuclear fuel. It has a mass of approximately 1.5 $M_{\odot}$ (solar masses), a radius of approximately three thousand kilometers, a central density near 10^{10} gm/cm^3, and a central temperature near ~ 0.5 MeV (approximately equivalent to 6×10^9 K). Embedded inside the massive star (envelope mass > 6.5 $M_{\odot}$), which has an outer radius (photosphere) of no less than 30 million kilometers, the core would seem insignificant. However, as the exhausted core reaches the critical "Chandrasekhar" mass of $\sim$1.5 $M_\odot$, it can no longer support itself against persistent gravity. After eons of stability, the core becomes dynamic and collapses "under its own weight." Note that the rest of the star does not collapse with the core. It is still unaware of its impending death, and its photosphere is quiet. In less than one second, parts of the imploding core reach speeds of 70,000 kilometers per second, one quarter the speed of light. So strong is the gravitational pull of this compact imploding sphere, that collapse is halted only after nuclear densities (2.7×10^{14} gm/cm^3) and beyond are achieved. It is only then that the strong repulsive nuclear force can stiffen the core sufficiently to finally halt and reverse collapse. If the matter did not stiffen, the entire core would plunge into a black hole.

During collapse, the core marches though almost two decades in radius, five decades in central density, and more than one decade in central temperature to the most extreme thermodynamic conditions since the big bang. In bouncing, the inner core ($\sim$0.8 $M_\odot$) "pulls" as many as one hundred billion (10^{11}) "g's." It collides violently with the still-collapsing outer core of 0.7 $M_\odot$ and thereby generates a strong off-center, through spherically symmetric, shock wave. This shock is launched into the stellar envelope with a speed near ten thousand kilometers per second and is the supernova in its infancy. Though core collapse takes almost one second, rebound and shock-wave formation take only a few milliseconds. After launching the shock wave, the spent core does not reexpand, but quickly settles into hydrostatic equilibrium. This dense, hot (temperature $\sim$ 10^{11} K) and extended (radius $\sim$ 100 kilometers) "protoneutron-star" is not the cold, compact (radius $\sim$ 10 kilometers) neutron star of the textbooks, but an intermediate state through which the core must go in birthing a neutron star.

Having described core dynamics, we can now return to a general theoretical description of the neutrino signature. Compression during the early stages of collapse increases the electron energies above the threshholds (a few MeV) for electron capture on the heavy nuclei in the core. This weak interaction process, e^- (electron) + p (proton) $\rightarrow$ n (neutron) + ν_e (electron-neutrino), leads to the further loss of electron pressure and the conversion of protons into neutrons in the nuclei. Core nuclei are thereby made more neutron-rich and electron-neutrinos are liberated in substantial numbers for the first time. The above process assumes lepton conservation, which is now an important fixture of the standard theory of collapse, but is not etched in stone and may yield to future experiments. Nevertheless, since lepton conservation is assumed in current supernova calculations, it is the results of such calculations that we report here.

The electron capture accelerates as higher core densities are achieved. However, when the central density reaches and exceeds 10^{11} gm/cm^3, the product of the nuclear scattering cross section for the progressively more energetic capture neutrino and the matter density becomes so large that the electron-neutrino mean-free-path, its "interaction" length, reaches, then exceeds, the size of the core. Electron-neutrinos, that only hundreds of milliseconds earlier streamed freely out of the imploding core, are now trapped in the flow. Though no more than a few hundred kilometers in radius, the core quickly achieves the neutrino opacity of a "light-year of lead." Beyond 10^{11} gm/cm^3, decades in density before bounce, electron-neutrino capture on neutrons, the inverse of electron capture, stabilizes electron loss. If it were not for trapping, much of the supernova neutrino burst would be in electron-capture neutrinos emitted during the few hundred milliseconds of collapse. Because of trapping, "only" about 1% ($\sim 10^{51}$ ergs) of the neutrino burst is in such "infall" neutrinos. The lion's share of the energy has yet to be radiated.

The lepton-rich core continues to collapse beyond trapping, achieves nuclear densities ($>2.7 \times 10^{14}$ gm/cm^3), bounces, drives the shock wave into the outer core, and settles into the non-dynamical, hydrostatic PNS state. The shock is formed in a neutrino-opaque region near densities of 10^{13} gm/cm^3. However, within milliseconds, it plows to lower densities where the neutrino mean-free-paths are longer and the matter is transparent. The boundary between neutrino opacity and transparency is called the "neutrinosphere," in analogy with the more common photosphere. As the shock traverses the neutrinosphere, there is a brilliant burst of electron-neutrinos [3]. These electron-neutrinos are liberated by electron capture behind the matter-compressing shock, and are dammed-up until the shock "breaks out" of the neutrinosphere. However, this mini-burst lasts no more than a few milliseconds and also involves only a few times 10^{51} ergs. Though it is a distinctive signature of shock dynamics, the break-out burst is difficult to detect.

Most of the neutrino burst of a supernova is actually radiated during the non-dynamical transformation of the bloated PNS into the compact neutron star [4]. The PNS (again, "protoneutron-star") is energy- and lepton-rich and only marginally bound. A cold neutron star is so compact and dense and of such a large mass (~ 1.5 M$_\odot$) that it is tightly bound, with a large binding energy near 3×10^{53} ergs. Therefore, energy conservation alone demands that to form a neutron star this binding energy must be radiated, and theory concludes that it must be in neutrinos. Since the PNS is opaque to neutrinos (indeed, at this stage there are $\sim 10^4$ mean-free-paths from the center to the neutrinosphere!), the energy cannot stream out quickly, but must <u>diffuse</u> out slowly with the neutrinos. The PNS is like a hot ember that cools and shrinks via neutrino emission. Since the neutrino mean-free-paths are so short (meters to kilometers, inside to outside), diffusion takes not milliseconds, but <u>seconds.</u> Net electron capture and final neutronization (to form the "neutron" star) are paced by the slow diffusion and loss of capture ν_e's.[5)] In addition, so hot is the PNS (10-50 MeV) that neutrino pairs of all species (electron (ν_e) and anti-electron ($\bar{\nu}_e$) types, muon (ν_μ) and anti-muon ($\bar{\nu}_\mu$) types, and tauon (ν_τ) and anti-tauon ($\bar{\nu}_\tau$) types), are created. Therefore, neutrinos of all species, not just electron-type, carry away by slow diffusion the prodigious binding energy of the neutron star. The average energies of the electron-types are roughly 10-20 MeV, while those of the mu- and tau-types are roughly 25 MeV. However, each of the six neutrino species carries away roughly the same fraction (~one-sixth) of the binding energy. Curiously, theory has about two-thirds of the neutrino burst in the difficult-to-detect mu and tau channels. Importantly, theory also predicts that $\bar{\nu}_e$'s are radiated in respectable amounts. As stated previously, $\bar{\nu}_e$'s have the largest interaction cross sections in water and are expected to dominate the detected signals, despite the fact that they do not dominate the emissions. The different phases of neutrino emission are summarized in Table 1. Calculations show that more than 90% of the signal in water should be due to the $\bar{\nu}_e$ Cowan-Reines reaction, even though only 15% of the energy is in $\bar{\nu}_e$'s. The total number of events in one kilotonne of water at one kiloparsec ($\sim 3\times 10^{21}$ centimeters) is predicted to be between 10,000 and 20,000 [3]. This number can easily be scaled to any distance and to any detector size.

A few additional facts can illustrate the almost incredible magnitude of the ten-second PNS phase neutrino emission. The $\sim 3\times 10^{53}$ ergs radiated is equivalent to ($E=mc^2$) a mass of 0.15 solar masses, 50,000 times the mass of the Earth. Over the age of our galaxy, approximately ten million solar masses in neutrinos have issued from neutron star births. This is equivalent to the mass of ~10 giant globular clusters. Indeed, at any one time, due to the finite speed of light (and neutrinos), there are 10-100 solar masses of burst neutrinos in very thin expanding shells within our galaxy. Though neutrinos are notoriously weakly interacting, so brilliant is a neutrino burst that it is lethal to humans within a distance equal to the radius of Pluto's orbit around our sun (~40 astronomical units $\equiv 6\times 10^9$ kilometer). (However, given the supernova's photon radiation and blast wave, neutrino lethality is rather academic for civilizations near dying stars.)

Table 1. Neutrino Signature Sketch

	E (10^{51} ergs)	Δt (seconds)	Species
Collapse (infall)	~1.0	0.01→0.1	ν_e
Prompt burst	1-3	~0.003	ν_e
*Cooling and neutronization	250	~1.0→10.0	$\bar{\nu}_e, \nu_e, "\nu_\mu"$

Protoneutron-Star → Neutron Star
Shock Break-out → Prompt Burst

*<u>Inside</u>, Deg. 200 MeV ν_e ---> <u>Outside</u>, many, 10-30 MeV (All species)

$$\langle\epsilon_\mu\rangle \sim 25 \text{ MeV}$$
$$\langle\epsilon_{\bar{\nu}_e}\rangle \sim 15 \text{ MeV}$$
$$\langle\epsilon_{\nu_e}\rangle \sim 10\text{-}15 \text{ MeV}$$

$$2.5 \times 10^{53} \gg 10^{51} \gg 10^{49} \text{ ergs}$$
$$\uparrow \quad\quad \uparrow \quad\quad \uparrow$$
$$*(\nu) \quad (SN) \quad (\text{Light})$$

3. The IMB and KII Data

The epochal neutrino data gathered by the IMB [1] and KII [2] collaborations are shown in Table 2. Quite a bit of information has been derived about not only "collapse," but also neutrino and exotic particle properties. This paper will not recapitulate the detailed analyses of the author [5] or others that can be found now in many journals. Rather, we sketch the important conclusions concerning protoneutron-stars and "supernovae" and make some general remarks about the new status of the field.

Table 2 demonstrates that the problems of small-number statistics must play a central role in any but the most general conclusions. However, even those conclusions are quite useful to a field emerging from three decades of data starvation. The IMB and KII detections demonstrate above all else that neutrinos, or particles just like neutrinos, are indeed radiated from Type II supernovae.

The large angles of the events with respect to the LMC (shown in Table 2) imply that most were not ν-e^- scatterings, which are quite forward-peaked, but that most or all were indeed $\bar{\nu}_e$ absorptions. Positron emission following $\bar{\nu}_e$ absorption is almost

Table 2. Data from the Kamiokande II and IMB detectors

Event #	Time (sec)	Electron energy (MeV)	Angle with respect to Large Magellanic Cloud (degrees)
Kamiokande II			
1	0.000	20.0 ± 2.9	18 ± 18
2	0.107	13.5 ± 3.2	40 ± 27
3	0.302	7.5 ± 2.0	108 ± 32
4	0.323	9.2 ± 2.7	70 ± 30
5	0.507	12.8 ± 2.9	135 ± 23
6[a]	0.685	6.3 ± 1.7	68 ± 77
7	1.540	35.4 ± 8.0	32 ± 16
8	1.728	21.0 ± 4.2	30 ± 18
9	1.915	19.8 ± 3.2	38 ± 22
10	9.219	8.6 ± 2.7	122 ± 30
11	10.432	13.0 ± 2.6	49 ± 26
12	12.439	8.9 ± 1.9	91 ± 39
IMB			
1	0.000	38 ± 7	80 ± 10
2	0.411	37 ± 7	44 ± 15
3	0.650	28 ± 6	56 ± 20
4	1.141	39 ± 7	65 ± 20
5	1.562	36 ± 9	33 ± 15
6	2.683	36 ± 6	52 ± 10
7	5.010	19 ± 5	42 ± 20
8	5.581	22 ± 5	104 ± 20

isotropic. However, the IMB data show a marked preference for the forward hemisphere that may well be a statistical fluke, but is as yet unexplained [6].

The best inferred average source temperature is 3.0-5.0 MeV. There is a slight indication from the data that the source is actually cooling, as one would expect. The late-time events are all lower in energy. The shorter duration of the IMB signal (5.58 seconds) with respect to the KII signal (12.44 seconds) also suggests that the source is cooling, since a given decay in temperature implies an even more rapid decay in the high energy tail of a thermal, or near-thermal, spectrum.

The evolution of the signal can be fit reasonably well, not by a single exponential, but by two exponentials, one after the other, with τ's of ≤ 1.0 seconds and ~4.0

seconds, respectively. In other words, two phases, an early short one and a later long one, seem indicated. No neutrino mass, source pulsing, or neutrino oscillations are necessary to explain the data, though none of these exotica are absolutely eliminated. The total $\bar{\nu}_e$ energy radiated is ~3-5x10^{52} ergs, assuming a distance of 50 kpc. If we multiply by 6 to approximately account for the other five neutrino species, a total neutron star binding energy of 2-3x10^{53} ergs is derived. This is our first "direct" measurement of a neutron star's binding energy and it is surprisingly close to what was expected.

Both the KII and IMB data must be fit simultaneously. The two detectors must have sampled the same underlying source. The two major uncertainties in determining which model best represents the LMC remnant are our imprecise knowledge of D (±10%) and the inevitable $\sqrt{\mathcal{N}}$ statistical fluctuations in the sampled event number. The latter are, for 8 and 11 events, 35% and 30%, respectively. The resultant uncertainty in the fit of the data sets when taken individually is ~40% and when taken together is ~30%. In addition, though the KII signal is only weakly dependent on $\langle T_{\bar{\nu}_e} \rangle$ ($\propto \langle T_{\bar{\nu}_e} \rangle^{1.35}$ at T = 4.0 MeV), the IMB signal, sampling as it does the high energy tail, depends steeply on $\langle T_{\bar{\nu}_e} \rangle$ ($\propto \langle T_{\bar{\nu}_e} \rangle^4$ at T = 4.0 MeV). A 10% error in the calculation of $T_{\bar{\nu}_e}$ will result in a ~50% error in the predicted IMB signal. From this fact alone, we can conclude that $\langle T_{\bar{\nu}_e} \rangle$ is now known to better than ~20% and cannot be less than 3.0 MeV or greater than 5.0 MeV. Final baryon masses smaller than 1.2 $M_\odot$ or larger than 1.7 $M_\odot$ do not fit the data. From these considerations, we can conclude that M_G of the LMC neutron star can be 1.3-1.5 $M_\odot$ with little difficulty. It would be difficult to square with the neutrino data the accretion of more than 0.3 $M_\odot$ onto a protoneutron star whose initial mass is ~1.3 $M_\odot$ (baryon). The masses we here derive for the LMC neutron star are in the standard neutron star mass range. For these best-fit models, E_T(20 seconds) is 2.0-2.5x10^{53} (D/50 kpc)^2 ergs and $E_{\bar{\nu}_e}$(20 seconds) is 3.0-4.0x10^{52} (D/50 kpc)^2 ergs. Independently, the observed SN1987A ^{56}Ni mass of 0.075 $M_\odot$ and recent likely models for SN1987A progenitors have led NOMOTO et al. [7] to conclude that the residue mass is indeed ~1.6 $M_\odot$ (baryon).

4. The Fallout and the Future

The epochal detections by IMB and KII of a neutrino burst from a Type II supernova serve to verify the general, not the specific, features of stellar collapse. We now know that neutrinos (specifically, anti-electron neutrinos) are indeed important in such supernovae. This in itself is important since it forcefully suggests that our theories have not been devoid of content. From the detected events and the detector characteristics, we can infer a neutrinosphere temperature near 4.0 MeV (4.6×10^{10} K). This is ten million times hotter than the surface of our sun and the hottest emission temperature since the big bang (or the last stellar collapse). That the IMB and KII signal lasted seconds, not milliseconds, fits nicely into our current models which demand that the PNS is opaque to neutrinos, as bizarre as this seems. Opacity considerably (by factors of hundreds) lengthens neutrino escape times and, hence, the duration of the neutrino burst [4]. In fact, since a set amount of binding energy must be radiated to form a neutron star and the radius of the emitting surface is set by basic neutron star physics to be near ten kilometers, or only a few times ten kilometers, the duration of the cooling burst and the temperature of the neutrinosphere must be complimentary: If the signal duration is shorter, then the emission temperature is higher, the more quickly to radiate that set binding energy. A duration of ten milliseconds, a number from the 1960's, implies a temperature of a least 20 MeV, far in excess of what was observed. However, and gratifyingly, modern theoretical durations of seconds imply temperatures near 3-5 MeV, in precisely the temperature range observed. Hence, the detected neutrino energies and signal durations are mutually reinforcing observational facts.

Nevertheless, the capture of but nineteen events between the two multi-kilotonne detectors should humble even the most exuberant astrophysicist. The statistics of small numbers will hobble any attempt to write more than the first line on the final granite tablets of "stellar collapse." Little astrophysics beyond the important fundamentals cited above has been learned. What in fact is the mechanism of Type II supernovae? Is there a break-out burst? What is the neutrino spectrum and how does it evolve? Is lepton number trapped on infall? Are neutrinos of all species in fact radiated? What is the mass of the residue? What is the pressure-density relation for neutron star matter? What is the role of convection in PNS evolution? None of these important questions was directly answered by SN1987A.

However, there is a great deal of information in these sparse data about the properties of neutrinos themselves. The fact that a neutrino (strictly a $\bar{\nu}_e$) traveled for approximately 160,000 years before reaching Earth gives us our best limit on its lifetime and eliminates neutrino decay as a reason for the outstanding solar neutrino problem [8]. This is new fundamental particle physics information, garnered on the cheap. If $\bar{\nu}_e$s had a nonzero rest mass, they would not all travel at the speed of light, but at speeds that would depend on their energies. A spread in $\bar{\nu}_e$ energy would imply, therefore, a spread in speeds and, hence, an increased spread in arrival times to our northern hemisphere. Since the neutrino signal was dispersed over only a few seconds after traveling for 160,000 years, a good upper limit on the $\bar{\nu}_e$ mass of ~20 eV/c^2 can be derived, assuming little about burst theory [9]. This is 25,000 times smaller than the mass of the electron.

Furthermore, the properties (and existence) of a zoo of hypothetical particles, from majorons [10] to axions [11], each of which has been evoked to solve some outsanding problem in particle physics, can be constrained by the fact that, though these particles would have been created and emitted at the high temperatures in the PNS, they would also have competed with the neutrinos for the finite neutron star binding energy available. Since the standard neutrino burst alone can explain the signals and registered in full in IMB and KII, little room is left for the exotic particles to have carried away some of the energy. Assuming that exotica could be buried in the noise or statistics gives us usable limits on the coupling and properties of these particles, still inaccessible by standard laboratory experiments.

The above list of non-supernova conclusions from the SN1987A neutrino data illustrates the manifold and unexpected uses to which good data can be put. There is always much more than 19 bits of information in 19 events. However, a collapse not fifty, but five kilosparsecs away, in our own galaxy, promises to incite a revolution. A factor of ten decrease in distance leads to a factor of one hundred increase in integrated signal. Table 3 depicts predicted event totals from a collapse at the galactic center in proposed or extant neutrino telescopes (see this volume for details). What could not be learned about supernova physics and fundamental physics with one thousand events?

The first detection of neutrinos from a supernova has been an exhilarating experience for all those involved. Nevertheless, we were lucky. Both IMB and KII had undergone crucial upgrades only six months to one year before the epiphany of SN1987A. Had these upgrades not been successfully completed when they were, neither detector would have seen the neutrinos, even if they had been on-line. It is curious to note that the detection of neutrinos emitted long before the end of the last ice age, when Neanderthals still roamed Europe, should have depended on such recent serendipity. Furthermore, these detectors were not built to catch supernova neutrinos, but to observe proton decay. When proton decay was not seen, these huge tanks of water searched for monopoles or solar neutrinos. Supernova neutrino detection was rarely considered and, when considered, was not considered feasible by the

Table 3. Sample Future Detector Event Totals (from the Galactic Center (8.5 kpc))

	Total #	Prompt ν_e's ($\dot{E}_{\nu_e}/10^{51}$ ergs)	Infall ($E_{\nu_e}/10^{51}$ ergs)	"ν_μ"'s
KII (H$_2$O)	548	0.5	0.5	~20
SNO (D$_2$O+H$_2$O)	1179	~4.1	~4.1	~500
ICARUS (^{40}Ar)	169	~3.6	~3.6	~25
Homestake (^{37}Cl)	5.7	~0.15	~0.15	--

experimenters. To date, SN1987A has been each detector's greatest triumph.

The future looks good for supernova neutrino detection. Around the world, many large mass detectors are being built or planned, not just for burst detection, but for a variety of astrophysical and particle physics missions. The scientific community has been educated by SN1987A in the next simple steps: upgrade phototubes, expand data buffers, reduce dead times, maintain accurate clocks, and, importantly, coordinate and link the international network of detectors to ensure that at least one detector (preferably more) is on-line at all times. The mutually confirming data from the U.S. and Japan emphasize the importance and usefulness of such an international approach.

Acknowledgments

This work was supported by an NSF grant (No. AST87-14176) and the Alfred P. Sloan Foundation.

References

1. Bionta, R. M. et al., Phys. Rev. Lett., 58, 1494 (IMB Collaboration) (1987).

2. Hirata, K. et al., Phys. Rev. Lett., 58, 1490 (KII collaboration) (1987).

3. Burrows, A., Mazurek T. J., Nature, 301, 315 (1983).

4. Burrows, A. and Lattimer, J. M., Ap. J., 307, 178 (1986).

5. Burrows, A., Ap. J., 334, 891 (1988).

6. Matthews, J., in proceedings of the 4th George Mason Workshop in Astrophysics, ed. M. Kafatos and A. G. Michalitsianos (Cambridge University Press, Oct. 12-14, 1987).

7. Nomoto, K., Shigeyama, T. and Hashimoto, M., to appear in the proceedings of the IAU Colloquium 108 on Atmospheric Diagnostics of Stellar Evolution: Chemical Peculiarity, Mass Loss and Explosion, Tokyo, Japan, ed. K. Nomoto (Springer-Verlag 1987 (p. 319)).

8. Frieman, J. et al. (1988), preprint.

9. Burrows, A., Ap. J. (Letters), 328, L51 (1988).

10. Aharnov, Y., Avignone, F. T., and Nussinov, S., Phys. Rev. D, 37, 1360 (1988).

11. Burrows, A., Turner, M. S., Brinkemann, R. P., Phys. Rev. D, 39, 1020 (1989).

Implications of the SN 1987A Neutrinos for Supernova Theory and the Mass of ν_e

Thomas J. Loredo & Don Q. Lamb

The detection of neutrinos from supernova SN 1987A in the Large Magellanic Cloud by the Kamiokande II (KII) and Irvine-Michigan-Brookhaven (IMB) detectors was a landmark event in astrophysics [1-4]. Although only about two dozen of the $\sim 10^{28}$ neutrinos which passed through the Earth were detected, they provide us with the first glimpse of the collapse of a dying star, and hence deserve careful scrutiny.

There is already an extensive literature analyzing these epochal detections. Our work improves on previous studies in three important respects. First, our comparison of the data with parametrized models of the neutrino emission uses a consistent and straightforward statistical methodology. Second, our analysis uses an improved detector model which explicitly includes the empirically measured detector background spectra. Third, we compare the data with a much wider variety of neutrino emission models than was explored previously.

Our improved methodology allows a complete and rigorous comparison of the implications of the data with the expectations of the theory of neutron star formation, taking into account the effects of the strong correlations between the inferred neutrino emission model parameters. Further, it provides correct confidence regions for the electron antineutrino mass $m_{\bar{\nu}_e}$, unlike previously used methods that produce regions that do not enclose the unknown true value of $m_{\bar{\nu}_e}$ with the stated probability. Our inclusion of the background spectra in our analysis allows us to correctly account for the probability that some of the detected events are background events, and significantly weakens the constraint placed on $m_{\bar{\nu}_e}$ by the data. Our exploration of a wide variety of emission models ensures that our inferences regarding $m_{\bar{\nu}_e}$ are robust. The importance of an analysis exploring such a broad class of models has been emphasized by KOLB, STEBBINS, and TURNER [5].

A detailed discussion of our work is presented elsewhere [14-16], including a full comparison with earlier work; here we present our principal conclusions.

The class of neutrino emission models we have explored spans a wide variety of temporal and spectral behavior. Our calculations show that a simple exponential cooling model adequately explains the KII and IMB data when background is included, though more complicated models cannot be ruled out. In the exponential cooling model, the neutrinosphere has a fixed observed radius, $R_{\rm obs}$, and an exponentially decreasing $\bar{\nu}_e$ temperature, $T(t) = T_0 \exp(-t/4\tau)$, with initial temperature T_0 and luminosity decay timescale τ. The best-fit parameter values are $(R_{\rm obs}, T_0, \tau) = (22.5$ km, 4.17 MeV, 4.15 s). These parameter values are in remarkable agreement with the basic predictions of supernova theory. The implied number of $\bar{\nu}_e$ is comparable to that expected from degenerate ν_e diffusing out of the inner core and heating the outer core by neutral current scattering and absorption. The $\bar{\nu}_e$ energy $3.15\, T_0 \approx 15$ MeV is typical of that expected for neutral current diffusion of degenerate $\bar{\nu}_e$ out of the hot outer core. The cooling time scale $\tau \approx 4$ sec is of order that expected for the neutral current diffusion of ν_e out of the inner core.

Assuming the neutron star emits its binding energy equally into 6 species (3 flavors) of neutrino, the best-fit parameters imply a binding energy of $E_b = 2.85 \times 10^{53}$ erg. The best-fit observed radius and binding energy are unusually large, and it has been suggested that the observations therefore rule out soft equations of state [7,8]. However, the inferred parameter values have a large statistical uncertainty. More importantly, the parameter values are highly correlated; confidence volumes in the three dimension parameter space are very asymmetrical, as can be seen by examining their two dimensional projections [14,15]. To allow full comparison of the inferred parameter values with neutron star models, Fig. 1 shows the 95% confidence region projected onto the (R_{obs}, E_b)-plane. Also shown are (R_{obs}, E_b) curves for a representative set of equations of state from the compendium of neutron star models compiled by ARNETT and BOWERS [17]. Although the best-fit values of the radius and energy lie outside of the range permitted by these neutron star models, the projected confidence region comfortably overlaps all of the curves.

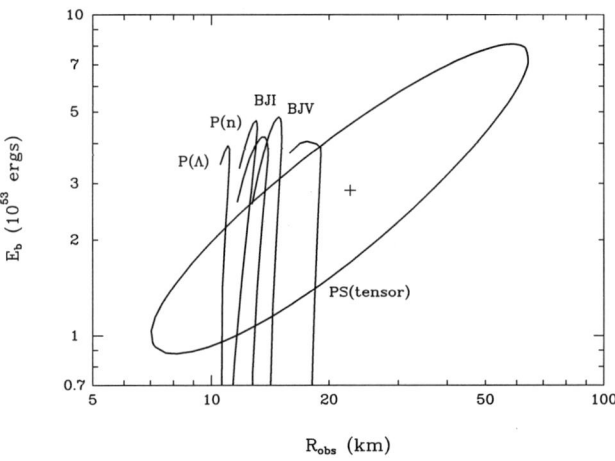

Figure 1. Comparison of the best-fit values and the 95% confidence volumes projected onto the (R_{obs}, E_b)-plane, and the (R_{obs}, E_b)-curves for neutron star models based on a representative set of equations of state.

The intersection of the projected confidence region with the (R_{obs}, E_b) curves defines the ranges of neutron star gravitational mass M_G that are permitted for each model. For each neutron star model, Fig. 2 shows the range of M_G bounded by the projected 95% confidence contour for the exponential cooling model including background. The allowed values of the neutron star mass are in remarkable agreement with the expected gravitational core mass $M \approx 1.4\ M_\odot$ expected from gravitational collapse and measured for neutron stars in binary systems.

To assess the implications of the data for $m_{\bar{\nu}_e}$, we include it as an additional parameter in our model. It enters the predicted rate function in a manner completely analogous to that of other model parameters, thus inferences regarding $m_{\bar{\nu}_e}$ are made simply by calculating best-fit parameter values and confidence regions in a larger parameter space.

All models considered give a best-fit mass at or near 0 eV. The exponential cooling model, with best-fit mass $m_{\bar{\nu}_e} = 0$ eV, gives the most conservative (i.e., highest) upper limit on $m_{\bar{\nu}_e}$, indicating that $m_{\bar{\nu}_e} < 25$ eV with 95% confidence. If this limit is calculated incorrectly by omitting the background spectra, it decreases to 18 eV. Thus proper inclusion of the background is crucial for obtaining the proper upper mass limit. Our 95% upper limit is 1.5 - 5 times larger than found previously using incorrect statistical methods and ignoring the background [10-13]. We note that our limit is not significantly better than current laboratory limits.

In conclusion, our calculations show that a simple exponential cooling model

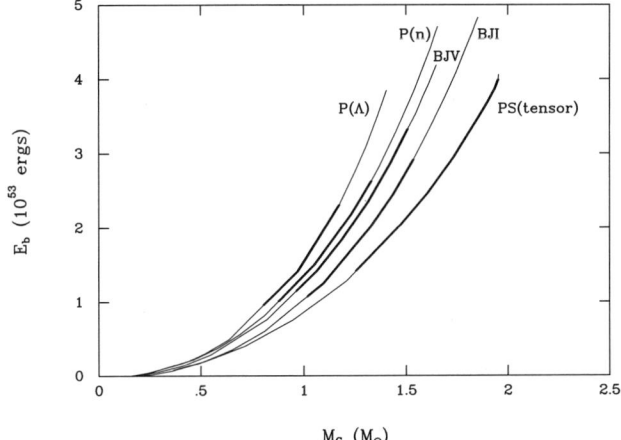

Figure 2. (M_G, E_b) curves for the neutron star models shown in Fig. 2, with the portion of each curve that lies within the projected 95% confidence volume drawn more thickly, indicating the allowed range of neutron star gravitational mass for each model.

adequately explains the KII and IMB data when background is included. The inferred characteristics of this model are in spectacular agreement with the salient features of the theory of gravitational collapse and neutron star formation that had developed over several decades in the absence of direct observational data. We have also shown that the data do not require a nonzero $\bar{\nu}_e$ rest mass, and that they place an upper limit on this mass of ≈ 25 eV at the 95% confidence level. Use of a correct and rigorous statistical methodology and inclusion of the detector background are crucial for obtaining complete and correct inferences, and our consideration of a wide variety of neutrino emission models ensures that our neutrino mass limit is robust.

This work was supported in part by NASA grants NAGW-830, NAGW-1284, and NGT-50189.

REFERENCES

1. K. Hirata, et al.: Phys. Rev. Lett. **58**, 1490 (1987).
2. R. M. Bionta, et al.: Phys. Rev. Lett. **58**, 1494 (1987).
3. C. B. Bratton, et al.: Phys. Rev. **D37**, 3361 (1988).
4. K. Hirata, et al.. Phys. Rev. **D38**, 448 (1988).
5. E. W. Kolb, A. J. Stebbins, and M. S. Turner: Phys. Rev. **D35**, 3598; **D36**, 3820 (1987).
6. L. M. Krauss: Nature. **329**, 689 (1987).
7. D. N. Spergel, T. Piran, A. Loeb, J. Goodman, and J. N. Bahcall: Science. **237**: 1471 (1987).
8. S. A. Bludman and P. J. Schinder: Ap. J. **326**, 265 (1988).
9. D. Q. Lamb, F. Melia, and T. J. Loredo: 1988. In Supernova 1987A in the Large Magellanic Cloud, Proceedings of the George Mason Workshop, ed. by M. Kafatos (Cambridge U. Press, Cambridge, England 1988), p. 204.
10. E. N. Adams: Phys. Rev. **D37**, 2047 (1987).
11. L. F. Abbott, A. DeRújula, and T. P. Walker: Nuc. Phys. **B299**, 734 (1988).
12. D. N. Spergel and J. N. Bahcall: Phys. Lett. **B200**, 366 (1987).
13. A. Burrows: Ap. J. (Letters)**328**, L51 (1988).
14. T. J. Loredo and D. Q. Lamb: In Proceedings of the Fourteenth Texas Symposium on Relativistic Astrophysics (New York Academy of Sciences, in press).
15. T. J. Loredo and D. Q. Lamb: Submitted to Phys. Rev. (1989).
16. T. J. Loredo and D. Q. Lamb: Submitted to Phys. Rev. (1989).
17. W. D. Arnett and R. L. Bowers: Ap. J. Suppl. **33**, 415 (1977).

Neutrino Signal from Rapidly Rotating Collapsed Stellar Iron Cores

H.-Thomas Janka

Rapid rotation (rotation periods of the order of milliseconds) causes a significant deformation of the collapsed stellar iron core and hot young protoneutron star (JANKA and MÖNCHMEYER [1]). The ratio of polar extension and equatorial extension was found to be typically of the order of $R_p : R_e \cong 1 : (1.5-2)$. It is reasonable to expect a similar deformation of the regions where neutrinos decouple from the core matter ('neutrino sphere').

Therefore we must conclude that the neutrino emission from a collapsed rapidly rotating stellar core is anisotropic. Observers at different inclination angles relative to the rotation axis will receive different neutrino luminosities. Taking into account the size of the visible area of the neutrino sphere as well as influences from the variation of the neutrino flux density with the position on the radiating 'surface' (for which the local density gradient can be taken as a rough measure) we end up with an estimate for the ratio of the observable fluxes of (JANKA [2]) $J^p_{obs} : J^e_{obs} \approx R_e^2 : R_p^2 \approx (2.25-4)$. This means that an observer in the equatorial plane will typically receive only 40–50% of the energy which is detectable from a position along the polar axis (JANKA and MÖNCHMEYER [1], [3]). Moreover, the result implies that drawing conclusions on the total energy release during the birth of a rapidly rotating neutron star from given experimental neutrino data can only be done within the uncertainty limits of about $+50\%$ and $-(30$–$40)\%$ of the measured value, when no independent information about the inclination angle relative to the rotation axis is available.

Due to the facts that most probably a neutron star in the gravitational mass range of 1.2–1.6 $M_\odot$ was formed and the total energy most likely to explain the neutrino detection is around $(3.2 - 3.8) \cdot 10^{53}$ ergs (JANKA and HILLEBRANDT [4]), the Kamiokande 2 data (HIRATA et al. [5]) suggest that if there is a rapidly rotating neutron star in SN 1987A we observe it from a position significantly outside the equatorial plane.

References
1. H.-T. Janka, R. Mönchmeyer: Astron. Astrophys. (1989), in press.
2. H.-T. Janka: in Proceedings of the 5th Workshop on Nuclear Astrophysics, ed. by W. Hillebrandt and E. Müller, (MPA/P1, Garching 1989) (p. 130).
3. H.-T. Janka, R. Mönchmeyer: Astron. Astrophys. 209, L5 (1989).
4. H.-T. Janka, W. Hillebrandt: Astron. Astrophys. (1989), in press.
5. K. Hirata, et al.: Phys. Rev. Lett. 58, 1490 (1987).

Implications of SN 1987A Neutrino Observations for Future Detections

John LoSecco

Introduction. We have learned a great deal from the neutrino observations[1,2] of the stellar collapse SN1987A in the LMC. In particular we have a much better idea about the time structure, energy spectrum and neutrino content of a stellar collapse neutrino burst. These factors can be taken into account in the design of future experiments.

In some cases the observations are indicative but not conclusive. The hope is that future experiments may be able to clarify questions raised by the current observations. It appears that there may not be one detector that combines all the qualities needed to improve our current knowledge. In that case it seems clear that a variety of complementary observation techniques will be needed.

Observations. Much has been said about the neutrino observations. Most analyses have *assumed* that the observed signal was entirely due to electron antineutrino interactions on hydrogen.

$$\bar{\nu}_e P \to e^+ n$$

The cross section for this particular reaction is very well known[3] and the observations can be understood with a minimum of assumptions. This cross section is the highest known for neutrino reactions of these energies. The flux can be estimated from the reaction rate. For SN1987A it was about 10^{10} neutrinos /cm^2. From the flux and the measured neutrino energy the total energy output into neutrinos can be estimated. The calculation[4] gives from 2 to 8 times 10^{53} ergs. This is a rather large range for such an important measurement. But the range reflects assumptions used and perhaps the bias of the calculator.

It is difficult to conclude that all interactions come from electron antineutrinos, as often assumed. The angular distribution of both the IMB and Kamioka samples has a very low probability of having come from *just* this reaction. While each of the two experiments has a probability 5%-10% of a random fluctuation producing the observed distribution the two experiments are in very good agreement with each other. This is strong evidence that other neutrino reactions are present[5] in the observed sample.

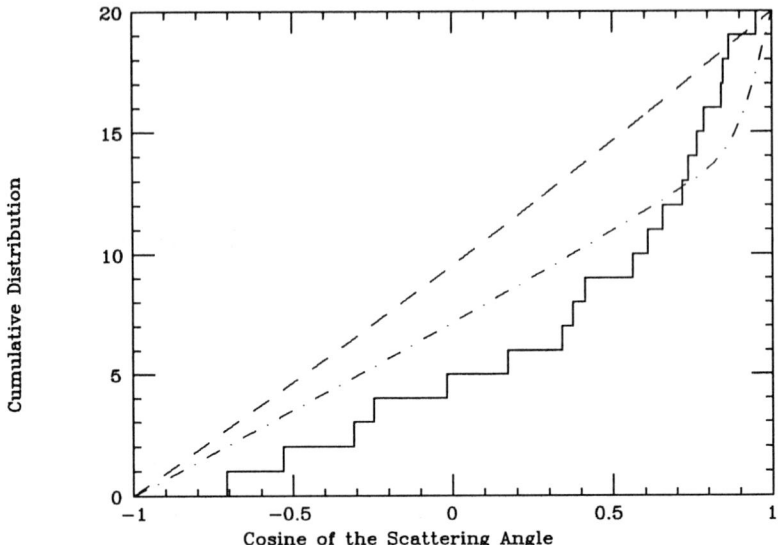

Figure 1: Comparison of Data with Expectations

Figure 1 compares the observed angular distribution with a distribution expected for purely electron antineutrino interactions (dashed curve) and with one expected if 25% of the interactions are due to neutrino electron scattering

$$\nu e \to \nu e$$

(dot dashed curve). The dot dashed curve is favored. The full argument and the likelihood is discussed in reference 5.

The presence of these additional reactions is not surprising. Since the pulse contains all neutrino types this is to be expected. But it is very difficult to draw quantitative results on these other components due to the very low data rate and the various possible reactions.

Implications. Idealy one would like to have a unique reaction for each of the possible components of the neutrino flux. But since the muon and tau neutrinos are below charged current reaction threshold they can only be observed by neutral current interactions. We do not know how to identify the type of neutrino involved in a neutral current reaction (except possibly by its cross section). The electron antineutrino is already well identified by its isotropic angular distribution and by the large fraction of the incident neutrino energy that can be measured in the recoiling positron.

It would be good to find a nuclear reaction in which only electron neutrinos can participate.

$$\nu_e N \to e^- X$$

The reaction needs to have a low energy threshold, so that interactions will occur for a substantial fraction of the flux. One can also hope for a large cross section since the detector may not be feasible for simple economic reasons if the cross section is too small.

The neutrino electron scattering reaction will record all neutrinos present in the pulse. But measurements with it are very difficult. In particular the emerging neutrino carries off some of the initial energy. Scattering and measuring errors make it very difficult to reconstruct the recoiling electron direction. Without an accurate direction the energy can not be measured.

With three measurements, the electron antineutrino spectrum through the proton reaction, the electron neutrino spectrum through the nuclear reaction and all neutrinos through the neutrino electron scattering reaction a good picture of the neutrino pulse can be reconstructed with minimal assumptions. The electron neutrino and antineutrino contribution to the neutrino electron scattering rate can be calculated and subtracted to yield a net signal from the other neutrino types.

Conclusions and Recomendations. It is important to have a well understood set of neutrino interactions to achieve the maximum astrophysics results from the next supernova neutrino observation. It would be prudent to use reactions that have been experimentally tested, and found to conform to expectations. We are fortunate that the muon decay neutrino spectrum is comparable in energy to the observed supernova neutrino pulse and can provide electron neutrinos and muon antineutrinos for a possible beam test.

An independent measurement of the electron neutrinos may confirm speculation[6] that this component carries as much as twice the energy of each of the others.

Acknowledgements. I would like to thank S. Woosley for organizing a great workshop. I would like to thank my colleagues on the IMB experiment for helpful advice and encouragement. This work was supported in part by the US DOE under Contract No. DE-AC02-87ER40366.A002.

References

1. R.M. Bionta, et al., Phys. Rev. Lett. **58**, 1494 (1987)
   C.B. Bratton, et al., Phys. Rev. **D37**, 3361 (1988).
2. K. Hirata, et al., Phys. Rev. Lett. **58**, 1490 (1987)
   K. Hirata, et al., Phys. Rev. **D38**, 448 (1988).
3. T.D. Lee and C.N. Yang, Phys. Rev. **126**, 2239 (1962)
   S. Bonetti, et al., Nuov. Cim. **38**, 260 (1977)
   C. Llewellyn-Smith, Phys. Rep. **3C**, 261 (1972).
4. S.A. Bludman and P.J. Schinder, Ap. J. **326**, 265 (1988)
   I. Goldman, et al., Phys. Rev. Lett. **60**, 1789 (1988).
5. J.M. LoSecco, Phys. Rev. **D39**, 1013, (1989).
6. H.-T. Janka, this conference.

SECTION VIII

SYNTHETIC SPECTRA OF SUPERNOVA 1987A, TYPE I'S, & OTHERS

Spectral Diagnostics of Type II Supernova
Peter Höflich

The investigation of the spectra of Type II supernovae (SN II) is important for different fields in astronomy and astrophysics. Firstly, SN II are one of the most luminous single objects and may reach the same brightness at maximum as a whole galaxy. Therefore, they can be used as candles (KIRSHNER and KWAN, [1]) to determine the distances of galaxies, in particular, to fix the cosmologically important Hubble constant H_o. Secondly, the observed spectrum gives direct information on the physical and chemical conditions of the supernova photosphere at a given time. Deeper layers of the expanding envelope are observable at later times. Therefore, a detailed spectral analysis of the time evolution is helpful in order to answer questions concerning the the overall structure of the envelope. In principle, this allows for an investigation of the explosion mechanism of SN II, for the test of hydrodynamic models and of the final stages of the evolution of massive stars.

Supernova 1987A in the Large Magellanic Cloud (LMC) has triggered a rapid development of tools for atmospheric diagnostics of SN II, because it has provide a lot of information due to the complete sample of observations. It has been shown that the spectra of SN1987A can be well understood by atmospheric models which take extention and NLTE effects into account. The total mass of the H-rich envelope was estimated to be about 10 $M_\odot$ both from the light curve (LC) (e.g. WOOSLEY[2]) and from the spectral analysis. Strong mixing processes of Co and Fe up to the hydrogen rich layers and of the inner few solar masses of hydrogen with the layers below are strongly indicated by the IR-lines of (RANK et al.[3]) and by the chemical analysis of the optical wavelength region, respectively. As a result of mixing hydrogen was observed at velocities of about 800 km/sec at the beginning of October 1987. In addition, the chemical abundances could be determined etc.(HÖFLICH[4,5,6,7]). The distance of SN1987A was derived by several groups (see paragraph III). A more detailed discussion of the atmospheric models for SN II and the diagnostics of SN1987A can be found in HILLEBRANDT and HÖFLICH[8]and the references therein.

In order to investigate scattering dominated atmospheres of SN II, we have extended our investigation of SN1987A to perform a more systematic study but by taking SN1987A as an example for spectral analysis. We want to show different aspects of the application of these models.

Type II SN show a wide range of individual variations of the light curves (LC) and details of the spectra (BRANCH, this volume). Therefore, detailed atmospheric models are needed for the determination of the properties of the expanding atmospheres, and the sensitivity of the observable features on the model parameters has to be investigated (paragraph II). The consequences are discussed for the use of SN II as distance indicators, and the practical usefulness of the models is demonstrated by the example of SN1987A (paragraph III). The LC of SN1987A is well understood and a lot of details concerning the progenitor and explosion of SN1987A could be derived by the LC using the grey flux limited diffusion approximation for the radiation transport. However, the explosion energy needed for the interpretation of the LC is only certain up to a factor of 2 ($1...2\ 10^{51} erg$). In paragraph IV the validity of the limited diffusion approximation is investigated and we discuss whether additional information can be derived by detailed atmospheric models from very early LC of SN1987A. Finally, consequences of the limb darkening effects are studied as an example in order to investigate the speckled data which are used for the determination of radii and of the geometrical structure of SN1987A (PAPALIOLIOS et al.[9]). We will show what additional information is needed in this specific case to allow for a detailed analysis, to prevent the investigation of the limb darkening from being a "marginally useful, somewhat academic investigation. ... in the absence of application".

I. The Model Construction

Stationarity and radiative equilibrium are generally assumed because the radiative timescales are much shorter than the hydrodynamic ones shortly after the expansion of the envelope begins. Spherical symmetry is adopted. The expansion of the envelopes are homologous soon after the initial acceleration. Therefore, the velocity is assumed to be a linear function of r. Power law density profiles as a function of the distance r (i.e. $\rho \propto r^{-n}$) are taken for the general investigation (paragraph II) according to WEAVER and WOOSLEY [10]. Homologous expansion of an initial stellar structure and power laws are assumed for the analysis of SN1987A for the first few months and at the later stages, respectively. Note, that the density, velocity and temperature profiles are taken from the hydrodynamic model in paragraph IV because the above assumptions are not valid for the very early stages.

Detailed atomic models are used for the three most abundant ionization stages of a number of elements (H, He, C, N, O, Ne, Mg, K, Ca, Ba). The statistical equations are consistently solved with radiation transport for the bound-bound and bound-free transitions. The radiation field is calculated by a comoving frame method very similar to that of MIHALAS et al.[11,12], but it includes line blending of the NLTE elements. Here, we presume complete redistribution for the individual line source functions but handle the blending effect between different lines as a partial redistribution of the

Spectral Diagnostics of Type II SN 417

total source function. The redistribution function is iteratively determined. Line blanketing of 5000 to 50 000 additional lines of heavy elements are taken into account by using either a two level or the pure scattering approximation for weak lines. The atomic data of the line transitions of these elements are taken from the compilation of KURUCZ [13]. See HÖFLICH [4-7] for more details of the atmospheric models.

II. Study of the Synthetic Spectra

The relation between the free model parameters and the synthetic spectra are discussed in some examples. Our models are characterized by the following free parameters (Table 1): a) the photospheric radius R_{ph}, b) the effective temperature T_{eff}, c) the exponent n of the density slope ($\rho \propto r^{-n}$), the expansion velocity v_{ex} and d) a statistical velocity field which is assumed to be 10% of v_{ex}.

Two types of models can be distinguished (Table 1). They are characterized by the recombination front R_{HII} which is located in or above the line forming region for *ionization bounded models* (IBM) and *density bounded models* (DBM), respectively. The location mainly depends on T_{eff}, and to a smaller amount on v_{ex} and on R_{ph} because their influence of the photon escape probability in lines and the scattering domination in the continua. Although hydrogen recombines inside the distance grid of the models with $T_{eff} = 7000K$, they should not be regarded as IBMs because R_{HII} is located above the line forming region.

Table 1. The distance R_{ph} at which the optical depth is 1 for true absorption at 5000 Å, the effective temperature T_{eff}, the particle density N_o, the value of n of the density profile ($N(r) \propto r^{-n}$), the expansion velocity v_{ex} and the Thomson optical depth τ_{sc} are given at R_{ph} in cgs. In addition, we show the the relative extention E of the continuum forming region (i.e. $r(\tau_{sc} = 1.)/R_{ph}$) and the distance R_{HII}, up to which hydrogen is mainly ionized. Solar composition is assumed.

No.	R_{ph}	T_{eff}	N_o	n	v_{ex}	E	τ_{sc}	R_{HII}
I	5.E14	5500.	4.6E11	3	1000.	1.10	25.	5.5E14
II	3.E15	5500.	1.3E11	3	1000.	1.13	64.	3.3E15
III	5.E14	5500.	5.0E11	5	1000.	1.07	21.	5.3E14
IV	1.E15	5500.	3.7E11	5	1000.	1.08	31.	1.08E15
V	3.E15	5500.	1.8E11	5	1000.	1.12	57.	3.3E15
VI	5.E14	5500.	7.0E11	8	1000.	1.06	19.	5.3E14
VII	3.E15	5500.	2.3E11	8	1000.	1.07	34.	3.2E15
VIII	5.E14	7000.	3.7E11	5	3500.	2.1	34.	1.1E15
IX	1.E15	7000.	2.5E11	5	3500.	2.3	46.	2.9E15
X	1.E15	7000.	2.5E11	5	7000.	2.3	45.	2.7E15
XI	3.E15	7000.	1.3E11	5	3500.	2.6	80.	1.1E16
XII	5.E14	10000.	5.3E11	5	3500.	2.3	50.	(2.7E15)
XIII	1.E15	10000.	3.5E11	5	3500.	2.5	69.	...
XIV	3.E15	10000.	1.6E11	5	3500.	2.9	99.	...
XV	1.E15	10000.	5.4E11	8	3500.	1.7	58.	...

The following qualitative consequences for the processes can be drawn which govern the spectra: a) scattering domination increases with flattening of the density (i.e. -n), with R_{ph} and T_{eff}. b) The extention effects as represented by E (Table 1) become substantial for the continuum forming region for all DBMs, but, in general, they are much smaller for IBMs and can be neglected for steep density slopes (n $\leq$-5...-6).

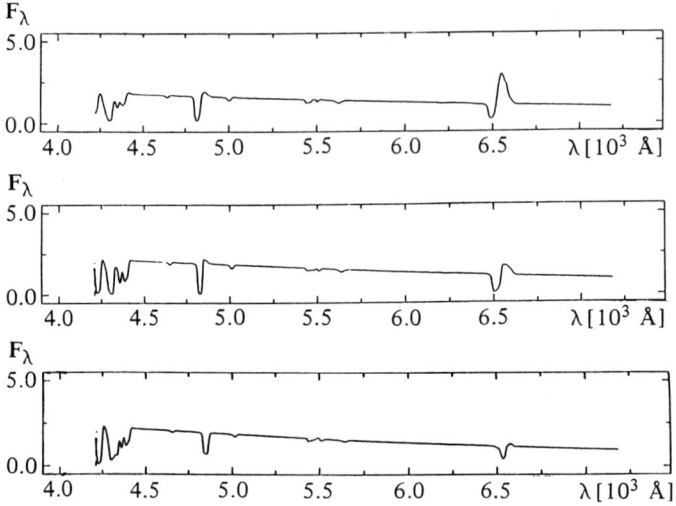

Figure 1. Synthetic optical spectra as calculated during the recombination phase (model III-V, Table 1).

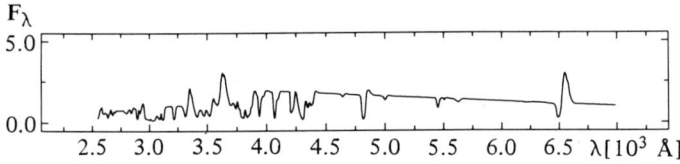

Figure 2. Synthetic spectrum of the UV to optical wavelength range as calculated by model V (Table 1).

The DBMs are already studied (HÖFLICH [14]). They show the following tendencies: The H line profiles are sensitive to v_{ex}, T_{eff} and the exponent n of the density profile. Generally, the line shift of the absorption feature decreases inside the Balmer series of H. The absorption minima of H_β and of weak lines of heavier elements occur at R $(\tau_{sc}) \approx 1$. Therefore, v_{ex} can be determined first in an analysis, then T_{eff} is derived by the energy slope of the continuum (but $T_{color} \neq T_{eff}$, see below) and n is fixed by the emission of H_α. However, the optical spectra are less sensitive to R_{ph}. The problem of a radius determination can be overcome for DBMs, if the UV flux including the Balmer jump (BJ) is measured. In particular, the BJ changes from absorption to emission with increasing radius (HÖFLICH et al.[15]).

The transition from the density bounded regime to the ionization bounded case is clearly marked by the occurance of strong optical lines due to heavy elements.

The hydrogen lines are very sensitive to T_{eff}, n and R_{ph} for IBMs. In particular, the emission components increase with T_{eff} and -n because of the larger excitation and higher cross section, respectively. In contrast to DBMs the emission of H_α is sensitive to R_{ph} (Fig.1). However, the v_{ex} by the absorption minima of the H Balmer series differs significantly from $v_{ex}(R_{ph})$ and they sensitivly depend on R_{ph}. E.g. $v_{ex}(R_{ph})$ equals $1400 km/sec$ in the models IV and V but the absorption minima of H_α & H_β correspond to 3200 & 2600 and 2600 & 2000 km/sec, respectively. In addition, the H lines of the higher Balmer series are strongly blanketed by transitions of heavier elements, causing serve problems for the determination of v_{ex}. Therefore, the expansion of the photosphere can hardly be determined by the absorption minima to a good accuracy. The UV flux increases with R_{ph}, T_{eff} and n whereas the IR flux of the continua and the lines increase with lower n. Line blanketing becomes most prominent in the UV (Fig.2). The opacity is mostly given by a large number of weak scattering lines which exceed the Thomson scattering opacity by orders of magnitude and which form a more or less smooth quasi continuum. Conclusively, observations during the recombination phase of hydrogen provides more information than the earlier phase and, in principle, allow for a more accurate analysis. Furthermore, the relation between v_{ex} and R_{ph} at a specific time can be used even if the time of the initial event is not well known, because of the increasing time base. However, the coupled influence of the different free model parameters on the synthetic spectra causes complications for the analysis. A detailed discussion of the subject of this paragraph will be given in a forthcoming paper.

Most observations of SN II are measurements of the brightness in the UBV-filter system, and the black body approximation is used for the interpretation. However, the color temperature bases on the color index (B-V) differs significantly from T_{eff} (Table 2). This is even true if the U-B and B-V color excess follows the relation as given by a black body. The physical reason is due to extention effects and the domination of the (grey) Thomson scattering which results in a dilution of the emitted fluxes but hardly redistribute the photons. The black body approximation results in a systematicly overestimation of the V flux by about 35 to 45 % during the DBM phase, with a small dependence on the model parameters. Note that the V flux may be underestimated during the recombination phase because the line blocking in the B filter is much more pronounced than in the visual wavelength range. This should not be regarded as a systematic effect because its dependency on the density structure, the metalicity, the velocity field etc. .

III. Type II SN as Distance Indicators

SN1987A has been taken as a examination of accuracy of the calculated absolute fluxes. We have used those models which allow for the best representation of the observed spectra of SN1987A. A distance of 48 ± 4 Kpc has been derived on the basis of the monochromatic optical fluxes (Table 3, HÖFLICH, [4,5]). This value is in good agreement with those infered from other distance indicators for the LMC (RR-Lyrae:

Table 2. Comparison of the calculated fluxes (see Table 1) δF in the V-filter band (at 5500 Å) with those as infered by a black body for the same color index B-V.

No.	R_{ph}	T_{eff}	n	B-V	T_{BB}	δF
IV	1.E15	5500.	5	0.58	5900	1.26
IX	1.E15	7000.	5	0.50	6500	0.85
XII	5.E14	10000.	5	0.09	10750	0.65
XIII	1.E15	10000.	5	0.08	11000	0.6
XIV	3.E15	10000.	5	0.06	11250	0.55
XV	1.E15	10000.	8	0.12	10250	0.6

48.7 ±1.1 kpc, 48.3±1.3 kpc, WALKER and MACK [16]; δ Cep.: 49.4 ±3.3 kpc; WALKER [17]; 54.9 kpc, MARTIN et al., [18]; 51.8±1.2 kpc, WELCH et al.[19]) but it clearly tends to the lower values. Our distance of SN1987A compares well with those deduced from detailed atmospheric models by other groups which used the UV flux (43 ± 4 kpc, CHILUKURI and WAGONER [20]) and which, recently, used the optical wavelength range (46 kpc, SCHMUTZ et al.[21]; 49 ± 5 kpc EASTMAN, this volume).

Table 3: The distance in Kpc of SN1987A as derived by comparison between the calculated (HÖFLICH [5]) and observed monochromatic absolute fluxes (mean value ±30 Å). A reddening of $E_{B-V} = 0.15^m$ is assumed.

No.	Date	5000	5300	5500	5700	6000	6300	at H_α
Mar. 23	53.	44	49	46	52	52		46.5
May 14	48.	50.	48.	49.	51.	50.		45.
June 02	48.	52.	46.	46.5	45.	50.		52.

In the last few years several distances of SN II have been determined using the Baade-Wesselink method, black body fits and taking the minima of the absorption features as v_{ex} at the photosphere (e.g. SN 1969L: $12 \pm 4 kpc$ and SN 1970G: $7 \pm 2 kpc$ KIRSHNER and KWAN [1]; SN1979C: $23 \pm 3 kpc$, BRANCH et al. [22]). A Hubble constant H_o of $57 \pm 4 kms^{-1} Mpc^{-1}$ is implied (BRANCH[23]). Our calculations have shown that the line shift of the absorption features of weak line transitions (see above) are good first order indicators for $v_{ex}(\tau_{sc} = 1)$ before the recombination phase and, therefore, allow for the determination of the velocity at a certain distance in the envelope if the exact time of the initial explosion is well known. However, the absolute visual flux is overestimated by about 15 to 45 %, causing a systematic error of the distance in the order of 10 - 20 % and indicating a correction of H_o (65 ± 10 km $s^{-1} Mpc^{-1}$). The problem with the inaccuracy due to the initial event can be significantly reduced if late stages are considered. However, the difficulties of the parameter deduction for IBMs should be noted. Therefore, detailed analyses of different stages are really needed to minimize the error for the use of SN II as distance indicators. Besides the uncertainties due to the spectral analyses in respect to H_o, note that up to now only very few spectra of SN II have been measured which are in the Hubble flow (see WAGONER, this volume).

IV. Analysis of the Early Light Curve of SN1987A

In order to investigate the fluxes as emitted from the expanding envelope of SN1987A during the first day, we have used the hydrodynamic model 14E1 of NOMOTO et al.[24](Table 4). The atmospheric models correspond to the times when the shock breaks through the photosphere (A), when the first photons where detected in the V filter band (B) and when the first UBV magnitudes where available (D).

Table 4. The absolute visual brightness M_V, the color indices U-B and B-V in Johnson's filter system and the bolometric luminosity L_{bol} are given for model 14E1 of NOMOTO et al.[24](He core mass: 6 $M_\odot$, envelope mass: 10 $M_\odot$; $E_{kin} : 10^{51} erg$) for different times as calculated by the atmospheric models. The correction factors C_V and C_{bol} give the ratio between the visual and bolometric fluxes, respectively, as calculated by atmospheric models in comparison with the extended grey atmosphere (EGA). In addition, the electron temperature T, the distance R and the particle density N_o are given at the distance where the Thomson optical depth equals 2/3. All quantities are given in CGS except for the brightness.

Model	time [s]	$T[K]$	$R[cm]$	$N_o[cm^{-3}]$	M_V	U-B	B-V	L_{bol}	C_V	C_{bol}
A	6916.	820000.	3.34E12	1.2E15	-11.26	-1.12	-0.28	8.9E44	0.60	0.25
B	10798.	69000.	1.60E13	6.3E11	-10.51	-1.08	-0.27	2.0E42	0.18	0.12
C	43254.	20800.	7.80E13	1.1E11	-12.73	-0.99	-0.23	2.8E41	0.23	0.26
D	129587.	10300.	1.85E14	4.4E10	-13.31	-1.02	-0.16	1.6E41	0.38	0.43

The LC of SN1987A is well understood by hydrodynamic models which use a flux limited diffusion approximation or a grey LTE solution for the radiation transport equation. However, there are several major differences between the detailed NLTE calculations and the diffusion approximations which have strong implications on the interpretation of the early observed data and the use of the measurements as tests for the hydrodynamical calculations: i) L_{bol} is smaller by a factor C_{bol} of between 0.12 and 0.43. ii) L_V is reduced by a factor C_V of between 0.18 and 0.6. iii) L_V shows a strong local minimum, i.e. in the very first stages not only the bolometric luminosity decreases but also the visual one. iv) The correction factors C_V and C_{bol} show a strong time dependence which can be well understood as a consequence of the change of the densities and temperatures at the photosphere. The reduction of the luminosities in respect to the EGA solution is a consequence of line blanketing effect and of the Thomson scattering domination at the photospheres.

Although the general observed trend is reproduced by the calculations (Fig.3), two major differences between the observed and calculated visual brightness m_V are obvious: i) The calculated m_V is just at its local minimum (i.e. 1.7^m fainter, model B) than the observation of McNaught. ii) The calculated luminosity is somewhat too low. iii) At day 1.5 (model D) the reddening corrected observed color index B-V (-0.235^m) is significantly lower than the calculated value of -0.16^m, indicating a too low local temperature in the hydrodynamic models. This interpretation is also supported by the absence of the optical HeI triplet line at Feb.24, 1987,in the synthetic spectra.

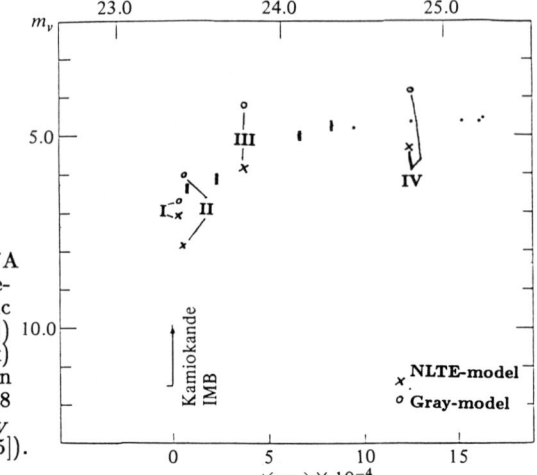

Figure 3. Observed m_V of SN1987A in comparison with those as predicted by Nomoto's hydrodynamic model 14E1 (NOMOTO et al.[24]) by using atmospheric models (x) and the grey LTE approximation (o). The distance is taken to be 48 kpc. A reddening correction E_{B-V} of $.15^m$ is applied (WAMPLER [25]).

All this strongly indicate a larger kinetic energy than $10^{51} erg$ as used for this hydrodynamic model. A quantitative estimate can be derived by the difference of the visual luminosities of model B showing that the minimum of the calculated L_V occur too late. The time of the increase of the very early light curve mainly depends on the shock travelling time through the initial stellar structure and it is approximately proportional to the square root of E_{kin} (SHIGEYAMA and NOMOTO [26]). Therefore, E_{kin} can be estimated to be 20 to 40 % larger than 10^{51} erg.

Note, that detailed atmospheric diagnostics of hydrodynamic models are needed to allow for a more accurate determination of the total kinetic energy. Furthermore, such analyses should be done for different initial stellar models. E.g. the general slopes and effects turned out to be qualitatively the same for the Arnett's stellar model but quantitative differences occur. These problems and the interpretation of the initial UV light flash are under investigation.

V. Limb Variation Effects

We want to discuss the effects of the limb variation at the example of model V (Table 1) which has typical parameter for type II SN during the recombination stage. This phase occurs some time after the initial expansion. Therefore, the envelope most likely can be resolved by speckle observations.

The normalized intensity distribution functions (IDF) differ significantly from those of a disk of constant intensity (i.e. a step function) at all frequencies (Fig.4; HÖFLICH [27]). At 6700 Å the IDF shows a relatively sharp outer boundary, because the R_{HII} is just 12 % (Table 1) above the Thomson scattering dominated photosphere. Note, that a sharp outer boundary does not occur at times earlier than the recombination phase of hydrogen. The opacity in the UV is mainly dominated by a large number of weak lines which form a quasi continuum. This results in a similar global behaviour of the IDFs as in the case of the Thomson scattering but at larger distances (HÖFLICH[27]). However, this global structure of the IDF profile cannot be generalized. In particular, even ring structures in the IDFs occur if the opacities are strongly frequency dependent in the comoving frame.

Several speckle measurements are performed in the H_α-line of SN1987A. Therefore, we want to discuss the wavelength dependence over this line in some detail (Fig. 4). Near the rest wavelength, secondary maxima of the IDFs appear which strongly depend on the wavelength of both the size and radial location. The maxima occur if a specific projected Doppler shift in the spectrum corresponds to a specific radial distance. Note that even a difference of 15 Å is sufficient to shift the position of the secondary maximum by about 20 % in distance, and a shift of 140 Å would result a radius change by a factor of 80 % . This implies that the transmission function of the filter have to be known quite well to use the correct IDF.

However, the frequency variation of the IDFs have some severe consequences not only for the determination of the radii but also for the reconstruction of images on the basis of two dimensional speckle observations. Even a small deviation from sphericity of the velocity, the density or chemical structure may imply very different radii for two orthogonal directions of a slit which is layed over the disk, because two different IDFs are seen.

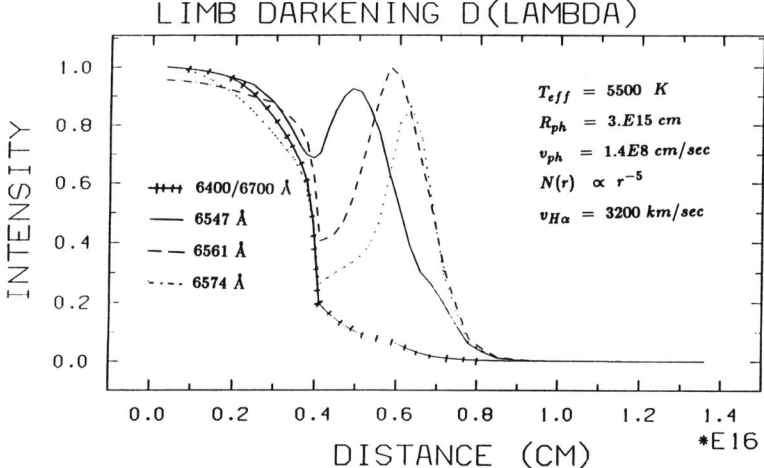

Figure 4. The calculated normalized intensity distribution (IDF) in the region of the H_α line as calculated by model V (Table 1).

The observed large frequency and time dependent axis ratio for SN1987A as proposed by PAPALIOLIOS et al.[9] may be explained as a consequence of the frequency dependent IDFs. See HÖFLICH [27] for more details.

References

1. R. Kirshner, J. Kwan: Astrophys. J. 193, 27 (1974)

2. S.E.Woosley: Astrophys.J. 330, 218 (1988)

3. D.M.Rank, J.Gregman, F.C.Witteborn, M.Cohen, D.K.Lynch, R.W.Russell: Astrophys.J. 325, L1 (1988)

4. P.Höflich: Lect.Notes in Phys. 287, ed. W. Hillebrandt, Springer, p.307, (1987)

5. P.Höflich: Proc.Astron.Soc.Austral. 7, 434 (1988)

6. P.Höflich: IAU Symp.108, ed.K.Nomoto, Springer, p.388 (1988)

7. P.Höflich: Proc.MPA P1, 111 (1989)

8. W.Hillebrandt, P.Höflich: Rep.on Prog. in Phys. (1989) in press

9. C.Papaliolios, M.Karovska, L.Koechlin, P.Nisenson, C.Standley, S.Heathcote: Nature 338, 565 (1989)

10. T.A.Weaver, S.E.Woosley: Astrophys.J. 289, 198 (1984)

11. D.Mihalas, R.B.Kunasz, D.G.Hummer: Astrophys.J. 202, 4 (1975)

12. D.Mihalas, R.B.Kunasz, D.G.Hummer: Astrophys.J. 206, 5 (1976)

13. R.L.Kurucz: Proceedings of the IAU conference, Baltimore (1989) in press

14. P.Höflich: *Particle Astrophysics Workshop*, ed. C. Pennypacker, (1989) in press

15. P.Höflich, R.Wehrse, G.Shaviv: Astron. Astrophys. 163, 105 (1986)

16. A.R.Walker, P.Mack: Astron.J. 96, 872 (1988)

17. A.R.Walker: M.N.R.A.S. 225, 627 (1987)

18. W.L.Martin, R.P.Warren, M.W.Feast: M.N.R.A.S 188, 139 (1979)

19. D.H.Welch, R.A.McLaren, B.F.Madore, C.W. McAlary: Astrophys.J., 321, 162 (1984)

20. M.Chilukuri,R.V.Wagoner: IAU Symp.108, ed.K.Nomoto, Springer, p.295 (1988)

21. W.Schmutz, C.Russell, D.C.Abbot, U.Wessolowsky: preprint (1989)

22. D.Branch, S.Falk, M.McCall, P.Rybski, A.K.Uomoto, B.J.Will: Astrophys.J. 244, 780 (1981)

23. D.Branch: Proc. of the Symp.on Extragalactic Distance Scales, ed. van den Bergh, (1988) in press

24. K.Nomoto et al.: ed. Hayakawa& Sato, Universal Academy Press (1988) in press

25. E.J.Wampler: SN1987A: One Year later, ed. M.Greco, Ed. Frontiers, p.17 (1988)

26. T.Shigeyama; K.Nomoto; M.Hashimoto: Astron.Astrophys. 196 141 (1988)

27. P.Höflich: Astron. Astrophys. (1989) submitted

Synthetic Spectrum Calculations of the Type II Supernova SN 87A

Ronald G. Eastman

I. Introduction

Hydrodynamic calculations of Type II supernova (SNII) explosions have been highly successful at reproducting the major observational properties of these events, particularly in the case of SN87A (e.g. [1], [2], [3]) Basic properties which can be determined from the data, such as the gas velocity and the bolometric luminosity are reasonably well fit by the hydrodynamic models. What makes these calculations feasible however is a compromise treatment of details concerning the radiation field. Most hydro codes treat the radiation transport by a simple flux limited radiative diffusion scheme and use a Lagrangian mass grid which is too course to yield up more than crude information on details of the emergent spectrum. Ultraviolet, optical and infrared spectrophotometry of supernovae are pregnant with information about their source, but in order to decipher most of this information it is first necessary to perform more refined calculations of the gas excitation/ionization and the radiation field structure in the photospheric and overlying layers. These calculations, which are becoming increasingly more elaborate and sophisticated, are themselves compromises in that most often the explicit time dependent behavior of the atmosphere and radiation field are ignored. The properties of the gas and radiation field are treated as being in a *quasistatic steady state*. Such an approximation may introduce errors in the transfer solution of $10 - 30\%$, which may or may not be acceptable, depending on the intended application.

The intrinsic properties which can be learned about supernovae through detailed modeling of their atmosphere and spectra are myriad, and include the mass, chemistry and energetics of the ejecta. One very important application of model supernova atmospheres concerns the use of SNIIs as distance indicators to external galaxies. The spectra of SNII's contain enough information, subject to simple interpretation, to deduce their intrinsic luminosities and thus their distances. Supernovae are the brightest stars in the Universe, and are observable well into the Hubble flow at distances greater than 30 Mpc, making them the ideal candidate for use in determining the scale and age of the Universe.

In this contribution I would like to present some results of model atmosphere calculations for SN87A during the first few days of its existence, and show how model atmospheres of Type II supernovae may be combined with SNII observations to derive highly accurate distance estimates.

II. Model Atmospheres of SN87A

Robert P. Kirshner and I have modeled the atmosphere of SN87A for times $t \leq 10$ days. The density structure through the atmosphere was approximated as $\rho(v,t) = \rho_0(v/v_0)^{-\gamma}(t/t_0)^{-3}$, which is an excellent description of the outer, hydrogen rich layers. Homologous expansion was assumed, so that $dv/dr = v/r = 1/t$, where t is the time since the onset of expansion.

The code we have developed performs a simultaneous solution of the transfer equation and equations of gas excitation/ionization. The transfer equation solved is given by

$$\mu \frac{\partial I_\nu}{\partial r} + \frac{1-\mu^2}{r}\frac{\partial I_\nu}{\partial \mu} + \frac{1}{ct}\left(3 - \frac{\partial}{\partial \ln \nu}\right)I_\nu = -\chi_\nu I_\nu + \sigma_\nu J_\nu + \eta_\nu, \qquad (1)$$

where I_ν is the specific intensity at frequency ν, σ_ν is the monochromatic (and isotropic) scattering opacity, $\chi_\nu = \sigma_\nu + \kappa_\nu$ is the total monochromatic opacity, including both scattering and true absorption, $J_\nu \equiv 1/2 \int_{-1}^{1} I_\nu d\mu$ is the angle averaged mean intensity, and η_ν is the emission term. All quantities in equation (1) are measured in the local gas rest frame. If equation (1) was explicitly time dependent, there would be a term $(1/c)(DI_\nu/Dt)$, which is the Lagrangian time derivative, on the right hand side. In these calculations all explicit time dependence has been suppressed, and so this term was set equal to zero.

The atmosphere calculations were performed in two steps. In the first step, the gas equation of state for all elements was assumed to be given by the Saha-Boltzmann equation. Thermal balance between gas and radiation field was assumed. The temperature distribution through the atmosphere was computed by linearizing the thermal balance constraint and radiative transfer equations at each frequency. Once convergence was obtained, the temperature distribution obtained in the first step was then used in the next step where the detailed equations of excitation/ionization were solved for hydrogen and helium. Besides H and He, a complete contingent of heavy elements was included at an abundance relative to solar of 1/3. The effects of line blanketing in the UV were substantial in SN87A, and were accounted for in the calculations by the inclusion of 63,000 lines of heavy elements. The excitation and ionization of all elements heavier than helium was calculated with the Saha-Boltzmann equation.

The lower boundary condition to the transfer equation was given by specifying the radiative diffusion flux. For models of SN87A at a particular time, the value chosen was such that the bolometric luminosity at the photosphere would equal the observed value for SN87A. For more details, see Eastman and Kirshner [4].

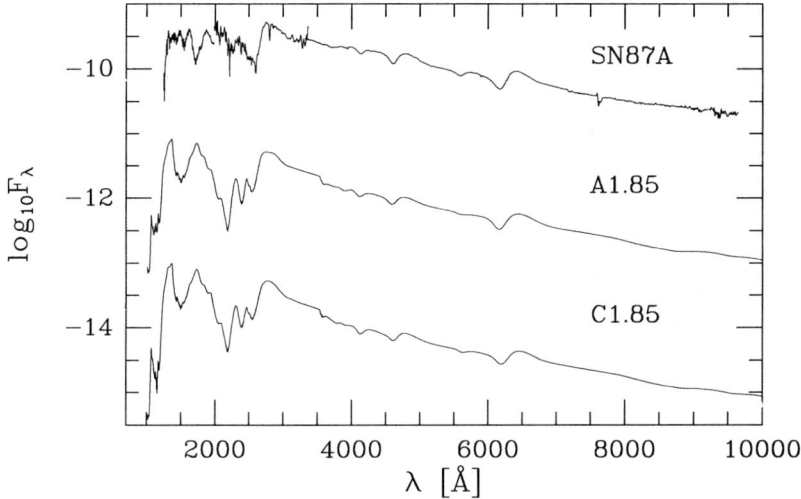

Figure 1 - Comparison of optical and ultraviolet observations of SN87A at $t = 1.85$ days with synthetic spectra of two model atmospheres.

Figure 1 compares combined CTIO optical (BLANCO et al. [5]) and IUE ultraviolet (KIRSHNER et al. [6]; WAMSTEKER et al. [7]) spectra of SN87A at $t = 1.85$ days with synthetic spectra computed for two models. The two models shown, A1.85 and C1.85, differ only in that the former has $\gamma = 9$ while the latter has $\gamma = 7$. The overall agreement between the two models and the data is not bad, with the exception of several strong features in the UV. Almost all of the strong features in the ultraviolet come from transitions in heavy elements (Mg, Si, Al, Ti, Fe, Co) which we have calculated using the Saha-Boltzmann equation, and I believe that this explains much of the discrepancy. Such an approximation is more suited for some elements than for others. Lucy [8] has obtained much better agreement between calculated and observed UV spectra by making a the nebular approximation and explicitly calculating the ionization balance for each species. Figures 2 and 3 compare synthetic spectra of models with observations of SN87A at 7.7 days and 10 days, respectively. In general, the spectra of these models agree well with the data, especially the stronger Balmer

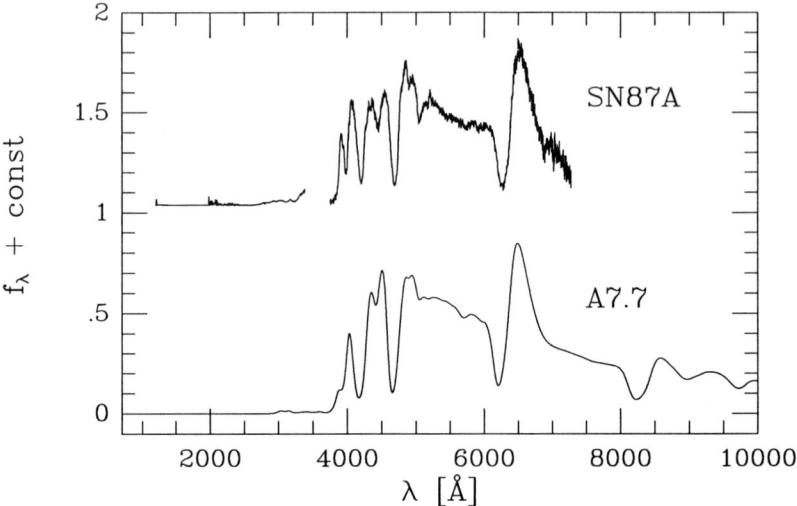

Figure 2 - Comparison of model atmosphere spectrum with optical and ultraviolet observations of SN87A at $t = 7.7$ days.

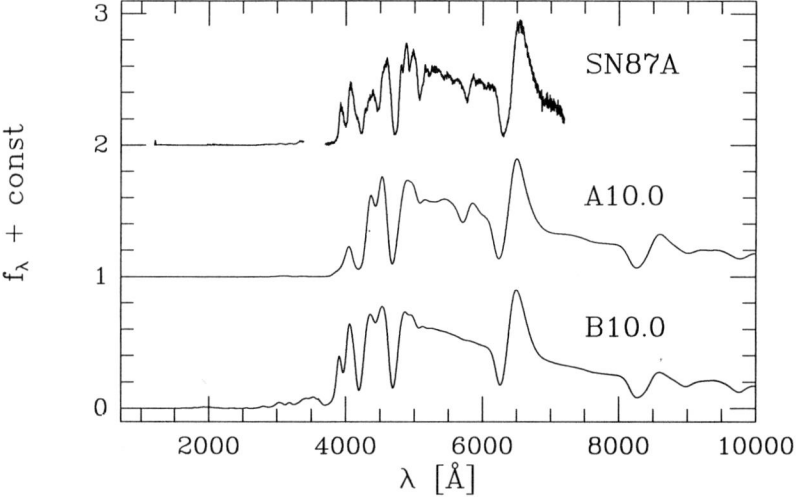

Figure 3 - Comparison of optical and ultraviolet observations of SN87A at $t = 10$ days with synthetic spectra of two model atmospheres.

lines and the overall continuum distribution. Again, the strength of some features calculated with the Saha-Boltzmann equation are not quite right. One troublesome disagreement between models A7.7 and A10.0 with the data is that there is not enough flux at around $\lambda 4000$ Å. These models have about the same luminosity as SN87A, but it turns out that their effective temperatures are slighly lower because their photometric radii are larger. Consequently, in model B10.0 the density has everywhere been decreased by a factor of 4. This has the effect of moving the photosphere inward, and for constant luminosity gives a higher effective temperature. Both the hydrogen Balmer lines and continuum of model B10.0 agree better with the observed spectrum than does model A10.0. However, the Na I D line at $\lambda 5892$, which is well matched in model A10.0, is too weak in model B10.0. This is an indication that the Saha-Boltmann equation used to calculate the Na ionization overestimates the ionization of species above the photosphere.

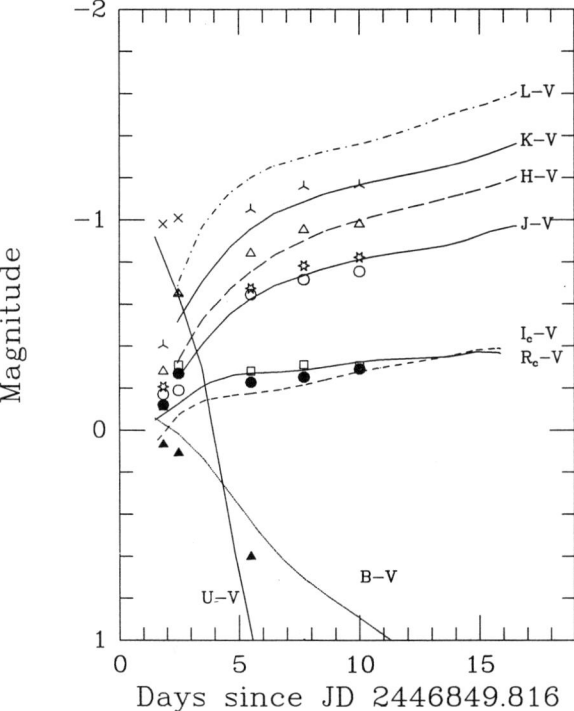

Figure 4 - Comparison of observed and computed photometric colors, $M_\lambda - V$, versus time. Labeled curves are observed colors dereddened by $E(B - V) = 0.18$. Symbols correspond to colors computed from synthetic spectra of model atmosphere. They are $L - V$ ($\wedge$), $K - V$ ($\triangle$), $H - V$ ($\star$), $J - V$ (o), $R_c - V$ ($\square$), $I_c - V$ ($\bullet$), $B - V$ ($\blacktriangle$), and $U - V$ ($\times$).

Figure 4 shows a comparison between optical and infrared broad band photometry of SN87A, with photometry computed for a sequence of model atmospheres. The data are displayed as colors, and have been dereddened by an amount $E(B - V) = 0.2$. The agreement is adequate, with the largest deviations of ~ 0.3 magnitudes occuring between the computed and observed $U - V$. Although the computed infrared to V flux ratios do appear to be systematically shifted downward relative to the observations, the infrared-infrared colors are in excellent agreement with the observations. This is explained by the fact that, because the free-free opacity in the infrared is high, the infrared continuum most nearly matches that of a blackbody at the effective photospheric temperature.

III. The Distance to SN87A

An important application of supernovae observations and models is in the use of supernovae as distance indicators via the Expanding Photosphere Method (KIRSHNER and KWAN [9]; KIRSHNER [10]; BRANCH [11]; WAGONER [12]; EASTMAN and KIRSHNER [4]). The basic idea is that if the size of the photosphere, R_{ph}, is known, and the flux emergent from the photosphere, $\mathcal{F}_\nu$, is known, then observations of the observed flux f_ν^{obs} can be used to solve for the distance. The efficacy of this method derives from the fact that one can determine the photospheric velocity and the age of the supernovae by observing the change in apparent angular diameter with time, and from the fact that the emergent flux is observed to be very nearly Planckian.

The flux emergent from the photosphere may be written as

$$\mathcal{F}_\nu = \xi_\nu \pi B(T_{c,\nu}) \qquad (2)$$

where B is the Planck function and $T_{c,\nu}$ is the continuum color temperature at frequency ν, which can be determined from spectrophotometric observations. The correction factor, ξ_ν, accounts for the fact that the emergent flux, although Planckian in its distribution, is perhaps dilute. In the analysis which follows, we will assume that $T_{c,\nu}$ is constant with frequency, and just write T_c for the color temperature and ξ for the correction factor.

Broad band photometry is often easier to obtain that spectrophotometry. Good results can be obtained using BVR_cI_c photometry, although we have also applied the method using just V and I_c. In terms of the observed, dereddened photometric magnitude, m_λ, the approximation becomes

$$m_\lambda \approx -2.5 \log \Pi - 2.5 \log \pi B_\lambda(T_c) + C_\lambda, \qquad (3)$$

where $\Pi \equiv \xi \theta^2$ and $\theta \equiv R_{ph}/D$ is the angular size of the photosphere, with D being the distance from observer to supernova. We have computed an evolutionary

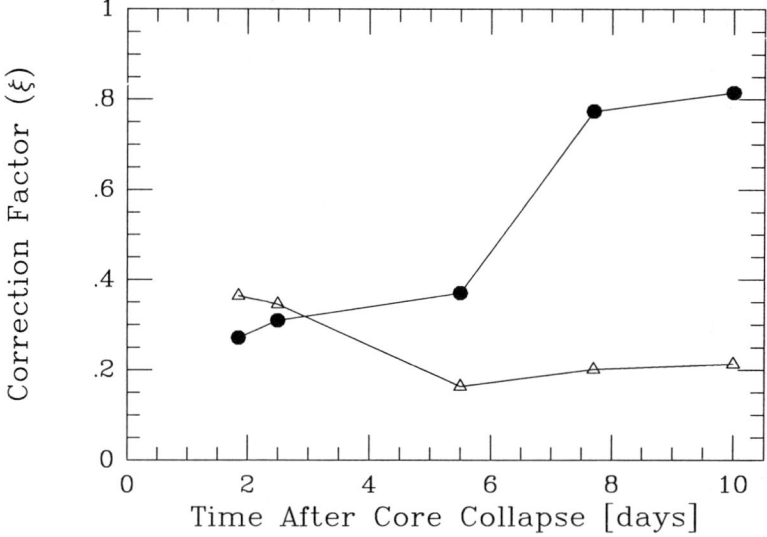

Figure 5 - Time variation of correction factors derived by fitting photometry from model atmospheres to equation (3). The filled circles correspond to correction factors derived from the BVR_cI_c magnitudes, while the triangles correspond to correction factors defined for the $(V - I_c)$ color temperature (see text).

sequence of models based on a single power law density distribution and possessing surface bolometric luminosity equal to that of SN87A. For each of these model atmospheres, we then derived a value of ξ from the computed spectrum. Figure 5 shows how the value of these correction factors change as the atmosphere expands, and both the density and the effective temperature decrease. The two curves in this figure correspond to two different sets of photometric magnitudes employed in the fit. In one case, BVR_cI_c colors were used to determine ξ (circles). At $t \lesssim 2-3$ days when the effective temperature is $\sim 10^4$ K, the emergent spectrum is highly diluted. As the photosphere cools the correction for dilution becomes less important, and the BVR_cI_c temperature fit approaches the true effective temperature of the supernova. If only the V and I_c magnitudes are used, a somewhat different behavior is found. This is shown in fig. 5 by the triangles. The explanation for this is that both the B and R bands are heavily absorbed at $t \gtrsim 5$ days, and their inclusion in the temperature fit leads to a lower value of T_c than the value obtained from just V and I_c. The lower value obtained in the former case is closer to the true effective temperature of the supernova, and so the corresponding Planck function is less dilute.

We have fit equation 3 to photometric observations of SN87A which were dereddened by an amount $E(B_V) = 0.2$. The fit gives a value for Π and T_c. The size of the photosphere was set equal to $v_{ph}t$, where t is the time since the onset of

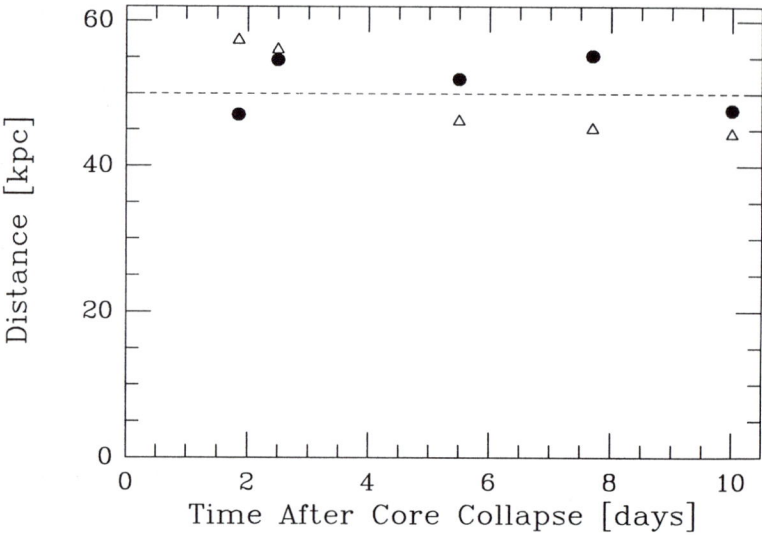

Figure 6 - Time variation of the distance derived to SN87A. The filled circles correspond to distances derived from observed BVR_cI_c magnitudes, while the triangles correspond to distances derived using only the V and I_c magnitudes. The dashed line represents the mean distance of 50 kpc obtained by the first method.

expansion and v_{ph} was determined from spectroscopic observations. The distance is given by

$$D = \sqrt{\frac{\xi}{\Pi}} v_{ph} t. \tag{4}$$

The results are shown in fig. 6, which displays the derived distance to SN87A from BVR_cI_c photometry (circles) and from just V and I_c (triangles). In the former case, the mean distance determination is 50 ± 5 kpc, while in the latter case it is 49 ± 6 kpc. These values are in good accord with the recent results of WALKER and MACK [13] who observed RR Lyrae stars in NGC 1786 and obtained an LMC distance of 49.8 kpc, and of WALKER [14], who found the distance to LMC Cepheids to be 49.4 kpc. The fact that there appears to be no strong systematic trend in the calculated distance is encouraging, especially since over the period considered, T_c changed from ~ 13000 K to ~ 6000 K, the age of the supernova increased by a factor of 5, the density dropped by a factor of 1000, and ζ varied by a factor of 4.

References

[1] Woosley, S. E., Pinto, P., and Ensman, L. 1988, *Ap.J.*, **324**, 466.

[2] Arnett, W. D. 1987, *Ap.J.*, **319**, 136.

[3] Nomoto, K., Shigeyama, T., and Hashimoto, M. 1987, in *SN 1987A*, ed. I.J. Danziger, (Garching bei Munchen: ESO), p325.

[4] Eastman, R. G. and Kirshner, R. P. 1989, *Ap.J.*, **347**, in press.

[5] Blanco, V. M. *et al.* 1987, *Ap.J.*, **320**, 589.

[6] Kirshner, R. P., Sonneborn, G., Crenshaw, D. M., and Nassiopoulos, G. E. 1987, *Ap.J.*, **320**, 602.

[7] Wamsteker, W., Panagia, N., Barylak, M., Cassatella, A., Clavel, J., Gilmozzi, R., Gry, C., Lloyd, C., van Santvoort, J., Talavera, A. 1987, *Astr. Ap.*, **177**, L21-24.

[8] Lucy, L. 1987, in *SN 1987A*, ed. I.J. Danziger, (Garching bei Munchen: ESO), p417.

[9] Kirshner, R. P. and Kwan, J. 1974, *Ap.J.*, **193**, 27.

[10] Kirshner, R. P. 1985, in *Supernovae as Distance Indicators*, ed. N. Bartel, (Berlin:Springer-Verlag), p171.

[11] Branch D. 1987, *Ap.J. (Letters)*, **320**, L23.

[10] Wagoner, R. V. 1988, in *Proceedings of the Berkeley Workshop on Particle Astrophysics*, ed. C. Pennypacker (in press).

[13] Walker, A. R. and Mack, P. 1988, preprint.

[14] Walker, A. R. 1987, *MNRAS*, **225**, 627.

Modelling the Late-Time Optical Spectra of Supernova 1987A

Douglas Swartz

Supernovae consist of up to tens of solar masses of material freely expanding into nearly empty space. This gas will rapidly cool and quickly fade from view. However, if even a fraction of a percent of this material happens to be radioactive ^{56}Ni, then the situation changes dramatically. The cold gas is now permeated with high energy photons. These γ-rays travel nearly unhindered through the gas but eventually they may strike one or several electrons and accelerate them to relativistic energies. The electrons, in turn, rip through the gas, stripping more electrons from atoms and heating the surrounding material. Eventually, when these hot electrons have lost most of their energy, they become indistinguishable in the sea of free electrons they have created. The cold gas, in the mean time, attempts to maintain its low energy state. Electrons recombine with ions, excited atoms radiate their excess energy in returning to the ground state, and thermal energy is equally partitioned among all the nearby particles. The heating by the high energy decay products is distributed among all the particles in the gas and eventually escapes through thermal processes. The spectrum we observe, therefore, is the signature of this thermal gas and contains a wealth of information about the physical state of the atmosphere.

If the equations governing these and other relevant atomic processes are solved for a model of such an atmosphere, then the physical state can be determined and the resulting spectrum computed. Spectra are then compared to observations. By implication, models which are best able to reproduce the observations represent most correctly the conditions within the supernova atmosphere. Observations of supernovae at the late-time stage of evolution are particularly useful in this regard. At late times the supernova ejecta is highly tenuous and even the deepest layers should be directly observable, at least in principle.

As a specific example, such a method is applied to SN 1987A in an effort to determine the physical characteristics of this supernova and as an independent means of testing conclusions drawn by others concerning this event.

Initial models based on hydrodynamic models discussed in the literature have been used here. These provide the density, velocity, and composition structure of the atmosphere. They represent the best currently accepted representations of SN 1987A

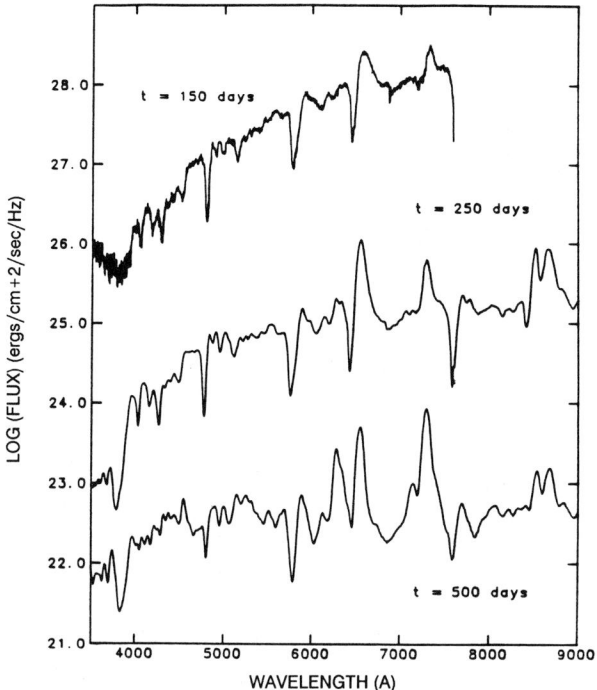

Figure 1: Observed optical spectra of SN 1987A. Spectra courtesy N. Suntzeff, CTIO.

through their ability to reproduce the known characteristics of the progenitor, the observed bolometric light curve and other properties. In the present work, these models will be shown to quantitatively reproduce the optical spectrum from 200 to 500 days. Other possible input models, such as models with different envelope masses or density distributions, have not been examined here. The effects of composition mixing and of the distribution of ^{56}Co on the emergent spectra have, however, been considered.

Figure 1 shows the observed time evolution of SN 1987A from 200 to 500 days. The spectra do not change appreciably during this time frame even though the total luminosity decreases by a factor of ≈ 20. P-Cygni type absorption features are evident indicating the presence of an underlying continuum component existing up to t>500 days. Many of the features remain at the same strength relative to the continuum throughout this phase while some strengthen ([OI] 6300-6365) and others weaken (CaII infrared triplet). All the identifiable lines are due to neutral and singly ionized species and most are associated with low lying energy levels. The electron temperature of the gas is therefore less than about 7000 to 10,000K.

Three quantities are allowed to vary in the models. These are the distribution of the elements in velocity (radial) coordinate, the distribution of radioactive ^{56}Co, and the position of a continuum emitting lower boundary. The mass distribution in velocity space is taken from the models in the literature.

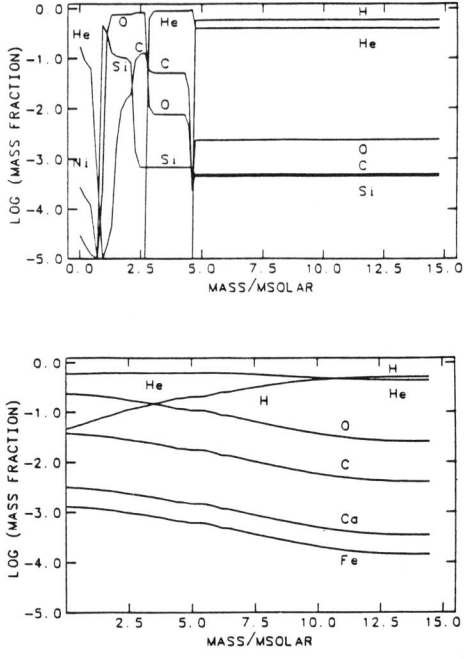

Figure 2: Composition (in mass fraction) for two models of SN 1987A.

Figure 2 illustrates the composition plotted logarithmically against the mass coordinate for a stratified (WOOSLEY [8]) and mixed (PINTO and WOOSLEY [3]) version of an $\approx 16\ M_\odot$ star containing a 6 $M_\odot$ core. The neutron star has been removed from this plot and the mass coordinate appropriately rescaled. The total mass of each element is identical in the two models.

The radioactive cobalt distribution is chosen independently of the distribution of the remaining elements as another parameter. The mass of radioactive substance is constrained to be 0.075 $M_\odot$ based on the bolometric light curve and known distance to the LMC. Radioactive cobalt (initially ^{56}Ni) is the only source of energy.

The placement of a lower, opaque, continuum-emitting boundary is also a free parameter. The use of this boundary helps to determine where the emission lines are formed by replacing line emission in the region below this boundary with a continuum flux (under the constraint of energy conservation). Implicitly, the lower boundary represents the effect one expects of many weak lines which are undoubtedly present in the optical (but which are not modelled in detail in this work) and the effect of electron scattering of radiation in broadening the lines in the observer's frame (WITTEBORN, ET AL. [7]) The shape of the continuum photon energy distribution is represented in the models as a blackbody spectrum at 5000K. The strength of the continuum is determined by the local heating rate and hence by the cobalt distribution (thus maintaining energy conservation).

Details of the models computed for comparison to observations made at 200 days, emphasizing the results for different cobalt distributions and different photosphere positions, have been discussed elsewhere (SWARTZ, HARKNESS, WHEELER [5]). Here we reiterate the basic conclusions and extend the work to later times. The best fit to the observed spectrum at 200 days occurs when the cobalt is distributed out to a Lagrangian mass point greater than 10 $M_\odot$ (corresponding to material velocities $v > 2.5 \times 10^3$ km/sec) and when the lower boundary is placed at the core/envelope interface, thus effectively obscuring the core from direct view. The cobalt is always assumed uniformly distributed below some parameterized mass point in the models. A more precise analysis using non-uniform cobalt distributions has not been undertaken.

Figure 3 illustrates the spectrum at 200 days for the mixed and unmixed models compared to the observed spectrum. There has been no scaling of the data nor the theoretical spectra, however, note the logarithmic scale. The distance to the LMC is assumed to be 50 kpc. Both models shown assume the ^{56}Co is uniformly distributed below mass point 14 $M_\odot$ and the lower boundary is placed at the core/envelope interface. These parameter values provide the best fit to the observations in both the mixed and unmixed models (SWARTZ, HARKNESS, WHEELER [5]).

The differences in the two model spectra arise from the different envelope compositions. There is a larger mass fraction of intermediate and high mass elements in the mixed model than in the stratified model. (The difference in hydrogen and helium abundance is not very significant, see Fig. 2). Metals are more efficient coolants than either hydrogen or helium and the mixed model tends to be 1500 to 2000 K (about 20 %) cooler than the unmixed model in the envelope. This shifts the bulk of the emission to lower lying energy states. This factor, combined with the increased metal abundance, is reflected in the theoretical spectrum. For example, the hydrogen H_α line is weaker in the mixed model due to the lower temperature. The [OI] 6300 Å line, in contrast, is stronger in this model because of the increased abundance and the cooler temperature which favors emission in this line. Other examples include the [CaII feature at 7300 Å which is strengthened in the cooler, higher metallicity, mixed model.

There are some features which are poorly fit in both models. Most notable is the feature at 4571 Å a semi-forbidden line of neutral magnesium. This feature is very strong in both models but is not found in emission in the observations at 200 days. The entire spectrum blueward of this feature is also poorly reproduced by the models. This is partially an artifact of the continuum shape (5000K blackbody) which was chosen principally on the basis of the observed continuum redward of 5000 Å.

The spectrum of both models are again compared to observations in Figs. 4 through 6 at 300, 400, and 500 days, respectively. The important changes occurring in the models are the decrease in density with time and the increased transparency to γ-rays. These factors act in opposition in their effect on the temperature structure. A decreased density with the same γ-ray heating rate per unit volume tends to drive the equilibrium temperature upward. The escape of γ-rays reduces the local heating rate and hence the equilibrium temperature. Prior to 500 days, neither of these factors are particularly troublesome and the spectrum evolves rather smoothly instead of shifting to the extremely low energy fine structure transitions in the far IR (AXELROD [2]). As has been described elsewhere in these proceedings, the supernova fades rapidly in the optical after 550 days and an increasing fraction of the total energy is observed at long wavelengths due in part to this effect and partially to dust.

As early as 300 days, the mixed model severely underestimates the strength in the H_α feature. The unmixed model produces a better representation of all features with the possible exception of the CaII infrared triplet at 300 days, compare particularly the FeII

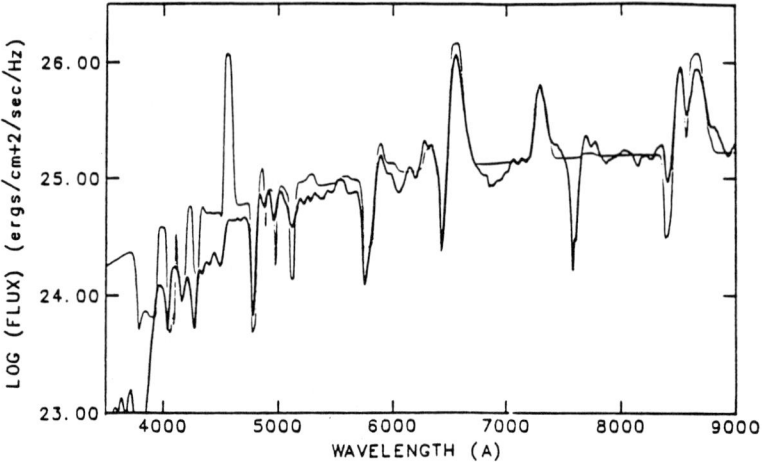

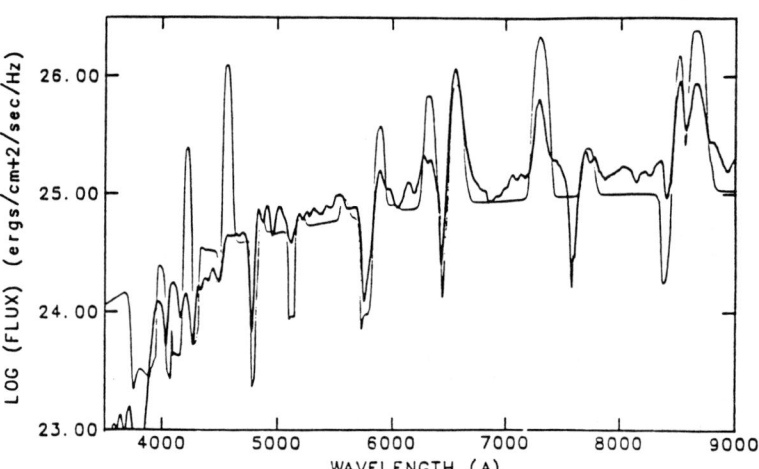

Figure 3: Spectra at 200 days comparing observations (heavy line) to unmixed (top) and mixed composition models.

Modelling Late-Time Optical Spectra

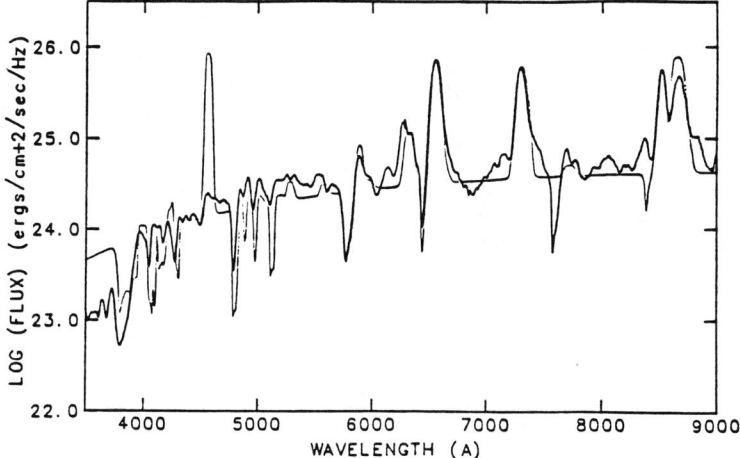

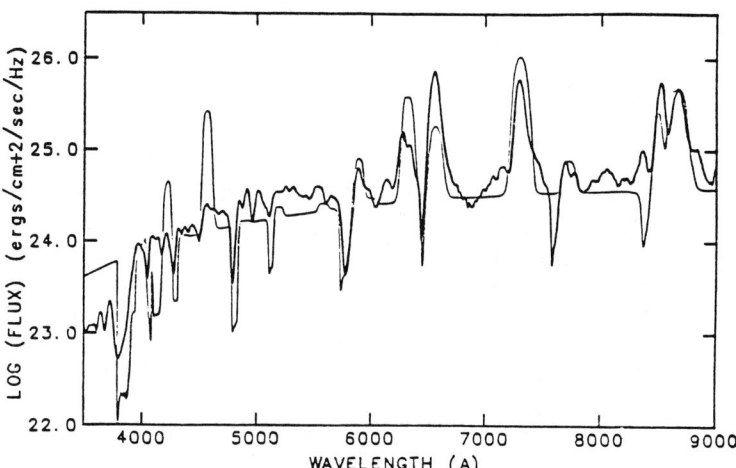

Figure 4: Spectra at 300 days

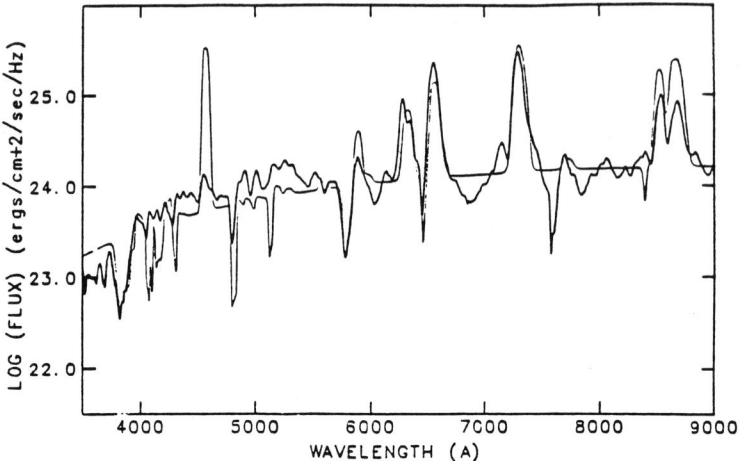

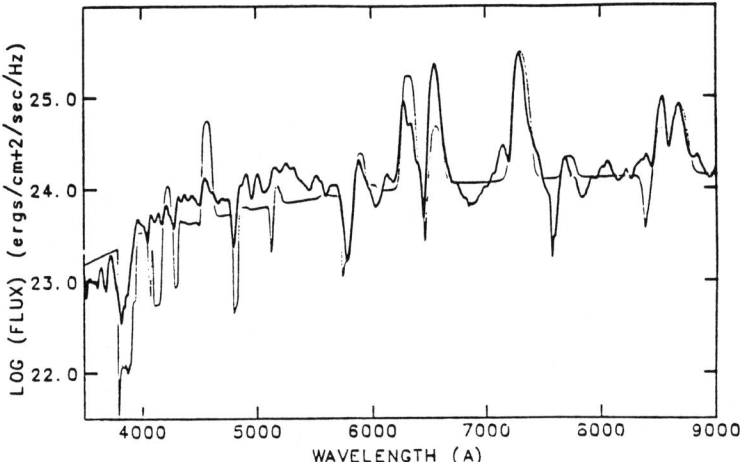

Figure 5: Spectra at 400 days

Modelling Late-Time Optical Spectra

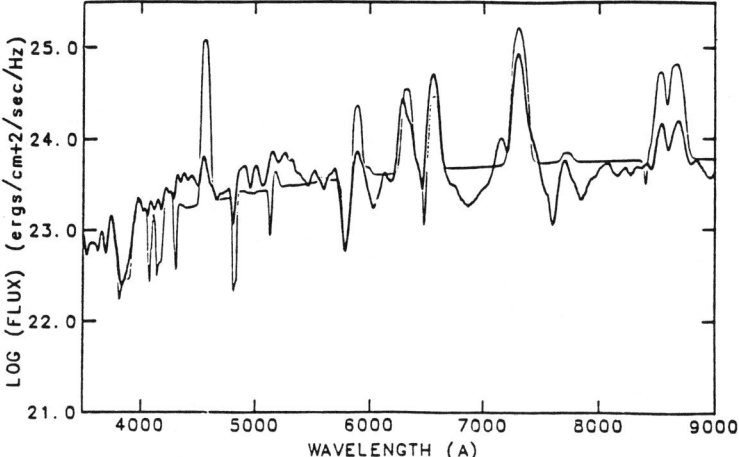

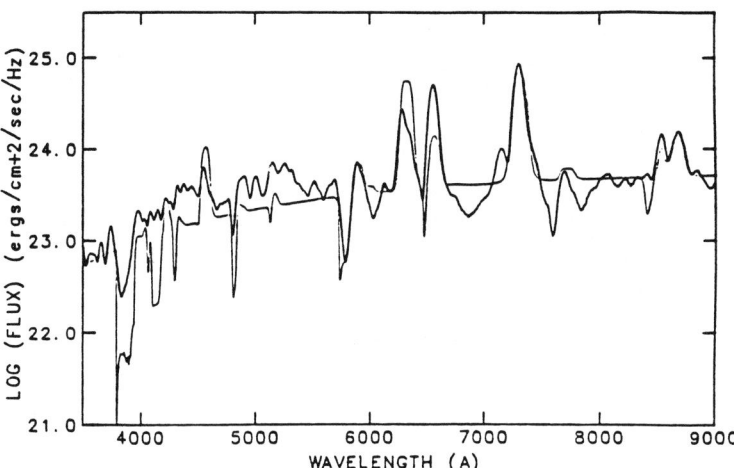

Figure 6: Spectra at 500 days

features near 5000 Å and the spectrum between 6000 and 8000 Å. The CaII infrared feature improves in the mixed model at 400 and 500 days while the stratified model fit to this feature worsens. This is also true of the NaI 5890 Å line. The opposite trend is apparent in the OI 6300 Å CaII H and K, and H_α lines. It is impossible to exclude either of the two composition mixing prescriptions on the basis of these comparisons. The unmixed model, however, provides the best overall fit during the time frame modelled here and is the preferred model in this work.

Supernova SN 1987A is the most thoroughly investigated supernova in history and the conclusions made here are discussed in context with those based on other independent research of this object.

The models assume radioactive decay of ^{56}Co is the sole source of heating in SN 1987A at late times. From observations, and the known distance to the LMC, the total mass of this element (originally ^{56}Ni) is 0.075 $M_\odot$. A sufficient amount of energy is supplied by this material to account for the observed spectrum. A similar conclusion has been reached previously for Type Ia supernovae (AXELROD [1]) and has been inferred from observations of the H_α line profile of SN 1980K (UOMOTO and KIRSHNER [6]). It has long been known that shock heating alone will not maintain the observed optical display into the late-time stage. This work shows, for the first time, that the cobalt decay energy source alone can account for the observed late-time spectrum of a Type II supernovae.

To reproduce the observed optical spectrum of SN 1987A, the cobalt must be distributed throughout a substantial fraction of the atmosphere and cannot reside in the deepest layers where it was created. This result was anticipated from investigations of the γ-ray and X-ray spectral evolution of SN 1987A, but this is the first time mixing of the cobalt has been deduced from models of the optical spectrum. For distant supernovae, the γ-ray and X-ray flux is not detectable (PINTO and WOOSLEY [4]). The optical spectrum, on the other hand, has been observed from many such supernovae. Thus models of distant supernovae using the methods presented here can determine if mixing is occurring in these objects as well or if the phenomenon is unique to events such as SN 1987A.

The novel approach of using a continuum emitting lower boundary in late-time supernova atmosphere models has led to the conclusion that the observed optical line profiles of SN 1987A arise solely from material in the envelope and that the core regions are somehow obscured from direct view (at least until 500 days). Furthermore, the best fit is obtained if the envelope retains its original composition and has not been enhanced, particularly in intermediate mass elements, through a mixing of core and envelope material.

Composition mixing was introduced in the literature in efforts to obtain better fits to the observed light curve. Mixing of ^{56}Co and other iron group elements was specifically invoked to explain the γ-ray and X-ray flux. Mixing of iron group elements into the envelope cannot be discounted in the present analysis due to the oversimplified models of the iron group ions used in this work. Based on the conclusions reached here, it appears that some mechanism exists which has enabled the radioactive material to be mixed into the envelope without disturbing the original stratification of the remaining elements. This conclusion narrows the possibilities of what that mechanism might be. If all the material were mixed, then large-scale Rayleigh-Taylor mixing could be responsible. The fact that at most only a few elements, and these originally located in the deepest layers of the ejecta, have been mixed points toward the formation of energetic Ni-rich clumps which have been able to penetrate to the outer layers.

SN 1987A shows distinctive blue-shifted absorption in the late-time spectra. These features were reproduced by placing a lower boundary in the models at the base of the hydrogen-rich envelope and this implies the existence of broad-band opacity sources which obscure the core region. Other Type II supernovae do not show the blue-shifted absorption but otherwise are very similar to SN 1987A in spectral features and in the time evolution of those features. It has been commonly assumed that the evolution of many of these features, for example the [OI] 6300 Å line, indicates the exposure of deeper layers (namely the oxygen-rich core) as the supernova expands. We have shown that this is not the case for SN 1987A. Instead, this and other features evolve in response to changes in the heating and cooling rates brought about by changes in local conditions in the envelope. That similar evolution of these features occurs in other Type IIs suggests the same mechanism is responsible in those cases as well.

This research is suppored in part by the R. A. Welch Foundation and by NSF Grant 8717166. The computations were done on the Cray X-MP of the University of Texas System Center for High Performance Computing.

References

[1] Axelrod, T.S., (1980a) PhD Thesis Univ. Calif. Santa Cruz

[2] Axelrod, T.S., (1980b) in *Type I Supernovae* ed. J.C. Wheeler (Austin:UT Press), p. 80.

[3] Pinto, P.A., Woosley, S.E., (1988a) Nature **333**,534.

[4] Pinto, P.A., Woosley, S.E., (1988b) Astrophys. J. **329**,820.

[5] Swartz, D.A., Harkness, R.P., Wheeler, J.C., (1989) Nature, **337**,439.

[6] Uomoto, A., Kirshner, R.P., (1986) Astrophys. J. **308**,685.

[7] Witteborn, F.C., Bregman, J.D., Wooden, D.H., Pinto, P.A., Rank, D.M., Woosley, S.E., Cohen, M., (1989) in press.

[8] Woosley, S.E., (1988) Astrophys. J. **330**,218.

Late Time Spectrum of SN 1987A
Yueming Xu & Richard McCray

I. Introduction

At late times ($\gtrsim$ 200 days), when the photosphere of continuum emission has disappeared from the envelope, the radiation of the supernova 1987A is powered by γ-rays resulting from ^{56}Co decays. The spectrum formation at such a late time is a highly non-linear process (XU [1]). The γ-ray photons first lose their energy due to Compton scattering and photoelectric absorption, generating non-thermal energetic electrons. These energetic electrons are then slowed down by Coulomb scattering or ionizing and exciting different ions in the envelope. The ions will recombine and de-excite, radiating away their energy in infrared (IR), optical and primarily ultraviolet (UV) wavebands. Most of the UV photons may be absorbed by photoelectric ionizations or split into photons of longer wavelengths by resonance line scatterings as they propagate through the supernova envelope. These processes continue until most of the internal luminosity is converted into optical or IR photons which can escape without further interactions. The self-consistent modeling of these processes is a coupled problem of the thermal equilibrium, ionization equilibrium and radiative transfer. No satisfactory model is available yet because the necessary atomic data set is not complete and because the envelope dynamics (such as mixing or clumping) is not clear at present.

In this paper we emphasize the importance of charge transfer, line trapping and line splitting in the spectrum formation of late-time supernovae. In §II we show that the observed hydrogen ionization of SN1987A can be explained by the photoionization from the $n = 2$ state, which is over-populated because of the Lyα trapping. Charge transfer is the main process by which hydrogen recombines and heavy elements become singly ionized. In §III we show that the line splitting process is the dominant source of opacity for photons of wavelengths less than 2000Å. Finally, in §IV we discuss the general theory of spectrum formation in late-time supernovae.

II. Envelope Ionization

The infrared continuum ($> 4\,\mu$m) emission of SN1987A in November 1987 requires an emission integral (MOSELEY et al. [2]):

$$EM^+ = \sum_z z^2 \int n_e n_z dV = 3 \times 10^{64} \text{ cm}^{-3}, \qquad (1)$$

where n_z is the number density of the ions with charge z, and n_e is the electron number density. The infrared hydrogen recombination line emissivities also require a comparable value (XU [1]).

For a homogeneous model with the chemical abundances of the model 10H given by WOOSLEY [3], the emission integral can be written as

$$\int n_e n(H^+) dV = (3.4 \times 10^{68} \text{cm}^{-3}) t_2^{-3} M_{15}^{7/2} E_{51}^{-3/2} \left(\frac{n(H^+)}{n_H}\right)^2. \quad (2)$$

where t_2 is the supernova age in units of 100 days, M_{15} is the envelope mass in units of $15 M_\odot$, and E_{51} is the total kinetic energy of the supernova in units of 10^{51} ergs. By equating (1) and (2), we estimate the hydrogen ionization fraction at ~ 300 days:

$$\frac{n(H^+)}{n_H} = 0.05 \, M_{15}^{-7/4} E_{51}^{3/4}.$$

A temperature of $T \approx 5000$ K would be sufficient to account for this ionization level in LTE, according to the Saha equation; but LTE would require a blackbody radiation field of 5000 K, which is clearly not there.

The rate of impact ionization of hydrogen atoms by thermal electrons at $T = 3000$K is far too low to explain this ionization level. The ionization cannot be explained by the non-thermal electrons resulting from γ-ray degradation, either. In fact, the total γ-ray energy available is

$$L_{Co} = (5 \times 10^{53} \text{ eV s}^{-1}) M_{Co} \exp\{-0.88 t_2\},$$

where M_{Co} is the initial mass of ^{56}Ni in units of $0.07 M_\odot$. A fraction η_i of the energy can be used to ionize hydrogen atoms. $\eta_i \leq 0.3$ for pure hydrogen gas (SHULL and VAN STEENBERG [4]), and it should be smaller for the supernova ejecta which is enriched by heavy elements. However, the hydrogen recombination rate implied by the observed recombination line strength is $R_C = \alpha^{(3)}(T) EM^+ = 4.5 \times 10^{51} T_4^{-0.92}$(s^{-1}) for Case C recombinations (McCRAY [5]; XU [1]). Therefore, the energy available for each hydrogen ionization is at most $\zeta_I = L_{Co} \eta_i / R_C = 4.2 \eta_i$(eV), which is much less than the hydrogen ionization potential 13.6 eV.

The fact that $\zeta_I \leq 4$ eV is a strong hint that the H^+ comes from excited $H^*(n = 2)$ rather than ground state hydrogen atoms. If this is true, the necessary energy per ionization is 3.4 eV, thus the fraction of fast electron energy used for hydrogen ionization must be $\eta_i \gtrsim 0.83$. This cannot happen in a pure hydrogen and helium gas where more than 30% fast electron energy is deposited as heat by Coulomb scattering (SHULL and VAN STEENBERG [4]) and there is no efficient way to turn the heat into hydrogen ionization.

In a metal-rich region, however, the radioactive energy can be used more efficiently to ionize hydrogen atoms. Most of the fast electron energy is deposited first in the excitation and ionization of heavy elements, such as Fe, because these elements have more atomic states and larger cross sections for electron collisions. The metal atoms and ions will give away the absorbed energy by emitting mostly UV photons. These photons cannot escape directly (§III), and will finally be turned into heat or hydrogen ionization. The energy deposited as heat can also excite some UV lines of metals. Thus, it is most likely that H^* is photoionized by near-UV lines ($3.4 < h\nu < 5$ eV) produced by electron impact excitation of metals such as Mg IIλ2800 (CHUGAI

[6]) and Fe II. This indirect ionization mechanism makes it possible to increase the efficiency η_i of hydrogen ionization; it is more effective than direct electron impact ionization of H^* because the metal ions are more abundant than H^* (by factors $\gtrsim 10^3$) and because the cross-sections for electron impact excitation of metals are greater than the cross-section for electron impact ionization of H^*.

The indirect ionization equilibrium can be approximated with a three-level atomic model, i.e., the ground state, the first excited state (n=2) and the continuum of hydrogen atoms. The ionization equilibrium can be written as

$$\Gamma \frac{1}{\zeta_H} n(H^0) + \xi n(H^*) = \chi_e \alpha(H^+) n(H^+), \tag{3}$$

where $\chi_e = n_e/n_T$ is the fractional number density of electrons, n_T is the total ion number density, $\alpha(H^+)$ cm^3 s^{-1} is the radiative recombination rate coefficient of H^+, ξ is a parameter representing the ratio of the UV radiation field to total density n_T, defined such that $\xi n_T n(H^*)$ is the rate of photoionization of hydrogen from the $n = 2$ state, and Γ is the ratio of energy deposition rate to atomic number density, defined such that the rate of the collisional ionization of fast electrons is $\Gamma n_T n(H^0)/\zeta_H$, ζ_H is the hydrogen ionization potential in units of eV. Assuming that about half of the γ-ray energy is deposited to ionizations, we have the collisional ionization rate coefficient:

$$\Gamma \approx (2.4 \times 10^{-16} \text{ eV cm}^3 \text{ s}^{-1}) t_2^3 M_{Co} M_{15}^{-7/2} E_{51}^{3/2} \exp\{-0.88 t_2\}. \tag{4}$$

The equilibrium equation of hydrogen excitation to the $n = 2$ state can be written as

$$\Gamma \frac{1}{\zeta_H} n(H^0) + \chi_e \alpha(H^+) n(H^+) = (\xi + \xi_c) n(H^*), \tag{5}$$

where the first term is the approximate collisional excitation rate to the $n = 2$ state by fast electrons, the second term is the radiative recombination to the $n = 2$ state, the first term on the right hand side represents the photoionization from the $n = 2$ state, and $\xi_c = \chi_e C_{21} + n_T^{-1}(A_{21}/\tau_{L\alpha} + A_{2\gamma})$ is the rate of collisional and radiative de-excitation from $n = 2$ state, C_{21} is the rate coefficient for collisional de-excitation by thermal electrons, $A_{2\gamma}$ is the two-photon emission rate from the 2s to 1s state of hydrogen atoms (NUSSBAUMER and SCHMÜTZ [7]), and $A_{21}/\tau_{L\alpha}$ is the effective Lyα emission rate corrected for resonant trapping when the Lyα optical depth $\tau_{L\alpha} \gg 1$. By solving (3) and (5), we obtain

$$\frac{n(H^+)}{n(H^0)} = \frac{\Gamma(2\xi + \xi_c)}{\zeta_H \xi_c \chi_e \alpha(H^+)}.$$

As a result, if the radiation field is weak, i.e., $\xi \ll \xi_c$, we have $n(H^+)/n(H^0) \approx 3 \times 10^{-3}$ at 300 days, which is about an order of magnitude smaller than the observations, as we have already seen from the earlier discussion of the energy budget problem. On the other hand, if the UV radiation field is strong ($\xi \gg \xi_c$) and is approximately a diluted black body emission of 5000K, we have $n(H^+)/n(H^0) \approx 0.8W$ at 300 days, where W is the dilution factor. Therefore, in order to explain the hydrogen ionization at 300 days, we need a UV radiation field within the hydrogen-metal mixed region. If this radiation can be fitted by a diluted 5000 K blackbody spectrum, the dilution factor cannot be smaller than $W = 0.06$. We know that Sobolev thick lines at the line center can have the same emissivity as a blackbody ($W = 1$) if they are effectively thick, *i.e.*, if $n_e C_{ul} \tau / A_{ul} > 1$. It is possible that there are enough thick UV lines to build the required ionizing radiation field.

The two-step mechanism of hydrogen ionization described here cannot work without the help of heavy elements. Moreover, the effect of charge transfer of hydrogen with the mixed heavy elements is to exacerbate the already puzzling problem of understanding the hydrogen ionization. Once a hydrogen atom is photoionized, it can be neutralized by charge transfer to heavy elements. If the charge transfer recombination rate is fast enough, the hydrogen ionization will be largely suppressed.

The rates of the charge transfer recombination and ionization of hydrogen can be written $C_M^r n(M) n(H^+)$ and $C_M^i n(M^+) n(H^0)$, respectively. The equation of the ionization equilibrium (3) becomes

$$\Gamma \frac{1}{\zeta_H} n(H^0) + \xi n(H^*) + C_M^i n(M^+) n(H^0) = \chi_e \alpha(H^+) n(H^+) + C_M^r n(M) n(H^+). \quad (6)$$

Thus, if the metal number density $n(M)$ is large, so that $C_M^r n(M) \gg \chi_e \alpha(H^+)$, the hydrogen ionization will be suppressed to a level much lower than would obtain without charge transfer. Even if the ionizing UV radiation field is very strong ($\xi \gg \xi_c$), the hydrogen ionization could saturate to a low value:

$$\frac{n(H^+)}{n(H^0)} = \frac{2\Gamma/\zeta_H + C_M^i n(M^+)}{C_M^r n(M)}.$$

Figure 1 shows some model calculations for the hydrogen ionization. We have assumed that the electron temperature $T = 3000$K and $\Gamma = 10^{-15}$ cm^3 s^{-1}. The model without charge transfer shows that the hydrogen ionization increases with the ionizing radiation. The totally mixed homogeneous model 10H, on the other hand, has too much charge transfer, which leads to very low hydrogen ionization, $n(H^+)/n(H^0) \lesssim 2 \times 10^{-4}$. The observed hydrogen ionization can be obtained if hydrogen atoms are mixed with only 10% of the heavy elements in the model 10H. Detailed calculations (XU [1]) show that the mixed heavy elements can be singly ionized for a long time by the charge transfer to hydrogen.

We conclude that a large fraction of the radioactive energy must be absorbed in the hydrogen-rich material, and some heavy elements must be mixed with the hydrogen gas to provide an ionizing UV radiation field, but the mass ratio of heavy elements to hydrogen cannot be larger than 5% in the mixed region. How can this model be possible? According to standard supernova models, most of the γ-ray sources, ^{56}Co nuclei, are within the central region which is enriched in heavy elements. Most of the UV photons ($h\nu > 3.4$ eV) cannot avoid photoabsorption in this metal-rich layer, thus the hydrogen atoms in the outer layers would not be exposed to enough photoionizing flux to maintain the observed hydrogen ionization. The probable solution to this puzzle is that most of the heavy elements (including ^{56}Co) in the supernova ejecta are clumped and the hydrogen is mixed into the interior region; thus γ-rays generated in the ^{56}Co knots can escape directly to the hydrogen-rich gas and deposit energy there by Compton scattering. Actually, the fact that the heavy element knots are observed in some supernova remnants, such as Cas A, support this clumpy model of the supernova ejecta. X-ray observations of this supernova also show properties of a clumpy model (KUMAGAI *et al.* [8]; XU [1]).

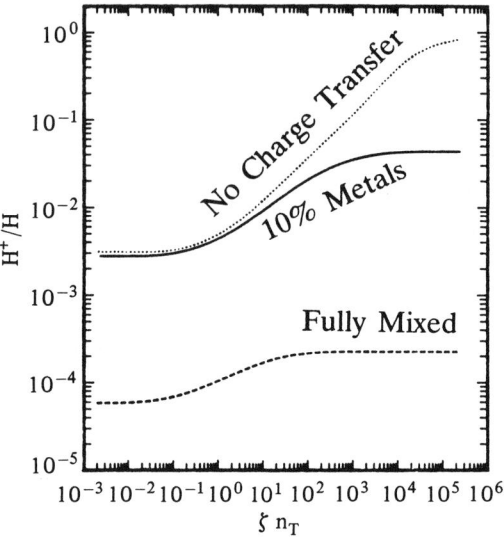

Figure 1: Hydrogen ionization.

III. Emergent Spectrum

In the late-time supernova envelope, strong EUV ($\lambda < 2000$Å) lines, such as He I $\lambda 584$ and H Lyα, are generated by the collisions of fast electrons (XU [1]). These photons cannot escape because the envelope has a large scattering opacity produced by many broad overlapping resonance lines of species such as Fe I and Fe II (McCRAY [5]; XU [1]). In fact, a photon of wavelength λ can be scattered by all lines with wavelength $\lambda' \in [\lambda, \lambda + \lambda_{exp}]$, where $\lambda_{exp} = \lambda v_{exp}/c$ is the redshift at the surface of the expanding envelope. In the Sobolev approximation (MIHALAS [9]), the direct escape probability through the resonant scattering region of line i is $P_i = \exp\{-\tau_i\}$, where τ_i is the Sobolev optical depth of the line i. Thus, the probability for a photon of wavelength λ to escape directly from the envelope can be written as

$$P_0(\lambda) = \exp\left\{-\sum_{\lambda_i > \lambda}^{\lambda_i < \lambda + \lambda_{exp}} \tau_i\right\}. \tag{7}$$

In general, photons can escape after resonant scatterings if the destruction probability in Sobolev layers is small. Since the effect of the multiple scatterings in a geometrically thin Sobolev layer is the same as that of one scattering at a point in space, we can assume that the effective number of the resonant scatterings by line i is $1 - \exp\{-\tau_i\}$ as far as the spatial diffusion is concerned. Thus, the mean redshift before the next scattering, $\delta\lambda$, of a photon of wavelength λ can be defined such that

$$\sum_{\lambda_i > \lambda}^{\lambda_i < \lambda + \delta\lambda} \left(1 - e^{-\tau_i}\right) = 1. \tag{8}$$

As a result of the diffusion process, the total wavelength redshift $\Delta\lambda$ of an emergent photon can be much larger than λ_{exp}. The redshift $\Delta\lambda$ can be calculated as follows. We use (8) to calculate the mean free path $\delta\lambda_0 = \delta\lambda$ of a photon with initial wavelength $\lambda_0 = \lambda$, and then obtain the mean wavelength after one scattering, $\lambda_1 = \lambda_0 + \delta\lambda_0$. With this procedure, we calculate the wavelength after n scatterings, $\lambda_n = \lambda_{n-1} + \delta\lambda_{n-1}$ for $n = 2, 3$, etc. Photons will diffuse out from the envelope when

$$\left(\frac{v_{exp}}{c}\right)^2 = \sum_{i=0}^{n_s}\left(\frac{\delta\lambda_i}{\lambda_i}\right)^2, \qquad (9)$$

where n_s is the total number of scatterings. UV radiation becomes transparent only if the total redshift $\Delta\lambda = \sum_{i=0}^{n_s}(\delta\lambda_i) < \lambda$. n_s decreases rapidly with the envelope temperature because the Sobolev depths of the lines corresponding to transitions between excited states decrease exponentially with the temperature. n_s also depends on the initial photon wavelength. The envelope will first become transparent at some wavelength "windows", where scattering lines are neither numerous enough nor thick enough to scatter UV photons.

In Figure 2, we plot the number of resonant scatterings n_s calculated from (9) for temperatures of 3000K and 500K. Here, we considered all the abundant element in the model 10H, but we artificially homogenized the chemical abundances throughout the envelope. We took the ionization fractions from the calculations in the last section except for Fe atoms, which we took the observed value, 50% (OLIVA et al. [10]). We used $\sim 58{,}000$ lines of the 20 important ions from the line list of ABBOTT and LUCY [11]. But, most of the important lines are from Fe I and Fe II. At 3000K, photons with wavelength less than 5800Å cannot escape without scattering, and thus the fast pulsations of a possible central source (if it exists) would be smeared out. However, the redshift of UV photons is not large enough to shift the photons to the optical waveband. In fact, the scattering number is $n_s \approx 200$, and thus the total redshift is $\Delta\lambda/\lambda \approx \sqrt{n_s}v_{exp}/c \sim 0.1$. At 500K, UV photons can escape directly through the windows at wavelengths $\lambda > 2500$Å.

Photons can be destroyed during the Sobolev scattering. Once an atom is excited by absorbing a UV photon, it may cascade down, splitting into several different photons. We find that the radiative splitting is the dominant destruction process. For simplicity, we assume that scatterings of the surviving photons are coherent in the comoving frame of the expanding envelope. XU [1] proved that the escape probability of a photon from the resonant region of the line i is given by

$$P_i = e^{-(1-\eta_i)s_i}, \qquad (10)$$

where s_i is the survival probability of the photon in one scattering. Thus, the total probability for a photon of wavelength λ to escape from an expanding envelope is

$$P_{esc}(\lambda) = \exp\left\{-\sum_{\substack{\lambda_i > \lambda}}^{\lambda_i < \lambda + \Delta\lambda}(1-\eta_i)\tau_i\right\}. \qquad (11)$$

In Figure 3, we plot the total escape probability (11) together with the escape probability (10) of single lines at 3000K. One sees that no photon with wavelengths less than 4500Å can escape directly from the envelope at 3000K. However, the envelope will become more transparent when the temperature decreases. We compared

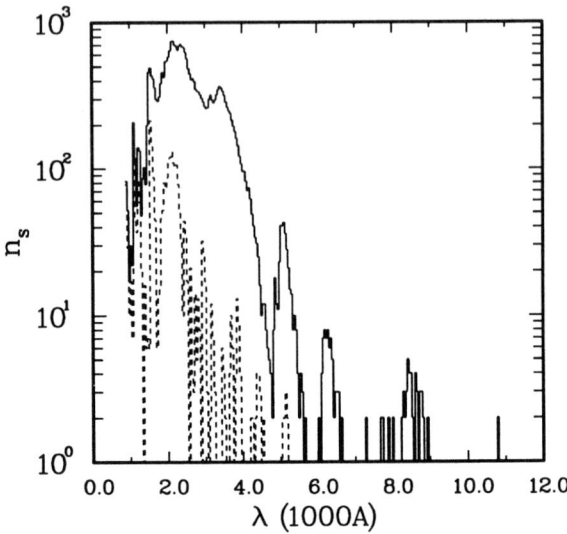

Figure 2: Number of resonant line scatterings in the envelope with expansion velocity $v_{exp}/c = 0.01$. Solid line: T = 3000K, $n_b = 2.4 \times 10^{10} \text{cm}^{-3}$; Dashed line: T = 500K, $n_b = 2.7 \times 10^9 \text{cm}^{-3}$.

P_{esc} with P_0 and found only small differences, which means that photon splitting is a much more common process than coherent line scatterings, *i.e.*, most photons are destroyed by line splitting during resonant scatterings.

We simulated the line scattering and splitting processes in the envelope of the homogenized model 10H by use of the Monte Carlo technique. We assumed that the envelope has a baryon number density of $n_b = 2.4 \times 10^{10} \text{cm}^{-3}$, and the level population of the ions is in LTE at the temperature of 3000K. We believe that these conditions are representative of the inner ejected material of SN1987A at 300 days. In our calculation, the line source function consists of the thermal emission, recombination lines and lines excited by fast electrons. We used the Bethe approximation to estimate the latter (XU [1]). The emergent spctrum (Figure 4) shows no strong source lines at wavelengths less than 2000Å. These lines have split and the energy has been redistributed to the wavelength range $\gtrsim 3000$Å as a quasi-continuum. The observed spectrum (PHILLIPS [12]) in December 1987 showed a similar quasi-continuum emission in the waveband of 4000Å to 5500Å but was black at the wavelength less than 4000Å. In fact, the photons of wavelength less than 3646Å shown in Figure 4 provide a necessary ionizing UV radiation field for hydrogen ionization as discussed in the last section. In the Monte Carlo calculation, we did not include the continuum absorption due to the photoionization of hydrogen atoms from the $n = 2$ state.

The three predominant lines in the wavelength range 6000Å to 9000Å in Figure 4 correspond to the observed strong lines: [OI]$\lambda\lambda$6300 and H$\alpha\lambda$6563, Ca II]$\lambda\lambda$7324 and Ca II $\lambda\lambda$8662. However, the calculated line ratios do not agree with the observations because our one-zone model is too simple. In fact, since Hα is very thick at 300 days,

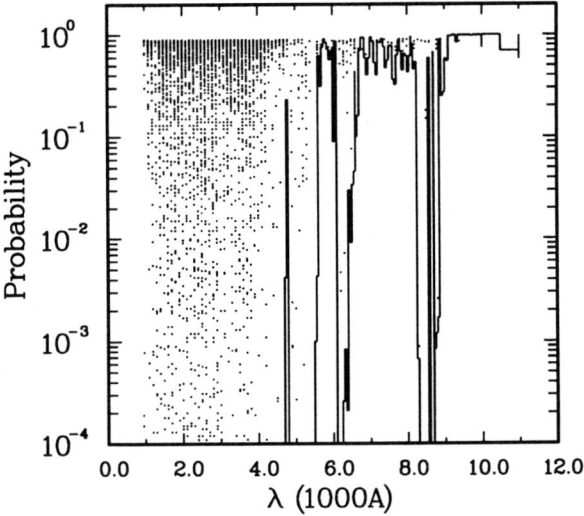

Figure 3: Total escape probability from the envelope with expansion velocity $v_{exp}/c = 0.01$. T = 3000K, $n_b = 2.4 \times 10^{10} \text{cm}^{-3}$. Solid line is the probability from the envelope; dots are for single lines.

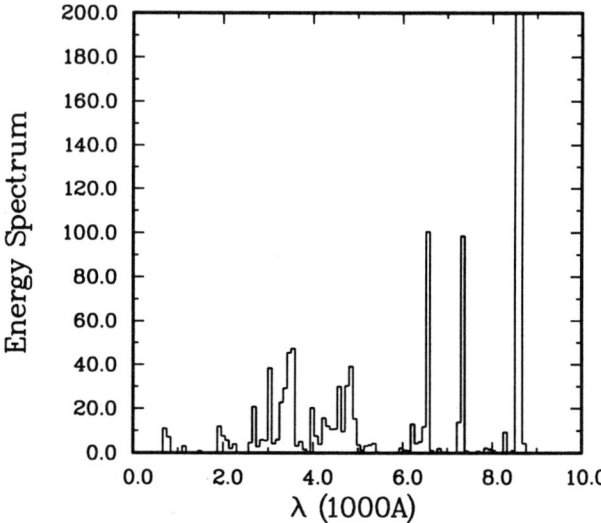

Figure 4: Emergent spectrum calculated for a typical model at 300 days.

it can be emitted from a much larger region than the Ca II lines, and so can be much stronger than in our model calculation. An alternate explanation is that Ca II is not so abundant in the main emission region, so the Ca II lines can be weaker than the model calculation. [OI]$\lambda\lambda$6300 and Ca II]$\lambda\lambda$7324 are forbidden lines connected to ground states. These lines can be thermally excited. Ca II $\lambda\lambda$8662 can also be thermally excited because Ca II H, K lines are trapped, or it can be pumped by the Ca II H, K lines ($\lambda\lambda$3968) or other high energy processes, such as fast electron excitations. If Ca II $\lambda\lambda$8662 is thermally excited, its line ratio to Ca II] $\lambda\lambda$7324 must depend on the electron temperature.

In summary, our simple model calculation has shown the basic features of the observed spectrum. The photon splitting process will destroy all photons of wavelengths less than 2000Å and redistribute the energy to the wavelength range $\gtrsim$ 3000Å. Photons of wavelengths greater than 2000Å cannot be destroyed by splitting because even if a photon splits, it will result in a photon with similar wavelength, and so it must diffuse out if there is no other absorption processes. However, the photoionization of hydrogen atoms from the $n = 2$ state can absorb all photons of wavelengths $\leq$3646Å. The emission of Ca II $\lambda\lambda$8662 is an example of the line splitting.

IV. Discussion

Up to now, the charge transfer and line splitting processes have been neglected in the theory of the spectrum formation in late-time supernovae. We have shown that both of these processes are crucial to the envelope structure and the emergent line spectrum, although our calculations are very preliminary. The current theory of the spectrum formation includes four basic problems: (1) how γ-rays deposit their energy within the supernova envelope; (2) how the subsequent fast electrons deposit their energy among excitations, ionizations and heating; (3) how charge transfer affects the ionization equilibrium; and (4) how the line splitting affects the radiative transfer with non-local coupling.

The former two are basic physics problems, and can be solved separately and accurately. The γ-ray energy deposition can be accurately calculated by the Monte Carlo simulation of the Comptonization (XU et al. [13]; SHULL and XU [14]). The key to the accuracy of the γ-ray deposition function is the spatial distribution of ^{56}Co, which can be inferred from the light curves of X-rays and γ-rays. The energy degradation of fast electrons can be calculated from the Spencer-Fano equation (SPENCER and FANO [15]; XU [1]), although the accuracy of the calculation is limited by the lack of knowledge of the cross sections for collisional excitations and ionizations, especially for heavy elements. In future research, more detailed work needs to be done in this field, including the collection of the cross sections.

The thermal and ionization equilibria are closely coupled with the radiative transfer of spectral lines. The charge transfer and line splitting processes add complexity to this already non-linear problem. The charge transfer tends to suppress the hydrogen ionization and to keep the heavy elements singly ionized. It is clear that more accurate atomic data for charge transfer are required to improve the calculation of the ionization equilibrium in supernovae. The incoherent line scattering will destroy all EUV photons ($\lambda <$ 2000Å) and redistribute the energy into longer wavelengths, which makes the radiative transfer harder to calculate accurately. Since there is no continuum radiation field in late-time supernova envelope, the Monte Carlo technique

(ABBOTT and LUCY [11]) is not efficient for solving iteratively the radiative transfer here. RYBICKI and HUMMER [16] developed a Sobolev approach to treat the line transfer with non-local coupling. This approach may be generalized to include the continuous absorption and line splitting processes.

The ultimate goal of the theory of spectrum formation in late-time supernovae is to calculate the emergent spectrum and its evolution from basic principles. However, the purpose of theoretical modeling is not just to fit the observational data, but to understand the physics implied by the observations. The comparison of theories and observations can help us to understand the structure and the chemical abundances of the ejected material. But, given the incompleteness of atomic data and the uncertainties about the interior dynamics of the supernova, we do not think that it would be successful to try a pure theoretical modeling at present. Therefore, in our future research, we should continue to work from observations of line ratios and line profiles to deduce more information about the properties of the supernova interior.

References

1. Y. Xu: *Ph. D. Thesis*, University of Colorado, Boulder (1989).
2. S. H. Moseley, E. Dwek, R. F. Silverberg, W. J. Glaccum, J. R. Graham, R. F. Loewenstein: *Ap. J.*, (1989), in press.
3. S. E. Woosley: *Ap. J.*, **330**, 218 (1988).
4. J. M. Shull, M. E. Van Steenberg: *Ap. J.*, **298**, 268 (1985).
5. R. McCray: In *Molecular Processes in Astrophysics*, ed. by T. H. Hartquist, (Cambridge University Press, 1989), in press.
6. N. N. Chugai: *Soviet Astron. Lett.*, **13**(4), 282 (1987).
7. H. Nussbaumer, W. Schmütz: *Astron. Astrophys.*, **138**, 495 (1984).
8. S. Kumagai, T. Shigeyama, K. Nomoto, M. Itoh, J. Nishimura, S. Tsuruta: *Ap. J.*, (1989), submitted.
9. D. Mihalas: *Stellar Atmosphere*, (San Franciso: W. H. Freeman and Company, 1978).
10. E. Oliva, A. F. M. Moorwood, I. J. Danziger: In *Proc. 22nd ESLAB Symp. on Infrared Spectroscopy in Astronmy*, ed. by H. Glasse, M. S. Kessler, and R. Gonzales-Riesta, (ESA SP, 1988) p. 270.
11. D. C. Abbott, L. B. Lucy: *Ap. J.*, **288**, 679 (1985).
12. M. M. Phillips: In *Supernova 1987A in the Large Magellanic Cloud*, ed. by M. Kafatos, and A. Michalitsianos, (Cambridge: Univ. Press, 1988), p. 16.
13. Y. Xu, P. G. Sutherland, R. McCray, R. R. Ross: *Ap. J.*, **327**, 197 (1988).
14. J. M. Shull, Y. Xu: In *Supernova 1987A in the Large Magellanic Cloud*, ed. by M. Kafatos, and A. Michalitsianos, (Cambridge: Univ. Press, 1988), p. 371.
15. L. V. Spencer, U. Fano: *Phys. Rev.*, **93**, 1172 (1954).
16. G. H. Rybicki, D. G. Hummer: *Ap. J.*, **219**, 654 (1978).

A Comparison of Carbon Deflagration Models for SN Ia

Robert Harkness

The observational properties of Type Ia supernovae can be qualitatively explained in terms of the explosion of a carbon-oxygen white dwarf. For several years this hypothesis has gained support although there seems to be no clear understanding of how the white dwarf evolves to the appropriate conditions. Furthermore, the details of how degenerate carbon ignition occurs, and how the burning propagates are quite controversial. Recent studies on very fine mass scales tend to show that detonation is inevitable for one-dimensional models. Such a detonation, once formed, incinerates the entire star, leaving no significant quantity of the intermediate mass elements which are required in quantity to reproduce the observed spectra for the first two to three weeks following the explosion.

Carbon deflagration models are attractive because the subsonic burning allows the white dwarf to expand ahead of the burning front so combustion occurs at lower densities. This results in a partially burned layer surrounding the core and can also cause the nuclear burning to cease before reaching the surface of the star.

Four carbon deflagrations are considered here, two models computed by WOOSLEY and WEAVER [1] (models G7 and F7, corresponding to their models 2 and 3, respectively), and two computed by NOMOTO, THIELEMANN and YOKOI [2], (models C6 and W7), incorporating the revised nucleosynthesis calculations of THIELEMANN, NOMOTO and YOKOI [3]. These two sets of models each use a different prescription for the propagation of the deflagration front. In Woosley's models the burning velocity is determined by limiting the rate of increase of the convective luminosity coupling the burning zone and the next unburned zone. This tends to produce a deflagration which propagates at a roughly constant fraction of the sound speed. In the models of Nomoto et al. the flame speed is determined by a time-dependent mixing-length theory, where the mixing length is taken to be a constant fraction of the pressure scale height. This has the consequence that the deflagration wave propagates initially very slowly and accelerates towards the surface of the white dwarf. In both cases the prescription is arbitrary and amounts to no more than a convenient parameterization of the front velocity. Details of the four models are given in the table below.

At first glance it might seem that there is little to choose between these four explosion models, particularly if one examines the abundance distribution as a function of the mass coordinate. If, however, one examines the abundance distribution as a function of velocity (or radius) after the expansion becomes homologous, there are clear distinctions and these are reflected in the emergent spectrum near maximum light (see Figures 1 to 4).

The emergent spectrum is dependent upon not only the abundance distribution, but also on the gamma ray deposition function (which in turn is dependent on the ^{56}Ni distribution, the total mass of ^{56}Ni, the density profile and the expansion velocity). In earlier calculations of the maximum light spectrum of model W7, BRANCH et al. [4] found that their synthetic spectra could be improved if the partially burned matter with expansion velocity greater than about 10,000 km/s was homogenized. Calculations by HARKNESS [5] of model atmospheres based on model W7 reached the same conclusion and similar prescriptions for mixing are considered for each of the models presented here.

Model	C6	W7	G7	F7
E_k ($\times 10^{51}$ ergs)	0.91	1.30	1.04	1.73
ρ ($\times 10^9$ gm/cm^3)	1.5	2.6	2.1	2.1
$M/M_\odot$	1.366	1.378	1.40	1.40
M_{Ni}	0.48	0.58	0.51	0.89
$M_{C/O}$	0.4	0.08	0.4	0
$M_{Ni/Fe}$	0.66	0.89	0.85	1.25
$V_{partial}$ (km/s)	6500-10000	9000-15000	9500-11000	14300-17000

All of the explosion models provided by their authors were terminated at a few seconds after the explosion. Their subsequent evolution was computed with a Lagrangian hydrodynamics code with flux-limited diffusion, using Rosseland mean opacities calculated from the detailed composition of the model. The gamma ray deposition is calculated from a solution of the radiative transfer equation in co-moving coordinates, assuming the gamma ray opacity is purely absorptive with $\kappa = 0.03$ cm^2/gm.

The spectrum of each model was then computed at 14 days after the explosion using the supernova radiative transfer code described in HARKNESS[5] and WHEELER and HARKNESS [6]. The effects of mixing were simulated by artificially homogenizing the composition above a particular expansion velocity, usually taken to be at the point where the composition changes from the products of nuclear statistical equilibrium (NSE) to the products of partial burning. Approximately 400 of the strongest resonance lines are included in the calculations described here.

Model W7 provides an excellent match to the maximum light spectrum of SN1981B. The combined IUE and McDonald Observatory data (BRANCH et. al [7]) span the wavelength range 1500 - 8500Å and model W7 is in excellent agreement throughout this range (see figure 5). All of the observed spectral features can be accounted for using the original composition profile. When the matter with expansion velocity in excess 11,000 km/s is homogenized the fit in the near ultraviolet is improved, although the optical potion of the spectrum fits slightly less well. This is principally due to the effects of mixing a small amount of iron and cobalt from the NSE region out to high velocity. The observed absorption feature at 3300Å is most easily accounted for by a number of Co II lines. Unfortunately, this feature is located near the ground-based optical cutoff and slightly beyond the long wavelength sensitivity of IUE. Confirmation of this absorption in other SN Ia should be considered a high priority.

Calculations performed after the conference indicate that when sufficient numbers of

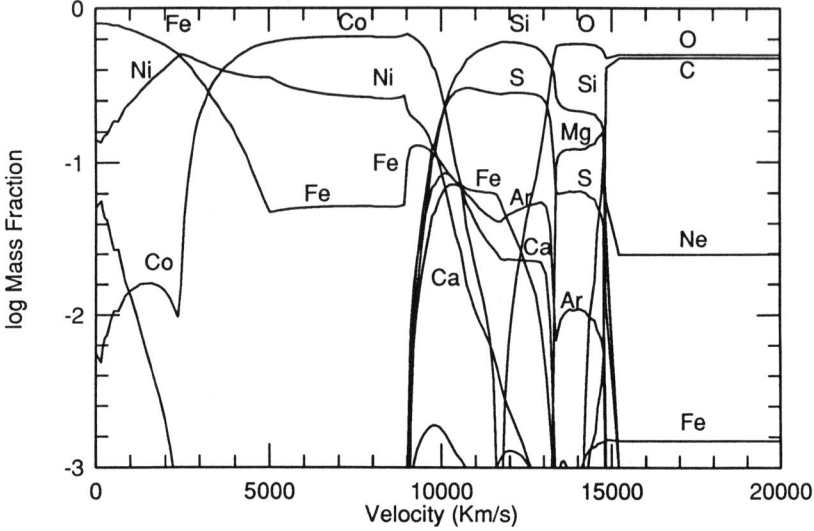

Figure 1: Abundance profile at 14 days for unmixed model W7.

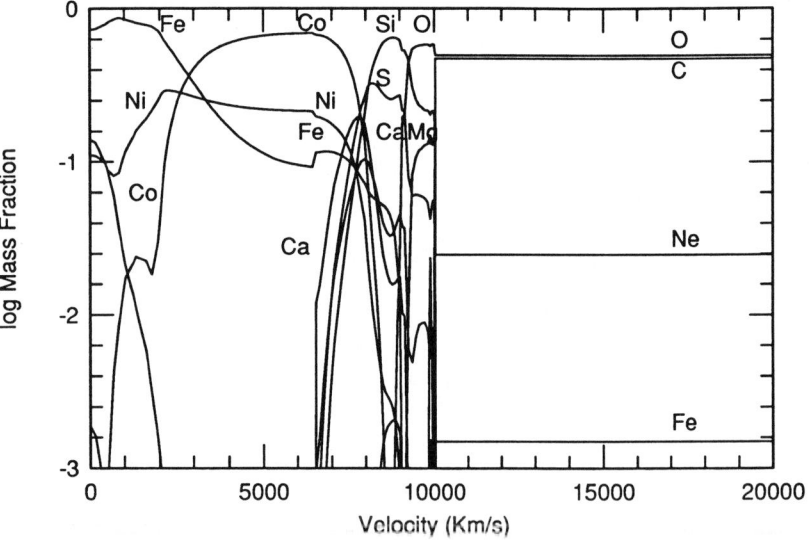

Figure 2: Abundance profile at 14 days for unmixed model C6.

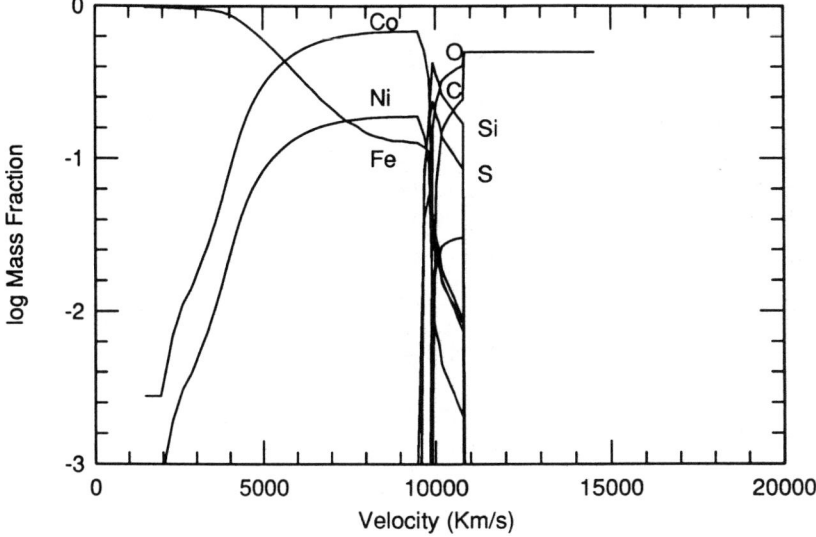

Figure 3: Abundance profile at 14 days for unmixed model G7.

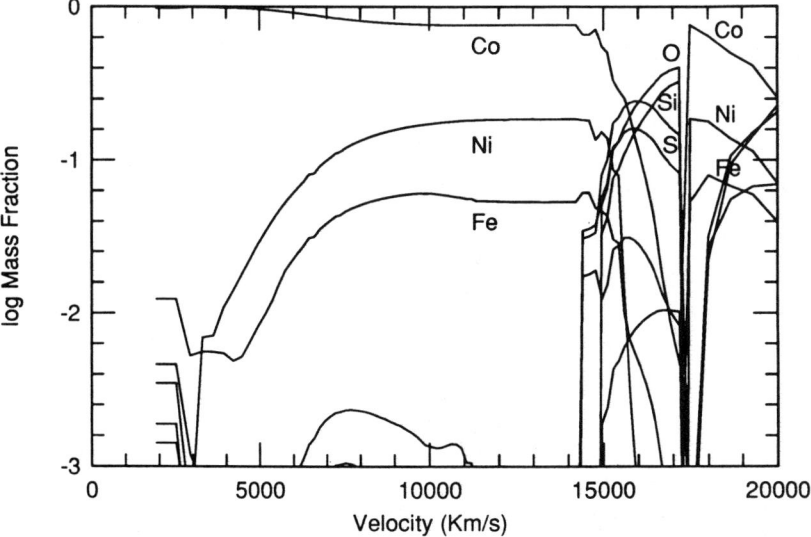

Figure 4: Abundance profile at 14 days for unmixed model F7.

spectral lines are included in the ultraviolet, the emergent spectrum of the *unmixed* W7 model may be superior at all wavelengths to the version which is mixed for velocities greater than 11,000 km/s. This is in contradiction to the previous results of BRANCH et. al [4] and HARKNESS [5].

The spectral evolution of model W7 has been computed in some detail, and will be presented elsewhere. The spectra change slowly from 4 days to around 16 days, when the NSE region is uncovered. The spectrum then changes extremely rapidly to become totally dominated by lines due to Fe II, together with minor features due to Co II and other iron-group elements.

Model C6 gives a good optical spectrum only when the intermediate mass elements are mixed for expansion velocities greater than 6,500 km/s (see figure 6). In the unmixed case the large mass of unburned C/O ($0.4 M_\odot$) provides a greater number of free electrons per gram and the electron scattering surface is situated in this unburned layer. While the mixed model accounts for the presence of most of the observed spectral features, the lines all occur at longer wavelengths than observed in the case of SN1981B. It is possible that the mixed C6 model could be a decent fit to some of the slow SN Ia.

Comparing figures 2 and 3, one might expect the spectra of models C6 and G7 to be quite similar, but this is not the case. Like C6, model G7 has a large amount of unburned C/O and the unmixed spectrum shows essentially a continuum with a few weak line of oxygen and carbon. The principal differences between C6 and G7 are the density structure and the relative distribution of the Ni^{56}. G7 has a higher density in the unburned layer than C6, and the Ni^{56} is located in a shell immediately below this layer, and the local heating rate is higher. The intermediate mass elements lie in a very narrow shell which is much too restricted in velocity space. Even when the model is mixed from the base of this layer (V > 9,500 km/s) it provides an unsatisfactory spectrum because the kinetic energy of the outer layers is too low (figure 7).

The final model, F7, provides an interesting constraint. The intermediate mass elements occur at high expansion velocity, which alone might be expected to produce a spectrum incompatible with observations. However, as the shock wave propagated through the outer layers of this model, the deflagration became a detonation, burning the outer layers to NSE at very high expansion velocities (V > 17,000 km/s). The net result is a high velocity layer of the intermediate mass elements sandwiched between the core NSE region, and a very high velocity surface NSE region. The resulting large mass of Ni^{56} produces the largest gamma ray deposition of the four models. The spectra of the unmixed model and a model mixed from the base of the partially burned region are almost indistinguishable because the spectra are always dominated by iron group elements and Fe II in particular (figure 8). Furthermore, the spectrum evolves far too rapidly to be a viable model for normal SN Ia.

From this comparison of four current deflagration models we can draw the following conclusions:

1. The amount of Ni^{56} produced in the explosion should probably not exceed $\approx 0.8 M_\odot$, and should not be thoroughly mixed with the partially burned matter. Model W7 also produces an excellent light curve, so around $0.6 M_\odot$ may be optimum.

2. It seems a major reason for the success of model W7 is that the partial burning extends almost to the surface. As it is, W7 would be even better if the burning DID extend to the surface, producing more magnesium. In this case it appears that the artificial mixing may prove to be unnecessary. Clearly, a large mass of C/O should not remain.

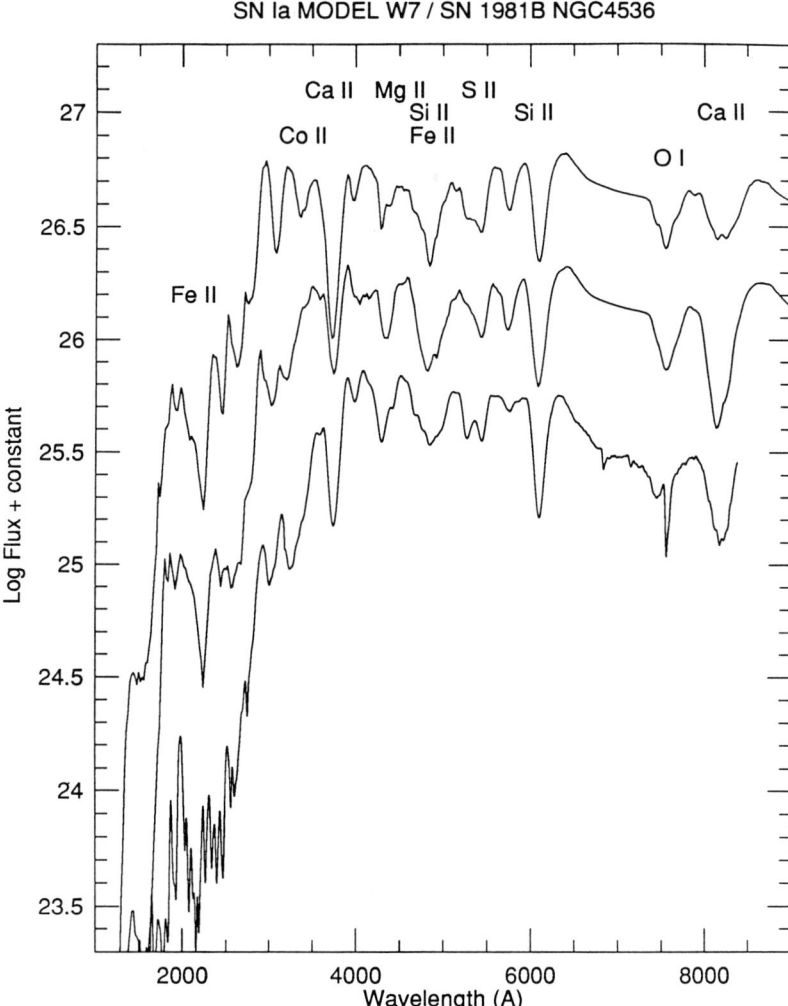

Figure 5: Emergent spectra of model W7 at 14 days, with no mixing (top) and mixing for V > 11,000 km/s (middle) compared with the maximum light spectrum of SN1981B.

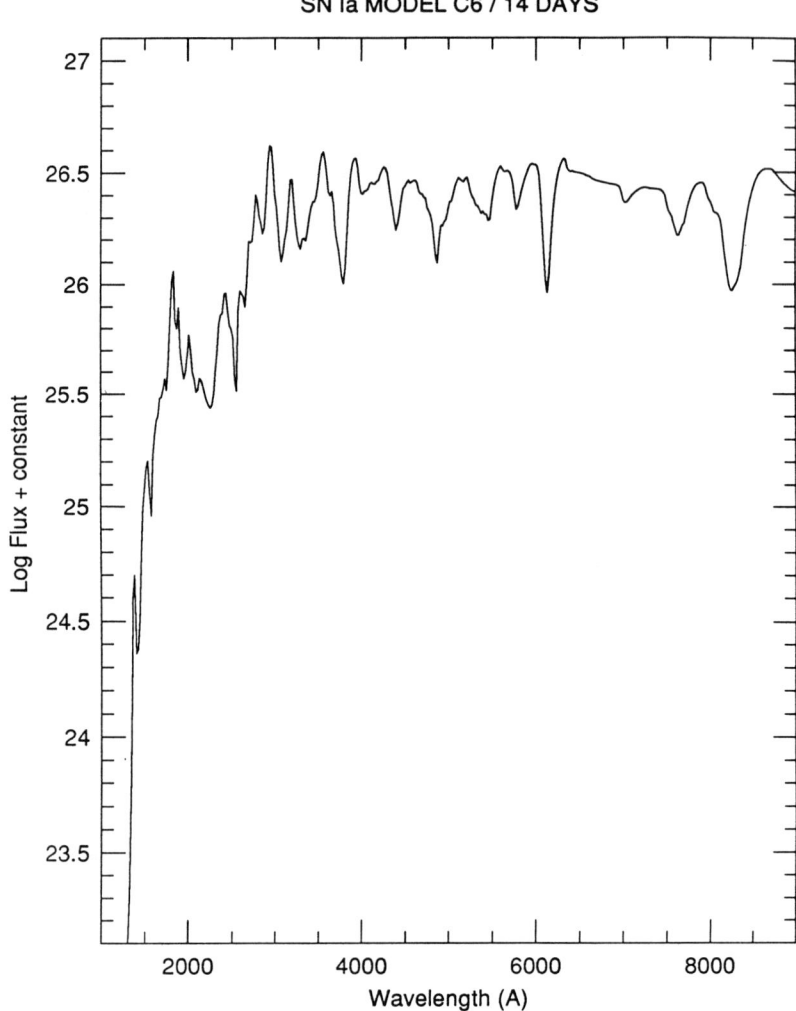

Figure 6: Emergent spectrum of model C6 at 14 days, with mixing for V > 6,500 km/s.

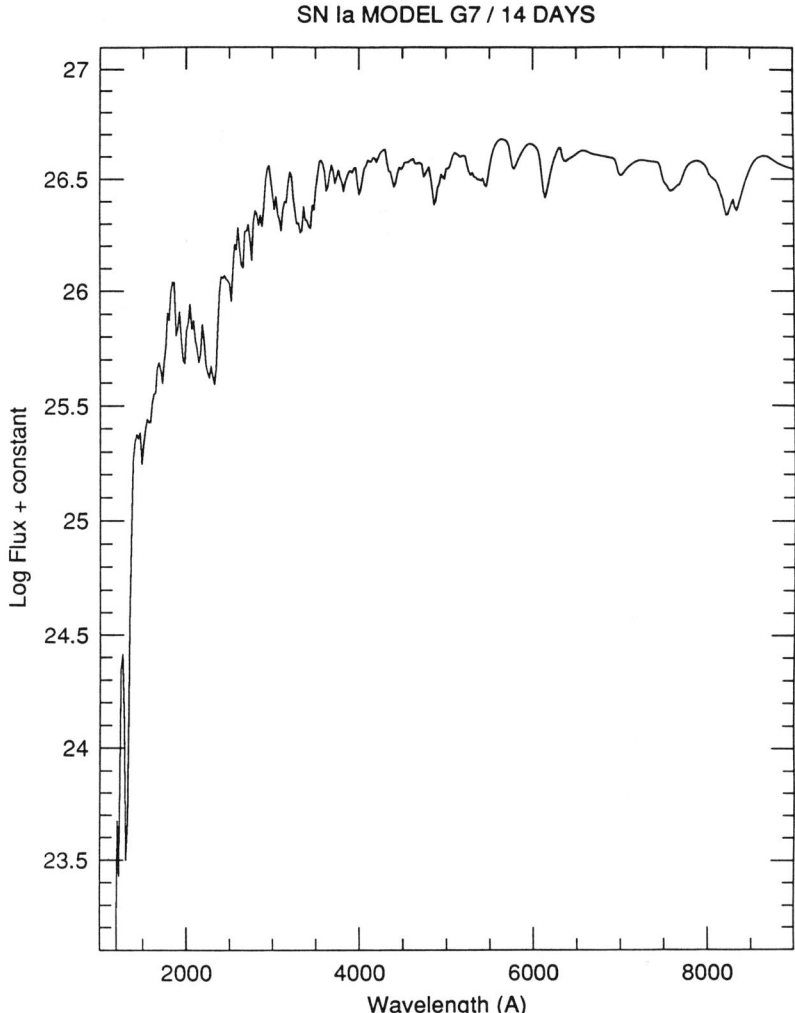

Figure 7: Emergent spectrum of model G7 at 14 days, with mixing for V > 9,500 km/s.

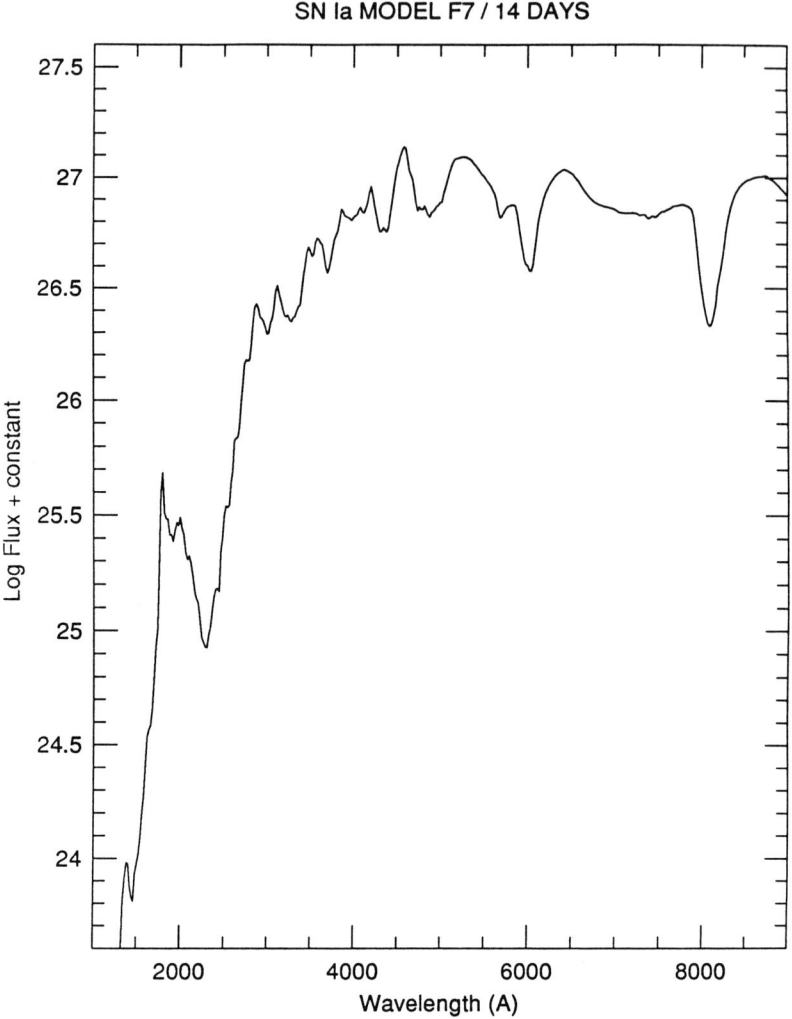

Figure 8: Emergent spectrum of model F7 at 14 days, with mixing for V > 14,000 km/s.

3. The intermediate mass elements resulting from the partial burning must be distributed over a large range of expansion velocity, with minimum velocity $V > 8$-$10,000$ km/s. The NSE products should occur at lower velocity. The more gradual transition from NSE seen in models C6 and W7 seems to produce better spectra.

I would like to thank Dr. K. Nomoto and Dr. S. Woosley for providing their explosion models.

All of the computations described here were performed on the Cray X-MP/24 and Cray EA X-MP/14se computers at the University of Texas System Center for High Performance Computing.

References

[1] Woosley, S.E., and Weaver, T.A., in *IAU Colloquium 89, Radiation Hydrodynamics in Stars and Compact Objects*, ed. by D. Mihalas and K.-H.A. Winkler (Berlin:Springer-Verlag),p. 91 (1986).

[2] Nomoto, K., Thielemann, F.-K., and Yokoi, K., Astrophys. J. **286**,644 (1984).

[3] Thielemann, F.-K., Nomoto, K., and Yokoi, K., Astron. Astrophys. **158**,17 (1986).

[4] Branch, D., Doggett, J.B., Nomoto, K., and Thielemann, F.-K., Astrophys. J. **294**,619 (1985).

[5] Harkness, R.P., in *IAU Colloquium 89, Radiation Hydrodynamics in Stars and Compact Objects*, ed. by D. Mihalas and K.-H.A. Winkler (Berlin:Springer-Verlag),p. 166 (1986).

[6] Wheeler, J.C., and Harkness, R.P., submitted to Reports on Progress in Physics (1989).

[7] Branch, D., Lacy, C.H., McCall, M.L., Sutherland, P.G., Uomoto, A., Wheeler, J.C., and Wills, B.J., Astrophys. J. **270**,123 (1983).

SECTION IX
OBSERVATIONS OF RECENT SUPERNOVAE (NOT SN 1987A)

Supernovae: Fabulous Results and Stories

Alexei V. Filippenko

1. Introduction

When I opened the printed program for this workshop and saw that Bob Kirshner, the chairman of the session on "Supernova Classification and Observations of Recent Supernovae (not 87A)," had entitled my talk "Fabulous Results and Stories," I was somewhat concerned that people would think this was the title I personally had chosen. After all, what right do I have to call my own results fabulous? On the brighter side, though, the title (and Bob's introduction — in which he referred to the "tall tales" I would tell) clearly gave me a chance to relate some interesting tidbits that might indeed entertain and amaze you. I love describing supernovae (SNe); they are often so different from one another. I wish Fritz Zwicky were alive today, so that he could see the bizarre spectra our wonderful new detectors make available to us.

2. Type Ib Supernovae: A Distinct New Subclass

It has been clear for many decades [1] that a useful way to classify SNe is to look at their optical spectra, usually near maximum brightness when the spectra are easiest to procure, and check whether there is strong evidence for hydrogen (other than from underlying H II regions) in them. If there's *no* hydrogen the SN is Type I, and if there *is* hydrogen the SN is Type II; that's all there is to it! Sure, one can also look for correlations among SN spectra and light curves, but those are all secondary characteristics. In part, the presence or absence of hydrogen is thought to be of fundamental importance because it naturally leads us to consider two different types of progenitors: white dwarfs (SN I) and supergiants (SN II). The other observed properties of SNe — such as the great homogeneity among the spectra and light curves of most SNe I, and the great heterogeneity among SNe II — seem to corroborate this simple scheme.

Long ago, though, BERTOLA and collaborators [2, 3] had noticed that *some* SNe I (specifically SNe 1962L and 1964L) lack the deep absorption trough generally seen at about 6120 Å within the first month past maximum brightness. For two decades there were few, if any, new examples of such objects, and they were simply labeled as "peculiar SNe I" (SNe Ip). Interest in them was revitalized in the mid-1980s by the studies of several newly-discovered SNe Ip made by UOMOTO and KIRSHNER [4], WHEELER and LEVREAULT [5], SRAMEK, PANAGIA, and WEILER [6], and ELIAS et al. [7]. Particularly influential was the thorough, much referenced (but still unpublished) optical and ultraviolet investigation of SN 1983N done by

Nino Panagia and collaborators. As summarized by PORTER and FILIPPENKO [8], SNe Ip seemed to constitute a distinct subclass, characterized by their (a) lack of the 6120 Å absorption trough, thought to be blueshifted Si II $\lambda\lambda 6347, 6371$ in normal SNe I, (b) preference for galaxies having Hubble types Sbc or later, (c) proximity to H II regions, (d) rather low luminosity, typically 1.5 mag fainter than classical SNe I, (e) distinct IR light curves having no secondary maximum around 1 month past primary maximum, (f) reddish colors, and (g) emission of radio radiation within a year past maximum. The subclass was named "Type Ib" [7] to distinguish it from normal SNe Ia. At least one of the earliest studies [5] had concluded that the explosion mechanism might be more closely related to that of SNe II than to SNe Ia, but nobody was really sure because the spectroscopic appearance of SNe Ib near maximum resembled that of somewhat older SNe Ia ($\sim$ 1 month past maximum). More clues to the nature of SNe Ib were needed!

On 28 February 1985 UT, during a spectroscopic survey of nearby galaxies with the Hale reflector at Palomar Observatory, Wal Sargent and I "accidentally" discovered SN 1985F near the nucleus of the peculiar SBbc galaxy NGC 4618 [9, 10]. That is, we saw a starlike object close to the end of the central bar of H II regions in NGC 4618, and thought it odd that such a bright nucleus would be present in a late-type galaxy. We guessed that it was either a starburst nucleus or a Galactic foreground star, but its spectrum proved otherwise. In addition to the narrow emission lines produced by the surrounding "fuzz" (the H II regions), we saw very strong, broad emission lines that were later identified as [O I] $\lambda\lambda 6300, 6364$, Mg I] $\lambda 4571$, and Na I D. Additional spectra obtained during the next two months revealed emission lines of [Ca II] $\lambda\lambda 7291, 7324$, the Ca II infrared triplet, O I $\lambda 7774$, [C I] $\lambda\lambda 8727, 9823, 9849$, and other low-excitation lines of neutral or singly ionized species (Fig. 1).

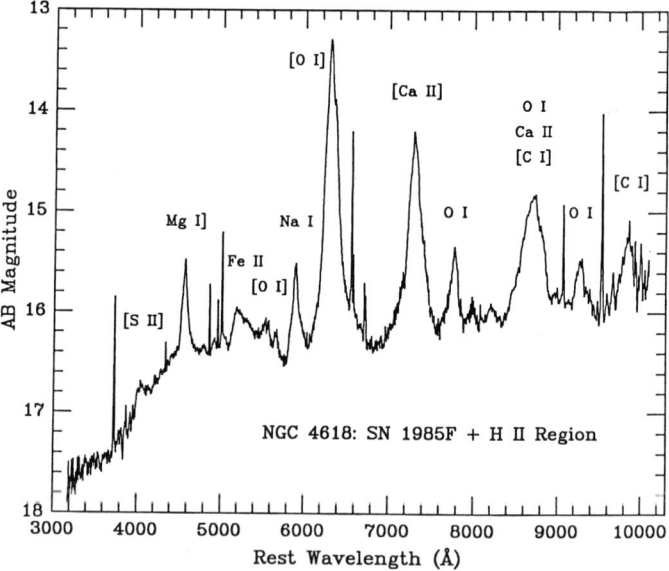

Figure 1: Spectrum of SN 1985F in NGC 4618, obtained with the Palomar Hale (5 m) and Lick Shane (3 m) reflectors in March and April 1985. Only broad (SN) lines are labeled; narrow lines are from the superposed H II regions. AB magnitude $= -2.5 \log f_\nu - 48.6$, where the units of f_ν are erg s^{-1} cm^{-2} Hz^{-1}.

The emission-line spectrum of SN 1985F, dominated by forbidden lines, suggested that we were looking at an old SN, as did the exponential decline of the derived light curve [11]. The complete absence of hydrogen led to a formal classification of SN I, although no known spectra of SNe I at *any* stage of development resembled that of SN 1985F. Given the physical conditions implied by a rough analysis of the emission-line intensity ratios, it was likely that lines of hydrogen would have been visible had hydrogen been present in appreciable quantities [9, 10]. This, along with the dominance of intermediate-mass elements, the crude estimates of at least several solar masses of ejecta, and the apparently close association with an H II region, suggested that we were looking at the explosion of a massive star that had rid itself of hydrogen prior to exploding, somewhat like the progenitor long ago proposed for Cas A by CHEVALIER [12]. The *San Francisco Chronicle* thus reported that we had "peeked at a stripteasing star," although I don't think I actually ever used those terms. Several theorists did more detailed calculations which agreed that the progenitor was probably quite massive [13, 14].

So, here was yet another new puzzle in the overall picture of SNe I, long thought to be nearly homogeneous in their observed properties. On the one hand there were the SNe Ib, which appeared to differ from SNe Ia in several ways, but which had not definitely been linked to massive stars or to a different explosion mechanism. On the other hand there was SN 1985F, spectroscopically distinct from SNe Ia (aside from the absence of hydrogen), and most likely the explosion of a massive star. It seemed that SNe I, far from being all the same, were breaking up into several distinct subclasses.

A crucial "unification" occurred when the Texas group [15] showed that a spectrum of the Type Ib SN 1983N, obtained 8 months past maximum, was very similar to that of SN 1985F at the time of its discovery. Moreover, Bob Kirshner (quoted in CHEVALIER [16]) found that a late-time spectrum of the Type Ib SN 1984L also resembled that of SN 1985F. (His spectrum is now published in [17]). Thus, SN 1985F was probably a SN Ib discovered long after maximum and, conversely, SNe Ib eventually turn into objects whose spectra really are vastly different from those of SNe Ia (Fig. 2). This provided much-needed evidence that SNe Ib constitute a physically separate subclass of SNe I, possibly having a fundamentally different explosion mechanism. It is interesting that CHUGAI [18] had, in fact, already suggested that SN 1985F might be a SN Ib discovered long after maximum.

Based on a comparison between the spectroscopic appearance of SN 1983N and SN 1985F, GASKELL et al. [15] deduced that Sargent and I had discovered SN 1985F 8–9 months past maximum. This was later confirmed by TSVETKOV [19], whose inspection of pre-discovery plates taken at the Crimean Station of the Sternberg State Astronomical Institute showed that SN 1985F had reached maximum brightness at $B = 12.1$ mag about 260 days prior to our discovery. In fact, the earliest plate had been obtained when SN 1985F was still on the rise, and it is sad that the object was not recognized at that time. It would have been among the brightest SNe, and certainly the brightest SN Ib, in many years. On the other hand, it is unlikely that I personally would have become so interested in supernovae had Sargent and I not stumbled across SN 1985F. Such is the nature of serendipity in astronomy!

Not having a complete series of spectra of SN 1985F over the course of its development, we must resort to other SNe Ib to see how they evolve. At present, the most complete long-term series of spectra is that of FILIPPENKO, PORTER, and SARGENT [20] for SN 1987M. The data are shown and discussed in the contribution by PORTER [21] in this volume. Of significance is the relatively early emergence of the [O I], [Ca II], and Ca II infrared triplet emission lines; they are already very prominent at $t = 2$ months. It is interesting that at this time, [O I] $\lambda 6364$ is approximately as strong as [O I] $\lambda 6300$, because both lines are near the intensity of the Planck function at the appropriate temperature.

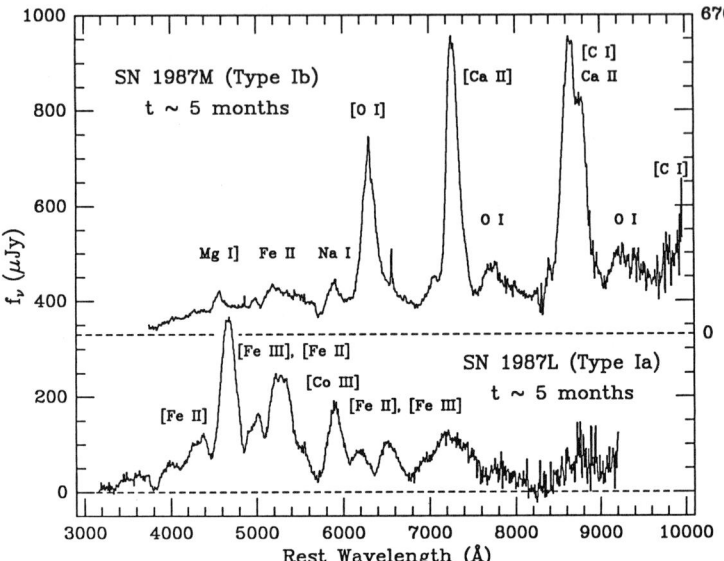

Figure 2: Spectra of SN 1987M (Type Ib) and SN 1987L (Type Ia), each obtained about 5 months past maximum brightness. Although both objects exhibit strong emission lines, the spectra could hardly be more dissimilar.

It is now becoming clear that SNe Ib may constitute a rather heterogeneous subclass, with large variations in the observed strengths of helium absorption lines in spectra obtained around maximum brightness [22, 23]. HARKNESS and WHEELER [24] even suggest that SNe Ib should actually be divided into two separate categories: SNe Ib are those showing strong He lines (e.g., SNe 1983N, 1984L), and SNe Ic are those in which He is weak or absent near maximum (e.g., SN 1987M). Perhaps a larger sample of SNe Ib should be observed before SNe Ic are formally introduced into the nomenclature. It is quite possible, for example, that there exists a continuum of helium relative strengths among SNe Ib, and that He-rich objects are not fundamentally different from He-poor objects — just as B-type main-sequence stars are not fundamentally different from A-type main-sequence stars. If a continuum is indeed found, a satisfactory classification scheme can later be developed.

3. What are the Progenitors of SNe Ib?

During the period 1984–1987 many authors [5, 10, 13, 14, 15, 16, 21, 22, 23, 25] had come to the conclusion that SN 1985F and other SNe Ib were the explosions of massive stars that had peeled off (either by winds or by mass transfer) their outer layers of hydrogen prior to exploding. In this case, the explosion mechanism was generally thought to be core collapse, as in SNe II. One of the most recent, and persuasive, arguments is that of FRANSSON and CHEVALIER [26] (see also [27] and [28]). They show that a 25 $M_\odot$ (zero-age main sequence) star that evolves to a 8 $M_\odot$ helium core develops, 9–10 months after its explosion, an emission-line spectrum remarkably similar to that of SN 1985F. The predicted line intensity ratios are in good agreement with the observed ones, but the calculated line profiles are much too flat-topped, or "boxy." This suggests that mixing of different layers occurs during the explosion. Ample evidence of such mixing has in fact been found in SN 1987A; see the review by ARNETT et al. [29].

Despite the evidence for massive SN Ib progenitors, there are problems to be addressed. PANAGIA and LAIDLER [30], for example, claim that SNe Ib generally occur at greater distances from H II regions (as measured by them) than do SNe II (as measured by HUANG [31]). If there really is a significant difference in distance, it implies that the progenitors of SNe Ib are probably less massive, on average, than those of SNe II — they have more time to wander away from their birth places before exploding. This interesting result must be verified with a carefully chosen sample of SNe Ib and SNe II, all measured in a consistent manner. (At least one SN Ib [SN 1985F] directly superposed on a bright H II region seems to have been excluded from the study reported in [30].) Another potential difficulty, discussed by ENSMAN and WOOSLEY [32], is that the light curve produced by iron core collapse in an 8 $M_\odot$ helium core is too broad to be consistent with that of a typical SN Ib. Even 6 $M_\odot$ helium cores yield rather broad light curves [32] (see also [33]); most SNe Ib rise and decline at about the same rate as SNe Ia during the first few months.

The above problem with light curves, however, might not be serious. Recent calculations of evolving stars by LANGER [34] suggest that the final helium core of a very massive star can be substantially smaller than that predicted in earlier studies, if mass loss is properly taken into account. This is at least partially supported by observational studies of Wolf-Rayet stars in binary systems (MOFFAT et al. [35]). Moreover, ENSMAN and WOOSLEY [32] point out that clumping of the ejecta can lead to smaller gamma-ray deposition, and hence to a narrower light curve. Evidence for clumping has been found in SN 1987A, of course [29], and more recently in the Type Ib SN 1985F [36]. As shown in Figure 3, both of the [O I] $\lambda\lambda 6300, 6364$ lines in SN 1985F showed small-scale structure at the same relative velocities within the line profiles (thereby confirming the reality of the features), and this structure became more pronounced with time.

As emphasized by BRANCH [37], it is nevertheless possible that at least some SNe Ib represent the explosions of white dwarfs [38, 39, 40]. The most widely discussed model, that of BRANCH and NOMOTO [38] (see also [37]), invokes an off-center detonation at the base of the helium layer in a white dwarf that is slowly accreting hydrogen from the wind of a companion star. Naively, I expect that the resulting light curve should decline *faster* than that of SNe Ia, since the detonation only occurs in the outer few tenths of a solar mass; this is supported by the calculations in [41]. In addition, the predicted late-time spectrum [26, 27] does not exhibit sufficiently strong emission lines of intermediate-mass elements, and the relative intensities of certain lines (such as [C I] $\lambda 8727$ and [O I] $\lambda\lambda 6300, 6364$) differ from the observations. More recently, though, WOOSLEY [42] has suggested that a slow-flame carbon deflagration in a white dwarf may explain some SNe Ib; the light curve is fainter and broader, and the late-time spectrum may be consistent with observations. Further study of white dwarf models should prove illuminating.

Of course, the question of low-mass versus high-mass progenitors could be settled if the mass of the SN Ib ejecta were measured accurately. During the late-time "supernebular" phase this might seem to be an easy task with the help of standard nebular diagnostics of temperature and density [13, 17, 25, 26, 43]. In particular, the strength of [O I] $\lambda 5577$ could be compared with that of [O I] $\lambda\lambda 6300, 6364$ to get the electron temperature, and in the high-density limit ($n_e \gtrsim 10^6$ cm^{-3}, almost surely present at $t \lesssim 1$ year) the oxygen mass is easily computed (e.g., [25]). The problem is that the mass depends exponentially on T_e, and T_e is very difficult to measure because the weak [O I] λ5577 line is heavily blended with Fe II and other contaminants; see Figure 1, and the spectra of SN 1987M shown in [20] and [21]. For example, if the distance of SN 1985F is 7.1 Mpc and the measured flux of [O I] $\lambda\lambda$6300, 6364 in February 1985 was 2.2×10^{-12} erg s^{-1} cm^{-2} [9], then we find that $M_O = 0.11\ M_\odot$ if $T_e = 10\,000$ K, $M_O = 1.1\ M_\odot$ if $T_e = 5000$ K, and $M_O = 11\ M_\odot$ if $T_e = 3300$ K. Clearly, an accurate measurement of T_e is needed if we are to directly determine the mass of the ejected oxygen!

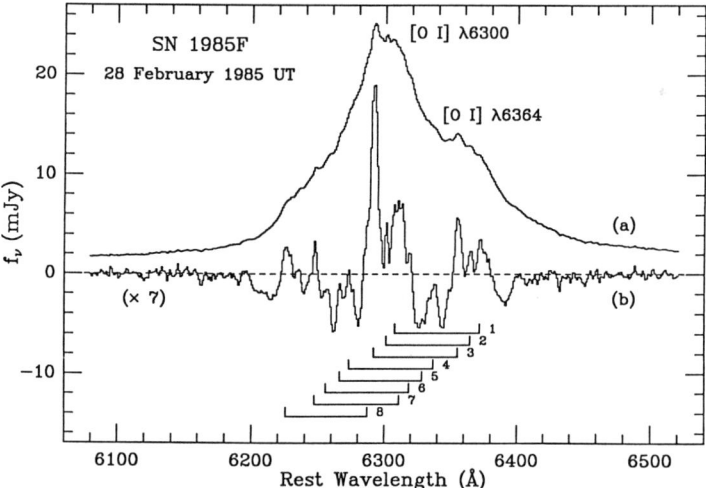

Figure 3: (a) [O I] blend in SN 1985F, roughly 9 months past maximum. (b) A heavily smoothed version of (a) was subtracted from (a) to obtain this residual spectrum, scaled by a factor of 7. Pairs of [O I] $\lambda\lambda$6300, 6364 "peaks" having the same relative velocity are indicated.

4. The "Missing Link" Between SNe Ib and SNe II?

In late July 1987, a supernova which may play a particularly significant role in our understanding of SNe Ib was discovered [44] by the Berkeley Automated Supernova Search Team [45] in the Virgo spiral galaxy NGC 4651. The first few spectra of SN 1987K showed it to be a SN II, with a P Cygni profile of Hα, and I dutifully reported its spectral type to the *IAU Circulars*. However, Hα did not seem as prominent as in most SNe II having well-developed low-excitation absorption lines elsewhere in the spectrum. Furthermore, the object was atypical in that the relative strength of the Hα emission line did not grow during the next two weeks. Anyone who has tried to observe the Virgo cluster in August knows that it's quite tough to do, as the Sun tends to get in the way; sadly, the object was subsequently lost for a few months.

When I reobserved it in December 1987, I was astonished to find that, unlike previously observed SNe II, it had lost all traces of the broad Hα emission line [46]. Instead, the spectrum exhibited broad [O I] $\lambda\lambda$6300, 6364 and [Ca II] $\lambda\lambda$7291, 7324 — the defining characteristics of *Type Ib SNe* long after maximum! These results were confirmed by a spectrum obtained in February 1988 (Fig. 4). Such a metamorphosis is unprecedented, but would undoubtedly have pleased Fritz Zwicky.

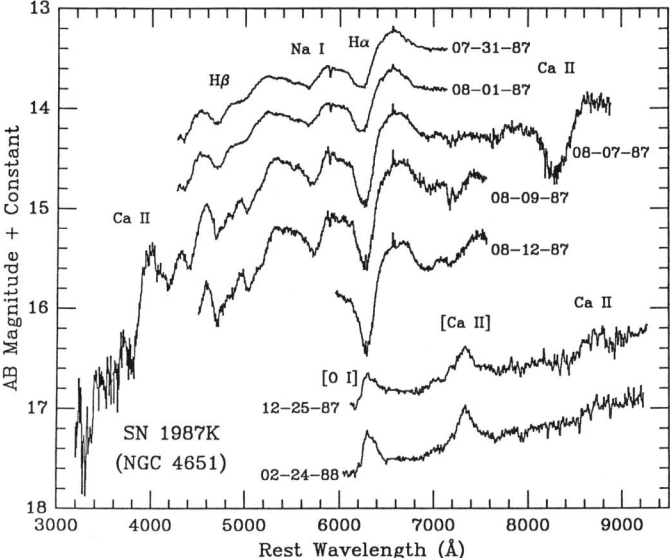

Figure 4: Series of spectra of SN 1987K, showing its transformation from a SN II into a SN Ib. Narrow Hα and other emission lines from the underlying H II region have been excised in the last two spectra, for clarity. Constants added to the spectra before plotting were (top to bottom) −0.85, −0.45, 0.0, 0.15, 0.0, 0.3, and 0.2 mag.

Apparently, Bob Kirshner and Eric Schlegel had not obtained an early spectrum of SN 1987K, but observed it for the first time in April 1988. They, too, found the spectrum to be that of a SN Ib [17]. Not knowing my new results, over which I was still pondering because they were so unexpected, Bob telephoned me and said that I had mistakenly called SN 1987K a SN II, when actually it was a SN Ib. I assured Bob that SN 1987K had undergone the supernova equivalent of a sex-change operation, and that my early classification was indeed correct. Bob, naturally, seemed skeptical, but I think that now, having seen the full set of spectra, he's a believer.

The simplest interpretation of SN 1987K, of course, is that it was a massive star that lost *most*, yet not all, of its outer layer of hydrogen prior to its explosion as a regular core-collapse SN [46, 47]. This could occur if the star were not sufficiently massive (say, 25–35 $M_\odot$?) for its wind to blow away all of the hydrogen and become a helium giant, or if the star were less massive but dumped much of its atmosphere onto a binary companion. If it had a thin hydrogen shell at the time of its explosion, it would masquerade as a SN II for a while, and as the expanding ejecta thinned out the spectrum would become dominated by emission from the deeper and denser layers. A completely different conjecture is that there was plenty of hydrogen in the atmosphere of the star, but at late times it was poorly heated, perhaps because radioactive nuclides were not mixed sufficiently well with the hydrogen.

It is interesting that, in the early models of SN 1987A, WOOSLEY *et al.* [48] suggested that the progenitor might have undergone much mass loss, leaving behind a very thin hydrogen shell. They dubbed such an object a SN IIb — having the spectroscopic properties of SNe II initially, and of SNe Ib later on. In fact, we now know that SN 1987A had a massive hydrogen envelope (5–10 $M_\odot$), but the idea is nevertheless a potentially valid one for other SNe. Notably, VAN DEN BERGH [49] had previously argued that the difference between SNe Ib and SNe II might be only skin deep. Further evidence for this point of view is provided by the detailed analysis of Cas A ejecta done by FESEN, BECKER, and GOODRICH [50].

If the above hypothesis of a thin hydrogen skin is correct, we expect several observable consequences. First, the expansion velocities of the oxygen and calcium ejecta in SN 1987K should be larger than those in typical SNe II many months after core collapse, since SN 1987K didn't have a massive hydrogen envelope tamping the inner layers. This is indeed the case, as shown in Figure 1 of FILIPPENKO [51], where a comparison is made between the late-time line widths in SN 1987K and in the Type II SN 1986I. Second, SN 1987K should have had a *broader* light curve than typical SNe Ib, because of the hydrogen recombination wave traversing the remaining envelope in SN 1987K. The light curve illustrated in [46] seems to confirm this, although the evidence is not conclusive because the data were taken through a red (rather than visual or blue) bandpass. Finally, some SNe Ib should exhibit a *very* weak Hα line near maximum brightness, to complete the mass-loss continuity between SNe Ib and SNe II. In retrospect, we do see local maxima near Hα in the spectra of a few SNe Ib (e.g., SN 1988L [46]), but the mere presence of a local maximum at the right position in a very bumpy spectrum does not constitute proof that hydrogen is present. It would be more convincing if a shallow P Cygni profile were present at the correct position. Such might be the case in SN 1989O [52], as shown in Figure 5. SN 1989O appears to be a SN II, but Hα is very weak, even compared with Hα in SN 1987K. (The Ca II lines in SN 1989O seem even weaker.) Unfortunately, this object was so distant ($z \approx 0.064$) and faint at maximum ($m \approx 18$) that it was not possible to follow for a long time.

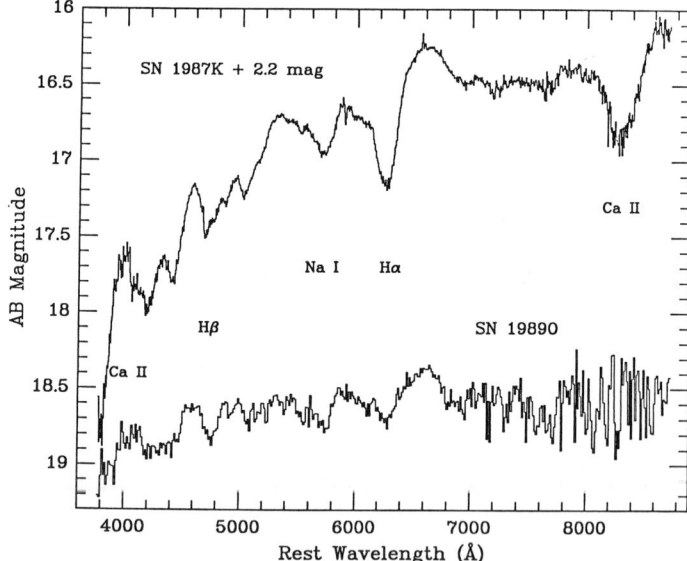

Figure 5: Spectrum of SN 1989O in MCG 6-1-26, obtained at Lick Observatory 5–6 days after discovery, compared with that of SN 1987K. Note the weak Hα and Ca II in SN 1989O, and the overall similarity of the spectra.

Despite the superficial success of my naive interpretation of SN 1987K, what we really need is detailed models which show that the spectrum of a massive star having a thin hydrogen envelope really does resemble that of SN 1987K, and evolves in the observed manner. Robert Harkness and Craig Wheeler are currently attempting to do the requisite calculations, and the preliminary results are not encouraging. The theoretical spectrum seems to show deep features produced by the heavy elements that would naturally be present (with roughly solar abundances) in the hydrogen and helium shells of a massive star, yet these are not observed. I am not yet sure whether this represents a flaw in the calculations, in the specific assumptions, or in the basic hypothesis; further theoretical work is needed to clarify the situation. More observations of SNe like SN 1987K are also crucial, but these objects are apparently quite rare. Aside from the questionable case of SN 1989O, no known SN since SN 1987K has shown similar properties. Given its relatively broad light curve [32], SN 1985F may have actually been a SN II near maximum (like SN 1987K), but we will probably never know. Unlike the case for SN 1987A, the light echoes of SN 1985F are much too faint to observe, let alone get spectra of; in this case we can't "play it again, Sam" (to quote Bob Kirshner).

5. A Distinct Subclass of Type II Supernovae?

I would now like to mention a topic similar to that discussed by Eric Schlegel at this workshop — namely, the gradual emergence of a new, distinct subclass of SNe II. Most SNe II show prominent P Cygni profiles of hydrogen in their spectra, but in some objects the absorption component is either very weak or entirely absent. These SNe exhibit strong Hα emission whose equivalent width grows to astoundingly high values as they age. The Hα line is sometimes superposed on a much broader component of Hα emission. Their continua seem bluer than normal, they stay bright for a very long time, and their late-time spectra ($t \approx 1$ year) indicate extremely high densities in the ejecta. Some of them are also unusually luminous at maximum, compared with other SNe II. Finally, a few show strong evidence of fairly dense circumstellar matter, probably ejected prior to the explosion.

An excellent example of such an object is SN 1987F, which occurred in a bright H II region in a spiral arm of NGC 4615 (FILIPPENKO [53]). When first observed, broad Hα emission was superposed on a luminous ($M_V \approx -19.3$ mag), nearly featureless continuum, but its profile did not have the characteristic P Cygni shape, and its centroid was blueshifted by $\gtrsim 1500$ km s^{-1} with respect to the systemic velocity of the parent galaxy (Fig. 6). The near-maximum spectrum of SN 1988I, also discussed in [53], was similarly dominated by broad hydrogen Balmer lines, but the SN was too faint to monitor for an extended period of time. Many months later, the broad Hα in SN 1987F was more luminous, and had much larger equivalent width; Fe II, Ca II, and O I emission were detected as well. Forbidden lines, normally quite strong at this phase, were very weak. The narrow component of Hα, initially quite luminous, was now much less prominent. At early times it may have been produced by material previously ejected by the progenitor, but this gas was eventually engulfed by the expanding SN ejecta, as in the case of SN 1984E (GASKELL [54]; HENRY and BRANCH [55]).

The derived electron density in the ejected envelope of SN 1987F at late times was $\gtrsim 10^9$ cm^{-3}. This, together with the observed flux of Hα emission, can be used to derive the mass of the emitting hydrogen: $M \lesssim 0.1$ $M_\odot$ if $H_0 = 75$ km s^{-1} Mpc^{-1}. (An earlier calculation [53] gave $M \gtrsim 5-30$ $M_\odot$, but clumping of the ejecta had unfortunately been neglected. In fact, I find that the filling factor of clumps is $\lesssim 0.01$ if the ejecta are expanding at $v \gtrsim 6000$ km s^{-1}.) Although this does not seem like a large amount of gas, it is likely that the progenitor was massive; the light curve declined very slowly at both early and late times. With a few small but probably significant exceptions, the overall optical spectroscopic properties of SN 1987F closely resemble those of type 1 Seyfert nuclei and QSOs, whose emission-line spectra are thought to be produced by high-density clouds irradiated by a flat ultraviolet continuum.

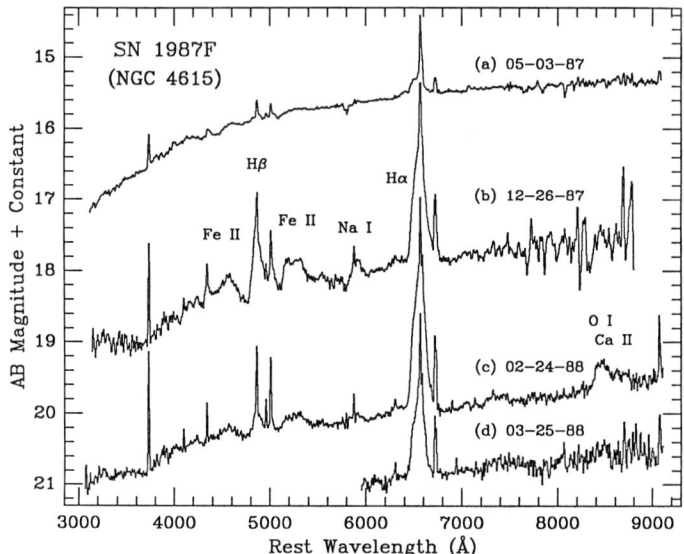

Figure 6: Spectra of SN 1987F in NGC 4615, plus the surrounding H II region. Offsets of 0.2, 1.9, and 2.8 mag have been added to spectra (*b*), (*c*), and (*d*), respectively. Spectrum (*b*) is very noisy at $\lambda \gtrsim 7300$ Å due to incomplete removal of interference fringes; also, broad Hα is too weak relative to broad lines at $\lambda \lesssim 6000$ Å.

Another, more recent, object of this type is SN 1988Z in MCG 03-28-022. As discussed by Joe Shields during the "supernova swap meet," the early-time spectra of SN 1988Z showed very narrow [O III] λ4363 and [O III] $\lambda\lambda$4959, 5007 emission lines whose relative intensities indicate $n_e \gtrsim 10^{6.9}$ cm^{-3}, *regardless* of the electron temperature. The actual electron density may be substantially greater, but in any case it is much higher than that of the normal interstellar medium. Although careful measurements are still in progress, the flux of [O III] λ5007 may have grown with time, at least during the first month. Moreover, the helium abundance of this gas appears to be abnormally high. The obvious conclusion is that the progenitor of SN 1988Z expelled a shell of dense material, and this material became ionized by the flash of ultraviolet radiation emitted by the SN as the shock wave broke through the stellar surface, as in SN 1987A (FRANSSON et al. [56]).

Even after several months, SN 1988Z remained remarkably blue. Moreover, as in SN 1987F, the density of the actual SN ejecta was very high: forbidden lines were weak or absent, and very strong lines of Fe II, Ca II, and O I emerged (Fig. 7). The blend of O I λ8446 and the Ca II infrared triplet, in particular, became stronger than the very broad (FWHM $\approx$ 15 000 km s^{-1}) component of Hα, yet little or no [Ca II] $\lambda\lambda$7291, 7324 was present.

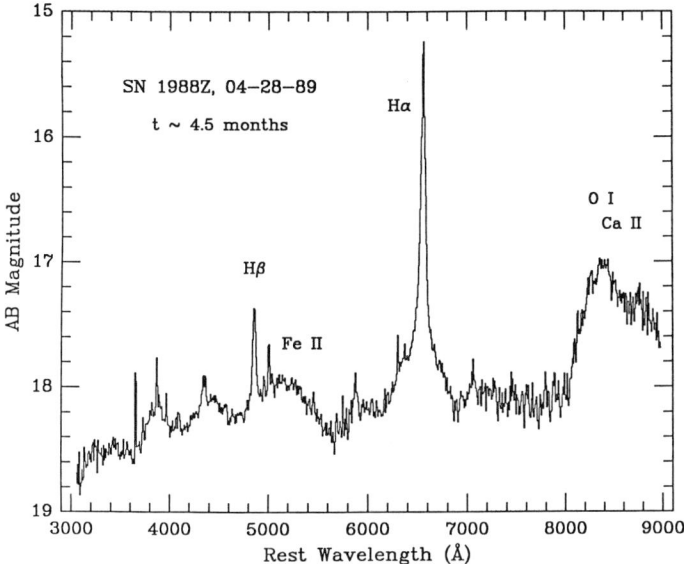

Figure 7: Spectrum of SN 1988Z, obtained with the Shane reflector at Lick Observatory. The narrow [O III] lines reveal the presence of a dense circumstellar shell. Balmer lines of intermediate and great width are also present. Note the broad undulations in the blue-green part of the spectrum, which are probably produced by Fe II.

But SN 1988Z has a lot more in store for us than this! Perusal of the spectra shows that an intermediate-width component of the Balmer lines (FWHM ≈ 1600 km s^{-1}) became visible after about 1 month, and its flux steadily grew with time. As shown in Figure 7, the Balmer decrement of this component is very steep, indicating that some sort of collisional excitation might be operating. Is this another shell of matter, ejected at high velocity from the progenitor of SN 1988Z immediately prior to the titanic explosion? Its origin is not yet clear, but analysis of the old spectra — as well as new data — is continuing. SN 1988Z has remained so bright that it is still easily observed, nearly one year after discovery, despite its relatively large distance ($z \approx 0.022$). The new spectra reveal the dominance of the intermediate component; the equivalent width of Hα is enormous. In fact, the optical spectrum resembles that of the radio-loud SN 1986J (RUPEN *et al.* [57]), and an attempt should be made to observe SN 1988Z with the VLA.

6. Future Prospects

We now see that ZWICKY [58] was probably right when he said that there are actually many classes of SNe; with sufficiently good spectra, we are finding all sorts of interesting differences among objects. However, we probably shouldn't further subdivide SNe into new subclasses (other than Ia, Ib, II-L, and II-P) until we have a much more extensive data base. It would be good to choose observable characteristics that are most fundamental from a *physical* point of view. Perhaps, for example, those objects having strong Hα emission, but little or no absorption, always experience pre-supernova winds; on the other hand, SN 1987A went through a prominent phase of gas ejection, yet it developed Balmer lines having normal P Cygni profiles.

To achieve such a data base, it is clear that observers need to start pooling their data — especially their spectra, which do not depend on site-specific bandpasses of various filters. Although obtaining one spectrum of each available SN is still useful for statistical purposes, we can take a major step beyond this by getting relatively full coverage of the spectral evolution of a few well-placed objects. This is difficult for one observer, or even a team of astronomers at one observatory, to achieve because of ever-present time constraints and the rapid fading of most SNe. However, by working together we can obtain high-quality data for many objects other than SN 1987A. Fortunately, recent progress in the use of electronic (computer) mail and standardized software has made our task considerably easier.

I am grateful to the entire local organizing committee of this workshop for making our stay in Santa Cruz so pleasant, and especially for asking Mother Nature to postpone the big earthquake until well after we had departed. Special thanks also go to Stan Woosley for his astonishing patience; my contribution must be the very last one to be submitted. I also thank my collaborators on various projects for allowing me to discuss results prior to formal publication elsewhere. This work is partially funded by a Presidential Young Investigator Award (NSF grant AST–8957063), as well as by the Center for Particle Astrophysics, an NSF Science and Technology Center operated by the University of California at Berkeley under Cooperative Agreement AST–8809616. Support from the California Space Institute (grant CS–41–88) is also appreciated. Lick Observatory receives partial funding from NSF through Core Block grant AST–8614510.

References

1. R. Minkowski: *Pub. A. S. P.*, **53**, 224 (1941).
2. F. Bertola: *Ann. d'Ap.*, **27**, 319 (1964).
3. F. Bertola, A. Mammano, and M. Perinotto: *Contrib. Asiago Obs.*, **174**, 51 (1965).
4. A. Uomoto and R. P. Kirshner: *Astr. Ap.*, **149**, L7 (1985).
5. J. C. Wheeler and R. Levreault: *Ap. J. (Letters)*, **294**, L17 (1985).
6. R. A. Sramek, N. Panagia, and K. W. Weiler: *Ap. J. (Letters)*, **285**, L59 (1984).
7. J. H. Elias, K. Mathews, G. Neugebauer, and S. E. Persson: *Ap. J.*, **296**, 379 (1985).
8. A. C. Porter and A. V. Filippenko: *A. J.*, **93**, 1372 (1987).
9. A. V. Filippenko and W. L. W. Sargent: *Nature*, **316**, 407 (1985).
10. A. V. Filippenko and W. L. W. Sargent: *A. J.*, **91**, 691 (1986).
11. A. V. Filippenko, A. C. Porter, W. L. W. Sargent, and D. P. Schneider: *A. J.*, **92**, 1341 (1986).
12. R. A. Chevalier: *Ap. J.*, **208**, 826 (1976).
13. M. C. Begelman and C. L. Sarazin: *Ap. J. (Letters)*, **302**, L59 (1986).
14. R. Schaeffer, M. Cassé, and S. Cahen: *Ap. J. (Letters)*, **316**, L31 (1987).
15. C. M. Gaskell, et al.: *Ap. J. (Letters)*, **306**, L77 (1986).
16. R. A. Chevalier: *Highlights Astron.*, **7**, 599 (1986).
17. E. M. Schlegel and R. P. Kirshner: *A. J.*, **98**, 577 (1989).
18. N. N. Chugai: *Pis'ma Astron. Zh.*, **12**, 461 (*Sov. Astron. Letters* **12**, 192) (1986).
19. D. Yu. Tsvetkov: *Pis'ma Astron. Zh.*, **12**, 784 (*Sov. Astron. Letters* **12**, 328) (1986).
20. A. V. Filippenko, A. C. Porter, and W. L. W. Sargent: submitted (1990).

21. A. C. Porter: These *Proceedings*.
22. J. C. Wheeler, et al.: *Ap. J. (Letters)*, **313**, L69 (1987).
23. R. P. Harkness, et al.: *Ap. J.*, **317**, 355 (1987).
24. R. P. Harkness and J. C. Wheeler: In *Supernovae*, ed. by A. Petschek (Springer-Verlag, Berlin 1989), in press.
25. A. Uomoto: *Ap. J. (Letters)*, **310**, L35 (1986).
26. C. Fransson and R. A. Chevalier: *Ap. J.*, **343**, 323 (1989).
27. C. Fransson: In *Atmospheric Diagnostics of Stellar Evolution*, IAU Colloquium No. 108, ed. by K. Nomoto (Springer-Verlag, Berlin 1988), p. 385.
28. T. Axelrod: In *Atmospheric Diagnostics of Stellar Evolution*, IAU Colloquium No. 108, ed. by K. Nomoto (Springer-Verlag, Berlin 1988), p. 319.
29. W. D. Arnett, J. N. Bahcall, R. P. Kirshner, and S. E. Woosley: *Ann. Rev. Astr. Ap.*, **27**, 629 (1989).
30. N. Panagia and V. G. Laidler: In *Supernova Shells and their Birth Events*, ed. by W. Kundt (Springer-Verlag, Berlin 1989), in press.
31. Y.-L. Huang: *Pub. A. S. P.*, **99**, 461 (1987).
32. L. M. Ensman and S. E. Woosley: *Ap. J.*, **333**, 754 (1989).
33. K. Nomoto, T. Shigeyama, and M. Hashimoto: In *Atmospheric Diagnostics of Stellar Evolution*, IAU Colloquium No. 108, ed. by K. Nomoto (Springer-Verlag, Berlin 1988), p. 319.
34. N. Langer: *Astr. Ap.*, **220**, 135 (1989).
35. A. F. J. Moffat, et al.: *A. J.*, **91**, 1386 (1986).
36. A. V. Filippenko and W. L. W. Sargent: *Ap. J. (Letters)*, **345**, L43 (1989).
37. D. Branch: In *Atmospheric Diagnostics of Stellar Evolution*, IAU Colloquium No. 108, ed. by K. Nomoto (Springer-Verlag, Berlin 1988), p. 281.
38. D. Branch and K. Nomoto: *Astr. Ap.*, **164**, L13 (1986).
39. A. M. Khokhlov and E. V. Ergma: *Pis'ma Astron. Zh.*, **12**, 366 (*Sov. Astron. Letters*, **12**, 152) (1986).
40. I. Iben, K. Nomoto, A. Tornambé, and A. Tutukov: *Ap. J.*, **317**, 717 (1987).
41. S. E. Woosley, R. E. Taam, and T. A. Weaver: *Ap. J.*, **301**, 601 (1986).
42. S. E. Woosley: In *Supernovae*, ed. by A. Petschek (Springer-Verlag, Berlin 1989), in press.
43. N. N. Chugai: *Sov. Astron. Circular* No. 1469 (1986).
44. C. Pennypacker: *IAU Circular* No. 4426 (1987).
45. S. Perlmutter, et al.: In *Instrumentation for Ground-Based Optical Astronomy*, ed. by L. B. Robinson (Springer-Verlag, Berlin 1988), p. 67.
46. A. V. Filippenko: *A. J.*, **96**, 1941 (1988).
47. A. V. Filippenko: *Proc. Astr. Soc. Aust.*, **7**, 540 (1988).
48. S. E. Woosley, P. A. Pinto, P. G. Martin, and T. A. Weaver: *Ap. J.*, **318**, 664 (1987).
49. S. van den Bergh: *Ap. J.*, **327**, 156 (1988).
50. R. A. Fesen, R. H. Becker, and R. W. Goodrich: *Ap. J. (Letters)*, **329**, L89 (1988).
51. A. V. Filippenko: In *Particle Astrophysics: Forefront Experimental Issues*, ed. by E. B. Norman (World Scientific, Singapore 1989), p. 177.
52. A. V. Filippenko and J. C. Shields: *IAU Circular* No. 4851.
53. A. V. Filippenko: *A. J.*, **97**, 726 (1989).
54. C. M. Gaskell: *Pub. A. S. P.*, **96**, 789 (1985).
55. R. B. C. Henry and D. Branch: *Pub. A. S. P.*, **99**, 112 (1987).
56. C. Fransson, et al.: *Ap. J.*, **336**, 429 (1989).
57. M. P. Rupen, et al.: *A. J.*, **94**, 61 (1987).
58. F. Zwicky: In *Stars and Stellar Systems*, Vol. 8, ed. by L. H. Aller and D. B. McLaughlin (Univ. of Chicago Press, Chicago 1965), p. 367.

A Spectroscopic Glance at the CfA Supernovae Atlas

Eric M. Schlegel

Supernovae have traditionally been difficult to study. These objects are transient events, hence unpredictable. The scheduling of telescope time for observations, particularly to cover a sizable portion of the evolution, is impossible. The obvious alternative is to request observations by the available observers, using the available equipment. This approach usually works near maximum, as most spectroscopists are at least somewhat curious about supernova spectra. However, it usually proves difficult to maintain interest, particularly as the supernova fades, which is when the observations become difficult. Consequently, a few, stray spectra of a particular supernova, near maximum, are obtained, and either published or left to rot on a data tape. There are two cures for this problem. First, interested observers can migrate to those institutions which have good facilities, and subsequently make use of them. Second, one can "arrange" to blow up a nearby star, and raise the interest level of many observers. The workshop has demonstrated that SN 1987A produced the second cure. This contribution describes a program which tackles the first.

Data for all supernovae other than SN 1987A are relatively sparse. A program exists at the Center for Astrophysics to observe as many supernovae as possible as often as possible. The observations consist of CCD photometry and spectroscopy, using a variety of telescopes and instruments. The telescopes used include the 0.6m for CCD photometry, the 1.5m Tillinghast reflector, both on Mt. Hopkins, and the Multiple Mirror Telescope. The instruments used include the "Z-machine" (DAVIS and LATHAM [1]) (a Reticon spectrograph built for the CfA redshift survey), occasionally the Faint Object Grism Spectrograph on the MMT, and more recently, the MMT "Red Channel" spectrograph (SCHMIDT et al. [2]). The wavelength coverage is generally 4000Å to 7000Å, at about 5-10Å resolution. It should be noted that the Z-machine flux calibration is sometimes poor (too much operator experience with the redshift survey). The desire for good flux calibration indicates a need for good photometry with which to calibrate the spectroscopy.

A supernova data base is slowly being assembled, and will eventually be made available to all. Table 1 lists the objects present to date (this review written in August 1989), with the number of spectra obtained on each object. This type of data base can be as useful as the vast pile of data on SN 1987A, simply because of the wider range of supernova properties sampled. Numerous questions can be addressed with

Table 1
Supernovae Atlas by Type: Spectra Available

SN II		SN Ia		SN Ib		Unknown	
SN 80K	19*	SN 81F	1	SN 83I	1	SN 82D	1
SN 81E	1	SN 81G	3	SN 83N	5	SN 82V	1
SN 82F	3	SN 82C	1	SN 84L	12*	SN 82X	1
SN 84E	6?	SN 85A	9*	SN 85F	4*	SN 82Y	1
SN 85H	2	SN 85B	8*	SN 87K	2	SN 88W	1
SN 85L	1	SN 86A	5	SN 87M	4		
SN 85O	13	SN 86N	5	SN 88L	1		
SN 85R	5	SN 86O	6	SN 89E	1		
SN 86B	1	SN 87D	3				
SN 86E	6	SN 87L	6				
SN 86I	4	SN 87N	5				
SN 86K	7	SN 88B	2				
SN 87B	5	SN 88C	2				
SN 87C	3	SN 88F	2				
SN 87F	2	SN 88V	4x?				
SN 88A	13x	SN 89B	15x				
SN 88H	4	SN 89D	8				
SN 88Q	1	SN 89M	2x				
SN 88S	1						
SN 88Y	1						
SN 88Z	5x						
SN 89A	5						
SN 89C	11x						
SN 89F	2						
SN 89K	1						
SN 89L	3x						

* = data published, or data published by others and donated
x = still following (August 1989)

these data, including the few listed below:
- spectroscopic differences between SN Ia in E, S, and Irr galaxies;
- spectroscopic differences between SN II-L and SN II-P;
- velocity behavior of particular lines, for example, the Si II 6150[Å] absorption

line seen in SN Ia;

- the net H_α flux evolution.

A typical collection of spectra for the SN Ib SN 1984L, at late times, is shown in Figure 1 (next page). Numbers listed in the upper right-hand corner are the age in days past maximum (if known; otherwise, the age in days past discovery), and the vertical offset to separate the data. The offset is the value given by

plotted vertical position = log(data value) + offset.

Note the large [O I] 6300/6363Å emission lines, a characteristic of the late-time spectra of SN Ib. The SN 1984L data indicate the benefit of late-time supernova data: the 385-day spectrum, while noisy (the "technical" term is "herbaceous"), provided the connection between SN 1983N and SN 1985F, thereby establishing the subclass of SN Ib. SN 1983N was relatively well-observed at early times (PANAGIA et al. [3]), but was not observed beyond about 100 days. SN 1985F, the Filippenko-Sargent object (FILIPPENKO and SARGENT [4]), was discovered about 9 months past maximum. SN 1984L was well-observed at early times (HARKNESS et al. [5]), and was observed at late times. The early-time data on SN 1983N and SN 1984L showed that some supernovae of Type I belonged in a separate subclass, and the late-time data have indicated what types of object may be the progenitors for these supernovae (SCHLEGEL and KIRSHNER [6]). A summary of the late-time data on SN 1984L is included elsewhere in this volume (SCHLEGEL [7]).

Figure 2 (second page after this one) is a spectrum of SN 1988S, discovered by C. Pollas and workers (POLLAS [8]). I include this spectrum, the only one I know of, because it appears to show a bump in the H_α profile at the same location as that seen in SN 1987A, and described there as the "Bochum event" (CRISTIANI et al. [9]). I point out this feature in the SN 1988S spectrum for two reasons. First, the Bochum event, described as the photospheric breakout of ^{56}Ni (PHILLIPS and HEATHCOTE [10], LUCY [11], HANUSCHIK et al. [12]), could also be studied in distant supernovae, thereby providing a wider range of behavior to aid in understanding what this event is. Second, high-resolution spectroscopy is not a waste of time, if that is what you as an observer can contribute. The only thing which must be considered with high-resolution spectroscopy is what bandpass in which to work. The bandpass will be most useful if it is matched to the supernova type. For a Type II, working near H_α is best.

Figure 3 (third, fourth pages after this one) shows a series of early-time spectra of the recent Type Ia supernova SN 1989B. The SN Ia characteristic Si II 6150Å absorption is present, and can be followed for about the first 25 days. Note that a feature is present in the core of the line, and that it appears to vanish after a few days. If the line persists for a few days in the cores of the Si II lines of all SN Ia, then it could bias the velocity centroid of the line. This *might* lead to the variations of the sort discussed in BRANCH et al. [13]. A larger discussion of the Si II line for all SN Ia observations included in the database will be published elsewhere.

Two patterns that I believe are present in the data, and which were discussed at the Workshop as "work in progress", have not been included in these proceedings.

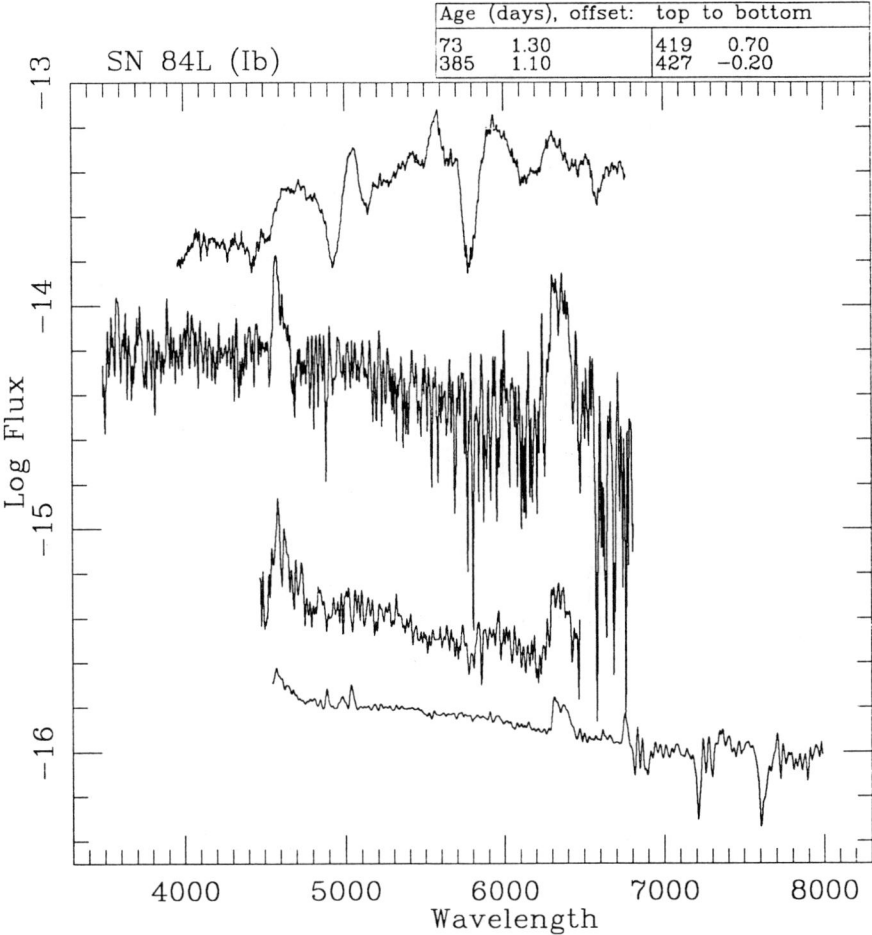

Figure 1: The late-time spectra of the Type Ib SN 1984L. Note the [O I] 6300-6363Å lines, which characterize the late-time emission of this subclass.

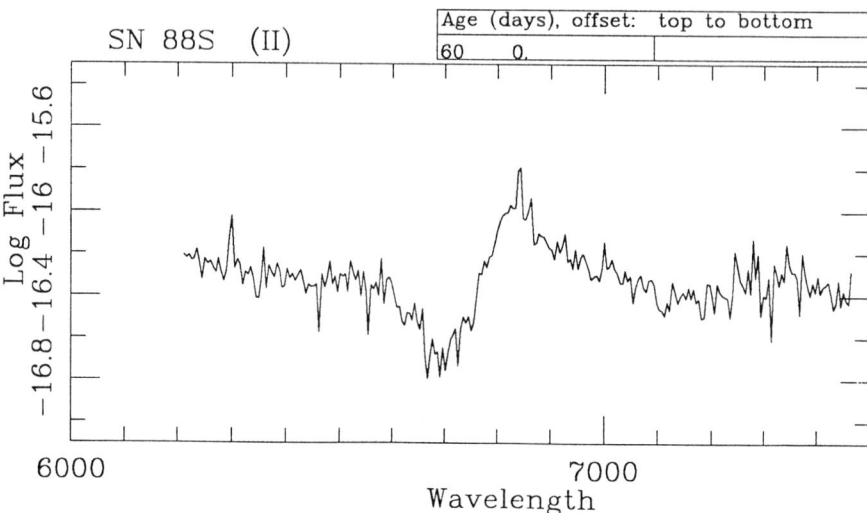

Figure 2: A high-resolution spectrum of the Type II SN 1988S, about 60 days past maximum. Note the feature on the blue edge of the emission component, just redward of 6800Å. A similar feature, called the "Bochum event", was seen in SN 1987A. This raises the possibility that such an event, whatever its cause, can be studied in distant supernovae.

The two patterns, a possible spectroscopic distinction between SN II-L and SN II-P, and a pattern of velocity behavior in the H_α lines, are still being worked on, and will be reported in detail at another time.

Finally, recent data on some Type II supernovae point to the possibility of a new subclass. These supernovae are characterized by having weak H_α profiles (relative to the typical Type II, such as SN 1986I). The profiles are often asymmetric, with the red portion of the profile missing. The broad base generally lies blueward relative to the narrow portion of the line. The narrow lines are often resolved, and appear to be wider than the lines from neighboring H II regions. Table 2 lists the candidate objects, and Figure 4 shows two spectra of SN 1987F. SN 1987F has been described by FILIPPENKO [14], where he labels these objects "Seyfert I supernovae". I prefer the label "SN IIn (n = narrow)", which describes the most apparent feature in the spectrum without invoking a particular model. A somewhat larger discussion of these objects has been submitted for publication (SCHLEGEL [15]). These objects may be related to SN 1984E (e.g., HENRY and BRANCH [16]) and SN 1983K (Niemela et al. [17]). Some data on SN 1984E are being resurrected for comparison. The published spectra of SN 1984E appear to be superficially related in that one or two of the spectra look similar to the proposed SN IIn spectra. However, the SN 1984E data show a broader H_β line, while the SN 1983K data show He II 4686Å in emission, and absorption at relatively early times at H_α. Both features are not seen in the proposed SN IIn subclass. Perhaps there is a continuum in some parameter, and SN 1983K and SN 1984E sit a one end, while the proposed SN IIn subclass objects sit at the other end. Further analysis will indicate how likely this idea is.

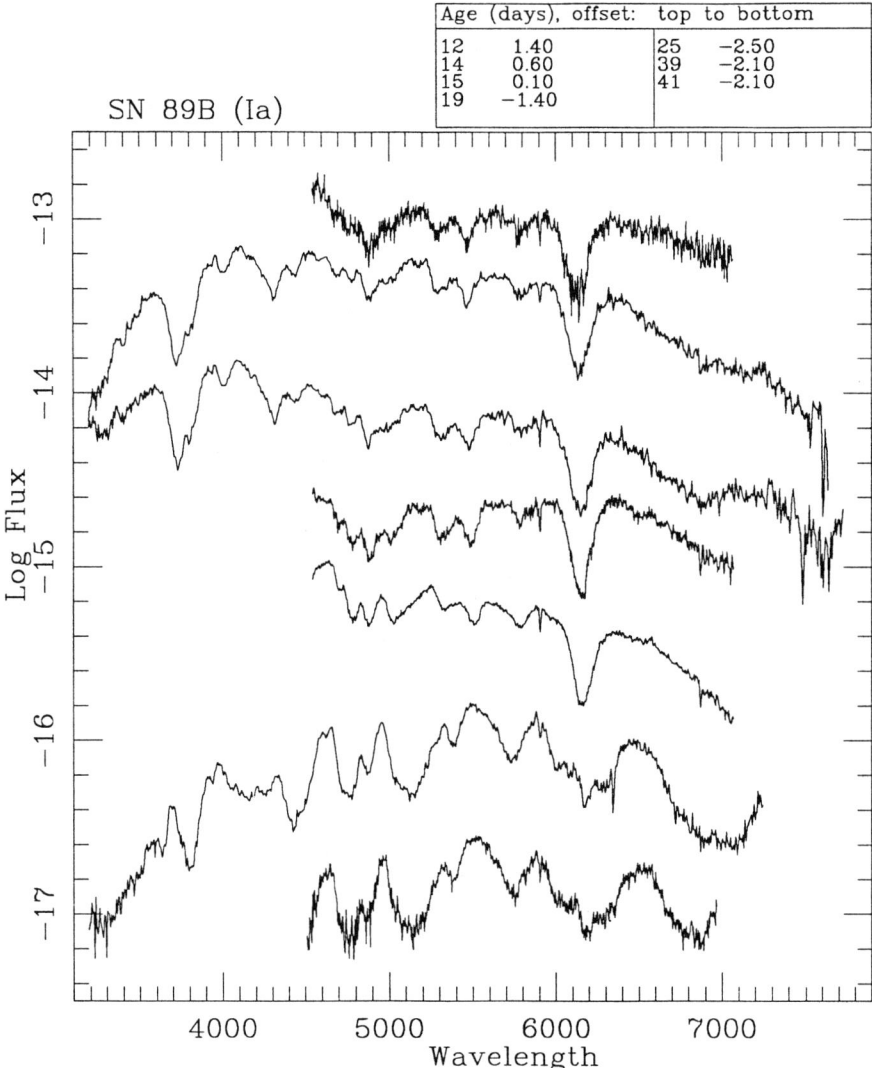

Figure 3. A series of early-time spectra, out to day 100, of the Type Ia SN 1989B. The characteristic 6150Å absorption is present. Note the presence of an emission-like component just redward of the core of the line near day 15. This core emission could distort the velocity behavior attributed to the line. A large database similar to the one being assembled here will investigate such behavior.

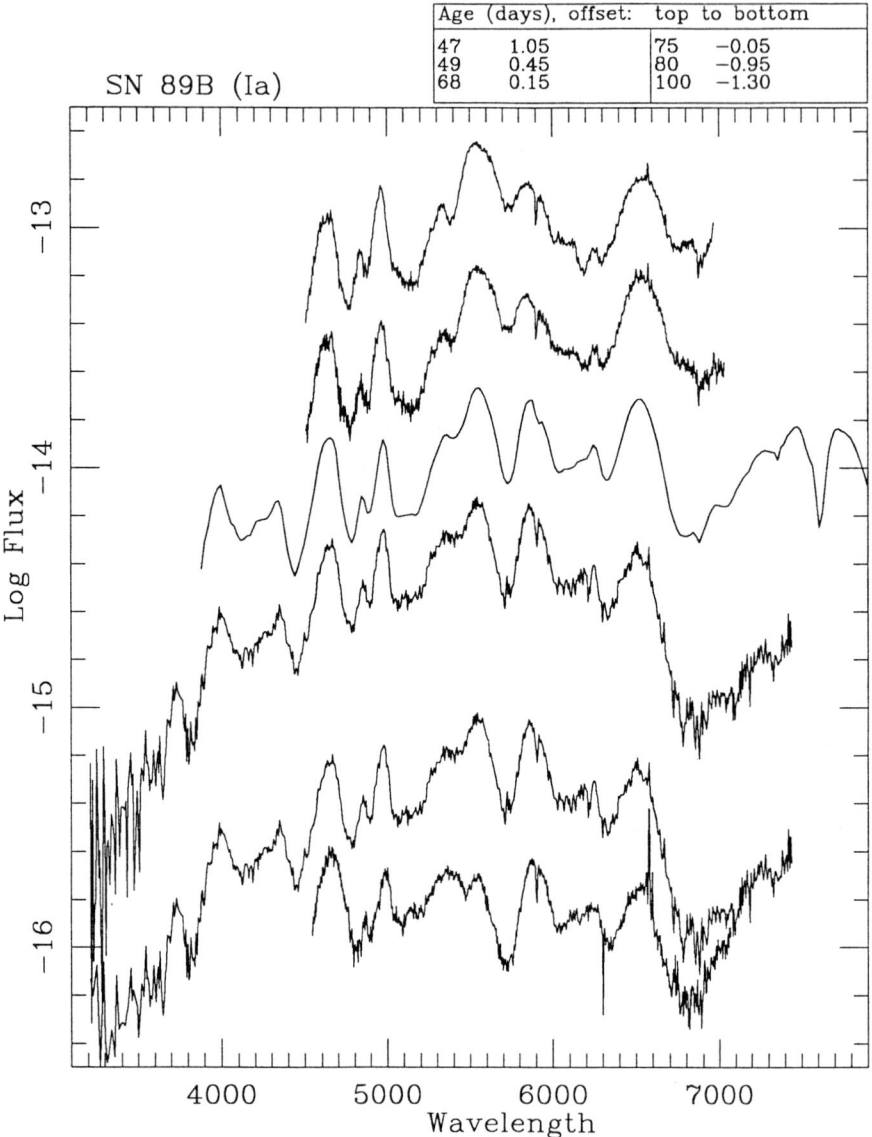

Figure 3. A series of early-time spectra, out to day 100, of the Type Ia SN 1989B. The characteristic 6150Å absorption is present. Note the presence of an emission-like component just redward of the core of the line near day 15. This core emission could distort the velocity behavior attributed to the line. A large database similar to the one being assembled here will investigate such behavior.

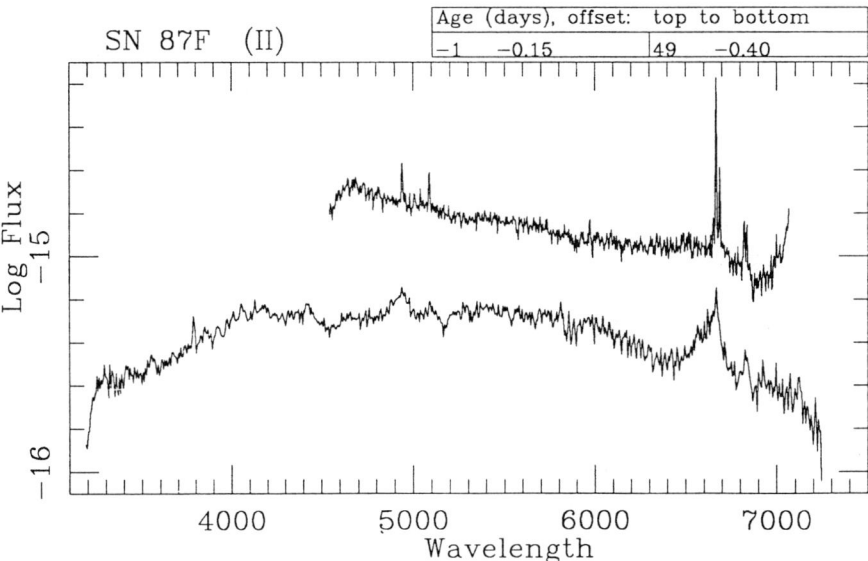

Figure 4: Spectra of SN 1987F, representative of the possible new subclass of Type II supernovae. The narrow lines are prominent in many of the candidate members of this subclass. In addition, the evolution of the spectra is relatively slow.

Table 2
Supernova Members of Proposed Subclass

SN	Galaxy	Type	Offsets (arc secs)
78G	IC 5201	SBcd	W96, N42
87B	NGC 5850	SBb	W75, S145
87C	Mk 90	???	E12.6, S16.8
87F	NGC 4615	Sd	E24, S6
88I	1018+3554	Sc(?)	E6, N1.1
88Z	MCG+3-28-22	Sa(?)	E11, S1
89C	UGC 5249	SBcd	???
89L	NGC 7339	Sbc	E38, N1

Acknowledgments

I thank the following people for contributions to this project: Robert Kirshner, Ed Horine, John Huchra, Ron Marzke, Charles Maxson, April Michel, Doug Mink, Jim Peters, Rudy Schild, Chris Smith, Susan Tokarz, William Wyatt.

References

1. Davis, M. and Latham, D. L. 1979, *SPIE Proceedings*, Tucson.
2. Schmidt, G., Weymann, R., and Foltz, C. 1989, *Preprint*.
3. Panagia, N. *et al.* 1989, *Preprint*.
4. Filippenko, A. V. and Sargent, W. 1985, *Nature*, **316**, 407.
5. Harkness, R., Wheeler, J. C., Margon, B., Downes, R., Kirshner, R., Uomoto, A., Barker, E., Cochran, A., Dinerstein, H., Garnett, D., and Levreault, R., 1987, *Ap. J.*, **317**, 355.
6. Schlegel, E. M. and Kirshner, R. P. 1989, *Astr. J.*, **98**, 577.
7. Schlegel, E. M. 1989, *Proceedings of the Santa Cruz Summer Workshop on Supernovae*, this volume.
8. Pollas, C. 1988, *IAU Circular*, 4651.
9. Cristiani, S., Gouiffes, C., Hanuschik, R., and Magain, P., 1987, *IAU Circular*, 4350.
10. Phillips, M. and Heathcote, S., 1989, *Publ. Astr. Soc. Pac.*, **101**, 137.
11. Lucy, L., 1988, in *Supernova 1987A in the Large Magellanic Cloud*, ed. M. Kafatos and A. Michalitsianos, (Cambridge: Cambridge University Press). p. 74.
12. Hanuschik, R., Thimm, G., and Dachs, J. 1988, *M. N. R. A. S.*, **234**, 41P.
13. Branch, D., Drucker, W., and Jeffrey, D. 1988, *Ap. J. (Letters)*, **330**, L117.
14. Filippenko, A. V. 1989, *Astr. J.*, **97**, 726.
15. Schlegel, E. M. 1989, *Preprint*.
16. Henry, R. B. C. and Branch, D. 1987, *Publ. Astr. Soc. Pac.*, **99**, 112.
17. Niemela, V., Ruiz, M. T., and Phillips, M. 1985, *Ap. J.*, **289**, 52.

Late Time Photometric Behavior of Supernova

Enrico Cappellano, Roberto Barbon, Massimo Della Valle, Sergio Ortolani, Leonida Rosino, & Massimo Turatto

In a previous paper BARBON et al. [1] have shown, from the analysis of the light curves of few well studied supernovae (SNe), that the blue luminosities of SNe in the range 200–400 days after maximum light fade linearly with a decline rate which seems a characteristic for each SN type. The average decline rates in the blue band were found $\gamma_{SNI} = 1.52$, and $\gamma_{SNII} = 0.81$ $[mag/100^d]$. Due to the scanty material available no distinction was made for the different subtypes of SNe, neither was possible to analyze the behaviour in different photometric bands. To improve that work, we started a program of photometric observations of SNe at late stages, using the ESO telescopes at La Silla (DELLA VALLE et al. [2]). In the first run, we observed a sample of ten SNe, i.e. 1985P, 1986G, 1986E, 1986I, 1986L, 1986N, 1986O, 1987D, 1987F, 1987K, that, at the time of observations, were at phase ranging from six months to two years. A full account of the observations and of the reduction technique will be presented elsewhere (TURATTO et al. [3]), while the detailed photometric and spectroscopic study of three SNe of the sample (SN 1986E, SN1987D and SN 1987F) has been given in a previous paper (CAPPELLARO et al. [4]).

In order to study the photometric behaviour of as many SNe as possible, all SN photometry obtained in B and V bands later that 100 days from maximum light was collected from the literature. The complete description of the late time light curves will be given elsewhere ([3]). In the following, we will focus on two general aspects: the late time absolute luminosities and the late time decline rates.

I. Late Time Absolute Luminosity

In Fig. 1 we report the absolute V magnitudes, in the phase range $100 \div 400$ days, of 5 SNe which are representative of different subclasses of SNe.

These objects were chosen because, they have a good coverage and a photometric behaviour typical of their subclass. Absolute magnitudes were calculated using the parent galaxy distance moduli from TULLY [5] and no correction for extinction was applied, since, for all five SNe, it has been estimated to be very low.

Although this should be checked with a more complete sample, Figure 1 shows that, in the considered phase range, the absolute V luminosities of all types of SN have a very little scatter. In particular, we stress the very close match of the light curves of all subclasses of SN II, despite of the very large differences exhibited at earlier

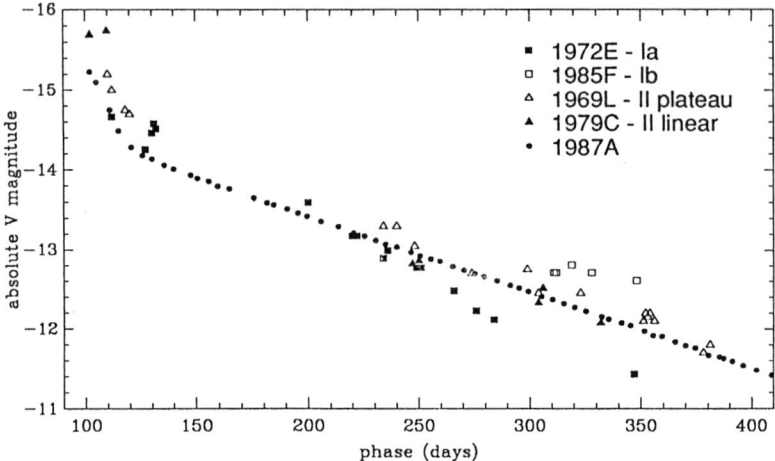

Figure 1: Absolute V light curves of 5 SNe representative of different subclasses in the phase range 100 ÷ 400 days after maximum.

phases, which, in the framework of the radiactive decay input energy model, could argue in favour of the production of a similar amount of ^{56}Ni in the different subclasses of SNII. It appears also that due to the different decline rates, the V luminosity of SN Ia is equal to that of SN II around phase 200. In the radioactive decay context, this is explained assuming that SNI produce a larger amount of ^{56}Ni but, because of a less massive envelope compared to SNII, an increasing fraction of the produced γ-ray escapes from the envelope without being thermalized and giving no contribution to the optical luminosity. Although only few data are available for SNIb, it seems that, while at maximum SNIb are fainter than SNIa due to the slower light curve SNIb are brighter than SNIa after about 300 days.

II. Late Time Decline Rate

Using data collected from the literature together with our observations, we derived the decline rates γ_B, γ_V for all SNe of our sample. The decline rates have been computed with regression lines through all points with phase 150 ÷ 400 days. The lower phase limit was chosen by taking into account two conflicting requirements: to include the largest number of SNe in order to have a fair sample of objects, and, in the meantime, to avoid the early phases in which the light curves show different behaviours peculiar to the different SN types. The upper limit, instead,, was chosen to restrict our analysis to the constant decline regions as shown by SN 1987A (CATCHPOLE et al. [6]).

In Fig. 2 we show the histograms of the observed decline rate in B and V bands, in unit of magnitude per 100 days. In the upper panel also three well studied SNI, for which only γ_{pg} is available, are included [1]. Two more SNII, for which the decline rates have been calculated using photometry at phases later than 400 days are also included. These objects are marked with the symbol * and they have not been used in the computation of the average decline rates reported in Table 1. The Table and Figure confirm that the rate of decline of SNI is in the average higher than for SNII.

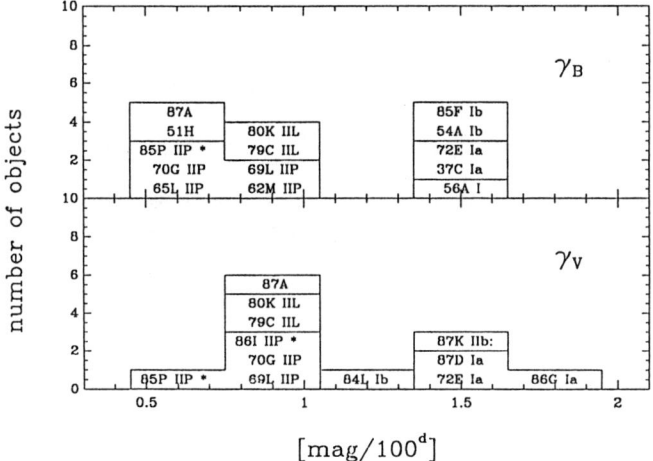

Figure 2: Histograms of the observed decline rates ($[mag/100^d]$) for a sample of SNe of different subclasses, in B (upper panel) and V (lower panel) bands.

A closer inspection, taking into account the different subclasses of SNe, shows that SNIa and SNII *Linear* exhibit the same decline rate in V and B bands, whereas SNII *Plateau*, SN 1987A and SN 1951H (whose late light curve is very similar to that of SN 1987A [3]) appear, in the average, significantly slower in B compared to the V band. For the SNIb it seems that $\gamma_V < \gamma_B$, but we stress again that photometric data on SNIb are scanty. In the lower panel of Fig. 2 the peculiar SN 1987K is classified IIb as suggested by Filippenko [8]. Its late time photometric behaviour appears close to that of SNIa. Finally, it is worth noting that for SN 1987A the V and the bolometric late decline are very close (WHITELOCK et al. [7]), and that the decline rate in the V band for all SNII is very close to that expected from the radioactive decay of ^{56}Co, i.e. $\gamma = 0.976$ $[mag/100^d]$.

Table 1: Average decline rates, $\gamma[mag/100^d]$, in B and V bands for different subtypes of SNe. The number of SNe in each subclass is indicated by n..

	γ_B	n.	γ_V	n.
SNIa	1.52	2	1.59	3
SNIb	1.52	2	1.06	1
SNI total	1.51	5	1.46	4
SNII *Plateau*	0.67	4	0.92	2
SNII *Linear*	0.84	2	0.87	2
1987A-like	0.72	2	0.97	1
SNII total	0.73	8	0.91	5

References

1. Barbon, R., Cappellaro, E. and Turatto, M. 1984, *Astr. Ap.* **135**, 27
2. Della Valle, M., Cappellaro, E., Ortolani, S., Turatto, M. 1988, *ESO Messenger* **52**, 16
3. Turatto, M., Cappellaro, E., Barbon, R., Della Valle, M., Ortolani, S., Rosino, L. in preparation
4. Cappellaro, E., Della Valle, M., Iijima, T., Turatto, M. 1989, *Astr. Ap.* in press
5. Tully, B. R. 1988 *Nearby Galaxies Catalog* Cambridge University Press
6. Catchpole, R. M. et al. 1988, *Mon. Not. R. astr. Soc.* **237**, 55P
7. Whitelock, R. M. et al. 1988, *Mon. Not. R. astr. Soc.* **234**, 5P
8. Filippenko, A. V. 1988, *Astron. J.* **96**, 194

Mean Evolution and Characteristics of Type I Supernova Spectra

Stefano Benetti & Roberto Barbon

The growing interest on the issue of type I supernova homogeneity (see e.g. BRANCH et al. [1] and references therein) has suggested us to use all the spectroscopic material obtained at Asiago Observatory in the past years, through a fairly homogenous set of instrumentation, to give a contribution to the understanding of this important problem. Our first goal was to produce a temporal sequence of spectra defining a standard evolution for SNeI to be used as reference in search for peculiarities and, afterwards, to correlate these ones with other SN features such as the photometric parameters.

I. Type Ia supernovae

We have examined 140 spectra (40% of which collected at Asiago) for a total of 15 supernovae. The Asiago observations have been made either with the 122 cm reflector (prism spectrograph and RCA image tube) or with the 182 cm telescope (grating spectrograph and ITT/VARO image tube). The plates have been digitized with a PDS microphotometer and intensity calibrated. Wavelength calibration has been made through IHAP commands at the HP working station of Asiago Observatory. Although the intrinsic error of the measurements, as derived by wavelength fits to night sky lines, is of the order of 2-3 Å, the central wavelength of the broad SN features has been given with an error of the order of 5-10 Å. No correction for spectral response of the detector has been applied since it is not essential at this stage of the work.

Using the best Asiago data, we have assembled a spectroscopic Atlas showing the mean spectral evolution of SNeIa from 5 days before maximum to 53 days past maximum. Characteristics phase intervals have been found and the common spectral behaviour has been described, deriving also some useful methods to date the spectra independently of the photometry.

We have also found that some features, as the Fe II bands at 4800-4900 Å, do not fit to the normal scheme since in some supernovae (e.g 1986G) these bands appear quite early, whereas in other objects (e.g. 1968E) they develop some weeks after maximum. A full account on the spectral evolution of SNeIa will be given in a forthcoming paper (BENETTI and BARBON [2]); here we anticipate some of the results.

Following [1] we show in Fig.1, for various SNe, the evolution of the photospheric velocity, corrected for the parent galaxy recession, as derived from the SiII λ6355 absorption. The data plotted in the Figure should be accurate and fairly homoge-

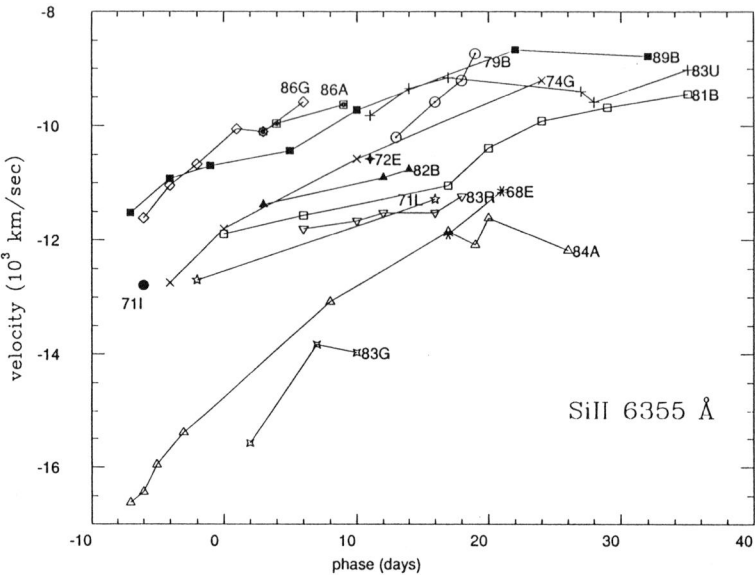

Figure 1: Kinematical evolution, in the frame of the parent galaxy, of the SiII λ6355 absorption feature for 15 supernovae.

neous since they refer to well studied supernovae and half of them come from Asiago spectra. We confirm the velocity evolution found in [1] and moreover, we argue that the inhomogeneity shown by the different objects may decrease with increasing phase. The scatter in Fig.1, from maximum to phase $+20 \div +25$ days, decreases of about 2000 Km/s.

In Fig.2, the same kind of data are given as derived from the MgII λ4481 absorption band. The velocity correlates linearly with phase and, most important, although the error bar is larger than in Fig.1 (670 Km/s against 470 Km/s) the scatter appears smaller. In Fig.2 the kinematically fast SNe 1984A and 1983G behave normally, whereas the data for SN 1989B, which define the low velocity end of our sample, suffer for uncertainty on the date of maximum which has been preliminary set on February 6.

Both Figures 1 and 2 confirm the existence of kinematical differences among SNeIa as recently found, but they also seem to suggest that the amount of this discrepancy depend on the particular spectral feature used and, moreover, that it decreases as the SNe get older.

We have also investigated whether the properties of some spectral features (e.g. phase of appearance, wavelength, etc.) correlate with the photometric parameter β which gives, in mag/100^d, the rate of the initial decline in the B light curve.

Firstly, we checked the correlation between β and the wavelength of the SiII λ6355 absorption at phase $+12^d$, already found by PSKOVSKII [3] and BRANCH [4], using a larger sample of objects and with better values of the parameter β (PSKOVSKII [5]). The data are shown in Fig.3, and no correlation is apparent.

Secondly, we studied the behaviour of the FeII emission bands at 4800 Å and 4900 Å which, as stated above, do not fit to the standard spectral evolution. Relating the phase of appearance of such bands with the same photometric parameter β, we found

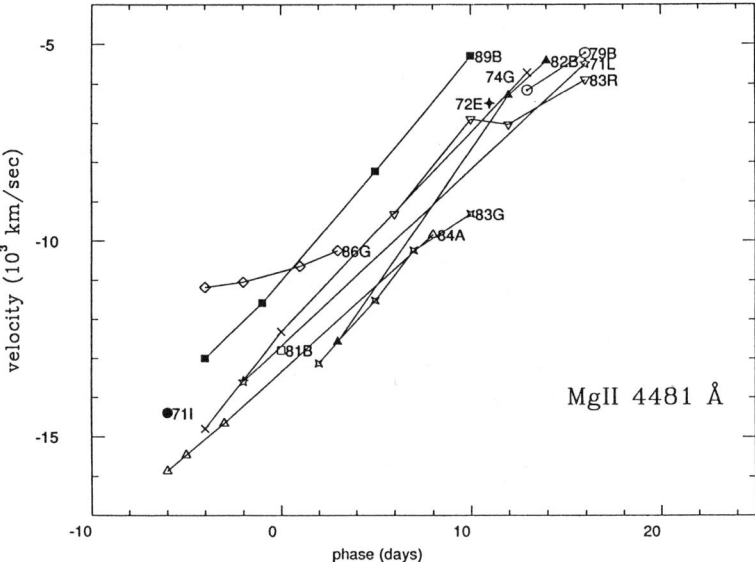

Figure 2: Kinematical evolution, in the frame of the parent galaxy, of the MgII $\lambda 4481$ absorption feature for 12 supernovae.

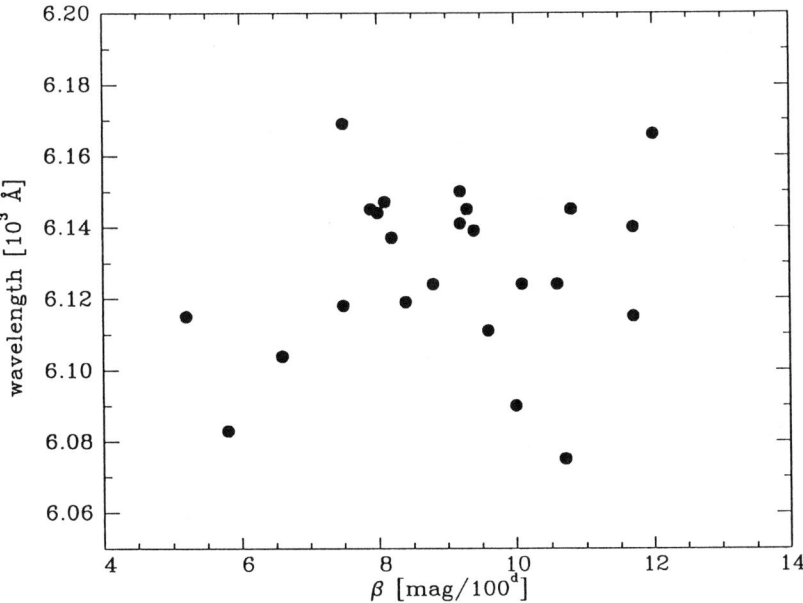

Figure 3: Wavelength of the SiII $\lambda 6355$ absorption, measured at phase $+12^d$, is plotted against the rate of the luminosity decline β.

that, in the average, SNeIa showing large β values (~ 10) develop such bands at early phases, whereas objects with smaller β (~ 5) show these features appreciably later on. Since the rate of luminosity decline depends on the transparency of the ejected supernova envelope, these findings may suggest that such bands are signatures of (processed?) material in the internal layers of the supernova.

II. Type Ib supernovae

A similar study for SNeIb is not yet possible since few such objects have been thoroughly studied: 1962L, 1964L (observed at Asiago), 1983N and 1984L.

However, one result may be anticipated. Taking the behaviour of SN 1984L and 1983N as representative of the subclass, we noticed, respect to SNeIa, a higher degree of peculiarity, such as the lack of the redshift of the spectral features in 1962L and the anomalous behaviour of the absorption doublet at 6300-6500 Å in the same object as well as in SN 1964L. Due to the small sample, more observation of SNeIb are necessary to confirm the large spectral inhomogeneity of this subclass.

Finally, concerning the discrimination between type Ia at late phases and Ib at early epochs, we found that the latter objects exhibit a much faster shift to longer wavelenghts.

References

1. Branch, D., Drucker, W., and Jeffery, D. J., 1988, Ap. J.(Letters), 330, L117.
2. Benetti, S. and Barbon, R. 1989, in preparation.
3. Pskovskii, Y. P. 1977, Soviet Astr., 21, 675.
4. Branch, D. 1981, Ap. J., 248, 1076.
5. Pskovskii, Y. P. 1984, Soviet Astr., 28, 658.

IUE Observations of Supernovae
Nino Panagia & Roberto Gilmozzi

1. Introduction

The launch of the International Ultraviolet Explorer (IUE) satellite in early 1978 marked the beginning of a new era for SN studies because of its capability of measuring the ultraviolet emission of objects as faint as $m_B = 15$. Moreover, just around that time other powerful astronomical instruments have become available, such as the Einstein Observatory for X-ray measurements, the VLA for observations at radio wavelengths and a number of new telescopes either dedicated to infrared observations (*e.g.* UKIRT and IRTF at Mauna Kea) or equipped with new and highly efficient IR instrumentation (*e.g.* AAT and ESO observatories). As a result, a wealth of new information has become available which, thanks to the coordinated effort of astronomers operating at widely different wavelengths, has provided us with fresh insights as for the properties and the nature of supernovae of both types.

The first supernova observed with IUE was SN 1978G in IC 5021, just toward the end of the first year of IUE operation. It was a type II SN discovered somewhat after maximum so that the observations could not be carried out for any long time.

In 1979 a joint ESA-SERC target-of-opportunity program was started for observing bright supernovae, defined such as *i.e.* $B_{max} < 12$. And sure enough, in April 1979 a bright supernova, SN 1979C in NGC 4321, was discovered, promptly observed and followed with IUE in a collaboration across the Atlantic, for more than three months (PANAGIA *et al.* [1]). Since then, IUE has observed all bright supernovae plus a number of fainter ones: a total of 15, out of which 6 are of Type II, 7 Type Ia and 2 Type Ib. However, only five SNe, namely 1979C, 1980K, 1981B, 1983N and, obviously, 1987A, were bright enough to obtain high quality ultraviolet spectra and/or to follow their time evolution in detail.

A summary of the IUE observations is presented in Table 1. The data of the first 6 SNe have been collected in an atlas compiled by BENVENUTI *et al.* [2]. A paper containing IUE, optical and IR observations of the SNIb prototype 1983N will eventually be completed this year (PANAGIA *et al.*, [3]), soon followed by an analogous paper on SN 1980K. A preliminary discussion of both SNe can be found in PANAGIA [4]. The observations of SN 1987A have already been discussed in part in a number of papers which I am not going to refer to here. The relevant references can be found

Table I

Summary of *IUE* Observations of Supernovae

SN	Type	B_{max}	Galaxy	Observing Period	# SW	# LW	Station
1978G	II	<12.9 V	IC 5201	78/11/30–78/12/11	–	2	G
1979C	II	11.6	NGC 4321	79/04/21–79/08/04	12	19	V,G
1980K	II	11.6	NGC 6946	80/10/30–80/12/09	12	24[a]	V,G
1980N	Ia	~12.5	NGC 1316	80/12/11–81/01/16	1	8	V,G
1981B	Ia	12.0	NGC 4536	81/03/09–81/04/05	2	5	V
1982B	Ia	13.7	NGC 2268	82/02/18	1	2	V
1983G	Ia	12.9	NGC 4753	83/04/08–83/04/25	1	7	V,G
1983N	Ib	11.6	NGC 5236	83/07/04–84/07/31	12	16	V,G
1984J	II	13.2 V	NGC 1559	84/08/13	1	–	V
1985F	Ib	12.1	NGC 4618	85/05/18	–	1	V
1985L	II	<12.5	NGC 5033	85/06/28–85/07/17	1	2	V
1986G	Ia	12.5	NGC 5128	86/05/06–86/05/29	–	6	V,G
1987A	II	4.5	LMC	87/02/24–present[b]	207[a]	509[a]	V,G
1989B	Ia	11.8 V	NGC 3627	89/01/13–89/02/01	–	4	G
1989M	Ia	12.0 V	NGC 4579	89/07/06–89/07/20	–	7	V,G

[a] High resolution observations obtained as well.
[b] As of April '89 for GSFC, July '89 for Vilspa.

in the recent review by KIRSHNER and GILMOZZI [5]. Let me just mention here that the data collected in the first two years will be presented in an extensive atlas in preparation (KIRSHNER et al. [6]).

In addition to the obvious interest of observing SNe *per se*, *i.e.* to understand their nature and the mechanisms inducing their explosion, bright supernovae have been used as background sources to study the intervening interstellar medium, most remarkably the galactic haloes, with an accuracy impossible otherwise. Two such supernovae have been observed in the UV at high dispersion, namely SN 1980K in NGC 6946 (PETTINI et al. [7]) and, needless to say, SN 1987A in the LMC (DE BOER et al. [8], DUPREE et al. [9], BLADES et al. [10], [11]).

2. Type Ia Supernovae

Although 7 Type Ia SNe have been observed with IUE none of them has been followed for a long time either because of their intrinsic UV faintness or because of satellite pointing constraints. Therefore, for all of them we have observations concentrated around the epoch of their maximum light but we know little about their time evolution.

The UV spectrum is declining quickly with frequency, making it hard to detect any signal at short wavelengths. This aspect is illustrated in Figure 1, which displays the LW spectra of the first three Type Ia SNe observed with IUE, plus SN 1986G. In all cases the observing epoch is within three days from the optical maximum. It also appears that the spectrum is not a smooth continuum but rather consists of a number of "bands" which are observed, with somewhat different strength. The most prominent feature is the emission that peaks at ~ 2950 Å with a half-power width of ~ 100 Å, *i.e.* $\Delta v \simeq 10^4 \ km \ s^{-1}$. Alternatively, this band may be the result of strong absorptions occuring on both sides of the apparent emission, *i.e.* centered at ~ 2840 Å and ~ 3060 Å and having half-power widths of the order of 100 Å. A similarly prominent emission band is seen at $\lambda \sim 1890$ Å in the only one spectrum obtained at short wavelengths for SN 1981b. Several other absorptions features can be recognized, which are present at all epochs of observation. Although some of them might be identified with multiplets of Fe I, Fe II and Mg II, no detailed study has been made yet for the majority of the absorptions. Nevertheless, the very fact that the spectrum is so similar for the first three SNe and at all epochs when observations were made is already an important result. This support the idea of an overall homogeneity of properties of Type I SNe.

Confirmation of this result has come from observation of all of the other Type Ia SNe with the only clear exception of SN 1986G. This latter deviates from the main path in that the various UV features, such as the one around 2950 Å, are considerably less prominent relative to the continuum as compared with canonical Type Ia spectra (see Fig. 1). It is of interest to note that the rate of decline of the B light curve of SN 1986G was remarkably fast, corresponding to the infrequent Pskovskii class $\beta = 12$ (PHILLIPS et al [12]).

3. Type Ib Supernovae

SN 1983N in NGC 5236 (= M 83) is one of the best studied SNe with IUE. Preliminary results can be found in PANAGIA [4], while a complete account of the UV, optical and

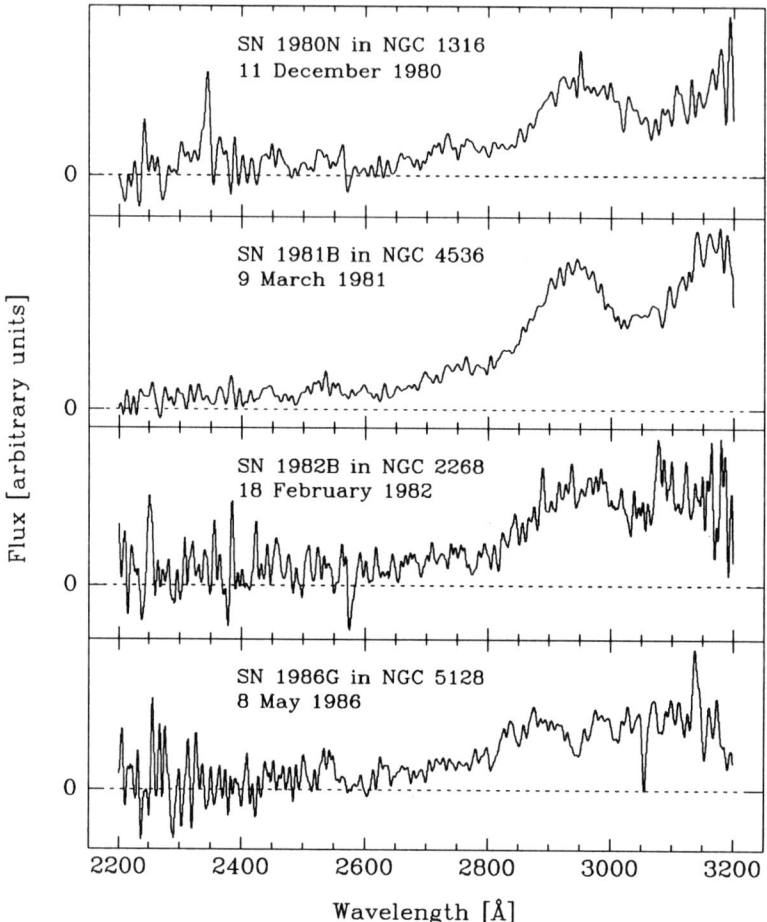

Figure 1 - The LW spectra of SN 1980N, 1981B, 1982B and 1986G at epochs near the optical maximum.

IR observations obtained in the first two months after discovery will be published soon (PANAGIA et al. [3]).

Its UV spectrum closely resembles that of Type Ia SNe at comparable epoch and, as such, only a minor fraction of the SN energy is radiated in the UV. In particular, only 13% of the total luminosity was emitted shortward of 3400 Å at the time of the UV maximum. Moreover, there is no indication of any stronger emission in the UV at very early epochs: this implies that the initial radius of the SN, i.e. the radius the stellar progenitor had when the shock front reached the photosphere, was definitely much less than 10^{13} cm and probably lower than 10^{12} cm, and rules out a red supergiant as a possible progenitor of this supernova. A WR star can equally well be excluded according to the stringent arguments summarized by PANAGIA and LAIDLER [13] The most likely scenario is that of a binary system in which both stars are relative massive ($> 5M_\odot$) in which the primary explodes after becoming a massive white dwarf ($M \sim 1.35\ M_\odot$) and accreting matter from the companion while it is a red giant (cf. SRAMEK, PANAGIA and WEILER [14]).

SN 1985F was discovered by FILIPPENKO and SARGENT [15] near the nucleus of NGC 4618. It was observed once with IUE, on 1985 May 18, and only with the long wavelength camera. At that time the SN was approximately a year old. The observed spectrum is essentially featureless and flat, with an average flux of $6 \times 10^{14}\ erg\ cm^{-2}\ Å^{-1}\ s^{-1}$. This is approximately one half of the optical continuum level and may entirely be due to the emission of the underlying HII region.

4. Type II Supernovae

Among the five Type II SNe which have been observed with IUE, only two, namely SN 1979C and SN 1980K, were bright enough to allow a detailed study of their properties in the UV.

The main characteristic is that the UV emission is rather strong for quite some time (PANAGIA et al. [1]). In particular, for both 1979C and 1980K the UV flux is higher than the extrapolation of the optical spectrum with a black body curve, with a clear excess shortward of $\lambda = 2000$ Å. Such an excess is found at all epochs although it is less pronounced at early times. FRANSSON [16] has shown that the UV excess may be photospheric radiation which has been Compton-scattered by energetic, thermal electrons ($T \sim 10^9\ K$) at the shock front where the ejecta interact with pre-existing circumstellar material. This model can explain both the extra radiation observed at short wavelengths and the high ionization implied by some emission lines (e.g. NIV] 1486 Å, CIV 1550 Å, etc.) observed in the spectrum of SN 1979C (PANAGIA et al. [1]).

Emission lines in the UV have been detected only for SN 1979C. From a comparison of the line profiles observed in the UV and in the visual with theoretical calculations (FRANSSON et al. [17]) concluded that the UV emission lines of highly ionized species are produced in the upper atmosphere, as well as Hα or Mg II λ 2800 Å, although just in the outermost layers where density is lower and the ionizing radiation flux is higher. The line profiles imply an expansion velocity of 8400 $km\ s^{-1}$ (FRANSSON et al. [17]), which is only marginally lower than that measured in the optical (i.e. 9200 $km\ s^{-1}$; PANAGIA et al. [1]). From an analysis of the NV 1240 Å, NIV] 1486 Å, CIV 1550

Å, NIII] 1750 Å and C III] 1909 Å line intensities the abundance ratio of nitrogen to carbon has been estimated to be N/C ∼ 8 (FRANSSON et al. [17]) i.e. ∼ 30 times higher than the cosmic value. This strong enhancement of nitrogen relative to carbon suggests that the pre-supernova star was a massive supergiant which had undergone a long period of mass loss, thereby exposing CNO processed material.

A similar overabundance of N has been found in the wind of SN 1987A progenitor (FRANSSON et al. [18]). This result suggests that a considerable N overabundance may be a signature of Type II supernovae.

References

1. Panagia, N., et al.: M.N.R.A.S., 192, 861, (1980).

2. Benvenuti, P., Sanz Fernandez de Cordoba, L., Wamsteker, W., Macchetto, F., Palumbo, G. C., Panagia, N.: ESA SP-1046 (1982).

3. Panagia, N. et al.: in preparation (1989).

4. Panagia, N.: in "Supernovae as Distance Indicators", ed. N. Bartel (Berlin: Springer), p. 14 (1985).

5. Kirshner, R. P., Gilmozzi, R.: in "Exploring the Universe with the IUE Satellite" (2nd edition), ed. in chief Y.Kondo, (Dordrecht: Kluwer), in press (1989).

6. Kirshner, R. P., Panagia, et al.: in preparation (1990).

7. Pettini, M. et al.: M.N.R.A.S., 199, 409 (1982).

8. de Boer, K., Grewing, M., Richtler, T., Wamsteker, W., Gry, C., Panagia, N.: Astron. Ap., 177, L37 (1987).

9. Dupree, A.K., Kirshner, R.P., Nassiopoulos, G.E., Raymond, J.C., Sonneborn, G.: Ap. J., 320, 597 (1987).

10. Blades, J.C., Wheatley, J.M., Panagia, N., Grewing, M., Pettini, M., Wamsteker, W.: Ap. J. (Letters), 332, L75 (1988).

11. Blades, J.C., Wheatley, J.M., Panagia, N., Grewing, M., Pettini, M.,Wamsteker, W.: Ap. J., 334, 308 (1988).

12. Phillips, M.M., et al.: P.A.S.P., 99, 592 (1989).

13. Panagia, N., Laidler, V.C.: this Conference.

14. Sramek, R. A., Panagia, N., Weiler, K. W.: Ap.J. (Letters), 285, L59 (1984).

15. Filippenko, A. V., Sargent, W. L. W.: Astr. J., 91, 691 (1986).

16. Fransson, C.: Physica Scripta, T7, 50 (1984).

17. Fransson, C., Benvenuti, P., Gordon, C., Hempe, K., Palumbo, G. G. C., Panagia, N., Reimers, D., Wamsteker, W.: Astr. Ap., 132, 1 (1984).

18. Fransson, C., Cassatella, A., Gilmozzi, R., Kirshner, R.P., Panagia, N., Sonneborn, G., Wamsteker, W.: Ap. J., 336, 429 (1989).

VLBI Observations of Supernovae and Their Remnants

Norbert Bartel

1. INTRODUCTION

The technique of Very-Long-Baseline Interferometry (VLBI) allows us to contribute uniquely to research of supernovae (SNe) and supernova remnants (SNRs). To illustrate the potential of SN VLBI, let us take as an example the VLA image of the SNR Cas A (BRAUN, GULL, and PERLEY [1]) and consider the wealth of information revealed in the details of the brightness distribution in each segment of the shell. Let us then take as an example any recent SN and imagine that we make a set of detailed maps of the radio brightness distribution. Not only would we have imaged the supernova shortly after the explosion, but we would also have monitored the two-dimensional expansion of the debris over a large fraction of the SN's lifetime and, perhaps, eventually revealed a pulsar nebula in the center of the expanding cloud. However, until recently, the reality of VLBI of SNe and SNRs only trailed our imagination and caused us to be more modest, especially in those cases where we not only failed to detect a SN but also failed to obtain any useful information on that SN. I do not really want to elaborate on these cases.

More rewarding were VLBI observations of SN1987A made only 5.2 d after the neutrino burst. We did not detect the SN, but we obtained important lower bounds on the angular radius and mean angular expansion velocity of the SN's radiosphere.

SN1980K in NGC6946 and an SNR in NGC4449 were detected in VLBI observations and allowed bounds on their angular radii to be determined. In the latter case, such a bound, when combined with a value for the distance of the galaxy and with information from optical spectroscopic data, led to an estimate of the age of the SNR.

SN1979C in M100 in the Virgo cluster of galaxies has been detected in VLBI observations at several epochs. For each epoch, an angular radius was determined. By virtue of the SN's having been monitored for a large fraction of its lifetime, and its relatively large distance from us, SN1979C has been, scientifically, one of the most rewarding supernovae of the ones observed with VLBI. The observations allowed estimates of the supernova's angular expansion velocity and of bounds on any deceleration or acceleration of it. Combined with a determination of the radial expansion velocity of the line-emitting and -absorbing gas, the distance to the Virgo cluster and Hubble's constant could be estimated (for the two latter estimates, see BARTEL, this volume).

Of the 23 hot spots in the starburst galaxy M82, six were detected in VLBI observations. For one of these sources, an image could be obtained. The image, combined with an estimate of the expansion velocity of the hot spot and earlier measurements of their luminosities and radio light curves, led to the conclusion that the hot spots are indeed SNe and SNRs. This result led to further conclusions about the SNe/SNRs' ages and about the SN rate in the inner 600 pc of M82.

SN1986J in NGC891 is the first SN imaged with VLBI. By virtue of the SN's relatively large flux density and relatively compact structure and of the VLBI array's recently increased sensitivity, we can now indeed hope to obtain a set of images of the expanding gas and make a movie of an exploding star.

In the remainder, I will review the observations and their results for the six SNe and SNRs investigated with VLBI, in the order of increasing information obtained and obtainable as outlined in this section. An earlier review is given in BARTEL [2].

2. SNe AND SNRs OBSERVED WITH VLBI

2.1 SN1987A: no detection – bound on θ

With an unprecedented promptness, the radio emission of SN1987A reached its maximum of ~ 140 mJy at 1.4 GHz (TURTLE et al. [3]) only three days after the neutrino burst (AGLIETTA et al. [4]; BIONTA et al. [5]; HIRATA et al. [6]). The only antennas in the southern hemisphere that were conceivably capable of resolving the expanding shell of SN1987A were one of the antennas in Tidbinbilla, Australia, and the 26-m diameter antenna in Hartebeesthoek, South Africa. After frantic organization, Mark III VLBI observations were made at 2.3 GHz at $t = 5.2, 6.2,$ and 7.2 d with the latter antenna and NASA's 34-m diameter DSS42 antenna in Tidbinbilla (SHAPIRO et al. [7]). Unfortunately, at the time of the observations, the SN was already too weak and too extended to be detected with the above interferometer. No fringes were found from the supernova's radio emission on any of those three observing days, although fringes were obtained for the calibrator sources on all three days with amplitudes agreeing (to within the corresponding combined standard errors) with those obtained from VLBI measurements made at the same resolution, but five years earlier (PRESTON et al. [8]; G. NICOLSON 1987, priv. communication).

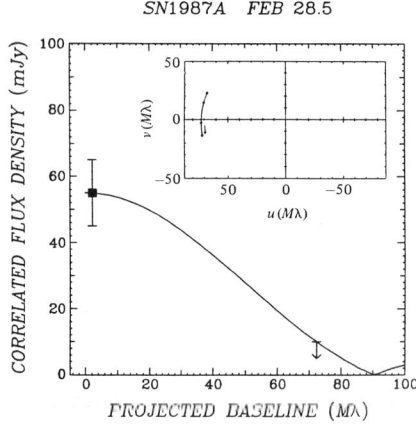

Fig. 1. The total flux density and an upper bound on the correlated flux density of SN1987A on ~ 28.5 Feb. 1987, together with the prediction of a model of an optically thin uniform sphere with a radius of 1.6 mas. The prediction is similar to that from a model of an optically thin shell with an outer angular radius of 1.25 mas. The u-v track for the VLBI observations is plotted in the inset.

The upper bound on the correlated flux density of SN1987A obtained on the first day of the VLBI observations was compared with the corresponding total flux density (Fig. 1) to derive a lower bound on the angular radius of the radiosphere (BARTEL et al. [9]; JAUNCEY et al. [10]; SHAPIRO et al. [7]). For an optically thin shell model with a shell thickness of $\sim 15\%$ of the shell's outer radius, the lower bound on the radius is $\theta_{radio} > 1.25 \pm 0.07$ mas. Here and hereafter, the quoted errors are meant to be standard errors (σ), with statistical and systematic contributions combined, unless otherwise stated. The use of any other physically plausible model would result in an up to $\sim 30\%$ larger lower bound (see, e.g., MARSCHER [11]). Given a distance to SN1987A of 50 ± 5 kpc (FEAST and WALKER [12]), the lower bound on the angular radius corresponds to a lower bound (with the combined 1σ error subtracted) on the linear radius, R_{radio}, of $R_{\text{radio}} > 8.3 \times 10^{14}$ cm $= 12 \times 10^3 \, R_\odot = 55$ AU, at $t = 5.2 \, d$. If one assumes that the radiosphere expanded linearly from zero size at $t = 0$, the lower bound on the radius corresponds to a lower bound on the expansion velocity, v_{radio}, of the radiosphere: $v_{\text{radio}} > 19 \times 10^3$ km s^{-1}.

Since the distance to the Large Magellanic Cloud is known to within about 10%, SN1987A allowed for the first time a comparison of the linear radii and the expansion velocities of a supernova's photosphere and radiosphere with those of the supernova's line-emitting and -absorbing regions. In Fig. 2, the lower bounds on the radius and expansion velocity obtained from the VLBI radio data are compared with the corresponding radii and velocities obtained from optical photometric (MENZIES et al. [13]) and spectroscopic (HANUSCHIK and DACHS [14]; BLANCO et al. [15]) data.

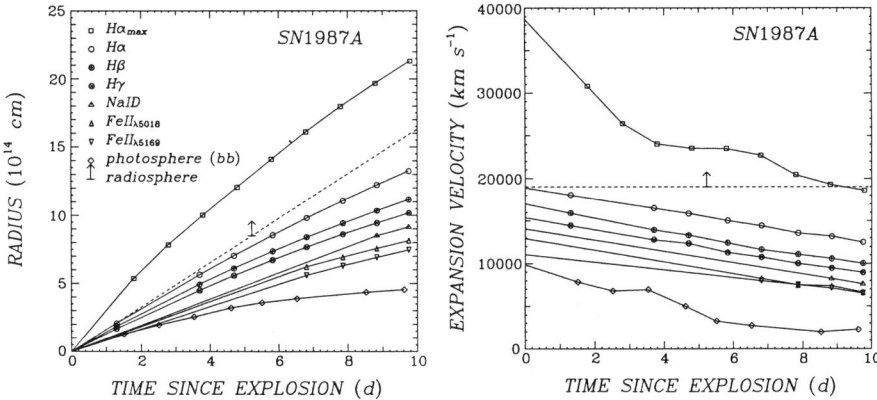

Fig. 2. Lower bounds on the radius and the corresponding (assumed uniform) expansion velocity of the radiosphere of SN1987A (dashed lines), compared with radii and expansion velocities of the blackbody photosphere and the line-forming regions. The radii of the line-forming regions were obtained from an integration of the velocities corresponding to the blueshifts of the absorption minima of the indicated lines and the largest observed blueshift, $H\alpha_{\text{max}}$, the latter from the blue edge of the $H\alpha$ absorption trough. The expansion velocities of the photosphere were obtained from a differentiation of the photosphere's radii. The uncertainties of the $H\alpha_{\text{max}}$ velocities are ~ 1000 km s^{-1} and those of the $H\alpha_{\text{max}}$ radii are smaller than the symbols. Other uncertainties were not given in the original papers but are believed to be not larger than those of the $H\alpha_{\text{max}}$ velocities and radii, respectively.

At the time of the VLBI observations, the radius and the expansion velocity of the radiosphere were both at least a factor 2.5 larger than those of the blackbody photosphere and, respectively, at least 10% and 25% larger than the radius and velocity inferred from the $H\alpha$-line absorption minimum. The results not only add to our knowledge of supernovae but are also important in limiting the uncertainties accompanying the use of supernovae as distance indicators (see, e.g., BARTEL [16], [17]; BARTEL et al. [18]), if the physical processes responsible for the radio emission from SN1987A are typical for SNe in general (see BARTEL, this volume).

2.2 SN1980K and SNR in NGC4449: detection – bound on Θ

The supernova SN1980K in the galaxy NGC6946 reached its maximum flux density of ~ 2.5 mJy at 1.5 GHz ~ 0.4 yr after the explosion that occurred on, or near, 1980 Oct. 17 (WEILER et al. [19]). VLBI observations were made at 2.3 GHz on 1983 May 7 with the sensitive NASA 64-m antennas at Goldstone, CA and Madrid, Spain. The supernova was detected in two out of three adjacent 13-min scans. The visibility amplitudes determined in the two scans, and an upper bound determined in the third scan, are shown in Fig. 3. Since the visibility amplitudes of the three segments are expected to be approximately Gaussianly distributed, we can compute their mean value and standard error and infer that SN1980K was unresolved at the epoch of our VLBI observations, 2.54 yr after the assumed date of 1980 Oct. 17 for the explosion. The value for the angular radius of a shell model is: $\Theta \lesssim 0.5 \pm 0.5$ mas, equivalent to $\Theta < 1$ mas (BARTEL [20]). The prediction from this model is also shown in Fig. 3.

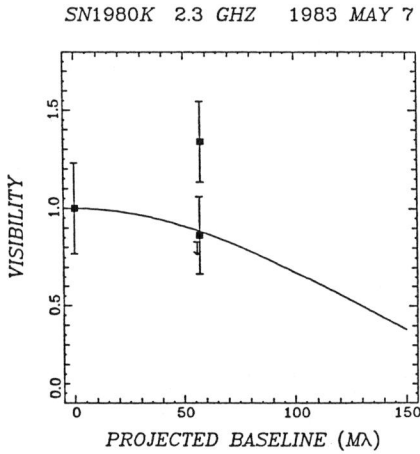

Fig. 3. Visibility amplitudes and the prediction from a shell model. The visibility amplitude at zero spacing was obtained from interpolating between several measurements made with the VLA by WEILER et al. [19] at 1.5 and 5 GHz only two days to seven weeks prior to our VLBI observations.

The SNR in the galaxy NGC4449 (SEAQUIST and BIGNELL [21]; BALICK and HECKMAN [22]) at a distance from Earth of a few Mpc shows a declining flux density that was ~ 15 mJy at 1.5 GHz in 1981 (DE BRUYN [23]). So far, only an upper bound on the SNR's angular radius of 38 mas (Cas A morphology assumed) has been determined (DE BRUYN [23]) with VLBI, but new data may some time allow an image of this source to be made (DE BRUYN 1988, priv. communication).

When the upper bound is combined with the galaxy's distance and the SNR's linear expansion velocity (KIRSHNER and BLAIR [24]), an upper bound on the SNR's age of ~ 200 yr can be estimated. There is some optical evidence for a lower bound on the age of ~ 60 yr. If this lower bound could be confirmed, the SNR in NGC4449 would be, together with the SNRs in M82, an important element for supernova VLBI research in bridging the gap of ages between extragalactic SNe with ages of up to ~ 10 yr and galactic SNRs with ages $\gtrsim 300$ yr.

2.3 SN1979C: detection – $\theta(t)$

The supernova SN1979C in the galaxy M100 in the Virgo cluster reached its maximum flux density at 1.4 GHz of ~ 10 mJy 3.7 yr after the explosion on, or around, 1979 Apr. 1 (WEILER et al. [19]). Figure 4 displays a radio map (BARTEL et al. [18]) of the galaxy with the supernova located in one of the galaxy's spiral arms.

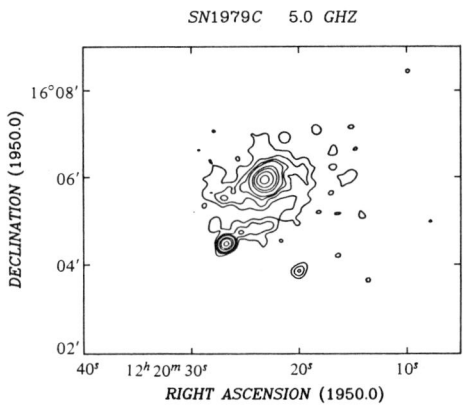

Fig. 4. Radio map of SN1979C, located at the southern edge of a spiral arm of the galaxy M100. The map was made with the VLA on 1982 Dec. 8.

VLBI observations commenced on 1982 Dec. 8 and have resulted in angular radius determinations at 5 GHz at four consecutive epochs. The measured visibility amplitudes and the predictions from a model for the supernova's brightness distribution are shown in Fig. 5.

The angular radius determinations, Θ, are plotted, as a function of the time since explosion, t, in Fig. 6. A weighted least-squares fit of the form $\Theta \propto t^m$ gives $\Theta = 0.42 \pm 0.03$ mas for the time of our first VLBI observations at $t = 3.69$ yr, and $m = 1.03 \pm 0.15$, consistent with uniform expansion.

These data provide the first direct measurement of the expansion of a supernova. The expansion is consistent with being uniform, as predicted on the basis of a fit of the circumstellar interaction model (CHEVALIER [25]) to the radio light curves at two frequencies (CHEVALIER [26]; WEILER et al. [19]).

VLBI observations from 1988 are still being analyzed. The results from these observations together with results from anticipated observations in the spring of 1990 could help to reduce the uncertainty in m considerably. A small uncertainty of m could lead to a model-independent distinction between a uniform or decelerated expansion ($m \leq 1$), as expected in the circumstellar interaction model, or an accelerated expansion, as could be expected if a central pulsar powers the nebula.

2.4 SNR41.9+58 and other SNRs in M82: image – $\dot{\Theta}$

The starburst galaxy M82 (Fig. 7) has been known for some time to contain more than ~ 20 radio hot spots in its central region of ~ 600 pc extent (KRONGERG, BIERMANN, and SCHWAB [27], [29]; UNGER et al. [30]). We assume the galaxy's distance from Earth to be 3.3 Mpc (TAMMANN and SANDAGE [31]; but see also SANDAGE [32] for a $\sim 50\%$ larger estimate). Since the hot spots' time variability (see, e.g., KRONBERG and SRAMEK [33]) and spectra (e.g., KRONBERG, BIERMANN, and SCHWAB [27]) also resemble those of SNe and since a high star-formation rate with a correspondingly high SN rate of ~ 0.3 yr^{-1} is expected for M82 on the basis of infrared observations (RIEKE et al. [34]), the hot spots in M82 were believed to be SNe or young SNRs (e.g., KRONBERG, BIERMANN, and SCHWAB [27], [29]; UNGER et al. [30]).

VLBI determinations of the sizes, morphologies, and expansion velocities of the hot spots further helped to clarify their nature and qualified earlier VLBI observations made by GELDZAHLER et al. [35] that seemed to support different interpretations of the nature of the hot spots.

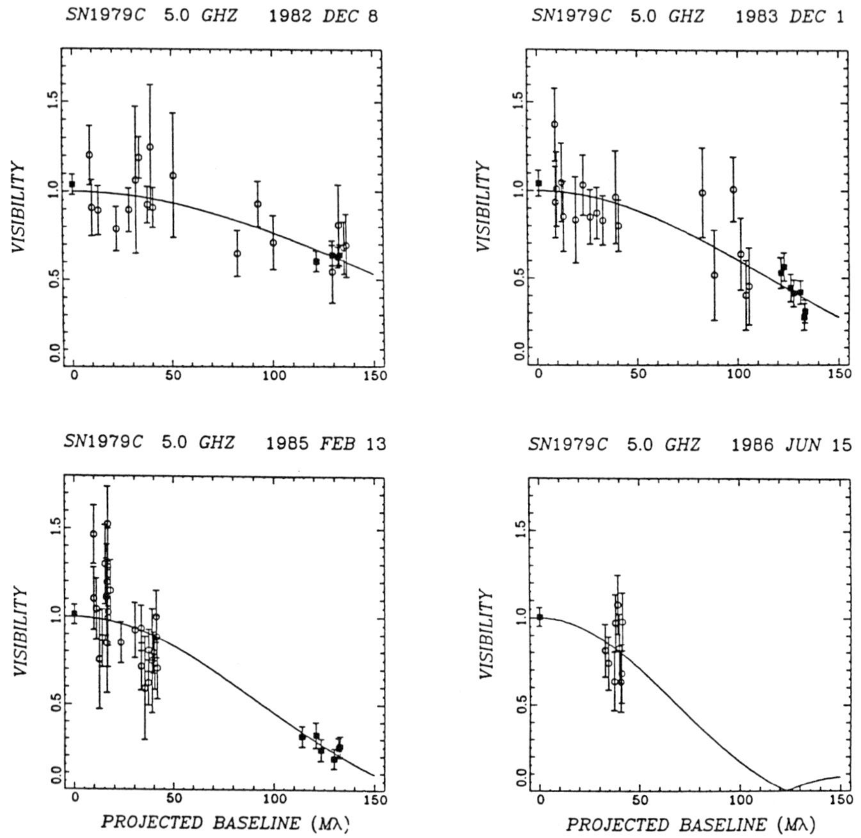

Figure 5. Measured visibility amplitudes at 5.0 GHz and predictions from the fit of a uniform sphere model. The filled squares show the most significant data points, obtained with the VLA alone and with the Bonn-VLA interferometer. At epoch 1986 June 15, the antenna at Bonn was malfunctioning and therefore prevented the recording of data from SN1979C with the transatlantic interferometers.

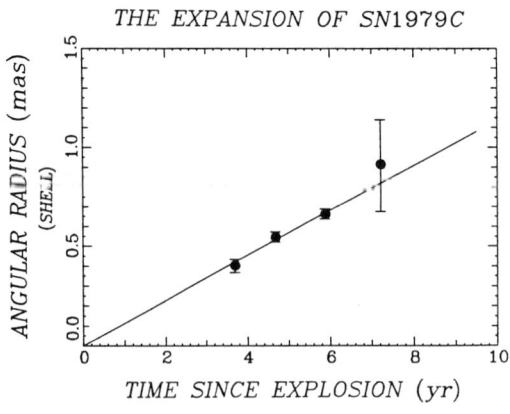

Fig. 6. The angular radius determinations for a shell model. For the extreme models of a ring and a uniform sphere, the ordinate scale has to be multiplied by 0.8 and 1.3, respectively. The solid line represents uniform expansion ($m = 1$), which is consistent with our weighted least-squares solution for m.

VLBI Observations

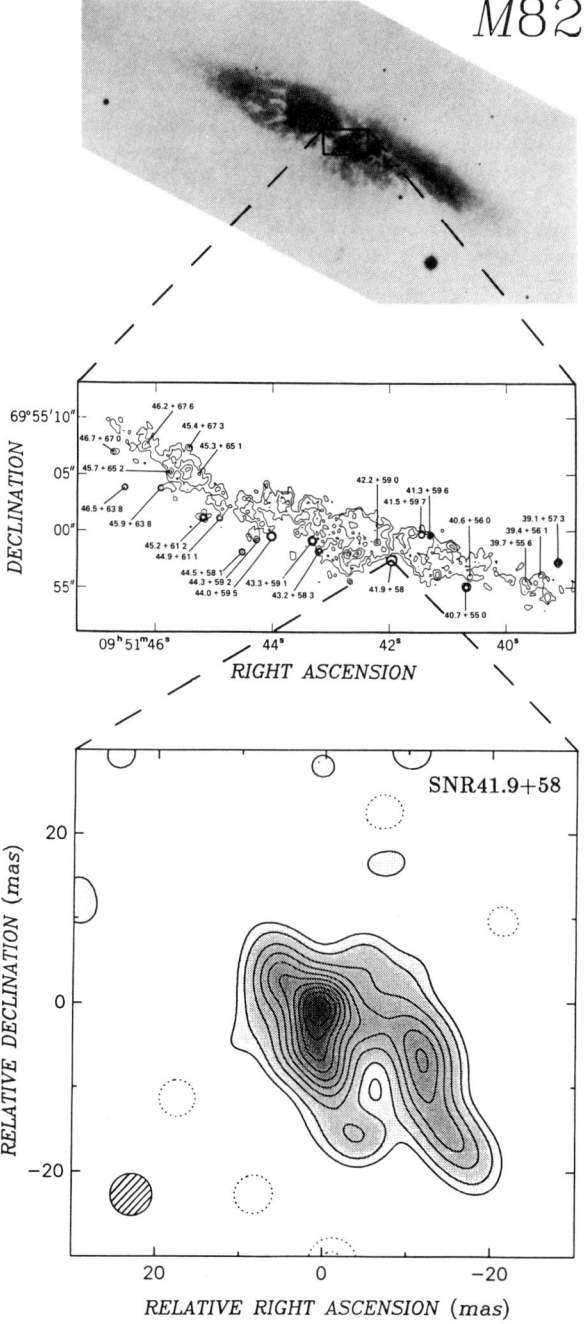

Fig. 7. A hybrid map at 2.3 GHz (lower part) of SNR41.9+58, the strongest compact component in the nuclear region of M82. The contours are at 90, 80, 70, 60, 50, 40, 30, 10, 5, −5% of the peak brightness of 25 mJy per beam area, equivalent to 4.4×10^8 K. The 50% contour of the restoring beam is shown as the striped circle in the lower left corner. The map is shown in relation to a radio map of the inner 600 pc of M82, made by KRONBERG, BIERMANN, and SCHWAB [27] with the VLA at a frequency of 4.9 GHz and with an angular resolution of 0.″34. The contours of the VLA map are shown at 40, 30, 20, 10, and 5% of the peak brightness of 102 mJy per beam area. All the sources we observed with VLBI, and analyzed, are labeled. For results from VLBI observations of the sources other than SNR41.9+58, which are presumably also SNRs, see BARTEL et al.[28]. The radio map is juxtaposed to an optical image of M82 taken from Sandage's Hubble atlas of galaxies. For each of the three images, north is up and east to the left.

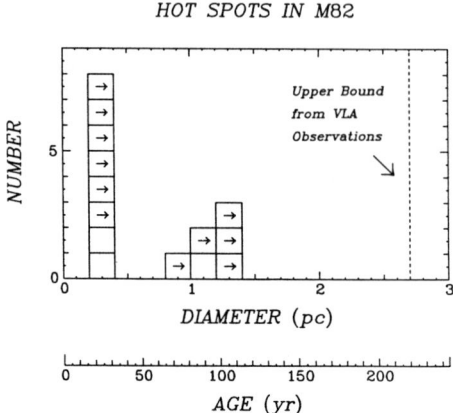

Fig. 8. A histogram of the FWHM-Gaussian diameters, or lower bounds on them (with arrows) of SNR41.9+58 and 13 other hot spots in M82. The second ordinate gives the hot spots' ages, given that they are all expanding with a velocity of 6×10^3 km s^{-1} for the HWHM points of a Gaussian, equivalent to a velocity of 8500 ± 4300 km s^{-1} for the outer parts of a shell. The bound on the diameters from VLA observations (KRONBERG, BIERMANN, and SCHWAB [27]) is between ~ 2.7 and ~ 5.4 pc ($d \equiv 3.3$ pc), depending on the observing frequency and the VLA configuration.

The lower part of Fig. 7 shows a map of the brightest hot spot, 41.9+58 (BARTEL et al. [28]; see also WILKINSON and DE BRUYN [36] for an image of 41.9+58 at 5 GHz resembling in several details ours at 2.3 GHz).

The map displays a shell-type morphology. The apparent deviation of the structure from circular symmetry may have been caused by relatively large Rayleigh–Taylor instabilities and by the relatively high pressure of the interstellar medium in the nuclear region of M82, which is estimated to be 30–300 times larger than the equivalent pressure in our Galaxy (LUGTEN et al. [37]). Further detailed imaging of 41.9+58 is of particular interest, since it promises to reveal the spectral evolution of each segment of the supernova's shockfront and its expansion into the dense ambient medium.

A value for the expansion velocity was found by fitting Gaussian models to the visibility data at several epochs. The expansion velocity was found by combining estimates of angular radii at epochs 1980 (WILKINSON and DE BRUYN [38]) and 1983 (BARTEL et al. [28]): 6000 ± 3000 km s^{-1} along the northeast–southwest axis. This value is equivalent to an expansion velocity of 8500 ± 4300 km s^{-1} for the outer part of a shell-like brightness distribution. Assuming uniform expansion, the date of explosion is 1955^{+10}_{-20}. A backwards extrapolation of the source's light curve to a time around the date of explosion suggests a maximum flux density at 1.5 GHz of the order of 1 Jy. The shell-like morphology of 41.9+58 and its large expansion velocity, combined with the previously found characteristics of 41.9+58 and those of the other hot spots, lead to the conclusion that 41.9+58 and most other hot spots, if not all, in M82 are indeed SNe and young SNRs.

Apart from SNR41.9+58, all other hot spots that were labeled in the VLA image in Fig. 7 were observed with VLBI. For 13 of these sources, sizes, or lower bounds on them, could be determined (Fig. 8). These values combined with upper bounds on their sizes from VLA observations (KRONBERG, BIERMANN, and SCHWAB [27]) indicate a radio SN rate in the inner 600 pc of M82 of 0.1 yr^{-1} (BARTEL et al. [28]). The rate for SNe in general could even be larger.

2.5 SN1986J: image – potential for movie

The supernova SN1986J in the galaxy NGC891 (Fig. 9), at 0.56 the distance to the center of the Virgo cluster (AARONSON et al. [39]), reached its maximum flux density of ~ 120 mJy at 1.5 GHz in mid 1987 (WEILER, this volume). This epoch occurred about one year after its discovery at the VLA (RUPEN et al. [40]) and several years after the (unobserved) explosion. On the basis of the supernova's light curve and a theoretical model for the interaction of a shell of the SN with its circumstellar material ejected in the pre-supernova phase (CHEVALIER [41]; WEILER, this volume), the explosion occurred sometime between 1982 and 1983.

VLBI observations were made at 1.7 GHz on 1986 Sep. 29 (BARTEL, RUPEN, and SHAPIRO [42]), at 10.7 GHz on 1987 Feb. 23, at 5.0 GHz on 1987 May 30 (BARTEL, RUPEN, and SHAPIRO [43]), and at 8.4 GHz on 1988 Sep. 29. Since each of the observations was made at a different frequency, and since only a sparse set of data was obtained for the two earlier observations, our sensitivity for determining any expansion was relatively small. Probably partly as a result, we have not yet detected any significant expansion.

The first three observations did not allow more complicated models than circular and elliptical Gaussians to be fit to the visibility data. For the 5.0 GHz data, we obtained a half-width at half-maximum of the major axis of 0.8 ± 0.1 mas with a position angle of $145° \pm 5°$ and a ratio between the minor and the major axis of 0.62 ± 0.05 (BARTEL, RUPEN, and SHAPIRO [43]).

The last observations so far were the most sensitive and most extensive ones and allowed us to make a VLBI image, the first one ever of a SN. The image of SN1986J is shown in the lower part of Fig. 9 juxtaposed to an image of the host galaxy NGC891.

SN1986J has a complex brightness distribution elongated in the direction indicated by the model in the earlier observations. An elongation could have been caused by a number of processes. First, it is conceivable that the flow pattern of the expanding gas is anisotropic due to rotation of the progenitor star (BODENHEIMER and WOOSLEY [44]) or to an asymmetric explosion (SHKLOVSKII [45]) or both. Second, the flow pattern of the expanding gas could be isotropic, but the combination of the rate of mass loss and wind velocity of the progenitor star could have varied angularly and given rise to an anisotropic density distribution of the circumstellar medium (EMMERING and CHEVALIER [46]). Third, the radio emission might not emanate from the shockfront region but rather from the amorphously shaped relativistic particle plasma emanating from a central pulsar (PACINI and SALVATI [47]). In this case, deviations from spherical symmetry of the brightness distribution of the supernova are a natural consequence. Because of the complexity of the brightness distribution, rotation of the progenitor star cannot be considered as the only cause for the SN's morphology.

Because of the limited angular resolution, the type of the morphology has been difficult to determine. Different mapping techniques give somewhat different results. Although mapping the outer structure with its jetlike extensions appears to be independent of the imaging technique, mapping the inner 2 mas is not quite independent. The clearest indication for a shell or composite structure in the brightness distribution of SN1986J, with a local minimum in its center, comes from the "maximum entropy" map as displayed in Fig. 9. A shell-type morphology would be expected (WEILER and SRAMEK [48]), since the radio spectrum of SN1986J around 8 GHz is steep, having an index $\alpha \sim -0.7$ ($S_\nu \propto \nu^\alpha$) (WEILER, this volume). It remains to be seen whether such a morphology becomes more apparent in SN1986J's further evolution with either mapping technique and how the morphology's complexity is linked to the velocity field of the expanding material. A sequence of detailed VLBI images may answer these and related questions. Such a sequence of images is indeed obtainable for SN1986J.

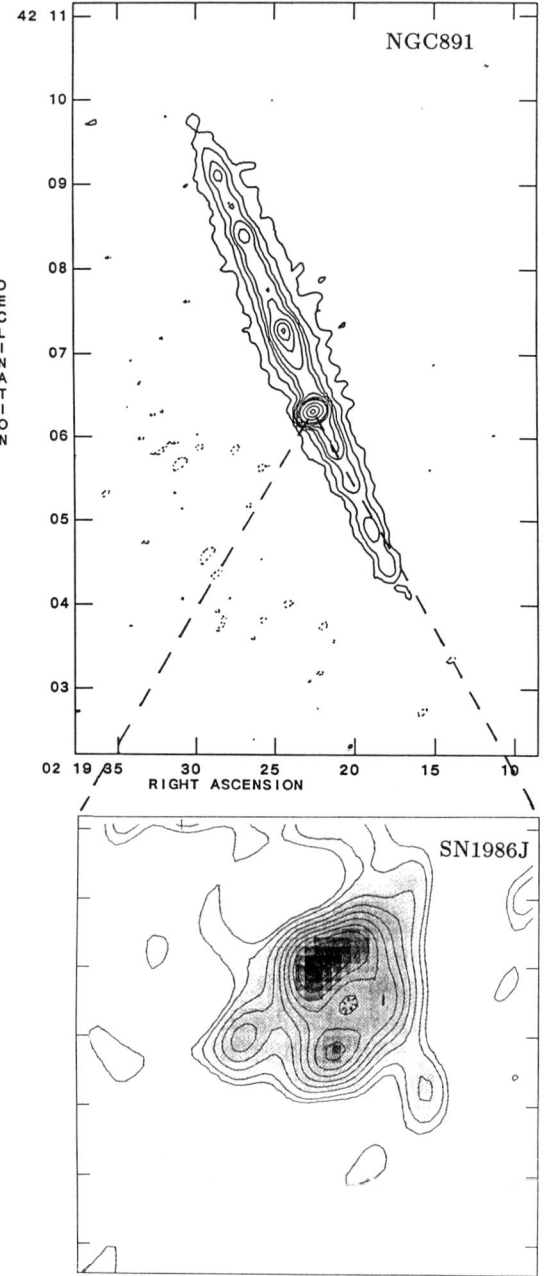

Fig. 9. A "clean" map of the galaxy NGC891 and its pointlike supernova SN1986J made with the VLA at the frequency and epoch of the VLBI observations on 1988 Sep. 29. The contours are −0.2, +0.2, 0.6, 1.1, 1.7, 2.9, 5.7, 8.6, 11.4, 28.6, 57.1, and 85.7% of 53 mJy per beam area. The negative contours are dashed. The coordinates are for epoch B1950.0. The lower part of the figure displays a preliminary VLBI "maximum entropy" image of SN1986J. The contours are 5, 10, 20, 30, 40, 50, 60, 70, 80, 90, and 99% of the peak brightness. Any angle of 1 mas on the sky is indicated by the separation of the tick marks on the left and right side of the figure. North is up and east to the left. There is a 180° ambiguity as to the orientation of the apparently shell-like inner structure of the map. The ambiguity is probably due to the lack of sufficient closure phase information from the intermediate and long baselines. There still remains some uncertainty as to the reality of the shell-like inner structure. For comparison, a "clean" map, made from convolving a set of δ-components, shows similar condensations to those shown here but not smoothly connected to a shell. Only indications of arcs are apparent. The final analysis is pending.

3. CONCLUSIONS

The most important results from VLBI observations of SNe and their remnants have been a) the imaging of a supernova (SN1986J) and a young supernova remnant (SNR41.9+58) and the estimate of the radio SN rate in the central region of the SNR's host galaxy (M82), b) the determinations of the angular expansion rate, and bounds on any acceleration or deceleration of it, of a supernova (SN1979C), c) the estimate of a useful lower bound on the size of the radio shell of a supernova (SN1987A) relative to the sizes of the line-forming regions, and d) estimates of the distance to the Virgo cluster of galaxies and H_0 (see BARTEL, this volume).

More observations of the supernovae discussed here and of supernovae yet to be discovered should allow, at least in some cases, investigations of:

— the detailed dynamic and spectral evolutions, over a large fraction of the SNe's lifetime, of different segments of the shockfront as it expands into the circumstellar medium;

— the relation between the dynamics of the shockfront and those of a) the outer jetlike features and b) the inner pulsar nebula, if the latter exists and can be detected;

— the correlation between radio/optical light curves and the properties derived from the VLBI images; and

— the method of determining distances to galaxies as far away as ~ 40 Mpc.

The VLBA, the new Green Bank 100-m class telescope, and other sensitive antennas together with space-based antennas will aid considerably in the realization of the projects discussed and afford us the intriguing opportunity to make movies, with unprecedented details, of exploding stars.

4. ACKNOWLEDGMENT

This research was supported in part by the NSF under grant No. AST-8902087.

5. REFERENCES

1. Braun, R., Gull, S. F., and Perley, R. A. 1987, Nature, **327**, 395.
2. Bartel, N. 1988, in Supernova Shells and Their Birth Events, Lecture Notes in Physics, ed. W. Kundt (Springer–Verlag, Berlin), **316**, 206.
3. Turtle, A. J. et al. 1987, Nature, **327**, 38.
4. Aglietta, M. et al. 1987, Europhys. Lett., **3**, 1315.
5. Bionta, R. M. et al. 1987, Phys. Rev. Lett., **58**, 1494.
6. Hirata, K. et al. 1987, Phys. Rev. Lett., **58**, 1490.
7. Shapiro, I. I. et al. 1988, in IAU Symposium 129, The Impact of VLBI on Astrophysics and Geophysics, eds. M. J. Reid and J. M. Moran (Reidel, Dordrecht), p. 185.
8. Preston, R. A., Morabito, D. D., Williams, J. G., Faulkner, J., Jauncey, D. L., and Nicolson, G. D. 1985, A. J., **90**, 1599.
9. Bartel, N. et al. 1988, in Supernova 1987A in the Large Magellanic Cloud, eds. M. Kafatos and A. Michalitsianos (Cambridge Univ. Press, Cambridge), p. 81.
10. Jauncey, D.L. et al. 1988, Nature, **334**, 412.
11. Marscher, A. P. 1985, in Supernova as Distance Indicators, Lecture Notes in Physics, ed. N. Bartel (Springer–Verlag, Berlin), **224**, 130.
12. Feast, M. W., and Walker, A. R. 1987, Ann. Rev. Astr. Ap., **25**, 345.
13. Menzies, J. W. et al. 1987, M. N. R. A. S., **227**, 39p.

14. Hanuschik, R. W., and Dachs, J. 1987, *Astr. Ap. Lett.*, **182**, L29.
15. Blanco, V. M. *et al.* 1987, *Ap. J.*, **320**, 589.
16. Bartel, N. 1985, in *Supernovae as Distance Indicators*, Lecture Notes in Physics, ed. N. Bartel (Springer-Verlag, Berlin), **224**, 107.
17. Bartel, N. 1986, in *Highlights of Astronomy*, ed. J. P. Swings (Reidel, Dordrecht), **7**, 655.
18. Bartel, N., Rogers, A. E. E., Shapiro, I. I., Gorenstein, M. V., Gwinn, C. R., Marcaide, J. M., and Weiler, K. W. 1985, *Nature*, **318**, 25.
19. Weiler, K. W., Sramek, R. A., Panagia, N., van der Hulst, J. M., and Salvati, M. 1986, *Ap. J.*, **301**, 790.
20. Bartel, N. 1988, in *IAU Symposium 129, The Impact of VLBI on Astrophysics and Geophysics*, eds. M. J. Reid and J. M. Moran (Reidel, Dordrecht), p. 175.
21. Seaquist, E. R. and Bignell, R. C. 1978, *Ap. J. (Letters)*, **226**, L5.
22. Balick, B. and Heckmann, T. 1978, *Ap. J. (Letters)*, **226**, L7.
23. de Bruyn, A. G. 1983, *Astr. Ap.*, **119**, 301.
24. Kirshner, R. P. and Blair, W. P. 1980, *Ap. J.*, **236**, 135.
25. Chevalier, R. A. 1982, *Ap. J.*, **259**, 302.
26. Chevalier, R. A. 1984, *Ann. NY Acad. Sci.*, **422**, 215.
27. Kronberg, P. P., Biermann, P., and Schwab, F. R. 1985, *Ap. J.*, **291**, 693.
28. Bartel, N. *et al.* 1987, *Ap. J.*, **323**, 505.
29. Kronberg, P. P., Biermann, P., and Schwab, F. R. 1981, *Ap. J.*, **246**, 28.
30. Unger, S. W., Pedlar, A., Axon, D. J., Wilkinson, P. N., and Appleton, P. N. 1984, *M. N. R. A. S.*, **211**, 783.
31. Tammann, A. and Sandage, A. R. 1968, *Ap. J.*, **151**, 825.
32. Sandage, A. 1984, *A. J.*, **89**, 621.
33. Kronberg, P. P., and Sramek, R. A. 1985, *Science*, **277**, 28.
34. Rieke, G. H., Lebofsky, M. J., Thompson, R. I., Low, F. J., and Tokunaga, A. T. 1980, *Ap. J.*, **238**, 24.
35. Geldzahler, B. J., Kellermann, K. I., Shaffer, D. B., and Clark, B. G. 1977, *Ap. J. (Letters)*, **215**, L5.
36. Wilkinson, P. N. and de Bruyn, A. G. 1988, in *IAU Symposium 129, The Impact of VLBI on Astrophysics and Geophysics*, eds. M. J. Reid and J. M. Moran (Reidel, Dordrecht), p. 187.
37. Lugten, J. B., Watson, D. M., Crawford, M. K., and Genzel, R. 1986, *Ap. J. (Letters)*, **311**, L51.
38. Wilkinson, P. N. and de Bruyn, A. G. 1984, *M. N. R. A. S.*, **211**, 593.
39. Aaronson, N. *et al.* 1982, *Ap. J. Suppl.*, **50**, 241.
40. Rupen, M. P., van Gorkom, J. H., Knapp, G. R., Gunn, J. E., and Schneider, D. P. 1987, *A. J.*, **94**, 61.
41. Chevalier, R. A. 1987, *Nature*, **329**, 611.
42. Bartel, N., Rupen, M., and Shapiro, I. 1987, IAU Circ. No. **4292**.
43. Bartel, N., Rupen, M. R., and Shapiro, I. I. 1988, *Ap. J. (Letters)*, **337**, L85.
44. Bodenheimer, P., and Woosley, S. E. 1983, *Ap. J.*, **269**, 281.
45. Shklovskii, I. S. 1970, *Soviet Astr.*, **13**, 562, transl. from *Astr. Zh.*, **46**, 715.
46. Emmering, R. T., and Chevalier, R. A. 1988, *A. J.*, **95**, 152.
47. Pacini, F. and Salvati, M. 1981, *Ap. J. (Letters)*, **245**, L107.
48. Weiler, K. W., and Sramek, R. A. 1988, *Ann. Rev. Astr. Ap.*, **26**, 295.

A Supernova with a Difference, SN 1986J
Kurt W. Weiler, Nino Panagia, & Richard Sramek

I. Introduction

A new radio source was discovered on 21 August 1986 by VAN GORKOM et al. [1] during their study of the nearby, edge-on, spiral galaxy NGC891. Because the source lay in the disk and had HI absorption features characteristic of the galaxy, they concluded that it was a supernova in NGC891 and their report assigned the designation SN1986J. A summary of the known properties of SN1986J is given in Table 1.

Table 1. Properties and references for SN1986J

Property	Value	Reference
Position		
Right Ascension	$02^h19^m22^s60 \pm 0^s02$	
Declination	$+42°06'18".9 \pm 0".2$	
Distance (NGC891)	12 Mpc	2,3
Explosion Date	13 Sept. 1982 ± ~250 days	
Discovery Date	21 Aug 1986	1
Optical/IR photometry		1,4,5,6
Optical/IR spectroscopy		4,7
Radio flux density meas.		1,4,7,8,9,10,11 12,13,14,15
Radio diameter measurements (Gaussian model, FWHM)	1.6 x 1.0 mas in 5/87	16
Physical diameter	$\geq 2.9 \times 1.8 \times 10^{17}$ cm	
Average expansion velocity	$\geq 9.6 \times 6.1 \times 10^3$ km s^{-1}	
Maximum line width	$\sim 10^3$ km s^{-1}	4
Apparent B magnitude at max.	$> 18^m$?	5
Absolute B magnitude at max.	$> -14^m.9$? for $A_B = 2^m.5$	
Peak flux density ($\lambda 6$ cm)	~130 mJy	
Average surface brightness at peak flux ($\lambda 6$ cm)	$\sim 3.5 \times 10^{-11}$ Wm^{-2}Hz^{-1}ster^{-1}	
Peak brightness temp. ($\lambda 6$ cm)	$\sim 4.5 \times 10^9$ K	
Peak spectral lumin. ($\lambda 6$ cm)	$\sim 2.1 \times 10^{28}$ erg s^{-1}Hz^{-1}	
Ratio to Cas A	~3,000	3
Ratio to SN1979C	~3	3

Optical spectral observations by RUPEN et al. [4] in 1984 and 1986 of an object at the position of SN1986J reveal the presence of hydrogen lines indicating classification as a Type II, but the lines are rather narrow, being only ~ 1000 km s^{-1} wide. A more detailed discussion of the properties of SN1986J in all wavelength ranges is given in WEILER, PANAGIA, and SRAMEK [17].

Since we are carrying out a long standing program of searching for and monitoring the radio emission from RSNe, we were asked by the collaborators on RUPEN et al. [4] to include SN1986J in our program. We report here on the results of this continuing series of observations and their meaning in terms of the type, nature, and physical properties of SN1986J.

II. Observations

Even though it, unfortunately, was not found optically so that its exact age is not well known, SN1986J is the most powerful RSN ever detected and there are extensive radio observations available. We have added 63 new measurements at the 5 different VLA wavelengths of λλ90, 20, 6, 2, and 1.3 cm over a period of more than two years. Including the measurements available from other observers and from the literature, there are now

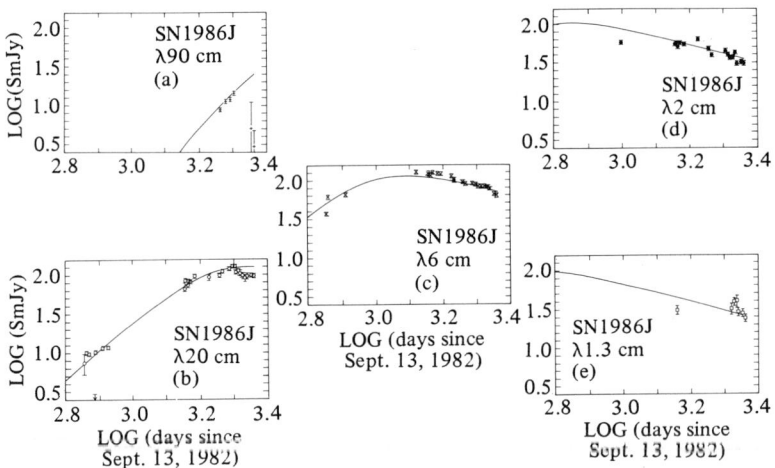

Figure 1. Radio "light curves" for SN1986J in NGC891 for the five wavelengths λλ90, 20, 6, 2, and 1.3 cm. The age of the supernova is measured in days from the best fit date of explosion on 13 September 1982. The solid lines represent the best fit light curves of the form $S(mJy) = K_1[\nu/(5\ GHz)]^\alpha [(t-t_0)/(1\ day)]^\beta e^{-\tau}(1-e^{-\tau'})\tau'^{-1}$, where $\tau = K_2[\nu/(5\ GHz)]^{-2.1}[(t-t_0)/(1\ day)]^\delta$ and $\tau' = K_3[\nu/(5\ GHz)]^{-2.1}[(t-t_0)/(1\ day)]^{\delta'}$ with $\delta = \alpha - \beta - 3$ and $\delta' = 5\delta/3$ from the CHEVALIER [18,19] model.

SN 1986: Supernova With a Difference   517

almost 100 flux density measurements available at these 5 wavelengths and
these are plotted in Fig. 1.

Examination of Fig. 1 shows some unusual features: a. the emission
turns on relatively slowly with time compared with SN1979C and SN1980K
(see WEILER et al. [20]) and b. the shortest wavelength for which there
is a reasonable data set (λ1.3 cm) shows roughly constant flux density
over the measurement interval.

One aspect which is perhaps not unusual, although it might appear so
at first sight, is the apparent disappearance of SN1986J at λ90 cm in
November and December 1988 after detection by SUKUMAR and ALLEN [11] of
strong and rising flux density in the period from September 1987 to March
1988. Given the high optical depth at λ90 cm still present in 1988, (see
models below) any fluctuation in this opacity would quickly blot out the
λ90 cm radiation since we are seeing such a small fraction of the total
emission. Such a flux density fluctuation in the same time interval is
also evident in the λ20 cm data. This opacity change can, in fact, be
quantified as has been done by WEILER, PANAGIA, and SRAMEK [17] who show
that an external absorption variation can explain the observed decrement.
Similar short term changes in the opacity of the external absorbing
medium were also observed in SN1979C (WEILER et al. [20]) and have been
interpreted by LUNDQVIST and FRANSSON [21] as due to variation in the
temperature and ionization of the presupernova stellar wind close to the
supernova blast wave.

Our extensive data set yields many determinations of the spectral
index α ($S \propto \nu^{+\alpha}$) both in time and between different pairs of frequencies.
These are plotted in Fig. 2. Examination of Fig. 2 shows that:
a. The spectrum from λ90 cm to λ20 cm through the end of 1988 is "in-
   verted" with a large positive index ($\alpha \sim +1.5$) indicating that
   SN1986J is still very optically thick to its λ90 cm emission.
b. The spectral index from λ20 cm to λ6 cm changes from a large
   positive index ($\alpha \sim +1.5$) initially, when the RSN was still optically thick to its λ20 cm emission, to a more "normal" negative
   index of $\alpha \sim -0.3$ for the most recent data as SN1986J has become
   almost optically thin at λ20 cm. The form of the change, however,
   is quite unlike the sharp decline of the spectral index followed by
   an asymptotic approach to the optically thin value as was seen for

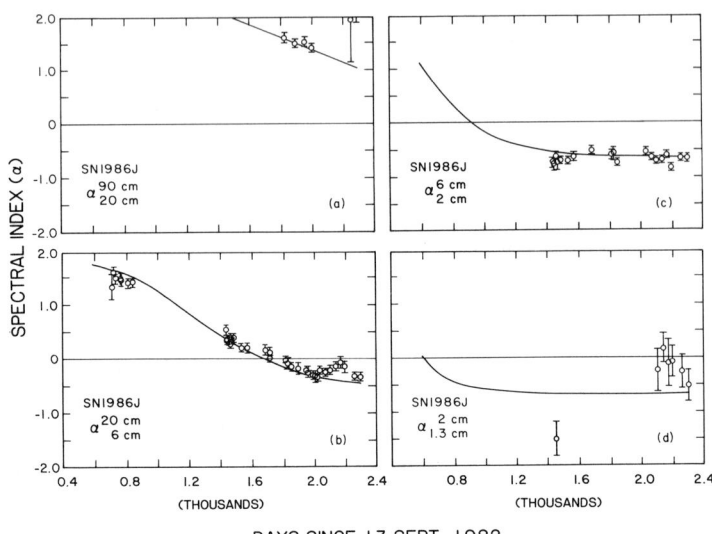

Figure 2. Spectral index α, ($S \propto \nu^{+\alpha}$) evolution for SN1986J between (a) λ90 cm -- λ20 cm, (b) λ20 cm -- λ6 cm, (c) λ6 cm -- λ2 cm and (d) λ2 cm -- λ1.3 cm plotted as a function of time in days since the explosion date on ~13 September 1982. The solid lines are calculated from the best fit theoretical "light curves" shown in Fig. 1 and described below.

SN1979C and SN1980K (WEILER et al. [20]). It is more of plateau at $\alpha \sim$ +1.5 followed by a slow decline to an optically thin value which may eventually reach $\alpha \sim$ -0.7.

c. At λ6 cm to λ2 cm, for the period where there is data, the RSN is optically thin to its emission at both wavelengths with an average index of α = -0.7 ± 0.1.

d. The spectrum between λ2 cm and λ1.3 cm, even though sparse and hampered by larger errors is, quite surprisingly, flat with an average index of only α = -0.2 ± 0.2 .

III. Discussion

1. Light Curves

In their study of a number of RSNe WEILER et al. [20] established several common properties:

a. non-thermal emission with high brightness temperature;
b. turn-on first at shorter wavelengths and later at longer wavelengths;

c. initial rapid increase of flux density with time at each wavelength;
d. power law decline in flux density at each wavelength after maximum is reached;
e. sharp initial decrease in spectral index between any two wavelengths as the longer wavelength goes from optically thick to optically thin, and
f. a final asymptotic approach of the spectral index α to an optically thin, non-thermal, constant negative value ($S \propto \nu^{+\alpha}$).

They showed that such behavior is best described by the change in optical depth of a external, thermal, absorbing screen and ruled out such absorbing processes as synchrotron self-absorption, Razin-Tsytovich effect, and mixed, internal, non-thermal emitting, thermal absorbing gas. They then modelled the radio "light curves" of the RSNe with the simple mathematical form:

$$S(mJy) = K_1 \left(\frac{\nu}{5\ GHz}\right)^{\alpha} \left(\frac{t - t_0}{1\ day}\right)^{\beta} e^{-\tau} \qquad (1)$$

with

$$\tau = K_2 \left(\frac{\nu}{5\ GHz}\right)^{-2.1} \left(\frac{t - t_0}{1\ day}\right)^{\delta}. \qquad (2)$$

This formulation assumes that both the flux density S and the optical depth τ are well described by power-law functions of the supernova age ($t - t_0$), with powers β and δ, respectively; that the absorption is purely thermal, free-free absorption in an ionized medium (frequency dependence $\nu^{-2.1}$) external to the emitting region with a radial dependence of r^{-2} from a constant speed, red supergiant wind; and that the intrinsic emission is due to the nonthermal synchrotron process with an optically thin spectral index α. The quantities K_1 and K_2 are two scaling factors for the units of choice of mJy, GHz, and days, and correspond formally to the flux density (K_1) and optical depth (K_2) at 5 GHz 1 day after the SN explosion.

While SN1986J certainly shares a number of common properties with other RSNe such as Points a, b, d, and f listed above, it is clearly different in its slow turn on at each frequency, early detection at low frequencies, and spectral index evolution. The purely external, thermal absorbing gas described by (1) and (2) provides a poor fit to our data set. Quantitatively, the best fit which could be obtained with the model of (1) and (2) still had a reduced $\chi_{red}^2 > 10$ even though a minimum measurement error of 14% was introduced into the calculations.

Since synchrotron self-absorption and the Razin-Tsytovich effect are still unlikely to be significant factors in a relatively extended emitter such as SN1986J, the most attractive alternative mechanism to describe its radio light curves is to add an additional component consisting of an expanding, mixed, thermal absorbing/non-thermal emitting gas undergoing a transition from optically thick to thin. This can be mathematically expressed by including an additional absorption term in (1) to give

$$S(mJy) = K_1 \left(\frac{\nu}{5\ GHz}\right)^\alpha \left(\frac{t - t_0}{1\ day}\right)^\beta e^{-\tau} (1 - e^{-\tau'}) \tau'^{-1} \quad (3)$$

where τ is still the external absorption described by (2) and

$$\tau' = K_3 \left(\frac{\nu}{5\ GHz}\right)^{-2.1} \left(\frac{t - t_0}{1\ day}\right)^{\delta'} \quad (4)$$

with τ', K_3 and δ' describing the properties of a thermal absorbing medium which is <u>mixed</u> with the nonthermal emitting gas. To limit the number of free parameters, we again adopt the CHEVALIER [18,19] model which determines $\delta = \alpha - \beta - 3$ and $\delta' = 5\delta/3$.

Searching parameter space for a minimum χ^2 with (2), (3), and (4) yields the values listed in Table 2. These values are then used to calculate the model curves which are shown as the solid lines in Figs. 1 and 2. As can be seen in the Figures, the fit to the data is quite satisfactory, especially considering the simplicity of the model, and describes quite well the changes in the flux density of SN1986J both with time and frequency.

As might be expected, the degree to which the several parameters are determined by the fitting process varies greatly. The spectral index (α) and rate of decline of the emitting process (β) are tightly constrained with the intrinsic intensity of the non-thermal emission (K_1) and the amount of internal absorption (K_3) somewhat less so. The solutions are not very sensitive to the explosion date (t_0), with indeterminacy of ~8 months earlier or later than the best fit date of 13 September 1982, or to the amount of external absorption (K_2). The external absorption

Table 2. Fitting parameters for SN1986J[1]

Parameter	Value	Deviation Range[a]
K_1	6.7×10^5	$(3.8 -- 9.2) \times 10^5$
α	-0.67	-(0.59 -- 0.71)
β	-1.18	-(1.16 -- 1.22)
K_2	3×10^5	$(0 -- 63) \times 10^5$
δ ($=\alpha-\beta-3$)	-2.49	-(2.19 -- 2.69)
K_3	4×10^{12}	$(2 -- 12) \times 10^{12}$
δ' ($=5\delta/3$)	-4.15	-(3.65 -- 4.45)
t_0	13 Sept. 1982	(25 Feb. '82 -- 10 Jul. '83)

Derived Quantities
$M_{dot} \sim 1.8 \times 10^{-4} (v/10 \text{ km s}^{-1}) M_\odot \text{ yr}^{-1}$
$M_{eject} \geq 5.5 M_\odot$

[1]With an additional error of 14% of the measured flux density to account for the fact that no simple model can completely describe such a complicated phenomenon, these parameters yield a $\chi^2_{red} = 0.96$.
[a]The Deviation Range is the range in which there is a ~67% probability that the true value lies. This is equivalent to a 1σ range for a one parameter solution.

could, in fact, be omitted entirely ($K_2 = 0$) and still obtain a reasonable description of the available data. However, $K_2 = 3 \times 10^5$ provides the best fit and there are other reasons for expecting an external absorbing medium to be present.

2. Models

As discussed above, SN1986J is more complex than a simple mini-shell model can describe. In addition to the presumed presence of an external absorbing medium surrounding the emission region there is an additional absorbing medium which is mixed with the emission regions [the additional terms in (3) and (4)]. We shall discuss these separately.

a. The external absorber

Because of the dominance of the mixed emitting/absorbing component, the properties of the purely external absorber are relatively poorly determined for SN1986J. Examination of the uncertainty for parameter K_2 in Table 2 (which specifies the initial amount of external absorption) shows that the external absorption could range from $0 < K_2 < 6.3 \times 10^6$ to within 1σ. In other words, the amount of external absorption could range from none to almost as much as was estimated for the next brightest RSN SN1979C ($K_2 = 5.1 \times 10^7$; WEILER et al. [20]).

However, as discussed above, shorter term variations in the optical depth at $\lambda\lambda 90$ and 20 cm imply the existence of an external absorbing medium of roughly this magnitude. Attributing this external absorber to the presence of a surrounding cocoon of matter established by mass loss from the SN progenitor in the last, presupernova stages of stellar evolution, one can estimate a mass loss rate (see WEILER et al. [20] for a discussion of the assumptions involved).

Following LUNDQVIST and FRANSSON [21], we adopt a temperature of 3×10^4 K for the circumstellar gas prior to the strong cooling episode. We also adopt an average expansion velocity of 7.8×10^3 km s^{-1} derived from VLBI observations in May 1987 (t ~ 1720 days; BARTEL, RUPEN and SHAPIRO [16]). Then, using Equation 16 of WEILER et al. [20], we obtain a mass loss rate of M_{dot}(absorption) = 1.8×10^{-4} (v/10 km s^{-1}) $M_\odot$ yr^{-1}. This value agrees quite well with the estimate one can make from the level of intrinsic emission as determined by the interaction of the SN ejecta with the circumstellar material. Using the simplified formulation of WEILER et al. [3] valid for Type II SNe, we obtain M_{dot}(emission) = 1.3×10^{-4} $M_\odot$ yr^{-1}. Although the excellent agreement of the two estimates may be coincidental, it is clear that the mass loss rate of the SN1986J progenitor was quite high. This implies that it was a red supergiant as massive as possible to lose mass at such a high rate, i.e., M(ZAMS) $\gg$ 8 $M_\odot$ which is the limit above which stars are supposed to be able to explode by core collapse. However, the original mass should not be too high, say $\leq$30 $M_\odot$, because otherwise the progenitor would have first become a Wolf-Rayet star before exploding and would have created a much less dense circumstellar envelope.

b. The mixed absorber

Even though the presence of an external, wind created absorbing medium of density comparable to that observed for SN1979C is indicated both by our parameter fits and by the observed short term light curve variations, the radio properties of SN1986J are dominated by an absorbing medium which is mixed with the non-thermal emitters. Equations (3) and (4) implicitly assume an expanding, filled, volume with uniformly mixed emitters and absorbers.

Adopting for the absorbing material mixed with the non-thermal gas a temperature of 3×10^4 K, the value of $K_3 = 4 \times 10^{12}$ implies an emission measure of $n_e^2 \Delta R = 1.9 \times 10^{26}$ cm^{-5}. In the case of a spherical structure with constant density, this indicates a total absorbing mass of M(internal abs.) ~ 3 $M_\odot$. The mass would be lower if the filling factor is significantly lower than unity but higher if the gas ionization is not complete.

Similarly, we can estimate the properties of the thermal gas which is emitting Hα radiation. From RUPEN et al. [4] the intensity of Hα in September 1986, corrected for an extinction corresponding to $A_V = 2^m$, is $I_{corr}(H\alpha) = 1.9 \times 10^{-13}$ erg cm^{-2} s^{-1} which, for a distance of 12 Mpc, becomes $L(H\alpha) = 3.2 \times 10^{39}$ erg s^{-1}. Since the expansion velocity of the Hα emitting region is about 10^3 km s^{-1}, its radius is about 1/7.8 of the radius of the radio emitting region. Therefore, extrapolating to May 1987, the average density turns out to be $n_{ave}(H\alpha) = 7.3 \times 10^6$ and the emitting mass to be ~2.5 $M_\odot$ (again assuming $T = 3 \times 10^4$ K). Since the density is so much higher than that of the radio emitting region and the radius so much smaller, we have direct evidence for a strong density gradient. Furthermore, it is likely that the two regions are spatially distinct, so that the total mass of the ejecta is essentially the sum of the two masses, i.e., ~5.5 $M_\odot$. In fact, this may even be just a lower limit to the true mass because it is quite possible that, similar to what is found in SN1987A, some dust may have condensed within the emitting gas and be absorbing a sizeable fraction of the Hα radiation.

3. What is SN1986J?

It is clear that SN1986J is different from all previously studied RSNe and may be the defining member of a new subclass of Type II SNe. For illustrative purposes, we sketch an estimate of its basic structure in Fig. 3. Since the origin and role of its apparently elongated radio structure (BARTEL, RUPEN, and SHAPIRO [16]) is not known at the present time, we represent it as spherically symmetric.

Although very speculative at this stage, we suggest that we may be witnessing the birth of a plerion -- a Crab Nebula. The possibly high mass progenitor star, the high abundance of He, the mixed thermal and non-thermal matter, the extensive filamentation, and the elliptical morphology all bear some similarities to the Crab Nebula. HOWEVER, it should be emphasized that emission from a mini-plerion is apparently not presently being observed at radio wavelengths although at optical wavelengths it may be (Chevalier [22]). A defining characteristic of a plerion is its flat spectrum ($\alpha > -0.3$) radio emission while SN1986J has a rather steep ($\alpha = -0.67$) spectrum. Although there is slight evidence in our data for flattening of the radio spectrum at the short wavelengths ($\lambda 1.3$ cm) that must still be confirmed. If a mini-plerion is indeed active and just becoming visible at the present time, one expects the radio light curves to begin to deviate from the description of (2), (3), (4) and Table 2 as the "new" emission becomes visible. Since quarterly monitoring of SN1986J is continuing, its full nature and the possible presence of additional emitting components should become clearer in time.

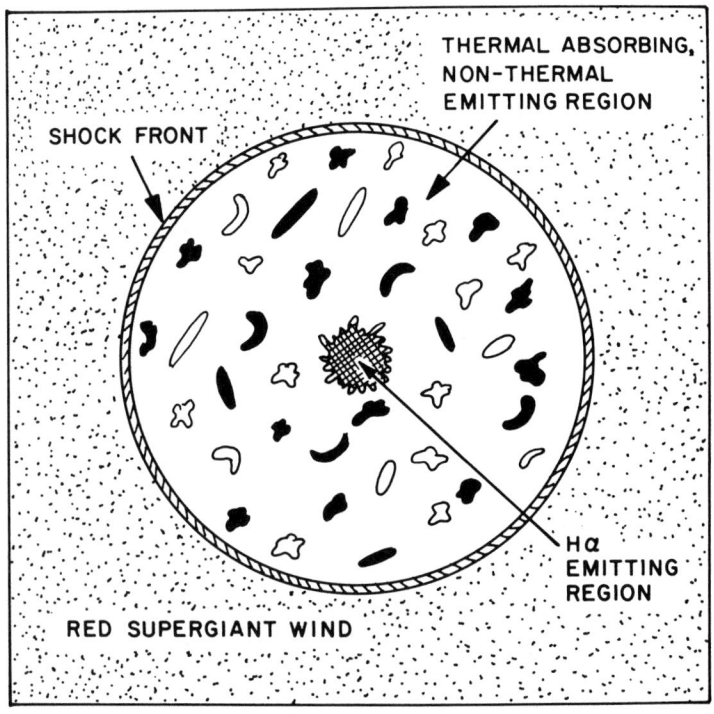

Figure 3. A spherically symmetric cartoon of the possible structure of SN1986J at the present epoch. The circumstellar cocoon from the red supergiant (RSG) wind phase of the presupernova star extends to an unknown distance. The supernova shock front presently forms the boundary between the RSG wind and the thermal absorbing/nonthermal emitting regions. The diameter of this shock front is equal to the VLBI size of the radio emission from SN1986J or $\sim 2.4 \times 10^{17}$ cm and it is expanding at $\sim 7,800$ km s^{-1}. The thermal absorbing/nonthermal emitting region appears to be heavily fragmented into thermal absorbing blobs or filaments co-mixed with numerous nonthermal emitting regions. The high density Hα emitting region is central, is expanding much more slowly (~ 1000 km s^{-1}), and is much smaller being $\sim 1/7.8$ of the VLBI size or $\sim 3 \times 10^{16}$ cm.

IV. Conclusions

Analysis of all of the available data for SN1986J leads us to conclude:

1. It is clearly different from previously known Type II RSNe and may represent a new class.
2. Its radio characteristics are dominated by a mixed thermal absorbing/nonthermal emitting medium which is evolving in a regular way with time.
3. An external absorbing medium, although contributing relatively less to the observed properties of the radio emission, is present with a magnitude similar to that seen in previous RSNe such as SN1979C and SN1980K. It is also probably responsible for the short term fluctuations seen in the radio light curves.
4. A presupernova stellar mass loss rate of $M_{dot} \sim 1.8 \times 10^{-4}$ $M_\odot$ yr^{-1} is needed to account for the most likely external absorbing medium.
5. A minimum ejected mass of $M \sim 5.5$ $M_\odot$ is needed to account for the observed absorption in the mixed emitting/absorbing region and the observed Hα emission.
6. The density of the presupernova stellar wind and the ejected mass which can be accounted for in the mixed thermal absorbing/non-thermal emitting region and the Hα emitting region imply a zero age main sequence stellar mass $M(ZAMS) \sim 20 -- 30$ $M_\odot$.
7. We may be witnessing the birth of a plerion like the Crab Nebula and it has been suggested by Chevalier [22] that pulsar driven optical emission has already been observed. However, the presently detectable radio emission is steep spectrum ($\alpha \sim -0.67$) and is not likely to be plerionic. A new, flat spectrum radio component <u>may</u> be emerging at the highest monitoring frequencies ($\lambda\lambda 2 -- 1.3$ cm), but must still be confirmed.

In summary, SN1986J is a very interesting and unusual object which has already revealed enough of its nature to allow us to model its physical structure quite well. As it evolves we are continuing to monitor it at regular intervals to confirm and refine those properties already established and to look for the possible development of new characteristics.

References

1. van Gorkom, J., Rupen, M., Knapp, G., and Gunn, J.: IAU Circ., No. 4248 (1986).
2. Aaronson, M., et al.: Ap. J. Suppl. 50, 241 (1982).

3. Weiler, K.W., Panagia, N., Sramek, R.A., van der Hulst, J.M., Roberts, M.S., and Nguyen, L.: Ap. J., 336, 421 (1989).
4. Rupen, M.P., van Gorkom, J.H., Knapp, G.R., Gunn, J.E., and Schneider, D.P.: Astron. J. 94, 61 (1987).
5. Cappellaro E. and Turatto, M.: IAU Circ., No. 4262 (1986).
6. Kent, S. and Schild, R.: IAU Circ., No. 4423 (1987).
7. Gunn, J.: IAU Circ., No. 4258 (1986).
8. Wehrle, A.: IAU Circ., No. 4260 (1986).
9. Sukumar, S.: IAU Circ., No. 4287 (1986).
10. Allen, R.J., Sukumar, S., and Beck, R.: IAU Circ., No. 4595 (1988).
11. Sukumar, S. and Allen, R.J.: Ap. J., 341, 883 (1989).
12. Gioia, I.M. and Fabbiano, G.: Ap. J. Suppl. 63, 771 (1987).
13. Condon, J.J.: IAU Circ., No. 4258 (1986).
14. Fabbiano, G. and Gioia, I.M.: IAU Circ., No. 4258 (1986).
15. van der Hulst, J.M., de Bruyn, A.G., and Allen, R.J.: IAU Circ., No. 4258 (1986).
16. Bartel, N., Rupen, M.R., and Shapiro, I.: Ap. J. Lett., 337, L85 (1989).
17. Weiler, K.W., Panagia, N., and Sramek, R.A.: Ap.J. (1990), in press.
18. Chevalier, R.: Ap. J. 251, 259 (1981).
19. Chevalier, R.A.: Ap. J. 259, 302 (1982).
20. Weiler, K.W., Sramek, R.A., Panagia, N., van der Hulst, J.M., and Salvati, M.: Ap. J. 301, 790 (1986).
21. Lundqvist, P. and Fransson, C.: Astr. Ap. 192, 221 (1987).
22. Chevalier, R. A.: Nature 329, 611 (1987).

Spectrophotometry and Photometry of SN 1987M
Alain Porter

Supernova 1987M was discovered in NGC 2715 by M. LOVAS [1] of Konkoly Observatory on September 21, 1987. Spectroscopy at Lick and Palomar Observatories in the following months showed that it was a Type Ib supernova, and provided the best coverage to date of the start of the supernebular phase in this class.

1. Spectrophotometry

The montage in Fig. 1 shows the spectrum between September 28, 1987, and February 25, 1988. The early spectrum is established as Type I by the absence of hydrogen lines, and as Type Ib by the absence of Si II λ 6355 absorption near 6150 Å. The classification is confirmed by the emergence of strong, broad emission lines of intermediate mass elements (O, Ca, Mg, Na) several months after maximum. The early and rapid onset of this supernebular phase was a bit of a surprise. No [O I] λ6300 emission is visible in the October 20 spectrum, but the calcium emission is already very strong only one month later. However, this behavior was predicted by CHUGAI [2].

Lacking He I λ5876 and λ6678 absorption lines, SN 1987M more closely resembles SNe 1983I and 1983V than the "prototypical" SNe Ib 1983N and 1984L. Wheeler *et al.* [3] give SN 1983I and 1983V a separate classification, "Type Ic." These objects certainly seem to have different abundances from other SNe Ib, and a comparison of published spectra suggests that they have continua which are redder (cooler) in the optical and near infrared region. This may significantly constrain the mechanism and ^{56}Ni mass of the explosion, and photometric and spectrophotometric tests of this possibility should be a top observing priority.

The rapid decrease in density of the remnant with time is traced by the increasing strength of forbidden relative to permitted calcium emission. It also appears that the Ca II H and K (permitted) absorption trough may be filled in by emission in the last spectrum, though by this time the star was becoming difficult to observe. In work in progress (FILIPPENKO *et al.* [4]), we hope to be able to estimate densities in the emitting regions using the calcium emission lines.

2. Photometry

Photometry of the supernova in the Thuan-Gunn g and r passbands was collected by several direct CCD observers using the 1.5 meter Oscar Mayer telescope at Palomar Observatory. Although the data are sparse, the light curve is consistent with a maximum near the discovery date and an inflection point about 30 days later. Except for a zero point shift, the g light curve agrees to within better than 0.3 magnitudes with the average Type Ia V light curve compiled by DOGGETT and BRANCH [5]. However, SN 1987M appears to have been subluminous. Assuming the Revised Shapley-Ames distance modulus of 32.4 magnitudes to NGC 2715, the maximum absolute magnitude in Gunn g (4950Å) was -16.8. Typical SNe I have maximum V

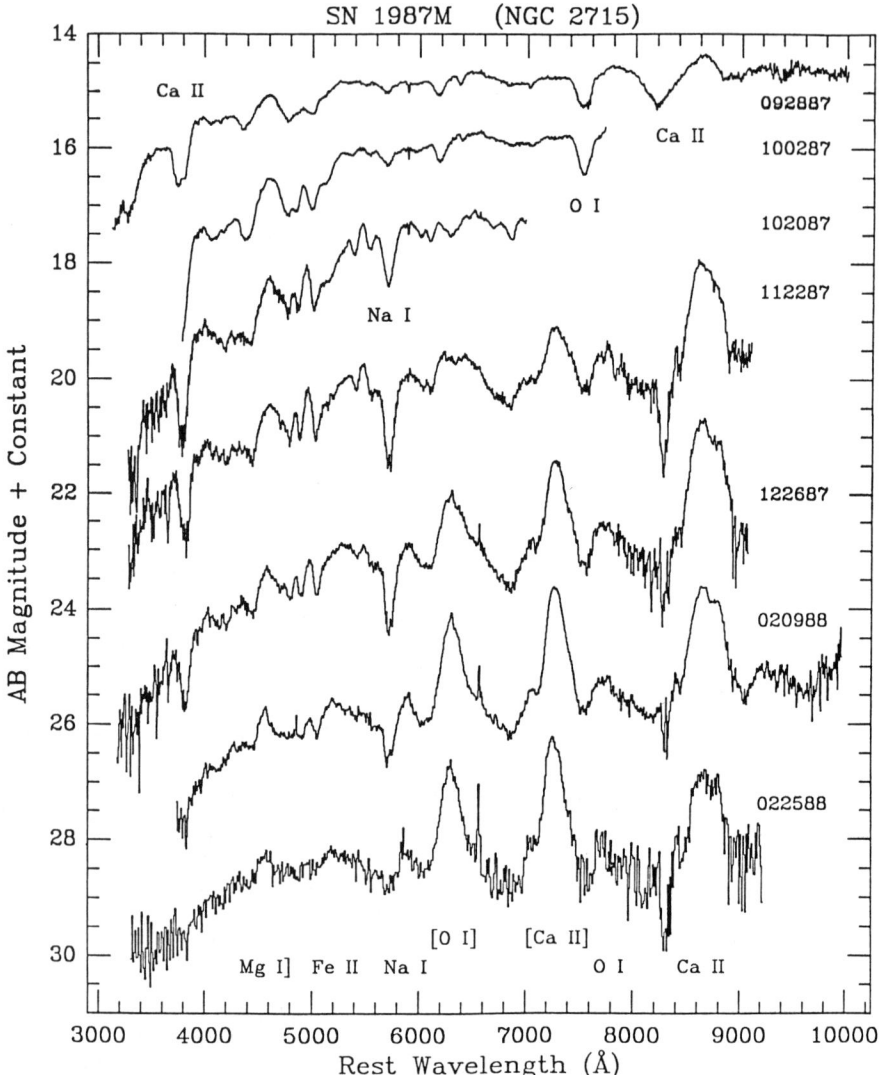

Figure 1. Spectra of SN 1987M.

(5500Å) magnitudes of -19.5 ($H_0 = 50$). It is unlikely that the $g - V$ color of the supernova and error in the distance modulus can account for this difference.

Could the supernova have been heavily obscured by dust? Na D absorption from NGC 2715 is visible in the early spectra, but its equivalent width is only 1.5 Å. PHILLIPS et al. [6] and RICH [7] found 3.6 Å of Na D absorption in the line of sight to SN 1986G in Cen A. They agreed closely on a reddening of $E_{B-V} = 0.9$ and a blue extinction of 3.6 magnitudes. ALLEN [8] also quotes a relation $A_V = 3.3 E_{B-V}$ for visual extinction. On this basis, the visual extinction to SN 1987M is likely to have been 1.2-1.4 magnitudes. This alone certainly does not account for the star's faintness. Extinction, distance error, and color together *might* explain it, but only with difficulty.

3. Of Progenitors

The similarity of the *shape* of the light curve of SN 1987M to the Ia template poses a problem for a favored model of Type Ib explosions. ENSMAN and WOOSLEY [9] have pointed out that the light curves of exploding Wolf-Rayet stars should have broader, shallower peaks than most SNe I show. On the other hand, white dwarf detonation models are either too luminous to be SNe Ib, or fade away too rapidly (BRANCH [10]). Light curves of large samples of supernovae on *uniform* photometric systems are as necessary as spectroscopy to choose between the models and measure the explosion energies.

SN 1987M differed from most earlier SNe Ib in that it was *not* superposed on a luminous H II/OB complex. This is evident, not only from the template image of NGC 2715, but from the weakness of the narrow Hα emission in the spectra, which is not visible until the end of 1987. PANAGIA and LAIDLER [11] have argued that SNe Ib are less closely associated with H II/OB complexes than are SNe II, and that they therefore have less massive progenitors–as also suggested by their light curves. Careful astrometry, photometry, and spectroscopy of H II regions in host galaxies is needed to solve this problem.

References

1. M. Lovas: I.A.U.Circular # 4451 (1987).
2. N. N. Chugai: Pis'ma Astron. Zh. 12 461 (1986).
3. J. C. Wheeler et al.: Astrophys. J. 313 L69 (1987).
4. A. V. Filippenko et al.: (1990), in preparation.
5. L. Doggett, D. Branch: Astron. J. 90 2303 (1985).
6. M. M. Phillips et al.: Pub. Astron. Soc. Pacific 99 592 (1987).
7. R. M. Rich: Astron. J. 94 651 (1987).
8. C. W. Allen: Astrophysical Quantities (London, Athlone Press 1973).
9. L. Ensman, S. Woosley: Astrophys. J. 333 754 (1988).
10. D. Branch: In Atmospheric Diagnostics of Stellar Evolution, IAU Colloquium # 108, ed. by K. Nomoto (New York, Springer-Verlag 1987).
11. N. Panagia, V. Laidler: preprint (1989).

The Type Ib Supernova SN 1984L in NGC 991
Eric M. Schlegel

SN 1984L in NGC 991 is a temporarily unique object for the Type Ib subclass of supernovae. It remains the only "fully" observed SN Ib to date, where "fully" means photometry *and* spectroscopy at early *and* late times.

The Type Ib subclass was only recognized about 1985, with the discoveries of SN 1983N and SN 1984L (e.g., UOMOTO and KIRSHNER [1], WHEELER and LEVREAULT [2]). The early-time observations of these supernovae showed an overall similarity with the typical SN Ia supernovae, of which the recent prime examples are SN 1981B (BRANCH et al. [3]) and SN 1989B (PHILLIPS et al. [4]). The obvious difference was the lack of the 6150Å absorption so characteristic of the first 20-30 days of the evolution of SN Ia. The discovery of SN 1985F, with its obviously strange spectrum dominated by [O I] 6300Å (FILIPPENKO and SARGENT [5]), and the late-time spectra of SN 1984L and SN 1983N (GASKELL et al. [6]), gave an indication of exactly what the late-time evolution was. Unfortunately, SN 1985F was not observed spectroscopically before about 250 days past maximum. SN 1984L, another Reverend Evans discovery (EVANS [7]), was observed near maximum, and again about 10 months later. It matched the appearance of SN 1983N at early times, and showed the [O I] lines now known to be characteristic of the late evolution of SN Ib. Subsequent Type Ib supernovae have generally been quite faint relative to SN 1983N and SN 1984L. The general properties have been summarized in SCHLEGEL and KIRSHNER [8].

The late-time light curve of SN 1984L was obtained from CCD images of the supernova taken about 300 to 500 days past maximum. An image of NGC 991 obtained at approximately 1250 days past maximum was used to remove the galaxy background. The resulting light curve is shown in Figure 1 (next page). The early-time points are from the literature (see SCHLEGEL and KIRSHNER [8] for the details). The overall light curve behavior does not match any of the standard light curves from DOGGETT and BRANCH [9]. The measured late-time slope for the V light curve falls almost embarrassingly on top of the e-folding time for ^{56}Co decay. Given that this is not a bolometric light curve, the agreement is perhaps surprising. No tricks or antics were used to get the light curve: a straight-forward, cross correlation of the "galaxy plus supernova" CCD frame with the galaxy frame was used to obtain the correctly subtracted image. The remaining pixels at the supernova's location were summed through a 7-arcsec aperture. Perhaps the visible light at 500 days past max-

Type Ib SN 1984L in NGC 991 531

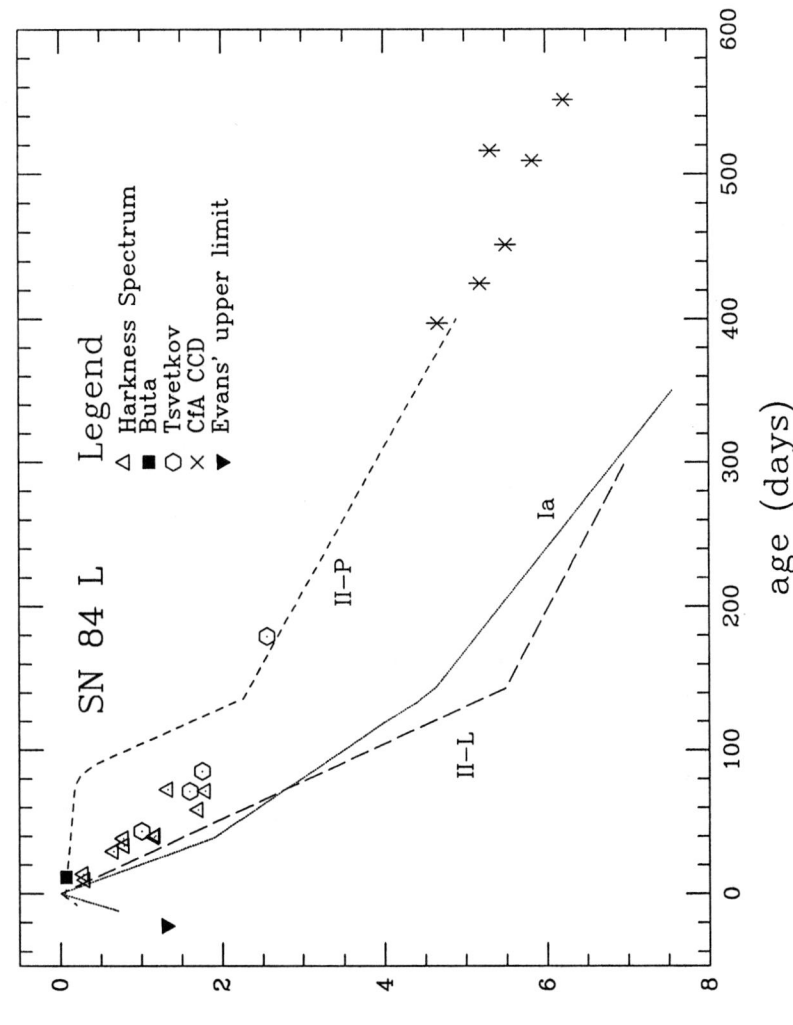

Figure 1. The V light curve for SN 1984L. The early-time points are from the literature. See [8] for citations and details.

imum is a crude approximation to the bolometric flux. Only a future, well-observed SN Ib will tell us.

The late-time spectra of SN 1984L are present in Figure 1 of SCHLEGEL (this volume) [10]. The characteristic [O I] 6300/6363Å emission is present, as well as Mg I] 4571Å emission. The presence of the oxygen emission in the debris implies a massive star has exploded. A spectrum, with poor S/N (presented in [10]), which extends to about 1μ, shows what may be the [C I] 9830Å complex. The ratio of the fluxes of the [C I] 9830Å to [C I] 8727Å provides a limit of about 3000[K] on the temperature of the debris. The number density is greater than about 10^6 cm^{-3}. These numbers lead to an estimate of the ejected oxygen mass of about $1M_\odot$. This number is about a factor of 3-5 greater than in the Type II SN 1980K (UOMOTO and KIRSHNER [11]).

Further details may be found in SCHLEGEL and KIRSHNER [5].

References

1. Uomoto, A. and Kirshner, 1985, *Astr. Ap.*, **149**, L7.
2. Wheeler, J. C. and Levreault, R. 1985, *Ap. J. (Letters)*, **294**, 117.
3. Branch, D., Lacy, C. H., McCall, M. L., Sutherland, P. G., Uomoto, A., Wheeler, J. C., and Wills, B. J. 1983, *Ap. J.*, **270**, 123.
4. Phillips, M. *et al.* 1989, *In preparation*.
5. Filippenko, A. V. and Sargent, W. 1985, *Nature*, **316**, 407.
6. Gaskell, C. M., Capellaro, E., Dinerstein, H., Garnett, D., Harkness, R., and Wheeler, J. C. 1986, *Ap. J. (Letters)*, **306**, L77.
7. Evans, R. 1984, *IAU Circular*, 3979.
8. Schlegel, E. M. and Kirshner, R. P. 1989, *Astr. J.*, **98**, 577.
9. Doggett, J. and Branch, D. 1985, *Astr. J.*, **90**, 2303.
10. Schlegel, E. M. 1989, in *Santa Cruz Summer Workshop on Supernovae*, ed. S. Woosley, (Springer-Verlag). in press.
11. Uomoto, A. and Kirshner, R. P. 1986, *Ap. J.*, **308**, 685.

SECTION X

TYPE Ia AND Ib SUPERNOVAE — PROGENITORS AND MECHANISMS

Evolution of Type Ia Progenitors
Ramon Canal, Jordi Isern, Javier Labay, & Rosario Lopez

Type Ia supernova (SNIa) progenitors are widely believed to be mass-accreting white dwarfs, growing toward Chandrasekhar's limit. Explosive ignition of the electron-degenerate material induces mass ejection and creates the radioactive nuclei whose decays power the light curve (COLGATE, PETSCHECK, and KRIESE [1]; ARNETT [2]; WOOSLEY and WEAVER [3]; see also WOOSLEY, this volume). Progenitor requirements can be summarized as follows:

a) According to the spectra, the object has to be devoid of hydrogen at the time of explosion. There is some debate as to the maximum amount of H that would still be compatible with the absence of Balmer lines. A current estimate is $M_H \leq 0.1 M_\odot$ (see WHEELER, this volume).

b) It has to be long-lived (ages up to several Gyr) to account for the occurrence of SNIa in elliptical galaxies, where major activity of star formation stopped long ago, and also in view of the lack of association with HII regions in spiral galaxies (MAZA and VAN DEN BERGH [4]).

c) The explosion has to produce a nickel mass $M_{Ni} \geq 0.5 M_\odot$ in order to explain the light curves (ARNETT [2]; ARNETT, BRANCH, and WHEELER [5]) and late-time spectra (WOOSLEY, AXELROD, and WEAVER [6]).

d) Intermediate-mass elements (O, Mg, Si, S, Ca) must be present in the outer layers, as deduced from the spectra at maximum light (BRANCH et al. [7]; WHEELER, HARKNESS, and CAPPELLARO [8]; see also HARKNESS, this volume).

e) The light curves of the explosions must be fairly homogeneous (CADONAU, SANDAGE, and TAMMANN [9]; see also both BRANCH and LEIBUNDGUT, this volume). Nonetheless, observed inhomogeneities (BRANCH [10]; PHILLIPS et al. [11]) may provide important diagnostics of progenitor characteristics and mechanism of explosion (CANAL, ISERN, and LOPEZ [12]).

f) In addition, of course, the progenitors must die at the observed rates of SNIa (see VAN DEN BERGH, this volume) and produce acceptable nucleosynthesis.

All of the preceding (but maybe the last point) lends strong support to the white dwarf hypothesis, and model explosions based on it do account fairly well for the general characteristics of SNIa outbursts even if important problems remain unsolved (see the above references). Finding a consistent scenario for evolution of the white dwarfs up to explosion is, however, a pending task.

Unless it were possible to revive some long-term mechanism for igniting single white dwarfs (such as the slow electron capture once proposed by FINZI and WOLF [13]), all evidence points towards white dwarfs in binary systems. There the clock is set by the evolution of the system up to the point when mass accretion by the white dwarf starts. All chemical compositions of the white dwarf are possible in principle: helium, carbon-oxygen, or oxygen-neon-magnesium. Most studies, however, have concentrated on C+O white dwarfs. He white dwarfs would almost certainly detonate (burn supersonically) after igniting. Their material would be completely incinerated (no intermediate-mass elements, then), and expansion velocities would be too large. At the other end, O+Ne+Mg white dwarfs have rather been thought to collapse after igniting O at high densities (MIYAJI et al. [14]; MIYAJI and NOMOTO [15], but see below). This leaves C+O white dwarfs, that can ignite carbon at lower densities than O+Ne+Mg ones and may, nonetheless, be able to sustain subsonic burning fronts through either the whole or a fraction of their mass (WOOSLEY [16]).

I. C + O White Dwarfs in Close Binary Systems

C+O white dwarfs can form in binary systems either by Roche-lobe overflow just before or just after ignition of He in *initially close binaries* or by Roche-lobe overflow during early asymptotic giant branch (AGB) phase or thermally pulsing AGB phase in *initially wide binaries*. In the last case, common envelope evolution should allow losing enough orbital angular momentum to change the wide binary into a close one. A problem arises as to which are the typical mass range and the upper mass limit for C+O white dwarfs formed this way. Observation of cataclysmic variables and of classical novae give average masses of $0.75 M_\odot$ and of $1.23 M_\odot$, respectively, and a recent model for the recurrent nova U Sco gives a mass of $\simeq 1.38 M_\odot$ (STARRFIELD, SPARKS, and SHAVIV [17]). But, as we will see, nor novae nor cataclysmic variables in general seem to be the progenitors of SNIa. Besides, the most massive white dwarfs found in those systems may well not be C+O white dwarfs but O+Ne+Mg ones.

Depending on the initial parameters of the system, the companion of the C+O white dwarf may either be:

1) A main-sequence star

2) A subgiant or a red-giant star

3) A He white dwarf (or a He nondegenerate star)

4) Another C+O white dwarf

Scenarios leading to the formation of those systems have been thoroughly studied by IBEN and TUTUKOV [18]. Depending on the type of companion, widely different time intervals may separate the onset of mass transfer from the epoch of white dwarf formation.

II. The Mass Growth Process

IIa. The outer layers

Mass accretion affects both the outer layers and the core of the white dwarf. Concerning the first, for the white dwarf to grow by a few tenths of a solar mass the material has not only to fall onto its surface but also to be incorporated into the degenerate core. This poses many problems and a fully satisfactory scenario has not yet been devised.

Accretion of *H-rich material* (from the two first types of companion listed above) should avoid its *explosive ignition* (as in novae) and also formation of a *red-giant envelope* (eventually engulfing the white dwarf and its companion together) on top of a H-burning shell or direct formation of a *common envelope*. Usually quoted values are:

$\dot{M}_H \leq 10^{-9} M_\odot yr^{-1}$ as leading to nova outburst

$\dot{M}_H \geq 10^{-6} M_\odot yr^{-1}$ formation of a red-giant envelope

$\dot{M}_H \geq \dot{M}_{Edd} \sim 10^{-5} M_\odot yr^{-1}$ direct formation of a common envelope

Especially concerning the first limit, one must note that it is based on calculations assuming spherically symmetric and "soft" accretion. Most likely, material will form a disk around the compact star and the accretion process will thus include angular momentum and kinetic energy dissipation. When those effects are included, the actual range of $\dot{M}_H$ producing nova explosions is ill-defined (SHAVIV and STARRFIELD [19]; SPARKS and KUTTER [20]). What seems clear, however, is that nova outbursts will reduce actual mass growth to, at most, 10% of $\dot{M}_H$ (TRURAN [21]).

Common envelope (either due to accretion above Eddington's limit or to formation of a red-giant envelope) should induce mass loss by the system as a whole and thus inhibit further growth of the white dwarf. Nonetheless, HACHISU, KATO, and SAIO [22] propose a model where stable mass transfer in common envelope is possible (through steady hydrogen burning) for a range of parameters of the binary system. Predicted mass-accretion rates are $\dot{M}_H \geq 10^{-7} M_\odot$.

There is good evidence that SNIa are not the descendants of novae nor of cataclysmic variables. One argument comes from the observation that in M31 the galactic bulge is ~ 20 times more efficient than the disk in producing novae whereas, on the contrary, galactic disks in general are more efficient than bulges in producing SNIa (RENZINI [23]). Also, the birthrate of cataclysmic variables (in the solar neighbourhood at least) is one order of magnitude lower than the SNIa rate (RITTER [24]).

Hypothetical close binaries where H were accreted at $10^{-9} M_\odot yr^{-1} \leq \dot{M}_H \leq 10^{-6} M_\odot yr^{-1}$ might burn it into He steadily or in weak flashes (and would thus not be novae nor cataclysmic variables). Anyway, those systems would be very luminous, and assuming that they had to accrete a few tenths of a solar mass there should now be ~ $10^4 - 10^5$ of them in the Galaxy to account for one SNIa event every ~ 100 years. No known object is a likely candidate. When igniting H they would appear as bright EUV sources. Between burning episodes their luminosities should equally be high, due to the energy released by accretion. Would they appear as symbiotic stars, or as emission-line variables? If they were long-period variables, observational selection effects would however be against their detection.

A further limitation is set by the fact that the He layer resulting from burning the accreted H will explosively ignite if it is accumulated at a rate $10^{-9} M_\odot yr^{-1} \leq \dot{M}_{He} \leq 5 \times 10^{-8} M_\odot yr^{-1}$. The lower limit, however, is only valid for initial masses of the C+O core: $M_{core} \leq 1.13 M_\odot$ (NOMOTO [25]). It is unclear to which extent detonation of the He layer would propagate into the C+O core, but no such outburst could be a valid model for SNIa: iron-peak instead of intermediate-mass elements would appear in the spectra at maximum light.

The same restriction applies to direct accretion of He from either a nondegenerate or a degenerate companion. Concerning the former, only 3-4 systems are known at present and in all of them the mass of the He star is exceedingly low. C+O plus He white dwarf binaries, on the other hand, would have very short lifetimes, and this is incompatible with SNIa statistics.

In recent years, the idea (Webbink [26]; IBEN and TUTUKOV [18]) that SNIa originate from double C+O white dwarf systems has become popular. Accretion of C+O material onto a white dwarf of the same composition does not pose the problems encountered in the accretion of H or He. Once the two C+O white dwarfs have formed, orbital angular momentum will be lost by emission of gravitational radiation, and the stars will get closer on the corresponding time scale. Roche-lobe overflow by the lower-mass component will eventually occur and have a runaway character: the secondary will be disrupted and its material will likely form a massive disk around the primary. It is not clear what should happen next. Very fast accretion ($\dot{M}_{C+O} \geq 5 \times 10^{-6} M_\odot yr^{-1}$) would induce carbon ignition close to the surface and the star would not explode as a SNIa but quasi-hydrostatically burn into a O+Ne+Mg white dwarf (NOMOTO and IBEN [27]), that might then collapse (or explode: see below). Lower accretion rates would allow increase in central density and entropy up to the point of explosive carbon ignition and a SNIa event might result. The actual rate depends on viscous dissipation in the disk (MOCHKOVITCH and LIVIO [28]), and the issue remains undecided (see MOCHKOVITCH, this volume).

An additional problem is the actual frequency of such white dwarf binaries in the Galaxy. Two independent searches (ROBINSON and SHAFTER [29]; BRAGAGLIA et al. [30]; see also BRAGAGLIA, this volume) have yielded none and only one double degenerates, respectively. The one found would need more than a Hubble time to merge and is probably a double He white dwarf system. Taking the two surveys together, the frequency of double degenerates in the white dwarf population would be $\nu_{DD} < 0.04$ (with 90% probability) or $\nu_{DD} < 0.02$ (with 70% probability): far too low to account for SNIa (the required frequency would be $\nu_{DD} \sim 0.1$). Observational bias has favored DA white dwarfs (84 out of 89), and one can argue that double C+O degenerates should rather be non-DA (RENZINI [23]). However, we know that (in single stars at least) non-DA may turn into DA (H finally floating at the surface), and thus the validity of this explanation is questionable.

Indirect evidence favoring the double white dwarf scenario might come from recent measurements of the [O/Fe] ratio in main-sequence dwarfs belonging to the old disk and halo populations of our Galaxy (ABIA and REBOLO [31]): to account for the variation of the ratio with Fe abundance, the start of the main production of this last element (by SNIa) should be delayed by an amount that agrees with the predictions from merging of two white dwarfs by emission of gravitational radiation (ABIA et al. [32]).

IIb. The core

We turn now to core evolution. It begins with the formation of the C+O white dwarf. Prior to mass transfer, it consists only of cooling. If the time interval between formation and the onset of mass transfer from the secondary is long enough (that depends also on the mass of the white dwarf), a first-order phase transition will take place: the star's core will *crystallize*, the ion sites forming a body-centered cubic lattice (bcc). This happens for a critical value of the plasma-coupling constant $\Gamma = Z^2 e^2 / r_s kT$ (where Z is atomic number, e the the electron charge, k Boltzmann's constant, T temperature, and r_s the *ion-sphere radius*: the radius of the sphere containing on average one ion). Monte Carlo calculations for the one-component plasma (OCP) give $\Gamma_{crit} = 155 \pm 5$ (SLATTERY, DOOLEN, and DE WITT [33]). The case of a C+O plasma or of a binary ion mixture (BIM) in general is more complex. We see, from the expression of Γ, that in a core cooling at constant density (constant r_s) Γ_{crit} will be reached first for oxygen. The question arises of whether carbon and oxygen are miscible in the solid phase. Early Monte Carlo simulations by LOUMOS and HUBBARD [34] seemed to support the idea that they actually were and that the crystallization temperature of the mixture (at a fixed density) should be the weighted (by mass fraction) mean of those of pure carbon and pure oxygen. Later, STEVENSON [35] proposed an *eutectic* phase diagram by adopting the *random alloy mixing* (RAM) model for internal energies in the solid phase: carbon and oxygen would separate when crystallizing, solid oxygen accumulating at the center and a pure oxygen core thus progressively growing (MOCHKOVITCH [36]). More recently, however, there have been new calculations of the phase diagram for BIM. On one hand, BARRAT, HANSEN, and MOCHKOVITCH [37], using a density-functional approach for calculating the energies, deduce a diagram of the *spindle* form: a *random* C+O alloy, only slightly more oxygen-rich than the fluid phase would result from crystallization. Transition to an *ordered* alloy of the ClCs type (bcc lattice with carbon and oxygen ion sites forming simple cubic sublattices) is predicted for values of Γ larger than Γ_{crit}. On the other hand, ICHIMARU, IYETOMI, and OGATA [38] find, by Monte Carlo simulations, that the *linear mixing* formula is more accurate than the *random-mixing* one for calculating the energies of both fluid and solid phases. They obtain an *azeotropic* phase diagram. Again, as in BARRAT et al. [37], only a moderate oxygen enrichment of the solid alloy is predicted. In the Monte Carlo simulations of the bcc lattice, ICHIMARU et al. [38] find the equilibrium final states to take *random* bcc-solid configurations. This does not necessarily exclude a transition to an ordered configuration at a value of Γ larger that those considered in these last simulations. Finally, GODON et al. [39] have also recently approached the problem by solid state physics methods (linear Muffin-Tin orbitals, LMTO). They conclude that, within 1% accuracy, microscopic separation requires no energy and that the issue cannot be decided. In the remainder of this discussion we will, however, mainly adopt the view that carbon and oxygen *do not* appreciably separate when freezing, and that they form a *random alloy*. Implications of the other two alternatives (phase separation or ordered crystal) will be pointed out in due course.

When mass accretion starts, whatever of the mass-transfer scenarios that we have previously considered works, the degenerate core will grow in mass and it will be heated by compression and (in the cases of either H or He accretion) also by the inward flow from the He-burning shell (but for the cases $\dot{M}_H \leq 10^{-9} M_\odot yr^{-1}$ or $\dot{M}_{He} \leq 10^{-9} M_\odot yr^{-1}$ and $M_{core} \geq 1.13 M_\odot$, where there would only be a H-burning shell in the first case and no shell at all in the second). Compressional heating will also affect the outer layers first and diffuse inward (NOMOTO [40]). The star's center will thus increase both in density and in entropy (the last by heat inflow from the outer core) up to the point of carbon ignition. An exception to this is when either the accretion rate is low ($\dot{M} \leq 10^{-10} M_\odot yr^{-1}$) or both M_{core} and $\dot{M}$ are large (HERNANZ et al. [41]). In the first case, heat inflow is quenched by thermal neutrino losses. In the second one, carbon ignition precedes the arrival to the center of the heat flow. In both cases the central layers of the white dwarf are compressed *adiabatically* (but for thermal neutrino emission). This is an important point, since in these cases a variable fraction of any solid core that forms during the cooling phase survives until carbon ignition.

III. Explosive Carbon Ignition

Most currently available calculations of C+O white dwarf evolution upon mass accretion (NOMOTO, THIELEMANN, and YOKOI [42]; SUTHERLAND and WHEELER [43]; WOOSLEY, AXELROD, and WEAVER [6]) have assumed combinations of initial mass and internal temperature plus accretion rate that lead to central carbon ignition at $\rho_c \simeq 2 - 3 \times 10^9 g\ cm^{-3}$ in an entirely fluid core ($T \simeq 2 \times 10^8 K$ and $\Gamma \ll \Gamma_{crit}$). Prior to runaway, the central layers become convectively unstable. Urca nuclei such as ^{23}Na are produced during carbon burning and electron Fermi energies are high enough at those densities for convectively driven Urca processes (PACZYNSKI [44]) to operate. IBEN [45] found that Urca neutrino losses would then delay thermonuclear runaway to higher densities. More recently, BARKAT and WHEELER [46] (see also BARKAT, this volume) have found that a steady state can be reached where convective Urca losses exactly balance the energy released by carbon burning. Subsequent evolution is unclear: it might lead to collapse or maybe to off-center ignition of carbon.

It must be noted, however, that if one considers the full spectrum of initial white dwarf masses, internal temperatures, and accretion rates, central carbon ignition densities (even without convective Urca losses) can span a range $2 - 3 \times 10^9 g\ cm^{-3} \leq \rho_c \leq 1.5 \times 10^{10} g\ cm^{-3}$, the highest values corresponding to cases where ignition (in the *pycnonuclear* regime) takes place inside a residual solid core (HERNANZ et al. [41]).

Assuming that a thermonuclear runaway still happens, it can propagate either supersonically, by the shock wave it initiates (*detonation*) or subsonically, by conduction and turbulent mixing (*deflagration*). Deflagration has been favored in recent years (see the above references and also WOOSLEY, this volume), since it simultaneously provides incineration of a fraction of the core (needed to produce the light curves and late-time spectra) and partial burning of another (outer) fraction (needed to produce the spectra at maximum). Its physical soundness has recently been questioned (BLINNIKOV and KHOKHLOV [47]; WHEELER et al. [48]). If an adiabatic (or even flatter) temperature gradient prevails close to the center, spontaneous ignition may simultaneously affect a region large enough to initiate detonation. WOOSLEY [16] disputes this on the basis that once runaway starts no large enough regions can remain isothermal to the required degree. A major objection to the detonation model has been that the star should be completely incinerated and no intermediate-mass elements would be produced. This might not be true if the detonation breaks down for densities $\rho \leq 10^7 g\ cm^{-3}$ (IMSHENNIK and KHOKHLOV [49]; KHOKHLOV [50]).

An unsolved difficulty in either case (detonation or deflagration) is that the calculated isotopic abundances for the iron group elements (of which SNIa are thought to be the main producers) do not agree with those measured in the solar system (THIELEMANN, NOMOTO, and YOKOI [51]): ^{58}Ni and ^{54}Fe are overproduced by factors $\simeq 5$ and $\simeq 2$, respectively. This results from incinerating the material at high densities, where a large amount of electron capture happens. In the framework of the deflagration model, conveniently varying the flame propagation speed (having it starting very slowly and later accelerating) might provide an initial expansion of the star that would then allow most incineration to happen at lower densities (WOOSLEY [16], and this volume). All the preceding is based on one-dimensional calculations, that unavoidably resort to parametrization. Two- or three-dimensional hydrodynamic simulations can not, however, be expected to provide reliable answers in the near future (see FRYXELL, MÜLLER, and ARNETT [52]).

Another possible way out of the excess neutronization would be to centrally ignite carbon at lower densities: $\rho_c \leq 1.0 - 1.5\ g\ cm^{-3}$ (NOMOTO [53]), or to leave gravitationally bound, as a result of central ignition in a partially solid core, the material that is incinerated at high densities (ISERN, LABAY, and CANAL [54]).

IV. The Branch − Pskovskii Correlation (?) and Off − Center Carbon Ignitions

In spite of their overall homogeneity, SNIa show some range of variation in their spectroscopic and photometric properties. Clear differences in photospheric velocities at maximum light have recently been confirmed (BRANCH [10]). The same is true of differences in the rate of postmaximum decline of the light curves (PHILLIPS et al. [11]). A correlation had earlier been proposed among maximum luminosity, photospheric velocity, and decline rate (PSKOVSKII [55]; BRANCH [56]): brighter SNIa would expand faster and decline more slowly. Varying only ^{56}Ni mass from explosion to explosion would give just the opposite correlation (NOMOTO, THIELEMANN, and YOKOI [42]). It would however find a natural explanation in models based on phase separation of carbon and oxygen at crystallization (LOPEZ et al. [57]): mass accretion would induce off-center carbon ignition at the bottom of the carbon-rich layers surrounding the central oxygen core and so the total mass involved in the explosion would no longer be fixed. As we have discussed above, recent calculations of the phase diagram for C+O mixtures do not confirm this picture. Off-center ignitions would still be possible, nonetheless, for an *ordered* C+O alloy (where $^{12}C + ^{12}C$ reactions are inhibited: see below): they would happen when melting of the initial solid core by heat inflow reached deep enough layers (with densities $\simeq 2 - 3 \times 10^9 g\ cm^{-3}$). A similar effect would be obtained for central carbon ignition in a (random) solid core at comparatively low densities (the last to avoid core collapse: see below), when the burning front emerged from the solid into the fluid layers (ISERN, LABAY, and CANAL [54]). Another equally speculative possibility is that off-center ignitions result from growth of a central convective core with burning stabilized by Urca losses (BARKAT and WHEELER [46]).

GRAHAM [58] recently proposed varying central ignition density in the "standard" deflagration model: for increasing densities a correspondingly larger "hole" of neutronized, nonradioactive material would form. ^{56}Ni (whose decay accounts for the luminosity peak down to the beginning of the exponential "tail" of the light curve) would thus be closer to the surface and the light curves would decay faster. CANAL, ISERN, and LOPEZ [12] have shown that, if this were the case, both higher luminosities at maximum and larger expansion velocities would correspond to faster decline of the light curve, contrary to the suggested correlation. BRANCH (this volume) now thinks that most likely maximum luminosity variations can be accounted for by differences in the amount of extinction in the parent galaxy. If only variation in photospheric velocities and rate of peak luminosity decline are intrinsic (but see LEIBUNDGUT, this volume), and correlated in the aforementioned way, the last conclusions would nonetheless be valid and some kind of off-center ignition should be involved in SNIa outbursts.

V. Collapse of C + O White Dwarfs

Accretion-induced collapse (AIC) of C+O white dwarfs does most likely not produce SNIa outbursts but its physics is closely related to that of the progenitors of such events. As we already pointed out, a central solid core can subsist up to carbon ignition for a range of initial masses, temperatures, and accretion rates. Carbon ignition then happens in the *pycnonuclear* regime (SALPETER and VAN HORN [59]), at central densities $9.5 \times 10^9 g\ cm^{-3} \leq \rho_c \leq 1.5 \times 10^{10} g\ cm^{-3}$ (HERNANZ et al. [41]). Besides, burning propagates conductively (at velocities of the order of 0.01-0.001 times the local sound speed) until it reaches the boundary of the solid core. This combination (high density plus relatively low propagation of burning) allows electron captures to remove energy and to decrease Chandrasekhar's mass faster than the energy release by carbon burning promotes expansion, and collapse ensues (CANAL and ISERN [60]; ISERN et al. [61]; CANAL, ISERN, and LABAY [62]). A complicating factor, however, are the neutrinos emitted by electron capture in the central, growing incinerated region: they heat up the solid layers ahead of the burning front and can melt them before the start of dynamical contraction, when Chandrasekhar's mass is still lower than the star's mass. The burning front should accelerate in reaching fluid layers, where hydrodynamic instabilities can grow. How severe this limitation on both ρ_c at ignition and on conductive velocities (within their range of uncertainty) is, for producing collapse, depends on the poorly known growth rate of hydrodynamic instability (the initial stages of formation of a turbulent flame front: see WOOSLEY [16]).

Once collapse starts, neutrino heating also induces carbon ignition further out than sole compression would otherwise produce, and it has therefore to be included in collapse models (see ISERN, his volume). The high entropy of these collapsing cores (as compared to the Fe-Ni cores of massive stars) should result in little mass ejection and produce only a "dim" event.

The (by now marginal) possibility of formation of an *ordered* C+O alloy when the fluid C+O mixture crystallizes would delay carbon ignition to still higher densities, since only $^{12}C +^{16}O$ (and $^{16}O +^{16}O$) reactions could take place in the solid (for $x_C \leq x_O$, x_i being fraction by number). It would happen at $\rho_c \simeq 2 \times 10^{10} g\ cm^{-3}$ and be triggered by electron captures on oxygen, provided that the core has not been melted before by heat inflow or off-center carbon ignition has not been induced by this last process (see the preceding paragraph).

Concerning carbon ignition in the random alloy case, the limited oxygen enrichment of the solid phase predicted by both BARRAT et al. [37] and ICHIMARU et al. [38] should be included together with the chemical stratification predicted in models for the evolution leading to formation of the white dwarf (MAZZITELLI and D'ANTONA [63]) (it is, however, dependent on the value of the $^{12}C(\alpha,\gamma)^{16}O$ cross-section). One should equally bear in mind the uncertainties in the *pycnonuclear* reaction rates.

VI. The Case of O + Ne + Mg White Dwarfs

Mass-accreting O+Ne+Mg white dwarfs should, on average, be more massive than C+O ones and thus would have to accrete less material before (in this case) Ne-O ignition at the center. Prediction that such ignition would happen at $\rho_c \simeq 2 \times 10^{10} g\ cm^{-3}$ (MIYAJI et al. [14]) was based on the assumption that Schwarzschild's criterion is adequate in determining the onset of convection in those cores. A convective core would already develop due to heating by electron captures on ^{24}Mg and ^{24}Na (at $\rho \simeq 4 \times 10^9 g\ cm^{-3}$). This ignored that electron captures not only heat up the core but also produce a negative Y_e-gradient that has a stabilizing effect. Applying Ledoux's criterion, MIYAJI and NOMOTO [15] find that convection is inhibited up to Ne-O ignition at $\rho_c \simeq 9.5 \times 10^9 g\ cm^{-3}$. Contention that semiconvective instability might develop and produce mixing (as in the "salt finger" instability in the oceans) disregards the fact that extra energy is needed to bring electrons from regions of lower Fermi level into regions of higher Fermi level, and also that the time scale of oscillations is here much shorter than the time scale of heat diffusion. The last ignition density should thus be a good estimate. MIYAJI and NOMOTO [15] predict collapse, but in their calculation they suppress any form of burning propagation. Conductive burning propagation can however not be averted, and both convective and Rayleigh-Taylor instabilities can develop from the beginning since the layers are always fluid (due, in last resort, to previous heating by electron captures on ^{24}Mg and ^{24}Na). When current estimates of hydrodynamic burning propagation velocities (WOOSLEY and WEAVER [3]) are adopted, the outcome is explosion, not collapse. The problem is again how fast hydrodynamic burning propagates in its initial stages. Explosion of O+Ne+Mg white dwarfs is thus an open possibility. Their nucleosynthesis would nonetheless yield excess neutron-rich isotopes. The corresponding outbursts have still to be modelled to see if they would produce viable SNIa (or maybe SNIb).

VII. Conclusions

While mass-accreting C+O white dwarfs are the most likely progenitors of SNIa, no consistent and observationally confirmed evolutionary path leading to the outburst is known. Possible progenitor systems include white dwarf / H-rich star binaries where slowly accreted H would somehow manage to burn into He and remain there, or a similar (well-hidden) pair where H would be accreted fast, or still equally elusive double C+O white dwarf binaries (either non-DA or rapidly merging DA, to be compatible with the statistics). In the last case, accretion from the massive disk resulting from disruption of the secondary should be finely tuned.

Confirmed inhomogeneity in the spectroscopic and photometric characteristics of SNIa would indicate some type of off-center ignition. This might be either due to growth of an Urca-stabilized convective core or to the presence of a central solid core.

The problem of a too neutron-rich nucleosynthesis stands. If it could not be solved by the dynamics of the burning front, this would mean that either white dwarfs manage to ignite at lower densities than it is currently thought or, on the contrary, that part of the ashes remains gravitationally bound. Collapsing models, however, do not seem able to produce viable outbursts.

References

1. Colgate, S.A., Petschek, A.G., and Kriese, J.T. 1980, *Ap. J. (Letters)*, **237**, L81

2. Arnett, W.D. 1982, *Ap. J.*, **253**, 785

3. Woosley, S.E., and Weaver, T.A. 1986, *Ann. Rev. Astron. Ap.*, **24**, 205

4. Maza, J., and van den Bergh, S. 1976, *Ap. J.*, **204**, 519

5. Arnett, W.D., Branch, D., and Wheeler, J.C. 1985, *Nature*, **314**, 337

6. Woosley, S.E., Axelrod, T.S., and Weaver, T.A. 1984, in *Stellar Nucleosynthesis*,

ed. C. Chiosi and A. Renzini (Dordrecht: Reidel), p.263

7. Branch, D., et al. 1982, *Ap. J. (Letters)*, **252**, L61

8. Wheeler, J.C., Harkness, R.P., and Cappellaro, E. 1987, in *Proc. 13th Texas Symposium on Relativistic Astrophysics*, ed. M.P. Ulmer (Singapore: World Scientific), p. 402

9. Cadonau, R., Sandage, A., and Tammann, G.A. 1985, in *Supernovae as Distance Indicators*, ed. N. Bartel (Berlin: Springer Verlag), p. 151

10. Branch, D. 1987, *Ap. J. (Letters)*, **316**, L81

11. Phillips, M.M., et al. 1987, *Pub. Astron. Soc. Pacific*, **99**, 592

12. Canal, R., Isern, J., and Lopez, R. 1988, *Ap. J. (Letters)*, **330**, L113

13. Finzi, A., and Wolf, R.A. 1967, *Ap. J.*, **150**, 115

14. Miyaji, S., Nomoto, K., Yokoi, K., and Sugimoto, D. 1980, *Publ. Astron. Soc. Japan*, **32**, 303

15. Miyaji, S., and Nomoto, K. 1987, *Ap. J.*, **318**, 307

16. Woosley, S.E. 1989, in *Supernovae*, ed. A.G. Petschek (Berlin: Springer Verlag), preprint

17. Starrfield, S., Sparks, W.M., and Shaviv, G. 1989, preprint

18. Iben, I., and Tutukov, A. 1984, *Ap. J. Suppl.*, **54**, 335

19. Shaviv, G., and Starrfield, S. 1987, *Ap. J. (Letters)*, **321**, L51

20. Sparks, W.M., and Kutter, G.S. 1987, *Ap. J.*, **321**, 394

21. Truran, J.W. 1989, private communication

22. Hachisu, I., Kato, M., and Saio, H. 1989, *Ap. J.*, in press

23. Renzini, A. 1989, private communication

24. Ritter, H. 1989, private communication

25. Nomoto, K. 1982, *Ap. J.*, **253**, 798

26. Webbink, R.F. 1979, in *White Dwarfs and Variable Degenerate Stars*, ed. H.M. Van Horn and V. Weidemann (Rochester: Univ. Rochester) p. 426

27. Nomoto, K., and Iben, I. 1985, *Ap. J.*, **297**, 531

28. Mochkovitch, R., and Livio, M. 1989, *Astron. Ap.*, **209**, 111

29. Robinson, E.L., and Shafter, A.W. 1989, in *White Dwarfs*, ed G. Wegner (Berlin: Springer Verlag), p. 492

30. Bragaglia, A., Greggio, L., Renzini, A., and D'Odorico, S. 1989, in *White Dwarfs*,

ed. G. Wegner (Berlin: Springer Verlag), p. 138

31. Abia, C., and Rebolo, R. 1989, *Ap. J.*, in press

32. Abia, C., et al. 1989, in preparation

33. Slattery, W.L., Doolen, G.D., and DeWitt, H.E. 1982, *Phys. Rev. A*, **26**, 2255

34. Loumos, G.L., and Hubbard, W.B. 1973, *Ap. J.*, **180**, 199

35. Stevenson, D.J. 1980, *Jour. Phys. Suppl.*, No 3, **41**, C2-53

36. Mochkovitch, R. 1983, *Astron. Ap.*, **122**, 212

37. Barrat, J.L., Hansen, J.P., and Mochkovitch, R. 1988, *Astron. Ap.*, **199**, L15

38. Ichimaru, S., Iyetomi, H., and Ogata, S. 1988, *Ap. J. (Letters)*, **334**, L17

39. Godon, P., Shaviv, G., Ashkenazi, J., and Kovetz, A. 1989, in *White Dwarfs*, ed. G. Wegner (Berlin: Springer Verlag), p. 85

40. Nomoto, K. 1982, *Ap. J.*, **257**, 780

41. Hernanz, M., Isern, J., Canal, R., Labay, J., and Mochkovitch, R. 1988, *Ap. J.*, **324**, 331

42. Nomoto, K., Thielemann, F.-K., and Yokoi, K. 1984, *Ap. J.*, **286**, 644

43. Sutherland, P., and Wheeler, J. C. 1984, *Ap. J.*, **280**, 282

44. Paczynski, B. 1972, *Astrophys. Lett.*, **11**, 53

45. Iben, I. 1982, *Ap. J.*, **253**, 248

46. Barkat, Z., and Wheeler, J. C. 1989, in preparation

47. Blinnikov, S.I., and Khokhlov, A.M. 1986, *Soviet Astron. Lett.*, **12**, 131; 1987, *ibid.*, **13**, 364

48. Wheeler, J.C., Harkness, R.P., Barkat, Z., and Swartz, D. 1986, *Publ. Astron. Soc. Pacific*, **98**, 1018

49. Imshennik, V.S., and Khokhlov, A.M. 1984, *Soviet Astron. Lett.*, **10**, 262

50. Khokhlov, A.M. 1989, *M.N.R.A.S.*, **239**, 785

51. Thielemann, F.-K., Nomoto, K., and Yokoi, K. 1985, *Astron. Ap.*, **158**, 17

52. Fryxell, B.A., Müller, E., and Arnett, W.D. 1989, in *Numerical Methods in Astrophysics*, ed. P.R. Woodward (New York: Academic Press), in press

53. Nomoto, K. 1989, private communication

54. Isern, J., Labay, J., and Canal, R. 1984, *Nature*, **309**, 431

55. Pskovskii, Y.P. 1977, *Soviet Astron.*, **21**, 675; *ibid.*, **28**, 658

56. Branch, D. 1982, *Ap. J.*, **285**, 35

57. Lopez, R., Isern, J., Canal, R., and Labay, J. 1986, *Astron. Ap.*, **155**, 1

58. Graham, J.R. 1987, *Ap. J. (Letters)*, **318**, L47

59. Salpeter, E.E., and Van Horn, H.M. 1969, *Ap. J.*, **155**, 183

60. Canal, R., and Isern, J. 1979, in *White Dwarfs and Variable Degenerate Stars*, ed. H.M. Van Horn and V. Weidemann (Rochester: Univ. Rochester), p. 52

61. Isern, J., Labay, J., Hernanz, M., and Canal, R. 1983, *Ap. J.*, **273**, 320

62. Canal, R., Isern, J., and Labay, J. 1989, in *Timing Neutron Stars*, ed. H. Ögelman and E.P.J. van den Heuvel (Dordrecht: Reidel), p. 631

63. Mazzitelli, I., and D'Antona, F. 1987, in *The Second Conference on Faint Blue Stars*, ed. A.G. Davis, D.S. Hayes, and J.W. Liebert (Schenectady: Davis Press), p. 351

Wolf-Rayet Stars as Supernova Precursors
Norbert Langer

Wolf-Rayet (WR) stars are thought to be massive stars which are burning helium in their centers and have lost all or most of their hydrogen rich envelope, consequently showing products of hydrogen burning (WN stars) or helium burning (WC stars) at their surface. The very intense stellar wind of those objects ($\dot{M}_{WR} > 10^{-5}\, M_\odot\, yr^{-1}$) is responsible for the dominance of emission lines in their spectra, which is their most prominent characteristic. All massive single stars with initial masses above a certain limit M_{WR} are supposed to evolve into WR stars, which represents their final hydrostatic evolutionary stage (cf. Chiosi and Maeder, 1986). Note that M_{WR}, which is of the order of $25 - 50\, M_\odot$ in our Galaxy (van der Hucht et al., 1988; Humphreys et al., 1985), may depend on the stellar metallicity (cf. Dopita, this volume).

As with massive stars, most WR stars, after core helium exhaustion, undergo central carbon-, neon-, oxygen-, and silicon burning, leading to the formation of an iron core, which eventually collapses. Whether this collapse can be reversed into a supernova (SN) explosion depends upon the maximum iron core mass $M_\uparrow$, which can be exploded by the core collapse mechanism (cf. Baron and Cooperstein, this volume; Mayle and Wilson, this volume). The iron core mass developed in a given WR star depends on its actual mass at the end of its evolution, which presumably does not change after core helium exhaustion because of the short amount of time left from this point on to core collapse. Therefore it is important that, because of the high mass loss rate of WR stars and of certain WR progenitors (esp. the Luminous Blue Variables, LBVs), the final WR mass is much smaller than the corresponding zero age main sequence (ZAMS) mass, and in most cases even much smaller than the helium core mass at hydrogen exhaustion. Both, $M_\uparrow$ and the initial-final mass relation for massive stars are rather uncertain at present (see below for latter), and therefore no general conclusion about the final fate of WR stars can be drawn. However, some WR stars (e.g. HD 152270: $5 \pm 2\, M_\odot$; St. Louis et al., 1987) are known to have a smaller total mass than the presumed helium core mass of the SN 1987A progenitor ($\sim 6\, M_\odot$), which implies that at least those are very likely to explode.

May each WR subclass contain pre-SN stars?

As mentioned above, there are two spectroscopic WR subclasses, the WN and the WC stars. Observationally determined surface abundances agree well with abundances resulting from partial or complete hydrogen burning for the WNs and incomplete helium burning for the WC-stars (cf. Maeder, 1983), which allows one to directly compare stellar models with appropriate surface abundances to stars of the respective WR subclass. Both WR subclasses are further divided into subtypes according to spectroscopic criteria (see van der Hucht et al., 1981). There is some evidence that the so called late WN stars (WNLs) still contain a considerable amount of hydrogen in there atmospheres, in contrast to the early WN stars (WNEs), where hydrogen seems to be very rare or absent (Willis, 1982). The correspondence of WN subtypes to the surface hydrogen abundance seems not to be strict (cf. Hamann, 1989); however, we shall designate hydrogenless WN stellar models as WNE stars and hydrogen containing ones as WNL stars in this work. Also the WC subclass is divided into subtypes (WCE, WCL, and WO), but a corresponding distinction of surface abundances could not be established observationally (Torres, 1988; Smith and Hummer, 1988). Therefore, this division can not be transposed to stellar models.

In any evolutionary scenario for WR stars, a WNL phase must precede the WNE phase. This is so because the hydrogen burning convective core is shrinking with time, i.e. in order to expose ashes of complete H-burning at the surface (= WNE-phase), ashes of incomplete H-burning have to be exposed earlier (= WNL-phase). Similarly, because the He-burning convective core is smaller than the H-burning convective core, a WC phase must be preceded by a WN phase. However, this does not necessarily imply, that the time sequence WNL $\to$ WNE $\to$ WC is followed up to the end by all massive stars which enter the WR stage (which would mean that only WC stars could be SN progenitors). Actually, the fact that the WR phase of any massive star has to start with a WN stage indicates, that at least stars with a ZAMS mass closely above the lower ZAMS mass limit for WR formation (M_{WR}) should terminate their evolution as WN stars: their ZAMS masses being closely larger than M_{WR} means that they reach the WR phase just at the end of their evolution, implying that no more time is left to further remove sufficient mass in order to reach the WC stage.

Stellar evolution calculations for the pre-WR phases of massive stars still contain far too large uncertainties (concerning $\dot{M}$ in the red supergiant or LBV phase, convection, etc.; cf. Langer and El Eid, 1986) in order to allow reliable estimates for the relative number of SNe to be expected from the different WR subtypes. However, qualitative conclusions may be drawn, though even most of them have to be regarded as tentative and preliminary.

WNL stars as progenitors of peculiar Type II SNe

The above argument for the existence of stars which terminate their evolution as WN stars seems to imply that stars with M_{ZAMS} closely above M_{WR} might explode as WNL star rather than WNE stars. Though this may be right in principle, the number of stars to which this applies may be small. Since massive stars in the ZAMS mass range considered (i.e. somewhere between 25 and 50 $M_\odot$) contain a steep hydrogen gradient above the H-burning shell, the mass range ΔM_r where the H mass fraction changes from 0 up to a value considered too high to apply to a WNL surface (e.g. ~ 0.3; cf. Maeder, 1983) is very small ($< 0.1 M_\odot$). Let $\dot{M}_{WNL}$ be a typical mass loss rate for WNL stars (say $3 \cdot 10^{-5} M_\odot yr^{-1}$), then $\Delta M_r / \dot{M}_{WNL}$ is an upper limit for the duration of the WNL phase τ_{WNL}, which, with above numbers, turns to $\tau_{WNL} < 3000\, yr$. This means that stars with the smallest ZAMS masses considered in this paper may, on becoming WR stars, almost immediately turn into WNE stars.

However, the concept of estimating the duration of the different WR phases on the basis of internal composition profiles and typical mass loss rates may lead to the conclusion, that the most massive stars terminate their lives as WNL stars (cf. Langer, 1987): the thickness (in mass) of the convective zone above the H-burning shell (i.e. also the thickness of the corresponding hydrogen plateau ΔM_{ICZ}) is an increasing function of the stellar mass. The H mass fraction established in this convective zone, X_{ICZ}, is a decreasing function of the stellar mass. For X_{ICZ} to be sufficiently small in order to correspond to the WNL phase, its duration will be $\tau_{WNL} \simeq \Delta M_{ICZ}/\dot{M}_{WNL}$, which, for sufficiently massive stars, may become larger than the post main sequence lifetime, meaning that the WNL phase is the final evolutionary phase in this case. The lower ZAMS mass limit for stars terminating their evolution as WNL stars according to this scenario is rather uncertain, but $M_{ZAMS} \simeq 100\, M_\odot$ may give an order of magnitude (cf. Langer and El Eid, 1986).

$M_{ZAMS} \simeq 100\, M_\odot$, on the other hand, is also a limiting mass concerning the final fate of massive stars: while stars of lower initial mass form an iron core, leading eventually to core collapse, higher mass stars perform a collapse due to the formation of $e^\pm$-pairs prior to central oxygen ignition, and subsequent explosive oxygen burning is able to disrupt the star, giving rise to the so called pair creation supernovae (PCSN) (cf. Woosley and Weaver, 1986). Towards still higher masses, explosive oxygen burning does not deliberate sufficient energy in order to reverse the collapse into an explosion (at least in nonrotating objects; see Glatzel et al.,1985 ; Stringfellow and Woosley, 1988), and the stars collapse to black holes; however, such massive objects are, if formed at all at the present epoch, extremely rare due to the steep decline of the initial mass function. Note that the fate of stars with masses close to the lower mass limit for PCSNe is still somewhat uncertain, some of them becoming pulsationally pair-unstable (see Woosley, 1986).

In summary, the most massive stars (i.e. $100\, M_\odot \lesssim M_{ZAMS} \lesssim 200\, M_\odot$) may end their evolution as WNL stars performing a PCSN. Herzig et al. (1990) performed numerical computations for lightcurves of pair-unstable exploding massive WR stars and investigated the dependence of the peak luminosity on the amount of synthesized radioactive nickel. They estimated the fraction of PCSN events among the observed supernovae to be of the order of 1%. This number is small, but taken at face it means, that two or three PCSNe could have already been observed, probably classified as peculiar Type II SNe. Herzig et al. argue, that a PCSN may be distinguished from a usual Type II SN by either very low or very high peak luminosity due to the fact that the amount of nickel synthesized may be somewhere in the range between 0 and several solar masses, depending on the mass of the progenitor star. Furthermore, the high mass loss rate of WR stars should result in a high radio luminosity of PCSNe. Possible candidates for PCSNe are SN 1961v (cf. discussion in Langer, 1987a) and SN 1986j (Rupen et al., 1987), while El Eid and Langer (1986) discussed the possibility of Cas A being a PCSN remnant. All three cases, which undoubtly have massive progenitor stars, have a very high radio luminosity, unusual lightcurves and/or peak luminosities, and show strong indications of considerable hydrogen deficiency and helium and nitrogen overabundance.

Hydrogenless WR stars: SN Ib progenitors?

The bulk of observed WR stars, i.e. most WNE and all WC stars, apparently contains no hydrogen at all. Concerning the stellar structure, it appears to be crucial whether the envelope of a WR star contains some amounts of hydrogen or not: its presence implies a hydrogen burning shell as a second nuclear energy source besides the He-burning stellar center. Consequently, the star has a larger radius and smaller surface temperature compared to hydrogenless stars of similar mass, which is also supported by the high radiative opacity and small mean molecular weight of hydrogen. Furthermore it is known, that a hydrogen containing envelope can prevent the WR star from being unstable due to radial pulsations according to the ϵ-mechanism. Maeder (1985) finds massive WR stars to be stable if their surface hydrogen mass fraction exceeds $\sim 8\%$.

In this context it is important to note that there is high observational evidence, that the most massive WR stars are WNL stars, while WNE and WC stars are found to have relatively low masses. Niemela (1983) made a statistic of masses of WR stars in binary systems and found a mean mass of $63\,M_\odot$ for WNLs but values of $8\,M_\odot$ and $15\,M_\odot$ for WNE and WC stars, respectively. This is consistent with estimates for the bolometric luminosity of WR stars (cf. Smith and Willis, 1983; Schmutz et al., 1989), indicating high values for WNLs but much lower ones for WNEs and WCs (note that luminosities can readily be transformed into masses for WR stars, since they obey a narrow mass-luminosity relation; see Maeder, 1983; Langer, 1989).

The recent data of Schmutz et al. indicates a mass interval of $17\,M_\odot \gtrsim M_{WNE} \gtrsim 9\,M_\odot$ for WNE stars and of $10\,M_\odot \gtrsim M_{WC} \gtrsim 4.5\,M_\odot$ for WC stars, and they notice the incompatibility of these data with standard stellar evolution calculations like that of Maeder and Meynet (1987). The basic contradiction is that WR stars have to originate from very massive stars, but (except the WNL stars) their masses are very small. This contradiction can be resolved only, when the massive WNE and WC stage is a very short phase during the evolution of a WR star. Langer (1989a), who computed WR evolutionary sequences assuming mass dependent mass loss rates for hydrogenless WR stars (instead of the standard assumption of a constant mass loss rate) found, that this discrepancy disappears for a mass dependence of the mass loss rate to a power of 1 or larger, which is motivated by WR structure calculations (Langer, 1989), and is in agreement with present observations of WR mass loss rates (cf. references in Langer, 1989a; see also Abbott et al., 1986). Moreover, WR evolution computed with mass dependent mass loss rates is found to account for observed WR subtype number ratios, observational indications for average progenitor ZAMS masses for WNE and WC stars, as well as an increased average total WR lifetime, which is required by the high observed number ratio of WR to O-stars in the Galaxy (Conti et al., 1983).

A further result of WR evolution incorporating mass dependent mass loss rates, which is most relevant to the topic of this paper, is **1.** the mean final mass of stars with $M_{WR} \leq M_{ZAMS} \lesssim 100\,M_\odot$ is very small (i.e. below $10\,M_\odot$), and **2.** the scatter in the final masses is very small ($\sim \pm 1\,M_\odot$), implying that stars originating from the above ZAMS mass range end up practically with the same final mass.

The general characteristics of WR evolution with mass dependent mass loss rates outlined above, which have been obtained by performing a large number of simplified evolutionary computations, are confirmed by elaborated calculations using a hydrodynamical stellar evolution code. E.g. a $60\,M_\odot$ population I star — which may be a typical WR progenitor — is found to end its evolution as a $5.8\,M_\odot$ WC star, using a mass loss rate for hydrogenless WR stars of the form $\dot M_{WR} \sim M_{WR}^{2.5}$. The final surface abundances, which were found to be similar within most of the considered ZAMS mass range, are 20% helium, and about 40% carbon and 40% oxygen by mass. The thickness of the radiative envelope in final He-burning stages was $\sim 2\,M_\odot$, indicating the amount of mass which contains noticeable amounts of helium.

Note that $5.8\,M_\odot$ is a mass which is certainly able to perform a supernova explosion after core collapse, since it is of the same size as the He-core of SN 1987A. Light curves of exploding low mass WR stars have been calculated by Ensman and

Woosley (1988) and are found to be compatible with observed SN Ib light curves for such low masses, while abundance constraints from SN Ib spectra are matched by the abundances mentioned above.

We conclude that some fraction of Ib supernovae may be related to WR stars. However, many problems remain to be solved. For ZAMS masses close to M_{WR} the envelope composition of the SN progenitor corresponds to WNE stars, i.e. to complete H-burning ashes. The ZAMS mass range, for which evolution ends in the WNE stage is not well known (for $M_{WR} = 30\,M_\odot$ Langer, 1989a, finds a range of $30\,M_\odot \leq M_{ZAMS} \lesssim 35\,M_\odot$). The spectroscopical display of WNE-supernovae is unknown. Furthermore, for M_{ZAMS} close to M_{WR}, the final WR mass is of the order of the He-core mass of a star of mass M_{WR}. For $M_{WR} > 30\,M_\odot$, this may be more than $10\,M_\odot$, which seems to be incompatible with SN Ib light curves (Ensman and Woosley, 1988; see also: this volume). Also, as mentioned above, it is unclear if such massive cores lead to SN explosions at all.

The structure of the presupernova configurations

Observations of WR stars can tell us almost nothing about the internal structure and surface conditions (except the chemical composition) of WR stars at the time of central collapse. The SN 1987a has impressively demonstrated, that stellar radius and surface temperature, and due to that also the mass loss rate, may change drastically during the last couple of $10^4\,yr$ of the evolution of hydrogenrich supergiants. The Kelvin-Helmholtz timescale for hydrogenless WR stars can be expressed as $\tau_{KH} \simeq 4.8 \cdot 10^4 (M/M_\odot)^{-0.38}$ (Langer, 1989), and is a good approximation for the time interval from central helium exhaustion up to central collapse. This time is too short in order to find more than 4% of the WR stars in post core helium burning phases, but sufficiently long in order to allow a global rearrangement of the stellar structure.

The low mass WC star originating from the $60\,M_\odot$ evolution as described in the previous section, e.g., finishes core helium burning with a luminosity of $\log L/L_\odot = 4.9$, and a surface temperature of $120\,000\,K$. In the following contraction phase, however, the luminosity increases up to $\log L/L_\odot = 5.2$, and the surface temperature increases first up to $165\,000\,K$ and decreases then to $140\,000\,K$. A similar situation is encountered in massive WR models (cf. Langer et al., 1988). Thus, the final values of luminosity, radius, and surface temperature can be predicted by stellar evolution calculations, but they cannot be compared to observations. Moreover, the dependence of the mass loss rate during the final hydrostatic evolutionary phases of WR stars cannot even be estimated theoretically, since there is no theory for WR mass loss.

We have to conclude that a qualitative comparison of wind properties derived from observed radio fluxes of Type Ib or Type II pec. SNe with observed WR wind properties may be meaningless.

Conclusions

The modeling of the evolution of massive stars still involves many large uncertainties (mass loss rates, convection, nuclear reaction rates, ...). Depending on the choice of physics used for stellar evolution calculations, quite different results concerning presupernova configurations may be obtained. The conclusions of this paper are based on stellar models, which were obtained with a physics compatible to that which successfully reproduced the progenitor evolution of SN 1987A (see Langer et al., this volume). A further basic ingredient is the concept of mass dependent mass loss rates for hydrogenless WR stars (Langer, 1989a). Our conclusions may be summarized as follows:

- WR stars of any subtype (WNL, WNE, WC) may be presupernova stars. WR progenitors may therefore give rise to Type II SNe (WNL) as well as to Type I SNe (WNE, WC).
- The most massive stars ($M_{ZAMS} \gtrsim 100\,M_\odot$) are supposed to explode during their WNL phase as peculiar Type II SNe due to the PCSN mechanism. About 1% of the observed SNe may be due to these objects.
- The bulk of very massive stars ($35\,M_\odot \lesssim M_{ZAMS} \lesssim 100\,M_\odot$) is supposed to end their evolution as low mass WC star ($M_{WC} < 10\,M_\odot$). Some of them certainly explode due to the core collapse mechanism, possibly being classified as Type Ib SNe.
- The wind properties of WR stars during their final evolutionary phases are unknown, which allows at most a qualitative comparison between observed and predicted radio fluxes of SNe related to those objects.

The above ZAMS mass limits are not very well known and should only be understood as order of magnitude estimates. Even at fixed input physics for stellar evolution calculations they would not be constant but rather a function of the stellar metallicity.

Acknowledgment. I am grateful to S. Woosley for valuable discussions and for his hospitality at Lick Observatory. This work has been supported by the Deutsche Forschungsgemeinschaft (DFG) through grants La 587/1-2 and La 587/2-1, by the Astronomische Gesellschaft through the Ludwig-Biermann award 1989, and by NASA through grant NAGW-1273.

References

Abbott, D.C., Bieging, J.H., Churchwell, E., Torres, A.V.: 1986, Astrophys. J. **303**, 239

Chiosi, C., Maeder, A.: 1986, Ann. Rev. Astron. Astrophys. **24**, 329

Conti, P.S., Garmany, C., de Loore, C., Vanbeveren, D.: 1983, Astrophys. J. **274**, 302

El Eid, M.F., Langer, N.: 1986, Astron. Astrophys. **167**, 274

Ensman, L.M., Woosley, S.E.: 1988, Astrophys. J. **333**, 754

Glatzel, W., El Eid, M.F., Fricke, K.J.: 1985, Astron. Astrophys. **149**, 413

Hamann, W.-R.: 1989, Proc. Hot Star Workshop, Boulder, C. Garmany, ed., in press

Herzig, K., El Eid, M.F., Fricke, K.J., Langer, N.: 1990, Astron. Astrophys., submitted

van der Hucht, K.A., Conti, P.S., Lundström, I., Stenholm, B.: Space Sci. Rev. **28**, 227

van der Hucht, K.A., Hidayat, B., Admiranto, A.G., Supelli, K.R., Doom, C.: 1988, Astron. Astrophys. **199**, 217

Humphreys, R.M., Nichols, M., Massey, P.: 1985, Astron. J. **90**, 101

Langer, N.: 1987, Astron. Astrophys. *Letter* **171**, L1

Langer, N.: 1987a, in: *Nuclear Astrophysics*, Lecture Notes in Physics **287**, W. Hillebrandt et al., eds., Springer, p. 180

Langer, N.: 1989, Astron. Astrophys. **210**, 93

Langer, N.: 1989a, Astron. Astrophys. **220**, 135

Langer, N., El Eid, M.F.: 1986, Astron. Astrophys. **167**, 265

Langer, N., Kiriakidis, M., El Eid, M.F., Fricke, K.J., Weiss, A.: 1988, Astron. Astrophys. **192**, 177

Maeder, A.: 1983, Astron. Astrophys. **120**, 113

Maeder, A.: 1985, Astron. Astrophys. **147**, 300

Maeder, A., Meynet, G.: 1987, Astron. Astrophys. **182**, 243

Niemela, V.S.: 1983, in: Proc. *Workshop on Wolf-Rayet stars*, Paris-Meudon, eds M.C. Lortet, A, Piltaut, p. III.3

Rupen, M.P., van Gorkom, J.H., Knapp, G.R., Gunn, J.E., Schneider, D.P.: 1987, Astron. J. **94**, 61

Schmutz, W., Hamann, W.-R., Wessolowski, K.: 1989, Astron. Astrophys. **210**, 236

Smith, L.F., Hummer, D.G.: 1988, M.N.R.A.S. **230**, 511

Smith, L.J., Willis, A.J.: 1983, Astron. Astrophys. Suppl. **54**, 229

St.-Louis, N., Drissen, L., Moffat, A.F.J., Bastien, P., Tapia, S.: 1987, Astrophys. J. **322**, 870

Stringfellow, G.S., Woosley, S.E.: 1988, preprint, UCRL-98066

Torres, A.V.: 1988, Astrophys. J. **325**, 759

Willis, A.J.: 1982, in: *Wolf-Rayet Stars: Observations, Physics, Evolution*, IAU-Symp. **99**, C. de Loore, A.J. Willis, eds., p. 87

Woosley, S.E.: 1986, in *Nucleosynthesis and Chemical Evolution*, Saas-Fee lecture, B. Hauck, A. Maeder, eds.

Woosley, S.E., Weaver, T.A.: 1986, Ann. Rev. Astron. Astrophys. **24**, 205

Type Ib Supernovae Wolf-Rayet Stars
Lisa Ensman & S. E. Woosley

Since Type Ib supernovae were identified as a class several years ago, the idea that their progenitors are massive stars that have lost their hydrogen envelopes has been quite popular. ENSMAN and WOOSLEY [1] calculated a series of numerical models to test this idea and found that, if SNIb do come from massive stars (as opposed to, say, white dwarfs), those stars must have masses between approximately 4 and 7 $M_\odot$ at explosion. For more massive stars, the long diffusion time produces too broad a light curve. Smaller stars, on the other hand, produce negligible ^{56}Ni, making the light curve too dim. It was estimated that *some* SNe Ib, such as SN 1985F, might have progenitors closer to 8 $M_\odot$, but the typical SN Ib seems to require a lighter progenitor. Since observed Wolf–Rayet stars have masses much larger than this, the derived mass constraint led us to conclude that the majority of SNe Ib probably do not come from single Wolf–Rayet stars. They might, however, come from hydrogen–stripped stars produced by mass transfer in interacting binaries.

Since [1], some interesting developments in the study of WR stars have led us to be somewhat less pessimistic about single WR stars as SN Ib progenitors. On the observational side, MOFFAT [2, 3] argues, from plots of WR subtype versus mass ratio q ($q = M(\text{WR})/M(\text{O})$, where $M(\text{O})$ is the mass of an OB binary companion), that, as expected on theoretical grounds, WR stars evolve from type WNL to type WNE as they lose mass, then perhaps make a jump over to the WC sequence at some point, finally ending up at type WO. The smallest WR stars (those at the ends of the WN and WC/O sequences) have a mass ratio of about 0.2, implying that they are indeed about 6 to 8 $M_\odot$. Note however that this does not mean that all WR stars must evolve through the whole sequence to 6 to 8 $M_\odot$. In principle, a supernova explosion could occur at any point, depending on the age and core structure. However, on the theoretical side, Norbert Langer (this volume), has found that with a mass-dependent mass loss rate for the WR stage, one obtains stars which are indeed on the order of 6 to 10 $M_\odot$ at death, independent of the main sequence mass. Furthermore, he finds that the mass loss affects the core evolution such that, even for a very small final mass, some helium may remain on the surface. (The burning volume shrinks leaving partially burned helium behind.) Helium is seen in the spectra of at least some SNe Ib and provides an important constraint on the progenitors. While neither of these works is the last word on the subject, they do both offer hope for the WR–Ib connection. As the WR and Ib observations and theory improve, we will know with more certainty.

As pointed out in [1], there is also the questionable role of clumping and mixing in supernovae of Type Ib. Either would be expected to have a salutory effect on the light curve leading to a narrower peak and greater peak to tail contrast. (The observed drop in magnitude between maximum and the start of the tail could not be matched by the models in [1].) To study the effects of mixing, two 6 $M_\odot$ models have been run – variations on Model 6A of [1]. The first was totally mixed (a homogeneous composition) after shock breakout, while the second was mixed only to 4000 km/s, roughly the base of the helium layer. In addition, these models had only half as much ^{56}Ni as Model 6A (i.e., 0.22 $M_\odot$). The results are shown in Fig. 1.

Although it allowed the rise to maximum to begin immediately, complete mixing of the ejecta had almost no effect on the full width at half maximum. This is probably due to the fact that energy deposition in the outer layers by the decay of ^{56}Ni kept the temperature from falling and hence the electron scattering opacity remained high, offsetting the decrease in diffusion time resulting from mixing the ^{56}Ni closer to the surface. However, the total gamma ray optical depth was diminished, causing the peak to tail contrast to increase, though not enough to match the SN 1983N data, even in this extreme and probably unrealistic case of complete mixing. In the case of partial mixing, the peak in the light curve is sharper and narrower because as soon as the recombination front reached the bottom of the helium layer, radioactive material was exposed, and the radioactive tail, at near 100% deposition, began almost immediately. There was no nickel in the outer layer to keep it ionized so that that mass did not have any effect on the width of the peak. But, again, the changes in

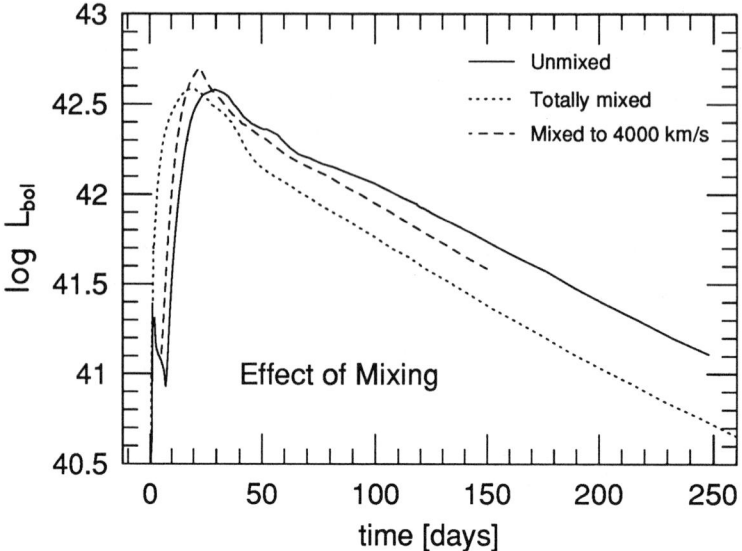

Figure 1. Effect of mixing on the light curve of a 6 $M_\odot$ model.

the light curve were not large enough to improve the fit to the data.

Models which include the effects of clumping have not yet been computed, but "holes" in the ejecta would indeed decrease the diffusion time and allow gamma rays to escape sooner. Whether a large effect on the light curve can be produced with a reasonable amount of clumping remains to be seen. (See [1] though for an extreme case in which the effective gamma ray opacity was decreased by a factor of 10 to roughly simulate the effect of clumping on gamma ray escape.)

References

1. L. Ensman, S. E. Woosley: Ap. J., **333**, 754 (1988).

2. A. Moffat: private communication (1988).

3. A. Moffat: A.J., **91**, 1386 (1986).

On the Nature of Type Ib Supernova Progenitors
Nino Panagia & Victoria G. Laidler

The realization that there is a separate subclass of Type I supernovae (SNe) to be denoted as Type Ib came after the detailed study of the SN 1983N in M83 (PANAGIA et al. [1]; see also PANAGIA [2], WHEELER and LEVREAULT [3], UOMOTO and KIRSHNER [4]). It was immediately clear that SN 1983N is distinctly different from the classical variety of Type I SNe (obviously denoted as Type Ia SNe) in a number of important aspects. Since then about a dozen SNe have been classified as Type Ib SNe, some newly discovered and others found just re-examining old spectra or paying due attention to the comments that the observers gave at the time when the original observations were made (*e.g.* BERTOLA [5]). In addition to the necessary condition to be called Type I SNe, *i.e.* the absence of hydrogen lines from the spectrum, the distinctive characteristics of Type Ib SNe can be summarized as follows (cf. PANAGIA et al. [6], WEILER and SRAMEK [7]):

- The 6150 Å feature is absent from the spectrum.

- The overall spectral distribution is redder (Δ(B-V)$\sim$ 0.5) and fainter ($\sim$ 1.5 magnitudes) than for Type Ia SNe.

- The optical light curve is essentially "normal", *i.e.* quite similar to that of Type Ia SNe.

- The IR light curve is single-peaked, the maximum occurring a few days after the optical maximum.

- They are strong radio emitters with a steep spectrum and a quick temporal decline.

- They are found only in spiral galaxies.

- They are located in spiral arms.

- They are possibly "associated" with (*i.e.* projected on, or near to) an HII region.

All these properties can be "read" in a rather simple manner and the picture that emerges is that of the explosion of stars which are "compact" (hence *not* a red supergiant) and have a small envelope similar to the case of Type Ia SNe (because of the similarity of the light curves), but have a chemical composition different from that of Type Ia progenitors (absence of the 6150 Å band) and a lower amount of ^{56}Ni synthetized in the explosion (redder and fainter emission).

Their radio emission requires the presence of a circumstellar envelope created by mass loss corresponding to $\dot{M}/v_{exp} \sim 3 \times 10^{-7} [M_\odot \ yr^{-1}]/[km \ s^{-1}]$ (WEILER et al. [8]). Such a flow would be so opaque as to create a *pseudo-photosphere* in the wind itself. For example, assuming a constant wind velocity, the radius at which the optical depth is of the order of unity would be (PANAGIA and FELLI [9]):

$$R \approx 3 \times 10^{12} \ (\kappa/\sigma_e)\{(\dot{M}/v_{exp})/10^{-7}\} \ [cm] \ > \ 9 \times 10^{12} \ [cm]$$

where κ is the average opacity, σ_e is the electron scattering cross section, $\dot{M}$ is in $M_\odot \ yr^{-1}$ and v_{exp} in $km \ s^{-1}$. It is clear that a radius so large is inconsistent with the hypothesis of a WR stellar wind. On the other hand the value of $\dot{M}/v_{exp} \sim 3 \times 10^{-7} \ [M_\odot \ yr^{-1}]/[km \ s^{-1}]$ is appropriate for a red supergiant: this implies the presence of a relatively massive companion (*i.e.* several solar masses; SRAMEK et al. [10]).

The lifetime of their progenitors must be shorter than 3×10^8 years, and, therefore their original mass larger than 5.5 $M_\odot$, in order to satisfy the condition posed by them being located in spiral arms. In fact, *if* Type Ib SNe are intrinsically associated with HII regions, their progenitors should be quite short-lived and, therefore, be much more massive. Since this is the only argument which may favor the idea that Type Ib SNe progenitors be very massive stars, we have considered this point in quite some detail.

First of all we have checked the validity of the "association" of Type Ib SNe with HII regions which is claimed for about 50% of them (WHEELER et al. [11]). By overlaying the best positions of Type Ib SNe [among those reported in the BARBON et al. Catalog of SNe [12] and those astrometrically determined either in the optical or in the radio] on the galaxy images with the use of the GASP[1] software, we find that 6 ± 1 out of 12 SNe appear to fall within 5" from the image of a knot (*i.e.* presumably an HII region). On the other hand, only in two cases (SN 1981I in NGC 4051 and SN 1985F in NGC 4618) the SN seems to fall on top of an HII region. Therefore, the "association" with an HII region actually means *close proximity*. And since 5" even at a distance as short as 4 Mpc corresponds to 100 pc, such a *proximity* may in fact be just fortuitous. For example, had the LMC been at 4 Mpc instead of 54 kpc, SN 1987A would appear to be *associated* with the 30 Doradus nebula while it is *not*.

A possible way to clarify this issue is to compare these results with a similar statistics made for the case of Type II SNe. Such an analysis is in progress but for the time being let us utilize the results of a similar study done by HUANG [13]. Out of 29 SNe for which there were good position measurements and good galaxy images to make the overlays, 25 objects were found to fall within an average distance of 5" from an HII. This immediately indicates that, independently on whether *any* such association is real in *any* case, the "association" of Type Ib SNe is *much* looser than for Type II

---

[1]GASP is the Guide Star Astrometric Support Program available at the Space Telescope Science Institute.

SNe. Assuming that this difference is entirely due to "evaporation" of the stars from their birth place, that difference implies lifetimes of the SN Ib progenitors considerably longer (3-10 times) than those of SN II progenitors and, consequently, original masses considerably lower (2-3 times for SN Ib than for SN II). Since Type II SNe are believed to originate from progenitors with masses in the range 8-20 $M_\odot$ (*e.g.* MAEDER [14]; see also VAN DEN BERGH, this Conference), the progenitors of Type Ib must have had masses within the possible range 5-10 $M_\odot$.

Such a range of progenitor's masses can be further narrowed down considering that the frequency of Type Ib explosions in spiral galaxies is about 1/3 that of Type II SNe (BRANCH [15], VAN DEN BERGH, MCCLURE, and EVANS [16]). Therefore, assuming that stars more massive than 8 $M_\odot$ make Type II SNe and adopting an initial mass function proportional to $M^{-2.35}$ the possible mass range for SN Ib progenitors turns out to be about 6.5-8 $M_\odot$. This agrees well with the direct estimate of $M > 6.5$ $M_\odot$ made by SRAMEK *et al.* [10] for SN 1983N on the basis of its radio emission. Also, a relatively "modest" mass for the progenitor can naturally explain why the mass ejected in the explosion (as implied by the "normal" optical light curve) is a few solar masses at most (BRANCH [17]).

We conclude that the only viable scenario to account for Type Ib events is that of a star with original mass around 7 $M_\odot$, which is member of a binary system in which the companion is slightly less massive (say, $\sim 5\ M_\odot$). The primary follows its evolution to the end becoming a rather massive degenerate star, which explodes when the secondary has reached the stage of red supergiant. The alternative hypothesis of a very massive progenitor (*i.e.* $M > 20\text{-}30\ M_\odot$) is ruled out on the basis of the mass loss characteristics required to account for the radio emission, the "light" envelope implied by the behaviour of the optical light curve and the "association" with HII regions which is much looser than for Type II SNe.

References

1. Panagia, N. et al: in preparation (1989).

2. Panagia, N.: in "Supernovae as Distance Indicators", ed. N. Bartel (Berlin: Springer), p. 14 (1985).

3. Wheeler, J.C., Levreault, R.: Ap. J. (Letters), 294, 17 (1985).

4. Uomoto, A., Kirshner, R.P.: Astr. Ap., 149, L7 (1985).

5. Bertola, F.: Ann. Ap., 27, 319 (1964).

6. Panagia, N., Sramek, R.A., Weiler, K.W.: Ap. J. (Letters), 300, L55 (1986).

7. Weiler, K.W., Sramek, R.A.: Ann. Rev. Astr. Ap., 26, 295 (1988).

8. Weiler, K.W., Sramek, R.A., Panagia, N., van der Hulst, J.M., Salvati, M.: Ap. J., 301, 790 (1986).

9. Panagia, N., Felli, M.: in "Wolf-Rayet Stars: Observations, Physics, Evolution", eds. C.W.H. de Loore and A.J. Willis (Dordrecht: Reidel), p. 203 (1982).

10. Sramek, R.A., Panagia, N., Weiler, K.W.: Ap. J. (Letters), 285, L59 (1984).

11. Wheeler, J.C., Harkness, R.P., Cappellaro, E.: Proc. 13th Texas Symposium on Relativistic Astrophysics, ed. M.P. Ulmer, (Singapore: World Scientific), p. 402 (1987).

12. Barbon, R., Cappellaro, E., Ciatti, F., Turatto, M., Kowal, C.T.: Astr. Ap. Suppl., 58, 735 (1984).

13. Huang, Y.-L.: P. A. S. P., 99, 461 (1987).

14. Maeder, A.: ESO Workshop "SN 1987A", ed. I.J. Danziger (Garching: ESO), p. 251 (1987).

15. Branch, D.: Ap. J. (Letters), 300, L51 (1986).

16. van den Bergh, S., McClure, R.D., Evans, R.: Ap. J., 323, 44 (1987).

17. Branch, D.: in Proc. IAU Colloquium No. 108, in press.

The Carbon Explosion Model
Zalman Barkat

The main theoretical characteristics of the carbon explosion model (more often authors use the names carbon deflagration or carbon detonation) are:

  a. A carbon/oxygen core grows from below towards the Chandrasekhar mass.

  b. In a single star which is able to retain its envelope the growth rate of the core is given by the luminosity-core mass relation and one can show [1][2] that the evolutionary tracks of growing cores converge to a unique track independent of initial mass.

  c. In binaries, the growth rate is determined by the companion star and by the geometry. We shall not comment on the reality of scenarios which allow cores to grow. Here we only note that *a priori* there is some freedom for different evolutionary tracks due to different growth rates and the combination of core mass and age (i.e. control temperature). It turns out, however, that for the range of accretion rates $3 \times 10^{-6} \lesssim \dot{M}/M_\odot \lesssim 4 \times 10^{-8}$ the possible differences are rather small, especially in regards to the character of the core at carbon ignition, e.g. central density and temperature [3].

  d. Note that in the above discussion the initial point from which the mass of the core is growing ("infant mass") is the phase of evolution where the core has already evolved past the point of maximum central temperature and would have been cooling at almost constant density unless forced to grow. One important aspect of this is associated with the fact that if the infant mass is larger than $\sim 1.05\ M_\odot$, at least some carbon must have already been burnt. Even though the evolutionary tracks of these cores are still almost identical to all the others, the *compositions* of the cores should be different and infant-mass-dependent.

  e. Beyond carbon ignition (which is defined as the point where energy generation by nuclear reactions become equal to neutrino energy loss) a convective core forms and grows around the center. Because of the high degeneracy the energy liberated does not affect the pressure so that the usual regulation of burning by expansion does not apply and the temperature increase is accelerated along with the nuclear energy generation rate [4].

f. The only mechanism ever suggested to prevent thermonuclear runaway, i.e. burning on a dynamical timescale, is the convective Urca mechanism, PACZYŃSKI [5]. We shall come back to discuss this issue, but first let us pretend, as has been done in recent years by most authors, that the effect is negligible.

g. One can show that the high sensitivity of the nuclear reactions to the temperature ($\sim T^{20}$) means that the burning proceeds in the form of a narrow front which advances from the center (if this is where it originates) outwards. In general the front can be described by the Hugoniot relations and it can be either a detonation or a deflagration. We shall not discuss here the question whether it is one of these or the other, we only mention that both incinerate matter all the way to nuclear statistical equilibrium as long as the density is higher than $\sim 10^7$ g cm^{-3}. The great advantage of a deflagration is that it is necessarily preceded by a shock which induces matter ahead of the front to expand. This expansion allows the deflagration to "die" at a point beyond which there remain a few tenths of a solar mass whereas in the case of detonation the corresponding amount is negligible. The point is that observations clearly say [6][7] that a significant amount of *partially* burned matter must be present. A detonation could possibly only be allowed if, for some reason, the core is already expanding when the detonation forms. This possibility will be discussed elsewhere.

The attractive thing about the models is the fact that at least some deflagration models [8][9] do produce spectra and light curves which fit observations of Type Ia supernovae amazingly well, and the fact that by their intrinsic nature they must be nearly identical.

The problems associated with the model are:

a. Single stars up to ~ 7 M$_\odot$ are thought to eject their envelopes in the form of planetary nebulae before their cores grow to the neighborhood of the Chandrasekhar mass [10].

b. If they should appear as Type Ia supernovae they must not possess an excessive hydrogen envelope at explosion.

c. The above two points could possibly be taken care of in a binary system. Again we shall not discuss the reality of such scenarios. We mention, however, that near explosion the luminosity, which is determined by the accretion rate, is, in the range of interest, many thousands of solar luminosities and the supernova progenitor should appear as a blue supergiant. Observationally, it appears that such stars are not abundant enough [11].

d. Single stars having main sequence masses in the range $7 \lesssim M/M_\odot \lesssim 10$ may, depending on some not yet resolved problems in stellar evolution theory, evolve to the point where their cores grow to the Chandrasekhar mass without losing the envelope. If these stars explode they will appear just before the explosion as *red supergiants* with a well defined luminosity ~ 60,000 K (the luminosity-mass relation) and will certainly show hydrogen in the spectrum. Again it is not clear that enough (if any) such stars are observed.

e. From the theoretical point of view, a major problem is associated with the treatment of convective Urca neutrino losses. Current successful models of carbon deflagration [8][9] use as pre-explosion models the structure at carbon ignition, where the central density is 3×10^9 g cm^{-3} and the central temperature ~ 2×10^8 K, on the basis that the runaway is imminent. In 1972 Paczyński has suggested that circulating relevant nuclei, e.g. Na^{23}, by the convective currents past a point in the core (the "Urca shell") where the Fermi energy of electrons matches the threshold energy for capture/emission of electrons produces a cyclic process known as the "Urca process" which constitutes an energy sink, since in both cases a neutrino (or antineutrino) carries away energy. He showed that this sink can become efficient enough to control carbon burning even for nuclei whose abundance is solar, i.e. as low as 10^{-5} (by mass). BRUENN [12], however, drew attention to the fact that in these Urca processes, matter is actually *heating* in spite of the neutrino losses. Over the years since 1972 several authors have discussed this problem which is complicated because of the role which convection is playing. COUCH and ARNETT [13] and IBEN [14][15] have argued that the heating is expended in moving electrons around by the convection, so that the net result of the Urca process is still cooling. Although the detailed treatment is different, both find that carbon burning runaway does not occur at ρ_c ~ 3×10^9 g cm^{-3}. As shown in Figure 1, Couch and Arnett find that Urca losses due to the pair Na^{23} – ^{23}Ne delay the runaway until ρ ~ 6×10^9 g cm^{-3} while IBEN [16] finds that the temperature first oscillates on a thermal timescale due to alternate cooling and heating phases, and then as the density rises to ~ 4×10^9 g cm^{-3} *drops* sharply due to the appearance of a new Urca shell associated with the pair ^{21}F – ^{21}Ne whose threshold energy is 5.7 Mev which corresponds to ρ ~ 3.5×10^9 g cm^{-3}. Oddly enough these results have not been taken into account in the existing carbon explosion models cited above. As can be seen from Iben's work, the problem is indeed quite complicated and the end result unclear.

Recently [17], we have reviewed the problem and believe we can clarify the way it should be treated. We find that the convective core must settle into a quasi-steady state where the Bruenn heating term is canceled by a current of electrons (together with the appropriate nuclei). In this case Urca losses can control the burning as originally suggested. We analyze the stability of the thermal balance and find:

1) The balance is *unstable* towards *cooling*. This is so because the heating depends on central entropy(s) and the cooling on the excursion of the convective zone beyond the Urca shell. These two variables are related in a complicated way which involves the manner in

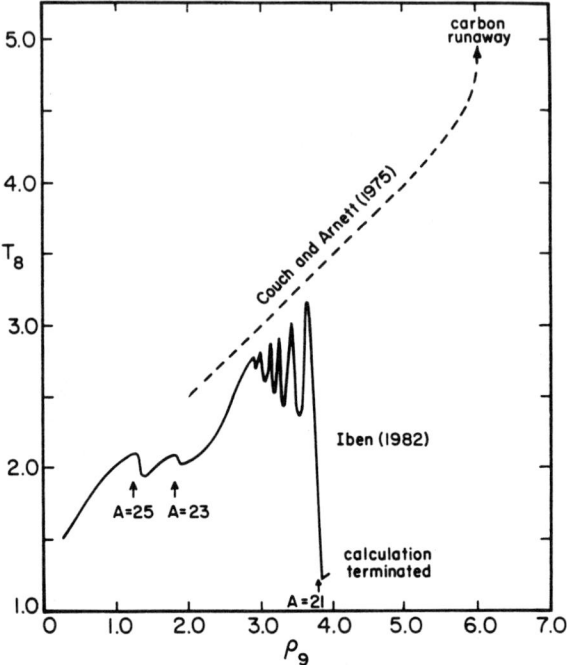

Figure 1. The evolutionary track, on the ρ,T plane, of the central conditions of the core near and following carbon ignition as obtained by IBEN [16] (full line), is compared with the track obtained by COUCH and ARNETT [13] (dashed line).

which the convective boundary retreats upon central entropy decrease on one hand and the outward advance of the Urca shell on the other. The latter is due to core contraction, which is induced by the continuous growth of the core as well as by electron capture on products of carbon burning (e.g. ^{24}Mg).

2) We show that the Urca losses can control burning only up to a limiting value of the nuclear luminosity $\sim 10^7$ $L_\odot$—the "maximal Urca power." If and when this limit is exceeded, the runaway will be revived.

Our analysis points out what we believe went wrong in Iben's treatment and suggests how to improve on it. At this time we can only conclude that the convective Urca process should not be ignored and speculate on the possible outcome:

1) Runaway at a much higher central density $\gtrsim 6 \times 10^9$ g cm^{-3}, which may at best lead to an explosion which is quite different from what the existing models give, especially since copious electron capture must occur on nickel-iron group nuclei behind the burning front. In fact, at densities above $\sim 10^{10}$ g cm^{-3} reimplosion can occur [18][3].

2) Runaway off center above a cool inner core. It is not impossible that the result in this case may not be too different from the successful current models.

References

1. B. Paczyński: *Acta Astr.*, **20**, 47 (1970).
2. Z. Barkat: *Ap. J.*, **163**, 433 (1971).
3. K. Nomoto: In *Proceedings of XXIth Rencoutre de Moriond VIth Astrophysics Meeting*, Les Arcs (1986).
4. F. Hoyle and W. A. Fowler: *Ap. J.*, **132**, 565 (1960).
5. B. Paczyński: *Ap. Letters*, **11**, 53 (1972).
6. D. Branch, J. B. Doggett, K. Nomoto, and F.-K. Thielemann: *Ap. J.*, **294**, 619 (1985).
7. R. P. Harkness: In *Radiation Hydrodynamics in Stars and Compact Objects*, ed. D. Michalas and K.-H.A. Winkler (Springer-Verlag, Berlin 1986 [p. 166]).
8. K. Nomoto, F.-K. Thielemann, and K. Yoki: *Ap. J.*, **286**, 644 (1984).
9. S. E. Woosley and T. A. Weaver: In *Radiation Hydrodynamics in Stars and Compact Objects* (Springer-Verlag, Berlin 1986 [p. 91]).
10. Y. Tuchman, N. Sack, and Z. Barkat: *Ap. J. (Letters)*, **225**, L137 (1978).
11. P. G. Sutherland and J. C. Wheeler: *Ap. J.*, **280**, 282 (1984).
12. S. W. Bruenn: *Ap. J. (Letters)*, **183**, L125 (1973b).
13. R. G. Couch and W. D. Arnett: *Ap. J.*, **196**, 791 (1975).
14. I. Iben, Jr.: *Ap. J.*, **219**, 213 (1978a).
15. _____. *Ap. J.*, **226**, 996 (1978b).
16. _____. *Ap. J.*. **253**, 248 (1982).
17. Z. Barkat and J. C. Wheeler: In preparation (1989).
18. S. W. Bruenn: *Ap. J.*, **186**, 1157 (1973a).

Explosion of Massive Wolf-Rayet Stars
Mounib F. El Eid

We have computed the final evolution of two Wolf-Rayet (W-R) stars of 61 $M_\odot$ (model A) and 44.86 $M_\odot$ (model B) through the carbon, neon, and oxygen burning phases using a one dimensional hydrodynamic code, and an extended network of nuclear reactions (El EID and PRANTZOS, [1]) to determine the nuclear energy generation rates, and the nucleosynthesis in such objects. In this contribution, only a brief summary of the main results is given; more details will be published elsewhere.

As described by LANGER and EL EID [2], the core masses above were obtained from evolutionary calculations of a 100 $M_\odot$ pop I star with mass loss and different assumption about convective overshooting (mixing beyond the boundary of the convective core as predicted by the Schwarzschild criterion for convection). According to these computations, model A resembles a W-R star of subtype WC/WO while model B resembles a WN star. Other evolutionary computations (MAEDER and MEYNET [3]) with mass los but a moderate amount of overshooting, show that the core masses above may originate from initial masses of $\approx$ 115 $M_\odot$ and $\approx$ 90 $M_\odot$ respectively.

At the end of core helium burning the oxygen mass was 50.67 $M_\odot$ in model A, and 36.36 $M_\odot$ in model B. Before central carbon ignition both models had a relatively short phase ($\approx 10^3$ years) of gravitational contraction during which the temperatures and densities increased steadily along with the energy losses due to neutrino processes [4]. Due to the small central carbon abundance, and the enhanced neutrino losses, the carbon burning phase proceeded in a radiative core in both models. Towards the end of neon burning, which also occurred in a radiative core, T and ρ have reached values that favour the production of electron-positron pairs ($e^\pm$) by the rediation field. The $e^\pm$ pair creation reduced the entropy of radiation, hence the radiation pressure, and the adiabatic index dropped below the critical value of 4/3. Consequently, both models above got dynamically unstable at the onset of central oxygen burning. A collapse phase followed during which oxygen burnt explosively on a time scale of typically 50 sec (cf. Fig. 1a).

We found that the oxygen burning phase marks the final phases of the present stellar models, but their behaviour during this phase was remarkably different due to their different masses. After oxygen ignition, model A collapsed within 50 sec to a peak central temperature $T_c = 3.73 \cdot 10^9$ K and density $\rho_c = 2.28 \cdot 10^6$ g cm^{-3} and burnt 7.82 $M_\odot$ of oxygen at this time. The nuclear energy release from explosive oxygen burning was sufficient to reverse smoothly (no shock formation) the collapse into explosion, which finally led to total disruption of the star. Since the total amount of burnt oxygen was 8.75 $M_\odot$, the maximum kinetic energy of the explosion attained the value $8.75 \cdot 10^{51}$ erg. The nucleosynthetic yield was dominated by oxygen and its burning products (Si, S, Ar, Ca), and 0.015 $M_\odot$ of ^{56}Ni was synthesized in this model. As we shall see below this amount of nickel has an appreciable effect on the bolometric light curve which may arise from such explosion.

The final evolution of Model B was more complicated, since it encountered the pair instability twice. Fig. 1a shows that the first infall reached a peak central temperature of $3.18 \cdot 10^9$ K and density $1.67 \cdot 10^6$ g cm^{-3} in a time of 50 sec after oxygen ignition. As displayed in Fig. 1b, the inner zones have left the pair instability domain due to the increased density, so that the collapse is halt there. The nuclear energy release from oxygen burning was than sufficient to reverse the collapse, again without shock formation, into explosion. A total amount 1.57 $M_\odot$ of oxygen was burnt, which led to $1.57 \cdot 10^{51}$ erg of explosion kinetic energy. However, during the expansion phase only the outer layers comprising 1.41 $M_\odot$ of unprocessed helium-rich material were ejected, while the total energy of the star remained negative.

After a time of 367 sec (counted from oxygen ignition), the central temperature was reduced to $3.59 \cdot 10^8$ K and the central density to $2.34 \cdot 10^3$ g cm^{-3}. An oscillation phase followed (cf. fig. 1a) with a total duration of about 2500 sec, after which the remaining core became pair unstable for the second time. The ensuing second infall was stronger, and proceeded to $T_c = 4.26 \cdot 10^9$ K and $\rho_c = 4.06 \cdot 10^6$ g cm^{-3} in 30 sec. During this phase, the oxygen mass decreased from 34.70 $M_\odot$ to 24.45 $M_\odot$. This high amount of burnt oxygen led to a stronger explosion which disrupted the star. The final ejected mass of oxygen was 24.01 $M_\odot$ and the maximum kinetic energy turned out to be $8.50 \cdot 10^{51}$ erg. Thus this model has burnt 12.35 $M_\odot$ of oxygen in total.

The composition of the ejecta was dominated by oxygen and its burning products like in model A. However, the ^{56}Ni yield from model B was 0.72 $M_\odot$, remarkably higher than from model A, since model B has achieved higher temperatures and densities during its second collapse phase.

We note that the only other computations which have shown the repeated occurrence of the pair instability were those of WOOSLEY and WEAVER [5] (see also WOOSLEY [6]). They called this process "pulsational pair-instability". According to them, the pair instability was encountered four times during the evolution of a 45 $M_\odot$ W-R star after oxygen ignition. At the end of their calculations, an iron core of 2.2 $M_\odot$ was formed surrounded by 39 $M_\odot$ of outside material. The final fate of such objects is still to be determined [5]. Clearly, this type of evolution is different from that of our model B. The reason is not clear yet. What we know (Woosley, private communication) is, that the initial oxygen of our model B is higher by $\approx 2\ M_\odot$. This may not be the only reason for the discrepancy, though it appears that the final fate of pair unstable stars is very sensitive to the oxygen mass if this mass is close to the limit of 30 $M_\odot$, below which a star may not become pair unstable at all [7]. We leave the clarification of this issue for a forthcoming work.

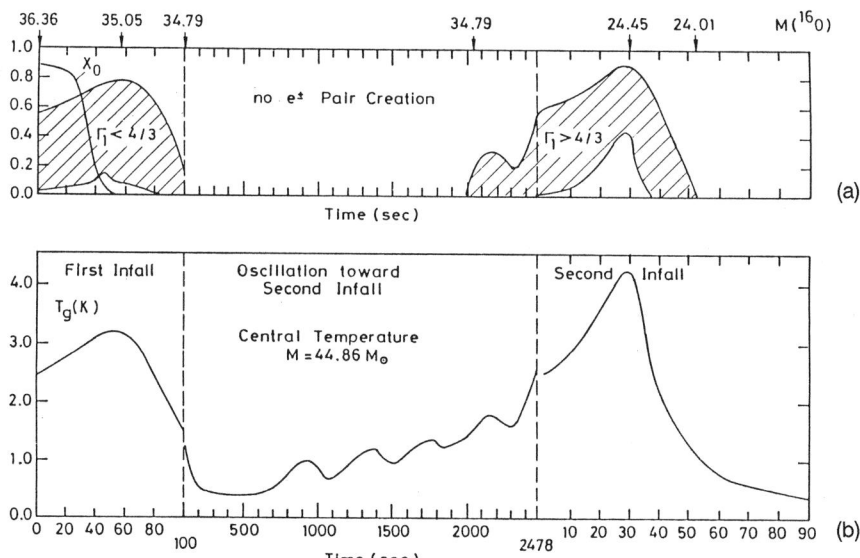

Figure 1. (a) Central temperature as a function of time for the pair unstable Wolf-Rayet star of the indicated mass. Time = 0 is taken at oxygen ignition (note the change of time scale). The Fig. shows that the star encounters the $e^\pm$ pair creation instability twice. (b) Development of the pair instability domain with time where the adiabatic index $\Gamma_1 < 4/3$. The variation of the oxygen mass with time is indicated at the top of the Fig. X_0 denotes the central abundance (mass fraction) of oxygen.

Finally, we mention that the bolometric light curve, which may be associated with the explosion of the present model A, has recently been calculated at Göttingen (HERZIG [8]; HERZIG et al. [9]). The light curve of model B is currently under study. Only some results will be mentioned here; the details will be given in [9]. In Fig. 2, two light curves of the 61 $M_\odot$ star are shown and compared with the light curve resulting from the exposion of the 8 $M_\odot$ W-R star according to ENSMAN and WOOSLEY [10]. The dotted light curve is calculated with 0.015 $M_\odot$ of ^{56}Ni synthesized in model A as mentioned above, while the dashed curve is obtained when the nickel mass is artificially increased to 0.50 $M_\odot$. The early shape of the light curves is dominated by the energy input from the oxygen recombination, which leads to the first peak, while the late shape is determined by the energy input from the radioactive decay of ^{56}Ni and ^{56}Co. The late influence of the radioactive decay on the light curves is a consequence of the large mass, hence the longer diffusion time scale, especially when nickel is concentrated near the center as in the high mass model. The comparison between the dotted curve and that of the 8 $M_\odot$ star reveals, that the former is less luminous and has a larger width. The larger width is due to the higher core mass, whereas the lower peak luminosity reflects the difference in the nickel mass. The effect of increased nickel mass is demonstrated by the dashed curve in Fig. 2. In this case, the peak luminosities become similar, simply because the nickel masses are now comparable. Thus, the remaining difference between the light curves is due to the different masses. Therefore, it appears possible to distinguish observationally between the two types of explosions on the basis of the bolmetric light curve alone.

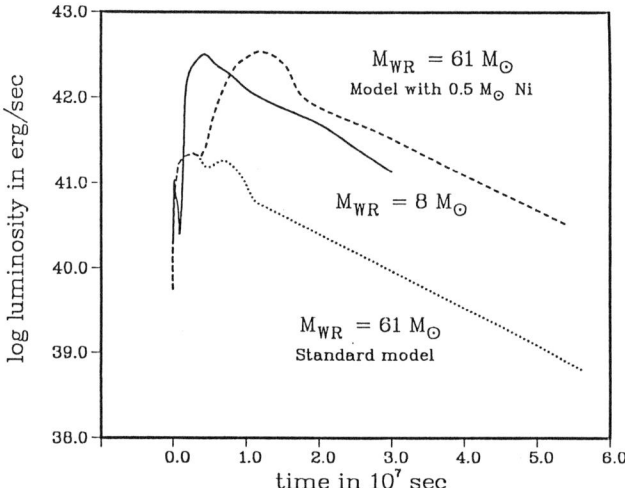

Figure 2. Comparison of the light curves of the exploding high and low mass Wolf-Rayet stars. The effect of the radioactive ^{56}Ni decay on the light curve of the 61 $M_\odot$ star (model A in the text) is illustrated by comparing the dotted and dashed curves. The light curve of the 8 $M_\odot$ is due to ENSMAN and WOOSLEY [10].

References

1. M.F. El Eid, N. Prantzos: in The Origin And Distribution of the Elements, ed. by G.J. Mathews (World Scientific, New Jersey 1988), p. 485
2. N. Langer, M.F. El Eid: Astron. Astrophys. **167**, 265 (1986)
3. A. Maeder, G. Meynet: Astron. Astrophys. **182**, 243 (1987)
4. H. Munakata, Y. Kohyama, N. Itoh: Ap. J. **226**, 197 (1985)
5. S. E. Woosley, T.A. Weaver: in IAU Colloq. No. 89, Radiation Transport and Hydrodynamics, ed. by D. Mihalas and H. Winkler (Reidel, Dordrecht 1986)
6. S. E. Woosley: in Nucleosynthesis and Chemical Evolution, ed. by B. Hack and A. Maeder (Geneva Observatory 1986), p. 1
7. J.R. Bond, W.D. Arnett, B.J. Carr: Ap. J. **280**, 825 (1984)
8. K. Herzig: Diploma Thesis, Univ. of Göttingen, 1988
9. K. Herzig, M.F. El Eid, K.J. Fricke, N. Langer: Theoretical light curves for exploding massive Wolf-Rayet stars, preprint, submitted to Astron. Astrophys., 1989
10. L.M. Ensman, S.E. Woosley: Ap. J. **333**, 754 (1988)

Theoretical Light Curves of Type I Supernovae
K. Nomoto & T. Shigeyama

1. Introduction

Type I supernovae (SN I) are identified from the absence of hydrogen lines in the maximum light spectra. SN I are further subclassified from the helium features in the spectra, namely, SN Ia (no helium), SN Ib (helium-rich), and SN Ic (helium-poor) [34].

The lack of hydrogen lines implies that the progenitors of SN I have lost their hydrogen-rich envelope at the time of explosion. Two cases are possible: (1) tidal mass loss during the evolution of a close binary system, and (2) stellar wind type mass loss. This implies that we have basically two candidates for the progenitor of SN I, i.e., white dwarfs and Wolf-Rayet stars. Because of the complicated mass loss processes, it has not been easy to identify the exact evolutionary origin of SN I. The currently popular models are the carbon deflagration of accreting C+O white dwarfs for SN Ia and the explosion of Wolf-Rayet stars for SN Ib. However, accreting white dwarf models for Ib and especially for Ic may be possible (e.g., helium detonation as speculated in [4]). Here we discuss to what extent these models can account for the observed light curves (§§2–3)

Since the origin of SN Ib, Ic, and variations of Ia have not been quite clear, we reexamine the fate of 8-10 $M_\odot$ stars, O+Ne+Mg white dwarfs, and solid C+O white dwarfs to explore other possible models for SN I (§4).

2. Type Ib and Ic Supernovae

2.1. Exploding Helium Stars

Wolf-Rayet stars form from massive stars by losing their hydrogen rich envelope and becoming helium stars. Such helium stars eventually undergo iron core collapse like SN II. Because of the lack of hydrogen-rich envelope, the Wolf-Rayet star is too compact to power the light curve by shock heating, thereby requiring the power of radioactive decays to become SN Ib. In fact, the exponential tails of the light curves and the IR emission line of iron at late times [13] show that decays of ^{56}Ni and ^{56}Co also work for SN Ib. The peak luminosity is lower than SN Ia by a factor of $\sim$ 2-4.

We calculated the light curves for the helium star models of masses $M_\alpha = 3.3\ M_\odot$, $4\ M_\odot$ and $6\ M_\odot$ (cooresponding main-sequence masses are $\sim 13 M_\odot$, $15 M_\odot$, $20 M_\odot$, respectively) assuming the production of $0.075\ M_\odot$ ^{56}Ni. the γ-ray opacity of 0.03 cm^2 g^{-1} and the optical opacity are calculated as done for the SN 1987A model [30]. For $M_\alpha = 3.3, 4$, and $6\ M_\odot$, the masses of the ejecta are $M_{\rm ej} = 2.1, 2.6$, and $4.4\ M_\odot$, and the neutron star residue are $M_{\rm ns} = 1.2, 1.4$, and $1.6\ M_\odot$, respectively [5].

The decline rate of the light curve depends largely on how fast γ-rays and X-rays escape from the star. The column depth to the ^{56}Ni-^{56}Co layer at time t is roughly proportional to (mass of the overlying layer)$^2/(Et^2)$. Accordingly the optical light curve declines faster, if the ejecta mass is smaller, ^{56}Ni is mixed closer to the surface, and E is larger.

2.2. Light Curves of Type Ib Supernovae

For SN Ib, two observed light curves are shown in Fig. 1: the slower curve is the visual light curve of SN 1984L [14] and the faster one is the bolometric light curve of 1983N [26]. The latter decline rate is close to that of SN Ia [17].

If all γ-ray energies are deposited in the star, bolometric light curve after the peak declines at the radioactive decay rate as shown by the dotted curve in Fig. 1. With $E = 1 \times 10^{51}$ erg and the original stratified composition structure (i.e., ^{56}Ni being confined in the central region), the tails of the calculated light curves for $M_\alpha = 4$ and $6 M_\odot$ are close to the dotted line (see also [29]). This seems to be slower than even the slowest SN Ib, SN 1984L, suggesting a mixing of ^{56}Ni into the outer layers.

The dashed line in Fig. 1 shows a light curve for rather extreme case of mixing where ^{56}Ni is uniformly distributed in the whole ejecta of $M_\alpha = 6\ M_\odot$. It is probably consistent with SN 1984L but its decline is slower than 1983N. The solid line calculated for $M_\alpha = 4\ M_\odot$ ($M_{\rm ej} = 2.6\ M_\odot$) with mixing of ^{56}Ni at $M_r < 2.2\ M_\odot$ is in good agreement with SN 1983N. (If we mix ^{56}Ni closer to the surface, the pre-peak dip in the light curve is too bright to be consistent with 1983N like the solid line in Fig. 2.)

Figure 1 shows that the light curves of SN Ib may be accounted for by the helium star models of $M_\alpha < 6\ M_\odot$ as far as ^{56}Ni is mixed out close to the surface. The variation of the decline rate of the light curve may be ascribed to the variation of the ejecta mass. Mixing of radioactive materials into outer layers might cause a large non-LTE excitation of helium lines [3].

However, the above constraint of $M_\alpha < \sim 6\ M_\odot$ leads to some problems. If the Wolf-Rayet stars are the progenitor of SN Ib, their main-sequence masses should be larger than $20\ M_\odot$ (and $M_\alpha > 6\ M_\odot$) because of the following reason. We know that SN 1987A is the explosion of a $20\ M_\odot$ star ($M_\alpha = 6\ M_\odot$) that produced $\sim 0.07\ M_\odot$ ^{56}Ni. On the other hand, SN Ib should produce $0.15 - 0.3\ M_\odot$ ^{56}Ni, because the peak luminosity of SN Ib is about 1/4 - 1/2 of SN Ia that are powered by the decay of $\sim 0.6\ M_\odot$ ^{56}Ni. Therefore the main-sequence mass of the Wolf-Rayet progenitor of SN Ib should be larger than that of the progenitor of SN 1987A. For smaller mass stars,

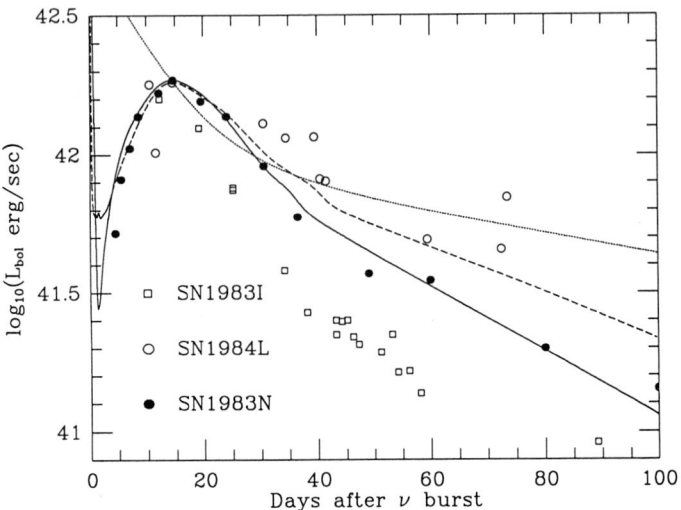

Fig. 1: Observed light curves of SN Ib (bolometric curve of SN 1983N and visual curve of SN 1984L) and SN Ic (visual curve of SN 1983I) are compared with the helium star models of $M_\alpha = 6\ M_\odot$ (with the ejected mass $M_{ej} = 4.4\ M_\odot$: dashed curve) and $4\ M_\odot$ ($M_{ej} = 2.6\ M_\odot$: solid curve). Both curves assume almost complete mixing of 0.075 $M_\odot$ ^{56}Ni in the ejecta. The dotted curve is the energy generation rate of the ^{56}Ni-^{56}Co decays.

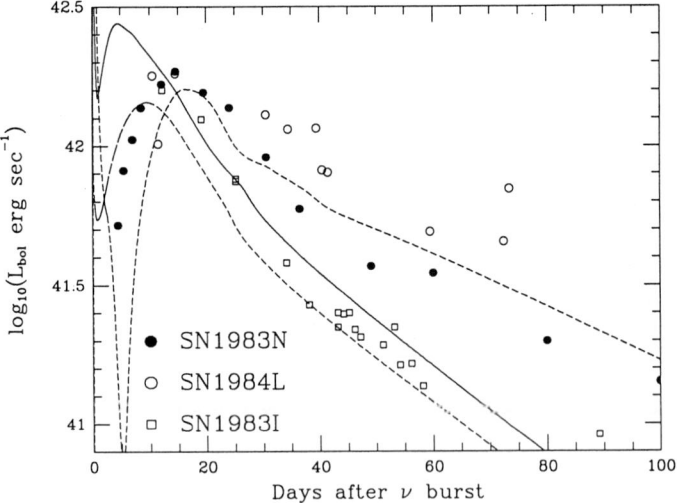

Fig. 2: Same as Fig. 1 but compared with the helium star models of $M_\alpha = 3.3\ M_\odot$ ($M_{ej} = 2.1\ M_\odot$) with mixing (solid curve) and $M_\alpha = 4\ M_\odot$ ($M_{ej} = 2.2\ M_\odot$) with and without mixing (dashed).

the density of the silicon and oxygen layers is too low to synthesize enough ^{56}Ni. This requirement could meet the constraint from the light curves only for relatively narrow range of stellar mass around main-sequence $\sim$ 20 - 25 $M_\odot$ [33, 9]. If the ejecta are highly clumpy, however, they are more transparent to γ-rays, thus being allowed to be more massive [9].

2.3. Light Curves of Type Ic Supernovae

For SN Ic the fast decline of the luminosity is more difficult to be reconciled with the peak luminosity. In Figures 1 and 2, the visual light curve of SN 1983I is shown since the visual curve is close to the bolometric one. This light curve of SN Ic declines significantly faster than SN Ia and SN Ib. It is clear from Fig. 1 that the two curves for $M_\alpha = 4$ and 6 $M_\odot$ can not be consistent with SN Ic even with extreme mixing. The large difference between the peak luminosity and the tail as well as narrow peak is difficult to reproduce with such a massive star model [9].

To reproduce the SN Ic light curve, the helium star mass should be as small as $M_\alpha = 3.3\ M_\odot$ ($M_{ej} = 2.1\ M_\odot$) as shown by the solid curve in Fig. 2. Almost complete mixing of ^{56}Ni is also necessary for this curve.

The ratio M_{ej}/M_α could be smaller than assumed above, if the helium star loses its helium envelope by mass loss. To explore such a case, we constructed the ejecta model with $M_{ej} = 2.2\ M_\odot$ from the helium star of $M_\alpha = 4\ M_\odot$ by removing the neutron star mass of 1.8 $M_\odot$. The calculated light curves are shown by the two dashed curves in Fig. 2 where the faster and the slower declines correspond to the cases with and without mixing. It is clear that mixing is required to reproduce the light curve of SN 1983I. If M_{ej} is significantly larger than 2.2 $M_\odot$ to be consistent with the ^{56}Ni mass, the effect of clumpiness to make the ejecta transparent to γ-rays should be significant [9].

The evolution of the photospheric velocity v_{ph} observed in SN Ic provides an another important clue to the nature of the progenitor. In SN 1983V, v_{ph} changes from $\sim$ 18000 km s^{-1} [3] to 7500 km s^{-1} [14] in 8 days, i.e., 1200 km s^{-1}/day near maximum light. On the contrary, SN Ib 1983N showed much slower decrease in v_{ph} with 400 km s^{-1}/day [28]. In Fig. 3, the change in v_{ph} is shown for several helium star models as well as the model for SN 1987A. Compared with SN 1987A, the helium stars have smaller envelope mass, thus having the smaller velocity contrast between the envelope and the core. Consequently the velocity gradient in the envelope and the change in v_{ph} are small. This is consistent with SN 1983N but cannot reproduce the observed feature of SN Ic 1983V. The SN Ic feature might better be explained by a model involving accreting white dwarfs (e.g., [4]). Certainly more quantitative studies of theoretical spectra and light curves (including the expansion opacity) are necessary to identify the SN Ib and Ic progenitors.

2.4. Mixing

For massive helium star models of SN Ib and Ic, mixing of ^{56}Ni and formation of clumps are required to explain the observed light curves. For SN 1987A, mixing during explosion

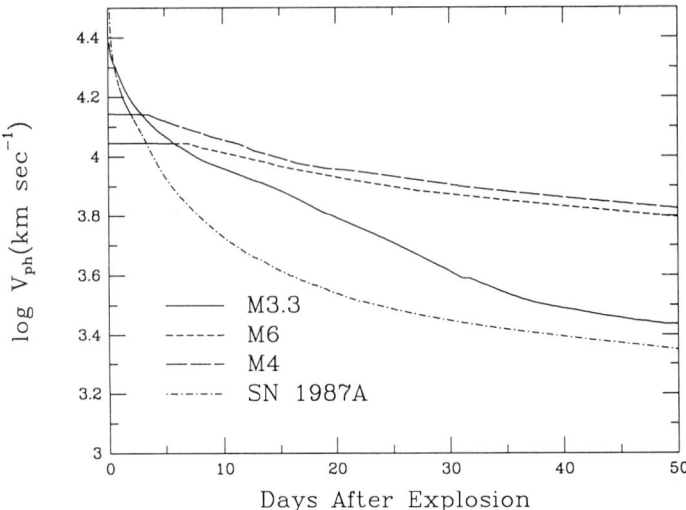

Fig. 3: Evolution of the photospheric velocity for several helium star models and the model for SN 1987A.

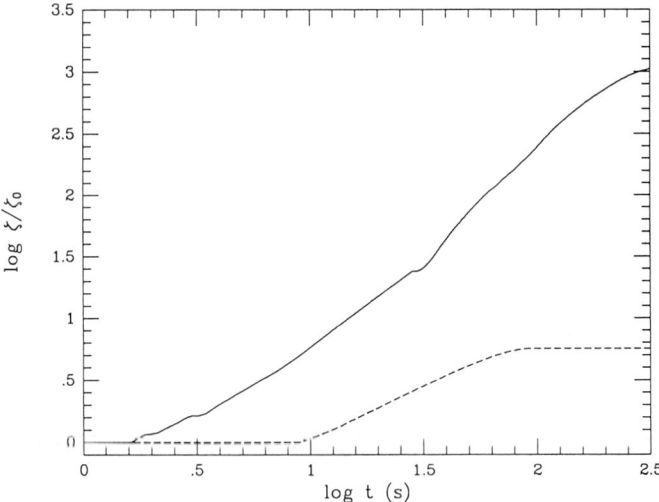

Fig. 4: The growth of the Rayleigh-Taylor instability at the He/C+O interface of helium stars. The amplification factor relative to the initial perturbation is plotted for the explosion of the helium star of $M_\alpha = 6\ M_\odot$ (dashed curve) and $4\ M_\odot$ (solid).

is found to be induced by the Rayleigh-Taylor instability at the composition interface. We have studied whether such a mixing occurs in the exploding helium stars as well by the linear stability analysis [8].

When the shock wave hits the helium envelope, the expansion of the inner core is decelerated. The resulting pressure inversion induces the Rayleigh-Taylor instability at the interface between the core and the helium envelope where the density steeply decreases outward. The growth of the initial perturbations is larger for the smaller mass helium star as shown for $M_\alpha = 3.3$ $M_\odot$ (solid) and 6 $M_\odot$ (dashed) in Fig. 4. The reason is as follows:

1) For smaller M_α the mass ratio between the helium envelope and the core (excluding the neutron star mass) is larger (i.e., 2.5, 2.7, 1.0, and 0.45 for $M_\alpha = 3.3$, 4, 6, and 8 $M_\odot$, respectively) so that the deceleration of the core is larger.
2) Smaller mass stars have steeper density gradient near the composition interface.
3) The stellar radius is larger for smaller M_α so that it takes longer for the shock wave to reach the stellar surface; then the instability grows for a longer time until the rarefaction wave from the surface makes the layer stable.

All these effects result in the shorter timescale of the growth and the larger amplification of the perturbation for the smaller mass helium star (Fig. 4). This implies that a large scale mixing would occur only for stars with masses smaller than a certain limit.

From the ^{56}Ni mass constraint, on the other hand, the mass of the helium star progenitor of SN Ib should be larger than 6 $M_\odot$. Compared with SN 1987A where the Rayleigh-Taylor instability starts to grow at the hydrogen/helium interface, the amplification at the helium/heavy-element interface in the 6 $M_\odot$ helium star is much smaller (dashed curve in Fig. 4). This is because the density gradient is less steep and, moreover, there is not enough time for the instability to grow before the shock wave reaches the surface. On the other hand, some clumpiness in SN Ib is suggested from observations [10]. Further 2D hydrodynamical calculation is necessary to see whether the two constraints of the progenitor mass can be consistent with each other.

3. Type Ia Supernovae

3.1. Carbon Deflagration in Accreting C+O White Dwarfs

The evolution of accreting white dwarfs in close binary systems is determined by the balance between compressional heating and radiative cooling and, thus, strongly depends on the mass accretion rate, $\dot{M}$. For intermediate accretion rates (2.7×10^{-6} $M_\odot$ yr^{-1} > $\dot{M}$ > 4×10^{-8} $M_\odot$ yr^{-1}), the C+O white dwarf can grow up to the Chandrasekhar mass [21, 22]. When the central density reaches $\sim 3 \times 10^9$ g cm^{-3}, explosive carbon burning starts in the white dwarf's center. A carbon burning front then propagates outward on the timescale for convective heat transport, which is called a convective deflagration wave. It takes about 1 sec for the deflagration wave to reach the surface region, during which the white dwarf expands [25].

Behind the deflagration wave, the material undergoes explosive nuclear burning of silicon, oxygen, neon, and carbon. In the inner layer, iron-peak elements, mostly ^{56}Ni, are produced. When the deflagration wave arrives at the outer layers, the density it encounters has already decreased due to the expansion, so that only Ca, Ar, S, and Si are produced. In the intermediate layers, explosive burning of carbon and neon synthesizes S, Si, and Mg. In the outermost layers, the deflagration wave dies and C+O remain unburned. The composition structure after freeze-out is seen in [32].

In the current standard model W7 [25], a carbon deflagration occurs in the white dwarf of mass 1.38 $M_\odot$ and synthesized 0.58 $M_\odot$ ^{56}Ni. The star explodes completely with the kinetic energy of $E = 1.3 \times 10^{51}$ ergs and no neutron star residue. The synthetic spectrum at maximum light is in excellent agreement with the observed optical spectrum of SN 1981B. The agreement implies that both explosion energy and nucleosynthesis in the carbon deflagration model are consistent with the observations near maximum light.

3.2. Optical Light Curve and Distribution of ^{56}Ni

Although most of SN I show similar tails in their light curves, there exists a certain variations in the declining rate as seen in the bolometric light curves of SN 1972E and SN 1981B [11] and the visual light curve of SN 1986G [27] in Fig. 5. SN 1986G shows significantly faster decline than SN 1972E and SN 1981B. We suggest that such a variation would mostly stem from the difference in the distributions of ^{56}Ni.

We calculate the light curves for three different distributions of ^{56}Ni as seen in Fig. 5. Assuming the optical opacity of 0.1 cm^2 g^{-1} and the γ-ray opacity of 0.03 cm^2 g^{-1}.
1) W71 (dashed): ^{56}Ni is confined in the central region of $M_r = 0 - 0.58$ $M_\odot$.
2) W72 (solid): ^{56}Ni is located at the intermediate region of $M_r = 0.28 - 0.86$ $M_\odot$ as in the original W7. At $M_r < 0.28$ $M_\odot$, more neutron-rich ^{58}Ni, ^{54}Fe and ^{56}Fe are produced.
3) W73 (dash-dotted): ^{56}Ni is distributed in the outermost layers of $M_r = 0.80 - 1.38$ $M_\odot$.

The calculated light curves are compared with observations in Fig. 5. The slow light curves of SN 1972E and SN 1981B are in good agreement with W72 (solid, i.e., the original W7), but W71 (dashed) is a little too slow. The fast decline of SN 1986G is well reproduced by W73 (dash-dotted) because γ-rays from the outer layer escape earlier. In order to reproduce SN 1986G with the same ^{56}Ni distribution as in W72, E/M should be 3 times larger than that of W7, which is impossible for carbon deflagration models. In fact, the expansion velocities of SN 1986G is even lower than SN 1981B [5].

This indicates that the light curve shape is more sensitive to the distribution of ^{56}Ni than E/M. This is consistent with the fact that the light curve of SN 1984A is similar to SN 1981B though its velocities are significantly higher [5].

3.3. Variations of Carbon Deflagration Models

Here we discuss the evolutionary origin of the difference in the abundance distribution as well as the effect of the initial metallicity (i.e., population) of the white dwarf. The distribution of ^{56}Ni depends on 1) the size of the neutron-rich core [12] if the carbon deflagration starts from the center and 2) the site of carbon ignition if an off-center deflagration occurs.

The neutronized core could not be very large, because it would lead either to the ejection of too much neutron-rich ^{58}Ni and ^{54}Fe or to the collapse due to rapid electron capture at high central density [22]. Thus as far as the carbon deflagration starts from the center, variation of the light curve would not be so large.

If the off-center carbon deflagration frequently occurs, larger variations are expected. This would take place if a solid oxygen core has formed in the white dwarf [7] or the convective Urca neutrino process efficiently cools down the inner core after carbon ignition [1, 15]. However, the former possibility has been ruled out by the recent findings that chemical separation between carbon and oxygen does not occur [2, 16].

The convective Urca process will not occur if the carbon ignition density, ρ_{ig}, is higher than the threshold densities of Urca process, i.e., $\rho_{th} = 1.3 \times 10^9$ g cm^{-3} for ^{25}Na - ^{25}Mg pair and 1.8×10^9 g cm^{-3} for ^{23}Ne - ^{23}Na pair. If the accretion rate is as high as $\dot{M} > \sim 10^{-6}$ $M_\odot$ yr^{-1}, ρ_{ig} would be lower than ρ_{th} for the A = 25 pair. Even for lower $\dot{M}$, the A = 25 Urca shell cooling would not operate if the white dwarf belongs to the old population and has low metallicity. In this case, $\rho_{ig} \sim 1.5 \times 10^9$ g cm^{-3} if $\dot{M}$ corresponds to the steady hydrogen burning as occurs in the AGB star or common envelope ($\sim 8 \times 10^{-7}$ $M_\odot$ yr^{-1}) [19]; this would induce the central deflagration without undergoing convective Urca cooling. For still lower $\dot{M}$, the convective Urca process would operate; however, nova-like explosions might reduce the occurrence frequency of this case.

Our speculation is that the majority of the SN Ia progenitor undergo rapid accretion to avoid nova-like explosions [21]. Then the central deflagration is induced without undergoing convective Urca cooling. Resulting SN Ia form quite a uniform class of light curves. This would be more likely the case for the white dwarfs with low metallicity. The variations of the light curves would result from the off-center carbon deflagration that occurs for slower accretion as well as high metallicity white dwarfs.

4. Possible Alternative Models

As discussed in §§2-3, the origin of SN Ib,c and variations of Ia have not been clarified yet. Thus it is worth exploring possible alternative models, which include O+Ne+Mg white dwarfs, and C+O white dwarfs having high ρ_c. Whether the stars related to these white dwarfs, e.g., 8-10 $M_\odot$ stars and some merging white dwarfs, can produce SN-I like events depends on whether these white dwarfs undergo collapse or explosion.

4.1. 8 - 10 $M_\odot$ Stars and O+Ne+Mg White Dwarfs

The stars in this mass range is distinct from other mass range because they develop a degenerate O+Ne+Mg core. If these stars are in close binary systems, they form O+Ne+Mg white dwarfs [20]. The initial masses of the O+Ne+Mg white dwarfs are as large as 1.2 - 1.37 $M_\odot$ which is favorable feature to produce short period recurrent novae. The abundances of the typical O+Ne+Mg white dwarfs may be consistent with the observed abundance of Neon Novae [35]. Furthermore, such recurrent novae on massive white dwarfs could easily grow the white dwarf mass [31].

When the core mass grows to 1.38 $M_\odot$, the central density reaches 4×10^9 g cm^{-3} and electron captures ^{24}Mg (e$^-$, ν) ^{24}Na (e$^-$, ν) ^{20}Ne and ^{20}Ne (e$^-$, ν) ^{20}F (e$^-$, ν) ^{20}O. The central density at which electron captures ignite a neon/oxygen deflagration could range from $1 - 2.5 \times 10^{10}$ g cm^{-3} depending on the timescale of material mixing in the electron capture region [18]. If the neon/oxygen deflagration is initiated at $\rho_c \sim 1 \times 10^{10}$ g cm^{-3}, whether it leads to collapse or explosion needs careful study.

4.2. C+O White Dwarfs

The accreting C+O white dwarfs could also either explode or collapse, depending on the conditions of the white dwarfs. Compression of the white dwarf by the accreted matter first heats up a surface layer and, later, heat diffuses inward [19]. If the initial mass of the white dwarf, M_{CO}, is smaller than 1.2 $M_\odot$, the entropy in the center increases substantially due to the heat inflow and carbon ignites at relatively low central density ($\rho_c \sim 3 \times 10^9$ g cm^{-3}). On the other hand, if the white dwarf is more massive than 1.2 $M_\odot$ and cold at the onset of accretion, the central region is compressed only adiabatically and thus is cold when carbon is ignited in the center. In the latter case, the ignition density is as high as 10^{10} g cm^{-3} (e.g., [6]) and the white dwarf may well have a solid core. For such a case, it is important to determine the critical condition for which a carbon deflagration induces collapse rather than explosion.

4.3. Collapse of C+O White Dwarfs Induced by Carbon Deflagration

Nomoto [23, 24] examined the critical condition for which a carbon deflagration initiated at the center of $\rho_c \sim 10^{10}$ g cm^{-3} leads to collapse of the white dwarf. The outcome depends on whether, behind the deflagration wave, nuclear energy release or electron capture is faster. The energy generation rate is determined mainly by the propagation velocity of the deflagration wave, v_{def}, while the electron capture rate depends on the density. If v_{def} is lower than a certain critical speed, v_{crit}, electron capture induces collapse. If v_{def} is sufficiently high, on the contrary, complete disruption results.

First let us start from the *conductive* deflagration in the solid C+O white dwarf. In the old calculation [23, 24], v_{def} obtained from the heat conduction calculation was too low in the very central region because of too coarse mesh points compared with the sphericity. To avoid this problem, we adopt a simpler approach assuming a constant ratio of v_{def}/v_s for conductive deflagration wave, where v_s denotes the local sound velocity.

Figure 6 shows the change in the central density of the C+O white dwarf starting from 9×10^9 g cm^{-3}. Three cases assume $v_{def}/v_s = 0.05$, 0.03, and 0.01, and the latter two slow cases undergo the collapse. This implies that the critical velocity, v_{crit}, that divides collapse and explosion is $v_{crit} \sim 0.03\, v_s$ for $\rho_c \sim 10^{10}$ g cm^{-3}. The realistic value of conductive deflagration speed is $v_{def} \sim 0.01\, v_s$ [36], thereby leading to the collapse of the solid white dwarf.

4.4. Collapse of O+Ne+Mg White Dwarfs Induced by Ne/O Deflagration

Next we discuss the deflagration in O+Ne+Mg white dwarfs. After electron capture on ^{24}Mg starts, resulting entropy production heats up the central region and forms a liquid core even if the white dwarf had initially a solid core [18, 5]. When electron capture on ^{20}Ne ignites a neon flash, therefore, a *convective* neon/oxygen deflagration wave forms. Since the propagation velocity of the deflagration wave, v_{def}, is highly uncertain, we apply a time dependent mixing length prescription with the ratio between the mixing length and the pressure scale height $\alpha = \ell/H_p = 0.7$, 1.4, and 2 [25].

Figure 7 shows the change in ρ_c associated with the propagation of the deflagration wave. The slowest case of $\alpha = 0.7$ goes into collapse, while the case with $\alpha = 1.4$ is marginal. For smaller α, the deflagration speed in the central region is so low that the *conductive* deflagration is faster. Thus the minimum v_{def} is set at $\sim 0.01\, v_s \sim 100$ km s^{-1}. Such a slow propagation is seen from the initial slow increase in M_r at the location of the deflagration front (Fig. 8). Consequently the fate of the convective deflagration wave depends mainly on whether v_{def} exceeds $\sim 0.03\, v_s$ in the central region of $M_r < \sim 0.1$ - 0.2 $M_\odot$.

If $\alpha < 1.4$ is the case, the O+Ne+Mg white dwarf collapses even if $\rho_c \sim 10^{10}$ g cm^{-3}. Since W7 model, which adopts $\alpha = 0.7$ for the carbon deflagration, can nicely account for the observations of SN Ia, $\alpha = 0.7$ may also be preferred for Ne/O deflagration and thus the collapse would be more likely.

If total disruption results from such high central density as 10^{10} g cm^{-3}, such an explosion may not be preferred because too much neutron-rich matter would be ejected. Moreover, the explosion energy is such low as $\sim 10^{50}$ ergs because of large neutrino losses, thereby cannot be consistent with any subclass of SN I.

Though the definite conclusion needs multi-dimensional calculation to determine the propagation speed, the deflagration initiated from $\rho_c \sim 10^{10}$ g cm^{-3} would make a collapse for both O+Ne+Mg and C+O white dwarfs. In other words, such white dwarfs and related stars may not become SN I but become a neutron star. Such an accretion-induced collapse of white dwarf may be necessary to account for the existence of a certain class of binary pulsar and low mass X-ray binaries [24].

K.N. would like to thank Dr. Ramon Canal for useful discussion on the white dwarf collapse.

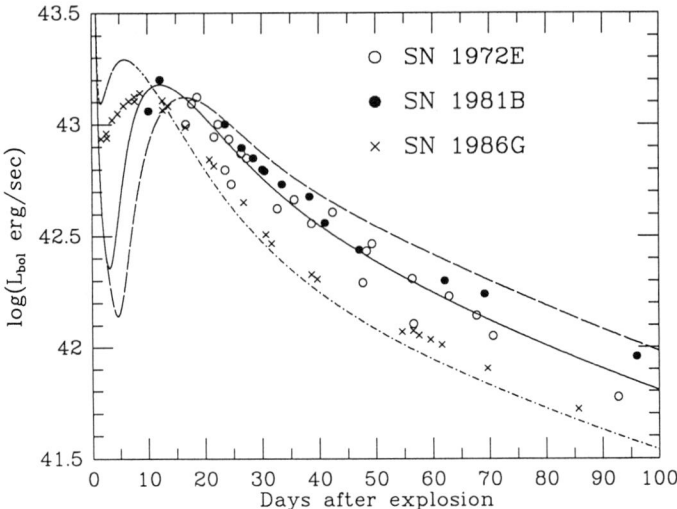

Fig. 5: Bolometric light curves for the different distribution of ^{56}Ni in W7 as compared with the bolometric light curves of SN 1972E and 1981B and the visual light curve of SN 1986G. 1) W71 (dashed): ^{56}Ni is confined in the central region of $M_r = 0 - 0.58$ $M_\odot$. 2) W72 (solid): ^{56}Ni is located at the intermediate region of $M_r = 0.28 - 0.86$ $M_\odot$ as in the original W7. 3) W73 (dash-dotted): ^{56}Ni is distributed in the outermost layers of $M_r = 0.80 - 1.38$ $M_\odot$. The optical opacity of 0.1 cm^2 g^{-1} and the γ-ray opacity of 0.03 cm^2 g^{-1} are assumed.

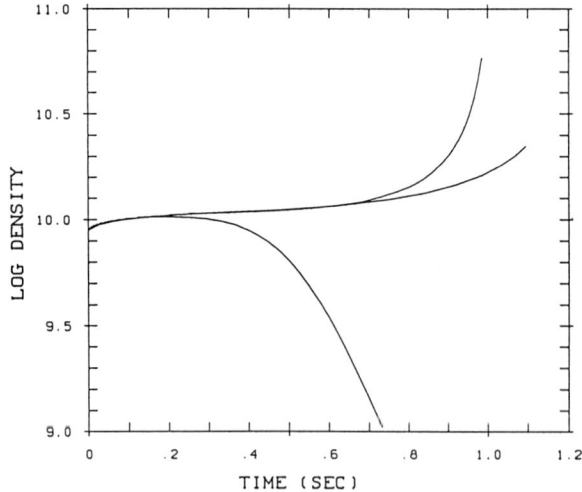

Fig. 6: Change in the central density of the C+O white dwarfs following the propagation of the conductive carbon deflagration wave in the initially solid core. Three cases with $v_{\rm def}/v_{\rm s} = 0.05$, 0.03, and 0.01 are shown and the latter two undergo collapse.

Theoretical Light Curves

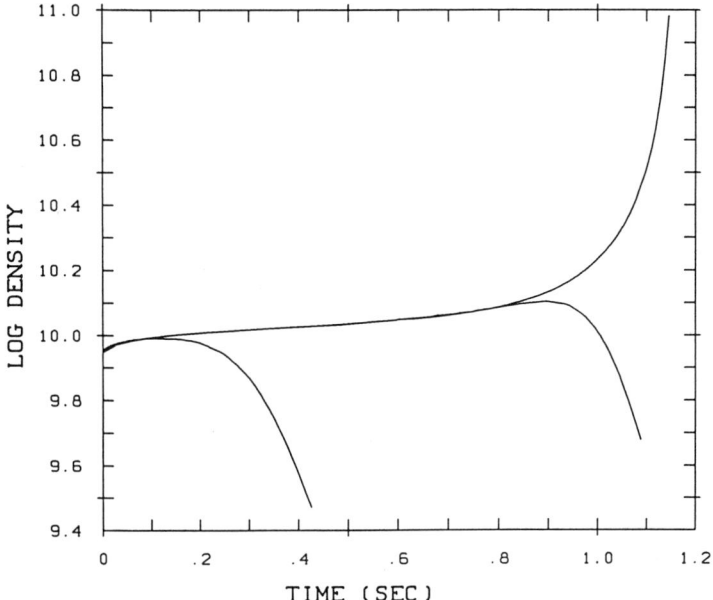

Fig. 7: Same as Fig. 6 but for the convective Ne/O deflagration wave in the O+Ne+Mg white dwarf for three cases with $\ell/H_p = 1.4$, 1.0, and 0.7. For the slowest case of $\ell/H_p = 0.7$, the white dwarf undergoes collapse.

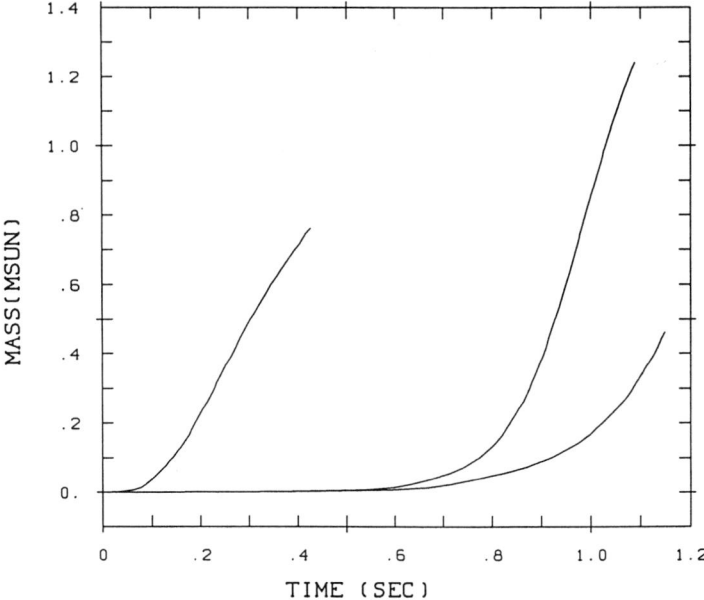

Fig. 8: Propagation of the convective Ne/O deflagration wave in the O+Ne+Mg white dwarf. The location of the deflagration front is plotted as a function of time for three cases with $\ell/H_p = 1.4$, 1.0, and 0.7.

References

1. Barkat, Z. 1990, in this volume.
2. Barrat, J.L., Hansen, J.P., and Mochkovitch, R. 1988, *Astr. Ap.*, **199**, L15.
3. Branch, D. 1988, in *IAU Colloquium 108, Atmospheric Diagnostics of Stellar Evolution*, ed. K. Nomoto, *Lecture Notes in Physics*, **305**, 281.
4. Branch, D., and Nomoto, K. 1986, *Astr. Ap.*, **164**, L13.
5. Branch, D., Drucker, W., and Jeffery, D.J. 1988, *Ap. J. (Letters)*, **330**, L117.
6. Canal, R. 1990, in this volume.
7. Canal, R., Isern, J., and Lopez, R. 1988, *Ap. J. (Letters)*, **330**, L113.
8. Ebisuzaki, T., Shigeyama, T., and Nomoto, K. 1989, *Ap. J. (Letters)*, **344**, L65.
9. Ensman, L., and Woosley, S.E. 1988, *Ap. J.*, **333**, 754.
10. Filippenko, A.V., and Sargent, W.L.W. 1989, *Ap. J. (Letters)*, **345**, L43.
11. Graham, J. 1987, *Ap. J.*, **315**, 588.
12. Graham, J. 1987, *Ap. J. (Letters)*, **318**, L47.
13. Graham, J. et al. 1986, *M. N. R. A. S.*, **218**, 93.
14. Harkness, R.P. et al.: 1987, *Ap. J.*, **317**, 355.
15. Iben, I.Jr. 1982, *Ap. J.*, **253**, 248.
16. Ichimaru, S., Iyetomi, H., and Ogata, S. 1988, *Ap. J. (Letters)*, **334**, L17.
17. Leibundgut, B. 1988, Ph.D. thesis.
18. Miyaji, S., and Nomoto, K. 1987, *Ap. J.*, **318**, 307.
19. Nomoto, K. 1982, *Ap. J.*, **253**, 798.
20. Nomoto, K. 1984, *Ap. J.*, **277**, 791.
21. Nomoto, K. 1986a, *Ann. NY Acad. Sci.*, **470**, 294.
22. Nomoto, K. 1986b, *Prog. Part. Nucl. Phys.*, **17**, 249.
23. Nomoto, K. 1987, in The Origin and Evolution of Neutron Stars, IAU Symp. 125, ed. D.J. Helfand and J.-H. Huang (D. Reidel), p. 281.
24. Nomoto, K. 1988, in Proc. 13th Texas Symposium on Relativistic Astrophysics, ed. M. Ulmer (World Scientific), p. 519.
25. Nomoto, K., Thielemann, F.-K., and Yokoi, K. 1984, *Ap. J.*, **286**, 644.
26. Panagia, N.: 1987, in *High Energy Phenomena Around Collapsed Stars*, ed. F. Pacini (D. Reidel), p. 33.
27. Phillips, M.M. et al. 1987, *P.A.S.P.*, **99**, 592.
28. Richtler, T., and Sadler, E.M. 1983, *Astr. Ap.*, **128**, L3.
29. Schaeffer, R., Casse, M., and Cahen, S. 1987, *Ap. J.*, **316**, L31.
30. Shigeyama, T., and Nomoto, K. 1989, *Ap. J.*, submitted.
31. Starrfield, S. 1990, in this volume.
32. Thielemann, F.-K., Nomoto, K., and Yokoi, K. 1986, *Astr. Ap.*, **158**, 17.
33. Wheeler, J.C., and Levreault, R. 1985, *Ap. J. (Letters)*, **294**, L17.
34. Wheeler, J.C., and Harkness, R. 1990a, in *Supernovae*, ed. A. Petschek (Springer-Verlag), in press.
35. Williams, R.E. et al. 1985, *M. N. R. A. S.*, **212**, 753.
36. Woosley, S.E., and Weaver, T.A. 1986, in *IAU Colloquium 89, Radiation Transport and Hydrodynamics*, ed. D. Mihalas and K.H. Winkler, *Lecture Notes in Physics*, **255**, 91.

Expansion Opacity, Type Ia's and the Question of Collapse vs Thermonuclear

Stirling A. Colgate

It is a difficult question whether Type Ia supernova are caused by collapse to a neutron star or a thermonuclear explosion. The density required to ignite carbon burning is only slightly less than that at which collapse occurs due to neutrino emission. In addition there is the question of the URCA shells that may stabilize carbon burning. Finally, there is an argument that a deflagration may turn into a detonation (Woosley 1989). The consequence of a detonation is that the strong shock causes almost the entire star to be synthesized to ^{56}Ni, which consequently overproduces ^{56}Fe and greatly under produces the lower atomic number elements necessary for producing the observed spectrum. On the other than, for the same reason the collapse model must eject the envelope slowly by the hot bubble (Colgate 1989) or overproduce iron relative to lighter elements. Despite this uncertainty, the thermonuclear model has gained credence as the "standard" model (Woosley and Weaver 1986). The principal calculation of the thermonuclear model motivating this perception is that of the light curve. The calculations of the explosion of a $1.4 M_\odot$ white dwarf performed using a constant opacity, $\kappa = 0.1 cm^2\ g^{-1}$ result in a light curve very close to the observed one. "How could the same kinetic energy in roughly one-third the mass – typical of collapse models ($1 M_\odot$ neutron star, $0.4 M_\odot$ ejected) result in the same light curve?" The purpose of this note is to show how nearly the same light curve results regardless of the mass or energy. The point is that when the opacity of the expanding nebula is corrected to first order for the expansion opacity (Karp et al. 1977), the optical thickness of the nebula remains nearly constant, contrary to intuition. This means that the simple observation of light maximum must be interpreted as a combination of the exponentially decaying energy source and the extremely complex process of line scattering where a statistically few large gaps between $\sim 10^5$ lines determine the Rosseland mean opacity. Colgate, Petschek and Kriese (1980) and Colgate and Petschek (1980a) have argued that the way to measure the thickness and hence, mass of the SNIa's is by the interpretation of the late light curve, 56-day half life, as due to the escape of the positrons of the ^{56}Co decay. Here "opacity" is due to the less complex and experimentally measured scattering and energy loss of high energy electrons (positrons). In this case the measured expansion velocity from the Doppler shift of the lines and the modification of the 77-day decay of ^{56}Ni to the 56-day observed leads to an interpreted ejected mass of $0.4 M_\odot$ rather than the thermonuclear model where $1.41 M_\odot$ is ejected.

Finally, we point out that this complex behavior of the expansion opacity in the interpretation of the light curves of supernovae is fortunate because recently Kirshner (1989) has published three early light curves of SNIb's that nicely overlap and show a rise time to maximum in 15 days. There is one observation 4^m below (2.6% of) maximum at 14 days before maximum so that there is small error in the estimate of the time (15d) to light maximum. On the other hand, since the "standard model" predicts that the presupernova mass of Type Ib's is 6 to 7 $M_\odot$, much larger than Type Ia's, and therefore the time to light maximum at constant opacity should be much larger contrary to observation. The time to light maximum should scale (at constant total energy) as $M^{3/4 \text{to} 1}$. Hence, one would therefore expect the time to light maximum of Type Ia's to be 3 to 5 days or a factor of at least 3 less than many observations. Hence, we need some effect that changes the opacity with mass, i.e. the expansion opacity, to explain Type Ia's versus 1b's regardless of collapse of thermonuclear.

This note will first discuss the effect of the expansion opacity on the light curve. Then the logic of the positron transparency modification of the ^{56}Co (77d) decay in Type Ia's is applied to the corresponding gamma ray transparency and resulting modification of the ^{56}Co (77d) decay in SN1987a.

Expansion Opacity

Karp et al. (1977) showed how the opacity of expanding media was different from static atmospheres due to the monotonic redshift of every photon, sometimes called "tired light." This redshift allows the possibility of a photon to scatter from a sequence of atomic states before Compton scattering from a background of free electrons. Hence, the opacity is enhanced above Compton scattering if the redshift — or expansion — is large enough in the time of one Compton mean free path and the cross section of the states large enough. This requires that the fractional energy gap between states be less than the redshift of the photons in the Compton mean free path time. This fractional redshift is measured as $1/s$ where s, the expansion parameter is $\kappa_c \rho c t$. Here t is the time since the beginning of the expansion or explosion and κ_c the Compton opacity. The calculations of Karp et al. used a set of 2.6×10^5 lines for temperatures between 6000 K and 30,000 K. The opacity enhancement became significant for $s \sim 10^3$ or fractional redshift between scatterings of $\sim 10^{-3}$. This is a measure of the significant gaps in the Rosseland mean in the 2.6×10^5 lines. When s is small, $100 < s < 500$, and over a limited range of temperature (6000 to 15,000 K) then the expansion opacity scales like $1/s$. This implies that as the density gets lower, the increase in fractional redshift of a photon between Compton scatterings just compensates by increased line scattering the reduction in Compton opacity. A larger line list would broaden in temperature and range of s the conditions at which this approximation is valid. In addition, Karp et al. used a solar mixture depleted in hydrogen, but still with helium 10 times that of the heavier elements. The ejecta of SNIa's is likely to contain less helium. Recognizing these uncertainties and that the $1/s$ approximation applies over a very limited range of parameter space, the scaling of the optical thickness of the supernova nebula can be estimated.

If we express s in terms of the ejected mass of a supernova, M_{eject}, and kinetic energy, E_{51}, as 10^{51} ergs, time t_6 in 10^6 seconds and atomic weight A, per free electron, we obtain

$$s = 2.4 \times 10^3 M_{eject}^{5/2} E_{51}^{-3/2} t_6^{-2} A^{-1}. \tag{1}$$

Hence, for a mean atomic weight of once ionized He of 4, at time of light maximum of 14 days, $M_{eject} = 1.41$, and $E_{51} = 1.6$, characteristic of thermonuclear models, we obtain $s = 420$ just at the boundary where the $1/s$ approximation to the opacity applies. On the other hand for a Type Ib, of $7M_\odot$, 10^{51} ergs and $t = 15$ days, $s = 2.7 \times 10^4$ well within Compton scattering. The collapse model would give $s = 37$, below the region of the $1/s$ approximation. Nevertheless, if we use for the smaller models, $\kappa = \kappa_c(s_o/s)$, then the optical thickness of the expanding nebula, τ_s becomes

$$\tau_s = \kappa \rho R = \frac{\kappa_c \rho R s_o}{\kappa_c \rho c t} \tag{2}$$

or

$$\tau_s = s_o(v/c) = s_o((10/3)E/M)^{\frac{1}{2}}/c \tag{3}$$

where R and v are the outside radius and velocity respectively. Hence, in this rough approximation the optical thickness is independent of time provided $s < s_o$ and becomes even greater with smaller mass! Here $s_o \simeq 700$, that is a value of s where the expansion opacity becomes roughly 2 times Compton opacity. This means that simple intuition is too simple indeed. Hence, the time to light maximum is a convolution of the optical thickness and a decaying exponential heat source. Since $s_o \simeq 700$ and $v/c \simeq 1/25$, τ_s is $\simeq 28$, the same as calculated for light maximum in the past (Colgate and McKee, 1979; Arnett 1982). However in this simple approximation, the collapse model will have a slightly longer time to light maximum than the thermonuclear. This will be difficult to calculate accurately because of the extreme sensitivity of the expansion opacity to composition, state conditions, and the completeness of the line list. By way of comparison, the optical thickness for Compton opacity alone and $A = 4$ becomes:

$$\tau_c = 26 M_{eject}^2 E_{51}^{-1} t_6^{-2}. \tag{4}$$

This is a factor of 2 smaller than the expansion opacity thickness for the two smaller mass models, but for Type Ib's the Compton opacity will dominate, and then the actual value of A becomes more critical. In general uncertainties in the composition and the line list will make this a continuing difficult problem so that it is difficult to use the light curve as a measure of the ejected mass.

The Gamma Ray Deposition Function Applied to 1987a

Even though SN1987a is a Type II supernova, the method for calculating the late light curve of Ia's can be applied to a modified late light curve of 1987a. Colgate, Petschek, and Kriese (1980a) calculated the gamma ray deposition from the ^{56}Ni decay in an expanding nebula of several models (mixed and unmixed) using an extensive Monte Carlo program. The emergent spectrum showed the early large x-ray flux expected from the gamma ray Compton scattering, which later was observed in 1987a. The numerical results were parameterized in a simple formula that was valid for any spherical expanding absorbing mass and an exponential path length radiation source. This generalization allowed the same formulation of deposition to be applied to positron energy deposition (from ^{56}Co decay) at a later time in the expansion because the peculiar combination of beta ray spectrum, multiple scattering and ionization loss leads (experimentally) to an exponential path length distribution. Hence, by scaling the effective range (0.1 $g\ cm^2$) to that of the gamma rays (35.5$g\ cm^{-2}$) the same deposition function could be used for the positrons as used earlier for the gamma rays. This assumed that any magnetic field was combed purely radially and/or that the initial magnetic field was less than 10^4 gauss.

When this deposition function is applied to an exponentially decaying source, a family of curves results of various differing decay rates from that of the original exponential, Fig. 1. The single parameter of each curve is the ratio of the expansion time, t_o, at which the deposition is one half (total thickness, $\tau = 1$) to the half life time t_1 (Colgate, Petschek, and Kriese 1980b). This ratio for our best fit model of SNIa's was 4.9 leading to an exponential decay time of the deposited fraction of the energy of 73% of the unmodified decay time or $0.73 \times 77d = 56.5d$. Transparency time is then $4.9 \times 77d = 377d$ at which $[\rho R]$ of the expanding nebula is 0.1 $g\ cm^{-2}$.

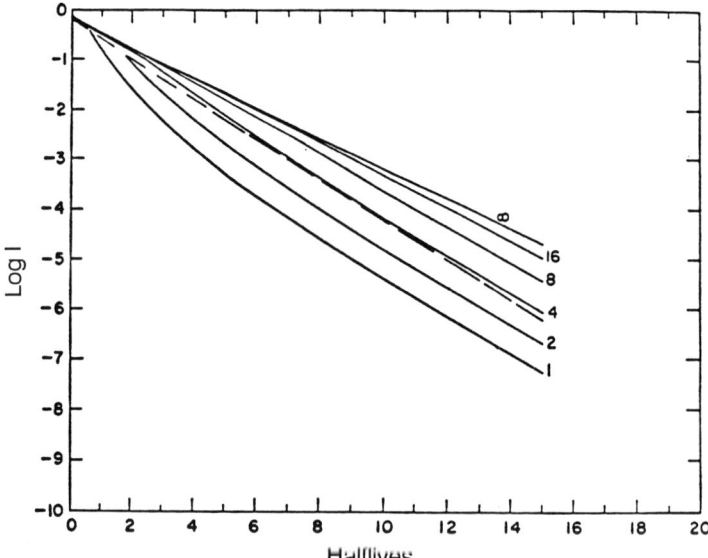

Fig. 1. We plot $D\ e^{-t\ell n2/t_1}$ for various values of t_0/t_1 where t_0 is the time at which deposition is $\frac{1}{2}$ (Colgate, Petschek, and Kriese 1980b)

For an expansion velocity of 1.4×10^9 cm s^{-1}, this corresponds to a mass of $0.42 M_\odot$. Hence, our claim that Type Ia's are collapse rather than thermonuclear.

The corresponding ratio for the gamma rays of 1987a where one half deposition of the gamma rays occurred at 660 days from Pinto, Woosley and Ensman (1988), is then $t_o/t_1 = 8.57$. From Fig. 1 the modified deposition function has a slope of 82.5% of the 77-day half life or 63.5 days. Figure 2 shows this drawn on the current bolometric light curve (Whitelock 1989). This early agreement is close enough to be a good argument for this interpretation of the 56-day decay observed in SNIa's. Of course later ^{57}Co and a possible pulsar will alter this agreement (Pinto et al. 1988).

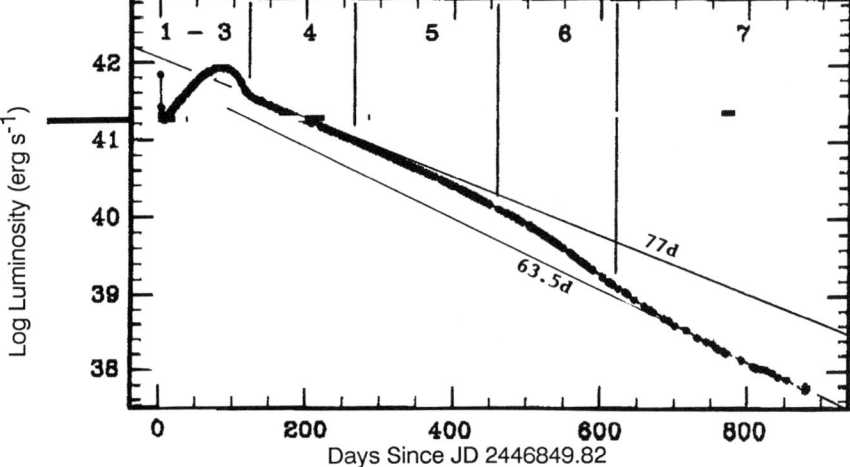

Fig. 2. Bolometric light curve from U to M photometry[6].
Courtesy of P. Whitelock, This Volume.

Since the light curve at this stage of calculation cannot be relied upon for a unique interpretation of the ejected mass because of the expansion opacity (Harkness (1989) expects to do such calculations), meanwhile it seems reasonable to use the positron range as a better measurement. The infrared emission was used by Axelrod (1980) to modify the late SNIa optical decay below the 77-day exponential, but this shows a "guillotine" effect or sharp cut off in time as opposed to the long exponential observed by Kirshner and Oke (1975) of over ten half lives.

Acknowledgements

I am indebted to discussions with Albert Petschek. This work was supported by the DOE.

References
1. S. E. Woosley: In Supernovae, ed. A. G. Petschek (Berlin: Springer-Verlag) (1989).
2. S. A. Colgate: Santa Cruz Workshop on Supernovae, ed. S. E. Woosley (1989).
3. S. A. Colgate, A. G. Petschek and J. T. Kriese: Ap. J. 239, L81 (1980a).
4. S. A. Colgate, A. G. Petschek, and J. R. Kriese: AIP Conf. Proc. 63 *Supernova Spectra*, ed. R. E. Meyerott, LaJolla Inst., LaJolla, CA, p.7 (1980b).
5. P. Whitelock: Santa Cruz Workshop on Supernovae, ed. S. E. Woosley (1989).
6. S. A. Colgate and A. G. Petschek: *Nature* 296, 804 (1982).
7. S. A. Colgate and C. McKee: Ap. J. 157, 623 (1969).
8. A. H. Karp, G. Lasher, K. L. Chan, and E. E. Salpeter: Ap. J. 214, 161 (1977).
9. R. V. Kirshner: In Supernovae, ed. A. G. Petschek (Berlin: Springer-Verlag) (1989).
10. S. E. Woosley and T. A. Weaver: Ann. Rev. Astron. and Ap. 24, 205 (1986).
11. W. D. Arnett: Ap. J. 253, 785 (1982).
12. P. A. Pinto, S. E. Woosley and L. M. Ensman: Ap. J. 331, L101 (1988).
13. T. S. Axelrod: Thesis, Univ. Calif., Berkeley and T. A. Weaver, T. S. Axelrod, and S. E. Woosley: In "Type I Supernova" ed. J. C. Wheeler, (Austin: Univ. of Texas Press) p. 113 (1980).
14. R. V. Kirshner and J. B. Oke: Ap. J. 200, 574 (1975).
15. Harkness, private communication (1989)

SN Ia Models by Coalescence of Two Carbon-Oxygen White Dwarfs

Robert Mochkovitch & Mario Livio

White dwarf coalescence models for type Ia supernovae (SNe Ia) have been recently proposed [1,2] as an alternative to the standard scenario in which a white dwarf accretes hydrogen rich material from a companion star. The need for new models appeared after it was realized that it might be difficult to increase the white dwarf mass up to the Chandrasekhar limit by accretion, at least in a sufficiently large number of systems to account for the SN Ia rate in the Galaxy. Indeed, mass loss during hydrogen and helium flashes and off-center helium detonation considerably restrict the range of values of the accretion rate, white dwarf and companion masses for which central carbon ignition is possible. Another difficulty is the risk of contamination of the spectrum by stripped hydrogen from the companion. Even if a small window of parameters giving a SN Ia explosion may remain (the theoretical modelling of all the processes involved in the presupernova evolution is too uncertain to draw definite conclusions) the search for a new class of progenitors may turn to be more promising.

I. Close Binary White Dwarfs

Very close white dwarf pairs result from the evolution of close binary systems of stars of intermediate mass after one or two episodes of non conservative mass transfer. If the two white dwarfs are formed with a separation of less than about 2 $R_\odot$, they will merge within a Hubble time due to gravitational radiation losses. For two carbon-oxygen (C-O) white dwarfs, the total mass of the system will be generally larger than the Chandrasekhar limit and some kind of violent outcome seems unescapable. Whether it will fit the observable properties of a SN Ia is however still a matter of discussion. Another problem concerns the statistics of the binary white dwarf (BWD) population. WEBBINK [1] and IBEN and TUTUKOV [2] estimated the birthrate of C-O/C-O pairs to be comparable to the SN Ia rate in the Galaxy. This was confirmed in a recent study by TORNAMBE [3] as long as the efficiency of the common envelope phase to reduce the orbital separation is not too large. The long timescale for merging by the emission of gravitational radiation then implies that BWDs should be quite common in the Galaxy. Several groups [4,5,6] have tried to detect them but the two objects which have been found until now, L 870-2 [4] and WD 0957 -666 [5] have periods larger than one day which corresponds to a timescale for merging much larger than 10^{10} years. Moreover, ROBINSON and SHAFTER [6] did not detect any BWD with a period between 30 s and 3 h in a sample of 44 catalogued white dwarfs. They concluded that the resulting upper limit for the space density of BWDs in the Galaxy is too small to account for the SN Ia rate. The origin of the present disagreement between the theoretical predictions and the observational status is unclear. We shall not discuss this point and rather focus on the evolution which follows the coalescence of the two white dwarfs. This problem will naturally remain of interest even if BWDs are not SN Ia progenitors (if at least one BWD able to merge within a Hubble time is finally discovered!).

II. Post-Coalescence Models

When the less massive white dwarf overfills its Roche lobe coalescence, i.e. dynamical merging occurs if its mass is not too different from that of the primary ($M_2 > 0.5$ $M_\odot$ for $M_1 = 1$ $M_\odot$). In a few orbital periods the secondary is tidally disrupted and forms a thick disk orbiting around the primary, as illustrated by the beautiful 3D hydrodynamical calculations of BENZ et al. [7]. We have used the self-consistent field (SCF) method developed by OSTRIKER and MARK [8] to compute the structure of the resulting configuration. Since we do not follow the evolution during the merging process, some parametrization for the final distribution of angular momentum in the disk must be assumed. We also constraint the pressure to be a function of the density only and use the results of [7] as a guide for the parametrization. The SCF method therefore relies on inputs from the 3D calculations but has the advantage of being more accurate in the outer parts of the disk where the density contrast relative to the center becomes large.

The post coalescence configuration is computed with conservation of the total mass, angular momentum and energy (less than 3% of the total mass is ejected in the case studied by [7]). The distribution of angular momentum in the disk is given by

$$j(m) = j_0 \frac{(m - M_1)}{(M_1 + M_2 + b(m - M_1))} \text{ for } m > M_1 \text{ and } j(m) = 0 \text{ for } m < M_1 , \quad (1)$$

where M_1 and M_2 are the original white dwarfs masses ($M_1 > M_2$) and m is the mass within axial cylinders; j_0 is determined by the value of the total angular momentum and b is a parameter. The pressure $P_e(\rho)$ of degenerate electrons is used until a transition density ρ_{tr}, below which the thermal pressure P_{th} becomes important. At $\rho < \rho_{th}$ a polytropic relation $P = K\rho^\gamma$ is adopted and $P_{th} = P - P_e$.

We computed the structure of the configuration resulting from the coalescence process considered in [7]. The central white dwarf of mass 1.2 $M_\odot$ is surrounded by a disk of 0.9 $M_\odot$. The transition density is $\rho_{tr} \approx 10^7$ g.cm^{-3}, $\gamma \approx 1.4$ and $b = 9.5$. The model isodensities are represented in Fig.1. The central density, polar and equatorial radii are $\rho_c = 1.75 \ 10^8$ g.cm^{-3}, $R_p = 3500$ km and $R_e = 26500$ km. As already discussed by MOCHKOVITCH and LIVIO [9] for a different model and in agreement with [7] we find that the temperature at the white dwarf–disk boundary is 5 – 10 10^8 K, i.e. possibly larger than the carbon ignition temperature. Off-center carbon burning would strongly affect the subsequent evolution which also critically depends on the viscosity in the disk.

III. Post-Coalescence Evolution

Let us first suppose that carbon was not ignited during merging or that carbon burning was rapidly quenched, for example by material expansion. The disk evolution will then be determined by the balance between heating by viscous dissipation and cooling by neutrino and radiation losses. If molecular viscosity is the only way to carry angular momentum in the disk, heating will be negligible and cooling will occur on a Kelvin-Helmholtz timescale (a few 10^6 years). The structure will become completely degenerate and there will be a slow increase in central density as rotational support is

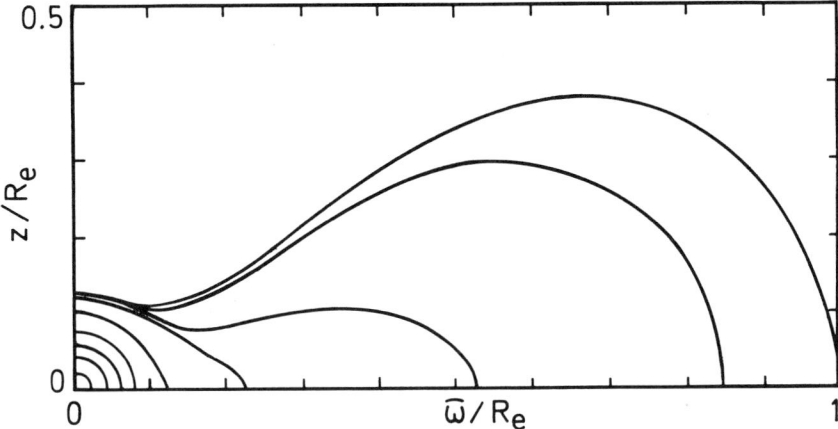

Figure 1. Isodensity contours ($\rho/\rho_c = 0.8, 0.5, 0.2, 0.1, 10^{-2}, 3\ 10^{-3}, 10^{-3}, 10^{-4}$ and 0) for a model with a central 1.2 $M_\odot$ white dwarf and a 0.9 $M_\odot$ disk.

progressively removed by transport of angular momentum (with a very long timescale $\sim 10^{10}$ years). Finally, central carbon ignition will take place and one may expect that most of the results of the carbon deflagration model [10] will be recovered. However, the high shear in the disk (even if it satisfies the Rayleigh criterion for stability) is likely to induce turbulence as indicated by the value of the Richardson number $Ri < 1/4$ in most of the disk ($Ri > 1/4$ is a sufficient condition for stability; $Ri < 1/4$ is a strong indication for turbulence even if it does not imply it). The α prescription for the viscosity then gives values which can be larger than 10^{12} cm^2.s^{-1}, producing a dissipation rate of 10^{13} erg.g^{-1}.s^{-1} or more in the boundary layer. This certainly leads to carbon ignition, even if it did not occur during the merging process itself.

As a result of carbon burning the object becomes more spherical as its radius increases (the "eccentricity" $e \propto R^{-1/2}$) and eventually adopts a giant-like structure with a carbon burning shell as in the models computed by KAWAI et al. [11]. The luminosity of such models is very close to the Eddington limit, with therefore the possibility of extensive mass loss. Another complication would be the inward propagation of a carbon burning front, incinerating the central white dwarf to O-Ne-Mg composition [12]. One can only speculate on the final outcome of the evolution. Will the central white dwarf finally collapse or explode? Or will mass loss be sufficiently important to reduce the total mass below the Chandrasekhar limit?

In conclusion, white dwarf coalescence still appears far from being a fully conclusive alternative to the standard model for SNe Ia. On the observational side, no BWD able to merge within a Hubble time has been discovered yet. In the theoretical models, it seems difficult to prevent off-center carbon ignition during coalescence or later by viscous heating in the disk. Nuclear burning in semi to non-degenerate material cannot directly produce a SN Ia and the evolution following carbon ignition is extremely uncertain. Clearly, much work will be needed either to confirm or eliminate the coalescence scenario.

References

1. R. F. Webbink: Ap. J. 277, 355 (1984).
2. I. Jr. Iben, A. V. Tutukov: Ap. J. (Suppl.) 54, 335 (1984).
3. A. Tornambe': M.N.R.A.S. 239, 771 (1989).
4. R. A. Saffer, J. Liebert, E. W. Olszewski: Ap. J. 334, 947 (1988).
5. A. Bragaglia, L. Greggio, A. Renzini, S. D'Odorico: Messenger 52, 35 (1988).
6. E. L. Robinson, A. W. Shafter: Ap. J. 322, 296 (1987).
7. W. Benz, R. L. Bowers, A. G. W. Cameron, W. H. Press: preprint (1989).
8. J. P. Ostriker, J. W. K. Mark: Ap. J. 151, 1075 (1968).
9. R. Mochkovitch, M. Livio: Astr. Ap. 202, 211 (1989).
10. K. Nomoto, F. K. Thielemann, K. Yokoi: Ap. J. 286, 644 (1984).
11. Y. Kawai, H. Saio, K. Nomoto: Ap. J. 328, 207 (1988).
12. K. Nomoto, I. Jr. Iben: Ap. J. 297, 531 (1985).

Collapse or Explosion of C+O White Dwarfs
J. Isern, R. Canal, D. Garcia, & J. Labay

The existence and the orbital parameters of low-mass binary x-ray sources suggest that a fraction at least of neutron stars have been produced by the accretion induced collapse (AIC) of a white dwarf (TAAM and VAN DEN HEUVEL [1]). Two types of candidates have been proposed thus far: carbon-oxygen white dwarfs (CANAL and SCHATZMANN [2]; CANAL and ISERN [3]; CANAL, ISERN and LABAY [4]), and oxygen-neon-magnesium white dwarfs (MIYAJI et al [5]; MIYAJI and NOMOTO [6]).

In the firt case, however, there is ample consensus that such stars are the progenitors of Type Ia supernovae. Current models (NOMOTO, THIELEMAN and YOKOI [7]; SUTHERLAND and WHEELER [8]; WOOSLEY and WEAVER [9]) do not predict the formation of any compact remmnant. A possible way out of this dilemma comes from consideration that white dwarfs are, in general, at least partially solid objects. Solidification has two main consequences: 1) Nuclear reaccions start in the pycnonuclear regime, this delaying the onset of thermonuclear runaway up to high densities ($\rho \simeq 10^{10}$ g/cm^3) (HERNANZ et al [10]) and 2) The propagation velocity of a burning front inside a solid likely corresponds to conduction only, that implying lower velocities ($v_{BF} \simeq 10^{-2} c_s$; c_s local sound speed) than in a fluid since Rayleigh-Taylor instabilities cannot develop, that allowing the energy loss by electron captures behind the front to win (CANAL & ISERN [3]) over the energy release by propagation of the burnig front.

It has been shown by ISERN et al [11] and by HERNANZ et al

[10] that central termonuclear runaway can indeed be delayed up to densities $\rho_c \geq 10^{10} g\ cm^{-3}$ in mass-acreting C+O white dwarfs, provided that they are initially cold and massive and the accretion rates are either $\dot{M} \geq 10^{-7}\ M_\odot\ yr^{-1}$ or $\dot{M} \geq 10^{-9}\ M_\odot\ yr^{-1}$. Central densities for which runaway happens inside a central solid core span the range $9.5 \times 10^9 g\ cm^{-3} \geq \rho_c \geq 1.5 \times 10^{10} g\ cm^{-3}$.

We have performed a parameter study of the dynamical evolution of a C+O white dwarf for a central ignition starting at $\rho_c = 1.13 \times 10^{10} g\ cm^{-3}$. Burning front velocities are 0.1, 0.03, 0.01, and 0.005 times c_s. The last velocity roughly corresponds to the estimate of conductive front velocities by WOOSLEY and WEAVER [9]. Electron capture rates ere calculated by means of EPSTEIN and ARNETT's [12] expressions, recalibrated by comparison with the rates of FULLER, FOWLER, and NEWMAN [13] at selected points in (ρ, T, Y_e) space. We see that transition from explosion to collapse takes place between 0.03 and 0.01 times c_s. Calculations were stopped when $\rho \simeq 10^{11.5}\ g\ cm^{-3}$ (in the cases of increasing density), and the star was already contracting homologously in a hydrodynamic time scale. Collapse to nuclear densities is thus the only possible issue. In a second series of calculations we have taken into account the change in burning propagation velocity that must follow from the emergence of the burning front outside of the central solid core into fluid layers. In this case the size of this core plays an essential role. We adopted, for the conductive velocities in the solid core, those derived from WOOSLEY and WEAVER's [9] expression. In the fluid layers, we switched to a turbulent front velocity given by SUTHERLAND and WHEELER's [8] prescription for the propagation of Rayleigh-Taylor instabilities. The solid core's size, however, does not stay at its initial value at runaway but changes in the course of burning propagation. A major effect in this is the absorption of neutrinos coming from the electron captures in the central, incinerated regions. The rates of energy deposition in the layers surrounding the central incinerated core are from CHECHETKIN et al [14], and IBAÑEZ et al [15].

Taking into account the latent heat, this typically gives $\simeq$ 1 s for survival of the solid layers. That, in turn, poses the most severe lower (upper) limits to central ignition density (burning propagation velocity). For a model with ρ_{ign} = 1.13 x 10^{10} g cm^{-3} and initial solid core of $M_{core} \simeq$ 0.6 M_{star}, and the burnig front velocity prescriptions given above, collapse also ensues, but the behaviour is quite diferent: whihout inclusion of the neutrinos, the incinerated mass when ρ_c = 10^4 g cm^{-3} would be $M_{inc} \simeq$ 0.07 M_{star} while with neutrinos included it is $M_{inc} \simeq$ 0.86 M_{star} when reaching the same density. The larger mass of the incinerated core in the second case partially arises from switching from conductive to turbulent (hidrodynamic) velocities when reaching the edge of the solid core, but to a much larger extent from ignition of overlying material by neutrino heating when the core has already entered dynamic contraction.

We thus conclude that AIC of C+O white dwarfs is possible but only for a limited range of ignition densities and solid core sizes. Minimum solid core size at ignition should be $\simeq$ 0.04 M_{star} that depending on the still uncertain values of conductive velocities. This, in turn, sets narrow limits to initial mass and temperature (at the star on accretion) and to mass accretion rates.

References
1. R.E.Taam and E.P.J. van den Heuvel: Ap.J. 305, 235 (1986)
2. R.Canal and E.Schatzmann: Astr. Ap.46, 229 (1976)
3. R.Canal and J.Isern: in White Dwarfs and Variable Degenerate Stars, ed. by H.M. van Horn and V.Weidemann (Rochester: Univ. Rochester Press 1979), p.53
4. R.Canal, J.Isern and J.Labay: Ap.J. (Letters) 241, L33 (1980)
5. S.Miyaji, K.Nomoto, K.Yokoi and D.Sugimoto: Publ. Astr. Soc. Japan 32, 303 (1980)
6. S.Miyaji and K.Nomoto: Ap.J. 318, 307 (1987)
7. K.Nomoto, F.Thielemann and K.Yokoi: Ap.J. 286, 644 (1984)
8. P.G.Sutherland and J.C.Wheeler: Ap.J. 280, 282 (1984)
9. S.E.Woosley and T.A.Weaver: Ann. Rev. Astr. Ap. 24, 205 (1986)
10. M.Hernanz, J.Isern, R.Canal, J.Labay and R.Mochkovitch:

Ap.J. 324, 331 (1988)
11. J.Isern, J.Labay, R.Canal and M.Hernanz: Ap.J. 273, 320 (1983)
12. R.Epstein and D.Arnett: Ap.J. 201, 202 (1975)
13. G.M.Fuller, W.F.H.Fowler and M.J.Newman: Ap.J.Suppl. 48, 279 (1982)
14. V.M.Chechetkin, Gershtein S.S., Imshennik V.S., Ivanova L.N., M.Yu. Khlopov: Ap. Space Sci. 67, 61 (1980)
15. J.M.Ibañez, J.A.Miralles, R.Canal, J.Isern and J.Labay: In preparation (1989)

Searching for Double Degenerates: One Out of Fifty

Angela Bragaglia, Laura Greggio, Alvio Renzini, & Sandro D'Odorico

1 − Observations and Results

Motivated by the theoretical suggestion that the precursors of type I supernovae may be binary white dwarfs (WD), also called double degenerates (DD), in 1984 we started a systematic search for binarity among spectroscopically confirmed WDs taken from the existing catalogues. If DDs are Type I SN precursors, we should find some systems which are close enough to merge in less than one Hubble time, i.e. with separations less than 3 $R_\odot$, implying orbital periods less than $\sim 10^h$ and orbital velocities $\gtrsim 300$ kms^{-1} (IBEN & TUTUKOV [1]). This holds, however, only if the bulk of DD are not initially formed much closer than 3 $R_\odot$.

In four observing runs at the ESO 3.6m telescope we have then obtained 155 useful spectra for a total of 49 WDs, all but one of the DA variety. This choice was primarily dictated by the larger number of suitable lines in the spectra of DAs that could be used to detect evidence of binarity by comparing 2÷4 spectra of the same WD with a cross-correlation algorithm, and then looking for a radial velocity variation Δv_r or for a change in line profile, if any. Apart from this, no other selection criterion for the target WDs was imposed (if one excludes apparent brightness, of course). So our sample was not biased towards WDs having *a priori* a larger chance of being double (e.g. exceptionally low gravity).

Details of the observational and reduction techniques are given elsewhere (BRAGAGLIA et al. [2]). The 1 σ error of our Δv_r determinations is ~ 20 km/s in the best cases; the whole set of Δv_r's (excluding 3 special cases) is well fitted by a gaussian with $\sigma \simeq 40$ km/s. Therefore, even in the worst cases we should have been largely able to detect a Δv_r as high as the minimum required for a type I SN precursor (a 15 σ effect!).

Till now we have found only one DD system (WD0957-666) and two WD + RD pairs (WD0034-211 and WD0419-487). We have also 2 dubious cases ($\Delta v_r \simeq 2 \sigma$) that we intend to reobserve.

For the confirmed DD we have till now obtained 17 spectra over a baseline of 15 months. Its radial velocity amplitude is 220 km/s, or $\sim 5 \sigma$. Of course we are trying to determine the period of this object. The available data indicate $P \simeq 1^d.17$, but alternative periods as long as $1^d.9$ cannot be excluded, as well as the possibility of the unseen companion being a red or brown dwarf. We plan to obtain several new spectra of this object during our next run (January 1990), so as to remove any residual ambiguity. We note that WD0957-666 is the object with the smallest gravity for which KOESTER et al. [3] have derived a mass: they found only $0.13 M_\odot$, while GUSEINOV et al. [4] obtained 0.16 $M_\odot$. Both groups assumed a mass-gravity relation for completely degenerate configurations. While this may actually result in a sizable underestimate of the mass (cf. Fig. 4 in IBEN & TUTUKOV [5]), still the extreme properties of this object were suggestive of a binary nature that we have now confirmed. Yet, we emphasize that the object was not included on purpose in the sample, and therefore it can be used for statistical considerations. Instead, in the statistics we will not consider WD0153-052 (SAFFER et al. [6]) as this latter DD was indeed observed specifically for its *special* properties.

2 – Discussion

Our result can be compared and combined with that of ROBINSON & SHAFTER ([7]; RS). They examined 44 WDs (40 DAs and 4 non-DAs). With their experimental set-up they could detect only short-period binaries (with $30^s < P < 3^h$); they found none. We are sensitive even to much longer periods: from about 20 minutes (twice our typical exposure time) to several days; very short period systems that we could miss must be very rare anyway, because of very rapid gravitational wave radiation shrinking of the orbit.

On the base of their data RS calculated an upper limit for the frequency of DDs among WDs:

$$\nu < 0.05 \qquad (90\% \text{ probability}) \qquad (1)$$

and the corresponding upper limit of field DDs:

$$N_{DD} < 3.0 \cdot 10^{-5} \text{pc}^{-3} \qquad (90\ \% \text{ probability}). \qquad (2)$$

We can now use a larger set of WDs by co-adding the two samples: we have a statistics on 89 WDs (4 are in common between the two sets) and the results are:

$$\nu < 0.04 \qquad (90\% \text{ probability}) \qquad (3)$$

$$N_{DD} < 2.4 \cdot 10^{-5} \text{pc}^{-3} \qquad (90\ \% \text{ probability}) \qquad (4)$$

If instead we use only our data (49 WDs) we obtain:

$$\nu < 0.07; \qquad N_{DD} < 4.3 \cdot 10^{-5} \text{pc}^{-3} \qquad (90\ \% \text{ probability}) \qquad (5)$$

The *a posteriori* probability of finding a DD with $P < 3^h$ is less than 4 % and with $P <$ few days is less than 7 % at the 90 % confidence level.

Is this consistent with the hypothesis that DDs are Type I SN progenitors? RS argue that the minimum space density of DD required to produce the observed SNI rate is $2.8 \cdot 10^{-5} \text{pc}^{-3}$, just about what they find for the *upper limit* to N_{DD}, so *all* DDs should produce a SNI. This seems impossible, since most DDs are not enough massive. They conclude that DDs *are not* the dominant progenitors of Type I SNe unless they form with a very short period and quickly merge.

Adding our data we *reinforce* this conclusion. The situation is only marginally more favorable if we choose to consider only our data, on the fact that RS's method is sensible only to very short periods.

3 – DAs or not DAs?

At this point it looks hard to escape the conclusion that type I SN precursors are not DD binary systems contained in catalogues of DA white dwarfs. This negative result has prompted us to give a closer look to the DD scenario, and indeed another possibility yet remains to be observationally tested: in fact this negative result does not exclude the possibility that non-DAs may do it! Only 5 out of 89 observed WDs are non-DAs and therefore very little statistics is available for them at this stage. Are there any plausible reasons why SNI precursors should in case be non-DA's? We now believe that actually there are rather convincing theoretical arguments supporting this notion. Keeping in mind that in case we presently observe the WD produced by the secondary binary component (the primary WD is most likely fainter), we distinguish four main cases concerning the initial mass of the secondary – M_2 – and its evolutionary phase at its final Roche-lobe contact.

Case 1: $M_2 \lesssim M_{HeF} \simeq 2.2 M_\odot$, contact of type B, i.e. during the shell hydrogen-burning phase of the secondary. Objects of this kind have a degenerate helium core at Roche-lobe contact; removing most of the envelope by Roche-lobe overflow will result in a helium WD with $M_{\rm WD} \lesssim 0.5 M_\odot$ and still some hydrogen at the surface (IBEN & TUTUKOV [5]), i.e. a DA white dwarf.

<u>Case 2</u>: $M_2 \lesssim M_{\rm HeF} \simeq 2.2 M_\odot$, contact of type **C**, i.e. during the AGB phase of the secondary. The contact can take place either during the early AGB phase (prior to the first thermal pulse) or just during one thermal pulse, when the star significantly expands in response to the pulse. In both cases Roche-lobe overflow leaves a star whose luminosity is powered by helium burning. This should ensure that the residual hydrogen-rich envelope (with an initial mass $\lesssim 10^{-3} M_\odot$) can be lost during the bright Post-AGB phase, thereby leaving a bare CO-WD, with a pure helium atmosphere (RENZINI [8]; IBEN [9]), i.e. a non-DA WD with $M_{\rm WD} \gtrsim 0.5 M_\odot$.

<u>Case 3</u>: $M_2 \gtrsim M_{\rm HeF} \simeq 2.2 M_\odot$, contact of type **B**. After most envelope is removed by Roche-lobe overflow, the NON-degenerate helium core is still able to ignite helium, thereby producing an almost bare core helium-burning star (envelope mass $\sim 10^{-3} M_\odot$, IBEN & TUTUKOV [10]). Even a modest mass loss rate during the helium burning phases is then able of removing the last vestiges of the hydrogen envelope, thus ultimately leaving a CO-WD ($M_{\rm WD} \gtrsim 0.5 M_\odot$) without hydrogen layers, i.e. a non-DA dwarf. Finally,

<u>Case 4</u>: $M_2 \gtrsim M_{\rm HeF} \simeq 2.2 M_\odot$, contact of type **C**. The case is practically very similar to Case 2, and therefore a non-DA C-O dwarf is left.

We conclude that in all cases but 1, non-DA WDs are most likely produced. However, in this first case a helium WD is formed, and therefore if SNIs are the product of the merging of two CO-WDs, then these should be searched ONLY among non-DAs. Therefore, at this stage we intend to discontinue our search of DDs among DAs, and will now shift only to non-DAs, in order to have a secure statistics also for this kind of degenerate dwarfs. In closing, we note that the three binary WDs that we have found among DAs (one DD and two WD+RD pairs, cf. [2]), and also the DD observed by SAFFER et al. [6], are all probably the result of Case 1-like evolution, as indicated by the small mass of the observed WD ($M_{\rm WD} < 0.5 \ M_\odot$).

In any event, on the base of the above arguments we predict that the He-WDs formed in interacting binaries should all be of the DA type, while the overwhelming majority of CO-WDs formed in such systems should be of the non-DA type. This is a prediction now subject of observational check.

<u>References</u>

1. I. Iben, A.V. Tutukov: *Ap. J. Suppl.* **54**, 335 (1984).
2. A. Bragaglia, L. Greggio, A. Renzini, S. D'Odorico: *The Messenger* **52**, 35 (1988).
3. D. Koester, H. Schulz, V. Weidemann: *Astron. Astrophys.* **76**, 262 (1979).
4. O.H. Guseinov, H.I. Novruzova, Y.S. Rustamov: *Astrophys. Space Sc.* **96**, 1 (1983).
5. I. Iben, A.V. Tutukov: *Ap. J.* **311**, 742 (1986).
6. R.A. Saffer, J. Liebert, E.W. Olszewski: *Ap. J.* **334**, 947 (1988).
7. E.L. Robinson, A.W. Shafter: *Ap.J.* **322**, 296 (1987).
8. A. Renzini: in <u>Stars and Star Systems</u>, ed. B. Weserlund (Dordrecht, Reidel), p. 155 (1979)
9. I. Iben: *Ap. J.* **277**, 333 (1984).
10. I. Iben, A.V. Tutukov: *Ap. J. Suppl.* **58**, 661 (1985).

Neon Novae, Recurrent Novae, and Type I Supernovae

S. Starrfield, W. M. Sparks, J. W. Truran, & G. Shaviv

Over the past few years, we have been investigating the effects of accretion onto massive white dwarfs and its implications for their growth in mass toward the Chandrasekhar limit, in attempts to identify a possible relationship between SN I and novae. In our studies we have considered accretion at various mass accretion rates onto a variety of different white dwarf masses. We have found that there is a critical white dwarf mass above which a significant fraction of the accreted mass can remain on the white dwarf after the outburst. Below this value of the white dwarf mass, all of the accreted mass, plus core material dredged up into the envelope, is ejected as a result of the explosion. Our latest results include accretion and boundary layer heating produced by the infalling material. From these studies, we have identified some members of the class of recurrent novae, those involving a thermonuclear runaway, as the novae that are occurring on very massive white dwarfs and evolving toward a SN I explosion. One of the outgrowths of our UV studies of novae in outburst has been the identification of a class of novae which eject material that is very rich in the elements from oxygen to aluminum. We have shown that these outbursts occur on ONeMg white dwarfs, which are necessarily very massive white dwarfs.

The assumption commonly made is that a classical nova system is a close binary with one member a white dwarf and the other member a cooler star that fills its Roche lobe. Because it fills its lobe, there is a flow of gas through the inner Lagrangian point into the lobe of the white dwarf. The high angular momentum of the transferred material causes it to spiral into an accretion disk surrounding the white dwarf. Some (unknown) viscous process transfers mass inward and angular momentum outward through the disk, so that a fraction (also unknown) of the material lost by the secondary ultimately ends up on the white dwarf. The accreted layer grows in thickness and is heated by compression until it reaches a temperature that is high enough for thermonuclear burning of hydrogen to begin at the bottom. The simulations show that, if the material is degenerate, a thermonuclear runaway (hereafter: TNR) occurs and the temperature in the accreted envelope can grow to values exceeding 10^8K.

The further evolution of nuclear burning on the white dwarf now depends upon the mass and luminosity of the white dwarf, the rate of mass accretion, and the chemical composition of the reacting layer (Truran 1982; Starrfield 1989; Starrfield, Sparks, and Shaviv 1988; and references therein). Observations of novae ejecta also imply that there is mixing of core material into the accreted layer, so that the chemical composition of the material that is ultimately ejected by the outburst reflects a combination of core plus accreted material (Sparks et al. 1988).

It was proposed some years ago that accretion onto white dwarfs in close binary systems could lead to SN I (Truran and Cameron 1971; Whelan and Iben 1973). There have always been difficulties with including novae in this scenario, however, since they have been thought to eject most of their accreted mass. Unfortunately, although there have been other proposals for close binary progenitors of SN I, none of these proposals has yet received observational confirmation. It is the purpose of this paper to show that there is a class of nova-like events in which the white dwarf component is probably increasing in mass and is already close to the Chandrasekhar limit. We also note that the core composition of this class of novae has been identified.

I. RECURRENT NOVAE AND "NEON" NOVAE

Over the past few years, there has been intensive study of a class of novae that is referred to as "recurrent" because they have been *observed* to go through more than one outburst. They experience low amplitude outbursts which repeat on time scales of 20 to 50 years although the shortest known recurrence time is that of U Sco, which underwent outbursts in 1979 and 1987. Recurrent novae eject very small amounts of material, $\leq 10^{-7}$ $M_\odot$, which represents only a *small* fraction of the amount of envelope mass necessary to initiate a TNR on a massive white dwarf. Presumably, the rest of the accreted material remains on the white dwarf.

The short recurrence times for this kind of outburst demands that the mass of the white dwarf exceed $1.3 M_\odot$ and the closer to $1.4 M_\odot$ the better (Starrfield, Sparks, and Truran 1985; Starrfield, Sparks, and Shaviv 1988; Truran et al. 1988). The simulations also show that the accreted envelope is burned to helium very rapidly, ensuring that the entire accreted envelope does not have to be ejected in order for the system to return to quiescence. In addition, abundance analyses of the ejecta of recurrent novae indicate that the heavy element abundances are not enhanced relative to a solar mixture (c.f., Williams et al. 1981; Starrfield 1988). We interpret these results as implying that this class of novae is neither mixing core material into the accreted envelope nor ejecting all of the accreted material. Therefore, it seems likely that the mass of the white dwarf, *in recurrent novae systems*, is growing as a result of the nova outburst. We have identified U Sco and V394 CrA as two recurrent novae which contain white dwarfs already close to the Chandrasekhar limit (Starrfield, Sparks, and Shaviv 1988). Finally, because the observed recurrence time scales require high $\dot{M}$ and because most of the material remains on the white dwarf, we predict that their mass must be growing at a very high rate ($\dot{M} > 10^{-7} M_\odot \text{yr}^{-1}$).

It is also possible to speculate on the internal composition of the white dwarfs in these systems. The basis of this speculation is the UV studies of novae done with the **IUE** satellite (Starrfield 1988) which show that many novae are ejecting significant amounts of core material into space as a consequence of the outburst. These are the classical novae that show large enhancements of helium and heavier nuclei over a solar mixture (Truran and Livio 1986). In this context, we have been able to identify a subclass of novae that must be occurring on ONeMg white dwarfs based upon abundance analyses of the ejected material. Currently, we have positive identifications for four such novae (V1370 Aql, V693 CrA, QU Vul, and Nova Vul 1987) and in all cases the intermediate elements are a major fraction of the ejecta.

Observations allow us to estimate what fraction of the ejected material is core material and they show that, in some cases, the fraction is large (Truran and Livio 1986; Sparks et al. 1988). In the most extreme case, that of V1370 Aql, the efficiency of this process is very high and it appears that most of the ejecta is core material.

The straightforward interpretation is that the white dwarfs in these nova systems are being eroded in mass as a result of the nova outburst. Therefore, *novae that show large enrichments of intermediate mass nuclei in their ejecta cannot be the progenitors of SN-like events.* We note that they must have been formed as high mass white dwarfs in order for the pre-white dwarf to survive carbon burning.

II. CONCLUSIONS

We draw the following conclusions:

(1) Those recurrent novae that are powered by thermonuclear runaways, such as U Sco and V394 CrA, must involve a very massive white dwarf, close to the Chandrasekhar limit. This is demanded by the short recurrence times characteristic of these systems and the fact that only massive degenerate dwarfs can accrete sufficient matter on the observed recurrence time-scales to initiate a runaway.

(2) The white dwarfs in recurrent nova systems appear to be growing in mass since the observed masses of the ejecta are less than the envelope masses necessary to trigger a TNR. This result is also consistent with the findings that the ejecta of recurrent novae show no evidence for high concentrations of heavy nuclei, so that dredge-up and ejection of white dwarf core matter cannot have occurred.

(3) The massive white dwarfs in these systems are most likely to be ONeMg white dwarfs. This prediction is consistent with stellar evolution calculations (Iben, private communication) which suggest that it is difficult to form CO white dwarfs in the mass range $M > 1.3 M_\odot$ necessary to understand the recurrent novae and is also consistent with observational evidence for the presence of ONeMg systems among the classical novae.

(4) Typical classical novae are very unlikely to be progenitors of supernovae, since it appears that the compact component in these systems is systematically being reduced in mass as a consequence of successive outbursts.

It thus seems reasonable that the recurrent nova systems, which experience TNR's, may indeed see their white dwarf components evolve to the Chandrasekhar limit, setting the stage for the occurrence of a more violent event. The explosion of an ONeMg white dwarf in a close binary system should be investigated to determine whether the formation of a neutron star in a close binary can be achieved in this manner. Williams(private communication) has suggested a possible relation between recurrent novae and low mass x-ray binaries, since both classes show evidence for helium enrichments in the material being transferred from the secondary. Studies of the long term evolution of recurrent nova systems and hydrodynamic studies of the evolution of the resulting ONeMg white dwarf at the Chandrasekhar limit can hopefully provide a clear statement regarding this matter.

We would like to express our thanks for many useful discussion to Drs. G. S. Kutter, K. Nomoto, S. Shore, E. M. Sion, L. Stryker, G. Sonneborn, R. Wade, R. M. Wagner, and R. E. Williams. S. Starrfield is grateful to Drs. S. Colgate, A. N. Cox, C. F. Keller, M. Henderson, and K. Meyer for the hospitality of the Los Alamos National Laboratory and a generous allotment of computer time. This work was supported in part by NSF Grants AST85- 16173 and AST88-18215 to Arizona State University and AST 86-11500 to the University of Illinois, by the Institute of Geophysics and Planetary Physics at Los Alamos, by NASA grants to Arizona State University and to the University of Colorado, and by the DOE.

REFERENCES

Sparks, W.M., Starrfield, S., Truran, J. W., and Kutter, G. S. 1988, in *Atmospheric Phenomena in Stellar Explosions*, ed. K. Nomoto, (Springer-Verlag: Heidelberg), p. 234.
Starrfield, S. 1988, in *Multiwavelength Astrophysics*, ed. F A. Córdova, (Cambridge: University Press), p. 159.
Starrfield, S. 1989, in *The Classical Nova*, ed. N. Evans, and M. Bode, (New York: Wiley), p. 39.
Starrfield, S., Sparks, W. M., and Shaviv, G. 1988, *Ap. J. Lett.*, **326**, L35.
Starrfield, S., Sparks, W. M., and Truran, J. W. 1985 *Ap. J.*, **291**, 136.
Truran, J. W. 1982, in *Essays in Nuclear Astrophysics*, ed. C.A. Barnes, D.D. Clayton, and D. Schramm (Cambridge: Cambridge U. Press), p. 467.
Truran, J. W., and Cameron, A. G. W 1971, *Astrophys. Space Sci.*, **14**, 179.
Truran, J. W., and Livio, M. 1986, *Ap. J.*, **308**, 721.
Truran, J. W., Livio, M., Hayes, J., Starrfield, S., and Sparks, W. M. 1988, *Ap. J.*, **324**, 345.
Whelan, J. A. J., and Iben, I. 1973, *Ap. J.*, **186**, 1007.
Williams, R.E., Sparks, W.M., Gallagher, J.S., Ney, E.P., Starrfield, S., and Truran, J. W. 1981, *Ap. J.*, **251**, 221.

SECTION XI
NUCLEOSYNTHESIS IN SUPERNOVAE

Explosive Nucleosynthesis in Type I and Type II Supernovae

Friedrich-Karl Thielemann, Masa-aki Hashimoto, Ken'ichi Nomoto, & Koichi Yokoi

1. Introduction

There exist many original and review articles about the mechanisms of type I and type II supernovae (SNI and SNII, e.g. Nomoto, Thielemann, Yokoi 1984; Nomoto 1986; Bruenn 1989; Cooperstein and Baron 1989; Wilson et al. 1986; Woosley and Weaver 1986) and a number of contributions to this conference (Nomoto, Woosley, Cooperstein and Baron, Mayle and Wilson), so that we do not intend to repeat this discussion here. We rather want to concentrate on the accompanying nucleosynthesis processes. This introduction contains a general presentation of the nucleosynthesis processes, while the application to both types of supernova events is given in sections 2 and 3. Section 4 includes a comparison of both contributions to the enrichment of heavy elements in the interstellar medium and a general conclusion. For a discussion of the nuclear physics input in the present nucleosynthesis calculations see Thielemann (1989) and Thielemann, Hashimoto, Nomoto (1990). One of the major free parameters in stellar evolution is the still uncertain $^{12}C(\alpha,\gamma)^{16}O$ reaction (see Filippone, Humblet, Langanke 1989; Caughlan et al. 1985; Caughlan and Fowler 1988). The present calculations were performed with the rate of Caughlan et al. (1985).

1.1 Explosive Si-Burning

Zones which experience temperatures in excess of 4.0–5.0×10^9K undergo explosive Si-burning. Temperatures beyond 5×10^9K lead to complete Si-exhaustion and produce only Fe-group nuclei. Explosive Si-burning can be devided into three different regimes: incomplete Si-burning and complete Si-burning with either a normal or alpha-rich freeze-out. Which of the three regimes is encountered depends on the peak temperatures and densities attained during the passage of the shock front (see Fig.20 in Woosley, Arnett, and Clayton 1973, and Fig.5 in Thielemann, Nomoto, Yokoi 1986). The most abundant nucleus in the normal and alpha-rich freeze-out is ^{56}Ni, in case the neutron excess is smaller than 2×10^{-2} or Y_e is larger than 0.49. For the less abundant nuclei the final alpha-capture plays a dominant role transforming nuclei like ^{56}Ni, ^{57}Ni, and ^{58}Ni into ^{60}Zn, ^{61}Zn, and ^{62}Zn in an alpha-rich freeze-out where also trace abundances of ^{40}Ca, ^{44}Ti, ^{48}Cr, and ^{52}Fe are obtained.

Incomplete Si-burning is characterized by peak temperatures of $4 - 5 \times 10^9$K. Temperatures are not high enough for an efficient bridging of the bottle neck above the proton magic number Z=20 by nuclear reactions. Besides the dominant fuel nuclei ^{28}Si and ^{32}S we find the alpha-nuclei ^{36}Ar and ^{40}Ca being most abundant. Partial leakage through the bottle neck above Z=20 produces ^{56}Ni and ^{54}Fe as dominant abundances in the Fe-group. Smaller amounts of ^{52}Fe, ^{58}Ni, ^{55}Co, and ^{57}Ni are encountered.

1.2 Explosive O-burning

Temperatures in excess of roughly 3.3×10^9K lead to a quasi-equilibrium among nuclei in the range $28 < A < 45$ in mass number (Woosley, Arnett, Calyton 1973). These conditions are accomplished in explosive O-burning. The main burning products are ^{28}Si, ^{32}S, ^{36}Ar, ^{40}Ca, ^{38}Ar, and ^{34}S. With mass fractions less than 10^{-2} also ^{33}S, ^{39}K, ^{35}Cl, ^{42}Ca, and ^{37}Ar show up. In zones with temperatures close to 4×10^9K there exists still a contamination by the Fe-group nuclei ^{54}Fe, ^{56}Ni, ^{52}Fe, ^{58}Ni, ^{55}Co, and ^{57}Ni.

1.3 Explosive Ne and C-burning

The main burning products of explosive neon burning are ^{16}O, ^{24}Mg, and ^{28}Si, synthesized via the reaction sequences ^{20}Ne$(\gamma,\alpha)^{16}$O and ^{20}Ne$(\alpha,\gamma)^{24}$Mg$(\alpha,\gamma)^{28}$Si, similar to the hydrostatic case. The mass zones in question have peak temperatures in excess of 2.1×10^9K. They undergo a combined version of explosive neon and carbon burning. Besides the major abundances, mentioned above, explosive neon burning supplies also substantial amounts of ^{27}Al, ^{29}Si, ^{32}S, ^{30}Si, and ^{31}P. Explosive carbon burning contributes in addition the nuclei ^{20}Ne, ^{23}Na, ^{24}Mg, ^{25}Mg, and ^{26}Mg.

1.4 r-Process

The operation of an r-process is characterized by the fact that 10 to 100 neutrons per heavy nucleus have to be available for the onset of substantial neutron capture. Such conditions are only existent after the freeze-out of charged particle reactions, in matter which experienced nuclear statitical equilibrium which was compressed to densities of $10^{11}-10^{12}$g cm^{-3}, undergoing electron captures until a beta equilibrium is attained (Cameron 1989). A different situation surfaces when the maximum temperatures are below freeze-out conditions for charged particle reactions with Fe-group nuclei. Then reactions among light nuclei which release neutrons, like (α,n) reactions on ^{13}C and ^{22}Ne, can sustain a neutron flux. The constraint of having 10-100 neutrons per heavy nucleus, in order to attain r-process conditions, can then be met by small abundances of Fe-group nuclei. Such conditions were expected when the shock front passes the He-burning shell and enhances the ^{22}Ne(α,n) reaction by orders of magnitude. However, Blake et al. (1981) and Cowan, Cameron and Truran (1983) could show that this neutron source is not strong enough for an r-process in realistic stellar models. Recent research based on additional neutron release via inelastic neutrino scattering (Epstein, Colgate, and Haxton 1988) can also not produce neutron densities which are required for such a process to operate (see also Woosley et al. 1989).

2. Type I(a) Supernovae

In the following we want to discuss in detail the burning conditions as they occur in a SNIa. We take the model W7 by Nomoto, Thielemann, and Yokoi (1984) and Thielemann, Nomoto, and Yokoi (1986) as a typical example for that class of exploding C-O white dwarfs in a binary system. There is still considerable uncertainty in the physics of propagating flame fronts (see e.g. Woosley and Weaver 1986b, Müller and Arnett 1986, Zeldovich et al. 1985, and Nomoto, Woosley, Canal et al. this volume) and open questions remain. The propagation of the burning front after central C-ignition has in published calculations only been treated in a parametrized way, fitting the mixing-length parameter in the time-dependent mixing-length theory of Unno (1967) to the observed supernova energy.

Temperatures in the burning front are increased by about a factor of 10, in comparison to the intitial values, leading to explosive burning of the C-O fuel. Fig.1

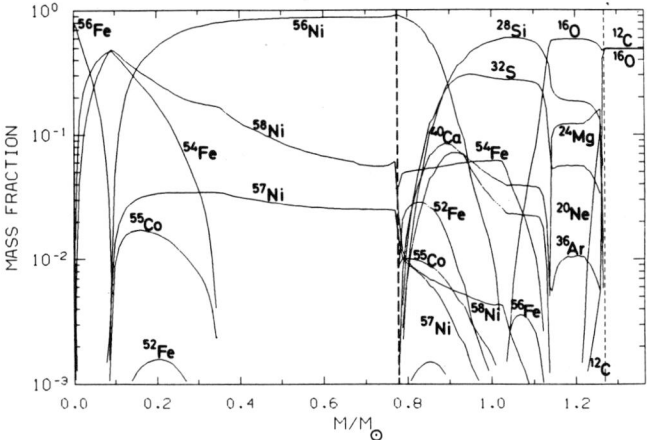

Fig.1: Major abundances after explosive processing. In the inner 0.8 $M_\odot$ only Fe-group nuclei are produced. The inner dashed line shows the transition to incomplete Si-burning, followed further out by products of explosive O, Ne, and C-burning. The outer dashed line marks the quenching of the burning front.

displays the mass fractions of a few major nuclei. We see that the outer zones experience explosive C and Ne-burning, where first the carbon fusion produces ^{20}Ne which photodisintegrates back to ^{16}O. Further towards the center, zones undergo explosive O-burning where also ^{16}O is burned by fusion reactions to ^{28}Si and ^{32}S. Even higher temperatures lead to the burning of Si. In incomplete Si-burning doubly-magic ^{56}Ni is produced together with intermediate nuclei like ^{40}Ca. Inside $0.8M_\odot$ only "Fe-group" nuclei exist with the dominant abundance of ^{56}Ni, which has the highest binding per nucleon for N=Z nuclei. The situation only changes towards the very center where the densities become high enough to cause Fermi energies of the electron gas in excess of several MeV, which enables appreciable amounts of electron captures on free protons (and to a minor extent on heavy nuclei $\approx$40%). This changes the total proton to neutron ratio and the most abundant nuclei become first ^{54}Fe and ^{58}Ni and finally ^{56}Fe. The region of complete Si-burning is devided into an inner zone of $0.35M_\odot$ with a normal freeze-out and an outer region with an alpha-rich freeze-out. We see the strong decline of ^{54}Fe and the dominance of ^{58}Ni in the alpha-rich freeze-out.

One of the major aspects of nucleosynthesis calculations is to understand the chemical evolution of galaxies and especially the present abundances in our galaxy, assuming that the solar system abundances give a good representation. Fig.2 shows the ratio of abundances produced in a SNI event to solar abundances. Displayed are abundance ratios after decay of unstable nuclei, normalized to unity for ^{56}Fe. If a SNI event always starts from the same configuration (a white dwarf with $M = M_{Ch}$), the same nucleosynthesis products are expected from each event and the comparison with solar abundances is actually meaningful without averaging over a complete sample. It is obvious from Fig.2 that the production of Fe-group nuclei in comparison to their solar values is a factor of 2 larger than the production of intermediate nuclei from Si to Ca. This shows that SNIs are the dominant production sites of Fe-group nuclei, while SNIIs have to fill in the intermediate nuclei.

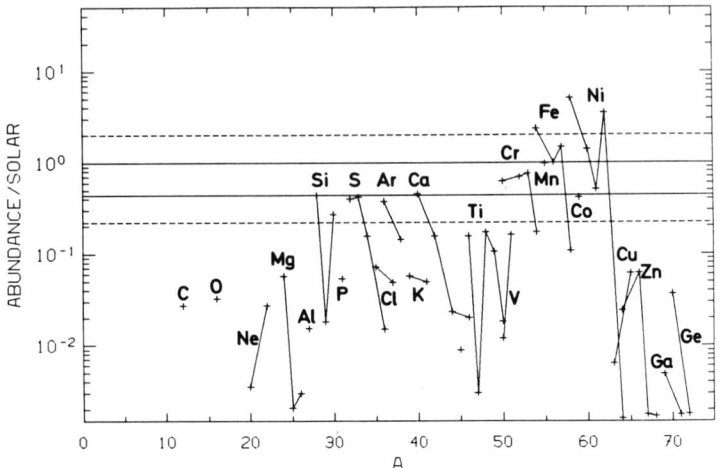

Fig.2: The abundances of stable isotopes formed in a SNI event are shown relative to their solar values. The ratio is normalized to ^{56}Fe. Note the strong overabundances of ^{58,62}Ni and ^{54}Fe.

One undesirable aspect is the large scale of deviations from solar abundances within the Fe-group, when SNIs are the main contributors of these nuclei to the interstellar medium. We notice here especially ^{54}Fe, ^{58}Ni, and ^{62}Ni (originating from ^{62}Zn-decay). All these nuclei come from a chain in the nuclear chart which is displaced by two units to the neutron-rich side from the N=Z chain and measures therefore the neutron excess of the material. Outside of $0.3M_\odot$, where electron capture is not effective, the neutron excess is only determined by the ^{22}Ne admixture to ^{12}C and ^{16}O in the original white dwarf, coming from ^{14}N in He-burning, which in turn originated from all CNO-nuclei in H-burning, i.e., the metallicity. Using time-averaged metallicities would reduce the overproduction of these nuclei by 25-40%. Probably more important is that the propagation of the burning front is not fully understood yet. A burning front which starts with a small velocity and then accelerates (Woosley and Weaver 1986b), could reduce the amount of material which is displayed in the mass zones between 0.05 to $0.3M_\odot$, where ^{54}Fe, ^{58}Ni, and ^{62}Ni are produced predominantly.

3. Type II Supernovae

While there exists encouraging progress in the understanding of the explosion mechanism of SNIIs (Mayle and Wilson, this volume), we still lack a complete understanding of self-consistant models for collapse and explosion, predicting the mass cut between neutron star and ejecta reliably (Cooperstein and Baron 1989, Myra and Bludman 1989, Bruenn 1989, Mönchmeyer 1989). Despite these open questions it is still possible to model supernova light curves with an artificially induced shock wave of the appropriate energy (see Arnett 1987; Shigeyama et al. 1988; Woosley, Pinto, Ensman 1988 for the case of SN1987A). The same approach has been taken in the past to calculate explosive nucleosynthesis in SNII explosions (Woosley and Weaver 1986a). The only assumption, made implicitly by running the shock wave through the initial model, is that matter which is finally ejected, did not experience significant changes between the onset of the collapse of the inner core and the arrival of the shock wave.

This is well justified for prompt explosions with time scales of 30 ms, but might be questionable for delayed explosions with time scales of seconds.

We want to discuss the general behavior at the example of a $20M_\odot$ star (Nomoto and Hashimoto 1988). The explosion energy used corresponds to a supernova energy of 10^{51} erg. As mentioned before, this treatment cannot predict the position of the mass cut between neutron star and ejecta, but the observation of $0.07 \pm 0.01 M_\odot$ of ^{56}Ni in SN1987A (a $20M_\odot$ star) gives an important constraint, because ^{56}Ni is produced in the innermost ejected zones. The explosive nucleosynthesis due to burning in the shock front is shown in Fig.3 for a few major nuclei. Beyond $1.6M_\odot$ all Fe-group nuclei are produced in *explosive* Si-burning during the SNII event. At $1.63M_\odot$ Y_e changes from 0.494 to 0.499 and leads to a smaller ^{56}Ni abundance further inside, where more neutron-rich Ni-isotopes share the abundance with ^{56}Ni.

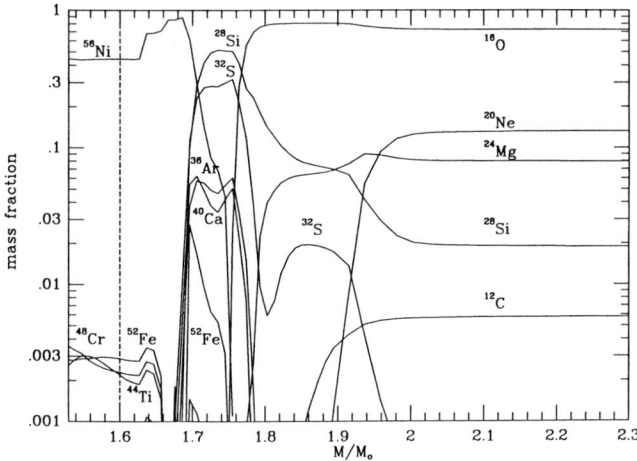

Fig.3: Mass fractions of a few major nuclei after passage of the supernova shockfront. Matter outside $2M_\odot$ is essentially unaltered. Mass zones further in experience explosive Si, O, Ne, and C-burning. In order to eject $0.07M_\odot$ of ^{56}Ni the mass cut between neutron star and ejecta is required to be located at $1.6M_\odot$.

Only alpha-rich freeze-out and incomplete Si-burning are encountered. Contrary to SNIs, densities in excess of 10^8gcm^{-3}, which would result in a normal freeze-out, are not attained in the ejecta of this $20M_\odot$ star. The most abundant nucleus in the normal and alpha-rich freeze-out is ^{56}Ni. For the less abundant nuclei the final alpha-capture plays a dominant role transforming nuclei like ^{56}Ni, ^{57}Ni, and ^{58}Ni into ^{60}Zn, ^{61}Zn, and ^{62}Zn. The region which experiences imcomplete Si-burning starts at $1.69M_\odot$ and extends out to $1.74M_\odot$. In the innermost zones with temperatures close to 4×10^9K there exists still a contamination by the Fe-group nuclei ^{54}Fe, ^{56}Ni, ^{52}Fe, ^{58}Ni, ^{55}Co, and ^{57}Ni. Explosive O-burning occurs in the mass zones up to $1.8M_\odot$. The main burning products are ^{28}Si, ^{32}S, ^{36}Ar, ^{40}Ca, ^{38}Ar, and ^{34}S. With mass fractions less than 10^{-2} also ^{33}S, ^{39}K, ^{35}Cl, ^{42}Ca, and ^{37}Ar are produced. Explosive Ne-burning leads to an ^{16}O-enhancement over its hydrostatic value in the mass zones up to $2M_\odot$.

Traditionally the r-process was assumed to occur close to the mass cut between neutron star and ejecta in matter with very high neutron excess. Using the ^{56}Ni constraint and assuming a spherical explosion led to a mass cut at $1.6M_\odot$. The most neutron-rich zones of the ejecta are located at this inner boundary with a Y_e of 0.494 which corresponds to a neutron excess $\eta = \sum_i(N_i - Z_i)Y_i/\sum_i A_iY_i = 1 - 2Y_e$ of 1.2×10^{-2}. These zones which experience temperatures in excess of 5×10^9K, produce predominantly nuclei in the mass range 50-60. The quoted value of η therefore indicates that each nucleus has about 0.5 more neutrons than protons. For that mass region this corresponds to a nucleus being still about 1.5 mass units *more* proton-rich than the stability line.

No r-process material is ejected from these zones close to the mass cut between neutron star and ejecta. This conclusion relies on the assumption that rotation is not strong enough to violate spherical symmetry, which could cause jet-like ejection (LeBlanc and Wilson 1970; Symbalisty, Schramm, and Wilson 1985). For reasonable ratios of rotational to gravitational energy of 1% before collapse, Mönchmeyer (1989) finds small jet-like circulations at the poles when the shock front is still close to the collapsed core, but obtains an almost spherical symmetry when the shock front reaches the Si-zone. This indicates that a $20M_\odot$ star does not eject r-process nuclei in its final supernova explosion, although SNIIs are strongly expected to be the dominant r-process source. SNIIs with smaller masses, however, could contribute r-process nuclei (Mathews and Cowan 1989).

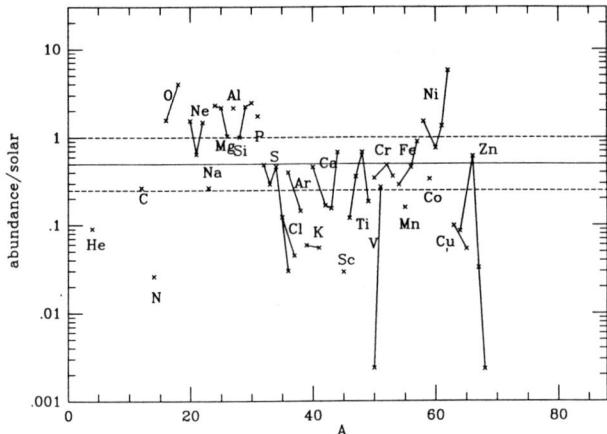

Fig.4: Composition of the supernova ejecta in comparison to solar abundances, normalized to ^{28}Si. Elements lighter than P have strong contributions from hydrostatic C and Ne-burning. Heavier nuclei originate from explosive processing and show similar ratios within a factor of 2 to 3. The ^{58,61,62}Ni abundances are strongly dependent on the mass cut, i.e., the neutron excess of ejected matter

In order to get a general feeling about the nucleosynthesis production in a $20M_\odot$ SNII we display the abundance ratio over solar (normalized to ^{28}Si) in Fig.4. Nuclei heavier than Si and P are on average produced by a factor of 2 to 4 less than ^{28}Si. P, Si, Al, Mg, Na, and Ne, while also produced in explosive burning, have large contributions from the zones of hydrostatic C and Ne-burning, which are unaltered during the explosion (see Fig.3). The reason is the existence of an extended shell of combined C and Ne-burning, ranging from 1.8 to $3.7 M_\odot$ in the progenitor star (see. Fig.10 in Nomoto and Hashimoto 1988). Essentially all heavier elements originate from explosive processing. Thus, the ratio between elements heavier than Si and P to lighter elements reflects mainly the size of hydrostatic zones to the explosively processed ones and is a function of stellar mass (and the methods used in stellar evolution calculations). This is evident when comparing to Woosley, Pinto, and Weaver (1988) who use a different treatment of convection (Ledoux vs. Schwarzschild) and have smaller C-burning cores. The amount of ^{16}O is closely linked to the "effective" ^{12}C$(\alpha,\gamma)^{16}$O rate during core He-burning. This effective rate is determined by three factors: 1. the actual nuclear rate, 2. the amount of semiconvection and overshooting, mixing fresh He-fuel into the core at late phases of He-burning, when the temperatures are relatively high and favor alpha-capture on ^{12}C, and 3. the stellar mass which determines the central temperature during He-burning. Our model calculations predict $1.48 M_\odot$ of ejected ^{16}O. Hopefully an improved analysis of observations for SN1987A can give better estimates for abundances of the elements discussed above and therefore help to put tighter constraints on the pre-collapse models.

The products of explosive burning from S to Cu originate mainly from mass zones up to $1.8 M_\odot$. They fall well along a line of constant overproduction (within reasonable errors). The nuclei ^{58,61,62}Ni, which show large overabundances, are produced in form of the neutron-rich species ^{58}Ni and ^{61,62}Zn. Their production is strongly dependent on Y_e and varies therefore with the position of the mass cut between ejected matter and the remaining neutron star. Especially for the Ni-abundances the position of the mass cut is crucial and one would expect lower mass SNIIs to eject more of these neutron-rich species. This could explain the observed very high Ni abundances in some supernova remnants like the Crab (Henry and Fesen 1988), if they are not explained away by atomic or other effects.

A few nuclei like ^{36}S, ^{37}Cl, ^{40}Ar, ^{58}Fe, and possibly some odd-Z nuclei, which are underabundant in Fig.4, are mainly produced by the weak s-process during core He-burning (Arnett and Thielemann 1985). They were not included in the 30 nuclei network for hydrostatic burning stages and consequently their s-process contribution is neglected. Haxton (1988), Woosley and Haxton (1988), and Woosley et al. (1989) examined the possible effect of inelastic neutrino scattering on explosive nucleosynthesis, an idea which was already introduced earlier by Domogatsky and Nadyozhin (1977). Inelastic neutrino scattering can populate excited states which are unstable against particle emission and produce neighboring nuclei. Outside the neutrino-sphere the scattering events will be rare and therefore this process will be mostly of importance for nuclei with very small abundances, which are not produced otherwise. We did not include this effect in the present calculations.

4. SNI and SNII Contributions to Nucleosynthesis

In order to compare the different contributions of SNIs and SNIIs to the interstellar medium, we display in Table 1 the masses involved in the different types of explosive burning for the standard model of SNI (W7) and a typical (?) representative for SNIIs, the $20 M_\odot$ star from section 3. The main difference is seen in the vastly differing amounts involved in explosive Si-burning, 1.03 vs. $0.15 M_\odot$. As the major products of Si-burning are Fe-peak elements, it is eminently clear that they are mainly produced by SNIs, as long as the frequencies of both events are comparable. Another difference is given by the fact that only SNIs seem to eject matter which experienced a normal freeze-out in complete Si-burning. This ensures also that the dominant abundances of e.g. ^{54}Fe and ^{55}Mn (from ^{55}Co-decay) come from SNIs, while their counterparts ^{58}Ni and ^{59}Co (from ^{59}Cu-decay) stem from a distorted Fe-peak composition in an alpha-rich freeze-out.

Due to the fact that the innermost matter from SNIs experienced strong electron captures and attained values of Y_e=0.46-0.47, while the $20M_\odot$ star only ejected matter as neutron-rich as $Y_e = 0.498$, the only stable ^{56}Fe – not being a decay product of ^{56}Ni – comes from SNIs. Similarly the contributions to ^{54}Fe and ^{55}Co, both nuclei with $N/Z > 1$, are enhanced. This statement is however very tentative, as we assume that less massive SNIIs can actually eject more neutron-rich material and even r-process nuclei, and the Y_e-values in SNIs depend strongly on the propagation speed of the deflagration front, which governs the amount of electron captures and is still somewhat uncertain.

Zones further out in SNIs and SNIIs have a Y_e determined by the original metalicity in form of ^{22}Ne, which was produced in hydrostatic He-burning from CNO-nuclei. Thus for the same metallicities the burning conditions barely differ but only the masses involved. For explosive O and Ne-C-burning those numbers lie within a factor of 2. While SNIs, consisting initially only of C and O, eject only products of *explosive* Ne and C-burning, SNIIs can have extended convective shells of C and Ne-burning which will only be partially processed explosively (see discussion in section 3) and thus a large amount of hydrostatic C and Ne-burning material will also be contributed from SNIIs.

TABLE 1
MASSES IN EXPLOSIVE BURNING

	SNI (TNY 1986)	SNII (THN 1990)
Si-burning	1.03	0.15
complete	0.77	0.10
normal alpha-rich	0.33 0.44	0.10
incomplete	0.26	0.05
O-burning Ne+C-burning	0.11 0.13	0.06 0.20

If we take the very premature approach of assuming that the $20M_\odot$ mass star can represent a typical SNII, one can try to derive a ratio of SNI to SNII events, necessary to produce a solar Si/Fe ratio in total

$$\frac{M(Si)}{M(Fe)}_\odot = \frac{R_I M_I(Si) + R_{II} M_{II}(Si)}{R_I M_I(Fe) + R_{II} M_{II}(Fe)}. \qquad (1)$$

Here M denotes the mass involved, R the supernova rate, I and II the types of supernovae. From here we can derive a ratio

$$\frac{R_I}{R_{II}} = -\frac{M_{II}(Si) - M(Si)/M(Fe)_\odot M_{II}(Fe)}{M_I(Si) - M(Si)/M(Fe)_\odot M_I(Fe)} = 0.22 \pm 0.03, \qquad (2)$$

if we adopt the appropriate values for M_I and M_{II} from Thielemann, Nomoto and Yokoi (1986) and Thielemann, Hashimoto, Nomoto (1990) [$M_{II}(Fe) = 0.07 \pm 0.01 M_\odot$], as well as $M(Si)/M(Fe)_\odot = 0.559$ (Cameron 1982). Such a ratio is quite uncertain, due to the fact that differences of uncertain numbers are involved. The results for SNIs seem, however, quite reliable since a number of tests comparing theoretical and observational light curves and spectra have been performed. The $20 M_\odot$ star is not necessarily typical for SNIIs, but its Si/Fe ratio seems to be (see Table 5 in Thielemann, Hashimoto, Nomoto 1990). R_I/R_{II} reflects the ratio of SNIs to all core collapse events. If SNIbs are interpreted as core collapse events of massive Wolf-Rayet stars (e.g. Wheeler and Levreault 1985, Ensman and Woosley 1988, Nomoto this volume) and one uses the respective observational rates for SNIa, SNIb, and SNII (van den Bergh, this volume), a remarkable agreement is obtained ($R_{Ia}/(R_{Ib} + R_{II})) = 0.214$).

When we take the value for R_I/R_{II} from Eq.(2), we predict $^{57}Fe/^{56}Fe=0.016-0.023$, the errors being due to the uncertainties of the mass cut in SNIIs between neutron star and ejecta. This compares well to a solar value of 0.024 and the ^{57}Fe contribution is dominated by SNIIs. Using the same ratio also results in $^{55}Mn/^{56}Fe=(8.6-9.3) \times 10^{-3}$ which compares well with the solar value of 1.1×10^{-2}. In this case the ^{55}Mn contribution is dominated by SNIs. Similarly we also obtain that the intermediate mass elements from Si to Ca (Si being representative) are produced to roughly 28% in SNIas, while Fe, i.e. ^{56}Fe, is produced to 66% in SNIas. It will be interesting to test similar predictions in the future also for other elements. In order to obtain, however, really meaningful results it will be necessary to have predictions of explosive nucleosynthesis in SNIIs also for masses different from $M = 20 M_\odot$ and to perform an integral over the IMF. This is underlined by the deficiency of overabundances in [S/Fe] through [Ca/Fe] for the $20 M_\odot$ star in comparison to average values for SNIIs (see Table 5 in Thielemann, Hashimoto, Nomoto 1990).

This research was supported in part by NASA grant NGR 22-007-272, NSF grant AST-8612647 and the National Center for Supercomputer applications at the University of Illinois (AST 890009N).

References

Arnett, W.D. 1987, *Ap. J.* **319**, 136

Arnett, W.D., Thielemann, F.-K. 1985, *Ap. J.* **295**, 589

Blake, J.B., Woosley, S.E., Weaver, T.A., Schramm, D.N. 1981, *Ap. J.* **248**, 315

Bruenn, S.W. 1989, *Ap. J.* **340**, 955

Cameron, A.G.W. 1982, in *Essays in Nuclear Astrophysics*, eds. C.A. Barnes, D.D. Clayton, D.N. Schramm, (Cambridge Univ. Press), p. 23

Cameron, A.G.W. 1989, in *Cosmic Abundances of Matter*, ed. C.J. Waddington, AIP Conf. Proc. 183, p.349

Caughlan, G.R., Fowler, W.A. 1988, *At. Nucl. Data Tables* **40**, 283

Caughlan, G.R., Fowler, W.A., Harris, M.J, Zimmerman, G.E. 1985, *At. Nucl. Data Tables* **32**, 197

Cooperstein, J., Baron, E. 1989, in *Supernovae*, ed A. Petschek, (Springer-Verlag, New York), in press

Cowan, J.J., Cameron, A.G.W., Truran, J.W. 1983, *Ap. J.* **265**, 429

Domogatsky, G.V., Nadyozhin, D.K. 1977, *M.N.R.A.S.* **178**, 33p

Ensman, L., Woosley, S.E. 1988, *Ap. J.* **333**, 754

Epstein, R.I., Colgate, S.A., Haxton, W.C. 1988, *Phys. Rev. Lett.* **61**, 2038

Filippone, B.W., Humblet, J., Langanke, K. 1989, *Phys. Rev. C*, in press

Haxton, W.C. 1988, *Phys. Rev. Lett.* **60**, 1999

Henry, R.B.C., Fesen, R.A. 1988, *Ap. J.* **329**, 693

LeBlanc, J.M., Wilson, J.R. 1970, *Ap. J.* **161**, 541

Mathews, G.J., Cowan, J.J. 1989, in *Heavy Ion Physics and Nuclear Astrophysical Problems*, eds. S. Kubono, M. Ishihara, T. Nomura, (World Scientific, Singapore), p.143

Mönchmeyer, R. 1989, Ph. Thesis, TU Munich, unpublished

Müller, E., Arnett, W.D. 1986, *Ap. J.* **307**, 619

Myra, E.S., Bludman, S. 1989, *Ap. J.* **340**, 384

Nomoto, K. 1986, *Prog. Part. Nucl. Phys.* **17**, 249

Nomoto, K., Hashimoto, M. 1988, *Phys. Rep.* **163**, 13

Nomoto, K., Thielemann, F.-K., Yokoi, K. 1984, *Ap. J.*, **286**, 644

Shigeyama, T., Nomoto, K., Hashimoto, M. 1988, *Astron. Astrophys.* **196**, 141

Symbalisty, E.M.D., Schramm, D.N., Wilson, J.R. 1985, *Ap. J. Lett.* **291**, L11

Thielemann, F.-K. 1989, in *Nuclear Astrophysics*, ed. M. Lozano, M.I. Gallardo, J.M. Arias (Springer: Berlin), p.106

Thielemann, F.-K., Hashimoto, M., Nomoto, K. 1989, *Ap. J.* **348**, in press

Thielemann, F.-K., Nomoto, K., Yokoi, K. 1986, *Astron. Astrophys.*, **158**, 17

Unno, W. 1967, *Publ. Astron. Soc. Japan* **19**, 140

Wheeler, J.C., Levreault, R. 1985, *Ap. J. Lett.* **294**, L17

Wilson, J.R., Mayle, R., Woosley, S.E., Weaver, T.A. 1986, in *Proc. 12th Texas Symp. on Relativistic Astrophysics, Ann. N. Y. Acad. Sci.* **470**, 267

Woosley, S.E., Arnett, W.D., Clayton, D.D. 1973, *Ap. J. Suppl.* **26**, 231

Woosley, S.E., Hartmann, D., Hoffman, R.B., Haxton, W.C. 1989, preprint

Woosley, S.E., Haxton, W.C. 1988, *Nature* **334**, 45

Woosley, S.E., Pinto, P.A., Ensman, L. 1988, *Ap. J.* **324**, 466

Woosley, S.E., Pinto, P.A., Weaver, T.A. 1988, *Proc. Astron. Soc. Australia* **7**, 355

Woosley, S.E., Weaver, T.A. 1986, *Ann. Rev. Astron. Astrophys.* **24**, 205

Woosley, S.E., Weaver, T.A. 1986, in *Radiation Hydrodynamics*, IAU Colloq. No 89, eds., D. Mihalas, K.H. Winkler, (Reidel, Dordrecht), p. 91

Zeldovich, Ya.B., Baerenblatt, G.I., Librovich, V.B., Makhviladze, G.M. 1985, *The Mathematical Theory of Combustion and Explosions*, (Plenum, New York)

On Supernovae Rates, Oxygen and Iron Abundances

F. X. Timmes

Recently the argument was advanced by Arnett, Schramm and Truran (1989) that there is $\sim 10^9$ $M_\odot$ of oxygen in the $\sim 10^{10}$ year old Galactic disk; that each Type II supernovae ejects ~ 1 $M_\odot$ of oxygen; and hence that Type II supernovae have occurred on the average of once every ten years. By further assuming that all Type II produce 1987A amounts of iron, they conclude that the bulk of iron in the Galactic disk originates from the core collapse of young massive stars. Their conclusions regarding the Type II supernovae rate and Type IIs being the dominant source of iron, even with a gratuitous factor of two, represents an excellent example of extrapolation beyond bound.

Type II supernovae events are the prime nucleosynthetic site for the mid atomic number elements. As the mass of the progenitor star is turned up, calculations by Arnett (1978) and more recently by Woosley (1986) demonstrate that the mass fraction of oxygen produced increases rapidly, soon becoming the dominant element produced. The mass fraction of iron produced by Type II supernovae is relatively small. On the other hand, the carbon deflagration wave front in an accreting carbon + oxygen white dwarf model of Type I supernovae is a copious nucleosynthetic site for the iron peak elements. The computations by Nomoto, Thielemann, and Yokoi (1984) and Woosley (1989) indicate that the mass fraction of iron peak elements produced by this model of Type I supernovae is about 0.7 $M_\odot$ while the mass fraction of oxygen produced is minimal. This suggests that Type I supernovae produce a significant fraction of the iron peak elements in the Galactic disk, which is quite complimentary to the nucleosynthesis of Type II supernovae.

The yield of any element produced by an entire generation of Type I or Type II supernovae is dependent of the birth rate of stars at a previous epoch, the initial mass function, the stellar mass-lifetime relationship, the nucleosyntheses prescriptions and the accretion of primordial material. It is not clear that all Type II events, on average, occur once every ten years and that they all produce 1987A amounts of oxygen and/or iron. To facilitate an understanding of the temporal evolution of the chemical elements and supernovae rates, the coupled, integro-differential system of equations governing the single zone was integrated, assuming the production matrix formalism of Talbot and Arnett (1971, 1973, 1975). The computational algorithms were derived from Press et al. (1986). The nucleosynthetic yields of the core collapse of massive stars follows Woosley (1986) while the prescription for intermediate mass stars follows Renzini and Voli (1981). The carbon deflagration model of Type I nucleosynthesis was taken from Nomoto et al. The methodology developed by Matteucci and Greggio (1986) for incorporating multiple types of supernovae into the basic equation of chemical evolution was adopted. Further assumptions include a Schmidt (1959) n=2 surface density birth rate, a Miller-Scalo (1974) initial mass function and Chiosi and Matteucci's (1982) functional form for the infall of primordial material.

A typical computation of the Type II and Type I supernovae rates are shown in Figure 1. The models indicate that over a physically reasonable range of model parameters that Type II core collapse events occur at present rate of about two every century and that the present rate of Type I supernovae is about half the rate of core collapse events. These results are in accord with the observational evidence summarized by Van der Bergh (this conference). Note that averaged over the age of the Galaxy, single zone models of chemical evolution yield a core collapse rate of about one every 25 years. As the Galaxy ages, a larger and larger percentage of the iron is attributable to Type I supernovae; the computations suggesting about 65 percent in the present epoch ($\sim$ 12Gy). A similar conclusion was reached by Matteucci and Greggio (1986). It is precisely for this reason, namely, that the bulk of the Galactic oxygen is produced by short lifetime massive stars and that the bulk of Galactic iron is produced by Type I's that produces the [O/Fe] versus [Fe/H] trends observed in F and G main sequence stars by Sneden, Lambert, and Whitaker (1979) and Clegg, Lambert, and Tomkin (1981).

Based on the relatively standard models of chemical evolution adopted here one would conclude that Type II supernovae occur at a present rate of about 2 per century and have occurred at an average rate of about 4 per century over the lifetime of the Galactic disk. Furthermore, Type II supernovae produce the majority of oxygen and other mid atomic weight elements while Type I supernovae produce the bulk of iron peak elements in the Galactic disk.

References

Arnett, W. D. 1978, Ap. J., **219**, 1008.

Arnett, W. D., Schramm, D. N., Truran, J. W. 1989, Ap. J., **339**, L25.

Chiosi, C., Matteucci, F. M., 1982, Astron. Astrophys., **105**, 140.

Clegg, R. E. S., Lambert, D. L., Tomkins, J. 1981, Ap. J., **250**, 262.

Matteucci, F. M., Greggio, L. 1986, Astron. Astrophys., **154**, 279.

Miller, G. E., Scalo, J. M. 1979, Ap. J., **41**, 513.

Nomoto, K., Thielemann, F. K., Yokoi, K. 1984, Ap. J., **286**, 644.

Press, W. H., Flannery, B. P., Teukolsky, S. A., Vetterling, W. T. 1986 Numerical Recipes: *The Art of Scientific Computing*, (Cambridge Univ. Press; Cambridge).

Renzini, A., Voli, M. 1978, Ap. J., **219**, 1008.

Schmidt, M. 1959, Ap. J., **129**, 243.

Sneden, C., Lambert, D. L., Whitaker, R. W. 1979, Ap. J., **234**, 964.

Talbot, R. J., Arnett, W. D. 1971, Ap. J., **170**, 409.

Talbot, R. J., Arnett, W. D. 1973, Ap. J., **186**, 151.

Talbot, R. J., Arnett, W. D. 1975, Ap. J., **197**, 551.

Woosley, S. E. 1986, *Nucleosynthesis and Chemical Evolution*, Hauk, B., Maeder, A., eds. (Geneva Obs.: Geneva), 1-195.

Woosley, S. E. 1989, *Supernovae*, Petschek, A. G., ed. (Springer-Verlag: Berlin), 1-25.

Van den Bergh, S. 1989, This Conference, preprint.

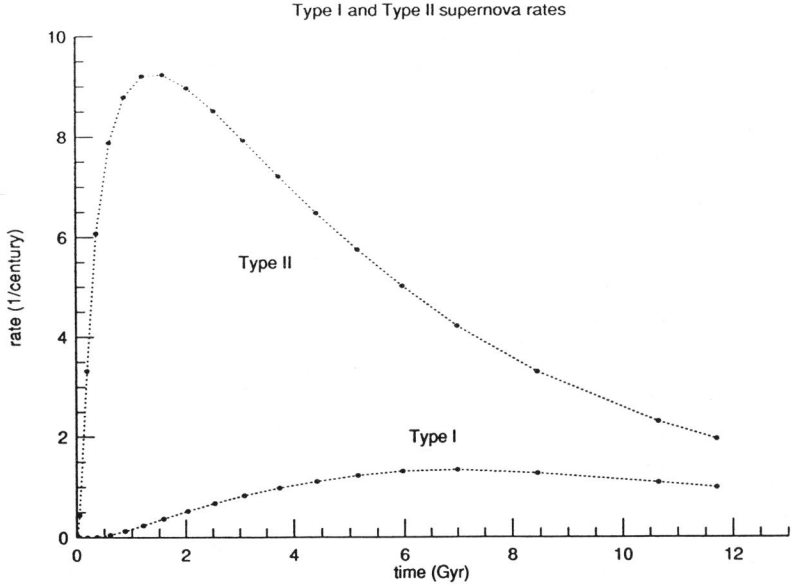

Fig. 1 - The evolution of the number of Type I and Type II supernovae events per century. The average Type II rate is between 3.5 and 5.0 per century, depending on the model parameters, while the average Type I rate is between 2.5 and 1.0 per century.

The p-Process in a Realistic Supernova Model

N. Prantzos, M. Hashimoto, M. Rayet, & M. Arnould

The astrophysically most plausible site for the synthesis of the ($Z \geq 34$) neutron deficient isotopes (the "p−nuclei") seems to be the deep interior of highly evolved massive stars. There, (γ, n) photodisintegrations of preexisting more neutron rich ($s-$ and $r-$) species, possibly followed by cascades of (γ, p) and (γ, α) reactions, lead to the production of $p-$nuclei for temperatures ranging roughly from 2 to 3.2×10^9 K. Such a $p-$process is expected to occur in O/Ne layers during a type II supernova explosion (Woosley and Howard, 1978), as well as during a presupernova hydrostatic oxygen burning phase (Arnould, 1976), where radiative proton captures might also contribute to the production of some light $p-$nuclei.

Recently, Rayet, Prantzos and Arnould (1989; henceforth RPA) reinvestigated the $p-$process in the oxygen rich layer of an exploding massive star using a parametrized model where the explosion is simulated by a sudden increase of temperature and density to peak values, followed by an exponential decrease. They used an extended network providing a reliable basis for a self-consistent calculation of a long suite of $12 \leq A \leq 210$ nuclides (see RPA for details) as well as background neutron, proton and helium concentrations. The seed nuclei abundance distribution was obtained by an $s-$process calculation during core helium burning (see e.g. Prantzos et al. 1987). With the simple assumption of six shells of equal mass and constant peak density of 10^6 g cm^{-3}, heated to peak temperatures between 2.2 and 3.2×10^9 K, RPA obtained a $p-$nuclei abundance pattern comparable to the solar system distribution within a factor 3, for 60% of the 35 $p-$isotopes.

In this work, we consider the $p-$process in a realistic type II supernova model recently proposed by Hashimoto et al.(1989) in order to compare their explosive nucleosynthetic yields with spectroscopic observations from SN1987A. The presupernova model, fully described in Nomoto and Hashimoto (1988), consists of an evolved 6 $M_\odot$ helium star, corresponding to the helium core of a 20 $M_\odot$ star, and containing in particular an oxygen/neon rich layer at 1.67 $M_\odot < M_r \leq 3.66\ M_\odot$. An explosion energy of 10^{51} erg is deposited at the inner edge of the ejecta and the changes in temperatures and densities, due to the shock wave propagation and nuclear burning, are calculated hydrodynamically (Shigeyama et al., 1988).

Inspired by previous $p-$process calculations, we select a zone in this layer, where the material is heated during the explosion to a peak temperature T_p ranging from 3.2 to 2.0×10^9 K. Such a zone is located towards the inner edge of the O/Ne layer, at 1.80 $M_\odot \leq M_r \leq 2.05\ M_\odot$, with peak densities ρ_p ranging from 7.2 to 1.9×10^5 g cm^{-3}. A $p-$process calculation was performed in this region with the same input physics as in RPA. For consistency however, seed nuclei abundances were first obtained by an $s-$process calculation during the He burning phase of the 6 $M_\odot$ helium core. Another difference with RPA comes from the use of realistic temperature and density profiles, $T(t)$ and $\rho(t)$. In RPA, T and ρ decayed with a constant timescale given (for ρ) by the hydrodynamic free expansion time $446 \times \rho_p$(g cm^{-3})$^{-1/2}$ s. Here

$T(t)$ and $\rho(t)$ decay also in an almost exponential manner, but with timescales which, systematically, are by a factor 2 smaller than the free expansion values obtained with the corresponding values of ρ_p. On the other hand, since ρ_p is as small as $2 \times 10^5\,\mathrm{g\,cm^{-3}}$ in our outermost shells (5 times smaller than in RPA), the decay times in both calculations are in fact comparable in the regions with small values of T_p, while in the inner region ($T_p \geq 2.4$) they become significantly smaller than in RPA.

Figure 1 shows the overproduction factors obtained for a sample of $p-$nuclei from ^{74}Se to ^{190}Pt as a function of T_p. It is seen that each species is produced in a very narrow range of temperature, lower mass nuclei requiring for their synthesis higher values of T_p than the heavier ones. The corresponding mass range involved in the O/Ne layer is also shown on Figure 1. The average overproduction factors $<X>/X_\odot$, where $<X>$ is the mass fraction averaged over the whole 0.25 $M_\odot$ considered layer, are plotted in Figure 2 for the 35 species usually classified as either pure or dominantly $p-$isotopes. This abundance pattern, obtained in realistic astrophysical conditions, essentially confirms the results obtained in the parametrized model of RPA. However, the mean overproduction factor for the 35 $p-$nuclei is only 26, which is small compared to the values $100 - 200$ obtained in RPA. This can be explained by the use of the LMC metallicity for calculating the $s-$process seed nuclei as well as by some dilution effect due to the inclusion in this calculation of a relatively thick layer with $2 \leq T_p \leq 2.2\,10^9$ K, where very few $p-$nuclei are produced.

On the other hand, ^{180}Ta is abundantly produced in these layers, which is the first successful attempt to synthesize this especially fragile odd-odd isotope in comparatively large quantities by photonuclear processes (see e.g. Woosley and Howard, 1978). Further investigations are needed to examine the role of the rather large background neutron concentrations obtained with our network in the present model.

Considering the underproduced species of Figure 2, our conclusions are the same as in RPA where their case was discussed in detail. Summing up, ^{113}In, ^{115}Sn, ^{152}Gd and ^{164}Er can in fact be considered as $s-$isotopes, some with slight $p-$process contributions, while other mechanisms are usually invoked to explain the synthesis of ^{138}La. The underproduction of the Mo and Ru $p-$isotopes, the most abundant in the solar system, remains, as expected, unsolved.

The production of ^{146}Sm in the $p-$process has been discussed several times (see e.g. Woosley and Howard, 1978), owing to its relation with the much debated existence of ^{142}Nd/^{144}Nd anomalies in meteorites. The interest in ^{146}Sm has recently been revived by Printzhofer et al. (1989) who have obtained clear evidence of such anomalies in 2 meteorites, from which they conclude to an abundance ratio $P = {}^{146}\mathrm{Sm}/{}^{144}\mathrm{Sm} = 0.015$ at the time of formation of the solar system. Our $p-$process calculation gives a ratio $P = 0.14$, where most of the contribution to ^{146}Sm comes from its short-lived, semi magic ($N = 82$), progenitor ^{146}Gd. Comparison of these two numbers has far reaching implications for the nucleosynthetic history of the galaxy, that will be discussed elsewhere. We only want to note here that, from RPA's calculations, a ratio $P = 0.56$ is obtained, which indicates the sensitivity of P to the detailed astrophysical conditions in which the $p-$process takes place.

We must finally mention that in order to evaluate the enrichment of the supernova ejecta in $p-$nuclei, one must consider the dilution of the latter in the 1.48 $M_\odot$ of oxygen emitted in Hashimoto et al. (1989) model. Since the $p-$nuclei are only produced inside a thin layer of 0.25 $M_\odot$, their mean overabundance will become as small as 0.03 when normalized to ^{16}O. This difficulty, which also arises whith the same acuity for several light elements (see Figure 4 of Hashimoto et al., 1989) might be much alleviated in the explosion of stars with, 1) lower mass (13 to 15 $M_\odot$), which develop relatively smaller oxygen layers (see e.g. Nomoto and Hashimoto, 1988) and, 2) higher metallicity. The $p-$process could occur in such conditions within a larger fraction of the oxygen layer and with a higher efficiency.

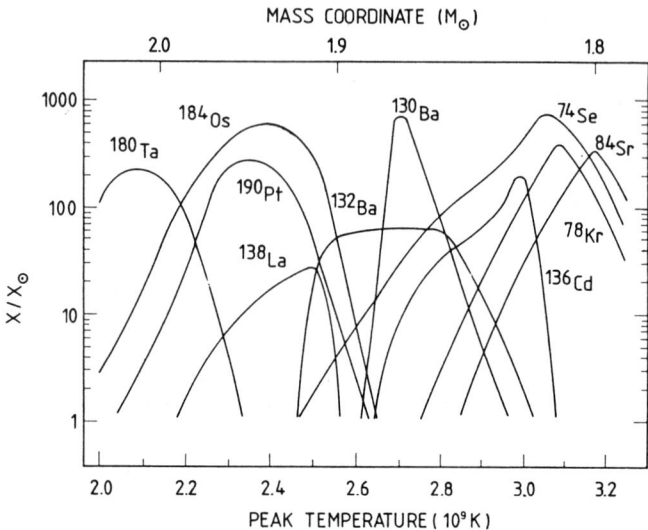

Fig. 1.—Overproduction factors for several p—nuclei as a function of T_p

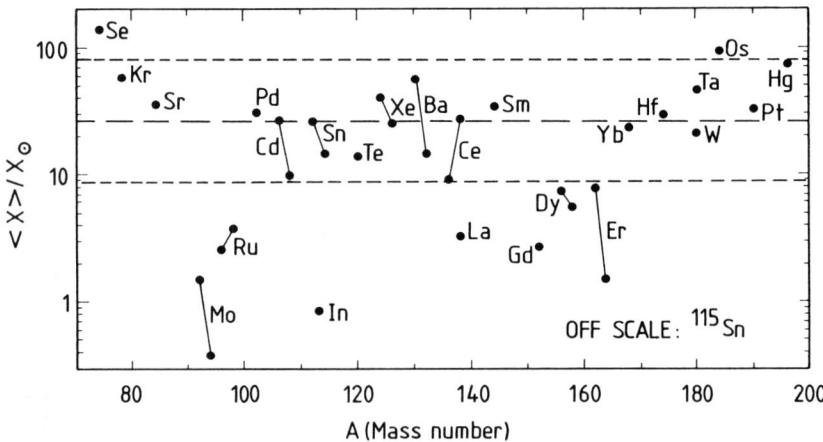

Fig. 2.—The p—nuclei overproduction factors averaged over the whole considered layer. The mean overproduction is shown by the long-dashed line. Solid lines join p—isotopes of the same element

References

Arnould, M. 1976, *Astr. Ap.*, **8**, 436.
Hashimoto, M., Nomoto, K., and Shigeyama, T. 1989, *Astr. Ap.*, **210**, L5.
Nomoto, K., and Hashimoto, M. 1988, *Phys. Rept.*, **163**, 13.
Prantzos, N., Arnould, M., and Arcoragi, J.-P. 1987, *Ap.J.*, **315**, 209.
Prinzhofer, A., Papanastassiou, D.A. and Wasserburg, G.J. 1989, to appear in *Ap.J.(Letters)*
Rayet, M., Prantzos, N., and Arnould, M., 1989, to appear in *Astr. Ap.*
Shigeyama, T., Nomoto, K., and Hashimoto, M., 1988, *Astr. Ap.*, **196**, 141.
Woosley, S.E., and Howard, W.M. 1978, *Ap.J.Suppl.*, **36**, 285.

Neutrino Nucleosynthesis in Massive Stars
Dieter Hartmann

Nucleosynthesis induced by the neutrino burst accompanying core collapse and neutron star formation in massive stars was first studied by DOMOGATSKII ET AL. [1] and WOOSLEY [2]. Since these pioneering studies significant improvements in our understanding of Type II supernovae and weak interactions as well as the direct observation of SN 1987A in ν–light have substantiated the arguments for this ν–process. Recent work by EPSTEIN, COLGATE, and HAXTON [3] and WOOSLEY and HAXTON [4] suggest that a large number of elements could owe their existence in nature to ν–reactions in supernovae. A study of this process including shock wave propagation was carried out by WOOSLEY ET AL. [5;WH^3] for selected zones of a 20 M$_\odot$ star. This paper describes essential features of the ν–process and discusses some of the results obtained by WH^3.

I. Core Collapse Neutrino Burst

The dynamic collapse of massive stars is initiated by photodissociation of iron peak nuclei and electron capture on free protons and heavy nuclei. The electron neutrinos generated by the capture process are trapped inside the collapsing core when $\rho \sim 10^{12}$ g cm^{-3}. In analogy to stellar photospheres one can define an energy–dependent neutrinosphere at which the total 'optical depth" is of order unity. This surface, located at r $\sim$ 50–100 km, radiates $\sim 10^{51}$ ergs during infall ($\sim$ 100 ms). When the core density exceeds nuclear matter density the repulsive nuclear force causes core bounce which drives a strong shock wave through the collapsing envelope [6]. When the shock front reaches the neutrinosphere a burst of $\nu\bar{\nu}$–pairs of all flavors is released. This spike ($\sim$ 4 ms), followed by a cooling tail ($\sim$ 10–20 ms), carries $\sim$ 3 10^{51} ergs. However, the total amount of energy lost due to neutrino emission during infall and shock breakout is small compared to the total binding energy of the neutron star that has to be released in the supernova event. Depending on the details of the nuclear matter equation of state the binding energy is approximately 3 10^{53} ergs (e.g. [7]). The bulk of this energy is emitted during the Kelvin-Helmholtz cooling phase of the proto neutron star lasting several seconds [8]. The energy is equipartitioned between all neutrino flavors. WH^3 assumed the neutrino energy spectrum to be of Fermi-Dirac form with an effective temperature T_ν and zero chemical potential. The mean neutrino energy is then related to the temperature by $\bar{\epsilon}_\nu = 3.15\ T_\nu$. Because the heavy lepton neutrinos (ν_μ, ν_τ) interact with matter only via neutral current interactions, their mean free path is much larger than that of the electron neutrinos. Consequently their neutrinospheres are located further inside the star resulting in a larger neutrino temperature. Expected values are T(ν_e) $\sim$ 4–5 MeV and T(ν_μ) $\sim$ T(ν_τ) $\sim$ 2 T(ν_e). Recent calculations of neutrino transport in Type II supernovae by JANKA and HILLEBRANDT [9] show that the mean neutrino energy remains approximately constant during the first $\sim$ 10 s following shock breakout, but indicate that the energy distribution is non-thermal. The total energy emitted in all neutrino flavors ($\sim$ 3 10^{53}

ergs) can be described by an exponentially decaying luminosity with time constant $\tau_\nu \sim 3$ s. At a radius r = 10^9 r_9 cm inside the star the neutrino flux is then given by

$$\Phi_\nu \sim 2.5\, 10^{38}\, r_9^{-2}\, E_{53}\, T_\nu\, \tau_\nu\, exp\left(-t/\tau_\nu\right)\, cm^{-2} s^{-1}. \tag{1}$$

Consider now ν–interactions in the various shells of heavy elements in the star.

II. Explosive Neutrino Nucleosynthesis

Because of their higher temperatures, μ– and τ–neutrinos can efficiently excite nuclei to particle unbound states by inelastic neutral current scattering: $(Z, A) + \nu \rightarrow (Z,A)^* + \nu'$. The excited nuclei then decay by n, p, d, t, α, or multiple particle emission. WH[3] also include charged current cross sections in their study. Nucleons and nuclei generated by neutrino spallation then continue the nucleosynthesis by reacting with the supernova environment. EPSTEIN ET AL. [3] suggest that neutron spallation off ^{4}He in helium-rich zones could significantly contribute to, or perhaps even generate, the elusive r-process. A realistic simulation of the ν–process must include full nuclear network calculations to take reactions due to ν–induced particles into account. Furthermore, a consistent treatment of the ν–irradiation and nuclear flows must also include effects due to the passage of the shock wave. Some stellar zones experience the neutrino flux during the cooling phase following shock ejection while in other zones the ν–induced modifications are already completed when the shock arrives. Explosive nucleosynthesis can be simulated assuming adiabatic expansion on the hydrodynamic time scale $\tau_{dyn} \sim 446/\sqrt{\rho}$ s. In the case of Type II supernovae, WEAVER and WOOSLEY [10] found that, at a time when the shock wave is traversing the mantel of heavy elements, the temperature jumps to its peak value

$$T_p \sim 2.4 \mp \gamma 10^9\, E_{51}^{1/4}\, r_9^{-3/4}\, K \tag{2}$$

where E_{51} is the total kinetic energy of the supernova in units of 10^{51} ergs. The peak temperature can also be estimated solving the Rankine-Hugoniot equations assuming, as detailed models suggest, that the portion of the supernova behind the shock is nearly isothermal and radiation dominated. Due to the radial expansion (v $\sim 5\, 10^3$ km s^{-1}) the neutrino flux during the post-shock phase declines more rapidly than the assumed exponential decay. The neutrino reaction rates after shock arrival are thus given by

$$\lambda_\nu = \sigma(T_\nu)\, \Phi_\nu\, b_c \left(1 + \frac{v_9}{r_9(0)}(t - t_0)\right)^{-2}, \tag{3}$$

where the shock arrival time t_0 can be estimated using the Sedov solution

$$t_0 \sim 0.7\, r_9 \left(\frac{M_{env}}{E_{51}}\right)^{1/2} s, \tag{4}$$

with M_{env} being the Lagrangian mass coordinate at radius $r_9(0)$ minus the remnant mass (1.4 $M_\odot$). For details of the calculation of the inelastic neutrino scattering across section $\sigma(T_\nu)$ and the branching ratio for emission of particle c we refer the reader to WH[3] and HAXTON [11]. The qualitative features of the nuclear response to neutrinos of energies up to $\sim$ 150 MeV are well understood. The threshold response is determined by allowed Gamow-Teller transitions. The allowed response should be weak for closed-shell nuclei like ^{4}He, ^{16}O, and ^{40}Ca, where such transitions are Pauli blocked, but relatively strong for nuclei located between closed shells. Because of first-forbidden operators the higher energy μ– and τ–neutrinos can strongly excite the supermultiplet giant resonances. These transitions are direct analogs of the giant E1 resonance observed in nuclear photoabsorption. WH[3] carried out full shell model calculations of neutral and charged current cross sections for a set of 18 "node nuclei" that included most of the abundant network spescies between ^{4}He and ^{80}Zr. Cross sections for non-node nuclei were obtained by interpolation. Theoretical uncertainties in the cross section calculations are estimated to be less than $\sim 10\%$.

III. Results

When one considers the declining number of stars of increasing mass and the fact that more massive stars exhibit greater absolute yields of heavy elements one arrives at a representative Type II supernova with M $\sim$ 25 M$_\odot$. Together with the relevance of SN1987A for determining the ν–properties of Type II supernovae a 10 M$_\odot$ star is motivated for a study of the dominant features of the ν–process. WH^3 adopted a model of WOOSLEY and WEAVER [12] that was evolved without mass loss. Because the stellar model carries only 13 major species a separate calculation using a much larger reaction network has to be carried out "off-line" to determine initial compositions for the various zones under consideration. Population I and II abundance sets were calculated using a scaled solar abundance distribution.

Consider the nucleosynthetic signature of the ν–process when various stellar zones of given initial composition are subjected to the thermodynamic conditions and neutrino flux described in previous sections. Here we emphasize only those elements that are produced by the ν–process in large enough amounts to account for their solar abundance. A large number of species experience significant production enhancements, such as the γ–ray line isotopes ^{26}Al and ^{22}Na, but an absolute calibration of their yield requires more accurate and complete stellar model calculations that include effects of convection in the presupernova star. Typically the ratio of the mass fraction of major elements in the ejecta to their solar mass fraction fall in the range P $\sim$ 5–10 ([10]). Thus for an isotope to be produced by the ν–process in significant amounts one requires

$$\int \frac{X}{X_\odot}(m)dm \sim P\, M_{ej}. \quad (5)$$

For example, an isotope created with a production factor $X/X_\odot = 200$ in 0.5 M$_\odot$ of the star would be equivalent to a production factor of ~ 5 in the entire star and would therefore be counted as a "success." Successful production of mass 7 and 11 elements results in the arguably most significant change of current nucleosynthesis paradigms. WH^3 find that ^{7}Li and ^{11}B (but not ^{6}Li, ^{9}Be, and ^{10}B) are produced by $^4He(\nu,\nu'n)^3He(\alpha,\gamma)^7Be(\alpha,\gamma)^{11}C$ and $^4He(\nu,\nu'p)^3H(\alpha,\gamma)^7Li(\alpha,\gamma)^{11}B$. The nuclei ^{7}Be and ^{11}C decay to ^{7}Li and ^{11}B, respectively. Mass 7,11 production requires high ^{4}He seed abundances. In the 20 M$_\odot$ model studied by WH^3 this occurs either in the helium shell or in the innermost shells to be ejected from the supernova which expand so rapidly that the freeze-out from NSF is rich in α particles. Lithium has been regarded as either a product of cosmic ray spallation (CRS) or Big Bang nucleosynthesis [13]. Boron is also traditionally a CRS product. However, ^{11}B is not well produced in past studies of CRS which has led to the hypothesis that cosmic rays might have an (unobservable) alternate low-energy component [13]. The results of WH^3 argue against such a contrivance.

Another isotope successfully produced by supernova neutrinos appear to be ^{19}F whose nucleosynthetic origin has traditionally been very uncertain. The results of WH^3 confirm those of WOOSLEY and HAXTON [4] who showed that fluorine is chiefly a product of the ν–process operating in the neon shell. Although fluorine can also be produced in the presupernova star by partial helium burning recent studies of the ν–process confirm the conclusion of WH^3 that ν–production of ^{19}F predominates in massive stars.

Perhaps the most intriguing implication of the ν–process is the possibility that spallation of neutrons off ^{4}He in the helium zone could provide the elusive site of the r-process [3]. WH^3

explored many circumstances in this respect but did not find a successful site in which the solar r-process might be produced. Although some simulations gave r-process like neutron exposures, the neutrons liberated in those cases were not due to ν–spallation but rather reflect the occurrence of explosive helium burning as the shock passes through a mixture of helium, iron, and ^{18}O or ^{22}Ne. However, for very small metallicities (less than 0.001 solar), compact stellar progenitors (helium shell at r $\sim$ 10^9 cm), and small neutron capture cross sections on major poisons (such as ^{12}C) a ν–induced r-process contribution could be significant. While these results suggest that a ν–r-process from low mass stars in the very early Galaxy might be observable in extremely metal deficient stars, the origin of the present day r-process must invoke other causes.

References

1. G. V. Domogatskii, R. A. Eramzhyan, and D. K. Nadozhin 1978, *Ap. Space Sci..,* **58,** 273.
2. S. E. Woosley 1977, *Nature,* **269,** 42.
3. R. I. Epstein, S. Colgate, and W. Haxton 1988, *Phys. Rev. Lett.,* **61,** 2038.
4. S. E. Woosley and W. Haxton 1988, *Nature,* **334,** 45.
5. S. E. Woosley, D. Hartmann, R. Hoffman, and W. Haxton 1990, *Ap. J.,* in press.
6. E. Baron, these proceedings.
7. J. Cooperstein 1988, *Phys. Rep.,* **163,** 95.
8. A. Burrows and J. Lattimer 1986, *Ap. J.,* **307,** 178.
9. H.-T. Janka and W. Hillebrandt 1989, *Astr. Ap. Suppl.,* **78,** 375.
10. S. E. Woosley and T. A. Weaver 1986, *Ann. Rev. Astr. Ap.,* **24,** 205.
11. W. C. Haxton 1988, *Phys. Rev. Letters,* **60,** 1999.
12. S. E. Woosley and T. A. Weaver 1988, *Phys. Rep.,* **163,** 79.
13. M. Arnould and M. Forestini 1989, in *Nuclear Astrophysics,* eds. M. Lozano, M. I. Gallardo, and J. M. Arias (Springer Verlag Berlin: Heidelberg), p. 48.

Possible Gamma-Ray Signatures of an r-Process Event

Bradley S. Meyer & W. Michael Howard

The r-(or rapid) process of neutron capture nucleosynthesis is responsible for the formation of roughly half of the abundances of the nuclei with mass greater than $A \approx 80$ and for all of the actinides. It is known that the r-process occurs in a hot ($T > 10^8 K$), high neutron number density ($n_n > 10^{20} cm^{-3}$) environment where neutron captures typically occur more *rapidly* than β-decays. The nuclei thus tend to follow a path in the neutron number-proton number plane many neutrons rich of the β-stability line. At closed neutron shells ($N = 50, 82,$ and 126), the β-decay rates are especially slow so that the nuclear abundances build up at these points along the r-process path. Once the r-process has stopped, the nuclei decay from the r-process path to the stability line, thereby giving the final abundances of the r-process. The large abundances built up at the closed neutron shells then yield the three well-known abundance peaks in the r-process abundance distribution at $A = 80, 130,$ and 195. For a general review of the r-process, see SCHRAMM [1] and MATHEWS and WARD [2].

Although the general features of the r-process are well known, the actual astrophysical environment or event in which the r-process occurs remains a great mystery. Supernova explosions are perhaps the most likely event, but there has as yet been no direct evidence to support this belief. In this paper we suggest several γ-ray lines as possible signatures of a recent r-process. If these lines were observed in the ejecta of SN 1987A, we would have direct evidence for supernovae as r-process events.

The question of γ-rays from cosmic radioactivity is well-studied (see, for example, CLAYTON [3] and WOOSLEY, PINTO, and HARTMANN [4]). Apart from ^{125}Sb [3] and some transbismuth elements (CLAYTON and CRADDOCK [5]), however, r-process nuclei have not been considered as sources of cosmic γ-rays. We consider in this paper γ-rays from r-process nuclei lighter than bismuth. Since the abundance of these nuclei is fairly well-known for the solar system, we can make estimates of the γ-ray flux resulting from their decay. If the r-process producing these nuclei is greatly different from the nucleosynthesis processes producing the solar system r-process nuclei, the flux estimates will be off. The sharpness of the solar system r-process peaks argues against strong variation among r-process events, however, so we expect flux estimates made from the solar system elemental abundance distribution to be reasonably reliable.

The γ-rays that would serve as r-process signatures would result from the β-decay of nuclei from the r-process path to the β-stability line. Near the r-process path, β-decay life-times are on the order of milliseconds. As the decaying nuclei approach the stability line, however, the decay life-times become greater, reaching in some cases tens of years to thousands of years or more. Since decaying parent nuclei in many cases leave daughter nuclei in excited states, the daughter nuclei will decay to their ground states by emitting γ-rays of specific energy, thus producing signatures of a recent r-process. The count rate at time t after the r-process for a γ-ray line of energy E from such a decay is given by

$$N(E) = N_A \lambda_A \Gamma(E) \exp(-\lambda_A t), \qquad (1)$$

where N_A is the total number of nuclei of mass A produced in the r-process, λ_A is the β-decay rate of the relevant decaying A-chain nuclide, and $\Gamma(E)$ is the branching ratio of β-decay to a level at excitation energy E in the daughter nucleus followed by γ-deexcitation to the daughter nucleus ground state. Equation (1) assumes that only one nuclide in a given A-chain has a long life-time and has a daughter that emits a γ-ray. If a long-lived nucleus does not emit a γ-ray upon β-decaying but a later, shorter-lived β-decay in that A-chain does emit a γ-ray, the count rate becomes

$$N(E) = N_A \lambda_{A_1} \Gamma_{A_2}(E) \exp(-\lambda_{A_1} t), \qquad (2)$$

where λ_{A_1} is the decay rate of the long-lived nuclide A_1 and $\Gamma_{A_2}(E)$ is the branching ratio for β-decay of the short-lived nuclide A_2 to an excitation energy E in its daughter nucleus followed by γ-deexcitation to the daughter nucleus ground state.

We now consider specific candidates for signatures of a recent r-process. We choose decay A-chains that have nuclides with life-times between 200 days and 100 yrs. Gamma-rays from decays with much shorter life-times will probably be obscured by the ejecta of the r-process event. Decays with much longer life-times would produce too low a flux of γ-rays due to the small decay rate. We present the candidate γ-ray decay lines in Table 1. In this table, we identify the relevant decay, the γ-ray energy, the $\tau_{1/2}$ for that line (i.e. $\ln 2/\lambda_A$ in equation (1) or $\ln 2/\lambda_{A_1}$ in equation (2)), and the coefficient B in the following expression for the γ-ray flux at Earth of r-process γ-rays, scaled to the distance of SN 1987A:

$$F(E) = B \exp(-t \ \ln 2/\tau_{1/2}) \left(\frac{50 \ kpc}{d}\right)^2 \left(\frac{M_r}{10^{-4} M_\odot}\right) \ cm^{-2} \ s^{-1}. \qquad (3)$$

In equation (3), d is the distance to the r-process event and M_r is the mass of the r-process material produced in the event. In order to compute B, we used life-times and branching ratios given in LEDERER and SHIRLEY [6] and the solar system r-process abundance distribution in HOWARD et al. [7]. To get an estimate of M_r, we consider the case that all r-process material was formed in all supernovae. There is approximately $3 \times 10^4 \ M_\odot$ of r-process matter in the Galaxy (inferred from the data in HOWARD et al. [7] and ANDERS and EBIHARA [8]). Since the Galaxy is roughly 10^{10} years old (for example, see FOWLER and MEISL [9]) and the supernova rate is probably between $0.1 - 0.01 \ yr^{-1}$ in our Galaxy (ARNETT, SCHRAMM, and TRURAN [10] and VAN DEN BERGH, MCCLURE, and EVANS [11]), we may estimate that M_r is roughly $10^{-4} \ M_\odot$. We note that we have assumed that all γ-rays produced escape the ejecta of the r-process event. This may not be true at early time but becomes a better and better approximation as the supernova nebula density falls due to expansion. Finally, we also note that we have not included in Table 1 lines from trans-lead α-decays and β-decays since we only have theoretical predictions of the abundances of these trans-lead nuclei in an r-process event. The theoretical predictions of the abundances of these nuclei are typically less than or roughly equal to the abundances of the nuclei in Table 1, so γ-ray fluxes from these trans-lead nuclei should be roughly comparable to or less than the fluxes in Table 1. Interesting cases are the decay A-chains 210, 227, 228, 241, 252, and 257. See also [5].

From Table 1 we see that there are a number of γ-ray lines which may serve as signatures of a recent r-process. We may now consider whether these lines might be observable from SN 1987A with current observational techniques. The Oriented Scintillation Spectrometer Experiment (OSSE) of the Gamma Ray Observatory is expected to have an experimental sensitivity of about $2 \times 10^{-5} cm^{-2} \ s^{-1}$ for 0.1-10 MeV γ-rays in a 10^6 second observing session [12]. The best rate we would expect for the lines in Table 1 in the 0.1-10 MeV energy range is about $10^{-8} \ cm^{-2} \ s^{-1}$. Clearly at present the best one can probably do with GRO is to set a rather large upper limit on the amount of r-process material that could have been produced by SN 1987A, namely, $M_r < 0.2 \ M_\odot$. This limit might help confirm or rule out an exotic

Table 1. Possible γ-ray r-process signatures.

Decay	E (keV)	$\tau_{1/2}(yr)$	B
$^{90}Sr \to ^{90}Y$			
$\to ^{90}Zr$	1761	28.8	8.9(-10)
$^{106}Ru \to ^{106}Rh$			
$\to ^{106}Pd$	622.2	1.0	1.6(-8)
	511.9	1.0	3.3(-8)
$^{125}Sb \to ^{125}Te$	428.0	2.7	2.0(-8)
	35.5	2.7	5.7(-8)
$^{137}Cs \to ^{137}Ba$	661.6	30.2	1.5(-9)
$^{144}Ce \to ^{144}Pr$			
$\to ^{144}Nd$	133.5	0.8	2.6(-8)
$^{151}Sm \to ^{151}Eu$	21.5	90	3.1(-12)
$^{155}Eu \to ^{155}Gd$	105.4	4.9	3.2(-9)
	86.5	4.9	1.7(-9)
$^{171}Tm \to ^{171}Yb$	66.7	1.9	2.3(-10)
$^{194}Os \to ^{194}Ir$	43	6.0	1.7(-8)
$^{194}Ir \to ^{194}Pt$	328.5	6.0	4.9(-9)

r-process associated with SN 1987A, such as the Mystery Spot being a massive chunk ($M \sim 0.1 M_\odot$) of the core that was ejected and then underwent some r-processing (PETRICH [13]). Better limits will require improvements in experimental sensitivity and, consequently, increases in detector size. Moreover in order even to see γ-ray lines from r-process nuclei in the ejecta of SN 1987A one would probably require at least a few thousand-fold increase in sensitivity. Such an improvement would be technologically extremely challenging, if not impossible. Nevertheless, let us point out that ^{137}Cs and the $A = 90$ decay chain have half-lifes of about 30 years, so there is time to try.

We thank Charles Dermer, Mark Leising, Loren Petrich, Phil Pinto, and Stan Woosley for useful discussions and comments. This work was performed under the auspices of the U. S. Department of Energy by the Lawrence Livermore National Laboratory under Contract No. W-7405-ENG-48.

References
1. D. N. Schramm: in Essays in Nuclear Astrophysics, ed. by C. N. Barnes, D. D. Clayton, and D. N. Schramm (Cambridge University Press, Cambridge 1983), p.325.
2. G. J. Mathews, R. A. Ward: Rept. Prog. Phys. 48, 1371 (1985).
3. D. D. Clayton: in Essays in Nuclear Astrophysics, ed. by C. N. Barnes, D. D. Clayton, and D. N. Schramm (Cambridge University Press, Cambridge 1983), p. 401.
4. S. E. Woosley, P. A. Pinto, D. Hartmann: Ap. J. (1989), in press.
5. D. D. Clayton, W. Craddock: Ap. J. 142, 189 (1965).
6. Table of the Isotopes, ed. by C. M. Lederer and V. S. Shirley (John Wiley and Sons, New York, 1978).
7. W. M. Howard, G. J. Mathews, R. A. Ward, K. Takahashi: Ap. J. 309, 633 (1986).
8. E. Anders, M. Ebihara: Geochim. Cosmochim. Acta 46, 2363.
9. W. A. Fowler, C. C. Meisl: in Cosmogonical Processes, ed. by W. D. Arnett, C. J. Hansen, J. W. Truran, and S. Tsuruta (VNU Press, Singapore 1986).
10. W. D. Arnett, D. N. Schramm, J. W. Truran: Ap. J. Letters 339, L25 (1989).
11. S. Van den Bergh, R. D. McClure, R. Evans: Ap. J. 323, 44 (1987).
12. Gamma-Ray Observatory Science Plan, March 1985.
13. L. Petrich: private communication.

SECTION XII
SUPERNOVA REMNANTS AND INTERACTION WITH THE ISM

Recent Optical Studies of Supernova Remnants
Robert A. Fesen

Although supernova remnants (SNRs) have been studied the longest time at optical wavelengths, such investigations continue to provide new information and insights into the properties of Galactic and extragalactic SNRs. One reason for this is that optical SNR research can provide data not easily obtainable at other wavelengths. For example, optical studies of SNRs can yield kinematic data (proper motions and radial velocities), gas temperatures and densities, plus elemental abundances relative to hydrogen and helium – information that is at present either difficult or impossible to derive from radio, infrared, or X-ray data. Optical studies also permit the investigation of SNRs over a wide-range of ionization states; from Fe I in S Andromedae (SN 1885; FESEN, HAMILTON, and SAKEN [17]) to [Fe X] and [Fe XIV] in Puppis A, IC 443, and the Cygnus Loop (TESKE and PETRE [37,38]; BROWN, WOODGATE, and PETRE [3]; TESKE and KIRSHNER [36]). Finally, while it is true that only about 25% of the 160 known Galactic SNRs have been detected optically, this list does include the six youngest Galactic remnants known: SN 1006, SN 1054 (the Crab Nebula), SN 1181 (3C58), SN 1572 (Tycho's SN), SN 1604 (Kepler's SN), and Cas A ($\approx$ 1680).

Recent optical research on SNRs has included work on: (1) young Galactic remnants having high-velocity, nonradiative shock emission, (2) young Galactic ejecta-dominated remnants such as the Crab Nebula and Cas A, (3) extragalactic remnant surveys and studies on individual objects, and (4) detection of young remnants associated with historical observed extragalactic supernovae (SNe). Below, I briefly review some of the recent work done in these areas.

I. Young Galactic SNRs with Nonradiative Shock Emission

Optical emission seen in the remnants of SN 1006 and Tycho's SN (SN 1572) consists of thin and very faint filaments which exhibit only hydrogen Balmer-line emission. Such Balmer-dominated shock emission is often referred to as nonradiative shock emission and is interpreted as being the result of a high-velocity shock moving through a low-density medium leading to the production of both broad and narrow emission-line components (CHEVALIER, KIRSHNER, and RAYMOND [4]). A narrow component is produced by the collisional excitation of neutral atoms passing through the collisionless shock front, while a broad component results from the charge exchange with high-velocity protons. The broad component has a width corresponding to the postshock temperature and thus can be directly related to the shock's velocity.

Recently, improved observations of Tycho's SNR as well as the detection of a broad Hα emission component in SN 1006's faint optical filaments have been carried out by KIRSHNER, WINKLER, and CHEVALIER [26]. These new data have significantly improved our knowledge of these remnants' distances and shock velocities. In Tycho's remnant, a bright eastern filament was observed and found to have a broad Hα component with a width of 1800 ± 100 km s^{-1} (FWHM). This, when combined with nonradiative model calculations [4] and filament proper motion studies (HESSER and VAN DEN BERGH [23]), suggests a shock velocity of 1930 – 2670 km s^{-1} and a kinematical distance of 2.0 – 2.8 kpc. SMITH and KIRSHNER [41] have obtained now even better spectroscopic data on Tycho's nonradiative emission filaments which indicate that the broad component and thus the remnant's derived shock velocity may vary among filaments, presumably as a function of filament density. This may mean that an accurate kinematic distance to the remnant requires care in obtaining both proper motion and spectroscopic data on the same filamentary position.

Kirshner, Winkler, and Chevalier were able also to successfully detect the faint broad 2600 km s^{-1} (FWHM) emission component in SN 1006's filaments at a level just below that of the earlier data of LASKER [27]. They derive a shock velocity of 2800 – 3870 km s^{-1} and a distance of 1.5 – 2.1 kpc using the proper motion value of 0.39 ± 0.06" yr^{-1} reported by HESSER and VAN DEN BERGH [23]. A somewhat smaller but more accurate value for SN 1006's proper motion has recently been measured by LONG, BLAIR, and VAN DEN BERGH [30] who find 0.30 ± 0.04" yr^{-1}. This revised value implies a larger SN 1006 distance of 1.7 – 3.1 kpc. A distance of around 1.7 kpc is indicated by an analysis of UV observations of a sdOB star lying behind the remnant (HAMILTON and FESEN [21]).

High-velocity, nonradiative emission has now been detected in Kepler's SNR (SN 1604). This remnant had previously been known to only exhibit bright radiative emission, meaning that it's emission knots show a variety of emission lines and ionization states characteristic of dense, cooling shocks like those commonly found in older remnants. Faint emission along the remnant's northern limb first detected by D'ODORICO et al. [9] has now been shown to be nonradiative emission (FESEN et al. [13]). This emission region exhibits both narrow and broad Hα components with the broad one suggesting a shock velocity in the range 1600 – 2800 km s^{-1}. Besides yielding a direct estimate of Kepler's shock velocity, this result also means that it is possible to directly measure shock velocities in SNRs having largely radiative filaments, and raises questions about remnant classification schemes based upon the presence or absence of nonradiative emission filaments (VAN DEN BERGH [43]).

Even more recent spectroscopic studies of Kepler's optical emission obtained by BLAIR and LONG [2] indicate that not only is the nonradiative emission not confined to just the remnant's northern section but also is emitted by several knots located near the remnant's projected center. Until now, all nonradiative shock emission, whether in young or old remnants like the Cygnus Loop (see HESTER, RAYMOND, and DANIELSON [24] and references therein) has exhibited a thin, faint filamentary morphology located along the tangential edge of a remnant. Blair and Long's new results may imply that the suspected circumstellar medium around Kepler consists of a wide range of densities. The lowest density material produces the northern thin faint nonradiative filaments like present in SN 1006 and Tycho, while slightly higher density clumps produce the observed knotty nonradiative emission, with the densest clumps producing the bright, radiative emission that has been long observed in the remnant. If this is correct, then it lends support to the idea that the medium surrounding Kepler contains circumstellar mass loss material from the SN progenitor (see BANDIERA [1] and references therein).

II. Young Galactic Ejecta Dominated Remnants

The Crab Nebula: As we approach the 1990's, the Crab Nebula remains the subject of much active optical research. Indeed, several recent studies have produced important and somewhat surprising results, running contrary to the widespread feeling that the Crab is a well understood remnant.

DAVIDSON [7] obtained an integrated spectroscopic scan of the whole nebula and found that estimates of the [O III]/continuum flux ratio taken over the last 25 yr are discrepant. He suggested that either the visual continuum of the Crab may be changing rapidly at about 2% yr^{-1} or that the nebula's [O III] flux may have changed. VÉRON-CETTY and WOLTJER [45] have questioned Davidson's results using CCD images taken in 1986 and 1988 which covered the central portion of the nebula. They place an upper limit to a decrease of 0.5% on the continuum's flux and suggest the real decrease is closer to 0.3%. According to Véron-Cetty and Woltjer, this last value would indicate the pulsar resupplies about half of the energy lost in the nebula's expansion, $\approx 10^{38}$ erg s^{-1}. However, DAVIDSON [8] maintains that, since Woltjer and Véron-Cetty's results were based upon imaging of only the central portion of the nebula, the question regarding possible rapid changes in the remnant's optical brightness remains open.

In an extensive new optical study of the remnant, MACALPINE et al. [31] present spectra and images of the Crab Nebula from which they make important new claims about the remnant. They interpret N-S oriented, long-slit spectra as suggesting bipolar 'bubbles' in the Crab's filamentary structure both above and below a band of helium-rich filaments which run across the center of the remnant. They find that many of the brighter, central filaments are composed almost purely of He, as much as 95% by mass. In addition, CCD images taken using an interference filter centered on the [Ni II] 7378 Å emission line show that the remnant's Ni II emission is not distributed like that of other lines but instead is stronger primarily in the northern filaments, coincident with the low He filaments. Strong [Ni II] line strengths can be interpreted as indicating an Ni abundance as much as 55 times over solar, although the true nature of the Crab's unusually strong [Ni II] is uncertain (HENRY and FESEN [22]). Furthermore, they propose that the high Ni and low He found in the northern filaments indicate an interaction of nickel-rich ejecta with an ambient interstellar cloud in this region. MacAlpine et al. conclude that the mass of the filaments + pulsar is closer to 8 - 9 $M_\odot$ rather than the 2 - 3 $M_\odot$ of previous estimates, thereby suggesting the precursor's intial mass was around 20 - 30 $M_\odot$. If true, this would have important implications regarding the mass range of SN II progenitors since such massive stars have been implicated as possible progenitors of the hydrogen-deficient SN Ib (VAN DEN BERGH [43]; WEILER and SRAMEK [46]).

Recent optical data is beginning to resolve some of the general properties of the Crab's peculiar northern 'jet'. WOLTJER and VÉRON-CETTY [47] have reported the detection of faint optical continuum while new kinematic studies of the Crab Nebula's jet by MARCELIN et al. [32] indicate it formed around the same time as the rest of the remnant. Marcelin et al. obtained long-slit spectra which show the jet to be expanding at a velocity of 260 km s^{-1} with random motions of 60 km s^{-1}. This, when combined with improved proper studies of the jet made by STAKER and FESEN [42] which show the jet's average proper motion is $0.27 \pm 0.04''$ yr^{-1}, suggest the jet formed coeval with the rest of the nebula and both have a homologous-like expansion. Marcelin et al. support the idea that the jet formed out of an instability in the Crab's filamentary shell rather than the plasma beam models of SHULL et al. [40] or the 'shadowed flow' model of MORRISON and ROBERTS [35].

Finally, although the presence of dust in the Crab had been suggested earlier from infrared observations (GLACCUM et al. [18]; MARSDEN et al. [33]; MEZGER et al. [34]), optical data now clearly supports the idea of dust inside the denser filaments. In 1987, WOLTJER and VÉRON-CETTY [47] reported evidence of optical absorption in one bright [O III] filament. More recently, FESEN and BLAIR [16] have found that dusty filaments are present throughout the remnant and coincide not with [O III] bright filaments but ones particularly strong in low-ionization emission lines, e.g. [S II], [O I], and [C I]. Dust condensation in the Crab probably occurred early in the evolution of the remnant when the filaments were denser and had cooled to below 1000 K. The presence of dust in the Crab indicates that it can form and survive in a relatively hostel environment around an active pulsar, and may help to explain the recent discovery of molecular hydrogen in some of the Crab filaments (GRAHAM, WRIGHT, and LONGMORE [20]).

Cassiopeia A: New deep optical CCD imaging and spectra of Cas A suggests that the Cas A progenitor star may have been a Wolf-Rayet star up to the moment it exploded. FESEN, BECKER, and BLAIR [14] and FESEN, BECKER, and GOODRICH [15] have discovered more than a dozen faint emission-line knots that lie outside of the remnant's main radio and X-ray emission shells. The new ejecta knots show strong [N II] emission lines, weak or no Hα emission, and possess ejecta in velocities between 7000 and 8600 km s^{-1}. These knots are called 'fast-moving flocculi' (FMFs) and indicate that the Cas A supernova had a maximum expansion velocity of at least 8500 km s^{-1}, a thin nitrogen-rich but hydrogen-deficient envelope, an explosion date around AD 1680, and a likely WN Wolf-Rayet star progenitor. The supernova explosion apparently left no visible stellar remnant or surviving binary companion behind. Deep images by VAN DEN BERGH and PRITCHET [44] taken under excellent seeing conditions have set better magnitudes limits on the presence of a stellar remnant of 23.5 in I and 24.8 in R corresponding to $M_I \gtrsim +8.9$ and $M_R \gtrsim +9.3$. The region around Cas A's center of expansion appears void of any detectable stars.

Recent follow-up images and spectroscopic data (FESEN and BECKER [11]) continue to support the notion of a thin hydrogen and nitrogen-rich layer on the progenitor at time of SN outburst. They report the discovery of an ejecta knot lying near the base of the remnant's NE jet which possesses both the hydrogen and nitrogen emission seen in the remnant's QSFs and FMFs but also shows strong [O I], [O III], and [S II] emissions like those seen in the remnant's oxygen and sulfur-rich FMKs (see Fig. 1). In addition, new images of Cas A (FESEN [10])

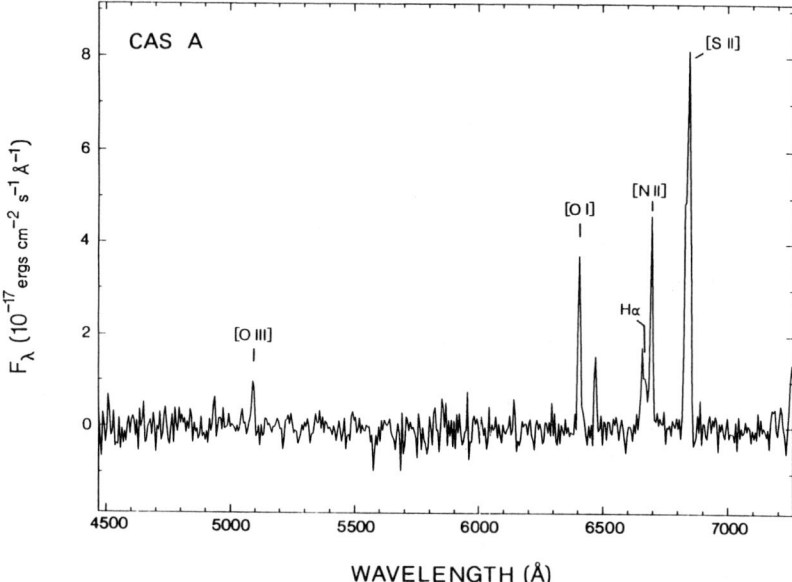

Figure 1: Optical spectrum of a 'mixed-ejecta knot' in Cas A. Knot exhibits the Hα and [N II] line emission like that of the remnant's QSFs and FMFs while also showing strong lines of [O I] 6300,6364 [O III] 4959,5007 and [S II] 6717,6731 like that seen in the FMKs.

show the remnant's NE jet of ejecta stretches out to at least a radial distance of 280″ from the center of expansion. If the explosion date is taken to be 1680 AD, then this angular separation implies an transverse velocity of nearly 13 000 km s^{-1}, assuming no deceleration. This, in turn, means that the jet, which consists largely of S and O-rich knots, was somehow ejected at velocities significantly greater than even those experienced by the progenitor's photosphere. Deep images indeed give one the impression of the jet as an eruption from the main optical shell. The origin of the jet is unknown but what is clear is that it represents an asymmetrical ejection of underlying material up through the progenitor's original surface layers. Finally, one notes that Cas A's jet, like that of the Crab Nebula, appears to lie very close to the plane of the sky thereby permitting us an excellent viewing angle.

III. Extragalactic Remnant Surveys

Although more difficult to study than Galactic SNRs due to increased distances, extragalactic remnants offer distinct advantages in the optical study of SNRs. Due to less extreme extinction variations particularly in face-on systems, it is easier to study an entire galaxy's SNR population. Moreover, while galactic remnants often have highly uncertain distances making meaningful comparisons of their optical morphologies difficult, remnants in a given galaxy are all located at approximately the same distance. Several studies of the LMC, SMC, and local group galaxies have identified now almost 100 optically visible SNRs. These have been detected largely based upon a comparison of [S II] and Hα interference images on which SNR shock emission produces larger [S II]/Hα ratios than for photoionized H II regions. Advances in the optical study of extragalactic SNRs promise to have important implications on general remnant studies.

CHU and KENNICULT [5] obtained long-slit Echelle spectra on nine LMC and SMC remnants from which they derive crude integrated velocity profiles and then use them to distinguish foreground nebula contamination from SNR spectra. They also outline a method to distinguish between SNRs and stellar wind-blown bubbles using kinematic information alone. KIRSHNER et al. [25], using spectra of the oxygen-rich LMC remnant 0540-69.3, find emission-line widths of 2735 km s^{-1} (FWZI) suggesting an expansion age of just 760 $\pm$ 50 yr. This would make it perhaps the second youngest SNR in the LMC behind SN 1987A. While this remnant is similar to Cas A in that is shows strong lines of O and S, 0540-69.3 exhibits emission of Fe, Ni, and probably Hα as well. They propose that 0540-69.3 is the young remnant formed by the core collapse of a massive star akin to SN 1987A.

One of the best galaxies to search for SNRs is M33, and LONG et al. [28] have recently completed an atlas of optically identified remnants in this galaxy. Long et al. mainly utilized the optical selection criterion of large [S II]/Hα ratios to identify remnant candidates. Their survey, which consisted of both images and spectra covering the galaxy's inner 15 arcmin region, found a total of 50 SNRs. This suggests that M33's total remnant count could be around 80. The cumulative number vs. diameter relation found for M33's SNRs appears to obey a $N(\leq D) \propto D^{2.1}$ function, substantially steeper than that indicated in previous M33 studies but suggesting an expansion law reasonably close to that of a Sedov expansion. Spectroscopic follow-up on these objects will yield electron densities and abundances which can be used with diameters to further study evolutionary effects and galactic abundance gradients.

IV. The SN–SNR Connection

Until very recently, no supernova had been observed past about 700 days after optical maximum. This led to severe difficulties in relating remnants to their parent SNe. Simply put, we observe extragalactic SNe with ages of 0 – 2 yr yet study young Galactic SNRs with ages of 300 - 2000 yr. Today this situation has changed: there are now 6 SN/SNRs known. These are SN1987A in the LMC, SN1986J in NGC 891, SN1980K in NGC 6946, SN1961V in NGC 1058, SN1957D in M83, and SN1885 in M31. The opening of the observational connection between SN and their remnants promises to be one of the most useful and active fields of SN/SNRs research.

SN 1980K: Recent optical CCD images of the SN site in NGC 6946 by FESEN and BECKER [12] revealed faint Hα emission nearly 8 years after initial outburst. This emission has remained constant to $\pm$0.2 mag between 1987.5 and 1988.6. A low dispersion 1988 spectrum shows both narrow and broad Hα line emission, broad [O I], [O III], [Fe II], and [Ca II] and/or [O II] emission, and a faint, underlying blue continuum at $\approx$ 24 mag (see Fig. 2). All broad emission lines appear to have

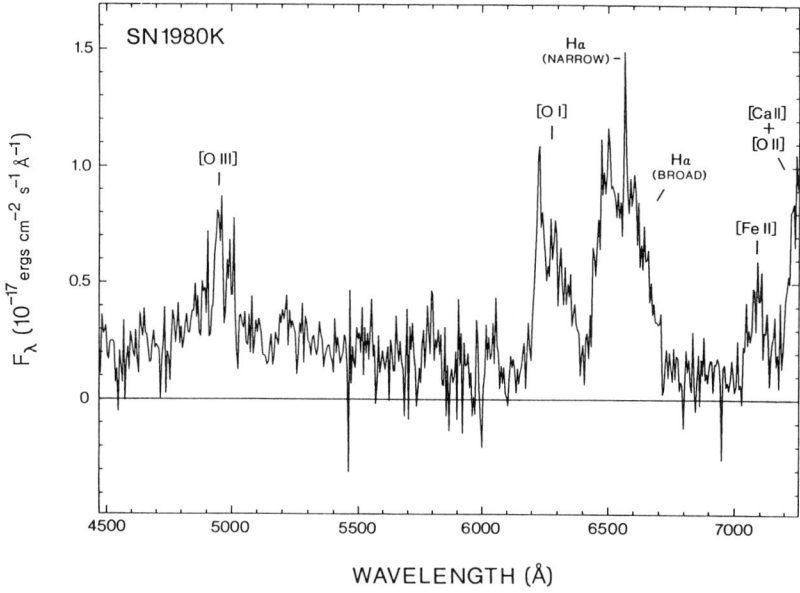

Figure 2: August 1988 spectrum of SN 1980K (Day 2844); from FESEN and BECKER [12].

mean blueshifted line centers possibly indicating the formation of dust within SN 1980K's ejecta. Expansion velocities suggest two distinct emission regions; i.e., a hydrogen-rich zone ($V_{exp} \approx 6900$ km s^{-1}) plus an oxygen- and iron-rich zone ($V_{exp} \approx 5300 - 5500$ km s^{-1}). The narrow Hα emission likely originates in the SN's circumstellar material with the faint blue continuum arising from the pre-SN's parent OB association. Detection of optical emission from the narrow Hα emission likely originates in the SN's circumstellar material with the faint blue continuum arising from the pre-SN's parent OB association. The answer to the key question of the origin of SN 1980K's late-time energy source may be the interaction of the SN's ejecta and shock wave with this circumstellar matter.

SN 1961V: Exhibiting perhaps one of the most unusual SN light curves, SN 1961V in NGC 1058 was classified as the prototype for Type V SNe by Zwicky. It showed narrow H emission lines ($V_{exp} = 2000$ km s^{-1}), and is the only SN other than SN 1987A to have been observed prior to outburst – in this case as an 18th mag star at least back to 1937. Spectra of the site reveals broad Hα emission (FWHM = 2100 km s^{-1}) with a luminosity of 2×10^{36} erg s^{-1} (GOODRICH et al. [19]). Goodrich et al. argue that SN 1961V was not a true SN event (i.e. the explosion of a massive star ending its life) but instead was an eta Car like outburst of a very massive star with the progenitor surviving having faded optically due to the formation of a dusty 1 - 10 M$_\odot$ circumstellar shell. They argue that the progenitor must be one of the most massive and luminous stars known with M$_{ZAMS} \gtrsim 240$ M$_\odot$ and believe it is currently of type Of/WN.

SN 1957D: LONG, BLAIR, and KRZEMINSKI [29], using deep interference filter images of the inner portion of M83, have detected the optical remnant of SN at the exact position where COWAN and BRANCH [6] had detected nonthermal radio emission. Spectra show broad [O III] emission (FWHM $\approx$ 2500 km s^{-1}) suggesting the formation of an oxygen-rich, Cas A-like remnant. Improved follow-up spectra have been obtained by TURRATO and DANZIGER [39] which reveal [O I] 6300 and possibly Hα and [S II] emission lines in addition to the [O III] line emission. Unfortunately, no spectra near outburst were taken, leaving its SN classification type unknown.

SN 1885: The first ever observed extragalactic SN, commonly known as S And, occurred in the nuclear bulge of M31, just 16" from the nucleus. Because this SN showed no bright hydrogen lines near outburst, the object has been classified as a SN I pec. If really a Type I and thus the probable explosion of a wd, then its remnant could be Fe-rich. Also, if S And occurred on the near side of M31's bulge, then its remnant might produce an observable patch of obscuration silhouetted against M31's bright nuclear bulge. FESEN, HAMILTON, and SAKEN [17] have successfully detected the remnant as an unresolved spot of obscuration located within 1" of S And's reported position by using a interference-filter centered on the Fe I resonance line at 3860 Å. This detection suggests SN 1885's remnant is iron-rich, relatively cool, expanding at $\approx$ 5000 km s^{-1} and is located on near side of the galaxy's bulge.

V. Summary

Future optical SNR research seems promising. In the study of Galactic remnants, further work on young objects such as Puppis A, 3C58, and G292.0+1.8 may provide valuable clues as to the nature of their progenitors and thus indicate the SN type involved. A more complete study of the properties of all young Galactic SNRs will help better define their differences and thus lead to an improved understanding on the variety of SN types.

The field of extragalactic SNR research has taken on a new importance in light of the recent detections of remnants associated with historic SNe thereby finally allowing us to directly connect SN events with SNR types. Although preliminary work indicates that such detections may be rare, the presence of optical emission from the quite normal Type II SN 1980K nearly 8 years after outburst indicates the formation of a young, bright supernova remnant. This raises hope that similarly detectable levels of optical emission may exist for at least some other young extragalactic SNe particularly those with detectable nonthermal radio emission.

REFERENCES

1. R. Bandiera: Ap. J. 319, 885 (1987).
2. W. P. Blair and K. S. Long: in preparation (1989).
3. L. W. Brown, B. E. Woodgate, and R. Petre: Ap. J. 334, 852 (1988).
4. R. A. Chevalier, R. P. Kirshner, and J. C. Raymond: Ap. J. 235, 186 (1980).
5. Y.-H. Chu and R. C. Kennicutt: A. J. 95, 1111 (1988).

6. J. J. Cowan and D. Branch: Ap. J. 293, 400 (1985).
7. K. Davidson: A. J. 94, 964 (1987).
8. K. Davidson: Sky and Telescope 78, 341 (1989).
9. S. D'Odorico, R. Bandiera, J. Danziger, and P. Focardi: A. J. 91, 1382 (1986).
10. R. A. Fesen: in preparation (1989).
11. R. A. Fesen and R. H. Becker: in preparation (1989).
12. R. A. Fesen and R. H. Becker: Ap. J. in press (1989).
13. R. A. Fesen, R. H. Becker, W. P. Blair, and K. S. Long: Ap. J. (Letters), 338, L13 (1989).
14. R. A. Fesen, R. H. Becker, W. P. Blair: Ap. J. 313, 378 (1987).
15. R. A. Fesen, R. H. Becker, R. W. Goodrich: Ap. J. (Letters) 329, L89 (1988).
16. R. A. Fesen and W. P. Blair: Ap. J. submitted (1989).
17. R. A. Fesen, A. J. S. Hamilton, and J. M. Saken: Ap. J. (Letters) 341, L55 (1989).
18. W. Glaccum, D. A. Harper, R. F. Loewenstein, R. Pernic, and F. L. Low: Bull. A.A.S. 14, 612 (1982).
19. R. W. Goodrich, G. S. Stringfellow, G. D. Penrod, and A. V. Filippenko: Ap. J., in press.
20. J. R. Graham, G. S. Wright, and A. J. Longmore: preprint (1989).
21. A. J. S. Hamilton and R. A. Fesen: Ap. J. 327, 178 (1988).
22. R. B. C. Henry and R. A. Fesen: Ap. J. 329 693 (1988).
23. J. E. Hesser and S. van den Bergh: Ap. J. 251, 549 (1981).
24. J. J. Hester, J. C. Raymond, and G. E. Danielson: Ap. J. (Letters) 303, L17 (1986).
25. R. P. Kirshner, J. A. Morse, P. F. Winkler, and W. P. Blair: Ap. J. 342 , 260 (1989).
26. R. P. Kirshner, P. F. Winkler, and R. A. Chevalier: Ap. J. (Letters) 315, L135 (1987).
27. B. M. Lasker: Ap. J. 244, 517 (1981).
28. K. S. Long, W. P. Blair, R. P. Kirshner, and P. F. Winkler: Ap. J. in press.
29. K. S. Long, W. P. Blair, and W. Krzeminski: Ap. J. (Letters) 340, L25 (1989).
30. K. S. Long, W. P. Blair, and S. van den Bergh: Ap. J. 333, 749 (1988).
31. G. M. MacAlpine, S. S. McGaugh, J. M. Mazzarella, and A. Uomoto: Ap. J. 342, 364 (1989).
32. M. Marcelin, M.-P. Véron-Cetty, L. Woltjer, J. Boulesteix, S. D'Odorico, and E. Lecoarer: preprint (1989).
33. P. L. Marsden, F. C. Gillett, R. E. Jennings, J. P. Emerson, T. De Jong, and F. M. Olnon: Ap. J. (Letters) 278, L29 (1984).
34. P. G. Mezger, R. J. Tuffs, R. Chini, E. Kreysa, and H.-P. Gemund: Astr. Ap. 167, 145 (1986).
35. P. Morrison and D. Roberts: Nature 313, 661 (1985).
36. R. G. Teske and R. P. Kirshner: Ap. J. 292, 22 (1985).
37. R. G. Teske and R. Petre: Ap. J. 314, 673 (1987).
38. R. G. Teske and R. Petre: Ap. J. 318, 370 (1987).
39. M. Turrato and I. J. Danziger: ESO Messeger, June 1989.
40. P. Shull, U. Carsenty, M. Sarcander, and T. Neckel: Ap. J. 285, L75 (1984).

41. R. Smith and R. P. Kirshner: in preparation (1989).
42. B. Staker and R. A. Fesen: in preparation.
43. S. van den Bergh: Ap. J. 327, 156 (1988).
44. S. van den Bergh and C. J. Pritchet: Ap. J. 307, 723 (1986).
45. M.-P. Véron-Cetty and L. Woltjer: Astr. Ap. 201, L27 (1988).
46. K. W. Weiler and R. A. Sramek: Ann. Rev. Astr. Ap. 26, 295 (1988).
47. L. Woltjer and M.-P. Véron-Cetty: Astr. Ap. 172, L7 (1987).

Supernova Remnants and Candidates in M33

R. Chris Smith, Robert P. Kirshner, P. Frank Winkler, Knox S. Long, & William P. Blair

I. Introduction

Supernova remnants (SNRs) provide fundamental information about stellar evolution and the properties of the interstellar medium. The galactic sample of optical SNRs is large, but severely limited by obscuration, and distances and sizes for these remnants remain uncertain. Extragalactic surveys provide samples for which sizes are more easily determined and for which obscuration is less vexing. Over 70 SNRs have previously been identified in local group galaxies; the largest sample consisting of the 25 remnants in the LMC (MATHEWSON et al. [1]). Here we describe the results from the first stage of our survey of M33. These results are based on the atlas of SNRs and candidates by LONG et al. [2].

Optical SNR surveys employ the large [S II] to Hα ratio found in typical SNRs compared to that in H II regions. Both models and observations show that SNRs usually have [S II]/Hα ratios greater than 0.4 (RAYMOND [3], FESEN, BLAIR, and KIRSHNER [4]), while the ratio in H II regions is usually ~ 0.1. M33 is ideal for such a survey because it is nearby (720 kpc, DE VAUCOULEURS [5]) and relatively face on (i=57°, CONSIDERE and ATHANASSOULA [6]). Previous optical surveys (see D'ODORICO, DOPITA, and BENVENUTI [7] and references therein) have identified 13 confirmed SNRs and several candidates from interference filter surveys using photographic plates. Less than eight of these SNRs have been detected at radio and X-ray wavelengths (GOSS and VIALLEFOND [8], TRINCHIERI, FABBIANO, and PERES [9], and references therein). Surveys in these bands have not yielded significant numbers of new SNRs in M33, although promising work is underway at the VLA (DURIC [10]), and should be feasible with ROSAT. We have therefore begun an optical survey of M33 using CCDs, taking advantage of their linearity and high quantum efficiency to search for fainter, more diffuse SNRs.

II. Observations and Remnant Identification

We have surveyed the inner 15 square arcmin of M33 with narrow-band interference filter CCD images using the 4m Mayall telescope at Kitt Peak National Observatory with the TI-2 CCD at prime focus. A grid of 18 overlapping 3.5 arcmin fields was used to map the nucleus and inner spiral arms of M33. For each field, images were taken in the light of Hα, [S II] $\lambda\lambda 6717, 6731$, [O III] $\lambda 5007$, and a continuum band at 6100 Å. The Hα, [S II], and continuum images distinguish ISM dominated

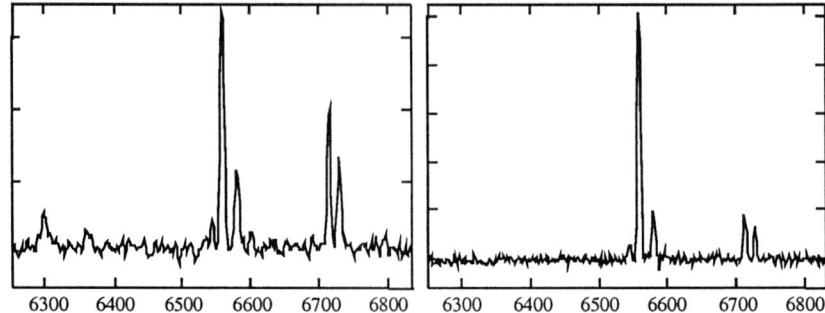

Figure 1: Spectra of a newly identified SNR (left) and a H II region (right) in M33. Note the high [S II]/Hα ratio in the SNR relative to the H II region, as well as the [O I] 6300,6363 emission in the SNR.

SNRs from H II regions and stars, and the [O III] images are used to identify young ejecta-dominated SNRs (see LONG, BLAIR, and KRZEMINSKI [11]).

The SNR candidates were identified in two steps. Objects were initially selected by blinking the Hα, [S II], and continuum images to identify nebulae which appeared to have high [S II]/Hα ratios. These candidates were then verified by measuring background subtracted fluxes from smoothed Hα and [S II] images to derive a quantitative [S II]/Hα ratio. Of more than 50 candidates identified by blinking, 42 were found to have [S II] to Hα ratios greater than 0.4, the dividing line between H II regions and SNRs. This sample includes every one of the 10 spectroscopically confirmed SNRs in our survey area, as well as 2 previously identified candidates which have not been confirmed spectroscopically. An atlas of the 42 objects, with positions, descriptions, and images, can be found in LONG et al. [2].

The next stage of our survey is spectroscopic examination of the candidates. We use the Multiple Mirror Telescope with a long slit CCD spectrograph to obtain ~ 5 Å resolution spectra of all of the survey objects. Preliminary reductions show that over 3/4 of the candidates (all those for which we have spectra) exhibit [S II] to Hα ratios $\gtrsim 0.4$, and most show [O I] $\lambda\lambda 6300, 6363$ emission, which is often present in SNRs but is weak in photoionized regions (see Fig. 1).

III. Results

In this survey, we have detected 30 NEW candidates in the central region of M33, more than doubling the number of candidates from previous surveys of this region. This confirms the advantages of CCD surveys over photographic techniques, and opens the possibility of pushing optical surveys for SNRs beyond the local group. Figure 2 shows the surface brightness of the 42 objects in our survey, plotted as a function of estimated diameter. Filled points are previously identified SNRs and candidates, and the open points are the newly identified objects. The new candidates are larger and have lower surface brightnesses than previous objects. The spectra show that most, if not all, of these candidates are SNRs.

With this sample, we can begin to study the evolution of SNRs. The distribution of remnants with diameter provides information on the expansion law for remnants.

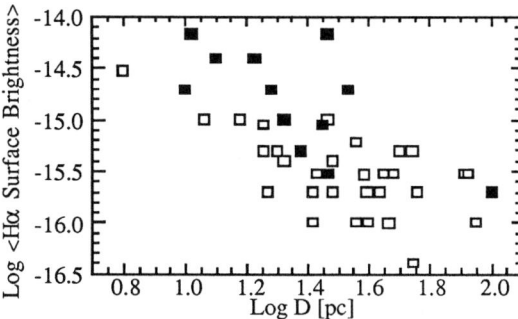

Figure 2: Surface brightness vs. diameter for our sample of SNRs and candidates. Filled squares are previously identified SNRs and candidates; open squares are new candidates. In general, we have identified larger and lower surface brightness objects than previous surveys.

The SEDOV [12] solution predicts $N(<D) \propto D^{2.5}$, in sharp contrast to the results of previous surveys of the LMC (MATHEWSON et al. [1]) and M33 (BLAIR and KIRSHNER [13]), which revealed exponents near 1 for this relation, consistent with free expansion of the remnants to their present size. The cumulative number vs. diameter relation for the objects in our survey is plotted in Fig. 3, which shows that the slope in the log-log relation is roughly 2 for diameters smaller than 30 pc in our sample. This slope is in reasonable agreement with the Sedov solution, although a more detailed analysis is required (GREEN [14], BERKHUIJSEN [15])

If the expansion law for remnants is known, we can estimate the supernova rate in M33. We assume that there are as many remnants outside our survey area as there are inside it. With 24 (candidate) remnants less than 30 pc in diameter in our survey, this would give 48 in the whole galaxy. Using $E \sim 10^{51}$ ergs, $n \sim 1$ cm^{-3}, and Sedov expansion, we obtain a rate of 1 SN every 300 years. This corresponds to 0.9 supernovae per 100 years per $10^{10} L_{B\odot}$, which agrees with the most recent estimates of the total SN rate for late type spirals by EVANS, VAN DEN BERGH, and MCCLURE [16] of $1.9h^2$, for H_0 of $\gtrsim 65$ km s^{-1} Mpc^{-1}.

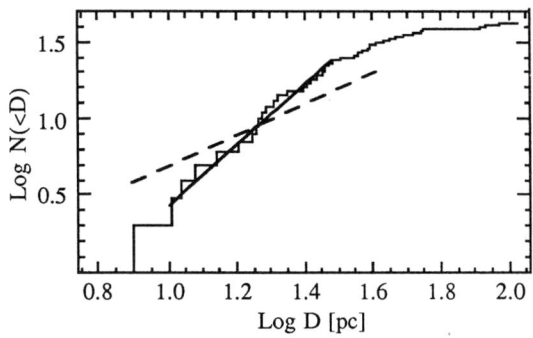

Figure 3: Cumulative number vs. diameter relation for our new sample of candidates and SNRs. The solid line, with a slope 2, is the best fit to the data for objects less than 30 pc in diameter. The dashed line has a slope of 1, the value previous samples gave for this relation.

These results are preliminary, as we are analyzing the images and spectra to quantify the completeness of the sample and perhaps discover a few candidates that were missed by the blink comparison method. The spectra will be used estimate abundances and to derive electron densities, which can be combined with the observed diameters to determine the thermal energy of each remnant (BLAIR, KIRSHNER, and CHEVALIER [17]). In addition, we plan to extend our survey to the whole of M33 with the new large format CCDs that are becoming available. Such a survey will provide a better estimate of the SN rate and facilitate the study of the relation of SNRs (and SNe) with spiral arms and giant star forming regions.

We would like to thank the staffs at Kitt Peak National Observatory and the Multiple Mirror Telescope Observatory for the considerable assistance in the execution of this project, and Tammy Smecker for assistance in the reduction of the image data. RCS and RPK acknowledge support from NSF grant AST 85-16537. PFW's research is supported by NSF grant AST 85-20557, and KSL and WPB acknowledge the support of the Johns Hopkins University Center for Astrophysical Sciences.

References

1. Mathewson, D.S., Ford, V.L., Dopita, M.A., Tuohy, I.R., Long, K.S., and Helfand, D.J. 1983, *Ap. J. Suppl.*, **51**, 345.
2. Long, K.S., Blair, W.P., Kirshner, R.K., and Winkler, P.F. 1990, *Ap. J. Suppl.*, in press for 1 Jan 1990.
3. Raymond, J.C. 1979, *Ap. J. Suppl.*, **39**, 1.
4. Fesen, R.A., Blair, W.P., and Kirshner, R.P. 1985, *Ap. J.*, **292**, 29.
5. de Vaucouleurs, G. 1978, *Ap. J.*, **223**, 730.
6. Considere, S., and Athanassoula, E. 1988, *Astr. Ap. Suppl.*, **76**, 365.
7. D'Odorico, S., Dopita, M.A., and Benvenuti, P. 1980, *Astr. Ap. Suppl.*, **40**, 67.
8. Goss, W. M., and Viallefond, F. 1985, *J. Astrophys. Astr.*, **6**, 145.
9. Trinchieri, G., Fabbiano, G., and Peres, G. 1988, *Ap. J.*, **325**, 531.
10. Duric, N. 1988, in *IAU Coll. 101: Supernova Remnants and the Interstellar Medium,* ed. by R.S. Roger and T.L. Landecker (Cambridge: Cambridge University Press), p. 289.
11. Long, K.S., Blair, W.P., and Krzeminski, W. 1989, *Ap. J. (Letters)*, **340**, L25.
12. Sedov, L.I. 1959, *Similarity and Dimensional Methods in Mechanics*, (New York: Academic Press).
13. Blair, W.P., and Kirshner, R.P. 1985, *Ap. J.*, **289**, 582.
14. Green, D.A. 1984, *M. N. R. A. S.*, **209**, 449.
15. Berkhuijsen, E.M. 1987, *Astr. Ap.*, **181**, 398.
16. Evans, R., van den Bergh, S., and McClure, R.D. 1989, *Ap. J.*, in press.
17. Blair, W.P., Kirshner, R.P., and Chevalier, R.A. 1981, *Ap. J.*, **247**, 879.

The Optical Structure of Cassiopeia A

Jeri E. Reed, A. C. Fabian, & P. F. Winkler

At a distance of 3 kpc and age of about 330 years, Cas A is one of the premier laboratories of the kinematic and chemical structure of supernova remnants. The material in its fast-moving ejecta is unusually rich in oxygen and the silicon-group elements and contains little or no hydrogen (PEIMBERT and VAN DEN BERGH [1], CHEVALIER and KIRSHNER [2]). Although photographic studies of Cas A have been continuing for over 30 years, in this work we present the first complete spectroscopic map of its optical structure.

The optical emission from Cas A consists of a faint, incomplete shell and a jet-like feature of unclear origin. Two major types of optical knots are seen: 1) slow-moving, 'quasi-stationary flocculi' (qsfs) containing nitrogen and hydrogen, which is thought to be circumstellar material lost prior to the explosion; and 2) the very fast-moving ejecta (4000-8000 km/s) containing heavier elements. Asymmetry in Cas A is implied by the existence of its jet, by asymmetric X-ray Doppler shifts (MARKERT et al. [3]), and by the lack of correlation between velocity and composition in optical data. Studies of a few bright knots indicated that some heavy material derived from the inner atmosphere is moving faster than the lighter oxygen-rich knots from the outer layers of the star (KAMPER and VAN DEN BERGH [4], CHEVALIER and KIRSHNER [5]), implying that radial mixing has occurred among the layers of the star. This inversion might be principally due to instabilities in the explosion itself, or could reflect interaction with the surrounding material.

In an effort to build a comprehensive map of the kinetic and chemical structure of Cas A, we have obtained optical observations of the face of the nebula and the inner parts of its jet using a CCD spectrograph on the 2.5m Isaac Newton Telescope. The frames were separated by 4 arcsec and covered the wavelength range from 6250 to 7600 Å. The slit width was 2.5″, the resolution along the slit was 0.64 arcsec/pixel and the spectral resolution was 100 km/s/pixel, sufficient to resolve the lines of [SII] and [OII]. The CCD frames were reduced using the FIGARO package, and the spectra corrected for a reddening of $A_v = 4.3$ magnitudes (SEARLE [6]). The complete data set contains about 25,000 spectra. We developed an automated method which allowed us to extract velocities and line strengths for each of the components present in each spectrum of the data set. In this first pass through the data we selected for analysis only lines of 4σ significance or larger. The flux in each line was estimated as the FWHM of the cross correlation peak times the peak line flux. In this way we have found the radial velocity, velocity width and position of every optical knot, and the fluxes of the most important lines needed to determine abundances. We have used this data to create the most complete map of Cas A's optical structure, and the first to show its overall three-dimensional chemical and kinematic structure.

In Fig. 1a we illustrate the correlation of velocity of the fast-moving knots with radial distance from the centre of expansion. It can be seen that the signature of a uniformly expanding shell is present with an expansion velocity of ~ 5000 km/s. Closer inspection of Fig. 1a shows a double arc structure which is also suggested by the radio and X-ray maps of Cas A. The arcs lie along a shell of radius 1.7 arcmin with a velocity centre red shifted by about 900 km/s. The quasi-stationary systems do not appear to be distributed in a shell (Fig. 1b). An expansion velocity of about 500 km/s leads to a 3-D map having major features which cover roughly the same extent as those in maps of the fast knots. A 'cloud' of faster qsfs seems to surround these features.

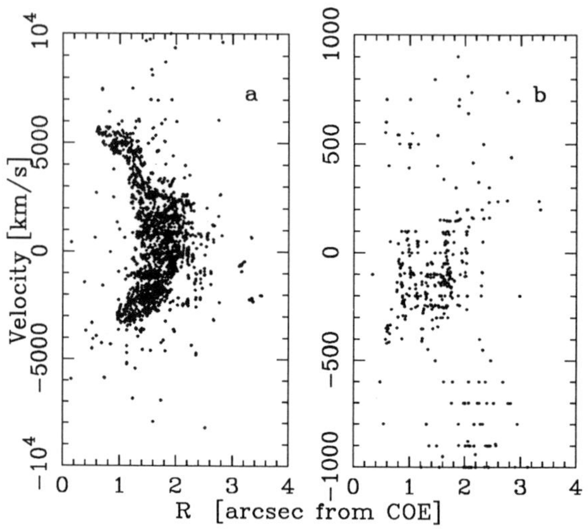

Figure 1. Radial velocity vs. distance from COE for
a) fast-moving knots; and
b) quasi-stationary flocculi.

Figure 2 shows the positions of the fast-moving optical knots, where the velocity has been scaled to be 5000 km/s at the radius of the X-ray ring. At least two emission lines had to be detected at 4σ or better for the emission feature to be included in these plots. For comparison, Fig. 2a is a CCD image of Cas A taken through an [OII] filter. Figure 2b is our map of the optical emission in the plane of the sky. The cross-hairs and dotted circle show the centre of expansion and the position of the main ring of X-ray emission at a radius of 1.7 arcmin. The linear appearance of the emission features simply reflects the slit positions on the sky. Figure 2c is the projected view from 'above' the remnant, and Fig. 2d is the projected view from the 'side'. In Fig. 2c and 2d, no correction has been made for the mean velocity of Cas A. Blue shifted velocities have negative values and the dotted line represents the projected X-ray ring as above. The plots do not distinguish between knots of different composition, but the spectra contain lines of O, S, A, and some Ca which we have tabulated for each knot. Lines of Fe and Ni have not been found at the 4σ level, but may be found when we combine the spectra of brighter knots.

The three-dimensional structure is quite asymmetric and seems to consist of a complex of interacting rings. The filaments near the low density region to the northeast, which include the prominent Baade and Minkowski's Filament 1, appear to be one-dimensional in the plane of the sky. When seen in Figs. 2c and 2d, however, they resolve into a fan of emission from which the jet itself emerges. Our data extends only to the nearest portion of the jet, but this also seems to be spreading in radial velocity with distance from the nebula. The chemical abundance distribution is confused, showing that mixing of knots did occur, but some patterns can be seen. For example, there is a large, blue shifted concentration of oxygen-rich material just east of the centre at a declination between 1 and 2 arcmin above the COE. The large ring seen in Fig. 2c seems to show a gradient from sulfur-rich materials inside towards oxygen-rich at the outer edge.

We are currently searching the data for evidence of very fast moving knots containing nitrogen and hydrogen, which have previously been reported in the outlying portions of the remnant and its jet, but not within the main shell (FESEN *et al.* [7]). (The existence of such knots might imply that material from the outer portions of the star was carried along with the exploding ejecta.) We are also examining the density structure of the nebula via the [SII] lines. Our comprehensive maps of the optical emission and density changes as a function of position and velocity promise to clarify the origin of the asymmetry in Cas A.

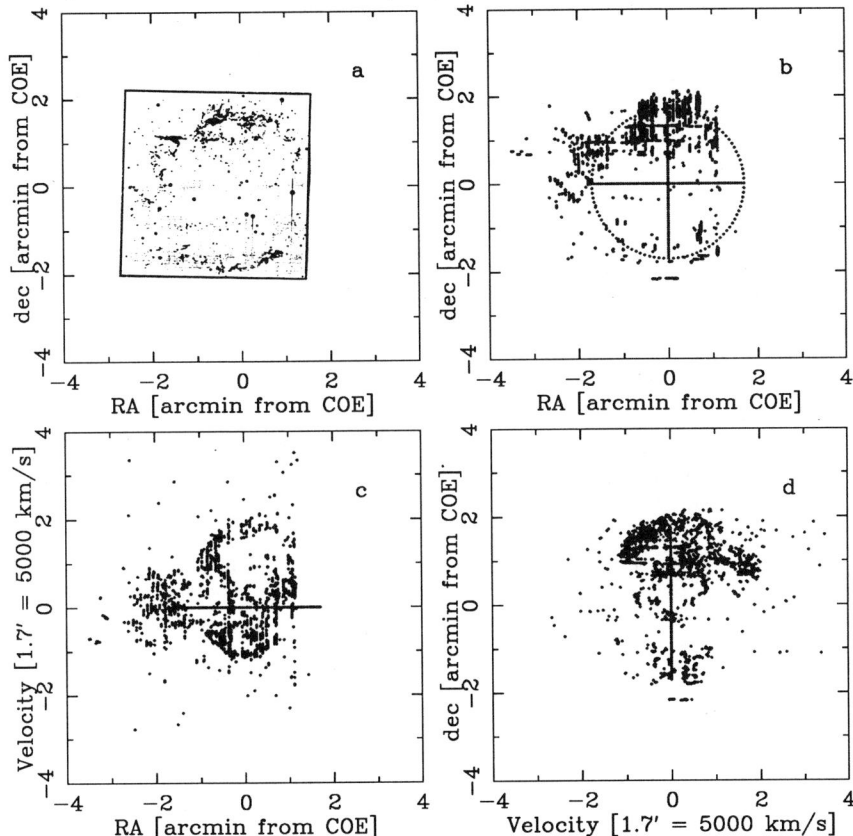

Figure 2. The positions of the fast-moving optical knots. Figure 2a is a comparison CCD image of Cas A in the light of [OII] 7325 Å, obtained at the prime focus of the KPNO 4m. The filter bandwidth is 200 Å, sufficient to include the entire velocity range of the Cas A knots. North is up, east to the left. Figure 2b represents the positions of the optical knots in the plane of the sky. The cross-hairs indicate the centre of expansion. In Figures 2c and 2d we have used the appropriately scaled velocity of the knots as a third dimension. Figure 2c shows the view from 'above' and Figure 2d the view from the 'side' of Cas A in the resulting space. The dotted circle or line represents the position of the X-ray shell at 1.7'.

References
1. M. Piembert and S. van den Bergh: *Astrophys. J.*, **259**, 198 (1971).
2. R.A. Chevalier and R.P. Kirshner: *Astrophys. J.*, **219**, 931 (1978).
3. T.H. Markert, C.R. Canizares, G.W. Clark, P.F. Winkler: *Astrophys. J.*, **268**, 134 (1983).
4. K. Kamper and S. van den Bergh: *Astrophys. J. Suppl.*, **32**, 351 (1976).
5. R.A. Chevalier and R.P. Kirshner: *Astrophys. J.*, **233**, 154 (1979).
6. L. Searle: *Astrophys. J.*, **168**, 41 (1971).
7. R.A. Fesen, R.H. Baker, W.P. Blair: *Astrophys. J.*, **313**, 378 (1987).

Spectrophotometry of Cas A: Implications for Nucleosynthesis in Massive Stars

P. Frank Winkler, Peter F. Roberts, & Robert P. Kirshner

Cas A is the prototype of supernova remnants (SNRs) in which fast-moving, chemically peculiar debris is found. The fast-moving knots have velocities 4000–8000 km/s and are composed entirely of products from advanced stages of nucleosynthesis, with essentially no hydrogen (PEIMBERT and VAN DEN BERGH [1], CHEVALIER and KIRSHNER [2]). Based on this evidence, the fast knots are generally believed to represent uncontaminated ejecta from the core of a massive star. Recent studies by FESEN *et al.* [3] find that the fastest knots in Cas A are very nitrogen-rich, which suggests the more specific identification of the progenitor as a WN star, and that the super-fast nitrogen knots are material from its surface. Along with the handful of remnants with similiar but less extreme properties, Cas A provides one of the few arenas where theoretical models for the evolution and explosion of massive stars can confront observational evidence VAN DEN BERGH [4]. Cas A has become all the more interesting in the wake of SN1987A, for the two objects appear to have many similarities.

We have used the Cryogenic Camera with the KPNO 4-m telescope to obtain long-slit spectra at several positions in Cas A. Three different spectrograph set-ups were used; we have combined the data to give composite spectra for some 20 knots covering the range 4500-10500 Å with approximately 15 Å resolution. Figure 1 shows one long-slit spectrum, taken with the slit oriented nearly E-W across the northern portion of the remnant shell. Velocity variations of several thousand km/s are apparent, even in material which is not resolved as separate knots in direct images. Equally dramatic (though less obvious in this display in which the strong lines are saturated in order to show the faint lines) are large variations in the relative line strengths from one knot to another. Lines from several elements are identified here for the first time in Cas A: [C I] 8727, 9824, and 9850, [Cl II] 8579, [Ni II] 7378, and numerous faint [Fe II] lines.

Figure 2 shows extracted 1-dimensional spectra for two knots of widely varying composition. Lines of oxygen in three different ionization states dominate the spectrum of Fig. 2*a*, and the products of oxygen burning: S, Ar, and Ca manifest themselves only in minute traces, if at all. Furthermore, permitted lines of O I, 7774 and 8446, are seen in addition to the usual forbidden lines. The presence of these lines in the ratio expected for O+ recombination further confirms an extreme oxygen abundance (WINKLER and KIRSHNER [5]). Oxygen lines are also apparent in the spectrum of Fig. 2*b*, but here the S and Ar lines are far more prominent. The contrasting pair of spectra typifies the spectroscopic range for

Spectrophotometry of Cas A 653

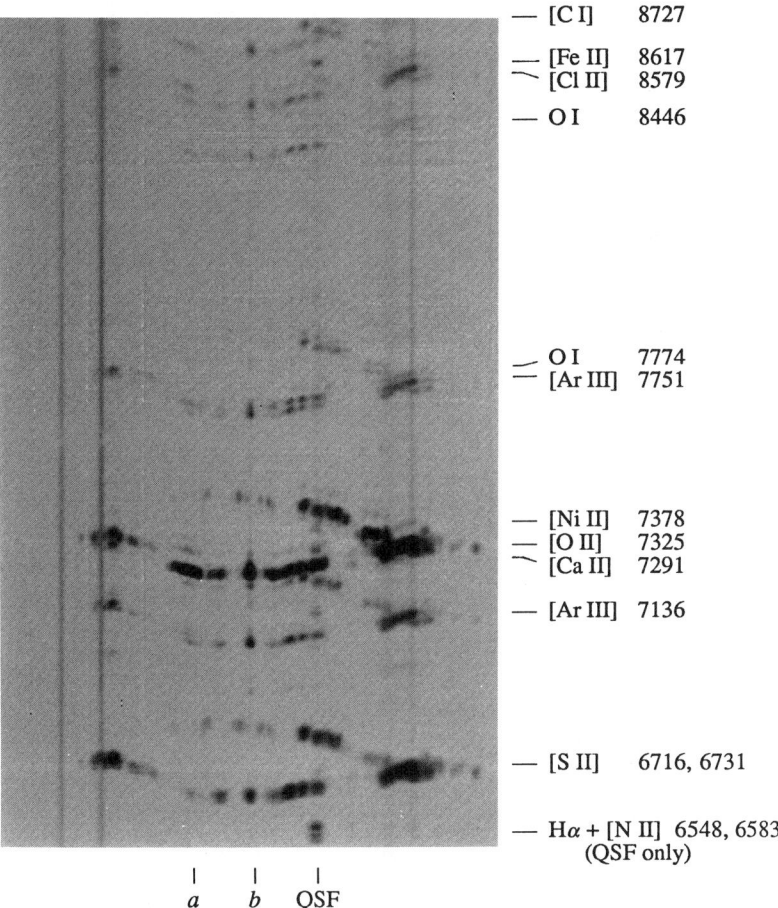

Figure 1. The near-infrared spectrum of Cas A, taken with a long slit crossing the northern portion of the remnant. Knots at the approaching and receding edges of the expanding shell differ in velocity by more than 8000 km/s. Line identifications indicate zero-velocity emission, which is approximately the case near the ends of the slit. Strong lines appear saturated in this display, in order to emphasize the fainter lines. Knots *a* and *b* refer to those shown in Fig. 2. Note the [Fe II] and [Ni II] lines, which are best seen in knot *a*. One quasi-stationary flocculus (QSF) lies on the slit as indicated.

the fast-moving knots in Cas A, from nearly pure oxygen to a mixture in which oxygen-burning products are most evident.

Does the spectroscopic contrast indicate the chemical make-up of these knots, or might unusual physical conditions masquerade as chemical differences? To avoid ionization effects we look at lines from different species that should coexist in the same physical volume, *i.e.*, ions with similar ionization potentials. We have compared the sulfur:oxygen line ratio in different knots for neutral and singly ionized species (Fig. 3a). While each ratio varies by almost 2 orders of magnitude among the 20 knots, there is an excellent correlation

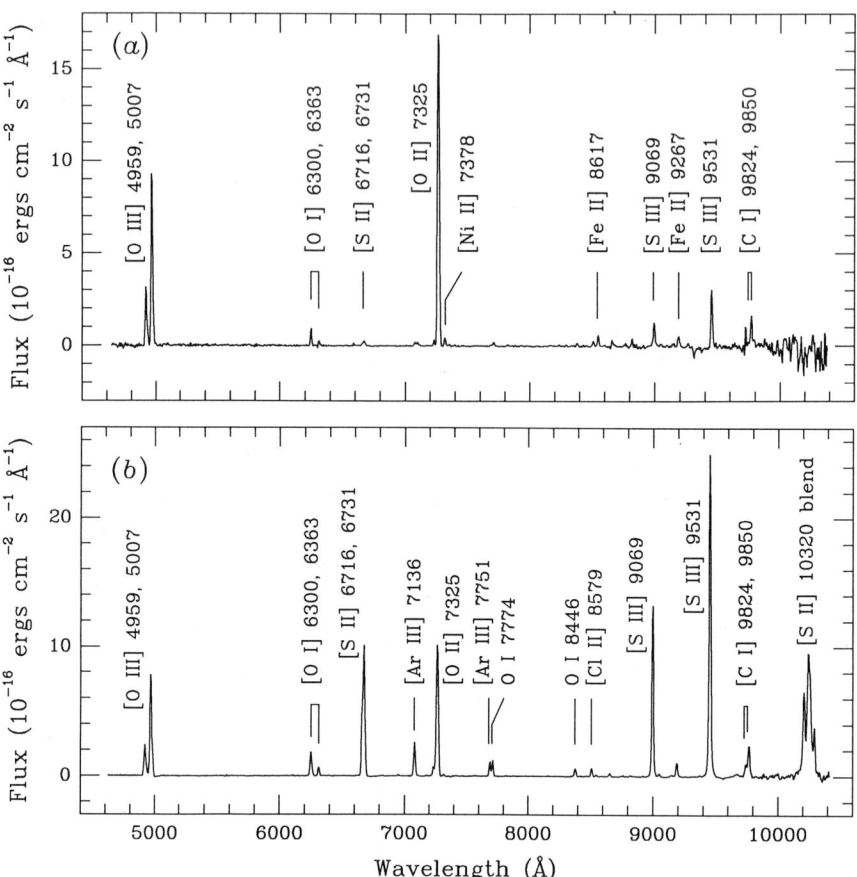

Figure 2. Optical-IR spectra of two fast knots in Cas A, illustrating differences in chemical composition: (a) A knot dominated by oxygen lines; note, however, the presence of iron and nickel. (b) A knot composed primarily of oxygen and oxygen-burning products. Note the absence of hydrogen emission in both knots.

between the two. A comparison of [S III]/[O II] vs [S II]/[O I] shows a similar correlation. Surely we are seeing true composition variations by large factors. By contrast, we have plotted the [Ar III]/[S III] line ratio vs [S II]/[O II] in Fig. 3b. The Ar/S ratio is roughly constant (to within a factor of 3), indicating that Ar and S are formed together in appproximately constant ratio during oxygen burning, while the S/O ratio variations by a factor of 100 represent different mixtures of oxygen and oxygen-burning products – a conclusion tentatively arrived at by CHEVALIER and KIRSHNER [6] based on only a few knots. The measured line strengths indicate that the relative *ionic* abundances of Ar^{++}/S^{++} are in the ratio ~1/8, a value which likely reflects the true *elemental* abundances.

The iron and nickel, though faint, are nevertheless noteworthy. These are most prominent in the "oxygen knot" of Fig. 2a (see also Fig. 1), and have the same velocity as the oxygen lines. The same lines are present in many other knots, but with strengths that are

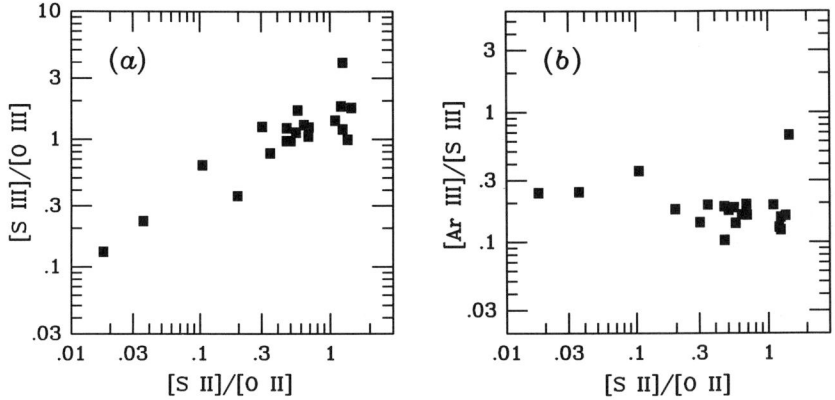

Figure 3. Correlations between flux ratios for pairs of lines as measured in 20 knots of Cas A. (a) [S III] 9069 Å : [O III] 5007 Å (vertical) vs [S II] 6716, 6731 Å : [O II] 7325 Å (horizontal). (b) [Ar III] 7136 Å : [S III] 9069 Å (vertical) vs [S II] 6716, 6731 Å : [O II] 7325 Å (horizontal).

much weaker relative to oxygen or sulfur. Thus iron-peak elements appear in varied concentrations both in material that is primarily oxygen and that composed predominantly of oxygen-burning products. These observations suggest that some of the iron-peak inner core of the progenitor was mixed by the supernova with overlying material, at least as far out as the oxygen zone. Similar upward mixing of an iron-peak core in SN1987A is widely invoked to explain the early escape of X- and γ-ray emission, as has been discussed by several participants in this workshop. The oxygen-rich SNR 0540-69.3 in the LMC also has iron and nickel at high velocities similar to those of oxygen, suggesting that here too the iron-peak elements are mixed with oxygen in the debris (KIRSHNER et al. [7]). Perhaps such mixing is a characteristic feature of massive supernovae.

We are grateful to the organizers of the UCSC workshop on Supernovae for a most interesting meeting, and to participants too numerous to mention individually for stimulating discussions. PFW and PFR acknowledge the support of NSF grant AST 85-20557, NASA grant NAG8-735 and the Middlebury College Faculty Research Fund. RPK acknowledges support from NSF grant AST 85-16537.

References
1. M. Peimbert, S. van den Bergh: *Ap. J.* **167**, 223 (1971).
2. R.A. Chevalier, R.P. Kirshner: *Ap. J.* **219**, 931 (1978).
3. R.A. Fesen, R.H. Becker, R.W. Goodrich: *Ap. J. (Letters)* 329, L89 (1988); also talk by Fesen at this meeting.
4. S. van den Bergh: *Ap. J.* **327**, 156 (1988).
5. P.F. Winkler, R.P. Kirshner: *Ap. J.* **299**, 981.
6. R.A. Chevalier, R.P. Kirshner: *Ap. J.* **233**, 154 (1979).
7. R.P. Kirshner, J.A. Morse, P.F. Winkler: *Ap. J.* **342**, 260 (1989).

Photoionization Models of Iron-Rich Ejecta in SN 1885

A. J. S. Hamilton & R. A. Fesen

1. Introduction

The recent discovery by Fesen et al. [1] of the remnant of S Andromedae, the historic supernova of 1885 observed a mere 16" from the nuclear center of M31, brings to two the number of supernovae whose ejecta have been observed successfully in absorption: SN 1006 (Type Ia; Wu et al. [2]; Fesen et al. [3]; Hamilton and Fesen [4]) and now SN 1885 (Type I peculiar; de Vaucouleurs and Corwin [5]). In the discovery image, SN 1885 appears as an unresolved spot of Fe I absorption silhouetted against the starry blaze of M31's bulge. From the observed absorption contrast, Fesen et al. [1] estimate that SN 1885 has an Fe I diameter of 0.3", corresponding to an expansion velocity of $\pm 5,000 \, \mathrm{km \, s^{-1}}$.

Absorption line observations of supernova ejecta can be tremendously powerful, since observed absorption line profiles yield directly the density and composition as a function of radius in the freely expanding ejecta. However, absorption observations are obviously limited to those young remnants which happen to have a suitable background source behind them. This is why most remnants have not been observed in absorption: a suitable background source just does not exist, or at least has not yet been noticed. *HST* may change this situation. In the case of SN 1006, the background object is a single subdwarf OB star (Schweizer and Middleditch [6]). For its part, SN 1885 occults some 10^5 bulge stars in M31.

SN 1885 promises some advantage over SN 1006 in regard to absorption observations. In SN 1006, a good fraction of the ejecta has been shocked, and of the unshocked ejecta only about $0.015 \, M_\odot$ remains as observable Fe II, the rest of the unshocked ejecta having been photoionized mainly to Fe III to Fe V mainly by UV and x-ray emission from the shocked ejecta (Hamilton and Fesen [4]). The resonance lines of Fe III and higher ions unfortunately all lie in the far UV inaccessible to current telescopes. By contrast, as discussed below, SN 1885 has probably collided with little ambient gas, and we expect that most of the ions in SN 1885 are still neutral and singly ionized. Thus almost all the ejecta in SN 1885 should still be observable in absorption. Such is the advantage of youth.

2. The Medium Around SN 1885

The absence of detectable emission from the site of SN 1885 in the radio (Dickel and D'Odorico [7]), in the optical (Ciardullo et al. [8]; Jacoby et al. [9]), or in x-rays (Van Speybroeck et al. [10]) implies that SN 1885 has not yet swept up a large mass of ambient gas. The tightest constraint comes from VLA observations (Dickel and D'Odorico [7]) which set an upper limit on the radio luminosity of SN 1885 at less than half the luminosity of Tycho's SNR. If the fractional energy density in relativistic particles and magnetic fields is the same in SN 1885 as in Tycho, then the ambient density must be less than $\sim 2\,cm^{-3}$ and the mass of shocked gas must be less than $\sim 0.2\,M_\odot$.

A low density of gas surrounding SN 1885 is consistent with what is known about conditions in the bulge of M31. The optical bulge of M31 is dominated by starlight from an old but metal-rich population (Walterbos and Kennicutt [11]; Roger et al. [12]; Kent [13]; Faber and French [14]) with a dynamically inferred mass of $\sim 3 \times 10^9\,M_\odot$ within the central 5′ ($=1\,kpc$) diameter (McElroy [15]). There are no OB stars (Welch [16]; Wirth et al. [17]), no Wolf-Rayets (Moffat and Shara [18], [19]), nor any other sign of recent star formation. Twenty-one centimeter (Bajaja and Shane [20]) and IRAS observations (Soifer et al. [21]) indicate only $\sim 1\text{-}2 \times 10^5\,M_\odot$ of neutral hydrogen gas within the central 5′ diameter. This gas is presumably associated with the dust extinction lanes observed optically (McElroy [15]; Ciardullo et al. [8]; Nieto et al. [22]), but no dust lane is evident at the position of SN 1885 (Fesen et al. [1]). X-ray observations (Fabbiano et al. [23]; Van Speybroeck et al. [10]) set upper limits of $\lesssim 0.02\,cm^{-3}$ and $\lesssim 10^4\,M_\odot$ to the density and mass of diffuse hot gas at temperatures $\gtrsim 10^6\,K$ in the central 5′ diameter. Diffuse nonthermal radio emission is nevertheless observed (Walterbos and Gräve [24]; Hjellming and Smarr [25]) with a minimum energy density $\gtrsim 2\,eV\,cm^{-3}$ in relativistic particles and magnetic fields, interestingly close to the maximum energy density of $\lesssim 2\,eV\,cm^{-3}$ of hot x-ray emitting gas. These numbers pose the novel possibility that the ambient pressure around SN 1885 may be primarily relativistic, in cosmic rays and magnetic fields.

3. Ambient UV Starlight

Fe I has an ionization potential of 7.87 eV, which is below the Lyman limit, so is relatively easily photoionized by ambient UV starlight. Fe I's photoionization cross-section (Lombardi et al. [26]; Hansen et al. [27]) averages about $3 \times 10^{-18}\,cm^2$ between threshold (1575 Å) and Lyman α (1216 Å), with a broad peak from many resonances between 1400 Å and 1250 Å.

IUE observations (Johnson [28]; Welch [16]) give a direct handle on the level of ambient UV light, although the actual UV flux experienced by SN 1885 depends on its geometry relative to the nucleus of M31. Between Fe I threshold (1575 Å) and Lyman α (1216 Å) the dereddened flux observed with *IUE* is more or less flat at about $2 \times 10^{-14}\,erg\,cm^{-2}\,s^{-1}\,Å^{-1}$ through the 178 arcsec^2 race-track-shaped aperture of *IUE*, centered on the nucleus. The flux is about half this at the position of SN 1885. The spectrum and spatial distribution of the observed UV light suggests that it probably arises from blue horizontal branch stars in the bulge of M31 (Welch [16]). If SN 1885 is half way through the bulge, that is, at a position closest to the nucleus, then it is experiencing a photoionizing flux of $\sim 5 \times 10^8$ phot cm^{-2} s^{-1} between 1575 Å and 1216 Å, summed over all directions. The photoionizing flux is smaller if SN 1885 is further from the nucleus.

Combining the UV flux with the photoionization cross-section of Fe I yields an ionization time of ~ 20 years, or more if SN 1885 is further than the minimum distance from the nucleus, for Fe I exposed to light from the bulge of M31. Optically thick inner layers of ejecta are however shielded, and remain neutral.

4. Photoionization Models of SN 1885

The estimates of the previous two sections suggest that the main source of ionization of ejecta in SN 1885 is photoionization by ambient UV starlight. Currently, inner layers of

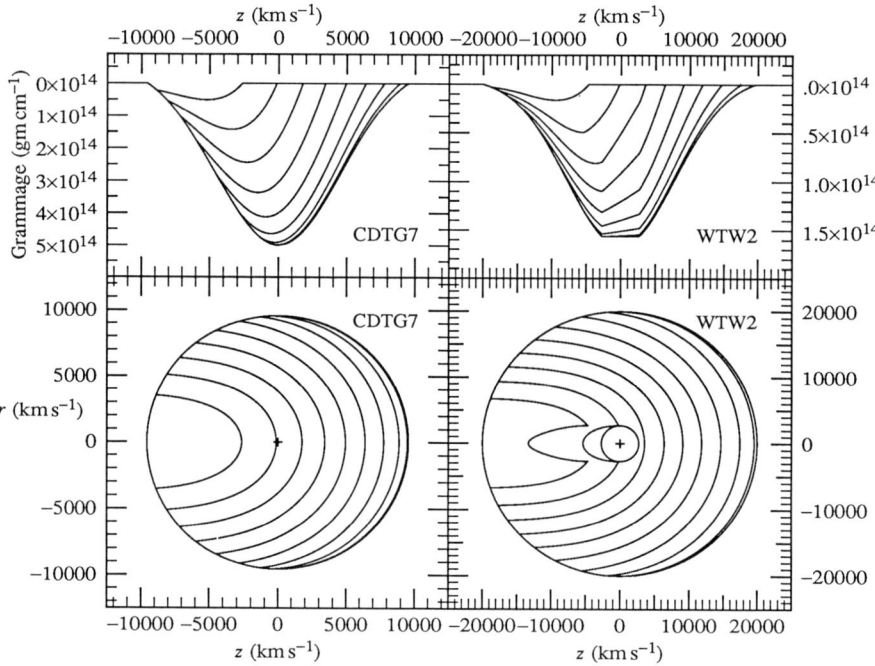

Figure 1. Lower panels show positions of Fe I to Fe II photoionization front in SN 1885, driven by one-sided UV stellar illumination coming from the right. The computations are based on the carbon-deflagrated white dwarf model CDTG7 of Woosley [29], [30], and the off-center helium detonation model 2 of Woosley, Taam and Weaver [31]. The photoionization front is plotted at equal intervals of time, and moves from right to left. Currently the front is about half way through the remnant. Upper panels show the resulting Fe I absorption line profiles expected in spatially unresolved observations, from the point of view of an astronomer observing from the left. As the photoionization front moves through the remnant, the Fe I absorption profile weakens and becomes more blueshifted. The center of WTW2 is composed of unburnt CO.

iron-rich ejecta should be mainly Fe I, but outer layers should have been photoionized to Fe II. One of the intriguing aspects of this photoionization is that SN 1885 is experiencing a one-sided tan — it is being photoionized mainly on the side nearest the bulge (see Fig. 1). If SN 1885 occurred on the near side of the bulge of M31, as the relatively high absorption contrast suggests (Fesen et al. [1]), then this one-sided tan should show up as a blue-shift of Fe I lines (Fig. 1), and a corresponding red-shift of Fe II lines. The observation of such a shift would in fact give an indication of SN 1885's position along the line of sight within the bulge of M31.

We have run some idealized models which illustrate the non-spherical ionization structure of SN 1885 which develops as a result of the one-sided photoionization. As examples, we took the carbon-deflagrated white dwarf model CDTG7 of Woosley [29], [30], and, since SN 1885 was after all a peculiar Type I, an off-center helium detonation model, model 2, hereafter WTW2, of Woosley, Taam and Weaver [31]. To simplify the calculations, we assumed (a) that SN 1885 is illuminated by a single UV point source at infinity, and (b) that this causes a sharp Fe I to Fe II photoionization front to propagate through the remnant.

Figure 1 shows the position of the Fe I to Fe II photoionization front at equally spaced intervals of time in models CDTG7 and WTW2 of SN 1885. Currently the photoionization front should be about half way through SN 1885's ejecta. The precise position of the front depends on how close SN 1885 is to M31's nucleus: the front moves faster if SN 1885 is closer to the nucleus, where the UV flux is fiercer.

Figure 1 also shows the resulting Fe I absorption line profiles expected for spatially unresolved (i.e. ground-based) observations of SN 1885. The profiles are shown from the point of view of an observer located the opposite side of the remnant from the photoionizing UV source, which would be a reasonable approximation if SN 1885 is in fact well to the near side of M31's bulge. The depth of the line profile is determined by the "grammage" of intervening Fe I, which is the Fe I density integrated over the transverse directions in the remnant. The off-center helium-detonation model WTW2 differs from the carbon-deflagration model CDTG7 in that the detonation model (a) shows higher expansion velocities, (b) has a lower overall density at any given time, and (c) has Fe in outer layers of ejecta, and unburnt CO on the inside, whereas it's vice versa in the deflagration model.

5. Conclusions

The main message of this paper is that we will learn a lot about the Type I peculiar supernova of 1885 from absorption line observations. Specifically, from observed absorption line profiles we will learn the density and composition of the ejecta as a function of radius. Unlike SN 1006, the only other supernova whose ejecta have so far been observed in absorption, most of the ejecta in SN 1885 are probably still freely expanding and in a low ionization state, mostly neutral and singly ionized. Currently, UV starlight from M31's bulge is driving a lop-sided Fe I to Fe II photoionization front, which has reached about half way through SN 1885's ejecta.

SN 1885's small size, about 0.5" in diameter, means that observations with *HST* will be essential to realize the full potential of absorption line observations of SN 1885.

References

1. R. A. Fesen, A. J. S. Hamilton, J. M. Saken: *Ap. J. (Letters)*, **341**, L55 (1989).
2. C.-C. Wu, M. Leventhal, C. L. Sarazin, T. R. Gull: *Ap. J. (Letters)*, **269**, L5 (1983).
3. R. A. Fesen, C.-C. Wu, M. Leventhal, A. J. S. Hamilton: *Ap. J.*, **327**, 164 (1988).
4. A. J. S. Hamilton, R. A. Fesen: *Ap. J.*, **327**, 178 (1988).
5. de G. Vaucouleurs, H. G. Corwin, Jr.: *Ap. J.*, **295**, 287 (1985).
6. F. Schweizer, J. Middleditch: *Ap. J.*, **241**, 1039 (1980).
7. J. R. Dickel, S. D'Odorico: *M. N. R. A. S.*, **206**, 351 (1984).
8. R. Ciardullo, V. C. Rubin, G. H. Jacoby, H. C. Ford, W. K. Ford, Jr.: *Astr. J.*, **95**, 438 (1988).
9. G. H. Jacoby, H. Ford, R. Ciardullo: *Ap. J.*, **290**, 136 (1985).
10. Van L. Speybroeck, A. Epstein, W. Forman, R. Giacconi, C. Jones, W. Liller, L. Smarr: *Ap. J. (Letters)*, **234**, L45 (1979).
11. R. A. M. Walterbos, R. C. Kennicutt, Jr.: *Astr. Ap. Suppl.*, **69**, 311 (1987).
12. C. M. Roger, J. P. Phillips, C. S. Magro: *Astr. Ap.*, **161**, 237 (1986).
13. S. M. Kent: *Ap. J.*, **266**, 562 (1983).
14. S. M. Faber, H. B. French: *Ap. J.*, **235**, 405 (1980).
15. D. B. McElroy: *Ap. J.*, **270**, 485 (1983).
16. G. A. Welch: *Ap. J.*, **259**, 77 (1982).
17. A. Wirth, L. L. Smarr, T. L. Bruno: *Ap. J.*, **290**, 140 (1985).
18. A. F. J. Moffat, M. M. Shara: *Ap. J.*, **273**, 544 (1983).
19. A. F. J. Moffat, M. M. Shara: *Ap. J.*, **320**, 266 (1987).
20. E. Bajaja, W. W. Shane: *Astr. Ap. Suppl.*, **49**, 745 (1982).
21. B. T. Soifer, W. L. Rice, J. R. Mould, F. C. Gillett, M. Rowan-Robinson, H. J. Habing: *Ap. J.*, **304**, 651 (1986).
22. J.-L. Nieto, F. D. Macchetto, M. A. C. Perryman, S. di Serego Alighieri, G. Lelièvre: *Astr. Ap.*, **165**, 189 (1986).
23. G. Fabbiano, G. Trinchieri, L. S. Van Speybroeck: *Ap. J.*, **316**, 127 (1987).
24. R. A. M. Walterbos, R. Gräve: *Astr. Ap.*, **150**, L1 (1985).
25. R. M. Hjellming, L. L. Smarr: *Ap. J. (Letters)*, **257**, L13 (1982).
26. G. G. Lombardi, P. L. Smith, W. H. Parkinson: *Phys. Rev. A*, **18**, 2131 (1978).
27. J. E. Hansen, B. Ziegenbein, R. Lincke, H. P. Kelly: *J. Phys. B.*, **10**, 37 (1977).
28. H. M. Johnson: *Ap. J. (Letters)*, **230**, L137 (1979).
29. S. E. Woosley: private communication (1987).
30. S. E. Woosley, T. A. Weaver: In *Proc. IAU Colloquium 89, Radiation Hydrodynamics in Stars and Compact Objects* ed. D. Mihalas, K.-H. A. Winkler (Springer-Verlag, Berlin 1987), p. 91.
31. S. E. Woosley, R. E. Taam, T. A. Weaver: *Ap. J.*, **301**, 601 (1986).

X-Ray Spectroscopy of Young Supernova Remnants: Mixing in the Ejecta of Type I and II Supernovae

John P. Hughes

I. Introduction

Supernova remnants (SNRs) are the product of stellar explosions. From them we can learn much about the late stages of stellar evolution, mass-loss processes in stars, and explosive nucleosynthesis. The events involve the ejection of several solar masses of material at velocities reaching 10^4 km s^{-1} into the circumstellar and interstellar medium. It is possible to observe radio, optical, and X-ray emission from SNRs with ages ranging from hundreds to tens of thousands of years old. Remnants represent a significant input of energy and matter into the galaxy as a whole and thus are important contributors to the overall dynamical and chemical evolution of the galaxy.

The X-ray spectra of SNRs are quite rich: they show strong emission lines from many elements (among which are oxygen, neon, silicon, sulfur, argon, calcium, and iron) with abundances that are often decidedly enhanced relative to the abundances in the sun or the interstellar medium (see Figs. 1, 2, and 4). The continuum emission in some cases is best described by a multi-temperature distribution. Furthermore the rapid evolutionary timescales for these objects influences the observed spectra in subtle ways, through nonequilibrium effects on the ionization states of the various elemental constituents and on the energy transfer between electrons and ions. These effects make SNR X-ray spectra difficult to interpret.

Many previous studies of SNR X-ray spectra have used detailed models for the underlying dynamical evolution to compare to the observational data (ITOH [1,2,3]; GRONENSCHILD and MEWE [4]; SHULL [5]; NUGENT et al. [6]; HUGHES and HELFAND [7]; HAMILTON, SARAZIN, and SZYMKOWIAK [8,9]). In general these models have been quite complicated with many parameters and assumptions; unfortunately this has tended to obscure some of the underlying important astrophysics. The models have been computationally expensive and as a result, full exploration of the multidimensional parameter space available has not been attempted. Furthermore no group has been able (or willing) to investigate more than one or two objects.

The limitations in previous analyses discussed above have motivated this investigation of SNR X-ray spectra. The intention was to carry out a consistent spectral analysis of data from several galactic SNRs using simple parametric models for the line and continuum emission. It was planned to utilize data from several satellites in order to have the broadest possible energy band available. The ultimate goal of the project is to obtain, for a number of SNRs, reliable values for the elemental abundances and information on the ionization and thermal state of the plasma. As we show below, some results have already been obtained for three young SNRs: Cassiopeia A, Tycho's SNR, and the remnant of SN1006.

The conclusions of this study are that the ejecta of the Type I remnants (Tycho and SN1006) have retained much of the stratification in their elemental composition to the present day. However the Type II remnant (Cassiopeia A) is much more completely mixed. These results are based on the measurements of line centroids and comparison to a simple nonequilibrium ionization model, which I describe below. I discuss these results in light of recent work on mixing in the ejecta of both Type I and II supernovae (SNe).

II. Nonequilibrium Ionization Model

The observable effects of nonequilibrium ionization (NEI) are most prominent in the comparison between line emission and continuum emission in the X-ray spectra of SNRs. The continuum arises principally from bremsstrahlung emission of electrons on highly ionized atomic species. It depends strongly on the electron temperature in the plasma and very weakly on the atomic species and the ionization state, through the Gaunt factor. In contrast, the line emission depends strongly on the latter; an increase or decrease in elemental abundance or ionization state will cause a proportional change in line intensity. Additionally, the observed line energy for a given transition depends on the ionization state. For example, the energy of the Kα line of iron, in which the principal quantum number changes from n = 2 to n = 1, varies from 6.96 keV for Fe XXVI, to approximately 6.66 keV for Fe XXV, to as low as 6.4 keV for ionization states below about Fe XIX, a consequence of the "screening" of the nuclear charge by innershell electrons. Clearly the line energy of a given electronic transition is a sensitive indicator of the ionization state of that atomic species. However, the ionization state also depends on the electron temperature, as well as whether the plasma is in equilibrium and not. Indeed the line energies of a lower temperature plasma in equilibrium may mimic the true line energies in a higher temperature plasma which is in the ionizing phase. However, given a broad energy band and detectors with sufficient energy resolution to isolate the line emission, it is possible to determine the electron temperature from the continuum emission.

The complications due to NEI effects make it clear that the ionization calculation must be included properly within the context of the evolution of supernova remnants in general. The model to be used in this study assumes a single component plasma that has been recently heated to a temperature of several keV by the passage of a strong shock. The time since the passage of the shock (actually the density times this time, called the ionization timescale) and the temperature of the plasma (assumed constant) become the two relevant parameters. I refer to this as the single temperature – single timescale model. Although in an actual remnant there is a range of temperatures and ionization timescales, this model should be an ideal first approximation to the average state of the plasma (HAMILTON and SARAZIN [10]).

I have coupled my matrix-based solution for the NEI fractions (see [7]) to the RAYMOND and SMITH [11] optically-thin plasma emission code. Additional emission lines appropriate to nonequilibrium conditions were included from MEWE and GRONENSCHILD [12]. For comparison to the fitted Kα line energies, I took the weighted average of all $n = 2$ to $n = 1$ transitions to determine a mean line energy for the NEI model corresponding to a given ionization timescale and electron temperature. This was done separately for each of the astrophysically abundant elements silicon, sulfur, argon, calcium, and iron.

III. Data Analysis

The data used in this project came from the solid state spectrometer (SSS) on the *Einstein Observatory* and the gas scintillation proportional counters (GSPCs) on the *Tenma* satellite. The SSS data covered the energy range from approximately 0.5 keV to 4.0 keV and the *Tenma* data covered the range from 1.5 keV to beyond 10 keV. The combined analysis of these datasets is a powerful technique for the study of line and continuum emission processes in SNRs. As a consequence of the relatively high resolving power of the *Tenma* GSPCs (a factor of two better than previous instruments in this energy range), the iron Kα line ($\sim$6.5 keV) can be studied to higher precision than ever before. In addition the line and continuum emission can be more easily separated to allow for a good determination of the electron temperature. However the *Tenma* GSPCs were not well suited to studying the silicon and sulfur Kα line region ($\sim$2 keV) or searching for low temperature ($<$1 keV) emission components. The *Einstein* SSS obtained some of the highest resolution data on SNRs to date, with energy resolution better than about 200 eV. The best data was obtained from the silicon and sulfur Kα line regions, while beyond about 4 keV the *Einstein Observatory* X-ray telescope cut-off and below about 1 keV there was the well-known problem of icing on the surface of the SSS. It was difficult to determine continuum temperatures above about 2-3 keV from the SSS data alone.

Thus these two types of data complement each other and joint fits allow for study of the silicon, sulfur, argon, calcium, and iron Kα lines. As discussed below, the average line energies are a sensitive probe of the ionization state of the plasma. Comparison among the different elemental species allows for investigation into the relative ionization histories. Joint fits also allow for a determination of the continuum temperature and searches for multiple components, such as the blast wave in the interstellar medium or the reverse shock in the metal rich stellar ejecta.

In this project I have followed closely the analysis of TSUNEMI et al. [13]. The approach is as model independent as possible with the use of parameterized forms for the continuum and line emission. I fitted the continuum emission with an exponential (including Gaunt factor) of two parameters: the normalization and kT. Emission lines were modeled as gaussian profiles with the parameters normalization, central energy, and energy width. The width was held constant at a value $\sigma = 0.050$ keV. Lines were included at energies appropriate to the Kα emission complexes of the elements Ne, Mg, Si, S, Ar, Ca, and Fe; Kβ lines were also included for Si and S; and, when apparently necessary, lines were included in the 1 keV region of the spectra to represent Fe L-shell emission. Absorption due to intervening material in the galaxy along the line of sight was also included. Due to the problem of ice absorption on the SSS, the column density was allowed to vary separately for the SSS and *Tenma* datasets. A relative normalization between the two datasets was also included, in part to account for differences in the fields of view. The field of view of *Tenma* was several degrees, while that of the SSS was only 3' in radius, smaller than the sizes of the three SNRs I studied. I assume that the SSS spectra are representative of the entire remnant. Multiple SSS observations of Tycho and SN1006 were done and since in each case the spectra were similar, I have averaged them.

Before carrying out the joint analysis, an initial program of fits to the individual datasets was done. Differences in the silicon and sulfur line energies between the SSS and *Tenma* were found for Tycho and Cassiopiea A. This is attributed to an error in the *Tenma* energy scale, which was nominally accurate to 30 eV. Assuming that the SSS data was more precise, I shifted the energy scale for the Tycho *Tenma* data up by 15 eV and shifted the Cassiopeia A data down by 70 eV. The shift for Cassiopeia A was uncomfortably large, but probably arose from confusion between one of the calibration lines at 8.04 keV and the source emission at this energy. The result of these shifts is to change the fitted emission line energies from the *Tenma* data, of which the most significant is the iron Kα line. Where appropriate, I discuss how this shift in energy scale influences the conclusions.

My conclusions differ from TSUNEMI et al. for reasons which arise purely from the inclusion of the SSS data and the shift of the *Tenma* energy scale as mentioned above. I was able to reproduce the fitted values of TSUNEMI et al. for line centroids and continuum temperatures using my analysis system and the *Tenma* data alone. The differences in conclusions can be attributed mainly to the improved errors on the silicon and sulfur line centroids, the recognition of multiple temperature components, and the different derived continuum temperatures.

IV. Results for Individual Remnants

SN1006

The remnant of the supernova (SN) explosion in 1006 shows a shell-like morphology in the X-rays with a radius of about 15' (PYE et al. [14]). For a time the X-ray spectrum was thought to be nonthermal, due to a lack of observed emission lines and a single power-law spectral form from 0.5 keV to beyond 10 keV (BECKER et al. [15]), in seeming contradiction with the imaging data. However an analysis of *Tenma*

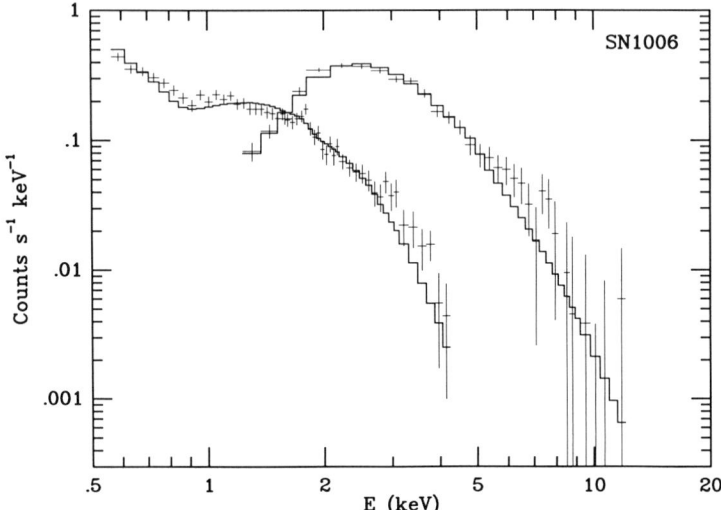

Figure 1. *Einstein* SSS and *Tenma* X-ray spectra for SN1006 and best-fit single temperature continuum model.

data (KOYAMA et al. [16]) showed the X-ray background emission in the vicinity of SN1006 to be dominated by a 7.5 keV thermal spectrum from the Lupus Loop (an older SNR). Since the 2-10 keV emission from SN1006 is rather weak, proper subtraction of this background component is essential. As I show below this *Tenma* spectrum, when analyzed with the SSS data, is more consistent with a single temperature thermal model than the earlier nonthermal, power-law form. In addition, VARTANIAN, LUM, and KU [17] discovered an oxygen emission line from SN1006, adding additional weight to a thermal interpretation of its X-ray emission.

The SSS and *Tenma* data are shown in Figure 1, with the best-fit model superposed. This is a pure thermal continuum model with $kT = 1.8$ keV and hydrogen column density of 4×10^{20} atoms cm². The χ^2 was 130 for 84 degrees of freedom. Introduction of a gaussian line at an energy of 1.86 keV improved the fit slightly, reducing χ^2 to 121. The best fitting power-law yielded a higher χ^2 value: 151 and in this case the column density was 24×10^{20} atoms cm². The 21 cm H I emission survey of HEILES and CLEARY [18] gives a column density of $6.5 \pm 0.6 \times 10^{20}$ in the direction of SN1006, a value which is more consistent with the thermal spectrum than the power-law one.

In the standard model of explosive nucleosynthesis, an iron-rich core is surrounded by layers of progressively lighter elements in an "onion-skin" structure. As the SNR evolves and the ejecta decelerates, a so-called reverse shock begins to propagate into the ejecta, heating the material to X-ray emitting temperatures. The shock travels backwards through the ejecta, progressing into material with increasing atomic number, until the iron core is reached. Much of this spatially stratified structure has been preserved to the present in SN1006. It is known that there are significant amounts of unshocked iron in the interior of the SNR from the presence of broad Fe II absorption lines seen in absorption against the remnant (WU et al.

[19]). Yet the only evidence for X-ray line emission is an oxygen line and some hint of a weak silicon line, implying that the reverse shock in this SNR has only recently begun to propagate into the silicon-rich layer of the ejecta.

Tycho

Tycho's SNR is the product of the supernova in 1572, which is widely believed to have been a Type I explosion. The X-ray image of the remnant shows a beautiful shell of emission about 8' in diameter (SEWARD *et al.* [20]). Three emission components were identified in the *Einstein* high resolution image: an outer shell of swept-up interstellar medium, a diffuse component of ejecta, and clumpy ejecta. The emission measures of these three components were determined to be in the ratios 1:0.25:0.61 and the temperatures were estimated to be 7 keV for the first two and 2 keV for the clumpy ejecta.

The X-ray spectra from the *Einstein* SSS and *Tenma* are shown in Fig. 2. The best fit model shown in the figure includes a number of lines as well as two thermal continuum components. The principle continuum component has a temperature of 1.9 keV; the second component, at a temperature of about 6 keV, has an emission measure nearly 20 times lower than the first. The statistical significance of the second component was not high, since the reduction in χ^2 was modest ($\Delta\chi^2 \sim 25$) when it was included. Taken together these results imply that the SNR is nearly isothermal over the energy band from 0.5 keV to 10 keV. Although the values of fitted temperatures are in agreement with the imaging analysis, SEWARD *et al.* require that the higher temperature component have about twice the emission measure of the cooler component. It would seem that the spectral analysis does not support this picture. I suggest that the emission measure of the hotter component, i.e., the blast wave and the diffuse ejecta, was overestimated in the imaging analysis. For example, the so-called diffuse ejecta component could just as easily be emission clumped at a spatial scale below the resolution of the X-ray image. Further study of the X-ray images from *Einstein* and new observations with ROSAT will help address this point.

With the electron temperature fixed at a value of 1.9 keV, I used the NEI model to determine the expected average Kα line energies for each elemental species as a function of ionization timescale. These are drawn as the smooth curves in Fig. 3; the boxes superposed on each curve are from the fits to the data and are at the 90% confidence level. The errors on the energy centroids for silicon and sulfur are of course quite small due to the excellent spectral resolution of the SSS data. The results on iron are also good because the line is relatively strong and isolated. However the argon and calcium lines are weaker and in the case of the SSS data, fall near the high energy cut-off of the *Einstein* X-ray telescope. As a consequence, the errors on the fitted line centroids are rather large.

It is clear that the ionization timescale derived from the iron line centroid is less than the timescale derived from the other elemental species. In fact the difference between the iron ionization timescale and that of silicon is significant at greater than 99% confidence. Note that this difference is not the result of the energy scale shift of the *Tenma* data. Without the energy shift the iron line centroid would be 0.015 keV *smaller*, which would *increase* the discrepancy. I believe that the difference is a result of the stratification of the ejecta into zones of different elemental composition. As was the case for SN1006, Tycho's SNR has also retained its stratified ejecta, while the main difference is that the reverse shock in Tycho's SNR has begun to enter the iron-rich core.

Cassiopeia A

With an age of approximately 300 years, Cassiopeia A is the youngest known supernova remnant in the Galaxy. The X-ray image (MURRAY *et al.* [21]) shows emission from an inclined ring geometry, which can be identified with the stellar

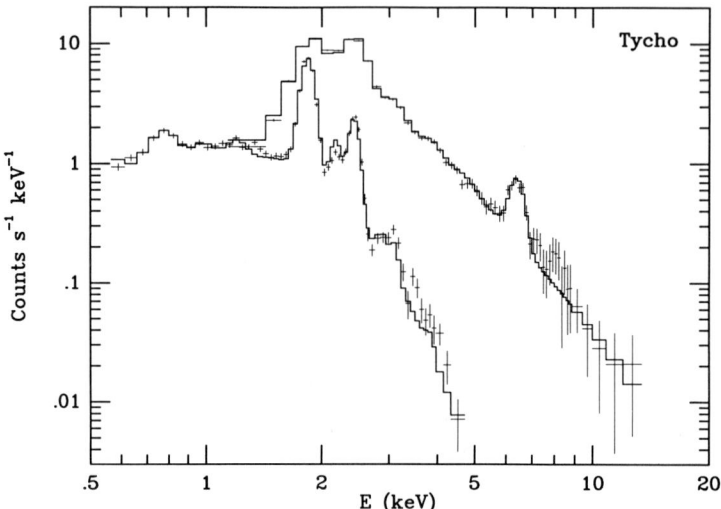

Figure 2. *Einstein* SSS and *Tenma* X-ray spectral data for Tycho's supernova remnant. Prominent lines at 1.9, 2.5 and 6.4 keV are emission from silicon, sulfur, and iron, respectively.

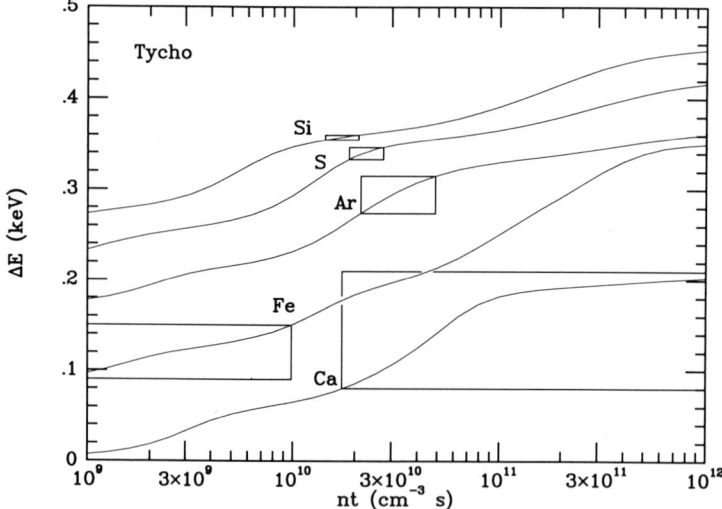

Figure 3. The variation of mean line energy for the Kα lines of silicon, sulfur, argon, calcium, and iron as a function of ionization timescale for Tycho's SNR. The electron temperature was fixed at a value of 1.9 keV. The boxes show the allowed timescales (at the 90% confidence level) derived from the fitted line energies. The reference energies corresponding to the zero of ΔE are: 1.5 keV (Si), 2.1 keV (S), 2.8 keV (Ar), 3.7 keV (Ca), and 6.3 keV (Fe).

ejecta, and an emission region surrounding that, arising from the expansion of the blast wave into the ambient circumstellar medium (CSM). The remnant is believed to be the explosion of a massive star.

The X-ray spectra from the *Einstein* SSS and *Tenma* are shown in Fig. 4 along with the best fit model which includes a number of lines as well as two thermal continuum components. The presence of two continuum emission components is highly significant. First, the χ^2 decreased by a factor of 3 when two components were included. Second, separate fits to the SSS and *Tenma* data using single temperature continua yielded very different temperatures: 1.4 keV (SSS) and 3.8 keV (*Tenma*). Finally, in these separate fits the fluxes for the silicon and sulfur $K\beta$ lines derived from the *Tenma* data were too large in comparison to the SSS data (where these lines are resolved). This "extra" flux from the $K\beta$ lines mimics a low temperature thermal component because of the poor spectral resolution of the *Tenma* detectors in the low energy range.

The derived continuum temperatures are $kT = 1.2$ keV and $kT = 4.7$ keV and there is no evidence for a significantly hotter (> 10 keV) emission component. The low temperature component has an emission measure which is 7.7 times larger than the high temperature one. I associate the low temperature component with the reverse-shocked ejecta and the high temperature component with the blast wave in the CSM. The ejecta is surely more dense than the CSM, and so the requirement for pressure-equilibrium through the contact interface implies that the ejecta emit at a lower temperature relative to the blast wave.

A deprojection of the high resolution X-ray image (FABIAN *et al.* [22]) showed that the emission measure of the ejecta region was about 6.2 times that of the outer plateau region, which is certainly in adequate agreement with the results quoted here from the spectral analysis. Although these authors do find that the plateau region is hotter than the ejecta region, there is no obvious bimodality in their temperature distribution, but rather an almost uniform distribution of emission measures from about 0.5 keV to 4.0 kev, with an additional few temperature values up to about 8 keV. Their analysis neglected nonequilibrium ionization effects and clumping of the ejecta, which should be significant. Nevertheless in future analyses I intend to investigate whether a continuous distribution of thermal continuum models can fit the X-ray spectra as well as the bimodal distribution presented here.

Comparison to the NEI model for this SNR is shown in Fig. 5. I assume that the line emission is produced almost entirely in the low temperature, ejecta component so I fixed the electron temperature at the derived value of $kT = 1.2$ keV. In contrast to Tycho's SNR (Fig. 3), the line centroids for the different elemental species are in good agreement with a single value of the ionization timescale $nt \sim 10^{11}$ cm-1 s. This is about a factor of 5 higher than the silicon and sulfur ionization timescales for Tycho, and thus consistent with the higher densities expected for the massive star progenitor of Cassiopeia A. (Note that if I use the higher temperature value of $kT = 4.7$ keV in the NEI model, the numerical value of the ionization timescale decreases, but the level of agreement among the different elemental constituents remains about the same.) If the shift of the *Tenma* energy scale were removed, then the iron line centroid would move to higher values and the ionization timescale would increase by almost an order of magnitude for the full 70 eV shift. Although I consider this unlikely, further analysis of the *Tenma* energy scale calibration is essential to eliminate this source of uncertainty.

What can one say about the structure of the supernova ejecta from the fact that a single ionization timescale seems to fit the data for Cassiopeia A? Perhaps it implies that the ejecta are stratified but that the reverse shock has passed through most of it or at least has propagated deeply into the iron-rich core. There are two objections to this picture: (1) it isn't clear that the ionization timescales will be the same since the layers of differing elemental composition would have been shocked at

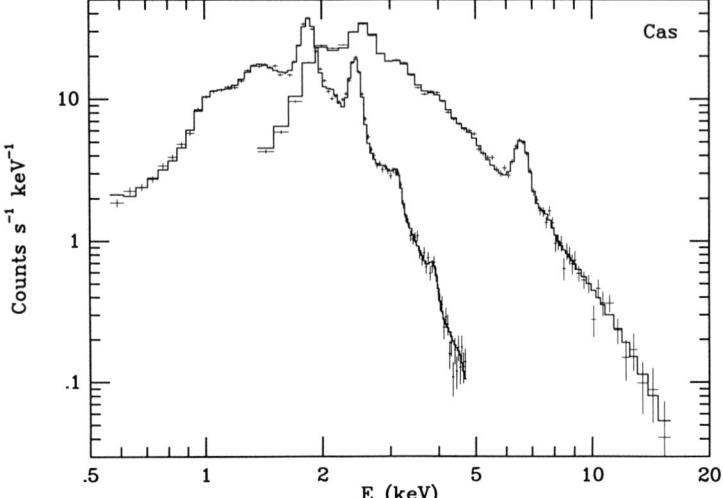

Figure 4. *Einstein* SSS and *Tenma* X-ray spectral data for Cassiopeia A. Prominent lines at 1.9, 2.5 and 6.4 keV are emission from silicon, sulfur, and iron, respectively.

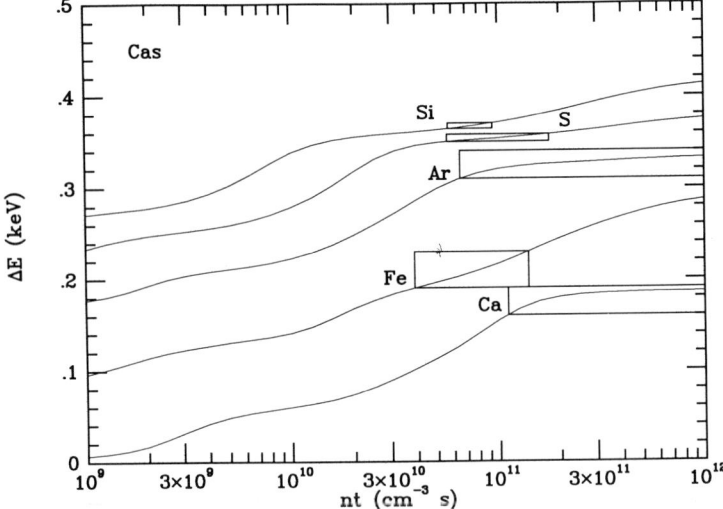

Figure 5. The variation of mean line energy for the Kα lines of silicon, sulfur, argon, calcium, and iron as a function of ionization timescale for Cassiopeia A. The electron temperature was fixed at a value of 1.2 keV. The boxes show the allowed timescales (at the 90% confidence level) derived from the fitted line energies. The reference energies corresponding to the zero of ΔE are: 1.5 keV (Si), 2.1 keV (S), 2.8 keV (Ar), 3.7 keV (Ca), and 6.3 keV (Fe).

different times and densities, and (2) the general appearance of the remnant is more consistent with incomplete thermalization of the ejecta, *i.e.*, more consistent with the remnant being in the free expansion phase than the Sedov phase. Consequently I prefer an alternative explanation wherein the iron-rich core was originally mixed at least as far as the silicon-group layer and the reverse shock is now propagating through a region of nearly homogeneous composition.

V. Conclusions

The two remnants of Type I supernovae which I have discussed in this paper, SN1006 and Tycho's SNR, show strong evidence for spatial stratification of their ejecta. In both cases an iron-rich core is separate from the silicon-group layer, and in the case of SN1006 another distinct region of oxygen or oxygen-group elements may be present. On the other hand, Cassiopeia A, the product of a Type II explosion, seems to have a spatially homogeneous composition.

Our best evidence for mixing in the ejecta of supernovae comes from studies of SN1987A in the Large Magellanic Cloud. These lines of evidence include the early appearance of soft X-rays and γ-rays and fits to the bolometric light curve (see numerous references in this volume). SN1987A was a Type II SN explosion. Evidence for mixing in other SNe is less well established. FILIPPENKO and SARGENT [23] recently observed evidence for inhomogeneities in SN1985F, a Type Ib. The presence of inhomogeneities may indicate the formation of Rayleigh-Taylor instabilities in the ejecta, which would imply significant mixing. However other explanations for clumping are also possible. BRANCH *et al.* [24] require mixing in the outer half of the ejecta of a Type I SN (SN1981B) to explain the early-time optical spectrum. In this case mixing was required to produce the observed velocity-broadening of several Si, S, Ca, and Co lines and to match their blueshifts and absorption depths. However, only about 16% (by mass) of the total iron-peak elements in the ejecta were mixed to higher velocities; the bulk of the iron-rich core was left undisturbed.

Recently two groups (ITOH, MASAI, and NOMOTO [25]; BRINKMANN *et al.* [26]) have compared compositionally-stratified models for a Type I explosion to the X-ray spectra of Tycho's SNR. Both groups started from the carbon deflagration model W7 of NOMOTO, THIELEMANN, and YOKOI [27] and evolved the hydrodynamic and ionization state of the remnant to the present age of Tycho. They found that significant amounts of iron must be mixed out from the interior in order to fit the equivalent width of the iron Kα line. However, neither group used the energy centroids of the lines to establish the relative ionization state between the silicon- and iron-group zones, as I have done here. (This was largely because they did not have access to the high spectral resolution *Einstein* SSS data.) Numerous effects can influence the equivalent width of the lines: clumping, thermal conduction, additional heating of electrons by collective plasma interactions, and not least of all, details of the initial conditions, in this case the W7 model. Further research along some of these lines may be necessary to reproduce accurately the broadband X-ray spectrum of young supernova remnants.

This research on the X-ray spectra of the remnants of historical SNe suggests that substantial amounts of mixing cannot have occurred in the ejecta of Type I SNe, while mixing is essential for Type II SNe. This conclusion is consistent with our present understanding of SN1987A as well as other supernovae. Further investigation along the following lines of research are indicated: (1) additional searches for evidence of mixing and/or inhomogeneities in the optical spectra of both Type I and II SNe, and (2) the extension of this analysis to the X-ray spectra of other historical remnants, such as Kepler's SNR, using existing X-ray data. Finally, a significant improvement in our ability to probe questions of the stratification of SN ejecta will come with the planned X-ray astronomy missions of the 90's.

VI. Acknowledgments

I would like to thank K. Koyama and H. Tsumeni for supplying the *Tenma* data and A. Szymkowiak for the SSS data. Special thanks are due to D. Yoon and S. Nolen who carried out much of the data analysis. This research was supported by NASA SADAP grant NAG8-670 and Smithsonian Institution funds.

VII. References

1. H. Itoh, *Pub. Astr. Soc. Japan*, **29**, 813 (1977).
2. H. Itoh, *Pub. Astr. Soc. Japan*, **30**, 489 (1978).
3. H. Itoh, *Pub. Astr. Soc. Japan*, **31**, 541 (1979).
4. E. H. B. M. Gronenschild and R. Mewe, *Astr. Ap. Suppl.*, **48**, 305 (1982).
5. J. M. Shull, *Ap. J.*, **262**, 308 (1982).
6. J. J. Nugent, S. H. Pravdo, G. P. Garmire, R. H. Becker, I. R. Tuohy, and P. F. Winkler, *Ap. J.*, **284**, 612 (1984).
7. J. P. Hughes and D. J. Helfand, *Ap. J.*, **291**, 544 (1985).
8. A. J. S. Hamilton, C. L. Sarazin, and A. E. Szymkowiak, *Ap. J.*, **300**, 698 (1986).
9. A. J. S. Hamilton, C. L. Sarazin, and A. E. Szymkowiak, *Ap. J.*, **300**, 713 (1986).
10. A. J. S. Hamilton and C. L. Sarazin, *Ap. J.*, **284**, 601 (1984).
11. J. C. Raymond and B. W. Smith, *Ap. J. Suppl.*, **35**, 419, (1977).
12. R. Mewe and E. H. B. M. Gronenschild, *Astr. Ap. Suppl.*, **45**, 11 (1981).
13. H. Tsunemi, K. Yamashita, K. Masai, S. Hayakawa, and K. Koyama, *Ap. J.*, **306**, 248 (1986).
14. J. P. Pye, K. A. Pounds, D. P. Rolf, F. D. Seward, A. Smith, and R. Willingale, *M.N.R.A.S.*, **194**, 569, (1981).
15. R. H. Becker, A. E. Szymkowiak, E. A. Boldt, S. S. Holt, and P. J. Serlemitsos, *Ap. J. (Letters)*, **240**, L33, (1980).
16. K. Koyama, H. Tsunemi, R. Becker, and J. P. Hughes, *Pub. Astr. Soc. Japan*, **39**, 437, (1987).
17. M. H. Vartanian, K. S. K. Lum, and W. H.-M. Ku, *Ap. J. (Letters)*, **288**, L5, (1985).
18. C. Heiles and M. N. Cleary, *Australian J. Phys., Ap. Suppl.*, **47**, 1, (1979).
19. C. C. Wu, M. Leventhal, C. L. Sarazin, and T. R. Gull, *Ap. J. (Letters)*, **269**, L5, (1983).
20. F. Seward, P. Gorenstein, and W. Tucker, *Ap. J.*, **266**, 287, (1983).
21. S. S. Murray, G. Fabbiano, A. C. Fabian, A. Epstein, and R. Giacconi, *Ap. J. (Letters)*, **234**, L69, (1979).
22. A. C. Fabian, R. Willingale, J. P. Pye, S. S. Murray, and G. Fabbiano, *M.N.R.A.S.*, **193**, 175, (1980).
23. A. V. Filippenko and W. L. W. Sargent, *Ap. J. (Letters)*, **345**, L43, (1989).
24. D. Branch, J. B. Doggett, K. Nomoto, and F.-K. Thielemann, *Ap. J.*, **294**, 619, (1985).
25. H. Itoh, K. Masai, and K. Nomoto, *Ap. J.*, **334**, 279, (1988).
26. W. Brinkmann, H. H. Fink, A. Smith, and F. Haberl, preprint, (1989).
27. K. Nomoto, F.-K. Thielemann, and K. Yokoi, *Ap. J.*, **286**, 644, (1984).

Infrared Knots Around SS433 – Results of Jets

Zhenru Wang, Yang Chen, Richard McCray, & Qinyue Qu

1. INTRODUCTION

SS433 is a famous exotic object in the center of radio source W50. It has been widely observed at various wavelengths and has attracted more and more attention since 1978. The most unusual feature of SS433 is two relativistic jets ejected at a velocity of 0.26c in opposite directions (MARGON [1]). This feature can explain the simultaneous presence of red and blue shifts of strong optical emission lines varying periodically as well as the two bright X-ray lobes stretched in the direction of the jets (SEWARD et al. [2]). In 1987, six infrared knots around SS433 were discovered from IRAS data by BAND [3]. They have similar infrared spectra except for the fifth one. Band suggested that the fifth one is a different kind of object [3], and we agree. But for the other five knots, we suggest a different model. We don't think it is accidental that five knots are all located in the direction of the jets and are within, or adhere to, the radio shell of W50. It is very probable that they result from the interaction between the jets and the interstellar medium. We assume that the knots consist mainly of dust grains and gas. Both are continuously heated by collisions of particles in the jets. Their spectra are explained by the thermal radiation of dust grains and the free-free emission of partly ionized hydrogen gases.

2. THE FITS OF SPECTRA

Suppose the thermal emission of dust is the main component of the steep spectra (from 100 to 60 µ). The dust radiation drops so quickly with frequency that the radiation between 25 and 12 µ can be considered as free-free emission only. The results of fitted parameters, electron density n_e (or n_p), and electronic temperature T_e for the five knots are listed in Table 1. The observed flux between 60 and 100 µ should contain two kinds of radiation. Subtracting the free-free emission contribution from the ob-

Table 1. Physical parameters of the knots from the spectra fits.

knot	1	2	3	4	6
$n_e [10^2 \text{ cm}^{-3}]$	3.0	1.5	1.7	1.9	0.55
$T_e [10^3 \text{ K}]$	3.3	1.1	0.67	2.1	0.81
$n_d [10^{-10} \text{ cm}^{-3}]$	24	1.2	0.62	1.5	0.91
T_d {K}	23	25	32	27	22

served fluxes, the fluxes of dust radiation at 100 and 60 µ are easily obtained from the observed data. The flux of dust grains is:

$$F_d(\nu) = 4\pi R^3 j_d(\nu)/3d^2 = 4\pi R^3 n_d \sigma_d Q_a B_\nu(T_d)/3d^2 \qquad (1)$$

where d is the distance of SS433, 5 kpc, R is the radius of the knots [3], $j_d(\nu)$ is the emissivity of the dust grains (SPITZER [4]), n_d is the number density of dust grains, σ_d is the geometrical cross section of a single grain, $\sigma_d = \pi a^2$, a is the grain radius. T_d is the temperature of dust grains and Q_a is the efficiency factor. Taking 2a = 0.3 µ and the index of refraction m = 1.3 - 0.02i (ALLEN [5]), then $Q_a = 1.45 \times 10^{-16} \nu$. Using (1) to fit the steep spectra, the values of n_d and T_d in the knots are obtained and also listed in Table 1. Figure 1 shows the infrared spectrum of knot 1 and its spectrum fit. Other knots are similar.

3. THE CONSISTENCY OF PHYSICAL PARAMETERS

We will now discuss whether the physical parameters of the knots are reasonable.

The hydrogen atoms in the knots are ionized by the bombardment of relativistic particles in the jets. The equation of ionization-recombination equilibrium is:

$$n_H(n_{je}+n_{jp}) v_j \sigma_{1c} = n_e n_p \alpha(2) \qquad (2)$$

where n_H is the number density of neutral hydrogen atoms of the knots, n_{je} and n_{jp} are the number densities of relativistic electrons and protons in the jets respectively, $n_{je} = n_{jp} = n_j$, $\alpha(2)$ is the recombination coefficient to all states except the ground state which is a function of T_e [4]. Let $v_j = 0.26c$, and σ_{1c} is the cross section for collision ionization of hydrogen atoms from ground state (LOTZ [6]). From (2) we can easily get the values of $n_H n_j$ for the knots as ~1 cm^{-6}.

Let us now discuss the cooling and heating of dust. The cooling rate of the dust is

$$\Lambda_d = 4\pi \int_0^\infty n_d \sigma_d Q_a B_\nu(T_d) d\nu = 2.64 \times 10^{-9} T_d^5 n_d \sigma_d \text{ [ergs cm}^{-3} \text{ s}^{-1}]. \qquad (3)$$

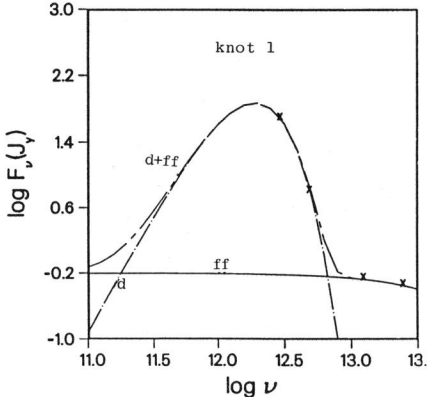

Fig. 1 The infrared spectrum of knot 1. Curve d is the thermal emission of the dust. Curve ff is the free-free emission of hydrogen. The observed data are shown by crosses.

The heating rate of the dust (DWEK [7]) by the jets' electrons is:

$$\Gamma_d^j = n_d \sigma_d n_j v_j [E_e \zeta(E_e) + E_p \zeta(E_p)] \tag{4}$$

where E_e and E_p are the energy of impinging electrons and protons respectively, $\zeta(E)$ is the fraction of E that is deposited in the dust grain [8]. In our case, $\zeta(E_e) = 0.16$ and $E_p \zeta(E_p) \approx E_e \zeta(E_e)$. Then

$$\Gamma_d^j = 70 \, n_d \sigma_d n_j \quad [\text{ergs cm}^{-3} \text{ s}^{-1}] \quad . \tag{5}$$

The heating rate of the dust by thermal electrons can be obtained by

$$\Gamma_d^T = n_d \sigma_d n_e \int_0^\infty v f(v) \frac{1}{2} m_e v^2 dv = n_d \sigma_d n_e 2 (\pi m_e)^{-1/2} (2kT_e)^{3/2} \tag{6}$$

where $f(v)$ is the Maxwell velocity distribution function. From the equation of energy equilibrium of the dust grains $\Lambda_d = \Gamma_d^j + \Gamma_d^T$, we derive values of n_j at the positions of knots $\sim 10^{20}$ cm from SS433 that range from 10^{-4} to 1.3×10^{-3} cm^{-3}. Compared with previous results (WATSON [8]), these results are consistent with $n_j \propto 1/r^2$. Further, the neutral hydrogen atom number density n_H, the ionization degree χ, and the gas-to-dust ratio $(n_p + n_H)/n_d$ are derived (see [10]).

As to the energy equilibrium of the gas there are two cooling mechanisms. One is thermal bremsstrahlung, the other is due to collision excitation of radiative transitions of trace elements by thermal electrons and atoms. They are represented by $\Lambda_{ff}(T_E)$ and Λ_{cc} (DALGARNO and MCCRAY [9]) respectively

$$\Lambda_{ff}(T_E) = 1.426 \times 10^{-27} n_e n_p T_E^{1/2} \langle g_{ff} \rangle \quad [\text{ergs cm}^{-3} \text{ s}^{-1}] \tag{7}$$

$$\Lambda_{cc} \simeq 4 \times 10^{-24} n_e n_H \text{ [ergs cm}^{-3}\text{ s}^{-1}\text{]} \quad . \tag{8}$$

The heating role is played by the net ionized electrons, and then

$$\Gamma(T_E) = 2 n_H n_j v_j \sigma_{1c} \bar{E}_2 - n_e n_p \alpha(2) \frac{3}{2} kT_E \tag{9}$$

where $\bar{E}_2$ is the mean kinetic energy of electrons released from the collision ionization. The average energy loss of the relativistic particles during a collisional ionization is $E_\ell = \bar{E}_2 + 13.6$ eV. Using the energy equilibrium equation $\Lambda_{ff}(T_E) + \Lambda_{cc}(T_E) = \Gamma(T_E)$ and (2) for the ionization equilibrium together with $T_E \simeq T_e$, we find that the value of E_ℓ is physically reasonable (see [10]).

4. CONCLUSION

Based on the infrared data of knots and the analysis here, it is probable that the five knots are physically related to SS433. The knots are mainly composed of dust and partly ionized hydrogen gas. Their infrared spectra are well fitted with the thermal emission of dust and the free-free emission. The knots are in a state of ionization-recombination equilibrium and energy equilibrium. The physical parameters derived from these physical processes are reasonable and consistent. In another paper (WANG et al. [10]), we further consider the stochastic heating of dust grains and a distribution of grain sizes. We find no important changes in the results, because for the interaction between the jets of SS433 and the interstellar medium, dust grains of larger size are more important and they are nearly in a state of equilibrium. The upper limit on surface brightness of H_α for the knots expected from our model is consistent with Becker's observation ([3],[10]).

This work is supported by the National Science Foundation in the U.S. and the National Natural Science Foundation of China.

References
1. B. Margon: Ann. Rev. Astr. Ap. 22, 507 (1984).
2. F. Seward, J. Grindlay, E. Seaquist, W. Gilmore: Nature 287, 806 (1980).
3. D. L. Band: Publ.A.S.P. 99, 1269 (1987).
4. L. Spitzer: In Physical Processes in the Interstellar Medium (Wiley, 1978).
5. C. W. Allen: Astrophysical Quantities (William Clowes, 1973).
6. W. Lotz: Ap. J. Suppl. 14, 207 (1967).
7. E. Dwek: Ap. J. 322, 812 (1987).
8. M. Watson, R. Willingale, J. Grindlay, F. Seward: Ap. J. 273, 688 (1983).
9. A. Dalgarno, R. McCray: Ann. Rev. Astr. Ap. 10, 375 (1972).
10. Z. R. Wang, Y. Chen, R. McCray, Q. Y. Qu: Astr. Ap. submitted.

The Radio Spectra of Supernova Remnants
John Dickel

1. General Characteristics

The radio emission from supernova remnants (SNRs) is synchrotron radiation by relativistic electrons in magnetic fields. One electron will produce radiation in a series of harmonics of its cyclotron frequency around a magnetic-field line but these harmonics will smear into a continuum with the frequency of peak emission dependent upon the energy of the electron. The radio frequencies of interest are generally well above the peak frequency. A collection of electrons with a power law distribution in energy, $N(E) = CE^{-\gamma}dE$ where $N(E)$ is the number of electrons with energy E, will then produce continuum radiation with a power-law spectrum of the form $S_f = \text{const } f^\alpha$, where S_f is the observed flux density (in Janskys where $1 \text{ Jy} = 10^{-26} \text{w m}^{-2} \text{ Hz}^{-1}$) at frequency f and the power, α, is called the spectral index where $\alpha = -(\gamma-1)/2$. Typical values of α range between -0.8 and -0.3 for shell SNRs. This means that they are brighter at lower frequencies.

The detailed formula for the intensity of the synchrotron emission is

$$I_f = \frac{A e^3}{mc^2} \left(\frac{3e}{4\pi m^3 c^5}\right)^{(\gamma-1)/2} B^{(\gamma+1)/2} L C f^{-(\gamma-1)/2} \tag{1}$$

where e is the charge of the electron, m its mass, c the speed of light, B the magnetic field strength, f the frequency, γ the energy index, L the depth of the radiating region along the line of sight, C the constant in the energy distribution given above is related to the density, and A is a complex function with a numerical value near 0.1 containing Γ functions of γ (GINZBURG and SYROVATSKI [1]). Evaluation of the spectrum will require knowledge of the magnetic fields and the relativistic electron distributions. The field can be diluted by expansion of the remnant but also compressed by shocks and thermal instabilities or amplified by turbulence. Electrons can suffer losses by radiation and work under adiabatic expansion but also gain energy by Fermi acceleration — first order by crossing shocks and second order in turbulent eddies created by expansion into an irregular medium with Rayleigh-Taylor and Kelvin-Helmhotz instabilities (DICKEL et al [2]). Crab-type or filled remnants appear to have continuous injection of particles from a neutron star and values of α near 0.0 (WEILER [3]).

2. Time Changes

How do the radio spectra of shell-type SNR behave under the various competing mechanisms? Observational data indicate that older remnants appear to have flatter spectra than young ones. Figure 1 might suggest that the change in slope is most rapid at young ages but the sample is too small to specify a trend. In addition, Cas A, the youngest known SNR in the Milky Way, is flattening with time (BAARS et al [9]); the annual decrease, d, in flux density of Cas A as a function of frequency:

$$d(f) \text{ [in \%/year]} = 0.97(\pm 0.04) - 0.30(\pm 0.04) \log f \text{ [in GHz]}. \qquad (2)$$

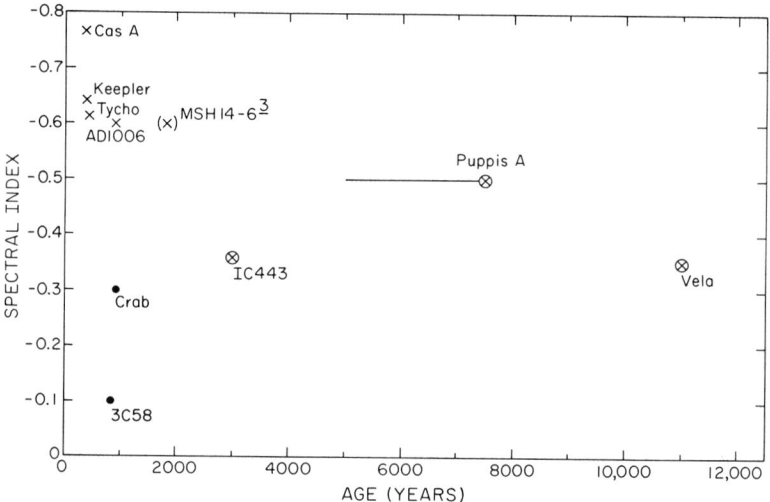

Fig. 1. Radio spectral indices of supernova remnants versus age. Spectral indices are taken from GREEN'S [4] list and references for the ages are: historical remnants (CLARK and STEPHENSON [5]; Puppis A (ARENDT [6]); IC 443 (PETRE et al [7]); and Vela (MANCHESTER and TAYLOR [8]).

It is difficult to include more galactic objects in the sample because of inhomogeneities in the database. We don't know how to obtain ages for most remnants and determination of consistent spectral indices is very difficult because of varying beam sizes, sidelobe responses, background removal, etc. at the different frequencies. To obtain a reasonably homogeneous sample we have used a survey of 19 SNRs in the Large Magellanic Cloud (MILNE et al [10]). All of these remnants were identified in the radio at 5 GHz and the data used for the spectral index evaluations extend from 0.4 to 14.7 GHz. Although the list does not contain all the SNRs known in the LMC, it should be an unbiased sample of objects. Because we do not know the ages of these objects, we have adopted the 1 GHz surface brightness, Σ, as an indicator of relative evolutionary age. The surface brightness should decrease with time because there is more acceleration at early epochs when the velocities and shocks are faster and, by later times, adiabatic expansion will cause a decrease in density and particle energy. The results, shown in Fig. 2, indicate a rather weak correlation with a value

$$\alpha = -2.25 - 0.09 \log \Sigma \qquad (3)$$

and a correlation coefficient of 0.62. The average index of the 19 remnants is -0.44. Thus the spectra appear to be steeper at greater surface brightness which implies they are flattening with age. This is contrary to what one would expect for energy losses alone as the most

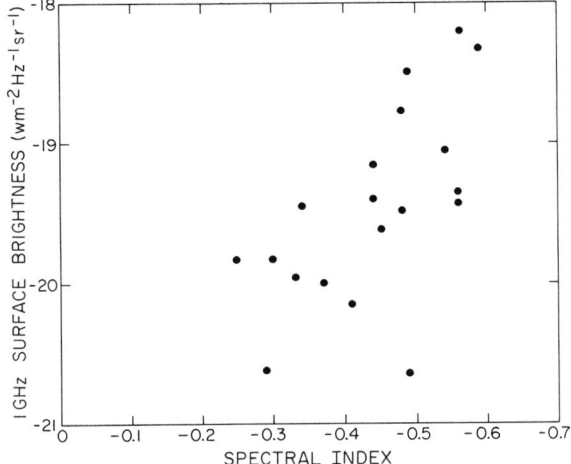

Fig. 2. Radio spectral index versus 1 GHz surface brightness of SNRs in the LMC. Brighter (younger) remnants have more negative (steeper) spectral indices so remnants should evolve toward the lower left.

energetic particles should lose energy fastest. However, COWSIK and SARKAR ([11]) have shown that continued stochastic acceleration of relativistic particles in turbulent regions will tend to decrease the number of particles near the peak in the energy distribution with some going to higher energies and some to lower energies. This will flatten the overall energy distribution and thus the spectrum of the observed radiation with time. The fact that this process continues at least well into the adolescent phase of SNR evolution after the blast has swept up many times the ejected mass, shows that acceleration processes are still important at these later times.

3. Spectral Variations Across a Remnant?

Because particle acceleration depends on turbulent instabilities and shock strength, changes in spectral index might be expected across a remnant as varying conditions are encountered. This does not appear to be the case, however, as there are no conclusive data on changes in spectral index across any shell remnant. Some early indications of such variations have been shown to be erroneous after careful removal of the confusing galactic background, and correction for differing beam resolution near the edges of some remnants, e.g. for IC 443 (ERICKSON and MAHONEY [12]) and Vela (MILNE and MANCHESTER [13]). It thus appears that the spectrum does not depend upon the magnitude of the particle acceleration and field amplification but only on the length of time the stochastic processes have been occurring.

Remnants which do show spectral variations are the composite objects consisting of a filled or Crab-type remnant with a flat spectrum and sharp boundary surrounded by a shell type one with a steeper spectrum, e.g. M5H 15-56 (MILNE et al [14]). Also, ERICKSON and PERLEY ([15]) reported a short lived "flare" in the brightness of Cas A at 38 MHz. They could not resolve the feature but its rapid decay required it to be small and thus a small-scale change in spectrum.

4. Changes in Spectral Index With Frequency?

Synchrotron radiation should have a constant spectral index unless the electrons themselves have a changing distribution with energy. Synchrotron losses will steepen a spectrum as they affect the highest energy electrons most significantly but the lifetime for such losses is much greater than 10^5 years, the age of the very oldest observed remnants. Spectra of the old remnants HB9 and the Cygnus Loop, however, suggest kinks near 1GHz with a steeper slope at high frequencies (DE NOYER [16]). These results need confirmation but, if true, might represent a balance between the reduced acceleration processes and compression of previously present ambient particles which are no longer being accelerated. The general galactic background has a change in its spectrum near 200 MHz (BRIDLE [17]) which could be shifted upward in frequency to near 1GHz by the compression. Finally, a number of remnants near the galactic plane show a decrease in brightness at frequencies $\leq$ 100 MHz. This can be attributed to free-free absorption by intervening ionized hydrogen and is not a property of the remnants themselves (e.g. KASSIM [18]).

References

1. V. Ginzburg, S. Syrovatski: Ann. Rev. Astr. and Ap. 3, 297 (1965).
2. J. Dickel, J. Eilek, E. Jones, S. Reynolds: Ap. J. Sup. 70, 497 (1989)
3. K. Weiler: In Supernova Remnants and Their X-ray Emission, ed. by J. Danziger and P. Gorenstein (Reidel, Dordrecht, 1983) p. 299.
4. D. Green: MN 209, 449 (1984).
5. D. Clark, F. Stephenson: The Historical Supernovae, (Pergamon Press, Oxford, 1977).
6. R. Arendt: Ph.D. Thesis, University of Illinois (1988).
7. R. Petre, A. Szymkowiak, F. Seward, R. Willingdale: Ap. J. 335, 215 (1988).
8. R. Manchester, J. Taylor: Pulsars, (Freeman, San Francisco, 1977).
9. J. Baars, R. Genzel, I. Pauliny-Toth, A. Witzel: Ast. Ap. 61, 99 (1977).
10. D. Milne, J. Caswell, R. Haynes: MN 191, 469 (1980).
11. R. Cowsik, S. Sarkar: MN 207, 745 (1984).
12. W. Erickson, M.J. Mahoney: Ap. J. 290, 596 (1985).
13. D. Milne, R.N. Manchester: Astron. Astrophys. 167, (1986).
14. D. Milne, J. Caswell, R. Haynes, M. Kesteven, K. Wellington, R. Roger, J. Bunton: Publ. Astron. Soc. Australia 6, 78 (1985).
15. W. Erickson, R. Perley: Ap. J. Lett. 200, L83 (1975).
16. L. De Noyer: A. J. 79, 1253 (1974).
17. A. Bridle: MN 136, 219 (1967).
18. N. Kassim: Ap. J. 347, in press, December (1989).

Observations of Molecular Clouds Associated with Supernova Remnants in the LMC

J. P. Hughes, L. Bronfman, & L. Nyman

I. Introduction

The Large Magellanic Cloud (LMC) has been systematically surveyed for CO line emission by COHEN *et al.* [1], who found a general correspondence between the CO emission and such Population I objects as supernova remnants (SNRs) and H II regions. However, because of the limited spatial resolution of the survey ($8\rlap{.}'8$), a detailed association between individual objects and molecular cloud complexes was not possible. Guided by the survey results, we have undertaken a study of SNR-molecular cloud associations using the Swedish-ESO Submillimeter Telescope (SEST) at La Silla, Chile. The SEST has good spatial resolution: at the CO J = 2 – 1 line (230.5 GHz) the half power beam width is only about 22″. We have obtained data on two LMC SNRs: N49 and N132D, both of which have CO line emission in their vicinities.

We mapped the CO J = 2 – 1 line emission with a grid spacing of 20″ starting at the approximate center of each remnant. The telescope was operated in frequency switched mode with a 21 MHz frequency throw, corresponding to a velocity shift of about 27 km/s. The total frequency range sampled was 87 MHz (about 110 km/s in velocity). In most cases we integrated for 30 min., although for the regions of stronger emission near N132D we used 10 min. integrations. The system temperature varied from about 800 K to 1000 K during the two days of observations of N49, and varied from 1000 to 1250 K for the N132D observations (done on a single day). The data were folded, third order baselines were subtracted, and the CO emission was integrated over velocity for mapping purposes. We also integrated over a line-free region of the spectra in order to assess our signal to noise and establish the level of possible systematic error in our baseline fits. In a 10 km/s wide velocity region adjacent to the CO line the RMS velocity-integrated emission was ±0.086 K km/s for N49 and ±0.082 K km/s for N132D.

II. N49

The *Einstein* high resolution X-ray image of N49 is shown in Fig. 1 in a grey scale presentation along with contours of the velocity-integrated CO emission (W_{CO}). The lowest contour in the figure is 8.7 times the RMS noise level determined from integrating an adjacent 10 km/s velocity region, as described above. The average velocity (LSR) of this cloud is about 286 km/s, in excellent agreement with the velocity of the SNR: 286 ± 1 km/s (SHULL [2]). There is little difference in average velocity from point to point in the cloud (< 1 km/s), although the width (FWHM) of the line varies from about 3.5 km/s to almost 7 km/s. We note that the peak antenna temperature (uncorrected for beam efficiency) was 0.36 K.

The agreement in position and velocity between this molecular cloud and the SNR N49 strongly suggest that the objects are physically related. In addition, the cloud is located near the brightest region of X-ray emission, where the optical emission is also bright. Further study of our data (e.g., searches for high velocity CO emission) and comparisons with optical and infrared observations should allow us to investigate the relationship between the cloud and SNR.

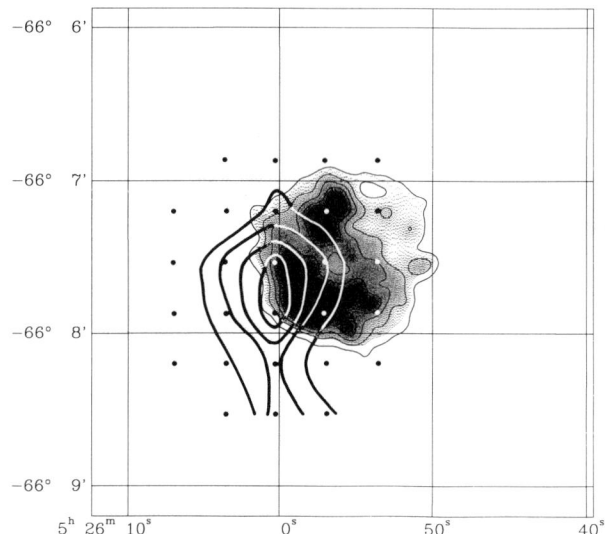

Figure 1. *Einstein* X-ray image of N49 overlaid with contours of the velocity-integrated CO emission. The grid pattern for the CO observations is shown. The contour levels are 0.75, 1.0, 1.25, and 1.50 K km/s and the spectra were integrated from 280 km/s to 290 km/s.

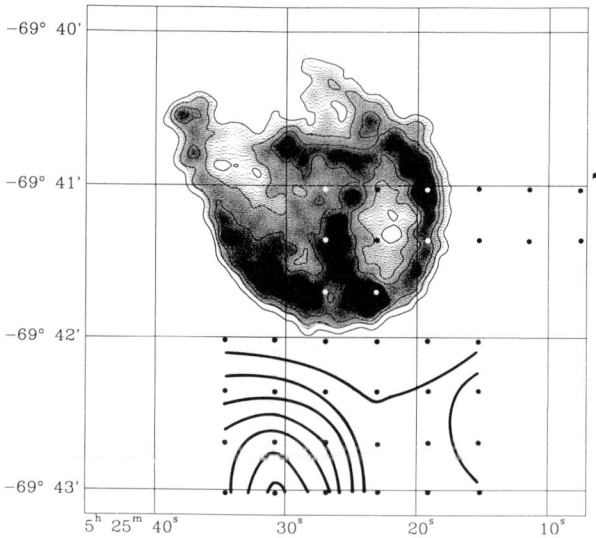

Figure 2. The same as Fig. 1, but for the SNR N132D. Here the contour levels are 3, 5, 7, 9, 11, 13, and 15 K km/s for a velocity integration range from 260 km/s to 270 km/s.

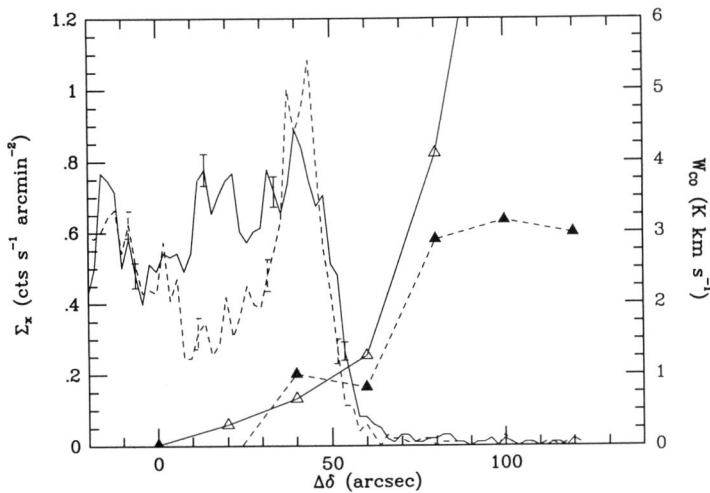

Figure 3. Comparison of X-ray surface brightness (curves on the left) with the velocity-integrated CO emission (curves rising to the right) for the SNR N132D. Two different strips through the remnant are shown.

III. N132D

Figure 2 shows the high resolution X-ray image of N132D and the contours of W_{CO}. The lowest contour in this figure is a factor of 37 times the RMS noise level and the peak antenna temperature is about 3 K. This molecular emission is significantly stronger than that in N49 by about a factor of ten. There is a strong velocity gradient across the CO emission region: the average velocity varies from 262 km/s in the east to about 268 km/s in the west. Although the uncertainty is large, it appears that the SNR lies at a different velocity (247 ± 16 km/s DANZIGER and DENNEFELD [3]). The velocity of the cloud and the SNR are both larger than that expected from the rotation curve of the LMC, which should be about 236 km/s at this point (DAME [4]).

Toward the south the match between the shape of the CO contours and the X-ray image is rather striking, even considering the incomplete CO coverage. This is shown in more detail in Fig. 3., where we plot the X-ray surface brightness and the W_{CO} emission for two slices through the SNR image. The slices correspond to $\alpha(1950) = 5^h\ 25^m\ 27^s$ (solid curves) and $\alpha(1950) = 5^h\ 25^m\ 23^s$ (dashed curves). The ordinate represents the distance in arcsec from declination value -69° 41' 2''. The anticorrelation between X-ray and CO emission is apparent, although there is CO emission near the shell of N132D (near $\Delta\delta = 50''$ in Fig. 3) at about the same level as observed for N49. It is the presence of a rather bright molecular cloud complex to the south which is striking. Note, however, that the slices which were mapped to the west show little or no CO emission.

HUGHES [5] proposed an evolutionary scenario for N132D in which the precursor star blew a cavity in the surrounding interstellar medium (ISM) before it became a supernova, and that the SN blast wave has now propagated to the walls of the cavity. The model requires a gradient in the local ISM density, in the sense of increasing from the northeast to the southwest, in order to explain the morphology of the remnant. This requirement could be satisfied if the SN occurred at the edge of a molecular cloud, as the present observations seem to indicate. In this case a significant interaction should be occurring between the remnant and the molecular cloud.

We thank the SEST program committee for granting observation time to this project and we thank T. Dame, H. Tananbaum, and D. Harris for useful discussions and comments. This research was supported in part by Smithsonian Institution funds.

IV. References
1. R. S. Cohen, T. M. Dame, G. Garay, J. Montani, M. Rubio, and P. Thaddeus, *Ap. J. (Letters)*, **331**, L95, (1988).
2. P. Shull, *Ap. J.*, **275**, 611, (1983).
3. I. J. Danziger and M. Dennefeld, *Ap. J.*, **207**, 394, (1976).
4. T. M. Dame, private communication, (1989).
5. J. P. Hughes, *Ap. J.*, **314**, 103, (1987).

The Interaction of Supernova Remnant in the Early Phase with a Circumstellar Shell

Tatsuo Yoshida & Hitoshi Hanami

The observations in the ultraviolet(IUE), the near infrared(speckle interferometry), and the soft X-ray(Ginga) of SN1987A suggest circumstellar shells(CSSs) exist. The shells have been formed when the fast blue supergiant wind sweeps the red supergiant wind.

If the supernova remnant(SNR) hits the CSS, hydrodynamical instability may arise in the acceleration of the high-density shell by the lower-density shocked circumstellar matter. In this paper, we give the numerical results of our two dimensional calculations to investigate how the instability develops.

Model

We use the spherically symmetric self-similar solution(CHEVALIER [1]) as a model of SNR, assuming that the envelope of the ejecta and the circumstellar matter(CSM) have power-law density profiles as $\rho \propto r^{-7}$ and $\rho \propto r^{-2}$, respectively. We start calculations from 0.5 yr after the explosion. The parameters are as follows: the explosion energy is 10^{51}erg and the mass of the ejecta is 10 $M_\odot$. The ratio of the progenitor's mass loss rate to the wind velocity is $2.4 \times 10^{-6} M_\odot yr^{-1} / 10$ kms^{-1} (YOSHIDA and HANAMI [2]).

The parameters of the shell are based on Masai's model (MASAI et al. [3]), which explains the flare in January 1988 of SN1987A. The shell and the CSM are assumed to be initially in pressure equilibrium. The surface of the shell is located at $r_c = 4.1 \times 10^{16}$ cm with a density of $\rho_{cloud} = \delta \cdot \rho_{CSM}(r_c)$ and a thickness d of 5.4×10^{15} cm. The shell covers $\Omega/4\pi \sim 15$ % of the spherical area. We assume that initially the surface of the shell has sinusoidal corrugations. The amplitude a_0 is 0.1d and the wavelength λ is $2\pi r_c / \ell$, where ℓ is the azimuthal wave number.

Numerical Results

Figure 1a and b show how the density distribution and the velocity field of the SNR and the CSS evolve at an interval of 1.0 yr for the case $\delta = 20$ and $\ell = 48$. We find that the corrugations grow and finger-like structures are formed.

In order to see how the instability develops, we pursue the motion of the marker particles, which are set on the surface of the shell initially. Figure 2a shows the positions of the marker particles at evolutionary stages. The particles are connected by a line at each stage. Figure 2b shows the time evolution of the corrugation amplitude. We find that there are three periods, which have different growth rates of the amplitude.

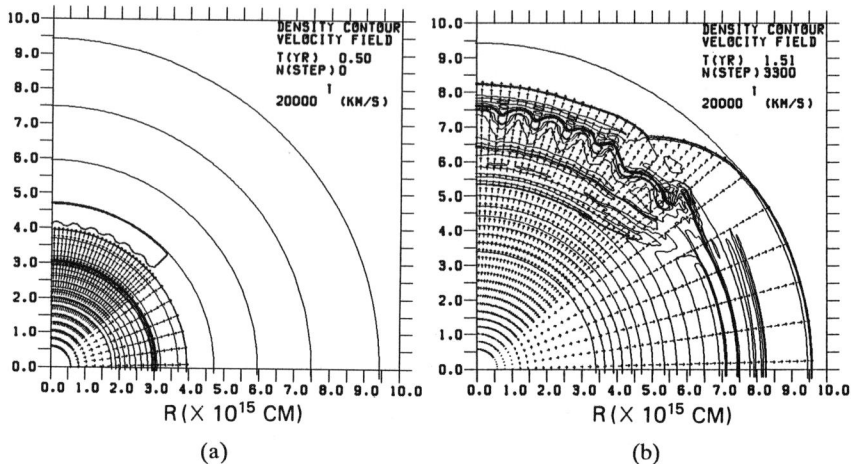

Figure 1. (a) Density contours and velocity vectors for the case $\delta=20$ and $\ell=48$ at the initial condition($t=0.5$ yr). Lines of constant density are logarithmically spaced with $\log\Delta\rho=0.2$. (b) The same as (a) except $t=1.5$ yr.

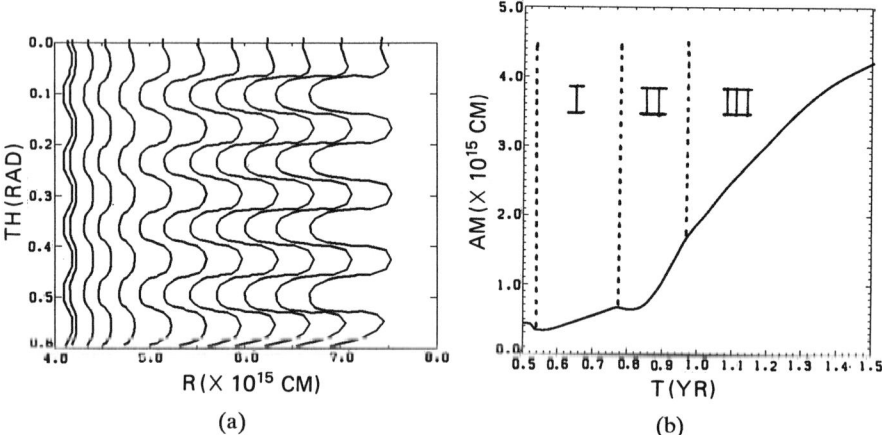

Figure 2. (a) The positions of the marker particles are shown. (b) Time evolution of the amplitude.

In the first period the amplitude grows linearly. Richtmyer [4] finds that, in systems which have been impulsively accelerated by a shock, the amplitude grows at a constant rate with time according to

$$a(t)/a(0)=1+\alpha t, \quad \alpha=\frac{2\pi}{\lambda}\left(\frac{\rho_{cl}-4\rho_0}{\rho_{cl}+4\rho_0}\right)\Delta v, \tag{1}$$

where Δv is the increment of the velocity imparted by the acceleration. If we know the value of Δv, we can estimate the value of α. Figure 3 shows the velocity history of the marker particle at a crest of corrugations. This figure shows after the particle is impulsively accelerated, the value of the particle velocity becomes nearly constant. Using this as the value of Δv, we can calculate the value of α. This calculated value of α is 1.6 times as large as one obtained from figure 2b. The discrepancy could be attributed to numerical diffusion.

In the second period, when the shock goes out of the dense shell, the growth rate increases rapidly. This is because rarefaction wave is formed and the shell compressed by the shock becomes subject to expansion. Figure 3 shows that the particle is accelerated again in this period. In the third period, the growth rate decreases slowly. However, the amplitude becomes comparable with the thickness of the shell since the growth rate in the second period is large.

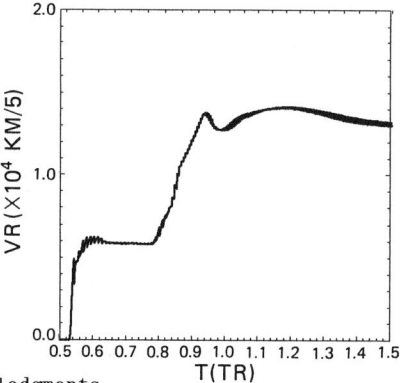

Figure 3. A velocity history of the marker particle at a crest of corrugations.

Acknowledgments

T.Y would like to thank Professor S.Sakashita, Dr.A.Habe, and Dr.T.Ebisuzaki for their valuable discussions T.Y. is grateful to the Nukazawa Memorial Foundation for financial support. The calculations were carried out on HITAC M-680H at the Center for Information Processing Education of Hokkaido University, HITAC S-820/80 at the Computing Center of Hokkaido University, FACOM VP200 at the Space Data Analysis Center, the Institute of Space and Astronautical Science, and FACOM VP50 at the Nobeyama Radio Observatory.

References

1. R. Chevalier: Ap.J. 258, 790(1982).
2. T. Yoshida, H. Hanami: Prog.Theor.Phys. 80, 83(1988).
3. K. Masai, S. Hayakawa, H. Inoue, H. Itoh, and K. Nomoto: Nature 335, 804(1988).
4. R. D. Richtmyer: Com.Pure.Appl.Math. 13, 297(1960)

Global Effects of Supernova Remnants on the Interstellar Medium

Christopher McKee

1. Introduction

The overall energetics of the interstellar medium (ISM) are governed largely by the outflow of energy from stars through the ISM to the intergalactic medium. This energy is in the form of radiation, winds, and supernova explosions; supernovae dominate the injection of kinetic energy into the ISM. Much of this energy is from massive stars, which are continually forming out of the ISM and which return most of their mass back to the ISM.

The ISM is observed to be highly inhomogeneous, with much of the mass concentrated in clouds—both atomic and molecular—which occupy a small fraction of the volume, whereas much of the volume is filled with warmer intercloud gas. Field, Goldsmith, and Habing (1969; hereafter FGH) provided a theoretical explanation of how such multiphase behavior is possible: the temperature dependence of the cooling rate of interstellar gas is such that cold ($T \sim 10^2$ K), neutral (H I) clouds can coexist in pressure equilibrium with warm ($T \sim 10^4$ K) intercloud H I only over a limited range of pressures, close to those observed in the ISM. Subsequently, Cox and Smith (1974) argued that supernova explosions in the Galaxy are sufficiently frequent that supernova remnants tend to overlap, forming a network of hot tunnels in the ISM with a filling factor of about 10%; numerical simulations of this model were carried out by Smith (1977). McKee and Ostriker (1977; hereafter MO) argued that the filling factor of the hot gas is substantially larger than this, so that it forms the background medium in which the two phases of the FGH model are embedded. The ISM thus consists of three phases: the cold neutral medium (CNM), taken to have a temperature of 80 K; the the warm medium at $T \sim 8000$ K, which has both neutral (WNM) and ionized (WIM) parts; and the hot ionized intercloud medium (HIM) at a calculated temperature $T \sim 5 \times 10^5$ K. The most obvious difference between the three–phase model and the two–phase model is that a large fraction of the volume of the ISM is predicted to be almost empty, filled with low–density, hot gas; as a result, mass exchange between the hot phase and the other phases, due to thermal evaporation and condensation, is crucial in determining the equilibrium. The thermal pressure in the ISM is determined dynamically by the evolution of supernova remnants (SNRs) in the ISM, permitting prediction of the distribution of the pressures in the ISM. The three–phase model remains controversial; in particular, Cox (1988) and Cox and Slavin (1989) have suggested that the filling factor of the hot gas is only about 10%. Determining the filling factor of the hot gas in the ISM is one of the critical observational problems in interstellar astrophysics (see Spitzer 1990).

Observations in the last decade have shown that the ISM extends much farther from the plane of the Galaxy than originally believed: Lockman (1984) has found a component of HI with a scale height of about 500 pc, Reynolds (1989a) has inferred a scale height for ionized gas of 1–2.5 kpc from observations of pulsar dispersion measures, and a number of investigators have studied halo gas far from the plane through its absorption lines (Savage 1987). The mass and scale height of the various components of the ISM have been reviewed by Bloemen (1987), Spitzer (1990), and McKee (1990a). A quantitative view of the vertical structure of the ISM is given in Table 1, taken from McKee (1990a). The densities are given in terms of $\bar{n}_H(z)$, the volume averaged density of hydrogen nuclei as a function of distance from the Galactic plane, z. The surface densities Σ include the mass of helium, which we take to be 10% by number. References for the various entries are given in McKee (1990a,b).

Some comments on the Table are necessary. The division of the H I into three components is based on the work of Lockman (1984). Kulkarni and Heiles (1987) identify the component with the lowest scaleheight with the HI clouds (the CNM) and the remaining two components with the intercloud HI (which we label as WNM_1 and WNM_2). One of the components (WNM_2) extends into the halo, as has been confirmed by ultraviolet observations of high latitude stars (Lockman, Hobbs, and Shull 1986). Ionized hydrogen near the Galactic plane is in two forms, photoionized (the WIM) and collisionally ionized (the HIM). The density and scale height of the WIM can be inferred from observations of pulsar dispersion measures (e.g., Kulkarni and Heiles 1987), which imply an electron distribution of the form given in the Table, with a scale height $H_w \simeq 1$ kpc. Allowing for the roughly 4% of the electrons contributed by helium (Mathis 1986), a correction more important in principle than in practice, gives the mean hydrogen density listed in Table 1. Observations of the WIM in emission lines (reviewed in Reynolds 1989b) also imply a thick disk of warm, ionized gas.

Table 1. Vertical Mass Distribution of the ISM

Component	$\bar{n}_H(z)$ (cm^{-3})	Σ ($M_\odot$ pc^{-2})
H_2	$0.54 \exp -\frac{1}{2}(z/60)^2$	2.80
HI: CNM	$0.39 \exp -\frac{1}{2}(z/135)^2$	4.54
WNM_1	$0.093 \exp -\frac{1}{2}(z/254)^2$	2.04
WNM_2	$0.053 \exp -(|z|/480)$	1.75
HII:[a] WIM	$0.96[0.015 \exp -(|z|/70) + 0.025 \exp -(|z|/H_w)]$	1.72/1.36
HIM	$0\ /\ 0.0015 \exp -(|z|/3000)$	0/0.31
Total		12.8

[a] Two cases are considered for the hot component of the ISM (HIM): (1) no HIM / (2) HIM based on MO. The second case accounts for some of the electrons observed in the dispersion measure of high altitude pulsars, thereby reducing the scale height of the WIM from 1 kpc for Case 1 to 780 pc for Case 2.

The characteristics of the HIM are more controversial, as indicated above. To gauge the effects of the HIM on the vertical structure of the ISM, two cases are considered: (1) The HIM is negligible, in the sense that its mean pressure is small compared to that of the other components. (2) The HIM is similar to that envisioned by MO, with a temperature of about 5×10^5 K, a density $n_H \simeq 3 \times 10^{-3}$ cm^{-3}, and a filling factor f_h of about 0.5 in the plane. A scale height of $H_h = 3$ kpc for the mean density has been adopted.

The accuracy of this inventory of the mass distribution is difficult to assess, but it is consistent with the available data on the column densities and scale heights of H$_2$, HI, and HII; the total column density of all the components in this model is 13 $M_\odot$ pc^{-2}, the same as that quoted by Kulkarni and Heiles (1987). Furthermore, the total midplane density is 1.1 cm^{-3}, in good agreement with the value 1.2 cm^{-3} found from an analysis of extinction data by Spitzer (1978). The question to be resolved is: why is the scale height as large as it is? This question has been addressed observationally by Kulkarni and Fich (1985), who concluded that the H I is sufficiently turbulent that it can support itself; McKee (1990a) has shown that this conclusion applies to the WIM as well. The question then becomes, why is the ISM so turbulent? We shall argue that this turbulence is due to energy injection by supernovae, and that the remnants of the supernovae must essentially fill the ISM in order to explain the observed level of turbulence.

Before addressing these issues, a brief comment on superbubbles is in order. One of the major advances in our understanding of the ISM in the past decade is the realization that the clustering of supernovae in stellar associations can have a dramatic effect on the ISM. HI shells far too large to have been created by individual supernovae have been observed throughout the Galaxy, with large shells and supershells occurring primarily outside the solar circle (Heiles 1979) and vertical structures ("worms") occurring inside (Heiles 1984). A number of authors, beginning with Bruhweiler *et al.* (1980), have attributed these structures to energy injection by associations of massive stars, leading to the creation of superbubbles in the ISM. A discussion of this topic is beyond the scope of this paper; a thorough review has recently been given by Tenorio-Tagle and Bodenheimer (1988). It should be noted that a number of the theoretical models of superbubbles assumed that the gas disk of the Galaxy is thin, so that the energy could easily break out into the halo; however, the observations discussed in §II above show that the gas disk is in fact rather thick, so that most superbubbles should remain confined (Cox 1989). Observationally, superbubbles appear to occupy only about 10–20% of the area of the Galactic plane in the solar neighborhood (Heiles 1980), leaving most of the volume available for a two- or three-phase ISM.

2. Isothermal Models for the Vertical Structure of the ISM

In view of the inordinate complexity of the observed ISM, it is instructive to pull back and develop simple toy models to see what the ISM would be like if only a few processes were operating. Here we shall consider isothermal models for the vertical structure of the ISM. Let $C \equiv (P/\rho)^{1/2}$ be the isothermal sound speed for the ISM, where P is the total pressure and ρ the density. In order that the model not be too unrealistic, we shall include a magnetic pressure and a pressure due to cosmic rays in P. Let $g(z)$ be the magnitude of the z-component of the gravitational acceleration, and let $\bar{g}(z)$ be the mean value,

$$z\bar{g}(z) \equiv \int_0^z g(z')dz'. \qquad (1)$$

Then the solution of the equation of hydrostatic equilibrium is

$$\rho(z) = \rho_0 \exp{-\left[\frac{z\bar{g}(z)}{C^2}\right]}. \qquad (2)$$

If the gas disk is sufficiently thin and has a small fraction of the total mass, then the acceleration will be approximately a linear function of height, $g(z) \simeq z g'_0$, with the midplane gradient g'_0 constant. In this case the density is a Gaussian,

$$\rho(z) = \rho_0 \exp{-\frac{1}{2}\left(\frac{z^2}{H^2}\right)}, \qquad (3)$$

where the scale height is

$$H = \frac{C}{g'^{1/2}_0} = 116 C_6 \quad \text{pc}, \qquad (4)$$

with $C_6 \equiv C/(10^6 \text{ cm s}^{-1})$. The numerical value for the scale height is based on an acceleration gradient $g'_0 = 2.4 \times 10^{-11}$ cm s^{-2} pc^{-1}; g'_0 is proportional to the total density in the Galactic plane, and the adopted value is intermediate between those corresponding to densities of 0.185 $M_\odot$ pc^{-3} (Bahcall 1984) or 0.1 $M_\odot$ pc^{-3} (Kuijken and Gilmore 1989).

2.1 One Phase: The Dead ISM

We begin with the simplest case, in which the rate of energy injection into the ISM is so low that the gas is all cold, say at a temperature of 80 K. If we assume that the thermal, magnetic, and cosmic ray pressures are all equal, then the isothermal sound speed in the medium is 1.25 km s^{-1}, and the scale height of the gas is only about 15 pc! Such an ISM is lifeless. The scale height is small even compared to that of the molecular gas in the Galaxy, so this model can be rejected outright.

2.2 Two Phases: The Quiescent ISM

Consider now a higher heating rate, so that some of the gas is at a temperature of order 10^4 K. It is generally possible for interstellar gas to have two phases, one warm and one cold, coexisting at the same pressure: The warm phase can be in equilibrium for thermal pressures less than $P_{th,max}$, whereas the cold phase can be in equilibrium for thermal pressures greater than $P_{th,min}$; a two-phase medium is possible provided $P_{th,max} > P_{th} > P_{th,min}$ (FGH; Begelman and McKee 1990). A recent calculation of the heating and cooling of the interstellar gas including heating due to the ejection of photoelectrons from grains and the damping of hydromagnetic waves found $\tilde{P}_{th,max} \simeq 2000$ cm^{-3} K (we use $\tilde{P} \equiv P/k$ for convenience; 2000 cm^{-3} K corresponds to 2.8×10^{-13} dyne cm^{-2}) and $\tilde{P}_{th,min} \simeq 150$ cm^{-3} K (Ferriere, Zweibel, and Shull 1989).

Provided the thermal pressure in the midplane exceeds $P_{th,max}$, gas in the midplane would lie in a cold, thin disk, as in the one-phase model described above; the disk would be about 30 pc thick. At a height above the plane at which the thermal pressure has dropped below $P_{th,max}$, a two-phase structure would become possible, with cold clouds embedded in a warm intercloud medium. The scale height of the warm gas would be about 130 pc. Clouds could continue to exist up to heights somewhat greater than this, until the thermal pressure dropped below $P_{th,min}$; for

$\tilde{P}_{th,min} = 150$ cm^{-3} K, this height is about 300 pc. At greater heights, the gas would be homogeneous and warm. If not supported by turbulent motions or magnetic fields, clouds which formed in the two–phase zone would rain down on the cold disk.

This model is a substantial improvement over the one–phase model, but it is a far cry from reality. The possibility that clouds could exist in the two–phase zone above the cold disk could increase the scale height of the cold gas somewhat above 15 pc, but it would still be much less than the observed 135 pc. Warm gas is observed to have an effective scale height $\Sigma/2\rho_0$ of 430 pc (see Table 1), several times greater than the model predicts. This discrepancy is due to the fact that the model has no turbulence; it is quiescent, in contrast to the observed ISM. We conclude that isothermal models without injection of kinetic energy cannot account for the observed ISM.

3. The Three Phase ISM

The actual ISM is rent by stellar winds and supernova explosions, leading McCray and Snow (1979) to term it the "violent ISM". Supernovae are the dominant source of energy; they heat large volumes of the ISM and agitate it, inflating the ISM to its observed height. Cold clouds have a scale height much greater than 15 pc because of their turbulent motions. The scale height for the hot gas at a temperature of 5×10^5 K, the temperature calculated by MO, is about 3 kpc (this is higher than implied by equation [4] because the hot gas extends well above the stellar disk, so that $g \ll g_0' z$). If magnetic fields or cosmic rays contribute to the support of the hot gas, the scale height would be yet higher. The hot gas can confine clouds far from the plane, as envisaged by Spitzer (1956); absorption line observations indicate that these clouds extend to about 3 kpc from the plane. What is the filling factor f_h of this gas near the Galactic plane? More specifically, what is the filling factor of this gas outside superbubbles?

Consider that subset of supernovae which are effectively random in space and time; this includes supernovae from low–mass progenitors (Type Ia) and those supernovae from high–mass progenitors which are not in large associations. The rate of these supernovae per unit volume is denoted by S. Let $V(t)$ be the volume of an isolated SNR as a function of its age t. For a one–phase or two–phase ISM, this volume first increases as the remnant expands, and then decreases as the hot gas cools off. In a three–phase ISM, the remnants cannot be approximated as isolated; the SNR expansion is well defined, but thereafter the remnant merges into the hot medium. Let $dQ(t)$ be the probability that a given point is in a remnant of age between t and $t + dt$; in terms of the SN rate, we have $dQ(t) = SV(t)dt$. The expected number of SNRs younger than t encompassing a given point is then

$$Q(t) = S \int_0^t V(t')dt'. \qquad (5)$$

The expected number of SNRs of *any* age which encompass a point is $Q(t \to \infty)$; we denote this by Q, without an argument. Q is sometimes termed the "porosity" of the medium (Cox and Smith 1974). Since $V(t)$ is not well-defined for an SNR in a three–phase medium after its expansion stops, Q is not precisely defined in such a medium, but it is large: any point may be regarded as being in an SNR of some age. In the absence of interactions among the SNIts, the probability of not being in any remnant is $\exp(-Q)$, and the probability of being in at least one SNR is $1 - \exp(-Q)$.

Observe that Q is directly proportional to the *volume in space–time*, or four-volume, occupied by an SNR, $\mathcal{V} \equiv \int V dt$. We can estimate this four–volume with a simple model in which the SNR expands as a power-law in time, $R \propto t^\eta$, until it reaches a radius R_m at time t_m; at this point, its expansion velocity v_m is a factor β times the ambient isothermal sound speed C_0,

$$v_m = \frac{\eta R_m}{t_m} \equiv \beta C_0. \tag{6}$$

If the filling factor of the hot gas is not large, the SNR will subsequently contract (the importance of this contraction was emphasized by Heiles [1987] and by B.-C. Koo, private communication). Under the assumption that this contraction occurs at a constant velocity over a time $t_{\rm con}$, the total four-volume of the SNR is

$$\mathcal{V} = \left(\frac{V_m t_m}{3\eta + 1} + \frac{V_m t_{\rm con}}{4} \right) \equiv q V_m t_m, \tag{7}$$

where $V_m = (4\pi R_m^3/3)$ and q is a numerical coefficient of order unity. If the contraction occurs at the velocity v_m, we have

$$q = \frac{1}{3\eta + 1} + \frac{1}{4\eta}. \tag{8}$$

This model is certainly over-simplified: it ignores the transition from expansion to contraction, which is accompanied by an overshoot in which the internal pressure drops below the ambient value (e.g., Ostriker and McKee 1988), and which would tend to increase Q; and it does not include the effects of the embedded clouds, which tend to destroy the remnant from within toward the end of its evolution, and which would tend to decrease Q.

Cioffi, McKee, and Bertschinger (1988) have studied the late evolution of spherically symmetric SNRs in a uniform medium. They found that the expansion can be approximated with $\eta = 0.3$ at late times. The maximum radius of the remnant is

$$R_m = 77.3 \left(\frac{E_{51}^{0.316}}{n_0^{0.153} \zeta_m^{0.051} \beta^{0.429} \tilde{P}_{04}^{0.214}} \right) \text{ pc}, \tag{9}$$

which is reached at a time

$$t_m = 2.97 \times 10^6 \left(\frac{E_{51}^{0.316} n_0^{0.348}}{\zeta_m^{0.051} \beta^{1.429} \tilde{P}_{04}^{0.714}} \right) \text{ yr}, \tag{10}$$

where n_0 is the ambient density of hydrogen nuclei, $\tilde{P}_{04} = \tilde{P}_0/(10^4 \text{ cm}^{-3} \text{ K})$, and ζ_m allows cooling rate to depend on the metallicity of the gas; we shall take $\zeta_m = 1$ in our numerical estimates. With $q = 1.36$ from equation (8), the SNR four-volume is

$$\mathcal{V} = 7.82 \times 10^{12} \left(\frac{E_{51}^{1.26}}{n_0^{0.110} \zeta_m^{0.204} \beta^{2.72} \tilde{P}_{04}^{1.36}} \right) \text{ pc}^3 \text{ yr}. \tag{11}$$

This result is quite close to the value found by MO over a decade ago, aside from the factor $q \simeq 1.36$. Note in particular that $\mathcal{V}$ is insensitive to the ambient density n_0. On the other hand, the four-volume is sensitive to the parameter β; for the case in which the interstellar magnetic field does not dominate the pressure, we assume that the SNR expansion stops when the velocity drops to the ambient isothermal sound speed, so that $\beta = 1$. For a two–phase ISM in which the mean intercloud density is 0.3 cm^{-3} and the ambient pressure is $\tilde{P}_{04} = 0.62$ (comprised of a thermal pressure $\tilde{P}_{th} = 3600$ cm^{-3} K and a magnetic pressure corresponding to a 3 μG field), the four–volume of an SNR is $\mathcal{V} = 1.7 \times 10^{13} E_{51}^{1.27}$ pc^3 yr. If the magnetic field is signficantly higher, say 5 μG as envisaged by Cox and Slavin (1989), then the four–volume is reduced by a factor of about 3 (McKee 1990b).

The porosity of the ISM is simply $Q = S\mathcal{V}$, the product of the SN rate per unit volume and the SNR four–volume. Evidence from historical SN and from the observed rate of massive star formation suggests that 0.022 yr^{-1} is a conservative estimate of the Galactic SN rate (McKee 1990b). This value is identical to van den Bergh's (1983) estimate of the Galactic SN rate, and it is consistent with the rate estimated from extragalactic SN by Tammann (1982) and by van den Bergh (1990) provided the Hubble constant is in the range 50–70 km s^{-1} Mpc^{-1}. Under the assumption that the SN rate per unit area is proportional to the surface density of disk stars (Ratnatunga and van den Bergh 1989), the SN rate per unit area at the solar circle is 2.6×10^{-11} pc^{-2} yr^{-1}.

To determine S, we must determine the fraction of the SN that are effectively random in space and time, and their scale height. According to Evans, van den Bergh, and McClure (1989), almost 90% of SN are of Types Ib or II, so we focus on them. These stars are believed to have massive progenitors. Humphreys and McElroy (1984) surveyed over 5000 OB stars, and found them to be nearly evenly divided between those in associations and those in the field; we therefore assume that about half of the supernovae are random. Heiles (1990) comes to the same conclusion based on an analysis of the size of an association required to create a superbubble. The observed scale height of OB stars is about 60 pc (e.g., Allen 1963). The scale height of these stars when they die might be somewhat larger; indeed, the scale height of the youngest pulsars is about 150 pc (Taylor and Manchester 1977). We shall adopt the latter value to be conservative; this gives

$$S = 0.5 \left(\frac{2.6 \times 10^{-11} \text{ pc}^{-2} \text{ yr}^{-1}}{300 \text{ pc}} \right) = 4.4 \times 10^{-14} \text{ pc}^{-3} \text{ yr}^{-1} \quad (12)$$

for the solar neighborhood. This is about half the nominal rate $S = 10^{-13}$ pc^{-3} yr^{-1} adopted by MO, primarily because we are excluding correlated SN from the rate. Note that the conversion from the SN rate per unit area to the SN rate per unit volume, S, is essentially the same for SN Ia as for the massive SN: for SN Ia, all the SN contribute to the porosity, but their scale height is larger (Heiles [1987] estimates 325 pc). Thus, if SN Ia make a larger contribution to the SN rate than estimated by Evans et al., the value of S in equation (16) would be unaffected.

For the typical two–phase medium described below equation (11), the resulting porosity is $Q = S\mathcal{V} = 0.75$. For such a large value of Q, the ISM will be a three–phase medium rather than a two–phase medium, and interactions among the SNRs will tend to increase the filling factor of the hot gas above the value it would have in the absence of interactions (Smith 1977). On the other hand, in the highly magnetized ISM considered by Cox and Slavin (1989), the porosity is considerably smaller, $Q \simeq 0.23$ (assuming $E_{51} = 1$). It appears that additional evidence, both observational and theoretical, must be brought to bear in order to determine the filling factor of hot gas in the ISM; new theoretical evidence will be presented in §4.

4. Interstellar Turbulence and the Porosity of the ISM

The observations of the ISM described in §1 show that the scale height of the gas is several times greater than can be explained in one– or two–phase models of the ISM (§2). Observationally, the large scale height is associated with a high degree of turbulence in the ISM (Kulkarni and Fich 1985). Here we show that the level of turbulence in the ISM is directly associated with the porosity of the ISM (McKee 1990a).

Consider supernovae occurring randomly at a rate S per unit volume. Assume the porosity Q is small, so that interactions can be neglected and the SNRs expand into the warm intercloud medium. Furthermore, assume that thermal pressure forces dominate the evolution of the SNRs; the remnants are small compared to a scale height, so that gravity may be neglected, and the magnetic field does not dominate the pressure. After becoming radiative, the SNRs slow down until they merge with the ISM, carrying a radial momentum $(\rho_0 V_m)\beta C_0$ (see §3). This momentum is approximately conserved, and is concentrated in a thin shell which expands at about the sound speed (see Landau and Lifschitz 1959), which we take to be βC_0. The shell overlaps another shell at a radius R_{ov} (corresponding to a four–volume $\mathcal{V}_{ov}$) given by

$$S\mathcal{V}_{ov} = \frac{S}{4}\left(\frac{4\pi R_{ov}^3}{3}\right)\left(\frac{R_{ov}}{\beta C_0}\right) \equiv 1, \tag{13}$$

from equation (7); in this case, $\eta = 1$. We assume that the momentum is annihilated at R_{ov}. We obtain an upper limit on the turbulent pressure by assuming that the momentum flux is carried by the dynamic pressure, ρv^2. Approximating the shell as a delta function, we can express the momentum flux density as

$$\rho v^2 = \left(\frac{\rho_0 V_m \beta C_0}{4\pi r^2}\right)\delta\left(t - \frac{r}{\beta C_0}\right). \tag{14}$$

Averaging this over space and time yields

$$\int \rho v^2 dV dt \equiv \langle \rho v^2 \rangle \mathcal{V}_{ov} = \frac{\langle \rho v^2 \rangle}{S} = R_{ov}\rho_0 V_m \beta C_0. \tag{15}$$

Since

$$Q = S\mathcal{V} = qSV_m t_m = qSV_m \left(\frac{\eta R_m}{\beta C_0}\right) \tag{16}$$

from equations (6) and (7), we find

$$\frac{\langle \rho v^2 \rangle}{\rho_0 C_0^2} = \frac{\beta^2}{q}\left(\frac{QR_{ov}}{\eta R_m}\right). \tag{17}$$

The turbulent pressure is proportional to the one–dimensional velocity dispersion, $P_{turb} = \langle \rho v^2 \rangle/3$; eliminating R_{ov}/R_m with the aid of equations (13) and (16), we find

$$\frac{P_{turb}}{P_{th}} = \frac{4^{1/4}\beta^2}{3}\left(\frac{Q}{q\eta}\right)^{3/4} \simeq 0.9Q^{3/4}, \tag{18}$$

where the numerical evaluation is for the values used in §3. This estimate of the turbulent pressure does not include the contribution of the motions due to SNRs prior to merging with the ISM or during their subsequent collapse (§IV a), but one can show that this contribution is of higher order and does not alter the result in equation (18) when Q is small. We conclude that *the turbulent pressure is significant if and only if the porosity due to explosive energy injection is large.* Thus, provided the interstellar magnetic field is not too strong, the observation that the gas disk of the Galaxy is thick and highly turbulent implies that the porosity of the ISM is large. In their calculation of the turbulent velocity of the clouds, MO found $P_{turb} \simeq P_{th}$, consistent with the large porosity they inferred; at such a large Q, the simple estimate in equation (18) cannot be assumed to be quantitatively correct, however. It is unlikely that the conclusion that Q is large can be avoided by appealing to superbubbles to produce the turbulence: the fact that the ISM extends to great heights implies that most superbubbles are confined within the ISM (Cox 1989), so the relation between the turbulent pressure and the porosity given above should apply to them as well, at least approximately. Since superbubbles are observed to have a small filling factor (Heiles 1980), they cannot account for the observed level of interstellar turbulence.

What if the interstellar magnetic field is large? In that case, a fraction of the energy from the supernovae can be stored in the oscillations of the field (Cox 1988). However, if the interstellar field is large, it must be tangled on scales $\lesssim 100$ pc, since the mean field observed toward pulsars is $\lesssim 2.5$ μG, and perhaps as low as 1.6 μG (Rand and Kulkarni 1989). Such a tangled field contributes a pressure of only 1/3 that of an ordered field, so it is difficult to see how such a field could inflate the ISM to the required height. Further observations of the Galactic magnetic field are required to clarify this point.

5. Concluding Remarks

It has long been recognized that the injection of energy by supernovae plays an essential role in the structure and dynamics of the ISM. Indeed, as the simple isothermal models developed in §2 demonstrated, one and two–phase models without substantial energy injection bear little resemblance to the observed ISM. Recent observations have shown that the ISM extends well above its natural scale height (even allowing for magnetic and cosmic ray pressure), and that this is accompanied by a high degree of turbulence. An enormous injection of kinetic energy is required to account for the observed turbulence; since supernovae are the dominant source of kinetic energy in the ISM, their remnants must essentially fill space if they are to supply the required turbulence (§4). Direct observational tests of this prediction, which underlies the three–phase model of the ISM, should be possible in the next decade as increasingly sophisticated and powerful instruments become available.

Acknowledgments: I wish to thank Stan Woosley for organizing such a stimulating conference and for inviting me to speak. The material in this article is taken from work reported on in McKee (1990a,b). My research is supported in part by NSF grant AST–8615177.

REFERENCES

Allen, C.W. 1963, *Astrophysical Quantities* (2d ed.;London: Athlone Press), p. 241.
Bahcall, J.N. 1984, *Ap. J.*, **276**, 169.
Begelman, M.C., and McKee, C.F. 1990, *Ap. J.*, in press.
Bloemen, J.B.G.M. 1987, *Ap. J.*, **322**, 694.

Bruhweiler, F.C., Gull, T.R., Kafatos, M., and Sofia, S. 1980, *Ap. J. (Letters)*, **238**, L27.
Cioffi, D.F., McKee, C.F., and Bertschinger, E. 1988, *Ap. J.*, **334**, 252.
Cox. 1988, in *Supernova Remnants and the Interstellar Medium*, ed.R.S. Roger and T.L. Landecker (Cambridge: Cambridge University Press), p. 73.
———. 1989, in *Structure and Dynamics of the Interstellar Medium*, eds. G. Tenorio-Tagle, M. Moles, and J. Melnick (Berlin: Springer–Verlag), in press.
Cox, D.P., and Slavin, J.D. 1989, in *EUV Astronomy*, eds.R.F. Malina and S. Bowyer (New York: Pergamon), in press.
Cox, D.P., and Smith, B.W. 1974, *Ap. J. (Letters)*, **189**, L105.
Evans, R., van den Bergh, S., and McClure, R.D. 1989, *Ap. J.*, **345**, 752.
Ferriere, K.M., Zweibel, E.G., and Shull, J.M. 1988, *Ap. J.*, **332**, 984.
Field, G.B., Goldsmith, D.W., and Habing, H.J. 1969, *Ap. J. (Letters)*, **155**, L149 (FGH).
Heiles, C. 1979, *Ap. J.*, **229**, 533.
———. 1980, *Ap. J*, **235**, 833.
———. 1984, *Ap. J. Suppl.*, **55**, 585.
———. 1987, *Ap. J.*, **315**, 555.
———. 1990, *Ap. J.*, in press.
Humphreys, R.M., and McElroy, D.B. 1984, *Ap. J.*, **284**, 565.
Kuijken, K., and Gilmore, G. 1989, *M.N.R.A.S.*, **239**, 651.
Kulkarni, S.R., and Fich, M. 1985, *Ap. J*, **289**, 792.
Kulkarni, S.R., and Heiles, C. 1987, in *Interstellar Processes*, ed.D. Hollenbach and H. Thronson (Dordrecht: Reidel), p. 87.
Landau, L.D., and Lifschitz, E.M. 1959, *Fluid Mechanics* (Reading: Addison–Wesley).
Lockman, F.J. 1984, *Ap. J.*, **283**, 90.
Lockman, F.J., Hobbs, L.M., and Shull, J.M. 1986, *Ap. J.*, **301**, 380.
Mathis, J.S. 1986, *Ap. J.*, **301**, 423.
McCray, R., and Snow, T.P. 1979, *Ann. Rev. Astr. Ap.*, **17**, 213.
McKee, C.F.. 1990a, *Ap. J.*, to be submitted.
———. 1990b, in *The Evolution of the Interstellar Medium*, ed. L. Blitz (San Francisco: Astronomical Society of the Pacific), in press.
McKee, C.F., and Ostriker, J.P. 1977, *Ap. J.*, **218**, 148 (MO).
Ostriker, J.P., and McKee, C.F. 1988, *Rev. Mod. Phys.*, **60**, 1.
Rand, R.J., and Kulkarni, S.R. 1989, *Ap. J.*, **343**, 760.
Ratnatunga, K.U., and van den Bergh, S. 1989, *Ap. J.*, **343**, 713.
Reynolds, R.J. 1989a, *Ap. J. (Letters)*, **339**, L29.
———. 1989b, in *Galactic and Extragalactic Background Radiation*, ed.S. Bowyer and C. Leinert, in press.
Savage, B.D. 1987, in *Interstellar Processes*, ed.D.J. Hollenbach and H. Thronson (Dordrecht: Reidel), p. 123.
Spitzer, L. 1956, *Ap.J.*, **124**, 20.
———. 1978, *Physical Processes in the Interstellar Medium* (NewYork: Wiley).
———. 1990, *Ann. Rev. Astr. Ap.*, **28**, in press.
Tammann, G. 1982, in *Supernovae: A Survey of Current Research*, ed. M.J. Rees and R. Stoneham (Reidel: Dordrecht), p 371.
Taylor, J.H., and Manchester, R.N. 1977, *Ap. J.*, **215**, 885.
Tenorio–Tagle, G., and Bodenheimer, P. 1988, *Ann. Rev. Astr. Ap.*, **26**, 145.
van den Bergh, S. 1983, *Pub. A.S.P.*, **95**, 388.
———. 1990, in *Supernovae*, ed.S. Woosley (Berlin: Springer–Verlag), in press.
van den Bergh, S., McClure, R.D., and Evans, R. 1987, *Ap. J.*, **323**, 44.

The Effect of Supernova Remnants on Interstellar Clouds

Richard I. Klein, Christopher F. McKee, & Philip Colella

INTRODUCTION

The interaction between supernova remnants (SNRs) and interstellar clouds in the galaxy is known to play a major role in determining the structure of the interstellar medium (ISM). We know that the ISM is highly inhomogeneous, consisting of both diffuse atomic clouds (T~100K) and dense molecular clouds (T~10K) surrounded by a low density warm ionized gas (T~10^4K) and by a very hot coronal gas (T~10^6K). Next to radiation directly from stars, supernova explosions represent the most important form of energy injection into the ISM; they determine the velocity of interstellar clouds, accelerate cosmic rays, and can compress clouds to gravitational instability, possibly spawning a new generation of star formation. The shock waves from supernova remnants can compress, accelerate, disrupt and render hydrodynamically unstable interstellar clouds, thereby ejecting mass back into the intercloud medium. Thus, while the interaction of the SNR blast wave with cloud inhomogeneities can clearly alter the appearance of the ISM, the cloud inhomogeneities can similarly have a profound effect on the structure of the SNR.

Recent observations of SNR of enhanced emission in the Balmer line filaments show evidence of cloud shock interactions for Tycho (Braun, 1988). Velusamy (1987) finds evidence of the remnant cloud interaction in his radio observations of W28 and W44 taken at 327 MHz. These observations clearly show the distortion of the radio shell as the remnant begins to wrap around a dense cloud. The observations of the SNR IC443 by Braun and Strom (1986) show the later evolution of the cloud shock interacting with the outer layers of the cloud stripped off at high velocity.

Given the importance of the interaction of the supernova shocks with clouds for understanding the structure and the dynamics of the ISM as well as the potential importance of the interaction as a means of triggering new star formation, the problem has been studied both analytically and numerically over the past decade. All of the previous work on this important problem leave unanswered several questions of key importance: What is the ultimate fate of clouds that have been impacted by SNR shocks? What is the total momentum delivered to the cloud? How much mass is lost from the cloud? What are the mechanisms by which clouds are disrupted and to what extend does disruption take place? How does cloud morphology scale with cloud density, shock Mach number and cloud size? Is the cloud driven to gravitational instability or is the cloud destroyed? What is the effect of the interstellar magnetic field on the evolution? What are the observable consequences of the interaction?

We have recently found (Klein, Colella and McKee, 1989a,b) that highly complex shock-shock interactions and instabilities and shear flow motions play a major role in determining the morphology of the cloud. To address these physical complexities, we have used the local adaptive mesh refinement techniques with second order Godonov methods for 2-D axisymmetry developed by Berger and Colella, 1989 (cf. Klein, Colella, and McKee, 1989a,b). We assume that the cloud and intercloud gas are both adiabatic, although we allow the cloud and intercloud medium to have different values of the adiabatic index γ.

From the point of view of being able to resolve detailed complex physical structures with reasonable amounts of supercomputer time and memory, the most important feature of our code is that it employs a dynamic regridding strategy known as local Adaptive Mesh Refinement (AMR) to dynamically refine the solution in regions of interest or excessive error.

This is effected by placing a finer grid over the region in question with the grid spacing reduced by some even factor (typically) in each spatial dimension. Multiple levels of grid refinement are possible with the maximum number of nested grids supplied as a parameter in the calculation. Typically our calculations employ two nested grids over the initial coarse grid.

CLOUD SIZE SCALES

As the SNR expands through the ISM, it drives a shock into any cloud it encounters. Assuming that these are strong shocks, the pressure behind the blast wave and the pressure behind the transmitted cloud shock are comparable, and one finds that (McKee and Cowie, 1975)

$$v_s \approx (\rho_i/\rho_c)^{1/2} v_b , \qquad (1)$$

where v_s and v_b are the cloud shock and blast wave velocities and ρ_c and ρ_i the initial cloud and intercloud densities, respectively. Following McKee (1988), we define characteristic timescales for the cloud-shock interaction. Let $\chi \equiv \rho_c/\rho_i$ be the density contrast and assume that $\chi >> 1$. Assume that the cloud is a sphere with radius a at a distance R_b from the supernova explosion. The blast wave in the Sedov-Taylor phase will expand as $R_b \propto t^{2/5}$, so the age of the SNR is,

$$t \equiv \frac{dR_b}{dt} = \frac{2}{5} \frac{R_b}{v_b} . \qquad (2)$$

The blast wave in the intercloud medium crosses the cloud in a time

$$t_{ic} \equiv \frac{2a}{v_b}, \qquad (3)$$

whereas the cloud shock crushes the cloud in a time

$$t_{cc} \equiv \frac{a}{v_s} = \frac{\chi^{1/2} a}{v_b} . \qquad (4)$$

The cloud crushing time t_{cc} is of the order of the sound crossing time in the crushed cloud; it is also about the timescale for the growth of large scale Rayleigh-Taylor instabilities. Finally, the cloud accelerates up to the velocity of the intercloud gas in a characteristic drag time t_d defined by $\rho_i v_b t_d = \rho_c a$, or

$$t_d = \frac{\chi a}{v_b} = \chi^{1/2} t_{cc} . \qquad (5)$$

In this paper, we will consider only clouds that can be characterized as "small", so that the SNR does not evolve significantly during the time for the cloud to be crushed:

$$t > t_{cc} \Rightarrow a < \frac{0.4R}{\chi^{1/2}} . \qquad (6)$$

Indeed, we shall focus on the case in which the cloud is "very small", so that $t >> t_d$, and a $<< 0.4R/\chi$. In either case, we have a $<< R$ so that the blast wave may be treated as a planar shock. In the opposite limit of a shock interaction with a large cloud, the SNR blast wave will undergo substantial weakening over the time it takes to cross the cloud. We expect substantial disruption for the small clouds, but only impulsive effects for large clouds.

CLOUD EVOLUTION

a. Cloud Crushing

Since there are no intrinsic scales in the problem, it is parameterized by the Mach number of the SNR blast wave M and the density ratio χ. Our calculations assumed 2-D axisymmetry for an inviscid fluid with no magnetic field. Two cases were considered for the cloud: $\gamma =1.1$ and $\gamma = 5/3$. The intercloud gas was assumed to have $\gamma = 5/3$. Several calculations have been made for Mach numbers in the range 10-1000 and density ratios 10-400.

It is useful to follow the morphological evolution of the cloud through several cloud crushing times to obtain a sense of the different stages of development. We present the time-development of the isodensity contours of the cloud for the case γ (cloud) = γ (intercloud) = 5/3, $\chi=10$, $M=10$. At t=0.84 t_{cc} (Fig. 1), the transmitted shock is compressing the cloud from the front, secondary shocks have enveloped the sides of the cloud as the blast wave passes over the cloud, and a reflected bow shock moves upstream into the intercloud medium. The reflected shock becomes a standing bow shock and eventually a weak acoustic wave carrying away a small amount of energy from the supernova shock (Spitzer, 1982). At t=1.05t_{cc} (Fig. 2) the blast wave behind the cloud reflects off the axis giving rise to a Mach reflected shock back into the cloud. Substantial flattening of the cloud is observed at t=2.1t_{cc} from the strong shocks which have squeezed it like a vise. The pressure maximum on the nose of the cloud exceeds the pressure minimum on the sides and the cloud begins to expand laterally (Fig. 3). We note the growth of Richtmyer-Meshkov instabilities (Richtmyer, 1960) on the cloud nose which grow more slowly than the classic Rayleigh Taylor modes and evidence of Kelvin Helmholtz instabilities on the sides of the cloud.

b. Shear Flow and Vortex Production

At 3.78t_{cc} a prominent shear layer exists due to the motion of the cloud through the ICM. The shear produces copious vortex rings along the shear flow layer. The cloud consists of a distorted unstable axially flattened core component and a severely disrupted halo of cloud material. Over 70% of the original cloud mass is in small fragments which, in the absence of cooling, should merge with the intercloud medium. The unstable break up is dominated by large scale differential shear. At t=9.7 t_{cc}, the cloud is completly destroyed (Fig. 4) and consists of several thousand fragments. At 4.2 t_{cc} the strong supersonic vortex rings align along the shear flow layer produced in the dominant arm of cloud material that has been pulled from the main core of the cloud as well as along a second substantially fractured mass of cloud that has been fragmented from the arm. In Fig. 5 we show the associated flow field alongside of isodensity contours of the cloud and intercloud gas at t=4.2 t_{cc}. It is clear that regions of strong circulation (high vorticity, numbered 1-5) are associated with positions along the shear flow layer where the cloud has undergone severe fragmentation. As vortex rings are formed in the shear layer and move away from the initial cloud are, the vortex rings are broken off. The process is called vortex shedding. It is suggestive of the possibility that the vorticity in the intercloud matter is acting to enhance the cloud break-up along the differential shear layer, thus acting as a mix-master aiding the development of the Kelvin-Helmholtz instabilities. This interesting possibility is worth further study.

The vorticity depends upon a baroclinic term which is the major source of vorticity in the cloud-shock interaction. The shock is curved as it interacts with the cloud surface and produces surfaces of constant pressure that are not coincident with surfaces of constant density at the interface of the cloud and intercloud matter. This gives a non-zero cross product of gradients. The vorticity in the ICM is greater than that in the cloud because of the higher velocities in the lower density material. Our calculations show that most of the vorticity remains concentrated near the cloud boundary, where it originated. An additional term that can be important is vortex diffusion. If the gas has a frictional force due to viscosity, F/ρ, it can be represented as $F/\rho = \nu\nabla^2 u$ where ν is the viscosity; then $\nabla \times (F/\rho)$ ~ $\nu\nabla^2\omega$. This represents the diffusion of vorticity from regions of high to low concentration. It is proportional to the amount of numerical viscosity in the finite difference approximations. Given the importance of vorticity as a possible observational diagnostic of the remnant cloud

SN Remnant Effects on Interstellar Clouds

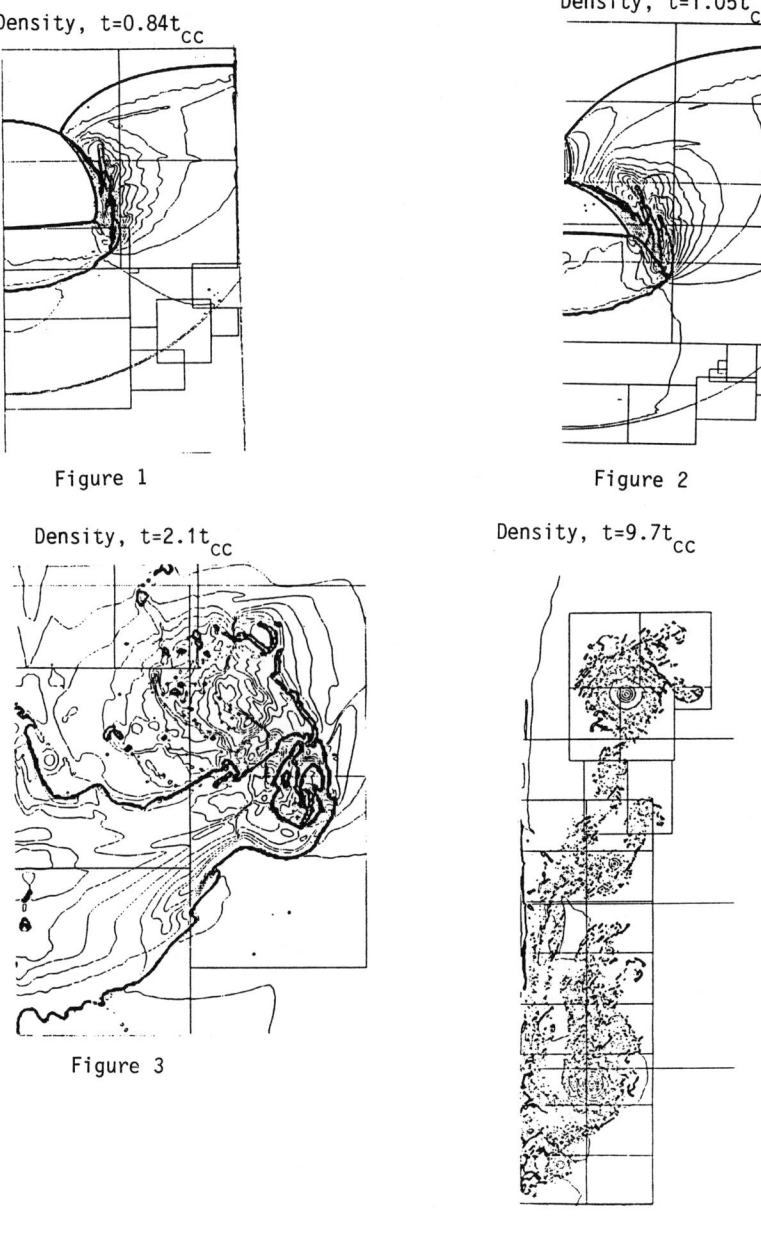

Figure 1 — Density, $t=0.84 t_{cc}$

Figure 2 — Density, $t=1.05 t_{cc}$

Figure 3 — Density, $t=2.1 t_{cc}$

Figure 4 — Density, $t=9.7 t_{cc}$

Figures 1-4 Isodensity contours of cloud and intercloud matter at different times.

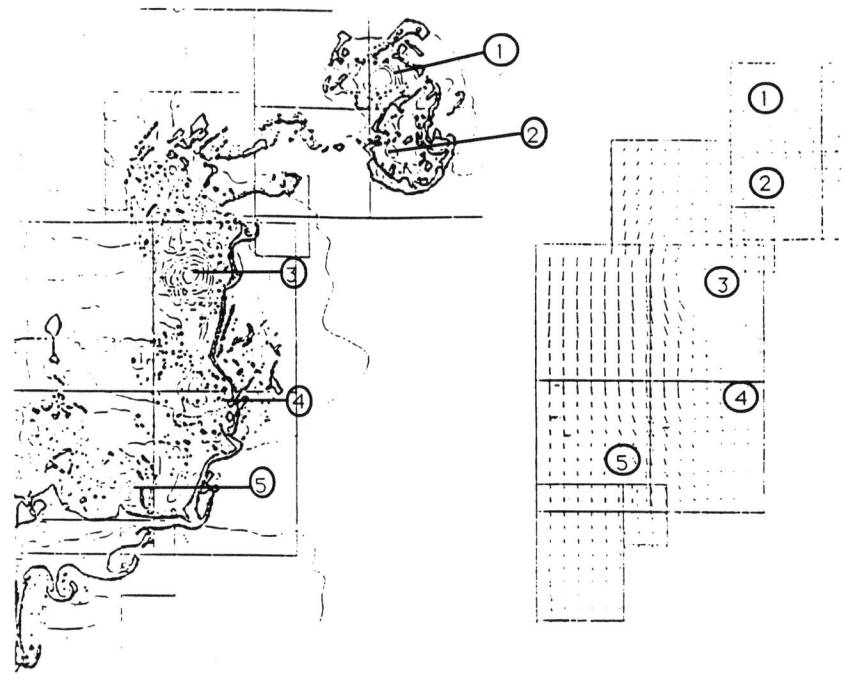

Figure 5 Isodensity contours (on left) at t=4.2 t_{cc}, flow field (on right). Numbers are sites of vorticity maximums.

SN Remnant Effects on Interstellar Clouds

Figure 6   Isodensity contours for $\chi=100$, $M=100$ at $t=4.0$ t_{cc}

interaction as well as its possible role in the cloud fragmentation, it is of great importance to demonstrate that numerical viscosity does not play a role in determining the amount of vorticity production. We have computed the time evolution of the cloud for four increasingly resolved initial grids, doubling the number of cells in both Δr and Δz with each increase in resolution. We have found that the time evolution of the vorticity for even the coarsest mesh tracks to a remarkable degree of accuracy the vorticity of the finest grid resolution, which is equivalent to a 7×10^6 zone calculation for a fixed grid method. This clearly establishes that numerical viscosity, which is proportional to grid resolution, does not affect the production of vorticity for the adaptive grid techniques we are using. This type of calculation is a powerful check on the conservation of vorticity.

Let us consider the characterization of the evolution of the interstellar cloud in more detail. In Table 1, we display the results of adiabatic calculations for three models in which $\gamma = 5/3$ in both the cloud and ICM. The calculations are done for two models ($M=10$ and 100) for density contrast $\chi = 10$ and one model ($M=100$) for density contrast 100. The first entry in the table is the time normalized to the intercloud crossing time. The second entry gives the time normalized to the cloud crushing time and the drag time, $t_d = \chi^{1/2} t_{cc}$. The next column is the sound speed behind the cloud shock normalized to the blast wave velocity. The shocked intercloud gas moves at a velocity $(3/4) v_b$ relative to the cloud for $\gamma = 5/3$, so the next entry measures the ratio of the current cloud/intercloud relative velocity Δv to its initial value; in the frame of the shocked intercloud gas, this is a measure of cloud deceleration. The next column is a characterization of the cloud's aspect ratio in the radial and axial direction weighted by its half mass distribution. Here $r_{1/2}$ is the radial half-mass distance and $Z_{1/2}$ is the axial half-mass distance. The last column gives the radial $\dot{r}_{1/2}$ and axial $\dot{Z}_{1/2}$ expansion velocities of the cloud. These velocities are computed by using the half mass distance distributions at the two final times in the calculation.

Table 1

	t/t_{ic}	t/t_{cc} t/t_{drag}	c_c/v_b	$\frac{4}{3}(\Delta v / v_b)$	$r_{1/2}(t)/r_{1/2}(0)$ $Z_{1/2}(t)/Z_{1/2}(0)$	$\dot{r}_{1/2}/v_b$ $\dot{Z}_{1/2}/v_b$
$\chi=10$						
$M=10$	6.7	4.2 / 1.3	0.18	0.16	1.8 / 3.2	~0.0 / 0.35
	15.3	9.66 / 3.0		0.074	2.38 / 5.69	~0.0 / ≤0.045
$M=100$	6.7	4.2 / 1.3	0.18	0.14	2.0 / 2.6	~0.0 / 0.32
$\chi=100$						
$M=100$	21.3	4.3 / 0.43	.056	0.25	3.7 / 8.4	~0.0 / 0.42

Several conclusions can be drawn from these results. Comparing the results at the same normalized "final" time $t \sim 4.2 t_{cc}$ for clouds of the same density $\chi \sim 10$, but subjected to blast waves of different Mach number, 10 and 100, we note that both clouds have decelerated to about 0.15 of their initial velocities. Thus, these clouds have almost stopped, leading to a small pressure differential between the front of the cloud surface and the sides so that there is little force driving further radial expansion; hence the clouds have a radial expansion velocity $\dot{r}_{1/2} \approx 0$. The strong shear flow in the cloud is still dominant, however, and both clouds are supersonically shearing apart at about the same axial expansion velocity $\dot{Z}_{1/2}$ of 3 times the cloud velocity. The physical extent of the stretching in both the radial and axial direction

$$\frac{r_{1/2}(t)}{r_{1/2}(0)}, \frac{Z_{1/2}(t)}{Z_{1/2}(0)}$$

is essentially the same for the two cases. The remarkable agreement of these features of the clouds and their similar morphological structure leads one to suspect that the cloud evolution may scale similarly with the Mach number of the SNR shock. This Mach scaling can be clearly seen if we scale the time, velocity and pressure as $t' = t/M$, $v' = vM$ and $P' = PM$. Substituting these scaled quantities into the Euler equations, we find that Euler equations are invariant under this transformation. Thus, we find that for fixed γ and density contrast χ, the morphological evolution is a function of t/t_{cc} only, in the limit of large M.

Clouds with greater density contrasts χ show greater expansion in both the radial and axial directions, as shown both by the results in Table 1 and by Fig. 6, which portrays the state of a shocked cloud with $\chi = 100$ at 4 t_{cc}. This follows from the fact that the characteristic expansion time for the cloud is the sound crossing time (which, as remarked above, is about t_{cc}), whereas the time for the cloud to decelerate is the drag time $t_d = \chi^{1/2} t_{cc}$. The lateral expansion of the cloud is due to the lower pressure on the sides of the cloud caused by the Venturi effect (Nittman et al. 1982). This pressure difference decays on the drag time; by the time shown in Fig. 6, this expansion has stopped. At $t = 4$ t_{cc}, the axial expansion velocity is a substantial fraction of v_b for both $\chi = 10$ and $\chi = 100$; since t_{cc} is larger for $\chi = 100$, the length of the cloud is greater in this case. We expect the axial expansion of the cloud to stop within a few drag times. This has been verified for the $\chi = 10$ case, but not the $\chi = 100$ case.

c. Cloud Fragmentation

At late times (several t_{cc}) the clouds is turbulent with many fragments reduced to a foam on the scale of grid resolution. It is of great interest to follow the mass loss of the cloud as it fragments, and to understand how the fragmentation scales with varying cloud density. In Fig. 7, we show the mass of the cloud core as a function of time for clouds with density contrasts $\chi=10,100,400$. The cloud core is defined to be the most massive cloud fragment. The mass loss vs time has been fitted with a exponential to determine the fragmentation time t_f, defined as the time for each cloud to be left with 1/e of its original mass. We find for $\chi=10$ that the cloud fragments initially into two roughly equal mass fragments. The mass fragments then begin a series of further fragmentation stages into smaller pieces due to combined Rayleigh Taylor and Kelvin Helmholtz instabilities. In Fig. 4 we show isodensity contours of the cloud at $t=9.67$ t_{cc} where the cloud is completely destroyed. The final fate of this cloud consists of a quasi-static halo of fragments of which 50% of the mass resides in an axially elongated distribution stretched out 5-6 times its initial shape, and the rest of the mass resides in a multitude of fragments much less dispersed.

For clouds with $\chi >> 10$, the stripping process proceeds differently. For $\chi=400$, the cloud fragments gradually, with a continuous erosion by loss of small fragments (cf. Fig. 7, Fig. 8). Since small fragments rapidly become comoving with the intercloud medium whereas the cloud core decelerates gradually, small fragments trail far behind the massive cloud core until the core itself is destroyed by Kelvin-Helmholtz instabilities as it drags through the intercloud medium. The cloud core mass at $t = 2t_{cc}$ (Fig. 8) is 26% of the original cloud and we see that the cloud has the distinct morphology of a dense cloud core trailed by a multitude of fragments in a narrow tail.

Our results show that clouds are fragmented in a time $t_f \sim (1.5 - 4)$ t_{cc} as χ ranges from 400 to 10; recall that t_{cc} is of order the Rayleigh Taylor timescale. The numerical coefficient is smaller for the higher density contrasts, presumably because the relative velocity of the cloud remains greater.

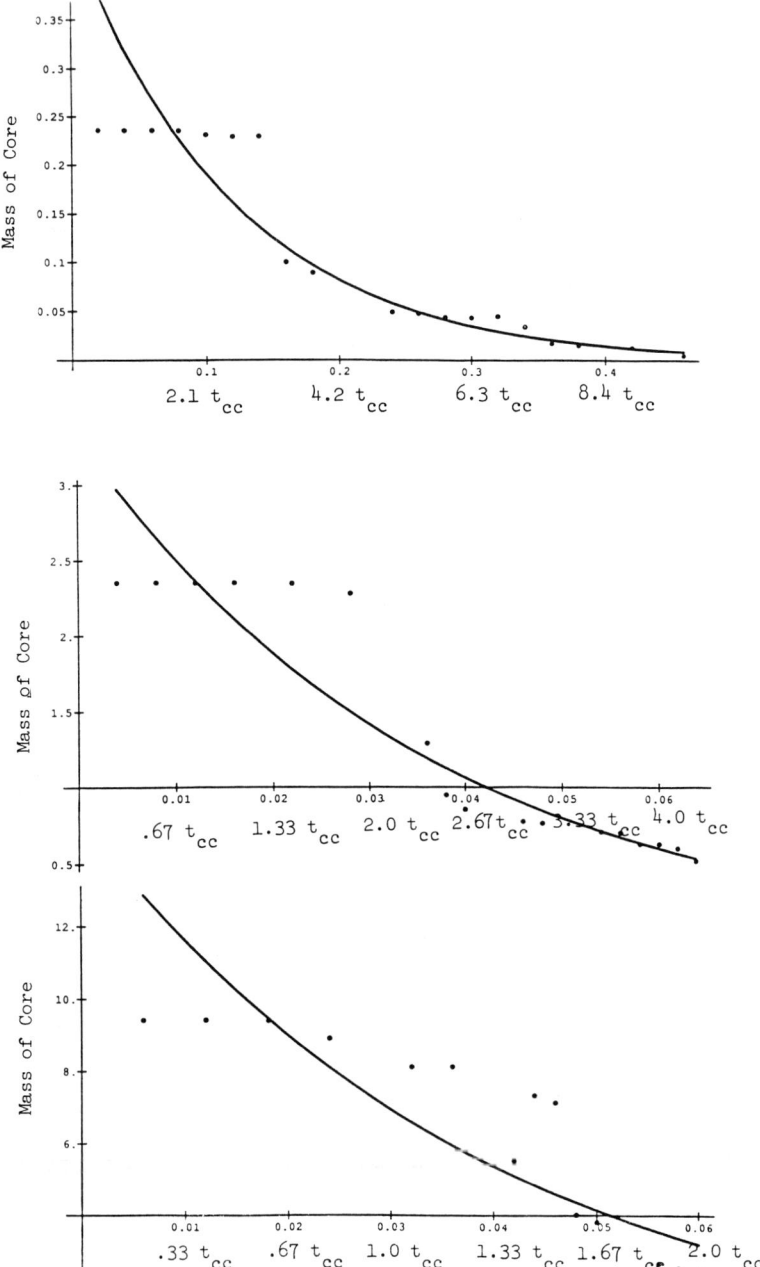

Figure 7 Core mass vs time for χ=10, 100, 400

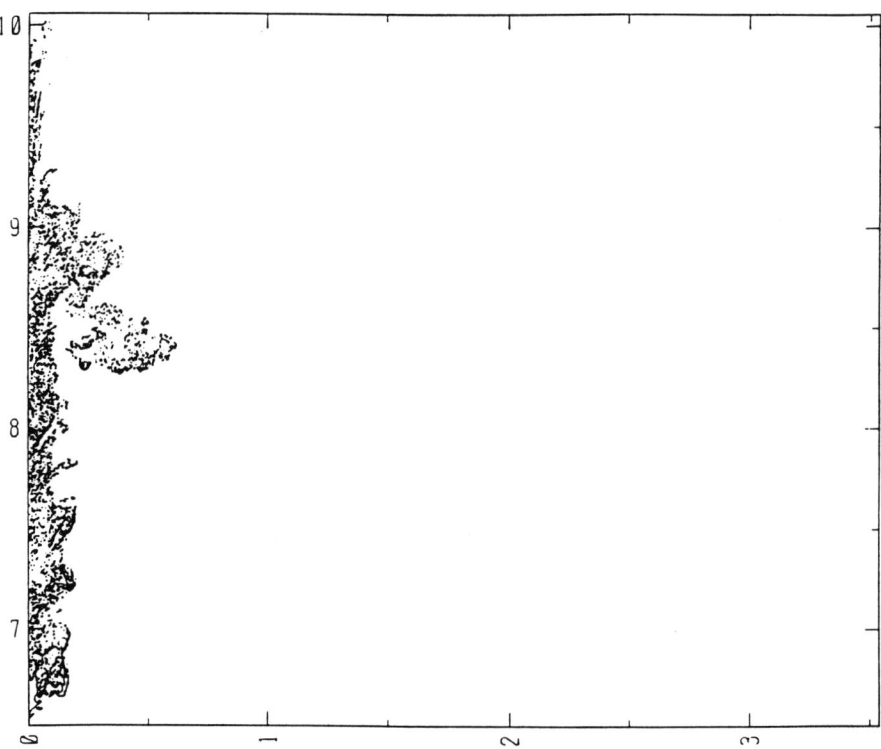

Figure 8   Isodensity contours for $\chi=400$, $M=100$ at $t=2.0\ t_{cc}$. Note morphology of cloud consisting of a dense "head" followed by a trail of several thousand fragments with an aspect ratio of 20 to 1.

This conclusion is consistent with those of Nittman et al. (1982), who concluded that the cloud would be destroyed in a time $\sim 3\ t_{cc}$ due to the combined effect of lateral expansion and strong fluid rotation behind the cloud. Because of the increase in the cross section of the cloud due to the lateral expansion, the time for the fragmented cloud to accelerate up to a velocity comparable to that of the shocked ICM is several times less than the initial drag time $t_d = \chi\ a/v_b$. For $\chi \lesssim 10^2$, the fragmentation time and the acceleration time are comparable; on this point, our conclusion differs from that of Nittman et al. In an analytic study of the related problem of the stripping of gas from a galaxy moving through an intracluster medium, Nulsen (1982) concluded that the stripping time is of the order of the drag time t_d; in the absence of gravitational effects (which he found to be generally small), our results indicate that stripping will occur substantially more rapidly.

We have performed calculations for several similar models for $\gamma=1.1$ in the cloud. This softer equation-of-state is more representative of clouds that are radiative, although it should be pointed out that truly radiative clouds can get rid of their stored energy efficiently, and we would expect substantially more shock compression than the models considered here. We note that these "radiative" clouds move substantially more rapidly than their $\gamma=1.67$ counterparts. These clouds are significantly more radially compressed, and thus experience far less drag than the $\gamma=1.67$ clouds. This can again be understood by consideration of the sound speed in these clouds. We find that the scaling of sound speed c_c with γ is such that $c_c(\gamma=1.1) << c_c(\gamma=5/3)$, so that these "radiative" clouds expand laterally more slowly. We note that the high density "radiative" cloud is still experiencing large supersonic axial shearing. As with the previous $\gamma=5/3$ models Mach scaling appears to be established.

OBSERVATIONAL CONSEQUENCES

An outcome of these calculations that may be potentially very important for observations of SNR is the discovery of the copious production of vortex rings distributed along the strong shear flow layer (Fig. 5). Approximating the rotation of these vortices by rigid body rotation, we can relate the vorticity ω in an individual vortex ring to the pressure differential across the vortex ΔP, and we find that $\omega = (8\Delta P/\rho)^{1/2}/r$. This appears to be an excellent approximation when compared to our detailed calculations. Those rings with large aspect ratio may be subject to non-axisymmetric instabilities and break up into yet smaller vortex structures (Saffman and Baker, 1979). "Fat" rings, with small aspect ratio, are likely to remain intact. Recent high resolution radio observations of the Cas A SNR (Tuffs 1986) have revealed several hundred intense compact radio emission peaks distributed throughout the remnant. We have demonstrated that strong shear flows associated with shock-cloud interactions result in the production of many supersonic vortex rings. These vortex rings can be expected to wind up ambient magnetic fields present in the interstellar clouds until equipartition between the energy in the field and the vortex is achieved. It is quite possible that the resulting intense wound up magnetic field and the associated betatron acceleration could account for the synchrotron emission of electrons, thus explaining the observations in Cas A. Equipartition magnetic fields are often involved in astrophysics to explain non-thermal emission; our results suggest that the fields may indeed reach equipartition, but only in a small fraction of the volume. Chevalier (1976) postulated the presence of turbulent vortices, acting as magnetic scattering centers in SNRs to explain particle acceleration by a second-order Fermi mechanism. We conjecture that the radio hot spots may indeed be indirect observational evidence of the presence of vortex rings produced behind the shocked clouds. The vortex rings would have low density and pressure at the center, thus appearing weak in optical, UV and x ray emission.

Finally, the cloud morphology itself is a important signature. The clouds can be expected to be elongated structures with aspect ratios ~5-6, and multitudes of fragments trailing behind the cloud core. A possible example of this has been observed by Braun and Strom (1986).

CONCLUSIONS

We have performed second order accurate, high resolution local adaptive mesh refinement calculations of the interaction of a supernova shock with interstellar clouds. These extremely powerful hydrodynamic techniques have enabled us to calculate exceedingly complex flows much more rapidly and much more accurately, and much further in time than previous work with standard fixed grid hydrodynamics. We have followed the evolution of interstellar clouds well into the regime of fragmentation. Our calculations have demonstrated high accuracy with 80,000 grid cells in the cloud that would only be achievable with fixed grid high order accurate hydrodynamic schemes with >1,000,000 grid cells. We find:

1) Small non-radiative interstellar clouds are efficiently destroyed in a few cloud crushing times times by combined Rayleigh-Taylor and Kelvin Helmholtz instabilities dominated by large scale shear flow. Clouds that have the same density but are enveloped by strong shocks of differing Mach number exhibit scaling behavior in their morphological evolution.

2) Small clouds are highly fragmented by non-radiative shocks. Cloud fragments will most likely eventually feed their mass back into the ISM by thermal evaporation.

3) Small adiabatic clouds fragment to such an extent that it is unlikely that fragments large enough to become gravitationally unstable and form stars will survive. The cloud destruction proceeds more rapidly than the free fall time.

4) Clouds evolve toward a elongated structures with aspect ratios of five to six, consisting of multitudes of fragments.

5) Our calculations indicate the copious production of supersonic vortex rings. These vortex rings may be effective in winding up the ambient magnetic field in clouds, increasing the magnetic field strength and enhancing the synchrotron emission of cosmic ray electrons. This could explain the recent observations of numerous compact radio hot spots in Cas A.

In the future, we shall use adaptive mesh refinement hydrodynamic techniques to investigate a broad range of astrophysical gas dynamical phenomena.

ACKNOWLEDGEMENTS

The calculations presented in this paper were performed on the XMP416 and YMP832 at the Lawrence Livermore National Laboratory. This work was performed under the Auspices of the U.S. DOE by LLNL under Contract W-7405-Eng-48, supported in part by the Applied Mathematical Science Program of the office of energy research, and was also performed in part under the auspices of a special NASA astrophysics theory program which supports a joint Center for Star Formation Studies at NASA Ames Research Center, University of California, Berkeley, and University of California, Santa Cruz. The work of CFM is supported by NSF grant AST 86-15177.

BIBLIOGRAPHY

Berger, M. J., and Colella, P., 1989, to appear in J. Comp. Phys.

Braun, R. and Strom, R.G., 1986, Astronomy and Astrophysics 164, 193.

Braun, R., 1988, IAU Coll. 101, Supernova Remnants and the Interstellar Medium, Ed. R. S. Roger and I. L. Landecker, Cambridge Univ. Press, 227.

Chevalier, R. A., 1976, Ap.J., 207, 450.

Colella, P. and Woodward, P., 1984, J. Comp. Phys. 54, 174.

Glaz, H. M., Colella, P., Glass, I.I., Deschambault, R. L., 1985, Proc. Roy. Soc. Lond. A 398, 117.

Hornung, H., 1986, Ann. Rev. Fluid Mech., 18, 33.

Klein, R. I., Colella, P. and McKee, C. F., 1989, Ap. J. in preparation.

Klein, R. I., Colella, P., and McKee, C. F., 1989a, "The Physics of Compressible Turbulent Mixing International Workshop", Princeton University, Ed. W. Dannevik, 1989, Springer Verlag, New York Inc., Lecture Notes Series.

Klein, R. I., McKee, C. F. and Colella, P., Proceedings of the Astronomical Society of the Pacific, 100th Centennial, Berkeley, Calif., Ed. L. Blitz, 1989b.

McKee, C. F. and Cowie, L. L., 1975, Ap.J., 195, 715.

McKee, C. F., 1988, IAU Coll.101, Supernova Remnants and the Interstellar Medium, Ed. R. S. Roger and I. L. Landecker, Cambridge Univ. Press, 205.

Nulsen, P.E.J. 1982, M.N.R.A.S., 198, 1007.

Richtmyer, R.D., 1960, Comm. Pur. Appl. Math., 13, 297.

Saffman P. G., Baker, G. R., 1979, Ann. Rev. of Fluid Mech. 11, 95.

Spitzer, L., 1982, Ap.J., 262, 315.

Tuff, R. J., 1986, M.N.R.A.S., 219, 13.

Velusamy, T., 1988, IAU Coll 101, Supernova Remnants and the Interstellar Medium, Ed. R. S. Roger and I. L. Landecker, Cambridge Univ. Press, 265.

SECTION XIII

SUPERNOVA RATES, SEARCHES, AND USE AS STANDARD CANDLES

Galactic and Extragalactic Supernova Rates
Sidney van den Bergh

1. Introduction

Supernova explosions are rare events. Only 5 supernovae [Lupus (1006), Crab (1054), Tycho (1572), Kepler (1604) and Cas A (1658 ± 3)] are known with certainty to have occurred in the Galaxy during the last millenium. Other Galactic supernovae, no doubt, occurred during this period but escaped detection because of heavy obscuration.

Most extragalactic supernovae are discovered serendipitously, or during the course of large surveys of rather poorly-defined galaxy samples. Such data are, of course, ill-suited to the determination of supernova rates. Surveys designed to maximize the supernova discovery rate by observing rich clusters will be strongly biassed in favor of early-type galaxies. Some other recent surveys have concentrated on study of supernova-prone ScI galaxies. Finally serendipitous discoveries in spiral galaxies tend to be biassed in favor of pretty face-on spirals, which are photographed more frequently than esthetically less-pleasing edge-on spirals!

2. Extragalactic Supernova Rates

At the New Delhi IAU meeting the Rev. Robert EVANS [1] gave a lecture on amateur observations of supernovae. During the period 1980-84 Evans discovered a total of 10 supernovae. While listening to his talk I was struck by the thought that there must also be a large amount of useful information in the tens of thousands of observations of galaxies in which Evans did not find a supernova. Fortunately Evans kept a detailed record of all of his observations. A first attempt to extract information on supernova rates from this material is given in VAN DEN BERGH,

MCCLURE and EVANS [2], and MCCLURE, VAN DEN BERGH and EVANS [3]. These authors derive supernova rates from ~50000 observations of 748 Shapley-Ames (SANDAGE and TAMMANN [4]) galaxies, including 15 supernova discoveries, by Evans during the period 1980-85. More recently EVANS, VAN DEN BERGH and MCCLURE [5] have used ~75000 observations of 855 Shapley-Ames galaxies, during which 24 supernovae were discovered, to re-derive supernova rates for various types of galaxies. These results obviously suffer from small-number statistics, but have the advantage that they deal with a homogeneous, and well-observed, galaxy sample.

To determine supernova frequencies one first has to establish a "control time" (ZWICKY [6]) for each galaxy. In other words one needs to know the total period of time during which supernovae of a certain type would have been observable in a given galaxy. For any individual galaxy the control time will depend on (1) the distribution and frequency of the observations, (2) the limiting magnitude of the search, (3) the lightcurve shape and maximum magnitude for the supernova type considered, and (4) the distance of the target galaxy. Control time does not, however, depend on the numerical value of the Hubble parameter. This is so because both the distance of a galaxy, and the M(max) values for each type of supernova, depend on the adopted value of H. Within any class of supernovae the lightcurves of individual objects exhibit considerable variation. The mean shapes of the lightcurves adopted for each type of supernova are shown in VAN DEN BERGH, MCCLURE and EVANS [2]. EVANS, VAN DEN BERGH and MCCLURE [5] adopt the following values for the luminosity at maximum light for the three types of supernovae that are presently recognized:

Type Ia M(max) = -19.79,
Type Ib M(max) = -18.19,
Type II M(max) = $-17.8 + 0.65 \, (M^{oi}_{B_T} + 20.9)$.

All of these relations assume H = 50 km s^{-1} Mpc. Since $(B - V)_{max} \approx 0.0$ the difference between $M_B(max)$ and $M_V(max)$ has been ignored. VAN DEN BERGH [7] has speculated that the apparently significant correlation (r = 0.45 ± 0.14) between M(max) of SNII and the absorption-free, inclination corrected parent galaxy luminosity $M^{oi}_{B_T}$ (SANDAGE and TAMMANN [4], is due to a dependence of the M(max) values of individual SNII on the metallicities of their progenitors. Such a relationship might be understood by assuming that SNII progenitors in luminous galaxies have higher metallicities than do those that occur in less luminous systems. It was also assumed that all supernovae in Shapley-Ames galaxies suffered the same absorption $A^o + A^i$ (SANDAGE and TAMMANN [4]) as their parent galaxies. (This may result in a systematic underestimate of absorption for young massive supernovae in dusty star forming regions). Finally V(lim) ≈ 14.5 was adopted for Evans' 1980-85 observations with a 25cm telescope, and V(lim) ≈ 15.4 for his observations with a 41cm telescope during the period 1985-88. The latter assumption is, perhaps, somewhat suspect because no supernovae fainter than V = 14.5 were discovered by Evans during the last three years of his survey. This lack of discoveries of faint supernovae might well be due to the vagaries of small number statistics. Alternatively the completeness limit of Evans' visual search may have been overestimated, and the supernova frequency might therefore have been slightly underestimated by EVANS, VAN DEN BERGH and MCCLURE [5].

For an average Shapley-Ames galaxy these authors find the following rates:

SNIa $(0.28 \pm 0.10)h^2$ SNU,
SNIb $(0.27 \pm 0.15)h^2$ SNU,
SNII $(1.04 \pm 0.30)h^2$ SNU.

In these relations h = H/100 km s^{-1} Mpc, and 1 SNU is defined as one supernova per 10^{10} $L_B(\odot)$ of parent galaxy luminosity per century. The relatively large errors quoted for these rates are due to the fact that they are based on rather small number statistics. These results were derived from a total surveillance time of 12267 years for SNIa, 5091 years for SNIb and 4608 years for SNII. [For a galaxy of luminosity L_B the surveillance time is defined as the control time multipled by $L_B/1 \times 10^{10} L_B(\odot)$]. Supernova frequencies in galaxies of differing Hubble type, that were derived from Evans' survey, are collected in Table I. The high frequency derived for SNII in galaxies of types Sm + Im is entirely due to the fact that SN1987A occurred in the LMC during the survey period!

3. The Theoretical Galactic Supernova Rate

In the Shapley-Ames Catalog 528 galaxies have types earlier or equal to Sab, and 426 have types Sc or later. The Galaxy, which is generally

TABLE I. Extragalactic Supernova Rates

	No. observed			SN rate*		
Type	SNIa	SNIb	SNII	SNIa	SNIb	SNII
E+S0	2	0	0	$0.3h^2$	–	–
Sa	2	0	0	$0.6h^2$	–	–
Sab, Sb	2.5	1.5	6	$0.3h^2$	$0.6h^2$	$1.8h^2$
Sbc-Sd	2	2	5	$0.2h^2$	$0.4h^2$	$1.3h^2$
Sm+Im	0	0	1	–	–	$(31h^2)$

* Expressed in supernovae per century per $10^{10}L_B(\odot)$

believed to be of type Sbc, is therefore close to being an "average" Shapley-Ames galaxy. It follows that the supernova rates listed in §2 can, once the luminosity of the Galaxy is known, be used to calculate the Galactic supernova rate. Unfortunately the luminosity of our own Milky Way system is still quite uncertain. Recent estimates for the luminosity of the Galaxy range from $1.6 \times 10^{10}L_B(\odot)$ [$M_B = -20.1$] (DE VAUCOULEURS and PENCE [8]) to $3.9 \times 10^{10}L_B(\odot)$ [$M_B = -21.1$] (TAMMANN [9]). In a review of presently available data, DE VAUCOULEURS [10] derives a face-on absolute magnitude $M_B^o = -20.2 \pm 0.15$ for the Galaxy. A correction $A_B \approx 0.3$ mag has to be applied to this value to transform it to the dust-free magnitude $M_{B_T}^{oi}$ of SANDAGE and TAMMANN [4]. A value $M_{B_T}^{oi} = -20.5 \pm 0.2$ corresponds to a blue luminosity $(2.2 \pm 0.4) \times 10^{10} L_B(\odot)$. This result is consistent with $L_B = (1.8 \pm 0.3) \times 10^{10}L_B(\odot)$ that VAN DER KRUIT [11] recently obtained for the Galactic disk. Adding a spheroid luminosity of $(1.5 \pm 0.5) \times 10^9 L_B(\odot)$ yields a total blue luminosity of $(1.95 \pm 0.3) \times 10^{10}L_B(\odot)$ for the Galaxy. Both this determination, and that by de Vaucouleurs, are based on the assumption that the Sun is located at a distance $R_o = 8.5$ kpc from the Galactic center. For other Galactocentric distances the Galactic luminosity (and supernova rate!) scales approximately as $(R/0.5)^2$. In the subsequent discussion it will be assumed that $L_B = (2.0 \pm 0.3) \times 10^{10}L_B(\odot)$. With this value the Galactic supernova rates become: SNIa $(0.56 \pm 0.22)h^2$, SNIb $(0.54 \pm 0.31)h^2$ and SNII $(2.08 \pm 0.68)h^2$ per century. These values correspond to rates of 0.6, 0.5 and 2.1 per century if $H = 100$ km s^{-1} Mpc^{-1}, and to 0.14, 0.14 and 0.5 per century if $H = 50$ km s^{-1} Mpc^{-1} for SNIa, SNIb and SNII, respectively. The total Galactic supernova rate is therefore predicted to be $(3.18 \pm 0.78)h^2$ per century; corresponding to 0.8, 1.8 and 3.2 per century for Hubble parameters of 50, 75 and 100 km s^{-1} Mpc^{-1}, respectively.

VAN DEN BERGH [12] has reviewed the evidence on masses of supernova progenitors. He concludes that the progenitors of SNIb are stars with masses greater than those of the progenitors of SNII. If the hypothesis that SNIb have very massive progenitors is correct then the total Galactic core collapse rate of supernovae with massive progenitors (SNIb + SNII) is $(2.62 \pm 0.75)h^2$ per century.

Major fluctuations in the Galactic star formation rate probably occur on a timescale $>1 \times 10^8$ years. Since the progenitors of core-collapse supernovae have main sequence lifetimes $<1 \times 10^8$ years it is (neglecting effects of mass-transfer in close binaries!) safe to assume that the birthrate of these objects is approximately equal to their death rate. The total rate at which massive stars die in the Galactic disk is therefore equal to the rate at which they form, which is

$$N(M_{min}) = 2\pi \int_{M_{min}}^{M_{max}} \int_{R_{min}}^{R_{max}} \psi(M) \frac{\sigma(R)}{\sigma(R_o)} R dR dM \quad . \tag{1}$$

In Eqn. (1) M_{min} is the minimum mass of stars that are still capable of becoming supernovae by core collapses and M_{max} is the largest observed stellar mass. $\psi(M)$ is the present stellar birthrate function (initial mass function), integrated perpendicular to the Galactic plane, for stars in the range M to $M + dM$. In Eqn. (1) $\sigma(R)/\sigma(R_o)$ is the (azimuthally averaged) stellar surface density, as a function of Galactocentric radius R, normalized to its value at the solar radius. Adopting the $\psi(M)$ relation found by SCALO [13], and assuming ψ is the same throughout the Galactic disk, RATNATUNGA and VAN DEN BERGH [14], find that the core-collapse supernova frequency is approximated (to an accuracy of ~5 percent) by the relation

$$N(M_{min}) \approx A\, 10^{-1.9 \log M_{min} - 1.3 \pm 0.3} \tag{2}$$

With the assumption of an exponential radial profile, the integral of the surface density over radius is

$$A(kpc^2) = 2\pi H_R^2 \exp(R_o/H_R). \tag{3}$$

Eqn. (3) gives the area that the star forming Galactic disk would have if it were of uniform surface density equal to that in the solar neighborhood. Adopting H_R = 4 kpc and R_o = 8.5 kpc Eqn. (3) yields an equivalent surface area of 842 kpc^2 for the Galactic disk. The regions beyond 15 kpc and interior to 3 kpc, in which there is probably not much current star formation, contribute only 11% and 17%, respectively, to the integral over radius. Assuming a scale-length H_R = 8 kpc would yield an equivalent area A = 1163 kpc^2. Adopting A = 1000 ± 250 kpc^2 one finds $1.0^{+1.5}_{-0.6}$ stellar collapses per century for M_{min} = 8 $M_\odot$ and $2.2^{+2.7}_{-1.6}$ stellar collapses per century for M_{min} = 5 $M_\odot$. Clearly supernova frequencies in the range one per 45 years to one per 100 years are disappointing to those who hope to observe neutrinos from Galactic corecollapse supernovae! The supernova rates quoted above are consistent with a rate of (2.62 ± 0.75)h^2 Galactic core collapse supernovae per century that was derived from Evans' supernova survey. Equating the extragalactic rate of SNIb + SNII to the rate of Galactic core collapse events yields 0.34 < h < 1.15 for M_{min} = 8 $M_\odot$ and 0.42 < h < 1.62 for M_{min} = 5 $M_\odot$.

4. Observational Estimates of Galactic Supernova Rates

KATGERT and OORT [15] and TAMMANN [9] have used the distribution of nearby historical supernovae to derive the Galactic supernova rate. Such estimates of supernova frequencies are, of course, wrought with uncertainty because of incompleteness in the historical record, uncertainties in supernova distances, and the vagaries of small-number statistics. From the data on recent supernovae Tammann obtains a rather high rate of 6.3 ± 2.5 supernovae per century.

According to CLARK and STEPHENSON [16] three supernovae (the Crab, 3C58 and Tycho) have occured in the region with 100° < ℓ < 260° during the last two millennia, yielding an observed rate of 0.15 ± 0.09 per century. From the fact that 16 out of 20 radio SNR's in this longitude zone suffer so little obscuration that they can be seen optically (VAN DEN BERGH [17]) it follows that historical supernova discoveries in the Galactic anti-center direction are probably ~80% complete. [As seen from

Beijing the region with $\ell < 210°$, $b = 0°$ culminates above 10° altitude now, and 15° above the horizon in the first century AD]. The corrected supernova rate in the anti-center direction is therefore $\sim$0.19 ± 0.11 per century. The Galaxy contains 46 SNR's with a surface brightness $>3.0 \times 10^{-20}$ W m^{-2} Hz^{-1} Sr^{-1} at 408 MHz; of these 4 are located in the anti-center region with $100° < \ell < 260°$. The total Galactic supernova rate may therefore be estimated to be 0.19 x 46/4 ≈ 2 per century.

The currently favored scenario for the formation of SNIa (WOOSLEY and WEAVER [18]) involves an accreting white dwarf that is pushed over the Chandrasekhar limit. [But see HACHISU, KATO and SAIO [19] for an alternate view in which novae and SNIa are alternate evolutionary paths for stars that are initially embedded in a common envelope]. Classical novae are also believed to be due to accretion onto a white dwarf in a close binary system. It therefore seems reasonable to assume that novae and SNIa occur in similar stellar populations. The ratio of the number of novae to the number of SNIa might therefore be expected to be a constant. From observations of 8 novae in Virgo cluster ellipticals by PRITCHET and VAN DEN BERGH [20] the nova rate in E galaxies is 18 ± 6.5 per year per $10^{10}L_B(\odot)$ of parent galaxy luminosity. This value assumes a Virgo distance modulus m - M = 31.5, corresponding to a distance of 20 Mpc. According to TAMMANN [15] the supernova rate in E galaxies is $(0.88 ± 0.24)h^2$ per $10^{12}L_B(\odot)$ per year. With h = 0.67 km s^{-1} Mpc^{-1} (VAN DEN BERGH [21]) this yields a supernova rate of 0.4 ± 0.1 per $10^{12}L_B(\odot)$ per year. The nova to SNIa ratio is therefore (18 ± 6.5) x 100/0.4 ± 0.1 ≈ 4500 ± 1800. Note that this ratio is independent of the Hubble parameter, but that it does depend slightly on the adopted infall velocity into the Virgo cluster.

According to CAPACCIOLI et al. [22] the nova rate in M31 is 29 ± 4 per year, while that in M33 is found to be 4 ± 2 per year (DELLA VALLE [23]. From these data CAPACCIOLI et al. [22] derive a Galactic nova rate of 15 ± 5 per year. It then follows that the Galactic SNIa rate is 100 x (15 ± 5)/(4500 ± 1800) = 0.33 ± 0.17 per century. According to EVANS, VAN DEN BERGH and MCCLURE [5] $\sim$18% of all supernovae in the Shapley-Ames Catalog are of type Ia. If the same ratio applies to the Galaxy then the expected Galactic supernova rate is $\sim$1.8 per century. This value is in satisfactory agreement with the other estimates of Galactic supernova frequency that have been given above.

5. Summary and Conclusions

(a) Evans' discovery of 24 supernovae in Shapley-Ames galaxies during the period 1980-1988 are used to derive the following supernova rates in an average Shapley-Ames galaxy:

SNIa $(0.28 \pm 0.10)h^2$ SNU,
SNIb $(0.27 \pm 0.15)h^2$ SNU, and
SNII $(1.04 \pm 0.30)h^2$ SNU.

In these relations $h = H/100$ km s^{-1} Mpc, and one SNU is one supernova per century per $10^{10} L_B(\odot)$ of parent galaxy luminosity. The total supernova rate in an average Shapley-Ames galaxy is therefore 1.59 ± 0.35 SN per century for $h = 1.0$ and 0.40 ± 0.09 SNU for $h = 0.5$. Of these supernovae ~82 percent are of the core-collapse type which have massive progenitors.

(b) From the extragalactic supernova rate and the assumption that the Galaxy is an "average" Shapley-Ames galaxy with $L_B = (2.0 \pm 0.3) \times 10^{10} L_B(\odot)$ the following Galactic supernova rates are obtained: SNIa $(0.56 \pm 0.22)h^2$, SNIb $(0.54 \pm 0.31)h^2$ and SNII $(2.08 \pm 0.68)h^2$. The corresponding total supernova rates in the Galaxy are 3.2 ± 0.8 for $h = 1.0$, and 0.8 ± 0.2 for $h = 0.5$.

(c) From SCALO's [13] mass spectrum of star formation RATNATUNGA and VAN DEN BERGH [14] find a rate of $1.0^{+1.5}_{-0.6}$ supernovae per century in the Galaxy if the minimum mass for core-collapse is 8 $M_\odot$. For a minimum core-collapse mass of 5 $M_\odot$ the Galactic rate of supernovae with massive progenitors is found to be $2.2^{+2.7}_{-1.6}$. These figures assume that the Galactic disk has an equivalent area, with a star formation rate equal to that near the Sun, of 1000 ± 250 kpc.

(d) From a comparison of the fraction of all supernova remnants in the anti-center direction with the total number of Galactic SNR's, with the historical rate of optical supernovae in the anti-center region, a rate of ~2 Galactic supernovae per century is derived.

(e) Scaling from the nova rate in M31 and M33, and adopting $N(novae)/N(SNIa) = 4500 \pm 1800$, yields a SNIa rate of 0.33 ± 0.17 per century. If the Galaxy is a typical Shapley-Ames object then ~18% of all supernovae are of type Ia. It then follows that the total Galactic supernova rate is ~1.8 per century.

References

1. R. Evans: Highlights of Astronomy 7, 579 (1986).
2. S. van den Bergh, R.D. McClure and R. Evans: Ap.J. 323, 44 (1987).
3. R.D. McClure, S. van den Bergh and R. Evans: Pub. Dom. Ap. Obs. 16, 281 (1987).
4. A. Sandage and G.A. Tammann: A Revised Shapley-Ames Catalog of Bright Galaxies (Washington, Carnegie Institution) (1981).
5. R. Evans, S. van den Bergh and R.D. McClure: Ap.J. 343, xxx (1989).
6. F. Zwicky: Ap.J. 96, 28 (1942).
7. S. van den Bergh: A.J. 96, 701 (1988a).
8. G. de Vaucouleurs and W.D. Pence: A.J. 83, 1163 (1978).
9. G.A. Tammann: in Supernovae: A Survey of Current Research, eds. M.J. Rees and R.J. Stoneham (Dordrecht, Reidel) p.371 (1982).
10. G. de Vaucouleurs: Ap.J. 268, 451 (1983).
11. P.C. van der Kruit: A.Ap. 157, 230 (1986).
12. S. van den Bergh: Ap.J. 327, 156 (1988b).
13. J.S. Scalo: Fund. Cosmic Phys. 11, 1 (1986).
14. K.U. Ratnatunga and S. van den Bergh: Ap.J. 343, xxx (1989).
15. P. Katgert and J.H. Oort: Bull. Astr. Inst. Netherlands 19, 239 (1967).
16. D.H. Clark and F.R. Stephenson: in Supernovae: A Survey of Current Research, eds. M.J. Rees and R.J. Stoneham (Dordrecht, Reidel) p.355 (1982).
17. S. van den Bergh: in IAU Symposium No. 101, Supernova Remnants and Their X-Ray Emission, eds. I.J. Danziger and P. Gorenstein (Dordrecht, Reidel) p.597 (1983).
18. S.E. Woosley and T.A. Weaver: Ann. Rev. A. Ap. 24, 205 (1986).
19. I. Hachisu, M. Kato and H. Saio: Ap.J. (Letters) 342, L19 (1989).
20. C.J. Pritchet and S. van den Bergh: Ap.J. 318, 507 (1987).
21. S. van den Bergh: A.Ap.Rev. 1, xxx (1989).
22. M. Capaccioli, M. Della Valle, M. D'Onofrio and L. Rosino: A.J. 97, 1627 (1989).
23. M. Della Valle: in The Extragalactic Distance Scale, A.S.P. Conference Proceedings Vol. 4, eds. S. van den Bergh and C.J. Pritchet (Provo, Brigham Young University Press) p.73 (1988).

The Asiago Supernova Catalog
Roberto Barbon, Enrico Cappellaro, & Massimo Turatto

The large number of supernovae (SNe) discovered in the last years, i.e. since the publication of the Revised Supernova Catalogue [1] which contained all SNe discovered up to 1983, led us to publish a new version including all SNe discovered up to 1988 December 31. The number of listed supernovae amounts to 661, of which 267 have been classified.

The Catalogue is intended as a quick reference for statistical studies, so only the main data relative to all extragalactic SNe and their parent galaxies are presented.

Besides the inclusion of the newly discovered supernovae, a great effort has been devoted to update the information relative to all objects already included in the 1984 edition of the Catalogue by collecting new data either from the literature, private communications, further inspection of archival material and by new observations. The Catalogue has also been cross-checked with all major extragalactic files in order to improve data on parent galaxies.

Some differences in the data presentation have been suggested us by the experience of investigators in the field, in order to improve the quality of the information.

The main differences with respect of the past version are as follows:

- asterisks preceding the SN designation denote now all supernovae in that same parent galaxy;

- morphological types of the parent galaxies include Sm subtypes. Intermediate spirals, once classified SAB, have been put in either class by careful searching, through galaxy catalogues, for a more accurate classification. This will help when doing statistics with small numbers. Finally, peculiarity has been also marked;

- anonymous galaxies are coded as in the RC2 [2] for easier identification;

- when available, the integrated B magnitudes of the parent galaxies are given, instead of the m_{pg} from ZWICKY et al. [3] which are not of high accuracy and, moreover, present systematic errors expecially for low latitude fields;

- supernova types include the recent subclasses Ia and Ib, whereas type III, IV and V have been kept mostly for historical reasons, although they are, very likely, spectroscopically similar to type II;

- to better discriminate between *epoch of maximum* and *date of discovery*, an asterisk marks this latter one for poorly studied supernovae;

-name(s) of the discoverer(s) is given.

The symbol "-" in the first column indicates that some modification with respect to the previous version, either correction or implementation, has been applied to that data line.

Asiago SN Catalog

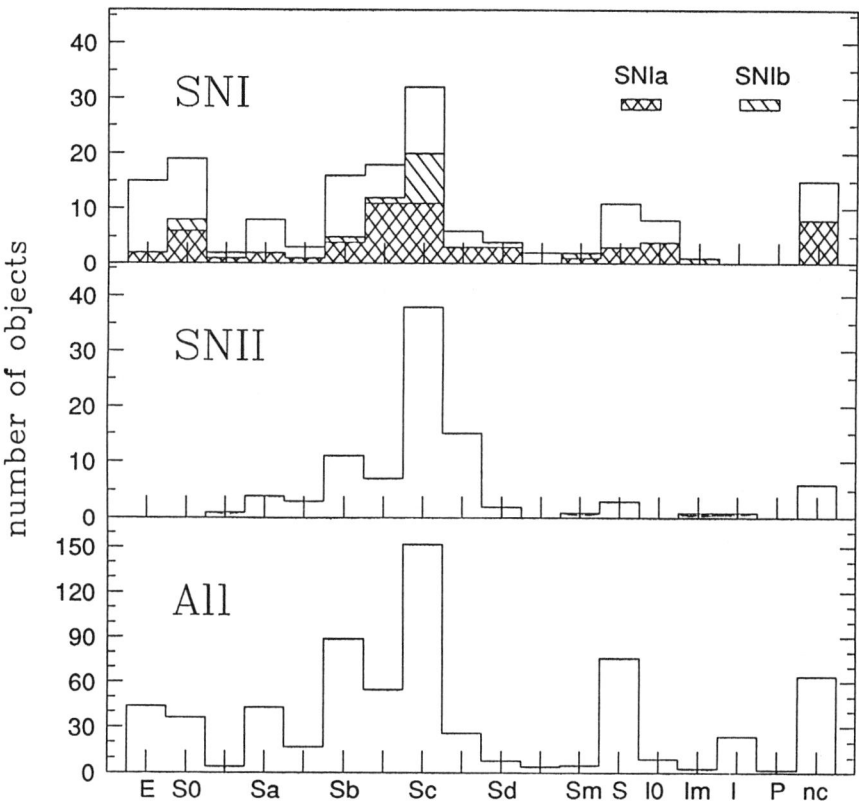

Figure 1: Frequency distribution of supernovae according to the morphological types of their parent galaxies. The bottom panel includes classified (255) and unclassified (406) objects.

The meaning of the different columns in Tables is similar to that of the previous edition [1].

Figure 1 shows the frequency distributions of the various types of classified supernovae with respect to the different morphological types of their parent galaxies, nc meaning parent galaxies without classification. In the Figure, normal and barred spirals have been binned together.

In Figure 2, the productivity of the worldwide SN search since 1970 is shown, where the shaded region refers to classified SNe. From this Figure the efforts of the observers to provide full information on each new object is outstanding, thus revealing the growing interest in such field of research.

Table 1 gives an example of the data presentation. The whole Catalogue will appear in a forthcoming issue of Astronomy and Astrophysics Supplement Series.

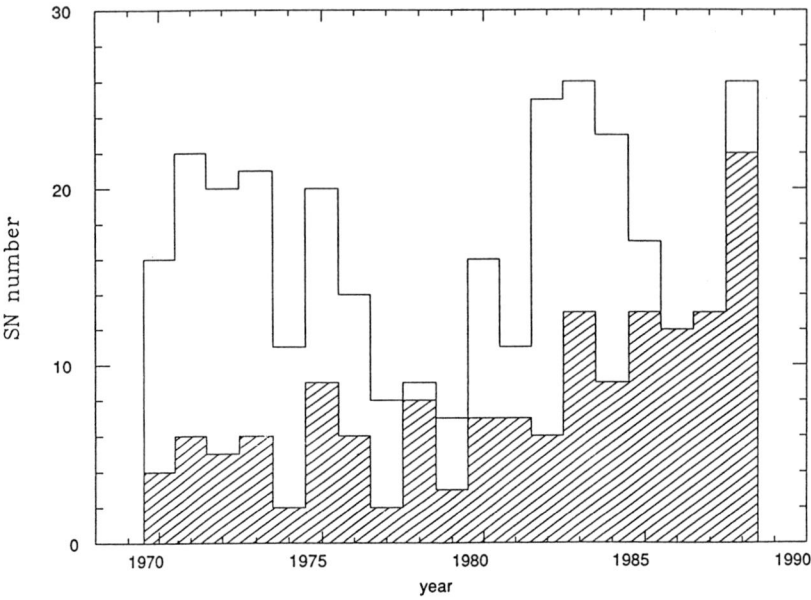

Figure 2: Productivity of the worldwide SN search since 1975. The dashed area represents the number of classified objects.

References

1. Barbon,R., Cappellaro,E., Ciatti,F., Turatto,M., Kowal,C.T.: 1984, *Astron. Astrophys. Suppl. Ser.* **58**, 735
2. de Vaucouleurs,G., de Vaucouleurs,A., Corwin,H.G.Jr.: 1976, *Second Reference Catalogue of bright galaxies* (RC2) (The University of Texas Press, Austin)
3. Zwicky,F., Herzog,E., Karpowicz,M., Kowal,C.T., Wild,P.: 1960-1968, *Catalogue of Galaxies and Clusters of Galaxies* (California Institute of Technology, Pasadena) Vol. 1-6

Table 1. The Asiago Supernova Catalogue by date.

SN	Galaxy	α (1950.0) h m.0	δ ° '	type	GALAXY DATA Lc	inc	V_{hel}	mag	log D	SUPERNOVA offset	mag	type	DATA date	discoverer
· 1885 A	NGC 224	00 40.0	+41 00	Sb	2	69	-299	B 4.4	3.25	15W 4S	V 5.9	I	Aug21	Hartwig (S And)
* 1895 A	NGC4424	12 24.7	+09 42	Sa P	5:	59	439	B12.3	1.57	75E 11S	12.5*	I	Mar*	Wolf (VW Vir)
· 1895 B	NGC5253	13 37.1	-31 23	I0 P		-	403	B11.0	1.60	16E 23N	8.0	I	Jul 6	Fleming (Z Cen)
· 1901 A	NGC2535	08 08.2	+25 21	Sc P	1:	54	4135	B13.1	1.47	19E 7N	14.7*	I	Jan*	Reinmuth
· 1901 B	NGC1331	12 20.4	+16 06	Sc	1	27	1568	B10.1	1.84	110W 4N	15.6*	I	Mar	Curtis
· 1907 A	NGC4674	12 43.5	-08 23	SB0		67	1301	14.5	1.28	10W 11N	13.5:		May10	Luyten
· 1909 A	NGC5457	14 01.5	+54 36	Sc	1	12	266	B 8.2	2.43	620W 408N	B13.5		Feb:	Wolf (SS Uma)
* 1912 A	NGC2841	09 18.5	+51 11	Sb	1	62	631	B10.1	1.91	50W 20N	13.0*	I	Feb*	Pease, Curtis
* 1914 A	NGC4321	12 20.4	+16 06	Sc	1	27	1568	B10.1	1.84	24E 11S	15.7*	I	Mar*	Curtis
* 1915 A	NGC4527	12 31.6	+02 56	Sb	3	69	1738	B11.3	1.80	44E 8S	15.5*	I	Mar*	Curtis
* 1917 A	NGC6946	20 33.8	+59 59	Scd	1	27	46	B 9.6	2.04	37W 105S	14.6*	II	Jul	Ritchey
· 1919 A	NGC4486	12 28.3	+12 40	E0 P		-	1258	B 9.6	1.56	15W 100N	12.3	I	Feb26	Balanowsky
· 1920 A	NGC2608	08 32.2	+28 39	SBb:	3	50	2119	B12.8	1.40	19W 5N	11.8*	I	Jan	Wolf
· 1921 A	NGC4038	11 59.3	-18 35	SBm P		46	1650	B11.3	1.41		13.5	II:	Mar*	Hubble, Duncan
· 1921 B	NGC3184	10 15.3	+41 40	Scd	1	12	418	B10.4	1.84	32E 160S	11.0	I	Apr:	Zwicky, Hubble
* 1921 C	NGC3184	10 15.3	+41 40	Scd	1	12	418	B10.4	1.84	79E 236S	B12.4:	II	Dec11	Jones
· 1923 A	NGC5236	13 34.3	-29 37	SBc	2	24	506	B 8.2	2.05	109E 58N	14.2	II	Feb20:	Lampland
* 1926 A	NGC4303	12 19.4	+04 45	Sc	1	24	1566	B10.2	1.78	11W 69N	14.8*	II	May 5	Wolf, Reinmuth
* 1926 B	NGC6181	16 30.1	+19 56	Sc	1	60	2158	B12.5	1.41	0 48N	13.6:	·	Jun *	Van Maanen
* 1934 A	IC4719	18 29.0	-56 41	I		-				6E 13S	15.0*		Oct11	Boyd
1935 A	IC4652	17 22.0	-59 41	Sbc									Jun *	Boyd, Huruhata
· 1935 B?	NGC3115	10 02.7	-07 29	S0		68	698	B10.1	1.92	36W 60N			Apr *	Samaha
· 1935 C	NGC1511	03 59.3	-67 46	Sab		27	1525	B12.1	1.52	55E 8S	12.5:		Sep19:	Boyce
· 1936 A	NGC4273	12 17.4	+05 37	SBc	3	47	2378	B12.4	1.36	0 29N	14.9	II	Jan26	Hubble, Moore
· 1936 B	M+02-04-29	01 18.4	+15 26	SBc:		41		15.6	1.03		14.0*		Sep *	Zwicky
· 1937 A	NGC4157	12 08.6	+50 47	Sbc	3:	76	916	B11.6	1.84	42E 42N	15.5	II	Jan19	Zwicky
· 1937 B	M-04-52-18	22 07.8	-22 54	Sbc		17	9337	14.8	1.28	29E 31S	15.3*		Aug *	Zwicky
1937 C	IC4182	13 03.5	+37 52	Sm	8	21	225	B11.5	1.76	30E 40N	8.4	Ia	Aug24	Zwicky
· 1937 D	NGC1003	02 36.1	+40 39	Scd	5	67	585	B12.1	1.73	48E 1S	12.9	Ia	Sep18	Zwicky
· 1937 E	NGC1482	03 52.4	-20 39	S0		42	1655	14.4	1.19	24W 51N	15.0*	I:	Dec:	Zwicky
* 1937 F	NGC3184	10 15.3	+41 40	Scd	3	12	418	B10.4	1.84	5E 149S	13.7	II	Dec15	Zwicky, Jones
· 1938 A	M+06-06-68	02 34.6	+34 13	SBa	5:	45	4800	B14.2	1.17	6W 28S	15.2:	I:	Nov	Zwicky
· 1938 B	NGC2672	08 46.5	+19 16	E1		-	4223	B12.6	1.41		15.5*			Wachmann
1938 C	Anon1313+25	13 13.7	+25 26	I:		-				31E 20S	17.7*	I	May *	Klein
· 1939 A	NGC4636	12 40.3	+02 58	E1		-	979	B10.5	1.79	26W 20N	12.6	I	Jan25	Zwicky
· 1939 B	NGC4621	12 39.5	+11 55	E4		-	424	B10.8	1.71	0 53S	12.0	I	May 1	Zwicky
· 1939 C	NGC6946	20 33.8	+59 59	Scd	1	27	46	B 9.6	2.04	215W 24N	13.4*	I:	Jun:	Zwicky
· 1939 D	NGC 321	00 54.9	-05 18	SBcd	3:	46	5775	14.5		9W 11N	16.0*		Nov *	Zwicky
· 1940 A	NGC5907	15 14.6	+56 30	Sc	3:	82	535	B11.0	2.09	137E 310S	14.3	II	Feb22	Johnson
* 1940 B	NGC4725	12 48.0	+25 46	Sab P	1	44	1114	B10.0	2.04	95E 118N	13.1	II	May 8	Johnson
· 1940 C	IC1099	15 05.6	+56 42	Sbc	3	32		15.0	1.15		16.3*	II:	Apr:	Zwicky

Views from the OCA Schmidt Telescope
Christian Pollas

Fifteen SNe were found with this 90/152/360 cm telescope in the South-East of France near Grasse [1] and announced in Circulars of UAI. The rate of discoveries has been seven a year for the last two years. Most were between 17 and 20 magnitude, i.e. faint SNe with z up to 0.05. Since early 1987 the Palomar and the OCA Schmidt Telescopes have together provided fifty percent of the SNe production.

This is not new, as Zwicky and Kowal, Wischnjewsky more recently [2] produced record-numbers of faint SNe. Multiple discoveries were predicted and observed by Mnatskanian in 1968 [3]. We confirmed this, with two then three SNe on one plate. But today many observations are possible on large telescopes or with CCD, allowing classification and discoveries of some peculiarities. We especially need spectral observations on our faint objects,the position of which we can rapidly provide by means of electronic mail.

But our research is not a specific SN program and is not exhaustive for all the galaxies in our view. These discoveries have been made in the run of other regular astronomical programs on our Schmidt telescope. The method used is only an ocular comparison between the images of galaxies on our plates and on the Palomar Observatory Sky Survey prints. Sometimes direct examination of brighter galaxies of 14-15 magnitude (between one and 50 galaxies on each plate) provides 1 or 2 SN/y. 1984 P, 1987 J, 1988 A, 1988 Z, 1989 J were found this way. Other times a binocular scanning provides a localisation of galaxies with star image nearby that are compared in a second step with the red Poss print then with the blue if necessary. This second method may produce from 100 to 800 of candidate galaxies (up to eighteenth magnitude) for further examination. Any big schmidt can do it!

Since July 1987, 13000 to 20000 galaxies provided 7 detected SNe on our plates. Our annual plate production is only two hundred, with 0 to a thousand of examinable galaxies by plate. This work can take quite a long time: between 0 and 8 hours per plate. Nevertheless only a few stars around galaxies are examined perhaps to 7000 on a plate. It is fast in regards of the very high number of objects present to 22 magnitude on a 5dx5d field.

The most often used emulsion is Kodak Technical Pan Plate 15301 which has a very high signal to noise ratio. Its spectral sensitivity extends from UV to 7000Å including an interesting but dangerous detection of H alpha . It includes all the images that may be faint enough to be visible on only one of either the blue or red POSS prints which are used for comparison. The best resolution and detection quality of this 15301 plate drive us to abandon sometimes up to 3 faint possible SNe on a plate. Collaboration work has started with French astronomers on imagery and photometry with 2m-T and 1m-T of Pic du Midi and 1.2m-T of OHP, and the development of this working relationship between spectroscopics observers and theoricians is expected [4],[5].

Locally, we hope to replace expensive plates by film and to build a videoblink [6]. A specific Sne research program on a circumpolar field or on a chosen cluster of galaxies should be planned.

We will continue production of accurate positions of faint Sne and nearby stars in the field of observational cooperations as made with A. Filippenko and as suggested at this workshop.

References

1 J-L. Heudier: The INAG Schmidt Telescope in Proceedings of the IAU Colloquium 48 Modern Astrometry (1978).

2 R. Barbon, E. Cappellaro, M. Turatto: The Asiago Supernovae Catalogue A&A (1989) in press.

3 R.G.Mnatsakanian: IBVS 785 (1973).

4 C.Pollas, J-L.Heudier: Journal des Astronomes Français 32 (1988).

5 C.Pollas, R.Moschkovich, P.Prugniel: JAF 35 (1989).

6 A.Maury: Observatoire de la Cote d'Azur Technical report (1988).

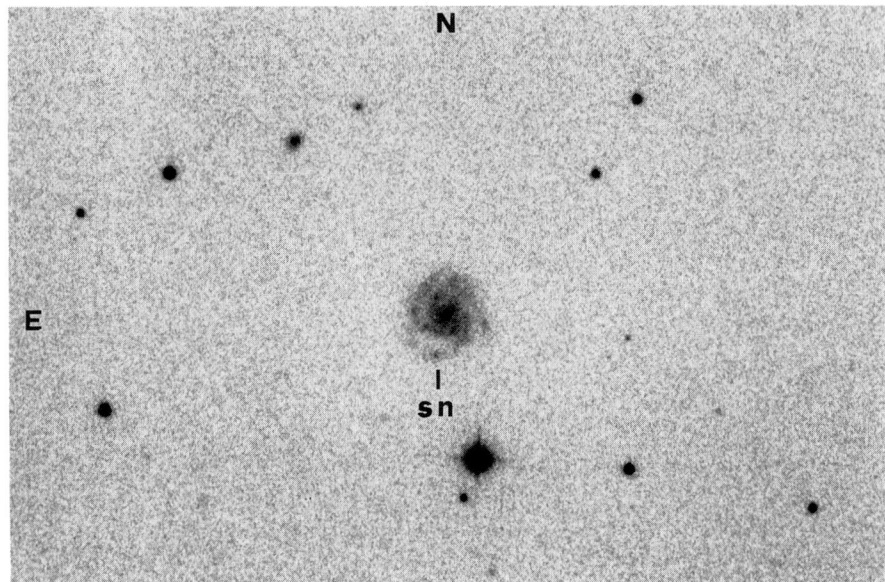

Fig. 1. Supernova 1989 H in MCG +6-30-64 discovered on a February 7 plate at Bj=20. The image obtained on 1989 March 12 shows the object in the 15301 emulsion spectral band, probably fainter than the 22 magnitude. It is superimposed on a blue region visible on the POSS print. Offset from nucleus 3.6" E and 16.3" S . Exposure: 40 mn. ©OCA.

Progress and New Directions for the Berkeley Supernova Search

Saul Perlmutter, Heidi J. Marvin, Richard A. Muller, Carlton R. Pennypacker, Timothy P. Sasseen, Craig K. Smith, & Li-Ping Wang

1. Review of Real-Time Automated Search

The Berkeley Automated Supernova Search is a systematic search for supernovae in a known galaxy set. The primary goals of our experiment are to discover close supernovae early in their light curves (before maximum light) and to discover a large number of supernovae which can be used for statistical purposes. To aid in the study of supernova explosions and their classification, we are conducting VRI photometry on supernovae discovered in our data set (including those found by other observers). The supernova discoveries themselves will eventually be used to determine the supernova rates for various supernova types, galaxy types, and positions within the galaxy. With this in mind, we keep an extensive data base of all observations, their results, and characteristics of each galaxy.

The automated search system consists of a 30" Ritchey Chretien reflecting telescope, an RCA CCD, and a network of computers and software. The software generates galaxy observation lists, controls telescope motion and data acquisition, compares the galaxy image with a previous image of the same galaxy, archives images, stores the results of its analysis in a database, and notifies scientists at LBL of the possible supernova candidates. Apart from maintenance and constant improvements, the search requires one person to start up and shut down the telescope every night and one person to check the search results for supernovae every morning.

The automated search allows more prompt reporting of supernovae and less human effort than the previous generation "semi-automated" supernova search which utilized human scanners to search for supernovae in subtractions of a reference image from a recent image. The software searches for supernovae as the images are taken. Then, if a candidate is detected, a second image is taken immediately to rule out the possibility that the candidate is a cosmic ray. If the potential supernova is still present, a third image is taken one hour later to verify that it is not an asteroid (which would move in the space of an hour). Therefore, we have three images of a supernova to examine the following morning (Figure 1) and can report the discovery to the IAU that very day. Using these procedures, the Berkeley team has never falsely reported a supernova. (See PERLMUTTER et al. [1] for a more detailed description of our search).

2. Current Progress and Recent Discoveries

This second generation search is currently capable of imaging about 300-600 fields per night to a limiting detection threshold of 17th magnitude. In the eighteen months it has been in operation since January 1987, the automated search has accumulated 960 galaxy years of observations (unnormalized for galaxy luminosity) and has added four supernova discoveries to the list of four found previously by the semi-automated search. The more recent discoveries were SN 1988H, 1988L, 1989A, and 1989L (PERLMUTTER and

PENNYPACKER [2,3,4,5]. The last two of these were discovered at or before maximum light. During this same period, two additional supernovae were discovered in our data set (Table 1 gives the complete list of supernova discoveries in our galaxy set). One of them, 1989B, was "re-discovered" at a later time by our automated search. The second, 1989M, was not discovered due to an inadequate reference picture of the galaxy. Although this

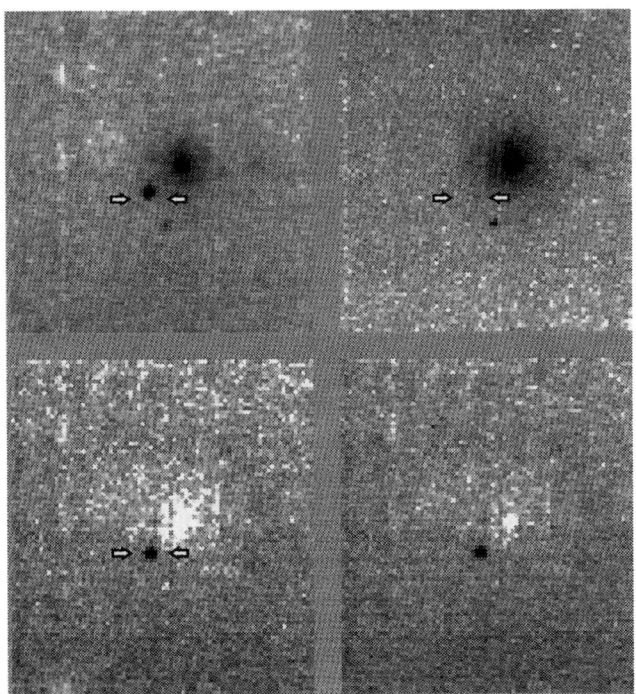

Figure 1. Sample morning report printout. This is the discovery printout for supernova 1989A. This shows the January 19 image (top left), the reference picture (top right), the subtraction used by the supernova search to identify the supernova (bottom left), and a version of the subtraction used to aid the eye in verifying supernovae (bottom right). The arrows point to the spot where the software has found the supernova.

represents a real inefficiency in our search, events such as this one will not ultimately effect our statistics because these inefficiencies will be noted when we characterize our reference image set for statistical analyses (and also eliminated whenever possible). From these supernovae, we find approximate rates consistent with the recent supernova rates of VAN DEN BURGH, MCCLURE, and EVANS [6,7] (type II supernovae must be calculated with a lower effective number of galaxy years due to its dimmer absolute magnitude).

An automated filter wheel is now incorporated into our search, and was used to collect VRI photometry of 1989A, 1989B, 1989L, and 1989M. These data will be published when the supernovae have faded and low noise reference images can be taken in three colors. We intend to continue collecting such follow-up photometry on all discoveries in our galaxy set. In addition, it is our standing policy to notify observers immediately upon our detection of a supernova event so that early spectra can be taken and the supernova can be typed. For one of these supernovae, 1989A, we are organizing a collaboration to publish the spectra and light curve.

Table 1.
Supernovae Discovered
in the Galaxy Set of the Berkeley Supernova Search

Supernova	Galaxy	Discovery Observation	Discovery Magnitude	Type	Discovered By Us	Follow-up Photometry
1986I	M99	May 17	14	II	Y	Y
1986N	NGC 1667	Dec 11	15	Ia	Y	N
1986O	NGC 2227	Dec 24	14	Ia	Y	N
1987K	NGC 4651	July 28	~15	II/I	Y	N
1988H	NGC 5878	Mar 3.5	15.5	II	Y	N
1988L	NGC 5480	May 3.4	16.5	Ia	Y	N
1989A	NGC 3687	Jan 19.5	15.3	Ia	Y	Y
1989B	NGC 3627	Jan 30.5	13	Ia	N	Y
1989L	NGC 7339	Jun 1.4	16	II	Y	Y
1989M	NGC 4579	Jun 28.8	12.2	Ia	N	Y

3. New Telescope

We plan to increase the sensitivity and number of images per night by moving our supernova search to new site. We are considering sites with improved seeing and much lower sky background than our present Leuschner Observatory, which is located only 12 miles into the Berkeley hills. For this purpose, we have purchased a 30" Ritchey Chretien (f/6.75) telescope which has been delivered to us at Lawrence Berkeley Laboratories and is being fitted with our own motion controller and search hardware.

Currently, our processing time is about 70 seconds per image. With a new computer, we can reduce the processing time by a factor of about three. However, we will have to move to a site with better conditions to reduce the imaging time. At a new site with 1" seeing and 21st magnitude sky background, we will cut our time in half while finding supernovae three magnitudes fainter. In addition, we will operate many more nights due to better weather. We are in the process of further automating our observatory so that it can be operated at a remote site.

4. Deep Supernova Search

One of the original motivations for our search for supernovae was to measure the deacceleration parameter of the universe, q_o, and thus determine whether the universe is open, flat, or closed. It appears that it may now be possible to achieve this, with the apparent constancy of the peak absolute magnitude of type Ia supernovae (LEIBUNDGUT [8]; CADONAU, SANDAGE, and TAMMANN [9]) and the recent discovery of a distant type Ia supernova by a Danish group at ESO (NORGAARD-NIELSEN *et al.* [10]). We have set up a collaboration with Warrick Couch and Brian Boyle at the AAO and Shane Burns at Harvey Mudd to attempt to find a statistically significant number of distant supernovae. Thus while we are expanding our search for nearby supernovae, we are also beginning an entirely new search for supernovae of redshifts out to about z=0.3.

The deep search will utilize the prime focus of the AAT 3.9 meter telescope in Coonabarrabran, Australia. We have installed and are testing f/1 reducing optics and a Thomson 1024x1024 pixel CCD, which allow us to image a 16'x16' field with a pixel scale of 1 arcsec/pixel. With 5-10 minute exposures, we should be able to detect supernovae to about 23rd magnitude. With 100-200 interesting galaxies per field and one type Ia supernova every 300-400 galaxy years, we should discover about one supernova per night of observation.

This work has been supported in part by the National Science Foundation, the Ann and Gordon Getty Foundation, and the U.S. Department of Energy under contract number DE-AC03-76SF00098

REFERENCES

1. Perlmutter, S., Crawford, F.S., Muller, R.A., Pennypacker, C.R., Sasseen, T.S., Smith, C.K., Treffers, R., and Williams, R., "The Status of Berkeley's Real-Time Supernova Search," *Instrumentation for Ground-Based Optical Astronomy*, ed. L. B. Robinson, New York: Springer-Verlag, p. 674-680 (1988).

2. Perlmutter, S., and Pennypacker, C.R., IAU CIRCULAR #4560, March 8, 1988.

3. Perlmutter, S., and Pennypacker, C.R., IAU CIRCULAR #4590, May 5, 1988.

4. Perlmutter, S., and Pennypacker, C.R., IAU CIRCULAR #4721, January 24, 1989.

5. Pennypacker, C.R., and Perlmutter, S., IAU CIRCULAR #4791, June 3, 1989.

6. Evans, R., van den Bergh, S., and McClure, R.D., "Revised supernova rates in Shapely-Ames galaxies," submitted to *Astrophysical Journal*, (1989).

7. van den Burgh, S., McClure, R.D., and Evans, R., *Astrophysical Journal*, **323**, 44-53 (1987).

8. Leibundgut, B., "Supernovae Ia as standard candles," this volume.

9. Cadonau, R., Sandage, A., Tammann, G.A., "Type I supernovae as standard candles," in*Supernovae as Distance Indicators*, ed. N. Bartel, Berlin:Springer, p.151-165, (1985).

10. Nørgaard-Nielsen, H.U., Hansen, L., Jørgensen, H.E., Salamanca, A.A., Ellis, R.S., Couch, W.J., *Nature*, **339**, 523-525, (1989).

Searching for Supernovae in Starburst Galaxies
Michael Richmond & Alexei V. Filippenko

1. Introduction

A number of explanations have been suggested to account for the strong emission lines seen in "starburst galaxies," the most successful of which postulates that a short-lived, but intense, period of star formation yields the high-energy photons needed to excite the lines. Several different measurements (e.g., the luminosity of a hydrogen Balmer line or the far-infrared continuum) can be used to estimate the number of O and early-B main-sequence stars in such galaxies. We are currently monitoring nearby starburst galaxies to look for the many supernovae (SNe) that ought to be produced in these star-forming regions. Within the next year or so, we will be able to check quantitatively whether most of the massive stars end their lives as normal SNe, subluminous SNe, or some other objects such as black holes. If the observed SN rate is too low, it is even possible that vigorous star formation is *not* responsible for the energetic phenomena in some of these peculiar galaxies.

2. Expectations: a Supernova Per Year?

Based on extensive visual observations by Robert Evans in Australia, the supernova rate in "normal" spiral galaxies has been estimated as roughly $1.8\,h^2$ SNU for all types of SNe combined (VAN DEN BERGH et al. [1]). Here, $h = H_0/(100 \text{ km s}^{-1} \text{ Mpc}^{-1})$, and a SNU (SuperNova Unit) is defined as one supernova per $10^{10}\,L_B(\odot)$ per century (TAMMANN [2]). More recent work by VAN DEN BERGH [3], reported at this meeting, refined this rate to $(1.59 \pm 0.35)\,h^2$ SNU, where about two-thirds of the SNe are of type II and one-sixth each of types Ia and Ib. For our Milky Way Galaxy, with an assumed $L_B = 2 \times 10^{10}\,L_B(\odot)$, the total rate is only about two SNe per century ($h = 0.75$, used throughout this paper).

But there are many relatively nearby galaxies whose predicted SN rates are much higher, per unit blue luminosity, than in normal galaxies. In particular, the observed phenomena in "starburst" galaxies, which are characterized by a bright, compact nucleus and spectra containing strong, narrow lines of H I, [O III], [N II], and other species, can be explained by a vigorous, recent burst of star formation. A population of many hot, young stars emits high-energy photons that ionize the interstellar medium and produce spectra very similar to those observed. Because so many massive stars are formed, however, many SNe should follow some $10^6 - 10^7$ years after the onset of activity. In such galaxies, the SN rate can be one or two orders of magnitude greater than in "normal" galaxies.

For example, (WEEDMAN et al. [4]) studied the galaxy NGC 7714 at many wavelengths and found that there must be 10^4 supernova remnants within the inner 280 pc in order to explain the observed X-ray and radio fluxes. Since a typical remnant lifetime is of order 10^4 years, they estimated that the SN rate in NGC 7714 must be about *one per year* in the inner regions alone! This agrees with the rate they calculated from the number of massive stars needed to produce the measured, dereddened luminosity of Hα in NGC 7714. Not all starburst galaxies are so active, but SN rates of $0.2 - 0.5$ yr^{-1} must be fairly common. A set of 150 such galaxies, observed for a year, might yield $30 - 75$ SNe *if* obscuration is negligible.

3. The Sample

Our sample comes primarily from two sources: the list of starburst galactic nuclei of BALZANO [5], and a group of *IRAS*-bright galaxies (SOIFER et al. [6]). Balzano selected galaxies with strong blue and UV continua from the lists of Markarian. All Markarian galaxies are fainter than magnitude 13, so she added a number of bright galaxies from the *Second Reference Catalog* (DE VAUCOULEURS et al. [7]) to fill the gap at small distances. She chose galaxies with a bright, stellar or semi-stellar nucleus; those with diffuse inner regions were excluded. She took spectra of her final sample of 102 galactic nuclei through either a circular ($4''$ diameter) or a rectangular ($8'' \times 3''$) aperture. The Hα fluxes, together with the galaxy redshifts, yield intrinsic luminosities of 10^{40} to 6×10^{42} ergs s^{-1} in Hα, from which she concluded that the galaxies were in the process of forming $10^7 - 10^9 M_\odot$ of massive stars.

The *IRAS* sample consists of all extragalactic *IRAS* sources with a 60 μm flux of more than 5.4 Jy, a Galactic latitude of $|b| > 30°$, and declinations generally larger than $-15°$. For a total of 324 such sources, with identifications and redshifts, SOIFER et al. [6] fit a single-temperature Planck function to the 60 μm and 100 μm fluxes and compute a total far-infrared (FIR) luminosity. Most of the galaxies are very luminous in the far IR, with the peak of the sample distribution at $L_{FIR} \approx 10^{10.5} L_\odot$. According to BECKLIN [8], at luminosities greater than $10^{10} L_\odot$ it is likely that star formation is the dominant form of energy generation in IR-bright galaxies; moreover, a study of the 56 galaxies shared by both samples (DEUTSCH and WILLNER [9]) showed that the Hα luminosity correlates well with the *IRAS* FIR luminosity. Thus, the *IRAS*-bright galaxies may be expected to have high SN rates as well. On the other hand, considerable quantities of dust are present in most of these galaxies, making it more likely that the SNe will be heavily obscured.

It is significant that in all six of the *IRAS* galaxies that had previous IR photometry through a $50''$ circular aperture, 1.3 to 5 times more FIR emission was detected through the larger $[(1.5' - 3') \times 5']$ effective aperture of *IRAS*. This implies that in these galaxies, and probably in many of our sample, there are comparable amounts of star formation occurring both near the nucleus and well outside it — an important point for our search.

The total sample we chose from these sources is somewhat heterogeneous, but it does consist of several complete subsets. All of the galaxy redshifts (z) are relatively low, so normal SNe should easily be detected in our survey. From the Markarian galaxies of BALZANO [5], we took all galaxies with an *observed* Hβ luminosity greater than 10^{40} ergs s^{-1} and $z \leq 0.025$; in addition, some galaxies with $z \leq 0.03$ were included. Comparison with the NGC 7714 calculation of WEEDMAN et al. [4] indicates that these galaxies should have an *observed* SN rate of 0.03 yr^{-1}. Their *intrinsic* SN rate, determined from the extinction-corrected Hβ luminosity, is ~ 0.2 yr^{-1}. From the *IRAS* sample, we included all galaxies with $L_{FIR} \geq 10^{10.5} L_\odot$ and

$z \leq 0.0125$, as well as all galaxies with $L_{FIR} \geq 10^{11.0} L_\odot$ and $z \leq 0.03$. Once again, the intrinsic SN rates are predicted to be high ($\gtrsim 0.5$ yr^{-1}). We also added a small number of somewhat less luminous galaxies in areas of the sky which were sparsely populated by galaxies, so that throughout the year there would always be objects to examine at reasonable airmass. This was done primarily in the range $16^h \lesssim \alpha \lesssim 23^h$, where the Milky Way blocks extragalactic views. We ended up with a total of about 150 galaxies, whose distributions with distance and absolute blue magnitude can be seen in Figure 1.

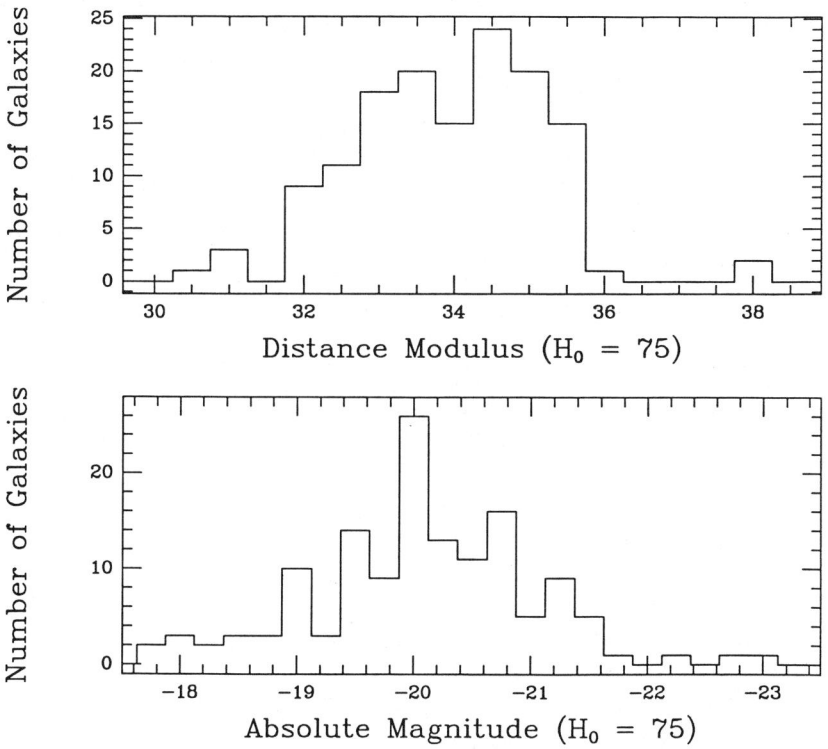

Figure 1: Starburst galaxies in the current survey ($H_0 = 75$ km s^{-1} Mpc^{-1}).

Using the SN rates of VAN DEN BERGH [3] for *normal* galaxies, we can calculate the *minimum* number of SNe we expect to see per unit time in our sample of *starburst* galaxies. If we adopt the *observed* blue luminosities as our basis, then extinction by dust in the parent galaxy should not seriously affect our calculations: in general, if the blue photons from hot stars can reach us, so ought the blue photons from SNe. Simply binning our sample by absolute blue magnitude and adding up the rates from each bin should provide a rough estimate of the minimum *observable* SN rate. We find that our sample should yield about $160\,h^2$ SNe per century, so we may expect to see about one SN per year, assuming all 150 galaxies are observed throughout the year (i.e., 150 galaxy-years of coverage). If starburst galaxies produce *more* SNe per unit blue luminosity than normal galaxies, then our observed rate should be significantly higher. This is true even if some of the SNe are partially obscured, because most of our images go several (and in some cases, many) magnitudes deeper than the expected unobscured magnitude of a SN at maximum brightness.

4. The Search Method

At present, our search for SNe is a simple one. We use the 1-m Anna Nickel reflector at Lick Observatory to take short (two to seven minute) CCD exposures of each galaxy. During the first eight months we used no filters, hoping to gain an extra magnitude, but recently we have begun taking all images through the "Spinrad red" filter (similar to the one described by DJORGOVSKI [10]). We find that the sky is so bright in the shorter visual wavelengths, due to nearby San Jose and to scattered moonlight, that the benefits of being able to perform accurate photometry more than make up for the little signal lost with the filter in place.

We attempt to take an image of each galaxy that is well placed in the sky once every two weeks, near the night of quarter moon, although the region in right ascension from 11^h to 14^h is so crowded that for some galaxies a full month elapses between images. Immediately after each picture is taken, the frame is flattened and displayed on a computer screen in the telescope control room. The observer then compares, by eye, the image with a hardcopy version of a previous picture of the same galaxy. If he notices a difference, he takes one or more additional images before the end of the night so that we can distinguish defects and slowly-moving objects from SN candidates. Several asteroids have been found in this manner, but usually we have too little data to calculate their orbits.

We also take regular pictures, through a number of wide-band filters, of any SNe in the sky which are bright enough to remain visible for an extended period of time — generally those which reach sixteenth magnitude or brighter. The resulting light curves can be used in conjunction with spectra obtained during other observing programs to study the physical processes at work in SNe. Typically, there are only three or four visible on any given night, so we don't lose much time from our search.

Although our visual comparison is less sophisticated than computer analysis of CCD images, we have found that it is adequate to detect SNe which occur outside the nucleus of galaxies in our sample. Preliminary tests indicate that a trained comparator can distinguish an object of magnitude $m \lesssim 17.5$ within $5'' - 10''$ of the nucleus (but not within $3''$), $m \lesssim 18 - 18.5$ in the disk of a spiral galaxy, and $m \lesssim 19$ in a typical arm. The limit of detection in "the field" of our exposures ranges between $m = 19.5$ and $m = 21$. Since almost all our galaxies have distance moduli $\lesssim 36$, and about half have $m - M \lesssim 34$, a typical SN will exceed our detection limit of $m \lesssim 17.5$ for at least twenty days around maximum, and usually for several months (see Table 3 of VAN DEN BERGH et al. [1]). We are likely to miss a SN only if it is superposed directly on the galactic nucleus (but see §6). As pointed out above, however, certain galaxies in our sample, especially the IRAS-bright galaxies, experience star formation over an extended region. With this simple approach, we therefore hope to find at least some of the SNe that may be produced in starburst galaxies.

5. Preliminary Results

Up through September 1989, we have been searching for ten months, during which we observed 21 clear (or relatively clear) nights. We have a total of 691 images. To get a rough idea of how many galaxy-years we have covered, we subtract the initial image of each galaxy, leaving about 540 images, and estimate that each of those images covers two weeks of time. This is likely to be an underestimate, since we can detect a majority of SNe for much longer after maximum; on the other hand, most images of a given galaxy are taken just two weeks after the previous image. We therefore have about twenty galaxy-years of images. With an assumed average rate of one SN every three years for our galaxies, and neglecting obscuration, to date we may expect to have found seven SNe associated with starbursts, including the *nuclear* starbursts that we have not yet thoroughly checked. The most likely expected number, if some dust extinction is included, is probably $1-2$ SNe. If the VAN DEN BERGH [3] rate for normal galaxies is used (§3), the corresponding estimate is only $0.5\,h^2$ SNe, or about 0.3 SNe ($h = 0.75$).

Our current SN count is two (see Appendix) — SN 1988ab (RICHMOND [11]) and SN 1988ac (RICHMOND [12]). However, SN 1988ac (which breaks the record of 28 SNe found in 1954!) should probably not be included in our starburst statistics; it occurred in NGC 3995, a *companion* to one of our sample starburst galaxies (NGC 3994) that just happened to fall within our CCD field of view. It can also be argued that SN 1988ab does not affect our *starburst* statistics, making the actual starburst-SN count equal to zero. SN 1988ab was located at the outer edge of a spiral arm about 33″ from the nucleus of NGC 762 (Mrk 1012), a galaxy from the list of BALZANO [5] whose starburst characteristics are strongly confined to its *nucleus*.

So, while it is still too early to make any definitive statements about the frequency of SNe in starburst galaxies, we suspect that the rates may be lower than theoretical predictions. We plan to extend this project for at least another year, by the end of which we should accumulate over fifty galaxy-years of observations. If we continue to see very few SNe associated with starbursts during this interval, we may be able to significantly constrain models of the end states of stellar evolution. Some of the SNe in such galaxies might be subluminous, or perhaps certain types of massive stars can end their lives as black holes. At the current time, though, a plausible explanation for our low observed rate may be the concentration of SNe in the central few *arcseconds* of each galaxy, since many of our galaxies have luminous starbursts in the *nuclear* region.

6. Future Prospects

To detect SNe which occur in the central parts of galaxies and are hidden by the glare of bright nuclei, we must perform a more quantitative analysis of our CCD images. Accurate photometry of the innermost 5″ of each galaxy could identify normal SNe in many of our galaxies. For example, WEEDMAN *et al.* [4] calculated that a SN going off in the magnitude 13.8 nucleus of NGC 7714 would increase its brightness by about 10%, which could easily be seen. Our images, about 4′ on a side, usually contain two or more reasonably bright ($m \lesssim 18$) stars as well as the target galaxy; these stars may serve as relative calibrators so that we can derive useful differential photometric measurements of the galactic nuclei, even on nights which are not completely cloud-free. This requires a substantial amount of work, however, and it will take a number of months to go through the backlog of data.

Another possibility for improving our search is the acquisition of a dedicated telescope. There is a good chance that within the next year we may have a fully-automated observatory with a 0.8-m telescope, imaging CCD, and autoguider. This observatory will open and close its dome, schedule observations, find galaxies, and guide long exposures all by itself. We plan to reach mag 21 in deep images, through standard *UBVRI* filters. Such an instrument will free human operators the chore (and expense) of travelling to the mountain and spending long hours watching a TV screen. It will also take images every clear night, extending our coverage of galaxies and making much more frequent observations; this should increase our chances of finding SNe before they reach maximum light. Finally, and most importantly, it will allow us to *monitor* SNe, and many other types of variable or ephemeral objects (e.g., Seyfert nuclei, quasars, faint variable stars, novae), on an almost nightly basis. Indeed, discovering new SNe is not the major goal of our group; we wish instead to complement the efforts of the existing Berkeley Automated Supernova Search Team (PERLMUTTER et al. [13]). By making long-term follow-up observations of all available SNe, we will construct the accurate light curves badly needed for a more thorough understanding of the processes which lead these massive stars to explode, light up the sky, and then slowly, quietly, fade away.

This work is partially funded by a Presidential Young Investigator Award (NSF grant AST-8957063) to AVF, as well as by the Center for Particle Astrophysics, an NSF Science and Technology Center operated by the University of California at Berkeley under Cooperative Agreement AST-8809616. Support from the California Space Institute (grant CS-41-88) is also appreciated. Lick Observatory receives partial funding from NSF through Core Block grant AST-8614510. We thank our colleagues at U.C. Berkeley, especially Joseph Shields, for obtaining some of the data used in our survey.

Appendix: Supernovae Discovered Thus Far

SN 1988ab was detected at mag 15.6 (red) in an image obtained on 4 December 1988 UT, the very first night devoted to this search. Through a stroke of bad luck, we did not recognize it as a SN for over eight months. Since it appeared in our *initial* image of NGC 762, which was adopted as the comparison standard, its subsequent appearance in an image taken on 3 January 1989 UT did not attract our attention, despite its considerably fainter magnitude of 17.9 (unfiltered). Unfortunately, shortly thereafter the galaxy became unobservable due to its position in the sky, and the next image was not obtained until August 1989. Although we quickly realized that the "missing" star was a SN, by that time it had faded below our detection limit.

Our other discovery, SN 1988ac, also has no spectroscopic classification. We have determined that SN 1988ac brightened to at least 16.5 mag (unfiltered) sometime between 15 December and 30 December 1988 UT. Unfortunately, we only noticed it in October 1989, while going back through all our images during the course of reductions. Because it was superposed on a bright H II region, it was difficult to detect in images taken long after maximum. A spectrum of the H II region, obtained with the 3-m Shane reflector at Lick Observatory, also did not reveal the old SN.

References

1. S. van den Bergh, R. D. McClure, and R. Evans: *Ap. J.*, **323**, 44 (1987).
2. G. A. Tammann: In *Supernovae: A Survey of Current Research*, ed. by M. J. Rees and R. J. Stoneham (Reidel, Dordrecht 1982), p. 371.
3. S. van den Bergh: these *Proceedings* (1990).
4. D. W. Weedman, et al.: *Ap. J.*, **248**, 105 (1981).
5. V. A. Balzano: *Ap. J.*, **268**, 602 (1983).
6. B. T. Soifer, et al.: *Ap. J.*, **320**, 238 (1987).
7. G. de Vaucouleurs, A. de Vaucouleurs, and H. G. Corwin: *Reference Catalog of Bright Galaxies*, 2nd ed. (University of Texas Press, Austin 1977).
8. E. E. Becklin: In *Star Formation Galaxies*, ed. by C. J. Persson (U.S. Government Printing Office, Washington D.C. 1987).
9. L. K. Deutsch and S. P. Willner: *Ap. J. (Letters)*, **306**, L11 (1986).
10. S. Djorgovski: *Pub. A. S. P.*, **97**, 1119 (1985).
11. M. Richmond: *IAU Circular* No. 4836 (1989).
12. M. Richmond: *IAU Circular* No. 4900 (1989).
13. S. Perlmutter, et al.: In *Instrumentation for Ground-Based Optical Astronomy*, ed. by L. B. Robinson (Springer-Verlag, New York 1988), p. 67.

The Value of the Hubble Constant Through Novae and Supernovae

Massimo Della Valle, Massimo Capaccioli, Enrico Cappellaro, & Massimo Turatto

The reliability of novae as standard candles has been questioned on several occasions, particularly in relation to the determination of the distance of M31 (COHEN [1]). This problem has been recently re-discussed by CAPACCIOLI et al. [2]; they found, through a new calibration of the galactic maximum magnitude *vs.* rate of decline relationship (=MMRD), a distance modulus of M31 in agreement with the values given by other indicators. We apply here these results to the sample of novae discovered by PRITCHET and VAD DEN BERGH [3] in Virgo to determine the distance of the Virgo cluster.

On the same time, the distance of the Coma cluster in units of the Virgo has been derived by comparing the average magnitudes at maximum of selected samples of SNI-a. Finally, we give a value of the Hubble constant of $H_o = 59 \pm 13 \: [kms^{-1}Mpc^{-1}]$, nearly independent of the assumption on the values of the Virgo–infall correction and of the mean galactocentric redshift of Virgo cluster. In the following we give a short account of the different steps involved in this analysis whereas, the complete discussion will be given elsewhere (CAPACCIOLI et al. [4]).

I. The Distance of the Virgo Cluster

The best fit (Fig. 1) between the new MMRD calibrated through M31 novae and seven novae discovered in Virgo cluster [3], yields a differential distance modulus $(m_{Vir} - m_{M31})_o = 7.0 \pm 0.35$; with $(m - M)_o^{M31} = 24.30 \pm 0.20$ the distance modulus for the Virgo cluster is $(m - M)_o = 31.30 \pm 0.40$.

In principle, using this number, we can soon derive the Hubble constant; however, because of the present uncertainties on both the infall correction toward Virgo $\Delta V \simeq 100 \div 400$ kms^{-1} (DRESSLER et al. [5]) and the average recession velocity of this cluster $\langle V \rangle \simeq 900 \div 1200$ kms^{-1} (KRAAN-KORTEWEG [6], HUCHRA [7]), the global error on the value of H_o would be rather closer to 35% than to 20%, this latter figure results taking into account the only uncertainty on the distance modulus.

II. The Distance Virgo–Coma from SNI-a

To avoid the afore mentioned uncertainty we decided to determine the relative distance Virgo–Coma using SNI-a as distance indicators. The selected supernovae are listed in Table 1. Epoch (col. 5) and magnitude of maximum light (cols. 6 and 7) of each SN result from a new critical analysis of the original observations and by best fitting the revised light curves to the average light curve for type I SNe (BARBON et al.[8]).

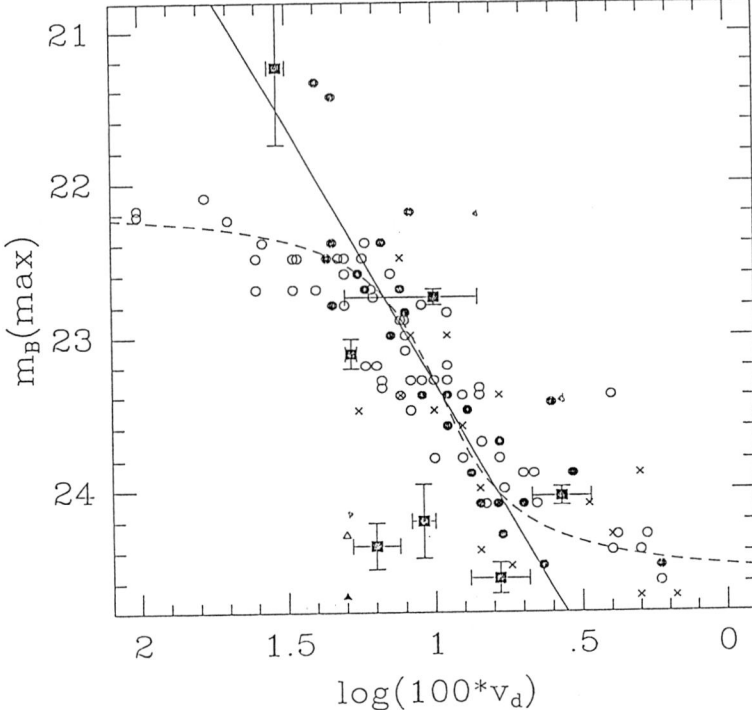

Figure 1: Maximum magnitude versus rate of decline for seven novae (*filled squares*) discovered in two Virgo E galaxies (NGC 4365 and NGC 4472). Smaller symbols are M31 novae, the dark circles refer to objects with observed maxima. The magnitudes have been corrected for color term, internal and galactic extinction, and reduced to the *adopted distance* of the Virgo cluster $((m_{Vir} - m_{M31})_o = +7.0)$. The *dashed* curve reproduces equation 2 of CAPACCIOLI et al. [2], with the zero point adjusted to give the best fit of Virgo novae. The *solid* line is the linear fit of the central part of the MMRD.

Table 1: Photometric data for type I SNe

SN		Parent Galaxy				SN Photometry		
iden.	type	iden.	type	J.D.	B_{max}	V_{max}	$(B-V)_{max}$	$E(B-V)$
					VIRGO			
1919 A	I	NGC 4486	E	22016	12.25 ± 0.15 (pg)			
1939 A	I	NGC 4636	E	29289	12.60 ± 0.10 (pg)	12.25 ± 0.15 (pv)	0.29 ± 0.15	0.33
1957 B	I	NGC 4374	E	35967	12.20 ± 0.10 (pg)			
1960 R	I	NGC 4382	S0 P	37288	11.90 ± 0.20			
1961 H	I-a	NGC 4564	E	37428	11.80 ± 0.10		0.25 ± 0.30	0.29
1963 I	I	NGC 4178	SBdm	38155	13.30 ± 0.20			
1965 I	I-a	NGC 4753	I0	38929	12.50 ± 0.10	12.40 ± 0.15	0.50 ± 0.30	0.54
1981 B	I-a	NGC 4536	Sbc	44673	12.00 ± 0.05	11.90 ± 0.05	0.10 ± 0.18	0.14
1983 G	I-a	NGC 4753	I0	45431	12.85 ± 0.10	12.65 ± 0.10	0.10 ± 0.07	0.14
1984 A	I-a	NGC 4419	SBa	45716	12.45 ± 0.10	12.15 ± 0.10	0.20 ± 0.14	0.24
							0.30 ± 0.14	0.34
					COMA			
1961 D	I	M+05-30-101	E	37305	16.00 ± 0.30 (pg)	16.30 ± 0.30 (pv)	-0.01 ± 0.31	0.00
1962 A	I	M+05-31-102	S0	37685	15.20 ± 0.20 (pg)	15.40 ± 0.15 (pv)	0.08 ± 0.21	0.00
1963 C	I	M+05-31-32	E	38056	15.60 ± 0.15 (pg)	16.00 ± 0.10 (pv)	-0.09 ± 0.15	0.00
1963 M	I:	M+05-31-35	Sa	38195	15.70 ± 0.30 (pg)	15.90 ± 0.30 (pv)	0.08 ± 0.36	0.11
1973 F	I	NGC 4944	S0	41782	15.70 ± 0.15	15.80 ± 0.15	-0.10 ± 0.21	0.00

When necessary, maximum magnitudes were reduced to the B, V photometric bands using standard relations (see [4] for references).

In order to evaluate the global extinction, we make the assumption that all SNeI-a have the same intrinsic color at maximum and we adopt as reference $(B-V)_o = -0.02$, corresponding to the average color of the 5 SNeI-a discovered in early-type galaxies of Coma. The observed color and the derived $E(B - V)$ for each SN are listed in Table 1, cols 8 and 9 respectively. The extinction is then computed from the relation $A_B = R_B \times E(B - V)$ where the value of R_B is not well established [4]. Assuming $R_B = 4$, we derive a $(m - M)_{Coma} - (m - M)_{Virgo} = 4.1 \pm 0.3$, $(m - M)_o^{Coma} = 35.4 \pm 0.5$ and $\langle M_B \rangle SNI - a = -19.7 \pm 0.5$.

III. The Value of the H_o

The mean galactocentric radial velocity for the Coma cluster, reduced to the motion of the centroid of the Local Group is $\langle V \rangle = 6890\ [kms^{-1}]$ [5], with a correction of 240 $[kms^{-1}]$ to account for a Virgocentric infall velocity of $\simeq 250\ [kms^{-1}]$, the cosmological expansion velocity turns out $V_o = 7130 \pm 200\ [kms^{-1}]$.

The Hubble constant results $H_o = 59 \pm 13\ [kms^{-1} Mpc^{-1}]$.

We like to stress the fact that this determination of H_o does not depend from the assumptions on the values of the Virgo-infall and mean galactocentric redshift of Virgo cluster, and the attached error ($\sim 20\%$) reflects the present uncertainty on the distance modulus of Coma cluster (~ 0.5 mag).

References

1. Cohen, J.G. 1985, *Astrophys. J.*, **292**, 90.
2. Capaccioli, M., Della Valle, M., D'Onofrio, M., and Rosino, L. 1989, *Astron. J.*, **97**, 1622.
3. Pritchet, C.J., and van den Bergh, S. 1987a, *Astrophys. J.*, **318**, 507.
4. Capaccioli, M., Cappellaro, E., Della Valle, M., D'Onofrio, M., Rosino, L., Turatto, M. 1989, *Astrop J.*, in press.
5. Dressler, A., Lynden-Bell, D., Burstein, D., Davies, R., Faber, S.M., Terlevich, R., and Wegner, G. 1987, *Astrophys. J.*, **313**, 42.
6. Kraan-Korteweg, R.C. 1981, *Astron. Astrophys.*, **104**, 280.
7. Huchra, J.P. 1985, in *"The Virgo Cluster"*, O.G. Richter and B. Binggeli eds., ESO: Garching, p. 181.
8. Barbon, R., Ciatti, F. and Rosino, L. 1973, *Astron. Ap.*, **25**, 241.

From the Expansion of SN 1987A to the Expansion of the Universe

Robert V. Wagoner

1. THE EXPANDING PHOTOSPHERE METHOD OF DISTANCE DETERMINATION

Sixty-three years ago Walter BAADE [1] proposed a method for directly determining the distances of oscillating stars. But, as Robert Kirshner has emphasized, it was Leonard Searle who realized that an extension of this method could be applied to supernovae. His direction led to the pioneering work of BRANCH and PATCHETT [2] and KIRSHNER and KWAN [3]. As more sophisticated atmospheric models have been employed, the power as well as the limitations of this method have become more apparent. For a review, see WAGONER [4]; for other recent results see the contributions of Höflich (denoted by H) and Eastman and Kirshner (denoted by EK) in these proceedings, as well as HÖFLICH [5], CHILUKURI and WAGONER [6] (denoted by CW), and EASTMAN and KIRSHNER [7].

We will summarize in Section 5 how well this method has passed its most critical test, afforded by the unique opportunity of SN 1987A (whose properties have been authoritatively reviewed by ARNETT et al. [8]). However, it must be remembered that for our ultimate task of mapping the Hubble flow, we will not have the luxury of a known progenitor and a flood of photons. Thus it is our philosophy that the detailed technique employed to extract the distance must be as model-independent as possible, with the minimum number of assumptions. The implementation of this philosophy is one of the focuses of this contribution.

In the next Section, we will argue that the early recombination phase is the optimum era within which to apply the method, with the only major assumption being spherical symmetry. The expansion has become homologous, with the matter velocity $v = r/t = const.$, with t the time since the matter was last accelerated (t_0). The density can then be specified in terms of conditions at some fiducial time t_* as

$$\rho = \rho_* \left(\frac{v}{v_*}\right)^{-\gamma(v)} \left(\frac{t}{t_*}\right)^{-3}. \tag{1}$$

Since by this epoch the photosphere can be considered as quasi-static, the second input is the depth-independent luminosity $L(t)$; or equivalently, the effective temperature at some fiducial photospheric radius, $T_e(r_p)$. The remaining quantities to be specified are then t_0 and the effective heavy-element abundance Z_* (which controls the line opacity).

With this input, a radiative transfer program can then output the spectral luminosity $L_\nu(t)$. Comparing a catalog of such spectra with the shape of the observed continuum can then determine the model parameters $T_e(r_p)$ (mainly from the optical region), ρ_* (mainly from the Balmer jump), and Z_* (mainly from the UV region). The line profiles determine the remaining effective model parameters $v(r_p)$ $[= r_p/t \Rightarrow r_p]$ and $\gamma(r_p)$, if the photosphere is sufficiently sharp. Once we have thereby determined the model appropriate to each observation of the spectral flux $f_\nu(t)$, the distance can be obtained from $L_\nu(t)$ if the redshift of the parent galaxy has been measured. We will address the two major problems, the effects of extinction and asymmetry, in Sections 3 and 4.

2. Advantages of the Early Recombination Phase

We have chosen to employ this method of distance determination during this particular phase for the following reasons.

- As shown by CW, the effective thickness of the photosphere $\delta r(\nu)$ is reduced by the abrupt drop in the electron density at a temperature $T \approx 6000$ K. This sharpening reduces the dependence of the computed spectrum on the density profile function $\gamma(v)$. In addition, the weaker P-Cygni line profiles will have sharper mimima, allowing a more accurate determination of the velocity $v(r_p)$.

- The complications introduced by the evolution of the atmosphere during the time it takes a photon to traverse the photosphere (EK) become negligible after $t \approx (\delta r)\tau_m/c$, typically a few days. [$\tau_m \sim 10$ is the maximum (frequency-dependent) thermalization optical depth.]

- For the luminous Type II supernovae that will be observed in the Hubble flow, this phase begins a few weeks after the explosion. Thus the uncertainty in the explosion time t_o affects the determination of r_p less than if earlier epochs were employed.

- As shown in Fig. 1 (from PEREZ and WAGONER [9]; see also KARP et al. [10]), the effective continuum (scattering) opacity produced by the $\sim 10^5$ Doppler-broadened lines is an important contribution mainly at wavelengths $\lambda < 4000$ Å. Thus the effects of the uncertainties in this opacity (incorporated partially in our parameter Z_*) are reduced because the fraction of the underlying flux at these wavelengths has become small at the recombination temperature.

- The emitted flux is less affected by (large or small scale) deviations from spherical symmetry during recombination because the photospheric temperature evolves relatively slowly.

An observational disadvantage of this era is obviously the reduced luminosity. The theoretical disadvantage is a more difficult radiative transfer problem, due to the near degeneracy of the equations of radiative and statistical equilibrium (mainly for the first excited state of hydrogen) if complete linearization is employed to achieve convergence.

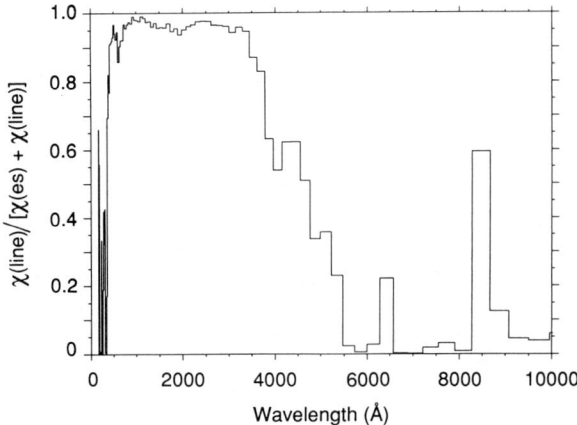

Figure 1. The ratio of the effective continuum opacity produced by lines to the total (electron plus line) scattering opacity is averaged over wavelength bands $\Delta \log \lambda = 0.02$. The parameters are $r/v = 10$ days, $\log \rho \, (\mathrm{g \, cm^{-3}}) = -13.5$, and $T = 6000$ K. The line list was provided by R. Kurucz.

3. REDUCING THE EFFECTS OF EXTINCTION

From the existing data on our galaxy, the Large Magellenic Cloud, and the Small Magellenic Cloud [11], there is no evidence that the wavelength dependence of interstellar extinction $A_\lambda = E_{B-V} \psi(\lambda)$ is not universal for those wavelengths $\lambda > 2600$ Å at which there is significant flux during recombination. Adopting this assumption of universality then allows us to employ the three-frequency indices

$$\Phi_{ABC} = 2.5 \left\{ \log \left[\frac{\Phi(\nu_B)}{\Phi(\nu_A)} \right] - \left[\frac{\psi(\nu_B) - \psi(\nu_A)}{\psi(\nu_C) - \psi(\nu_A)} \right] \log \left[\frac{\Phi(\nu_C)}{\Phi(\nu_A)} \right] \right\}, \qquad (2)$$

where Φ can be the observed flux f_ν or the emitted luminosity L_ν (simply generalized to broad bands). By employing an appropriate variety of such indices in comparing the observed and computed spectra, the values of the photospheric model parameters can be obtained in a manner independent of the value of the amount of extinction E_{B-V}. Of course, a Doppler correction of the form $\Delta \log L_\nu = (v/c) F (d \log L_\nu / d \log \nu)$ must be applied to the spectrum obtained in the comoving frame (CW).

The effect of the unknown extinction on the distance obtained is then minimized if L_ν / f_ν is employed at as long a wavelength as is feasible ($\lambda_0 \geq 3 \, \mu\mathrm{m}$).

4. Effects of Asymmetry

Supernova 1987A has provided us with the first observational evidence for deviations from spherical symmetry during the early expansion of the ejecta. However, as we shall see, there is no evidence that the matter that matters (near the photosphere during the early recombination phase: March 1–14, 1987) had significant asymmetries. Nevertheless, we shall illustrate via a simple model how large-scale deviations would affect the determination of distance, and how this might be detected.

The most relevant observation during this epoch is the March 7 polarization scan across the Hα line [12]. The only feature, representing a decrease in polarization of 0.2%, is seen at velocities approximately twice that of the matter at the photosphere. Since the otherwise constant level of polarization (0.8%) could be of interstellar origin, as indicated by nearby stars, the amount of asymmetry *at this epoch* could be small. The next scan, on May 5, shows much greater variations in polarization.

The other indication of large-scale asymmetry is the reported resolution of the supernova image by speckle interferometry [13]. Although an axis ratio of about 3/2 is inferred (especially in the Hα filter), the earliest observations were three months after the epoch of interest. Thus the claimed asymmetry referred to matter which was well below the photosphere during March 1–14. Although the position of the major axis is close to that of the polarization, radiative transfer effects in the line-producing region above the photosphere could enhance these observational consequences above the level expected from the photospheric asymmetry (H).

Evidence for smaller-scale asymmetries (mixing and clumping) come from the X-ray and γ-ray observations, as summarized by Nomoto in these proceedings (and [8]). However, the observational evidence again comes from much later epochs. In addition, the shells that appear to be Rayleigh-Taylor unstable or to be stirred by hot bubbles from Ni^{56} decay were well below the photosphere during the early recombination epoch [14,15].

It should be noted, moreover, that the more luminous Type II supernovae (which are thought to be produced by red supergiants) will be the ones used to determine cosmological distances. As CHEVALIER and SOKER [16] have pointed out, there are three reasons why these progenitors should produce more spherical supernovae: a) Their flatter density profile tends to reduce the asymmetry of the propagating shock; b) being more extended, they should have smaller rotational distortions; c) the probability of a companion close enough to significantly affect the flow or tidally distort the mantle remains small.

Nevertheless, we shall illustrate how asymmetry could affect this method of distance determination via a model (first employed by SHAPIRO and SUTHERLAND [17]) which incorporates the dominant factor. As shown in Fig. 2, we consider a sharp spheroidal supernova photosphere, but note that its matter velocity $\vec{v}(\theta)$ has become essentially radial by the epochs of interest. The 'radius' that is determined from the line profiles is then

$$R \equiv v_n t = (\vec{v} \cdot \hat{k}) t \quad . \tag{3}$$

The actual luminosity per unit solid angle directed toward the observer, and that which he would infer if he assumed that the photosphere was spherical, are given by

$$dL_\nu/d\Omega = \int I_\nu(\mu)\,\mu\,dA \quad (\mu = \hat{n}\cdot\hat{k} > 0) \;, \tag{4}$$

$$(dL_\nu/d\Omega)_s = R^2 F_\nu \;. \tag{5}$$

(Here $\hat{n}$ is the unit normal to the photosphere.) We shall take the ratio of flux F_ν to specific intensity I_ν to be that for pure scattering (a good approximation), and the flux to be constant over the surface (for the reason indicated earlier).

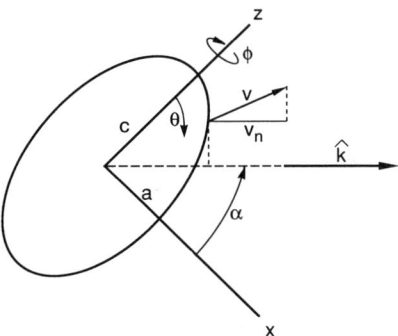

Figure 2. A radially expanding spheroidal photosphere with axis of symmetry (in the z direction) inclined at an angle $\pi/2 - \alpha$ from the direction $\hat{k}$ of the observer. The minima of weak P-Cygni lines are shifted by the velocity v_n.

The ratio of the actual distance to the 'spherical distance' of the supernova is then

$$Q(a/c, \alpha) = \left[\frac{dL_\nu/d\Omega}{(dL_\nu/d\Omega)_s}\right]^{\frac{1}{2}} . \tag{6}$$

This quantity is shown as a function of viewing angle α for various axis ratios a/c of prolate spheroids in Fig. 3a and oblate spheroids in Fig. 4a. We have also computed the mean and the r.m.s. deviation of Q for random viewing, shown in Figs. 3b and 4b.

From these results, we conclude that although the distance of a very distorted supernova can be significantly over- or underestimated, the average from many supernovae is remarkably accurate. On the other hand, the scatter ΔQ_{RMS} about the mean of N supernovae is a measure of the average degree of distortion. Finally, we note that the requirement that $L_\nu(t)/f_\nu(t)$ remain constant throughout the era of interest could eliminate very distorted supernovae from consideration, in addition to constraining the other parameters of the model atmosphere.

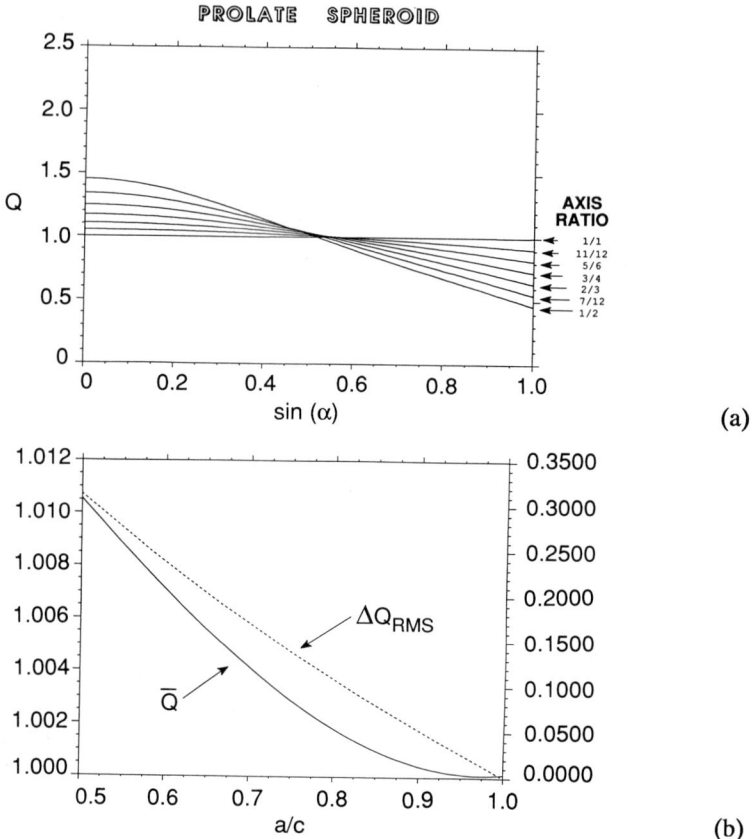

Figure 3. a) The dependence of the distance factor Q (6) on the orientation of prolate supernovae is shown for various axis ratios a/c. b) The average (left axis) and r.m.s. deviation (right axis) of the distance factor over random orientations.

5. The Distances of Supernova 1987A and the Large Magellenic Cloud

The supernova of February 23, 1987 has provided as one of its many gifts the first critical test of the expanding photosphere method of distance determination. Until then, no Type II supernova in a galaxy whose distance could be estimated by other methods had been observed with sufficient spectral range and line resolution to allow this method to be reliably employed.

(a)

(b)

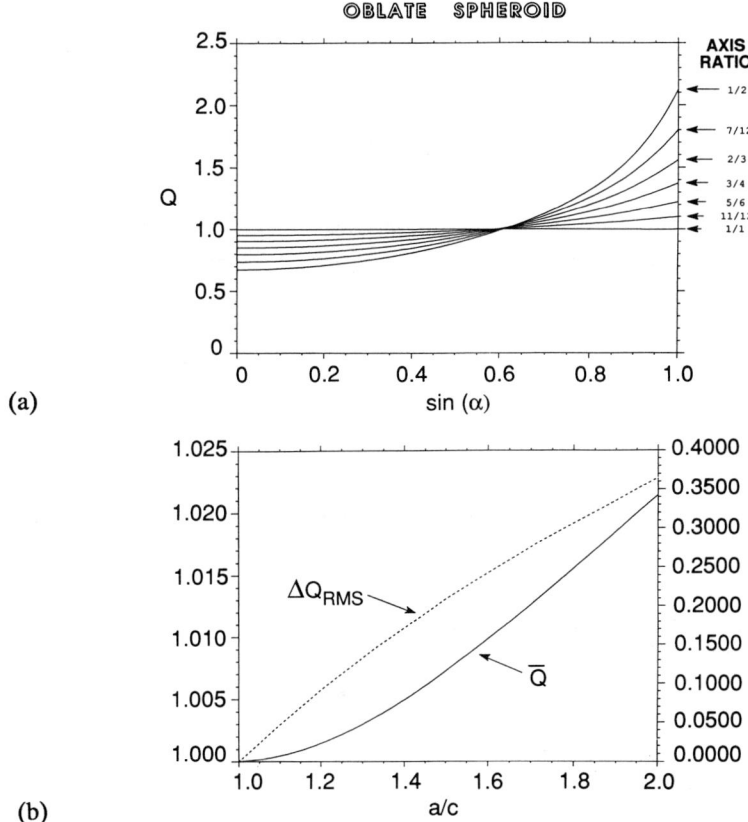

Figure 4. Same as Figure 3, for oblate spheroids.

Although BRANCH [18] obtained a distance of 55 ± 5 kpc (distance modulus 18.70 ± 0.20) by assuming that SN1987A emitted a blackbody spectrum at visible wavelengths, there have been three independent determinations from physically consistent models of the atmosphere. HÖFLICH [5] employed a nonLTE, static, extended atmosphere code which has since been enlarged (H) to include the blanketing effects of many lines (in LTE). He obtained good fits to many of the optical line profiles. EASTMAN and KIRSHNER [7] have applied a nonstatic code to the epoch 2–10 days after explosion, also obtaining good fits to many lines (see also EK). But in both cases, the fit to the UV continuum suffers from an incomplete line list.

CW employed a nonLTE, static, plane-parallel continuum code which incorporated the approximate line opacities of KARP et al. [10]. A comparison of their best-fitting model (corresponding to the values of the parameters indicated) with the March 1, 1987 spectrum is shown in Fig. 5. A blackbody spectrum characterized by the temperature $T_c = 6850$ K obtained by fitting the observed spectrum longward of the B band [19] is shown for comparison. Note the expected dilution of the flux produced by the dominance of scattering over absorption [20], as also indicated by the lower effective temperature $T_e = 5750$ K. Subsequently, a fit to the March 6 spectrum has been obtained, producing the same distance. In addition, a correction for extension has been derived by computing the increase in the radius of the photosphere (CW) at the flux comparison wavelength $\lambda_0 = 3.16\,\mu$m (due to a larger absorptive fraction of the opacity) over that at optical wavelengths, where it is determined by the line profiles. This correction is inversely proportional to the density profile parameter γ, as expected.

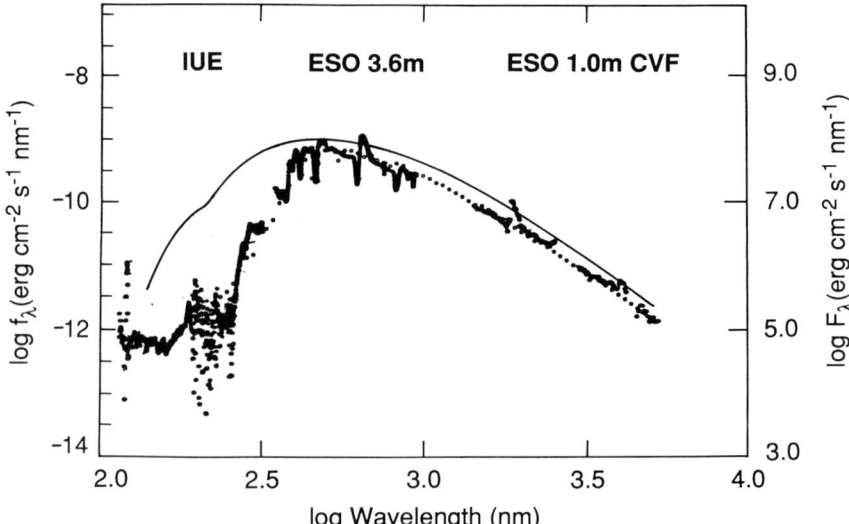

Figure 5. A composite spectrum of SN 1987A observed on March 1, 1987 [22] is compared with the best-fitting model of CW (small dots) and a blackbody of $T_c = 6850$ K [19]. An extinction corresponding to $E_{B-V} = 0.19$ has been applied to both emitted fluxes F_ν. The parameters of the CW model are $T_e = 5750$ K, $\log \rho_p (\text{g cm}^{-3}) = -11.8$, and $Z_\phi = 0.01$

A survey of the distances to the LMC obtained from a variety of methods has been included in a recent review of Cepheids as distance indicators [21]. In Table

1, we compare the determinations of the distance modulus $m - M$ of the supernova with that of the LMC. This comparison is probably reasonable because the LMC is believed to be flattened roughly along our line of sight.

Table 1. Comparison of distances.

Supernova 1987A	$m - M$
Chilukuri and Wagoner (1988)	$18.20 \pm 0.20 + 0.7/\gamma$
Höflich (1988)	18.41 ± 0.18
Eastman and Kirshner (1989)	18.45 ± 0.22
Large Magellenic Cloud	$m - M$
Cepheids and other variables	18.47 ± 0.15
Old clusters	$18.42 \pm 0.2?$
Intermediate-age clusters	18.35 ± 0.35
Young clusters	18.45 ± 0.25

If we adopt the value $\gamma \cong 7 - 11$ obtained by fitting the line shapes (EK), the three supernova distances are remarkably consistent with a value that agrees with those to the LMC. This agreement provides strong evidence that this new method of distance determination is reliable. In particular, the results presented in the previous Section indicate that the photosphere of this supernova did not have a large-scale distortion during the first two weeks, unless our direction of viewing (or possibly the distribution of flux) was fortuitous.

However, before we venture into the Hubble flow, progress in three directions would reduce the uncertainties that will arise. It would be desirable to obtain more frequent polarization observations on another nearby Type II supernova, hopefully of the more luminous variety. This could give us important constraints on the degree of large-scale asymmetry. Secondly, more sensitive infrared detectors are needed (eventually in space) because of the importance of such wavelengths, as indicated above. Finally, we (and others) plan to include more of the relevant physics in our models of the atmosphere and improve the convergence of our radiative transfer codes.

6. ACKNOWLEDGMENTS

Important contributions were made by Chris Perez in the production of Figs. 1, 3, and 4; and by Robert Kurucz, who provided his new line list. This work was supported in part by NSF (grant PHY 86-03273) and by NASA (grant NAGW-299).

References

1. W. Baade: Astr. Nach. 228, 359 (1926).
2. D. Branch, B. Patchett: M. N. R. A. S. 161, 71 (1973).
3. R. P. Kirshner, J. Kwan: Ap. J. 193, 27 (1974).
4. R. V. Wagoner: In Theory and Observational Limits in Cosmology, ed. by W. R. Stoeger, S.J. (Vatican Observatory, 1987, p. 345).
5. P. Höflich: In Atmospheric Diagnostics of Stellar Evolution, I.A.U. Colloquium 108, ed. by K. Nomoto (Springer-Verlag, Berlin, Heidelberg, 1988, p. 288).
6. M. Chilukuri, R. V. Wagoner: In Atmospheric Diagnostics of Stellar Evolution, I.A.U. Colloquium 108, ed. by K. Nomoto (Springer-Verlag, Berlin, Heidelberg, 1988, p. 295).
7. R. G. Eastman, R. P. Kirshner: Ap. J., in press (1989).
8. W. D. Arnett, J. N. Bahcall, R. P. Kirshner, S. E. Woosley: Ann. Rev. Astron. Ap. 27, 629 (1989).
9. C. Perez, R. V. Wagoner: in preparation (1989).
10. A. H. Karp, G. Lasher, K. L. Chan, E. E. Salpeter: Ap. J. 214, 161 (1977).
11. G. C. Clayton, P. G. Martin: Ap. J. 288, 558 (1985).
12. M. Cropper, J. Bailey, J. McCowage, R. D. Cannon, W. J. Couch, J. R. Walsh, J. O. Strade, F. Freeman: M. N. R. A. S. 231, 695 (1988).
13. C. Papaliolios, M. Karovska, L. Koechlin, P. Nisenson, C. Standley, S. Heathcote: Nature 338, 565 (1989).
14. W. D. Arnett, B. A. Fryxell, E. Müller: Ap. J. (Letters), in press (1989).
15. T. Ebisuzaki, T. Shigeyama, K. Nomoto: Ap. J., submitted (1989).
16. R. A. Chevalier, N. Soker: Ap. J. 341, 867 (1989).
17. P. R. Shapiro, P. G. Sutherland: Ap. J. 263, 902 (1982).
18. D. Branch: Ap. J. (Letters) 320, L23 (1987).
19. J. W. Menzies et al.: M. N. R. A. S. 227, 39P (1987).
20. R. V. Wagoner: Ap. J. (Letters) 250, L65 (1981).
21. M. W. Feast, A. R. Walker: Ann. Rev. Astron. Ap. 25, 345 (1987).
22. I. J. Danziger, R. A. E. Fosbury, D. Alloin, S. Christiani, J. Dachs, C. Gouiffes, B. Jarvis, K. C. Sahu: Astron. Ap. 177, L13 (1987).

Supernovae Ia as Standard Candles
Bruno Leibundgut

1. Introduction

The use of Supernovae (SNe) as a mean of distance measurements was proposed already in the early times of supernova research. An extensive study by Baade (1938) of all available data at that time illustrates how SNe were used to infer cosmological parameters.

Although the recognition of various subtypes of SNe (Minkowski 1964, Kirshner et al. 1973, Oke and Searle 1974, Wheeler and Levreault 1985, Uomoto and Kirshner 1985) hampers the use of SNe In general for distance determinations, the possibility remains of using SNe of type II as "custom yardsticks" (Kirshner and Kwan 1974, Höflich 1987, Wagoner 1988, Eastman and Kirshner 1989) and SNe of type Ia as standard candles (Tammann 1982, Leibundgut 1988, Leibundgut and Tammann 1989). The second method needs, of course, a good calibration of SNe Ia as objects with equal, if not identical, evolution of their light emission. Spectroscopic studies of SNe Ia have shown differences between individual events (Branch et al. 1988), but the photometric observations have exhibited astonishing uniformity (Leibundgut 1988). The exceptional case of the well studied SN 1986G in the peculiar galaxy NGC 5128 (Cen A; Phillips et al. 1987, Frogel et al. 1987, see also Canal et al. 1988) poses a strong challenge to the significance of standard candles for SNe Ia. We would like to understand what caused the differences, for instance in the infrared light curves of SN 1986G compared to standard SNe Ia like SNe 1972E, 1981B, 1980N (Leibundgut 1988) and the dispersion of the expansion velocities in SNe Ia (Branch et al. 1988), before we really may rely on distances from SNe. The little knowledge on extinction in external galaxies complicates accurate determinations even further, but as will be shown below, it might still be acceptable to neglect this contaminating effect for most SNe Ia.

We will first demonstrate the photometric uniformity of SNe Ia and then outline their possible uses for cosmology. The observations of SN 1988U (Norgaard-Nielsen et al. 1989) provide a first test of the predictions.

2. Evidence for Photometric Uniformity of SNe Ia

2.1 Light Curves

The light curves of SNe I exhibit, unlike those of SNe II, a much closer resemblance for individual events (Barbon et al. 1973, 1979). The normalization of data sets of different SNe to analyze the photometric light curves, however, suffers from the very inhomogeneous composition of the available observations and the photometric errors involved. The improvement on the photometry was demonstrated by Cadonau et al. (1985; their Fig. 1) who compared photographic, mostly old observations, with those in B (from more recent SNe). A much better definition of the light curves was found for the B data, although a wider sample of SNe I was considered. Some of the remaining dispersion can be attributed to SNe Ib which by themselves show a larger dispersion (Ensman and Woosley 1988, Leibundgut 1988).

Thus we concentrate on SNe Ia with sufficient observations to determine good light curves in the optical (UBV) and the near infrared (JHK) which are used to find the intrinsic deviations, if at all present, between the light curves. The only SNe Ia with suitable observations were SNe 1972E, 1980N, 1981B, and 1981D. In Table 1 we list the number of photometric observations as well as the scatter about a templet light curve as defined by Cadonau (1986; cf. Leibundgut 1988). The dispersion around a standard light curve from 5 days before until 110 days past B maximum are exceedingly small. The errors in the near infrared are dominated by SN 1972E. The more recent SNe show again very small deviations from the templet curves (Elias et al. 1981, 1985, Leibundgut 1988). We want to stress the need of more observations in the infrared to improve the available data. Especially the J filter in which a strong Fe absorption trough is observed (Graham et al. 1986, Frogel et al. 1987) might be sensible to differences between individual SNe.

Table 1: Standard SNe Ia

	1972E	1980N	1981B	1981D	all SNe
galaxy	NGC 5253	NGC 1316	NGC 4536	NGC 1316	
galaxy type	I0	Sa$_{pec}$	Sc	Sa$_{pec}$	
N_U	47	32	31	9	119
N_B	47	44	82	9	182
N_V	55	45	85	9	194
N_J	5	13	15	7	40
N_H	9	14	15	7	45
N_K	19	10	14	7	50
σ_U	0.12	0.18	0.19	0.19	0.16
σ_B	0.08	0.06	0.09	0.13	0.08
σ_V	0.09	0.07	0.11	0.08	0.10
σ_J	0.24	0.20	0.10	0.10	0.16
σ_H	0.06	0.08	0.05	0.04	0.06
σ_K	0.26	0.11	0.13	0.03	0.18

The accurate repetition of fiducial light curves in six filter over the entire optical and the near infrared wavelength range is a strong indication that we might consider SNe Ia as standard candles.

2.2 Colors at Maximum

Although extinction in galaxies is unknown colors of SNe Ia may show a small dispersion. To test the uniformity of SNe Ia colors the magnitudes at maximum in each observed filter were inter- or extrapolated for 24 SNe I by means of the templet light curves. The photometric data were taken Cadonau and Leibundgut (1989). The optical measurements were corrected only for foreground absorption (Sandage and Tammann 1987); no corrections were applied to the infrared data. Any intrinsic absorption in the parent galaxies was assumed to be negligible. In spite of this simplification the resulting dispersions are very small (Table 2). It is probably significant that the scatter decreases with increasing wavelength, i.e. with decreasing influence of any internal reddening. The infrared colors are given at 10 days past the B maximum because no observations at earlier phases are known for SNe Ia. This evaluation of a standard character of SNe Ia has the advantage of being independent of distances (Leibundgut and Tammann 1989).

Table 2: Colors of SNe Ia at maximum

color	mean	σ	N(SNe)
$(U-B)^{max}$	-0.26	0.21	13
$(B-V)^{max}$	0.02	0.22	24
$(B-H)^{(10)}$	-0.53	0.21	6
$(J-H)^{(10)}$	0.92	0.12	6
$(H-K)^{(10)}$	0.05	0.04	6

2.3 Uniformity of the Peak Luminosity

To compare the brightness at maximum of individual SNe one is forced to use at least relative distances and hence an appropriate Virgo infall model as long as not enough SNe Ia are observed in distant galaxies out in the Hubble flow. To check the dispersion of SNe Ia at maximum, however, the SNe I in Virgo offer the unique opportunity to compare a set of SNe at essentially the same distance - neglecting the depth of the cluster (Leibundgut and Tammann 1989). Only six SNe are suited for this test (SNe 1957B, 1960F, 1960R, 1961H, 1981B, and 1984A). The mean apparent magnitude at maximum in B is 11.91 with a dispersion of only $0.^m19$ (Leibundgut and Tammann 1989) probably enlarged by internal absorption. The new SNe Ia in Virgo (e.g. SN 1989M) will hopefully add more data.

The sample of SNe Ia in Virgo yields only a value for m_B^{max} due to the poor observations in other filters. To widen the set and extend the study to more filters we used a model for the virgocentric infall (cf. Schechter 1980, Aaronson et al. 1982, Kraan-Korteweg 1986) to determine relative distances of the parent galaxies. The distances were taken from Kraan-Korteweg (1986) and are based on an infall velocity of 220 km s^{-1}. All SNe magnitudes were reduced to the Virgo distance and in Table 3 we give the mean apparent magnitudes, the standard deviations and the number of SNe used in deriving these numbers. The values for the infrared bands refer to the phase 10 days past the B maximum. The scatters are once more extremely small regarding that in this sample the uncertainties in distances add to the partially poor photometry and the untreated internal extinction. This derivation does **not** depend on absolute distances, i.e. H_0, nor the Virgo distance (i.e. absolute magnitudes of SNe Ia; see below).

Table 3: Apparent magnitudes of SNe Ia at Virgo distance

filter	$<m_{Virgo}>$	σ	N
U^{max}	11.79	0.42	12
B^{max}	12.06	0.32	22
V^{max}	12.04	0.34	18
$J^{(10)}$	13.98	0.22	5
$H^{(10)}$	13.05	0.15	5
$K^{(10)}$	13.01	0.15	5

The photometric properties of SNe Ia are thus very uniform. The light curves in six filters are highly repetitive, the colors at maximum are identical within the uncertainties and the absolute peak magnitudes show quite small scatter which could well be due to mainly observational errors of the photometry. SNe Ia are hence standard candles to a high degree and suitable for distance determinations and fine tools for the measurement of cosmological parameters.

3. Use of SNe Ia as Standard Candles

With a sufficiently large sample of maximum magnitudes and galaxy redshifts it is possible to measure the Hubble constant H_0 *and* the deceleration parameter q_0 (we assume $\Lambda=0$ here) for Friedmann models of the universe. It will, however, be essential to obtain high quality photometry at peak light for many SNe Ia in galaxies within the Hubble flow (for H_0) and at high redshifts ($z \geq 0.5$; for q_0). In the following we will explore these possibilities and describe furthermore a test for the nature of cosmological redshifts (Leibundgut 1989).

3.1 H_0 from SNe Ia

The calibration of H_0 with SNe Ia is not new. Values determined have been mostly low ($H_0 \leq 70$ km Mpc^{-1} s^{-1} (Branch 1988, Tammann 1982, Tammann and Leibundgut 1989). The method described here rests on the SNe Ia in Virgo (cf. section 2.3) and the Hubble diagram of SNe Ia at maximum (Fig. 1). The velocities are corrected to the centroid of the Local Group, but *not* for the infall into Virgo. This causes the relatively large scatter at low velocities in addition to the reported effect of absorption in certain galaxies (Branch 1989). Model dependent velocities improve the picture considerably (Tammann and Leibundgut 1989). Thus only SNe with $v_0 \geq 2000$ km s^{-1} were considered. The determination of H_0 is now possible through the best fit of SNe Ia in the Hubble diagram. Using the formula

$$\log H_0 = 5\log v_0 - m + 25 + M \qquad (1)$$

we can calculate H_0 by averaging over all SNe with well observed maximum provided the absolute magnitude is known. Given a distance modulus to the Virgo cluster of $(m-M)_0=31.70\pm0.09$ (Tammann 1988, Leibundgut and Tammann 1989) an absolute magnitude of $M_B^{max}=-19.79\pm0.12$ is derived for SNe Ia. This together with the nine SNe with $v_0 \geq 2000$ km s^{-1} yields a value of $H_0=54\pm1.5$. The error includes the uncertainty in the Virgo distance modulus, the scatter of the SNe Ia in Virgo, and the scatter of the distant SNe about the Hubble line in the diagram.

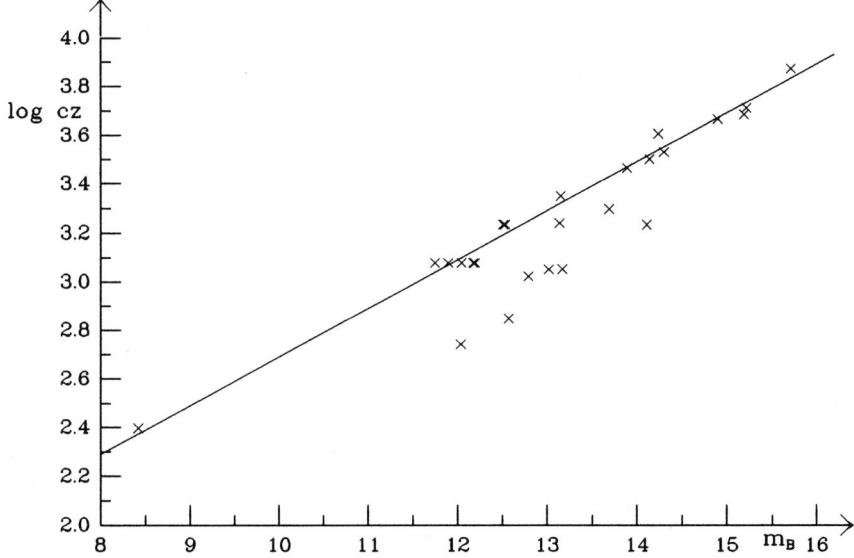

Figure 1: The Hubble diagram of SNe Ia at maximum

3.2 The Use of SNe Ia to Measure q_0

SNe Ia might open a new way to q_0. The small dispersion in absolute magnitude will allow to confine the range of q_0 (and Ω_0) to theoretically interesting values ($0<q_0<1/2$). With a few SNe Ia with well observed maxima at redshifts of ~ 0.5 a distinction between these two extreme cases of Friedmann universes should be feasible.

The effects of redshift on the apparent magnitudes at maximum, i.e. the K-corrections, were studied for this purpose for the V filter (Leibundgut 1989). Figure 2 shows the expected Hubble diagram for SNe Ia at maximum for $q_0=0$ and $q_0=1/2$. As a comparison also the uncorrected line for an empty universe ($q_0=0$) is drawn. The K_V-corrections are negative for small z due to the blue flux shifted into the V passband and the blue colors of SNe Ia at maximum. This effect is stopped as soon as the ultraviolet flux is redshifted into the V and the flux drops significantly ($z\geq0.6$) which drives the curves across the uncorrected predictions. In other words SNe Ia appear brighter at small redshifts (0.1<z<0.6) than "local" SNe Ia, but fainter beyond. This is a prediction due to the fact that they *are* standard candles! If SNe Ia do not follow this predictions then they are either effected by evolutionary effects and/or are not suitable as cosmological probes.

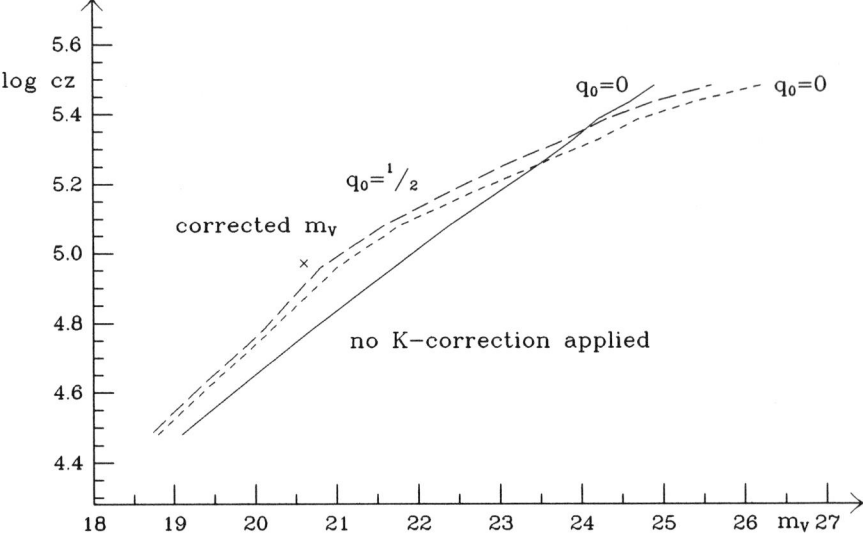

Figure 2: The predicted Hubble diagram for SNe Ia. The cross marks SN 1988U.

The observations of SN 1988U in the Abell cluster AC118 (Norgaard-Nielsen et al. 1989) at a redshift of z=0.31 unfortunately did not cover the maximum of the supernova. Although it supposedly was of type Ia (due to spectroscopic evidence) the lack of the maximum definition precludes an accurate test with this SN. Nevertheless we tried to fit the observations on a templet of an expected V curve of SNe Ia at z=0.3 (Leibundgut 1989; cf. next section). The inferred maximum value is shown in Fig. 2. The uncertainties in the determination are very large, for both the maximum estimate - which is $0.^m9$ brighter than derived by Norgaard-Nielsen et al. - and the curves based on an assumed M_V^{max}=-19.8. The validity of the corrections, however, is supported by this measurement. With more SNe and well defined maxima this potentially will be a route to measure q_0.

3.3 A Test to the Nature of Cosmological Redshifts

The identical photometric evolution in time provides a further clue to the nature of our universe. The explosion of a SN starts a clock, the ticks of which we measure relative to local clocks by comparing the shapes of the light curves. To illustrate this point the expected curve of SNe Ia at z=0.3 is drawn in Fig. 3 with and without the correction for time dilation (Leibundgut 1989). The differences are obvious and easily measurable as they are $\approx 0.^m6$ at 20 days past maximum or $\sim$30% in time to fade by the same amount. Thus SNe Ia provide an easy test to probe the nature of cosmological redshifts, i.e. a differentiation between expansion versus tired-light models. This method is much easier to perform than the well known test using the surface brightness within linear diameters of galaxies (Sandage 1988).

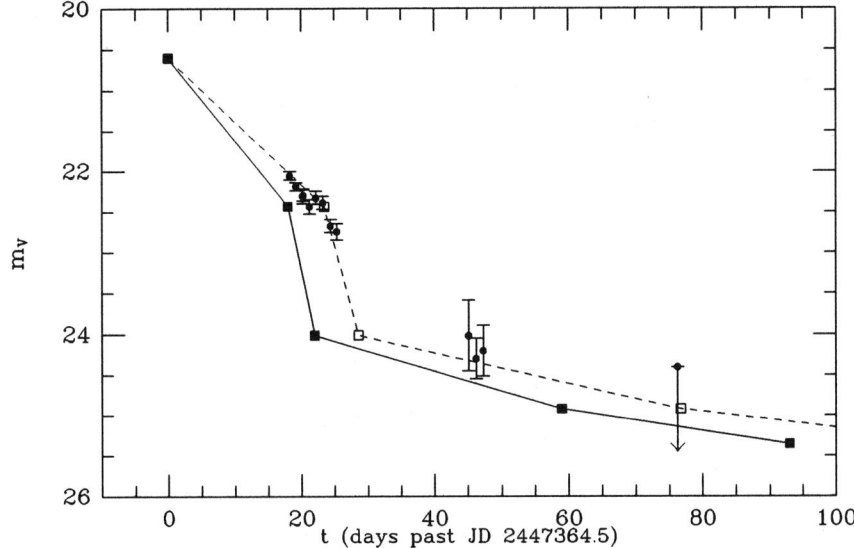

Figure 3: Comparison of the observations of SN 1988U and the predicted light curves.

The observations of SN 1988U allow us to carry out this test. The slope of the light curve after maximum clearly distinguishes between the models ($0.^m12$/day for expanding universes versus $0.^m15$/day for non-expanding models). The observations indicate a slope of $\sim 0.^m10$/day and clearly favor the curve corrected for time dilation (Fig. 3) and hence give evidence that the cosmological redshifts are due to an expansion of the universe and are not caused by tired light or equivalent models. To our knowledge this is the first clear prove of this assumption.

4. Conclusions

The conjecture of SNe Ia being standard candles is based on several independent determinations. The few well observed SNe Ia with light curves in six filters (UBVJHK) are identical to within the photometric errors (Leibundgut 1988) over the entire observed range (i.e. in time and in wavelengths), the colors at maximum are very similar for many SNe Ia and, in regard of the contamination by internal reddening, they are probably identical (Leibundgut and Tammann 1989), and finally their absolute magnitudes are identical to within $0.^m1 - 0.^m2$ in all six filters (Leibundgut and Tammann 1989, Leibundgut 1988).

Nevertheless a few question marks remain in this picture. SN 1986G (Phillips et al. 1987, Frogel et al. 1987), one of the closest SN Ia, clearly did not follow the standard photometric evolution of SNe Ia (cf. Leibundgut 1988). How much this is caused by the very strong extinction in Cen A is unclear, but we certainly do not understand this SN in the context of normal SNe Ia. Also the spectroscopic differences, e.g. expansion velocities (Branch et al.1988) contrast with the photometric uniformity of SNe Ia.

The confined behaviour of most SNe Ia requires a narrow explosion scenario, like the proposed deflagration or detonation of white dwarfs (Nomoto et al. 1984, Woosley and Weaver 1986).

The small dispersion in absolute magnitudes makes SNe Ia the best standard candles known. As cosmological probes they have several advantages over first-ranked cluster galaxies, e.g.

- SNe are point sources which facilitates the photometry considerably. The contribution by background galaxy light can be handled by careful reduction of the observations.
- no obvious luminosity evolution is present. The physics of an exploding white dwarf are set by natural constants and even chemical changes should not alter the explosion energies by much.
- no dynamical evolution, like the one of galaxies in clusters (mergers, interaction, etc.), introduces a secular term.

To check on the latter two assumptions it is imperative to observe many SNe Ia at various redshifts. The close correspondence of the predictions and the observations of SN 1988U indicate that such effects, if present, are probably small. This supernova also supports the fundamental assumption of the expansion of the universe, demonstrating the potential they bear as standard candles, not only for distance measurements.

Hence, although SNe Ia are transient objects, they provide us with a superb tool to determine the cosmological relevant parameters H_0 and, in the forseeable future, q_0.

Acknowledgement: It is a pleasure to thank Prof.Dr. G.A. Tammann for many enlightening discussions on the cosmological implications of SNe Ia. I would like to thank the Swiss Society for Astronomy and Astrophysics for travel support and the Swiss National Science Foundation which partially financed the research.

References

Aaronson, M., Huchra, J., Schechter, P.L., Tully, R.B.: 1982, Astrophys.J. **258**,64
Baade, W.: 1938, Astrophys.J. **88**,285
Barbon, R., Ciatti, F., Rosino, L.: 1973, Astron. Astrophys. **25**,241
Barbon, R., Ciatti, F., Rosino, L.: 1979, Astron. Astrophys. **72**,287
Branch, D., Drucker, W., Jeffery, D.J.: 1988, Astrophys.J. **330**,L117
Branch, D.: 1988, in *The Extragalactic Distance Scale*, eds. S. van den Bergh and C.J. Pritchet, San Francisco: Astron.Soc.Pacific,p146
Branch, D.: 1989, this workshop
Cadonau, R.: 1986, Ph.D. Thesis, University of Basel
Cadonau, R., Leibundgut, B.: 1989, submitted to Astron.Astrophys.Suppl.Series
Cadonau, R., Sandage, A., Tammann, G.A.: 1985, in *Supernovae as Distance Indicators*, ed. N.Bartel, Berlin:Springer, p.151
Canal, R., Isern, J., Lopez, R.: 1988, Astrophys.J. **330**,L113

Eastman, R.G., Kirshner, R.P.: 1989, Astrophys.J., in press
Ensman, L.M., Woosley, S.E.: 1988, Astrophys.J **333**,754
Elias, J.H, Frogel, J.A., Hackwell, J.A., Persson, S.E.: 1981, Astrophys.J **251**,L13
Elias, J.H., Matthews, K., Neugebauer, G., Persson, S.E.: 1985, Astrophys.J. **296**,379
Frogel, J.A., Gregory, B., Kawara, K., Laney, D., Phillips, M.M., Terndrup, D., Vrba, F., Whitford, A.E.: 1987, Astrophys.J. **315**,L129
Graham, J.R., Meikle, W.S.P, Allen, D.A., Longmore, A.J., Williams, P.M.: 1986, Mon.Not.R.Astr.Soc **218**,93
Höflich, P.: 1987, in *Nuclear Astrophysics*, eds. W. Hillebrandt, R. Kuhfuss, E. Müller, J.W. Truran, Berlin:Springer,p.307
Kirshner, R.P., Oke, J.B., Penston, M.V., Searle, L.: 1973, Astrophys.J. **185**,303
Kirshner, R.P., Kwan, J.: 1974, Astrophys.J. **193**,27
Kraan-Korteweg, R.C.: 1986, Astron.Astrophys.Suppl.Ser. **66**,255
Leibundgut, B.: 1988, Ph.D. Thesis, University of Basel
Leibundgut, B.: 1989, Astron.Astrophys., in press
Leibundgut, B., Tammann, G.A.: 1989, submitted to Astron.Astrophys.
Minkowski, R.: 1964, Ann.Rev.Astron.Astrophys. **2**,247
Nomoto, K., Thielemann, F.-K., Yokoi, K.: 1984, Astrophys.J. **286**,644
Norgaard-Nielsen, H.U., Hansen, L., Jorgensen, H.E., Salamanca, A.A., Ellis, R.S., Couch, W.J.: 1989, Nature **339**,523
Oke, J.B., Searle, L.: 1974, *Ann.Rev.Astron.Astrophys.* **12**,315
Oke, J.B., Sandage, A.: 1968, Astrophys.J. **154**,21
Phillips, M.M. et al.: 1987, Publ.Astron.Soc.Pac. **99**,592
Sandage, A.: 1988, *Ann.Rev.Astron.Astrophys.* **26**,561
Sandage, A., Tammann, G.A.: 1987, *A Revised Shapley-Ames Catalog of Bright Galaxies*, 2nd edition, Washington: Carnegie Institution of Washington
Schechter, P.L.: 1980, Astron.J. **85**,801
Tammann, G.A.: 1982, in *Supernovae: A Survey of Current Research*, eds. M.J. Rees and R.J. Stoneham, Dordrecht:Reidel,p.371
Tammann, G.A.: 1988, in *The Extragalactic Distance Scale*, eds. S.van den Bergh and C.J. Pritchet, San Francisco:Astron.Soc.Pacific,p.282
Tammann, G.A., Leibundgut, B.: 1989, in preparation
Uomoto, A., Kirshner, R.P.: 1985, Astron.Astrophys. **149**,L7
Wheeler, J.C., Levreault, R.: 1985, Astrophys.J. **294**,L17
Woosley, S.E.,Weaver, T.A.: 1986, *Ann.Rev.Astron.Astrophys.* **24**,205

An Estimate of the Distance to M100 in the Virgo Cluster via VLBI of SN1979C: Updates and Prospects

Norbert Bartel

1. METHOD

A VLBI determination, at time t after the explosion, of the angular radius, Θ, of a supernova's radiosphere, coupled with an optical-spectroscopic determination of the radial expansion velocity v_{shock}, at time t_0 after the explosion, of the supernova's shockfront allows estimates to be made of the distance, D, to the supernova's host galaxy and of Hubble's constant (BARTEL [1]; BARTEL et al. [2]; see also BARTEL [3], for a comparison of this method with other methods (e.g., BRANCH [4]) that use supernovae as distance indicators):

$$D = \frac{v_{shock}\, t\, \mu\, \eta}{\Theta\, m\, \kappa} \left[\frac{t}{t_0}\right]^{m-1} \tag{1}$$

$$H_0 = \frac{v_{redshift} + v_{infall}}{D}. \tag{2}$$

The parameter m is a measure of the deceleration (or acceleration) of Θ, with $\Theta \propto t^m$, η is the ratio between the expansion velocity of the radiosphere and that of the shockfront, and κ the model dependence of Θ. We define the parameter κ so that $\kappa = 1.0$ for a supernova having a shell-like brightness distribution with a shell thickness of $\sim 15\%$. The parameter μ describes the effect of any deviation from spherical symmetry on the distance determination. For spherically symmetric SNe, $\mu = 1$. The parameter $v_{redshift}$ denotes the redshift velocity of the host galaxy, and v_{infall} its correction due to local peculiar velocities. For a uniformly expanding, spherically symmetric supernova shell eq. (1) becomes simply: $D = v_{shock} \cdot t\eta/\Theta$.

The goal is to determine observationally each of the parameters in eq. (1) and thereby to estimate a host galaxy's distance and H_0. Since 1982, we have made VLBI observations of SN1979C in the galaxy M100 in the Virgo cluster at several epochs and combined the results with those from optical spectroscopic observations. In the remainder, I will describe the results and uncertainties and indicate prospects for more accurate determinations of M100's distance via additional VLBI observations.

2. PARAMETER DETERMINATIONS

For SN1979C, three of the six parameters in eq. (1) have been determined and a useful lower bound on a fourth parameter can be estimated from our VLBI observations of SN1987A. From VLBI observations of SN1979C, we obtained $\Theta = 0.42 \pm 0.03$ at $t = 3.69$ yr and $m = 1.03 \pm 0.15$ (BARTEL, this volume). From optical spectroscopic observations (BRANCH et al. [5]), the parameter v_{shock} can be estimated.

Since the largest unambiguous value for the expansion velocity is $\sim 12000 \pm 200$ km s^{-1}, determined from the blue edge of the absorption trough of the NaD line profile 0.24 yr after the explosion, and since the blue edge of the Hα emission profile, which is equivalent to 10500 km s^{-1}, remains constant until the last date of Branch et al.'s spectroscopic observations, 0.65 yr after the explosion, we take $v_{shock} = 12000 \pm 200$ km s^{-1} at $t_0 = 0.65$ yr.

A lower bound on the parameter η can be estimated from our VLBI observations of SN1987A (BARTEL et al. [6]; JAUNCEY et al. [7]; SHAPIRO et al. [8]), if the physical processes responsible for the radio emission from SN1987A are typical for SNe in general. Are these processes typical for SNe in general? In Fig. 1, I plot the spectral luminosity at 1.5 GHz of SNe and young SNRs versus the time since their explosions. Since the spectral luminosity of SN1987A is two to four orders of magnitude smaller than the spectral luminosities of other recent SNe, and since its peak was reached at least an order of magnitude faster than for the other SNe, it was speculated that the prompt radio burst was perhaps a precursor of, and quite distinct from, a more prominent outburst. Such a precursor would have been undetectable for more distant supernovae and, moreover, because of its likely occurrence well before maximum light, unobservable from other SNe discovered well after the epoch of explosion.

However, two and a half years have passed without SN1987A's flaring up again at radio frequencies (0.8-8 GHz). Further, the circumstellar interaction model was quite successful in fitting the evolution of the prompt burst's light curve and spectrum. Also, the shape of the prompt burst's light curve and the evolution of its spectrum resembled those of other supernovae in detail. A fit of the circumstellar interaction model to the radio flux densities observed at four frequencies (STOREY and MANCHESTER [19]; CHEVALIER and FRANSSON [20]) suggested a density of the circumstellar medium two to three orders of magnitude lower than the corresponding densities for SN1979C and SN1980K. This lower density is consistent with the progenitor of SN1987A having been a blue supergiant (wind velocity ~ 500 km s^{-1}), in contrast to the progenitors of SN1979C and SN1980K, believed to have been red supergiants (wind velocities ~ 10 km s^{-1}) (CHEVALIER and FRANSSON [20]).

Thus, it appears now that the relatively low radio luminosity and the early turn-on of radio emission were caused by the relatively low density of the circumstellar medium encountered by the SN1987A shockfront. Further, it appears that the physical processes responsible for the radio emission were indeed typical for SNe in general and that a lower bound on the parameter η can be estimated from our VLBI observations of SN1987A. The lower bounds on the size and velocity of the radio shell relative to, respectively, the radii and velocities inferred from the absorption minimum and the blue edge of the Hα-profile imply that $\eta > 0.9$ for the values for SN1979C (see, e.g., BARTEL, this volume). The upper bound on η is model dependent. The circumstellar interaction model predicts $\eta = 1.2$ for $0.9 \lesssim m < 1$ (CHEVALIER [21]). Based on these values, we assume $\eta = 1.0^{+0.2}_{-0.1}$.

Since we have not yet determined the brightness distribution of SN1979C, any estimate of the SN's angular radius is somewhat model-dependent. With $\kappa = 1.0$ for an optically thin, shell-like brightness distribution with a shell thickness of $\sim 15\%$ of the shell radius, κ can vary between ~ 0.8 for the distribution as a ring and ~ 1.3 for it as an optically thin uniform sphere. The variation of κ as a function of the shell thickness itself is smaller: $\pm 4\%$ for a thickness between 25% and $\lesssim 5\%$ (e.g., MARSCHER [22]). There are reasons to believe that the morphology of SN1979C is indeed shell-like. First, $\sim 90\%$ of all known SNRs with discernible morphology have a shell-like structure (GREEN [23]). Second, SNRs with steep radio spectra like that of SN1979C are shells, in contrast to SNRs with flat spectra like that of the centrally powered Crab nebula, which are plerions (WEILER and SRAMEK [24]). Since, further, a ring of emission is most likely unphysical for SNe, we adopt $\kappa = 1.00^{+0.15}_{-0.05}$, which allows for a morphology between that of a thin shell of emission and that of a composite between a shell and a plerion. Such a value for κ is also consistent with the

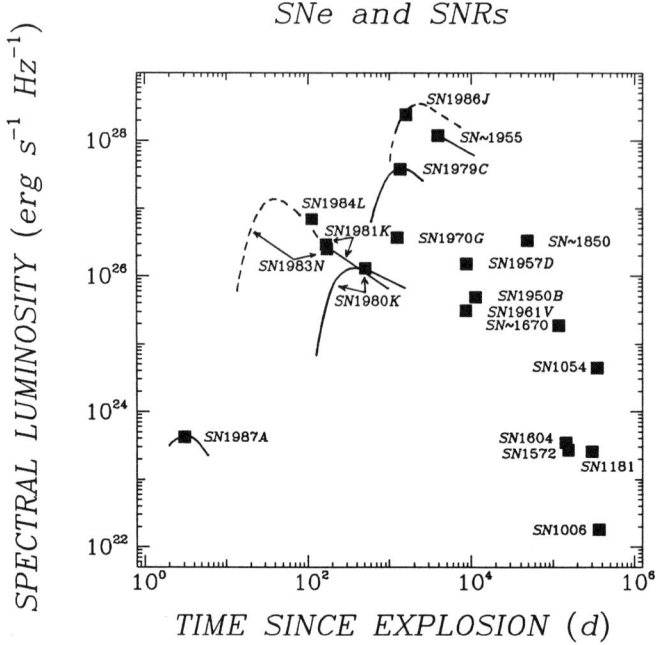

Fig. 1. The spectral luminosity at 1.5 GHz and, for SN1987A only, at 1.4 GHz, vs. the age of radio supernovae and young supernova remnants. The squares indicate the largest measured spectral luminosities of the corresponding sources, the solid curves represent all measured spectral luminosities, and the dashed curve predicts spectral luminosities according to CHEVALIER [9]. The time at which the flux density of a SN reaches maximum is frequency-dependent, typically threefold shorter at 8 than at 1.5 GHz. Note that SN~1955 (SNR41.9+58) is the brightest source among more than 20 hot spots in M82, which are most likely also SNe or SNRs. Their spectral luminosities are a few times to hundredfold smaller than the spectral luminosity of SN~1955, and their ages range from a few years to a few hundred years (UNGER et al. [10]; KRONBERG, BIERMANN, and SCHWAB [11]; KRONBERG and SRAMEK [12]; BARTEL et al. [13]). Their data are not plotted here. The data for SN1987A are from TURTLE et al. [14], for SN1986J from RUPEN et al. [15], BARTEL et al. [6], and WEILER, this volume, for SN1961V from COWAN, HENRY, and BRANCH [16], for SN~1955 (SNR41.9+58) in M82 from KRONBERG, BIERMANN, and SCHWAB [11] and BARTEL et al. [13], and for SN~1850 in NGC4449 from DE BRUYN [17]. The data from all other sources are from WEILER et al. [18] and references therein.

circumstellar interaction model for SNe (CHEVALIER [25] and, e.g., LUNDQVIST and FRANSSON [26]).

As to the parameter μ, we have not yet been able to determine with useful accuracy how much, if at all, the brightness distribution of SN1979C deviates from circular symmetry. The relatively small declination of the source of $\delta = 16°$ and the locations of the four telescopes used in the observations caused the u-v coverage to be rather elongated (see Fig. 2) and limited our sensitivity in modeling the SN in two dimensions. For now, we therefore have to rely on the assumption that SN1979C is approximately circularly symmetric and adopt $\mu = 1.0 \pm 0.15$.

Estimate of Distance to M100

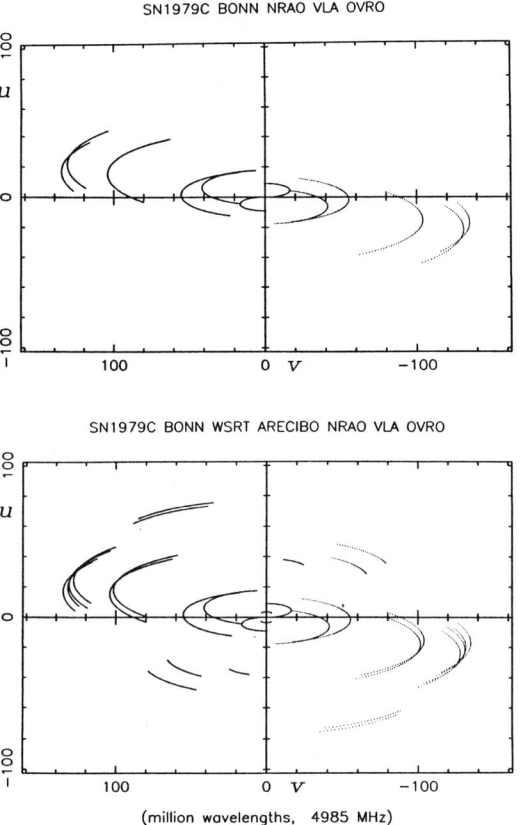

Fig. 2. The upper part of the figure shows the u-v coverage when SN1979C is observed with a four-station array, as during the first three sessions of our monitoring program. The four stations are: the 100-m antenna near Bonn, West Germany; the 43-m antenna in Green Bank, WV; the 27 × 25-m VLA near Socorro, NM; and the 40-m antenna near Big Pine, CA. The lower part shows the equivalent coverage when the array is enlarged by the 305-m antenna in Arecibo, PR, and the 14 × 25-m array at Westerbork, The Netherlands. The dotted curves show reflected tracks.

With these values and uncertainties, we get

$$D_{\rm M100} = 22^{+7}_{-6} \text{ Mpc} \ .$$

For estimating H_0, we take $v_0 + v_{\rm infall} = 1250 \pm 150$ km s^{-1} for the Virgo cluster center (see 12 references in Bartel et al. 1985). If we assume that the distance to M100 is within 10% of the distance to this center, since M100 is within 5° of the center and has a redshift consistent with other Virgo cluster members, we get

$$H_0 = 60 \pm 20 \text{ km s}^{-1} \text{ Mpc} \ ,$$

with the uncertainties of both estimates representing 1–2σ. A more complete error analysis is pending.

3. PROSPECTS

We anticipate making more and more extended VLBI observations of SN1979C to determine the parameters m, κ, and μ more accurately. In the spring of 1990, we will add the upgraded Arecibo telescope and the phased Westerbork array to our presently east–west oriented VLBI array of four antennas (Owens Valley Radio Telescope, VLA, Green Bank telescope, and Effelsberg telescope). Each of these additional antennas will add significantly to the sensitivity of our array and counterbalance to some degree the combined effects of SN1979C's decreasing flux density and increasing size on the rising difficulty of measuring the SN's angular size. Apart from determining the parameter m more accurately, we may also be able to distinguish whether the emission region has the morphology of a ring, an optically thin shell, or an optically thin uniform sphere; thereby we can also obtain an estimate of the parameter κ independent of our present educated guess. Further, the inclusion of Arecibo into the array will broaden the u-v coverage twofold (see Fig. 2) and should allow a useful estimate to be made on the bounds on μ.

4. CONCLUSIONS

VLBI observations of SN1979C in the galaxy M100 in the Virgo cluster were made to determine the angular radius Θ of the SN's radiosphere at several epochs and its deceleration parameter m. VLBI observations of SN1987A revealed a useful lower bound on the ratio η between the size of the radiosphere and that of the Hα line-forming region. Combined with a) a model-dependent upper bound on η, b) an educated guess of the possible range of values κ for the morphologies of SN1979C, and c) the assumption of approximate spherical symmetry of SN1979C, the distance to M100 could be determined with an uncertainty of about 30%.

Anticipated new observations could allow a more accurate measurement of the deceleration parameter m, and, for the first time, determinations of SN1979C's morphology and of a bound on any deviation of circular symmetry of its brightness distribution. With such determinations, the uncertainty of M100's distance could perhaps be limited to about 20%.

5. ACKNOWLEDGMENT

This research was supported in part by the NSF under grant No. AST-8902087.

6. REFERENCES

1. Bartel, N. 1985, in *Supernovae as Distance Indicators*, Lecture Notes in Physics, ed. N. Bartel (Springer–Verlag, Berlin), **224**, 107.
2. Bartel, N., Rogers, A. E. E., Shapiro, I. I., Gorenstein, M. V., Gwinn, C. R., Marcaide, J. M., and Weiler, K. W. 1985, *Nature*, **318**, 25.
3. Bartel, N. 1986, in *Highlights of Astronomy*, ed. J. P. Swings (Reidel, Dordrecht), **7**, 655.
4. Branch, D. 1985, in *Supernovae as Distance Indicators*, Lecture Notes in Physics, ed. N. Bartel (Springer–Verlag, Berlin), **224**, 138.
5. Branch, D., Falk, S. W., McCall, M. L., Rybski, P., Uomoto, A., and Wills, B. J. 1981, *Ap. J.*, **244**, 780.
6. Bartel, N. et al. 1988, in *Supernova 1987A in the Large Magellanic Cloud*, eds. M. Kafatos and A. Michalitsianos (Cambridge Univ. Press, Cambridge), p. 81.
7. Jauncey, D. L. et al. 1988, *Nature*, **334**, 412.
8. Shapiro, I. I. et al. 1988, in *IAU Symposium 129, The Impact of VLBI on Astrophysics and Geophysics*, eds. M. J. Reid and J. M. Moran (Reidel, Dordrecht), p. 185.

9. Chevalier, R. A. 1984, *Ap. J. (Letters)*, **285**, L63.
10. Unger, S. W., Pedlar, A., Axon, D. J., Wilkinson, P. N., and Appleton, P. N. 1984, *M. N. R. A. S.*, **211**, 783.
11. Kronberg, P. P., Biermann, P., and Schwab, F. R. 1985, *Ap. J.*, **291**, 693.
12. Kronberg, P. P., and Sramek, R. A. 1985, *Science*, **277**, 28.
13. Bartel, N. *et al.* 1987, *Ap. J.*, **323**, 505.
14. Turtle, A. J. *et al.* 1987, *Nature*, **327**, 38.
15. Rupen, M. P., van Gorkom, J. H., Knapp, G. R., Gunn, J. E., and Schneider, D. P. 1987, *A. J.*, **94**, 61.
16. Cowan, J. J., Henry, R. B. C., and Branch, D. *Ap. J.*, **329**, 116.
17. de Bruyn, A. G. 1983, *Astr. Ap.*, **119**, 301.
18. Weiler, K. W., Sramek, R. A., Panagia, N., van der Hulst, J. M., and Salvati, M. 1986, *Ap. J.*, **301**, 790.
19. Storey, M. C. and Manchester, R. N. 1987, *Nature*, **329**, 421.
20. Chevalier, R. A. and Fransson, C. 1987, *Nature*, **328**, 44.
21. Chevalier, R. A. 1985, in *Supernova as Distance Indicators*, Lecture Notes in Physics, ed. N. Bartel (Springer–Verlag, Berlin), **224**, 123.
22. Marscher, A. P. 1985, in *Supernova as Distance Indicators*, Lecture Notes in Physics, ed. N. Bartel (Springer–Verlag, Berlin), **224**, 130.
23. Green, D. A. 1984, *M. N. R. A. S.*, **209**, 449.
24. Weiler, K. W., and Sramek, R. A. 1988, *Ann. Rev. Astr. Ap.*, **26**, 295.
25. Chevalier, R. A. 1982, *Ap. J.*, **259**, 302.
26. Lundqvist, P. and Fransson, C. 1988, *Astr. Ap.*, **192**, 221.

Hard X-ray Radiation from Supernova 1987A. The Results of Kvant Module in 1987–1989

R. A. Sunyaev, A. S. Kaniovsky, V. V. Efremov,
S. A. Grebenev, A. V. Kuznetsov, J. Englhauser,
S. Doebereiner, W. Pietsch, C. Reppin, J. Truemper,
E. Kendziorra, M. Maisack, B. Mony, & R. Staubert

For the first time during two years observations of the Supernova 1987A in 1989 June the Roentgen observatory aboard the Mir-Kvant module was not able to detect its hard X-ray radiation during current series of observations. Radiation flux in energy band 45-105 keV decreased more than 8.5 times in comparison with maximal flux detected in 1988 January.

The results obtained during two years of the Supernova 1987A observations were given in the papers (Sunyaev et al., 1987a,b, 1988, 1989). By the present time we have succeeded in calibration of the third and fourth detectors of the HEXE device using the results of the Crab Nebula observation. These detectors have lower energy resolution in comparison with the first and the second ones. Therefore we reprocessed all the obtained data about SN1987A hard X-rays using the results of all four detectors of the HEXE device once more that is increased data significance and decreased statistical errors.

Paper not presented at Workshop; Late manuscript accepted by editor

In Fig.1a,b spectra of SN1987A hard X-ray radiation are presented. They were obtained in seven series of intense observations carried out by the Roentgen observatory during two years. The spectra demonstrate an increase of the flux from 1987 August to 1988 January. This increase is connected with rapid decreasing of the envelope transparence. From 1988 January to 1989 June a continuous decline of the flux is observed which is mainly connected with decreasing of ^{56}Co amount in the envelope. Already in 1988 September a strong change of the spectral shape was detected. This is explained by decreasing of the envelope optical thickness with respect to Thomson scattering. The number of successive scatterings experienced by majority of photons became insufficient to decrease energy of the ^{56}Co decay gamma-photons due to multiple recoil effect up to value $h\nu \leq 50$ keV.

Note the sharp cutoff of flux at the energies below 20 keV in 1987 August and 1988 January was connected with photo-absorption by heavy elements. At that time the photon diffusion in the envelope accompanied by the recoil effect moved majority of photons in the band $h\nu \leq 20$ keV where the photoabsorption dominated.

In Fig.2,3 light curves of the SN1987A emission in three energy bands: 15-45, 45-105, 105-200 keV (see also Table 1) are presented. Note here especially the point corresponding to observations on June 16, 1987 when the hard X-ray flux in the 45-105 keV spectral channel was detected at four standard deviation level (first it was noticed by Englhauser et al., 1989).

The light curves (Fig.3) testified to hard X-ray flux from the supernova changed smoothly in accordance with predictions of the model of this radiation appearance due to radioactive cobalt decay in opaque envelope. For two years of observations we have not been able to observe neither traces of a shock wave generated due to collision between expanding envelope of the supernova and a stellar wind emitted by the presupernova on a red giant stage of the evolution nor traces of X-ray radiation of the stellar remnant - a young pulsar or an accreting object, nor any manifestations of emission connected with cosmic rays.

Mixing of Radioactive Elements in the Expanding Envelope. Early detection of the SN1987A hard X-ray radiation by the Ginga satellite and the Kvant module (Dotani et al., 1987, Sunyaev et al., 1987a,b) was the first evidence of a radioactive ^{56}Co strong mixing over the envelope volume (Ito et al., 1987, Ebisuzaki and Shibazaki, 1988, Grebenev and Sunyaev, 1988, Pinto and Woosley, 1988). At present this conclusion is confirmed by direct observations of a velocity dispersion of infrared lines of the iron and cobalt ions(Ericson et al., 1988) and also by a broad spectral width of the ^{56}Co direct escape gamma-lines (Matz et al., 1988, Rester et al., 1989). These direct observations testify to presence of radioactive cobalt in the envelope layers having expansion velocities from 400 up to 3000 km/s. This would be impossible if a strongest mixing of envelope material due to generation of the Rayleigh-Taylor instability was not occured (Hachisu et al., 1989, Arnett et al., 1989).

The supernova hard X-ray light curve gives a possibility to estimate the distribution of radioactive cobalt over the envelope using the simplest assumptions. The ^{56}Co distribution (mass-fraction) consistent with the observed light curve is shown in Fig.4 by crosses (vertical line of a cross corresponds to error at one standard deviation level). The problem of reconstruction of cobalt distribution over the envelope is considerably simpler if cobalt radial distribution is searched as a superposition of two Gaussians: narrow one localized near the envelope centre and an extensive one with broader ^{56}Co distribution over the envelope. The regions of ^{56}Co distribution consistent with the observed light curve in this simple model are also presented in Fig.4.

It is obvious that two different approaches give quite close results. About 60% of cobalt is in central region of the envelope having low velocities. And about 40% is mixed over all the envelope volume. Note that the data of only two hard energy bands 45-200 keV were used during the cobalt distribution reconstruction. The flux at lower energies strongly depends on photoabsorption in the envelope but the photoabsorption efficiency strongly depends on degree of the cobalt mixing.

All the calculations the results of which were presented above and will be discussed below were carried out on the basis of the velocity and density distribution model resulted from hydrodynamics simulations by Arnett (1988).

In Fig.3 it is shown how the accepted model of cobalt distribution coincides with the observed X-ray light curve. Deviations are maximal at the beginning of the supernova X-ray observation in a soft 15-45 keV band. This points out at more strong photoabsorption in comparison with photoabsorption in the used model. It may be connected with the enhanced cobalt concentration in outer envelope layers. High X-ray and gamma-ray radiation from these layers appeared at early stages of the envelope expansion before the beginning of the Roentgen observatory systematical observations.

Abundance of ^{57}Co. By the beginning of the second year after the explosion a ^{57}Co isotope will be able to become an important energy source in the supernova envelope as it decays

3.5 times moreslowly than ^{56}Co. The simulations of explosive nucleosynthesis (Woosley et al., 1986, Hashimoto et al., 1989) predicted a ratio of ^{57}Co/^{56}Co abundances 2 times exceeding the ratio of ^{57}Fe/^{56}Fe abundances at the Earth. There are two ways to define the abundance of ^{57}Co in the SN1987A envelope: the first, by direct determination of flux in the ^{57}Co lines of 12? and 136 keV in the supernova spectrum and the second one, by determination of a ^{57}Co photon portion in the X-ray continuous spectrum in the 45-105 keV energy band. We means the photons emitted in the ^{57}Co lines 122 and 136 keV but undergoing to multiple scatterings in the envelope and decreasing their energy due to recoil effect. Because of relatively low energy resolution of Phoswich detectors the HEXE device aboard Mir-Kvant module gave considerably better results when the second method was used.

The results presented below depend on an accepted envelope model (the Arnett's model (1988) is used) and on a cobalt distribution over the envelope (the distribution presented in Fig.4 is used). It is also supposed that ^{57}Co is distributed similarly to ^{56}Co.

For the whole period from 1988 September to 1989 June the Roentgen observatory has not detected a statistically significant enhancement of X-ray luminosity in the 45-105 kev energy band over the model predictions in which the whole observed flux is connected with the ^{56}Co decay. The upper limits at three standard deviation level for the ratio of ^{57}Co/^{56}Co relative abundance in the supernova envelope to the Earth's ^{57}Fe/^{56}Fe relative abundance were equal to 2.4 in 1988 September, 3.3 in 1988 December and 1.8 in 1989 June at the accepted assumptions. Note that the ratio of ^{57}Fe/^{56}Fe abundances at the Earth is 0.024 (Cameron, 1986). All the data obtained from 1988 September to 1989 June allowed us to obtain a limit at three standard deviation level for a portion of ^{57}Co decay photons in the light curve of the SN1987A hard X-ray radiation. This limit corresponds to the ^{57}Co/^{56}Co abundance in 1.5 times exceeding the Earth's ^{57}Fe/^{56}Fe relative abundance. The observations in 1989 May-June gave upper limit on the cobalt 122 keV line flux $3.9 \cdot 10^{-4}$ photons$\cdot$cm^{-2}s^{-1} (at 3σ level). This limit corresponds in frames of the model being discussed to the ^{57}Co/^{56}Co abundance 6 times exceeding the Earth's abundance of ^{57}Fe/^{56}Fe.

The data obtained in 1989 May-June give also a possibility to set up an upper limit on a fraction of the ^{22}Na and ^{44}Ti radioactive photons in the X-ray 45-105 keV flux from SN1987A in 830 days after the explosion. The corresponding upper limits at three standard deviation level on mass of ^{22}Na and ^{44}Ti contained in the envelope at the moment of explosion are $1.3 \cdot 10^{-3} M_\odot$ and $9 \cdot 10^{-3} M_\odot$. These limits exceed the amount of ^{44}Ti, $M_{44} \sim 1.2 \cdot 10^{-4} M_\odot$, and ^{22}Na, $M_{22} \sim 3 \cdot 10^{-5} M_\odot$, predicted by Hashimoto et al. (1989) and Woosley et al. (1986) on basis of the explosive nucleosynthesis calculations at one order of magnitude.

Limits on the Stellar Remnant Luminosity. The observations of the Roentgen observatory in 1989 May-June set up strong restrictions on X-ray luminosity of a stellar remnant produced during the explosion L_x(1-6 keV) $\leq 3.6 \cdot 10^{36}$, L_x(6-15 keV) $\leq 5.4 \cdot 10^{36}$ and L_x(15-105 keV) $\leq 1.35 \cdot 10^{37}$ erg/s for the assumed distance 55 kpc (Sunyaev R.A. et al., 1990, Table 1). At that time a Thomson optical depth of the envelope yet exceeded 3-4, and a X-ray spectrum of the remnant was considerably distorted by a photoabsorption and a compton scattering. The absorbed energy went on the envelope heating and were reemitted in the infrared, submillimeter and optical bands. The measurements by Bouchet et al. (1990) showed that emission of a dust in the envelope had a black body spectrum with $T \approx 160K$ and the supernova bolometric luminosity in 1030 days after the explosion were equal to $(2.0 \pm 0.1) \cdot 10^{38}$ erg/s. Using the data of Monte-Carlo calculations, the upper limit on the hard X-ray flux in the 15-105 keV band obtained by the HEXE device on the 830th day and the information on the envelope emission at low frequencies rather interesting restrictions on an intrinsic spectrum of the stellar remnant may be obtained. For example, assuming that the remnant (pulsar) has a power law spectrum in 1-1000 keV energy band, $I_\nu \sim \nu^{-\alpha}$ [photons$\cdot$cm^{-2}s^{-1}keV^{-1}], and using the 3σ upper limit presented above for the X-ray 15-105 keV flux escaping the envelope on the 830th day we obtain the 3σ upper limit on the pulsar luminosity in the 1-1000 keV energy band $L_B \leq 2.4 \cdot 10^{38}$ and $\leq 4.4 \cdot 10^{38}$ erg/s for two spectral indexes α - 1.5 and 2.1. In neglecting the pulsar spindown and its luminosity changing we may find the upper limit on the energy absorbed in the envelope that is its low frequency luminosity on the 1100th day $L_{IR} \leq 1.0 \cdot 10^{38}$ and $\leq 3.5 \cdot 10^{38}$ erg/s for α - 1.5 and 2.1 correspondingly. It is clear that in case when the spectral index is 1.5 such a spectrum is not able to give the observed low frequency luminosity of the envelope. It may be easily shown that any spectrum with $\alpha \leq 1.75$ does not coincide with the data obtained by Bouchet et al. (1990).

The presented example shows a possibility for using our data to obtain restrictions on parameters of a pulsar hidden inside the expanding envelope. In the case when an accreting object is situated in the envelope centre our estimates are less definite. Nevertheless such an analysis with using the

HEXE data presented above for the object with spectrum similar to the spectrum of the wellknown source Cygnus X-1 in a low state (Sunyaev and Truemper, 1979) also demonstrates the impossibility to satisfy the low frequency data. If the infrared radiation is the result of dust reprocessing of a central object hard emission the X-ray spectrum of the stellar remnant should be soft enough.

Another way to explain the excess of infrared radiation detected by Bouchet et al. (1990) is that radioactive isotopes ^{57}Co, ^{22}Na and ^{44}Ti are more abundant in the envelope than it was assumed. Their hard radioactive emission transforms in the opaque envelope into the low frequency emission which was observed. As the excess luminosity on the 1100th day after the explosion was equal to $2 \cdot 10^{38}$erg/s it was necessary that about $4 \cdot 10^{-2} M_\odot$ of ^{57}Co (that is the ^{57}Co/^{56}Co ratio exceeded the Earth's ^{57}Fe/^{56}Fe ratio about 22 times), or $9 \cdot 10^{-4} M_\odot$ of ^{22}Na, or $9 \cdot 10^{-3} M_\odot$ of ^{44}Ti were hidden inside the envelope. Comparing these values with the HEXE upper limits for ^{57}Co, ^{22}Na and ^{44}Ti abundances, $M_{57} \leq 2.8 \cdot 10^{-3} M_\odot$, $M_{22} \leq 1.3 \cdot 10^{-3} M_\odot$ and $M_{44} \leq 9 \cdot 10^{-3} M_\odot$, we come to conclusion that the assumption about the radioactive nature of excess has failed in the case of ^{57}Co and is unlikely in the case of ^{44}Ti and ^{22}Na.

Discussion. All the data obtained by the four HEXE detectors in 1987 August - 1988 January confirm the identification of the hard X-ray source in the Large Magellanic Cloud having an unusual spectrum (see Fig.5) with SN1987A. The upper limits at 3σ level obtained during this localization on the X-ray fluxes from LMC X-1 and 50-millisecond pulsar PSR 0540-693 are presented in Table 2.

In 1989 May-June the Kvant module did not detect a statistically confident signal from the SN1987A region in spite of other X-ray sources LMC X-1 and PSR 0540-693 having been in the HEXE field of view. Taking into account the deviations between the direction of the telescope axis and directions on these X-ray sources an efficiency of the flux detecting from different sources differed. The upper limits on the fluxes from SN1987A and other sources are presented in Fig.1,6 and also in Table 3.

The weakness of the hard X-ray flux from LMC X-1 in 1989 May-June (Sunyaev et al., 1989) and the closeness of the upper limit on the LMC X-1 hard emission obtained by the HEXE device to limits obtained during the HEAO A2 (Wait and Marshall, 1984) and HEAO A4 (Matteson and Peterson, 1987) experiments testify to a small portion of the LMC X-1 flux to the flux detected by the Kvant module during 1987 August - 1988 April. Note that the flux detected in 1988 January exceeds the upper limits obtained in 1989 May-June about one order of magnitude.

Note in conclusion that the supernova light curve in 45-105 keV energy band did not show a single sharp statistically confident burst similar to the burst observed by the Ginga satellite in 1988 January in the softer energy band. In hard X-rays the light curve was smooth as it was expected for the light curve of the source connected with radioactive decay.

The authors are grateful to V.D.Blagov, V.M.Loznikov, V.G.Rodin, A.M.Prudkoglyd, the team headed by Yu.P.Semenov and the cosmonauts working aboard the Mir space station for the observatory control.

REFERENCES

Arnett W.D.//Astrophys.J., 1988, V.331, P.377.

Arnett W.D., Fryxell B.A. and Muller E.//Astrophys.J. Letters, 1989, 341, L63.

Bouchet P., Danziger I.J. and Lucy L.B.//IAU Circ., N°4933, 1990.

Cameron A.J.W.//Nuclear Astrophysics (ed. Barnes C.A., Clayton D.D. and Schramm D.N.), Moscow, Mir, 1986, P.33.

Clark D.H., Tuohy I.R., Long K.S. et al.//Astrophys.J, 1982, V.255, P.440.

Dotani T., Hayashida K., Inoue H. et al.//Nature, 1987, V.330, P.230.

Ebisuzaki T. and Shibazaki N.//Astrophys.J. Letters, 1988, V.327, P.L5.

Englhauser J., Doebereiner S., Pietsch E. et al.//23d ESLAB Symp. Proc., 1989.

Erickson E.F., Haas M.R., Colgan S.W.J. et al. //Astrophys.J. Letters, 1988, V.330, P.139.

Grebenev S.A. and Sunyaev R.A.//Soviet Astron. Letters, 1988, V.14, P.675.

Hachisu I., Matsuda T., Nomoto K. and Shigeyama T.// Astrophys.J. Letters, 1990, in press.

Hashimoto M., Nomoto K. and Shigeyama T.//Astron. Astrophys., 1989, V.20, P. L5.

Itoh M., Kumagai S., Shigeyama T. et al.// Nature, 1987, V.330, P.233.

Matteson J.L. and Peterson L.E.//1987, private communication.

Matz S.M., Share G.H., Leising M.D. et al.//Nature, 1988, V.331, P.416.

Pinto P.A. and Woosley S.E.//Astrophys.J, 1988, V.329, P.820.

Rester A.S., Coldwell R.L., Dunnam F.E. et al.//Astrophys.J. Letters, 1989, V.342, P.L71.

Seward F.D., Harnden F.R. and Helfand D.J.//Astrophys.J. Letters, 1984, V.287, P.L19.

Sunyaev R.A., Kaniovsky A.S., Efremov V.V. et al.//Nature, 1987a, V.330, P.227.

Sunyaev R.A., Kaniovsky A.S., Efremov V.V. et al.//Soviet Astron. Letters, 1987b, V.13, P.1027.

Sunyaev R.A., Efremov V.V., Kaniovsky A.S. et al.//Soviet Astron. Letters, 1988, V.14, P.579.

Sunyaev R.A., Kaniovsky A.S., Efremov V.V. et al.//Soviet Astron. Letters, 1989, V.15, P.291.

Sunyaev R.A., Gilfanov M.R., Churazov E.M. et al.//Soviet Astron. Letters, 1990, V.16, in press.

Sunyaev R.A. and Truemper J.//Nature, 1979, V.279, P.506.

White N.E. and Marshall F.E.//Astrophys.J., 1984, V.281, P.354.

Woosley S.E. and Weaver T.A.//Nuclear Astrophysics (ed. Barnes C.A., Clayton D.D. and Schramm D.N.), Moscow, Mir, 1986, P.359.

Table 1. The SN1987A X-ray flux evolution in accordance with da a of the HEXE device observations in 1987-1989.

Day since the outburst	Fluxes and 1σ errors [10^{-6} phot·cm^{-2}s^{-1}keV^{-1}] in the energy bands					
	15 - 45 keV		45 - 105 keV		105 - 200 keV	
143.9 - 144.1	2.	34.	51.	12.	18.	17.
169. - 182.	68.2	5.7	46.7	2.1	21.3	3.3
186. - 204.	96.7	8.5	50.9	3.5	26.0	5.2
231. - 247.	83.1	8.3	57.4	3.3	24.3	7.2
258. - 266.	85.	10.	55.2	4.4	12.8	9.7
291. - 309.	97.	11.	66.1	5.6	30.4	8.9
328. - 343.	100.	10.	62.6	3.5	25.1	4.8
413. - 426.	63.	9.5	51.1	3.8	27.9	6.1
444. - 446.	46.	27.	24.	12.	24.0	16.
559. - 569.	17.2	9.6	20.5	4.1	7.2	6.5
590. - 599.	21.4	6.1	14.5	3.0	8.2	4.7
630. - 648.	12.2	4.1	10.6	2.6	14.5	7.0
820. - 840.	8.2	7.0	3.8	2.9	-2.8	4.2

Table 2. The upper limits on the X-ray fluxes (in photons·cm^{-2}s^{-1}keV^{-1}) from LMC X-1 and PSR 0540-693 at three standart deviation level in accordance with the HEXE data obtained in 1987 August - 1988 January. They were reconstructed during localization used a number of offset observations.

Source	15-45 keV	45-105 keV
LMC X-1	$5.5 \cdot 10^{-5}$	$8.0 \cdot 10^{-6}$
PSR 0540-693	$2.9 \cdot 10^{-5}$	$6.8 \cdot 10^{-6}$

Table 3. The average efficiencies of the observatory Roentgen pointing and the corresponding upper limits at three standard deviation level on the X-ray fluxes (in photons$\cdot$cm^{-2}s^{-1}keV^{-1}) from the LMC sources observed by the HEXE device in 1989 May-June.

Source	Efficiency	15-45 keV	45-105 keV
SN1987A	52 %	$2.1 \cdot 10^{-5}$	$8.6 \cdot 10^{-6}$
LMC X-1	32 %	$8.5 \cdot 10^{-5}$	$1.2 \cdot 10^{-5}$
PSR 0540-693	45 %	$3.4 \cdot 10^{-5}$	$9.5 \cdot 10^{-6}$

Figure 1. The SN1987A X-ray spectra obtained by the Roentgen observatory in 1987 August (1) and October-November (2), 1987 December-1988 January (3), 1988 April (4), September-October (5) and November (6), 1989 May-June (7) (diamonds and crosses-the HEXE and Pulsar X-1 data respectively, crosses marked by circles - the TTM telescope upper limits). The errors correspond to one standard deviation, the upper limits - to three standard deviations (in the last graph the HEXE upper limits are shown by triangles). Results of the Monte Carlo calculations carried out according to the envelope model accepted in the present paper are presented by solid lines (time after the outburst is shown near each curve). In graphs 5,6,7 a ^{56}Co portion in the total ^{56}Co and ^{57}Co emission is shown by dotted lines. The relative abundance of ^{57}Co/^{56}Co is equal to two-abundance of ^{57}Fe/^{56}Fe at the Earth.

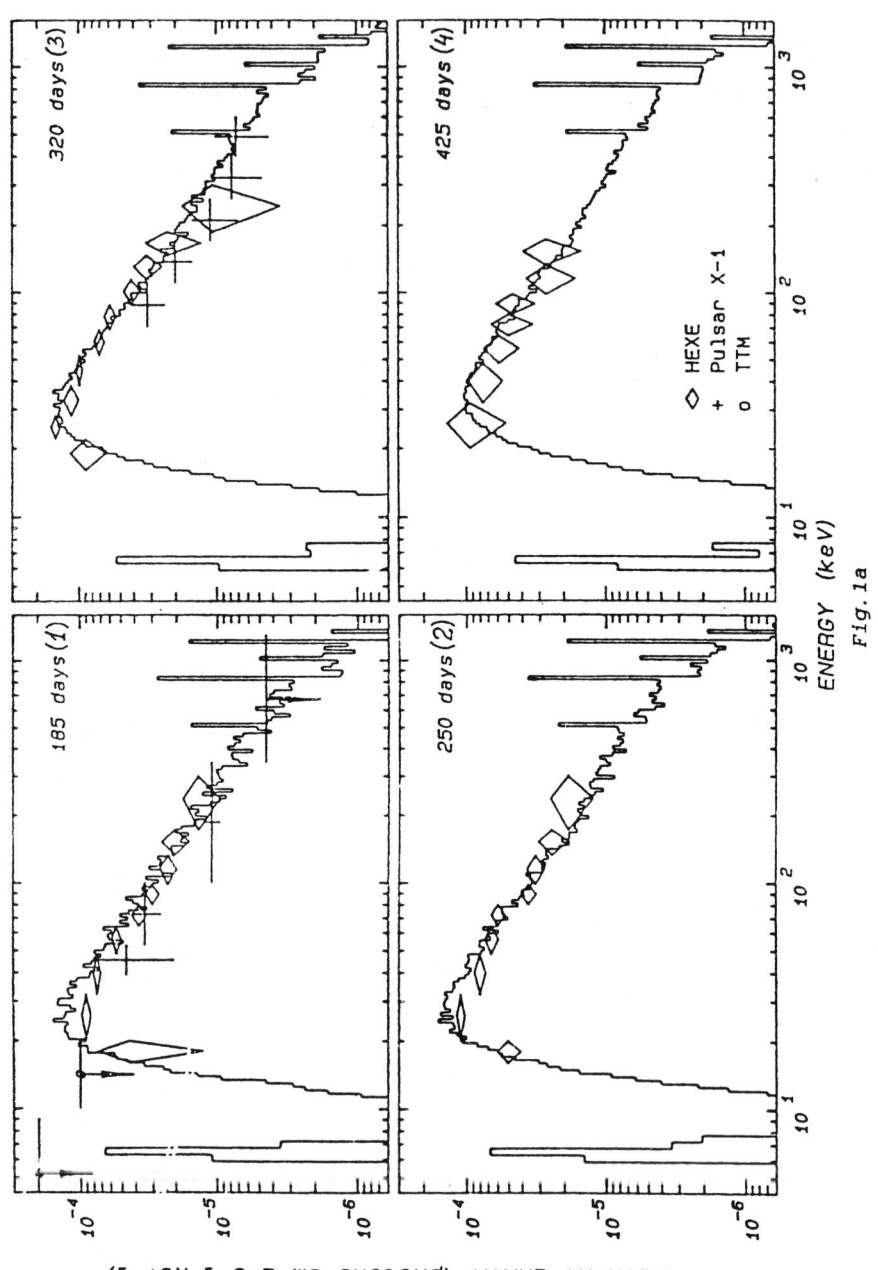

Fig. 1a

X-Ray Radiation from SN 1987A

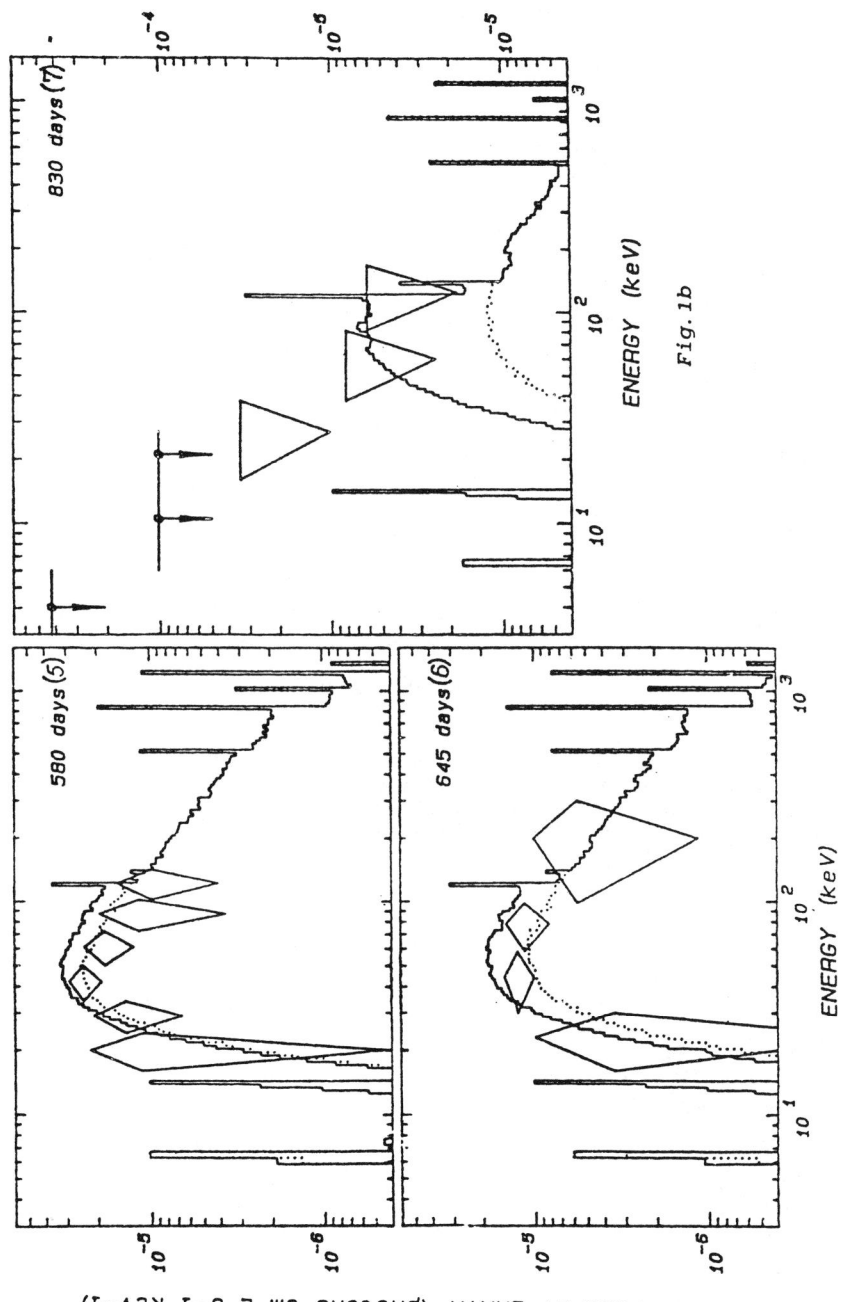

Fig. 1b

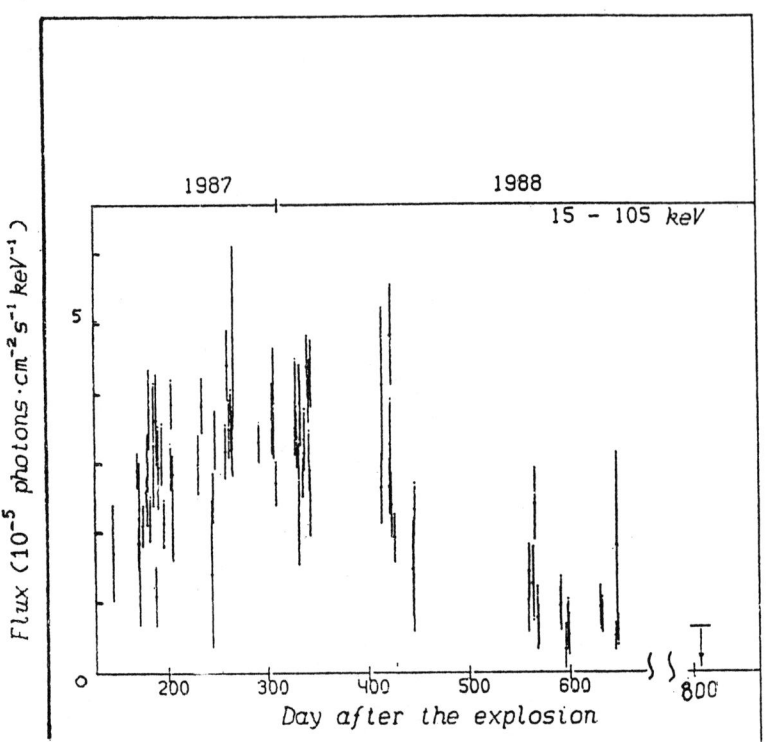

Figure 2. The SN1987A X-ray 15-105 keV flux as a function of time according to the HEXE observations. Each point corresponds to one observational day, the errors correspond to one standard deviation. Three sigma upper limit on the flux observed in 1989 May-June is presented.

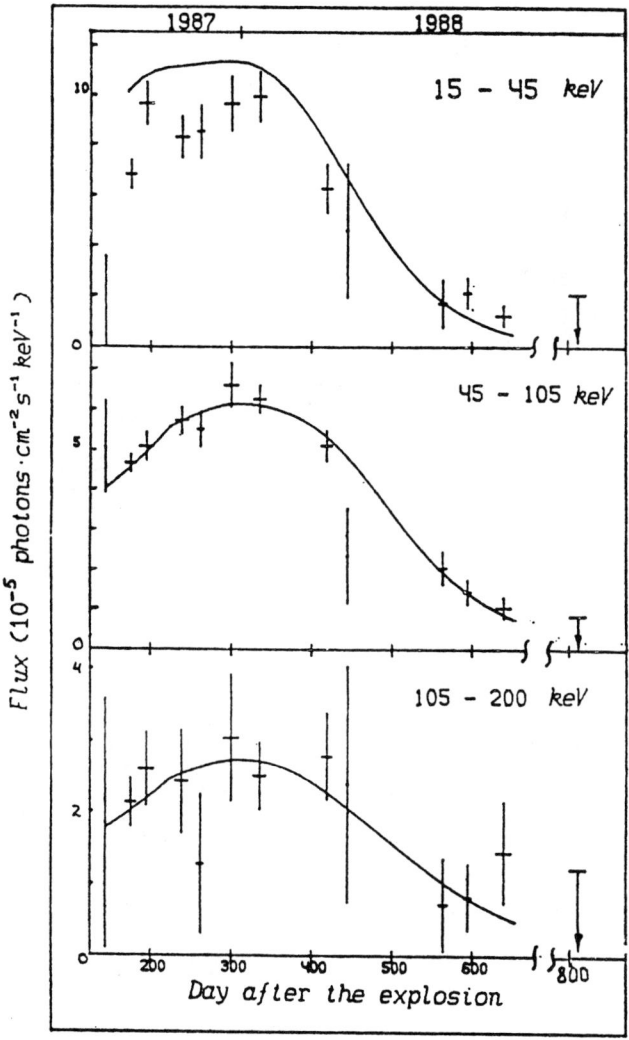

Figure 3. The SN1987A X-ray fluxes as functions of time according to the HEXE data in three colors 15-45, 45-105 and 105-200 keV. Each point presents data averaged over long period of observations. The errors correspond to one standard deviation. The results of Monte-Carlo simulations carried out for the envelope model accepted in the present paper are shown by solid lines.

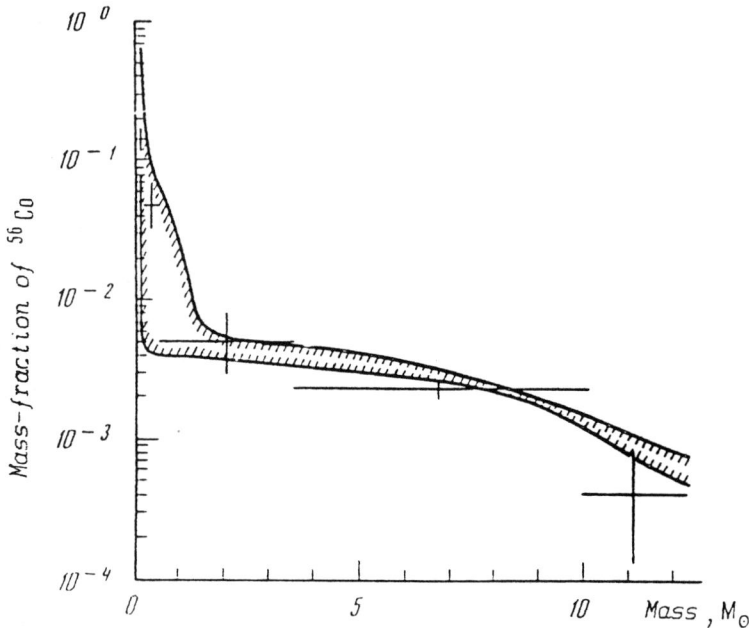

Figure 4. Region of the most probable ^{56}Co distribution (mass fraction) over the SN1987A envelope which gives a possibility to simulate the observed X-ray light curves of the source. The results of two independent approaches are presented. In the first approach it is assumed that cobalt is uniformly distributed over five spherical layers of the envelope (crosses, errors of the cobalt concentration in each layer are given at one sigma level). In the second approach the 67% confidence level region of the distribution described by superposition of two Gaussians is obtained. It is clear that both approaches give similar results.

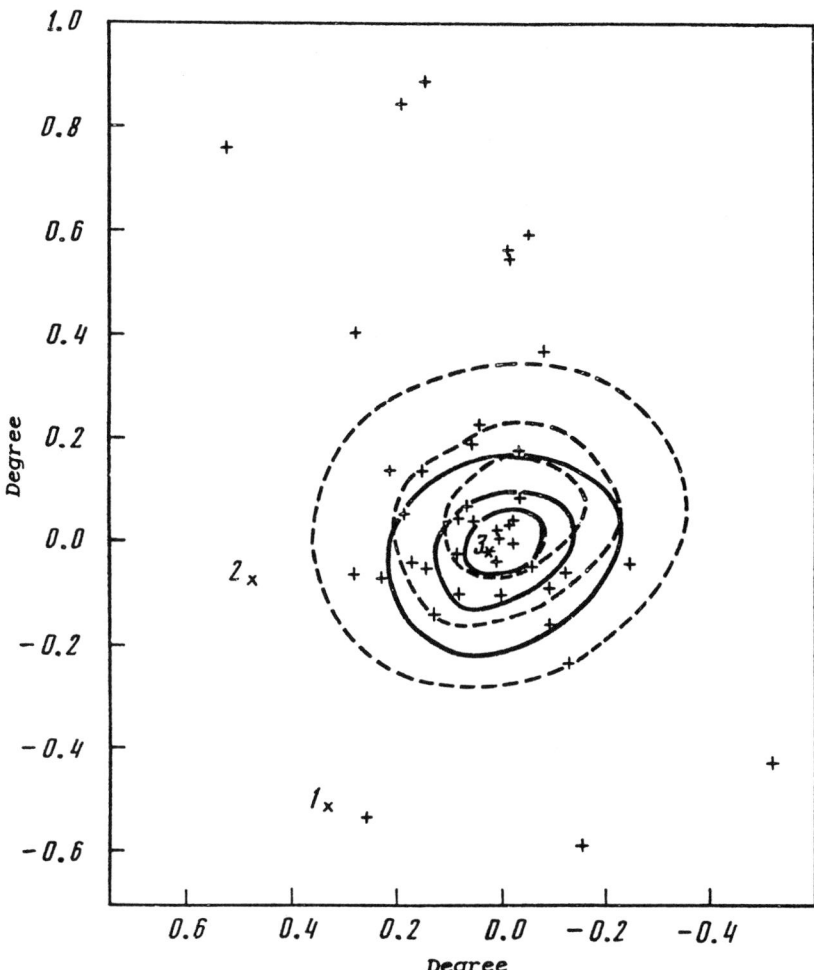

Figure 5. Localization of the hard X-ray source in the Large Magellanic Cloud according to the HEXE data obtained from 1987 August to 1988 January. The contours of 67%, 99%, and 99.9% significance for the energy bands 15-45 (Dotted lines) and 45-105 keV (solid lines) are presented. Positions of the sources LMC X-1 (1), PSR 0540-693 (2), SN1987A (3) are marked. Pointings of the HEXE device in different series of observations are shown by small crosses.

Figure 6. (a) Spectrum of LMC X-1 according to the HEAO A2 experiment (crosses) (Wait et al., 1984). The upper limits on the hard X-ray flux from this source according to the HEXE data. The analytical approximation of the TTM instrument data is shown by a solid line (Sunyaev et al., 1990). (b) Spectrum of PSR 0540-693 (a power law approximation) in accordance with the observatory Einstein (Clark et al., 1982, Seward et al., 1984) and the upper limits on the hard X-ray flux according to the HEXE data. The spectrum obtained by the TTM instrument (Sunyaev et al., 1990) coincides with the presented power law approximation within the limits of experimental data errors.

Figures 6a and 6b on next page

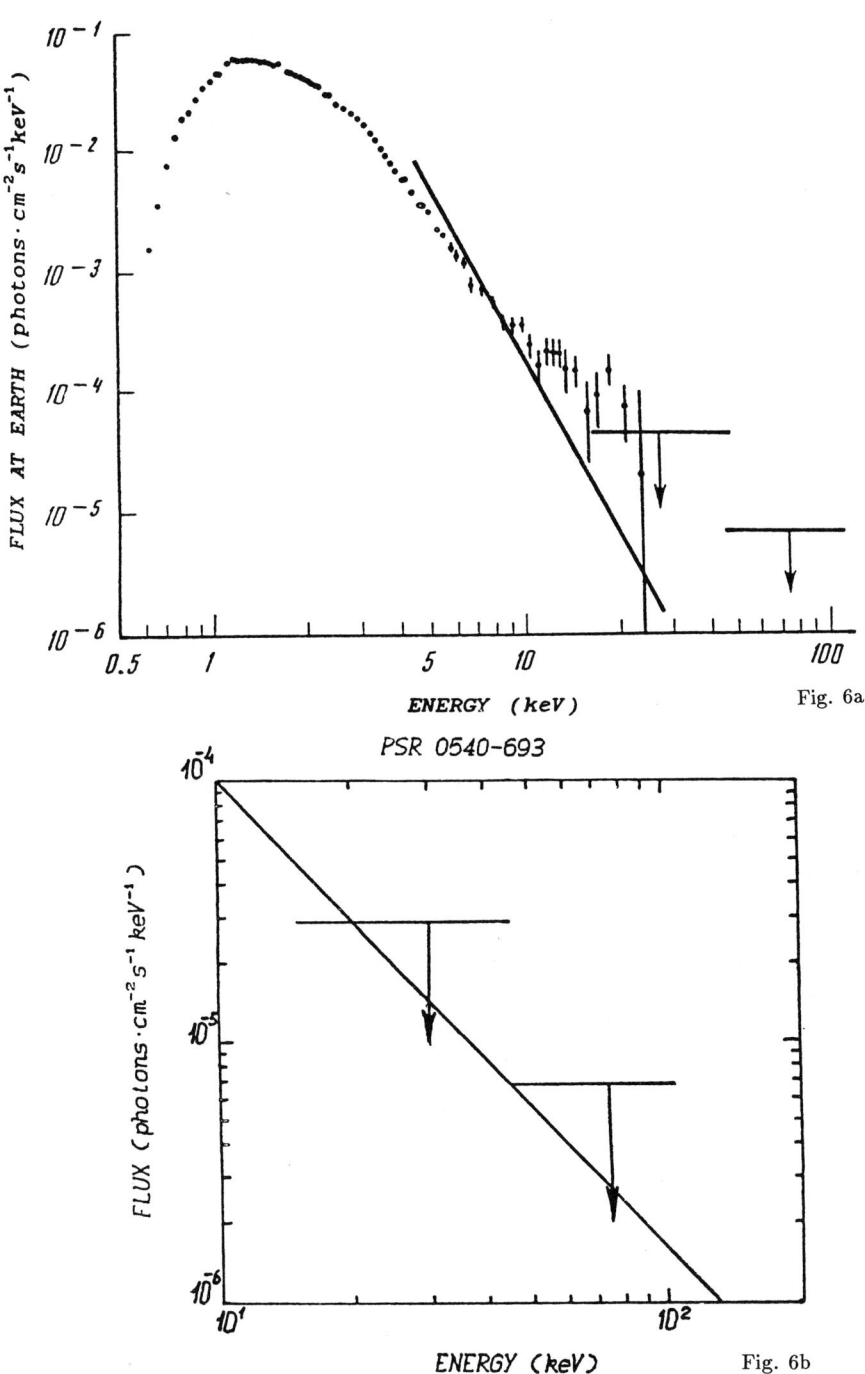

Fig. 6a

Fig. 6b

POSTSCRIPT

The "Supernova Song," such as it is, as performed by Woosley at the Conference Dinner.

```
D     D₇   A    D         D₇       A    A₇
```
Su-per nova, su-per nova; Super-no-va over you.

```
D            D₇
```
I just can't believe it,

```
      G                G₇
```
But before Reverand Evans sees it,

```
      D             A    A₇   D    G  D   A₇
```
Gotta get this telegram off to the IAU.

Supernova, supernova, your models are best it's plain to see.
You've got a great big Cray,
And it does, what you say,
In three dimensions and non-LTE.

Supernova, supernova, will we ever know you?
You live so far away,
Beyond the Milky Way.
I bet you've still got a secret or two.

And if you're not tired by this point repeat the first verse. The tune is very much like the song "Freedom" (with apologies to Odetta).

OHIO UNIVERSITY LIBRARY

Please return this book as soon as you have finished with it. In order to avoid a fine it must be returned by the latest date stamped below.

JUN 1 2 1999

SEP 0 7 1999

FEB 0 5 1992